Contents

◄◄ Ngorongoro Conservation Area ◄ Iringa market

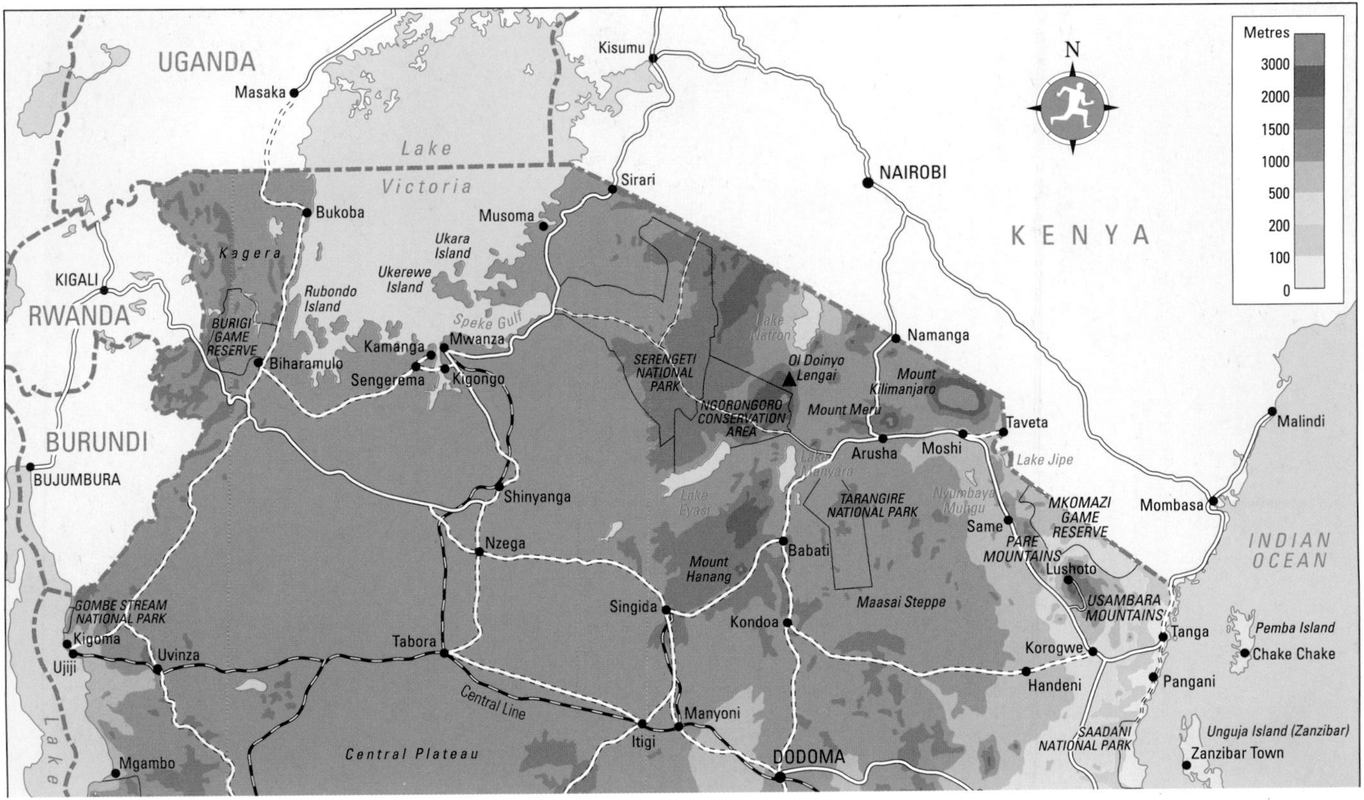
Metres
3000
2000
1500
1000
500
200
100
0
N
UGANDA
KENYA
RWANDA
BURUNDI
INDIAN OCEAN
Lake Victoria
Masaka
Kisumu
NAIROBI
Sirari
Bukoba
Musoma
Ukara Island
Ukerewe Island
Rubondo Island
Kagera
KIGALI
Speke Gulf
BURIGI GAME RESERVE
Kamanga
Mwanza
Biharamulo
Sengerema
Kigongo
SERENGETI NATIONAL PARK
NGORONGORO CONSERVATION AREA
Lake Natron
Ol Doinyo Lengai
Namanga
Mount Kilimanjaro
Mount Meru
Taveta
Arusha
Moshi
Lake Jipe
Malindi
Lake Manyara
Lake Eyasi
TARANGIRE NATIONAL PARK
Nyumbaya Mungu
MKOMAZI GAME RESERVE
Mombasa
Same
PARE MOUNTAINS
Lushoto
BUJUMBURA
Shinyanga
Nzega
Babati
Mount Hanang
USAMBARA MOUNTAINS
Maasai Steppe
GOMBE STREAM NATIONAL PARK
Singida
Kondoa
Tanga
Pemba Island
Chake Chake
Kigoma
Ujiji
Uvinza
Tabora
Korogwe
Handeni
Pangani
Central Line
Manyoni
Itigi
SAADANI NATIONAL PARK
Unguja Island (Zanzibar)
Zanzibar Town
Central Plateau
DODOMA
Mgambo
Lake

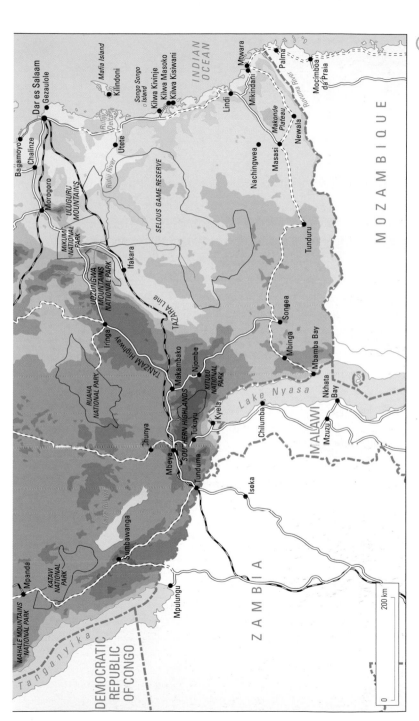

Introduction to

Tanzania

Lying just south of the equator, Tanzania is East Africa's largest country, and an immensely rewarding place to visit. Filling the brochures are several world-famous attractions: the plains of the Serengeti, Ngorongoro Crater, snow-capped Mount Kilimanjaro (Africa's highest mountain) and Zanzibar, with its idyllic palm-fringed beaches and historic Stone Town. Yet there's a whole lot more to Tanzania than these obvious highlights. Almost everywhere you go you'll find interesting wildlife and inspiring landscapes ranging from forest-covered volcanic peaks to dusty savannah populated by elephants, antelopes, lions, leopards and cheetahs. Tanzania is one of the four most naturally diverse nations on earth: it contains Africa's second-largest number of bird species (around 1500), the continent's biggest mammal population and three-quarters of East Africa's plant species (over ten thousand). Add to this the country's rich ethnic diversity, some superb hiking, and other activities like snorkelling and diving, and you have the makings of a holiday of a lifetime.

Tanzania's best asset is its people: friendly, welcoming, unassumingly proud and yet reserved – you'll be treated with uncommon warmth and courtesy wherever you go, and genuine friendships are easily made. The best known tribe are the Maasai, a pastoralist cattle-herding people who inhabit the region around the safari parks in the north, yet there are at least 127 other tribes in Tanzania, perhaps not as visually colourful as the red-robed, spear-carrying Maasai warriors, but with equally rich traditions, histories, customs, beliefs and music, much of which survive despite the ravages of colonialism, modernity and Christianity. For many years, only those with months on their hands had the privilege of really

▲ Dhow

getting to know these people, but since 1995, an award-winning cultural tourism programme has broken new ground in enabling tourists to experience local life in an intimate and inevitably fascinating way.

Where to go

Many visitors make a beeline for Tanzania's best-known protected areas, encompassed by the so-called **Northern Safari Circuit**. For many, the enormous volcanic caldera of **Ngorongoro Crater** is the highlight, providing a year-round haven for wildlife in a glorious setting. It's also the starting point for a wild hike to Tanzania's only active volcano, **Ol Doinyo Lengai**, and on to **Lake Natron**, an immense soda lake that appeals to flamingos and desert fanatics alike. The **Serengeti**, west of Ngorongoro, needs no introduction: its well-documented annual migration of over a million wildebeest, zebra and antelope provides one of the world's most awesome wildlife spectacles. Less well-known northern parks include **Tarangire**, fantastic for elephants, whose size is amply complemented by forests of gigantic baobabs; **Lake Manyara**, at the foot of a particularly spectacular section of the Rift Valley escarpment; and **Arusha National Park**, which contains the country's second-highest mountain, **Mount Meru**. The main base for Northern Circuit safaris is the attractive town of **Arusha**, home to hundreds of safari companies and with a good handful of cultural tourism programmes within easy reach.

7

Fact file

• Tanzania was created in 1964 by the union of mainland Tanganyika (former German East Africa) and Zanzibar, which was an Omani colony for several centuries before the British made it a protectorate. Covering 945,203 square kilometres, Tanzania is almost four times the size of the UK and twice that of California. The population is estimated at 36 million, and grows annually at a rate of around three percent. Population density is generally thin, apart from in the urban sprawl of Dar es Salaam and around the shoreline of Lake Victoria.

• Tanzania is among the world's poorest countries, with an average salary of $50 a month for those in work; taking the unemployed into account (almost thirty percent of urban youths), the average annual income comes out at barely $250 per person of working age. A third of the population live below the UN's dollar-a-day poverty line; over half lack access to safe water; one in seven children die before the age of five; and life expectancy, albeit high by African standards, is falling – it's now under fifty years. Tanzania receives over $1 billion annually in aid. Fortunately, these depressing statistics do not paint the full picture or reflect traditional modes of life, many of which – such as subsistence agriculture and cattle herding – carry on outside the official economy. And with the G8 having announced debt relief packages in 2005, things are definitely looking up, and growth in GDP is expected to reach ten percent a year by the end of the decade.

• Tanzania has been a multi-party democracy since 1995, although the ruling CCM party still receives the lion's share of media coverage. Zanzibar remains semi-autonomous and has its own parliament and president.

East of the Northern Circuit parks are the **Northern Highlands**, dominated by the snow-capped **Mount Kilimanjaro**, the challenging ascent of which is one of the classic African adventures. Further east, Kilimanjaro's foothills give way to the much older granite formations of the **Pare** and **Usambara mountains**, repository of some of the earth's most biologically diverse rainforests, especially at **Amani Nature Reserve** near the coast, which well deserves its nickname of "the Galapagos of Africa".

Much of **central Tanzania** is dry and semi-arid woodland, and natural attractions are fewer. **Dodoma**, Tanzania's capital, is a hot and dusty planned city, though it makes a good starting point for excursions to the fabulous prehistoric rock paintings of the **Irangi Hills**, the oldest of which date back some

◀ Children in local bus, Zanzibar

eighteen thousand years. **Morogoro** is the liveliest of central Tanzania's towns, and offers hikers access to the **Uluguru Mountains**, another place notable for its high species diversity. Heading south, the **Udzungwa Mountains** provide similar riches: the eastern flanks are especially good for primates, while the centre and west are a bird-watcher's paradise. **Iringa**, to the west, is one of Tanzania's more attractive towns and gateway to **Ruaha National Park**, whose wealth of wildlife is the equal of the Northern Circuit parks, but without the crowds.

The **far south**, for long ignored, has been opened to tourism through a number of cultural tourism programmes. The mountainous towns of Mbeya and Tukuyu are the bases for hikes and day-trips in the **Southern Highlands**, with its rainforests and crater lakes, and Tanzania's newest national park enclosing the flower-bedecked **Kitulo Plateau**. The highlight for many visitors to the region is **Lake Nyasa**, the southern-most of the Rift Valley lakes and home to hundreds of species of colourful cichlid fish, a trip on the weekly ferry along the Tanzanian side of the lake is one of the country's classic journeys.

North from here is the immense **Lake Tanganyika**, the world's longest (and second-deepest) freshwater lake

Hey, Mzungu!

Mzungu (plural *wazungu*) is a word white travellers will hear all over East Africa – children, especially, take great delight in chanting the word whenever you're around. Strictly speaking, a *mzungu* is a white European, although Afro-Europeans and Afro-Americans need not feel left out, being known as *mzungu mwafrikano* (Asian travellers will have to content themselves with *mchina*, and Indians *mhindi*). The term was first reported by nineteenth-century missionaries and explorers, who flattered themselves to think that it meant wondrous, clever or extraordinary.

The real meaning of the word is perhaps more appropriate. Stemming from *zungua*, it means to go round, to turn, to wander, to travel, or just to be tiresome. However weary you may grow of the *mzungu* tag, you should at least be grateful that the Maasai word for Europeans didn't stick: inspired by the sight of the trouser-wearing invaders from the north, they christened the newcomers *iloridaa enjekat* – those who confine their farts.

and scene of another unforgettable ferry ride aboard the vintage MV *Liemba*. The lakeshore provides the scenic setting for two remote nature reserves – **Mahale Mountains** and **Gombe Stream** national parks – both of which are home to troops of chimpanzees. Access to either is from the harbour town of **Kigoma**, close to **Ujiji**, where Stanley uttered his famous words, "Dr Livingstone, I presume?"

Northwest Tanzania is dominated by the shallow **Lake Victoria**, the world's second-largest freshwater lake. The views are magnificent, and the lake's

9

◀ Giraffes, Tarangire National Park

southwestern corner contains the little-known **Rubondo Island National Park**, which harbours a number of endangered species and immense colonies of birds. There are three main towns on the Tanzanian part of the lake, each with its own distinctive personality and attractions: **Musoma** in the east; the burgeoning city of **Mwanza** in the south; and **Bukoba** in the west, which is connected to Mwanza by ferry and provides overland access to Uganda.

The **Indian Ocean** coastline offers an altogether different Tanzanian experience. Especially recommended is **Zanzibar**, one of Africa's most famous and enticing destinations, comprising the islands of **Unguja** and **Pemba**, which have idyllic beaches and multicoloured coral reefs aplenty, perfect for both diving and snorkelling. There's a whole lot more to Zanzibar than beaches and tropical languor, however. The archipelago's capital, **Stone Town**, is a fascinating Arabian-style labyrinth of narrow, crooked alleyways packed with nineteenth-century mansions, palaces and bazaars. South from Zanzibar, the remote **Mafia Archipelago** has its own share of historical ruins, as well as stunning coral reefs which offer superlative snorkelling and diving.

On the mainland coast, the biggest settlement is **Dar es Salaam**, the country's former capital and still its most important city. Though it's usually only visited en route to Zanzibar, Dar is well worth spending some time in, especially for its music scene and exuberant nightlife. Tanzania's **north coast** features a series of beach resorts, the coastal **Saadani National Park**, and three towns which were involved in the nineteenth-century slave trade with Zanzibar – **Tanga**, **Pangani** and atmospheric **Bagamoyo**, which preserves a wealth of haunting old buildings and ruins. Tanzania's **south coast** is much wilder and less accessible. Historical colour is provided by the ruins of the island-state of **Kilwa Kisiwani** – at its height the wealthiest and most important of the Swahili coastal trading towns. In the far south are a trio of towns: workaday **Mtwara** and **Lindi**, and the smaller **Mikindani**, like Bagamoyo an attractively tumbledown reminder of the slave trade.

When to go

Tanzania's coast and lakeside regions are almost always hot and humid; highland regions have a more temperate climate; and the semi-arid central plateau is hot and dry. Divided into two rainy seasons and two dry seasons, much of the country's **climate** is controlled by the Indian Ocean's **monsoon winds**, which bring with them two rainy periods – the "**long rains**" (*masika*) from March to May, and the

▲ Women wearing kangas

Ujamaa

With 128 officially recognized tribes Tanzania boasts more distinct cultures than any other country in Africa apart from Congo. Yet unlike Congo, Tanzania remains a peaceful oasis amidst the continent's wars. Although Tanzania's borders were drawn up in the interests of colonial Europe rather than along socio-cultural lines, the country is unique in having successfully forged a healthy sense of unity within those artificial borders – and one which encompasses both tribal and national identities. Undoubtedly, part of the reason for this success is that none of the nation's tribes comes close to forming a majority (the biggest, the Sukuma, comprises no more than thirteen percent of the population), while the brutal period of German colonization also played a part, in that the Germans introduced Kiswahili as the national language, so that every tribe could converse with every other. More than anything, however, Tanzania's uncommon unity owes its existence to the country's first president, Julius Nyerere, and his experiment in African socialism, known as *Ujamaa*, or "togetherness". Although economically disastrous, *Ujamaa* threw everyone together during the 1960s and 1970s, when over eighty percent of the rural population were moved from their ancestral lands and relocated in collective villages. *Ujamaa* is Nyerere's lasting legacy to the Tanzanian people, and for this reason alone, he deserves his unofficial title of *Baba wa Taifa*, the Father of the Nation.

lighter **"short rains"** (*mvuli*) between November and December. At high altitudes it can rain at almost any time. The period from July to October is dry and starts cold, before becoming progressively warmer and more humid; it's also usually dry in June and from December to February. Western Tanzania, while broadly following the sequence outlined above, has a scattered rainfall pattern influenced by the presence of lakes Victoria, Tanganyika and Nyasa, and is always humid. **Dry-season travel** has a number of advantages, not least of which is the ability to actually move around the country – many roads become impassable during the rains. The dry season is also better for spotting wildlife, when animals congregate around the diminishing water sources.

Temperatures are determined largely by altitude; reckon on a drop of 6°C (or 11°F) for every 1000m you climb from sea level. Daytime temperatures in most places average 22–30°C, although tropical humidity on the coast and by the lakes makes the air feel hotter than it really is. The hottest period is from November to February; the coolest from May to August.

The month of **Ramadan** (see p.60 for dates) has little effect on travel in mainland Tanzania, but isn't the best time to visit Zanzibar, as most restaurants close by day and the mood in Stone Town especially isn't at its best.

Daily temperature ranges and average rainfall

	Jan	Feb	Mar	Apr	May	Jun	Jul	Aug	Sep	Oct	Nov	Dec
Arusha (altitude 1400m)												
°C	14–28	14–29	15–28	16–25	15–23	13–22	12–22	13–23	12–25	14–27	15–27	14–27
Rainy days/mm	8/70	8/75	12/140	19/225	12/85	4/15	3/10	2/6	2/10	4/25	10/125	11/100
Dar es Salaam (sea level)												
°C	23–32	23–32	23–32	22–31	21–30	19–29	18–29	18–29	18–30	20–31	21–31	23–32
Rainy days/mm	7/80	5/60	12/130	19/265	13/180	5/40	5/30	4/25	5/25	6/60	8/120	9/110
Kigoma (altitude 781m)												
°C	19–28	19–28	19–28	20–28	19–29	17–29	16–29	17–30	19–30	20–29	19–28	19–28
Rainy days/mm	9/75	8/75	9/60	11/100	6/20	0/0	0/0	1/10	2/20	9/70	12/120	12/155
Mbeya (altitude 1700m)												
°C	14–23	14–24	13–24	12–23	9–22	5–22	5–22	6–23	9–25	12–27	13–26	13–24
Rainy days/mm	20/200	18/170	18/170	14/110	4/20	0/1	0/0	0/0	1/5	2/15	7/65	8/180
Zanzibar (sea level)												
°C	22–32	24–32	25–32	25–30	23–28	23–28	22–27	22–28	22–28	22–30	23–31	24–31
Rainy days/mm	5/75	5/60	8/150	11/350	10/280	4/55	2/45	2/40	3/50	4/90	9/170	8/145

18

things not to miss

It's not possible to see everything that Tanzania has to offer in one visit, and we don't suggest you try. What follows is a selective taste of the country's highlights — outstanding scenery, exciting wildlife, memorable hikes — arranged in five colour-coded categories. All highlights have a page reference to take you straight into the guide, where you can find out more.

02 Beaches, Zanzibar Page **691** • There's no better place to relax after a hot and dusty safari than on Zanzibar's beaches.

01 Cultural tourism Page **64** • Often tacked on to the end of a trip as an afterthought, Tanzania's cultural tourism programmes end up being the highlight of many a holiday.

13

04 Stone Town Page **629** •
Stone Town's labyrinthine network of narrow streets is magically atmospheric, with opulent nineteenth-century palaces and poignant reminders of the slave trade at every turn.

03 Mount Kilimanjaro Page **334** • Africa's highest mountain and the world's tallest free-standing volcano, Kilimanjaro draws hikers from all over the world – although fewer than a third of them get to Uhuru Peak at the very top.

05 Serengeti Page **469** • The legendary Serengeti is home to Africa's highest density of plains game and the backdrop to one of the greatest wildlife spectacles on Earth each year, when over a million animals set off on their annual migration.

06 Bull-fighting, Pemba Page *Tanzania in Celebration* • The annual bull-fighting festivals held on Pemba Island are a reminder of Portuguese occupation; the bulls aren't killed, just mightily annoyed.

08 Kilwa Kisiwani Page **211** • The spectacular ruins of the island city-state of Kilwa Kisiwani are testimony to the immense riches that were made first from gold, then from ivory and slaves.

07 Forodhani Gardens, Stone Town Page **650** • Stone Town's waterfront Forodhani Gardens are a paradise for street-food enthusiasts, with a bewildering array of seafood, snacks and even roast bananas covered in melted chocolate – and all for no more than a dollar or two.

09 Ngorongoro Conservation Area Page **460** • The enormous caldera of an extinct volcano provides the spectacular setting for Ngorongoro's abundant plains game and their predators – close-up encounters with lions, buffaloes and rhinos are virtually guaranteed.

10 Makonde carvings Page **242** • The Makonde tribe of southern Tanzania are famed for their abstract wood carvings, including remarkable "trees of life" which perfectly illustrate the archetypal African concepts of remembrance and continuity.

11 Seafood, Zanzibar Page **650** • Seafood features prominently in Swahili cooking, especially in Zanzibar, where fish, prawns, squid and lobster are served with subtle spices and blended with sauces.

12 Tingatinga painting Page **126** • Tingatinga painting uses bold and bright bicycle paints to illustrate its eye-catching and humorous designs, many of which are based on *sheitani* spirit mythology.

13 Kondoa-Irangi rock paintings

Page **266** • The Irangi Hills of central Tanzania are home to a remarkable complex of painted rock shelters, the oldest dating back some 18,000 years.

14 Chimpanzees at Gombe Stream and Mahale

Mountains Page **544** • Studies of wild chimp populations at Mahale Mountains and Gombe Stream national parks have shed light on many fascinating aspects of chimp life.

15 Scuba-diving Page **61** • The coral reefs off Tanzania's coast at Zanzibar and Mafia Island offer some of the world's finest scuba-diving.

16 Tarangire National Park Page **430** • In the dry season Tarangire is the best place in all of Africa for seeing elephants – though even these mighty beasts are dwarfed by the park's huge baobab trees, many of them over a thousand years old.

18 Indian Ocean flights

Page **199** • Any flight from the mainland to Zanzibar or Mafia Island offers an unforgettable bird's-eye panorama of the coral reefs of the Indian Ocean.

17 Hiking in the Usambara and Udzungwa mountains

Pages **358** & **307** • Ancient rainforests, rare plant and animal species, and eyeball-to-eyeball encounters with primates; hiking in the Usambara and Udzungwa mountains is one of Tanzania's foremost pleasures.

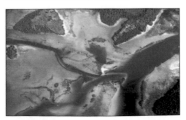

Basics

Basics

Getting there

Flying is the only practical way to reach Tanzania from outside East Africa – there are direct or one-stop flights from Europe to Dar es Salaam, Kilimanjaro (between Moshi and Arusha) and Zanzibar. Travellers from North America, Australia and New Zealand will have to change planes in Europe or South Africa. The main airlines flying into Tanzania are KLM, Emirates, Ethiopian, Kenya Airways and South African Airways. Overland routes from the north, other than from Uganda and Kenya, are impassable for all but the most foolhardy, but coming from southern Africa is possible by road or train.

Getting there from the UK and Ireland

The only **direct flights** from the UK are on British Airways (daily from Heathrow to Dar es Salaam). **One-stop flights** include KLM (daily from Heathrow and London City via Amsterdam to Kilimanjaro and on to Dar, arriving at night, or via Nairobi with the onward leg via Precisionair/Kenya Airways); South African Airways (from London via Johannesburg, usually in conjunction with other airlines); EgyptAir (weekly to Dar via Cairo); Ethiopian (Kilimanjaro and Dar via Addis Ababa, with a stopover of up to 30hr; also from Frankfurt, Paris and Rome); and Emirates (to Dar via Dubai – long flight times but comfortable planes). One-stop **flights from Ireland** are on BA (via London) and KLM (via Amsterdam).

Flight times are eight to nine hours direct from London, eleven to fifteen hours for most one-stop flights, and up to twenty hours for most two-stop routings. **Low season fares** (roughly Sept–Nov and April–June) offered by the airlines themselves can be under £400 (€800 from Ireland), but count on around £1000 (€ 1800) in high season (roughly July–Aug, Dec–Jan and possibly on to March). The most competitive are usually Emirates, EgyptAir and KLM (from London City, not Heathrow).

Airlines

British Airways UK ☎ 0870/850 9850, Republic of Ireland ☎ 1800/626 747, ⓦ www.ba.com.
EgyptAir UK ☎ 020/7734 2343, ⓦ www.egyptair .com.eg.

Plane tickets

Before **buying a plane ticket**, find out how easy it will be to **change your flight dates**, and what refund you'll get if you need to cancel. **Fares** for July, August and December are the most expensive; the best prices are usually available well in advance, meaning six or even eleven months before travel. Shop around: the cost of the exact same seat can vary between agents. **Discount flight agents**, the majority of them online, generally have the best prices but their tickets may be non-refundable and non-changeable (read the small print). Some agents offer reductions for **students and under-26s**.

If your visit to Tanzania is part of a multi-continent trip, consider a **round-the-world (RTW)** ticket, valid for six months or a year. As a general rule you'll have to select your itinerary and stopovers in advance, travelling either eastbound or westbound with no backtracking. Tanzania itself seldom features on RTW tickets: Nairobi is the closest city that does, but also useful are Johannesburg and Harare. Prices start at £1500/$2500: try the **online route planner** at ⓦ www .airtreks.com.

Seasons and prices

Rates at Tanzania's **beach resort hotels** and **safari lodges** can fall significantly out of high season, with anything up to fifty percent off.

Peak season: Mid-December to early January; rates may be quoted as Christmas and New Year supplements, over the high season rates.

High season: July to September or to mid-December, sometimes also January to March or Easter. Mainly hot and sunny weather, though there's a chance of rain between October and December.

Low season: Always April and May, sometimes March to June, coinciding with the long rains, or the "Green Season", as some hoteliers prefer to call it. October, November and sometimes early December, coinciding with the short rains, may also be considered low season, depending on the location and the hotel.

Emirates UK ☎0870/243 2222, ⓦwww.emirates.com.

Ethiopian Airlines UK ☎020/8987 7000, ⓦwww.flyethiopian.com.

Kenya Airways UK ☎01784/888 222, ⓦwww.kenya-airways.com.

KLM UK ☎0870/507 4074, Ireland ☎1850/747 400, ⓦwww.klm.com.

South African Airways UK ☎0870/747 1111, ⓦwww.flysaa.com.

Discount flight and travel agents

Apex Travel Republic of Ireland ☎01/241 8000, ⓦwww.apextravel.ie.

Co-op Travel Care UK ☎0870/112 0085, ⓦwww.travelcareonline.com.

Joe Walsh Tours Republic of Ireland ☎01/676 0991, ⓦwww.joewalshtours.ie.

North South Travel UK ☎012/608 291, ⓦwww.northsouthtravel.co.uk. Friendly and competitive; profits support projects in the developing world, especially the promotion of sustainable tourism.

McCarthys Travel Republic of Ireland ☎021/427 0127, ⓦwww.mccarthystravel.ie.

Rosetta Travel Northern Ireland ☎028/9064 4996, ⓦwww.rosettatravel.com.

STA Travel UK ☎0870/1600 599, ⓦwww.statravel.co.uk. Worldwide specialists in low-cost flights and tours for students and under-26s; other customers are welcome. Several branches.

Top Deck UK ☎020/8879 6789, ⓦwww.topdecktravel.co.uk.

Trailfinders UK ☎0845/0585 858, ⓦwww.trailfinders.co.uk; Republic of Ireland ☎01/677 7888, ⓦwww.trailfinders.ie.

usit NOW Republic of Ireland ☎01/602 1600, Northern Ireland ☎028/9032 7111; ⓦwww.usitnow.ie. Student and youth specialists with seven branches across Ireland; good fares on KLM.

ⓦ**www.ebookers.com** Low fares from the UK and Europe.

ⓦ**www.expedia.co.uk** Discount and standard fares.

ⓦ**www.gohop.com** From Ireland.

ⓦ**www.kelkoo.co.uk** Price comparisons.

ⓦ**www.opodo.com** Low fares on BA and KLM.

ⓦ**www.travelbag.co.uk** Efficient site with alluring deals and masses of search results.

Tour operators

See also the overland tour operators listed on p.26.

Abercrombie and Kent UK ☎0845/070 0610, ⓦwww.abercrombiekent.co.uk. UK arm of upmarket US long-haul specialists; see p.23 for review. From £250–300 a day.

Africa Select UK ☎01670/787646, ⓦwww.africaselect.com. Upmarket spins all over the country, including chimp-tracking, Kili climbs and scuba-diving, and safari accommodation in small but very luxurious tented camps. £200–300 a day.

Africa Travel Resource UK ☎01306/880770, ⓦwww.africatravelresource.com. These guys came from nowhere a few years back to become one of the leading mid-range and upmarket "outfitters" for both Tanzanian safaris and Zanzibar beach breaks, on the back of their superlative website – the most comprehensive resource about Tanzanian tourism on the Web. All tailor-made: give them an itinerary and see what they suggest.

African Initiatives UK ☎0117/915 0001, ⓦwww.african-initiatives.org.uk. A registered charity working to bolster the rights of pastoralists and related hunter-gathering communities in northern Tanzania (and in Ghana). Their sponsored trips (monies raised fund local projects) are run through Arusha's recommended Dorobo Safaris (p.406). A two-week trip, including stays with Maasai and

Package tours

Only a handful of overseas **tour operators** actually operate their own trips in Tanzania, usually through local subsidiaries. The rest piece together their offerings using hopefully carefully selected Tanzanian companies, hotels and lodges. Of course, you could do the same thing by using the information in this book, but the disadvantage is that you won't get the often hefty discounts on accommodation available to agents, some of which they may pass on to you. It's also much easier to pay just one overall price than have to deal with each lodge and company individually.

Whilst many companies offer **pre-packaged tours**, often with set departure dates, all offer **tailor-made trips**. What this means is that you either take a sample itinerary from them and send it back marked with your preferences, or – better but time-consuming – work out exactly what you want beforehand in terms of so many nights here or there and in what kind of accommodation, then suggest the itinerary to several operators and contrast and compare the results. Tours offered by UK operators can usually also be booked in the US, Canada, Australia and New Zealand, and vice-versa, so don't necessarily limit yourself to companies in your own country.

Lastly, don't forget **Tanzanian safari companies**, many of whom can also arrange packages: see p.404 for Arusha, and p.133 for Dar es Salaam.

Hadzabe, a Serengeti safari, and a hike in the Crater Highlands, costs £2200 including flights.

Baobab Travel UK ☎0870/382 5003, ⓦwww
.baobabtravel.com. A responsible and ethical operator offering tailor-made packages all over. Locally owned ground operators are given preference, and cultural tourism also features strongly. A fourteen-day "honeymoon" safari with Zanzibar starts at £1450, excluding international flights.

Encounter Zanzibar UK ☎020/7514 5836, ⓦwww.encounterzanzibar.com. That this originally South African company are nuts about Zanzibar is beyond question: their supremely detailed website, with its extensive and impartial hotel reviews, stands as proof – prices depend on where you stay.

Gane & Marshall UK ☎020/8445 6000, ⓦwww
.ganeandmarshall.co.uk. A small company involved in Africa for two decades, offering small-group tours using ethically and environmentally sound ground operators, and Tanzania's cultural tourism programmes. Includes less-trampled routes up Kilimanjaro (£1500–1600 over eight nights), and walking and cycling trips in the Rift Valley between Longido and Lake Natron.

IntoAfrica UK ☎0114/255 5610, ⓦwww
.intoafrica.co.uk. If you don't like the idea of a colonial-style safari, this Tanzanian-British outfit is the one for you. One of few to run their own Tanzanian operations (from Arusha, p.405), IntoAfrica promotes fair-trade trips, walks and mountain hikes (especially Crater Highlands treks), and makes good use of cultural tourism programmes and its own community-based projects. £130–200 a day.

Natural High Safaris UK ☎0845/456 1384, ⓦwww.naturalhighsafaris.com. Small, specialist operator focusing on hyper-luxurious (and expensive) private mobile camp safaris. They're particularly knowledgeable on Tanzania's south and west, and also offer ornithological tours.

Simply Tanzania Tour Company UK ☎020/8986 0615, ⓦwww.simplytanzania.co.uk. Recommended ethically run specialist covering less-travelled areas, including the southern highlands, and a lot of cultural tourism. Fourteen-day packages from £1250, excluding international flights.

Tanzania Odyssey UK ☎020/7471 8780, ⓦwww
.tanzaniaodyssey.com. Specializing only in Tanzania (and Zanzibar) for over a decade, this is a good company for tailor-made safaris: prices are at cost, meaning their profit lies in agents' commissions (which you wouldn't get booking direct). Lots of scanned hotel brochures online.

Tribes UK ☎01728/685971, ⓦwww.tribes
.co.uk. Off-the-beaten-track tours with community involvement – especially Maasai – across a range of luxurious yet adventurous trips away from the crowds. £1000–1500 a week excluding flights.

Zanzibar Travel UK ☎01242/222027, ⓦwww
.zanzibartravel.co.uk. Does what it says on the tin, plus Kili climbs and Kenyan safaris. All tours are tailor-made: a twelve-night mid-range Zanzibar holiday starts at £1000, including flights, or £1400 if staying in top-notch hotels. Add £300 for a short safari.

Getting there from the US and Canada

There are **no direct flights** from North America to East Africa. The fastest **one-stop** routings are New York (JFK) to Dar es Salaam

on Northwest/KLM via Amsterdam, or on British Airways via London, taking under twenty hours. Taking around thirty hours are Ethiopian Airlines via Addis Ababa (also from Toronto at Christmas), EgyptAir (via Cairo), and South African Airways (via Johannesburg), which can be routed into Zanzibar via Air Tanzania. Coming **from Canada**, single-ticket fares can be hugely inflated compared to buying two separate tickets: one from Canada to Boston or JFK, the other from there. High season **return fares** from JFK to Dar cost $2000 to $5000 depending on season and availability. If you're late in booking and prices are high, you could make an overall saving by **flying to London**, stopping over for a day or two, and picking up a last-minute (or Internet) flight from there. New York–London returns can be had for under $500: try Virgin Atlantic.

Airlines

British Airways ☏ 1-800/AIRWAYS, ⊛ www.ba.com.
EgyptAir US ☏ 1-800/334-6787 or 1-212/315-0900, Canada ☏ 1-416/960-0009, ⊛ www .egyptair.com.eg.
Ethiopian Airlines US ☏ 1-800/445-2733 or 1-212/867-0095, ⊛ www.flyethiopian.com.
Kenya Airways ☏ 1-866/KENYA-AIR, ⊛ www .kenya-airways.com.
Northwest/KLM ☏ 1-800/447-4747, ⊛ www .nwa.com, ⊛ www.klm.com.
South African Airways US ☏ 1-800/722-9675, Canada ☏ 1-800/387-4629, ⊛ www.flysaa.com.
Virgin Atlantic ☏ 1-800/862-8621, ⊛ www .virgin atlantic.com.

Discount flight and travel agents

STA Travel US ☏ 1-800/329-9537, Canada ☏ 1-888/427-5639, ⊛ www.statravel.com. Worldwide specialists in independent travel.
Travel Cuts US ☏ 1-800/592-CUTS, Canada ☏ 1-888/246-9762, ⊛ www.travelcuts .com. Popular, long-established student-travel organization, with worldwide offers.
Air Brokers International ☏ 1-800/883-3273, ⊛ www.airbrokers.com.
Flightcentre US ☏ 1-866/WORLD 51, ⊛ www .flightcentre.us; Canada ☏ 1-877/478-8747, ⊛ www.flightcentre.ca.
Travelosophy US ☏ 1-800/332-2687 or 1-248/557-7775, ⊛ www.itravelosophy.com.
⊛ **www.expedia.com & expedia.ca**. Discount and standard fares.

⊛ **www.orbitz.com** Returning lots of relevant results with better connections and prices than most, and great customer service.
⊛ **www.qixo.com** US-only: a rather lazy search engine (only KLM/Northwest for Tanzania), but competitive fares.
⊛ **www.skyauction.com** Auctions tickets and travel packages using a "second bid" scheme, like eBay. Bid the maximum you're willing to pay, since if you win you'll pay just enough to beat the runner-up, regardless of your maximum bid.

Tour operators

See also the UK tour operators reviewed on pp.20–21, most of whom also deal with North American clients; the overland tour operators listed p.26; and "Package tours" on p.21.
Abercrombie & Kent US ☏ 1-800/554-7016 or 1-630/954-2944, ⊛ www.abercrombiekent.com. Leading upmarket operator with a comprehensive and flexible Tanzanian programme operated through a local subsidiary. They have good vehicles and back-up, but group sizes can be large on the more popular options. On Kilimanjaro climbs, they carry oxygen cylinders and portable altitude chambers. From $400 a day.
Africa Safari Specialists US ☏ 1-800/456-8950, ⊛ www.safaris.com. Small group departures and tailor-made safaris including family packages, for around $2000 a week. Full details and prices online.
Africa Travel Resource US ☏ 1-866/672 3274 or 1-831/338 2383, ⊛ www.africatravelresource.com. Sales office for this flexible UK-based company; see review on p.20.
African Horizons US ☏ 1-888/212-6752, ⊛ www .africanhorizons.com. Tailor-made safaris, including bush walking options, particularly strong on the southern and western parks. Mid-range lodges to luxury mobile tented camps.
African Portfolio US ☏ 1-800/700-3677 or 1-203/637-2977, ⊛ www.onsafari.com. Highly regarded US/Zimbabwean outfit offering a range of customizable packages, for instance an eleven-day camping safari including birding and hiking from $3000.
Bestway Tours & Safaris Canada ☏ 1-800/663-0844 or 1-604/264-7278, ⊛ www.bestway.com. Small group cultural forays, better value and more off-beat than most, with a sixteen-day walking trip through northern Tanzania (Kilimanjaro, Ngorongoro and Tarangire) costing around $3000. Also covers family travel, voluntary working holidays, and Indian Ocean island extensions.
Born Free Safaris US ☏ 1-800/372-3274 or 1-720/524-9683, ⊛ www.bornfreesafaris.com.

Covering Tanzania since the 1970s, this lot offer a full range of trips from affordable camping to ultimate bush luxury, both in group departures and private tours. They have an excellent "safari planner" online, and are also happy just supplying a car, driver and camping equipment.

Good Earth Tours US ☎ 1-877/265-9003 or 1-813/615-9570, ⓦ www.goodearthtours .com. Specializing in Kenya and Tanzania, they're slow in replying to emails, but deliver the goods – with competitive prices. A private camping or mid-market lodge safari can be as little as $1000 per person a week, though staying in well-chosen upmarket lodges or camps will cost more than twice that.

Mountain Madness US 1-800/328-5925 or ☎ 1-206/937-8389, ⓦ www.mountainmadness .com. Pioneers of Kilimanjaro's Shira and Western Breach routes, and also offering the Umbwe route, this long-established Seattle-based climbing outfit comes highly recommended for Kilimanjaro (their Tanzanian arm is African Environments), and indeed is used by many an upmarket operator for their climbs. A portable altitude "chamber" (pressurizable bag), oxygen cylinders and water filters come as standard; a sixteen-day trip combining a climb with a wildlife safari will relieve you of $5500–6000.

Naipenda Safaris US ☎ 1-888/404-4499 or 1-830/238-4066, ⓦ www.naipendasafaris.com. Also has a Tanzanian subsidiary (same name), with twice-monthly departures for camping and lodge safaris, and an unusual array of custom-made trips that can include tribal culture, art, village volunteer programmes and even cooking. From $230 a day.

Premier Tours US ☎ 1-800-545 1910 or 1-215/893-9966, ⓦ www.premiertours.com. Set departures for budget camping and Kilimanjaro climbs, but mostly tailor-made. A six-day camping safari costs $1200, whilst a more comfortable week-long mobile camping safari ducks under $2000.

Getting there from Australia and New Zealand

There are **no direct flights** from Australia and New Zealand to Tanzania – all require a stopover either in Asia, southern Africa or the Middle East. From Australia, the best deals are on EgyptAir via Bangkok and Cairo. More direct but more expensive would be to go via Harare with Air Zimbabwe (A$2500–3000/NZ$2500–3500) or to Johannesburg on Qantas (A$2500–4000) and change there. Agents offering **package tours** tend to use companies based in the UK or US.

Airlines

Air New Zealand Australia ☎ 132476, New Zealand ☎ 0800/247 764, ⓦ www.airnewzealand.com.
Air Zimbabwe Australia ☎ 02/8272 7822, New Zealand ☎ 09/309 8094, ⓦ www.airzimbabwe.com.
British Airways Australia ☎ 1300/767 177, New Zealand ☎ 09/966 9777, ⓦ www.ba.com.
EgyptAir Australia ☎ 02/9241 5696, ⓦ www .egyptair.com.eg.
KLM Australia ☎ 1300/303 747, New Zealand ☎ 09/302 1792, ⓦ www.klm.com.
Qantas Australia ☎ 131313, New Zealand ☎ 09/357 8900 or 0800/808 767, ⓦ www.qantas. com.
South African Airways Australia ☎ 1800/221 699, New Zealand ☎ 09/977 2237, ⓦ www.flysaa .com.

Discount flight and travel agents, and tour operators

See also the UK tour operators reviewed on pp.20–21, most of whom also deal with clients from down under; the overland tour operators listed p.26; and "Package tours" on p.21.

Abercrombie & Kent Australia ☎ 02/9241 3213, New Zealand ☎ 0800/441 638, ⓦ www .abercrombiekent.com.au. Branch of the long-established US upmarket operator – see the review on p.23. Upwards of A$600 a day.
The Adventure Travel Company New Zealand ☎ 09/379 9755, ⓦ www.adventuretravel.co.nz. Agents for lots of package and specialist safari companies.
African Wildlife Safaris Australia ☎ 1300/363 302 or 03/9696 2899, ⓦ www .africanwildlifesafaris.com.au. Specialists in tailor-made safaris to southern and eastern Africa, from budget to flying and luxury "camping".
The Classic Safari Company Australia ☎ 1300/130 218 or 02/9327 0666, ⓦ www .classicsafaricompany.com.au. Luxury, tailor-made safaris to southern and eastern Africa.
Gecko's Holidays Australia ☎ 02/9290 2770, ⓦ www.geckos.com.au. Wide range of Tanzanian trips in all price ranges.
Holiday Shoppe New Zealand ☎ 0800/808 480, ⓦ www.holidayshoppe.co.nz. General travel agent.
OTC Australia ☎ 1300/855 118, ⓦ www.otctravel. com.au. Online flight and holiday agent.
STA Travel Australia ☎ 1300/360 960, ⓦ www .statravel.com.au; New Zealand ☎ 09/309 9273, ⓦ www.statravel.co.nz. Worldwide specialists in independent travel.

Trailfinders Australia 1300/780 212, ⓦwww
.trailfinders.com.au. Well-informed and efficient
agents for independent travellers.
World Expeditions Australia ☎1300/720 000,
ⓦwww.worldexpeditions.com.au; New Zealand
☎0800/350 354, ⓦwww.worldexpeditions.co.nz.
A reasonable choice of Tanzanian options, including a
thirteen-day family package, and ethically responsible
hiking: Kilimanjaro with safari over two weeks, or "twin
peaks" – Kili with Mount Kenya.
ⓦ**www.travel.co.nz** Comprehensive site for flights.
ⓦ**www.travel.com.au** The same from Oz.

Getting there from Africa

International flights within Africa can be
expensive, but as long as you're prepared to
use Kenya's capital, Nairobi, as an alternative destination in case there's nothing direct
to Tanzania, the country can be reached in
a hop or skip from most of the continent.
Major African **airlines** operating to and
from Tanzania are Kenya Airways, Ethiopian
Airlines and South African Airways (partnered
with the very minor Air Tanzania). The main
Tanzanian airlines, often using mono-prop
light aircraft, are Coastal Aviation, Precisionair and ZanAir, who together cover most of
the country: for information about routes,
see the "Arrival" and "Moving on" sections
throughout this guide, and "Travel details" at
the end of each chapter. If Tanzania is part
of a longer southern African trip, consider
buying a place on an **overland truck safari**:
taking three to twelve weeks from Nairobi to
Cape Town, they can be rather hurried affairs
given the wealth of things to see and do
along the way, and are often dominated by
party animals who could be on Mars for all
they cared, but do provide a handy means
of getting an initial feel for the place.

From Kenya, there are daily flights from
Nairobi and Mombasa to Arusha, Kilimanjaro, Dar es Salaam and Zanzibar (Precisionair, Regional Air and Air Tanzania are the
main operators, partnered with several international airlines), and good road connections, including "shuttle buses" from Nairobi
to Arusha (4–6 hours) and on to Moshi (5–7
hours), and normal buses from both Nairobi
and Mombasa to Arusha and Dar. The
safest are Scandinavian Express (ⓦwww
.scandinaviagroup.com) and Akamba.

From Uganda, options are limited to
uncomfortable local **buses** into Tanzania's

Kagera Region (Bukoba), unless you travel
via Kisumu or Nairobi in Kenya (again, Scandinavian and Akamba are safest). Air Tanzania **fly** from Entebbe to Dar; there may be
flights to Mwanza in future.

From Malawi, Scandinavian Express from
Lilongwe is the best **bus** service, taking just
over thirty hours to reach Dar es Salaam.
At the time of writing, **ferries** across Lake
Nyasa (Lake Malawi) into Tanzania had been
discontinued, but if you don't mind roughing
it there are still local boats connecting Malawi's Nkhata Bay with Tanzania's Mbamba
Bay, to and from either of which are weekly
ferries: on the Malawian side the MV *Ilala*
sails all the way up from Monkey Bay (and
beyond Nkhata Bay to Chilumba), and on
the Tanzanian side the MV *Songea* from
Mbamba Bay to Itungi Port in the north. See
p.614 for more details. **Flights** to Dar from
Blantyre and Lilongwe are operated by Air
Malawi.

From southern Africa and Zambia, flying
is quickest, on South African Airways in
conjunction with Air Tanzania from Johannesburg. One or two **overland truck**
companies run safari trips from South Africa to
Nairobi via Tanzania (try Drifters ☎011/888
1160, ⓦwww.drifters.co.za), but most head
up empty to pick up their clients in Kenya
– it may be possible to arrange a lift with the
drivers at the *Backpackers' Ritz* in Johannesburg: 1A North Rd (off Jan Smuts Ave),
Dunkeld West (☎011/327 7125, ⓦwww
.backpackers-ritz.co.za). The journey is also
feasible by public transport: it's a sealed road
all the way, and you can also travel by **train**
from Cape Town. The last leg – from New
Kapiri Mposhi in Zambia to Dar es Salaam
– is the TAZARA Line (see p.47). Coming by
bus, there are no really safe companies from
Zambia, but with a little luck you'll get from
Lusaka to Dar in one piece in around 35
hours. More fun is the weekly **ferry** on Lake
Tanganyika (either the historic MV *Liemba*,
or the MV *Mwongozo*) from Mpulungu in
Zambia to Kigoma, taking two nights; see
p.542.

From Central and northern Africa,
things are much more complicated and
mostly not recommended, given the eternal strife and/or instability in those regions.
At the time of writing, **Rwanda** is safe, but

Burundi limps on under the strain of bandit and rebel attacks, and the eastern section of the **Democratic Republic of the Congo** (DRC) remains the disaster area it always has been. Both the **Republic of the Congo** and **Central African Republic** are potentially volatile, too, due to internal dictatorial politics, whilst southern **Sudan** – although blessed with a peace accord in 2005 – gives seasoned observers little to feel optimistic about, especially given the situation in Darfur. Southern **Ethiopia** (for crossing into Kenya via Moyale) is passable, but there's always a risk of bandit attack on either side of the border, whilst **Somalia** has effortlessly won the "the world's most dangerous place" contest since its government disappeared in 1991 – reformed in 2004, the new executive has little control over anything.

African airlines

Air Malawi ⓦ www.airmalawi.com.
Air Tanzania ⓦ www.airtanzania.com.
Coastal Aviation ⓦ www.coastal.cc.
EgyptAir UK ⓣ 020/7734 2343, ⓦ www.egyptair.com.eg.
Ethiopian Airlines UK ⓣ 020/8987 7000, ⓦ www.flyethiopian.com.
Kenya Airways UK ⓣ 01784/888 222, ⓦ www.kenya-airways.com.
Precisionair ⓦ www.precisionairtz.com.
Regional Air ⓦ www.regional.co.tz.
South African Airways ⓦ www.flysaa.com.
ZanAir ⓦ www.zanair.com.

Overland truck tours

Organized, so-called **overland tours** through Africa generally use converted trucks, taking a set number of weeks or months to travel across all or a part of the continent. The classic trans-Africa trip went from the UK to Cape Town via Cairo, but continuing conflicts all over the place mean that most tours now come from the west and finish in Cameroon, continuing – one flight later – from Nairobi. The operators listed below all cover the Nairobi to Cape Town run via Tanzania, taking three to twelve weeks. When getting quotes, find out whether flights are included, what the optional extras are (eg Zanzibar beach breaks or additional safaris), and how much your contribution to the communal "kitty" will be, as this can add up to thirty percent to the total cost. Be aware that your fellow passengers will tend to be around 25 years old and very much in road-trip mentality: you'll either love or loathe it. Expect to pay £30–50 a day.

Absolute Africa UK ⓣ 020/8742 0226, ⓦ www.absoluteafrica.com.
African Trails UK ⓣ 020/8742 7724, ⓦ www.africantrails.co.uk.
Bukima Adventure Tours ⓦ www.bukima.com: UK ⓣ 0870/757 2230; Australia ⓣ 1800/215009 or 07/4776 0062; New Zealand ⓣ 09/235 8234; Canada ⓣ 1-604/892 2240.
Exodus Expeditions UK ⓣ 020/8675 5550, Republic of Ireland (Worldwide Adventures) ⓣ 01/679 5700, ⓦ www.exodus.co.uk.
Guerba Expeditions UK ⓣ 01373/826611, ⓦ www.guerba.com.
Kumuka Expeditions UK ⓣ 0800/068 8855, ⓦ www.kumuka.co.uk; Australia ⓣ 1800/804 277 or 02/9279 0491, ⓦ www.kumuka.com.
Phoenix Expeditions UK ⓣ 01509/881818, ⓦ www.phoenixexpeditions.com.

Red tape and visas

Most foreign nationals need a visa to enter Tanzania. Single-entry three-month visas can be bought on arrival, or beforehand from a Tanzanian embassy, consulate or high commission. Ensure your passport is valid for six months beyond the end of your stay. Yellow fever vaccination certificates are no longer required, though it's probably best to get the jab anyway, especially if you'll be travelling elsewhere in Africa. However, rules regarding visas have a habit of changing, so do check requirements with a Tanzanian diplomatic mission beforehand.

Visas

A **three-month single-entry visa** costs $50 (or £50 for Britons if bought in London). If buying on arrival, it's best to pay in dollars cash, as Euro and Sterling prices are significantly higher. **Multiple-entry visas** can be difficult to obtain. To extend your stay beyond three months, the trick is to leave the country and re-enter with a new visa. Rules regarding **transit visas** for Kenya and Uganda change frequently (and seemingly from border post to border post): in theory, they cost $20 and give you 24 hours to cross the country or reach passport control at an airport.

Tanzanian embassies, consulates and high commissions

Tanzanian **diplomatic missions** are listed on Ⓦ www.tanzania.go.tz/embassies.htm. Opening hours for **visa applications** are generally Monday–Friday 10am–12.30pm (closed on Tanzanian public holidays; see p.600). You'll need two passport-size photos and – sometimes – an air ticket out of the country. Processing takes 24 hours, although same-day processing can be obtained for a small additional fee.

Australia See Ⓦ www.tanzaniaconsul.com for the list of Honorary Consuls.
Canada High Commission, 50 Range Rd, Ottawa, Ontario K1N 8J4 ☏ 1-613/232-1509, Ⓔ tzottawa@synapse.net.
Ireland – see UK.

Italy Embassy, Via Cesare Beccaria 88, 00196 Rome ☏ 06/3600 5234, Ⓦ www.tanzania-gov.it.
Kenya High Commission, 9th Floor, Reinsurance Plaza, Taifa Rd, PO Box 47790 Nairobi ☏ 02/331056–7, Ⓔ tanzania@africaonline.co.ke.
Mozambique High Commission, Ujamaa House, PO Box 4515 Maputo ☏ 01/490110–3, Ⓔ ujamaa@zebra.eum.mz.
New Zealand – no representation.
South Africa High Commission, 822 George Ave, PO Box 56572 Arcadia, Pretoria 0007 ☏ 012/342 4371, Ⓦ www.tanzania.org.za.
Uganda High Commission, 6 Kagera Rd, PO Box 5750 Kampala 041/256272, Ⓔ tzrepkla@imul.com.
UK High Commission, 43 Hertford St, London W1Y 8DB ☏ 020/7499 8951, Ⓦ www.tanzania-online. gov.uk.
US 2139 R St NW, Washington DC 20008 ☏ 1-202/939-6125, Ⓦ www.tanzaniaembassy-us.org.
Zambia Ujamaa House, 5200 UN Ave, PO Box 31219-10101 Lusaka ☏ 01/253320, Ⓔ tzreplsk@zamnet.zm.

Customs and duty-free

The **duty-free allowance** for visitors entering Tanzania is one litre of spirits, 200 cigarettes, 50 cigars or 250g of tobacco and 250ml of perfume. Unless you're carrying a mountain of gear, items for personal use, like binoculars, cameras and laptops, pose no problem with **customs**. At worst you'll just have to sign (and pay) a bond which is redeemed when you leave the country with all your stuff. If you're taking items into Tanzania as presents, however, you're likely to have to pay duty if you declare them.

Information, maps and websites

The Tanzanian Tourist Board has no overseas offices. No matter though, if you've got the Rough Guide to hand you have all the information you need.

Maps

The best general **maps of Tanzania** are Reise Know-How's waterproof *Tanzania* (1:1,200,000; ISBN 3-8317-7126-X, 2004), packed with detail and showing relief using contours and colouring, and – almost as detailed, and just as accurate – harms-ic-verlag's *Tanzania, Rwanda and Burundi* (1:1,400,000; ISBN 3-9274-6826-6, 2nd edition 2004). A good alternative, if you can't find these, is Nelles' *Tanzania, Rwanda, Burundi* (1:1,500,000; ISBN 3-8861-8559-1, 2003). For **Zanzibar**, the best is harms-ic-verlag's *Zanzibar* (ISBN 3-9274-6818-5, 2nd edition 2004), which shows Unguja at 1:100,000 and has insets of Pemba and Stone Town. **Zanzibar's dive sites** are nicely presented on Giovanni Tombazzi's *Zanzibar at Sea* (Maco Editions; no ISBN), an attractive compilation of painted maps.

The **northern safari circuit** is also beautifully covered by Giovanni Tombazzi's painted maps, the most useful being *Arusha National Park*, *Kilimanjaro*, *Lake Manyara*, *Ngorongoro*, *Serengeti* and *Tarangire* (Maco Editions; no ISBN numbers). All are double-sided: the wildlife ones come with a dry-season version on one side and wet-season on the other (showing the changes of vegetation and illustrating commonly seen plants and trees), whilst the ones for *Arusha National Park* (Mount Meru) and *Kilimanjaro* have various insets useful to hikers. The most accurate northern park maps are harms-ic verlag's *Ngorongoro Conservation Area* (1:230,000; ISBN 3-9274-6820-7, 1999) and *Lake Manyara* (1:100,000; ISBN 3-9274-6821-5, 2001); sadly, promised additions to the series (Tarangire and Serengeti especially) appear to have been abandoned.

Apart from Tombazzi's plan, other good maps for **Kilimanjaro** are ITMB's *Kilimanjaro Trekking Map* (1:62,500; ISBN 1-5534-1553-1, 2nd edition 2004), which contains masses of hiking-related information and shows altitude with 100m contours and tinting, and Andrew Wielochowski's *Kilimanjaro Map & Guide* published by West Col Productions (1:75,000 and 1:30,000; ISBN 0-9062-2766-6, 5th edition 2001), also packed with useful information.

For completely **off-the-beaten-track hiking**, you need the 1:50,000 topographical sheets available at the Government's Mapping & Surveys Division in Dar es Salaam (Kivukoni Front; Mon–Fri 8am–3.30pm; ☎022/212 4575), which cover the whole country. They've run out of the more popular sheets, but it may be possible to buy photocopies. Most of them were produced between 1959 and 1962, so whilst the topographical detail remains more or less accurate (don't expect the forest cover to be as extensive though), things like roads and villages will have changed. The office also has regional maps at 1:250,000.

Buying maps

Whilst Giovanni Tombazzi's hand-painted maps can bought through the retailers listed below, his updated "New Map of..." versions are difficult to obtain outside Tanzania, so buy them when you get to Arusha, Dar es Salaam or Stone Town. The following stock most of the maps we've reviewed, with the exception of the government's 1:50,000 topographical plans. You can also order maps through your local bookshop using the ISBN numbers quoted above.

Stanfords Ⓦ www.stanfords.co.uk: 12–14 Long Acre, London ☎ 020/7836 1321; 39 Spring Gardens, Manchester ☎ 0161/831 0250; 29 Corn St, Bristol ☎ 0117/929 9966. Stocks most of the maps we've reviewed.

110 North Latitude Ⓦ www.110northlatitude. com: 4915-H High Point Rd, Greensboro NC, USA ☎ 336/369-4171. Awkward search engine; search by map title.

harms-ic-verlag @ www.harms-ic-verlag.
de: Industriestrasse 3, Kandel, Germany ☎ +49
(0)7275/957440. Sells its own output.
Map World (Australia) @ www.mapworld.net.
au: Jolimont Centre, 65 Northbourne Ave, Canberra
☎ 02/6230 4097; 136 Willoughby Rd, Crows Nest,
Sydney ☎ 02/9966 5770; 280 Pitt St, Sydney
☎ 02/9261 3601; 900 Hay Street, Perth ☎ 08/9322
5733. No online shopping.
Map World (New Zealand) @ www.mapworld.
co.nz: 173 Gloucester St, Christchurch
☎ 0800/627967. No online shopping.
NetStoreUSA @ http://maps.netstoreusa.com: US
& Canada ℻ 1-800/329-6736 or 1-602/532-7038;
UK ℻ 020/7681 1463; Australia ℻ 02/9475-0047.
International orders accepted.
Omni Resources @ www.omnimap.com: 1004
South Mebane St, Burlington NC, USA ☎ 1-
336/227-8300. Comprehensive Tanzania coverage;
international orders accepted.

Tanzania online

The following are some of the more informative and interesting websites on **Tanzania**.
Sites specific to places and tribes are
mentioned in the guide.

Official

The United Republic of Tanzania @ www
.tanzania.go.tz. The official national website, prim
and proper and aimed at businesses; also has visa
information and the like.

Governmental travel advisories

Australian Department of Foreign Affairs
@ www.dfat.gov.au.
British Foreign & Commonwealth Office
@ www.fco.gov.uk.
Canadian Department of Foreign Affairs
@ www.dfait-maeci.gc.ca.
Irish Department of Foreign Affairs @ www
.irlgov.ie/iveagh.
New Zealand Ministry of Foreign Affairs
@ www.mft.govt.nz.
US State Department @ www.state.gov/travel.

News and current affairs and magazines

allAfrica.com @ http://allafrica.com/tanzania.
Comprehensive and up-to-date news portal for the
continent, collating articles from both mainstream
and not so common sources, including UN agencies.
Most articles are available on-site, and the enormous
archive is fully searchable.

Africa Confidential @ www.africa-confidential
.com. Online presence of the highly respected weekly
broadsheet for African current affairs; it doesn't beat
about the bush when covering corruption and other
political shenanigans, and is consequentially usually
banned in its paper form. A few articles are posted
online, together with summaries of the main news.
Amnesty International @ www.web.amnesty
.org/library. What the government won't tell you, and
so especially useful for the background to Zanzibar's
political woes.
Arusha Times @ www.arushatimes.co.tz. News
and some laughs from up north.
BBC News @ http://news.bbc.co.uk/1/hi/world/
africa. Reliable daily coverage of Africa, with a useful
search engine for older stories.
The East African @ www.nationaudio.com/
eastafrican. The main articles and features from the
week's issue of one of Africa's leading newspapers,
plus an archive going back to 2001.
IPP Media @ www.ippmedia.com. Home of
Tanzania's *Guardian* newspaper and the Kiswahili
Nipashe.
The Norwegian Council for Africa @ www
.afrika.no. Brief summaries of the day's news with
links to full versions, a searchable archive, and free
email news service providing a more or less daily
selection of articles from papers around the continent.
There are also four thousand good-quality African
weblinks covering most subjects.

Tourism

There are hundreds of safari companies on
the Web – don't necessarily believe them, or
recommendations in newsgroups; Internet
addresses for companies we recommend
are given on p.133 (Dar es Salaam) and
pp.405–407 (Arusha), and in the "Getting
there" sections at the start of this chapter.
Africa Travel Resource @ www
.africatravelresource.com. Travel "outfitter" offering
not just bookings and holidays but a staggeringly
comprehensive and mostly accurate website for
most of Tanzania, with hugely detailed and copiously
illustrated accommodation reviews plus a good deal of
useful background reading too.
rec.travel.africa The best newsgroup for advice
from fellow travellers, and self-appointed experts,
about travel practicalities.
Tanzania National Parks @ www.tanzaniaparks
.com. Almost everything you need to know, with
wildlife photos to make a lion's mouth water.
Should hopefully have up-to-date entry fees.
The marine parks and reserves are covered on
@ www.marineparktz.com.

Tanzania Tourist Board Ⓦwww
.tanzaniatouristboard.com. Comprehensive travel
showcase covering all the main tourist destinations
and towns, lists of licensed safari operators and many
hotels, but not much on culture – at least for now.
Zanzibar.net Ⓦwww.zanzibar.net. A good portal
dedicated to Zanzibar with loads of links and sections
on tourism and the arts.

Music and culture

Africanhiphop Ⓦwww.africanhiphop.com. Rap
and hip-hop from across the continent, with news,
reviews and audio streams. A two-hour webcast of
fresh talent is published every two months at Ⓦwww
.africanhiphopradio.com; the older versions remain
available.
Afropop Ⓦwww.afropop.org. Lots of excellent
features, and reviews of gigs and festivals.
BongoFlava Ⓦwww.bongoflava.com. All you
wanted to know and more about Tanzania's current
music craze. Includes audio and video clips, and
listings of upcoming events.
Dhow Countries Music Academy Ⓦwww
.zanzibarmusic.org. Zanzibar's musical pulse, this
doesn't yet have an awful lot online, but does briefly
cover the Isles' main sonic styles, and provides
information on courses and the annual Sauti za
Busara festival.
East African Music Ⓦhttp://members.aol.com/
dpaterson/eamusic.htm. Devoted to popular East
African music, with lots of essays, plus discographies
and CDs for sale.

The Kamusi Project Ⓦwww.yale.edu/swahili. An
immense online English–Kiswahili and Kiswahili–
English dictionary, also downloadable, plus lots of
language resources and excellent links covering East
and Central Africa.
nTZ Ⓦwww.ntz.info. Thousands of searchable
extracts from books and articles about northern
Tanzania covering absolutely everything.
Rhythms of the Continent Ⓦwww.bbc
.co.uk/worldservice/africa/features/rhythms. A
short and limited if well done and visually attractive
introduction to African music from the BBC World
Service, complete with sound clips. East Africa is
represented by a good page on *taarab*.
Swahili Language and Culture Ⓦwww.glcom
.com/hassan. A modest selection of linguistic
resources, including *kanga* proverbs, poems, and
short lessons.
Tingatinga and his Followers Ⓦwww.art-bin
.com/art/atingae.html. A thoughtful essay about
Eduardo Tingatinga and the painting style named after
him, with plenty of images.
Traditional Music & Cultures of Kenya Ⓦwww
.bluegecko.org/kenya. Although this principally
covers Kenya's tribes, the Luo, Maasai, Kuria,
Makonde and Digo (who can also be found in
Tanzania) are represented, and there are hundreds of
images and hours of sound clips.
Zanzibar International Film Festival Ⓦwww
.ziff.or.tz. Digital home of the fantastic Zanzibar
International Film Festival.

Insurance

It's essential to take out an insurance policy before travelling to cover against
theft, loss, illness or injury. Before paying for a new policy, however, check whether
you're already covered: some all-risks home insurance policies may cover your
possessions when overseas, and many private medical schemes include cover
when abroad. In Canada, provincial health plans usually provide partial cover for
medical mishaps overseas, while holders of official student/teacher/youth cards
in Canada and the US are entitled to limited accident coverage and hospital in-
patient benefits. Students will often find that their student health coverage extends
during the vacations and for one term beyond the date of last enrolment.

After checking out the possibilities above,
you might want to contact a specialist travel
insurance company, or consider the travel
insurance deal Rough Guides offer (see

Rough Guides Travel Insurance

Rough Guides has teamed up with Columbus Direct to offer you **travel insurance** that can be tailored to suit your needs. Readers can choose from many different travel insurance products, including a low-cost **backpacker** option for long stays, a typical **holiday package** option, and annual **multi-trip** policies for those who travel regularly. Rough Guides travel insurance is available to the residents of 36 different countries with different language options to choose from via our website – ⓦ www .roughguidesinsurance.com. Alternatively, UK residents should call ☎ 0800/083 9507; US citizens should call ☎ 1-800/749-4922; Australians should call ☎ 1-300/669 999. All other nationalities should call ☎ +44 870/890 2843.

box above). A typical policy usually provides cover for the loss of baggage, tickets and – up to a certain limit – cash or cheques, as well as cancellation or curtailment of your journey. Most of them exclude so-called **dangerous sports** unless an extra premium is paid: in Tanzania this can mean bush walks, Kili climbs and scuba-diving, though probably not standard game drive safaris. Many policies can be chopped and changed to exclude coverage you don't need. If you take **medical coverage**, check whether benefits will be paid as treatment proceeds or only after you return home, and whether there's a 24-hour medical emergency

number (note that you can't make reverse/ collect calls from Tanzania). When securing **baggage cover**, ensure the per-article limit – typically under £500/$750 and sometimes as little as £250/$400 – will cover your most valuable possession. If you need to make a claim, keep receipts for medicines and medical treatment; in the event you have anything stolen, you must obtain an official statement from the police. If you're going to be travelling off the beaten track for any length of time and want extra peace of mind, you can buy temporary membership of AMREF's **flying doctors** service: in Tanzania, call ☎ 027/254 8578, or see ⓦ www.amref.org.

Health

Tanzania isn't a particularly dangerous place healthwise, and with sensible precautions you're unlikely to suffer anything more than minor tummy trouble – just as well, given the scarcity of well-equipped hospitals and clinics: the better ones are reviewed in the "Listings" sections of larger town accounts in this guide. For further information, the *Rough Guide to Travel Health* offers a comprehensive and practical account of the health problems which travellers face worldwide.

Medical resources for travellers

Websites

ⓦ **www.cdc.gov/travel** Precautions, diseases and preventive measures by region, from the US government's Center for Disease Control.
ⓦ **www.fitfortravel.scot.nhs.uk** From the Scottish NHS – travel-related diseases and how to avoid them.

ⓦ **www.istm.org** The International Society of Travel Medicine lists clinics, publishes outbreak warnings, suggests inoculations and precautions, and provides other background information.
ⓦ **www.tmvc.com.au** Lists all travellers' medical and vaccination centres in Australia and New Zealand, plus general information on travel health.
ⓦ **www.travelvax.net** Everything you probably didn't want to know about diseases and vaccines.

@ **www.tripprep.com** Comprehensive online database of necessary vaccinations for most countries, plus destination and medical service provider information.

@ **http://health.yahoo.com** Information and advice on specific diseases and conditions, drugs and herbal remedies.

In the UK and Ireland

British Airways Travel Clinics @ www .britishairways.com/travel/healthclinintro /public/en_gb: 213 Piccadilly, London W1J 9HQ (@ 0845/600 2236; walk-ins Mon–Fri 9.30am– 5.30pm, Sat 10am–3.30pm); 101 Cheapside, London EC2V 6DT (@ 0845/600 2236; by appointment, Mon–Fri 9am–4.30pm). Vaccinations and travel health care products.

Glasgow Travel Clinic 3rd floor, 90 Mitchell St, Glasgow G1 3NQ @ 0141/221 4224. Advice and vaccinations; walk-in clinics Wed–Fri 10am–6pm, otherwise by appointment .

Hospital for Tropical Diseases Travel Clinic 2nd floor, Mortimer Market Centre, off Capper St, London WC1E 6AU @ 020/7388 9600, @ www.masta.org. Mon–Fri 9am–5pm by appointment only; consultations £15, waived if you have your injections here.

Liverpool School of Tropical Medicine Pembroke Place, Liverpool L3 5QA @ 0151/708 9393, @ www.liv.ac.uk/lstm. Walk-in Mon–Fri 9am–noon, otherwise appointments .

Nomad Travel Stores and Medical Centres @ www.nomadtravel.co.uk: 3–4 Wellington Terrace, Turnpike Lane, London N8 0PX @ 020/8889 7014; 40 Bernard St, Russell Square, London WC1N 1LJ @ 020/7833 4114; Terminal House, 52 Grosvenor Gdns, Victoria, London SW1W 0AG @ 0207/823 5823; 43 Queens Rd, Clifton, Bristol BS8 1QH @ 0117/922 6567. Vaccinations, medication and equipment.

Travel Health Centre Department of International Health and Tropical Medicine, Royal College of Surgeons, Mercers Medical Centre, Stephen's St Lower, Dublin 2 @ 01/402 2337, @ www.mwhb.ie. Pre-trip advice and inoculations.

Travel Medicine Services 16 College St, Belfast BT1 6BT @ 028/9031 5220. Pre-trip medical advice and help afterwards.

Tropical Medical Bureau Grafton Buildings, 34 Grafton St, Dublin 2 @ 01/671 9200, plus thirteen other locations in Ireland; call @ 1850/487 674 or visit @ http://tmb.exodus.ie for details. Advice and vaccinations.

In the US and Canada

Canadian Society for International Health 1 Nicholas St, Suite 1105, Ottawa, ON K1N 7B7

Fleet Street Travel Clinic

29 Fleet Street, London EC4Y 1AA

020 7353 5678

www.travellershealth.com

❏ Africa specialists

❏ Yellow Fever centre

❏ Vaccines, malaria medicines, kits & supplies

❏ Post-travel healthcare

❏ Leading independent centre

❏ Official medical advisors to ATTA (The African Travel & Tourism Association)

Can't come to Fleet Street? - Read our book!

Travellers' Health:
How to stay healthy abroad

- Dr Richard Dawood

(Oxford University Press)

@ 1-613/241-5785, @ www.csih.org. Distributes a free pamphlet, *Health Information for Canadian Travelers*, containing an extensive list of travel health centres in Canada.

Centers for Disease Control 1600 Clifton Rd NE, Atlanta, GA 30333 @ 1-800/311-3435 or 404/639-3534, @ www.cdc.gov. Publishes outbreak warnings, suggested inoculations, precautions and other background information for travellers. Useful website plus International Travelers Hotline on @ 1-877/FYI-TRIP.

International SOS 3600 Horizon Blvd, Suite 300, Trevose, PA 19053, USA 19053-6956 @ 1-800/523-8930, @ www.intsos.com. Members receive pre-trip medical referral info, as well as overseas emergency services designed to complement travel insurance coverage.

MedjetAssist @ 1-800/963-3528, @ www .medjetassistance.com. Annual membership programme for travellers that, in the event of illness or injury, will fly members home or to the hospital of their choice in a medically equipped and staffed jet.

Travelers Medical Center 31 Washington Square, New York, NY 10011 @ 212/982-1600. A consultation service on immunizations and disease treatment.

In Australia and New Zealand

Travellers' Medical and Vaccination Centres
ⓦ www.tmvc.com.au: 27–29 Gilbert Place, Adelaide, SA 5000 ☎ 08/8212 7522; 1/170 Queen St, Auckland ☎ 09/373 3531; 5/247 Adelaide St, Brisbane, Qld 4000 ☎ 07/3221 9066; 5/8–10 Hobart Place, Canberra, ACT 2600 ☎ 02/6257 7156; 270 Sandy Bay Rd, Sandy Bay Tas, Hobart 7005 ☎ 03/6223 7577; 2/393 Little Bourke St, Melbourne, Vic 3000 ☎ 03/9602 5788; Level 7, Dymocks Bldg, 428 George St, Sydney, NSW 2000 ☎ 02/9221 7133; Shop 15, Grand Arcade, 14–16 Willis St, Wellington ☎ 04/473 0991. Vaccination, general travel health advice, and disease alerts; call ☎ 1-300/658 844 for details of travel clinics countrywide.

Inoculations

Whilst a **yellow fever vaccination certificate** is no longer required for entering Tanzania, if you're planning to visit other African countries except Kenya and Uganda, it would be wise to have a jab – and the certificate – just in case. Recommended inoculations are **typhoid** (the water supply of several towns is contaminated), **tetanus** and **polio** boosters, and **hepatitis A**. For the latter, Havrix is commonly prescribed – it lasts for ten years if you have a second, booster jab within six months. The much cheaper gamma-globulin (or immunoglobulin) shots are only effective for a few months, if at all. The series of **rabies** jabs is painful and cases of the disease are extremely rare. Start taking **malaria tablets** before departure (see below). In **Britain** your first source of advice and probable supplier of jabs and prescriptions is your GP. Family doctors are often well informed and are likely to charge you a (relatively low) flat fee for routine injections. However, for yellow fever and other exotic shots you'll normally have to visit a specialist clinic.

Malaria

Malaria is endemic in tropical Africa and accounts for at least one in seven deaths among children under five, and is the second-biggest cause of death amongst Tanzanian adults after HIV/AIDS. The disease, which is not infectious, is caused by a parasite carried in the saliva of female *Anopheles* **mosquitoes**, which tend to bite in the evening and at night. Malaria has a variable incubation period of a few days to several weeks, so you can develop the disease some time after you've been bitten. The destruction of red blood cells caused by the *Plasmodium falciparum* strain of malaria prevalent in East Africa can lead to **cerebral malaria** (blocking of the brain capillaries) and is also the cause of **blackwater fever**, in which the urine is stained by excreted blood cells. Malaria can be avoided by taking prophylactics and trying not to get bitten, although no method offers one hundred percent protection.

The disease is most prevalent in low-lying areas and around bodies of still water, meaning along the coast, on Zanzibar, around lakes and in areas of heavy banana cultivation, as the plants hold pools of stagnant water. The risk of contracting the disease decreases as you gain **altitude**, becoming minimal over 1400m and non-existent over 1800m. Unless you're spending an extended period in the northern or southern highlands, don't break your course of prophylactics, as it's vital to keep your parasite-fighting level as high as possible. The risk of infection increases during the rains, peaking in April.

Avoiding bites

The best way to avoid contracting malaria is to **avoid getting bitten**. You can greatly reduce bites by sleeping under a **mosquito net**, provided by virtually every hotel and guest house in the country, and by burning **mosquito coils**, which are readily available in Tanzania.

After dark, keep your limbs covered if there are mosquitoes, and consider using mosquito repellent. Most repellents contain **Deet** (diethyltoluamide), a nasty but effective oily substance that gets everywhere and corrodes most artificial materials, especially plastic (it's supposedly harmless to humans). If you're bringing a net, it's worth impregnating it with insecticide as well. If you don't like all this synthetic protection, natural alternatives based on **pyrethrum** flower-extract also work. Other repellents (which do not appear to have been clinically tested) are **citronella** or **lemongrass** oil; be careful: too much and you'll sting your face.

Prophylactics

Before leaving for Tanzania, get a course of **anti-malaria tablets**. They're freely available in the US, but require a prescription in the UK. Prophylactic drugs are rarely used by Tanzanians, though generic versions of all the main drugs are readily available in larger towns without prescription.

The cheapest and most-often prescribed drug is **mefloquine** (tradenames **Lariam** or Mephaquin), which can cause nasty psychological side effects ranging from mild depression and sleep disturbances to full-blown hallucinations and paranoia, together with mild bouts of nausea, dizziness and rashes. Mefloquine is unsuitable for pregnant women, people with liver or kidney problems, epileptics, or infants under 3 years. The dose is one 250mg tablet per week, starting two weeks before entering a malarial zone and continuing for at least two weeks after leaving. Test your reaction to the drug by taking it three rather than two weeks before departure. Some travellers report that side effects can be minimized by taking half a tablet at four-day intervals, though this hasn't been clinically tested. In Tanzania, a pack of four tablets costs under $10.

The antibiotic **doxycycline** (tradename Vibramycin) is recommended by some doctors, but the major side effect is that it causes an exaggerated sensitivity to sunlight in both skin and eyes, so use a strong sun cream. It can also cause thrush in women, reduces the effectiveness of contraceptive pills and is unsuitable for children or during pregnancy. Tablets are taken daily, starting one day before arrival and ending four weeks after you leave.

The newcomer to this inglorious pharmacopoeial collection is **Malarone**, a combination of atovaquone and proguanil. The known side effects are benign compared to the competition, and Malarone's newness means that no strains of malaria resistant to it have yet developed. In addition, you only need to start taking the tablets one day before entering a malarial zone, and for just seven days after. The disadvantage is that it costs a fortune, cannot be used by children, and should only be taken for a maximum of four weeks. It's extremely expensive locally, at upwards of $10 a tablet.

If you can't or won't take any of the above, a combination of **chloroquine** (2 weekly) and **proguanil** (2 daily) provides a modest level of protection, although chloroquine on its own is useless. Take the first pills a week before arriving, and the last four weeks after returning. The dose is best taken at the end of the day, and never on an empty stomach, or it will make you feel nauseous. Proguanil, bought locally, is expensive at around $0.50 a tablet; chloroquine is no longer sold in Tanzania.

Treatment

Common **symptoms** of malaria include waves of flu-like fever, shivering and headaches. Joint pain is also characteristic, and some people also have diarrhoea after the first week. If you think you've caught malaria, get to a doctor as soon as possible and have a **blood test** (note that using mefloquine as a prophylactic can lead to an inconclusive result). Most cures are based on **quinine**, found naturally in plants, but to avoid malarial parasites becoming resistant to it, pure quinine is only ever used in dire emergencies. Instead, there's a welter of competing remedies. **Sulfadoxine pyrimethamine (SP;** sold under various names including Fansidar, Malostat, Falcidin, Crodar, Laridox and Metakelfin), has long been used by Tanzanians. Severe side effects are rare, but you shouldn't take it if you're allergic to sulphur. An alternative treatment is **amodiaquine hydrochloride** (brand names: Basoquin, CAM-AQ1, Camoquin, Flavoquin, Fluroquine and Miaquin) – take 600mg to start, then 200mg after six hours, and 400mg daily on each of the two following days. Do not administer amodiaquine to children. **Malarone** (four tablets a day for three days) is also effective if you haven't been taking it as a prophylactic. An effective local remedy is a foul-tasting brew made from the quinine-rich leaves of the **muarabaini** tree.

All these treatments will leave you feeling very much under the weather: take plenty of fluids, and keep eating, but avoid milk-based products.

Sexually transmitted diseases

HIV is easily passed between people suffering relatively minor, but ulcerous, sexually transmitted diseases, and the prevalence of these is thought to account for the high incidence of heterosexually transmitted HIV: at least one in ten Tanzanians are infected. Areas along the Tanzam highway from Zambia to Dar es Salaam via Mbeya, Iringa and Morogoro, as well as tourist areas like Moshi and Arusha, are especially badly affected, with infection rates over twenty percent. Rates among prostitutes can top fifty percent. Standard advice is to avoid sexual contact or use **condoms**. A reliable local brand, sold in pharmacies throughout the country, is Salama.

Water and bugs

In most places the **tap water** is considered safe to drink by locals (exceptions, where known, are mentioned in the guide), though most tourists choose to give it a wide berth. If you're only staying a short time, it does make sense to be scrupulous, especially as locals happily quaffing tap water will have acquired some resistance to the most common bugs. So, for short trips, use either bottled or purified water (sold throughout Tanzania), or purify drinking water, easiest with iodine (four drops per litre), or – giving a vile taste – chlorine tablets. For longer stays, **re-educate your stomach** rather than fortifying it; it's virtually impossible to travel around the country without exposing yourself to strange bugs from time to time. Take it easy at first, don't overdo the fruit (and wash it in clean water) and be very wary of salads served in cheap restaurants, as well as the pre-cooked contents of their ubiquitous display cabinets. That said, the fruit and veg in most restaurants, even the cheapest, is generally perfectly fine.

Travellers' diarrhoea is the most common affliction, best weathered rather than blasted with antibiotics. Twenty-four hours of sweet, black tea and nothing else may rinse it out. The important thing is to replace your fluids. Make it easier on your body by sipping a **rehydration mix**: four heaped teaspoons of sugar or honey and half a teaspoon of salt in a litre of water. Commercial rehydration remedies contain much the same, and flat Coca-Cola is quite a good tonic, too. Avoid coffee, strong fruit juice and alcohol. Most upsets resolve themselves after two or

three days. If you continue to feel bad, see a doctor. If you have to travel a long distance, any pharmacy should have anti-diarrhoeal remedies, but these shouldn't be overused. Avoid jumping for **antibiotics** at the first sign of trouble: they annihilate your gut flora (most of which you want to keep), don't work on viruses, and may result in long-term bacterial disequilibrium in your digestive system.

If you catch **giardia** (from water polluted with faecal matter) you'll know – apart from making you feel generally ill and drowsy, it makes you pass wind – from both ends of your body – that smells worse than a sewer. The bug generally works itself out after two or three days, but may recur a few weeks after. The definitive treatment for it, and **amoebic dysentery**, is **metronizadole** (tradename Flagyl).

You're most unlikely to catch **cholera**, although isolated outbreaks – affecting a few dozen to a hundred people a year – are a regular occurrence, usually coinciding with heavy rains when flooding can mix sewage with drinking water. Areas lacking basic sanitation and sewerage systems are most at risk. The cholera **vaccine** is ineffective. The symptoms are fever and chronic diarrhoea; most attacks are relatively mild, and clear up naturally after a few days, but if left untreated the sudden and severe dehydration caused by the disease can be fatal. **Treatment** is simple: lots of oral rehydration therapy (salt and sugar in water; as above) or, in severe cases, rehydration fluid administered through a drip. Antibiotics (usually tetracycline or doxycycline) can also help, but are not essential.

Injuries, bites and stings

Take more care than usual over minor **cuts and scrapes**. In the tropics, the most trivial scratch can quickly become a throbbing infection if you ignore it. Take a small tube of antiseptic with you, or apply alcohol or iodine.

Otherwise, there are potentially all sorts of bites, stings and rashes which rarely, if ever, materialize. **Dogs** are usually sad and skulking, posing little threat. **Scorpions and spiders** abound but are hardly ever seen unless you deliberately turn over rocks or logs: scorpion stings are painful but almost

Medicine bag

There's no need to take a mass of drugs and remedies you'll probably never use, and can buy in Tanzania's larger towns in any case. Various items, however, are worth buying in advance, especially on a longer trip.

Alcohol swabs For cleaning wounds and infections.

Antibiotics Given the often disease-specific recommendations for the dozens of antibiotics out there, buying a course beforehand isn't recommended unless you're allergic to penicillin, in which case ask your doctor for a general-purpose "broad spectrum" course.

Antihistamine cream To treat insect bites. Or simply spread toothpaste on the bite. You heard it here first.

Antiseptic cream Avoid metal tubes – they risk springing leaks. Mercurochrome or iodine liquid also work but dye wounds brown or red.

Aspirin Mild pain, inflammation and fever relief. Not to be taken if you're prone to bleed easily, as it thins the blood.

Codeine phosphate Emergency anti-diarrhoeal pill, in some countries only on prescription. Loperamide (tradename Imodium) is also useful.

Iodine tincture or water-purifying tablets The chlorine-based tablets make water taste horrific; iodine is quite delicious by comparison, much cheaper, and can also be used to disinfect wounds and keep fungal infections in check. Some people are allergic to chlorine, others to iodine (especially if seafood gets to you); neither are recommended for long-term use.

Lip-salve/chapstick.

Natural alternatives You can avoid some of the other stuff in this list with the following natural products: tea tree oil (fungicide and disinfectant); fresh garlic (natural antibiotic and vampiricide when taken daily); menthol-and-camphor-based essential oil (eg Olbas oil; for colds, relieving headaches, and aromatic pick-me-up); olive oil (for keeping skin trim).

Sticking plaster (fabric rather than synthetic, as it sticks better and also lets the wound breathe), steri-strip wound closures, sterile gauze dressing, micropore tape.

Zinc oxide powder Useful anti-fungal.

never fatal (clean the wound and pack with ice to slow down the spread of the venom), while spiders are mostly quite harmless. **Snakes** are common, but again, the vast majority are harmless. To see one at all, you'd need to search stealthily; walk heavily and most species obligingly disappear. Victims of snake bites should be hospitalized as quickly as possible in case the bite is venomous , but whatever you do don't panic: more snake bite deaths are caused by shock rather than the venom itself. Venomous snake bites are usually treated with hydrocortisone and an anti-inflammatory and, in an emergency, with adrenaline injections. Local medicine, especially *jiwe ya punju* ("snake bite medicine stone"), apparently works very well if applied to the wound immediately after the bite as it sucks up moisture and, hence, the venom; you can buy it in markets everywhere. Another local remedy, from the bark of a shrub, is called *mkingiri*.

Stings from sponges, corals, fish (including catfish) and **jellyfish** can usually be treated with vinegar, or sometimes tiger balm. Don't use alcohol to treat the wound. For stings from cone shells (which have neurotoxic darts), immobilize the limb, apply a non-constrictive compress, and seek medical attention immediately. Spines from sea urchins, crown of thorns starfish, stingrays and surgeonfish are treated by applying scalding water (just under 50°C) to break down the poison.

Other complaints

Bilharzia (schistosomiasis) is a dangerous but curable disease which comes from tiny flukes (schistosomes) that live in freshwater snails and which, as part of their life cycle, leave their hosts and burrow into animal (or human) skin to multiply in the bloodstream. The symptoms are difficult to diagnose properly: a rash or itchy skin appears a few days after infection, and you may also feel severe fatigue and pass blood. After that you won't experience any further symptoms until a month or two later, when fever, chills, coughs and muscle aches may kick in. If left untreated, internal organs including the liver, intestines, lungs and bladder can be permanently damaged, and paralysis is also known, although all these effects are thankfully rare. The snails only favour stagnant water, and the chances of picking up bilharzia are small. The usual recommendation is never to swim in, wash with, or even touch, fresh lake water that can't be vouched for. Sea water is fine, as are well-maintained swimming pools.

Fungal infections can be avoided by not using used soap in cheap hotels, or towels if unwashed, badly washed or still damp. Antifungal cream is the best treatment for infections; alternatively, douse affected skin in iodine, though this will likely only keep the infection in check, not eliminate it. Many people get occasional **heat rashes**, especially at first on the coast, particularly between December and March. A warm shower (to open the pores) and cotton clothes should help. It's important not to overdose on **sunshine** in the first week or two. The powerful heat and bright light can mess up your system, and a hat and sunglasses are strongly recommended. Some people **sweat** heavily and lose a lot of salt. If this applies to you, sprinkle extra salt on your food.

To alleviate **sunburn**, aloe vera cream, calamine lotion, yoghurt, or a mixture of olive oil and lemon juice helps. **Coral ear** – an inflammation of the ear canal and tympanic membrane – is treated with antibiotic drops or an antiseptic solution.

One critter you might catch is a **jigger**, being the pupa of a fly that likes to burrow into your toes. More horrible than it sounds, this is best treated by physically removing all of the bug, and then repeatedly dousing the cavity left with iodine or other disinfectant. The cavity should heal itself in three or four days.

Finally, make sure you get a thorough **dental check-up** before leaving home, and take extra care of your teeth while in Tanzania. Stringy meat, acidic fruit and sugary tea are some of the hazards. There are reliable dentists in Arusha, Dar es Salaam, Dodoma and Stone Town. For **acute toothache**, the antibiotic Ampicillin works well, plus paracetamol for pain. Diclofenac helps reduce swellings. If you have a history of tooth inflammation or a dodgy tooth take a course of the analgesic and anti-inflammatory nimesulida (tradename Aulin) with you.

Money and costs

Tanzania's currency is the shilling (abbreviated to "Tsh"). Kiswahili words for money are colonial legacies: pesa (from Portuguese), hela (from German times) and bob (from the Brits). Cash comes in denominations of Tsh500, 1000, 2000, 5000 and 10,000 banknotes, and Tsh5, 10, 20, 50, 100 and 200 coins. Exchange rates have depreciated steadily over the years, to your advantage. At the end of 2005, exchange rates were: £1 to Tsh2000 (up from Tsh1300 in 2002), $1 to Tsh1100 (Tsh900 in 2002), €1 to Tsh1350, C$1 to Tsh900, A$1 to Tsh850, and NZ$1 to Tsh750. For the latest rates, see the Bank of Tanzania's website, Ⓦ www.bot-tz.org.

For most **tourist services** – such as mid-range and upmarket hotels, safaris, park entry fees and some ferry fares – tourists are quoted "non-resident" rates in dollars, often substantially more than the "resident" rates paid by locals. Try to think of it as positive discrimination rather than the daylight robbery it too often feels like. Excepting park entry fees and the Lake Tanganyika ferry, dollar prices can be paid for in shilling equivalent, albeit at inferior rates of exchange. Throughout this guide we've given prices in whichever currency they've been quoted in.

Average costs

Tanzania can be very expensive if you want to rent a car or go on safari, and very cheap if you don't, especially if you avoid staying too long in the main tourist areas of Dar es Salaam, Arusha and (particularly) Zanzibar, where even "budget" accommodation starts at $20 a night for a double. On the mainland, solo budget travellers can scrape by on around $15 a day, while couples can survive on even less. For $20–50 a day you can stay in good hotels and enjoy a few luxuries, whilst for upmarket travellers the sky really is the limit – if you really want to part from your cash as quickly as possible you'll even find a few hotels charging over $1000 a night.

Obviously, activities like hiking, snorkelling, scuba-diving and safaris, will significantly hike up your budget. For a standard budget camping **safari**, count on a minimum of $85–100 per person per day. Mid-range camping or lodge safaris go for between $120 and $200 per person per day, and top-end trips range from $250 up to $600 a day. A day's **scuba-diving** costs around $70–100 per person, whilst a four-day Open Water diving course averages $350–400 (not including accommodation).

Getting around by **bus and daladala** is very cheap (rarely more than Tsh1000 for an hour's journey). Unfortunately, they can't drive you around the game parks, and **renting a vehicle** – and paying for fuel – will add around $100–200 a day to your costs (or $50–70 on Zanzibar), though this isn't so cripplingly expensive if shared between two or more people.

With the exception of food, most things in Tanzania are **bargainable**, especially anything that a tourist might want – like accommodation, safaris and souvenirs.

Youth and student discounts

The various **student/youth ID cards** may get you reductions on flights, but won't get you discounts in Tanzania, and there are no student rates for park entry fees, accommodation or transport either. Full-time students are eligible for the **International Student ID Card** (**ISIC**, ⓦ www.isiccard.com); for Americans it also comes with up to $3000 in emergency medical coverage and $100 a day for 60 days in hospital, plus a 24-hour emergency hotline. The card costs $22 in the USA; C$16 in Canada; A$18 in Australia; NZ$20 in New Zealand; £7 in the UK; and €13 in the Republic of Ireland. The **International Youth Travel Card**, available to anyone aged 26 or under, costs the same.

What to take

It's wise not to rely on one source of money alone: take along a mixture of dollars in cash, dollars or sterling travellers' cheques, and a Visa or MasterCard with PIN number for fast withdrawals from ATMs, or for use in emergencies. **US dollar** banknotes are widely accepted and generally rapidly changed. $100 denominations attract better rates, but **$500 bills and old-style notes** may be refused, given the risk of forgery. **Sterling** and **Euro** cash is less widely accepted, and given that most tourist services are priced in dollars, you'll lose out on the conversion. Try to avoid carrying mainly Tsh10,000 notes outside tourist areas, as they're difficult to change in small villages.

Travellers' cheques

Travellers' cheques are the safest way to carry money, and the lower exchange rates you'll get for changing them (compared to cash) are the price you pay for peace of mind. American Express and Thomas Cook travellers' cheques are widely accepted by banks, at most foreign exchange bureaux, and for payment at the larger and more expensive hotels. The best rates tend to be for **US dollar** cheques, for which the equivalent cash rates differ least. When changing travellers' cheques, you'll need to show your passport and the **purchase receipt** you received when you bought the cheques (the one that includes the cheques' serial numbers). The importance of keeping your receipt in a safe place and in a legible state cannot be overstated; make photocopies and stash them away. In the event that cheques are lost or stolen, the issuing company will expect you to report the loss immediately – details are given when you buy the cheques; both American Express and Thomas Cook claim to replace lost or stolen cheques within 24 hours.

Credit cards and ATMs

Whilst it's theoretically feasible to use only **credit cards** while on holiday in Tanzania (for direct payments and, more usefully, in ATMs for cash advances), blips in the system – whether local or back home – mean that plastic should definitely not relied on as your primary means of accessing money. That said, by far the easiest means of getting cash (shillings) on a credit card is through one of the **24hr ATMs** run by NBC bank at over thirty branches nationwide, and which accept international Visa and MasterCard as long as you have the PIN number. Other banks with similarly enabled ATMs include Barclays (Dar es Salaam, Arusha and Stone Town), and Standard Chartered (Dar es Salaam, Arusha, Moshi and Mwanza). The maximum daily withdrawal is Tsh400,000, approximately $400. **Security** isn't much of a concern if you're using ATMs as most are either inside the bank, or in individual cubicles guarded by *askaris* (security guards). If you're overly worried, get a friend to come along and look out for you. The **additional costs** charged by your card supplier for ATM withdrawals should be no more than £2–3/$3–4 on a £200/$300 withdrawal – assuming, of course, that you've set up a monthly standing order to cover monthly charges and interest repayments.

Over-the-counter **cash advances** through the banks mentioned above are possible, if for some reason your PIN doesn't work, as long as your account has not been blocked. You can usually withdraw up to your card limit, although large transactions may entail an interrogation to screen for potential fraud, and note that your credit card company will charge you for the service: anything up to four percent including a "conversion fee" included in the exchange rate.

Direct payments using Visa, MasterCard, JCB or Diners Club for tourist services such as upmarket accommodation and restaurants, flights, safaris and car rental, are not always accepted, but when they are, will attract a premium of five to ten percent. American Express users often pay an additional fee. **To avoid abuse**: if you're in shillings, make sure that the voucher specifies the currency before you sign. In addition, fill in any empty boxes on the slip with zeroes, and be especially careful not to let the card leave your sight to ensure that only one slip is filled in.

A compromise between travellers' cheques and plastic is **Visa TravelMoney**, a disposable pre-paid debit card with a PIN that works in all ATMs that take Visa cards. You load up your account with funds before leaving home, and when they run out, you simply throw the card away. You can buy up to nine cards to access the same funds – useful for couples or families travelling together – and it's a good idea to buy at least one extra as a back-up in case of loss or theft. The card is available in most countries from branches of Travelex (@ cardservices@travelex.com), or from North America via calling ☎1-877/394-2247. For more information, see ⊛http://international .visa.com/ps/products/vtravelmoney.

Changing money

You can **exchange hard currencies** in cash or travellers' cheques at banks and foreign exchange bureaux ("forex") all over the country, at the international airports, and at most large hotels (though at substantially poorer rates). In theory you should keep exchange receipts until you leave the country, though they're rarely – if ever – asked for. **Do not change money on the street**, whether in a city or at border crossings: there's no need for a black market, and you're guaranteed to get swindled. Banks pay far better rates than foreign exchange bureaux, but the downside is that transactions can take an hour or more. **Exchange rates** are pretty uniform across the country, the main exception being Zanzibar, where you'll receive ten to fifteen percent less for your money than elsewhere.

Branches of **banks** in major towns and cities are usually open Monday to Friday 8.30am to 4pm and Saturday 8.30am to 1pm. Rural branches open Monday to Friday from 8.30am to 12.30pm and Saturday from 8.30 to 10.30am. Always ask first what commission and charges will be deducted, as they vary mysteriously even within branches of the same company (you shouldn't pay more than 2 percent). Virtually every town will have a branch of NBC, NMB or CRDB. NBC is by far the least inefficient, averaging 30–45 minutes to complete a transaction, and most of its branches have ATMs that accept international Visa cards. NMB is popular with farmers, so the queues can be long. CRDB is best avoided. Arusha, Dar and one or two other places also have branches of Stanbic and Standard Chartered: they're fast, but you'll lose out commission-wise .

Forex bureaux (usually Mon–Fri 9am–4.30pm, Sat 9am–noon or later, occasionally Sun mornings) in Arusha, Dar es Salaam, Moshi and Zanzibar are fast and convenient, usually taking little more than five minutes and rarely charging commission or other fees, but their exchange rates are lower than those in banks, and not all will change travellers' cheques – and if they do, the rate may be five to ten percent less than for cash.

Money transfers

Wiring funds to Tanzania is never convenient or cheap, and should be considered a last resort. Funds sent via **Western Union**

(US and Canada ☎1-800/CALL-CASH, Australia ☎1800/501 500, New Zealand ☎0800/005 253, UK ☎0800/833 833, Republic of Ireland ☎1800 395 395, ⓦwww.westernunion.com; customers in the US and Canada can send money online) can be picked up at any branch of the Tanzania Postal Bank, which are usually found in or combined with the post offices of even small towns. **MoneyGram** (US ☎1-800/444-3010, Canada ☎1-800/933-3278, UK, Ireland and New Zealand ☎00800/6663 9472, Australia ☎1800/6663 9472, ⓦwww.moneygram.com) funds can be collected at the National Bureau de Change on Samora Avenue in Dar es Salaam, and at a handful of offices elsewhere. It's also possible to have money **wired from a bank** in your home country to a bank in Tanzania, although this is distinctly unreliable. If you use this route, your home bank will need the address of the branch bank where you want to pick up the money and the address and telex number of the head office in Dar es Salaam, which will act as the clearing house; money wired this way normally takes two working days to arrive, and costs around £25, $40, C$54, A$52, or NZ$59 per transaction.

Getting around

The usual way of getting around Tanzania is by bus. Though they can be slow, uncomfortable and driven with breathtaking lack of road sense, they reach pretty much every part of the country, and are a good way of mixing with the locals. Alternatively, two railway lines cross the country, both originating in Dar: one runs south via Mbeya to New Kapiri Mposhi in Zambia, and the other heads west to Kigoma and Mwanza via Tabora. Lakes Victoria, Tanganyika and Nyasa all have ferry services. On the coast, ferries connect Dar es Salaam to both Unguja and Pemba on Zanzibar, and to Mtwara in the far south; there may also be ferries from Tanga to Zanzibar Air travel is a relatively affordable option if you're in a hurry.

Tanzania's main asphalt artery is the **Tanzam Highway**, which runs across the country from Zambia though Mbeya, Iringa, and Morogoro to Dar es Salaam, and then up to Tanga, Moshi and Arusha. Apart from

this, however, Tanzania's **roads** are in a pitiful state, some becoming impassable in the rains, which are heaviest from March to May. We've given descriptions of road conditions throughout the guide, but be aware that conditions can change radically after particularly heavy rains, and another El Niño – which in East Africa generally leads to catastrophic flooding and washed-out roads – is due any time.

Whether you're travelling by bus or driving, you'll quickly appreciate the reality behind Tanzania's abysmal **road safety record**, one that would be much worse were there any more surfaced roads. The main causes of accidents are speeding and reckless driving (encouraged by irresponsible timetables). The most **dangerous routes** are from Arusha to Moshi, and along the Tanzam Highway south of Iringa, especially down to Songea.

Buses, minibuses and pick-ups

For most Tanzanians, buses, minibuses ("Coasters" or smaller daladalas) and pick-ups are the normal way around, getting you close to almost anywhere you might want to go. All are prohibited from travelling between 10pm and 4am because of the risk of accidents and (very rare) attacks from bandits, so if you're on a long-distance bus that gets delayed, expect to sleep in your seat or in a local guest house before arriving the following day. Given the country's appalling road safety record, **safety** is a nagging concern, especially on fast sealed roads: always seek unbiased local advice before buying a ticket, but be aware that for some people "the best bus" is the fastest, not necessarily the safest. If you're really worried, you could try to minimize the damage in the event of an accident by sitting in the middle of the vehicle, and away from the windows. Head-on collisions while overtaking , and catastrophic rolls are the main causes of fatalities, with suicidal driving being the main culprit The main routes are served by **buses** that generally leave on time (6am is the norm). The better and more expensive ones don't allow standing passengers and may benefit from slightly saner drivers. The safest company overall is Scandinavian Express (though even they have been known to speed), which covers the entire surfaced road network but nothing off it. You can book online at Ⓦwww .scandinaviagroup.com. Other recommended companies, and **companies to avoid**, are mentioned throughout the guide in the "Moving on" sections. Except for some Scandinavian Express coaches, most buses lack **toilets** – instead, buses stop every few hours for passengers to scurry into the bush to relieve themselves (empty your bowels and bladder before setting off). You don't have to bring mountains of food for the journey: there's plenty available from hawkers at bus stations and villages, and long-distance buses also stop for lunch at a roadside restaurant.

Public vehicles at the smaller end of the spectrum have a similarly gruesome safety record; this is especially true of **minibuses** along main routes, most notoriously between Arusha and Moshi, where fatal crashes are common. In very rural areas, where roads are frequently in a terrible state, transport may be by **pick-up**, often Land Rovers ("one tens") or open-backed pick-up trucks. These, and all road transport on unsurfaced roads tend to be extremely **crowded**, deeply uncomfortable on bottoms and liable to mechanical failure, which is why they also carry their own mechanics (*fundis*). Despite this, they can be an enjoyable way of getting about, giving you close contact – literally – with local people, and often providing the only means of getting off the beaten track.

Most buses and minibuses depart from a central **bus stand** (bus station), which is

Drugging

Long a problem in Kenya, the drugging of bus passengers in order to rob them has occasionally been reported in Tanzania. The ruse involves someone befriending a traveller and then offering food, drink or cigarettes laced with knock-out drugs. By the time victims wake up, their luggage, money and other valuables will have disappeared. The simple way to avoid falling victim is not to accept such gifts from strangers, even if this might offend. You should also take care on ferries and trains, where the same trick might be used.

usually where the ticket offices are located; exceptions, and stands for pick-ups if different, are noted in the guide. On less-travelled routes, or for seats with safer companies along surfaced roads, you generally need to **reserve seats** a day or two in advance (and arrive at least thirty minutes before departure, or you may find your seat gets sold to someone else). **Tickets** normally have seat numbers indicated (on the bus, marked on the *back* of the seats they refer to). When choosing your seat, it's worth considering which side will be shadier, since the combination of a slow, bumpy ride, dust and fierce sun can be trying (remember that in the southern hemisphere, the sun travels in the northern half of the sky). On rough roads, choose a seat in the middle or front of the bus – away from the axles – to avoid the worst of the bumps.

Fares are Tsh1000–2000 for an hour's travel, depending on the route and standard of service. As a tourist you may be overcharged a little, but no more than a local who doesn't know the price either. Baggage charges aren't normally levied unless you're transporting commercial goods, though plenty of touts will try and convince you otherwise. For pick-ups, passengers should only pay some time after the journey has begun. This isn't a question of being ripped off but too often the first departure is just a cruise around town rounding up passengers and buying petrol (with your money) and then back to square one – a rigmarole which could go on for hours.

Hitching

Hitch hiking is not recommended, especially for lone female travellers, but may be unavoidable in more remote areas. Beckon the driver to stop with your whole arm; a modest thumb is more likely to be interpreted as a friendly, or even rude, gesture than a request for a lift. If you do hitch, expect to pay.

Urban transport: daladalas and taxis

Daladalas (usually battered Toyota Hiace minivans) are the standard way of getting around large towns. Fares are Tsh200 for a short journey, which can be up to 10km. Daladalas run along pre-determined routes, often – but not always – colour-coded, with destinations marked on the fronts of vehicles. Daladalas have the advantage of being plentiful and reasonably quick; the downside is that they can get amazingly crowded; 25 people in a vehicle with just twelve seats is common. When boarding a vehicle at a **daladala stand**, choose a vehicle that's full and about to leave, or you'll have to wait inside until they are ready to go. Competition is intense and people will lie unashamedly to persuade you the vehicle is going "just now".

Rather more comfortable are **taxis**, which are also the only safe way of getting around at night. They lack meters, so settle on a fare before getting in. A ride around town averages Tsh2000, sometimes less, though drivers will invariably try for more – haggle hard and, if you get nowhere, try another, but bear in mind that drivers rarely own their cars and pay a hefty slice of the day's takings to the owner.

Car rental

Renting a car has definite advantages: most of Tanzania's wildlife parks are open to privately rented vehicles, and there's a lot to be said for the freedom of having your own wheels. There are plenty of **car rental companies** in Dar, Arusha, Mwanza and Stone Town, and one or two in Morogoro, Moshi and Karatu. Tanzania's only multinational franchises – Avis and Hertz, both in both Dar and Arusha – are

Buying a second-hand car

With 4WD hire averaging $3000 per month, if you're going to be in Tanzania for some time, buying a second-hand vehicle in Arusha or Dar es Salaam is a possibility, though prices are inflated and you'll need to be mechanically confident. Rental companies sometimes have vehicles to dispose of, and the *Advertising in Dar* freesheet (that you can also find in Arusha, and on the Internet at Ⓦ www.advertisingdar.co.tz) carries classifieds. A used Land Rover 110 TDI in good condition shouldn't be more than $5000; you should be able to sell it at the end for little less than you paid.

pricey and capable of rolling out some real clunkers. Given Tanzania's awful roads, most companies insist you hire a **driver** as well – no bad thing, as they tend to double as safari guides with the unerring ability to spot things like a leopard's tail dangling from a tree a mile away. You may have to leave a hefty deposit, roughly equivalent to the anticipated bill. Credit cards are useful for this, but you'll need to trust the company. Much easier, if you just need an ordinary saloon for a day or two, is to rent a **taxi**: Tsh40,000–60,000 for a full day is reasonable depending on the distance covered. Bear in mind that most taxis are battered old saloons and, although there's little left to break, rough roads are not exactly their forté. For entering the **national parks**, any company offering a rental vehicle driven by a Tanzanian but mostly occupied by tourists officially needs a valid TALA safari licence – we've mentioned this in our rental company reviews, but do check it out before booking.

Choosing a vehicle

Off tarred roads, **high clearance** is useful, thanks to the dire state of many roads, even in dry weather. A **four-wheel-drive (4WD)** is essential for wildlife parks, mountainous areas and on minor roads during the long rains. **Land Rovers** and **Toyota Land Cruisers** are the most widely available 4WDs. Most mechanics – even in the middle of nowhere – are perfectly at ease with diesel-powered Land Rovers; Land Cruisers and petrol engines are trickier. Land Rovers use less fuel, and their springs are easier to repair than a Land Cruiser's coils; the newer Land Rovers, like the 110 series, also have Turbo Direct Injection (TDI), which gives more power and makes them more economical on surfaced roads. One of two rental companies still have diminutive **Suzuki jeeps**, which are light, rugged and capable of amazing feats. Don't expect them to top more than their legal limit of 80kph, however, and beware of their notorious tendency to fall over on bends or the dangerously sloping gravel hard shoulders that line many roads.

Costs

Hiring a decent **4WD with driver** averages $100–120 per day from Dar es Salaam and $130 from Arusha, including 100–120km free mileage. **Self-drive** isn't necessarily any cheaper: the saving on not paying a driver (usually $15 a day) is offset by having to pay insurance premiums. Saloon cars, for use within cities, towns and on sealed roads, cost around $70 a day self-drive, or $50–60 on Zanzibar. Rates are always cheaper by the week, and many firms are prepared to negotiate a little as well, especially off-season.

When given quotes, allow for VAT (nineteen percent) if not included, and always read the small print; check whether the driver's daily allowance is included, and – especially – **insurance** arrangements when self-driving. Always pay the daily collision damage waiver (CDW) premium: even a small bump could be very costly otherwise. Theft protection waiver (TPW) should also be taken. However, even with these, you'll still be liable for **excess liability** (anything from $500 to $3000) if you total the car, though if the accident was not your fault you shouldn't have to pay anything. Some companies are distinctly cagey about setting these terms out in black-and-white – as a rule of thumb, high excess liability is the trademark of dodgy companies hoping for punters to crash so they can earn some quick cash.

Fuel is available everywhere except the very smallest villages, and also along major highways, though it's worth filling up before heading out on a long drive. Fuel gets more expensive the further inland or away from a major town you get. In Tanga and Dar es Salaam, diesel costs Tsh1000 ($0.90) a litre and petrol Tsh1100 ($1); in some of the national parks, you'll pay over Tsh1600, though as global oil prices continue to rise, it's likely these prices will be history by the time you read this. You should get 10–14km per litre out of a Land Rover TDI, depending on its condition, less in a Land Cruiser. If you're intending to do a lot of driving in remote areas you should carry spare fuel in cans.

Before setting off

Don't automatically assume your rental vehicle is roadworthy: **check out the vehicle** before signing anything, and insist on a test drive – it's amazing how many vehicles "fresh from the mechanic" have weak brakes, dodgy clutches, leaky radiators or wobbly wheels. Things to check include wheel tread, a full complement of wheel nuts (many cars have wheels held on with only two or three) and cracks in the gearbox and engine mounts (you'll have to get under the car to check this). The vehicle should also have at least one spare tyre (with good tread and no punctures), preferably two, also a spanner that fits *all* the wheel nuts, and a jack.

If you're planning to spend any time off surfaced roads, the carburettor intake has to be close to roof height to avoid clogging things up with splashed mud or dust; most safari vehicles are customized with a "snorkel" for this purpose. A working mileometer is also helpful even if you're not paying by the kilometre, as navigating using map distances is often the only way to avoid missed turnings.

Other items you should carry, certainly for longer drives, are a shovel for digging your way out of mud or sand, a machete (*panga*), small bottles of engine oil and brake fluid (which can also be used as clutch fluid), a spare fan belt and possibly brake pads, tow rope, spare fuel and plenty of drinking water. Finally, try if you can to stay close to the place you rented the car from for the first day and night, as the first day's drive will give you a chance to spot any mechanical problems without the hassle of being miles from anywhere.

Regulations and fines

Officially, traffic drives on the left, although on rough roads you'll find people driving on whichever side of the road has fewer potholes (or mud pools in the rains). The **speed limit** is 50kph in populated areas and between 80kph and 120kph on major highways. Tourist drivers must be between 25 and 70 years old and have held a licence for at least two years. Zanzibar requires a valid **international driving licence** which must be endorsed by the police on arrival. If you don't have one, a temporary fifteen-day permit can be obtained on production of your national licence and a small fee. On the mainland, an international driving licence is recommended but not legally required. When driving, police may ask for a **PSV (passenger service**

vehicle) licence, which is usually displayed in one of the windows of rental vehicles. Some PSV certificates restrict the vehicle's movements to a particular region, and this will leave you open to an array of spot fines should you stray outside the region(s) on the permit. Check this out with the company before you leave.

Police checkpoints are generally marked by low strips of spikes across the road with just enough room to slalom round. Always slow down, and stop if signalled; on Zanzibar, always stop outside a police station until waved on. If you're pulled over, the usual reason given is that you were speeding, although Tanzania's notoriously corrupt cops are quite capable of finding something, anything, wrong with your car (broken wing mirror, flat spare tyre) so that they can fine you. Tourists are not immune. Do not, under any account, let them keep your passport or driving licence, as it gives them a most unfair advantage when negotiating a fine. **Spot fines** should be Tsh20,000, less if you're happy foregoing the official receipt (ie a bribe). This might reduce the fine to a few thousand shillings but is of course illegal.

Incidentally, the barriers slung across roads outside smaller towns and villages are maintained by local authorities for the purpose of extracting taxes from commercial vehicles. You should be let through without any payment

Driving hazards and etiquette

When driving, **expect the unexpected**: rocks, ditches, potholes, animals and people on the road, as well as lunatic drivers. It's accepted practice to honk your horn

Motoring organizations

Australia AAA ☎ 02/6247 7311, ⓦ www .aaa.asn.au.
Canada CAA ☎ 613/247-0117, ⓦ www .caa.ca.
Ireland AA ☎ 01/617 9999, ⓦ www .aaireland.ie.
New Zealand AA ☎ 0800/500 444, ⓦ www .nzaa.co.nz.
UK AA ☎ 0870/600 0371, ⓦ www.theaa.com; RAC ☎ 0800/550 055, ⓦ www.rac.co.uk.
US AAA ☎ 1-800/AAA-HELP, ⓦ www.aaa.com.

Tips and tricks for rough roads

Rough roads should be treated with respect and patience. Driving in the dry season is rarely too difficult, and following the most worn vehicle tracks should see you through without any problems. Driving in the rains, however, is a challenge that you'll either love or hate. The following tips should come in useful.

First off, know that **low range 4WD** is for steep inclines, whilst high range (if 4WD can't be disengaged completely) is for normal conditions. Driving on **loose sand and mud**, keep your speed down to minimize skidding and give yourself more time to deal with a skid if your car loses traction. On a consistently slippery surface your steering needs constant play to avoid sliding. In other words, even if you're driving in a straight line, repeatedly move the steering wheel a small distance left and right – you'll feel the increased traction between the ground and the wheels (though obviously, too much play and the car will begin lurching). If you do start sliding to one side, try to avoid the natural reaction of steering in the opposite direction; instead, steer briefly in the direction of the slide to bring the car back under control, then gradually steer the car back to its correct course. If you do inadvertently steer in the opposite direction, be ready to turn the wheel back abruptly when the car regains traction or you risk spinning out of control or ricocheting in the opposite direction. Deflating tyres a bit can also help, though this is a pain if you then have to drive 200km to the nearest foot pump.

Whereas slippery roads are mentally tiring over long distances, the art of crossing **mud pools** offers a more immediately nerve-wracking experience. First off, get out of the car and use a stick (or your feet) to gauge the depth. If the depth is less than about 50cm you should be fine (if it's more than that and you're inexperienced, turn back, as there might be worse to come). The usual rule is to make a line straight through the centre, as the surface under the water is more likely to be firm and settled than at the edges, which can get treacherously muddy. If there are tyre tracks, your best bet is to follow them both into and out of the pool. The crossing itself is easiest in second gear at a slow but steady speed (too fast and you'll drench the car in mud). Some drivers recommend first gear, but the disadvantage is that you risk getting stuck much faster should you run into difficulty (spinning wheels when you're stuck just gets you stuck even more). For deeper or muddier pools, engage 4WD first.

The most treacherous of wet season driving hazards is **black cotton soil**, called *kindiga* in Kiswahili (areas of *kindiga* are called *mbuga*). *Kindiga* quickly becomes waterlogged and has little traction, forming a perilous trap which should be completely avoided in the rains. If you have no choice, a combination of the techniques described above might help you through. The problem is that at low speed the vehicle may lack the momentum to get through particularly tricky sections, whilst at higher speed you run the risk of losing control and ending up in a ditch.

If you do get stuck and aren't completely off the beaten track, the next lorry along should be able to haul you out. Local villagers may also be willing to help you out, whether from the goodness of their hearts or (more likely) the prospect of payment.

stridently to warn pedestrians and cyclists of your approach. Beware also of **speed bumps**. These are sometimes signposted, but more usually the first you'll know of them is when your head hits the roof. They are found both in rural areas, wherever a busy road has been built through a village, and on the roads in and out of nearly every large town. **Be especially wary of buses** – which seldom slow down for anything – and also be careful when overtaking heavy vehicles, even more so when passing lorries groaning uphill: sometimes a line of them churning out diesel fumes can cut off your visibility without warning – extremely dangerous on a narrow mountain road. Avoid **driving after dark**, but if you must, be alert for stopped vehicles without lights or hazard warnings, and also for one-eyed vehicles: when what looks like a motorbike suddenly turns into a truck at full speed.

It's common practice to flash oncoming vehicles, especially if they're leaving you little room or their headlights are blinding you, and to signal right to indicate your width and deter drivers behind you from overtaking. Left-hand signals are used to say "Please overtake" – but don't assume that a driver in front who signals you to overtake can really see whether the road ahead is clear.

If you **break down** or have an accident, the first thing to do is pile bundles of sticks or foliage at fifty-metre intervals behind and in front of your car. These are the red warning triangles of Africa, and their placing is always scrupulously observed (as is the wedging of a stone behind at least one wheel). When you have a puncture, get it mended straight away so that you're never without a spare tyre – it's very cheap (Tsh500) and can be done almost anywhere. Spare parts, tools and proper equipment are rare off the main routes, though local mechanics (*fundis*) can work miracles with minimal tools. Always settle on a price before work begins.

Lastly, when **parking** by day in the central business districts of Dar es Salaam and Arusha, you need to buy a ticket from an attendant dressed in an orange jacket – they'll find you.

Foreign-registered vehicles

If you're arriving overland in your own vehicle, a **carnet de passage** is highly recommended to avoid a potentially time-consuming paper chase when you eventually leave the country. With a carnet, you may still have to pay road fund ($5) and $20 for a one-month foreign-vehicle permit or insurance. Without a carnet you'll have to leave a deposit equivalent to the tax payable on cars, which can be several thousand dollars. The deposit is paid back when you leave the country, although arranging this with the authorities can be a hassle. The carnet is valid for a year, and is available from motoring organizations in your home country (see box on p.44): you pay a deposit of several thousand pounds, euros or dollars, plus an annual fee in the hundreds. **Motorbikes** are eligible for a temporary import permit (free for one month, extensible each fifteen subsequent days).

Trains

Tanzania has two railways: the **Central Line**, which runs west from Dar es Salaam to Kigoma and Mwanza with branches to Singida and Mpanda; and the **TAZARA Line**, which heads southwest across the country and into Zambia. There are no passenger services along the lines from Dar es Salaam to Arusha or Tanga, and the connection to Kenya was discontinued years ago after a dispute over rolling stock.

There are four kinds of ticket. **First-class** on the Central Line is in compartments with just two bunks each; ideal for couples. On the TAZARA Line, they have four bunks. **Second-class** is in compartments with

---

Train security

Overnight trains are obvious targets for opportunistic thieves. If you have a compartment, keep the door and windows locked when you're asleep or outside, or ensure that there's always someone there to look after bags (locals are just as wary). Be especially careful when the train pulls in at main stations, especially Dodoma and Tabora on the Central Line. You should also be wary of people looking for a spare seat in second-class (genuine passengers always have numbered tickets corresponding to a particular compartment) and of passengers without bags – they may leave with yours. If you really get suspicious stay awake until the ticket inspector comes round. In third-class you'll probably have to stay awake all night or else stash your valuables out of reach (in a bag under your seat hemmed in by other people's bags, for example). All this is not to say that you should be paranoid, but just that you shouldn't drop your guard.

six berths each. Compartments are segregated by sex unless you book and pay for all bunks; both first- and second- class have washbasins, bed linen and blankets. Both kinds should be reserved in advance; ticket offices take bookings several weeks ahead. **Second-class seating** is also in compartments, and **third-class** consists of open carriages of reserved seats, but can become extremely crowded and uncomfortable, what with all the suitcases, boxes, baskets, chickens, children and *mama kubwas* ("big ladies"). All trains have a **dining car** (which mainly sees use as a dissolute bar), and food can also be ordered from a roving waiter. On long journeys the train stops at trackside villages whose inhabitants set up stalls where you can sample some of the best street food in the country.

The Central Line

The main section of the **Central Line**, running 1254km from Dar es Salaam to **Kigoma**, on the shores of Lake Tanganyika, was laid by the Germans just before World War I. The line isn't in the best condition: derailings involving freight trains are common, and an accident in 2002 claimed 281 lives when a train's brakes failed. Nonetheless, the line remains safer than road transport. The branch from Tabora to **Mwanza** on Lake Victoria was added in the 1920s. There are two other branches: south to **Mpanda** from Tabora, and north to **Singida** from Dodoma. Trains on all lines run three times a week: details are given in the "Moving on" boxes of this guide. Delays are frequent, so don't count on arriving at your destination at the scheduled time. The official **schedule** is on the Tanzania Railways Corporation website, Ⓦ www.trctz.com. For an idea of **prices**, Dar to Kigoma costs Tsh45,200 ($41) first-class, Tsh33,100 ($30) in a second-class bunk, and Tsh15,000–Tsh18,000 ($14–16) in second-class seating or third-class.

The TAZARA Line

If you thought the Central Line was unreliable, the **TAZARA Line** from Dar es Salaam to New Kapiri Mposhi in northern **Zambia** is a total shambles. The line, which is the northernmost extension of the railway from

Cape Town, was constructed in the 1960s to provide an outlet for Zambian copper exports without going through the racist regimes of Southern Rhodesia and South Africa. Whilst outbound schedules from Dar are reasonably reliable, northbound services from Zambia, or from **Mbeya** in southern Tanzania, are notoriously capricious. On the positive side, the route passes through some especially beautiful and wild landscape, including part of the Selous Game Reserve (antelopes, buffaloes and giraffes are frequently seen). Trains run three times a week from Dar es Salaam, one all the way to New Kapiri Mposhi (38hr, in theory), the other two terminating in Mbeya (19hr). **Fares** from Dar to Mbeya are currently Tsh22,200 (roughly $20) first-class, Tsh14,700 ($13) second-class and Tsh8300 ($7) third-class; first-class to New Kapiri Mposhi costs Tsh47,600 ($43), and second-class Tsh31,600 ($29) – third class isn't recommended.

Flights

Tanzania has a number of reasonably priced **internal air services** and it's well worth seeing the country from above at least once: the flight from Dar es Salaam or Stone Town to Pemba, over spice and coconut plantations, reefs, sandbanks and creeks, is especially beautiful. Flight schedules are given at the end of each chapter. The best local airlines – all operating propeller planes – are Coastal Travels, Precisionair and ZanAir, and can usually be relied on to keep to their schedules. Both Coastal Travels and Precisionair use single-engine planes for less busy routes, worth bearing in mind if mono-props give you the heebie-jeebies, although these companies have good reputations regarding safety. The national carrier, Air Tanzania (ATC), has – since its takeover by South African Airways – finally shed its "Any Time Cancellation" nickname, if only because it currently only flies four routes. It owns just one 737, but leases a few more. **Baggage limits** are usually 15kg, with additional weight carried at the pilot's discretion (and possibly at extra cost).

Ticket prices for tourists ("non-residents") are quoted in dollars but payable in shillings if you prefer. If you've been around for a while, you may be able to wangle significantly cheaper "resident" fares on less touristy routes – it all depends on the guy or gal in the office, as resident status is not checked at the airports. Fares vary little between the airlines. Some sample non-resident **fares**: Dar–Arusha $190; Dar–Zanzibar $50–60; Arusha–Zanzibar $160; Dar–Selous $120; Dar–Ruaha $300. An **airport tax** of $5 (or Tsh5000) and a $1 **airport safety tax** are payable on all domestic flights, and are only rarely usually included in the fare.

Charter flights – mainly useful for getting to remoter national parks in a hurry – are offered by several companies in Arusha, Dar, Mwanza and Zanzibar – see those cities' "Listings" sections. **Prices** depend on the destination and the type of aircraft, but you'll always pay more per person than a standard fare.

Ferries

On the **coast**, there are several daily ferries between Dar es Salaam and Stone Town (Unguja) or Pemba, and weekly ones from Dar to Mtwara, and from Tanga to Pemba. On **Lake Victoria**, steamers sail several times a week from Mwanza to Bukoba, and daily to Ukerewe Island. On **Lake Tanganyika**, there's a weekly ferry from Kigoma to Mpulungu in northern Zambia – with luck, aboard the marvellous MV *Liemba*, a pre-World War I relic. On **Lake Nyasa**, a weekly ferry runs from Itungi Port to Mbamba Bay, but not – at present – across to Malawi (this section is covered by rickety local boats).

Dhows

Though discouraged by the authorities, getting passage on a commercial **dhow** is a legal and feasible – if adventurous and potentially dangerous – way of getting along parts of the coast and from the mainland to Zanzibar. Be aware, however, that dhows do occasionally capsize, and there's little chance of being rescued should that happen.

The main hassle if you want to take a dhow to Zanzibar is dealing with the potential **paperwork**. In theory, this irksome paper chase shouldn't be required at all as Zanzibar is of course part of Tanzania, but in practice – and depending, it seems, on the current political situation in the Isles – you may need to navigate around obstructive and/or corrupt officials. **Journey times** given in this book are very approximate, so take plenty of food and water and remember that although the thought of a dhow trip is undeniably romantic, the reality can be rather different, with choppy seas, cramped seating and rudimentary toilet facilities.

The main **ports for catching dhows to Zanzibar** are Bagamoyo, Pangani and Tanga. Finding something in Dar es Salaam is virtually impossible. Dhow-hopping along the south coast of Tanzania is also a possibility if you're not in a hurry. The nearest main port to Dar is at Kisiju, 90km south of the city, from where you can get to Mafia Island or south to Songo Songo Island. From there, with luck, you'll find an onward connection to Kilwa Kivinje (or sometimes Kilwa Kisiwani), and then on to Lindi and Mtwara. From Mtwara, dhows occasionally head on to Mozambique.

Cycling

Tanzania's climate, varied terrain and reckless drivers make it challenging **cycling** country. Given time, you can cycle to parts of the country that would be hard to visit by any other means except on foot, and of course people will treat you in a completely different way – as a traveller rather than a tourist. And what would take several days to hike can be cycled in a matter of hours. Most towns have bicycle shops selling both trusty Chinese "Phoenix" three-speed roadsters and mountain bikes.

Bringing your own bicycle by air is fairly straightforward, but check with your airline in advance in terms of what you'll be charged and whether they have any special packing requirements. Few airlines will insist your bike be boxed or bagged, but it's best to turn the handlebars into the frame and tie them down, invert the pedals and deflate the tyres. Whatever you take, it will need low gears and strongly built wheels; you should also carry essential spare parts.

Buses carry bicycles for about half-fare (even if flagged down at the roadside), and trucks will often give you a lift for a small payment: trains also take bikes for a low fixed fare. You'll need to consider the **seasons**, however; you won't make much progress on dirt roads during the rains when chain-sets and brakes become totally jammed with mud. Obviously, you also need to be cautious when **cycling on main roads**. A mirror is essential and, if the pavement is broken at the edge, give yourself plenty of space and be ready to leave the road if necessary – local cyclists wisely scatter like chickens at the approach of a bus. That said, cycle tourists are a novelty in Tanzania: drivers often slow down to look and you'll rarely be run off the road.

Accommodation

Tanzania has a wide range of accommodation to suit all tastes and pockets, ranging from cheap local guest houses to wildlife lodges and luxurious tented camps in the bush. Camping is possible on the mainland (but not on Zanzibar), costing $3–5 per person (not much more than you'd pay in a decent guest house). Zanzibar's hotels are expensive by mainland standards, with the cheapest double rooms starting at $20, though this should be bargainable, especially in low season.

Types of room

Single bedrooms have one bed (*kitanda moja*); in some towns cheaper hotels let couples use singles for the same price as a solo traveller. A **double** has a larger bed suitable for couples, or two beds (*vitanda viwili*), which we've called a **twin**. A **common** room (or *sisolfu*) shares showers and toilets with

Accommodation price codes

Most mid-range hotels, almost all upmarket accommodation, and all hotels on Zanzibar, have two tariffs, one for **"non-residents"** (tourists) priced in dollars but payable in shilling equivalent (albeit at bad rates), the other for **"residents"** (Tanzanians and expats), usually quoted in shillings and invariably much cheaper. Their rates also vary according to the season.

All accommodation listed in this guide has been graded according to the **price codes** given below, based on the cost of a **standard double or twin room** charged at non-resident tourist rates in high (but not peak) season (see p.20). For dormitory accommodation, hostels and campsites (which all charge per person), exact prices have been given where possible. In more modest places, it should be possible to bargain the price down when things are slow.

Price code ❶ covers very basic guest houses with shared bathrooms. Price codes ❷–❹ include progressively more comfortable guest houses or lower-end hotels with private showers and toilets, and breakfast included. Price codes ❺–❼ denote tourist-class hotels or lodges, often with half- or full-board. At the top end of the price range (❽–❾) are luxury hotels and lodges with full-board and special facilities.

❶ Under $5 (under Tsh5500)
❷ $5–10 (Tsh5500–11,000)
❸ $10–20 (Tsh11,000–22,000)
❹ $20–40 (Tsh22,000–44,000)
❺ $40–70 (Tsh44,000–77,000)
❻ $70–100 (Tsh77,000–110,000)
❼ $100–150 (Tsh110,000–165,000)
❽ $150–250 (Tsh165,000–275,000)
❾ Over $250 (over Tsh275,000)

other rooms, whilst an **en-suite** or **self-contained** room (*self-container* or *selfu*) has a private bathroom. A **suite** has a bathroom and a lounge, usually with a horrid three-piece suite and often with a TV and fridge, and sometimes also a kitchen or kitchenette. A **banda** is a small cottage, usually with a thatched roof; a **rondavel** is similar but round.

Security

In both the budget and mid-range categories, **security** is an important factor: obviously, the more an establishment relies on its bar for income, the less secure it will be. Room keys are often so simple that they'd open every other door in the country; you could bring your own padlock, but it won't fit all doors. Whilst all hotels disclaim responsibility for thefts from bedrooms, **leaving valuables in rooms** is usually safe enough, but use your judgement, don't leave stuff lying around too temptingly, and try to take the key with you when you go out. If you decide to leave things with the management, ensure you get an **itemized receipt** for everything, including banknote serial numbers – rumours circulate of real notes being replaced by forgeries. Also ensure it is the management you're leaving stuff with rather than just the receptionist.

Hostels and guest houses

Nearly every town in Tanzania has at least one clean and comfortable **guest house** (a *gesti* or *nyumba ya kulala wageni* – "house for sleeping guests"). These vary from mud shacks with water from a well to little multi-storey buildings containing rooms with private bathrooms, plus a bar and restaurant. Guest houses are usually fairly quiet, though street noise and the proximity of mosques might wake you up earlier than you want, whilst a bar or disco nearby (or inside the guest house) may keep you from sleeping until after midnight. The less reputable places maximize their potential by admitting couples on "short time", though they're rarely too tawdry. The more puritanical display belligerent signs stating that "women of immoral turpitude" are not welcome. Similar in standards

to guest houses, but with a more cloying atmosphere and often with overly narrow beds intended to hinder the more carnal pleasures, are **church-run hostels** (there are no youth hostels). These have no membership requirements, but revellers and night owls should look elsewhere. Virtually all hostels and guest houses have **security guards** (*askaris*) at night, who you'll need to wake up if you're staggering home after the doors or gates are locked.

Except in Dar es Salaam and Zanzibar, where upwards of $20 (Tsh22,000) for a double room is the norm, **costs** are rarely more than Tsh8000 (Tsh5000 for a single), whilst in rural areas many places charge half that. It's always worth trying to bargain, especially if a place doesn't seem particularly busy or if you'll be staying more than a night or two. It's worth checking several places, testing the lights and fans (and electric socket if you need it), running water, the toilets, and the size and condition of mosquito nets – it's amazing how many don't cover the whole bed, or have more holes than a Gruyère. It's a good idea to bring toilet paper, a towel and soap, as well as pillow cases and two thin cotton sheets (a *kanga* or *kitenge* will do) to replace the ubiquitous nylon sheets, many of which are too small for the beds, especially in the hostels.

Hotels

Expect to pay Tsh8000–55,000 ($50) for a decent double or twin room in a **town hotel**, with private bathroom, hot water and breakfast included, often enough satellite or cable TV, and air conditioning rather than a ceiling fan. These places – the equivalent or two- or three-star hotels – can be bristlingly smart and efficient, or bland and boozy: price is not a reliable guide. It's worth reserving in advance at the more popular establishments, especially from December to February, and in July and August in touristy areas. At the top of the range, costing between $100 and $300 a night, are **four- and five-star style hotels** (though there's no official grading system), especially in larger towns and cities such as Arusha, Dar and Stone Town, though again price isn't necessarily a good indicator of high quality – read our reviews carefully.

Beach bungalows and resorts

Whilst several coastal areas have become quite developed in terms of tourism, particularly north of Dar es Salaam and on Zanzibar's Unguja Island, **coastal hotels** are almost all low-key and low-rise, anything over two storeys being an exception. Rooms tend to be in **bungalows**, either individual, or containing two or more guest rooms perhaps sharing the same verandah or balcony. It's worth spending a little more to be sure of a sea view, if there is one, and for air conditioning, especially between December and March when the heat and humidity are sapping. **Costs** can be surprisingly reasonable: from $30 or so per night in Zanzibar for two people, though some "exclusive" places, catering for one or two dozen guests at a time feel justified in charging over $500.

Wildlife lodges and luxury tented camps

At the top of the scale are the lodges and luxury tented camps in and around Tanzania's **national parks and game reserves**, which can charge pretty much what they like as demand far outstrips availability: indeed, when **reserving rooms** in the more popular parks, such as Serengeti and Ngorongoro, you need a degree of flexibility regarding dates even if you book months or over a year in advance. The more remote of these places tend to be closed in April and May during the long rains.

The **lodges** are the mainstay of mid-range and "cheaper" upmarket safaris, and are essentially large four- and five-star hotels transported into the bush. The better ones can feel quite intimate, but by and large this is package tour land, and they lack that wilderness feeling you might be hankering for. For that, either camp on a budget (see next column), or drain your bank account ($300–1200 for a couple) and stay at one of an ever-growing number of **luxury tented camps** (or "tented lodges"). Accommodation in these is usually large, walk-in tents pitched on raised wooden platforms, and

with a bathroom plumbed in at the back – not exactly camping in the wild. There's invariably also a thatched restaurant, bar and lounge area, and an atmosphere that tends to be neo-colonial in the extreme, dominated by "white hunter" type wildlife guides, tall tales around evening camp fires, and minimal if any local involvement beyond the employment of menial staff and perhaps a Maasai warrior or two to lend some tribal colour to the experience. Bush walks are often possible, and are – together with game drives – usually included in the "all inclusive" price.

Camping

Camping is illegal on Zanzibar, but mainland Tanzania has enough **campsites** to make carrying a tent worthwhile, and it's cheap too, at around $3–5 per person for a pitch. In rural areas, hotels may let you camp discreetly in their grounds.

The public campsites in most of Tanzania's **national parks** ($30 per person) offer the cheapest way of staying over, and don't require advance booking. The parks also have "special campsites" ($50 per person), usually restricted locations which you can reserve for your exclusive use. Some sites are especially attractive and can be fully booked up to a year in advance, but all are quite devoid of facilities. To book them, contact TANAPA in Arusha (p.403). Reliable travel agents can also book things for you, though they'll charge a premium and are likely to push their own safaris as part of the deal. **Collecting firewood** is not permitted in the parks; some provide firewood for a small fee, others insist you use gas cartridges (available in Arusha and Dar es Salaam).

When **camping rough** in more heavily populated districts, always ask before pitching a tent – a fire may worry locals and delegations armed with *pangas* sometimes turn up to see who you are. Out in the wilds, hard or thorny ground is likely to be the only obstacle (a foam sleeping mat is a good idea if you don't mind the bulk). During the dry seasons, you'll rarely have trouble finding wood for a fire, so a stove is optional, but don't burn more fuel than you need and take care to put out the embers completely before leaving. A torch is also useful.

Safety

Camping out is generally pretty safe, but there are some places you should avoid. Don't camp right by the road, in dried-out river-beds, or on trails used by animals going to water, and avoid areas where cattle-rustling is prevalent (the fringes of Maasai-land, for example), and anywhere on the Kenyan border: border clashes between different clans of the Kuria north of Musoma are common, whilst north of Lake Natron Somali bandits were operating until a few years ago. In addition, sleeping out on any but the most deserted of Indian Ocean beaches is an open invitation to robbers.

On the subject of **animals**, if you're way out in the bush, lions and hyenas are very occasionally curious of fires, but will rarely attack unless provoked. Nonetheless, listen seriously to local advice about **lions**, which have taken to sporadically terrorizing some districts, especially Kondoa and Babati north of Dodoma, Songea and Tunduru in the far south, and the whole region east of Selous Game Reserve. Usually more dangerous are **buffalo**, which you should steer well clear of (especially old solitary males), and lake- or river-side **hippo**, who will attack if they fear that you're blocking their route back to water.

Eating and drinking

Not surprisingly, perhaps, Tanzania has no great national dishes: the living standards of the majority of people don't allow for frills and food is generally plain and filling. That said, as long as you're adventurous and know what to look for, you could be pleasantly surprised. In cheaper places, lunch is typically served from noon to 2pm, and dinner no later than 8pm; at other times you may only have fare from the dreaded display cabinet to choose from. Having said that, restaurants leaning more towards expatriates and tourists tend to stay open all day.

Tanzanian food

In terms of culinary culture, only **the coast** has developed a distinctive style of regional cooking, influenced by its contact with Indian Ocean trade and dominated by seafood and rice, flavoured with coconut, tamarind and exotic spices. This is most memorably sampled in the fantastic open-air market held every evening at Forodhani Gardens in Stone Town. You can also find some very good fresh fish around the lakes, where another speciality is **dagaa** – tiny freshwater sardines that are fried in palm oil and eaten whole.

Wherever you are, you'll never go hungry. In any **hoteli** (a small restaurant, not a hotel), there are always a number of predictable dishes intended to fill you up as cheaply as possible, often for well under Tsh1000. **Rice** and **ugali** (a stiff cornmeal porridge) are the national staples, eaten with chicken, goat, beef, or vegetable stew, various kinds of spinach, beans and sometimes fish. Meals are usually served in a metal platter with hollows for each dish, so you can mix things as you wish.

Portions are usually gigantic, and half-portions aren't much smaller. But even in small towns, more and more **cafés** are appearing where most of the menu is fried – chips, eggs, fish, chicken, burgers and more chips. Indeed, chips have spawned one species of junk food that's peculiarly Tanzanian: **chipsi mayai** ("chips-eggs"): a Spanish-style omelette with chips replacing the boiled potatoes. **Snacks** include samosas (sometimes vegetarian), chapatis and stuffed chapati rolls ("Zanzibari pizza"), rice cakes, "chops" (battered meat or egg balls, sometimes with a mashed potato coating), miniature meat skewers, and roasted corn cobs. *Andazi* – sweet, puffy, deep-fried dough cakes – are made before breakfast and served until evening time, when they've become cold and solid.

The standard blow-out feast for most Tanzanians is a huge pile of **nyama choma** (grilled meat). *Nyama choma* is usually eaten at a purpose-built bar, with beer and music (live or otherwise) as the standard accompaniment, along with optional grilled bananas or *ugali*. You go to the kitchen or a booth and order by weight (half a kilo is plenty) direct from the butcher's hook. After roasting, the meat is brought to your table on a wooden platter and chopped into bite-size pieces with a sharp knife. The better places also bring you a small bowl of home-made **chilli sauce** – at their best, these are subtle and fresh, and laced with plenty of tomato, onion and lemon or vinegar. The more basic places simply cut up a green chilli pepper for you; these vary in strength from moderately hot to incendiary.

You'll usually find plenty of **street food** around bus stations and at night, dished up by a *mama lisha* or *baba lisha* ("feeding woman/man"). Their stock-in-trade is small skewers of grilled meat or fried chicken served with salt and (optional) chilli, grilled corn cobs and – inevitably – chips. Grilled cassava is also commonly available – it's usually mouth-drying, though it can occasionally be deliciously moist, especially when sprinkled with watery chilli sauce.

Fruit in Tanzania is a delight. Bananas, avocados, papayas and pineapples can be found in abundance all year round; mangos and citrus fruits are more seasonal. Look out for passion fruit (both the familiar shrivelled brown variety and the sweeter and less acidic smooth yellow ones), tree tomatoes, custard apples (sweetsops) and guavas – all distinctive and delicious. On the coast, roasted **cashew nuts** are popular, especially in the south around Lindi, Mtwara and Masasi, where they're grown and processed, while **coconuts** are filling and nutritious, going through several satisfying changes of condition (all edible) before becoming the familiar hairy brown nuts.

Breakfast

The first meal of the day varies widely. Stock **hoteli fare** consists of a cup of sweet milky *chai* and an *andazi* doughnut or chapati,

Being invited to eat at home

If you're invited to a meal at someone's home, do accept – it's something of an honour both for you and for the people whose home you visit. In any case, the food is likely to be much, much better than what you'll find in an average *hoteli*. Taking **small gifts** for the family is in order. Elder men often appreciate tobacco, whether "raw" (a piece of a thick, pungent coil that you can buy in markets everywhere) or a couple of packets of filterless *Sigara Nyota* cigarettes, nicknamed *sigara ya babu* – grandfather's cigarettes. Women appreciate anything that helps keep down their household expenses, be it soap, sugar, tea or a few loaves of bread. Kids, of course, adore sweets – but give them to the mother to hand out or you'll end up getting mobbed. Make sure you leave a big hole in your stomach before coming: your hosts will probably make a huge play out of the fact that you're not eating enough, even if you've just gobbled up twice what anyone else has.

Before eating, one of the girls or women of the house will appear with a bowl, soap and a jug of hot water to wash your hands with. Food is eaten by hand from a **communal bowl or plate** – though you may be presented with a plate and cutlery, it's best to try to eat with your hand: the gesture will be valued. When eating, use only your right hand. *Ugali* is eaten by taking a small piece with your fingers and rolling it in the palm of your hand to make a small ball. The ball is then dipped in sauce and popped into your mouth. And, finally, don't worry about making a mess – your hosts will be surprised if you don't.

occasionally with scrambled eggs or an omelette. At the other extreme, if you're staying in a **luxury hotel** or lodge, breakfast is usually a lavish expanse of hot and cold buffets that you can't possibly do justice to. In the average **mid-priced hotel**, you'll get an English-style "full breakfast" – greasy sausage, eggs and baked beans, with instant coffee (in a pot) and soggy toast.

Invariably tastier is **supu**, a light broth made from bony or gristly pieces of meat, chicken or fish, or indeed from boiled hooves (*supu ya makongoro*) or intestines (*supu ya utumbo*) – both much nicer than they sound. It can be spicy, and serves as a great hangover cure; it's usually eaten with chapati or rice. Other good and filling traditional breakfasts include *uji* (especially in Moshi), a porridge or gruel made of millet; and *mtori* (in Arusha and westwards), a light banana soup.

Restaurants

Eating out is not a Tanzanian tradition and few Tanzanians would consider it cheap. Standard tourist restaurants charge Tsh4000–5000, whilst fancier establishments can charge anything upwards of Tsh15,000 for a large spread of international-style dishes. The main concentration of these kinds of restaurants (including Indian, Chinese and Italian) is, predictably, in the tourist areas of Arusha, Moshi, Dar es Salaam and Zanzibar, with a few more in Dodoma, Iringa, Mbeya, Morogoro and Mwanza. Outside these places you're limited to whatever the *hotelis* happen to have prepared that day. The **bigger hotels and lodges** usually have buffet lunches ($12–15), which can be great value if you're really hungry.

Non-alcoholic drinks

The national beverage is **chai** – tea. Drunk at breakfast and as a pick-me-up at any time, it's a weird variant on the classic British brew: milk, water, lots of sugar and tea leaves, brought to the boil in a kettle and served scalding hot. Its sweetness must eventually cause diabolical dental damage, but it's curiously addictive and very reviving. Variants are laced with ginger (*chai tangawizi*) or other spices (*chai masala*). Ironically for a major coffee-producer, **coffee** is normally limited to instant, though fresh coffee – if you can find it – can be an utter delight.

Sodas are cheap, and crates of Coke and Fanta find their way to the wildest corners of the country. Local varieties worth tasting are Krest bitter lemon, and the punchy Stoney Tangawizi ginger ale. Fresh **juice** is available in towns, especially on the coast. Passion fruit is excellent, though it may be watered-down concentrate; you might also find orange juice, pineapple, sugar cane juice, water melon, mango, and sometimes tamarind (mixed with water) – very refreshing, and worth seeking out.

Vegetarians

If you're **vegetarian**, tourist-class hotels usually have a meat-free pasta dish available each day, and you can also eat remarkably well at Indian and Chinese restaurants in the larger towns (also available in Zanzibar). Local *hotelis* have plenty of choice, too, and not only the insidious chips and omelettes: most can be relied upon to supply beans and vegetables, and the better ones may be able to rustle up a salad.

Most Tanzanian staples are vegetarian, like *ugali*, cassava, *uji*, roast corn cobs, and all manner of bananas (*ndizi*), whether grilled, boiled, stewed (as in *mtori*), roasted or just plain. Many of these are served with *supu* – not the early morning broth, but a sauce. This can be vegetarian but is more likely to be based on a meat stock.

If you eat fish, you'll be in paradise in Zanzibar. Elsewhere, fish is generally limited to tilapia, dried and trucked in from the lakes in the west, which can be good depending on how it's cooked. Lastly, don't forget Tanzania's glorious fruits; mangos, bananas and coconuts can be found almost everywhere, and there are always seasonal specialities in each region.

Mineral or purified **water** is expensive, but can be bought everywhere. Tap water is usually drinkable if you're up to date on inoculations (especially typhoid), but heed local advice.

Alcoholic drinks

Tanzania has a strong drinking culture, inherited from the tradition of elders sharing drinks while sorting out the affairs of the day. Most tourists drink in bars; hard-up locals patronize *pombe* houses to partake of rough-and-ready local brews. So, *maisha marefu* – "long life" (cheers).

Beer and cider

Tanzanian **beer** is generally good. Prices vary according to where you drink it: from around Tsh700–800 for a half-litre bottle in local dives, up to Tsh2500 in the poshest establishments. Safari, Kilimanjaro and Tusker are the biggest selling **lagers**; other brands include Kibo Gold, Serengeti, and the more expensive Castle Lager. You can also find Pilsner Ice and Pilsner Extra, which apparently make your breath smell sweeter to the missus when you stagger back late. Everyone adopts a brand, even though you can't reliably tell the difference between any of them, and certainly not after you've drunk a few. More distinctive brews include Ndovu, which has a sickly-sweet smell which isn't to everyone's liking, and the infamous Bia Bingwa (seven percent alcohol) whose name means "Hero Beer", possibly because a few of these will see you flat out on the ground like Samson. A similarly lethal concoction found in Dar and Moshi is called, for no apparent reason, The Kick. Imported brands, or ones brewed locally under licence, include the Namibian Windhoek, Czech Pilsner Urquell, Miller, Carlsberg and Heineken.

There are also two **stouts**: a head-thumping version of Guinness which, at 7.5 percent, owes more to soya sauce in texture and flavour than pure genius (and which is sometimes mixed with Coca-Cola to make it more palatable); and Castle Milk Stout (six percent), a milder and more palatable competitor from South Africa. Alternatively, you could always try one of the country's two **fake ciders**: 49er and Redds Cool,

both sickly-sweet concoctions of fermented malt, sugar and artificial flavourings that have never been near a real apple.

When leaving a bar, never take your bottle with you as they carry deposits.

Pombe

Unlike Kenya, where home-brewing and distilling is illegal, things are laxer in Tanzania – to the extent that Kenyan revellers living near the border have taken to sneaking over to Tanzania for a cheap piss-up before staggering back into the arms of the Kenyan police. You can sample **pombe** (home-brewed beer) all over the country and under many different names: the versions available are as varied in taste and colour as their ingredients, which may include fermented sugar cane (*boha*), maize and honey (*kangara*), bananas and sorghum (*rubisi*), cashew fruit (*gongo*), bamboo juice (*ulanzi*), barley (*busa*) or just millet, all sometimes mixed with herbs and roots for flavouring and/or to kick off the process of fermentation. The results are frothy and deceptively strong, and can cause you to change your plans for the rest of the day.

On the coast, merely lopping off the growing shoot at the head of a coconut tree produces a naturally fermented **palm wine** called *tembo*. The drink remains popular despite the majority of people on the coast being Muslim, though there's usually a furtive discretion about *tembo* drinking sessions. And keep the Kiswahili proverb in mind. "If the maker of *tembo* is praised for his wine, he adds water to it" (*mgema akisifiwa tembo hulitia maji*).

Spirits and liqueurs

Whilst *tembo* and *pombe* are generally quite safe – and indeed still play an important part in traditional festivities – the same cannot be said for traditional spirits (**chang'aa**), treacherous and sometimes contaminated firewaters that regularly kill drinking parties en masse. As to more mainstream **spirits**, most bars stock a limited range of dodgy local whiskies and vodkas – often in plastic sachets called *kiroba* – plus a few imported brands. By far the most popular bottled spirit is the homegrown and very drinkable

Konyagi (35 percent) made from papaya, something between gin and lukewarm water with a kick. It's generally drunk to get drunk, often with bitter lemon, Indian tonic or soda water. Konyagi Ice is a mix of Konyagi and bitter lemon. **Liqueurs**, where you can find them, are pretty much the same as anywhere else in the world, though it's worth seeking out a chocolate and coconut liqueur called Afrikoko, and the South African Amarula, similar to Bailey's.

Wines

Tanzania produces some quite palatable **wines**, notably in West Usambara. These are produced by the Benedictine Fathers in Sakharani near Soni, under the name Sakharani Usambara (see p.365); quality varies from average to good. You can buy it in Lushoto, and in supermarkets or wine shops in Dar es Salaam, Arusha and even Stone Town in Zanzibar. Rather less tempting are the trio of wines produced by Tanganyika Vineyards in Dodoma, purveyors of what is widely considered to be among the world's worst plonk. Choose from Makutapora Rosé, Makutapora Red and Chenin Blanc.

Other alternatives worth trying are **papaya wine** and **banana wine** – look out for the latter especially in Moshi, Arusha and Lushoto (whose Doshi Banana Wine is produced by the Catholic Mission of the Montessori Sisters; see p.365). Both are an acquired taste, but it's one you might get used to quickly, since the stuff is both potent and much cheaper than imported wine.

Communications

Keeping in touch by post and telephone is easy if not fantastically reliable. Things do go missing, however – use a courier if you need to send valuables. Tanzania's terrestrial phone network is far from perfect but improving. Tanzanians have embraced mobile phones and the Internet with gusto.

Mail

There are **post offices** in all Tanzanian towns. Opening times are generally Monday–Friday 8am–4.30pm, Saturday 9am–noon. **Poste restante** is fairly reliable in major towns. Make sure people writing to you mark your surname clearly; it's also worth looking under your first (and any other) names. You'll have to show your passport to collect mail, and pay Tsh200 per item. Smaller post offices will also hold mail, but your correspondent should mark the letter "To Be Collected". Parcels can be received, too, but expect to haggle over import duty when they're opened. Ask the sender to mark packages "Contents to be re-exported from Tanzania", which might be helpful in your discussions.

Sending mail

Prepaid **aerograms** are the cheapest way of writing home, but can be difficult to find. **Airmail** takes about five days to Europe and ten days to North America and Australasia. For stuff you really don't want to lose, it's best to use an **international courier** – there are branches of DHL (☎022/286 1000, ⑩www.dhl.co.tz) and others in most towns and cities; details are given in "Listings" at the end of town accounts.

For **heavy parcels**, you'll pay Tsh60,000–70,000 ($55–65) for dispatching 20kg overseas by surface mail, but it's extremely slow (up to four months) and things go missing. The same 20kg parcel would cost Tsh142,400 ($130) to send to the US

Addresses in Tanzania

Tanzanian postal addresses are a post office box number (PO Box or SLP, its Kiswahili equivalent) except out in the sticks, where some are just given as "Private Bag" or "PO", followed by the location of the post office. There's no home delivery.

by airmail, or Tsh200,000 ($180) to New Zealand. Couriers charge about twice that. **Expedited mail** (EMS; called Datapost in the UK) can also be fast and may be cheaper. There's an EMS counter in most post offices. Parcels must be no more than 105cm long and the sum of the three sides less than 200cm; they must also be wrapped in brown paper and tied with string, but take whatever you want to send unwrapped to the post office, as the contents may have to be checked by a customs officer.

Telephones

Tanzania's terrestrial **telephone network** is run by TTCL. There are also six mobile phone operators. The terrestrial network is gradually getting more reliable, though power cuts, and thieves stealing wires for their copper, are perennial problems. Most of the country is covered by automatic exchanges, but there are still a few manual exchanges in more remote areas. For these numbers (generally two or three digits), dial the national operator (☎101) and give them the location and number (eg "Mbamba Bay

12"). The **dialling tone** is a continuous purring; a high-pitched interrupted tone means the number is engaged; a high-pitched continuous tone means there's no service for the number. It's not possible to make **collect calls** (reverse-charge) from Tanzania.

You can **phone abroad** from any TTCL office; these are invariably found in or close to the main post offices of towns. Avoid the time-consuming operator "assisted" rigmarole inside by using the direct-dial **card-operated** "Rafiki" phones (simu ya kadi) found outside all TTCL offices, at bus stations, and in some bars and hotels. The pre-paid cards (kadi ya simu) are sold at post offices, TTCL offices and in shops close to call boxes, and come in Tsh5000 and Tsh10,000 denominations. Also convenient are private telephone bureaux known as "**assisted call**" centres. Charges here are rarely much higher than TTCL's, and can sometimes be significantly cheaper. Cheapest of the lot, though, are the **Internet phone services** available at a growing number of Internet cafés in larger towns and cities, which cuts the price of calls by up to seventy percent, albeit at the

Phone numbers

Most **land lines** (TTCL) have seven-digit subscriber numbers plus a three-digit area code (022 to 028) that doesn't need to be dialled if calling from the same area. **Mobile phones** have ten digits including a four-digit company code (0741 to 0748, or 0787), which must be dialled wherever you are. **Calling from outside Tanzania**, omit the initial "0". **Tanzania's country code** is 255, unless you're calling from Kenya or Uganda, in which case dial ☎004.

Phoning abroad from Tanzania, dial ☎000 followed by the country code, followed by the subscriber's area code (minus the initial "0" if any) and the number itself. The exceptions are Kenya (☎005 followed by the area and subscriber number) and Uganda (☎006). Some **country codes**: Australia 61, Canada 1, Ireland 353, New Zealand 64, UK 44, USA 1.

Useful numbers

☎101 National operator (English)
☎0101 International operator (English)
☎135 Directory enquiries (and general queries)
☎112 Emergency services (but don't expect them to come in a hurry)

expense of low sound quality, drop-outs and a stuttering line.

In 2005, standard **costs** for local calls were Tsh72/minute ($0.06); national calls over 50km Tsh156–192/minute; and ringing mobiles from a land line Tsh354/minute ($0.32). International rates were $1.14/minute to Western Europe and North America, and $2.02/minute to New Zealand and Australia. Avoid using **hotel phones** unless you're absolutely sure of the rates: you could end up paying anything up to $50 a minute to the US.

Mobile phones

Tanzania's **mobile phone operators** use GSM 900/1800 networks. The best is **Celtel** (@www.celtel.com), covering virtually all towns and major roads, whilst winkling out a bit more coverage on Zanzibar is **Zantel**, who are partnered with Vodacom on the mainland. Obviously, there's no signal in the middle of nowhere. **Handsets** can bought virtually everywhere for around $60, and a Tanzanian **SIM card** only costs a few dollars. **Top-up scratch cards** (ask for a *vocha*, a voucher), usually priced in dollars but payable in shillings, can be bought at kiosks up and down the country. Alternatively, if your own phone is GSM, you should be able to use it in Tanzania. The simplest and cheapest method is just to replace the SIM card: unlock it at home, or through a "phone mechanic" (*fundi ya simu*) in

Tanzania for a few hundred shillings. Roaming services provided by your home operator are expensive.

Internet, email and faxes

Given the expense and unreliability of other forms of communication, the use of the **Internet and email** in Tanzania is rocketing. Most of Tanzania's larger towns are blessed with surprisingly fast broadband connections, and the proliferation of **Internet cafés** may come as a surprise. At the same time, prices for Internet access are very reasonable (for tourists), averaging Tsh500–1000 per hour. The downside is the fact that most computers are completely infested with viruses, spyware, trojans and the like, so if you're planning on using Internet banking, for instance, we'd recommend you take installable versions of the following software with you on CD: Sygate Personal Firewall (@www.sygate.com), Ad-Aware (to clean up most of the malware; @www.lavasoft.de), and Firefox (to avoid using Internet Explorer; @www.firefox.org). Details of Internet access are given in the "Listings" sections of major towns. Some of the larger hotels offer Wi-Fi connections, or provide modem or broadband sockets in bedrooms, often at no extra charge. @www.kropla.com is a useful website giving details of how to connect your laptop when abroad. The advent of email has largely kicked **faxes** into oblivion; if you need a machine, go to a post office or private telephone office.

The media

Tanzania is a nation absorbed in its press, with many lively and outspoken newspapers, though, unfortunately for the visitor, most are in Kiswahili. Local TV is rather staid but remains popular for its Kiswahili programming; many hotels and bars have satellite or cable TV. Radio is best for swotting up on the latest music craze.

The leading **English-language dailies** are *The Guardian* (and *Sunday Observer*), whose independence relies on the financial and political clout of tycoon Reginald Mengi,

and *The Citizen*, which can at times be more incisive, but at other times ruined by overly slack editing and reliance on dubious pieces culled from the Internet. Others include the government-owned *Daily News* (and *Sunday News*), strong on eastern and southern African news and with some syndicated international coverage, but spoiled by its slavish bias in favour of the ruling CCM party, which becomes outrageous around election time. There's also the *Business News* – at times one of mother earth's most tedious reads, but occasionally blessed with one or two interesting non-financial features.

Best of the **weekly papers** is *The East African*, whose relatively weighty, conservatively styled round-up of the week's news in Kenya, Uganda, Tanzania, Burundi and Rwanda is shot through with an admirable measure of justified cynicism. Its reporters and columnists are consistently incisive, articulate and thought-provoking, and it also carries the cream of the foreign press' news features. Less substantial but equally impartial is *The African*, combining an admirably combative and occasionally scurrilous editorial line with syndicated articles from Britain's *Guardian* newspaper. *The Express* is more downmarket but still entertaining. *The Financial Times* is almost totally occupied by business news.

Of the **foreign press**, the *Daily Telegraph*, *USA Today* and the *International Herald Tribune* get to all sorts of expatriate bastions: availability largely depends on what passengers left on the plane when arriving. *The Times*, *Express*, *Daily Mail* and, more occasionally, *The Guardian* can usually be found in Arusha and Dar.

One of the best of the **locally published magazines**, *Femina* is a women's magazine with the balls to address issues like AIDS and wife-beating directly; *Tantravel*, published by the tourist board, carries interesting features as well as saccharine holiday blurb; and *Tanzania Wildlife*, published in both English and Kiswahili (*Kakakuona*), contains superb in-depth articles on wildlife, ecology, people and conservation. All are published quarterly. There are lots of Kiswahili magazines available too, from smutty cartoons to music and women's affairs. **International magazines** often available include *Time, The Economist, Newsweek* and the BBC's *Focus on Africa*.

Worth picking up, if you're in Dar es Salaam, Arusha or Stone Town, are a trio of free glossy **listings booklets** that often carry interesting features of interest to visitors: the *Dar es Salaam Guide*, *What's Happening in Dar es Salaam* and *The Swahili Coast*.

Radio and TV

Zanzibari **radio and television** are particularly noxious examples of state control. Much more enlightening are mainland Tanzania's stations. The government-run Radio Tanzania broadcasts mainly in Kiswahili but is good for getting to know traditional music. The station competes with several **independent networks**, most of them on a diet of imported soul and home-grown "Bongo Flava". The **BBC World Service** and **Voice of America** provide newsfeeds for local FM stations, and also have their own frequencies: see Ⓦwww.bbc.co.uk/worldservice and Ⓦwww.voa.gov.

Until 2000, Tanzania was one of few countries not to have a **government-run television station**. Rather staid at times, and amateurish by international standards, **TVT** (Televisheni ya Taifa) is now the country's most popular channel, thanks to a preference for Kiswahili and a popular blend of political propaganda, religious material (Muslim on Friday, Christian on Sunday), Nigerian and home-grown dramas, interviews, and all kinds of Tanzanian music. Its main competitor, **ITV** (Independent Television) screens locally produced soap operas and syndicated American sit-coms, and carries BBC and CNN newsfeeds throughout the day. Despite its name, it's none too impartial in the run-up to general elections. The other national stations, Channel 10 (CTN) and Pulse Africa, mainly screen imported sit-coms. There are also some none-too-memorable regional stations. **Satellite TV** – usually provided by DSTV – is ubiquitous in bars, restaurant and hotels, piping up to sixty different channels, ranging from BBC World and Discovery to Iranian stations featuring Islamic clerics and sermons, and a ton of Bollywood action flicks and musicals.

Opening hours, public holidays and festivals

In larger towns, shops usually open Monday–Friday from 8.30am to 5pm, sometimes to 7pm, and sometimes with a lunch break; they're also open on Saturday mornings. Supermarkets may open later, as do local stores and kiosks in residential or rural areas. Government office hours are generally Monday–Friday 7.30am–2.30pm (or 8am–3pm). Post offices are open Monday–Friday 8am–4.30pm and Saturday 9am–noon. Banks in major towns and cities open Monday–Friday 8.30am–4pm and Saturday 8.30am–1pm; rural branches close at 12.30pm weekdays, and at 10.30am on Saturday.

Public holidays

Both Christian and Muslim **public holidays** are observed, as well as secular national holidays. Government offices, banks, post offices and other official establishments are closed at these times. **Public holidays with fixed dates** are as follows: January 1 (New Year); January 12 (Zanzibar Revolution Day); April 26 (Union Day between Zanzibar and Tanganyika); May 1 (Workers' Day); July 7 (Industrial Day); August 8 (Farmers' Day); December 9 (Independence Day); December 25 (Christmas); December 26 (Boxing Day). If a holiday falls on a weekend the holiday is taken the following Monday. Another special day, if not yet a holiday, is October 17, which marks the death of Tanzania's much-loved first President, Julius Nyerere. **Public holidays with variable dates** are: Good Friday, Easter Sunday and Easter Monday, and the Islamic festivals of Idd al-Fitr, Idd al-Haj and Maulidi (see dates below).

Islamic festivals

The lunar Islamic **Hegira calendar** is followed in Muslim communities throughout Tanzania. The Muslim year has either 354 or 355 days, so dates recede in relation to the Western calendar by ten or eleven days each year. Precise dates for Islamic festivals are impossible to give as they depend on the sighting of the moon; if the sky is cloudy, things are put on hold for another day.

Only the month of fasting, **Ramadan**, will have much effect on your travels. This holy month is observed by all Muslims, who may not eat, drink or smoke between dawn and dusk during this period. Visiting the coast and (especially) Zanzibar during this month might leave a slightly strange impression, as most stores and restaurants are closed by day, though the evenings are much livelier than usual, and stores and restaurants stay open late. Public transport and official businesses continue as usual, however, and you can usually find a discreet non-Muslim restaurant serving food, but you'll offend sensibilities if you're seen eating, drinking or smoking on the street by day. **Idd al-Fitr** (or *Idd al-Fitri*), the two- to four-day holiday that follows the sighting of the new moon at the end of Ramadan, is a great time to be in Zanzibar, with feasting, merrymaking and firecrackers. Another good time to be on the coast or in Zanzibar is for **Maulidi** (or *Maulid an-Nabi*), the Prophet Muhammad's birthday. Also fascinating, so long as the sight of blood leaves you unfazed, is the **Idd al-Haj** (or *Idd al-Adha*) – the one-day feast of the sacrifice – during which every family with the means sacrifices a sheep or goat to commemorate the unquestioning willingness of Ibrahim (Abraham) to sacrifice his son Ishmael (Isaac) for the love of God. Rooms fill up quickly for these festivals, so arrive a few days early or book in advance.

Approximate dates for these events over the next few years are as follows:
Maulidi April 11, 2006; March 31, 2007; March 20, 2008; March 9, 2009; February 26, 2010.
Start of Ramadan September 24, 2006; September 13, 2007; September 2, 2008; August 22, 2009; August 11, 2010.
Idd al-Fitr October 24, 2006; October 13, 2007; October 2, 2008; September 21, 2009; September 10, 2010.
Idd al-Haj December 31, 2006; December 20, 2007; December 9, 2008; November 28, 2009; November 17, 2010.

Outdoor activities

Tanzania has huge potential for outdoor activities, including hiking, diving, snorkelling and birding. For information about cycling, see p.48; safaris are covered on pp.67–71, and cultural tourism on pp.64–66.

Hiking

Hiking gives you unparalleled contact with local people and nature, and you'll sometimes come across animals out in the bush. Don't ignore the dangers, however, and stay alert – especially in the far south and in the region between Dodoma and Arusha, where lion attacks are frequently reported.

Regulations restricting walking in **national parks and nature reserves** have recently been eased, making hiking safaris a real – and exciting – possibility, so long as you're accompanied by a guide (and sometimes an armed ranger). Parks which allow access on foot are: Arusha, Kilimanjaro, Kitulo, Udzungwa Mountains, Katavi, Mahale Mountains, Gombe, Selous and Ngorongoro. Other superb hiking areas include the rainforest at Amani Nature Reserve in East Usambara, the Uluguru Mountains, the Pare Mountains and Usambaras, the Southern Highlands and Mount Hanang, near Babati to the south of Arusha. If you prefer **organized walking safaris**, a number of safari companies in Arusha and Moshi can sort things out.

Diving

There are excellent **scuba-diving reefs** along much of Tanzania's 800-kilometre coastline, though unless you've plenty of money and time to arrange a long trip, you're limited to places within easy reach of dive centres.

Pemba is generally considered the country's best dive centre, offering vertiginous drop-offs, largely unspoiled reefs and a stupendous variety of marine life; Misali Island is a particular gem. The waters around **Unguja Island (Zanzibar)** are shallower and sandier, and visibility is less, especially outside the November–March peak season. On the plus side, the corals here are excellent, there are many sheltered sites suitable for novices, and also a few wrecks

within reach. Often forgotten, but also good, are the handful of islands – protected as marine reserves – off the coast **north of Dar es Salaam**, though some of the reefs were badly damaged in the 1990s by dynamite fishing. There are also some good coral-fringed islets off Bagamoyo. To the south of Dar, the reefs around **Mafia Island** rival Pemba's, and are reckoned by some connoisseurs to be among the world's most beautiful: they're protected as Mafia Island Marine Park. In the far south, **Mnazi Bay–Ruvuma Estuary Marine Park** on the border with Mozambique is barely known, and its reefs are in superb condition. For more information, contact Tanzania Marine Parks & Reserves, Olympio St, Upanga West, PO Box 7565 Dar es Salaam (☏022/215 0621, ⓦwww.marineparktz.com).

Diving is possible all year round, although the *kusi* monsoon (strongest June–Sept) is accompanied by choppy seas and strong currents that make the more exposed reefs inaccessible. There can also be strong winds in December and January. **Visibility** is best from November to March, before the long rains set in. Except for the east coast of Pemba, you'll always find good reefs for **beginners** (and most dive centres offer PADI-certified courses), whilst **experienced divers** can enjoy night dives, drift dives and deep drop-offs. On any dive you can expect to see a profusion of colourful tropical fish in extensive coral gardens, together with giant groupers, Napoleon wrasse and larger pelagic gamefish, including barracuda, kingfish, tuna and wahoo. Dolphins are frequently sighted, as are marine turtles (mainly green and hawksbill), blue spotted rays, manta rays and sometimes even whale sharks. Blue whales, though rarely seen, are sometimes heard on their northward migration towards the end of the year.

Responsible diving and snorkelling

Coral reefs are among the most fragile ecosystems on earth, consisting of millions of individual living organisms called polyps. Solid though it seems, coral is extremely sensitive, and even a small change in sea temperature can have disastrous effects – even now, many sections of Tanzania's reefs show the scars of the mass coral bleaching that followed the 1997–98 El Niño event, which killed up to ninety percent of coral in places. You can minimize the impact that you have on a reef when diving or snorkelling by following the following common-sense rules.

Dive and swim carefully. Never touch the corals. Some polyps can die merely by being touched, and all suffocate if covered with silt or sand stirred up by a careless swipe of fins (flippers). For this reason, some companies don't provide fins for snorkellers. If you do wear fins, always be aware of where your feet are, and use your hands to swim when you're close to anything. If you're inexperienced, keep your distance from the coral to avoid crashing into it if you lose your balance. If you haven't scuba-dived for a while, take a refresher course and practise your buoyancy control in a swimming pool first.

Do not touch, handle or feed anything. This is both for your own safety (many corals and fish are poisonous or otherwise dangerous) and to avoid causing stress to fish and interrupting feeding and mating behaviour. Although several companies encourage it, do not feed fish. In some species, feeding encourages dependence on humans and upsets the natural balance of the food chain.

Do not take anything. Collecting shells, coral and starfish for souvenirs disrupts the ecosystem and is illegal, both in Tanzania and internationally. Getting caught will land you in serious trouble. Similarly, do not buy shells, corals or turtle products. With no market, people will stop collecting them. Taking a beautiful seashell might also deprive a hermit crab of a home, and certainly deprives other visitors of the pleasure of seeing it after you.

When mooring a boat, ensure you use established mooring points to avoid damaging corals. If there are no buoys, drop anchor well away from the reef and swim in.

Costs, courses and dive centres

Costs vary between dive centres. A standard dive for qualified divers averages $40 ($50 for night dives), increasing to $70 if they involve a long boat ride. Things work out cheaper if you buy a package, usually six or ten dives, which can bring the price down to $25 a dive. The Professional Association of Diving Instructors – PADI (ⓦ www.padi.com) sets the minimum standards for **scuba-diving** lessons. The standard training for beginners is a four- or five- day Open Water course ($300–400), completion of which gives you the right to dive to 18m with any qualified diver worldwide. It can be followed up with a three- to five- day Advanced Open Water course ($200–300). Details of other courses are given on PADI's website. Unless otherwise stated, the **dive centres** reviewed in this book were **PADI-accredited** at the time of writing. PADI accreditation doesn't guarantee **safety**, but does provide at least a minimum level of standards. Many operators wisely refuse to take clients down further than 25–27m, given the lack of decompression facilities in Tanzania – the nearest decompression chambers are in Mombasa (Kenya) and South Africa. Nonetheless, one or two companies do offer deeper dives, but only for very experienced divers. Most dive centres are based in mid- to upper-range hotels: though you're not obliged to stay there, some places have little in the way of alternative cheap accommodation nearby. In theory, a **medical certificate** is necessary before taking a beginner's course, though few companies ever ask for one.

Dive boats vary greatly. Some are state-of-the-art inflatables equipped with oxygen, radio and powerful engines; others are converted dhows; whilst many are just normal boats with outboard motors. The especially safety conscious should check for life jackets and whether boats have two motors (better than one). There's a live-aboard operator in Pemba. You don't need to bring your own **equipment**, though there's often a discount of about ten percent if you do. In-house equipment is usually fine, though bringing specialist gear like dive computers and waterproof cameras or camera housing is a good idea as renting them can be expensive, if you can even find what you want. Wetsuits aren't essential, although most companies routinely offer them and some recommend a thin wetsuit from June to September. Only two dive centres have **Nitrox facilities** (for deeper and longer dives, averaging 40min at 30m): Sea Breeze Marine Dive Centre at Jang-wani Beach near Dar es Salaam (p.135), and Sensation Divers at Nungwi on Zanzi-bar (p.695). For **further information**, Anton Koornhof's *The Dive Sites of Kenya and Tanzania* (New Holland) is highly recom-mended, and also covers a good number of snorkelling sites.

Snorkelling

If the idea (or cost) of scuba-diving scares you, **snorkelling** is an excellent and cheap way of discovering the fantastic underwater world of East Africa. Snorkelling is possible virtually everywhere off the coast, and whilst some reefs are close enough to swim out to (especially off Unguja), it's worth getting a boat to reach the more beautiful but less accessible reefs. All the dive sites mentioned above, with the exception of eastern Pemba, have shallow reefs suitable for snorkel-ling: **Chumbe Island** and **Mnemba Atoll** off Unguja, and Misali Island off Pemba are especially recommended. There are also good snorkelling reefs off **Pangani** and **Ras Kutani** on the mainland, as well as freshwater snorkelling at the north end of **Lake Nyasa** near Matema, remarkable for its extraordinary number of colourful cichlid fish species.

It's definitely worth bringing your own gear if you plan to do much snorkelling, since it costs $2–10 to rent equipment for a day, and a mean $40 to buy in Dar es Salaam. The price of **renting a boat** is equally vari-able: some fishermen will happily take you out for Tsh2000 ($2) per person, while dive centres and beach hotels might charge fifteen times as much.

Birding

Tanzania boasts over 1100 **bird species**, including dozens of endangered "Red Book" species and endemics, often only found in a particular forest or mountain range. The best time for birding is from November to March, when resident species are joined by Eurasian and Palaearctic winter migrants. It's impos-sible to recommend one area over another, as every place has something special. Highlights include Tarangire National Park and the adjacent Conservation Area (see p.439), which contains over 550 recorded species; Lake Natron for immense flocks of flamingoes and rare raptors; Lake Manyara, also for flamingoes and almost four hundred other species; and Rubondo Island in Lake Victoria, paradise for hundreds of species of water birds. For endemics, the rainforest at Amani Nature Reserve in East Usambara is the place to head for, while other Eastern Arc mountain ranges – like Uluguru and Udzungwa – also contain endemics, as does the Kilombero floodplain close to Udzungwa.

A recommended Tanzanian company for avid twitchers is the East African Safari and Touring Company in Arusha (p.406), which has enthusiastic guides and includes Tarangire, Udzungwa, Uluguru Mountains, the Usambaras and Ruaha National Park in its itineraries (from $130–200 per person per day). Three good **websites** for Tanzanian birding are: Ⓦwww.tanzaniabirdatlas.com, Ⓦwww.tanzaniabirding.com and Ⓦwww.africanbirdclub.org.

Cultural tourism

Whilst many tourists come to Tanzania to see wildlife, lounge on a beach and perhaps climb Kilimanjaro, an increasing number of visitors find that mixing with local people is the real highlight of their holiday.

Tanzania's pioneering **cultural tourism programme** was set up in 1995 by the Netherlands Development Organisation (SNV) following a request from a Maasai community in Longido for assistance in establishing a form of tourism that would allow them to benefit from the daily influx of visitors coming in from Kenya, rather than the safari companies and lodges reaping all the profit. The idea was to provide

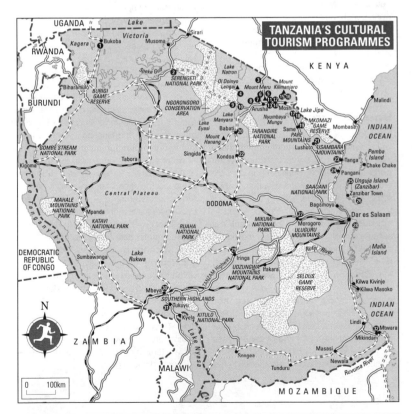

TANZANIA'S CULTURAL TOURISM PROGRAMMES

PROGRAMMES		Machame	**15**	Morogoro	**27**	North Pare (Usangi)	**18**	Tukuyu	**31**
Bukoba	**1**	Iringa **29**	Marangu	**16**	Mto wa Mbu	**10**	Pangani	**24**	West Usambara	
Engaruka	**4**	Karatu **9**	Mbeya	**30**	Mulala	**14**	South Pare (Mbaga)	**19**	(Lushoto)	**21**
Gezaulole	**28**	Kisangara **17**	Mikindani	**32**	Ng'iresi	**12**	Sukumaland	**2**	Zanzibar – Jambiani	**26**
Ilkiding'a	**11**	Kondoa **22**	Mkuru	**5**	Ngaramtoni		Tanga	**23**	Zanzibar – Nungwi	**25**
Ilkurot	**6**	Longido **3**	Monduli Juu	**8**	(Osotwa)	**7**	Tengeru	**13**		

visitors with a parallel rather than competing experience to standard wildlife safaris, and the programme – and its concept – has grown in leaps and bounds, now offering dozens of **community-based** experiences in over thirty locations (mainly in northern Tanzania), giving visitors the opportunity of getting to know local people, their cultures, ways of life, history and environment in a friendly, intimate, respectful and invariably memorable way. The villagers, in turn, benefit directly from tourists in form of services paid for (local guides, food, accommodation, entrance fees), and through modest "development fees" which go into community funds for local projects. Costs are extremely reasonable: a typical trip averages $15–30 for a full day, a little more if you stay overnight.

The various programme "modules" range from two hours to over a week. They can be visited under your own steam (private vehicle or public transport), or through a safari company as an option tacked on to a standard wildlife safari. Projects in the list below marked with asterisks are affiliated to the (original) national programme, now co-ordinated by the Tanzania Tourist Board in Arusha (see p.385), which provides informative leaflets and handles bookings for many. A quick **word of warning**: ensure your guide carries photo ID, as the project's success has inevitably attracted the attention of a motley crew of scammers and dupers. For **more information**, the tourist board website ⓦ www.tanzaniatouristboard.com should eventually have all the information you'll need. In the meantime, try either ⓦ www.infojep.com/culturaltours or ⓦ www.earthfoot.org/guides/tctco.htm.

Cultural tourism programmes in Tanzania

The Coast and Zanzibar

Gezaulole* A traditional fishing village just south of Dar: history and culture of the Zaramo, plus beaches, dhow and snorkelling trips, and homestays. See p.140.
Mikindani An atmospherically tumbledown former slave-trading town close to Mozambique, where an NGO offers walks and bike rides, and overnight trips to a forest and hippo lakes. See p.236.

Pangani* Former slave-trading entrepôt on the north coast; beaches, history, coconut and sisal plantations, dinosaur remains, river cruises, dhow and snorkelling trips. See p.179.
Tanga Village walks and trips to the Amboni Caves and medieval Tongoni ruins; also coordinates an overseas volunteer project. See p.174.
Zanzibar Not much cultural tourism yet on the Isles, the exceptions being short village walks offered at Jambiani (p.688) and in Nungwi (p.699), both on Unguja.

Central Tanzania

Babati* A few hours south of Arusha: encounters and homestays with the traditional Sandawe and Barbaig tribes, hikes up Mount Hanang, canoeing on Lake Babati, rock paintings in the Irangi Hills and much more. See p.270.
Kondoa Stepping stone for the Irangi Hills: prehistoric rock art, Rangi culture, birding, honey-harvesting, hiking and homestays. See p.263.
Morogoro* Explore the forests, streams, waterfalls and birdlife of the ancient Uluguru Mountains, and meet the matrilineal Luguru – among Tanzania's finest musicians. See p.281.

Northern Tanzania (Pare, Usambara and Kilimanjaro)

Kisangara* At the foot of the Pare Mountains: hikes up Mount Kindoroko, sacred and ritual sites, Nyumba ya Mungu reservoir for bird-spotting, canoeing and fishermen, dancing, even cookery lessons. See p.354.
Machame* On the slopes of Kilimanjaro, waterfalls, hot-water springs and sites of spiritual and historical significance to the Chagga. See p.333
Marangu* Hikes through Kilimanjaro's rainforest belt, traditional Chagga house construction, potters, coffee farms and homestays. See p.332.
North Pare (Usangi)* Glorious mountain hiking, sacred rainforests (monkeys and birds), visits to farms, a women's pottery co-operative and traditional healer, lots of Pare culture, and camping. See p.253.
South Pare (Mbaga)* Set in a former missionary station high up in the South Pare mountains, loads of walks to experience Pare life and culture first hand. Also former sites of child sacrifice, viewpoints, waterfalls, development projects, and a speaking rock. See p.355.
West Usambara (Lushoto)* One of the best: friendly locals, glorious nature (especially rainforest and waterfalls), spectacular vistas, and – continuing the weird rock theme – one that grows. See p.367.

Around Arusha

Ilkiding'a* Traditional Il Larusa dancing, craftsmen, a healer and homestays on the south flank of Mount Meru; half- to three-day hikes or bike trips to forests, caves, hills and markets. See p.415.

Ilkurot* Life among the Maasai: visits to (or overnights in) *bomas*, and walking or riding treks over several days by camel or donkey. See p.418.

Longido* The oldest cultural tourism programme: walks with Maasai along buffalo trails up Mount Longido, camping, village (*boma*) visits, and wildlife. See p.419.

Mkuru* A Maasai settlement famed for camels; rides from a few hours to a week-long expedition to Ol Doinyo Lengai volcano and Lake Natron, plus bird-watching guided by warriors. See p.415.

Monduli Juu* Two projects in the Monduli Mountains west of Arusha, amidst a cluster of Maasai villages: an official one, and a better one run by a culturally inclined NGO, which offers short visits, lengthier immersions in Maasai culture, and courses in anthropology, indigenous knowledge, medicine and environmental studies. See p.421.

Mulala* Inhabited by the Meru, this is run by a women's group: visits to development projects including a cheese dairy, also dancing, school and farm visits, and walks in forest and along rivers for monkeys, birds and bats. See p.415.

Ng'iresi* On the southern slope of Mount Meru, an Il Larusa village in transition from semi-nomadic cattle-herding to settled agriculture. Half-day walks to three-day camping trips, including forest, waterfalls and viewpoints, visits to development projects, and a traditional healer. See p.416.

Ngaramtoni (Osotwa)* Encompasses nine Il Larusa villages: markets, traditional healers, crafters, a sacred fig tree, a walk along the Ngarenaro River, and up Sambasha Hill for views, monkeys, birds and butterflies. See p.418.

Tengeru* Close to Lake Duluti (good birdlife): village life, traditional healers, coffee farms and production, tree-planting, hikes along the Malala River, and horse-riding. See p.416.

Northern Safari Circuit

Engaruka* An oasis at the foot of the Rift Valley escarpment amidst unremittingly dry terrain; Maasai culture, the enigmatic ruins of a stone settlement abandoned in the eighteenth century, and hikes up Ol Doinyo Lengai volcano. See p.451.

Karatu Encounters with Iraqw, Barbaig and Maasai, trips to the Iraqw heartland to see rock paintings and climb Mount Guwangw, and short forays to bat-filled caves on the edge of the Rift Valley. See p.459.

Mto wa Mbu* In the Rift Valley beside Lake Manyara, various short hikes and bicycle rides among Mto wa Mbu's plethora of ethnic groups: farm tours, hot-water springs, and canoeing. See p.442.

Northwestern Tanzania

Bukoba A wealth of cultural and historical trips in Kagera Region run by an ethically aware, locally owned tour company: rock art, hippo-watching, ruined palaces of former Haya kingdoms, messing about in boats on Lake Victoria, and a lake that (allegedly) emerged from a cooking pot. See p.521.

Sukumaland A fledgling set-up on the east side of Lake Victoria, just outside Serengeti National Park, that aims to become a centre of cultural tourism in Sukumaland. See p.476.

Southern Tanzania

Mbeya* Tons of trips in the Southern Highlands, including hikes, a massive meteorite, volcanic crater lakes and bat caves, plus homestays. See p.597.

Tukuyu* In the heart of the Southern Highlands, yet more crater lakes, a lava-stone bridge, rainforests, hikes up Mount Rungwe volcano (and – with luck – into Kitulo National Park), and homestays. See p.605.

Iringa Nothing formal as yet, but walks in the forested Western Udzungwa Mountains and elsewhere are now possible, the emphasis as much on culture (especially ethno-botany) as on nature. See p.583.

Safaris

Tanzania has more designated wildlife areas than any other country on earth, with almost one third of its land given over to national parks, game and forest reserves, and others forms of protected area.

Central to its wildlife crown are fourteen **national parks**: unfenced wildlife sanctuaries with no settlements other than a modest number of tourist lodges, tented camps and campsites. There are no surfaced roads, and consumptive utilization of wildlife and other natural resources is prohibited. The classic parks like Serengeti mostly occupy plains, and are where you'll get to see the animals you probably came to Tanzania for, albeit mostly from inside a vehicle, though some now allow limited hiking in designated areas if arranged as part of an organized tour. Getting around the more mountainous and forested parks – prime primate habitat – is always on foot, usually accompanied by an official guide or armed ranger. Acting as

ecological buffers around the parks are over sixty **game reserves**, in which human settlement and limited consumptive resource utilization is permitted; in some of them, wildlife viewing can be as good as inside the parks, especially if they cover land used by annual wildlife migrations. Parks and reserves levy entry fees, included in the cost of organized safaris.

Organizing your own safari

Whilst going with a safari operator (see following section) is the safest and easiest way of getting to see Tanzania's national parks, it's perfectly feasible to **organize your own safari**, either by renting a 4WD

Park regulations and guidelines

Driving Most of the plains parks have a speed limit of 50kph; 25kph is recommended. Keep only to authorized tracks and roads; off-road driving is illegal and causes irreparable damage to fragile vegetation via an erosion fuelled chain reaction. Ask your driver to stay on designated tracks, even if it means you won't get the best photographs. Leaving your vehicle is only allowed at designated points. Driving is only permitted 6am–7pm.

Do not disturb So much is made of spotting the "Big Five" – elephant, lion, leopard, cheetah or buffalo, and rhino – that safari drivers feel obliged to drive off-road in search of classic close-up shots; in fact watching a family of warthogs can be much more rewarding (and amusing) than crowding around a pissed-off leopard in a tree, but you will need to tell your driver – most tourists, indeed most people, prefer the "but just me doing it won't make a difference" vision of their impact on the environment. Harassment by vehicles also interferes with feeding, breeding and reproductive cycles: cheetahs, for instance, only hunt by day, and if they or their prey are disturbed by vehicles, will be deprived of a meal. Be quiet when viewing, switch off the engine and keep a minimum distance of 25m. If you really need to eyeball animals, bring a pair of binoculars, watch a documentary, or go to a zoo.

Do not feed animals This leads to unnecessary dependence on humans; habituated baboons and vervet monkeys, especially, will become violent if refused handouts.

Take only memories Do not uproot, pick, cut or damage any plant, and take care putting out campfires and cigarettes; don't chuck them out of your window – dozens of bush fires are started this way every year. Littering is equally stupid.

vehicle with or without a driver, or – for a limited number of parks – getting there by public transport. Arranging your own trip has the advantage of flexibility and of being able to choose your travelling companions, but isn't necessarily cheaper than going through a company unless you can fill all the seats in a rented vehicle (usually five or seven). You'll also have to pay full-whack "walk-in rack rates" on upmarket accommodation (the prices quoted in this guide), which might otherwise be discounted if booked as part of an organized safari.

Details on how to get to and around the national parks in a hire car, or by **public transport** wherever possible, are given in the "Arrival" sections of each park throughout this guide. Advice on **car rental** is given on pp.42–46, and recommended rental companies are reviewed on p.132 (Dar es Salaam), p.404 (Arusha), and p.500 (Mwanza). As to **costs**: count on $120–200 a day for the vehicle including driver, fuel, and the driver's allowance and his park fees, then you'll need to add your own park entry fees (see opposite), maps and

Scams, dodgy companies and flycatchers

Be extremely careful when choosing a **safari company** not reviewed in this book, especially at the budget end. Of over three hundred companies operating from Arusha and Dar es Salaam, barely one third are properly licensed, meaning that the rest are operating illegally if they take you inside a national park. If you choose to go with a company that hasn't been reviewed in this book (a new set-up, for example), the travellers' grapevine is the best way to get the latest recommendations, though even bad companies sometimes get it right. The following advice should help avoid getting stung.

TALA licence All safari companies must possess a Government-issued "TALA licence" to take clients into the national parks: the "Safari operator" and "Tour operator" licences are valid for all but Kilimanjaro National Park, and theoretically guarantee that the operator possesses a minimum of five vehicles, although this is not always the case. The "Mountaineering" licence applies to Kilimanjaro alone, and enables the company to use their own guides for a summit attempt. New or dodgy safari companies tend to have only the Mountaineering licence, as it doesn't require five vehicles and is available to virtually anyone with $2000 to spare. However, it is not valid for wildlife parks, no matter what the operator might say. Without these licences, companies will either be operating illegally (gaining admission to parks via bribes) or will be passing clients on to other companies, something over which you may have little control. Demand to see the original copy of the licence certificate before booking, and do not accept a photocopy. It should show the current year, the correct company name, and the official seal. The deadline for paying licences is June, so there might be cases where the operator is still using last year's licence: in these cases check with the tourist board.

Tanzania Tourist Board (TTB) The board's tourist information offices in Arusha and Dar es Salaam maintain lists of TALA-licensed companies, and also keep – far from comprehensive – blacklists of particularly noxious ones. Be sure to check the PO Box number of your choice (if not in this book) against blacklisted ones, as bad companies, even if they change their name, rarely change their address. Don't necessarily believe recommendations from the tourist offices themselves (and the same goes for the ads on the wall); low wages can make some of them partial to accepting bribes.

TATO membership Companies that belong to the independent Tanzania Association of Tour Operators (TATO; PO Box 6162 Arusha ☎027/250 4188; ⊛www.tatotz. org) are marked as such throughout this book. Whilst its members are generally reputable in terms of services and relations with clients, they do include a number of hunting companies and others deemed by us to operate unethically. Nonetheless,

guidebooks, food and accommodation: at the very least, $30 per person camping or staying in park *bandas* (very basic rooms; you'll need to be entirely self-sufficient for these and for camping), or $100–1200 for a double room in a lodge or tented camp depending on their standard, exclusivity and whether they're inside or outside of the park. You don't need to pay the driver for his accommodation when staying at lodges – they pay a few thousand shillings for a bunk at the back somewhere. You might also invest in an official guide for game

drives: $10–20 per group for a few hours, though prices aren't fixed.

Entry fees are paid on arriving at the park or reserve gates; tourist rates are quoted in US dollars and must be paid in **hard currency** (bad rates for sterling and euros). Recent proposals to insist on payment in bankers' cheques mean you'd do well to check the situation regarding cash or travellers' cheques **before leaving** Arusha or Dar es Salaam. Fees are per person and for 24 hours: $25 for the less-visited parks and reserves, $50–60 for Serengeti and Kilimanjaro, and $80–100

membership does offer a modicum of quality, and room to manoeuvre if you've reason to complain.

Who's really running the safari? Most overseas tour companies "specializing" in Tanzania don't run their own trips here at all, but pass you on to a local "ground handler" (safari company). At the very least, you should be informed of the names of local operators before booking, and be given a chance to back out. The same applies when booking locally. In all cases, check the credentials of the local company – either through this book, the TTB (see above), or – for upmarket safaris – with a search through the "Talk" section of Ⓦwww.fodors.com.

Booking ahead (and the Internet) Book or pay ahead only with companies reviewed in this book, as unwary first-timers can get ripped off by phantom or otherwise dodgy companies, especially those with flashy websites. Indeed, some truly awful companies are quite adept at plugging themselves (and rubbishing the opposition) with postings on Internet newsgroups and forums, so don't believe everything you read.

Flycatchers A "flycatcher" (or *papasi* in Zanzibar) is a tout who approaches tourists on the street, in bus stations, train stations, airports and even hotels, with offers of cheap safaris, money changing, drugs and pretty much anything else a tourist might conceivably want. The advice is simple: never buy a safari from a company touted by flycatchers, as any company worth its reputation will not use them. Likewise, be wary of any company offering you a free ride from the airport, whether they're Tanzanian or European, and no matter how slick their appearance or patter.

Appearances Companies whose offices comprise just a desk and a chair in a rented room should be avoided. And no electricity means unpaid bills, which means you should look elsewhere. These jokers are known as "briefcase companies"

Off-road driving Driving off-road in Tanzania's parks is illegal and destructive. Plenty of companies do it though, even some of the bigger ones (excluded from this book). To check a company's morals, ask them innocently whether it would be possible to drive off-road for that perfect shot of a lion or leopard.

Comments book Even the worst companies are eager to show you comments books overflowing with praise. All wildly positive, of course – no company will ever ask a dissatisfied or complaining punter to add their opinions. Ripped-out pages are a dead give-away for something they don't want you to read. Here's a trick that works though: ask the company what kind of complaints they receive. There isn't a single safari company in any price range that doesn't receive complaints from time to time, so if they tell you they never receive complaints, they're lying.

for Mahale Mountains and Gombe Stream. **Children** under 16 pay $5–30; under-5s get in free. **Vehicle permits** (under two tons) cost Tsh10,000 (roughly $9), or $40 if foreign-registered. Entry fees for Tanzanians, for example your driver, are just a few thousand shillings.

Safari companies

Recommended safari operators are reviewed in the Dar es Salaam chapter (see p.133; mainly for the central, southern and western parks) and in Arusha (pp.404–407; mainly for the north). See also the overseas tour operators reviewed at the start of this chapter. All have been thoroughly checked for reliability, reputation, licences, and methods of dealing with complaints, and should be among the most responsible, ethical, and – within reason – best-priced. Should you disagree, please let us know. Be wary of companies not listed in this book – whilst some may be perfectly kosher, some have been deliberately excluded, for anything from offering hunting safaris (Tanzania's holy gruyère of corruption) to those that might be racist in their staff policies or employ unsustainable environmental practices.

Types of safari

The kind of safari depends on your budget, what level of comfort you're expecting, and whether you want a neo-colonial "bush tracker" experience or something more authentic. **Vehicles** used are usually Land Rovers or Land Cruisers, sometimes with roof hatches handy for taking pictures. Travel by minibus is increasingly rare and not recommended due to increased group sizes: ensure at least that it has a pop-up roof (better than roof hatches as they provide shade), and that a window seat is guaranteed. Safaris are cheaper if you **share** with other travellers; in a group of four or five, you might pay half what you would have paid in a couple.

When on a safari, don't take too passive an attitude. Although some of the itinerary may be fixed, it's not all cast in stone, and daily routines may be altered to suit you and your fellow travellers – if you want to go on an early game drive, for example, don't be afraid to suggest you skip breakfast, or take sandwiches. As long as they know there will be reasonable tips at the end of the trip, most staff will go out of their way to help. **Tipping**, however, is often a cause of misunderstanding. There's no hard-and-fast rule about this: $40 from the group for the trip, or $15 per day, to both the driver and the guide (if there's a separate one), plus $20 per trip to the cook, seems about right, though if your group size is large, it would be fair to double those figures. On the other hand, if the driving was dangerous and the service awful, tip less or don't tip at all – but do explain why. Lack of wildlife is no reason to tip less, however – animals don't keep to schedules. Other **additional costs** are alcoholic drinks and, sometimes, bottled water.

Bear in mind that a "three-day safari" actually means two nights, and that most of the first and last days are likely to be **driving time** to and from the parks, so you'll only get one full day in wildlife areas; for this reason, two-day trips are not normally recommended. In terms of **group size**, the smaller the group, the more expensive the safari; on most trips you're likely to find yourself travelling with up to seven other people. For some people this doesn't matter, and indeed the larger operators (catering almost exclusively to US tour groups) are commonly seen in convoys of half a dozen vehicles. Nonetheless, group relations among the passengers can assume surprising significance in a very short time. You can avoid this by spending more on a "tailor-made" private safari.

Camping safaris

At the lower end, so-called "budget" **camping safaris** are far from cheap at around $100–120 per person per day. Any national park safari offered for under $90 is likely to be cutting corners and best avoided. Budget safaris mostly involve staying under canvas, often small dome tents, either in public campsites inside the parks, or in cheaper ones outside. Expect to pitch in with the crew for some of the work, like putting up tents and washing up, and be prepared for a degree of discomfort: thin mattresses and sleeping bags, not having a shower every night, and basic food. More expensive mid-range camping trips feature better tents and food but are otherwise pretty similar.

Lodge safaris

More upmarket is a **lodge safari**, with accommodation in – you guessed it – safari lodges or "tented camps". The cheaper trips ($130–200 per day) use lodges and tented camps that can be far from intimate (if perfectly comfortable) and which lack that "in the wild" feeling. Spending over $200 a day, you have the run of the more upmarket lodges and some of the better tented camps. Establish what the maximum group size is if you're on a shared safari, and the type of vehicle that will be used. Also be aware that maximum group sizes may become irrelevant if you end up travelling in a convoy of half a dozen vehicles, as frequently happens with the larger operators.

Luxury flying safaris

A so-called "**flying safari**" – getting to and from the parks by light aircraft – can add enormously to the cost of a trip (upwards of $300 a day), but does of course dispense with the dusty discomfort and time wasted in getting to places, and gives spectacular views to boot. You'll also be treated to luxurious touches like champagne breakfasts, fly-camps in the bush (set up in advance of your arrival by a support crew), and expert expat guides (who seem to model themselves on the white hunter types in *Out of Africa*). The main disadvantages to such Hemingwayesque capers are the cost (up to a blistering $1000 a day) and the almost total exclusion of Tanzanians from both the safari and its profits – most of these outfits are owned by Europeans and South Africans.

Complaints

First off, it's best to avoid **complaints** by choosing a reputable company – you've only yourself to blame if an $85-a-day safari bought off the street turns sour. Also, be understanding about things outside a company's control – like bad weather, a lack of animals (unless they explicitly promised sightings), and breakdowns caused by unforeseeable things like broken fuel-injection pumps, which even the best mechanics cannot predict. For justified complaints, the best operators in all price ranges should at least offer a partial refund or a replacement trip.

Should the operator not be forthcoming, there's unfortunately very little you can do to get a refund. You can, however, make things awkward for them in future. Alerting the tourist board may result in the company being blacklisted, and TATO (see p.68) can expel errant members – not that this castigation is worth much. Some people have even set up Web pages warning of their experiences and written to newsgroups, bulletin boards and the like, but the best way to get revenge is to write to the guidebooks: we're at ⓦwww .roughguides.com.

Photography

Tanzania is immensely photogenic, and the temptation is to takes loads of equipment. However, SLR cameras and lenses are heavy and relatively fragile so, except in the game parks (where some kind of telephoto is essential if you want pictures of animals rather than savannah), don't bother with cumbersome lenses. Indeed, given the sometimes awkward lighting conditions, it's probably best to take a digital camera so you can retake shots that didn't work the first time. If you want lots of people snaps, lugging a Polaroid along with your normal camera is useful: it's always helpful (and polite) to give subjects an instant snap.

Whatever you take, ensure you have a dust-proof **camera bag** (if dust had value, Tanzania would be rich beyond belief), and take **spare batteries**: keep them in their original packaging, wrap them in foil and bury them deep in a suitcase or rucksack. **Film** is not especially expensive, but bring all the slide and black-and-white film you'll need, which can be difficult to find in Tanzania. Keep film cool by wrapping it in foil, either individually in each canister, or around the inside of a sealable plastic box. You could also carry it stuffed inside a sleeping bag, clothes, or in a (dry) towel. Debates still rage about the **best film to take**: on a two-week holiday, you might just get away with using professional film (such as Fuji Provia) that would otherwise require refrigeration, but on a longer journey where exposing undeveloped film to some degree of heat is inevitable, you'd be better with standard (non-professional) film unless you can be sure about keeping your stock cool at all times. **Film processing** within Tanzania is not recommended, even though many towns now have automatic one-hour-service machines, as chemicals may not be changed as frequently as they should be, and – for slides – cutting and mounting can be a disaster. **Digital photography** is the way to go. For this, invest in a few spare high-capacity memory cards and a **memory card reader**: most Internet cafés run Windows XP and have computers with USB ports, so making back-ups onto a spare card is easy, as is sending the images home by email (but do "cc" yourself a copy before deleting the original – computers and connections are not always reliable).

Subjects

Animal photography is principally a question of patience: if you can't get close enough, don't waste your film, and always turn off the engine when taking photos from a vehicle. The question of **photographing people** is more tricky: you should never take pictures of people without asking their permission. The Maasai – Tanzania's most photographed people – are usually prepared to do a deal (at monopoly prices), and in some places you'll even find professional posers making a living at the roadside. If you're motivated to take a lot of pictures of people, you might consider lugging along a Polaroid camera – most people will be very pleased to have a snap. Or you could have a lot of photos of you and your family printed up with your address on the back, which should at least raise a few laughs when you try the exchange.

One thing is certain: if you won't accept that some kind of interaction and exchange is warranted, you won't get many pictures. Promising to send the subject a copy of the photo when you get home might work, but is decreasingly popular with subjects who look on the photo call as work and have fixed rates. Blithely aiming at strangers is arrogant; it won't make you any friends and it may well get you into trouble. Note also that in Islamic areas, popular belief equates the act of taking a picture with stealing a piece of someone's soul.

It's also a bad idea to take pictures of anything that could be construed as strategic, including any military or police building, prisons, airports, harbours, bridges and His Excellency the President. It all depends who sees you, of course – but protesting your innocence won't appease small-minded officials.

Shopping

Woodcarvings are ubiquitous in Tanzania, including walking sticks, Maasai spears and figurines, combs, animals and (especially) the intricate and abstract Makonde carvings, named after the largest tribe of southern Tanzania and northern Mozambique – though they're nowadays more likely to have been made by craftsmen of the Zaramo tribe around Dar es Salaam. See p.242 for more about the Makonde and their wood-carving tradition.

Also well worth buying are the colourful **Tingatinga paintings**, found anywhere there are tourists; see the box on p.126. Also ubiquitous are **tie-dye batiks**, annoyingly so in Arusha, where you'll have reams of them shoved under your nose by street vendors. The country's distinctive **toys** also make good souvenirs: most worthwhile are the beautifully fashioned buses, cars, lorries and even motorbikes made out of wire.

Other frequently seen items include a huge variety of **sisal baskets**, **beadwork** (especially Maasai) and **soapstone carvings** imported from Kisii in Kenya (though the bowls and plates are for decoration only, since the dye that is used in their manufacture can be toxic). **Traditional crafts** – weapons, shields, drums, musical instruments, stools, headrests and metal jewellery – are common as well. With the notable exception of Makonde "helmet masks", **masks** are mostly reproductions based on central and western African designs, and even the oldest-looking examples may have been made specifically for the tourist market, no matter how much congealed cow dung appears to fill the crevices.

Textiles, notably a profusion of printed women's wraps in cotton (*kanga*) and the heavier-weave men's loincloths, are really good buys on the coast, and older ones represent collectable items worth seeking out. *Kangas* are always sold in pairs and are printed with intriguing Swahili proverbs.

Lastly, remember that purchasing or exporting **ivory**, **turtleshell** ("tortoiseshell"), **seahorses** and **seashells** encourages the destruction of wildlife and is in any case illegal, both in Tanzania and abroad – penalties include heavy fines or even imprisonment. Similarly, avoid anything like animal skins or game trophies; possession of these is illegal in Tanzania without the requisite paperwork, and may be completely illegal in other countries.

Bargaining

Bargaining is an important skill to learn, since every time you pay a "special price" price for goods or services, you contribute to local inflation (or, rather, to tourists after you having to pay inflated prices). This is especially prevalent (and deeply annoying) on Zanzibar, where even basic foodstuffs are first offered on a "hey, my friend" basis. It's impossible to state prices in this guide for everything, so before splashing out, ask a few disinterested locals about the real price – as what's sometimes initially offered may be literally ten times what the vendor is prepared to accept. The bluffing on both sides is part of the fun; don't be shy of making a big scene, and once you get into it, you'll rarely end up paying much more than the going rate. Where prices are marked, they are generally fixed. In general though, if you're happy paying a certain price, then it's a good price, irrespective of what locals would have paid.

Trouble

Tanzania is a largely safe and peaceful country: crime levels are low, and outside the main tourist areas, you're unlikely to come across much hassle either. If you stick to the following common-sense precautions, you're unlikely to run into trouble.

There are a few places in the country's larger towns and cities that should be avoided at night, and sometimes by day – these are mentioned in the guide. More general areas that you should be wary of, if not avoid completely, are parts of the **northwest** close to Burundi and Rwanda, and **Loliondo** and the area around **Lake Natron**, which saw a spate of bandit attacks by Somali gunmen in the 1990s. These fizzled out after a spectacular police chase over the border into Kenya, but you should be aware that the region is by its very nature difficult to control and things could start up again at any time.

The only other substantial risks on the mainland are some stretches of **beach**, especially north of Dar (including Bagamoyo), where valuables often disappear from the beach or occasionally get grabbed. Local hotels routinely advise their guests not to walk unaccompanied on the beach, or to carry valuables.

Wherever you are, avoid **political rallies and demonstrations** – the infamously bloody police crack-down on demonstrations in Zanzibar and Dar es Salaam in January 2001 was the worst political violence that Tanzania has ever experienced, and political unrest is a constant theme in Zanzibar, especially on Pemba and in the Ng'ambo area of Zanzibar Town (and also be aware that publicly airing your own opinions about Tanzanian politics isn't always such a great idea either).

Hassle

There's virtually no **hassle** outside the main tourist centres of Arusha, Moshi, Dar es Salaam and Stone Town. In these places, your **appearance** goes a long way to determining the extent to which you'll attract attention. It's impossible not to look like a tourist – local expats are known by all – but

you can dress down and look like you've been travelling for months, so that people will assume you're streetwise. Avoid wearing anything brand-new, especially white clothes, and make sure your shoes aren't overly shiny. Some tourists swear by sunglasses to avoid making unwanted eye-contact; while this usually works, it still marks you out as a tourist and also puts a barrier between you and everyone else, not just hasslers.

Beggars and street children

Beggars are fairly common in Arusha, Dar es Salaam and Dodoma, but rare elsewhere. Most beggars are visibly destitute; many are cripples, lepers or blind, or are homeless mothers with children, and they are harassed by the police and often rounded up. Some have regular pitches; others keep on the move. Tanzanians often give to the same beggar on a regular basis in fulfilment of the Islamic requirement to give alms to the poor. A Tsh100 coin suffices, and Tsh200 will often delight.

Much more common, especially in Arusha, are the hundreds of **street children**, many of them glue-sniffing boys aged 8–14. They're responsible for much of the city's petty crime and are mostly ignored by Tanzanians. Pitiful as they are, they offer a disturbing insight into one of the realities of Tanzanian life. The children are forced onto the streets by a variety of reasons, most commonly to escape physical abuse and domestic violence. Others come from homes decimated by AIDS. With no prospect of employment (the situation is chronic enough for adults), the children's only option is the street.

Some people argue that giving street children money encourages a culture of dependency (the logic being that the supposedly rich pickings to be made on the streets will only encourage more kids to join them). If you want to help, it's probably best to give food.

Misunderstandings

Whilst most Tanzanians will go out of their way to help out visitors, in tourist areas it's easy to fall prey to **misunderstandings** with young men and boys who offer their services as guides or helpers. You shouldn't assume anything they do is out of simple kindness. It may well be, but if it isn't, you must expect to pay something. If you have any suspicion, it's invariably best to confront the matter head on at an early stage and either apologize for the offence caused by the suggestion, or agree a price. What you must never do, as when bargaining, is enter into an unspoken contract and then break it by refusing to pay for the service. If you're being bugged by someone whose "help" you don't need, just let them know you can't pay anything for their trouble. It may not make you a friend, but it's better than a row and recriminations.

Driving

It's never a good idea to leave even a locked car unguarded if it has anything of value in it – in towns, there's usually someone who will guard it for you for a tip (Tsh500 is enough). While **driving at night** in a town or a city – especially Arusha and Dar es Salaam – local advice is to keep the doors locked and windows up to avoid grab-and-run incidents.

Snatch-and-run robberies, **car-jackings** and **armed hold-ups** – though extremely rare – are on the rise, especially at night (never a good time to be driving). Areas to be wary of are Arusha, and – more seriously – remoter parts of the northwest along the borders with Burundi and Rwanda, where armed incursions from rebel factions and other bandits have been reported in the past. Other roads along which armed robberies have been reported are the unsurfaced seventy-kilometre stretch between Tanga and the Kenyan border (soon to be sealed), and the highways between Morogoro and Mikumi, and between Chalinze and Segera (part of the road between Dar and Moshi), which was targeted by highway bandits

before the road was resurfaced. You should be extremely wary of stopping for anyone along these stretches outside villages.

In **Zanzibar**, robberies at fake police roadblocks have been reported. For tips on avoiding hassle with the police when driving, see p.44.

Police – and bribes

Though you might sometimes hear stories of extraordinary kindness and of occasional bursts of efficiency that would do credit to any constabulary, in general the **Tanzanian police** are notoriously corrupt, and it's usually best to steer clear of them. If you need to deal with them, patience and politeness, smiles and handshakes always help, and treat even the most offensively corrupt cop with respect (greeting him with "Shikamoo, Mzee" for starters). Having said this, in unofficial dealings the police can go out of their way to help you with food, transport or accommodation, especially in remote outposts. Try to reciprocate. Police salaries are low – no more than $50 per month – and they rely on unofficial income to get by.

Unless you're driving a car, police are rarely out to solicit **bribes** from tourists, though there have been cases of them taking advantage when the law's not totally clear: swimming at Coco Beach after a man-eating shark scare in 2000 earned one policeman Tsh20,000 from a traveller who hadn't noticed the "no swimming" signs by the roadside, which in any case were in Kiswahili. If approached by policemen asking for money for alleged offences, insist on identification before going to a police station to make any payments.

If you know you've done something wrong and are expected to give a bribe, wait for it to be hinted at and haggle over it as you would any payment; Tsh2000 or so is often enough to oil small wheels, though traffic police may expect something more substantial from tourists. Be aware, of course, that bribery is illegal – if you know you've done nothing wrong and are not in a rush, refusing a bribe will only cost a short delay until the cop gives up on you and tries another potential source of income. If you're really getting nowhere, you can always kick up a loud fuss – it usually works wonders.

Drugs

If you spend any time in Dar, Arusha or Zanzibar, you'll probably be offered **drugs**, usually by flycatchers also offering batiks, dodgy safaris and money change. **Grass** (*bangi*) is widely smoked and remarkably cheap. However, it's also illegal, and the authorities do make some effort to control it: if you're caught in possession, you'll be hit with a heavy fine, and possibly imprisoned or deported. Anything harder than marijuana is rarely sold and will obviously get you in much worse trouble if you're caught in possession.

The use of and attitudes to grass vary considerably, but you should be very discreet if you're going to indulge, and watch out who you get high with. Never buy marijuana on the street – you're guaranteed to be ripped off or shopped to the police, who may or may not be amenable to bribes. There are also a number of **scams** associated with buying drugs, the most common one being approached by fake (or real) policemen shortly after buying, who will shake you down for everything you have.

Unseemly behaviour

Failure to observe the following points of **official etiquette** can get you into trouble. Stand in cinemas and on other occasions when the national anthem is playing. Stand still when the national flag is being raised or lowered. Don't take photos of the flag. Pull off the road completely when scores of motorcycle outriders appear, then get out and stand by your vehicle (for it's the President, or else the burly chief of police). Never tear up a banknote, of any denomination, and don't urinate in public.

Robbery and theft

Your chances of being **robbed** in Tanzania are pretty slim, but you should nonetheless be conscious of your belongings and never leave anything unguarded even for a second. In addition, you should be careful of where you walk, at least until you're settled in somewhere. Also be alert in bus stations, especially when arriving. If you can't help walking around with valuables and are in a town for more than a couple of days, vary your route and schedule to avoid creating temptation. Note also that there are always more **pickpockets** about at the end of the month, when people are carrying the salaries they've just been paid. Finally, beware of **doping scams** on public transport; see box on p.41 for more details.

Muggings

The best way to avoid being **mugged** is to not carry any valuables, especially anything visible. It should go without saying that you don't wear dangling earrings or any kind of chain or necklace, expensive-looking sunglasses or wristwatches; even certain brands of sports shoes (sneakers) can be tempting. Similarly, try to avoid carrying valuables in those handy off-the-shoulder day bags or even small rucksacks, as these provide visible temptation. Old

Carrying money safely

First off, carry as little cash as possible and put whatever money you are carrying in several different places: a money belt tucked under your trousers or skirt is invisible and thus usually secure for travellers' cheques, passports and large amounts of cash. The best money belts are cotton or linen, as nylon ones can cause skin irritations if you sweat a lot. For the same reason, wrap up your things in a plastic bag before placing them in the belt. Make sure that your money belt lies flat against your skin; the voluminous "bum bags" worn back-to-front by many tourists over their clothing invite a mugging, and are only one step short of announcing your stash with flashing neon lights. Equally dumb are pouches hanging around your neck, and ordinary wallets are a disaster.

Put the rest of your money – what you'll need for the day or your night out – in a pocket or somewhere more accessible: somewhat perversely, you're safer with at least some money to hand, as few muggers will believe you have nothing on you whatsoever.

plastic bags (nicknamed "Rambo", courtesy of the dim-witted action hero whose likeness is printed on millions of them) are a much less conspicuous way of carrying cameras. If you clearly have nothing on you, you're unlikely to feel, or be, threatened.

If you do get mugged, **don't resist**, since knives and guns are occasionally carried. It will be over in an instant and you're unlikely to be hurt. You'll have to go to the nearest police station for a statement to show your insurance company, though you may well be expected to pay a "little something" for it. You can usually forget about enlisting the police to try and get your stuff back.

As angry as you may feel about being robbed, it's worth trying to understand the desperation that drives men and boys to risk their lives for your things. Thieves caught red-handed are usually mobbed – and often killed – so when you shout "Thief!" ("*Mwizi!*" in Kiswahili), be ready to intercede once you've retrieved your belongings.

Theft from hotel rooms

Thefts from locked **hotel bedrooms** are extremely rare, except in a handful of backpackers' lodgings in Arusha and Dar. Petty pilfering by hotel staff is also uncommon. Other than – judiciously – depositing valuables with the hotel management, the best way to avoid either scenario is not to leave things lying about openly. Burying stuff in the bottom of your rucksack and closing all bags deters temptation, and hiding stuff between a mattress and bed frame is also usually safe – at least judging by the amount of accumulated grime under most hotel mattresses.

Cons and scams

An incredible number of newly arrived visitors get **ripped off** during their first day or two, perhaps because, with pale skin, new luggage and clean shoes, they stick out a mile. Most scams are confidence tricks, and though there's no reason to be paranoid (indeed, one or two scams play on a tourist's paranoia), a healthy sense of cynicism is helpful.

Ferry tickets

The process of buying **ferry tickets** between Dar es Salaam and Stone Town is a firm favourite with scammers both on the mainland and in Zanzibar. The scam basically involves someone selling you a ferry ticket at the discounted rates available to Tanzanians or bona fide residents. If you fall for it, you may well be let on the ferry, whence – cometh the ticket inspector, bent policeman and assorted heavies – you'll be made to buy another ticket at the full tourist price plus a bribe to smooth things over. A variation on this scam is to be offered a ticket at the discounted price paid by tourists travelling with overland trucks. The ticket inspector has a list of these clients, and if you're not on it, it's the same outcome.

An even cruder scam is to be sold a ticket for a ferry departure that doesn't even exist – especially the "night ferry" from Dar to Stone Town (there isn't one, but there is an overnight sailing in the opposite direction). All these scams are easily avoided by buying your ticket at the tourist rate and either at the ferry company's office or from a reputable travel agent.

Although we've received no reports about the same scam being tried on **bus tickets**, it's probably only a matter of time before it is.

Money-changers

Another old favourite is the offer to **change money** on the street at favourable rates. Given that the Tanzanian shilling is floated freely against hard currencies, there's no possible reason for a black market to exist, so it doesn't take a genius to realize that by changing money on the street you're just setting yourself up to get ripped off.

In its most obvious form, the money-changer simply dashes off with your money, sometimes aided by the timely appearance of a "police officer". Much more subtle – and common – is to trick you by sleight of hand: the scammer lets you count the shilling notes, takes your money, then proceeds to roll up the shillings and tie them with a rubber band. When you open the bundle it's been switched for one containing only low-value notes or even paper.

In addition, if you're entering the country overland, be aware that there are no regulations saying that visitors need to have Tanzanian shillings to be allowed in: it's just a line that con-men feed you.

Other scams

Approaches in the street from "school children" or "students" with **sponsorship forms** are usually just scams and best shrugged off, and if a man who has just picked up a wad of money in the street seems oddly willing to share it with you down a convenient nearby alley, you'll know you're about to be robbed... Lastly, several travellers report having had **marijuana planted** on them and then being nabbed by cops, real or fake, with hefty bribes being the way out. So, check your pockets in Dar and Stone Town if a stranger started chatting to you in the street, and if you do get "caught", insist on going to the police station to sort things out, where you'll be able to kick up a fuss with the officer's superior, threaten legal action against the corrupt cop, demand legal assistance and so on – a time-consuming rigmarole that hopefully won't be worth the corrupt cop's time, or his job if he gets shopped.

Customs and beliefs

Tanzanians are known for their tactfulness and courtesy, qualities that are highly valued right across the social spectrum and by all the nation's tribes. The desire to maintain healthy relationships with both neighbours and strangers epitomizes the peaceful and non-tribalistic nature of Tanzanian society, and expresses itself in the warm welcome given to visitors. As such, you'll be treated as an honoured guest by many people, and if you make the effort, you'll be welcomed to a side of Tanzania that too few tourists see.

Appearance and behaviour

There are no hard-and-fast rules about public behaviour so long as you respect local customs, cultural and religious beliefs. Apart from **indecent dress**, a few things are generally considered offensive: these include **public displays of intimacy** (though a couple holding hands is fine); **immodesty**, both verbal and material (don't flaunt wealth); and open displays of **bad temper and impatience**, which will not endear you to anyone. There are exceptions to this, of course: if you're a woman being pestered by a man, expressions of anger should result in embarrassed bystanders coming to your rescue. Lastly, it is insulting and invasive to take **photographs of people** without their permission. Always ask, and respect their refusal, or cough up if they ask for money in return.

Dress

Tanzanians make an effort to appear well dressed, and so should you. The simple rule is to wear comfortable and decent clothes; they should also be clean, within reason. Although Islamic moral strictures tend to be generously interpreted, in Muslim majority areas – mainly the coast and Zanzibar – men and women should **cover up** when not on a beach frequented by tourists. This means long trousers for men, and a long dress, skirt, *kanga* or trousers for women. Sleeves don't have to be too long, only enough to cover your shoulders. There's no need for headgear, though you'll probably be wearing a sun hat anyway. Although people are far too polite to admonish strangers, tourists who ignore the dress code – which is posted up in pretty much every hotel in Zanzibar – are viewed with scorn. The other very good reason for covering up is simple: you'll attract much less hassle from touts and flycatchers, and won't be treated as a dumb tourist.

Sadly, gross ignorance or wilful disregard of local customs by tourists appears to be on the increase, especially in Zanzibar as it gets swamped by mass tourism. The idea seems to be that spending a fortune on a two-week beach holiday also buys you the right to ignore local feelings and traditions. It doesn't.

Greetings

Lengthy greetings – preferably in Kiswahili – are extremely important, and people will value your efforts to master them. Elderly men and women are invariably treated with great deference. The word for greeting anyone older than you is *Shikamoo*, best followed by an honorific title: *Babu* (grandfather) for an elderly man, *Bibi* (grandmother) for an elderly woman, *Baba* (father) for a man, *Mama* (mother) for a woman and *Mwalimu* for a teacher or someone intelligent. The standard acknowledgement is *Marahaba*. If you're addressed with *Shikamoo* – usually children in rural areas – do respond with the requisite *Marahaba* (pulling a silly face goes down a storm, too). For some **common greetings**, see the "Language" section on p.779.

As well as the verbal greeting, younger women do a slight **curtsy** when greeting elders, while men invariably shake hands both at meeting and parting. Among younger people especially there are a number of more elaborate handshakes that anyone will be happy to teach you. You should always use your right hand to shake or to give or receive anything; it's especially polite to clasp your right forearm or wrist with your left hand as you do so. Incidentally, if someone's hands are wet or dirty when you meet, they'll offer their wrist instead. It's impolite to discuss a man's work or financial standing unless you know him well.

Gifts

When invited into someone's home, it's usual to bring small **presents** (see box on p.53) for the family if you've been invited to lunch or dinner. If you're staying longer, slightly more elaborate presents are in order. Increase the amount of practical presents you bring (a few of kilos of sugar, more tea), and bring a *kanga* or *kitenge* for the mother and grandmother. Ballpoint pens and writing pads will always find a use, and the kids will be fascinated by books (Tanzania's literacy rate, though down from a peak of ninety percent-plus which it reached in the 1980s, is still high by African standards). Most bookshops sell gorgeously illustrated children's books in Kiswahili. For other gift ideas, ask your host before coming – and insist beyond their polite insistence that the only presents you need to bring is your own presence.

Lastly, **do not give coins, sweets or pens to children**: it encourages begging, as you'll notice in the chorus of "*Mzungu* give me money/pen/sweet" that accompanies you anywhere where tourists ignoring this rule have been in the past. If you really want to give something, hand it to an adult who will share it out, or – even better – make a donation to the local school. If you'll be travelling or staying for some time and really want to prepare, get a large batch of photos of you and your family with your address on the back. You'll get lots of mail.

Sexuality

Sexual mores in Tanzania are refreshingly hedonistic and uncluttered. The downside of this openness is that sexually transmitted diseases are rife. At least one in ten Tanzanians carries **HIV**, and four out of five deaths among 25- to 35-year-olds are AIDS-related. It goes without saying that casual sex without a condom is a deadly gamble and you should assume any sexual contact to be HIV-positive. Despite this, female **prostitution** flourishes quite openly in urban areas.

Plenty enough **female tourists** arrive expecting sexual adventures to make flirtatious pestering a fairly constant part of the scene, irritating or amusing as it strikes you, though **machismo** is rare and male egos are usually softened by reserves of humour. If you are a woman looking for a holiday affair (Zanzibar is the main place), be aware that your cute dreadlocked lover more likely than not does this for a living.

Male homosexuality is an accepted undercurrent on the coast, although it's officially illegal. Public displays of affection are guaranteed to offend (though men holding

Sexual harassment

Women, whether travelling alone or together, may come across occasional **persistent hasslers** but seldom much worse. Universal rules apply: if you suspect ulterior motives, turn down all offers and stonily refuse to converse, though you needn't fear expressing your anger if that's how you feel. You will be left alone – eventually. Really obnoxious individuals are usually on their own, fortunately. A useful trick if you're unmarried and travelling alone is to wear a "wedding" ring (silver ones feel safer than gold in terms of tempting robbery), though for this to work it would be helpful to take along a picture of a burly male friend à la Mike Tyson with a suitably husband-like message written on the back as "proof".

These tactics are hardly necessary except on the coast, particularly in Zanzibar. Blonde women suffer more, though cutting your hair short or dyeing it seems drastic, and anyway you'll still look like a tourist.

hands is perfectly normal), and – in theory – could even get you 25 years in the slammer. Few hotels will let two men share a room; women sharing is usually fine. *Shoga* is Kiswahili for gay man; *msagaji* is a lesbian.

Religion

The majority of mainland Tanzanians are **Christians** – if sometimes only in name. Varieties of Catholicism and Protestantism are dominant but, as with Kenya, there are also many minor Christian sects and churches, often based around the teachings of local preachers. **Sunni Islam** dominates the coast and Zanzibar, and is in the ascendant throughout the country. Many towns have several mosques (or, on the coast, dozens). The Aga Khan's Ismaili sect is also influential,

with powerful business interests, the profits from which are often used in development projects. Unless you're given permission, **mosques** should only be entered by Muslims. **Hindu** and **Sikh** temples are found in most large towns, and there are adherents of **Jainism** and the **Bahai** faith, too.

Indigenous religions (mostly based around the idea of a supreme god and intercession between the living and the spirit worlds by deceased ancestors) survive in more mountainous and otherwise remote terrain, as well as among pastoralists like the Maasai and Barbaig, but is increasingly under threat from Christian missionaries, thanks to whom much of the cumulative wisdom, customs and traditional music of neighbouring Kenya has already been destroyed.

Working in Tanzania

It's illegal to obtain income in Tanzania while staying on a tourist visa, and unless you've lined up a job or voluntary work before leaving for Tanzania, you have little chance of getting employment. Wages are extremely low – school teachers earn about $80 a month – and there's serious unemployment in the towns. Particular skills are sometimes in demand – mechanics at game park lodges, for example, and teachers – but the employer or school will need good connections to arrange the required papers. Travel magazines often have a jobs section. ⓦwww.studyabroad. com has useful listings and links to study and work programmes worldwide.

Teaching English

There are two options: find or prepare for finding work before you go, or just wing it and see what you come up with while you're out there, particularly if you already have a degree and/or teaching experience. Teaching English is the way many people finance their way around the greater part of the world; you can get a **CELTA** (Certificate in English Language Teaching to Adults), a **TEFL** (Teaching English as a Foreign Language) or a **TESOL** (Teaching English to Speakers of Other Languages) qualification before you leave home. Strictly speaking, you don't need a degree to do the course, but you'll certainly find it easier to get a job with the degree/certificate combination. Certified by the RSA, the course is very demanding and costs about £1025/$2500/A$2550 for the month's full-time tuition; you'll be thrown in at the deep end and expected to teach right away. In **Canada**, try the Vancouver English Centre (☎604/687 1600, ⓦwww.vec.ca) where the four-week TEFL Certificate course costs C$1440, with occasional twenty percent off deals in the winter. New Zealand's Communicative Language Training International (☎03/377 8157, ⓦwww.cltintl.com) offer a six-week TEFL course for NZ$3720. The **British Council's** website, ⓦwww .britishcouncil.org/work/jobs and the **TEFL** website ⓦwww.tefl.com, both have a list of English-teaching vacancies.

Study and work programmes

For travellers from the UK and Ireland

British Council 10 Spring Gardens, London SW1A 2BW ☎020/7930 8466, ⓦwww .britishcouncil.org/work/jobs. Produces leaflet which details study opportunities abroad. The Council's Central Management of Direct Teaching (☎020/7389 4931) recruits TEFL teachers for posts worldwide (check website for vacancies), and its Central Bureau for International Education and Training (☎020/7389 4004, ⓦwww .centralbureau.org.uk) enables those who already work as educators to find out about teacher development programmes abroad. It also publishes a book, *Year Between*, aimed principally at gap-year students detailing volunteer programmes, and schemes abroad.

Changing Worlds Hodore Farm, Hartfield, East Sussex TN7 4AR ☎01892/770000, ⓦwww .changingworlds.co.uk. A small and friendly organization for volunteer teachers in Arusha and elsewhere.

Earthwatch Institute ☎01865/318 838; see under US and Canada.

Frontier Conservation Expeditions 50–52 Rivington St, London EC2A 3QP ☎ 020/7613 2422, ⓦwww.frontier.ac.uk. Paying volunteers are usually gap-year students working on environmental projects. Their Tanzanian involvement included much of the research that led to the establishment of Mafia Island and Mnazi Bay-Ruvuma Estuary marine parks. They're also involved in the Eastern Arc Mountains.

Trade Aid Burgate Court, Burgate, Fordingbridge, Hants SP6 1LX ☏01425/657774, ⓦwww .tradeaiduk.org. Heavily involved in Mikindani in southern Tanzania (they're based at the *Old Boma* hotel, see p.237), Trade Aid welcome volunteers with any kind of useful or professional developmental skills.

Voluntary Service Overseas (VSO) 317 Putney Bridge Rd, London SW15 2PN ☏020/8780 7200, ⓦwww.vso.org.uk. A British government-funded organization that places volunteers on various projects around the world.

For travellers from the US and Canada

Earthwatch Institute 3 Clock Tower Place, Suite 100, Box 75 Maynard, MA 01754 ☏1-800/776-0188 or 1-978/461-0081, ⓦwww.earthwatch .org. Long-established not-for-profit with offices in the US, UK and Australia, organizing environmental and archeological "research" projects worldwide, although many of them are really nothing more than thinly veiled safaris. Participation mainly as a paying volunteer (pricey), but fellowships for teachers and students available.

Peace Corps 1111 20th St, NW, Washington DC 2052 ☏1-800/424-8580, ⓦwww.peacecorps.gov.

Places Americans with specialist qualifications or skills in two-year postings in Tanzania.

Volunteers for Peace Tiffany Rd, Belmont, Vermont 05730 ☏1-802/259-2759, ⓦwww .vfp.org. Not-for-profit with links to a huge international network of "workcamps", in Tanzania meaning two-week volunteer programmes in all fields. Most workcamps are in June to August, with registration in April–May. Annual membership costs $20.

Voluntary Service Overseas Canada 806-151 Slater St, Ottawa, ON K1P 5☏1-888/VSO-2911 or 613/234-1364, ⓦwww.vsocanada.org. Canadian-based organization affiliated to the British VSO.

For travellers from Australia and New Zealand

Australian Volunteers International 71 Argyle St (PO Box 350), Fitzroy VIC 3065 ☏1800/331 292 or 03/9279 1788, ⓦwww.ozvol.org.au. Concerned with pressing social issues primarily in southern Africa, especially teachers and health professionals; postings up to two years.

Travellers with disabilities

Although by no means easy, Tanzania doesn't pose insurmountable problems for people with disabilities. While there is little government involvement in improving access, staff in the tourist industry – not to mention passers-by – will usually help where necessary. Wheelchair-users will find that many hotels have ground-floor rooms, while a number on the coast have ramped access walks to public areas, and larger hotels in Arusha and Dar es Salaam have elevators. Safari vehicles can usually manage wheelchair-users. If you're looking for an all-in tour, contact the upmarket specialists Abercrombie & Kent (see p.23), who have some experience in working with disabled passengers.

Attitudes to disabled people in Tanzania are generally good – there are always willing hands to help you over any obstacle. **Getting around** the cities, however, is difficult in a wheelchair: there is little ramping of pedestrian areas, and pavements are often pot-holed or blocked by parked cars and hawkers. Taxis are invariably small saloon cars.

Safari vehicles have superb springing, an advantage somewhat offset by the skills of the average driver, so taking a pressure cushion is wise. Even then, off-road trips can be very arduous, especially on the awful roads in and around Selous and in any other parks outside the Northern Safari Circuit, where flying in is recommended. If you're determined, most of the luxury lodges and tented camps should be accessible, with help, making a proper safari quite feasible. Only on the most adventurous trips, with temporary camps set up in the bush, and long-drop toilets, would wheelchair-users really have problems.

The sleeper trains from Dar es Salaam to Kigoma or Mwanza sound improbable but, again, are possible. On these, though, you would have to be carried – which might prove difficult – from your cabin (first-class is the only feasible choice) to the toilets and dining car, as the corridors are very narrow. Your wheelchair would go in the luggage van too, so expect a delay in retrieving it on arrival. With the exception of the "Royal Class" **coaches** operated by Scandinavian Express (ⓦwww.scandinaviagroup.com), public road transport isn't at all wheelchair-friendly.

Contacts for travellers with disabilities

In the UK and Ireland

Holiday Care 2nd floor, Imperial Building, Victoria Rd, Horley, Surrey RH6 7PZ ⓣ0845/124 9971 or ⓣ0208/760 0072, ⓦwww.holidaycare.org. uk. Provides free lists of accessible accommodation abroad, and information on financial help for holidays.
Irish Wheelchair Association Blackheath Drive, Clontarf, Dublin 3 ⓣ01/818 6400, ⓦwww.iwa.ie. Useful information provided about travelling abroad with a wheelchair.
Tripscope The Vassall Centre, Gill Ave, Bristol BS16 2QQ ⓣ08457/585 641 or 0117/939 7782, ⓦwww .tripscope.org.uk. Registered charity providing a

national telephone information service offering free advice on transport.

In the US and Canada

Access-Able ⓦwww.access-able.com. Useful website for travellers with disabilities.
Directions Unlimited 123 Green Lane, Bedford Hills, NY 10507 ⓣ1-800/533-5343 or 1-914/241-1700. Travel agency specializing in bookings for people with disabilities.
Mobility International USA 451 Broadway, Eugene, OR 97401 ⓣ1-541/343-1284, ⓦwww .miusa.org. Information and referral services, access guides, tours and exchange programmes.
SATH (Society for the Advancement of Travelers with Handicaps) 347 5th Ave, New York, NY 10016 ⓣ1-212/447-7284, ⓦwww.sath.org. Not-for-profit educational organization that has actively represented travellers with disabilities since 1976. Annual membership $45; $30 for students and seniors.
Twin Peaks Press PO Box 129 Vancouver, WA 98666-0129 ⓣ360/694-2462, ⓦⓦwww.home. pacifier.com/~twinpeak. Publisher of the *Directory of Travel Agencies* for the Disabled, listing more than 370 agencies worldwide; *Travel for the Disabled*; and *Wheelchair Vagabond*, loaded with personal tips.
Wheels Up! ⓣ1-888/38-WHEELS, ⓦwww .wheelsup.com. Provides discounted airfare, tour and cruise prices for disabled travellers, and publishes a free monthly newsletter. Comprehensive website.

In Australia and New Zealand

ACROD (Australian Council for Rehabilitation of the Disabled) PO Box 60, Curtin ACT 2605; ⓣ02/6282 4333 (also TTY), ⓦwww.acrod.org.au. Provides lists of travel agencies and tour operators for people with disabilities.
Disabled Persons Assembly 4/173–175 Victoria St, Wellington, New Zealand ⓣ04/801 9100 (also TTY), ⓦwww.dpa.org.nz. Resource centre with lists of travel agencies and tour operators for people with disabilities.

The environment and ethical tourism

Tourism may soon become the world's largest industry. It can play an important part in maintaining indigenous cultures, and also provides an invaluable source of foreign currency for many African countries. Although there are many benefits, there are also some irreversible and detrimental consequences. Tourism's growth in Tanzania has been spectacular, having increased five-fold over the last decade to approach one million visitors each year. It has been a boon for the economy, but with serious and potentially disruptive effects environmentally, socially and culturally. Zanzibar is a textbook case: some coastal villages have been all but bought out by large, all-inclusive package resorts surrounded by tall walls or electric fencing, and who contribute little to the local economy. And whilst ten years ago it was unheard of to have a kid asking tourists for presents, you're now just as likely to hear "Give me my money!" as you are "Jambo!" said in greeting.

Contacts

Campaign for Environmentally Responsible Tourism (CERT) Ⓦ www.c-e-r-t.org. Lobbies to educate tour operators and tourists in a sensitive approach to travel, focusing on immediate practical ways in which the environment can be protected.
Partners in Responsible Tourism (PIRT) Ⓦ www.pirt.org. An organization of individuals and travel companies promoting responsible tourism to minimize harm to the environment and local cultures. Their website features a "Traveler's Code for Traveling Responsibly."
Tourism Concern ☎ 020/7753 3330, Ⓦ www .tourismconcern.org.uk. Campaigns for the rights of local people to be consulted in tourism developments affecting their lives, and produces a quarterly magazine of news and articles. Also publishes the *Good Alternative Travel Guide*.

Eco-tourism: myth and reality

Most of the lodges and tented camps in Tanzania's wildlife areas claim to be "eco-friendly". Although some are genuine about this, many have simply appropriated the **eco-tourism** tag for business purposes. For a start, however eco-friendly they may claim to be, it's worth remembering that the very existence of a lodge or hotel inevitably has a negative impact on the **environment**, no matter how many safeguards are used. Equally, although many establishments boast that they are built entirely from natural or local materials, the very scale of many of these places means that the collection of materials for their construction was itself a huge blow to the environment: many coastal lodges, for instance, are constructed from a mixture of endangered tropical hardwoods, mangrove poles and coral ragstone, all of which continue to be exploited in a wholly unsustainable fashion. In short, don't believe the hype, and if a really ecologically sound holiday is important to you, steer clear of the big tourist places and stay instead in local guest houses.

We've tried, so far as possible, to mention ecological factors in our reviews, and have also excluded establishments that were built or are maintained in ways that damage the environment. The main exception to this rule – reluctantly so – are most of the lodges around the rim of the Ngorongoro Crater, which have been accused for many years of unecological practices, but cannot practically be excluded due to the huge number of tourists who stay there. We've also **excluded** a number of lodges, tented camps and safari companies that, in our opinion, operate unethically. All this is not to say that all the hotels and companies reviewed in this guide are guaranteed to be ethical – and feedback from travellers is always welcome.

On the positive side, a recent and very encouraging trend in lodges and tented camps outside national parks has been to involve local communities as owners and managers, as well as staff; these places are noted in the guide.

Directory

Clothes Bring loose cotton clothes, comfortable flip-flops (or suede shoes, plus boots for the highlands), and at least one really warm sweater or a jacket. See the "Mount Kilimanjaro" section (p.340) for advice on what you need at high altitudes. Don't bring mounds of clothes, though: cheap clothes, both new and second-hand, are available in markets throughout the country.

Contraceptives Condoms are freely sold in pharmacies and supermarkets; a reliable local brand is Salama. Bring oral contraceptives with you.

Departure tax The $30 international departure tax is included in ticket fares. There's also an $8 safety charge, which should eventually also be included. On national flights, the taxes are $5 and $1 respectively, and not normally included.

Electricity Like Britain, most of Tanzania uses square three-pin plugs on 220–240V, at least in theory: in practice, unstable supplies, power surges and drop-offs widen the range considerably; Arusha's supply varies from 160V to 260V. If you're using sensitive electronic equipment, ensure that it or the transformer accepts the whole of this range. A few places use thick round two-pin plugs, though adapters can easily be bought for about Tsh500. All but the very cheapest hotels tend to have sockets in the rooms. Apart from the unstable current, Tanzania is also subjected to frequent power cuts (blackouts). Things are worse at the end of particularly dry spells, when reservoirs are too low to adequately power the nation's hydroelectric stations. At these times, power rationing is common. Many rural places are not connected to the national grid, so electricity in these places – if any – is powered by local oil-fired power stations or else by generators belonging to hotels and businesses.

Laundry There are no laundromats in Tanzania and it's usually easiest to wash your own clothes: you can buy packets of soap powder, and things dry fast. Beware of New Blue Omo – it's very strong and wrecks clothes if you use it for long. Otherwise, there's often someone wherever you're staying who will be prepared to negotiate a laundry charge.

Time Tanzania is three hours ahead of Greenwich Mean Time, which means two hours ahead of Britain during the summer and three in winter;

seven or eight hours ahead of US Eastern Standard Time; and 6.5–7.5 hours behind Australian time. Remember that the hours in "Swahili time" run from 6am to 6pm rather than noon to midnight, so that 7am and 7pm Western time equate to 1 o'clock in Swahili (*saa moja*), whilst midnight and midday are *saa sita* (six o'clock). It's not as confusing as it first sounds – just add or subtract six hours to work out Swahili time. People and things are usually late in Tanzania, though trains heading out from Dar nearly always leave right on time, and buses often depart punctually as well (it's the arriving on time bit that they have trouble with).

Tipping The average salary is $50 (Tsh55,000) a month. In local hotels, bars and restaurants, tipping is not the custom, albeit always appreciated. If you're staying in tourist-class establishments, staff may expect to be tipped: Tsh1000 wouldn't be out of place for portering a lot of luggage, but Tsh500 is adequate. For small services, Tsh200–500 is fine. On safaris, tips are considered part of the pay; expectations vary widely, though anything less than $10–20 per person would be considered stingy. See p.341 for tipping advice on Kilimanjaro climbs.

Toilets Tanzania's lavatories (ask for the *choo*; *wanawake* is ladies, *wanaume* is for gents) are either "Western" sit-down style, or Asian-style "squats". Mid-range and upmarket hotels, restaurants and bars generally have Western toilets and flushing mechanisms, and should have toilet paper to hand. In lowlier places, they'll often lack seats and paper, and may need to be flushed with a bucket. Squat toilets, often in the same cubicle as showers, are mostly quite hygienic, and may also have flushing mechanisms. Locals rarely if ever use toilet paper, and there's a reason: in the tropical heat, rinsing your nether regions with water (using your *left* hand) is much cleaner than wiping with tissue, as long as you wash your hands properly afterwards. There's invariably a tap to hand, with a bucket for flushing and a plastic jug for rinsing. If you can't or won't adapt, buy toilet paper (available in all towns) as few cheap hotels provide it. Public toilets are a mixed bag: at their worst, they're horrid long-drops, meaning a deep hole in the ground covered by two slabs of concrete for positioning the feet.

Guide

Guide

Dar es Salaam and around

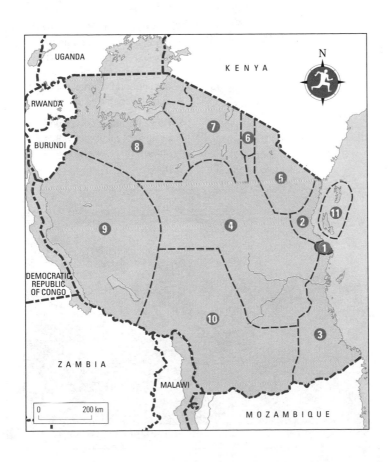

CHAPTER 1 # Highlights

✳ **National Museum** Small but perfectly formed, covering every angle on Tanzanian culture and history, from Nutcracker Man and a prehistoric fish to wooden bicycles and xylophones. **See p.107**

✳ **Kariakoo Market** A feast for the senses, selling everything from baobab seeds and trussed-up chickens to dodgy electronics. **See p.104**

✳ **Nightlife** With bars, nightclubs and dance halls galore, Dar is heaven for night owls. **See p.120**

✳ **Radio Tanzania Dar es Salaam** RTD's shops sell copies of over two hundred

archive recordings of traditional and modern music – a national treasure. **See p.124**

✳ **Beaches** The beaches in the north have all the amenities you might want; those in the south are quieter and more personal. **See p.134 and p.138**

✳ **Gezaulole** A traditional fishing village whose community-based cultural tourism programme blends history, culture and beaches, all at minimal cost. **See p.140**

✳ **Pugu Forest** A rare remnant of tropical rainforest within a stone's throw of the city. **See p.142**

△ Children and boat, Kunduchi Beach

Dar es Salaam and around

From a moribund settlement of three thousand people a little over a century ago, **DAR ES SALAAM** ("Dar" for short) has grown to become East Africa's largest city. Its present population, pushing four million, has an annual growth rate of almost ten percent, thanks to massive immigration from rural areas, and over seventy percent of its inhabitants live in non-planned housing, often little more than slums lacking electricity, water and sanitation. Their nickname for the city is **Bongo**, meaning "smart" or "clever", suggesting the skills that are needed to survive in an urban expanse this size.

In spite of having lost its capital status to Dodoma in 1974, Dar es Salaam remains Tanzania's industrial and commercial heart. Much of its wealth is based on a lively import trade conducted through the city's port, which also handles transit goods bound for Central Africa. This commercial ethos expresses itself best in the city's colourful shops and markets, especially in Kariakoo, in the heart of the city's African district, where you're likely to find anything from trussed-up chickens and counterfeit electronics to magical charms and concoctions sold by traditional healers.

Barely a century old, the city remains true to the old cliché of being a "melting pot", a vibrant blend of traditional tribal cultures and immigrant communities from Europe and Asia. In the European-planned streets of the centre, hawkers, smart businessmen, and women dressed in shrouding black *buibuis* jostle for elbow room under balconied Indian façades, whilst the wealthy – or corrupt – drive by in air-conditioned 4WDs. In the predominantly Asian area west of the centre, Indian traders lord it over colourful reams of cloth, spices, sweets and tourist trinkets; in the African areas further west, sprouting high-rises dwarf the few surviving mud-walled structures; whilst in the harbour you can still see wooden dhows whose design hasn't changed for a thousand years bobbing alongside freighters and oil tankers. For all its incongruities, everything seems to fit: Dar es Salaam is a cosmopolitan city.

For the traveller, the city boasts all the modern amenities you can think of. It's also home to a modest collection of museums and cultural attractions, as well as being a mecca for lovers of **East African music**, eclipsing even Nairobi in the number and quality of live acts on offer. **Kariakoo Market**, at the heart of the African area, is one of the continent's busiest and brashest, providing a welcome

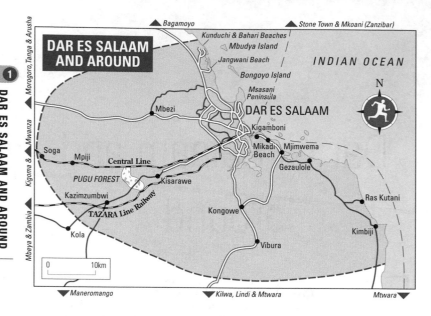

assault on the senses. For many though, Dar's northern **beaches** are the main draw – and if the prospect of fully fledged holiday resorts puts you off, there's an almost undeveloped stretch of coast to the south. Other attractions around Dar include **Pugu Forest**, a remnant of tropical rainforest; the atmospheric medieval ruins of the trading town of **Kunduchi**; and the village of **Gezaulole**, whose excellent community-based tourism programme blends history, culture, dhows and beaches.

Some history

Dar es Salaam dates from 1862, when the small Zaramo fishing village of **Mzizima** – where the present-day Ocean Road Cancer Hospital and State House are located – was chosen by Zanzibar's **Sultan Seyyid Majid** to be the site of his new summer palace and administrative headquarters, which he hoped in time would become the base of the Busaidi dynasty. The location was ideal, with its fine natural harbour strategically placed to take advantage of the flourishing **slave and ivory trade** from the Great Lakes to the coast, while the site had the additional advantage of being untroubled by warlike tribes, unlike Bagamoyo and Kilwa Kivinje, whose caravan routes were routinely pillaged and disrupted.

Sultan Majid named his palace **Bandur ul Salaam**, meaning the "Palace of Peace", a phrase nowadays happily mistranslated as the "haven" or "heaven" of peace. The palace's foundation stone was laid in 1865, and by September 1867 it was sufficiently complete to serve as the stage for a lavish banquet held in honour of the British, French, German and American consuls, whose economic and military influence the Sultan openly courted. Hadhramaut Arabs from Yemen were invited to develop coconut plantations around the small hamlet, and with the arrival of Indian merchants, who bought in slaves in exchange for imported goods, the fledgling city seemed set to flourish. Unfortunately, the Sultan died in 1870 – from a broken neck sustained in a fall in his new palace – before his plans could be fully realized. His successor, Sultan Barghash, had little interest in the site and abandoned the project. Economically too, the city seemed to have been stillborn: in 1873, the British forced Barghash to sign a decree prohibiting the sea-borne slave trade, and three years later they banned the trade on the mainland, too, effectively robbing Dar es Salaam of its purpose.

Decline was swift: the traders left, the dhows returned to Bagamoyo and Kilwa Kivinje, and Dar became little more than a small village with an outsize palace. So it remained for fourteen years until, in 1887, the **German East Africa Company** established a station there. Four years later, with the German colonization of Tanganyika in full swing, the capital of German East Africa (Deutsch Ostafrika) was transferred from Bagamoyo to Dar and the construction of the city resumed in earnest. The renascent city attracted Benedictine and Lutheran missionaries, who built churches and the Kaiserhof Hotel (now the site of the *New Africa*), hoping to use the city as a base from which to continue the evangelism of East Africa. In 1894, Dar es Salaam's new-found importance was confirmed by the surveying of the **Mittelland Bahn** – the present-day Central Line railway – which was to connect the city with Lake Tanganyika. Begun in 1905, the 1250-kilometre line finally arrived in Kigoma on the shore of Lake Tanganyika nine years later, becoming the colony's primary commercial conduit and allowing trade to flourish.

Unfortunately for the Germans, **World War I** resulted in their expulsion by Allied forces in September 1916. The new British overlords retained Dar as their commercial and administrative centre and began construction of the modern city proper, dividing it into three racially segregated "classes". **Uzunguni** (now comprising the city centre east of Maktaba Street), was designated for Europeans, and benefited from asphalt streets, shady trees, stone buildings, a hospital, a botanical garden inherited from the Germans and other amenities. The more compact **Uhindini** area, to the west of Uzunguni, was reserved for Asian immigrants brought by the British to work as coolies in the construction of the new colony; its shops and bazaars still form the city's retailing centre. Lastly, the **Uswahilini** district, between the Asian area and the swampy floodplain of the Jangwani River, was left open to Africans. This area, of which Kariakoo was the heart, lacked – and in places continues to lack – even the most basic of facilities.

As the city and its African population grew, the **Tanganyika African Association**, an ethnically diverse welfare agency and social club, was founded in Dar in 1927 to advocate the betterment of the African lot. It soon spread to rural communities, where it ultimately merged with the Tanganyika African National Union (TANU) to become the driving force behind the successful push for independence after World War II. Throughout this period, the city expanded relentlessly, and following **Independence** in 1961 became the capital of Tanganyika and, subsequently, Tanzania.

The failure of President Nyerere's collectivist **Ujamaa** policy (see p.733), and the consequent collapse of the country's economy led to a reverse in the city's fortunes, however. By the 1970s, Dar's economy had fallen into the doldrums, not helped by the loss of its capital status to Dodoma in 1974. Yet the city today is a far cry from its run-down state in the early 1980s. The election in 1985 of the reformist president, **Ali Hassan Mwinyi**, ushered in an era of economic liberalization which continues to this day. Many of Dar's formerly potholed streets have been patched up, new highways built, and the city's basic infrastructure is expanding.

But the pace of change is slow. Less than one third of Dar's inhabitants have running water, power cuts are a daily feature (more often than not caused by thieves stealing transformer oil to sell as superior diesel fuel and, weirdly, skin bleach), and poverty is entrenched. That said, Dar es Salaam is also one of the friendliest and most easy-going of large African cities, and definitely worth the effort of getting to know it better.

Arrival and information

Arriving, particularly by ferry or bus, can be disorienting, given the attention of hustlers and safari touts. If you're at all nervous (there's little reason to be – see "Avoiding trouble" below), catch a taxi.

By air

Dar es Salaam's **airport** lies 11km southwest of the city along Nyerere Road, a 25-minute drive. **International flights** use Terminal 2, which has a bar and restaurant, car-rental agencies, post office, foreign exchange bureaux (bad rates for travellers' cheques), and a none-too-useful tourist counter. Avoid the safari operators here unless we've reviewed the companies, as some are blacklisted (see box on pp.68–69), and be wary of safari touts in the arrivals hall. Most **domestic flights** use Terminal 1, whose facilities are limited to a snack bar, toilet and charter airline offices.

Taxis try to charge tourists upwards of Tsh12,000 to the city centre, particularly at the booking desk; locals and more wily travellers negotiate with individual drivers and pay Tsh8000. Fares to the northern beach resorts start at Tsh20,000, though these too can be talked down. **Daladalas** to the city (Tsh200) run along the highway 500m from the international terminal at the end of the slip-road, though clambering aboard one with tons of luggage won't endear you to your fellow passengers.

Avoiding trouble

Although Dar es Salaam is a relatively **safe** city, keep your wits about you, especially if you've just landed and have yet to develop that "worn-in" appearance.

Most obviously, offers of **marijuana** and **money-changing** on the street should be refused – you're guaranteed to get conned or worse. Equally, **safari touts** (flycatchers) should be given a wide if friendly berth: any operator worth its salt shouldn't need to tout for trade. For the low-down on scams involving **ferry tickets**, see p.77.

As to **specific areas**, it's fine to walk around anywhere by day, even in the crowded suburbs, as long as you stick to busy roads and are not visibly nervous, or carrying equally visible valuables. However, be on your guard for pickpockets and bag-snatchers in Kariakoo's crowded market area, and at transport terminals. Be equally careful along the beach beside Ocean Road if there aren't many people around. **At night**, it's always wise to catch a taxi, though the central business district, including Kisutu, has plenty of *askaris*, so walking short distances should be fine; heed local advice though, and beware of strangers suggesting places to eat – some people have been robbed. The general rule is the more people, traffic and lights, the lower the risk.

Lastly, reports of petty theft in some **budget hotels** mean you should deposit valuables with the management (not the receptionist), especially if your room key looks like it could open any other door in town; ensure you get an itemized receipt, including banknote serial numbers.

△ The Central Line Railway

By bus

Most buses finish at **Ubungo Bus Station**, 8km west of the city along Morogoro Road. The terminal is relatively calm, though there are still enough hawkers and touts to keep you on your toes – watch your bags and pockets, especially outside the terminal. **Taxis** charge around Tsh6000 from here to the city centre. **Daladalas** run to Kariakoo or Posta stands (Tsh200). The *Terminal Hotel* inside the bus station has decent en-suite rooms with a/c (❸).

Some buses – including Dar Express, Royal and Takrim – continue on to their old terminals in Kisutu district, close to the main budget hotels. Scandinavian Express also pass through Ubungo before finishing at their terminal on Msimbazi Street, on the edge of Kariakoo. Almost opposite is the terminal for Akamba Bus, if you're coming from Nairobi.

By train

Coming from Zambia or the southwest, the **TAZARA Line** terminates 5km west of the centre at the TAZARA Station, at the corner of Nyerere Road and Nelson Mandela Expressway. There are lots of daladalas outside, serving the city and the coast immediately south of Dar (both Tsh200), and taxis, which shouldn't charge more than Tsh4000 into the centre. Trains on the **Central Line** from Kigoma and Mwanza terminate at the **Central Line Railway Station**, just off Sokoine Drive. The Stesheni daladala stand, one block east of the station, has services to the south and west as well as to Kariakoo, from where there are daladalas to almost every corner of the city. There are also plenty of taxis outside the station.

By car

Driving into Dar is simple – Kilwa Road heads in from the south, and becomes Msimbazi Street in Kariakoo; turn right 20km before Dar at Kongowe to get to the beaches south of the city. Coming from elsewhere (except Bagamoyo), you'll arrive along Morogoro Road. **Parking** is problematic as there are few spaces in the centre – most upmarket hotels have their own parking lots but others tend to have reserved street spaces, used at your own risk. When parking in the centre, buy a daily ticket from one of the attendants wearing orange bibs.

By sea

The **ferry terminal**, where boats from Zanzibar and Mtwara dock, is on Sokoine Drive. Daladalas pass by frequently until around 9pm, heading south or on towards Kariakoo. Alternatively, it's perfectly safe to walk from here into the city by day, though you may be accompanied by flycatchers.

Information and tours

Dar's **tourist office** (Mon–Fri 8am–4pm, Sat 8.30am–12.30pm; ☎022/213 1555, ✉ttb2@ud.co.tz) is on the ground floor of Matasalamat Mansions on Samora Avenue, four blocks southwest of the Askari Monument. They have useful price lists for the main hotels, a register of licensed safari operators, train timetables, some brochures, and a good city map (free). If you need a really comprehensive plan, the excellent *Dar es Salaam City Map and Guide* (Tsh5000) is available in better bookshops and at the government's Surveys & Mapping Division on Kivukoni Front (Mon–Fri 8am–3.30pm; ☎022/212 4575).

For information about **forthcoming events**, especially those aimed at expatriate types, plus restaurant reviews and practical listings, pick up one of two monthly free booklets: the *Dar es Salaam Guide* (packed with useful info, including tide tables) or *What's Happening in Dar es Salaam*. Both can be found at the tourist office, major travel agents, better bookshops, and in large hotels and restaurants.

A number of travel agents (see p.129) offer guided **city tours**, usually a half-day ride around the main sights – essentially car hire with an English-speaking guide. At $30–70 per person, they're not cheap – much better to negotiate a half-day fare with a taxi driver who speaks your language; Tsh25,000 should suffice, plus any entry fees. The Wildlife Conservation Society of Tanzania (WCST) on Garden Avenue (℡022/211 2518, ✉wcst@africaonline.co.tz) organizes a **bird walk** from their office on the first and last Saturday of each month at 7.30am.

City transport

Most tourists use **taxis**, which are cheap by non-African standards. Even cheaper are **daladalas** – hectic, packed minibuses, covering every corner of the city.

Taxis

Taxis can be found almost everywhere, especially outside hotels, clubs, restaurants, bars, and at major road junctions. Licensed cabs are usually white, carry white number plates, and have a number painted on the side; others risk being pulled up by the police, at your inconvenience. Trips within the city shouldn't cost more than Tsh2000, journeys to the inner suburbs (this includes most of the jazz clubs) Tsh2500–4000, and Tsh4000–6000 to Msasani Peninsula or Mwenge, both to the north of the city. Hourly or daily rates can also be negotiated: Tsh40,000 for a full day is fine. Obviously, prices depend on how hard you bargain – if you're not in the mood, you could end up paying fifty percent more.

Daladalas

Despite periodic complaints in the press about dangerous driving, dirty uniforms and unsociably loud music, Dar es Salaam's **daladalas** – shared mini-buses – are surprisingly efficient and will get you almost anywhere within a twenty-kilometre radius of the city for only a few hundred shillings. Services run from 5am to 9pm, and the vehicles are usually battered old Hiace minibuses or slightly larger DCMs and Coasters. Each is **colour-coded** (the thick band painted around the middle) according to the route, and the terminals that it runs between are clearly marked on the front, together with details of which route it goes by if there are alternatives. The standard **fare** for all but the longest journeys is Tsh200; you're issued a ticket, and are unlikely to be ripped off. The only potential hassle is at the main terminals, where you'll have to contend with turnboys (*manangas*) competing to get you on their vehicle. If there are several daladalas going the same way, choose the one that's fullest, since it's most likely to leave first.

Most daladalas start and finish at one of two main terminals in the city centre, called stands or *stendi*: **Posta**, along Maktaba Street; and **Kariakoo**, 2km to the west along Msimbazi Street. The busiest routes out of the city have services from both stands.

Other useful city-centre stands include **Kivukoni** (or "Ferry"), at the east end of Kivukoni Front, and **Stesheni**, one block east of Central Line Railway

Station off Sokoine Drive, both of which have mainly west- and south-bound services. **Mnazi Mmoja**, on the section of Uhuru Street crossing the gardens east of Kariakoo, also has west-bound services to Ilala, TAZARA and the airport; most of these go via Kariakoo. Outside the city centre, you may find yourself having to change if there's no direct service to where you're going. **Mwenge** stand, 9km northwest of the city at the junction of Bagamoyo and Mandela roads, has daladalas heading north, whilst **Ubungo**, a few hundred metres beyond the main bus terminal at the junction of Morogoro and Mandela roads, covers the western outskirts and the university. There are plenty of daladalas from the city centre to both of these.

Accommodation

Dar's **accommodation** ranges from basic guest houses and Christian-run hostels, to a growing number of business-class hotels and beach resorts. **Prices** are higher than elsewhere in mainland Tanzania, and cheap rooms – anything under Tsh10,000 a double – are often little more than a bed in a cell.

The main area for **budget accommodation** is a cluster of hotels in the Asian-dominated Mchafukoge and Kisutu districts, both within walking distance of the centre. Kariakoo, further west, also has cheap options and a number of mid-range high-rises, some rather better than others. A popular alternative is to head to the **beaches** south of the city (see p.138) while the beach hotels north of the city (see p.134) are worth considering if you're looking for a resort-style stay. The former European quarter between the centre and the coast houses the city's main **luxury hotels**, and there are more on Msasani Peninsula to the north. All four- and five-star hotels have **wheelchair access**, and ones with specially designed rooms are noted in the reviews. At the budget end of things, the cheapest place with lift access is the *Concord Hotel* in Kariakoo, or the *Salvation Army Hostel*, which is all ground level. In our reviews, **safe parking** means the hotel has an enclosed or guarded area for guests' vehicles.

The nearest **campsites** are at Mikadi and Mjimwema beaches south of the city (see p.139); there are less-accessible pitches at *Jangwani Seabreeze Lodge* (p.136) and *Silver Sands Beach Resort* (p.137), both over 20km to the north.

City centre: east from India Street and Upanga Road

This area, occupying the former European quarter of Uzunguni, benefits from wide streets and, east of Maktaba Street, plenty of trees.

Harbour View Suites 10–12th floors, JM Mall Centre, Samora Ave ☎022/212 4040, ⓦwww.harbourview-suites.com. Large, modern, very good-value rooms, particularly for the harbour views at the back (other rooms overlook the city). All have fully equipped kitchens, huge satellite TVs and broadband sockets. Choose between four-poster nets or having your room sprayed. Rooms on the 11th floor have balconies, whilst the executive suites have enough space for a harem. Breakfast available. ❻

Holiday Inn Garden Ave ☎022/213 7575, ⓦwww.holiday-inn.com/daressalaam. Crammed into a small plot beside the Botanical Gardens, this modern five-storey hotel has 152 double rooms

(some with disabled facilities), all with satellite TV, phone, a/c, safe, bathtub, and local artwork. Facilities include a curio shop, Internet access, travel centre, swimming pool, gym, bar and restaurant. Safe parking. Buffet breakfast included. ❽

Kilimanjaro Kempinski Hotel Kivukoni Front ☎022/213 1111, ⓦwww.kempinski-daressalaam .com. This 180-room 1960s monolith has been transformed into Dar's leading hotel, enjoying both the Kempinski chain's high standards and great harbour and sea views from its front rooms, all with a/c, minibar, safe, Internet access and pay TV. Facilities include two restaurants, three bars (one on the roof), a health spa, infinity swimming pool, and casino. Safe parking. ❾

Luther House Centre Hostel Sokoine Drive
℡022/212 0734 or 6247 (after hours),
Ⓔluther@simbanet.net. A good, if pricey, Christian-run backpackers' haunt (though you do get a/c). Rooms are en suite – some at the back have glimpses of the harbour – and are adequate if not sparkling, with narrow beds, box nets, a chair and table, and cotton sheets. An extra $5 gets you a TV, fridge and hot water. There's also a good restaurant, the *Dar Shanghai*. Safe parking ❹

Mövenpick Royal Palm Ohio St ℡022/211 2416, Ⓦwww.moevenpick-hotels.com. Dar's classiest abode, with 251 luxurious rooms with all modcons. Rooms higher up at the back have sea views over the golf course. Amenities include no-smoking rooms, two restaurants, a business centre, safari offices, swimming pool, sauna and gym. Breakfast included. Safe parking. ❽

New Africa Hotel Azikiwe St ℡022/211 7050, Ⓦwww.newafricahotel.com. Rather bland compared to the competition, this large and still luxurious hotel remains good value, especially for its harbour-facing rooms ($10 more). Amenities include no-smoking floors, room service, business

centre, a bar and two restaurants, casino, swimming pool and gym. Free airport transfer. Street parking spaces. Breakfast included. ❼–❽

YMCA Youth Hostel Upanga Rd ℡022/213 5457. This has all the charm of an army blockhouse, in spite of its small courtyard garden, and the staff are unusually gloomy. Its rooms, with shared bathrooms, are ragged but clean, and have nets and fans. There's secure parking and a cafeteria (preorder) that also sells beer. Breakfast included. ❸

🏃 **YWCA** Maktaba St, entrance on
Ghana Ave ℡022/212 2439, Ⓔywca.
tanzania@africaonline.co.tz. A recommended budget choice if you don't mind the racket from Posta daladala stand from 5am to 10pm. It's cheap by Dar's standards, especially for singles, admits men and couples, and is friendly if the matriarchal *mama kubwas* ("big ladies") take a shine to you. The rooms are a bit tatty but clean (though for some, "en suite" means a sink), have nets and fans, and there's a laundry service and good cheap restaurant. The *askari* will let you in after the 11pm curfew. Also has flats: Tsh15,000 for two beds, Tsh20,000 for three. Reservations advisable. Paltry breakfast included. ❷

City centre: Kisutu and Mchafukoge

The predominantly Asian areas of **Kisutu** and **Mchafukoge** west of the centre contain Dar's main backpackers' hotels (and irritating if harmless safari touts), though in case you're wondering, all have signs forbidding "women of immoral turpitude". Half-decent doubles go for upwards of Tsh15,000, but you can still find a basic room for half that – though it's likely to be in a horrible fleapit with uncertain security. Note that between November and February, rooms get exceedingly hot; get one with a balcony, or consider investing in a/c (around Tsh25,000 a double). Walking around at night shouldn't pose any problem as long as you're sensible.

Continental Nkrumah St ℡022/212 3253. Rundown and unexciting, but a cheap mid-range option near the Central Line Railway Station. Rooms are en suite and have a/c, satellite TV and phone; more expensive ones have a minibar. There's also 24hr room service, two restaurants and a bar playing Indian music. Parking on street. ❹

Holiday Hotel Jamhuri St; reception on 2nd floor ℡022/211 2246, Ⓔyasinmjuma@hotmail .com. A secure and perfectly decent backpackers' choice, and cheaper than the *Jambo* and *Safari* nearby. Doubles are good, especially those with street-facing balconies higher up, and some have bathrooms, but singles are tiny and horrendously stuffy. ❸

Jambo Inn Libya St ℡022/211 4293, Ⓦwww .jambohotel.8m.com. The most popular backpackers' haunt, but ask to see a selection of rooms as they vary greatly: all are en suite, some with good-

sized nets, but others are hot and badly kept, with small beds, nylon sheets and no nets. Rooms at the front are noisier but the balconies are a boon. Also has triples. Luggage storage is Tsh500/day per item and there's an Internet café and overpriced restaurant downstairs. A mediocre breakfast is included and parking is available on the street. Fans ❸, a/c ❹

Kibodya Hotel Nkrumah St ℡022/211 7856. The large ground-floor bar makes for a distinctly intimidating atmosphere, especially for women, but the rooms themselves (all doubles) are OK, and come with bathrooms and fans. ❷

Safari Inn Off Libya St ℡022/211 9104, Ⓔsafari-inn@lycos.com. Another backpackers' haunt, along a narrow side alley, with small but bright, clean and airy en-suite rooms with big double beds, fans and nets. The bathrooms are smelly however, and the welcome at times

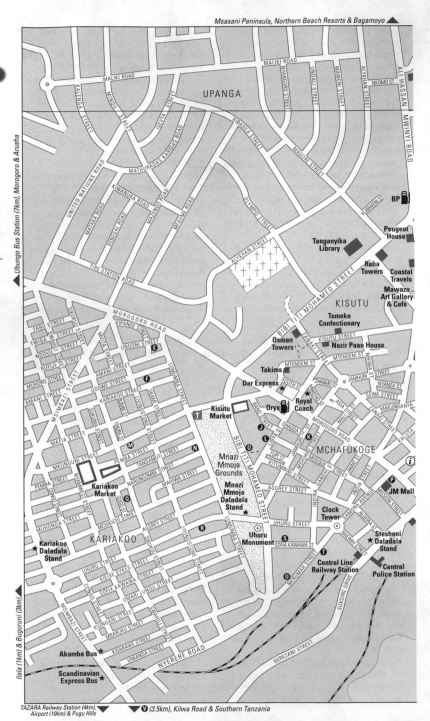

Msasani Peninsula, Northern Beach Resorts & Bagamoyo ▲

UPANGA

MALIKI ROAD
MALIKI ROAD
KALENGA STREET
MINDU STREET
ISSYA STREET
STREET
NYANGORO STREET
UNDALI STREET
MAWENI STREET
ALYKHAN STREET
NKOMO ST
ALI HASSAN MWINYI ROAD

KIBASILA STREET
MAGORE STREET

MATHURADAS KARIAS ROAD
UNITED NATIONS ROAD
KWANUKA ROAD
MATAKA ROAD
SENEGAL ROAD
MAZENGO ROAD
MFAUME ROAD
OLYMPIO STREET
VUBENENI ST

BP

Peugeot House

FIRE STATION ROAD

ALYKHAN STREET

Tanganyika Library

Raha Towers

Coastal Travels

Mawazo Art Gallery & Café

MOROGORO ROAD
KIPANDE STREET
UNGONI STREET
FARI STREET
TWIGA STREET
SIVUKILE STREET
NDOVU STREET
RUFIJI STREET
MUHORO STREET
AMANI STREET
NYATA STREET
UDOWE STREET
KARIAKOO STREET
BAMBI STREET
LIVINGSTONE STREET
LUMUMBA STREET
BIBI TITI MOHAMED STREET

KISUTU

Temeke Confectionary

Osman Towers

Nazir Paan House

KISUTU STREET
ZANAKI STREET
MTENDENI ST
MTENDENI ST
MRIMA STREET

Takims

Dar Express

SOUTH ST
ZARAMO ST
JAMHURI
NYANZA ST
SEWA STREET
MAKUNGANYA
KAUTA

Kisutu Market

E

Oryx

Royal Coach

CHAGGA ST
RAMLA STREET
ASIA STREET
MALI STREET

J
L
K

MCHAFUKOGE

AMANI STREET
MSIMBAZI STREET
SUKUMA STREET
CHAMBI STREET
MAFIA STREET
MUHORO STREET
PEMBA STREET
TANDAMUTI STREET
NARUNGOMBE STREET
MAHIWA STREET
NKRUMAH STREET
INDIRA GANDHI STREET
JAMAT ST

F

M

Kariakoo Market

N

FUPI ST
MSIKITI STREET
MOSQUE ST
KITUMBINI STREET
AGGREY STREET

Mnazi Mmoja Grounds

D

Mnazi Mmoja Daladala Stand ★

Clock Tower

JM Mall

P

i

MKUNGUNI STREET
NYAMWEZI STREET
CONGO STREET
GOGO ST
MCHIKICHI STREET
AGGREY STREET
SIKUKUU STREET
LUMUMBA STREET
KARIAKOO
Q
R
Uhuru Monument
S
UHURU STREET
SOFIA KAWAWA ST
SAMORA AVENUE
ALGERIA STREET
MISSION STREET

Kariakoo Daladala Stand ★

MUHONDA STREET
UHURU STREET
KICHE SYKES STREET
SOFIA KAWAWA STREET
OMARI LUNDU STREET
SIKUKUU STREET
MSIMBAZI STREET
CONGO STREET
KIUNGANI STREET
MBARUKU STREET
SWAHILI STREET

T

Stesheni ★ Daladala Stand

U

Central Line Railway Station

Central Police Station

NKRUMAH STREET
RAILWAY STREET
SOKOINE DRIVE

Akamba Bus ★

Scandinavian Express Bus ★

KISARAWE STREET
VIWANDA STREET
NYERERE ROAD
GEREZANI STREET

Ilala (1km) & Buguruni (3km) ▲

Ubungo Bus Station (7km), Morogoro & Arusha ▲

TAZARA Railway Station (4km),
Airport (10km) & Pugu Hills ▼

▼ V (3.5km), Kilwa Road & Southern Tanzania

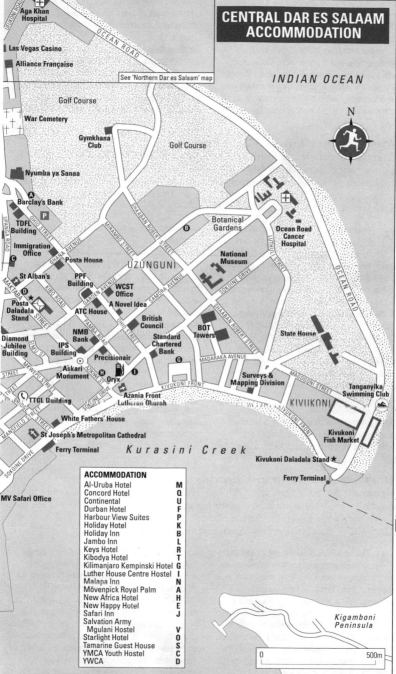

CENTRAL DAR ES SALAAM ACCOMMODATION

INDIAN OCEAN

See 'Northern Dar es Salaam' map

N

Aga Khan Hospital

Las Vegas Casino

Alliance Française

OCEAN ROAD

Golf Course

War Cemetery

Gymkhana Club

Golf Course

Nyumba ya Sanaa

Barclay's Bank

TDFL Building

Immigration Office

Posta House

St Alban's

PPF Building

WCST Office

A Novel Idea

ATC House

NMB Bank

IPS Building

Precisionair

Askari Monument

Oryx

TTGL Building

Azania Front Lutheran Church

White Fathers' House

St Joseph's Metropolitan Cathedral

Ferry Terminal

Diamond Jubilee Building

UZUNGUNI

Botanical Gardens

National Museum

British Council

Standard Chartered Bank

BOT Towers

Ocean Road Cancer Hospital

State House

Surveys & Mapping Division

KIVUKONI

Tanganyika Swimming Club

Kivukoni Fish Market

Kivukoni Daladala Stand ★

Ferry Terminal

MV Safari Office

Kurasini Creek

Mikadi Beach (2km), Mjimwema (7.5km) & Gezaulole (14km)

Kigamboni Peninsula

ACCOMMODATION

Al-Uruba Hotel	M
Concord Hotel	Q
Continental	U
Durban Hotel	F
Harbour View Suites	P
Holiday Hotel	K
Holiday Inn	B
Jambo Inn	L
Keys Hotel	R
Kibodya Hotel	T
Kilimanjaro Kempinski Hotel	G
Luther House Centre Hostel	I
Malapa Inn	N
Mövenpick Royal Palm	A
New Africa Hotel	H
New Happy Hotel	E
Safari Inn	J
Salvation Army Mgulani Hostel	V
Starlight Hotel	O
Tamarine Guest House	S
YMCA Youth Hostel	C
YWCA	D

0   500m

perfunctory. There's an Internet café and cheap restaurant downstairs. Good breakfast included. Fans ❸, a/c. ❹

Starlight Hotel Bibi Titi Mohamed St, also accessible from Libya St ☏ 022/211 9387, ✉ starlight@acexnet.com. An eight-storey block with 150 rooms, some overlooking Mnazi Mmoja Grounds. It's getting frayed but remains good value, especially compared to the *Peacock* next door. All rooms are en suite, and have both a/c and fan, TV,

phone and fridge, but the beds are small and lack nets. Amenities include a foreign exchange bureau, gift shop and restaurant. Safe parking. Breakfast included. ❺

Tamarine Guest House Sofia Kawawa St ☏ 022/212 0233. One of Dar's cheapest, and perfectly decent if you can cope with the idle men at the entrance. Choice of private or shared bathrooms. The *Pop Inn*, opposite, is similar. Security at both places appears to be loose, however. ❶, en suite ❷.

West of the centre: Kariakoo

Over the last decade, the former mud-and-thatch district of **Kariakoo**, sprawling westwards from Mnazi Mmoja Grounds, has been utterly transformed by mushrooming high-rises, some of them hotels. Many are surprisingly dingy and overpriced, however – the better ones are reviewed below. Walking around Kariakoo at night isn't safe, so use taxis.

Al-Uruba Hotel Mkunguni St ☏ 022/218 0133, ☏ 022/218 0135. Easily the best of the city's budget hotels, not to mention much cooler than those in Kisutu, with friendly staff and good if small en-suite rooms, complete with cotton sheets, desk and chair, ceiling fan, window nets (some also have box nets), hot water, and even satellite TV. An additional Tsh1500 gets you a/c. Busy restaurant downstairs (no alcohol). ❷

Concord Hotel Sikukuu St ☏ 022/218 2547. A high-rise with lift access, friendly staff, and bright modern rooms, all with large windows, TV, phone and good-sized beds, but no nets (rooms are sprayed). There's also a restaurant and two bars. ❹

Durban Hotel Udowe St ☏ 022/218 0555, ⓦ www.durbanhotel.co.tz. Cool and calm, offering good en-suite rooms with either fans or a/c. The restaurant-cum-bar (no smoking) makes up for its

bland appearance with good cheap food. Breakfast included. ❹

Keys Hotel Uhuru St ☏ 022/218 3033, ✉ abcclick@raha.com. Big place offering cheap en-suite doubles with fans as well as a/c suites. It also has a large if hot and gloomy restaurant, and two bars, with tables on a terrace at the back. Breakfast included. Rooms ❸, suites ❹

Malapa Inn Lumumba St ☏ 022/218 0023. Very basic and far from clean, but cheap by Dar's standards for couples. Rooms have big double beds, small round nets, ceiling fan, and sorry-looking bathrooms (no hot water). ❷

New Happy Hotel Ungoni St ☏ 022/218 0505. Good-value if stuffy rooms, all with fans, though many beds lack nets. The main attraction is the rooftop bar; there's also a restaurant-cum-bar on the ground floor, and the excellent *Royal Chef* restaurant around the corner. ❷

North of the centre: Upanga

Upanga ("Sword") area, from Ocean Road to Selander Bridge, contains a handful of mid-range options, though none are on the beach or have sea views. Catch a daladala along Ali Hassan Mwinyi Road from Posta towards Kawe or Mwenge, or from Stesheni to Mwananyamala/Nyamala.

The Courtyard Ocean Rd ☏ 022/213 0130, ✉ courtyard@raha.com. With its bougainvillea-festooned balconies, this three-storey hotel looks like part of New Orleans, rebuilt around a small swimming pool in, yes, a courtyard. The location is odd, flanked by high-rise, low-cost housing, and the nearby beach isn't recommended because of pollution, but no matter – service and standards are high. Standard rooms have a/c, phone, satellite TV, bathtub, safe and minibar, but smell of bug spray (no nets); more expensive rooms are larger but other-

wise identical. Amenities include the superb *Langi-Langi* restaurant, snack bar and bar, room service and travel desk. Safe parking. Breakfast included. ❼

Palm Beach Hotel 305 Ali Hassan Mwinyi Rd ☏ 0741/222299, ⓦ www.pbhtz.com. Recently renovated 1950s hotel, with 32 simple and smallish but good value en-suite rooms, each with a/c, Wi-Fi, phone, TV and safe. Triples are also available. There are no palm trees or beach, incidentally, but there is the excellent *305* restaurant and bar with plenty of shady seating. Safe parking. Breakfast included. ❻

North of the city: Msasani Peninsula

Msasani Peninsula, roughly 6km north of the city centre, is Dar's upmarket residential district. Daladalas from Posta to Masaki run up Haile Selassie Road, then along Chole Road to Oyster Bay and up to the *Sea Cliff Hotel*; taxis charge Tsh4000–6000.

Coral Beach West of the *Sea Cliff Hotel* ☏022/260 1928, ⓦwww.coralbeach-tz.com. A rather bland stab at a beach resort, hampered by a lack of beach (it's on a low headland), little shade and closely spaced buildings. However, the rooms are well-appointed and most have sea views, as does the fine swimming pool. There's also a gym and sauna (included in the price), two restaurants and two bars. Safe parking. ➐

Golden Tulip Touré Drive ☏022/260 0288, ⓦwww.goldentuliptanzania.com. This huge, over-the-top Arabian-style beach hotel is flogged as "a corporate hotel in resort surroundings", amply betraying its rather impersonal nature. The spacious standard rooms have balconies with sea views, and facilities include a huge swimming pool, poolside bar and grill, restaurant, Jacuzzi with sea view, fitness area, shopping mall and coffee shop. Safe parking. Breakfast included. ➑

Karibu Hotel Haile Selassie Rd ☏022/266 8458, ⓦwww.hotelkaribu.com. Clean and well-maintained, all rooms have satellite TV, a/c and minibar, and the big bonus of a swimming pool. Also has a poolside bar and two restaurants. ➍

 Q-Bar & Guest House Off Haile Selassie Rd ☏0744/282474, ⓔqbar@hotmail.com.

There are two good reasons to stay here: Msasani's liveliest (if noisiest) nightlife downstairs, and cheap dorm beds ($12 per person). The standard rooms are also good value, with satellite TV, a/c, fridge and window nets (cheaper ones share bathrooms). Also has triples. Laundry and breakfast included. ➍–➎

Sea Cliff Hotel Touré Drive ☏022/260 0380, ⓦwww.hotelseacliff.com. Perched on the tip of the peninsula, this 86-room hotel is a graceless thatched concrete block on the outside but very stylish inside. You've a choice of well-appointed en-suite doubles or twins, and for $20 more you get a sea view. Amenities include expensive bars and restaurants, a casino, bowling alley, shopping centre, gym and swimming pool. The downside is no beach (it's on a cliff), and the almost entirely non-African clientele. Safe parking. Breakfast included. ➑

The Souk The Slipway, Msasani Peninsula ☏022/260 0893, ⓦwww.slipway.net. Modern creature comforts wrapped in classic Arabian styling, on three floors around a glass-covered atrium. The spacious rooms and apartments all have a/c and satellite TV, and The Slipway's restaurants and bars are within walking distance. Safe parking. ➏

Outside the city

As well as the places below, accommodation outside Dar can be found in the Pugu Hills, and at the beaches both north and south of the city.

Mediterraneo Off Kawe Rd, Kawe Beach, 10km north of the centre ☏022/261 8359, ⓦwww.mediterraneo-tz.com. A cluster of low, Mediterranean-style buildings set in gardens within walking distance of the beach, with eleven of its fifteen well-priced, en-suite rooms facing the sea, all with cable TV. Amenities include a beach bar and Italian restaurant, a small pool, tennis and volleyball, and free Internet access. There's a boat for visiting islands, but no water sports. Safe parking. Catch a Posta–Kawe daladala. Breakfast included. ➎–➏

Salvation Army Mgulani Hostel Kilwa Rd, Mgulani, 3.5km south of the centre ☏022/285 1467, ⓔdavid_burrows@tnz.salvationarmy.org. Excellent value for single travellers (Tsh6000), with 68 individual bungalows, all with bathrooms, fans, pure nylon sheets and towels, and most with box nets. The canteen is humdrum; there's cheaper food at roadside bars on Nelson Mandela Expressway nearby. To get there, catch a taxi, or a daladala from Kariakoo, Stesheni or Posta to Mbagala, Temeke or Rangi Tatu marked "via Kilwa Road". Safe parking. Breakfast included. ➌

The City

Dar es Salaam is a patchwork of influences, from the vibrant **Asian district** to the more sedate European quarter of **Uzunguni**, although to find any authentically

African streetlife you'll have to head to **Kariakoo Market**, just west of the centre. In general it's the contrasting flavours of these different districts which provide the city's main interest, since conventional tourist attractions are thin on the ground. For a bird's-eye **view** of the city, head for the *Sawasdee* restaurant on the ninth floor of the *New Africa Hotel*, or to the 25th floor of Mafuta House on Maktaba Street – if ever it gets finished.

The Asian district

The western end of the city centre – a rough triangle bounded by India and Bibi Titi Mohamed streets – is occupied by the city's **Asian district**, a bustling quarter containing hundreds of shops, tea rooms, restaurants, goldsmiths and sweet shops, along with Hindu, Sikh, Jain and Muslim places of worship. This is the heart of historical **Uhindini**, the area reserved by the British for Indian coolies (indentured labourers) shipped in to help build the modern city. Despite a multiplicity of religions, cultures and languages, the individual communities have retained strong individual characters. You're not allowed into the mosques unless you're Muslim (the main concentration is on Mosque Street and the streets off it), but both the Sikh and Hindu communities will be happy to show you around their temples: start on Kisutu Street.

There's no real centre to the district, nor any specific sights – the pleasure of the place lies in unexpected details, such as the wrought-iron swastikas (an auspicious symbol of prosperity and good fortune for Hindus, Buddhists and Jain) adorning the Hindu temples on **Kisutu Street**, men selling beautifully arranged flower petals outside them, the luridly coloured pyramids of Indian sweets (Temeke Confectionery and Bhog 56, almost next door on Kisutu Street, are particularly good), the *paan* shops, and the beautiful balconied houses on **Uhuru Street**, which is well worth heading to anyway for its colourful blaze of printed cloth *kitenge* panels, sold by shops and hawkers at its western end – watch for the *mama kubwas* ("big ladies") squinting at their reflections in mirrors and window panes as they drape one ream after another over their hefty shoulders. In addition, don't miss **Kisutu Market** (daily 8am–5pm) on Bibi Titi Mohamed Street, an atmospheric if insalubrious little place selling fruit and vegetables, honey, beans and pulses, as well as baskets of squawking chickens, dried fish and some gorgeously pungent herbs.

Kariakoo

West of the Asian district, on the far side of the grassy Mnazi Mmoja Grounds, lies **Kariakoo**, the city centre's most African district. Kariakoo is made up of a dusty grid of streets, of which only some are surfaced, but whose mud-walled "Swahili houses" topped with corrugated-iron roofs have in recent years been

---

Dar's paan shops

One of the most distinctive features of Dar es Salaam's Asian area are the Indian *paan* shops, often doubling as tobacconists and corner shops. *Paan* is essentially a mildly narcotic dessert: you choose from a range of sweet spices, chopped nuts, bits of vegetable, syrup and white lime, which are then wrapped in a hot, sweet betel leaf (*mtambuu*), which is the mildly narcotic bit – it tastes as exotic as it sounds. *Paan* is chewed and sucked but not swallowed: pop the triangular parcel in your mouth and munch, then spit out the pith when you're finished. Good places to try it are Shehenai Paan House on Mrima Street, and Nazir Paan House at the west end of Kisutu Street.

giving way to mushrooming high-rises (the old style is still largely intact west of Msimbazi Street). Occupying much of the area set aside by the British for the city's African population, its name dates from World War I, when, after the expulsion of the Germans, thousands of Tanzanians were conscripted into the hated British **Carrier Corps** to serve as war porters. Their barracks were erected on a patch of ground that had been earmarked for a ceremonial park in honour of Kaiser Wilhelm II. After the war, Kariakoo (along with the Ilala district further west) was left to the African population. No amenities were provided – and indeed many parts of the area still lack the most basic of facilities.

In spite of the poverty, Kariakoo exudes a solid sense of community that manages to combine both tribal and religious identities. In many ways, the district is a microcosm of the country, and its pan-Tanzanian nature has resulted in one of the most fascinating and headily colourful markets in Africa. **Kariakoo Market** (daily sunrise–sunset), whose bizarre roof resembles a forest of upturned black parasols, occupies the site of the former barracks. In the maze of shops and stalls surrounding it, you'll find everything from exotic fruits, vegetables, fish and freshly cooked meat, to aromatic spices, herbs, coffee, handicrafts, textiles, local brews (*pombe*), and children's toys made from wire and recycled tin cans. Old men sell medicinal herbs, potions and powders in little bottles salvaged from hospitals, as well as bundles of tree bark, dried lizards and seashells with curative properties. Elsewhere, great squawking bundles of trussed-up chickens create a clamour, whilst in other parts of the market you might be offered tart baobab seeds, snuff tobacco or dodgy imported electronics. What's most striking though, is the care with which everything is displayed, whether pieces of cloth rolled into tight cones and propped up on the ground, oranges and other fruits balanced atop one other in *fungas* (geometrical piles) or fresh flowers artistically inserted between mounds of coconuts. Visitors are welcome, of course, but take precautions against pickpockets, particularly in the packed streets south of the main building, where the second-hand clothes (*mitumba*) area gives you little more than elbow room.

For a breather, join the locals at the famous **DDC Kariakoo Social Hall** on Muhonda Street. Tanzania's oldest African bar, it also serves up a wide range of tasty and dirt-cheap Tanzanian dishes, before – on Tuesdays, Thursdays and especially Sundays – turning into one of Dar's best-loved live music venues.

The Askari Monument, Kivukoni Front and the fish market

The eastern edge of the Asian district merges almost imperceptibly with the broad planned streets of **Uzunguni** district, the area in which the Germans (and subsequently the British) settled after taking control of the city. The centre of this area – the roundabout between Samora Avenue, Maktaba and Azikiwe streets – is marked by the **Askari Monument**. The first statue on this spot was erected in 1911 and depicted Hermann von Wissmann – the soldier, explorer and governor who played a key role in the German development of the city. The present statue, cast in bronze and designed by James Alexander Stevenson (who signed himself as "Myrander"), was erected in 1927 to commemorate the African soldiers and members of the Carrier Corps who lost their lives in the war, and depicts an *askari* standing with rifle at the ready.

Dar es Salaam's first buildings, erected during Sultan Majid's rule in the 1860s, faced the harbour along Kivukoni Front and what is now Sokoine Street, 150m southeast of the Askari Monument. Though most have long since disappeared, a notable exception is the **White Fathers' House**, near the corner with Bridge Street, which served as the Sultan's harem until being put to more holy uses by the Society of Missionaries of Africa, a Roman Catholic order founded by French Algerians in 1868, and who founded their first East African mission in Zanzibar in 1878.

Nearby, **St Joseph's Metropolitan Cathedral**, consecrated in 1897, is a major city landmark and a good place to experience Dar's vibrant church music (*kwaya*), best heard during Sunday Mass. The cathedral is notable for its twin confessionals facing the altar, one in Baroque style, the other Gothic. The squat, whitewashed **Azania Front Lutheran Church**, 200m to the east, is unmissable thanks to its fanciful tower, which looks like it should really be adorning a Rhineland castle. The *kwaya* here rivals that of St Joseph's.

Heading east along the bay, **Kivukoni Front** leads past a number of graceful German colonial buildings, most adorned with Indian-style wooden balconies, which are nowadays occupied by various government ministries and offices. At the eastern end of Kivukoni Front is the ferry (*mvuko*) terminal for Kigamboni and, almost opposite, **Kivukoni Fish Market** – not that you need directions to get there: the smell is unmistakable. Unsurprisingly, this is the best place in Dar – indeed probably the best place along the entire coast – for seafood, with red snapper, kingfish, barracuda, squid, crabs, lobster and prawns all usually available if you get there early in the morning. Should you feel peckish, plenty of women are on hand working their magic over wide frying pans, or putting muscle into huge pots of *ugali* and cassava porridge. On the other side of the road is the fruit and veg section with yet more street food, hidden behind a row of stalls selling beautiful seashells, starfish and other marine curios. Don't succumb to the temptation to buy souvenirs, since the collecting of shells and other marine life, especially endangered seahorses, has a direct and immediately damaging impact on coral reef ecology. The export of many species is illegal, both in Tanzania and abroad, even if they're openly for sale here.

Ocean Road

The **beach** starts just north of the fish market, a small part of which is enclosed by the members-only **Tanganyika Swimming Club**. There's nothing to stop you swimming just outside the club, of course, but pollution may deter you; the nearest clean stretches of sand are at Coco Beach on Msasani Peninsula (though the sand there is mixed with coral ragstone), and at Mikadi and Mjimwema in the south – catch the ferry at the fish market and then a daladala. Still, heading up Ocean Road from Kivukoni, you'll see a few brave souls stripping off for a dip, though most people are content to sit around and feel the breeze, sip coconuts bought from nearby vendors, or wander out onto the extensive flats that appear at low tide.

The big, white, heavily guarded building on your left is the **State House**. Originally dating from German times, it was damaged by British shelling during World War I and partially reconstructed thereafter. Its ornate structure blends elements of African and Arabian architecture, and currently houses the Office of the President – which means no photography. Five hundred metres along is **Ocean Road Cancer Hospital**, built in 1886 as the German Malaria Research Laboratory. This was where **Richard Koch**, who in 1905 was awarded a Nobel Laureate for his discovery of tuberculin (wrongly believed to be the cure for TB), developed the standard laboratory method for preparing pure bacterial strains, the Koch Method. Using his method, he went on to discover that flea-infested rats were responsible for the bubonic plague, and that the tsetse fly was the vector for sleeping sickness. As well as cancer research, the hospital is involved in the fight against malaria.

The National Museum and Botanical Gardens

A five-minute walk southwest from the Cancer Hospital is Tanzania's **National Museum** (daily 9.30am–6pm; $3, photography $10), on Shaaban Robert Street. Established in 1940 as the King George V Memorial Museum, this is rather smaller than you'd expect for a national showcase, but worth a visit nonetheless, since it briefly covers pretty much every aspect of Tanzanian culture and history, from prehistoric hominid fossils through to colonialism and Independence. The exhibits of tribal culture are especially fascinating, and it's a pity that no one has ever bothered to expand them, given that many of Tanzania's traditional cultures are now on the verge of disappearing.

The **Entrance Hall** is occupied by temporary exhibitions, often showcasing local artists, and a dusty Rolls Royce that was used by colonial governors and later Nyerere. To the left of the entrance, the **Hall of Man** succinctly traces mankind's evolution with displays of stone tools, a cast of Ngorongoro's famous Laetoli footprints that showed that mankind's ancestors were walking upright long before anyone had imagined, and fossilized hominid skulls from Oldupai Gorge and elsewhere, including the 1,750,000-year-old partial skull of *Australopithecus boisei*, whose impressive jaw led to him being dubbed "Nutcracker Man". Don't miss the hilarious letter from an irate newspaper reader in 1958 fuming about the "hideous" suggestion that man might have evolved from animals.

The **History Room** upstairs is something of a hotchpotch, with fragmentary displays on the colonial period, short biographies of nineteenth-century explorers, mementos from the Abushiri War and Maji Maji Uprising, a nineteenth-century Portuguese ship's figurehead, photographs tracing the road to Independence, the original Uhuru Torch planted atop Kilimanjaro on December 9, 1961, and bits of moon rock from the Apollo landings. Part of the room is dedicated to finds from the medieval coastal trading town of Kilwa Kisiwani, including glazed Chinese porcelain removed from graves, Indian trading beads, oil lamps, pottery, stone friezes and coins.

In the older building at the back of the grounds, the **Biology Hall** contains a large collection of seashells (including a truly enormous giant clam), corals, a couple of dull fish tanks, and – more interesting – an enormous pickled **coelcanth** caught off Tanzania's Songo Songo island in 2003. Until 1938, when a specimen was caught off South Africa, coelcanths were believed to have died out some 65 million years ago, when their fossil record ceased. Largely unchanged since their assumed genesis 350 million years ago, coelcanths have also been sighted in the Comoros, and off Sulawesi in Indonesia. Unlike most fish, coelcanths give birth to live offspring, and are considered to be the closest living relative of the first fish that wandered ashore to become the ancestors of all of us land lubbers.

In the same room is an overly stuffed dugong, which – like the ancestors of other aquatic mammals, such as dolphins and whales – was, some time along its evolutionary safari, lured back into the sea. Sailors' tales of sirens and mermaids were apparently inspired by this rather portly creature – no accounting for some tastes.

The museum's real gems are in the adjacent **Ethnography Room**, its entrance marked by display cabinets containing grotesque clay figurines from the Pare and Sambaa tribes. These were used in male and female initiation ceremonies and to educate children, and are as bizarre as they are abstract. The beaded leather skirt from Lake Eyasi is strikingly beautiful, as is the carved door from the Fipa tribe, made from a single piece of wood, and incised with geometric zigzags and concentric circles. Kids will adore the brilliant wooden bicycles, of which similar examples – fully functional – can still be seen in parts of the country. The musical instruments are also a delight, including an intricately carved wooden ceremonial horn from the Kimbu tribe, a giant Nyamwezi drum made from a hollow tree trunk, and a gorgeous-sounding Zaramo xylophone.

There's a small **cafeteria** in one of the outbuildings selling sodas and cheap lunches for Tsh700–800. Lastly, don't forget to look through the books on sale at the shop, most of which you won't find anywhere else: Fidelis Masao's booklet on the prehistoric rock art of Kondoa and Singida is especially recommended.

The **Botanical Gardens** (daily sunrise–sunset; free), opposite the museum at the eastern end of Samora Avenue, date from German times and offer a shady oasis of peace and a wonderful escape from the city. The gardens are reasonably kept, and contain dozens of species of palm trees and primeval, fern-like cycads, as well as a raucous population of peacocks. If you're in luck, the explanatory leaflet (Tsh500) covering the plants and the garden's history may have been reprinted – ask at the gardener's office

Nyumba ya Sanaa (Nyerere Cultural Centre)

At the top end of Ohio Street next to the *Mövenpick Royal Palm*, **Nyumba ya Sanaa** (shops Mon–Fri 8am–8pm, Sat & Sun 8am–4pm; workshops Mon–Fri 8am–3pm; free; ☎022/213 1727), the "House of Arts", also known as the Nyerere Cultural Centre, is a unique handicrafts venue in which artists, most of them young, create and sell their work. Their output is generally of high quality and includes jewellery, textiles, pottery and ceramics, etchings, paintings, and the inevitable Makonde woodcarvings. Rather somnolent these days, you can still try your hand at painting, drawing, batik and etching. **Traditional dances** are performed most Fridays at 7.30pm (Tsh2000), and there's a small bar and a modest restaurant where you can have lunch.

North from the centre

Heading north from the city, Ali Hassan Mwinyi Road crosses the mangrove-lined Msimbazi Creek at the mouth of the Jangwani River before reaching **Msasani Peninsula**, the city's most affluent residential district. On the west side of the road here is **Kinondoni** district, home to the city's most vibrant nightlife, while a short distance further on is **Msasani Village**, another lively nightlife venue. Further north, the suburbs thin out, though there are still a couple of attractions, including the **Mwenge Handicraft Centre** and the **Village Museum**, before you hit Kawe and Mbezi and the first of the northern beaches.

Msasani Peninsula and Bongoyo Island

Some 6km north of Dar is **Msasani Peninsula**, a crooked finger of land protruding inquisitively into the Indian Ocean. With the exception of the fishing village of Msasani itself, now completely engulfed by the city, the peninsula seems to have been uninhabited until the arrival of the Europeans, who set up their first homes from home in the Oyster Bay area, on the peninsula's eastern side. The peninsula is now the address of choice for diplomats, civil servants, NGOs and the otherwise rich, privileged or corrupt, their homes surrounded by buzzing electric fences and guarded by armed *askaris*, many of them Maasai. Most of the mansions, beachfront hotels,

△ Coconut vendor, south of Dar es Salaam

upmarket bars and restaurants were constructed after the economic liberalization and attendant corruption that followed President Mwinyi's election in 1985. It's actually illegal to build on the seaward side of the shoreline road, though you'd never guess it.

Things acquire a more human face on the southwestern part of the peninsula, where the mansions give way to the more earthy district of **Msasani Village** (also called Namanga), which manages to blend a host of cheap eateries, bars and street food joints with posher restaurants and nightclubs. **Public transport** to the peninsula is limited to purple-banded daladalas from Posta to Masaki, which turn up Haile Selassie Road, then right along Chole Road to Touré Drive, north along the shoreline to the *Sea Cliff Hotel*, and back.

The peninsula's only substantial stretch of sand, and rather rocky at that, is **Coco Beach** – the main draw for the masses (and packed during holidays), attracting a refreshingly Tanzanian crowd compared to the tourist resorts further north, together with a number of enterprising street food purveyors – grilled cassava, *mishkaki*, corn cobs and coconuts. A spate of shark attacks closed the beach a few years ago (see box on p.112), and although things have returned to normal, perhaps it's something you should bear in mind. *Coco Beach Bar* at its northern end is a handy place to chill out in.

Also popular is the beautiful stretch of sand surrounding **Bongoyo Island** (ⓦwww.marineparktz.com), 6km north of the peninsula. Uninhabited other than by a handful of fishermen, it receives a few hundred picnickers most weekends. Motorized dhows ($10 return) leave daily from The Slipway shopping centre at 9.30am, 11.30am and 1.30pm for the thirty-minute crossing, returning at 12.30pm, 2.30pm and 5pm. The island has some nature trails, and good snorkelling – see p.129 for shops selling equipment. Snacks and drinks are available, but most people bring a picnic.

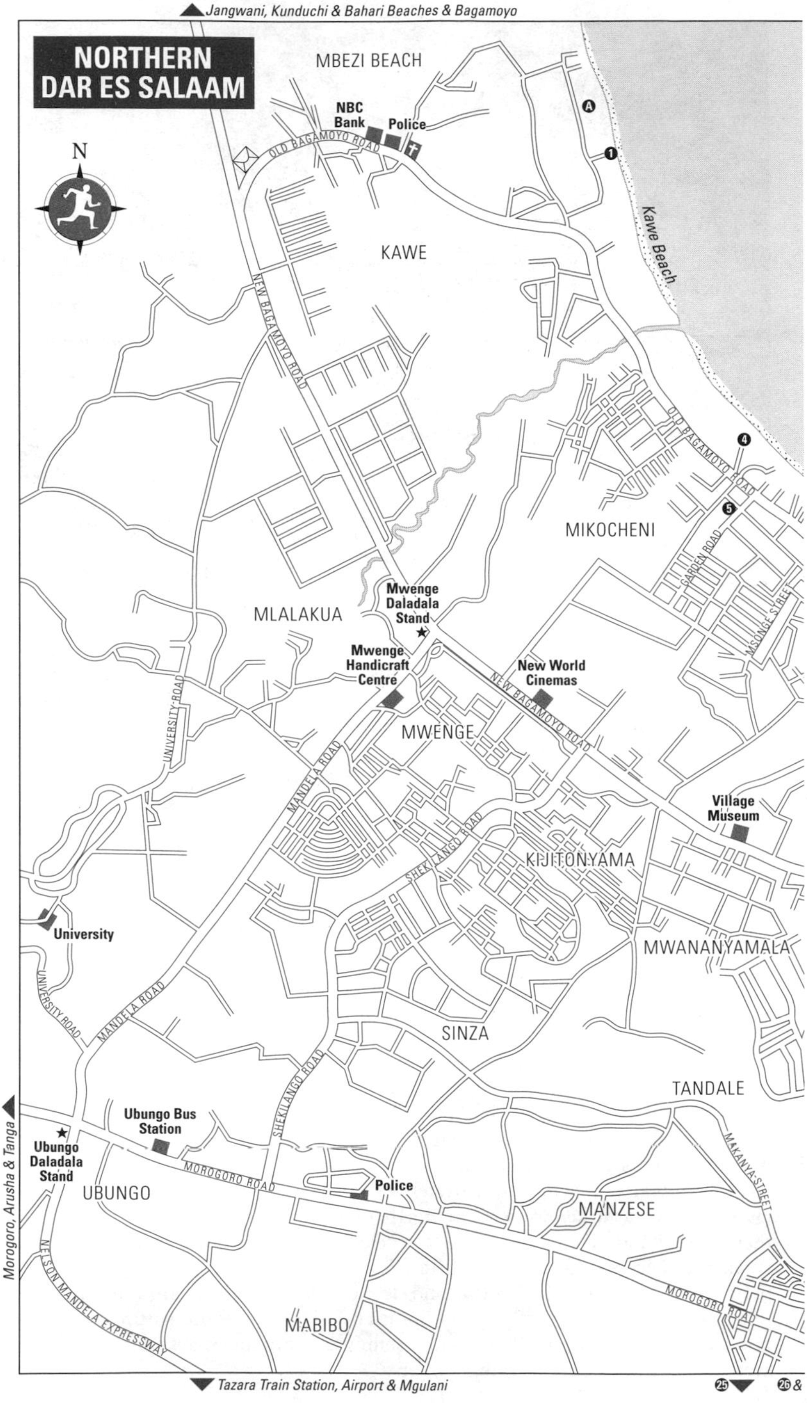
Jangwani, Kunduchi & Bahari Beaches & Bagamoyo
NORTHERN DAR ES SALAAM
N
MBEZI BEACH
NBC Bank
Police
OLD BAGAMOYO ROAD
A
1
KAWE
Kawe Beach
NEW BAGAMOYO ROAD
4
OLD BAGAMOYO ROAD
5
MIKOCHENI
GARDEN ROAD
MSONGE STREET
MLALAKUA
Mwenge Daladala Stand
Mwenge Handicraft Centre
New World Cinemas
NEW BAGAMOYO ROAD
MWENGE
UNIVERSITY ROAD
MANDELA ROAD
Village Museum
KIJITONYAMA
SHEKILANGO ROAD
University
MWANANYAMALA
UNIVERSITY ROAD
MANDELA ROAD
SINZA
SHEKILANGO ROAD
TANDALE
Morogoro, Arusha & Tanga
Ubungo Bus Station
Ubungo Daladala Stand
MOROGORO ROAD
Police
UBUNGO
MAKANYA STREET
MANZESE
NELSON MANDELA EXPRESSWAY
MOROGORO ROAD
MABIBO
Tazara Train Station, Airport & Mgulani
25
26 &

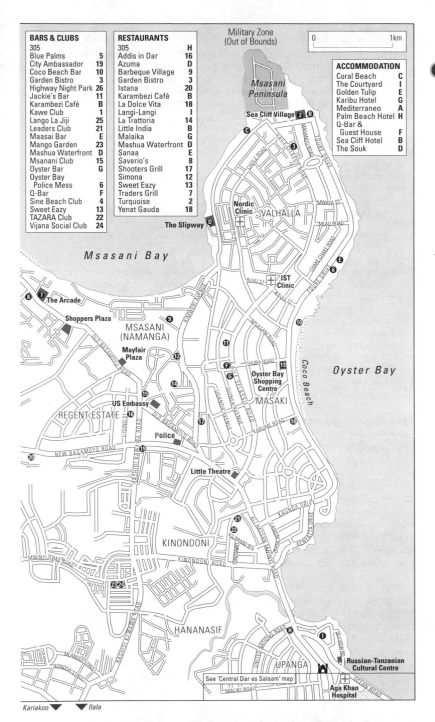

BARS & CLUBS

305	
Blue Palms	5
City Ambassador	19
Coco Beach Bar	10
Garden Bistro	3
Highway Night Park	26
Jackie's Bar	11
Karambezi Café	B
Kawe Club	1
Lango La Jiji	25
Leaders Club	21
Maasai Bar	E
Mango Garden	23
Mashua Waterfront	D
Msanani Club	15
Oyster Bar	G
Oyster Bay Police Mess	6
Q-Bar	F
Sine Beach Club	4
Sweet Eazy	13
TAZARA Club	22
Vijana Social Club	24

RESTAURANTS

305	H
Addis in Dar	16
Azuma	D
Barbeque Village	9
Garden Bistro	3
Istana	20
Karambezi Café	B
La Dolce Vita	18
Langi-Langi	I
La Trattoria	14
Little India	B
Malaika	G
Mashua Waterfront	D
Sanaa	E
Saverio's	8
Shooters Grill	17
Simona	12
Sweet Eazy	13
Traders Grill	7
Turquoise	2
Yenat Gauda	18

ACCOMMODATION

Coral Beach	C
The Courtyard	I
Golden Tulip	E
Karibu Hotel	G
Mediterraneo	A
Palm Beach Hotel	H
Q-Bar & Guest House	F
Sea Cliff Hotel	B
The Souk	D

Military Zone (Out of Bounds)

0   1km

Msasani Peninsula

Msasani Bay

Sea Cliff Village

The Slipway

Nordic Clinic   VALHALLA

IST Clinic

The Arcade

Shoppers Plaza

MSASANI (NAMANGA)

Mayfair Plaza

Oyster Bay

Coco Beach

Oyster Bay Shopping Centre

MASAKI

US Embassy

REGENT ESTATE

Police

Little Theatre

KINONDONI

HANANASIF

See 'Central Dar es Salaam' map

UPANGA

Russian-Tanzanian Cultural Centre

Aga Khan Hospital

Kariakoo ▼   ▼ Ilala

1

Shark attacks at Coco Beach

For reasons unknown, in January 2000 man-eating sharks migrated north from their customary haunts off Mozambique and South Africa to the Tanzanian coast, joining their octopus-eating brethren. A series of gruesome attacks off Coco Beach claimed five lives, terrorized beach-goers, and led to the government prohibiting swimming on Coco Beach (as well as, strangely enough, sunbathing or even walking on the beach).

The story of the sharks and attempts to capture them became something of a soap opera, much enlivened by the appearance of Dr Taratonga of the Kunduchi Beach Marine Research Institute, who was introduced on the National Television Network as a "warrior and marine science consultant". "You should expect to see a man-eating fish and then a fight between me and the fish," he announced, as crowds waited eagerly to watch the impending drama on huge screens set up in the city's Mnazi Mmoja Grounds. "But don't think it doesn't eat women. Unfortunately, it does" he added, before slipping into a dapper chain-mail suit which an assistant proceeded to stab with a knife to demonstrate its efficacy.

Sadly, when the crunch came, the "man-eating fish" was nowhere to be seen. The next development came when Hugo "Grub" van Lawick – owner of a deep-sea-fishing-safari outfit – claimed that he had caught the killer shark. Unfortunately, the Zambezi River Shark he hooked is not believed to have been the man-eater, and a post-mortem showed no traces of human flesh in the shark's stomach. Meanwhile, local astrologer Sheikh Yahya Hussein – always ready with a word to say on anything of national importance – insisted that the deaths had been caused by a demon appearing in the shape of a fish, suggesting that an offering be made to appease the spirits of the dead. The government's offering was a $5000 "monitoring station" equipped with satellite antennae and fast patrol boats, though predictably enough, nothing ever came of this.

The entire episode was treated as freak event, but you'd be wise to enquire about the latest before putting toe to water.

The Mwenge Handicraft Centre and Village Museum

Further north are a couple of cultural attractions which are invariably included in organized tours of Dar, though both are also accessible by public transport. The **Mwenge Handicraft Centre** (daily 8am–6.30pm) is 12km from the city on Mandela Road in Mwenge. There are frequent daladalas to Mwenge terminal from both Posta and Kariakoo, leaving you with a six-hundred-metre walk. The centre, founded in 1984, comprises almost a hundred shops, most of them selling identical Makonde woodcarvings, reproductions of studded Zanzibari chests, soapstone carvings from Kisii in Kenya, and Zambian malachite. Spend some time looking around, however, and you'll turn up some more unusual items, including traditional wooden stools, bao games, Christian idols, masks, sisal baskets and bags, coconut shredders, batiks, cow bells, Makonde masks and paintings.

Heading 3km back towards the city along Bagamoyo Road (catch a dala-dala from Mwenge terminal), the **Village Museum** in Kijitonyama (daily 9.30am–6pm; $4; ☎022/270 0437) nicely complements a visit to the handicraft centre. If you're coming from town, catch a Posta–Mwenge daladala as far as "Makumbusho" (Museum). The museum was founded in 1966, in an attempt to preserve some of the architectural and associated material traditions of traditional Tanzanian societies, thus educating future generations about their heritage. Spread out over the open-air site are nineteen replicas of houses built in the architectural styles of different tribes, each furnished with typical household items and utensils, and surrounded by small plots of local crops and animal pens. Although laudable, the aims of the museum became grimly ironic in the years following its establishment, when Nyerere embarked on his economically disastrous policy of "Villagization" in which the majority of rural Tanzanians were forcibly moved out of their villages to begin new lives as collective labourers in planned townships. By the time the experiment collapsed in the mid-1970s, the Tanzanian economy was in ruins.

Traditional crafts and arts, such as carving, weaving and pottery, are demonstrated by resident "villagers", whilst a blacksmith explains the intricacies of his craft, which has existed in East Africa for at least two millennia. The finished products are sold in the museum shop, which also stocks books and other souvenirs. There's a small café serving drinks and Tanzanian food, performances of **traditional dance** (Tues–Sun 2–6pm), and storytelling sessions on Tuesday and Thursday, primarily for groups of school children. March, June, November and December are also good times to visit, when the museum hosts **Ethnic Days** dedicated to a particular Tanzanian tribe or region, featuring song and dance, recitals of oral history and poetry, and traditional food. Ring ☎022/270 0437 for details, or see the *Dar es Salaam Guide*.

Eating

Dar es Salaam has no shortage of **places to eat**, with enough high-quality establishments to stimulate even the most jaded of palates. The larger **hotels** all have restaurants, often several, with some offering eat-all-you-want lunchtime buffets and others rotating through alternating theme nights. Although not cheap (upwards of Tsh12,000 is the norm), you're pretty much guaranteed good food.

There's also a good range of **top-end restaurants** at which you can eat well for upwards of Tsh10,000, as long as you're happy adding a taxi fare to the bill, as most places are north of the centre. In this price bracket you'll find dozens of Chinese, Indian and Italian places, plus more unusual culinary experiences like Ethiopian, Japanese, Malaysian, and even Croatian fare. More affordable and

Street food

You won't find much traditional Tanzanian fare on the menus of Dar's posher restaurants. Out on the streets, however, you'll find some truly superb and often dirt-cheap local food, especially around markets and transport terminals. **Kivukoni Fish Market** has some of the finest grilled fish on the coast. For fuller **meals**, try one of the *mama lisha* ("feeding ladies") in the Swedish-built buildings on the harbour side of Kivukoni Front, who dish out rice and *ugali* with stew or beans, fried fish or *mishkaki* (skewers of grilled goat meat), chicken kebabs wrapped in chapatis, bananas cooked in coconut milk, all delicious and costing under Tsh1000. On Kivukoni Front itself are hawkers aplenty, peddling **snacks** such as samosas, rice cakes, roasted maize cobs, mangos (which are peeled for you), and delicious roast cassava doused in light chilli sauce, a far cry from the usual mealy, mouth-drying tuber.

In addition, *mama* (and some *baba*) *lisha* at the west end of Garden Avenue serve full meals, as do handfuls of stalls at most road junctions in Kisutu. To cap a meal on the move, look for the **coffee vendors** (also in the morning), especially in the Asian district, Kariakoo, and at the daladala stands, who sell scalding Turkish-style coffee in small porcelain cups from shiny brass samovars.

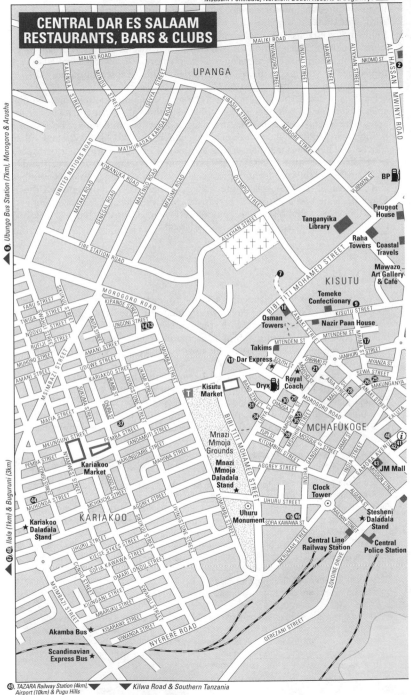

Msasani Peninsula, Northern Beach Resorts & Bagamoyo

CENTRAL DAR ES SALAAM RESTAURANTS, BARS & CLUBS

UPANGA

Ubungo Bus Station (7km), Morogoro & Arusha

Tanganyika Library

Peugeot House

Raha Towers

Coastal Travels

Mawazo Art Gallery & Café

KISUTU

Temeke Confectionary

Nazir Paan House

Osman Towers

Takims

Dar Express

Kisutu Market

Oryx

Royal Coach

MCHAFUKOGE

Mnazi Mmoja Grounds

Mnazi Mmoja Daladala Stand

Kisutu Market

Kariakoo Market

JM Mall

Clock Tower

Aggrey Street

Uhuru Monument

Uhuru Street

Stesheni Daladala Stand

KARIAKOO

Central Line Railway Station

Central Police Station

Kariakoo Daladala Stand

Ilala (1km) & Buguruni (3km)

Akamba Bus

Scandinavian Express Bus

TAZARA Railway Station (4km), Airport (10km) & Pugu Hills

Kilwa Road & Southern Tanzania

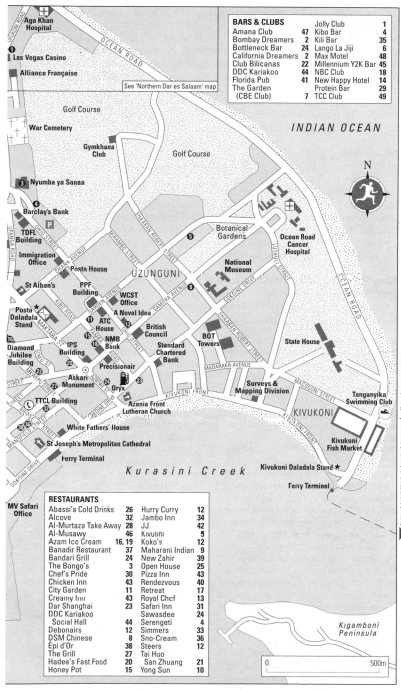

BARS & CLUBS

Amana Club	47	Jolly Club	1
Bombay Dreamers	2	Kibo Bar	4
Bottleneck Bar	24	Kili Bar	35
California Dreamers	2	Lango La Jiji	6
Club Bilicanas	22	Max Motel	48
DDC Kariakoo	44	Millennium Y2K Bar	45
Florida Pub	41	NBC Club	18
The Garden		New Happy Hotel	14
(CBE Club)	7	Protein Bar	29
		TCC Club	49

Aga Khan Hospital
Las Vegas Casino
Alliance Française
OCEAN ROAD
UPENKONI ROAD
See 'Northern Dar es Salaam' map

Golf Course
War Cemetery
Gymkhana Club
Golf Course

INDIAN OCEAN

N

Nyumba ya Sanaa
Barclay's Bank
TDFL Building
Immigration Office
Posta House
UZUNGUNI
St Alban's
PPF Building
WCST Office
A Novel Idea
ATC House
British Council
Posta Daladala Stand
NMB Bank
IPS Building
Precisionair
Standard Chartered Bank
BOT Towers
Diamond Jubilee Building
Askari Monument
Oryx
Azania Front Lutheran Church
TTCL Building
White Fathers' House
St Joseph's Metropolitan Cathedral
Ferry Terminal
MV Safari Office

Botanical Gardens
National Museum
Ocean Road Cancer Hospital
State House
Surveys & Mapping Division
MADARAKA AVENUE
MAGOGONI STREET
KIVUKONI FRONT
Tanganyika Swimming Club
KIVUKONI
Kivukoni Fish Market
Kivukoni Daladala Stand
Ferry Terminal

Kurasini Creek

Mikadi Beach (2km), Mjimwema (7.5km) & Gezaulole (14km)

Kigamboni Peninsula

0   500m

RESTAURANTS

Abassi's Cold Drinks	26	Hurry Curry	12
Alcove	32	Jambo Inn	34
Al-Murtaza Take Away	28	JJ	42
Al-Musawy	46	Kivulini	5
Azam Ice Cream	16, 19	Koko's	12
Banadir Restaurant	37	Maharani Indian	9
Bandari Grill	24	New Zahir	39
The Bongo's	3	Open House	25
Chef's Pride	30	Pizza Inn	43
Chicken Inn	43	Rendezvous	40
City Garden	11	Retreat	17
Creamy Inn	43	Royal Chef	13
Dar Shanghai	23	Safari Inn	31
DDC Kariakoo		Sawasdee	24
Social Hall	44	Serengeti	4
Debonairs	12	Simmers	33
DSM Chinese	8	Sno-Cream	36
Épi d'Or	38	Steers	12
The Grill	27	Tai Huo	
Hadee's Fast Food	20	San Zhuang	21
Honey Pot	15	Yong Sun	10

less fancy are **mid-range restaurants** in the Tsh5000–10,000 range, which you can find more or less everywhere, and which serve mainly European- and Indian-inspired food. Choose carefully, however, as quality and standards of hygiene are far from uniform. A host of small, **cheap restaurants** are scattered throughout the city, dishing up Indian, Swahili and European dishes for under Tsh5000, often for half that, with the very cheapest – in places like Kariakoo and Ilala – filling you up for under Tsh1000.

In addition, most **local bars and nightclubs** provide large and filling portions of *nyama choma*, *chipsi mayai*, *ndizi* and, more rarely, *ugali*. The busier the place, the better the food.

Markets

For your own supplies, all of the city's **markets** are great places to stock up. Apart from Kariakoo (p.105), Kivukoni (p.106) and Kisutu (p.104), the claustrophobic **Ilala Market**, to the west of Kariakoo on Uhuru Street, just before Kawawa Road, is worth a visit, mainly for the reams of second-hand clothes and shoes – most daladalas from Kivukoni and Kariakoo to Buguruni run straight past the entrance. In the city centre, **fruit stalls** can be found at the top end of Zanaki Street north of Jamhuri Street, though you'll pay much more than in the markets. **Supermarkets** are listed on p.129.

City centre: east from India Street

In addition to the following, there's a good unnamed *nyama choma* garden on Ohio Street just north of ATC House, with plenty of shady chairs, scrawny cats, Indian crows and cheap eats.

Alcove Samora Ave. Long-established but pricey Indian and Chinese restaurant, sometimes excellent, other times bland. There's a good choice, including tandoori and masalas, Indian kebabs, inventive seafood, sizzlers, fresh salads, pizzas and vegetarian dishes. Expect to pay at least Tsh10,000 for two courses, plus (expensive) drinks, and watch out for VAT. Live music Sun evening. Closed Sun lunch.

Bandari Grill 1st floor, *New Africa Hotel*, Azikiwe St. Best for its all-you-want lunchtime buffets (Mon–Fri; Tsh13,650), though you could always go à la carte for Indian dishes, flambées and prawns.

The Bongo's Nyumba ya Sanaa, Ohio St. In the courtyard of the arts centre, but hot whenever the electricity is down, this has a reasonable choice of snacks and Tanzanian meals (Tsh3000–4000), including grilled prawns. Lunchtimes only.

City Garden Corner of Garden Ave and Pamba Rd. The central, outdoor location is the main reason to eat here, with loads of seats under thatch, parasols and trees. The lunchtime buffets are good, though à la carte – including a range of fresh salads, seafood and pizza – is also reasonably priced (mostly Tsh4000–5000). Slow service, and no alcohol.

Dar Shanghai *Luther House Hostel*, Sokoine Drive. Unquestionably tasty Chinese and Tanzanian food, with soups around Tsh1500, and most dishes (including rice or noodles – for which read

spaghetti) costing Tsh3500–5000. Also has good juices. Closed Sun lunch.

DSM Chinese NIC Investments House, Samora Ave. In the basement, this looks like a cafeteria but serves up some delicious quasi-Chinese meals and snacks with not a pinch of MSG in sight. Busy at lunchtime. There's not a huge choice, but a full meal won't cost more than Tsh4500, soups cost Tsh1500, and a vegetable stir-fry with cashews and rice just Tsh2300. Closed Sun.

Épi d'Or Samora Ave. A friendly Lebanese bakery and café, perfect for breakfast or a light lunch. The Mediterranean influence shows in the wonderful fresh salads, snacks like *baba ghanouj* (aubergine and tahina purée) and paninis. Coffee is the real thing, so are the juices, and they even bake croissants. No smoking or alcohol. Mon–Sat 7am–6pm.

Hadee's Fast Food Maktaba St. No frills breakfasts, snacks and full meals, handily placed close to the Askari Monument, with CNN news on the TV in the morning. No alcohol

Honey Pot Pamba Rd. Cheap snacks and light meals (under Tsh1000) – popular at lunchtimes with office workers. Closed Sun.

JJ Samora Ave. A very cheap lunchtime place, serving acceptable, unspectacular Tanzanian grub (rice, *ugali* or chips with various stews, fish and meat) for Tsh1000–2000. Also does breakfast.

Kivulini *Holiday Inn*, Garden Ave. A swish venue specializing in Swahili seafood, with mains spiralling upwards of Tsh5000, and buffet breakfasts or lunches for around Tsh10,000.

Rendezvous Samora Ave. Split-level a/c place with harmless muzak serving up generous portions of local nosh (around Tsh4000), including good kingfish. Licensed. Closed Sun.

Sawasdee 9th floor, *New Africa Hotel*, Azikiwe St. Highly recommended rooftop restaurant, evenings only, with beautiful harbour views and fabulous buffets: Thai (lots of seafood; Tues & Fri) and Italian (Wed) both cost Tsh13,650, and Indian (Thurs) is Tsh12,000. There's also a Saturday barbecue. Thai dominates the à la carte, everything characteristically aromatic and delicious, and there's a good wine list too. Ideal for a romantic tête-à-tête.

Serengeti *Mövenpick Royal Palm*, Ohio St. Good for pig-out buffets if you've Tsh15,000-plus to spend , including lavish breakfasts. "Neptune's

Kingdom" is the fishy name for Thursday evening's theme, which includes lobster, crab claws, smoked sailfish and prawns. Their other themed evenings include Italian (Mon), game meat (Tues), oriental (Wed), Indian (Fri), African (Sat) and South African "Cape Malay" (Sun).

Sno-Cream Mansfield St. Scrummy ice creams at European prices served up in a f-f-freezingly cold interior. There's another branch at the north end of Alykhan Rd near *Palm Beach Hotel*.

Steers, Debonairs, Hurry Curry & Koko's CDTF Building, corner of Samora Ave and Ohio St. Four flavours from the Islamic South African fast-food chain, a kind of Halal-meets-McDonald's concept that works surprisingly well. *Steers* offers the usual junk plus toasted sandwiches, salads, milk shakes, juices and great toffee ice cream; *Debonairs* has expensive pizzas; *Hurry Curry* sells itself; and *Koko's* does Chinese. All four do takeaways and home delivery (☎022/212 2855). No alcohol.

City centre: Kisutu and Mchafukoge

Abassi's Cold Drinks Zanaki St. A friendly Indian place for breakfast, with a wide selection of refreshing fruit juices and snacks including samosas and rice cakes. No alcohol.

Al-Murtaza Take Away Asia St. Cheap meals and snacks including a great lunchtime chicken pilau, and chicken biriani on Sunday. No alcohol.

Al-Musawy Corner of Indira Gandhi and Sofia Kawawa streets. No-frills snacks like *andazi* doughnuts, samosas and chapatis. The fish and chips are a filling bargain at Tsh1000. No alcohol.

Azam Ice Cream Two branches in this area: one at the corner of Morogoro Rd and Bibi Titi Mohamed St, the other at the roundabout between Jamhuri and India streets and Upanga Rd. Both offer fixes for gelato junkies. No alcohol.

Chef's Pride Chagga St. A busy and deservedly popular split-level Tanzanian restaurant offering an embarrassment of choice, most of it freshly cooked, whether Zanzibari-style fish in coconut, biriani curry, tender roast chicken or pizza. It also dishes up fast-food favourites, snacks and great breakfast combos, with nothing much over Tsh3000. Open until 11pm.

The Grill Mkwepu St. A large and oddly plush place with attentive waiters, pressed tablecloths and icy a/c. The extensive menu majors on Indian, particularly Balti – lots of caraway and coriander – and you'll also find fajitas and enchiladas, Korean (Wed evenings), tandoori and teppinyaki, and a dozen ways of serving steak (Tsh9000 for 400g). The Tsh5000 lunchtime buffet is good value, otherwise it's expensive. There are also seats outside,

and a fast-food counter. Finish with a *shisha* water pipe.

Hong Kong Tai Yong Sun Corner of Bibi Titi Mohamed and Zanaki streets. Some of the best Chinese food in the city, but you'll pay through the nose (count on Tsh15,000 for a two-course meal with drinks), and the Tsh5000 lunchtime specials are too small to fill you up. Good for a treat. Closed Sun lunchtime.

Jambo Inn Libya St. Good food, mainly Indian plus some Tanzanian, but portions are stingy and it gets expensive given than rice, salad or even vegetables cost extra. From Tsh5000 a plate.

Maharani Indian Kisutu St. Modest but highly recommended, with fresh and tasty food featuring a huge vegetarian choice, either à la carte (around Tsh2500) or in the famous lunchtime buffet, a bargain at Tsh3500 (Tsh4000 with meat).

New Zahir Mosque St. A favourite with Kisutu's Muslims, this does reasonable curries and birianis for under Tsh2000, plus some Tanzanian dishes and real espresso, but juices aren't the real thing and hygiene is questionable. That said, it's handy for a quick bite. Arrive early at lunch to be sure of a table. Closed Fri 12.20–1.20pm for prayers.

Open House Sewa St. Large and imposing place with an extensive Indian and Chinese menu. The shredded chicken and chicken tikka masala are both good, and they also do pizzas, but the noodles are really just spaghetti, and it's pricey, with starters up to Tsh4000 and mains around Tsh5000 (watch out for VAT).

Pizza Inn, Chicken Inn, Creamy Inn Corner of

Samora Ave and Mission St. Three spick- and-span fast-food outlets, the latter for ice cream. Open until midnight.

🏃 **Retreat** Mrima St. Don't let the stark cafeteria-like dining room put you off – this vegetarian place serves up seriously good South Indian food, plus a small selection of more average Chinese dishes. A full meal with drinks shouldn't cost more than Tsh5000, and the lunchtime *thalis* are good value at Tsh3000–3500. No smoking. Closed Mon.

Safari Inn Off Libya St. Cheap eats in a cavernous but hot dining hall around the back, with mains at around Tsh1500–2000, and also snacks. Daily 4–10pm.

Simmers Jamhuri St, under the *Holiday Hotel*. A friendly, locally run place on two levels dishing up some of Kisutu's best food, whether liver stew, coconut fish and beef, or simple things like rice with beans and vegetables. Big portions, small prices – mains under Tsh3000. They also do good breakfasts.

Tai Huo San Zhuang Jamhuri St. The cream-themed dining room is the first impression here, something like a Victorian powder room. This serves up genuine Chinese cuisine, and depending on what you choose will lighten your pocket by Tsh5000–10,000. Lunchtime specials cost Tsh3500.

West of the centre: Kariakoo

Apart from the following, Kariakoo has loads of cheap no-frills eateries, especially along the unsurfaced streets west of Msimbazi Street.

Banadir Restaurant *Al-Uruba Hotel*, Mkunguni St. Busy Somali-run place, both for snacks and full meals. Choose at the counter from various kinds of stews (including the superb ratatouille), meat and fish. Tsh3000 will get you a filling meal. Also has fresh juices and fruit. No alcohol

DDC Kariakoo Social Hall Muhonda St. Dar's longest-running bar and live music venue is also one of the best places for a really cheap eat, packing them in with metal platters of pilau, beans and

stews for a mere Tsh600. Also has great *supu* for breakfast.

Royal Chef Lumumba St. Run by the same folks as *Chef's Pride*, and also highly recommended; this is one of the city's best cheap restaurants. The tasty food, both Tanzanian and Western, grills, meat, seafood or vegetarian, comes quickly and in huge portions, with an attractive streetside verandah to boot. Even the T-bone steaks and prawn dishes cost little more than Tsh3500.

North of the centre: Upanga

305 *Palm Beach Hotel*, 305 Ali Hassan Mwinyi Rd. A popular and recommended outdoor restaurant, set under tall shady trees and boasting an eclectic menu covering everything from Indian, vegetarian and seafood to Greek, including various kinds of souvlaki (stuffed pitta bread rolls). It's also good value for money, with light meals costing about Tsh2000, and more substantial main courses

under Tsh5000. A full cooked breakfast goes for Tsh6000.

Langi-Langi *The Courtyard Hotel*, Ocean Rd. Classy French, Indian and continental cuisine in a sophisticated ambience, with a popular Sunday brunch (11.30am–3pm; Tsh8000, including use of the swimming pool). Live music every evening.

North of the city: Msasani Peninsula

Msasani contains dozens of upmarket restaurants, of which the following is just a selection – new places open and old ones close constantly, so ring ahead before going. Unless otherwise stated, expect to part with upwards of Tsh15,000 for a full meal with drinks. See also the reviews of Msasani's bars, many of which serve (decidedly cheaper) food.

Azuma The Slipway ☎022/260 0893. Authentic Japanese and Indonesian cuisine – the sashimi (raw fish) is superb. Lunchtime specials go for around Tsh8000. Closed all day Mon, Sat & Sun evenings.

Barbeque Village Off Kimweri Ave, Namanga ☎022/266 7927. A flashy hotchpotch of styles

– Indian, Chinese and continental. The seafood buffets (Fri & Sat) include lobster, crab masala and seafood fondue, and there are barbecues the rest of the time. Evenings only. Closed Mon.

Garden Bistro 498 Haile Selassie Rd ☎022/260 0800. Lots of closely packed tables under thatch and trees offering fine Indian cuisine in its

Shamiyana Restaurant, plus continental food, a lounge for smoking shisha pipes, and popular bar.

Karambezi Café Sea Cliff Hotel, Touré Drive ☎022/260 0380. Beautifully located on the cliff edge with fine ocean views, the huge menu centres on steaks, pizzas and other Mediterranean dishes (Tsh5000–9000). Open 24hr.

La Dolce Vita Touré Drive ☎0741/782497. Genuine Italian fare, including pizzas (Tsh4500–6000), with sea views across the road. Open from 4pm, closed Sun.

La Trattoria Jan Off Kimweri Ave, Namanga ☎0744/282989. Consistently good and reasonably priced Italian and other Mediterranean food, with live music Thurs–Sat.

Little India Sea Cliff Hotel, Touré Drive ☎022/260 0380. Fine seafood and North Indian à la carte, with a weekly tandoori night on Wednesdays. Evenings only.

Malaika Karibu Hotel, Haile Selassie Rd ☎022/260 1767. One of the finest Indian restaurants in town, best sampled via their buffet dinner (Tues–Sun). Live Indian music after 8.30pm. Go à la carte for continental and Chinese.

Mashua Waterfront The Slipway ☎022/260 0893. The location's the thing here, with lovely views over Msasani Bay – chow down on pizzas and grills, or just take a drink.

Sanaa Golden Tulip Hotel, Touré Drive ☎022/260 0288. Another hotel offering theme nights (and expensive buffet lunches), including pasta (Wed), vegetarian (Thurs), steak and a live band (Fri), and a fun champagne brunch (Sun), with plenty of activities for kids like face-painting and a bouncy

castle (Tsh14,000 including use of pool; kids under 8 free).

Shooters Grill Kimweri Ave, Namanga ☎0744/304733. Styled after a bush camp, with safari chairs, fake game trophies and plenty of wood and thatch, this is primarily for carnivores, and especially good for steaks (including a whopping 1kg T-bone). Live music Sun.

Simona Kimweri Ave, Namanga ☎022/266 6935. Perhaps Africa's only Croatian restaurant, frequently recommended for its seafood, and with a well-stocked bar. Live music Fri & Sat. Closed Sun.

Sweet Eazy Oyster Bay Shopping Centre, Ghuba Rd ☎0745/754074. An offshoot of its Stone Town namesake, but not as atmospheric and more expensive too. The food – African and Thai – is excellent though, especially the marinated raw tuna jodari as a starter. Eat in the a/c dining room, or outside on the terrace. There's also a pricey bar. Inafrika play Thurs from 7pm, and there's jazz on Sat.

Turquoise Sea Cliff Village, next to Sea Cliff Hotel ☎022/260 0979. Excellent Turkish restaurant dishing up great kebabs and mezze, loads of vegetarian specialities, and delicious home-made cakes and sweets. Closed Sun.

Yenat Gauda 1 Touré Drive ☎0741/324057. Sharing the plot with La Dolce Vita, this is a rather pricey Ethiopian restaurant with most dishes costing Tsh5500–7000. The basic staple is injera, a huge soft pancake that you share with your partner, from which you tear bits off, to eat with a variety of highly spiced sauces and stews. Good coffee. Closed Sun.

North of the city: Mikocheni and Kawe

By day, frequent daladalas run from Posta to Kawe: those marked "via A.H. Mwinyi" drive along Bagamoyo Road; ones marked "via Old Bagamoyo Rd" go along the coast past The Arcade and pass Mikocheni. Taxis charge Tsh 4000–6000 each day.

Addis in Dar 35 Ursino St, off Bagamoyo Rd, Regent Estate ☎0741/266299. Even if you've eaten north Ethiopian food before, don't miss this place. Attention to detail is everything, from the traditional decor – even outside under the parasols – to the wafting incense. There's lots of choice for vegetarians, they also brew an excellent cup of coffee, and sell colourful Ethiopian art and beautiful silverwork. A little pricey, but thoroughly recommended. Closed Sun.

Istana Ali Hassan Mwinyi Rd, Mnananyamala ☎022/276 1348. Welcoming and friendly place serving a small range of spicy Malaysian, Chinese and Indian dishes, most for under Tsh5000, and lots of vegetarian choice too. Meals are dished up

on banana leaves, if you like, and served at tables in garden huts – try the nasi lemak (steamed coconut rice) with sambal ikan bilis (anchovies), boiled eggs, fried peanuts and cucumber. It's also famous for its eat-all-you-like buffets (Tsh7800), with Malay (Mon), Chinese (Tues), seafood (Wed), Satay (Thurs) and Indian (Sun) all featuring. Evenings only.

Saverio's Old Bagamoyo Rd, opposite The Arcade, Mikocheni ☎022/270 0393. Delicious wood-fired pizzas (under Tsh3500) plus seafood, steaks and an ice-cream parlour. Deservedly popular. Closed Mon.

Traders Grill The Arcade, Old Bagamoyo Rd, Mikocheni ☎0748/706188. Designed like an English country pub, the T-bones and rump steaks here (from Tsh10,000) satisfy any appetite, though the chicken, fish and seafood – especially prawns – are better value at around Tsh6000 (or Tsh11,500

for eat-all-you-want on Wed, Fri & Sun); wash it all down with Pilsner Urquell. Live music most nights. Evenings only.

Drinking and nightlife

Given its large Muslim population, Dar es Salaam isn't at first glance the most promising place for **bars and nightlife**. But head out into the suburbs to places like Kariakoo, Sinza, Ilala and Kinondoni, and you'll discover a wealth of **clubs** and **dance halls** brimming over with people dancing to live bands, or drowning their sorrows in any one of a thousand bars. If the local scene isn't to your liking, upmarket areas like Msasani have more than their fair share of places too, as glitzy, brash or downright expensive as you like, though they also attract a lot of prostitutes on the prowl. Oddly enough, while bars and clubs popular with locals don't tend to change all that much, the more upmarket crowds are fickle with their favours, so you'd do well to check on a venue's popularity before heading out there.

Taxis are the usual way of **getting around**, although you can use daladalas before around 9pm – details are given where appropriate. Getting back is no problem as even the smallest bar or club will have cabs waiting outside for customers, even at the most unsociable hours.

Bars

See also the reviews of live music venues, most of which operate as bars when not hosting bands. In addition, all big hotels have bars, usually expensive and rather anodyne affairs screening sports on large screens, and with extensive snack and cocktail menus. These include *Bottleneck Bar* at the *New Africa*, *Kibo Bar* at the *Mövenpick Royal Palm* (with live music Fri–Sun), *Maasai Bar* at the *Golden Tulip* (with karaoke on Fri), *Oyster Bar* at *Karibu Hotel*, and – with a matchless sea view – *Karambezi Café* at the *Sea Cliff Hotel*.

City centre

Florida Pub Mansfield St. Dark and pricey a/c bar with Dar's haughtiest barmaids – pay for your drinks straight off as they're not averse to overcharging later. There's Castle Lager on tap, a mute TV, two pool tables, and reasonable food (around Tsh3500). Closed Sun.

The Garden (CBE Club) College of Business Education, Bibi Titi Mohamed St. A pleasantly down-to-earth refuge for an afternoon (or evening) drink outdoors, with rickety tables under trees, *nyama choma*, and pool tables. Live music, especially rap, most Fridays.

Kili Bar Mshihiri St, Kisutu. One of three main boozers in the backpackers' area; it's uninviting by day, but better in the evening when tables appear on the pavement.

Jolly Club Next to Las Vegas Casino, Ufukoni St. A huge, partially outdoor bar, with fancy lighting, TVs all over, tables in cosy thatched nooks, and zillions

of prostitutes – things get really steamy at weekends, when there's a band (free). Food available, including *nyama choma*.

Millennium Y2K Bar Sofia Kawawa St. Best of the bunch in this area, a friendly local bar with tables on a shaded streetfront terrace and in a courtyard at the back. There's a pool table, cheerful Congolese music, full meals until 4pm and snacks and *mishkaki* thereafter.

NBC Club Pamba Rd. A famous unmarked bar in the central business district, with two distinct sections, one inside with a TV, the other outside with a dartboard. Good soup, *nyama choma* and *ndizi*.

New Happy Hotel Ungoni St. The rooftop bar here is popular with locals, with a good atmosphere, views over part of the city, and a TV usually showing UK football. The grilled goat meat is succulent, but beware of overcharging – pay as you order.

Protein Bar Jamhuri St, facing *Holiday Hotel*. Barmaids alternating between boisterous and sulky, seasoned drunkards, the occasional tourist and attendant flycatchers all make for an eclectic – if usually agreeable – evening cocktail, when tables appear on the pavement.

Outside the centre

Some of Msasani Peninsula's restaurants – including the *Garden Bistro*, *Mashua Waterfront* and *Sweet Eazy* – also double as bars; see the restaurant reviews.

305 *Palm Beach Hotel*, Ali Hassan Mwinyi Rd, Upanga. A relaxing place to while away your time, with plenty of tables under shady trees and canvas at the front, though drinks attract a premium. Good food. Catch any northbound daladala from Posta marked "via A.H. Mwinyi Road".

Coco Beach Bar Touré Drive, Msasani Peninsula. The most popular of Msasani's local joints, hardly surprisingly given its beachfront location (swimming possible). Beers are cheap by Msasani's standards (Tsh1000), and a wide range of food is served. Pool tables, and a Sunday disco from 4pm onwards (Tsh500).

Highway Night Park 3km along Morogoro Rd at Magomeni-Mapipa, before Rashidi Kawawa Rd. Dar's most exuberant 24hr dive, with live music some evenings (free entry) and dancers every night, including an acrobatic couple of polio victims on Sunday – amazing stuff. It gets packed at midnight when the music really gets going, and slowly fizzles out around 4am. Food is available here, at neighbouring kiosks and at basic restaurants in the area. The language barrier means that the prostitutes for which the place is infamous tend to leave tourists alone. Catch an Ubungo daladala from Posta or Kariakoo stands.

Jackie's Bar Haile Selassie Rd, Msasani Peninsula. Calm but nonetheless popular nocturnal respite from the nearby *Q-Bar*'s hordes and whores, with plenty of outdoor tables by the roadside.

Kawe Club 650m off Old Bagamoyo Rd, Kawe. An old colonial club established in 1952 by the Tanganyika Packers (lapsed purveyors of corned beef), now totally dilapidated and run by a cheerful bunch of young Tanzanian rap fans. The beach is the main attraction, but there's also a wonderful broken piano, an equally sorry-looking flint snooker table, and chips with chicken or beef in you're hungry. Catch a daladala to Kawe from Posta or Kariakoo.

Oyster Bay Police Mess Touré Drive, Msasani Peninsula. Astride a low ragstone headland, this huge bar no longer stages live music (something worth asking about though; Fri was the big day) and is consequently rather quiet, but has a nice bayside location.

Q-Bar Haile Selassie Rd, Msasani Peninsula. A popular place for locals, expatriates and tourists, as well as with a welter of well-dressed prostitutes. It's liveliest Wednesday and Friday, when Roots Rockers band play. Also has good food, pool tables, sports on the TV, cocktails and shooters. Catch a Posta–Masaki daladala.

Sine Beach Club Old Bagamoyo Rd, between TANESCO and Kawe village, Mikocheni. Popular for its beach with locals (and families) at weekends, with good food and occasional bands on Sunday from mid-afternoon, and live bands (Thurs & Sat). Swimming possible at high tide. Catch a daladala to Kawe from Posta or Kariakoo.

Nightclubs

Entrance fees average Tsh2000–5000. Some places admit women for free, especially on Wednesdays ("Ladies Night"); others are free for all on weekdays. Things really get going after 10pm.

Blue Palms Garden Rd, Mikocheni. Bright and cheerful bar, formerly *the* place for a Saturday night boogie until the *Garden Bistro* arrived. Currently more laid-back, though it still hosts the disco, and there's sometimes live music (Tues & Thurs; free). Food available. Catch a Posta–Kawe daladala. Closed Mon.

Bombay Dreamers Las Vegas Casino complex, Ali Hassan Mwinyi Rd. One of Dar's more unusual nightspots – an Indian-themed nightclub combin-ing cabaret, live music and dancing every evening from 9pm – with an equally individual door policy: couples and women are charged admission at weekends to discourage prostitutes.

California Dreamers Las Vegas Casino complex, Ali Hassan Mwinyi Rd. Along with *Club Bilicanas*, this is Dar's flashiest disco, with a good lighting and sound system, dancy modern music and loose ladies. Daily from 9pm, but the big night is Saturday.

Big names in live music

Dar is the best place in East Africa for catching **live music**. There are over twenty professional dance bands in the city, most playing three or four times a week on an ever-changing circuit of clubs and dance halls around the suburbs. On Sundays, the bands usually play on their home turf, generally a bar, club or social hall. For up-to-date **listings**, the weekend edition of the *Uhuru* newspaper has a small box on the inside back page announcing gigs that weekend; you might also try the evening *Alasiri* tabloid. More upmarket events are covered in either of Dar's listings booklets, or in the Friday edition of *The Citizen* newspaper. For a full round-up of Tanzania's most popular performers – mostly based in Dar – and for a history of the nation's effervescent music scene, see Contexts.

The city's biggest draw is its **dance bands**, also called jazz bands. It would be well worth extending your stay to catch the legendary OTTU Jazz Band (also known as "Msondo", after their *mtindo* or dance style), or their great rivals, DDC Mlimani Park Orchestra ("Sikinde"). Another eminently danceable rival couple of bands are the African Stars ("Twanga Pepeta"), and their stable-mates, African Revolution Band ("Tam Tam"). Also good are the mellow Vijana Jazz; the Congolese-influenced FM Academia; and the guitar-rich Mchinga Sound.

For something completely different, search out a **taarab** orchestra – the definitive musical expression of coastal Swahili culture. Dar's two big rivals are East African Melody and Zanzibar Stars Modern Taarab. A third one, TOT Taarab, is shamelessly pro-government (TOT also have a jazz band, TOT Achimenengule).

Reggae has virtually vanished in the face of rap and hip-hop, though two outfits still occasionally perform – Jah Kimbute's Roots & Culture, and Jhiko Man. **Rap and hip-hop** are hugely popular among the youth, as is the fusion of these styles with R&B, known as **Bongo Flava**. Unfortunately, catching any of this live is difficult – performers come and go with sprite-like frequency, and rarely perform more than once a month in any case: ⓦwww.bongoflava.com has an events section, as well as audio and video clips. *Club Bilicanas* occasionally features live crews, and can be relied on to play Bongo Flava in any case. Radio is your best bet for picking up on gigs: tune in to Radio Free Africa, Clouds FM, Radio One or Radio 5 .

Traditional music (*ngoma ya kiasili*) is best caught at the Village Museum (Tues– Sun 2–6pm; $4) or at Nyumba ya Sanaa (Fri 7.30pm; Tsh2000).

Club Bilicanas Simu St. Right in the centre, this is Dar's foremost, brashest and most popular nightclub, with good lighting and sound and, yes, prostitutes. Nights include the African Stars band (Wed), discos (Thurs–Sat), and rap, hip-hop and Bongo Flava (Sat). Women free on Friday. There's a jam session on Sunday afternoon (4–8pm), followed by a disco with the latest Bongo Flava until the next morning.

Garden Bistro 498 Haile Selassie Rd, Msasani Peninsula. The same crowd as for *Q-Bar* on Friday piles into this place on for the weekly disco on Saturday, with the prostitutes never lagging far behind. They also have DJs on Friday.

TAZARA Club Kilimani Rd, Kinondoni. The disco half of the live music venue, *Leaders Club*, *TAZARA* is a great place on Saturdays, when it heaves with sweaty bodies dancing to Congo's latest craze and rap.

Live music venues

Dar's live music venues are scattered through the city's suburbs, and sampling their delights is really what it's all about. Most are semi-open-air, with a dance floor between the tables and the band. Many venues are known by more than one name – both are listed where this is the case – and entrance fees aren't normally more than Tsh3000. Sundays have the advantage of starting earlier (3–4pm as opposed to 8–9pm), and can have a more family-oriented feel.

△ Mlimani Park Orchestra, Dar es Salaam

There are two **annual festivals** to coincide with if you can. For the latest in street, underground and otherwise youthful styles (rap, hip-hop and Bongo Flava, plus traditional *ngoma* and poetry), there's the two-day **B-Connected Festival** in the city's Mnazi Mmoja Grounds at the end of May, networked live via the Internet (and big video screens) with similar festivals elsewhere. For more information, see the Music Mayday website,  www.musicmayday .org. In July or August you might also catch the **Summer Jam Festival**, which attracts big-name bands from all over East Africa; for more information check out  www.cloudsfm.co.tz.

Amana Club (*OTTU Social Club*) Uhuru St, Ilala, past Kawawa Rd. A long-established social hall run by the Organization of Tanzanian Trade Unions, this is a superb place to be on Sunday, when home boys OTTU Jazz Band draw the masses, and the dancing goes on almost without stop until midnight. *Taarab* music is also played (Wed).

City Ambassador (*Gogo Hotel*) Morocco Rd, Kinondoni. Good local place hosting lesser-known bands. Saturday is the main night, with Kilimanjaro Connection strumming their *njenje* style into the early hours.

DDC Kariakoo (*DDC Social Hall*) Muhonda St, just off Msimbazi St, Kariakoo. This vast bar tucked under a vaulted roof is Dar's oldest, and home turf to the famous DDC Mlimani Park Orchestra (Sun). Tuesday features Zanzibar Stars Modern Taarab, and DDC Kabisa Ngoma Troupe plays traditional music on Thursday.

Lango La Jiji (*Club La Petite*) Magomeni. A major *taarab* venue: stomping ground for East African Melody (Mon), also with live *taarab* (Sun).

Leader's Club Tunisia Rd, Kinondoni. A major venue favoured for big, one-off music industry functions. It's also the home base of TOT's *taarab* orchestra (Sat), whilst the popular "Leaders Bonanza" bash on Sunday showcases a different band each week.

Mango Garden Mwinyijuma Rd. One of the best live venues, with FM Academia (Wed), Extra Bongo (Fri), African Stars (Sat), and Vijana Jazz (Sun).

Max Motel Ilala. Features lively jazz bands (Wed), African Revolution (Thurs), *taarab*, which is especially popular with women (Sat), and other bands (Sun).

Msasani Club Rashidi Kawawa Rd, Namanga. Occupying a huge and largely empty outdoor plot, this comes alive on Sunday when FM Academia are at home.

Buying recorded music

For traditional music (*ngoma ya kiasili*), get out to one of the **Radio Tanzania Dar es Salaam** (RTD) shops: the main one (daily 6am–4pm) is at the entrance of its studios on Nyerere Road, on the left just before the TAZARA railway station (daladalas from Mnazi Mmoja or Kariakoo towards Vingunguti), but often better stocked is the one inside Ubungo bus station (Mon–Fri 8am–3.30pm), on the first floor of the white build-ing closest to the entrance. Both sell cassettes (*kandas*) from around sixty Tanzanian tribes, plus over one hundred tapes of popular Tanzanian music from the 1950s to 1990s. The tapes cost Tsh1000 each, the quality is generally good, and the music itself – some of which is now no longer played – is a national treasure. Even if you have only a fleeting interest in traditional or popular African music, these shops are unmissable – try the superlative and totally hypnotic recordings from the Gogo, the Luguru, the Haya and Kuria.

If it's just dance music you're after, **Dar es Salaam Music & Sports House** (Mon–Fri 9am–5pm, Sat 9am–1pm) on Samora Avenue in the city centre, opposite JM Mall, has a huge selection of Tanzanian and Congolese tapes from the 1950s to the present day. But far and away the biggest money-spinners in recorded music are **Bongo Flava** (Kiswahili rap), and Christian **kwaya** (gospel and hymns, spiritually uplifting or cheesily irritating, depending on your mood). Tapes of both genres are sold at kiosks and carts throughout the city.

The Slipway This upmarket seafront shopping centre hosts The Tanzanites – playing a pleasant if none too exciting mix of styles – every Thursday (free).
TCC Club Off Chang'ombe Rd, Chang'ombe, between Kilwa Rd and Nyerere Rd 5km south of the centre The tireless African Stars perform here on Sunday.
Vijana Social Club (*New Vijana Club* or *Vijana Hostel*) Next to *Mango Garden*, Mwinyijuma Rd, Kinondoni. Home turf to Vijana Jazz (Sun). Saturday features African Stars.

Film, theatre and the plastic arts

Cultural events are pretty thin on the ground, with neither film nor theatre having much prominence, though there is the annual Euro African Film Festival to look forward to in November. The plastic arts fare better, with the output of contemporary Tanzanian artists showcased in a number of galleries, and also along-side their East African counterparts in the East African Art Biennale. For **informa-tion** on what's happening and where, have a talk with Rachel Kessi at Mawazo Gallery, or with Yves Goscinny at La Petite Galerie. You may also have some joy with the monthly *Dar es Salaam Guide* or *What's Happening in Dar* booklets.

Film

Dar es Salaam has just one **cinema**, the New World Cinemas multiplex (☎022/277 2178; Tsh6000) on New Bagamoyo Road in Mwenge, where entrance comes complete with popcorn. It screens recent blockbusters from both Hollywood and Bollywood, and hosts the annual **Euro African Film Festival** in the second and third weeks of November. The **British Council** screens British movies every Wednesday at 6.30pm (☎022/211 8255; free).

Theatre

Theatre is limited to the Little Theatre, off Haile Selassie Road near Ali Hassan Mwinyi Road, home of the Dar es Salaam Players who put on a production roughly once a month. The plays cater mainly for English-speaking expats and the Europhile Tanzanian elite, though the Christmas pantos are always a laugh. Details through ☎0748/277388, or ✉daressalaamplayers@raha.com, or see the weekly *Advertising in Dar* freesheet. The British Council (☎022/211 8255), on Samora Avenue, has also been known to indulge a thespian bent, having staged inventive cross-cultural events.

Galleries and exhibitions

The internationally acclaimed **East African Art Biennale** exhibition (next ones in December 2007 and 2009; ☎0741/261663, ✉eastafab@yahoo.co.uk) provides a major showcase for contemporary Tanzanian, Kenyan and Ugandan artists. The event assembles works by over a hundred painters, sculptors, photographers and cartoonists. Much of their output is extraordinarily powerful and beautiful – there's a collective eye for colour and movement that has long been absent in Western art – as you're free to judge; the exhibition also features works by Europeans resident in East Africa. The superb exhibition catalogue ($20) can be found in Dar's better bookshops. The catalogues of the Biennale's predecessor, "Art in Tanzania", may also still be available.

Dar has few **arts centres** or galleries, but what there is is worth seeing. You might also enquire at the National Museum about their long-standing plans to establish a gallery of contemporary art.

Alliance Française Off Ali Hassan Mwinyi Rd, next to Las Vegas Casino ☎022/213 1406, ✉afdar@africaonline.co.tz. There's always something on here, often involving artists or performers from Francophone Africa, including Congo.
La Petite Galerie Oyster Bay Shopping Centre, Ghuba Rd, Msasani Peninsula ☎022/260 1970 or 0741/261663. East African paintings and sculptures in Yves Goscinny's gallery – his tireless efforts are largely to thank for the astonishing vitality of the contemporary plastic arts scene. Mon–Sat 10am–5.30pm, Sun 10am–4pm.
Mawazo Gallery & Art Café Next to the *YMCA*, Upanga Rd ☎0748/782770, ⊛www.mawazo -gallery.com. A leading arts centre, also taking

an interest in traditional music. Apart from semi-permanent exhibits (mainly sculptures), it stages temporary exhibitions and the odd concert. Lunch available Mon–Fri (Tsh4000), plus juices, cakes and coffee. Daily 10am–5.30pm (to 8.30pm on Wed).
Russian-Tanzanian Cultural Centre Sea View Rd, off Ocean Rd ☎022/213 6577. Regularly hosts exhibitions and other cultural events.
Wasanii Art Centre The Slipway, Msasani Peninsula ☎0748/682878 or 0744/572503. Run by the painter Aggrey Mwasha, this gallery has monthly exhibitions of contemporary East African art, often showcasing young (and hopefully up-coming) artists. Mon–Fri 1–8pm, Sat 1–6pm.

Shopping

Given the city's size and cosmopolitan nature, you can find pretty much anything you might need, either in the centre or in several modern shopping centres, most on the outskirts. The usual souvenirs you'll see elsewhere in Tanzania can also be found, and although the choice isn't as wide (or bewildering) as in Arusha, prices can be lower. For **food markets**, see p.116; for **recorded music**, see the box on opposite.

Souvenirs

Dar has a handful of excellent curio shops, as well as the Mwenge Carvers, Nyumba ya Sanaa, and a trio of contemporary art galleries (see preceding section). Apart from the shops listed below, you'll find souvenir stalls throughout the city: the ones on Bridge Street opposite the Tanzania Curio Shop have a

Tingatinga paintings

Dar es Salaam is a great place to buy **Tingatinga paintings** – vibrantly colourful tableaux of cartoon-like animals and figures daubed in bicycle paint and sold virtually everywhere. The style takes its name from the artist **Eduardo Saidi Tingatinga**, who was born in the 1930s in Mindu village in southern Tanzania to a rural Makonde family, and moved to Dar es Salaam when he was sixteen. He worked on building sites, and in his spare time made paintings and signboards for shops. In the mid-1960s, he began selling his paintings from **Morogoro Stores** in Dar es Salaam. His Makonde heritage is echoed in his use of *sheitani* ("spirit") imagery – often amusingly grotesque beings. Tingatinga was shot dead in 1972, when police mistook him for a criminal.

Modern Tingatinga paintings are usually more geared to tourists, depicting safari animals, baobab trees, Kilimanjaro and rural scenes. This is not to dismiss them – they make singularly cheerful and attractive souvenirs. Prices are generally very reasonable, and a large A3-sized painting shouldn't cost more than Tsh10,000, depending on your bargaining skills.

great selection of **Makonde carvings**. For the colourful **kitenge and kanga cloths** worn by women, the section of Uhuru Street between the clock tower and Bibi Titi Mohamed Street is excellent, with dozens of shops and street vendors to choose from.

Karibu Art Gallery Bagamoyo Rd, Mbezi Beach area ☏022/264 7587. A huge choice of souvenirs at very reasonable prices (marked, but still negotiable), with no pressure to buy. Choose from Tingatinga paintings, the city's best selection of wood carvings, Kisii soapstones (from Kenya), and some marvellous Makonde *Mapiko* helmet masks and metre-tall *sheitani* sculptures. You can sometimes see the carvers at work in the gallery grounds. There's traditional music Sat 3–5pm, and a bar round the back. Catch a Mwenge–Tegeta daladala. Closed Tues.

Kangas and kitenges

The colourful printed cotton wraps worn by many Tanzanian women are called **kangas** (the name means "guinea fowl", as one of the first designs was a series of light polka dots on a dark background that resembled that bird's plumage). A double-pane *kanga* is called a **doti**, and is often cut in two, one part being worn around the body, the other around the head or shoulders. *Kangas* were introduced to Tanzania by Portuguese merchants in the mid-nineteenth century, though it was only at the start of the twentieth century that they began to acquire the **proverbs and riddles** (*neno*, literally statements) which are now such a characteristic feature of the design. The proverb is a way of making public sentiments that would be taboo expressed in any other form. So, for instance, a wife wishing to reprimand her husband for infidelity or neglect might buy a *kanga* for herself with the proverb, "The gratitude of a donkey is a kick" (*Fadhila ya punda ni mateke*), while one reading "A heart deep in love has no patience" (*Moyo wa kupenda hauna subira*) might be bought for a woman by her lover, expressing his desire to get married.

Similar to a *kanga*, but without the proverb or riddle, is a **kitenge**, made of thicker cloth and as a double-pane; their size also makes them ideal for use as bedlinen. **Prices** for simple *kangas* range from Tsh3000 to Tsh5000 depending on the design and where you buy it, while *doti* and *kitenges* go for Tsh5000–8000. Women will be happy to show you some ways of tying it. For more ideas, winkle out a copy of *Kangas: 101 Uses*, by Jeanette Hanby and David Bygott, or *The Krazy Book of Kangas* by Pascal Bogaert.

Morogoro Stores Haile Selassie Rd, Msasani Peninsula. Famous for Tingatinga paintings (it was here that Eduardo Tingatinga first sold his work) but other handicrafts are also available, from canvasses to crockery. Catch a Posta–Masaki dala-dala marked "via A.H. Mwinyi Rd".

The Slipway Msasani Peninsula. Several upmarket crafts shops, an enjoyable handicrafts bazaar (Sat & Sun to around 6pm), and the Wasanii Art Centre.

Tanzania Curio Shop Corner of Bridge and Mansfield streets. Attractively poky store selling a mixture of pure kitsch, malachite figurines, modern and antique Zanzibari silver (the dagger sheaths and heavy necklaces are especially attractive), coins and some beautiful reproduction Zanzibari chests. Closed Sat afternoon & Sun.

Bookshops

Dar's best **bookshop** is A Novel Idea (Ⓦ www.anovelidea-africa.com), with branches at The Slipway and Sea Cliff Village, both on Msasani Peninsula (Mon–Sat 10am–7pm, Sun noon–6pm), and in town on Ohio Street (daily 10am–7pm) next to *Steers*. All three have a lavish choice of imported coffee-table books, novels, academic tomes, guidebooks and maps, but are lamentably poor on Tanzanian-published titles. Other bookshops are very poorly stocked, though you may turn up the occasional locally published gem. Try Abacus Books on Nkrumah Street; the Tanzania Publishing House on Samora Avenue, one block west of the Askari Monument; Dar es Salaam Printers on Jamhuri Street, just east of Zanaki Street; and the University Bookshop, out of town on the campus ("The Hill") on University Road. There are **second-hand bookstalls** throughout the city centre, especially along Samora Avenue on both sides of the Askari Monument, at the corner of Samora Avenue and Mkwepu Street, and – with the best choice of Tanzania-related works – Sokoine Drive between Ohio Street and Pamba Road, as well as around the corner on Pamba Road itself.

Shopping centres

The handful of modern **shopping centres**, most on the outskirts of the city, are no competition for markets in terms of atmosphere or price, but do stock a fairly good range of products. The main ones are: Sea Cliff Village, at the north end of Touré Drive, Msasani Peninsula; The Slipway, on the west side of the peninsula; and Maytair Plaza – Tanzania's largest – on Old Bagamoyo Road in Mikocheni.

Listings

Air charters Tanzanair, *Mövenpick Royal Palm*, Ohio St ☎022/211 3151, Ⓦ www.tanzanair.com. Coastal Aviation (see "Coastal Travels", p.133) and Precisionair (see below) also do charters.

Airlines Air Malawi, TDFL Building, Ohio St ☎022/212 7746, Ⓦ www.airmalawi.com; Air Tanzania, ATC House, corner of Ohio St and Garden Ave ☎022/211 7500, Ⓦ www.airtanzania.com; British Airways, *Mövenpick Royal Palm*, Ohio St ☎022/211 3820, Ⓦ www.ba.com; Coastal Aviation, Ⓦ www.coastal.cc (see Coastal Travels, p.133); EgyptAir, Matasalamat Mansions, corner of Samora Ave and Zanaki St ☎022/211 3333, Ⓦ www.egyptair.com; Emirates, Haidery Plaza, corner of Upanga and Kisutu streets ☎022/211 6100, Ⓦ www.emirates.com; Ethiopian Airlines, TDFL Building, Ohio St ☎022/211 7063, Ⓦ www.flyethiopian.com; KLM / Kenya Airways, Peugeot House, corner of Bibi Titi Mohamed and Upanga streets ☎022/211 3336, Ⓦ www.kenya-airways.com/ Ⓦ www.klm.com; Precisionair, Pamba Rd ☎022/213 0800, Ⓦ www.precisionairtz.com; South African Airways, Raha Towers, Bibi Titi Mohamed St ☎022/211 7044, Ⓦ www.flysaa.com; Swiss, Lutheran Centre, Sokoine Drive ☎022/211 8870, Ⓦ www.swiss.com; ZanAir, Airport Terminal 1 ☎022/284 3297, Ⓦ www.zanaironline.com.

Airport information ☎022/284 4239 or 4211.

Ambulance ☎112 for emergencies. More reliable private ambulances are operated by AAR

0744/760790, Knight Support ☎0744/777100, and Ultimate Security ☎0741/123911.

Banks and exchange Don't change money on the street. Most foreign exchange bureaux are located along Samora Ave and India St, especially between Morogoro Rd and Bridge St (generally Mon–Fri 9am–4.30pm, Sat 9am–12.30pm). They're handy for changing cash quickly at reasonable rates but pretty lousy for travellers' cheques, if they accept them at all. Exceptions include Crown Forex, on the corner of India and Zanaki streets, and the one inside *Mövenpick Royal Palm*, which has better hours (Mon–Sat 8am–8pm, Sun 10am–1pm). Banks give better rates but take longer; the best are National Bureau de Change, Samora Ave, and NBC, corner of Azikiwe St and Sokoine Drive, neither of which charge commission. NBC has a 24hr ATM for Visa/MasterCard (also at the airport). There are other ATMs at Barclays' TDFL Building (Ohio St) and The Slipway (Msasani Peninsula) branches, and at Standard Chartered's branches at NIC Life House, corner of Sokoine Drive and Ohio St; International House, corner of Garden Ave and Shaaban Robert St; JM Mall, Samora Ave; and Shoppers Plaza, Old Bagamoyo Rd. If you don't have a PIN, cash advances (up to $500 a week into shillings or dollars) on Visa, MasterCard, Delta and JCB cards can be made through Coastal Travels on Upanga Rd (Mon–Fri 9am–4pm, Sat 9am–noon). Advances on Amex cards are made through Rickshaw Travels at Peugeot House, Upanga Rd.

Car rental See p.132.

Car repairs CMC Land Rover, Maktaba St ☎022/211 3017, near Bibi Titi Mohamed St.

Courier services DHL, 12b Nyerere Rd ☎022/286 1000, with branches at JM Mall on Samora Ave, and Peugeot House, corner of Bibi Titi Mohamed and Upanga streets ☎022/211 3171. FedEx is also in Peugeot House ☎022/213 3112.

Dentists Nordic Dental Clinic, Valhalla Estate, Msasani Peninsula ☎022/260 1650; Three Crowns Swedish Dental Clinic, 259 Ali Hassan Mwinyi Rd, Namanga ☎022/213 6801; ZAMU International French Dental Clinic, 9 Ali Hassan Mwinyi Rd ☎022/277 5958.

Embassies and consulates Burundi, 1007 Lugalo Rd, Upanga ☎022/211 7615; Canada, 38 Mirambo St ☎022/211 2831; Germany, Umoja House, corner Mirambo St and Garden Ave ☎022/211 7409; Ireland, 353 Touré Drive ☎022/260 2355; Italy 316 Lugalo Rd, Upanga ☎022/211 5935; Kenya, 14 Ursino St, Regent Estate ☎022/270 1747; Malawi, NIC Life House, Sokoine Drive ☎0748/481740; Mozambique, 25 Garden Ave ☎022/211 6502; Netherlands, Umoja House, corner Mirambo St and Garden Ave ☎022/211 0000; Rwanda, 32 Ali

Hassan Mwinyi Rd ☎022/213 0119; Uganda, 7th floor, Extelcoms House, Samora Ave ☎022/266 6286; UK, Umoja House, corner Mirambo St and Garden Ave ☎022/211 0101; US, 25 Msasani Rd, off Old Bagamoyo Rd ☎022/266 8001; Zambia, corner Ohio St and Sokoine Drive ☎022/211 8481 (visa applications Mon, Wed & Fri only).

Football Dar's big rivals, Simba and Yanga, share the National Stadium on Nelson Mandela Rd in Mgulani. Catch a daladala from Kariakoo to TAZARA, and from there to Mgulani.

Hospitals and clinics Best in an emergency is the modern Aga Khan Hospital, Ocean Rd ☎022/211 5151. Also good is TMJ Hospital, Old Bagamoyo Rd, Mikocheni ☎022/270 0007. Recommended clinics include Nordic Clinic, Valhalla Estate, Msasani Peninsula ☎0741/325569 (24hr) or 022/260 1650, ⩊www.nordic.or.tz; and the Dutch-run IST Clinic, International School of Tanganyika Campus, Ruvu St, Masaki ☎0744/783393 (24hr) or 022/260 1307, who offer a full travel health service including vaccines. Consultations cost $24.

Immigration Opposite Posta House, corner of Ohio St and Ghana Ave ☎022/212 6811, ℱ022/211 3297.

Internet Dar has hundreds of Internet cafés, so you should be able to find one within a block or two of wherever you are. Rates average Tsh500 an hour. Be wary of banking or using credit cards online as computers are often infested with malware.

Language courses KIU, Salvation Army complex, Kilwa Rd ☎022/285 1509, ⩊www.swahilicourses .com (Mon–Fri 8am–3.30pm) offers various Kiswahili courses both here and in town. A 3-week, 4-hours-a-day (Mon–Fri) beginners' workout costs $180, and two weeks $120; a personal tutor charges $5 an hour. Catch a daladala from Posta or Kariakoo to Temeke or Rangi Tatu marked "via Kilwa Rd", and get off at Mgulani, just before the radio mast.

Libraries Tanzania's main public library (*maktaba*), currently also housing the National Archives, is the Tanganyika (or Central) Library, Bibi Titi Mohamed St (Mon–Sat 9am–6pm; daily membership Tsh500; ☎022/215 0048). The British Council Library is at the corner of Samora Ave and Ohio St (Tues–Fri 10am–6pm, Sat 9.30am–1pm; monthly membership Tsh7000; ☎022/211 6574). The Wildlife Conservation Society of Tanzania, Garden Ave (Mon–Fri 8.30am–4.30pm; ☎022/211 2518), is outstanding for environmental and ecological matters.

Opticians Eyeline, Sewa St ☎022/212 1869; Vision Plus, Shoppers Plaza, Old Bagamoyo Rd ☎022/270 0841.

Pharmacies Mansoor Daya Chemicals, IPS Building, corner of Samora Ave and Maktaba St ☎022/212 2517 (Mon–Fri 8.30am–12.30pm & 2–5pm), is well stocked. There are several more along Samora Ave, and at The Slipway on Msasani Peninsula. On Sundays, a number of basic pharmacies are open in Kariakoo, for example along Mkunguni St.

Photography Number One Color Lab, Haidery Plaza, on the corner of Upanga and Kisutu streets, is well equipped and has a 1hr service, but if you need anything other than simple prints, wait till you get home.

Police ☎112 for an emergency, but don't expect a quick response. To report a theft and get paperwork done for an insurance claim, go to the Central Police Station on Sokoine Drive near the railway station ☎022/211 7362.

Post The main office is on Maktaba St, with customs officer for parcels. There's also a branch at Sokoine Drive near Mkwepu St.

Safaris See p.132.

Snorkelling equipment Masks, snorkels and fins are available at the Oyster Bay and Sea Cliff Village shopping centres; at $45–50 a set, they're not cheap.

Sport Hash House Harriers ("the drinking club with a running problem") organizes weekly runs at 5.30pm on Monday, followed by – or sometimes preceded by – vast quantities of beer. The venue changes weekly; details in the *Dar es Salaam Guide* or *What's Happening in Dar es Salaam* booklets. A 5km time trial is organized by the Hare and Tortoise Running Club, leaving at 5.30pm Thursday from the Little Theatre. Modern gyms include FitZone Health Club, Ghuba Rd, Msasani Peninsula (☎022/260 1953), and Elite City in Acacia House, Samora Ave (☎022/212 1079). The golf course at the Gymkhana Club on Ghana Ave (☎022/213 8445) covers both sides of the avenue, but its "greens" are made from sand and engine oil, and membership is expensive – enquire at the *Möven-*

pick *Royal Palm* hotel. For something less strenuous, try the state-of-the-art Cosmic Bowling Alley at *Sea Cliff Hotel*, Touré Drive, Msasani Peninsula (Tues–Thurs 5pm–2am, Fri–Sun 11am–2am). For a spot of yoga, there are sessions at The Slipway (Wed 6pm) and the *Golden Tulip Hotel* (Fri 6pm), both on Msasani Peninsula.

Supermarkets Dar's supermarkets stock an expensive selection of mainly imported goods, with prices for fresh food especially outrageous. The most central are ShopRite (Mon–Fri 9am–6pm, Sat 10am–3pm) at JM Mall, Samora Avenue, and Imalaseko (Mon–Fri 9am–7pm, Sat 9.30am–4pm, Sun 10am–4pm) in Pamba House, on the corner of Garden Avenue and Pamba Road. There's another ShopRite on Lumumba Street facing Mnazi Mmoja Grounds, one at The Slipway on Msasani Peninsula, and one – the largest of the lot – on Nyerere Road just west of Msimbazi Street, all with similar hours.

Swimming pools *Golden Tulip* charges Tsh6000, and has aqua aerobics on Monday at 5.30pm. You should be able to use the pools at the *Karibu*, *Mövenpick Royal Palm* and *Sea Cliff* hotels for a similar fee, or if you buy a meal.

Telephones There are cardphones throughout the city, in shopping centres, and outside post offices; cards can be bought at nearby kiosks. The main TTCL office is on Bridge St, off Samora Ave (Mon–Fri 7.45am–midnight, Sat & Sun 8.30am–midnight). The cheapest way of calling internationally is the Net2Phone Internet service offered by some Internet cafés, including Millennium on Jamhuri St (Mon–Sat 9am–9pm; around Tsh200 per minute); the line can be interrupted, but no complaints at the price.

Travel agents Easy Travel & Tours, Raha Towers, Bibi Titi Mohamed St, corner with Maktaba St ☎022/212 1747, ⑩ www.easytravel-tanzania.com; Kearsley Travel & Tours, Makunganya St ☎022/211 5026, ⑩ www.kearsleys.com; Takims Holidays Tours & Safaris, Mtendeni St ☎022/211 0346, ⑩ www.takimsholidays.com.

Moving on from Dar

Dar es Salaam lies at the hub of Tanzania's road, rail and air networks, so you can get to pretty much anywhere in the country in one or two hops. For **frequencies and journey times**, see "Travel details" at the end of this chapter.

By bus

Dozens of bus companies operate out of Dar, most starting at or passing through **Ubungo Bus Station**, 8km from the centre along Morogoro Road; ticket offices are in booths just outside, under an enormous billboard displaying schedules and the corresponding ticket office number. Buy your **ticket** the day before when you're unencumbered by luggage, and when you'll also have a wider choice of companies. If you can't do this, arrive at Ubungo no later than 5.30am, as the first buses to almost everywhere leave at 6am. Ensure you buy your ticket from a bona fide company office, not from some guy on the street (unless it's the ticket man and you're next to the bus). The only buses that don't go through Ubungo are those to Kilwa and villages near the eastern side of Selous, which depart from the amorphous **Temeke bus stand** south of the city. Given the early starts of these (4–5am), get your ticket the day before and catch a cab in the morning.

A handful of companies also have offices in town, where you might also be able to board their buses.

Safety should be a major concern when choosing a company. **Companies to avoid** – basically those with persistent reputations for reckless driving – include Abood, Air Bus, Air Msae, Amit, Buffalo, Hood, Kilimanjaro Express, Tashriff and Tawfiq. Takrim can be OK, but sometimes not. At the time of writing, the safest mainline operators from Dar were the following (for other destinations, consult the "moving on" boxes in the relevant chapters of this book, where recommended companies – if any – are mentioned).

Akamba Terminal: Msimbazi St, Kariakoo ☎022/218 5111; office also at Ubungo bus station. Buses to Moshi, Arusha, Mwanza (via Nairobi), and extensive onward connections in Kenya.
Dar Express Office: Africa St, between Morogoro Rd and Libya St, Kisutu ☎0748/276060; office also at Ubungo bus station. Buses to Moshi, Arusha and Karatu.
Royal Coach Office: corner of Libya and Mwisho streets, Kisutu ☎022/212 4073; office also at Ubungo bus station. Services to Moshi and Arusha.
Scandinavian Express Terminal: junction of Msimbazi St and Nyerere Rd, Kariakoo ☎022/218

4833 or 0748/218484; office also at Ubungo bus station. All major sealed roads in Tanzania are served (Arusha highway, Tanzam highway, Songea, Tanga and Dodoma), as well as buses to the Zambia (Lusaka), Kenya (Mombasa and Nairobi) and Uganda (Kampala).
Shabiby Ubungo bus station ☎0744/753769. Serves Mbeya, Kyela and Songea via Morogoro and Iringa.
Sumry Ubungo bus station ☎022/218 0169. Services to Mbeya, and Sumbawanga and Songea via Morogoro and Iringa.

By train

Two passenger train lines converge in Dar. The **TAZARA Line** begins at TAZARA station (☎022/286 0344), 5km from the city centre at the corner of Nyerere Road and Nelson Mandela Expressway, and is served by frequent daladalas from Kariakoo. There are currently two weekly services to Mbeya via Fuga and Kisaki (both handy for Selous), Mang'ula (for Udzungwa Mountains National Park) and Ifakara, though these are only useful if the trains leave in the morning so as to arrive by day. There's also a weekly "express" which continues on to New Kapiri Mposhi in Zambia. Unfortunately, the TAZARA line's schedules are notoriously unreliable and change on an almost monthly basis. Dar's tourist office or any decent travel agent are the best sources of current information, as the station itself closes when there are no trains.

In spite of its often badly maintained tracks and rolling stock, which caused a catastrophic crash in 2002, the **Central Line** connecting Dar with Kigoma and Mwanza via Morogoro, Dodoma and Tabora, is much more dependable, with three weekly departures (roughly 38 hours to either destination). Trains leave Dar at 5pm on Tuesday, Friday and Sunday from Central Line Railway Station, on the corner of Railway and Gerezani streets (ticket office Mon–Fri 8am–1pm & 2–5pm, Sat & Sun 8am–1pm, and from two hours prior to departures; ☎022/211 0600 , ⓦwww.trctz.com). For an idea of **fares**: the 38-hour haul to

Steam train excursions

The Central Line railway operates a restored 1950s **steam train** on the last Saturday of the month, leaving at 9am for a pleasant six- to seven-hour trip to Soga (roughly 50km away) and back, passing through Pugu Forest. Tickets cost Tsh10,000, including a dance performance at Soga. You can buy food (barbecue) at Soga, or in the train's dining carriage. Information and tickets from the Customer Information Centre at the Central Line Railway Station.

Kigoma costs Tsh45,200 in first-class, Tsh33,100 in a second-class sleeper, and Tsh15,000–18,000 seated.

By boat

Passenger ferries connect Dar to Stone Town in Zanzibar (at least 7 daily), Mkoani on Pemba (1–2 daily), and Mtwara on the south coast (1 weekly). All leave from **Dar es Salaam Ferry Terminal** in the centre of town on Sokoine Drive, behind the ferry ticket offices. Double-check fares and times before buying a ticket, and whether the $5 **port tax** is included. For an extra $5, most travel agents can buy the ticket for you. For Zanzibar, advance bookings are not normally necessary, even during peak tourist season. Whichever boat you choose, be aware of **scams** connected with buying ferry tickets (see p.77), especially offers of resident rates to tourists.

You're almost certain to find daily sailings to **Stone Town** at 7.30am, 10.30am, noon, 4pm and sometimes also 2pm. Arrive an hour before departure. The most reliable boats are the *MV New Happy* ($20 including port tax), and the *MV Sea Express*, *MV Sea Star*, *MV Sea Bus* and *SMV epideh* (all $35 in economy or $40 first-class, including port tax), taking 1.5–2.5hr.

For **Pemba** (all via Stone Town), schedules change on an almost monthly basis. At the time of writing, the fastest was the *MV Sepideh* (Wed, Fri & Sun 7.30am; $50 in economy, $60 first-class, including port tax), arriving in Mkoani at 12.30pm. Cheaper ($30 economy, $35 first-class, including tax) but incredibly slow (the onward sailing from Stone Town is overnight) are the *MV New Happy* to Mkoani, and either one of the *MV Aziza I*, *MV Aziza II* or *MV Mudathir* to Wete, all leaving Dar at noon on Friday, arriving at 6am on Saturday.

For **Mtwara**, Africa Shipping Corporation (☎022/212 4506) operates the weekly *MV Safari*, which currently runs at 8am on Saturday, takes 22 hours and costs $25 (seats only). It fills up quickly, so book several days ahead. The office is west of the Ferry Terminal facing Mission Street.

It's virtually impossible to arrange **dhow** passage from Dar, although there's usually a dhow or two leaving daily for Kilindoni on **Mafia Island** from Kisiju village, 90km south of the city – see Chapter 3.

By plane

Dar es Salaam International Airport lies 10km southwest of the city – allow an hour by road in case you get stuck in traffic. Most domestic **flights** take off from Terminal 1, though some Precisionair flights leave from Terminal 2 – check beforehand. A departure **tax** of $5 plus $1 safety tax is levied on domestic flights (taxes on international flights are included in the fare). You can book directly with the airline or via a travel agent – see "Listings". A taxi from the city centre should be no more than Tsh8000. Alternatively, catch a daladala from Kariakoo to P/Kajiungeni or Vingunguti, or from Ubungo to G/Uboto.

By car

First, read the section on car rental in Basics. Prices in Dar are reasonable compared to Arusha, but still expensive in international terms. Self-drive is rarely offered. The following companies are reliable and have the requisite TALA licence for entering national parks if you're with a driver. Prices quoted include VAT, and insurance if self-drive.

Avis Skylink Travel & Tours, TDFL Building, Ohio St ☎022/211 5381, ⊛www.skylinktanzania.com; also at the airport (Terminal 2). Suzuki Vitara self-drive $125/day including 120km ($500 excess liability); Land Cruiser Prado $180/day ($1000 excess). With driver, $120 and $160 respectively, excluding fuel. **Green Car Rentals** Nkrumah St, next to M.D. Motors ☎022/218 2022, ⊛www.greencars.co.tz. Land Cruiser with driver $120/day including 120km and fuel. Self-drive negotiable.

Hertz Leisure Tours & Holidays, *Mövenpick Royal Palm*, Ohio St ☎022/212 2130, ⊛www.hertz.com. Land Cruiser self-drive $180/day including 100km. Excess liability $1200. **Takims Holidays Tours & Safaris** Mtendeni St ☎022/211 0346, ⊛www.takimsholidays.com. 4WD with driver $100/day including 100km and fuel. No self-drive.

Safaris from Dar

If you're contemplating a **Northern Circuit safari**, arrange things in Arusha, particularly if you're on a low budget, as you'll have loads more choice, it's cheaper, and you'll waste less time driving to the parks. Also, if you ignore this advice, you risk being farmed out to a blacklisted company – and then having to trek back to Dar to get anything done should things go wrong. The same applies to **Kilimanjaro hikes**, which are normally arranged through Moshi- or Marangu-based companies; the exception is Easy Travel & Tours, who have their own TALA licence for mountaineering. Where Dar's operators come into their own is for **Southern Circuit safaris**, including Selous Game Reserve, and the national parks of Mikumi, Ruaha and Udzungwa Mountains, particularly if you're looking at mid-range or luxury options.

   Budget camping safaris along the lines of those offered in Arusha are a rare breed in the Southern Circuit, and quite pricey at $130–150 per person per day. In fact, it's usually cheaper to arrange things yourself, especially if you can find a few people to share the cost – details are given in Chapter 4 (under "Mikumi, Selous and Udzungwa") and Chapter 10 ("Ruaha"). In any case, there are only a handful of budget companies that can be even half-recommended, whereas there are dozens of unreliable companies and associated flycatchers: if you decide to go with a company not reviewed below, follow our advice on how to choose a reliable operator (see pp.68–69).

   For **lodge and luxury tented camp safaris**, you'll save money by going on an organized safari, as the operators get reduced rates on what's otherwise often shockingly pricey accommodation. The problem though, is that safaris waste time getting from Dar to the parks and back – at least four hours' driving each way for Mikumi, more for the other parks. As such, even a three-day safari will only give you one full day, plus quick game drives on the first and last days. The solution is either to splash out on a longer trip (six nights recommended; with more time, you could also include the Kilwas or Mikindani), or consider a **flying safari** – getting there by light aircraft. An alternative is to do the outbound journey by **train**, returning by plane, and this certainly has the edge over just flying, if you want a sense of how the land changes as you approach the parks.

Costs for mid-range options, overnighting in cheaper lodges and tented camps, average $200–270 per person per day; more than that and you're looking at the better lodges, whilst $500 plus will get you all the pampered neo-colonial **luxury** you can dream of, complete with rifle-toting white-hunter types as wildlife guides, and the odd Maasai lending some tribal colour.

Safari operators

Be especially suspicious of budget safari companies operating in and around Kisutu, and those touting themselves at the airport, some of whom are little more than "briefcase companies". Bearing this in mind, it might be safer to avoid the budget companies altogether and spend an extra $30–40 per day for more reliable service and peace of mind. At the time of writing, the following companies all held TALA licences for the wildlife parks, and had reasonable to excellent reputations. Membership of TATO (p.68) gives you some leverage in case of complaints. Prices given are per person.

A Tent with a View Safaris 5th floor, Osman Towers, corner of Zanaki and Bibi Titi Mohamed streets ☎ 0741/323318, ⓦ www.saadani.com. A reliable and enthusiastic outfit concentrating on Selous (*Sable Mountain Lodge*) and Saadani (*A Tent With a View Safari Lodge*). An all-inclusive three-night trip to Selous, including train down and flight back, costs $500–600. TATO member.

Authentic Tanzania *Mediterraneo Hotel*, Kawe Beach, 10km north of Dar ☎ 0748/825899, ⓦ www.authentictanzania.com. A responsible operator organizing innovative itineraries throughout southern and western Tanzania, plus Zanzibar, Pemba and Mafia islands, whether tailor-made flying safaris, extended trips by Land Cruiser, or infrequently offered activities such as horse-riding, mountain biking and ornithology. TATO member.

Coastal Travels Upanga Rd, facing Barclays, and also at the airport ☎ 022/211 7959, ⓦ www.coastal.cc. Based around their own airline (Coastal Aviation) and lodges and camps in Selous, Ruaha, Mafia and Zanzibar, Coastal specialize in good-value mid- and high-end flying safaris. Wildlife trips average $270/day plus flights; they also offer alluring last-minute deals, such as two-day Zanzibar breaks for $120 including flights. TATO member.

Easy Travel & Tours Raha Towers, corner of Bibi Titi Mohamed and Maktaba streets ☎ 022/212 1747, ⓦ www.easytravel-tanzania.com. A large, reputable and well-informed operator offering a wide range of safaris, Kilimanjaro climbs (for which they're licensed), Zanzibar holidays, cultural tourism and scuba-diving. Prices for Southern Circuit camping safaris start at $135/day in a group of four, or $180 staying in lodges. There's an Arusha branch for the Northern Circuit, and another in Zanzibar. Online booking and payment facility. TATO member.

Foxes African Safaris ☎ 0748/237422, ⓦ www.tanzaniasafaris.info. Long-established English family affair, with an emphasis on luxurious but keenly priced off-the-beaten-track forays, often flying or by train (they operate the luxury "Safari Express" private train to Selous), based at their places in Mikumi (*Foxes Safari Camp* and *Vuma Hills*), *Ruaha River Lodge*, *Katavi Wildlife Camp* and elsewhere. From $250/day.

Hippotours Nyumba ya Sanaa, Ohio St ☎ 022/212 8662, ⓦ www.hippotours.com. A reliable operator that runs *Rufiji River Camp* in Selous – a four-day fly-in excursion costs $1040. They also do road safaris (from $200/day) staying in lodges or tented camps, and adventurous trips into Mozambique, with clients flying back to Dar.

Leopard Tours *Mövenpick Royal Palm*, Ohio St ☎ 022/211 9754, ⓦ www.leopard-tours.com. Huge yet efficient mid-market operation, often dealing with package tours, and reasonably priced for the quality – though in high season you risk travelling in convoy. Putting luggage in trailers is a clever touch. Southern Circuit options average $250–300/day. Also in Arusha for the Northern Circuit. TATO member.

Planet Safaris Nyumba ya Sanaa, Ohio St ☎ 022/213 7456, ⓦ www.planetsafaris.com. A newish Tanzanian outfit with a solid reputation so far, offering good-value camping trips for around $130/day and tours incorporating cultural tourism. More upmarket options are also available.

Takims Holidays Tours & Safaris Mtendeni St ☎ 022/211 0346, ⓦ www.takimsholidays.com. A large, long-established Indian company offering a huge range of lodge and tented camp safaris, mostly by road (minibuses or well-equipped Land Cruisers). Selous is the speciality, staying at *Rufiji River Camp*. From $250–300/day. Arusha branch for the Northern Circuit. TATO member.

North of Dar

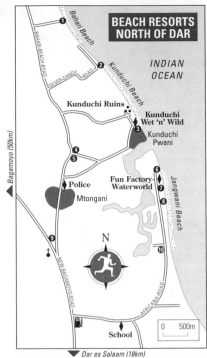

The beaches north of the city – **Kunduchi**, **Jangwani** and **Bahari** – are mainland Tanzania's busiest and most developed, and the resorts here offer all the amenities and standards you'd expect at the price (generally $100 and upwards for a double room), but there's little recognizably Tanzanian about them. For many visitors, the resort areas represent little more than sun, sand, sea and, even in the AIDS era, sex. That said, most of the development is low-key and well spaced out, with few if any buildings higher than three storeys. The downside of beach tourism in the developing world is startlingly obvious, however: **security** is a major concern, with frequent reports of muggings both on the beaches and along the access roads. Hotels routinely advise guests not to stray outside the usually well-guarded hotel compounds, nor to walk on the beach beyond the hotel strip without an *askari*. If you choose to ignore their advice – and plenty of visitors do – read the section on "Trouble" in Basics. You can, of course, have a wonderful time basking on the beaches doing nothing very much, but if you get bored with this there's the deeply atmospheric ruined medieval trading town of **Kunduchi** to explore.

ACCOMMODATION, BARS & RESTAURANTS

Bahari Beach Hotel	**1**	Jangwani Seabreeze Lodge **8**
Beachcomber Hotel Resort	**6**	Kunduchi Beach
Belinda Ocean Resort	**10**	Hotel & Resort **3**
Cris-Bagar Club	**9**	Silver Sands Beach Resort **2**
Green Palms	**4**	White Sands Hotel & Resort **7**
Ilembula 2000 Club	**5**	

Jangwani Beach

The most developed and accessible of the resort strips is **JANGWANI BEACH**, 21km north of the city. Apart from the beach itself, the main attraction is the flanking **coral reef**, whose six- to forty-metre drops make it ideal for **scuba-diving**. Jangwani's other attraction, especially for families, is the **Fun Factory–Waterworld** amusement park (daily 10am–6pm; Tsh3500), 250m beyond *White Sands Hotel & Resort*, which has several water flumes, four pools, beach volleyball, basketball, snooker tables and paddle boats, and is attentive to safety with kids.

Scuba-diving and snorkelling north of Dar

Most of Dar's **diving and snorkelling sites** are located along a double chain of coral reefs, the main concentration lying off Jangwani and Bahari beaches. The coral is in mixed condition (read the section on diving in Basics), many of the interior reefs having been extensively damaged by dynamite fishing. Still, the corals are recovering well, and after a successful and ongoing campaign by the Marine Action Conservation Trust (MACT), explosions from dynamite fishing are now infrequently heard. The trust is also involved in a coral transplanting programme, grafting live coral from healthier parts of the reef onto concrete bases.

The best **diving reefs** are roughly 7km offshore. **Fungu Yasini** ("Sand Bank") is the easiest to visit. Its wide variety of coral is home to crocodile fish, rays, pufferfish, lobsters, eels, lion fish, sea cucumbers, and a worryingly large population of the destructive crown-of-thorns starfish, which feed on coral. Much of the reef has also been damaged by dynamite fishing so there are few large fish other than the occasional barracuda. In contrast, the depth of the **Big T Reef** (also known as Mbudya Patches) further out has enabled it to survive dynamite fishing better, so you're more likely to see large game fish like kingfish and tuna, or occasionally bull and white-tipped reef sharks. Whales have occasionally been spotted, and heard – listening to their eerily powerful song through the water must rank as one of the world's most bewitching experiences. The reef is 45 minutes by *ngalawa* outrigger or fifteen minutes by speed-boat, but diving should only be attempted in calm seas as there are strong currents and swells: you stand a better chance of good weather in the morning. There's also a rarely undertaken **wreck dive** on the thirty-metre German freighter *Schlammerstadt* in Oyster Bay, which was towed out and scuttled in 1908 after it caught fire inside Dar harbour. The top of the wreck lies just three metres below sea level.

Trips to all these sites can be arranged through the PADI-accredited Sea Breeze Marine **dive centre** (℡0744/783 241, ⓦwww.seabreezemarine.org) at *White Sands Hotel* on Jangwani Beach, offering single dives ($50, also at night) and an array of courses from Discover Scuba ($80) and Open Water ($380) to Dive Master ($700). They also have Nitrox facilities for more experienced divers. It's best to book a few days in advance.

Snorkelling conditions are best around **Mbudya Island**, 3km offshore, which has shady casuarina, baobab and palm trees, and a rare population of endangered coconut crabs. Barbecued fish, sodas and sometimes beer are sold by enterprising locals, hence the island's nickname, "Mini Bar". Equally enterprising are the petty thieves and muggers: the mainland hotels post guards on the island, but take care not to leave stuff unattended. The main reefs here are the "Coral Gardens" (Mbudya West) which has staghorn and lettuce coral, but has been damaged by dynamite fishing, dragnets and careless anchoring; and the "Octopus Gardens" (Mbudya East), which has lots of moray eels but few if any octopus, despite its name. The reefs are part of a marine reserve which also encloses Bongoyo, Pangavini and Fungu Yasini islands: entrance fees (Tsh1000) are included in the cost of diving or snorkelling **boat trips** offered by Sea Breeze Marine, also bookable through other hotels. Count on $15 for a half-day's snorkelling, or $20 with a guide. Sea Breeze Marine rents snorkelling gear for $5 per day.

Arrival and accommodation

Frequent **daladalas** run throughout the day from Mwenge in Dar along New Bagamoyo Road to Tegeta, passing the turn-off to Jangwani Beach. However, there's no public transport from the turn-off to the beach (Africana Road) so, given the real risk of muggings, take a taxi from the junction (Tsh2500–5000 depending on your bargaining skills).

With the exception of the **campsite** at *Jangwani Seabreeze Lodge* ($7.50 per person), Jangwani's accommodation is expensive, with the cheapest doubles starting at around $100 half-board for a double room. The only **restaurants and bars** are in the hotels and at Waterworld; count on Tsh8000 for a full meal.

Beachcomber Hotel Resort 4.5km along Africana Rd ☏ 022/264 7772, ⊛ www.beachcomber.co.tz. A pleasingly informal package tour hotel, ideal for families, with an airy and cheerful design, friendly staff and comfortable rooms, all with a/c. Amenities include a swimming pool, a restaurant specializing in Indian and Chinese (the ginger-spiced chicken is especially succulent), children's activities, a health club with sauna and gym ($10/day), massage and Internet café. Water sports and boat trips to Mbudya Island can be arranged. The only gripe is the narrow beach flanked by unsightly breakwaters, though it extends north into wide sand banks on which you can walk if accompanied by an *askari*. Rates include transfer from Dar. Half-board ❼

Belinda Ocean Resort 2.8km along Africana Rd, signposted on the left ☏ 022/264 7549, ⊛ www.belindaoceanresort.com. A modern and attractive hotel, stylistically between a Roman villa and a Swahili town house, with nice touches like Makonde sculptures built into the staircases. The sixteen rooms, including triples, are clean and cool, and come with a/c, fans, box nets, satellite TV, phone and bathtubs; upper rooms have balconies, though the views aren't great. The staff are friendly and efficient, and there's a swimming pool in the cramped gardens. The drawback is the location, 300m from the beach. Breakfast included. ❻

Jangwani Seabreeze Lodge 3.8km along Africana Rd ☏ 022/264 7215, ⊛ www.jangwani.com. Long-established German-run hotel with a vaguely macho ambience (upmarket prostitutes frequent the bars and the street outside). Like the *Belinda*, it's on the wrong side of the road, though there's a beachfront annexe opposite with a beer garden and restaurant serving mainly north and central European food, with lots of pork, dumplings and stews, plus barbecue buffets on Saturday night in the gardens, and all day Sunday accompanied by a band. The 34 rooms in the main building, mostly doubles, are a mixed bunch, though all have box nets, satellite TV, a/c and fan, minibar and safe. Facilities include a Finnish sauna, two swimming pools and various water sports. A good laugh if drinking beer figures prominently in your plans. Breakfast included. ❼

White Sands Hotel & Resort 4.2km along Africana Rd ☏ 022/264 7620, ⊛ www.hotelwhitesands.com. Jangwani's largest and best-equipped hotel, and excellent value for money. The beachfront location is good, and the 88 bedrooms all have a/c, satellite TV, wireless Internet, and sea-facing verandahs, though some views are obscured by trees – get a room on the top away from the main building. There's a large octagonal pool, diving and kite-surfing, day-trips to Mbudya Island, and several bars and restaurants, with theme nights on Wednesday (Mediterranean), Friday ("Salsa Carnival"), Saturday (seafood), and a great Sunday lunch at the beach café with spit-roast lamb, live music and acrobats. There's also a nightclub (Fri & Sat) with a laser show. Breakfast and transfer from Dar included. ❼

Kunduchi and Bahari beaches

Slightly over a kilometre further along New Bagamoyo Road from the turning for Jangwani Beach, a signposted right turn takes you to two more beaches. **KUNDUCHI BEACH** takes its name from a fishing village and the nearby ruins of a Swahili trading town. **BAHARI BEACH** is the northern continuation of Kunduchi Beach, and at its furthest point lies some 28km from Dar. The beaches here are pretty similar to that at Jangwani, but there are far fewer hotels, and some good cheap accommodation.

Arrival

The easy but expensive way to reach the beaches is by **taxi**: seasoned bargainers might get the fare from Dar down to Tsh10,000, but Tsh15,000–20,000 is more usual (Tsh25,000 from the airport). You'll find it harder bargaining for the ride back into town as there's less competition. Cheaper but more fiddly is **public transport**. You have two options: catch a Tegeta-bound daladala from Mwenge, and get off at the turn-off to Kunduchi on the Bagamoyo Road, from where it's a Tsh2500 taxi ride along Bahari Beach Road to the beach; alternatively, catch a daladala from Mwenge to Mtongani, which is about 1km towards the beaches from New Bagamoyo Road, from where the cab fare shouldn't be more than Tsh2000. A bicycle taxi from the same place – if you can find one – should only cost a few hundred shillings.

Accommodation

There's a **campsite** at *Silver Sands Beach Resort* ($3 per person plus $2 per vehicle), which has good security, clean showers and the use of the hotel facilities included in the price.

Kunduchi Beach Hotel & Resort Next to Wet 'n' Wild ☎022/265 0050, ⊛www.kunduchiresort.com. Once threatened by coastal erosion, this reopened in 2005 on partially reclaimed land as a huge and, it must be said, kitsch resort à la Bollywood. Most of its 150-odd rooms are sea-facing, and there's a swimming pool, fitness centre, bags of noisy water-sports, a themed restaurant and a crèche. Breakfast included. ❽

🏃 **Silver Sands Beach Resort** 3.2km along Bahari Beach Rd, then 1km east ☎022/265 0567, ⊛www.silversands.co.tz. In a breezy beachfront location, this is the oldest of the north coast

hotels, still going strong after four decades, very good value, and nowadays also a popular port of call for overland tour trucks. As well as rooms (with fans or a/c), there are four-bed dorms ($9 with breakfast) with nets and shared bathrooms. Facilities include a bar and restaurant, swimming pool, snorkelling centre, and excursions, the best being the trip to Kunduchi-Pwani village and the Kunduchi ruins, followed by a dhow sail to Mbudya Island for snorkelling. The hotel boasts 400m of beachfront, though there's not too much of it thanks to erosion, which a number of unsightly breakwaters are attempting to stem. Breakfast included. ❹–❺

Eating, drinking and nightlife

You'll need a taxi to get to these places if you want to avoid the possibility of being mugged.

Bahari Beach Hotel 4.1km along Bahari Beach Road, then 400m east. Huge restaurant with a steel-vaulted *makuti* roof in a large package resort serving à la carte – the admission fee is recouped against the price of your meal. Musicians and snake dancers entertain diners on Wednesday, and there are live bands on Friday and Saturday nights from 9pm, and on Sunday from 4pm.
Cris-Bagar Club Near the Bagamoyo Rd junction. This is the main local club on this stretch of

the beach, and is worth checking out on weekend nights. There's the usual bar food available (mainly grilled meat and bananas).
Green Palms 2km along Bahari Beach Rd. A bar and restaurant with seating in shady *bandas* (huts) surrounded by bushes and low trees, good for an afternoon drink.
Ilembula 2000 Club 2km along Bahari Beach Road. Deceptively rough from the outside, it's actually a lively and friendly nightspot that gets packed at weekends when dance tunes reign.

Kunduchi Wet 'n' Wild

At the south end of Kunduchi Beach next to Kunduchi Pwani village, is **Kunduchi Wet 'n' Wild** (Tues–Sun 9am–6.30pm; Tsh4000; ☎022/265 0326, ⓔwetnwild@raha.com), East Africa's largest water park. With a spaghetti-like arrangement of 22 water chutes and tubes, a fake river, and seven swimming pools, this is very much tailored towards the affluent minority, and successfully manages to exclude anything that might spoil the Disney-like illusion. Past the heavy gate security, you'll also find slot machines, pool tables, a go-kart and quad-bike track, beach buggies, jet-skis, a miserable horse for rides and several restaurants. Access for visitors without transport is by daladala from Mwenge either to Kunduchi (with "7/20" displayed in the window) or Tegeta ("via Bagamoyo Road"). If you're driving or cycling, the turn-off is next to the police station in Mtongani, just under 2km along.

Kunduchi ruins

Just 600m north of Wet 'n' Wild are the infrequently visited but exceedingly atmospheric ruins of the Swahili trading town of **KUNDUCHI**, comprising a sixteenth-century mosque and various other ruined buildings set in a grove of baobab trees and bushes, together with graves dating from the eighteenth and nineteenth centuries. Little is known about the history of Kunduchi, other than like Kaole and Tongoni north of Dar (see Chapter 2) and Kilwa and Kua south of the city (Chapter 3), it was part of the medieval Swahili trading empire. Some of the graves bear distinctive obelisk-like pillars mounted on their heads, a style that's typical of the coast, whilst other tombs are made from ornately carved coral ragstone, inset with Chinese blue-and-white celadon porcelain bowls, one of the few sites where you can still see the bowls in their original settings. Different theories have been advanced to explain the presence of this porcelain. One suggests that the bowls were merely decorative, while another claims that they were indicators of the deceased's wealth and standing in the community. Either way, their presence is visible proof that East Africa was once part of a vast trading network that stretched as far afield as China.

Unfortunately, the site is a popular hang-out for muggers: the easiest and safest way to reach it is by car, but if you have a day to spare the combined trip with Mbudya Island organized by the *Silver Sands Beach Resort* is highly recommended – see p.137. If you can't find the site, ask for *magofu* – the "ruins" or "charmed place". There are two access roads. The easiest to follow is from Wet 'n' Wild, where you leave the sealed road and continue north. After 400m you come to a small crossroads under a tree. Dar es Salaam's university marine labs are on the right beside a water tower, whilst the main track veers off to the left. Ignore the track and continue 200m straight into the wood.

Less easy is the 2km route from the signs for Seamic and ESAMRDC Labs on the main Kunduchi Road, for which you really need a local guide. If you're walking, a police escort from Mtongani village is advisable. Although it's an informal arrangement, the *askari* will expect a decent tip (around Tsh2000 should do). There's a hut for the guard-cum-curator at the site, but he's usually absent.

South of Dar

The beaches south of Dar are much less frequented than those to the north, and just a short ferry and daladala ride away. Thankfully, the south coast has yet to see the kind of investment being sunk into Jangwani and Kunduchi, and at present the only facilities are a handful of modest hotels and campsites, plus – 25km further south at **Ras Kutani** – a couple of expensive lodges. There are no scuba-diving facilities. If hanging around on beaches isn't your thing, the community-run cultural tourism programme at **Gezaulole** village makes for a refreshing and humanizing change.

For something completely different, there's the easy day-trip from Dar to the **Pugu Hills**, 25km southwest of the city, which contain rare remnants of coastal monsoon forest, whose lush vegetation and relatively cool climate makes a pleasant break from the city's sweltering heat and humidity

Mikadi and Mjimwema beaches

Just to the south of Dar, Mikadi and Mjimwema beaches are a very different prospect from the northern resorts, with only three modest hotels to their name. **MIKADI BEACH**, just 2km from the city, is a coastal stop for trans-Africa truck tours, and can be a lot of fun if you're happy slipping into road-trip mentality. There are fewer dazed and dreadlocked *wazungu* at **MJIMWEMA BEACH**, 5km further south, which has a more intimate atmosphere.

To reach Mjimwema, catch the **ferry** (*mvuko*) at the east end of Kivukoni Front in Dar to Kigamboni Peninsula. It sails every thirty minutes or so between 5am and 1am (10min; Tsh100 per person, Tsh1000 per car). Watch your bags and pockets in Kigamboni, and don't allow yourself to be harried by daladala touts. Frequent **daladalas** (6am–8pm; Tsh200) cover the 7.5km from Kigamboni to Mjimwema, and there are hourly runs to Gezaulole. You could also catch a cab, which shouldn't cost more than Tsh2000 to Mikadi or Tsh3500 to Mjimwema. The last daladalas and cabs head off around 9pm. Don't walk the 2km to Mikadi from Dar – you risk getting mugged.

Accommodation, eating and drinking

Camping is possible at all the places listed below; the cost is Tsh3000–4000 per person.

Kipepeo Mjimwema: 7.5km south of Kigamboni, then 1.3km along a dirt track ☎022/282 0877, ⓦwww.kipepeocamp.com. Spread out along a huge sandy beach, *Kipepeo* ("butterfly") is friendly, relaxed, intimate and recommended whatever your budget, and walking unaccompanied on the beach to the south is fine. It's actually two places: *Kipepeo Camp*, with 14 simple but comfortable thatched beach *bandas* with large nets, fans and lights; and the more expensive *Kipepeo Village*, a row of twenty cosy, locally styled "chalets" flanking the beach, all en suite, with hot water and power. The chalets are raised on stilts, so catch sea breezes and give wonderful ocean views. Triple and family-size chalets and *bandas* are available. The bar and restaurant, in a colonial-era building, serves good snacks and meals (around Tsh5000), and barbecue buffets at weekends. There's also a beach bar. Beach *bandas* ❸, chalets (with breakfast) ❺.
Mikadi Beach Campsite Mikadi Beach: 2km from Kigamboni ☎0744/370269. Run by a friendly Australian, this is a major stopover for overlanders

on the Nairobi to Cape Town run. The bar (open most nights till 1am) is the main attraction, with US rock, techno, and even a Slush Puppy machine. There's also food. Most people camp, but there are also basic thatched *bandas* on stilts, the best on the beach, containing mattresses and smallish nets. Unfortunately, the beach is dangerous to walk along beyond the campsite, but there's a swimming pool and boat trips can be arranged. ❸
Sunrise Beach Resort Mjimwema: 7km from Kigamboni ☎022/282 0862, ⓦwww.sunrisebeachresort.co.tz. Another quirky place, this one an Indian-run resort built almost exclusively of *boriti* mangrove poles, wood and thatch. Though the buildings are too closely packed, the white sandy beach is a wow, and has plenty of recliners and parasols. The cheapest rooms share bathrooms, the most expensive right on the beach and with TV, fridge and plunge pool; all have electricity and Zanzibari four-posters. Add in a swimming pool, a restaurant specializing in flambées, two bars (one on the beach),

Gezaulole

Some 14km south of Kigamboni is the typical coastal settlement of **GEZAU-LOLE**, whose 4500 inhabitants survive through fishing and the cultivation of rice, sweet potatoes, mushrooms, maize and cassava. The whole place would be unremarkable were it not for its community-based **cultural tourism programme**, one of over twenty in Tanzania, which allows visitors to combine the hedonistic pleasures of beach, dhow and snorkelling trips, with local history, culture and village life. Prices are very reasonable, with a half-day tour costing around Tsh5000 (less per person if you're in a group) and no more than Tsh15,000 for 24 hours, including meals, accommodation and most activities. The price includes a guide. Proceeds from the programme directly fund local projects, such as provision of a clean and reliable water supply, a new dispensary, and the refurbishment of a primary school.

Guided walks

Gezaulole's history is well presented in the cultural programme's **Historical Places and Beach Walk**, which covers a number of historically important sites. The village's first inhabitants were Zaramo fishermen who used the site as a *dago* (temporary camp). After a while they decided to stay permanently and so – according to legend – went to their soothsayer for advice. He chillingly ordered that a young virgin be buried alive in sacrifice, and added, "then *gezau-lole* (try and see) whether you can stay here". The walk includes the unfortunate girl's tomb, as well as some early Muslim graves nestling – as in so many other coastal sites – in the shade of a large old baobab tree.

Gezaulole remained a village until the arrival of the Omani Arabs in the sixteenth century, when it changed its name to Mbwamaji and became a destination for ivory, hide and slave caravans travelling from the interior. Sadly, the ruins of the **slave depot** are on private land and cannot be visited, whilst the four-hundred-year-old Arab **mosque** – which for years lay in ruins – has recently been rebuilt, much to the anguish of archeologists. Mbwamaji changed its name back to Gezaulole in the early 1970s, when it became one of Tanzania's first collective agricultural villages under Nyerere's disastrous **Ujamaa** policy (see Contexts), during which the old tag of "try and see" once more became appropriate.

With the ivory and slave caravans now long since gone, Gezaulole survives on agriculture and fishing, as well as the small-scale harvesting of seaweed by women. Because of its *Ujamaa* past, Gezaulole's present population is now very mixed, comprising not only Zaramo but Chagga from around Kilimanjaro, Nyamwezi, Sukuma and Matumbi from the far west, Makonde from the south, and Ngindo from central Tanzania. This unusual cosmopolitan aspect of village life is explored by the **Village Life Walk**, which combines visits to local farms, tie-dyers, woodcarvers, an elderly female potter and women making mats and baskets. You can also have henna tattoos painted on your skin.

Sinda and Latham Islands

The **dhow trips** with local fishermen, also arranged by the tourism programme, are excellent value at Tsh5000 per person (minimum two people), and are the only way of visiting the uninhabited **Sinda Island**, 14km offshore, which has some superb snorkelling reefs. You'll have to bring your own snorkelling gear, but there's no time limit so you can stay as long as you like. You might also be able to arrange a lift to **Latham Island**, further south, some 26km offshore from Ras Kutani, which has a massive reef and a completely unspoilt beach. There's no vegetation or people, but the island offers brilliant diving if you have your own equipment.

Practicalities

Access to Gezaulole is quickest if you take the ferry from Dar to Kigamboni, and then catch a daladala to Gezaulole (ones running to Kimbiji also pass by); daladalas run roughly hourly between 7am and 6pm. The all-weather road from Kigamboni to Gezaulole is attractive, passing through a chain of small villages set amidst thick coconut, banana and mango plantations. On arrival, head for the cultural tourism programme's base at *Akida's Garden*, signposted 1km east of the village, where you'll find the project co-ordinator, the energetic and helpful Akida Mohammed Nzambah (℡0741/520264, ✉wcst@africaonline.co.tz). He can also arrange **bicycle** rental (Tsh1000 a day) – a great way to get around.

If you want **to stay** in the village, *Kali Mata Ki Jai's House* has two basic but adequate rooms (❶), one with four beds and the other with two, each with wonky raffia furniture, mosquito nets and cleanish sheets. Lodgings with other local families can be arranged through Akida. **Camping** is possible at *Akida's Garden* (Tsh1000 per person plus Tsh2000 for a night watchman; tents are available for Tsh1000). For **eating**, a good restaurant is the *Upendo*, in the village, whose *kisamvu* – cassava pounded in leaves, cooked in coconut milk and served with *ugali* – is absolutely delicious.

Ras Kutani

The *murram* road southeast from Gezaulole is usually in very bad condition, and frequently gets washed away in the rains, rendering road access impossible over the slippery black cotton soil. There's no public transport in any case – no problem for most visitors, since the only place of note is the promontory of **RAS KUTANI**, 30km south of Dar, which has only two expensive and exclusive **tourist lodges**, complete with their own airstrips – most guests fly in. The area badly needs some sanely priced accommodation, especially given the beautiful location, with kilometres of fine sandy beaches and crystalline waters protected by two coral reefs, the nearest 600m offshore. **Dynamite fishing** has decreased in recent years, but the effect of previous assaults is visible at Ras Kutani headland itself, where much of the cliff has collapsed into the sea as a result of stronger ocean currents unleashed against the coast by the destruction of protective coral.

Accommodation

Despite the beauty of the setting, the barbed wire and electric fences surrounding Ras Kutani's two **lodges** provide an unsettling atmosphere of neo-colonial exclusion.

Protea Hotel Amani Beach ℡0744/410033, ⓦwww.protea-hotels.co.za. Swahili-Arab themed resort set in extensive woodland grounds, offering stylish two-room cottages on a baobab-studded lawn, complete with a/c, satellite TV and Zanzibari four-posters. Facilities include a tennis court, a large swimming pool by the beach, windsurfing, snorkelling and mountain biking (all included in the price), but no boat trips. Full-board $150 per person. **❾**

Ras Kutani ☎022/211 1728, ⓦwww.selous .com. On an inlet close to a freshwater lagoon and coastal forest, this is more expensive than the *Amani* and shrouded in even more Colditz-like security, but has the edge with its rustic feel and wilder gardens, plus a good range of water sports, and walks with an armed *askari*. The fifteen bedrooms are huge and attractive, with bamboo walls, reed mats, open *makuti* roofs and spacious beds and hammocks. No children under 4. Closed mid-March to May. Full-board $195 per person. **❾**

The Pugu Hills

Ten million years ago the entire coast of East Africa, from Somalia to Mozambique, was covered with a thick belt of forest. The constant climate over this period, influenced by the Indian Ocean monsoon system, led to the development of a diverse ecosystem rich in endemic plants and animals. Sadly, over the last few centuries most of the coastal forests have disappeared, leaving only a few isolated patches which are now under intense pressure from a vastly increased human population. The most studied – and most disturbed – of Tanzania's coastal forests covers the **Pugu Hills**, roughly 25km southwest of Dar es Salaam. Fifty years ago it extended to within 10km of the city and was home to lions, cheetahs, hippos and black-and-white colobus monkeys, all of which have since disappeared. Despite official protection in the form of the forest reserves of Pugu and Kazimzumbwi, the forest's destruction continues unabated. By 1995, clearance for farmland and tree-felling for building materials, domestic fuel and charcoal had left just four square kilometres of natural forest in "reasonable condition" – there are no more recent figures. Accidental wildfires, started in neighbouring farms to clear stubble, haven't helped matters either. Despite all of this, Pugu still retains some 120 tree types and 120 bird species. The most commonly seen animals include giant elephant shrews, monkeys, bush pigs, suni antelopes and mongooses. Leopards, hyenas and pangolins also inhabit the area, but are rarely seen.

Practicalities

The official side of things is a mess: conservation projects have been abandoned, and little effort is being made to preserve what little is left of the original forest. So, the best approach is via the privately managed **Pugu Hills Nature Centre** (ⓦwww.puguhills.com), adjacent to the reserve's southeastern boundary, which has established a number of short **hiking trails** (guides are on hand) encompassing not just forest but a reservoir, a sacred cave replete with bats, a viewpoint over Dar es Salaam, a cattle market, and visits to Pugu School at which Nyerere taught before becoming President. Mountain biking from the centre is also possible. The centre's Tsh2000 entrance fee lets you use its swimming pool, if it has water. It also has a **campsite** ($6 per person), four comfortable bamboo **huts** on stilts with wooden floors (**❺**), and an excellent **restaurant** (meals Tsh7500, snacks from Tsh1500; you're not allowed to bring your own food unless you're camping). **Bookings** for all accommodation and activities are essential, even for day visitors.

To **drive** to the resort from Dar es Salaam, head southwest along Nyerere Road to the Oryx fuel station beyond **Kisarawe village** (roughly 20km), turn left, then right after 1km along a narrow dirt road. **Daladalas** can take you as far as the Oryx filling station (an hour's drive): catch them outside the TAZARA railway station on Nyerere Road, to where there are frequent daladalas from Kariakoo and Mnazi Mmoja. From Oryx, walk south for 1km, then right for the remaining 1.5km. The last daladala back from Kisarawe leaves around 6pm. Should you get stuck, there are rooms at *Kiki's Hotel* (❶) in Kisarawe.

Travel details

See pp.129–132 for more information on moving on from Dar.

Buses

Most bus services peter out by noon or early afternoon, so "hourly" in the frequencies below refers to services up to that time. Asterisks denote routes that are open in the dry season only; during the rains (usually Nov, Dec & most of March–May) these routes are often closed for days, weeks or even months at a time. Buses that do attempt these routes in the rains are subject to lengthy delays, often meaning days rather than hours.

Dar to: Arusha (20 daily; 9hr); Dodoma (hourly; 6–8hr); Ifakara (3 daily; 7hr); Iringa (hourly; 6–7hr); Kampala (3 daily; 26hr); Karatu (2 daily; 12hr); Kyela (4 daily; 13hr); Lindi (2–3 daily*; 22–28hr); Lushoto (3–5 daily; 5hr); Mahenge (2 daily*; 12hr); Mang'ula (2 daily; 6hr); Mbeya (10 daily; 11–12hr); Mohoro (3 daily; 7hr); Mombasa (3 daily; 10–12hr); Moshi (20 daily; 8–9hr); Mtwara (2–3 daily*; 24–30hr); Musoma via Kenya (2 daily; 27hr); Mwanza via Kenya (2 daily; 30hr); Mwanza via Singida (4 daily*; 35hr+); Nachingwea (1 daily*; 25–32hr); Nairobi (4 daily; 12–14hr); Newala (5–7 weekly*; 26hr+); Njombe (5 daily; 9hr); Singida (2 daily*; 24hr); Songea (3 daily; 9–11hr); Tanga (6–8 daily, 6hr).

Ferries

Dar to: Mwanza (1 weekly; 22hr); Pemba (5 weekly; 5–18hr); Stone Town (4–5 daily; 2–5hr depending on ferry).

Flights

Airline codes used below are: AE (Air Excel), AT (Air Tanzania), CA (Coastal Aviation), PA (Precisionair) and ZA (ZanAir). Where more than one airline flies to the same destination, the one with most frequent flights and/or shortest journey times is listed first.

Dar to: Arusha (PA, ZA, CT, AE: 6 daily; 1hr 15min–2hr 30min); Dodoma (CA: 3 weekly; 4hr 15min); Kigoma (PA: 6 weekly; 3hr 10min); Kilimanjaro (AT, PA: 2–3 daily; 1hr–1hr 15min); Kilwa (CA: daily; 1hr 20min); Lindi (PA: 2 weekly; 1hr 20min); Mafia (CA: daily; 30min); Manyara (CA: daily; 4hr); Mtwara (AT: daily; 55min); Mwanza (AT, PA: 3–4 daily; 1hr 30min–3hr); Pemba (ZA, CA: 3–4 daily; 1hr–1hr 30min); Ruaha (CA: daily; 3hr); Selous (CA, ZA: 3 daily; 30–45min); Serengeti (ZA, CA: 2 daily; 3hr 30min–6hr); Shinyanga (PA: daily; 2hr); Songo Songo (CA: daily; 1hr); Tabora (PA: 6 weekly; 1hr 50min); Tanga (CA: daily; 1hr 35min); Zanzibar (CA, ZA, PA, AE, AT: hourly; 20–25min).

Trains

All trains leave three times a week except to Tunduma and Zambia's New Kapiri Mposhi (once a week).

Dar to: Dodoma (14hr 30min); Fuga for Selous (3hr 40min–4hr 40min); Kigoma (38hr 30min); Kisaki (4hr 20min–5hr 15min); Makambako (14hr 15min–17hr 20min); Mang'ula (6hr 20min–7hr 45min); Mboya (18hr 10min–22hr 50min); Morogoro (6hr 30min); Mwanza (38hr 30min); New Kapiri Mposhi (38hr); Singida via Dodoma or Manyoni (26hr); Tabora (25hr 30min); Tunduma (21hr 45min).

2

The north coast

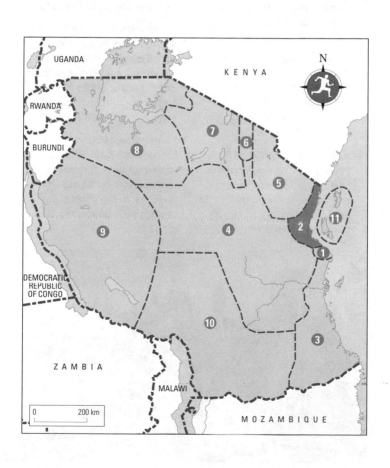

CHAPTER 2 # Highlights

* **Bagamoyo** Meaning "lay down my heart", this port was the most infamous transit point in the nineteenth-century slave trade, but now lies at the heart of Tanzania's contemporary arts scene, and is also a budding beach resort destination. **See p.148**

* **Freedom Village** Bagamoyo's Catholic Mission was founded in 1868 and the story of slavery and Christianity in Tanzania is adroitly told in the museum. **See p.153**

* **Kaole** The ruins of a medieval trading town, dating from the height of the Shirazi trading civilization, and now partly reclaimed by mangroves and the ocean. **See p.159**

* **Saadani National Park** Where bush meets beach; a unique shoreline wilderness combining marine, savannah, forest and riverine environments, together with the historic village of Saadani. **See p.161**

* **Amboni Caves** A great day-trip from Tanga: winding passageways, dripping stalactites, colonies of bats, an assortment of unlikely legends and a nearby forest and hot-water springs. **See p.175**

* **Pangani** Like Bagamoyo, a former slave-trading town, and delightfully somnolent and decrepit. It has superb beaches, and a good cultural tourism programme too. **See p.177**

△Holy Ghost Mission, Bagamoyo

The north coast

N orth of Dar es Salaam the beach resorts give way to a string of little-visited fishing villages interspersed by mangrove forests and sweeping sandy beaches, backed by a narrow fertile plain crossed by seasonal streams and the Ruvu, Wami and Pangani rivers. The main towns, all of historical significance, are Bagamoyo, Tanga and Pangani. **Bagamoyo** is easily visited on a day-trip from Dar, although it's worth staying longer. Wallowing in its infamous past as the coast's foremost slaving port, Bagamoyo is also the place where a host of explorers and missionaries set off into the African interior. Historic buildings from the slaving and colonial periods abound, including East Africa's first Catholic mission and a fort which served as the departure point for slaves being shipped out to Zanzibar. A few kilometres away, the ruins of the medieval Swahili trading centre of **Kaole** give a taste of what life was like almost eight centuries ago.

North of Bagamoyo, a strip of coastline and its bushy hinterland is protected as **Saadani National Park**, the only such coastal sanctuary in East Africa, which provides ample opportunities for spotting elephant, lion, leopard, zebra, antelope, giraffe and buffalo, as well as a plethora of birds and marine and riverine wildlife. Further north, at the mouth of the Pangani River, the delightful, laid-back fishing village and coconut-processing centre of **Pangani** blends the attractions of almost deserted beaches with atmospherically decrepit Swahili and colonial architecture. It's one of the nicest places on the coast to chill out for a few days of self-indulgent lethargy, and there's also an excellent cultural tourism programme in the village offering river cruises, dhow and snorkelling trips and historical tours.

Despite having Tanzania's second-busiest harbour, **Tanga**, 50km north of Pangani on the main road into Kenya, has a distinctly small-town feel. The beaches aren't brilliant and the town has clearly seen better days, but Tanga's proximity to the Amani Nature Reserve and Usambara Mountains (both covered in Chapter 5), as well as to Pangani, makes it an ideal base, while closer to hand there are the limestone caves at **Amboni** and the extensive Swahili ruins at **Tongoni** to explore.

The north coast is one of Tanzania's easier regions to travel around. **Transport** to the main towns is plentiful, and the main road up the coast from Dar es Salaam to Tanga is fast asphalt. The drawback is that for the most part the road passes around 100km inland. A more direct coastal road from Dar to Tanga via Bagamoyo, Saadani and Pangani has been on the drawing board for decades, but at present the only all-weather stretch is from Dar to Bagamoyo – the continuation to Saadani will remain impassable until or if the rope-pulled Wami River ferry, which was washed away in the 1998 El Niño floods, is replaced. The road

from Tanga into Kenya is also in an abysmal state, disintegrating every rainy season into a barely passable swill of mud, although work is currently underway to have it asphalted.

Bagamoyo and around

Set on a beautiful mangrove-fringed bay 72km north of Dar es Salaam, the attractive town of **BAGAMOYO** makes a popular day-trip from Dar, but has more than enough of interest to reward a longer stay. Though now little more than a large village, relying on fishing, coconuts and, to an increasing extent,

Bagamoyo: lay down my heart

The name **"Bagamoyo"** derives from the words *bwaga* (to put or throw down) and *moyo* (heart). As the exact meaning of Kiswahili depends on the context in which it is spoken, two theories have developed about the name. The first contends that the words were uttered by slaves on reaching the coast, where the impending sea voyage to Zanzibar signalled the end of any lingering hopes of escape. For them, Bagamoyo meant "crush your heart". An alternative and more likely explanation is that the words were spoken by caravan porters arriving on the coast after their arduous journey from the interior. In this context, *bwaga moyo* would have meant a place to "lay down the burden of your heart" – an expression of relief. This is supported by the existence of other places called Bagamoyo, one near Tanga, the other on the northern boundary of Rungwa Game Reserve in central Tanzania, both of which lay on caravan routes, and by a song that was sung by porters on the 1200km Ujiji–Bagamoyo route.

Be happy, my soul, let go all worries
soon the place of your yearnings is reached
the town of palms, Bagamoyo.
Far away, how was my heart aching
when I was thinking of you, my pearl
you place of happiness, Bagamoyo.

tourism for its survival, Bagamoyo's peaceful atmosphere conceals a very different past, when it was one of the richest and most important cities in East Africa. Its wealth stemmed from its role as a major conduit for the ivory and slave trade, being the place from which countless thousands of slaves were transported annually to the market in Zanzibar, whose lights can been seen twinkling over the water on clear nights. Bagamoyo's wealth of half-derelict buildings from slaving times are gradually being restored, and the town is slated for **World Heritage Site** status.

Bagamoyo is also Tanzania's **arts capital**, home to one of East Africa's leading arts colleges and a superb annual arts festival at the end of September and early October – if this is your cup of tea, it would be well worth timing your holiday to coincide.

For those with more time there's bird-watching and hippo-spotting in the **Ruvu River delta**, plus the ruins of **Kaole** a few kilometres to the south, which provide a vivid insight into medieval times, when the Shirazi trading civilization was at its height. Bagamoyo also has all the ingredients of a good **beach holiday**, with sandy shores, snorkelling trips and an increasingly broad choice of accommodation. Unfortunately, beach security is a concern: if the need to be watched over by hotel *askaris* turns you off, look elsewhere.

Some history

Bagamoyo's proximity to Zanzibar, 42km away across the Zanzibar Channel, is the key to the town's historical importance. During the eighteenth and nineteenth centuries, much of the Tanzanian coastline was ruled by the Omani Sultanate from Zanzibar, whose trading links with Arabia, Asia and Europe created one of the wealthiest dynasties ever seen in Africa. For much of this time, their riches came from the export of goods from the mainland, especially **slaves and ivory**, which were exchanged for cotton, beads and other manufactured goods. An estimated 769,000 slaves were transported from the East African coast during the nineteenth century, and countless more died, uncounted, along the caravan routes before reaching the ocean. Many of them passed through

Bagamoyo, which served as the major caravan terminus for routes coming from Lake Tanganyika and Lake Victoria, both over 1000km away.

Given its trading links, Bagamoyo was the logical starting and ending point for many European explorations of the continent. Stanley, Burton, Speke and Grant all passed through, as did a number of Christian missionaries and, most famously, the body of David Livingstone. In the 1880s, following the groundwork laid by the explorers and missionaries, the European **colonization** of East Africa began in earnest, and for the Germans – who had been accorded the territories now comprising Tanganyika, Burundi and Rwanda – Bagamoyo was an obvious choice for the capital of German East Africa. It was a status it enjoyed for less than a decade, however, as the **Abushiri War** of 1888–89, aimed against both Arab and German rule, prompted the Germans to move their capital to Dar es Salaam in 1891. Bagamoyo continued as provincial capital, but with the slave and ivory trades at an end and its shallow harbour eclipsed by new facilities at Dar es Salaam, Tanga and Mombasa, the town entered a long period of economic decline, and has nowadays effectively reverted to being the fishing village it once was.

Arrival and information

Bagamoyo is easily reached by road from Dar es Salaam. Other routes are difficult and unreliable, and the dhow trade has virtually ceased. **Buses** leave Dar's Ubungo bus station throughout the day, whilst **daladalas** leave from the Mwenge terminal north of the city. The journey takes about an hour. If you're loaded down with luggage, take a **taxi** once you've arrived both for security reasons and because the nearest beach hotel is a good fifteen minutes' walk away. Several tour operators in Dar offer Bagamoyo as a day-trip, though it certainly warrants more time than that: Takims (p.133) charge $55–85 per person, including lunch and a visit to the Kaole ruins.

The nearest thing to a **tourist office** is the Roman Catholic Mission Museum (see p.153), which should have a fold-out map and town guide available, and sells a wide range of booklets relating to the history of Bagamoyo, slavery and Catholicism – *Bagamoyo: a pictorial essay* by Jesper Kirknaes and John Wembah-Rashid (which you can also buy at the *Badeco Beach Hotel*) is particularly recommended.

Accommodation

The main **beach hotels** north of town actually garner a good chunk of their business from conferences (a welcome exception is *Travellers Lodge*), but there's little here that could be described as cheap. Budget travellers without tents are limited to **guest houses** in the town centre. **Camping** is possible in the grounds of *Badeco Beach Hotel* (Tsh7000 including breakfast), which has a grassy area with limited shade, and – in a lovely garden – at *Travellers Lodge* (Tsh5000, plus Tsh3500 for breakfast).

Beach safety

Bagamoyo's beaches may be most people's idea of a tropical paradise, but unfortunately **security** is a major concern, so heed the warnings given by your hotel about not walking unaccompanied on the beach, as reports of knife-point robberies of tourists are wearyingly familiar. The hotels should be able to provide an *askari* to keep an eye on you, though he'll appreciate a tip. As ever, don't take any valuables (which includes flashy sunglasses and running shoes) and if you are held up, don't resist.

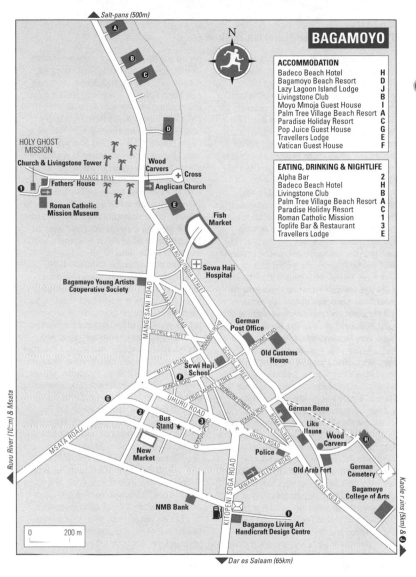

▲ Salt-pans (500m)

N

BAGAMOYO

ACCOMMODATION

Badeco Beach Hotel	H
Bagamoyo Beach Resort	D
Lazy Lagoon Island Lodge	J
Livingstone Club	B
Moyo Mmoja Guest House	I
Palm Tree Village Beach Resort	A
Paradise Holiday Resort	C
Pop Juice Guest House	G
Travellers Lodge	E
Vatican Guest House	F

EATING, DRINKING & NIGHTLIFE

Alpha Bar	2
Badeco Beach Hotel	H
Livingstone Club	B
Palm Tree Village Beach Resort	A
Paradise Holiday Resort	C
Roman Catholic Mission	1
Toplife Bar & Restaurant	3
Travellers Lodge	E

HOLY GHOST MISSION
Church & Livingstone Tower
Fathers' House
Roman Catholic Mission Museum
MANGO DRIVE
Wood Carvers
Cross
Anglican Church
Fish Market
Sewa Haji Hospital
Bagamoyo Young Artists Cooperative Society
OCEAN ROAD / DUNDA STREET
MANGESANI ROAD
MAKAANI ROAD
GEORGE STREET
MTONI ROAD
DUNDA ROAD
FRUIT MARKET STREET
UHURU ROAD
BOMANI ROAD
German Post Office
CUSTOMS ROAD
SCHOOL STREET
Old Customs House
Sewi Haji School
CAPUMA ROAD
Bus Stand
UHURU ROAD
GONGONI STREET
BOMA STREET
KAOLE ROAD
German Boma
Liku House
Wood Carvers
New Market
Police
Old Arab Fort
German Cemetery
Bagamoyo College of Arts
KITOPENI SOGA ROAD
MWANA KALENGE ROAD
MSATA ROAD
NMB Bank
Bagamoyo Living Art Handicraft Design Centre

◄ Ruvu River (10km) & Msata
Kaole ruins (5km) & ►
0   200 m

▼ Dar es Salaam (65km)

Town centre

Moyo Mmoja Guest House A few hundred metres east from the post office ☎023/244 0236, ©moyomdogo@hotmail.com. About ten minutes from the beach, this is the best of the budget hotels. There's a big garden and a kitchen for guests, but only three rooms (one with a private bathroom), so book ahead. Profits fund the adjacent children's home. ❷

Pop Juice Guest House Msata Rd ☎023/244 0318. A perfectly decent cheapie, with basic rooms sharing squat toilets and showers. ❶
Vatican Guest House Dunda Rd (no phone). Similar to *Pop Juice*, with the advantage of having some rooms with private bathroom. ❶

Beach

The following include breakfast in their rates.

Badeco Beach Hotel ☎023/244 0018, ⓦwww
.badecobeachhotel.de. A long-standing favourite
in need of an overhaul, with a pleasing clutter of
thatched buildings containing twelve rather dark
rooms, only two with sea views. The cheapest
share bathrooms and lack fans, more expensive
have bathrooms and a/c. Activities include historical town walks ($10) and dhow cruises ($50 per
person), and safaris can be arranged. There's also
a good restaurant and bar popular with locals.
❸–❹

Bagamoyo Beach Resort ☎023/244 0083,
Ⓔbbr@bagnet.com. French-managed place with a
welcoming atmosphere and efficient staff, making
it a popular choice with families. The eighteen
standard rooms are well back from the beach but
have large box nets, comfy beds and big patios;
more expensive rooms have a/c and are better
kept. There are also cheap *bandas* on the beach
which lack bathrooms or fans but have fantastic
views. Amenities include a swimming pool, bar
and restaurant, boat trips, sailing, windsurfing and
motor-boat rental, and mini golf. ❸–❹

🏃 **Lazy Lagoon Island Lodge** 20km south of
Bagamoyo by road; access also possible by
plane ⓦwww.tanzaniasafaris.info (book through
Foxes African Safaris in Dar; see p.133). A stylish
British-run place on its own island replete with
bushbabies, wild pigs, genets, baboons, duiker
and suni antelopes, this consists of a spectacular
vaulted main building and twelve wooden thatched
en-suite beach *bandas* with lofts (good for kids).
Each comes with solar-powered water and light,
and a large shaded verandah. There's also a
restaurant and a bar with panoramic views and a
swimming pool. The price includes boat transfer,
kayaking to explore the lagoon and mangroves,
windsurfing, Laser sailing and snorkelling, but
excludes dhow trips and excursions. Full-board ❽

🏃 **Livingstone Club** ☎023/244 0059,
ⓦwww.livingstone.ws. An impressive two-
level entrance sets the tone for Bagamoyo's classiest hotel, combining modern comforts with attractive Swahili style. Accommodation is in colourful
two-room bungalows, all with a/c, minibar, fan, box
net, a safe and verandah, though some of them
smell of air freshener. The beach, unfortunately, is

narrow and bounded by mangroves. Water sports
include canoeing, windsurfing, boat excursions,
snorkelling and a PADI diving school, and there's
also a tennis court, two swimming pools, a Jacuzzi,
and mountain bikes for guests' use. ❻

Palm Tree Village Beach Resort ☎023/244
0245–6, ⓦwww.palmtreevillage.com. This one is
run by Omanis, but is decidedly plain (and the palm
trees have yet to grow tall enough to give much
shade), though the big, bright and airy en-suite
rooms (46 in all) are attractive enough, all with a/c,
and some with huge, four-poster Zanzibari beds.
There are also five self-catering family cottages for
the same price. Facilities include a swimming pool,
windsurfing, and dhow and motor-boat trips; the
downside is the rather lifeless atmosphere, and no
alcohol during Ramadan. ❺

Paradise Holiday Resort ☎023/244 0000,
ⓦwww.paradiseresort.net. Shoehorned into a
rather narrow plot, this Indian-run place is good
value, and the best of several large resorts at the
north end of the beach, with a friendly welcome
and 83 rooms in thatched cottages. The "garden
view" ones may actually overlook the car park,
and are small and nothing special; much better are
the "superior" rooms, some with ocean views. All
have a/c, satellite TV, phone and minibar, and are
cheerfully decorated. Facilities include a swimming
pool (no sea views), tennis court, fitness centre,
two bars and an excellent restaurant, and activities
include windsurfing and dhow trips to Mambakuni
Island and the Ruvu delta for snorkelling, birds and
wildlife. ❺–❻

🏃 **Travellers Lodge** ☎023/244 0077 or
0744/855485, ⓦwww.travellers-lodge.com.
Run by an engaging German and South African
couple, this is Bagamoyo's best mid-range place.
Indeed, the friendly and easy-going atmosphere,
lush gardens and gorgeous gently sloping sandy
beach (reason enough to stay) recommends it over
pricier options. Rooms are in 26 attractive and
secluded en-suite cottages, all with verandah, a/c
or fan, the best on the beach. There's also an excellent restaurant-cum-bar whose fantastical carved
Makonde-style decor is simply mind-boggling, a
wild playground for kids and a motorboat for trips.
Busy at weekends, so book ahead. ❹–❺

The Town

Bagamoyo's rich history is embodied in a wealth of buildings dating from the
slaving era and subsequent German colonization – many of them ruined, some
achingly poignant, all of them photogenic, especially with the slender coconut

trees and glimpses of the ocean that frame most views. It's perfectly safe to walk around the town centre, but be wary of areas with a lot of tree or mangrove cover, especially along the shoreline, as muggings do occur. Read the box on "Beach Safety" (see p.150) and leave valuables in your hotel.

Holy Ghost Mission and Museum

At the north end of town in what used to be a slave-worked coconut plantation, the Catholic **Holy Ghost Mission** occupies a collection of whitewashed buildings whose plain appearance belies their historical importance. Also called **Freedom Village**, the mission was founded in 1868 by the French Holy Ghost Fathers, whose priests were instructed to spend as much as they could afford on buying slaves their freedom. The first transport of ransomed slaves, fifty boys, arrived on December 10, 1868 from Zanzibar. Eleven months later, 46 girls arrived, and by 1872 the village housed over three hundred children and young adults. Of course, the former slaves were expected to embrace the new religion, but the priests were open-minded enough to tolerate those who continued to follow their traditional beliefs. Although the immediate impact of the mission was limited to the freedom of a few hundred souls, the moral boost given to the anti-slavery movement by this pioneering mission could be said to have heralded the beginning of the end for the East African slave trade. In 1873, Sultan Barghash, under pressure from the British, reluctantly abolished the slave trade between Zanzibar and the mainland, although the trade continued illicitly for several decades more.

The **church** itself, built in the midst of the 1872 cholera epidemic, is now the oldest Catholic building in East Africa and attracts a variety of pilgrims from all over the region. It is dominated by a squat tower – the so-called **Livingstone Tower** – topped with a combination of arches and pinnacles resembling a mitre and named after the explorer-cum-missionary David Livingstone, whose preserved body was laid out here for a night on February 24, 1874, having been carried by foot on an epic eleven-month journey from Chitambo, in present-day Zambia, by his servants Susi and Chuma. The following morning it was carried to the shore to be taken to Zanzibar aboard the wryly named MS *Vulture*, and thence to England, where Livingstone was buried as a national hero in London's Westminster Abbey. For more on Livingstone, and his "discoverer" Stanley, see pp.536–537.

The colonnaded, three-storey **Fathers' House** facing the church was completed in 1873, and in 1876 a small chapel (also called the Grotto) was erected in the centre of Freedom Village and dedicated to Our Lady of Lourdes, who had made her miraculous appearance in France in 1858. Over the following years, especially during a second cholera outbreak during the Abushiri War (see p.161 and p.183), Freedom Village's population increased as people sought refuge, and it is from these refugees that many of Bagamoyo's present-day inhabitants are descended.

The story of the mission and its fight against the slave trade is told in the **Roman Catholic Mission Museum** (daily 10am–5pm; free, but donations welcome), housed in the Sisters' House of 1876. There's a small collection of woodcarvings, books and booklets for sale, and plenty of material documenting not only the arrival and progress of Christianity, but also much of Bagamoyo's pre-history, with extensive explanations in English. Other items on display include Indian and Arab door frames and a sewing machine, along with shackles, chains and whips which were used to restrain slaves, though even these are not as disturbing as the photographs of slaves tied together with chains around their necks.

△ Livingstone Tower, Bagamoyo

The big baobab tree outside the mission office was planted in 1868. Look carefully at its base and you'll see a short piece of metal **chain** protruding. This has nothing to do with slavery. Instead, the story goes that sometime after 1895 a certain Madame Chevalier, who had been running a dispensary in Zanzibar, came to the Bagamoyo mission as a volunteer. She fastened a chain around the tree in order to tie her donkey to it, and eventually forgot all about it. Since then, the tree's circumference has swelled by over seven metres, engulfing all but a foot or so of the chain.

The Anglican church

At the junction of the Holy Ghost Mission's driveway and Ocean Road are a cluster of pushy woodcarvers and the small **Anglican church.** A sign over the church door reads, "Through this door David Livingstone passed", a particularly fine example of linguistic sophistry, since although Livingstone did indeed pass through it, at that time the door was 1200km away on the shores of Lake Tanganyika. It was donated by an Anglican parish in 1974 following the construction of the present church, which is thought to occupy the site of the tree under which Livingstone's body was laid whilst awaiting the high tide to carry him to Zanzibar. Set in a small garden by the shore is a **stone cross**, not without its own touch of sophistry: though the inscription reads "First Cross of the RC Church in East Africa planted 17.6.1868", the cross itself is entirely modern.

South along Ocean Road to Liku House

Five minutes' walk south along Ocean Road from the Anglican church brings you to the **fish market**, busiest in the morning when the boats set out, and in the afternoon on their return. There are lots of simple but good restaurants here. South of here is **Sewa Haji Hospital**. Built in 1895, this is one of several public works in Bagamoyo that owe their existence to Sewa Haji, a Pakistani trader whose unstinting philanthropy was later rewarded with a knighthood from Queen Victoria. His condition for financing the hospital was that it would admit people of any race or religion. Some 500m further south along Ocean Road is the old **German Post Office** and, just inland, another of the Pakistani philanthropist's gifts: the three-storey **Sewa Haji School**. Built in 1896, it was donated to the colonial German government on condition that it remained multi-racial. The Ismaili branch of Shiite Islam to which Sewa Haji belonged has long enjoyed a commendable tradition of trans-religious altruism, most visible these days under the patronage of the Aga Khan Foundation (Ⓦ www .akdn.org) – it funded and is still funding most of the costs for the renovation of Zanzibar's Stone Town. Close by on the shore is the **Old Customs House**, with its keyhole arches.

Continuing south along Ocean Road brings you to the **German Boma**, Bagamoyo's most striking edifice. Built in 1897 to replace Liku House (see below) as the seat of the German regional administration, it's flanked by twin crenellated towers similar to the single-towered Boma at Mikindani on Tanzania's south coast, and has a heavily defensive feel despite the touches of arabesque in the arches of its balconies. Long-neglected, its roof collapsed in the El Niño rains of 1997; there are all sorts of plans for its future but nothing concrete as yet.

Just south of the Boma, **Liku House** was built in 1885 and served as the headquarters of German East Africa until 1891, when the capital was transferred to Dar es Salaam. It continued functioning as the regional headquarters until 1897, when the offices were moved to the Boma. The building currently houses the immigration department. Liku House is known for its connection with **Emin Pasha**, a Silesian Jew originally called Eduard Schnitzer, who adopted a Turkish name and Muslim way of life while serving as the Ottoman governor of northern Albania during 1870–74. In 1878 he was appointed *pasha* (governor) of Equatoria by the British Governor General of the Sudan, **General Charles Gordon**, though he later had to be reluctantly "rescued" (against his own wishes) from the "mad Mullah's hordes" by **Henry Morton Stanley**

Arts and crafts in Bagamoyo

Bagamoyo is Tanzania's leading centre for **arts**, with the Bagamoyo College of Arts and a number of artists' collectives to its name, as well as the annual **Bagamoyo Arts Festival**. This takes place over five days in late September and early October (contact the College of Arts for exact dates), showcasing theatre, music, dance and fine arts, and featuring both college students and artists and performers from abroad, notably Scandinavians – the college was partly funded with Norwegian money.

Bagamoyo College of Arts (BCA; Chua Cha Sanaa) Kaole Rd, 900m south of the Boma, PO Box 32 Bagamoyo ☎023/244 0032, ⓦwww.sanaabagamoyo.com (Mon–Sat 8am–3pm). Founded in 1981, this esteemed college – the first of its kind in Tanzania – teaches drama, fine arts (including the sculptures for which Bagamoyo has become famous), handicrafts, African and European music and dance, and even acrobatics. Free performances are held most evenings from 5–7pm except during Ramadan. You're welcome to watch classes, where you can also buy items. For a more hands-on experience, $6 an hour gets you a personal tutor in whatever takes your fancy, from wood sculpture and dance to lessons in how to play the lyre, Zaramo xylophone, drums and bamboo flute. Fifteen-hour week-long courses cost $75. Long-term foreign students are also welcome for up to three years; the fees aren't fixed, but shouldn't be prohibitively expensive.

Bagamoyo Young Artists Cooperative Society (BYACSO) Mangesani Rd, PO Box 67 Bagamoyo ☎023/244 0277. An inspired collective comprising mainly former students of the sculpture school. Starting off by producing life-size heads in both wood and cement (the entrance is marked by two cement sculptures of Nyerere), some of the collective's members have gained the confidence to progress to much more abstract – not to mention surreal – work, with deeply expressive, fluid and often hugely pleasingly grotesque results. Of the artists, Dula Bute is outstanding. Also worth checking out are Abdallah Ulimwengu, Mohamed Maulidi, Rama Marunda, Zakaria Mweru and Mwandale Mwanyekwa. You're welcome to drop by, but they prefer visitors in the evening when they're not so busy. The price of their work depends as much on the finish as the size and the theme of the object. Expect to pay between Tsh150,000 and Tsh200,000 for a well-finished life-size wooden head, or Tsh50,000–80,000 for a cement cast. There are plenty of cheaper alternatives, too, starting with key rings at Tsh1000. Avoid objects made from the endangered African blackwood tree (ebony) – the co-operative is aware of the problem and has pioneered sculpture in several other kinds of wood, including coconut, which has a coarse but unusually hard grain.

Bagamoyo Living Art Handicraft Design Centre (BLACC) Facing the post office, PO Box 163 ☎0744/834430 or 0744/463585, ⓦwww.jamani.nl/site/BLACC.html (daily 9am–4.30pm). A locally run NGO training disadvantaged women in handicraft and business skills, including basic computer knowledge. Their showroom sells a variety of items including pottery and ceramics, textiles, embroidery, basketry and clothes. You're welcome to visit the women at work, and there's a shop where you can buy their crafts. The centre has little outside support and is a laudable venture, currently training around sixty women a year.

following the Mahdist uprising. Evidently in need of another journalistic scoop to cap his meeting with Livingstone, Stanley subsequently published *In Darkest Africa, or The Quest, Rescue and Retreat of Emin, Governor of Equatoria*. Together with their sizeable entourage (albeit reduced to 196 from an original 708), Stanley and Emin Pasha arrived in Bagamoyo in December 1889. To celebrate their safe passage, the Germans threw a lavish party at Liku House, at which Emin Pasha became so carried away that, in the words of Evelyn Waugh, he accidentally took "a header off the balcony". He recovered from his fractured skull, but was murdered two years later in Congo.

Old Arab Fort
Just south of Liku House at the turn-off for the *Badeco Beach Hotel* is the **Old Arab Fort**, a large whitewashed and unadorned building. Its serene location, set amidst coconut palms overlooking the Indian Ocean, is rendered grimly ironic thanks to its nineteenth-century history as a holding place for slaves awaiting transportation to Zanzibar. Held in small, dark and overcrowded cells, the slaves would be led blindfolded through the courtyard and up a treacherously steep flight of stairs to the upper level of the fort, from where they were led back down along another stairway and out of the fort to the waiting dhows. The disorienting procedure was intended to deter any last-minute attempts at escape. The original structure dates from 1856, but was totally remodelled and fortified in the 1870s during Sultan Barghash's reign. It subsequently served as a German military camp (from 1894), a British prison (after World War I), and as a customs office and police headquarters. Following extensive restoration, it's now the base for the government's Antiquities Department: it should be possible to have a look around if you ask nicely.

The German Cemetery and the "Hanging Tree"
A short walk east of the fort are a couple of poignant memorials to the bloody Abushiri War of 1888–89, in which thousands of Africans died. The **German Cemetery**, down a path next to the *Badeco Beach Hotel*, contains the graves of eight German soldiers who lost their lives during the uprising and over the following years when the colonial *Schutztruppe* was almost constantly engaged in quelling resistance. The African dead are commemorated by a small plinth just inside the gate to the hotel which reads: "Here is the place where the German colonialists used to hang to death revolutionary Africans who were opposing their oppressive rule." Popularly called the Hanging Tree, the site was actually a scaffolded gallows where the leader of the rebellion, Abushiri ibn Salim al-Harthi, may have been executed in December 1889 (a sad distinction also claimed by Pangani; his grave site is unknown).

Eating

The beach hotel restaurants offer a good range of **seafood** including lobster and prawns, and both Italian and Indian favourites, though at tourist prices (Tsh5000–10,000 a meal). You'll find cheaper and more basic fare in town, and street food in the evenings around the market.

Badeco Beach Hotel Enjoys a sterling reputation for seafood, especially the day's catch; high standards and low prices also make it popular with locals.
Livingstone Club Brews up what some consider the best cappuccino in Tanzania, along with great

pasta (also with lobster), plus slightly more expensive meat dishes, and three-course set menus for under Tsh15,000.
Palm Tree Village Beach Resort Very good full English breakfast, and they rustle up some pretty decent main courses, too.

Paradise Holiday Resort Another good hotel restaurant, with cheaper à la carte dishes than other places and plenty of choice. Especially recommended are their themed buffet lunches (most days except in low season), currently including Oriental (Tues), Mediterranean (Wed), Italian (Thurs), African (Fri) and spicy food on Sunday. Saturday evenings feature barbecues.

Roman Catholic Mission The small area with thatched *bandas* at the rear of the mission buildings is good for cheap lunches and soft drinks.

Toplife Bar & Restaurant Corner Uhuru and Caravan roads. Good cheap local food – dishes like *ugali*, rice with grilled meat skewers (*mishkaki*) or stewed goat, fish or roast chicken won't cost more than Tsh1500–2000.

Travellers Lodge Open-air restaurant in tropical gardens dishing up consistently good food (Tsh5000–12,500), both local and international, including a famous Fisherman's platter (Tsh30,000 for two people). The astonishing Makonde-style woodcarvings are worth a visit alone.

Drinking and nightlife

There's a reasonable selection of **bars** both in the centre and at the beach hotels. The most popular local joint is the friendly, relaxed and eminently recommended *Toplife Bar & Restaurant*. *Alpha Bar* sometimes has discos, as does the *Livingstone Club*. The *Badeco Beach Hotel's* bar is popular with locals and is liveliest from Thursday to Sunday. If you're into **live music**, ask for performances of *ngoma ya kiasili* (traditional music) at the arts college. Two long-established cultural music bands worth tracking down are Mlutso (attached to the college), and Chibite, founded by the late Hukwe Ubi Zawose, who introduced the extraordinarily beautiful and complex "thumb piano" music of central Tanzania's Gogo tribe to the world stage.

Listings

Banks NMB, on the road opposite the post office, changes travellers' cheques and has a 24hr Visa/MasterCard ATM.

Hospital District Hospital, India St (℡023/244 0008). For a doctor, ask at the Huruma Dispensary, near *MM Guest House* in the centre of town.

Internet access 4MSK, beside Bagamoyo Living Art Handicraft Design Centre, facing the post office.

Language classes Kiswahili lessons with a personal tutor are given at the arts college for $6 an hour.

Pharmacy The Holy Ghost Mission has a well-stocked pharmacy, or try Huruma Dispensary near *MM Guest House* in the centre of town.

Police Kaole Rd ℡023/244 0026.

Post office Kitopeni Soga Rd.

Moving on from Bagamoyo

If you're heading north in the dry season, it's quickest to go straight to **Msata** rather than backtrack to Dar. In reasonable weather, this route is covered by occasional daladalas, a journey of around two hours – they're best caught in the morning, but check at the bus and daladala stand near the water tower the evening before you plan to leave. There's no direct access to Saadani National Park at present, as there's no way to cross the Wami River.

Given Bagamoyo's proximity to **Zanzibar**, it's a wonder that there isn't any regular transport to the island. If you want to try to get a passage on a **dhow**, the manager of the *Bagamoyo Beach Resort* can help you out. Alternatively, talk to local boat owners and captains headed to Kizimkazi at the southern tip of Zanzibar. If you strike a deal, you *may* need to visit Liku House to clear formalities, though the procedure varies according to the political state of affairs on Zanzibar – officials aren't particularly keen on tourists taking the crossing, as dhows do occasionally capsize and there's little chance of rescue. The trip takes 6–8 hours by motorized dhow: bring everything you'll need.

Kaole

The ruins of the once prosperous Shirazi town of **KAOLE**, 5km south of Bagamoyo, provide a fascinating and atmospheric complement to the historical sights of Bagamoyo. Founded in the thirteenth century, the ruins include what is thought to be the oldest mosque on the East African mainland, as well as a collection of unusual pillar tombs. The town went into decline following the arrival of the Portuguese in the 1500s, and by the time the Omanis gained control of Bagamoyo in the eighteenth century, Kaole had been abandoned. Kaole's original name was Pumbuji, but was renamed "Kalole" by the Zaramo after the town's desertion, meaning "go and see" what had been left behind. The attribution is similar to that of Gezaulole, south of Dar es Salaam (p.140), which means "try and see". No one knows for sure the reasons why the town was deserted, but the fact that much of it has now been reclaimed by sea and mangroves suggests environmental change or a tidal wave as possible causes.

There's **no public transport** to the site, and given the risk of being mugged if you walk, you'll need either to take a taxi (up to Tsh6000 for a return trip) or rent a bicycle. Either way, head for the modern village of Kaole, 4km south of Bagamoyo, which is notable for a couple of glaringly phallic **pillar tombs** on the right-hand side of the road as you come in, all quite different from the pillar tombs found in the main archeological site.

The archeological site

The **archeological site** itself (daily 8am–5.30pm; Tsh2000) is 1km beyond Kaole village. The entrance fee includes admission to a small but interesting **museum** containing pottery shards, oil lamps and other artefacts, some of them Chinese. There are two helpful guides who appreciate a small tip for their services. The museum office sells beautiful ocean shells, but bear in mind that the trade in these is illegal both in Tanzania and internationally.

Once you've seen the museum, the first stop is the thirteenth-century **mosque**, which was excavated from its sandy tomb in 1958 by the archeologist Neville Chittick. Although the ceiling of the building collapsed long ago, probably before the second mosque to the east of the site was erected in the fifteenth century, the fact that most of the walls are still standing attests to the strength of the coral, lime and sand mortar which was typical of the time – the *mihrab* (the alcove indicating the direction of Mecca) is especially well preserved. Outside, the steps up the wall were used by the muezzin for calling the faithful to prayer. Next to these is a well for ablutions which still contains water, its freshness proved by the frogs which have taken up residence in it. Beside the well is a much burnished stone which was used for washing feet.

Beside the mosque, and spread out throughout the site, are twenty-two **tombs**, some with tall pillars rising from their headstones, a feature found in many other sites in East Africa. These "pillar tombs" date from the fourteenth to nineteenth centuries, and the most intact one bears traces of an Arabic inscription recording Ali bin Juma, who died in 1270 aged 55 (the date relates to the Muslim Hegira calendar, equating to around 1854 of the Christian era). The pillar has five depressions which formerly held Chinese porcelain bowls. Sadly, three were stolen, and the other two are now in the National Museum in Dar es Salaam.

②

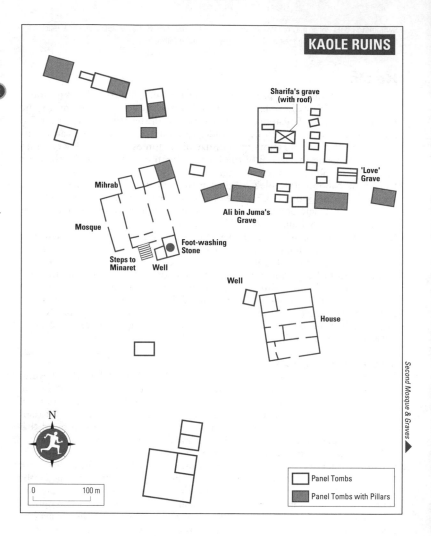

Second Mosque & Graves ▶

Also worth looking out for is the remarkable **Sharifa's grave**, the "hut tomb" of a holy woman who is still venerated by local women who pray to her for help and leave small offerings in a small metal bowl inside the tomb (which, like the pillar tomb, was originally decorated with Chinese porcelain bowls). Lastly, note the "**Love Grave**" nearby – a single structure containing two graves laid side by side, which house the remains of a couple believed to have drowned at sea.

The Ruvu River

The road to Msata, which is mostly graded, was the last leg of the old slaving route, and the start of many an explorer's journey into the interior of the "dark continent". It heads west out of Bagamoyo and then down into the **Ruvu River delta**, a reedy saltbush marshland which offers superb bird-watching.

Amazingly, even the swamp isn't enough to deter human habitation, as shown by the tiny houses perched improbably above it on stilts. **Bird-watching** and **hippo-spotting** are possible: although there are no organized tours, the owner of the *Bagamoyo Beach Resort* might be able to arrange a guide and a vehicle. Alternatively, rent a bicycle in town (there's no formal outlet – just ask anyone with a bike), and then hire a local once at the river to track down wildlife – be cautious of hippos however, as they can be extremely dangerous. You'll need a tent if you plan on doing anything more than a day-trip, since there are no guest houses in any of the small villages dotted about the delta. The Ruvu River itself, 10km from Bagamoyo, is now spanned by the narrow **Federici Bridge**.

Saadani National Park

Located 45km north of Bagamoyo, the 1062-square-kilometre **SAADANI NATIONAL PARK** is one of the most fascinating, and least visited, of Tanzania's

Bwana Heri and the Abushiri War

The small and tranquil village of **Saadani**, in the heart of the park, was formerly an important harbour town and slave-trading centre which, under the charismatic leadership of the legendary slave trader **Bwana Heri**, played an important role in the Abushiri War. During the nineteenth century, Saadani – under the control of the Zigua tribe – was one of only a few mainland coastal towns to retain its political independence from the Omani sultans, and grew wealthy on the slave trade with Zanzibar. A missionary writing in 1877 mentioned seeing slave caravans passing daily into Saadani, each with around a hundred children in chains. The profits from the trade were used to buy firearms from Zanzibar, which further served to strengthen Saadani's independence. Bwana Heri, who ruled Saadani from the early 1870s, achieved considerable power in this way, and also enjoyed considerable influence with the chiefs of the hinterland, especially with his own Zigua people and the Nyamwezi tribe from the Central Plateau (see p.555); he also became a valued ally of European traders and missionaries hoping to travel into the interior.

All this changed in 1884 with the arrival of a young German, **Karl Peters**, who set off from Saadani in November 1884 to make a series of bogus treaties with tribal chiefs that effectively gave Peters control of their land. Nonetheless, it was not until 1888 that Bwana Heri and the coastal people saw their political and economic power directly threatened, when the sultan of Zanzibar granted the Germans the right to extract customs duties on the mainland coastal strip. With local passions already inflamed by what many perceived as German arrogance (notably the desecration of mosques; see box on p.183), armed resistance was formed under the leadership of Bwana Heri in Saadani and Abushiri ibn Salim al-Harthi at Pangani, and the Germans were quickly expelled from much of the coast, signalling the beginning of the **Abushiri War**.

The German response took time to arrive, but was brutal when it did. In April 1889, **Major Hermann von Wissmann** and his army (the majority of whom were Nubians from Sudan, and Zulus from South Africa) quickly recaptured the towns north of Dar es Salaam. In June 1889 Saadani was bombarded and taken, and Bwana Heri was forced to flee inland, where he built a series of forts. These were destroyed one after the other by Wissmann, however, and Bwana Heri finally surrendered at Saadani in April 1890. Perhaps because of his previous hospitality to Wissmann, whom he had treated as an honoured guest in 1883, he was spared the fate of Abushiri (who was hanged at Bagamoyo), and was even left in control of Saadani. In March 1894 he tried to regain more substantial political power, but once more was defeated.

game parks. Its unique ecosystem combines marine, terrestrial and fluvial environments, which – together with historic **Saadani village** – make for an attractive and unusual destination.

Although touted as a place to see **big game on the beach**, such sightings are rare indeed, though you may well see waterbuck and baboons there by day and, at night, mongooses in search of crabs. Dolphins are sometimes seen off the coast, and Madete Beach in the north is one of Tanzania's few protected turtle nesting sites. Shoreline birdlife is profuse. The **plains and swamps** behind the shore are home to around thirty species of large mammal, although many are both rare and shy, so don't come expecting a wealth of wildlife photo-ops. That said, their very elusiveness makes spotting them all the more thrilling. Denizens include warthog, elephant (most likely in the north), buffalo, zebra and enormous herds of giraffe, as well as antelopes: Liechtenstein's hartebeest, wildebeest, waterbuck, dikdik, eland, oryx and the rare Roosevelt and Roan sables. The abundance of **warthogs** is thought to be the result of local Islamic beliefs which see them to be a form of swine and so *haram* – forbidden. The park is also home to some non-indigenous herbivores which were released into the wild when a translocation camp was closed in 1977. Of these, eland and zebra adapted best, though neither population has grown large enough to endanger the previous ecological balance. The most numerous **predators** are leopards, though lions are more visible thanks to the nocturnal leopard's preference for dense bush. **Birds of prey** include palmnut and white-backed vultures, yellow-billed kites, and various species of eagle. In the south, the **Wami River** also attracts fabulous **birdlife**, as well as hippos and crocodiles, whilst the low hills are covered with rare remnants of **coastal forest** – of which Zaraninge in the southwest is the jewel, with several primate species and yet more birds.

Arrival

Visiting Saadani can't be done on the cheap, as there's no accommodation other than three expensive lodges, and driving time – over four hours from Dar – precludes day-trips unless you delve in quickly from Pangani in the north: rather pointless as you'll have no time to really enjoy the place

By plane

Most visitors come by **plane**. Daily scheduled flights to and from Dar ($70) and Zanzibar ($50) are operated by ZanAir, whilst Coastal Aviation ($80) will stop "on inducement" along their daily Zanzibar–Dar–Selous routing; the fare to or from Selous is $130.

By road

The long-promised coastal highway via Bagamoyo is still a mere dream, and the Wami River ferry washed away in the 1997–98 El Niño rains was never replaced, so there are only three approaches.

From Dar, *A Tent With A View Safari Lodge* charges $200 per vehicle each way; shopping around with car rental companies, you should be able to find something for $150. If you're driving yourself, the shortest approach is to cut off the highway at Mandera 2km beyond the Wami River (149km from Dar), from where a decently graded dirt road goes straight to Saadani village (58km; 2hr). Longer is the road from Mkata, 59km north of Mandera, which skirts the park's northern fringes and takes you to the park headquarters. Approaching **from Bagamoyo**, drive 66km northwest to Msata on the highway, then north 16km to Mandera.

From **Pangani** (2hr; 4WD recommended), it's a bumpy ride down to Mkwaja village and the park headquarters. Public transport is limited to the daily "chicken bus" (Tsh1500), a green bus that leaves Bweni, on the south bank of the Pangani River facing Pangani town, every day between noon and 1pm, finishing at Mkwaja from where the lodges will pick you up. **Car rental** in Pangani can be arranged informally (try the cultural tourism office or *Pangadeco Bar & Lodge*), but might be as much as $200 for a full day there and back.

Entrance fees and information

Entrance fees are currently $20 for 24 hours; included if you're staying at *Saadani Safari Lodge*, otherwise payable at the **park headquarters** near Mkwaja (daily 7.30am–5.30pm; ⓔsaadani@bushlink.co.tz), or through the other lodges if you enter the park on a game drive. A vehicle permit costs Tsh10,000. The park's official **Internet site** is ⓦwww.tanzaniaparks.com/saadani.htm, but ⓦwww.saadani.com is a better source of information. The best **guidebook** is the colourful *Saadani and Bagamoyo*, published by TANAPA.

The **best time to visit** is the dry season, from June to October, when the animals converge on the river. January and February, after the short rains, are visually rewarding, as much of the park is painted in lush hues of green. Saadani can be inaccessible during the long rains, which are heaviest in April and May, and occasionally during November and December.

Accommodation

In the absence of official **campsites** (something that may well change – ask at the park headquarters; expect to pay $30 per person), Saadani's **accommodation** is limited to three upscale choices: one inside the park, two just outside, each with its own individual style and allure.

A Tent with a View Safari Lodge Outside the park's northeastern boundary, 7km south of Mkwaja ⓦwww.saadani.com (book through A Tent With A View Safaris in Dar; see p.133). On the beach in a former coconut plantation, this is stylish without being over the top, the emphasis as much on barefoot relaxation as activities, most at extra cost if you're on full-board only. On offer are guided bush walks ($20, also at night), strolls through Saadani village to see a ruined Shirazi mosque with its celadon china inlays intact ($15), canoeing on the mangrove-lined Mafue River to spot birds, a day's boating on the Wami ($70), walks along Mkwaja–Madete Beach (a green turtle nesting ground), as well as "traditional" game drives ($35). The beach itself allows blissful swimming, as long as you dodge the baboons. Accommodation is in eight simple but comfortable, individually styled solar-powered tents, pitched along the beach on raised wooden platforms and under thatched roofs, complete with inventive use of driftwood, amusing semi-outdoor showers, and large balconies (and hammocks) overlooking the ocean. The restaurant (mainly seafood) has similar views, and there's also a hide overlooking a waterhole. No children under 6. Closed April & May. Full board ($175 per person including transfer from Saadani airstrip, or $265 including all activities and park fees). **⑨**

Kisampa Camp Kisampa Wilderness Area, adjacent to the park's southwestern boundary near the Wami River ☎022/261 8277, ⓦwww.sanctuary-tz.com. At last, a "luxury" camp that won't ever be colonized by the Condé Nast brigade. "Rustic simplicity" perhaps, "bare necessities" definitely. The lack of creature comforts isn't for everyone – no electricity, no cold drinks, showers under buckets hung from trees, and toilets being long-drops covered by wooden seats – but this is an authentic bush experience, with accommodation in seven comfortable "star gazer" tents with transparent roof panels. The Wilderness Area is run in partnership with local villagers, who together with the resident former Australian SAS doctor, provide lots of activities to keep you busy: butterfly walks and birding, courses in bush survival and safari guiding, visits to a beekeeping project, school and village, fly camping, wobbling around in dugouts, river safaris, fishing, and game drives (at extra cost, also possible at night). All-inclusive ($160 per person) **⑨**

Saadani Safari Lodge In the park, 1km north of Saadani village ☎022/277 3294, ⓦwww.saadanisafarilodge.com. The most traditional of the three, with nine completely refurbished "tented cottages" strung along the beach – large and airy, with wooden floors, big Zanzibari four-posters, lots of draperies, and ocean-view verandahs. Activities, at additional cost (mostly $35), include fishing, forest walks, Wami River cruises, visits to Saadani village, snorkelling off a sandbank, and game drives. There's also a tree house overlooking a waterhole, a swimming pool, bar and library, and an excellent restaurant for seafood, prawns especially. Closed April & May. Full-board ($135 per person including park fees) **9**

The park

The park contains a multitude of **drives** but no decent map, so hiring a ranger at the park headquarters is recommended if you're not on an organized safari (count on $200 per day). Both the northern and southern sections are accessed from a crossroads about 5km west of Saadani village on the road to Mandera. Without your own transport, the best way around is on a **game drive** (3–4 hours), which cover a variety of habitats; these can be arranged by a lodge, if they're not too busy with other clients. A more intimate – though at times nerve-wracking – way to experience the park is on a **walking safari** or, to see the Wami River at its best, on a **boat safari**; both can be arranged through the lodges.

The coast

As East Africa's only coastal wildlife refuge, a lot has been made of "**bush-meets-beach**" wildlife encounters, though sadly those alluring stories of elephants and lions on the white sands are a mite exaggerated: few animals need venture to the coast except perhaps during the rains, when salt licks can become flooded. Nonetheless, the area's marine wildlife is second to none, and includes nesting sites for the endangered **green turtle** at Madete Beach in the north. The sites have been protected since 1993, and can be visited through *A Tent With A View Safari Lodge*, who also maintain a turtle egg incubation and hatching centre. Contact them in advance for likely dates for the next "hatch-out" (year-round).

If you're out snorkelling, bottle-nosed **dolphins** are common off the park's southern coast, and **humpback whales** have been reported passing through the Zanzibar Channel in October and November. Small **sharks** can also be found, though these are believed to content themselves with a diet of prawns rather than humans. The proximity of the silty Wami River means that some species, such as the **sea catfish**, have adapted to the muddy flats.

Birdlife is particularly rich, with both marine and freshwater birds frequently observed fishing. Particularly eye-catching is the majestic African fish eagle, which perches up in trees waiting for prey to be carried up on the high tide.

Saadani's human-wildlife conflict

Despite Saadani having repeatedly been increased in size, some of its migratory mammals – like sable antelope, kudu, buffalo and elephant, and a few hungry lions – still seasonally pass beyond the park and its protection. This is a constant worry for ecologists, as the most acute threat to Saadani's ecosystem other than destructive land use around its margins is what conservationists call **poaching**, and what villagers consider to be **subsistence hunting**. In the west of the park, the abundance of firearms led to game scouts dubbing the area "Kosovo".

Relations between villagers and the authorities have long been strained (the villagers also suffer crop damage from wildlife), and as the new national park status promises nothing new, all three tourist lodges have been at pains to involve locals in their operations, and in some of their profits.

Waders include the woolly-necked stork, yellow-billed stork, open-billed stork, common sandpiper and grey heron.

The northern sector

The park's **northern sector**, which includes the former Mkwaja cattle ranch, sustains a small population of around fifty **elephants**, though you'll be lucky to spot more than a couple, as their memories of poaching are still fresh. Two rare types of antelope can also be found in the north: **greater kudu**, which are well camouflaged and rarely seen (they spend much of the day resting in the shadow of bushes); and **sable antelope**, found mainly to the southwest of Mkwaja. They're smaller and lighter in colour than the common sable, and have shorter horns, which for a long time led zoologists to class them as a separate species. While you're around the area, don't forget to pay your respects to the lugubrious inhabitants of Madete Hippo Pool.

The southern sector

Inland, the park's southern sector comprises dense **acacia woodland**, another good place for birds: colourful lilac-breasted rollers, fork-tailed drongos, grey hornbills, bee-eaters, flocks of Meyer's parrots and red-cheeked cordonbleus can all be seen. In the far southwest, the woodland turns into **Zaraninge Forest**, home to black-and-white colobus and blue monkeys. There's a nature trail there too. Giraffes here tend to keep away from humans, but can be seen gliding between the acacia trees and around Saadani village. Closer to the river, Eastern Bohor reedbuck can be seen in reedbeds near swamps, whilst bushbuck are quite common, though they hide by day in dense bush alongside the river.

The whole area is best for wildlife during the dry season (June–Oct), when many animals migrate towards the perennial waters of the **Wami River**. The ideal way to experience it – a highlight for many visitors – is by boat ($35 per person from *Saadani Safari Lodge*, $70 from *A Tent With A View* for a full day). The boat heads down the coast before entering the Wami's mangrove-lined estuary, often frequented by large flocks of flamingos. In the river itself, look out for the pink backs of **hippo** lounging about in the water, and the log-like forms of **Nile crocodile** in the reeds along either bank – one particularly intrepid croc swam across the Zanzibar Channel a few years ago, much to everyone's surprise. Nowadays, it's mainly illegally produced charcoal that "floats" across to the Isles. High above in the forest canopy you might, if you're lucky, catch glimpses of black-and-white colobus monkeys.

Tanga and around

Located on a large, pear-shaped bay 200km due north of Dar es Salaam (but 350km by road), **TANGA** is Tanzania's second-busiest port and the country's third largest town, with a population of around two hundred thousand. Despite the town's size it's a refreshingly friendly and laid-back place, and surprisingly safe. In many respects, Tanga resembles Lindi on the south coast, with which it shares a similar feeling of decaying grandeur. In Tanga's case, decline started when its economy was eclipsed by that of Dar es Salaam in the early twentieth century, and was accelerated by the collapse of world sisal prices after World War II, when synthetics took away much of the demand for what is still the region's major cash crop. By 1999 Tanga had slipped from being the country's second most powerful economic region to the sixteenth.

△ Sisal plantation

The beaches are disappointing, since much of Tanga Bay is lined with mangroves, and there's not a whole lot to see in Tanga itself either, but an aimless wander around town is always fun. An excursion to the **Amboni Caves** and **Galanos Sulphur Springs** makes a good day-trip, and Tanga also serves as a springboard for longer trips to the wonderful beaches at the historic village of **Pangani**, 54km to the south; the atmospheric fourteenth-century ruins of the Swahili trading town of **Tongoni** en route; and the fantastic rainforest at **Amani Nature Reserve** in the East Usambaras (see p.372).

Some history

Tanga was founded in the fourteenth century by Persian traders, but little remains of this period except for graves and ruined mosques on Toten Island in Tanga Bay, and at Tongoni, and the town's name – which is Persian for "green valley" or "road beside a mountain". Tanga remained small until the eighteenth century, when it was occupied by **Omani Arabs**, under whose tutelage the town grew to become a major entrepôt for slaves and ivory, which were shipped into the Omani capital in Zanzibar. The town's trading links began to attract German missionaries, who started operating here in 1876, and by the early 1880s the town and its harbour had become a major centre for the **German conquest** of the interior. By 1888 the Germans had effectively become rulers of the region, although in the same year their brutal and often tactless rule led to the spontaneous uprising which became known as the Abushiri War (see box on p.000).

Following the end of the war in 1889, the Germans imposed a "protectorate" and began the military conquest of the hinterland. As their regional headquarters, Tanga looked set to prosper, especially when construction began on a railway linking Tanga with Moshi and the Kilimanjaro region. The driving force behind Tanga's renaissance was **sisal**, a major source of fibre for making ropes and sacks, which had been introduced to Tanzania by the German botanist

Richard Hindorf in 1892. Despite only 62 of the thousand plants originally taken from Florida surviving the journey, sisal proved to be spectacularly well adapted to the land and climate – by 1908 there were over ten million sisal plants in Tanzania, and at its height the region was producing 250,000 tonnes of sisal fibre a year (compared to 20,000 tonnes in 2000). The plantations, which stretch westwards from Tanga along much of the plains edging the Usambara Mountains, still constitute the region's major export crop.

Tanga saw **World War I**'s first land engagement in East Africa when, on November 2, 1914, Britain's General Aitken rashly issued the order that "Tanga is to be taken tonight." It wasn't to be, as the 48-hour delay in landing troops gave the Germans plenty of time to organize their defences. When confrontation finally came, some two thousand Allied troops, mostly Indian, found themselves pitted against a thousand Germans and their well-trained African *askaris*, who were lying in wait on the other side of the railway cutting. Although some Allied forces fought their way as far as the town centre, others were ambushed at the railway, were stung by bees (enraged at having had their hives pierced by stray bullets) or got lost in the rubber and sisal plantations and long grass. The inept nature of the assault was typified by the story of the 25 **cattle** stolen by the British to feed their beleaguered troops. The following night, the African cattle herders snuck in behind British lines and took them back, without anyone even noticing. The battle – most of which was fought in what is now Ras Kazone suburb – was a disaster for the British, who after three days and 795 casualties were forced to retreat to Mombasa, leaving behind sixteen machine guns, 455 rifles and six hundred thousand rounds of ammunition – enough for a year's fighting.

The Germans were finally ejected in 1917, and under **British rule** the railway connecting Tanga with the Central Line was finally completed. With sisal already proving its worth, Tanga's harbour was expanded in anticipation of a massive export trade, and the interwar years saw the town's heyday. Goans, Indians and Greeks – as well as Swahili and British merchants and administrators – descended on the town in the expectation that it would rival both Dar es Salaam and Mombasa in importance. Sadly, the invention of synthetic textiles such as nylon after World War II caused the sisal market to collapse, and the town entered a period of rapid decline from which it still shows precious little sign of emerging.

Arrival and information

Tanga is well connected with the rest of the country by good sealed roads, reasonably graded *murram* to Pangani, and not so reasonable dirt and mud to the Kenyan border. The **bus stand** is a ten-minute walk from the town centre along Pangani Road. It's relatively hassle-free as far as bus stations go. The **dala-dala stand** is nearby, also on Pangani Road.

Tanga's unofficial **tourist office** is the commendably energetic – and hugely knowledgeable – **Tour Care** on Mkwakwani Street (℡027/264 4111 or 027/264 4116), who are clued up about most things concerning northeastern Tanzania, including Amani Nature Reserve. Their main business is both community-based tourism and day-trips (for which see p.174), and co-ordinating the Tanzania eco-Volunteerism (TeV) project, which receives volunteers from overseas.

Accommodation

Tanga has plenty of **accommodation**, especially in the budget and mid-range categories. More luxurious options are thin on the ground and tend to have

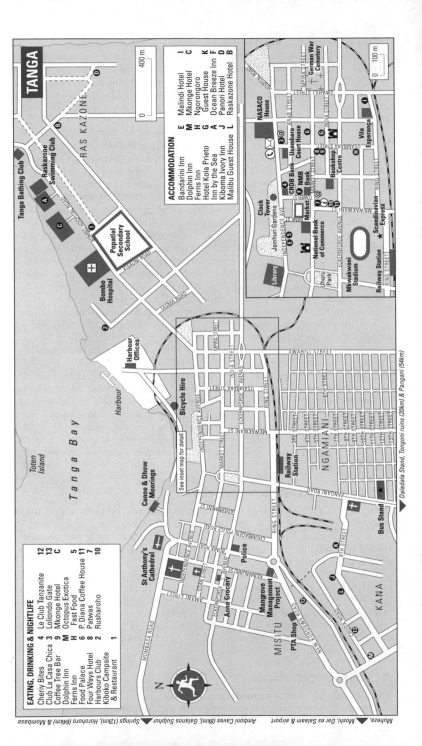

TANGA

ACCOMMODATION

Bandarini Inn	I	Malindi Hotel	E
Dolphin Inn	C	Mkonge Hotel	M
Ferns Inn		Ngorongoro	H
Hotel Kola Prieto		Guest House	G
Inn by the Sea	K	Ocean Breeze Inn	A
Kiboma Ivory Inn	F	Panori Hotel	J
Malibu Guest House	D	Raskazone Hotel	L
	B		

EATING, DRINKING & NIGHTLIFE

Cheriy Bites	4	Le Club Tanzanite	12
Club La Casa Chica	3	Loliondo Gate	13
Coffee Tree Bar	C	Mkonge Hotel	C
Dolphin Inn	M	Octopus Exotica	
Ferns Inn	H	Fast Food	5
Food Palace	6	P. Diana Coffee House	11
Four Ways Hotel	8	Patwas	7
Harbours Club	2	Rusharoho	10
Kiboko Campsite & Restaurant	1		

seen better days – *Mkonge Hotel* is the exception. **Camping** is possible at *Raskazone Hotel* ($4), and at the Swiss-run *Kiboko Campsite & Restaurant* off Bombo Hospital Road (T027/264 4929 or 0748/424292), which has a small lawn. Tour Care (see p.167) run two **hostels** ($5 per person), useful if you're really into their work. All places listed below include breakfast in their rates unless otherwise indicated.

Town centre

Bandarini Inn Independence Ave (no phone). Closed for years but due to reopen in 2006, this should once again be a great backpackers' choice, not least for the superb bay-facing views from its top-floor rooms. ❷

Ferns Inn Usambara St, near Ring St T0741/481608 or 0748/481609. Run by a sweet Goan, this has nine clean twin-bed en-suite rooms with fans and nets, though the ones with a/c are overpriced. There's a bar, and good food. ❷–❹

Hotel Kola Prieto India St, close to Custom Rd T027/264 4206, kolaprieto@tanga.net. Tanga's best business-class hotel, a modern four-storey affair with 24 clean and attractive en-suite rooms, each with carpet, big double beds, satellite TV, phone, fridge and a/c (which can be loud). There's a formal restaurant (no alcohol), but no lift. ❹

Malindi Hotel Ring St T027/264 2791 or 0741/332984. Another modern four-storey affair offering excellent value for money, with sixteen rooms, all with clean cotton sheets. A/c costs extra. ❸

Ocean Breeze Inn Clock Tower St, facing the market T027/264 4545. Another high-rise, this one seemingly under eternal reconstruction. The staff are desultory and not everything works, but there are sea views from some rooms (though some balconies are screened by trees), private bathrooms and fans throughout, plus a/c and TV (local stations) on the first floor. There's a bar next door, but no restaurant. ❷–❸

Ras Kazone

Tanga's main tourist-class hotels lie along and off Bombo Hospital Road in the affluent **Ras Kazone** suburb, the peninsula to the east of the centre. Unfortunately there's no real beach to speak of (the nearest is a cleared patch of mangroves occupied by two bathing clubs; see "Swimming" on p.174). Frequent daladalas run up and down Bombo Hospital Road from the main stand (Tsh200).

Inn by the Sea 1.5km along Bombo Hospital Rd T027/264 4614. Perched on a low cliff among lush bougainvillea hedges, this rather tatty establishment sees little trade, while the rooms (no singles; a/c extra) are well past their prime, especially the saggy beds. Even so, at the price this is the best value of the bay-side hotels, and you can swim in the sea. There's also a restaurant and a bar selling soft drinks. ❷–❸

Mkonge Hotel 1250m along Bombo Hospital Rd T027/264 3440, mkongehotel@kaributanga. com. Tanga's only international-class hotel, set in a baobab-studded lawn by the bay, though the fringing mangroves inhibit swimming. The main building, containing the bar and restaurant, is an oddly attractive and sensitively restored hulk dating from the happier days of the sisal industry; less enticing is the 1970s accommodation block accessed along a long dark corridor, although its large, newly refurbished rooms – with polished parquet – are cheerfully furnished and equipped with a/c (no

fans or nets however), satellite TV, phone, spotless modern bathroom and small terrace. The better ones (same price) have fine views over the bay and Toten Island, albeit through trees and a fence; best from the top floor. ❺

Panori Hotel 3km from the centre T027/264 6044, panori@africanline.co.tz. A poor location, being close to a stretch of beach owned by the military and over 1km from the bathing clubs and public transport, but the welcome is warm, and all rooms have private bathrooms and a/c, though the smell of bug spray is pervasive. Forget the four Old Wing rooms and take one in the New Wing, which have parquet floors, TVs and big bathrooms. There's also a bar and a good, if expensive, restaurant. ❹

Raskazone Hotel 200m off Bombo Hospital Rd near Tanga Bathing Club, 2km from the centre T0741/670790, raskazone@hotmail.com. Offers a warm reception if you can actually find anyone around, though the rooms (with either fan or a/c) are collapsing and the nets are too small to cover the beds. Some have satellite TV, and the food is good (and there's a bar), plus there's the bonus of an unusual garden with (dry) pools and artificial waterfalls adorned with sculptures of monsters and wildlife. Half-price in low season. **❸–❹**

Misitu and Kana

The **Misitu** and **Kana** areas, just east of the railway south of Ring Street, have a number of decent budget-range guest houses, as well as some popular bars and nightclubs. Walking around with a backpack is safe by day. The hotels are a ten- to twenty-minute walk west of the bus and daladala stands; alternately, if you're arriving in Tanga by public transport, you could ask the driver to let you off in Misitu by the Mangrove Management Project office. From here, cross the road, and take the path over the railway by the large mango tree. The *Ngorongoro Guest House* is about 300m along on the left, with the others down the road to your right.

Dolphin Inn Just east of the railway tracks on the signposted road to Pangani ☏027/264 5005. Probably the best hotel in this district, this modern and efficiently run establishment has thirteen rooms with nets, fans, tiled bathrooms, big beds and cotton sheets. There's also a hair salon. **❷**

Kiboma Ivory Inn 8th St ☏027/264 3578. Cheap and secure, but do check the mosquito nets for size. A handful of more expensive singles have private bathroom. Also has a quiet bar and very slow restaurant. Breakfast not included. **❶**

Malibu Guest House 8th St ☏027/264 7251. This is the same price as *Kiboma Ivory Inn* with the bonus of breakfast included, though not all rooms have bathrooms. Staff are reasonably friendly once you get past the language barrier, and there's a restaurant (but no alcohol). **❶**

Ngorongoro Guest House 8th St ☏027/264 3512. An excellent budget choice with large, clean rooms with private bathroom, fans, good showers, huge comfortable beds with cotton sheets and suitably sized nets. There's also a quiet bar, but the food is pretty average and the fish truly awful. **❷**

The Town

Apart from the harbour, there's no real focus to the older, colonial part of town, with most restaurants, hotels and businesses more or less evenly spread out over the four or five blocks inland from the bay. At times the place can feel almost deserted, incomprehensibly so until you realize that the main commercial centre is now the grid of colourful, crowded streets and haphazard structures around the bus station, 1km inland across the railway tracks, where the bulk of the population live and work.

In the colonial centre there's little to dispel the gently mouldering atmosphere, with a wealth of colonial-era buildings gradually succumbing to woodworm and verdigris, despite the sterling efforts of the Tanga Heritage Project (ⓦwww .geocities.com/urithitanga) to rescue Tanga's more impressive buildings. An

---

The Swahili People's Carnival

It's early days yet, but the first annual **Swahili People's Carnival**, held at Tanga's Mkwakwani Stadium over four days at the end of August and early September 2005, went off with a bang. Organized by Tanga-based NGO Tanzania ecoVolunteerism (TeV), it featured poetry, sports, and traditional music and dance (including *taarab* and Kidumbak), but also tackled a series of social concerns in workshops and conferences, from discussions on democracy and gender issues to the future of Kiswahili literature. All great fun, as well as enlightening. For more information, contact Tour Care in Tanga; see p.167.

aimless wander is always rewarding, as most streets contain a least a handful of beautiful and photogenic old buildings.

The German period is perhaps best represented by the restored neo-Gothic **Usambara Court House** on Usambara Street, formerly the German Governor's House. Other reminders of German times include the **clock tower** (1901), close by on Independence Avenue, and the **obelisk** in the adjacent Jamhuri Gardens, whose plaques commemorate German marines who died in the Abushiri War. The subsequent wars that the Germans were almost constantly engaged in are recalled by the **German War Cemetery**, at the corner of Swahili and Mpira streets, which contains the graves of 48 African soldiers and porters and sixteen German soldiers, including that of **Tom von Prince**, who commanded the German army's bitter 1894–98 campaign against Chief Mkwawa of the Hehe (see p.583), and died during the unsuccessful British assault of November 1914.

The British period, which coincided with the town's heyday between the two world wars, is represented by the attractive green-and-white gabled **railway station** on Ring Street, dating from 1930. Sadly, the dozens of rusty steam locos and carriages in the shuntings and sheds behind are currently fenced off, but the stationmaster should be amenable to the pleadings of ardent train buffs.

The cosmopolitan aspect of British rule is also reflected in the dozens of buildings throughout the town whose architectural style was influenced by Asians brought over by the British as coolies, who later became merchants and traders. The 1930 **Vila Esperança** (Villa of Hope) at the east end of Ring Street is a particularly fine example of this cross-cultural pollination, gracefully combining Goan and Art Deco styles with a hint of Portuguese. Its name reflects the wealth and high aspirations that Tanga enjoyed in the interwar years, before the collapse of the sisal market brought a sudden end to the town's golden age.

If you need a rest, there are two small parks: **Jamhuri Gardens**, overlooking the bay, benefits from a sea breeze and a children's playground, whilst two blocks inland, **Uhuru Park** has a few surviving benches under the trees arranged around a bizarre missile-like monument celebrating Independence.

Eating

Street food in the town centre is restricted to a handful of fruit stalls, coconut juice vendors and peanut and cashew pedlars rhythmically marking their presence with seed rattles. The area around the bus station has much more choice, and the narrow beach beside the canoe and dhow moorings just east of St Anthony's Cathedral is the best place for fried fish. The Anna Grocery on Chumbageni Police Road may not look like much but stocks occasional treats like feta cheese and pork. As for **restaurants**, there's not a huge choice, but what there is can be unusually good, and you can also find (rather average) *nyama choma* and *chipsi mayai* in most of the bars.

Cheriy Bites Independence Ave, next to CRDB bank. Basic snacks but great *supu* in the morning. Closed Sat afternoon and all day Sun. No alcohol.
Coffee Tree Bar Corner of Usambara and India streets. Local bar serving filling Tanzanian dishes like *ugali* with fish, or meat and banana stew (all around Tsh1000), with tables on a wide verandah outside.
Ferns Inn Usambara St. Friendly Goan-run place offering chips or *ugali* with meat, fish or squid (all

Tsh1000), prawns (Tsh2000) and curried or roast octopus (Tsh1500). A bargain.

Food Palace Market St. Always popular with expats and Asians, the menu isn't particularly extensive but the food is reliably good, including pizzas and Indian dishes (try the *nylon bhajia*, potato slices in batter), and there's a famous outdoor barbecue in the evening. It's good value too, with most mains under Tsh2500. Closed Mon evening.

Kiboko Campsite & Restaurant Off Bombo Hospital Road. A new Swiss set-up that's already garnered excellent reviews, particularly for its prawns. The tables are under individual thatched shelters in the garden.

Mkonge Hotel Bombo Hospital Rd. A surprisingly affordable restaurant given the surroundings, with most mains under Tsh6000, including fish and prawns, some pork, cheaper Tanzanian dishes, but boring vegetarian options. Don't forget the VAT.

Octopus Exotica Fast Food In the shipping crate next to the *Bandarini Inn* on Independence Ave. Serves up some truly delicious and cheap food, including octopus, prawns, kingfish and curry rice. Daily from 6pm.

P. Diana Coffee House Mkwakwani St. Up the narrow external staircase, this is a lovely breezy terrace (good street views) dishing up some rather good inexpensive nosh, including a number of Omani-style seafood dishes featuring cinnamon, cardamom and ginger. There's also a TV, and alcohol.

Patwas Mkwakwani St. Over forty years old, this famous Indian-run place is located in a bright and breezy old factory, and serves up good juices, milk shakes and snacks, but make sure they're fresh, as some sit around for days. Also full meals, including curries, for around Tsh4000. Closed Sun. No alcohol.

Rusharoho Mkwakwani St. Run by Tour Care next door, this new place has Swahili style at its heart, from food to decor, and also has an Internet café above.

Drinking and nightlife

You'll find plenty of **drinking** holes throughout town. The main **nightlife** focus is a cluster of lively bars and clubs in the Misitu and Kana areas between the railway and bus stand. At dusk and at night, take a taxi. Apart from the following, there are also sleepy bars at the *Mkonge*, *Raskazone* and *Panori* hotels in Ras Kazone. Most get busy after 8pm, and stay open until at least midnight.

Club La Casa Chica Top floor, Sachak House, Independence Ave. This popular, Western-style disco keeps out the rabble with its Tsh2000 entry fee (Tsh3000 for couples), though it has the worrying appearance of a fire trap. Wed & Fri–Sun from 9pm.

Coffee Tree Bar Corner of Usambara and India streets. Nice sleepy bar for an afternoon drink, with TV inside and tables on a wide verandah outside. Also serves decent food (see "Eating"), and has a pool table.

Dolphin Inn Around the corner from *Loliondo Gate*. A popular alternative to the *Loliondo* judging from the quantity of gold jewellery adorning the matron; also serves good *nyama choma*.

Ferns Inn Usambara St. Quiet place with seats outside in a small garden by the road; friendly and hassle-free.

Four Ways Hotel Market St. Large local dive on the first floor, especially busy on Wed & Fri–Sun when it rocks to cheerful Tanzanian and Congolese sounds. Food is limited to *nyama choma* and chip omelettes.

Harbours Club Off Bombo Hospital Rd. A pleasant bay-side venue that becomes really lively whenever they host a visiting band, whether *taarab* or *muziki wa dansi* (usually Fridays; around Tsh3000 entrance).

Le Club Tanzanite Chuda Rd, Misitu/Kana. A good place on Sunday evening for the latest in Bongo Flava and a smattering of hardcore hip-hop, interspersed with trashy US soul.

Loliondo Gate Facing the railway tracks in Misitu/Kana. A two-storey affair popular at night; its fresh *nyama choma* and live band (Wed & Fri–Sun from around 8pm) attract plenty of inebriated revellers of both sexes.

Listings

Airlines Coastal Aviation, airport ☏027/264 6548, town office at Hekim Travel Agency, Sachak House, Independence Ave facing the post office ☏027/264 6060.

Banks Quickest, but for cash only, is Boma Forex on Independence Ave, facing the post office. Better rates, for travellers' cheques too, but very slow are the banks: NBC, corner of Bank St and Sokoine Ave, is fastest and distinguishes itself with a 24hr Visa/MasterCard ATM.

Bicycle rental Bicycles can be rented throughout town, and via Tour Care. Standard price is Tsh2000/day.

Car repairs Akhtar Service, Mkwakwani St opposite *Patwas Restaurant*, has Land Rover spares.

Moving on from Tanga

By bus and daladala

Most **buses** depart early in the morning, the last ones generally leaving shortly after noon. The bus stand, along Pangani Road, has clearly defined bays signposted by destination, making the attentions of ticket touts easier to resist, but as ever it's best to buy your ticket the day before, when unencumbered by luggage – most ticket offices are around the bus stand. The safest bus company is Scandinavian Express, who run two buses a day to **Dar es Salaam**, and one to **Mombasa** (Kenyan visas are easily obtained at the border; $50 cash). Their office and "terminal" is on the south side of Mkwakwani Stadium on Ring Street (☏027/264 4337).

For other long-distance destinations, namely **Arusha**, **Dodoma**, **Morogoro** and **Moshi**, ask around beforehand as to the safest buses. At the time of writing, Simba Video Coach had a reasonable reputation (daily to Arusha via Moshi, and three times a week to Dodoma). The wildest route from Tanga is across the Maasai Steppe to Kondoa in central Tanzania: Mwambao Bus cover this twice a week in the dry season, taking over 24 hours (there's an overnight stop along the way).

To reach **Amani Nature Reserve**, you first need to get to Muheza on the Dar highway, either by catching any southbound bus along this route, or a daladala. Onward travel from Muheza is detailed at the end of Chapter 5. **Lushoto** is also covered by daladalas, whilst five buses a day ply between Tanga and **Pangani**.

By air

The easiest way to Zanzibar is by **plane**. Coastal Aviation have a daily service at 4pm, costing $55 to Pemba and $80 to Unguja. It finishes at Dar es Salaam ($100). A $5 departure tax is payable at the airport, off the Dar es Salaam highway 4km south of town. A taxi there costs Tsh3000.

By ferry or dhow

Tanga's **harbour** isn't the most user-friendly place on earth. The men hanging around waiting for casual labour can seem threatening, and you may even have trouble entering the place without paying a little *chai* to the guard on the gate. The best tactic is just to stride in with a purposeful air and, if stopped, explain that you have an appointment with the harbour master, who you will indeed be seeing.

Ferries to Wete (Pemba) are reliable only for being unreliable. At the time of writing, Mkunazini Shipping Enterprises was the only company operating the route regularly, using MV *Aziza I* or *II*, or the MV *Mudathir*. Departure days and times have stayed constant for some time (the inconsistency being cancellations), currently Tuesday at 10am, arriving in Pemba at 4pm the same day ($20 including port tax), before carrying on overnight to Stone Town ($30). It might also be worth enquiring about the MV *New Happy*, which occasionally extends its Dar–Stone Town–Pemba sailing to Tanga. There are no ferries to Mombasa (though this might change). The next sailing is usually chalked up on a board outside the harbour gate, or ask the harbour master.

The alternative is to arrange passage on a motorized **commercial dhow**, though this likely entails a joyless paperchase, and may not be possible at all if there's been political unrest on Zanzibar. It's also at your own risk, as engines frequently conk out, and dhows do occasionally capsize. For information, speak to the harbour master (☏027/264 3078), who should know which boats are going where, and when. The only payment, other than the fare to be negotiated with the dhow captain, is a $5 harbour tax. There's little chance of catching a dhow to Mombasa, as the immigration office – also at the port – is particularly obstructive about exit stamps.

Courier services DHL, Market St, opposite *Food Palace* ☎027/264 6523.

Hospitals Bombo Hospital, Bombo Hospital Rd ☎027/264 2997. Private clinics include Fazal Memorial Hospital, Independence Ave ☎027/264 6895, and Tanga Medicare Centre Hospital on the same avenue, which also has a dental clinic ☎027/264 6920.

Internet access There are Internet cafés all over, but many computers are infested with spyware or suffer from slow connections. Among the better ones (Tsh500/hr) are: TCCIA, Independence Ave facing Nasaco House (Mon–Sat 8am–8pm, Sun 10am–5pm); and Impala Internet Café, Market St (Mon–Sat 8.30am–10pm, Sun 9am–9pm).

Library Tanga Library (George V Memorial Library), in a lovely Arab-inspired building on Independence Ave, is surprisingly well stocked (Mon–Fri 9am–6pm, Sat 9am–2pm; daily membership Tsh500).

Police Off Independence Ave near Tanga Library ☎027/264 4519.

Post The general post office is on Independence Ave (Mon–Fri 8am–12.45pm & 2–4.30pm, Sat 9am–noon).

Shopping Woodcarvers sell their work in stalls facing the north side of the small produce market, between Market St and Independence Ave. The main market area is in the streets behind the bus station. There's a lively clothes market at the junction of Pangani Rd and 8th St on Tues, Thurs & Sat.

Swimming Tanga lacks a public swimming pool, but there are two swimming clubs along Hospital Rd: the Raskazone Swimming Club (Tsh500), with a tiled platform over the bay as well as a bar and restaurant, and the similar Tanga Bathing Club (same price), 300m further along. You can also reach the ocean from the roadside between the two clubs, down some short steep paths to a very narrow strip of sand, though being close to the town and still within the bay, the water is less than crystal clear. The closest clean stretch of shoreline is a few kilometres east of town at the end of Eckernforde Ave.

Telephones TTCL, at the post office on Independence Ave.

Travel agents Hekim Travel Agency, Sachak House, Independence Ave facing the post office ☎027/264 6060; Karimjee Travel, Nasaco House, corner of Independence Ave and Custom St ☎027/262 1099.

Around Tanga

There are a number of rewarding half-day trips in the vicinity of Tanga. Natural attractions include educational visits to nearby mangrove forests and the amazing limestone **Amboni Caves**, which can be combined with a soak in the **Galanos Sulphur Springs**. For a glimpse into Tanga's medieval past, a visit to the ruins and Shirazi tombs of the Swahili trading town of **Tongoni** is well worth the effort, while there are more Shirazi ruins on **Toten Island**, just off Tanga in the middle of the bay, though getting to the island can be a hassle (ask at Tour Care).

It's well worth taking a **guide** for Amboni and Galanos, as the access roads are poorly marked – Tour Care on Mkwakwani Street (see p.167) is the place to go. It's recommended that you combine your visit with a spot of **cultural tourism** with nearby communities. The additional cost is Tsh14,000 per

Mangrove forests around Tanga

Tanga's **mangroves** have been heavily depleted over the last few decades for use as building poles and fuel, as well as for the wood-intensive practice of boiling sea water to obtain salt. Working to counteract this trend is the **Mangrove Management Project** on New Korogwe Rd (Mon–Fri 7.30am–3.30pm; ☎027/264 2684), whose aims include protecting and replanting mangroves, and finding sustainable alternatives to mangrove use. They also help educate local communities about the importance of the forests, explaining their role as fish nurseries and filters for the fish-rich offshore reefs, and their function in preventing coastal erosion. The project is happy to arrange trips to existing or replanted mangroves and has two boats in Tanga and one in Pangani; you're expected to pay for fuel and, of course, a tip or donation would be appreciated – talk to the Zonal Mangrove Officer.

person per day, which includes the guide, lunch (with a local family), and visits to community projects including weavers and, curiously, the construction of ingenious fly-free toilets (the secret resides in blocking a "chimney"). If you're up to it, cycling is probably the best way around, though leave early to avoid the worst of the sun.

The Amboni Caves

With their winding passageways and galleries, dripping stalactites, weirdly shaped stalagmites, bat colonies and assortment of unlikely legends, the limestone **Amboni Caves** ("Mapango ya Amboni") are for many visitors one of the highlights of Tanzania. The caverns are thought to have formed during the Bathonian Period (176–169 million years ago), when sea levels were much higher than they now are, leading to inland limestone deposits. The caves cover an area of approximately fifteen square kilometres, making them the most extensive known cave complex in East Africa, and contain at least ten networks of caverns and passageways, one or two of which can be visited. There's no light, and even with a torch (the guide will have one) it takes a few minutes for your eyes to adjust to the obscurity. Bats (*popo*) live in the caves in colonies numbering tens of thousands, hanging upside down in enormous bunches for most of the day. If you hang around the entrance at sunset, you'll see clouds of the creatures fluttering out of the caves to feed. In most of the chambers the ground is very soft, the millennial product of accumulated bat droppings, which support numerous other animals including crickets, moths and spiders.

One cavern was allegedly used as a hide-out by a pair of local Robin Hoods during the 1950s Mau Mau insurrection in Kenya – Osale Otango (or Otayo) and Paulo Hamis – who, according to local legend, used to rob from the Europeans to give to the Africans. Otango was shot dead by the British in 1958. Your guide will probably show you the **Mombasa Road Cavern**, which is said to go all the way to the Kenyan port, and other passages which are rumoured to lead to Nairobi and Kilimanjaro. The last of these rumours originates from the tale of two Europeans who tried to explore the caves after World War II. They disappeared without trace, but their dog was found dead a few months later, 400km away outside another cave near Kilimanjaro. Sadly, these stories were scotched by a German–Turkish survey in 1994, which concluded that the longest of the caves extended no further than 900m from the entrance.

Of more genuine significance is the **Chamber of the Spirits** (*Mzimuni*), which is sacred to local people, who believe it to be inhabited by a force, represented by a snake, which can grant fertility to childless women, who come here to pray and leave offerings of food, money, flowers, goats or chickens. The floor of the chamber is littered with bottles, flags, charcoal and the remains of food. Another cavern, containing the chillingly named **Lake of No Return** (not always included in tours), is said to have been the place where the Digo tribe threw albino babies, which were believed to be a bad omen. Other attractions you might be shown include a miniature Mount Kilimanjaro (10m tall) and two natural "statues", one of the Virgin Mary, the other of the Statue of Liberty.

The patch of **riverine forest** above and around the caves is also of great interest, affording good bird- and butterfly-watching, as well as the chance to see members of a rare population of black-and-white colobus monkeys.

Practicalities

The caves are located near **Kiomoni village**, 8km north of Tanga and 2km off the Mombasa road, and are open daily from 9am to 4pm. They're managed by Tour Care in Tanga (see p.167); the village receives ten percent of the receipts.

The standard tour ($5, plus transport from Tanga and optional guide) includes three caves and takes around two hours. The longer "adventure tour" includes all eight caves and costs $10. The village operates a **campsite** near the caves, equipped with water, shower and toilet.

Galanos Sulphur Springs

Some 3km east from the Amboni Caves are the **Galanos Sulphur Springs**. The track from the Mombasa road is very poorly marked and becomes impassable in the rains, so a guide comes in useful – the springs are in any case usually tacked on to guided tours of the caves. Named after a Greek sisal planter, the springs are rarely visited and the small spa beside them has been derelict for years. It's possible to bathe in the hot, green and stinky waters, which are believed to relieve arthritis and cure skin ailments. Coming from Amboni, you have to cross the **Sigi River** by dugout canoe – your guide will arrange this for you. Crocodiles are sometimes found in the river here, depending on the ocean tide: high tide tends to push the crocs upriver. Needless to say, don't swim (though the springs are fine).

Tongoni

The atmospheric ruins of **Tongoni** (meaning "deserted village") lie just off Pangani Road about 20km south of Tanga. Comprising a mosque and over forty graves, the ruins are all that remain of a small but prosperous town which peaked shortly after being founded in the fourteenth and fifteenth centuries.

Although much smaller than contemporary ruins at Kilwa Kisiwani, Tongoni contains the largest collection of **Shirazi tombs** in East Africa, an indication of the prosperity it enjoyed before the arrival of the Portuguese disrupted the trading routes on which coastal towns like Tongoni depended. The settlement of Tongoni was mentioned by **Vasco da Gama** in April 1498 en route to India, when one of his ships ran aground on Mtangata (or Tangata) shoal near present-day Tongoni. Before they set sail they were visited by "Moors" from Tongoni who brought oranges which, according to da Gama, were better than those in Portugal. During the return voyage the following year his fleet spent fifteen days here, during which they scuttled one of their ships, as disease had reduced the fleet's manpower, and obtained domestic fowl from Mtangata in exchange for shirts and bracelets. According to later Portuguese sources, Tongoni was still a power to be reckoned with during the seventeenth century, when its rulers were friendly to the Portuguese, as they shared an enmity against Mombasa, which had become the most powerful sultanate on the coast.

The ruins have recently been taken over by Tour Care in Tanga (see p.167), who offer half-day trips including a cultural tour of modern Tongoni (roughly $20 per person including transport, entry fees and a cultural tour of the modern village), though the ruins are also easily visited by yourself: either cycle (leave early though), or catch a Pangani-bound **bus or daladala** from Tanga and get off at the modern village of Tongoni (no more than Tsh500), from where the ruins are a ten-minute walk towards the shore – you'll need to ask for directions. Leave early in the morning to be sure of having enough time to explore the site at your leisure; the last bus back from Pangani passes Tongoni around 5pm, but it would be unwise to rely on it as there's no accommodation nearby. The site is open daily from 9am to 4pm, and entrance costs $5. There's a caretaker on site, who – with luck – should also have photocopies of the 1975 booklet *A Guide to Tongoni Ruins* (by A.A. Mturi) for sale.

The ruins

The bulk of **the town** appears to have been situated to the north and west of the mosque, where the foundations of stone walls and a considerable quantity of pottery have been found, although much has been reclaimed by the ocean. The ruined **mosque** was cleared and excavated in 1958, revealing glazed blue *sgraffito* shards from the fifteenth century and a large amount of nineteenth-century pottery in the *mihrab* which archeologists speculate may have been used as offerings. Although the building measured just 12m by 13m, it was large for its time, though nowadays you'll need a lively imagination to picture what it might have looked like six hundred years ago. The roof disappeared long since and the east wall has collapsed, leaving only the remaining pillars, coral ragstone walls and the finely arched *mihrab*. On the south side is a transverse room the same size as the mosque, which was probably used by women. To the west is an extra structure which may have been a verandah (*baraza*), with windows in its west wall serving as ventilation. On the east you can still see coral stone bosses which were used for standing on when performing ablutions; a pillar tomb stands next to the ablution area.

Tongoni's **graveyard**, surrounding the mosque on three sides, contains over forty **Shirazi tombs** (many more have evidently succumbed to coastal erosion). About half of the tombs have been dated to the fourteenth century, when the Shirazi–Swahili civilization was at its height. These are characterized by their pillars, some square, others octagonal, which are contemporary with the mosque, though only one of them still stands intact. As with Kunduchi and Kaole, the recesses in a number of these pillars originally held Chinese or Islamic ceramic bowls, of which no trace remains. Other tombs bear traces of fine relief work, all testifying to the town's former riches. The extent of Tongoni's trading links were shown by one tomb which bore an imported glazed tile with a Persian inscription – the only example of Persian script ever found in East Africa – though this has scandalously been "lost".

The other tombs are rather crude in comparison, and date from Tongoni's brief revival in the eighteenth and nineteenth centuries, when it was occupied by migrants from Kilwa who rebuilt the houses and renamed the place *Sitahabu*, meaning "better than there". The walled double enclosure near the tomb, whose pillar has collapsed onto the east wall of the mosque, also dates from this period. It is revered by local people, especially barren women, who make offerings at the base of the grave, claiming the tomb belongs to a descendant of the Prophet Muhammad.

Pangani and around

Located at the mouth of the Pangani River 54km south of Tanga, the small and historic trading town of **PANGANI** is (thankfully) one of Tanzania's most underrated coastal destinations, boasting attractive sandy beaches, a friendly and laid-back atmosphere, and a wealth of atmospherically decaying colonial buildings dating from the time of the slave trade and German occupation. The town is also home to a community-based **cultural tourism programme** which offers a variety of guided walks and river cruises, plus snorkelling trips on an outrigger dhow and visits to fossilized dinosaur remains – a perfect place for a few days of blissful languor.

Pangani and Rhapta

According to some, Pangani's origins can be traced back almost two thousand years to the trading centre of **Rhapta**, which was mentioned in the *Periplus of the Erythraean Sea* (c.130–140 AD), an anonymous commercial guide which vividly recounts the considerable trade that flourished along the coast at that time. A fuller account of Rhapta, based on a report by the Phoenician geographer Marinus of Tyre about the journey of a Greek merchant named Diogenes, was given in Claudius Ptolemy's *Geography*, written a century or so later, in which the metropolis of "Rhaptum" marked the end of the known world. Beyond it, according to Ptolemy, lived *anthropophagoi* – cannibals. The identification of Pangani with Rhapta is given credence by Diogenes' claim to have "travelled for a twenty-five days journey [from Rhapta] and reached a place in the vicinity of the two great lakes and the snowy mountains from where the Nile draws its sources". Although doubted by experts, who consider 25 days too short a time to have reached Lake Victoria (700km distant) or Lake Tanganyika (1200km), never mind the Ruwenzori Mountains, the account nonetheless has a ring of truth to it: the very mention of two great lakes and snowy mountains at the very least proves that knowledge of the interior – and of the source of the Nile, which is indeed fed by the Ruwenzori Mountains via Lake Victoria – was a great deal more advanced in those times than it was in the nineteenth century.

Arrival and information

Apart from the road up from Saadani National Park, there are two roads to Pangani, one from Tanga, the other from Muheza. None are surfaced, and may require 4WD in the rains depending on how recently they were graded, especially the Muheza road which passes over easily waterlogged black cotton soil.

Coming from Tanga, five daily buses lurch along the bumpy road at roughly two-hour intervals (8am–4pm). Buy your ticket early to be assured of a seat. The road itself winds some distance inland through sparsely populated marshland (look for herons and other waders) and the extensive Kigombe Sisal Estate, then past small farming communities surrounded by ragged coconut groves. If you're staying at one of the beach hotels north of Pangani, ask the conductor to

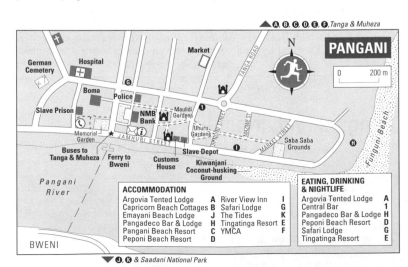

▲ **A**, **B**, **C**, **D**, **E**, **F**, *Tanga & Muheza*

PANGANI

N

0   200 m

German Cemetery

Hospital

Market

TANGA ROAD

Boma

Police

G

Slave Prison

NMB Bank

Maulidi Gardens

Uhuru Gardens

MAZ MU ST

MARKET STREET

Saba Saba Grounds

H

Funguni Beach

Memorial Garden

JAMHURI STREET

Buses to Tanga & Muheza

Ferry to Bweni

Customs House

Slave Depot

Kiwanjani Coconut-husking Ground

Pangani River

ACCOMMODATION

Argovia Tented Lodge	A	River View Inn	I
Capricorn Beach Cottages	B	Safari Lodge	G
Emayani Beach Lodge	J	The Tides	K
Pangadeco Bar & Lodge	H	Tingatinga Resort	E
Pangani Beach Resort	C	YMCA	F
Peponi Beach Resort	D		

EATING, DRINKING & NIGHTLIFE

Argovia Tented Lodge	A
Central Bar	1
Pangadeco Bar & Lodge	H
Peponi Beach Resort	D
Safari Lodge	G
Tingatinga Resort	E

BWENI

▼ **J**, **K** *& Saadani National Park*

drop you at the appropriate turning; otherwise stay on the bus until it reaches the ferry slipway by the river in town.

From Muheza, there's at least one daily bus during the dry season (2–3hr), plus a few battered Land Rover pick-ups and daladalas, which leave Muheza between 10am and 3pm – obviously, get there early to be sure of a ride. The Muheza road joins the Tanga road 4km north of Pangani; get off here for the beach hotels, which are to the north.

If you're heading to one of the lodges **south of the Pangani River**, the Shakila Bus leaves Tanga at noon and arrives in Pangani around 2.30pm, crosses the river to Bweni, and continues on to the fishing villages of **Sakara and Kipumbwe**. There's also a bus to **Mkwaja**, next to Saadani National Park, rumbling off from Bweni between noon and 1pm.

Information

You may well be met off the bus by guides, not all of them trustworthy. Ignore them as politely as you can and head 100m east to the **tourist office** (Mon–Sat 7.30am–4pm; no phone, ⓔ sekibaculturetours@yahoo.co.uk), which provides official guides and reliable advice about accommodation and restaurants. They can also arrange performances of traditional dancing on request, but the main purpose of the centre is to co-ordinate the town's highly recommended **cultural tourism programme**. In Pangani's case, the profits go to an educational trust which supports the district's neglected schools (there are currently 28 for a population of 44,000) and to build a hostel for schoolgirls who would otherwise be unable to afford both school fees and boarding.

The programme arranges a number of excellent **guided walks**, including a two-hour historical tour of Pangani, and an extensive agricultural and nature walk (which can be split into two separate walks), combining visits to local farmers, the coconut-processing area at the mouth of the river and the German fort on the opposite bank, sisal estates and the 200–300-million-year-old fossilized remains of dinosaurs, concluding with dinner in a local home. The walking tours cost Tsh6000 for the first person and Tsh3000 for each additional person up to a maximum of five (larger groups are assigned additional guides); the price includes guide fees and Tsh1000 per person for educational projects. Details of two boat trips organized by the programme are given on pp.185–187.

Pangani's **water supply** comes from two badly maintained boreholes: don't drink tap water as there have been cholera outbreaks in the past, though, having said that, it's a rare day when the water supply functions at all.

Accommodation

The **town centre** options are all pretty basic. If you're coming from Tanga, enquire with Tour Care there (p.167) about their hostel in Pangani, on the beach just south of *Pangadeco*, which costs $5 per person. Mid-range places are spread out along the coast **north of town** and are relatively accessible, whereas for the more upmarket options **south of town** you'll ideally have your own transport.

Four hotels allow **camping** in their grounds; rates include the use of toilets and showers. *Pangadeco* is the only central option, with an attractive plot right by the beach under plenty of shade (Tsh5000 per tent); 5km north, *Argovia Tented Lodge* has space for $5 per person, whilst least accessible but in by far the nicest location is the *Peponi Beach Resort* ($4 per person), 17km north of town, with a plot right on the sandy beach and with tents complete with bedding also available ($8–10).

Town centre

![runner icon] **Pangadeco Bar & Lodge** 1km east of the ferry at Funguni Beach ☎0748/369066 or 0748/504373. Pangani's best budget choice, on a large breezy beachside plot with plenty of tall trees, shaded seating and views over the ocean. Rooms, some en suite, are excellent value as long as you don't mind saggy beds. The Western-style toilets are reasonably clean, and the showers have Pangani's only guaranteed running water. There's also a good bar and food available to order. No single rates. ❶

River View Inn Jamhuri St, 500m east of the ferry ☎027/263 0121. A reasonable standby, though well past its prime, with nine basic and not totally clean rooms sharing grubby showers and squat toilets, and with nets and sheets too small for the larger double beds. The bars sells soft drinks only; meals available. ❶

Safari Lodge ☎027/263 0013. Very average, overpriced en-suite rooms, with Western-style toilets (but no seat or paper), shower and linoleum floors, though some rooms lack nets. The larger and more expensive rooms have huge beds and sofas, and there's also a (loud) bar and restaurant – see p.185. ❸

North coast

The following hotels are signposted off the Tanga road. Whilst they advertise themselves as "beach" hotels, all except *Capricorn* and *Peponi* occupy cliff-top locations, and the beaches below get covered at high tide. The water is clearer the farther north you go. All except the *YMCA* include breakfast.

Argovia Tented Lodge 6km north of Pangani on Mkoma Bay ☎027/263 0000, ⓦwww .argovia-lodge.com. This good-value and pleasingly idiosyncratic Swiss-run place occupies a breezy location with a stylish blend of traditional architecture and quirky modern touches. The cheaper rooms are in bunker-like prefabricated *bandas* with narrow twin beds and shared bathrooms. More expensive but more attractive (though they lack views) are the luxury tents on platforms under *makuti* roofs, each with a small verandah, box nets, table fans and attached bathroom. There's a swimming pool, a very good restaurant and a raft 1km out for swimming and sunbathing, while boating and snorkelling trips can be arranged (no fixed price). Half-board *bandas* ❺, tents ❻.

Capricorn Beach Cottages 17km north of town next to *Peponi* ☎0748/632529, ⓦwww .capricornbeachcottages.com. Relaxed and friendly, this has three secluded well-furnished self-catering cottages with ocean-facing verandahs, each with kitchen, hot water, showers, big beds with box nets and fans. Fresh flowers daily are a nice touch. Snorkelling and dhow trips can be arranged; there's also a barbecue area and email service, and of course *Peponi*'s excellent restaurant and bar is next door. ❻

Pangani Beach Resort Mkoma Bay, 4km north of Pangani ☎027/263 0088. A friendly place with ten clean if slightly musty and smallish en-suite rooms (no singles) in a motel-like environment, all with hot water, small twin beds (some triples also) and ripped linoleum floors, but no views. Also has a nicely sleepy bar, but no excursions. ❹

![runner icon] **Peponi Beach Resort** 17km north of Pangani, 30km south of Tanga ☎0748/202962, ⓦwww.peponiresort.com. A welcoming and well-run place offering comfortable and good-value two- to five-bed en-suite *bandas* set back from the beach, all constructed from mangrove poles, coconut leaves, fibre and sisal, each with a bathroom, standing fan and electricity, and most with box nets. There's also a gorgeously sited campsite on the beach (only one overland truck at a time), and delicious and reasonably priced food. The sandy beach is beautiful, there are mangroves nearby, and birding walks and *ngalawa* dhow snorkelling trips to a sandbank 6km out can be arranged ($8 an hour for the dhow plus $5 per person for equipment). ❺ (under 26s $14 each)

Tingatinga Resort Mkoma Bay, 4km north of Pangani ☎027/263 0022, ⓔtingatingapga@yahoo .com. Ten clean and very large circular rooms in semi-detached bungalows, all with twin beds, good bathrooms, plenty of furniture, fans and electricity, though they lack ocean views and nets (they're sprayed instead). Prices are negotiable, as indeed they should be given the starting price. ❹

YMCA 6km north of Pangani at Mkoma Bay ☎027/263 0044. Next to the *Argovia*, this place is getting pretty run-down and sees little trade, although the four large rooms are acceptable and good value; the better ones have private bathrooms (with showers and Western toilets), nets, twin beds, electricity, and verandahs with ocean views. No activities – arrange these at the *Argovia* or the tourist office. Simple food is available if ordered well in advance. No single rates. ❷

South coast

Facing Pangani across the river is the village of **BWENI**, to which a ferry (Tsh100) and small local boats cross frequently between dawn and dusk. Onward public transport to *Emayani Beach Lodge* and *The Tides* is limited to the noon bus from Tanga to Kipumbwe (leaves Bweni around 3pm), and the green "chicken bus" to Mkwaja, which heads off between noon and 1pm.

Emayani Beach Lodge 10km south of Pangani
℡027/264 0755, ⊛www.emayanilodge.com. A intimate and welcoming place set in a coconut grove on the beach with tidal pools, and plenty of activities including snorkelling, bird-watching (in nearby mangroves), river trips, windsurfing and sailing. All twelve cool and spacious thatched en-suite bungalows face the beach from their verandahs. Full-board. ❼

The Tides 16km south of Pangani
℡0741/325812, ⊛www.thetideslodge.com.

An intimate and frequently recommended place, classy but unostentatious, in a lovely beachfront location among palm trees. There are seven pale-blue, individually styled thatch-roofed chalets (all very attractive), a beachside bar, and an excellent open-sided restaurant with candlelit dinners. Activities include windsurfing and waterskiing, kayaking, river cruises, snorkelling, and licensed for game safaris to Saadani (book ahead). Free lift from Pangani. Closed May. Full-board. ❼

The Town

A walk in Pangani is always a pleasure – there are picturesque tumbledown buildings more or less everywhere, local children are invariably delighted to greet you (as are adults, for that matter), and the town's quiet and laid-back atmosphere makes for a pleasurably relaxing stroll at any time of day. All of which could hardly offer a greater contrast to Pangani's murky nineteenth-century history, when it served as a major slaving entrepôt – the town's very name, derived from the word *panga*, meaning to cut or divide, refers to the way in which auctioneers would separate slaves into groups before sale. Although Pangani is small enough to be walked around in an hour or so, it's sombre past is best understood as part of the cultural tourism programme's **historical walk** (see p.179).

The Boma and around

At the west end of town, the **Boma** – with its attractive carved doors – was built in 1810 by Mohamed Salim Breki, who decided that burying a live slave in each of its corners would ensure strong foundations (a belief that was also current in Zanzibar). The roof was added by the Germans, who used the building as their first district office, which remains its function today.

The **Slave Prison**, just to the southwest, was built by the Germans to house recalcitrant slaves (as well as tax evaders) – although the slave trade between the mainland and Zanzibar was officially abolished in 1873, slavery itself continued well into the British period, and was only completely eradicated in the 1920s. After this time, the building served as the district hospital, and is presently used as government offices and, once more, as a prison. There are plans to turn a couple of rooms into a local museum – ask at the tourist office.

The first Europeans to visit Pangani were the Portuguese in 1498, when a ship belonging to Vasco da Gama's fleet, the *São Rafael*, called in. The Portuguese met a chief called Makumba at Pangani's original centre at **Kumba**, 200m west of the Boma, and were well received and given food and water. The site of Kumba is now covered by the overgrown **German Cemetery**, containing several dozen graves. A handful were completely excavated a few years ago by locals in the belief that the Germans had buried treasure there, and most of the

△ Boy and girl in traditional Swahili doorway, Pangani

Pangani and the Abushiri War

Pangani's location at the mouth of Tanzania's second longest river, with its easy access to the interior, made it an obvious base from which to launch the German conquest of Tanganyika. In August 1888, a few days before the Muslim feast of Idd al-Hajj, **Emil von Zelewski** of the German East Africa Company appeared at the court of Abdulgawi bin Abdallah, the Omani governor of Pangani. To everyone's consternation, Zelewski proceeded to insult the governor by telling him that in a few days' time he, Zelewski, and not Abdulgawi would be the sultan's highest representative on the coast. True to his word, a few days later a small force of German soldiers entered Abdulgawi's quarters and removed the sultan's flag, taking it back to the German East Africa Company station house. Tensions rose, and the next day one hundred German marines landed and entered the mosque with their shoes and a hunting dog in their search of Abdulgawi, whom, not content with having humiliated, they now wanted to arrest.

The mosque's **desecration** (the very presence of non-Muslims, as well as dogs, would have been seen as such) not only turned people against the Germans, but undermined the credibility of the Omani rulers, who had failed to protect this sacred place from profanity. Deliberately or not, Zelewski further eroded Omani standing by breaking open the prison and releasing its inmates. By early September, local rage at both Omani impotence and the arrogant German presence had reached a point where the Germans had to be locked up by the Omanis in their company house for protection against the mob. They eventually slipped out to Zanzibar in the same week that they were expelled from Tanga. By the end of September, the Germans had been killed or expelled from all but two coastal enclaves – Dar and Bagamoyo.

The **expulsion of the Germans**, however, did nothing to placate local feelings against the Omanis, who now faced open rebellion. Having no military means of their own for putting down the rebellion, the Omanis tried to persuade the Germans to return and help restore Omani rule, even if only in diluted form. But by then the rebellion had turned into a fully fledged war against both Germans and Omanis, the **Abushiri War**, led in most towns by high-ranking Shirazis. The leader of the Pangani rebellion – by whose name the war is now known – was **Abushiri ibn Salim al-Harthi**, a wealthy Arab who united Arab traders and local tribes in a common effort to remove the Germans and the Omanis. By November, however, he had lost control of the rebellion and was forced to flee with a rump force to Bagamoyo, where he began a six-month siege of the town in a futile attempt to expel the Germans. In Pangani, the rebellion continued until July 1889, when it was brutally put down by German artillery. Abushiri was eventually captured by the Germans and hanged in Bagamoyo in December 1889. He was buried in an unmarked grave, some believe at Pangani, either in the grounds of the *Pangadeco Bar & Lodge*, or else in one of the mass graves which have recently been uncovered in the grounds of the Boma.

---

others have been vandalized. Some apparently date from the Abushiri War, but have lost their inscriptions.

The riverfront

Some 200m east of the Slave Prison, the small **memorial garden** facing the ferry slipway (where most guided walks start) contains a crumbling "pillar" commemorating the handful of Germans who died in the Abushiri War (surprisingly, no memorial exists to the thousands of African victims). The main building that survives from the German period is the **Customs House** on Jamhuri Street, five minutes' walk to the east along the riverfront. This imposing edifice took four years to build, opening in 1916 just before the Germans were kicked out. It's now used as a warehouse for coconuts, most of them from the Mauya plantations across the river – a legacy of the slave trade when cheap labour was plentiful – which constitute Pangani's main source of income. The Customs House's minor claim to fame is that the famous Swahili poet **Shaaban Robert** worked here as a customs official in the 1930s: his broken and rusty typewriter still sits in the office.

Almost next door, the **Slave Depot**, now derelict and close to collapse, used to have a whipping platform where slaves were punished, and a tunnel which led to the river for ferrying blindfolded slaves to the dhows. A particularly gruesome story about the building concerns the request of a slave-owner's wife to see an unborn child inside a woman's womb, for which a pregnant slave had her stomach sliced open while still alive.

The market and Uhindini Street

For an enjoyable detour, head up the street next to the Slave Depot to the **market**, a good place for buying an *mbuzi* – not a goat (though those are available too), but a coconut shredder. Properly called a *kibao cha mbuzi* ("goat board"), it resembles a small bookstand or foldable wooden chair, from one end of which – presumably resembling a goat's tail – protrudes a serrated metal spatula. You sit on the chair part and then grate off the flesh of half a coconut on the blade.

One street east of here is the road in from Tanga, whose southern continuation is called **Uhindini Street** (Indian Street). It's worth rummaging through the tailors' shops here, many of whose buildings date from the 1870s when Calcutta linen was the economic mainstay of the immigrant Indian community.

Kiwanjani and the beach

Back on the river, the area between Uhindini Street and the river mouth is called **Kiwanjani** ("the field"). This is where a team of around fifty workers dehusk giant mounds of coconuts with sharp iron crowbars, leaving behind a surreal debris of tens of thousands of coconut husks which are carried out to sea whenever the river floods. The dehusked coconuts are then stored in the Customs House before being transported by road to Dar es Salaam and other markets. The vast plantations in the area constitute about half of Tanzania's production.

Beyond the husking ground, either follow the shore itself as it curls north into Funguni Beach and the ocean proper, or follow the road a few hundred metres along to the *Pangadeco Bar & Lodge*, which also has access to the **beach**. Although the water doesn't look too enticing (the brown colour comes from the silt gathered along the river's 400km journey), it's apparently safe to bathe here. You should be extremely cautious of the river currents to your right however, as the Pangani pushes its waters out a good few kilometres before losing itself in the ocean. Local advice is to swim to the left of the beach, away from the river. At low tide you can walk almost 1km out to sea over the sand-flats, but keep an eye on the tide. It's apparently safe to walk up the beach to the *Pangani Beach Resort* (around 4km), but don't tempt fate by taking valuables or flashy sports shoes.

Eating and drinking

Apart from the rather pricey hotel restaurants north of town (for which you'll need transport in the evenings), **eating out** in Pangani itself is very limited, and unless you're content with chips or rice with fried chicken or fish, order early for specialities like prawns, lobster, octopus, parrotfish or kingfish. At the time of writing, Tanga-based Tour Care (see p.167) were planning to open a decent Swahili-themed restaurant on the riverfront, tentatively called the *Rusharoho* – it should be good, if indeed it happens. The cheapest eats are at the **foodstalls** along Jamhuri Street near the ferry, where you might find grilled octopus.

Given that Pangani is a mainly Muslim town, the ever-growing battalion of **bars** is quite a surprise, and source of considerable exasperation for the elderly **muezzin** of the main mosque, who is famous for his unusually blunt early morning exhortations to the not so faithful, starting with a strident series of loudspeakered "Amka!" ("Wake up!"), followed by a litany of colourful curses which invariably include the line "If you sleep now, your bed shall be your coffin and your sheets your shroud!"

Argovia Tented Lodge 6km north of Pangani. Slightly pricey but very good food, with light lunches at $5 and the full works at $12 for lunch or $15 for dinner (advance notice required for non-guests). There's the added bonus of genuine espresso and European and South African wines.

Central Bar Town centre. For good, cheap and filling portions of *nyama choma* (evenings), grilled chicken and *chipsi mayai*, this is definitely the place to be, and it stays open late. There are tables on the street corner verandah, a dartboard, cheerful music and satellite TV.

Pangadeco Bar & Lodge Funguni Beach. Enjoying an unbeatable beachfront location, this has plenty of tables under creaking trees in the gardens and a thatched main bar area, but without at least two hours' notice you're likely to find only chip omelettes, fried chicken and perhaps fried fish. Pre-ordered meat, fish or octopus or prawns cost Tsh2000–3000, depending on the season; *nyama choma* is available after 3pm. Also has cold beers, and hosts discos Wed, Fri & Sun (Tsh1500) playing an eclectic mix from *taarab* to Bongo Flava – there's a chilled-out if slightly tawdry atmosphere, thanks to the prostitutes who frequent the bar.

 Peponi Beach Resort 17km north of Pangani, 30km south of Tanga

⊤ 0748/202962, Ⓦ www.peponiresort.com. The region's best restaurant (and bar), especially for the glorious beachfront location, with its tables and chairs sinking into the soft sand under a broad *makuti* roof. The food's not half bad neither, and very reasonably priced for the quality (mains upwards of Tsh4500), with a great menu covering everything from toasts to Zanzibari-style coconut-sauced fish and a seafood platter (Tsh23,000 for two). There's also a dartboard, and a selection of South African wines. It's best to book ahead. Given the improvement of the road, it's possible to get there and back for lunch by public transport from either Tanga or Pangani.

Safari Lodge Town centre. Formerly the town's best restaurant, but nowadays mainly functioning as an (often loud) bar. The food remains reasonably priced though, with most dishes around Tsh2500–3500, all with fresh salad, or lobster or prawns for up to Tsh8000.

Tingatinga Resort Mkoma Bay, 4km north of Pangani. Good for seafood, though it's not cheap at upwards of Tsh6000 a plate for fish, Tsh7500 for prawns, and Tsh9500 for lobster. They also offer a seafood barbecue including lobster for Tsh15,000, for which you'll need to order a day in advance.

Listings

Banks NMB bank, 100m from the ferry, changes cash and travellers' cheques.

Bicycle rental This can be arranged via the tourist office; at the bicycle shop on Uhindini St; or at *Tingatinga Resort* north of town. Costs average Tsh2000 per day.

Hospital The reasonably well-equipped district hospital is 200m west of the *Safari Lodge*.

Post office On the same block as the tourist office, 100m east of the ferry.

Telephones TTCL, 200m west of the ferry on the riverfront.

Around Pangani

The cultural tourism programme's **Coconut Sunset Cruise** (Tsh30,000 up to eight people; 1–2hr) starts with a tour of the coconut husking grounds by the river mouth, then – boarding the boat on the beach – the cruise heads up

Moving on from Pangani

Leaving Pangani, the first **buses** and **daladalas** for both Tanga and Muheza leave between 6am and 6.30am. You should definitely catch one of these if you're heading to Muheza or south to Dar, to be sure of finding onward transport. Both the bus and daladala to Muheza arrive in time to catch the early buses from Tanga to Dar; spare seats are reserved on these for passengers getting on in Muheza, so buy your onward ticket as soon as you arrive. The last guaranteed vehicle to Muheza leaves at 8am. The last bus to Tanga departs at 4.30pm; it's best not to rely on it though. If you're **driving**, there's an adventurous and infrequently travelled route south of Pangani into Saadani National Park (see p.163 for details).

Getting a passage from Pangani on a **dhow to Zanzibar** (either to Mkokotoni or, more usually, Nungwi village, both at the northern tip of Unguja Island) is relatively straightforward, with at least two motorized dhows sailing each week, taking four hours if things run smoothly – ask at *Pangadeco Bar & Lodge*. The cost varies between Tsh10,000 and Tsh15,000 per person depending on the number of passengers. Dhows do occasionally capsize, however; it's only a slight risk but one to bear in mind nonetheless.

the Pangani River and past mangroves and coconut plantations. The mangroves are rich in birdlife, especially pied kingfishers, which are most active just before dusk. If you're lucky you might also see colobus monkeys and crocodiles, though the latter are less common since the El Niño floods of 1991 and 1997–98 widened the estuary and caused the waters to become more saline. Your best chance of spotting them is around noon, which is a bit awkward as most river cruises take place over the two hours before sunset, starting around 4pm, when it's cooler and you've more chance of spotting other wildlife. The tour concludes with juice from a freshly picked coconut (*madafu*) as the sun sets over the river.

Maziwe Island Marine Reserve

Maziwe Island, 8km southeast of Pangani, is a prime example of the effects of both mangrove clearance and rising sea levels. Until the 1960s the island was totally wooded with casuarina trees and fringed with mangroves, while its beaches served as East Africa's single most important nesting ground for three species of endangered marine turtles: the Olive Ridley turtle, green turtle and hawksbill turtle. By 1976, however, the last casuarina had been felled, and the final blow to the island's ecology came during the 1978–79 war with Idi Amin's Uganda, when the remaining mangroves were cleared away for security reasons, given the island's proximity to Pangani, Zanzibar and Pemba. Sadly, the mangroves have not rerooted, and the ensuing erosion means that the island is now submerged at high tide. The beaches are still being eroded, especially during the southeastern monsoon, though the island's disappearance is attributed by fishermen to rising sea levels.

The surrounding live **coral reef** has also been badly damaged by dynamite fishing and careless anchoring, though there are still some stunning coral heads providing food and shelter for dozens of beautiful tropical fish species (including moray eels, the poison-barbed lion fish, butterfly fish, clownfish, starfish and octopus), and the added attraction of a school of dolphins which can be seen feeding regularly a few hundred metres out.

Heading out to the island from Pangani, notice the **German fortress** at the mouth of the estuary on the south bank of the river, half-hidden by heavy tree cover and bush. A few kilometres out, you cross the unusually well-defined border between the brown estuarine waters and the clear blue of the ocean, a boundary which is also marked by a line of floating coconut husks and other debris from Pangani.

The trip out to the island is usually by motorboat (Tsh50,000 for the boat), although you could rent a *ngalawa* outrigger instead (Tsh10,000–15,000), albeit at your own risk. Outriggers take ninety minutes, the motorboat about half that. Mask and snorkel rental is Tsh2000. A **marine park fee** of Tsh1000 may be asked for. The trip can be arranged through the cultural tourism programme or the *Pangadeco Bar & Lodge*.

Travel details

Buses and daladalas

The bus companies Hood, Tashriff, Takrim and Tawfiq have particularly bad reputations for reckless driving and should be avoided. The long rains, when some services cease, are usually from March to May. Services may also be cancelled at times during the short rains (usually November, and sometimes October or December), though rarely for more than a day or two.

Bagamoyo to: Dar (hourly; 90min); Msata (1–2 daily except in the rains, 2–3hr).

Pangani to: Muheza (2 daily except in the rains; 2–3hr); Tanga (5 daily; 2–3hr).

Tanga to: Arusha (6 daily; 6hr); Dar (6–8 daily; 6hr); Kondoa (2 weekly dry season only; 26hr); Korogwe (hourly; 90min); Lushoto (every 2hr until mid-afternoon; 3hr); Mombasa (4 daily; 4–7hr); Mombo (hourly; 2hr); Morogoro (every 2hr until noon; 5–6hr); Moshi (3–4 daily; 5hr); Muheza (every 30min; 45min); Pangani (5 daily; 2–3hr).

Dhows

For information on catching dhows to Pemba or Unguja (Zanzibar), see the boxes under Bagamoyo (p.158), Pangani (opposite) and Tanga (p.173).

Ferries

Tanga to: Wete, Pemba (weekly; 6hr); Stone Town via Pemba (weekly; 20hr).

Flights

Airline codes used below are: CA (Coastal Aviation) and ZA (ZanAir).

Saadani to: Dar (ZA, 1–2 daily; 30min).

Tanga to: Dar (CA: daily; 1hr 35min); Pemba (CA: daily; 30min); Zanzibar (CA: daily; 1hr 10min).

3

The south coast

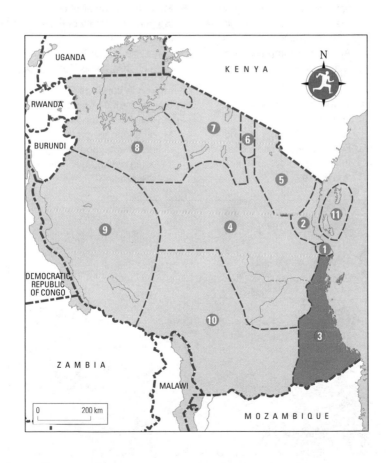

CHAPTER 3 # Highlights

✳ **Mafia Archipelago** This little-visited marine park protects superb coral reefs, justly famed for their superb scuba-diving. **See p.196**

✳ **Kilwa Kisiwani** In medieval times the wealthiest city on the Swahili coast, this ruined medieval island state is one of Africa's most impressive and historically significant sites. **See p.211**

✳ **Kilwa Kivinje** Atmospheric and very tumbledown nineteenth-century slaving harbour, whose rise signalled the demise of Kilwa Kisiwani. **See p.219**

✳ **Mnazi Bay-Ruvuma Estuary Marine Park** Superb beaches, snorkelling and scuba-diving along the border with Mozambique, and virtually no other visitors. **See p.233**

✳ **Mikindani** Another old slaving port with plenty of ruins, a pleasantly laid-back atmosphere and one of Tanzania's nicest hotels. **See p.235**

✳ **Makonde carvings** The Makonde tribe of southern Tanzania and northern Mozambique are famed for their abstract woodcarvings, including remarkable "trees of life". **See p.242**

△ Gereza Fort, Kilwa Kisiwani

The south coast

T he **south coast** is one of Tanzania's most fascinating and unspoilt regions, containing a wealth of infrequently visited natural and historical attractions, as well as beaches to dream about, although the lack of infrastructure and facilities makes exploring it a challenge.

Road access from Dar is still determined by the **Rufiji River**, which floods its delta – and part of the road – every year. The delta contains East Africa's largest mangrove forest, and would be a paradise for bird-watchers were travelling around not so difficult. Some 25km offshore, **Mafia Island** is home to some of the south coast's best beaches, as well as the stunning coral reefs of **Mafia Island Marine Park**, justly famed for superb diving.

Beyond the delta, the first settlements of note are the three Kilwas: the tumbledown town of **Kilwa Kivinje**, steeped in the history of nineteenth-century slavery and colonial oppression; **Kilwa Masoko**, the main base for visitors, now with a handful of beach hotels; and the island of **Kilwa Kisiwani**, whose ruined medieval city ranks amongst Africa's most impressive historical sites.

Further south are the pleasant harbour towns of **Lindi** and **Mtwara**, although a more atmospheric place to stay is **Mikindani**, a fishing village that retains a number of historic buildings, and whose German Boma has been converted into one of Tanzania's most attractive hotels. Mikindani is also the best base from which to explore **Mnazi Bay-Ruvuma Estuary Marine Park**, whether by road, boat, or underwater by diving or snorkelling.

Rising inland from Lindi and Mtwara is the **Makonde Plateau**, home of the famous woodcarving tribe. The main town here is **Newala**, its relatively cool climate a boon to those wearied by coastal heat and humidity.

The generally **abysmal roads** explain why the coast has largely been ignored by developers, and if creature comforts are important to you, it's best to look elsewhere. The roads will leave you literally battered and bruised, luxuries like electricity and running water are rare outside the major towns, **malaria** is rife (remember to pop those pills), and few places have more than a handful of rudimentary hotels. Indeed, even camping is not without its hazards – **man-eating lions** haunt patches of woodland and forest throughout the region, so seek local advice before pitching. But the rewards are many, and for the time being at least, any trip along the south coast retains a heady, dusty and bone-rattling aura of adventure.

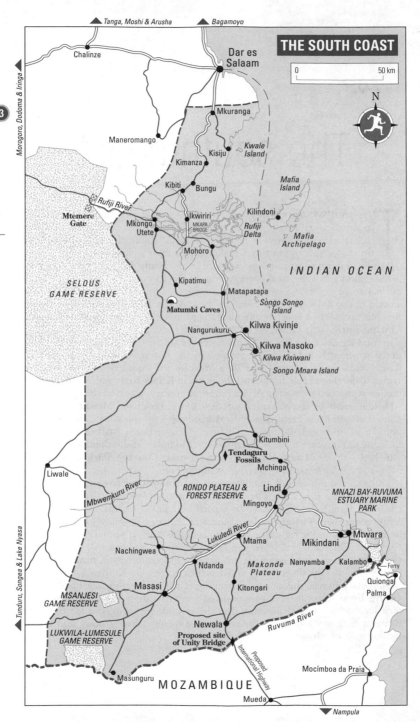

▲ *Tanga, Moshi & Arusha*   ▲ *Bagamoyo*

THE SOUTH COAST

0   50 km

N

Chalinze

Dar es Salaam

Morogoro, Dodoma & Iringa ▲

Mkuranga

Maneromango

Kisiju

Kwale Island

Kimanza

Mafia Island

Kibiti   Bungu

Rufiji River

Mtemere Gate

Mkongo Utete

Ikwiriri

MKAPA BRIDGE

Kilindoni

Rufiji Delta

Mafia Archipelago

Mohoro

INDIAN OCEAN

SELOUS GAME RESERVE

Kipatimu

Matumbi Caves

Matapatapa

Songo Songo Island

Nangurukuru

Kilwa Kivinje

Kilwa Masoko

Kilwa Kisiwani

Songo Mnara Island

Kitumbini

Tendaguru Fossils

Liwale

Mbwemkuru River

Mchinga

RONDO PLATEAU & FOREST RESERVE

Lindi

Mingoyo

MNAZI BAY-RUVUMA ESTUARY MARINE PARK

Tunduru, Songea & Lake Nyasa ▲

Lukuledi River

Mtama

Mikindani

Mtwara

Nachingwea

Ndanda

Makonde Plateau

Nanyamba

Kalambo

Ferry

Masasi

Kitongari

Quionga

Palma

MSANJESI GAME RESERVE

Newala

Proposed site of Unity Bridge

Ruvuma River

Proposed International Highway

LUKWILA-LUMESULE GAME RESERVE

Mocímboa da Praia

Masunguru

MOZAMBIQUE

Mueda

▼ *Nampula*

The Rufiji River delta and Mafia archipelago

The estuarine delta of Tanzania's largest river, the **Rufiji**, is one of the country's most important and sensitive ecological areas, containing East Africa's largest mangrove forest as well as seasonally flooded woods, saline swamps, tidal marshes and sandbanks. This largely unspoiled wilderness – recently declared a Wetland of International Importance under the RAMSAR Convention – forms an integral part of a much larger ecosystem running from the western woodlands of the Selous Game Reserve (see Chapter 4) to the coral reefs around **Mafia Island**, 25km offshore. The reefs, which are supported by fresh water and nutrients filtered through the Rufiji's mangroves, enclose what is probably East Africa's most diverse marine environment, offering near-perfect conditions for diving and snorkelling.

Unfortunately, neither area is easy to explore. **Road access** to the floodland south of the Rufiji is subject to the rains, whilst the Mafia archipelago is only reachable by **plane** unless you have the patience – and resilience – to brave the dhow crossing from Kisiju, 90km south of Dar. Still, both areas more than repay the inconveniences and costs of getting there and around.

The Rufiji River delta

The **Rufiji River delta** is one of East Africa's most beautiful and ecologically significant areas, though it's also every bit as hot, swampy and mosquito-infested as you might imagine. The delta contains seasonally flooded woods alive with the sound of frogs, birds and cicadas, along with East Africa's largest **mangrove forest**, covering some 5300 square kilometres. This acts as a gigantic sump, supplying the fragile reefs offshore with nutrients whilst protecting them against siltation. The delta and its floodplain support a population of over 150,000 people, the majority subsisting on cultivation, fishing and mangrove-pole extraction. During the long rains, the river can increase in width by up to fifteen kilometres: the silt carried by the floods fertilizes the land on either side of the river and feeds innumerable small lakes and pools in which a number of unique **fish** species have been found, while the waters around the mangroves themselves are an important breeding ground for prawns and shrimps. Commonly seen **birds** include the plain-backed sunbird, longbills, lovebirds and the majestic African fish eagle. Rarer species include the African pitta, found north of the river, and Livingstone's flycatcher, to the south.

Unsurprisingly, the delta's natural wealth has attracted the gaze of big industry, and the area is coming under increasing pressure from logging and fishing companies, something that the new $25 million **Benjamin Mkapa Bridge** over the Rufiji is likely to facilitate. The discovery of oil reserves north of the river also raises cause for concern. The greatest threat to the delta's environment came in the 1990s, however, when an Irish businessman proposed a $200 million **prawn farm**, the world's largest, which would have destroyed 1100 square kilometres of mangrove forest, degraded and polluted the land and water

△ Aerial shot of the Rufiji River

Transport along the south coast

The south coast's main problem is **transport**. Although work is under way to asphalt the Dar–Mtwara highway, the 2005 completion date passed by unnoticed, and even the revised 2007 target seems a mite optimistic. The trickiest section is the 50km stretch south of the Rufiji River to past Mohoro, which becomes extremely muddy and occasionally impassable during – and for a few days after – heavy rains. The accolade for the **worst road in Tanzania**, however, goes to the "highway" between Masasi and Songea in the far south, especially the second day's drive west from Tunduru – the route description is given in Chapter 10.

Off the north to south highway, you can get to most places in the dry season, although dirt roads can make for an exceedingly uncomfortable experience, especially if you're late in buying a bus ticket – get it 24 hours before to ensure you don't get plonked over the rear wheels, which is much worse than the meanest fairground ride. If you're **self-driving**, have your vehicle checked out thoroughly before setting out, and get it checked after particularly rough stretches – mechanics (*fundis*) can be found at bus stands. A degree of mechanical competence on your part is recommended, as is off-road experience; also read the advice on p.45. If it's likely to rain, check the state of the road with every driver you meet, and be prepared to stay wherever you are for at least an extra day after the rains stop to give the road time to dry out (or two or three days after a particularly heavy downpour).

In very heavy rains (usually March–May), roads are likely to be blocked. During this time, and until the asphalt ribbon from Dar is complete, **flying** from Dar or Zanzibar to Kilwa, Lindi or Mtwara, or catching the weekly **ferry** from Dar to Mtwara, are your only options.

---

supply on which 33,000 villagers depend, and displaced 6000 people. Despite the condemnation of the National Environmental Management Council, the government approved the project, prompting an international outcry. Local people took the company to the High Court and, after a four-year battle, the project was abandoned in 2001, to the jubilation of the villagers and environmentalists alike.

It's possible **to visit the delta by boat** from Mafia Island, but this needs to be arranged in advance, either with *Kinasi Lodge* (p.200) or with local boatmen in Kilindoni, who occasionally sail into the delta to collect mangrove poles. It isn't always plain sailing, in any sense, as the sea can become rough, especially when the monsoon changes direction between July and August. The best chance for calm seas is during the northerly *kaskazi* monsoon (Nov–March). On the mainland you might be able to rent a boat in Mohoro (see below). Both possibilities are very hit and miss, however.

South from Dar to Mohoro

Until the road south of the new bridge is fully surfaced, the south bank of the Rufiji is as far as you can travel by road from Dar during the heaviest of the long rains, usually from March to May. The road north of the river is mostly sealed, though some sections are in a pitiful state and can wreck a vehicle if you're not careful. There's a string of settlements along the way, all with small markets, bars, simple restaurants and guest houses, fuel "stations" (usually decanted into plastic bottles), and hawkers aplenty selling mangos, coconuts, smoked fish and improbably giant jackfruit.

The sealed road currently peters out 10km **beyond the Rufiji River**. The subsequent 50km of road – either very muddy or very dusty – is tiring to drive and can be impassable after heavy rain, as it crosses through a thick and swampy flood forest. Here and there you pass tiny, improbable settlements placed in small isolated clearings where the ground rises just a metre or two above the swamps, but for the most part the forest canopy is almost complete, providing a haven for plentiful **birdlife**, including pretty sunbirds.

The small Muslim village of **MOHORO** is the first place of any size beyond the river. Set on a creek on the southernmost branch of the delta, the village has plenty of *mgahawa* restaurants (but no petrol), and very basic, dirt-cheap **rooms** at the *6-Hotel* (❶), with nets, shared long-drops, and a large water barrel to shower with. Mohoro is potentially a perfect place from which to head off into the delta by boat, although you officially need a permit from the district commissioner in Utete; you could try asking at the village clinic, which has a number of boats. For **forest walks**, the tiny Forest Office on the road out towards Kilwa may oblige with an unofficial guide; a generous tip would be in order. The rough road continues for some 20km beyond Mohoro before reverting to a sealed surface, taking you all the way to Kilwa.

The Mafia archipelago

Lying 25km off the Rufiji delta, the **MAFIA ARCHIPELAGO** − consisting of Mafia Island, the smaller islands of Chole, Juani and Jibondo, and a host of minor isles and atolls − is surrounded by one of the world's richest marine habitats, much of it protected as **Mafia Island Marine Park**. The coral reefs here are among the world's most enthralling **scuba-diving** areas, while the archipelago's **beaches** provide an additional draw.

Mafia's attractions are not all marine, however: **terrestrial wildlife** includes duiker antelopes, monkeys, wild pigs, bushbabies and black-and-rufous elephant shrews, all of which might be seen in the few remnants of coastal forest that dot the islands. There are even some dwarf hippos, whose ancestors were presumably swept out to sea by the Rufiji's floods. **Birdlife** is plentiful too, with some 130 species, including falcons, fish eagles and waders. Historical interest is provided by a number of **ruins**, notably at Kua on Juani Island and Chole Mjini on Chole Island. Awkward **access** means that Mafia sees little tourism outside the main diving and sports-fishing seasons (Nov–March), and all the upmarket beach lodges are closed in April and May.

Some history

Excavations of **Iron Age forges** suggest that Mafia's earliest inhabitants were Bantu farmers who crossed over from the mainland no later than 200 AD, and from whom the present-day Mbwera tribe are believed to be descended. Around this time, the still-to-be-located mainland port and metropolis of **Rhapta** (possibly near Pangani, see box on p.178) was governed by a Yemeni people called the Ma'afir, who probably also ruled over Mafia, giving a possible source for the archipelago's name. An alternative is *maafya*, meaning "healthy place" in Kiswahili, but the most likely derivation is from the Arabic *morfiyeh* (archipelago), which appears misspelt as *monfiyeh* on sixteenth-century Portuguese charts.

The archipelago's geographical position made it a natural stopover for Arab and Persian dhows plying the ancient trade routes between Arabia and East Africa. Finds of pottery, coins and glassware indicate that Mafia was a regular part of the monsoon-driven Indian Ocean trading network which, in its

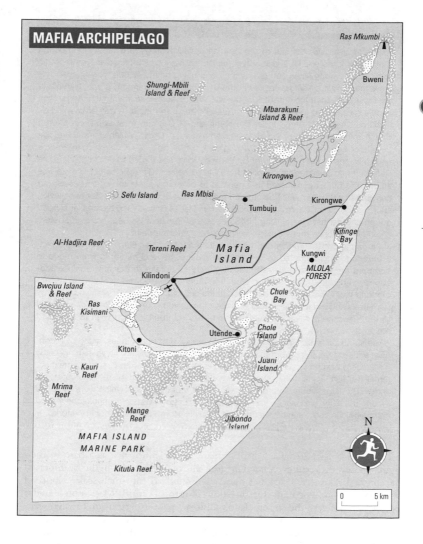

heyday, stretched as far as Malaysia, Indonesia and even Ming-dynasty China. Following the **conquest** of Mafia by the Portuguese captain Duarte Lemos in 1508, Mafia's fortunes entered a long period of decline, culminating in the destruction of Kua, the island's main town, by the cannibalistic Sakalava of Madagascar in 1829. The archipelago's fortunes revived briefly after 1840 under the control of the Zanzibari **Busaidi dynasty**, whose slaving and ivory trading interests left an indelible impression, not least in the establishment of slave-worked coconut plantations on Mafia Island, most of which survive today. But the days of the slave trade were numbered and the balance of power was shifting towards Europe; in 1890, the year Britain imposed a protectorate over Zanzibar, Sultan Seyyid Ali was forced to sell Mafia to Germany for four million marks.

The Königsberg's last stand

The Rufiji delta was the site of the German cruiser **Königsberg**'s last stand during World War I, the end of a pursuit by the British navy which lasted eleven months, tying down twenty ships and ten aircraft, and using nearly 40,000 tons of coal. The importance of the *Königsberg* lay in the fact that it was Germany's only warship in the Indian Ocean at the outbreak of the war, and as such was able to threaten British supply routes from Kenya, Zanzibar, Aden (Yemen) and India. A day after war was declared, the *Königsberg*, under the command of **Captain Max Looff**, captured a British freighter, the *City of Winchester*, off the coast of Oman, which was scuttled five days later. Despite taking on the *Winchester*'s coal supply, the *Königsberg*'s reserves were low, and at the beginning of September Looff was forced to seek shelter in the Rufiji delta, to await further supplies from Dar es Salaam. The choice of the delta was astute: the British considered its channels to be unnavigable to larger vessels, not knowing that the Germans had charted the delta just before the war. After two weeks, sufficient coal supplies had been brought from Dar es Salaam and the cruiser slipped out on another mission, sinking HMS *Pegasus* at Zanzibar on September 20, before engine failure once more forced the *Königsberg* into the delta.

It took the British a further five weeks to locate the cruiser, 8km upriver, after which a **blockade** was mounted to prevent her escape. Several attempts were made to bombard the ship using aircraft, but they were so unreliable that their main preoccupation appeared to be staying aloft. The much mythologized gentlemanly aspect of World War I was aptly demonstrated at the end of the year: "We wish you a Happy Christmas and a Happy New Year; we hope to see you soon," the HMS *Fox* signalled to the *Königsberg*. "Thanks, same to you," replied Looff, "if you wish to see me, I am always at home."

The stand-off lasted until July 1915, when a couple of brief battles, aided by recon-naissance planes flying from the recently captured Mafia Island, finally damaged the *Königsberg* beyond repair. The cruiser was scuttled on 11 July and sank into the mud, remaining visible until 1962, when the wreck was salvaged and the remains cut up for scrap. The largest surviving relics are a pair of four-inch guns which were removed before the ship was sunk, and used in Von Lettow Vorbeck's subsequent land campaign. One now stands outside Fort Jesus in Mombasa, the other in Pretoria.

The British seized Mafia from Germany in 1915, for use as a base in their fight against the cruiser *Königsberg* (see above), after which the archipelago became a backwater. Trade is nowadays limited to the small-scale export of fish, seaweed and coconuts. Despite this fall into obscurity, Mafia's present-day population reflects the archipelago's historic past. Apart from the Mbwera, inhabitants include Shirazis, Shatiri Hadhramaut Arabs, Omanis, Indians, assimilated descendants of traders from Madagascar and the Comoros Islands, and descendants of slaves from the Yao, Nyasa, Ngindo and Pokomo peoples, the latter originally from Kenya. More recent immigrants include Pakistani Baluchi on the south side of Mafia Island near Kitoni, who arrived in the nineteenth century as members of an expedition sent by the sultan of Zanzibar, and Makonde, who settled in Utende village as recently as 1991, having fled Mozambique's civil war.

Arrival and island transport

The Mafia archipelago is most easily reached **by plane** from Dar es Salaam, but with plenty of patience – and a strong enough stomach – you could arrange a lift by **dhow** from Kisiju on the mainland, to Kilindoni on Mafia Island. The **ferry** which used to connect Mafia with Dar es Salaam and Mtwara ceased operation years ago but it might be worth enquiring in Dar in case things change. It's best to change **money** before coming: the NMB bank in Kilindoni claims to change travellers' cheques, but you never know.

By air

Mafia airport is on the edge of Kilindoni, a five-minute walk away. Coastal Aviation (☎023/240 2552) have an office at the airport, and fly daily from Dar es Salaam ($80) via Kilwa, and have onward links to Dar, Kilwa ($70), Selous ($120), Songo Songo Island ($50) and Zanzibar ($100). **Hiring a plane** from Dar (see charter airlines on p.127) starts at $476 for a five-seat Cessna.

By dhow

The adventurous way of getting to Mafia is by dhow from the mainland fishing village of **Kisiju**, 91km south of Dar. You might have to deal with petty official-dom in Kisiju, who will try to discourage you with tales of missing or capsized boats, most of them true (if rare). **Getting to Kisiju** from Dar involves catching a bus towards Kibiti, Utete, Lindi, Mtwara or Masasi. Get off at Mkuranga, 46km south of Dar, where crowded and uncomfortable pick-ups run the remaining 45km to Kisiju along a sandy and bumpy road (2hr 30min). Several dhows sail to and from Kilindoni each day or night, depending on the tide, sometimes stopping en route at Kwale and/or Kome Islands, 1km and 10km from Kisiju respectively. **Departure times** depend on weather conditions and the tide, as the sandbar at the river mouth allows passage only at high tide, so you may well have to spend the night in Kisiju. There are a handful of rudimentary **guest houses**, but the village has a reputation for pickpockets and petty thieves, so take care. One last piece of advice: empty your bowels in Kisiju unless you fancy testing the cantilevered contraptions over the side of the vessels.

   Motorized dhows are quickest (8–12hr if the engines don't give out), but they're usually grimy. **Sailing dhows** take up to 24 hours, longer if the winds aren't right or the sea's rough: take more than enough food and water for the journey. **Fares** depend on what you arrange with the captain: locals pay upwards of Tsh3000-5000 for space on a sailing dhow or Tsh8000 on a motorized one.

Island transport

Public transport on Mafia Island is limited to a handful of **daladalas**, the main one of interest to tourists being the daily run between Kilindoni and Utende (Mon–Sat only), close to the Chole Bay beach hotels. It leaves Utende around 7am, and returns from Kilindoni at around 1pm. The Chole Bay hotels can arrange transport to meet flights ($10 per person if not included in room rates). If you're not being picked up, you could try catching a lift with one of these vehicles for the same price. Alternatively, *Mafia Pwani Camp* in Kilindoni offers a day-trip for $25 (excluding park fees), and *New Lizu Hotel*, also in Kilindoni, can fix you up with a **bicycle**, should you be immune to the wearying heat and humidity. Transport to Chole, Juani and Jibondo islands is from Chole Bay.

Accommodation and information

West is best if you're on a budget, with **Kilindoni** containing the archipelago's only cheap accommodation. Mafia's **beach hotels** (all closed April & May) are located on the eastern side of the island within the marine park boundaries, and are decidedly upmarket: three of them face **Chole Bay**, 14km east of Kilindoni and about 2km beyond Utende village; the fourth is on **Chole Island**, 1km inside Chole Bay. Chole Bay's sandy beaches and warm, reef-protected waters are ideal for swimming and water sports, and the islands of Chole, Juani and Jibondo are within easy reach. Check in advance exactly what is included in terms of excursions and water sports.

A $10 **entry fee** is collected by the beach hotels on behalf of the marine park. The hotels can fill you in about most things regarding the park, but for more specialized information – and to pay the entry fee if you're not staying at the hotels – contact the **marine park headquarters** at Utende, just behind the *Mafia Island Lodge* (Mon–Fri 7.30am–3.30pm; ☏023/240 2690 extension 116, Ⓦ www.marineparktz.com).

Camping is possible on the beaches – the glorious stretch of sand either side of Kilindoni is an obvious place to aim for – but seek local advice about safety. You'll need permission from the marine park headquarters in Utende if you want to camp inside the park, which includes Chole Bay.

Kilindoni

Bismillah Hotel 50m from the *New Lizu* in an unmarked blue building (no phone). Very basic and with horrid shared long-drops and bucket showers, but it's safe, and all rooms have ceiling fans – make sure you get one with a mosquito net. The *Kijuju Guest House*, 300m from the *New Lizu* along the Utende road, is very similar. ❶

Mafia Pwani Camp On the beach behind the hospital ☏0745/696067, Ⓔcarpho2003@yahoo.com.

Finally, a cheapish seaside option, this with five *bandas* all with sea views. Camping is possible. Breakfast included; lunch and dinner (both $6) to order. ❹

New Lizu Hotel In the town centre ☏023/240 2683. Rooms with private bathroom, but overpriced given that most lack mosquito nets (they do at least have fans). ❷

Chole Bay and Chole Island

Chole Mjini At the northern tip of Chole Island Ⓔ2chole@bushmail.net, Ⓦ www.cholemjini.com. One of Tanzania's most characterful hotels, with seven tree-houses on stilts (and one at ground level). Each has two floors with a double bed on each, and a bucket shower and composting toilet in a straw shelter at the base. Facilities include a comfy lounge, a bar and restaurant. There's no electricity and no beach, though beaches can easily be combined with the daily snorkelling or boat trips included in the rates. Local communities receive $10 per guest per night. Closed mid-March to mid-June. Full-board. ❾

Kinasi Lodge Chole Bay ☏0745/481033, Ⓦ www.mafiaisland.com. Relaxed and classy, with twelve large and airy *makuti*-roofed bungalows set on a hill facing the bay. Views are best from the six sea-facing ones. The open-plan lounge area is a delight, with a bar, satellite TV and superb reference library. Other facilities include Mafia's only swimming pool (guests only), hammocks slung between palm trees, a silty mangrove-flanked beach and lots of activities including windsurfing, kayaking and half-day excursions to Marimbani Sand Cay (all free), and – at additional cost – snorkelling, diving (through Blue World Diving) and

excursions on foot, by bike or by 4WD. Closed April & May. Full-board. ❾

Mafia Island Lodge Chole Bay Ⓦ www.mafialodge.com (book through Coastal Travels in Dar; see p.133). Refitted socialist-era government hotel with the best beach and sea views. The forty rooms and two suites, most with private verandahs overlooking the bay, are built of coral ragstone and are comfortable but nothing special, but good value at the price – especially if booked as part of a safari package (safaris to Selous, operated by Coastal Travels, can be booked here). All rooms have a/c, hot water, fans and nets. Facilities include a seafood restaurant and terrace bar (with recliners), scuba-diving centre (same as the one for *Pole Pole*), snorkelling trips and cruises by *ngalawa* outrigger, other excursions by boat or by vehicle, and Internet access. Closed April & May. Breakfast included ❺–❻, full-board ❼.

Pole Pole Resort Chole Bay ☏022/260 1530 (Dar es Salaam), Ⓦ www.polepole.com. This intimate Italian-run hotel is the most stylish and expensive of the lot, with attentive service and excellent food. There are seven exquisitely designed ocean-facing bungalows on stilts, two of which are for families. Although a patch of mangroves was cleared to make the beach (as at *Kinasi*), the lodge is run on sound principles and helps with local development projects. Activities revolve around their experienced dive centre (also snorkelling), actually based at *Mafia Island Lodge*, and rates include half-day boat trips within the bay and to Chole Island; excursions elsewhere, by land or sea, cost extra. Aromatic body massages also available. Closed April & May. Full-board. ⑨

Eating and drinking

Mafia's best **restaurants** are in Chole Bay's hotels, all of whom welcome day guests for lunch or dinner. Seafood is the predictable – and usually delicious – speciality; count on $10–20 per person. Given the Italian connection, *Pole Pole* is fittingly *eccellente*. Reservations are needed for *Kinasi Lodge*: you can radio them for free from the airport. In Kilindoni, food is available at the *New Lizu Hotel*, but unless you order well in advance for things like octopus, prawns or lobster, it's limited to the standard fried fish and rice found almost anywhere else in Tanzania. Much better is *Al-Watan*, just around the corner on the Utende road and run by a couple of friendly women who – if you order early enough – can prepare all manner of dishes. Also good are the foodstalls along the Utende road, by the market and at the harbour, where you can find various kinds of fish, octopus (*pweza*) and grilled goat meat. The only **bar** in town is at *New Lizu Hotel*, spartan and deeply uninspiring; much more atmospheric are the hotel bars at Chole Bay, though you'll pay around Tsh2500 for a beer.

Mafia Island

The low-lying **Mafia Island** is by far the largest of the archipelago's islands, spanning some 55km from northeast to southwest. Much of the island is covered by coconut plantations and other crops, of which pineapples and cassava are easiest to distinguish. The main town and major port is **KILINDONI** on the

Mafia's turtles and dugongs

Although the establishment of the marine park halted much of the destruction that previously threatened the area, the fate of the archipelago's marine turtles and dugongs remains a major concern. **Green** and **hawksbill turtles** nest at various sites on the archipelago, migrating from as far away as South Africa and Aldabra Atoll in the Seychelles. However, their populations have declined dramatically over the last two decades, a direct result of the introduction of *jarife* shark nets for fishing (which have also greatly reduced shark and ray populations), and subsequent habitat damage by the use of beach seine nets and dynamite fishing. Until recently, female turtles were also traditionally hunted during their nesting periods, whilst their eggs were taken by fishermen for food.

Mafia's **dugongs** – marine mammals that apparently provided the inspiration for seafarers' tales of mermaids, possibly because of the sight of their blubbery breasts bobbing on the water – are in an even more desperate situation. Also called manatees or sea cows, they breed – or used to breed – in the shallow **sea-grass beds** of the Majira Channel to the west and south of Mafia Island; sadly, commercial prawn trawlers and siltation are wrecking the sea-grass beds, and the continued use of *jarife* has now brought them close to extinction in East Africa. Although efforts are being made to eliminate the use of *jarife*, the handful of dugongs that are accidentally caught are pretty much all that researchers ever see of their subjects. For more information on the **Mafia Island Turtle & Dugong Conservation Programme**, contact the WWF office near the park headquarters in Utende (© wwfmafia@raha.com).

△ Hawksbill turtle, Mafia Island

southwest coast, a scruffy and dozy little place for most of the time (especially during the rains), though it does boast a stunning **beach**, an attractively poky market and an equally tiny but animated harbour. It's also useful for mundane things, as it has a bank, post office, telephones and pharmacy. If you can coincide with a **full moon**, however, the place really comes to life, when an age-old ritual **procession** takes place through the town's streets. The evening starts just after the full moon is seen rising in the east, with drumming announcing the start of the festivities. Over the next few hours, pretty much the whole town joins the milling crowd, headed by dozens of women singing to the rhythms of a brass band and drummers following behind, as local kids dash around in an excited frenzy. The music itself bears a resemblance to Swahili *taarab*, not only in terms of its rhythm and melody, but in the fact that it is women who control the words and therefore the mood of the occasion.

Although the new moon is important in Islam, marking the months of the Hegira calendar, the importance of the full moon appears to have its roots in pre-Islamic times, and so the celebrations are denigrated as heathen by some. The respect that locals have for more orthodox Islam (they're all Muslim, after all) is evident though; the procession falls silent as it moves past the Friday Mosque on the Utende road, only to pick up with even more exuberance on the other side.

If you're really into traditional music, ask around for **msanja** (played in the south of the island), a celebratory dance featuring drums and whistles, which can be danced by either sex but, like *taarab*, is mainly for women; or, in the north, the **mdatu dance**, which is played with a drum, bamboo whistles and oil drum lids for percussion, and features a mock fight by four men for the attentions of two women. Lastly, Utende village's sizeable Makonde population still play their own music, including the wonderfully theatrical **sindimba stilt dance**.

Ras Kisimani

Ras Kisimani – the "Headland of the Wells" – is Mafia Island's westernmost point, and as such proved useful in the past as a major port to the mainland. Much of the headland, together with the town of Kisimani, was washed away by a cyclone in 1872. Locals say that Kisimani, together with its rival Kua, were destroyed because of their wickedness. Potsherds and other remnants occasionally still turn up on the sandy beach, the oldest of which date to the twelfth century. *Pole Pole Resort* and *Kinasi Lodge* run trips to Kisimani for $200 per boat or $40–50 per person.

Chole Island

Just 1.5km east of Mafia Island's Utende Point, the tiny and lushly vegetated **Chole Island** is the archipelago's oldest continuously inhabited settlement,

---

Kinasi Nature Trail

Winding along the beach south from *Kinasi Lodge* on Chole Bay, the **Kinasi Nature Trail** (2hr) is a good way to explore the mangrove ecosystem and associated coastal forest, and also provides good opportunities for bird-watching – with patience you're likely to spot fish eagles and lilac-breasted rollers, whilst the shoreline is good for black kites, crab plovers and low-tide waders. Some of the plants are labelled and correspond to a free pamphlet available from *Kinasi Lodge*, who can also provide knowledgeable guides.

Snorkelling and diving in Mafia Island Marine Park

Established in 1995, **Mafia Island Marine Park** encloses 822 square kilometres of coastline, reefs and mangroves. The park includes **Chole Bay**, the islands of **Chole**, **Jibondo** and **Juani**, and a narrow strip running up much of the eastern shore of Mafia Island which covers most of the unbroken fringing reef, as well as the last remnants of Mafia's evergreen coastal forests. In this area can be found over four hundred species of fish, 53 genera of both hard and soft corals – including giant table corals, huge stands of blue-tipped staghorn, whip corals and delicate seafans – 140 forms of sponge, seven mangrove species, 134 species of marine algae, breeding grounds for hawksbill and green turtles, and a sea-grass area that is home to the highly endangered dugong.

Snorkelling

The isolated coral outcrops inside the warm shallow waters of **Chole Bay** range in depth from 2m to 8m, and boast underwater visibility of up to 40m – perfect for snorkelling and attracting a great number of colourful tropical marine life, including lion fish, damselfish, angelfish, sponges, sea cucumbers, crabs and other crustaceans. Other good snorkelling areas include **Okuta Reef** around Jibondo Island, the **Blue Lagoon** south of Juani Island and **Kifinga Bay** on the east coast of Mafia Island, which is also a nesting site for green turtles. **Kitutia Reef** also has good snorkelling, within swimmable distance of a lovely beach (on which, depending on the tide, you could have lunch). **Access** to the reefs is by *mashua* dhow or *ngalawa* outrigger, which can be rented on the beach facing *Mafia Island Lodge* ($20 per person including equipment), though sailing times mean that only Chole Bay and the Blue Lagoon are feasible to visit this way unless you leave early in the morning; this needs arranging in advance and a measure of luck with tides and winds. More reliable motorboat access for locations further out (minimum four or six people) is provided by the lodges: $40–60 for a full day's snorkelling with lunch.

Diving

Mafia and its surrounding reefs offers some of the best scuba-diving in East Africa. There are two PADI-accredited **dive centres**, both on Chole Bay: Blue World Diving at *Kinasi Lodge*, and The Dive Centre at *Mafia Island Lodge* but run by *Pole Pole*

having taken over Kua's mantle as Mafia's capital when the latter was sacked in 1829. Under Busaidi rule, Chole gained notoriety as one of East Africa's main **slave-trading** centres, so much so that for a time the main island of Mafia was known as Chole Shamba – Chole's Farm – as its slave-worked coconut plantations were planted and owned by slavers from Chole. But the boom was not to last. The slave trade was nearing its end and Chole soon fell into an irreversible decline – all that now remains of the wealthy nineteenth-century town is a picturesque collection of ruins overgrown with the twisted roots of strangling fig trees, and thick undergrowth inhabited by timid monitor lizards.

Access to Chole Island is by **boat**. Small local outriggers, basking in the grandiose title of ferries, shuttle between the beach in front of the *Mafia Island Lodge* and the island; the ten-minute trip costs Tsh200. Alternatively, the Chole Bay hotels can arrange a motorboat for $10. The boats land next to a church-like building on the beach, erected in the 1990s as a fish market but now used to sell high-quality woven mats, made from the fronds of Mafia Island's phoenix palm (*mkindu*). These colourful, naturally dyed mats have been made for centuries and come in two forms: large, rectangular floor mats (*mikela*) or oval prayer mats (*misali* or *misuala*).

Resort. Both are reliable, with Blue Ocean a little cheaper overall. Expect to pay $40–50 for a single dive inside Chole Bay (or $55–60 for a night or drift dive) including equipment, $400–430 for an Open Water course, and $300–350 for Advanced Open Water. **Diving conditions** are best during the northerly *kaskazi* monsoon (Oct/Nov to Feb/March), when there are calmer seas, weaker currents and better visibility. Diving from June to September and December to January is only possible within Chole Bay. **Sharks**, especially white-tipped, black-tipped and grey reef, are most commonly seen from November to January, whilst **whales** can occasionally be spotted – or heard – from November to December. Even at the best of times, however, visibility is generally poor on outgoing tides thanks to organic and granular matter in the water. The following are some of the most popular diving reefs.

Chole Wall Situated inside Kinasi Pass northeast of Chole Island, this goes down to 18m and is best on incoming tides. It has fewer big fish than Kinasi Pass Wall, but the coral is in pristine condition and you may see turtles close up.

Kinasi Pass Wall Between Chole Bay and the open sea, this is a long-standing favourite, with dense coral formations at depths of 6–26m and especially good coral cover between 10m and 15m, with a wealth of marine life including groupers up to 2m in length, large shoals of snappers, stingrays and ribbontail rays, moray eels, Napoleon wrasse, humphead parrotfish and occasional biggies like white-tipped reef and tiger sharks, barracuda and turtles. The reef is usually seen on a drift dive, although you can catch the slack between ebb and flow tides.

Kitutia Reef At the southern tip of the archipelago, Kitutia is visited as a day-trip by motorboat with a picnic lunch on the tidal sandbank. Diving is mainly on the seaward side, and whilst there isn't a great variety of marine life, there's a good range of corals.

Ras Kisimani Less frequently dived are the reefs off Ras Kisimani to the west of the archipelago, which are awkward and expensive to get to. The best are the relatively shallow Sefu Reef (average depth 12m), 15km northwest of Kilindoni, which offers good chances of seeing large schools of barracuda and other big game fish; and Belami Reef (average 17m depth), 4km west of Ras Kisimani, which has the added attractions of an exposed sandbank surrounded by coral heads (bommies) teeming with fish, and its proximity to Ras Kisimani itself.

Immediately behind the market and in the lee of a glorious stand of frangipani trees is Chole's most impressive ruin, consisting of a coral ragstone facade and associated foundations. It served as the **residence** of the German governor of Mafia between 1892 and 1913, after which the island's capital was moved to Kilindoni, since it offered a better anchorage for the newly introduced steamboat service. Prior to German colonization, the house was apparently owned by a rich Omani slave trader, and it is from this period that Chole's other ruins date. The old **prison**, almost next door amidst a fantastic tangle of fig-tree roots, has weathered the years somewhat better than its neighbour, with its eight small cells – said to have held up to fifty inmates each – still intact, though missing their roofs. The inmates were (presumably) mostly slaves, as the free population of Chole would never have needed so large a jail. Further along the broad "Market Street", which in the nineteenth century is said to have had lantern street lights arrayed along its length (something that's difficult to imagine now), a series of rectangular stumps within a low wall are said to have been the tethering pillars of the slave market, although some say the structure was actually just a warehouse. The ruins of a Hindu temple further on have, like the prison, acquired an impressive encrustation of fig-tree roots, which appear to be the only things keeping the walls upright. For those with more time, a mosque, various wells and other stone houses can also be seen.

Among Chole's other curiosities are its protected colonies of giant *Pteropus*, or **Comoros fruit bats** (also called flying foxes), that roost by day in big mango trees and which – unlike their cave-dwelling cousins – rely on eyesight rather than sonar for navigation. The colonies are included as part of the **Bat Trail** (1hr 30min; Tsh1000), whose winding pathways provide an ideal way of experiencing the island's lush vegetation. Leaflets detailing the trail and other walks can be picked up at the *Chole Mjini* lodge, and the local kindergarten – which the lodge can direct you to – has an exhaustive bird list. For more information, *The Chole Booklet* (Tsh5000), by Dudley Iles and Christine Walley, available at the *Chole Mjini* lodge, is an excellent guide to the island's history and wildlife.

Juani Island

Separated from Chole Island by a narrow waterway, **Juani** is the archipelago's second largest island, and is frequently visited by hotel guests as a half-day trip by *mashua* dhow to see the mangrove-lined Kua Channel at the south end of the island, and the ruins of Kua, believed to have been a base for the sultanate of Kilwa. Half- or full-day **boat trips** (roughly $15–20 per person) are offered by *Pole Pole Resort* and *Kinasi Lodge*.

The island's **wildlife** includes feral pigs (introduced by the Portuguese), monkeys and the diminutive blue duiker antelope, but the main attraction is

A short history of Juani Island and Kua

Recent finds of pottery and human remains in a collapsed coral cave on Juani prove that Juani's islanders were trading with other Indian Ocean peoples at least two millennia ago. But recorded history starts early in the eleventh century when – according to legend – the town of **Kua** was founded by Bashat, a son of the Shirazi founder of Kilwa. The archipelago's position between Kilwa and Zanzibar made Kua an important trading town, and before long, **Arab traders** were given the right to build their own settlement on the northern side of town; locals say they later seized power and began to rule unfairly.

Kua's rivalries were not confined to Shirazis and Arabs, but also with **Kisimani**, which was allied to Zanzibar. Legend tells of the launching of a *jahazi* dhow at Kisimani. The people of Kua were invited over for the celebrations, but on arriving, the children of Kua's elite were bound and laid on the ground in front of the dhow. The dhow was launched over their backs, killing the children. The people of Kua took their time to exact **revenge**. At Kua, they built a beautifully decorated chamber deep underground. When five or ten years had passed, they invited the people of Kisimani for a wedding. The people of Kisimani, having assumed that the Kua had forgiven them for killing their children, arrived unsuspecting. The wedding feast was held in the underground chamber. One by one, the people of Kua left the feast, until only an old man – who had volunteered to sacrifice himself – remained to entertain the guests. The entrance to the chamber was sealed off, and the occupants died.

Historians still debate the catastrophe that subsequently overtook Kua. According to one story, at the start of the nineteenth century Kua was ruled by a very harsh queen. Some opponents of the queen travelled to Madagascar, where they sought help from the **Sakalava people**. The Sakalava agreed to help overthrow the queen on condition that they be allowed to rule Kua, but when they arrived, in 1829, with a force of eighty canoes, they proceeded to sack the entire town regardless of allegiance, allegedly eating many of its inhabitants in the process. A good proportion of the three thousand survivors were sold into slavery, and by 1840 the last inhabitants had deserted Kua to start new lives on Kome Island, halfway between Mafia and Kisiju on the mainland.

undoubtedly the atmospheric **Kua ruins**, believed by locals to be haunted, which languish almost forgotten on the west side of the island among a dense tangle of undergrowth studded with baobab trees. Excavations in 1955 unearthed a rectangular grid of streets, along with Chinese and Indian coins from the thirteenth and fourteenth centuries. Kua appears to have covered about 1.5 square kilometres, and its ruins include a two-storey palace dating from the eighteenth century, two graveyards, at least fifteen houses and seven mosques, the oldest of which dates back to the fourteenth century. It's impossible to give a ruin-by-ruin description of the place, as what you see will depend on the state of the vegetation.

Jibondo Island

About an hour's sail south of Chole, **Jibondo Island** is the most traditional of the archipelago's settlements, and most of its two thousand inhabitants engage in fishing, especially for sharks, and octopus-baiting. The beaches facing the open ocean are important **turtle-nesting sites** – seaweed farming was introduced by NGOs in 1992 as an alternative source of income to killing turtles. Jibondo's craftsmen are famed for their skill in **boat building** without the use of iron, or even nails. With the onset of modern boats, their art is gradually becoming obsolete, although ongoing repairs and the small-scale construction of *mashua* dhows keeps some in business. A trip to Jibondo is usually included with a snorkelling trip from one of the Chole Bay hotels, and costs $20–25 per person in a group of four.

The Kilwas

Some 140km south of the Rufiji delta are the **KILWAS**, three settlements of exceptional historical interest whose atmospheric ruins represent a wide sweep of East African coastal history, from the dizzy heights of the Swahili and Shirazi trading civilization, to the darker days of slavery and the uprisings against German rule. At the neck of the Kilwa peninsula, **Kilwa Kivinje** ("Kilwa of the Casuarina Trees") was a major slave-trading centre and later a German garrison; nowadays little more than a fishing village, its historical core in a severely dilapidated if picturesque state. At the peninsula's southern tip, the modern town of **Kilwa Masoko** ("Kilwa of the Market") is the regional headquarters and the main base for travellers, as well as boasting a couple of beautiful beaches. It also offers easy access to the oldest and most fascinating of the Kilwas, **Kilwa Kisiwani** ("Kilwa of the Island"), situated on an island of the

---

Phoning Kilwa

No one really knows what happened to TTCL's promise to provide Kilwa with an automatic telephone exchange by 2002, so to ring land lines (eg "Kilwa Masoko 19") you'll have to go through the operator: call ☎100 unless you're in Lindi or Kilwa, in which case it's ☎961 for Kilwa Masoko and ☎968 for Kilwa Kivinje.

same name a couple of kilometres off the coast. Once one of Africa's wealthiest towns, Kilwa Kisiwani is now a UNESCO World Heritage Site, and contains the world's most extensive and best-preserved Swahili ruins. There are similar if smaller sites on the nearby islands of **Songo Mnara** and **Sanje ya Kati**.

Kilwa Masoko

For the handful of visitors who manage to make it down here, the small town of **KILWA MASOKO** is a handy base to either break the drive from Dar to

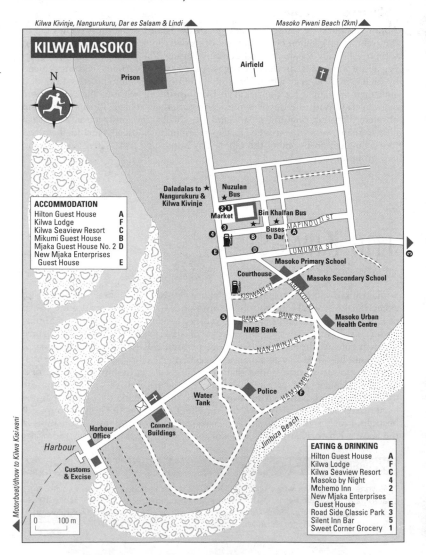

KILWA MASOKO

Kilwa Kivinje, Nangurukuru, Dar es Salaam & Lindi

Masoko Pwani Beach (2km)

Prison

Airfield

ACCOMMODATION
Hilton Guest House	A
Kilwa Lodge	F
Kilwa Seaview Resort	C
Mikumi Guest House	B
Mjaka Guest House No. 2	D
New Mjaka Enterprises Guest House	E

Daladalas to Nangurukuru & Kilwa Kivinje

Nuzulan Bus

Market

Bin Khalfan Bus

MAPINDUZI ST

Buses to Dar

LUMUMBA ST

Masoko Primary School

Courthouse

Masoko Secondary School

KISIWANI ST

KARAKACHO ST

Masoko Urban Health Centre

BANK ST

BANK ST

NMB Bank

NANJIRINJI ST

HamJambo ST

Water Tank

Police

Jimbiza Beach

Harbour Office

Council Buildings

Harbour

Customs & Excise

Motorboat/dhow to Kilwa Kisiwani

0   100 m

EATING & DRINKING
Hilton Guest House	A
Kilwa Lodge	F
Kilwa Seaview Resort	C
Masoko by Night	4
Mchemo Inn	2
New Mjaka Enterprises Guest House	E
Road Side Classic Park	3
Silent Inn Bar	5
Sweet Corner Grocery	1

Mtwara, or to visit the ruins of **Kilwa Kisiwani**, on the mangrove-rimmed island of the same name 2km offshore.

The first thing that strikes you about any of the Kilwas is their overpowering **lethargy**. Given the strength-sapping heat and humidity, siestas are unavoidable, and you'll see people sleeping almost anywhere, even flat out on the ground in front of their shops. Some locals say that the listlessness is a legacy of slavery; a more certain reminder of that trade can be seen in the dark skin of many of Kilwa's inhabitants, some of whom – from the Ngoni, Machinga, Mwera, Matumbi, Ngindo and Yao tribes – descend from slaves. People also seem rather reserved in their dealings with foreigners, and the long stares can feel unsettling at first, though once people get to recognize you, Kilwa is as welcoming as anywhere in the country, especially if you like kids – the Kilwan flavour have taken to greeting tourists with cheery choruses of "bye-bye"!

For long deprived of any but the most basic facilities, visitors now have a handful of modest tourist-oriented hotels on **Jimbiza Beach** to choose from – a broad expanse of sand deep enough for swimming at low tide, with fishermen and dhow builders at its northern end. **Masoko Pwani Beach**, 5km northeast, is more secluded, and contains another low-impact "resort", mainly used by (rare) overland truck tours. There's no problem donning swimming trunks or bikinis as long as you're not right next to fishermen – Kilwa, like most of the coast, is Muslim.

The daily **market**, under the mango trees on the north side of town, is always fun and continues well into the night, though the selection of fresh produce is limited.

Arrival and information

Completion of the bridge over the Rufiji has vastly improved access to Kilwa from Dar, and once the bridge's southern access road is sealed there'll be a surfaced road all the way, meaning a six- to seven- hour drive. For now, count on eight hours in good weather or twelve hours if it's been raining (assuming the road isn't blocked; read the box on p.195).

Excursions from Kilwa Masoko

Apart from the historical attractions of Kilwa Kisiwani, Songo Mnara and Sanje ya Kati, Kilwa Masoko also serves as a base for a handful of infrequently visited natural attractions. You may be able to arrange trips through *Kilwa Seaview Resort* (who also offer trips to the Selous Game Reserve), but having your own transport is recommended.

A particularly attractive destination is **Mutonyange Lake** on the way to Lindi, which contains literally thousands of hippo. Legend has it that should you try to hunt them, you'll never be seen again. To get there, turn off the main road to Lindi at Kiranjeranje and head west 17km to Makangaga. Park there and ask for the village chairman (*mwenyekiti wa kijiji*), who should be able to provide someone to guide you the remaining 3km to the lake.

Another excellent destination is the large **Matumbi Hills cave complex**, which saw service as a hide-out during the 1905–7 Maji Maji Uprising. Locals catch porcupines here, whose quills have medicinal and ritual significance. The name for the caves varies according to which entrance is used: choose from Nang'oma, Anduli, Nakitala or Nakinduguyu. To get there from Kilwa Masoko, head back towards Dar and turn west at Matapatapa, 53km north of Nangurukuru. The main entrance to the caves is at Kipatimu near Nandembo village, 60km further on.

A handful of rickety **buses and minibuses** ply the road from Dar every day, leaving at 5am from the amorphous Temeke bus stand: get a taxi there, buy your ticket a day or two beforehand, and be sure to know the exact point of departure. None are overly comfortable, but Bin Khalfan have the best reputation. Alternatively, catch a bus from Dar's Ubungo bus station to Lindi, Mtwara, Nachingwea or Masasi and get off in **Nangurukuru**, from where daladalas cover the remaining 30km throughout the day (Tsh1000). No bus company has a faultless reputation, but Akida's Coach is generally considered safest.

There are several petrol stations in Nangurukuru and Kilwa Masoko. Fill up here, as the next fuel isn't guaranteed until Lindi in the south or Kibiti in the north. Daily **flights** from Zanzibar ($130 one-way) via Dar ($110) are operated by Coastal Aviation (see p.127 for Dar, p.657 for Stone Town). The airfield is just north of Kilwa Masoko, within walking distance of the hotels.

For **local excursions** enquire at the *Kilwa Seaview Resort*. The **Antiquities Department**, in the council buildings opposite the post office (Mon–Fri 7.30am–3.30pm; ☎ Kilwa Masoko 16, 19 or 60), dispenses permits and practical advice on getting to the archeological sites of Kilwa Kisiwani, Songo Mnara and Sanje ya Kati. **Bicycle rental**, which can be arranged informally (just ask around), is handy for accessing Masoko Pwani beach.

Accommodation

Kilwa Masoko has some perfectly decent **guest houses**, and a handful of modest **beach hotels** aimed at tourists. **Camping** is possible at *Kilwa Seaview Resort* (Tsh10,000 per person). Low water pressure means that showers only work intermittently, and electricity is equally erratic.

Hilton Guest House Mapinduzi St ☎ 0748/677921. Best of the budget places – friendly, clean and safe. Its rooms are equipped with fans and electricity, the more expensive of which have bathrooms with clean long-drops (the shared ones aren't too salubrious). The downside is too-small bed sheets and mosquito nets – use plenty of repellent. ❶

Kilwa Lodge (*Kilwa Ruins Lodge*) Hamjambo Rd ☎ 0748/205586, ⓦ www.kilwa-lodge.com. Right on Jimbiza beach, this is a major big game fishing base, with four suitably equipped boats (around $600 a day per boat). There's plenty for other tastes too, including water-skiing, canoes and snorkelling. The cheaper rooms are in raised wooden *bandas* each with two single beds and standing fans (rather basic for the price); better are the modern cottages next to the beach, with terracotta tile floors but little furniture and no mosquito nets, though the combination of a/c and window screens should work. There's also a bar, restaurant and shaded pool. Half-board. ❻

Kilwa Seaview Resort 1.5km along Lumumba St ☎ 0748/613335, ⓦ www.kilwa.net. Perched on a scrubby plot atop a crumbling cliff at the end of Jimbiza beach, where fishermen repair their boats (the nearest swimmable section is a few hundred metres west), this has nice views of the

bay from its eight guest rooms, each occupying a vaulted *makuti*-roofed cottage fitted with one enormous double and one single bed, large box nets, fans, straw rugs, comfy furniture, satellite TV, and recliners on their verandahs (good views). Also has an open-sided restaurant (full-board $15 extra per person) and bar screening CNN, and a small murky swimming pool. Activities include boat excursions ($60–80 per boat), dhow trips to Kilwa Kisiwani ($10), and yachting ($300 per boat for 6–8hr). Breakfast included. ❺

Mikumi Guest House Mapinduzi St ☎ Kilwa Masoko 49. One of several really basic guest houses around here, all much of a muchness, with shared squat toilets and bucket showers. ❶

New Mjaka Enterprises Guest House On the highway ☎ Kilwa Masoko 89. Pricey compared to the *Hilton*, with two en-suite rooms (running water) in each of nine octagonal concrete *bandas*, with box nets, table fans and overly soft beds. Double your money for satellite TV, or spend less for a night in their annexe (the *No.2* on Lumumba St; ❶). Safe parking, a reasonable restaurant, and soft drinks – best taken on the terrace overlooking the mangroves at the back. Buses revving up may disturb light sleepers. ❷–❸

Moving on from Kilwa Masoko

Buses **to Dar** leave daily at 5.30am from beside the market or from their "offices" – usually a signboard and table – in nearby streets. Bin Khalfan's is on Mapinduzi Street, opposite *Mikumi Guest House*. Buy your ticket the day before to be sure of a seat.

Heading south, you'll have to catch a daladala to Nangurukuru and wait there for a bus from Dar (the first passes around 1pm). Arrive as early as possible, since buses from Dar don't always have spare seats. If it looks like you'll be stuck for the night, Nangurukuru has a basic guest house and loads of cheap eateries, but you'd be better off at Kilwa Kivinje, whose equally basic guest houses at least have the advantage of an atmospheric location. For information on moving on from the Kilwas by dhow, see the box on p.220.

Eating

Kilwa Masoko isn't the most gastronomically endowed place on earth, and few restaurants have more than a sackful of rice in their larders or days-old oily snacks in their display cases. Still, there are a handful of half-decent places at which you might strike lucky – especially if you order half a day in advance for things like prawns, lobster, squid, the meaty *kolekole* fish, or octopus, the latter stewed or grilled. For coconut juice and grilled dorado, try the market.

Hilton Guest House Mapinduzi St. The modest restaurant here sometimes has next to nothing, but is also capable of rustling up some prize nosh (under Tsh2000), including fresh squid and prawns, and even – should inspiration (and a can of cheese) strike, pizza. Also has cold soft drinks. No alcohol.

Kilwa Lodge Hamjongo Rd. A fantastic location right on the beach; a full meal with drinks shouldn't be more than Tsh10,000; order two or three hours before if you're not staying overnight.

Kilwa Seaview Resort 1.5km along Lumumba St. Rather average and slow-to-come but filling meals aimed at tourist palates for Tsh6000, plus a well-stocked bar built around a baobab tree, with satellite TV and views over Jimbiza Beach.

New Mjaka Enterprises Guest House On the main highway. Unexciting pre-fried fish and chicken served up with *ugali* or *pilau*, plus cold soft drinks.

Drinking

This mainly Muslim town has a surprising number of **bars**, one or two of which might even be described as lively at the weekend. Best located and well stocked are those at the *Kilwa Lodge* and *Kilwa Seaview Resort*, though you'll pay a premium for the views. In town, the large *Road Side Classic Park* on the highway has lots of shaded and secluded seating and a pool table (but terrible food), and vies in the evenings with *Masoko by Night* opposite, which wows the local boys and girls with live *taarab* every other Saturday, though its barmaids appear to double as prostitutes. One block north are two other busy bars, the *Mchemo Inn* and adjacent *Sweet Corner Grocery*, which tends to play lively music and also has food. Closer to the harbour, the *Silent Inn Bar* has a nice view of the sea inlet to the west, but only sells sodas.

Kilwa Kisiwani

Two kilometres across the water south of Kilwa Masoko are the spectacular ruins of the medieval city-state of **KILWA KISIWANI**, located on the northern shore of a small, mangrove-fringed island of the same name. At its height, Kilwa Kisiwani was the single most important trading centre on the East African coast, and the ruins here include several mosques, a fourteenth-century palace (in its time the largest stone structure in sub-Saharan Africa), dozens of Shirazi graves atmospherically set in groves of giant baobabs, and a well-preserved Omani fortress.

Some history

The oldest archeological remains at Kilwa Kisiwani date from the ninth century, part of an extensive settlement that pre-dated the arrival of the Arabs. According to legend, the **Sultanate of Kilwa** was founded in 975 by a Shirazi trader named Hassan bin Ali, who is said to have bought the island from the ruling chief for a quantity of cloth. Early Arab chronicles are clear that the inhabitants were Africans rather than Arabs or Asians, although the ruling class came to be dominated by immigrants from Persia and, later, from Arabia.

Kilwa reached its apogee in the fourteenth century, from when the bulk of the surviving ruins date. Kilwa's riches lay in its control of the **gold trade** from the Monomotapa kingdom in Zimbabwe: by 1300, Monomotapa's entire production was passing through Kilwa en route to Arabia, India and Europe. The most famous visitor to Kilwa during this period was the renowned Moroccan traveller **Ibn Battuta**, who in 1332 remarked that "Kilwa is amongst the most beautiful of cities and elegantly built". At the height of the gold trade, Kilwa boasted sub-Saharan Africa's largest stone building, its largest mosque and first mint. The ruling class lived in stone houses with indoor plumbing, wore silk and fine cotton, and ate off Chinese porcelain. The general population presumably lived in less durable mud-and-thatch dwellings, much as they do now, as only the palaces and mosques have survived.

The **arrival of the Portuguese** in 1498 marked the end of Kilwa's first golden age and triggered a long period of decline. Their first visit was innocuous enough, when Vasco da Gama's flotilla pulled into Kilwa's harbour on its way to discovering the sea route to India. They found a flourishing and powerful city, exporting not only gold and slaves but silver, precious stones, ivory, myrrh, animal skins, frankincense and ambergris, receiving spices and metal goods in exchange. But it was the gold trade that incited **Vasco da Gama's return** in 1502. After calling briefly at Sofala and Mozambique, da Gama sailed once more into Kilwa, this time ostensibly to avenge the "unfriendly" welcome that the ruler, Amir Ibrahim, had accorded Pedro Álvares Cabral a couple of years earlier (Cabral, with the characteristic tact of the Conquistadors, had refused to meet the Amir, had threatened war, and then proposed that Kilwa, which at the time was the most important Islamic settlement in sub-Saharan Africa, convert to Christianity). Da Gama threatened to burn the city and kill its inhabitants unless he was paid sufficient tribute. The Amir submitted and Kilwa effectively became a Portuguese possession.

In 1505 came the turn of the even more militaristic **Dom Francisco d'Almeida**, who had been made viceroy of the newly conquered territories of India. He quickly took a liking to the town: "Kilwa, of all the places I know in the world, has the best port and the fairest land that can be." Despite his fine words, d'Almeida set about plundering the town and triggering the collapse of much of the old coastal trading network, so much so that by 1513 the Portuguese saw no more reason to remain in Kilwa, and left. With its trading links destroyed, the town's fortunes nose-dived, brought to a brutal and gruesome end in 1587 by the massacre of forty percent of its population by the marauding **Zimba tribe**. Believed to have come from the Zambezi area (the name

Zimbabwe is a more than obvious clue), little is known of the Zimba other than their alleged cannibalistic habits. Their northward migration may have been precipitated by Portuguese attempts to control the gold mines of the central Zambezi the preceding decade; after Kilwa, they proceeded to sack Mombasa, and only finally disappeared when they were dispersed in Malindi on the Kenyan coast by the local Sheikh, supported by the Portuguese.

Kilwa's fortunes revived at the start of the eighteenth century, following the expulsion of the Portuguese from the African coast north of Mozambique. Kilwa gradually fell under **Omani control**, with slaves replacing gold as the coast's major commodity, and the following century saw a renaissance in Kilwa's fortunes, mostly though trade with the French. The latter part of this period also saw the establishment of Kilwa's semi-independent **ash-Shirazi dynasty**, whose first sultan was installed in 1776. The new sultan almost immediately signed a treaty with a French slave-trader, Jean-Vincent Morice, for the annual purchase of at least 1000 slaves. It was in this period that the present Gereza fort was constructed, but the upturn was not to last long. In 1842, Kilwa was captured by Zanzibar and the following year its last independent sultan was exiled to Muscat. With its trade eclipsed by the new mainland slaving centre of Kilwa Kivinje, Kilwa Kisiwani was finally abandoned and collapsed into the ruins that are now all that survives of the city.

Visiting the site

Visitors to Kilwa Kisiwani need a **permit** (Tsh1500 or $2) from the Antiquities Department in Kilwa Masoko, where you can also borrow a sketch map of the site. While you're there, ask to see or buy a copy of John Sutton's fascinating *Kilwa: A History of the Ancient Swahili Town*, also available in Dar es Salaam's better bookshops.

There are two ways of getting to Kilwa Kisiwani. The romantic option is to catch a local *mashua* **dhow** from Kilwa Masoko's harbour, most of which leave in the morning. If there are other passengers, it shouldn't cost more than Tsh500 each way, assuming you can get the captain to charge you the going rate, but if you want the dhow to yourself – as the captain is likely to assume you do – you'll pay anything from Tsh5000 to Tsh10,000 for the return trip. Less romantic but more reliable is the **motorboat** owned by the Antiquities Department, who charge Tsh25,000 for the return trip (Tsh60,000 to Songo Mnara), including the guide. There's a Tsh200 harbour tax at Kilwa Masoko; pay at the hut inside the gate.

Dhows usually drop you at the Gereza, where the captain will locate a **guide**. You're then shown around as many ruins as you want, and finish up (if you can face the walk) 2km east of the Gereza at Husuni Kubwa, where you're picked up for the return to Kilwa Masoko. The guides have improved markedly, but now expect to pay at least Tsh10,000 per group; it's negotiable, however.

If you fancy spending a night on the island, the Antiquities Department maintains a very basic **rest house**, equipped with beds and tattered sheets and nets. The *askari* can help collect water from a nearby well – it'll need purifying. The price is negotiable with the guide, but shouldn't be more than Tsh2500 per person. **Camping** is possible around the rest house – again, there's no fixed price.

The ruins

The **ruins** – recently spruced up with walkways and signboards – are scattered in and around the present-day settlement of Kilwa Kisiwani on the north side

△ Great Mosque, Kilwa Kisiwani

of the island, whose simple mud houses provide a stark contrast to the wealthy city that Kilwa once was. The bulk of the ruins, comprising the heart of the old city and the Gereza fort (where the boat deposits you), are in the northwest and cover little more than one square kilometre. Husuni Kubwa and Husuni Ndogo are 2km to the east, accessed by narrow footpaths wending between dusty plots of irrigated farmland, cashew plantations, shady mango groves and acacia and baobab thickets where, with a keen eye, you may spot bee-eaters and bulbuls.

The Gereza

The crenellated **Gereza** (also known as the fort or the prison) is Kilwa's most prominent building; boats from Kilwa Masoko drop you on the beach beside it. Built of coral limestone blocks, the Gereza occupies a commanding position, with unobstructed views over the harbours of both Kilwa Kisiwani and Kilwa Masoko, and sweeping vistas over the open ocean. Parts of the northern walls have crumbled into the waves, but the Gereza is otherwise in remarkably fine condition. Its name comes from the church (in Portuguese, *igreja*) it once contained, and it's said that construction of the complex took less than three weeks: in the florid words of Francisco d'Almeida, writing to the king of Portugal in 1505: "We built a fortress which if it were possible I would give years of my life for Your Highness to see, for it is so strong that the King of France could be awaited there, and it has lodgings in very fine houses for twice as many people as are left there now."

He rather overestimated its strength, however: when the Omanis gained control, they had to rebuild the entire fortress with the exception of the tower foundations, and this is the building you see today. In keeping with its defensive nature, there is only one entrance, though the door and frame are relatively modern. Above the entrance is a slot for muskets, and there are still more slits arranged along the parapet. The courtyard inside has a number of benches

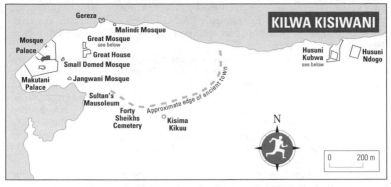

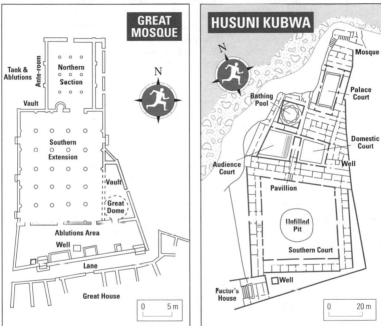

Adapted from John Sutton (1998), in Azania 33. Reproduced by permission of the British Institute in East Africa.

along the walls, and spyholes from the middle level of the surrounding three-storey edifice. The best-preserved rooms are in the southeast corner, on your left as you enter. The chamber set in the southern wall is believed to have been a gunpowder magazine. In the northeast corner, excavations have unearthed several cannonballs and musket shot, along with over three thousand trading beads.

The Great Mosque and Great House

The **Great Mosque** (or Friday Mosque), at the heart of medieval Kilwa, lies just to the south of the Gereza on the edge of the present-day village, in an area now frequented by goats. In its time the largest mosque in East Africa, it was excavated between 1958 and 1960 by Neville Chittick, who reconstructed parts of it and also somewhat carelessly left behind his own traces in the form of a short length of railway and an upturned carriage, which was used to clear debris during the excavations.

The mosque is a beautiful building, and the play of light and shadow on the mildewed archways and walls makes it supremely photogenic. Its architecture reflects Kilwa's rising prosperity over the centuries. The roofless **northern section** is the older, built in the twelfth century when the gold trade was in its infancy. Its flat, coral-concrete roof was supported by nine sixteen-sided wooden columns set in rows of three, on top of which were laid three beams running north to south. As the wood rotted away long ago, the only clues to this are the gaps left in the masonry into which the beams and pillars would have fitted.

As Kilwa prospered in the fourteenth century, the riches generated by the gold trade were reflected in the mosque's large **southern extension**, which was given an elaborately domed and vaulted roof supported by thin, octagonal stone pillars. Though elegant, they were unable to bear the weight of the roof, part of which collapsed in 1350. The pillars were subsequently replaced with coral limestone blocks, most of which still stand today. Some of the original stone pillars lie discarded by the eastern wall, and the domes are nowadays home to a small colony of bats.

At the southern end of the mosque is a porch which was used as the **ablutions area** by the faithful before entering the prayer hall. It was equipped with a well, a water trough, a bench and a piece of round sandstone where visitors would wash their feet before entering the mosque. At the eastern side of the ablutions area, a narrow door gave onto a large room under a single dome, which may have been used by the sultan for his prayers. On the south side of the ablutions area is the **Great House**, a complex of buildings now much overgrown (look for the huge fig tree growing into the walls), which apparently dates from the fourteenth century and included many dwellings and courts.

Next to the mosque is a very deep well. If you peer down, you'll see two **underground passages** leading off it about halfway down. The one on the eastern side leads to the Gereza and may have been used for moving slaves, whilst the one to the west heads to the Makutani Palace – a strange conjunction of privilege and servitude.

The Small Domed Mosque

The **Small Domed Mosque**, 150m southwest of the Great Mosque, is the best preserved of Kilwa's medieval buildings, with more than half its original roof intact, and it's certainly the most attractive. It dates from the middle of the fifteenth century when Kilwa's prosperity was at its height, though the thick fortifying buttresses supporting the walls from the outside bear a distinctly defensive air, perhaps foreshadowing the arrival of the Portuguese and the city's subsequent demise.

The first thing that strikes you about the mosque is the partly broken octagonal pillar that projects upwards from the central dome, which suggests comparison with the pillar tombs found at other Shirazi sites, such as Kaole and Kunduchi, and on Pemba Island. **Inside**, the mosque is an architectural gem. As with the Great Mosque, the African influence is visible in the overall form of the building, which is based on a rectangular prayer hall with a roof supported on numerous pillars, rather than the contemporary Arabian "pavilion" style featuring arcaded courtyards. The central dome was inlaid with circles of green-glazed ceramic bowls, some of which can still be seen, whilst some of the other surviving domes bear traces of blue paint. There's also an elegant *mihrab* in the north wall – like the domes, it's now home to a colony of easily startled bats. The **ablutions area** to the southwest is more complex than that in the Great Mosque, and contains a latrine and two water tanks. Like the Great Mosque, there are also some large flat circular stones which were used for scrubbing feet.

The Makutani Palace and around

At the western end of town next to the ocean is the **Makutani Palace**. The palace's name means "gathering place", hinting at the traditional African mode of rule in which a state's affairs were run by a council of elders rather than just a king or sultan. With the exception of the enclosing perimeter walls, however, much of the original fifteenth-century structure was demolished at the end of the eighteenth century to provide building material for the new palace. This is still largely intact, and occupies the south side of a roughly triangular area adjacent to the northeastern wall of the old palace, surrounded by enormous defensive outer walls which open only onto the shore.

The old palace consists of a **residential section** to the west and barracks or storerooms around a large **courtyard** to the east. The rusty cannon barrel in the courtyard adds to the impression that defence was a prime concern, as does the water cistern, which would have proved invaluable during a siege. Both wings of the palace had long, narrow rooms, their width limited by the length of the mangrove poles from which the ceilings were made. The reception rooms and living quarters were on the upper two floors, the latter provided with toilets. The decor of the rooms is hinted at by traces of pink plaster, which can be seen halfway up the walls of the corridor connecting the stores with the palace antechamber. While you're wandering around, have a closer look at the coral ragstone walls, some of which contain incredibly intricate natural patterns of cream and grey.

A few hundred metres southeast of the palace are the scanty remains of the **Jangwani Mosque**, of interest mainly to archeologists on account of the unique ablutionary water jars set into its walls just inside the main entrance. Passing the mosque, at low tide you can cut across the salt-crusted sands of the inlet just to the south to reach the so-called **Forty Sheikhs Cemetery**, part of which has been eroded by sea. Like the vast majority of known Shirazi grave sites, the tombs nestle in groves of **baobabs**, including one of the biggest you're ever likely to see. The presence of the trees is explained by the legend that when a sultan died, a pair of baobab saplings would be planted at either end of his grave; these would eventually grow together, effectively making the tomb part of the tree. The story certainly fits the atmosphere of the place, at once overpoweringly sacred and meditative.

Husuni Kubwa

Built on a protruding rocky spur high above the fringing mangroves 2km east of the Gereza, **Husuni Kubwa** (The Great Palace) was in its time the largest permanent building in sub-Saharan Africa, and remains one of the most enigmatic constructions on the Swahili coast. Walking along the footpath from the Gereza and the village, the undergrowth suddenly clears as your eyes meet a grey maze of courtyards, hallways, galleries, staircases and rooms up to three storeys high. Excavations suggest that the construction was never fully completed, nor lived in by more than three generations of sultans before the dynasty moved to the Makutani Palace. No one really knows why the building was abandoned, especially as the cliff-top location was ideal, benefiting from continuous sea breezes and a commanding position over the ocean and the channel running between the mainland and the island.

An inscribed plaque found in the palace lauded the praises of Sultan "al-Malik al-Mansur" ("the Conquering Ruler") al-Hasan ibn Sulaiman, which dates the bulk of the palace's construction to the 1320s, though its location outside the city has prompted much inconclusive speculation. The very size and ornateness of the building illustrates in spectacular fashion the wealth that was being made from the gold trade – if you've seen the display on Kilwa in the National Museum in Dar, with its Chinese porcelain bowls, elaborately engraved friezes, oil lamps, pottery and coins, it shouldn't be too difficult to imagine the opulence of the palace in the mid-fourteenth century. An inscription from the palace, also in the National Museum, reads: "Your good fortune is always new and with you, all days are festivals. Your Creator is glorious and protects you from destruction."

The palace complex had two main parts: the palace itself in the north, and a rectangular commercial section to the south, which is the first area you reach if walking here from the Gereza. Walking down a flight of steps, you pass a well and enter the large **Southern Court**, enclosed by a double range of rooms. No roof was found during the excavations, and as the walls of the rooms are uncommonly thick, they may have been intended to carry another storey. Near the centre of the courtyard is a large irregular pit which was either used as a quarry or may have been intended to form a large cistern.

North of the Southern Court is the **Palace** itself, occupying the north- and west-facing tip of the headland. Entering from the southern court, you pass through the **Domestic Court**, which is surrounded by terraces. To the west is the **Pavilion** in which the sultan would have received visitors and conducted public business. A short flight of steps below the Pavilion on the western edge of the complex is the **Audience Court**, flanked by wide terraces which may also have been used for receptions and dances, and which offer a fine view westwards over the coast and harbour. The niches in the walls here were possibly used for oil lamps.

North of the Audience Court is the octagonal **Bathing Pool**, set in an unroofed square enclosure; it's been estimated that this would have needed eighty thousand litres of water to fill, which – given the lack of channels – would have had to be hauled by hand from the well next to the Domestic Court, by an army of slaves or servants. The scale and opulence of palace fittings like these suggest why the site might have been abandoned prematurely, since the running costs of such a grandiose building must have been very much at the mercy of trading conditions, not just at Kilwa but at the Mozambican port of Sofala, the source of Kilwa's gold.

North of the Bathing Pool and through the rectangular **Palace Court**, steps lead down to a landing creek in the mangroves, where most dhows collect passengers before returning to Kilwa Masoko.

West of Husuni Kubwa, and separated from it by a deep gully, **Husuni Ndogo** (Small Palace) is believed to have been constructed in the fifteenth century, though archeologists are at a loss to explain much about the building. With the exception of its outer walls and turrets, it contains virtually no internal structures, and dense thorny shrubs render access difficult.

Songo Mnara and Sanje ya Kati

To the south of Kilwa Kisiwani are several more islands, including Songo Mnara and Sanje ya Kati, both of which contain Shirazi ruins. Those at **Songo Mnara** are the most impressive, mostly dating from the fourteenth and fifteenth centuries and comprising an extensive palace complex, at least four mosques and dozens of graves and houses, all surrounded by a defensive wall. **Sanje ya Kati**, formerly known as Shanga, is 3km to the west and contains the foundations of oblong houses and a tenth-century mosque, although they're little more than rubble.

You need a special **permit** from the Antiquities Department in Kilwa Masoko to visit Songo Mnara (Tsh1500 or $2), but it's unclear whether you need one just to visit Sanje ya Kati (it should be covered by the Songo Mnara permit in any case). If the cost of hiring a boat (see p.213) is prohibitive, Songo Mnara is also accessible by irregular *mashua* **dhow ferries** sailing between Kilwa Masoko and Pende; you'll have to wade through the water to get ashore. The journey to Pende costs Tsh800 for locals, though non-Kiswahili speakers will probably pay more. Be sure to double-check arrangements for your pick-up on the return trip, as there are no facilities on the island if you get stuck. Songo Mnara has a **guide** who will expect a tip (and may put you up for a night).

Kilwa Kivinje

Facing the ocean on the neck of Kilwa peninsula, 29km north of Kilwa Masoko, is the totally dilapidated but charming town of **KILWA KIVINJE**, a fascinating but rarely visited destination. In its brief period of prosperity in the mid-nineteenth century, the town was one of the main terminuses of the southern slave

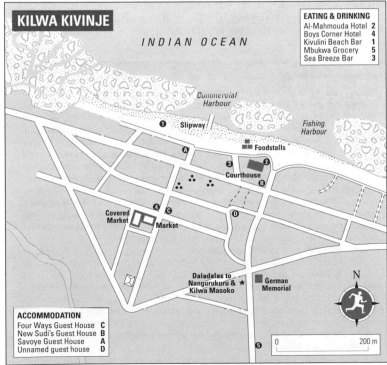

KILWA KIVINJE

INDIAN OCEAN

EATING & DRINKING
Al-Mahmouda Hotel	2
Boys Corner Hotel	4
Kivulini Beach Bar	1
Mbukwa Grocery	5
Sea Breeze Bar	3

Commercial Harbour

Slipway

Fishing Harbour

Foodstalls

Courthouse

Covered Market

Market

Daladalas to Nangurukuru & Kilwa Masoko

German Memorial

N

0   200 m

ACCOMMODATION
Four Ways Guest House	C
New Sudi's Guest House	B
Savoye Guest House	A
Unnamed guest house	D

Police Station (500m), Maji Maji Memorial (1km), Nangurukuru & Kilwa Masoko ▼

and ivory caravan route from Lake Nyasa, replacing Kilwa Kisiwani, which had been all but abandoned. Later on it became a garrison town for the Germans, from where they suppressed the Abushiri and Maji Maji uprisings.

With slaving long gone and road access from the rest of the country cut off for much of the year, Kilwa Kivinje is nowadays little more than a large fishing village, and most of its historical buildings, the majority of which date from the German and British periods, are rapidly crumbling away. Whilst there are no outstanding sights (the ruined **courthouse** facing the fishing harbour comes closest), Kilwa Kivinje is a great place just to wander around and absorb the atmosphere – the streets radiating from the market contain some beautiful balconies and carved doors, the latter invariably in better condition than the houses they guard. Whilst security isn't a worry by day so long as you're not dangling anything tempting, get a reliable local to escort you at night, as muggings have been reported.

Apart from the ruins and the somnolent **market** (coconuts, mangos and herbal remedies), there's not actually all that much to see or do, and if it's **beaches** you're after, Kilwa Kivinje isn't the best place, as mangroves line much of the coast, although at low tide the sea goes out almost 1km, making for fine walks along the shore.

Arrival and accommodation

There are no direct **buses** from Dar es Salaam, so your best bet is to head to Kilwa Masoko first and then catch a daladala back up the peninsula (Tsh800). Alternatively, skip Kilwa Masoko by getting off at Nangurukuru and catch a **daladala** (roughly hourly) there – the last leaves around 6pm. In Kilwa Kivinje, daladalas drop passengers opposite the German memorial on the road in. Note that most road maps of Tanzania get this area totally wrong – the road from

---

Dhows from Kilwa Kivinje

Kilwa Kivinje is one of the few remaining places on the coast where catching a **dhow** is a real possibility (for general advice on catching dhows, see p.48). The first place to head for is the harbour, which has two distinct areas separated by a clump of mangroves. The eastern harbour is for fishing boats, the western one for commercial dhows. As is the case along the whole of the south coast, your best chance of arranging lifts is between November and March or April. **Fishing dhows** will rarely give you a lift, as few of them land anywhere, though you could try to arrange an overnight trip with them to near Songo Songo Island, where they bait fish at night with lanterns, returning home at the crack of dawn. More promising if you actually want to get somewhere are the **cargo dhows** moored in the commercial harbour, which will usually take passengers for a fee. There are no fixed schedules, and the price depends on how wealthy the captain thinks you are. It's worth asking locally about the seaworthiness and the character of the skipper of any boat you decide to join.

There are boats to **Songo Songo Island** most days, some continuing to **Mafia Island**. Songo Songo Island itself has connections northwards, and occasionally all the way to **Zanzibar**, though you'll need an exit stamp to make this trip (ask at the regional offices in Kilwa Masoko; you'll need to be extremely patient). Failure to do this will land you in hot water with the Zanzibari authorities, who will require convincing explanations (or a bribe) to overlook your unorthodox entry. You'll also need to bring your own food and water. Heading south, there are less frequent dhows to **Lindi** – ask around, but be prepared to have to wait a few days or longer. There are no boats between Kilwa Masoko and Kilwa Kivinje.

Nangurukuru to Kilwa Masoko *doesn't* go through Kilwa Kivinje, but passes it 6km inland. **Leaving** Kilwa Kivinje, board the bus in Kilwa Masoko if you're aiming for Dar. Heading south, you have no choice but to go to Nangurukuru and wait for a spare seat on a passing bus. There's no **petrol** at Kilwa Kivinje, so fill up at Nangurukuru or Kilwa Masoko.

Kivinje has four cheap and basic **guest houses** (all ➊). By far the most pleasant, if you don't mind doing without electricity and a private bathroom, is the *Savoye Guest House* (☏ Kilwa Kivinje 4), beside the commercial harbour, which has cleanish rooms with mosquito nets, and friendly owners, though they don't speak English. Otherwise, there's the grotty *Four Ways Guest House* by the market, with dark and dingy but exceptionally cheap rooms with electricity; and the similar if even grubbier *New Sudi's Guest House*, which is accessed through a small bar. Equally basic but more atmospheric than any of these is the unnamed guest house on the little triangular square west of the market (it's on the second floor). Despite the modern facade, it's an old construction with thick walls, and still retains residual decoration (such as stuccowork and carved window frames) from more glorious times past.

The Town

The bulk of Kilwa Kivinje's nineteenth-century buildings lie along a couple of sandy streets flanking the shore, just back from the two harbours. Many date from Kilwa Kivinje's short but prosperous period in the mid-nineteenth century, when it was chosen by Zanzibar's Omani rulers to replace Kilwa Kisiwani as the major terminus for the southern **slave route** from Lake Nyasa. Slaves, ivory and other goods were transported along this route from the interior to Zanzibar, or directly to Madagascar and the French colonies of the Bourbon Islands (now Réunion) and Îles Maurice – it's estimated that over twenty thousand slaves were exported annually from Kilwa Kivinje during the 1860s.

Following the abolition of the slave trade in the 1870s (slavery itself only disappeared in the 1920s), decline was inevitable, and was swiftly followed by **German colonization** in 1888. On the strength of the town's trading links with the interior, Kilwa Kivinje was an obvious choice for the colony's southern headquarters. German rule was harsh and unforgiving, and their occupation – which lasted less than three decades – saw the German *schutztruppen* almost constantly engaged in quelling rebellions and uprisings all over the country: particularly the Abushiri War of 1888–89, and the Maji Maji Uprising of 1905–6. The **former courthouse**, an imposing two-storey building facing the fishing harbour, dates from this time. The **cannon** mounted on a replica carriage outside is from Omani times, and there are two more, unmounted cannons a few metres away on the grimy beach, which only appear at low tide.

Some 500m along the road to Nangurukuru from the fishing harbour in a square on the left is a small **German memorial**, with four cannons pointing downwards at its corners. It commemorates two Germans killed in September 1888 during the Abushiri War, defending, according to the inscription, "the house of the German East Africa Company in heroic fashion". Locals have another version of the story: the Germans, they say, had been hunting warthogs or wild boar, and after the hunt had skinned the animals and prepared the meat. Unfortunately for them, the meat was stolen by a local inhabitant, who proceeded to eat it with his family and friends. On discovering that what they had just eaten was a kind of pork and thus *haram* (forbidden), the good Muslim thief returned to lynch the hapless Germans.

Kilwa put up strong resistance during the rebellion, and was one of the last places to be "pacified" when its leader, **Hassan bin Omari Makunganya**, was captured in November 1895 and hanged from a mango tree. The tree has disappeared but the site of the hanging is still known as Mwembe-Kinyonga, "hangman's mango tree". It's located 1.5km further along the Nangurukuru road on the right, and is marked with another obelisk put up after Independence to commemorate both Makunganya and other local fighters who were hanged during the Maji Maji Uprising. The rebellion began in the Matumbi Hills near Kilwa, in the village of a soothsayer named **Kinjikitile**. Kinjikitile claimed to have discovered a spring from which magic water (*maji*) flowed. If sprinkled on a person, he said, the water would protect the wearer from bullets. Within months, word of the charm had spread and the entire south of the country rose up in arms against the Germans. Kinjikitile himself was one of the first victims of the German reprisal, and was hanged by troops from Kilwa. Surmounting the obelisk is a wooden statue of an old man, possibly Kinjikitile or Makunganya, though both his arms have broken off. The much-eroded painted inscription reads: "Mashujaa Walio Nyongwa na Mjerumani Vita Nya Maji Maji" ("Concerning brave people hanged by the Germans in the war of Maji Maji"). German rule ended during World War I, when they were ejected by British troops. If you look around the beach at the top of the slipway in the commercial harbour, you can still see a thick, armour-plated **gun hatch**. Where it comes from, nobody knows, though it's most likely to have turned up here sometime during World War I.

Eating and drinking

Kilwa Kivinje doesn't exactly roll out the carpet when it comes to food. Indisputably the best bites in town are at the ramshackle **foodstalls** on the beach facing the old courthouse, which serve up delicious grilled fish and squid, and also sell seasonal fruit. The ducks waddling around here don't appear to feature on anyone's menu, though. As to proper **restaurants**, the best of the bunch – which doesn't mean an awful lot – is the *Kivulini Beach Bar*, facing the mangroves at the northwest end of the port, which also has reasonably cool beers. Other choices are little more than eat houses: try *Al-Mahmouda Hotel*, to the left of the ruined courthouse looking from the beach, which offers cheap basic fare and is popular with locals; or the unnamed *hoteli* to the right of the courthouse, whose smoky atmosphere and grilled fish attracts old men. For breakfast, the best place is the friendly and dirt-cheap *Boys Corner Hotel* beside the market, with *andazi* doughnuts, scalding hot sweet tea, chapatis and *ugali* with sauce.

Beers and sodas are easy to come by. The "coldest" are at *Mbukwa Grocery*, the bamboo construction half a kilometre back along the road to Nangurukuru on the left, which also does snacks (mainly egg and chip omelettes). Coolish beers are also served at *Kivulini Beach Bar* near the port. The *Sea Breeze Bar* has warm beers in small thatched huts near the harbour inside a bamboo fence, but their food is abysmal.

Lindi, Mtwara and Mikindani

It must be said that the port towns of **Lindi and Mtwara**, 295km and 359km south of Dar respectively, whilst pleasant enough, aren't much of a draw in themselves, although if you've just arrived from Kilwa or have braved the overland route east from Lake Nyasa, they'll feel like veritable oases of civilization. As a bonus, both have access to some beautiful beaches, and have acquired – or will shortly be acquiring – a handful of tourist-oriented beach hotels.

A much more attractive destination is the former slave-trading town of **Mikindani**, on a bay just north of Mtwara, with picturesque ruins, a palpable sense of history, the best hotel in southern Tanzania, and a variety of walks and day-trips offered by a local NGO. In addition, the town is the base for the only **scuba-diving** centre between Mafia and Mozambique, the perfect way of exploring the coral reefs of the **Mnazi Bay-Ruvuma Estuary Marine Park**, southeast of Mtwara.

Lindi and around

Founded in the eighteenth century as a caravan terminus on the slave and ivory route from Lake Nyasa, the Indian Ocean port of **LINDI** ("Deep Channel") is capital of one of Tanzania's most impoverished regions, suffering both from geographical isolation (soon to end when the sealed road from Dar finally

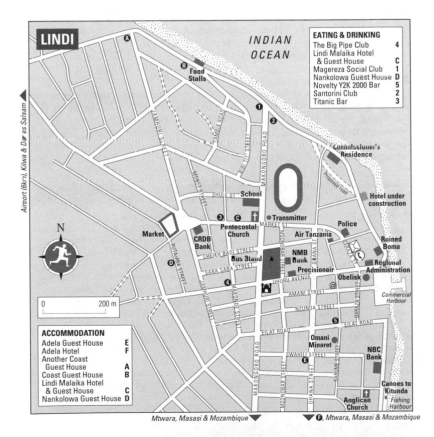

LINDI

INDIAN OCEAN

EATING & DRINKING
The Big Pipe Club	4
Lindi Malaika Hotel & Guest House	C
Magereza Social Club	1
Nankolowa Guest House	D
Novelty Y2K 2000 Bar	5
Santorini Club	2
Titanic Bar	3

Airport (6km), Kilwa & Dar es Salaam

Food Stalls

Commissioner's Residence

Proposed road

Hotel under construction

School

Transmitter

Police

Pentecostal Church

Market

Air Tanzania

Ruined Boma

CRDB Bank

NMB Bank

Bus Stand

Precisionair

Regional Administration

Obelisk

Uhuru Avenue

Commercial Harbour

Amani Street

Nzunda Street

Eilat Road

Omani Minaret

NBC Bank

Swahili Street

Canoes to Kitunda

Anglican Church

Fishing Harbour

N

0   200 m

ACCOMMODATION
Adela Guest House	E
Adela Hotel	F
Another Coast Guest House	A
Coast Guest House	B
Lindi Malaika Hotel & Guest House	C
Nankolowa Guest House	D

Mtwara, Masasi & Mozambique   Mtwara, Masasi & Mozambique

arrives) and depressed global market prices for cashew nuts, the region's major cash crop. There's a justified feeling of injured pride, too, at being ignored by the government whilst neighbouring Mtwara has matured into the south coast's most important trading centre and port, at Lindi's expense.

The feeling of abandonment is most obviously and mundanely expressed in Lindi's crumbling infrastructure. After the rains, especially, when clouds of mosquitoes and flies descend on the town, it's hard to imagine that Lindi was once home to a thriving expatriate community. Most of them cleared out after Independence and only a handful remain, mostly NGO workers and missionaries. Few people speak English, but the locals are unfailingly friendly if initially reserved, and the town itself enjoyable enough, with a host of attractive buildings dating from the first half of the twentieth century. The location is lovely, too, nestled on Lindi Bay at the mouth of the Lukuledi River, flanked by hills on both its landward and river sides, and by the ocean to the northeast, where dhows under sail are a common sight.

Arrival and accommodation

During the dry season there are at least three daily **buses** from Dar (Akida's Coach has the safest reputation), and buses to and from Mtwara, Masasi, Newala and Nachingwea also pass through. The **bus stand** is in the middle of town between Makongoro Road and Msonobar Street. Until the sealed road from Dar finally reaches town, access during the heaviest downpours (most likely March–May) is either by **plane** (Mon & Fri on Precisionair; the airport is 6km towards Kilwa – take a taxi or hitch a lift on arriving), or the weekly **ferry** from Dar to Mtwara, from where there are frequent buses and daladalas.

Accommodation

Lindi has a lot of cheap but often grim **accommodation**, and a couple of **beach hotels** in the works: one will replace the former *Lindi Club* along the coast road; the other, tentatively called *The Lindi Boma*, will be located in the colonial Commissioner's Residence, with the present road rerouted behind it to give it a nice beach. For information on the latter, contact the *Dolce Vita* restaurant in Dar (℗0741/782497, ⓔladolcevita@africaonline.co.tz).

Dhows from Lindi

Lindi has two harbours: the fenced-in **commercial harbour**, and the informal **fishing harbour**, 500m south past NBC bank. If you want to catch a lift in a dhow, talk your way into the commercial harbour and ask to be shown the Office of the Dhow Registrar (Mon–Fri 8am–4pm; ℗023/220 2162), which is the building on your right as you enter. The officer can tell you which dhows are due when, and – if any are in port – where they're headed to. The next step is to come to an arrangement with a dhow captain, after which the registrar will write your name on the passenger manifest and ask for payment of the Tsh200 harbour tax, and Tsh800 per item of "non-personal" luggage. Once through these formalities, see the Customs & Excise officer; if you're sailing to a Tanzanian port no fee should be levied.

The most frequent dhow connection is with **Kilwa Masoko** (which, bizarrely enough, exports boatloads of dried fish to Lindi). Dhows also sometimes go to **Kilwa Kivinje** and **Mafia**, though it's often quicker to take the first dhow headed north and proceed from there. There are no regular dhows to Mozambique or Mtwara, but there are occasional cargo boats to and from **Dar**, **Zanzibar** and **Mozambique**.

Adela Guest House Swahili St ☎023/220 2571.
A welcoming and safe budget option with dozens
of cell-like rooms with clean if stained sheets,
large box nets and quiet fans, sharing showers and
squat toilets. ❶

Adela Hotel Ghana St, four blocks south of Swahili
St ☎023/220 2310. Pricey but reasonable rooms,
all with tiled bathrooms (hot running water but
broken toilet seats), box nets and fans. There's a
quiet bar at the back (guests only), food to order,
and safe parking. Breakfast included. ❸

Another Coast Guest House Jamhuri St
☎0745/721486. Fresher rooms than at *Coast
Guest House* under the same owner, but the ocean
view is partially obscured by buildings on the opposite side of the road. ❶

Coast Guest House Facing the beach near the
top of Makongoro Rd ☎0745/721486. Pretty basic
but acceptable, as of course it's close to the sea,
with large double beds or two small ones in slightly
musty rooms, most sharing bathrooms, all with box
nets and fans. The two front rooms have sea views,
albeit through wire mesh windows. ❶–❷

Lindi Malaika Hotel & Guest House Market Ave
☎0744/057736. The best of the "budget" guest
houses, but a touch overpriced and still a tad basic.
All rooms have a shower and Western toilet, fan,
large box net(s) and TV, and there's also an "executive room" containing an enormous bed (too large
for its net), a desk, and a pleasingly horrendous
three-piece suite. Breakfast included. ❸

Nankolowa Guest House Rutamba St ☎023/220
2727. A safe and friendly budget choice with
single, double or twin-bed rooms (most sharing
bathrooms), all with ceiling fan and big box nets.
The en-suite rooms used to get musty, but lack of
running water at the time of writing had eliminated
that problem. ❷

The Town

Despite the loss of its economic importance, Lindi retains a lively and bustling
air, best experienced around the bus stand and at the main **market** at the west
end of Market Avenue. Heading east from here takes you to the Chinese-built
Stadium, from where a left turn along Makongoro Road heads up to the **beach**.
The coast road back into town skirts a pleasantly green and breezy part of Lindi,
favoured by colonial Europeans for their residences and offices, most of them
now in ruins. Notable among these – and planned to be converted into *The Lindi
Boma* hotel – is the marvellously dilapidated **Commissioner's Residence**, its
flags and bunting now replaced by festoons of ivy. If or when the hotel gets
built, the coast road is likely to be rerouted behind it. But the real highlight lies
further on. Just before the road turns back inland into Uhuru Avenue, on your
right is one of the most astonishing constructions in Tanzania. This is the old
Boma (the planned hotel's name is a bit of a fib), established by the Germans
as their headquarters, and now so dilapidated that a veritable forest of fig trees
has sprouted inside, and it's the trees rather than mortar that's holding the place
together. Catch it while you can – with the sealed road from Dar inching ever
closer, it surely won't be long before the place gives way to something else.

Another reminder of the colonial period is the **obelisk** in the garden outside
the commercial harbour. Although the obelisk has lost its plaques, its similarity
to the two obelisk monuments in Kilwa Kivinje suggests that it commemorates
Germans who died during the Maji Maji Uprising. Heading south from the
commercial harbour, you reach the small **fishing harbour**, which also has a
small market and stalls selling freshly grilled fish. Just behind this is the **Anglican Church**, a clumsy attempt at the formal proportions of Neoclassicism, not
helped by the battleship-grey cement. Heading back into town along Karume
Street, you'll come across what is arguably Lindi's oldest construction, a battered
and lop-sided domed **Omani minaret** dating from Zanzibari rule in the nineteenth century; it's just north of Swahili Street, beside a more recent mosque.

Local beaches

The town-centre **beaches** are mainly used by fishing boats, and for the most
part are lined with houses, offering you neither privacy nor – if you're a woman

– much chance to respect Islamic sensibilities. More suitable are the beaches north of town, which get better the further you go; the nearest, **Mtema beach**, is about 4km away in a beautiful sheltered cove, but a quarry on the headland beside it may have turned the water brown. Better, if you have time, would be to catch a motorized **canoe ferry** (Tsh200) across the Lukuledi River to the small farming village of **Kitunda**, from where a thirty-minute walk along the coast takes you to a beautiful sheltered beach. The canoes leave from Lindi's fish market, south of the harbour, and take about five minutes to cross the river. It should also be possible to rent a whole canoe (with its owner) to explore the wide river estuary, which contains a number of secluded beaches and bays, mangroves, outlandish limestone formations, crocodiles and the small island of **Kisiwa cha Popo** ("Bat Island"), which – as its name suggests – serves as a daytime roost for fruit bats

Eating and drinking

Lindi has a handful of half-decent restaurants, but what's really recommended is the row of **street vendors** inside the bus stand who every evening rustle up roast or fried chicken, eggs and chips for hungry travellers. There's the bonus of chairs and tables arranged out in front, so you can sit out under the stars watching the world go by in the flickering light of *kibatari* oil lamps. Waitresses from nearby bars bring sodas and beers, and the atmosphere is very friendly, with kids dancing about to the music which blares out from surrounding stores. Other street food can be found at kiosks at the fishing harbour (including prawns if you're lucky) and facing the beach just north of *Coast Guest House*, where you'll find especially good grilled fish.

There are plenty of **bars** to choose from, though, once again, for a different nocturnal experience, the bus stand beckons. Walking around at night is relatively safe, but being escorted by a reliable local would be wise.

The Big Pipe Club Corner of Uhuru Ave and Makonde St. A pleasantly quiet daytime haunt that gets busy on weekend nights for its discos (it occasionally also hosts live bands), with tables in a large covered courtyard and unspeakable toilets.

Lindi Malaika Hotel & Guest House Market Ave. Lindi's best restaurant, and with great breakfasts, but arrive early for lunch or dinner as the food is generally gone by 8.30pm. Portions are generous and prices low: Tsh1500 for *pilau* or banana and meat stew, Tsh2000 for their special biriani.

Magereza Social Club North end of Makongoro Rd. Operated by the prison authority, this is popular in the evenings for its coastal breezes. You can also drink in the nicely overgrown garden facing the bar – a lovely daytime refuge.

Nankolowa Guest House Rutamba St. Enjoys a good reputation and has an extensive menu to choose from, with most dishes under Tsh2500 (until 9pm), but order early to give them enough time to prepare things.

Novelty Y2K 2000 Bar Corner of Eilat Rd and Karume St. Looks like the novelty wore off, though this first-floor bar (with views towards the harbour) still gets busy on Friday and Saturday nights, when it plays a wide range of popular music. There's food from vendors in the courtyard downstairs.

Santorini Club On the coast at the top of Makongoro Rd. Mtwara's main nightspot, with heaving discos weekend nights, and a gaggle of prostitutes too.

Titanic Bar Market Ave. A good local place if you want to hit the beers and sink without a trace; the tables outside by the pavement are the main reason for coming.

Listings

Banks Change money before coming, as cashing travellers' cheques is uncommonly painful, taking hours. Best is NBC, south of the harbour, which also has a 24hr Visa/MasterCard ATM; CRDB is near the clock tower, facing the market.

Internet access Lindi Net, corner of Amani and
Karume streets (daily 8am–6pm; Tsh1000/hr).
Newspapers The only outlet is a kiosk on Msono-
bar St behind the bus stand; the day's papers

arrive in the evening or the next day.
Post office Baraza St.
Telephones TTCL, next to the post office; there are
card phones outside.

South and west of Lindi

The roads **inland from Lindi** can be tough-going in the dry season, and impassable in the rains. Yet, with a reliable 4WD (Land Rover pick-up drivers in Lindi should be happy to do a deal), an experienced driver and a healthy dose of curiosity, there are at least two destinations offering enough to reward the considerable effort of getting there.

Rondo Plateau Forest Reserve

The **Rondo Plateau Forest Reserve**, 77km due west of Lindi, provides a soothing contrast to the humid coastal swelter, and is relatively easy to access in your own 4WD, albeit in dry weather only. The reserve's eighteen square kilometres of semi-deciduous coastal forest offers **birders** the possibility of spotting the rare East Coast akalat, spotted ground thrush and the Rondo green barbet.

Those without wheels needn't fret: *The Old Boma at Mikindani* (see p.236) offers guided two-day trips for $95–150 per person depending on group size, all included, with the night spent in a former plantation manager's residence – oil lamps, a chorus of cicadas and frogs, a great view the next morning from the verandah, plus as much forest hiking as you want.

Tendaguru Hills

A more challenging target for a two-day trip (three or four days if combined with Rondo Plateau) is the **Tendaguru Hills** northwest of Lindi, 110km by road. These contain Africa's richest deposit of **late Jurassic fossils** – whose considerable similarities to those found at the Morrison Formation in the western USA vividly illustrate the existence, some 150 million years ago, of land bridges between the various post-Gondwanan continents.

The site was "discovered" by a German mining engineer, Bernhard Sattler, in 1907, while searching for garnet. Locals were already well acquainted with the gigantic fossilized bones that protruded from the ground, saying that they were the remains of a **man-eating ogre** whose toes had been slit open by warriors to release people that had been eaten.

The scientific excavation (and plunder) of the site began in 1909 under the auspices of Berlin's Museum für Naturkunde, which houses the finds. During the three-and-a-half year dig, an astonishing 225,000kg of fossils were removed by hand by up to five hundred labourers working simultaneously. Of the dozens of vertebrate species uncovered, including a mammal, crocodiles, sharks and bony fish, pterosaurs and dinosaurs, the glittering prize was the nearly complete skeleton of the giant sauropod, *Brachiosaurus brancai* – at 12m in height, the largest dinosaur ever to have been reconstructed (it still stands in the Berlin museum).

Practicalities are a pain, with access being the main problem – there's neither public transport nor accommodation, unless you can get *The Old Boma at Mikindani* to combine Tendaguru with a trip to the Rondo Plateau. Otherwise, you'll need to be totally self-sufficient, meaning a sturdy 4WD and driving skills to match. You'll need to leave Lindi before daybreak – in dry weather, it takes at least 5–6 hours each way, and you'll also need someone who knows the road. Camping probably isn't too clever given the ever-present if unlikely risk of attack by **lions**. But before all this, you'll need to obtain official **permission** from the Natural Resources Officer (Afisa ya Maliasili; ☎023/222 0501 or 0336) at the regional headquarters near Lindi's commercial harbour. If that's forthcoming, they should be able to suggest a suitable guide.

Arriving at the site, you'll see the trenches dug by more recent researchers (and looters) and slowly come to recognize the litter of smaller fossil fragments scattered about the place.

Mtwara and around

Heading south from Lindi, the road forks after 26km, one branch heading west to Masasi, the other south to Mikindani and Mtwara. **Mingoyo**, the village at the junction (also known as Mnazi Mmoja; "One Palm Tree" – in fact there are thousands), has hawkers aplenty peddling a variety of tasty snacks, from fruits and cashew nuts to all sorts of seafood, including octopus and succulent king prawns.

Eighty-two kilometres south of here, close to the border with Mozambique, is **MTWARA**, the south coast's largest town. Dubbed "Siberia" by civil servants thanks to its isolation from the rest of Tanzania, this modern town is something of an anomaly, and testimony to the failure of the **Groundnut Scheme**, a grand plan for regional development that the British put into action after World War II, and which saw the establishment of Mtwara itself in 1947. Unfortunately, the British seem not once to have considered whether the soil was suitable for growing groundnuts (peanuts) – it was not – and the project collapsed amidst colossal losses and bitter recriminations. The 211-kilometre railway from Mtwara to Nachingwea that had been built as part of the scheme was ripped up, leaving only the empty spaces which nowadays intersperse Mtwara's broad streets – it was to have become a city – to bear witness to the grandiose and short-sighted dreams of the past.

The cashew-nut economy that replaced the Groundnut Scheme has been the victim of fickle market prices, making Mtwara Region a net importer of food (prices here are steep by Tanzanian standards) and a favoured base for dozens of NGOs and aid organizations seeking to develop alternatives to this state of affairs. Still, things these days are looking up. Work on the **Mtwara Development Corridor** from Dar es Salaam has come a step closer to realization with the completion of the Rufiji River bridge, and work on the six-hundred-metre **Unity Bridge** over the Ruvuma River into Mozambique – for so long just a chimera – is finally about to kick off, with completion optimistically pencilled in for 2008 (the bridge will cross upriver, south of Newala). In addition, several million dollars have been spent modernizing Mtwara's harbour, Tanzania's third busiest, in anticipation of Mtwara being declared a free port. And with the Tarmac ribbon from Dar es Salaam finally becoming reality, it seems that Mtwara may at long last be able to emerge from its Siberian winter.

For visitors, Mtwara's modern origins mean that it lacks even a single building or sight of note. It does, however, sit on one of Tanzania's most beautiful stretches of coastline, while the **Mnazi Bay-Ruvuma Estuary Marine Park** to the south offers superlative swimming and snorkelling, some of Tanzania's best scuba-diving reefs, and miles of palm-fringed sandy beaches. The town is also a handy springboard for visiting **Mikindani**, 11km to the north.

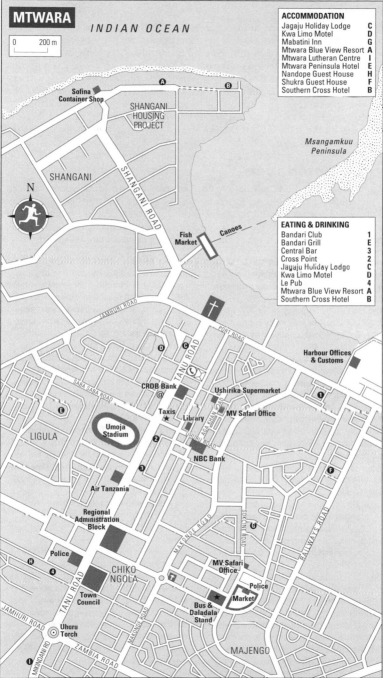

MTWARA

INDIAN OCEAN

0   200 m

ACCOMMODATION
Jagaju Holiday Lodge	C
Kwa Limo Motel	D
Mabatini Inn	G
Mtwara Blue View Resort	A
Mtwara Lutheran Centre	I
Mtwara Peninsula Hotel	E
Nandope Guest House	H
Shukra Guest House	F
Southern Cross Hotel	B

Sofina Container Shop

SHANGANI HOUSING PROJECT

Msangamkuu Peninsula

SHANGANI

SHANGANI ROAD

N

Fish Market

Canoes

EATING & DRINKING
Bandari Club	1
Bandari Grill	E
Central Bar	3
Cross Point	2
Jagaju Holiday Lodge	C
Kwa Limo Motel	D
Le Pub	4
Mtwara Blue View Resort	A
Southern Cross Hotel	B

TAMHURI ROAD

PORT ROAD

TANU ROAD

Harbour Offices & Customs

SABA SABA ROAD

CRDB Bank
@

Ushirika Supermarket

Taxis

Library

AGA KHAN

MV Safari Office

HURU ROAD

Umoja Stadium

LIGULA

NBC Bank

Air Tanzania

Regional Administration Block

MAKONDE ROAD

SOKOINE ROAD

RAILWAYS ROAD

Police

CHIKO NGOLA

MV Safari Office

Town Council

Bus & Daladala Stand

Police

Market

Uhuru Torch

MIKINDANI RD

TANU ROAD

JAMHURI ROAD

MAKONDE ROAD

ZAMBIA ROAD

MAJENGO

▼ *Airport (6km), Mikindani, Mnazi Bay-Ruvuma Marine Estuary Park, Lindi, Masasi, Mozambique & Newala (A19)*

Arrival

Buses from Dar take around twelve hours in dry weather, but potentially two or three days in the long rains, should the road be blocked by mud, trucks or floods. Once the surfaced road is complete (probably 2008), around ten hours is likely. Mtwara's **airport** is 6km south of town. Air Tanzania flies daily from Dar ($100–140 one-way, $220 return). The weekly **ferry** from Dar (currently departing at 8am on Saturday) docks in Mtwara the following morning.

Taxis can be rented at the corner of TANU and Uhuru roads, and there's a taxi rank on the south side of the bus stand. Rides cost Tsh2000 in the centre, or Tsh2500 to Shangani suburb.

Accommodation

There are some cheap and basic **guest houses** on the south side of the bus stand. Better places – some on the shore – are in the northern suburb of Shangani. They tend to fill up quickly during the cashew-nut buying season (roughly mid-Nov to Feb), so arrive early or book ahead by phone. Mtwara's **tap water** is unsafe to drink thanks to sediment contamination.

Jagaju Holiday Lodge TANU Rd ☎023/233 3380. A friendly place, although little English is spoken, with a choice of rooms with or without bathroom (all have nets and fans). ❶–❷

Kwa Limo Motel Off the top end of TANU Rd ☎0741/526320. Next to Mtwara's busiest bar and restaurant and a small and sometimes mosquito-infested pond, the fifteen self-contained doubles here all have fridges, but check the nets for holes, sheets and pillows for cleanliness, and see whether the shower works. Breakfast included. ❷

Mabatini Inn Signposted off Sokoine Rd, 500m north of the bus stand ☎023/233 4025. A friendly if slightly tatty family-run place with that musty smell so characteristic of Mtwara. It doesn't have the best rooms, and bathrooms are shared, but the bedrooms have box nets and fans, and they play good African music in the adjacent lean-to bar (though this might disturb light sleepers). ❶

🏃 **Mtwara Blue View Resort** Shangani (no phone). Worth asking taxi drivers whether it's still open as the seafront location is idyllic, with gorgeous sea views from both its en-suite cottages and restaurant-cum-bar. Breakfast included. ❸

🏃 **Mtwara Lutheran Centre** 100m south of Uhuru Torch roundabout ☎ & ☎023/233 3294. One of the nicest hotels in town, with a quiet and gentle atmosphere, and lots of clean rooms with box nets and standing fans, some also with bathrooms. Recommended as long as you don't plan on crawling back late after a night on the town, as there's a curfew. African food and soft drinks are available. Breakfast included. ❶–❷

Mtwara Peninsula Hotel West of Umoja Stadium ☎ & ☎023/233 3638. Mtwara's main business hotel, though its standard rooms (en suite, nets and fans) aren't much better than in cheaper places; for a few dollars more you get a better-value "superior" room with a/c and TV. Also has a restaurant, bar and safe parking. ❹

Nandope Guest House West off TANU Rd, near the police station ☎023/233 3362. One of Mtwara's best budget choices, with simple, colourful rooms painted in Rastafarian colours, reasonably clean shared showers and enclosed parking. The long-drops are smelly, though, and the nets a tad too small. ❶

Shukra Guest House Railways Rd, signposted on Port Rd opposite the Pax Filling Station ☎023/233 3822. One of the town's better cheapies, and more peaceful than the nearby *Mabatini Inn*. Most rooms (shared bathrooms only; twin or double) are huge, all with nets. ❶

🏃 **Southern Cross Hotel** Shangani ☎ & ☎023/233 3206. Mtwara's newest and most sophisticated lodging, and the first to be aimed at tourists, with nine high-ceilinged en-suite rooms in a sea-facing terrace, plus cottages, all with fans, window screens, useful furniture and attractive four-poster *semadari* beds. There's no beach as such – just lots of coral (some of which was thoughtlessly used for building the hotel) – though a sandy one is within walking distance. Also has an expensive but recommended restaurant, and a great terrace bar with grand views. Breakfast included. Currently ❹, may increase to ❻.

The Town and beaches

Mtwara's expansive street layout (which was intended to be filled by a city that never came) means it isn't overly conducive to walking – not that there's an awful lot to see. You could always rent a **bicycle** – ask around; it shouldn't cost more than Tsh2000 a day. The liveliest area is around the **market** near the bus station, but the rest of town is pretty somnolent. Probably the most interesting architectural sights are the terraces of the two-storey concrete stores facing one another on **Aga Khan Road**, the town's main commercial drag. Dating from the 1950s to 1970s, these pillared shop fronts are the modern equivalent of the traditional balconied Swahili town houses you can still see in Mikindani, Kilwa Kivinje and elsewhere.

The town's main beaches are in the NGO-colonized suburb of **Shangani**, a couple of kilometres north of town. There's no public transport so you'll have to walk, take a bike or grab a taxi. On the north (ocean-facing) side, the beach is narrow and you'll need sandals to walk out several hundred metres over the sharp coral plateau to deeper water at low tide; children will love rummaging around in the exposed pools in search of crabs and other animals. The beach on the east side of Shangani, facing Mtwara Bay, consists of fine gravel and sand and is better for swimming. The water at either place is pretty clean, though the beaches can get covered in seaweed. Basic supplies and sodas are available from Sofina Container Shop, just back from the beach; for proper meals and drinks, *Mtwara Blue View Beach Resort* and the more expensive *Southern Cross Hotel* duly oblige.

With more time, you could head across the bay to more attractive beaches at **Msangamkuu** – the "Big Sand" – a giant sandspit across the harbour entrance. Regular canoe ferries (around Tsh500) cross throughout the day from the jetty behind the Catholic church. People have camped here in the past without problems, but others – including a sizeable marine research expedition – have been robbed, so camping cannot be recommended.

Eating

For **eating out**, all bars or local *hotelis* will serve up perfectly acceptable *nyama choma*. For real restaurants, you're pretty much limited to the following.

Bandari Grill *Mtwara Peninsula Hotel*. Dine on decent continental and Indian grub in Arctic a/c. They don't always have meat, but can rustle up lasagne whenever they have mince. Mains around Tsh4000–5000.

Jagaju Holiday Lodge TANU Rd. Simple eats in the bar at the side of the guest house – the grilled fish is best.

Kwa Limo Motel Off the top end of TANU Rd. The row of double-parked Land Rovers outside testifies to *Kwa Limo*'s popularity with expatriates. There's a wide choice of food at reasonable prices (generally under Tsh2500), including banana soup.

Southern Cross Hotel Shangani. Haunt of tourists, expatriates and well-to-do Tanzanians, this has Mtwara's best if priciest restaurant (mains around Tsh5000, full meals upwards of Tsh10,000), with the menu consisting mainly of continental fare (steaks, pasta and seafood with chips).

Drinking and nightlife

Mtwara has plenty of enjoyable **bars** to choose from, including a couple on the beach in Shangani.

Bandari Club Port Rd. Mtwara's main nightspot, this lively and friendly place is host to a live band (Wed, Fri & Sat nights, Sun afternoons), with plenty of dancing. Tsh500 entry.

Central Bar TANU Rd. A pleasant place for a drink in the basement of a modern house hidden behind four fern trees.

Cross Point TANU Rd. Busy central boozer that stays open all night; also has good cheap food.

Kwa Limo Motel Off the top end of TANU Rd. Mtwara's biggest bar, with plenty of outdoor seating under trees. It's always popular, both in the daytime, when it catches a bit of a sea breeze, and at night – though it's next to a bug-infested pool which reeks during the rains.

Le Pub *Bondeni Hotel*, 100m from *Nandope Guest*

House. A popular bar which also has basic rooms (**1**) if you can't face the walk back.

Mtwara Peninsula Hotel Drinks, *nyama choma* and weekend discos under a huge *makuti* roof.

Mtwara Blue View Resort Shangani. Right on the coast, this is a lovely place in the afternoon, with a great ocean view, swimming once you've picked your way across the corals, and seats under trees.

Southern Cross Hotel Shangani. Another great seafront place with sweeping views, though with a more refined atmosphere and pricier drinks (beer Tsh1500). Also has satellite TV for sports.

Listings

Banks The slow but reliable NBC on Uhuru Rd, and the awkward CRDB on TANU Rd, can change travellers' cheques. NBC also has a 24hr Visa/MasterCard ATM.

Car rental *Kwa Limo Motel* has a Land Rover for rent, though the manager will wring every

last shilling out of you, so don that old bargaining hat.

Immigration The intransigent immigration office is on the ground floor of the Regional Administration Block on TANU Rd – boot-licking politeness and patience may pay dividends, but don't count on it.

Moving on from Mtwara

The **bus and daladala stand** is at the bottom of Sokoine Road near the market. Destinations for the various services are clearly marked on chalkboards by the parking bays, together with their Kiswahili departure times. The first buses for **Dar es Salaam** leave around 5am, with a second flurry at 7am. Safety – meaning (lack of) driving skills – is a perennial headache, especially now that there's more sealed roads: Akida's Coach is considered safest on account of it's taking two hours longer than the competition, but best enquire with several locals a couple of days before. Taqwa have a reputation for speeding. There are also hourly departures for **Lindi** via **Mikindani** throughout the day. Other destinations covered daily include **Newala**, **Masasi** and **Nachingwea**. For the **Kilwas**, catch a Dar-bound bus as far as Nangurukuru and catch a daladala.

Flights to Dar es Salaam are operated daily by Air Tanzania, whose office is on TANU Road (☎023/233 3417). Moving on by **ferry**, the MV *Safari* (☎023/233 3591; 22hr; $25) currently sails to Dar es Salaam every Tuesday at 10am. It fills up quickly, so book ahead, and is third-class only, so you might want to snatch some extra sleep before embarking. Tickets can be bought at several offices: the most reliable are on Aga Khan Road, and on Sokoine Road just north of the market.

By road or sea to Mozambique

The only official border crossing between Tanzania and **Mozambique** is at the mouth of the Ruvuma River, 40km southeast of Mtwara beyond the village of **Kalambo**, where a landing craft carries vehicles across the river (in theory at least – it's become unreliable of late; ask around at the bus stand). Several pick-ups and Land Rovers cover the 35km of rough *murram* road from Mtwara to Kalambo throughout the day (Tsh3000), but it's best to catch one early in the morning in case you're delayed in Kalambo or at the river. Kalambo is where you complete customs and immigration formalities, in that order. As a tourist travelling overland, you'll need to obtain a **Mozambique visa** in advance from Dar es Salaam – the procedure takes three days. Kalambo has plenty of bars and *hotelis* but no accommodation – more reason to arrive early.

Transport from Mtwara waits for its passengers to finish their paperwork before struggling on across the remaining 5km of floodplain to the river itself, assuming

Internet access The best is inside the post office (Mon–Fri 8am–4.30pm, Sat 8am–noon; Tsh500/hr). There's also DSTS Internet Café, TANU Rd, near the taxi rank.

Library "Mtwara Intellectual Service Station" is on Uhuru Rd (Mon–Fri 9.30am–6pm, Sat 9am–2pm; Tsh500/day).

Newspapers The day's press usually arrives in the afternoon: there are two good stands along Uhuru Rd near the library, and one at the post office entrance, which also has international magazines.

Pharmacy Bus Stand Pharmacy, in the bus stand ☎023/233 3359.

Post office Corner of TANU and Uhuru roads.

Souvenirs There's a stall selling Makonde wood-carvings on TANU Rd, next to an unnamed bar just north of the taxi rank.

Supermarket Ushirika Supermarket, north end of Aga Khan Rd; prices are particularly high during the rains.

Telephones TTCL, beside the post office (Mon–Fri 7.45am–4.30pm, Sat 9am–12.30pm). There are cardphones outside, also at the bus stand and at *Kwa Limo Motel*.

Mnazi Bay-Ruvuma Estuary Marine Park

Established in 2000, **Mnazi Bay-Ruvuma Estuary Marine Park** (🌐www .marineparktz.com) covers a large part of the land and ocean southeast of Mtwara between Msangamkuu Peninsula and the mouth of the Ruvuma River on the Mozambique border, encompassing a network of estuarine, mangrove, tidal, peninsular, island and coral reef environments. The last offer

the road is passable: the irregularly repaired narrow causeway frequently gets washed away. There are a handful of lean-tos down by the jetty selling warm sodas, tea and beer, but nothing else. The ferry operates at high tide (in effect, for a few hours twice in every 24hr) and occasionally runs at night. It costs Tsh1000 for passengers and Tsh5000 for a car. There should also be boys taking people over in canoes.

Once in Mozambique, clear customs and immigration at **Namoto**, 8km south of the river and connected to it by *chapas* (daladalas), which run from early morning to around 5pm. There's also a daily pick-up that goes all the way from the river to Mocímboa da Praia; ask in Kalambo about the departure time. There's no bank in Namoto, but you'll find informal money-changers both there and in Kalambo; try to check rates somewhere reputable first. The first major town in Mozambique is **Quionga**, 20km south of the river. The road to here, and the 30km continuation to Palma, is tricky sand, but the remaining 85km to the main coastal town of **Mocímboa da Praia** is good dirt. This whole area is prone to flooding, so ask any drivers you meet about road conditions.

Construction of the transfrontier **Unity Bridge** into Mozambique is scheduled for completion in 2008 (*Mungu akipenda* – God willing). However, access roads will likely require more time to complete. When ready, the approach from Tanzania will be via Newala.

There are neither ferries nor regular passenger-carrying **boats** to Mozambique from Mtwara, but with some luck you could find a **commercial dhow** headed for Mocímboa da Praia (at least 48hr) or Pemba (not to be confused with Pemba Island in Zanzibar or Pemba village near Mikindani), which leave roughly every two days from the dhow wharf by the fish market. Alternatively, enquire at the harbour office (Mon–Fri 8am–5pm; ☎023/233 3243) in the main port complex about the cargo-carrying **motorboat** to Pemba, which leaves once or twice a month. You should clear customs formalities in the main port complex in any case, and immigration at the Regional Administration Block on TANU Road – be prepared to grovel, as service with a smile is not their style.

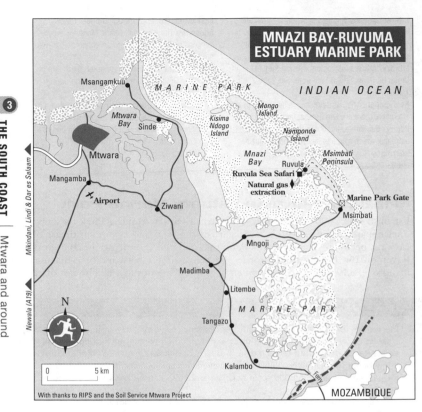

MNAZI BAY-RUVUMA
ESTUARY MARINE PARK

With thanks to RIPS and the Soil Service Mtwara Project

superb snorkelling and diving, especially on **Ruvula Reef**, off the north end of Msimbati Peninsula, which slopes steeply right up to the shore, whilst the **beaches** – with all the white sand, fringing palm trees and warm turquoise water you've dreamed of – are among Tanzania's most enthralling.

The easiest beach to access is just beyond **Msimbati** village and the park gate, though it's used by fishermen for peeling prawns and cleaning fish. Much nicer is the one after **Ruvula**, 6km northwest of Msimbati village on the tip of Msimbati Peninsula, and backed by thick vegetation. It's possible to arrange **dhow trips** with local fishermen at Ruvula to Namponda Island, 3km offshore; with more time, you could also explore Mongo Island and the diminutive Kisima Ndogo Island nearby. A word of caution when swimming: there's a dangerous **undertow** at Msimbati beach and possibly elsewhere at spring tide, and a few people get swept away every year, so seek local advice.

Practicalities

The heart of the park, **Msimbati Peninsula**, is roughly an hour's drive from Mtwara. To explore the park's amazing underwater world, though, it's best to go on a snorkelling or scuba-diving trip from Mikindani. For overnights, there's a basic lodge, and camping rough is possible.

Access

Msimbati Peninsula can be accessed by 4WD or daladala, though the latter leave you far from the best beaches. If **self-driving**, head south from Mtwara's Uhuru Torch roundabout for 900m and turn left. After 3.7km, turn left again off the tarmac on to the wide *murram* road that heads to Kalambo. The road takes you past the sizeable village of Ziwani, 8km from the junction and beautifully located in lush and shady coconut and mango plantations. Watch out for a dangerously slippery descent 3km further on. The turn-off for Msimbati is at Madimba, 17.5km from the junction; the road from here on is deep sand.

Daladalas from Mtwara run direct to Msimbati village, 2km before Msimbati beach. To get to Ruvula, at the tip of the peninsula, either walk the remaining 8km along a sandy track, or wait for a lift – you stand a better chance at weekends with Indian and European families. Alternatively, ask around for a lift at the *Kwa Limo Motel* in Mtwara, or with Mikindani's expatriates.

Access is easiest, however, on an **organized trip** from Mikindani: *The Old Boma at Mikindani* offers day-trips for $40–60 per person, including a lavish packed lunch. To really get to know the area, **snorkelling and scuba-diving** trips in and around the marine park are organized by eco2, also based in Mikindani (p.238). Access is usually by speedboat, taking an hour from Mikindani.

Park fees ($10 for 24hr) are paid either at the gate just beyond Msimbati village, or as part of the cost of trips from Mikindani. eco2 are the best source of **information**; in Mtwara, contact the Marine Parks and Reserves Unit in the Regional Block on TANU Road ☏023/233 3014.

Accommodation

Other than camping (see below), the park's only **accommodation** is *Ruvula Sea Safari Resort* at Ruvula beach (☏0748/367439; ❺), which has a handful of nice enough thatched cottages behind the beach sharing bathrooms. It's run more as a hobby than a business, and service can be slap-dash. It's also wise to ring up the day you're heading out to be sure someone's there. That said, the Belgian-Congolese couple running it are friendly when there, and the food is good.

Otherwise, **fly-camping** is the only choice (this can also be arranged through eco2), either on the beach at Msimbati or beyond Ruvula village. There are no facilities, so bring everything you'll need, though local fishermen will be happy to sell you fish and shellfish, including oysters, lobster, prawns and barracuda, and villagers can rustle up chickens and snacks for a barbecue. There are no security problems at present, but do ask permission before pitching a tent.

Mikindani

The contrast between the sprawling modern town of Mtwara and the tranquil fishing village of **MIKINDANI**, 11km back along the Lindi road, could hardly be greater – or more welcome. Beautifully set inside a sheltered, mangrove-lined bay, the village is home to some 12,000 people who rely on the ocean for their livelihood, catching fish and collecting cockles from the bay. Yet, as in so many other coastal villages, today's peaceful and languid atmosphere belies a turbulent and brutal past, when the town grew wealthy and powerful as one of the coast's major seaports for the ivory and slave caravans from the region of Lake Nyasa. Mikindani's many stone buildings, most of them in ruins, offer an eloquent and picturesque reminder of more prosperous times past, while beautiful beaches on the far side of the bay, a wide choice of excursions, a scuba-diving school, and one of southern Tanzania's most beautiful hotels make it a superb destination for a few days of getting away from it all.

Some history

Mikindani's sheltered location offered an ideal base for early traders sailing up and down the coast, and the town – or rather Pemba village, on the spur of land enclosing the bay's western entrance – was swiftly incorporated into the Indian Ocean trading network, as proven by some of Tanzania's earliest signs of Arab habitation. The arrival of **Islam** stimulated trade, and by the end of the fifteenth century – when Mikindani proper replaced Pemba as the main port – the town was trading inland as far as present-day Malawi, Zambia, Angola and Congo.

Decline set in with the arrival of the **Portuguese** in the sixteenth century and their disruption of the old trade links, but the town's fortunes picked up again in the middle of the following century when the Portuguese were ejected and the coastal slave trade fell under Omani and Zanzibari control. Mikindani's real boom began during the reign of **Sultan Seyyid Barghash**, whose rule saw the consolidation of the town's importance and the construction of several fine buildings, notably the Friday mosque. The legacy of the **slave trade** is also reflected in the village's tribal make-up, which includes the descendants of Yao, Makua and Mwera slaves, as well as Ngoni who first came as caravan porters working for the Arabs, and Makonde, some of whom had been slave traders themselves.

German rule was marked by the introduction of cash crops such as sisal, rubber, coconut and oil seed, though this failed to reverse the decline in the town's fortunes that had followed the abolition of the slave trade. Things changed little under **British rule** and by the 1950s Mikindani Bay had outlived its usefulness as a harbour, as it was too shallow for the vessels of the time. Mikindani's decline accelerated when the Mtwara–Nachingwea railway, built in 1949 for the Groundnut Scheme, was ripped up in 1962 following the scheme's spectacular collapse. Many of the colonial plantations subsequently fell to waste, as did many of the town's buildings, and Mikindani reverted to its original status as a humble fishing village.

Arrival, information and accommodation

Frequent **daladalas** run from Mtwara (Tsh200) throughout the day, whilst buses and daladalas from Lindi, Masasi and Dar es Salaam to Mtwara also pass through. You can get dropped off outside *Ten Degrees South Lodge* or at the start of the road to the *The Old Boma at Mikindani*; to catch **onward transport**; head to the square a few hundred metres south of *The Old Boma*. Dadadalas to Mtwara can be extremely full, with even the turn-boys unable to squeeze in more passengers, so get there early and be patient.

The Old Boma at Mikindani has a **tourist office** (daily from 8am to around 10pm), with dozens of informative sheets covering Mikindani and attractions in the Mtwara region, such as the Rondo Plateau and the Tendaguru Hills. **Trade Aid**, the British NGO that runs the hotel (ⓦwww.tradeaid.uk.org), is active both in bolstering local educational facilities, and in preserving the town's historical framework – part of its funding comes from hotel receipts, whilst locals also benefit directly by guiding (or sailing) tourists around.

Accommodation

Mikindani has only three **hotels**, none of them cheap; Trade Aid may open four guest rooms in Livingstone House once it gets renovated (probably around

$50–60 a double) – contact *The Old Boma at Mikindani* for details. If you're on a shoestring budget, the town is best visited as a day-trip from Mtwara, as there's no campsite. If you have at least six months free, and skills in either microfinance, self-help development, hospitality, accounts or teaching English, *The Old Boma at Mikindani* welcomes volunteers.

Makonde Beach Resort (also known as *Litingi's*) 3.5km south of Mikindani, 1.2km off the main road (no phone). The least attractive of the trio, with round brick *bandas* in a heavily fortified compound, though the rooms themselves are reasonable if tatty, with large double beds and nets, hot water, satellite TV and phones; more expensive ones have a/c. There's a bar and restaurant but no beach (it's all mangroves) – the nearest one is 1km away. Breakfast included. ❹

🏃 **The Old Boma at Mikindani** ☎0748/360110, ⓦ www.mikindani.com. Set inside the beautifully restored German Boma, this is southern Tanzania's best hotel by miles, with bags of atmosphere, outstanding accommodation, plus a wide range of activities and excursions (see p.238), a restaurant and bar, free Internet access, and a very welcome swimming pool (with lessons for local kids at 3pm Tues & Thurs). The eight

high-ceilinged rooms, four with balconies, have large timber beds and are decorated with local handicrafts. There's no a/c, but the thick walls, sea breeze and ceiling fans keep things cool. It's worth spending a little more for one of the corner rooms with sea views; the best is at the front under the parapet. All profits fund community projects. Credit cards accepted. Breakfast included. ❻–❼

🏃 **Ten Degrees South Lodge** On the bay by the roadside ☎0748/855833, ⓦ www.eco2.com. Set in a cool old house with thick walls, this informal, welcoming and affordable place has four comfortable rooms boasting solid Zanzibari beds with box nets and clean cotton sheets; all share bathrooms, though some en-suite *bandas* are planned for the hill behind. There's also free Internet access, Mikindani's best bar, and good food. Breakfast included. ❸

The Town

Mikindani is small enough to walk around, and the plentiful trees provide enough shade. If you want a guide, contact *The Old Boma at Mikindani*. As you're wandering along the narrow winding streets, look for the attractive first-floor wooden balconies (*uzio*) and the elaborately carved wooden doorways, both typical features of Swahili coastal settlements. Most of the stone buildings, many of them in ruins, date from the slaving era and are constructed of coral rock (ragstone) embedded in lime mortar. Much of the original lime stucco facing and cream or white limewash has disappeared, but where patches of limewash remain, the buildings make singularly photogenic subjects – kids are happy having their pictures taken, but most adults aren't, so ask before snapping.

Friday Mosque

Notable among the buildings dating from the reign of Sultan Barghash is the **Friday Mosque** in the centre of town. Its beautiful carved door was the work of an Ndonde slave called Gulum Dosa (the Ndonde are closely related to the Makonde), who belonged to an Indian customs officer in the Zanzibari government, which at the time also controlled Tanganyika's coastal strip. The three **stone graves** outside the mosque are believed to date from the fifteenth century, and face north towards Mecca. They are marked by baobab trees, which has led some to believe that the graves belong to sultans. Although there's no direct proof of this, a local legend says that when a sultan died, two baobab saplings would be planted at either end of his grave so that they would eventually unite to form a single tree.

Livingstone House and the Slave Market

At the bottom of the hill leading to the Boma, the nearly derelict **Livingstone House** has long been ear-marked for renovation by Trade Aid, but currently

Excursions from Mikindani

For landlubbers, *The Old Boma at Mikindani* offers a range of **guided walks**, from leisurely rambles around town ($5–10 per person) to longer forays, including the baobab-bedecked **Tingi Peninsula** (4km) on the eastern lip of the bay; **Pemba Village** (7km) on the west side; guided visits around a tree nursery; an evening's birding by canoe on **Kitere Lake**; and an overnight tour to **Rondo Plateau Forest Reserve** (see p.227; $95–150 per person). The shorter trips can also be done by bicycle, which can be rented informally in the village.

Mikindani's best-kept secret though is **eco2** (℡0748/855833, ⊛www.eco2.com) – a diving, marine research and marine education centre two doors along from *Ten Degrees South Lodge*, and run by the same people. As the only PADI-accredited **scuba-diving school** between Mafia Island and Mozambique, this is *the* place to head for if you want to experience the enchanting underside of **Mnazi Bay-Ruvuma Estuary Marine Park**, between Mtwara and the Mozambique border. Headed by a British marine biologist, eco2 offers a full range of snorkelling and scuba-diving trips in and around the marine park, and courses from Open Water ($400) to Dive Master ($700). Single dives cost $40, plus $45 a day for equipment, park fees and transport. Snorkelling is $30. A particular wow is **humpback whale watching** between August and November ($40; but no guarantees), when cetacean mothers-to-be return to the warm waters of East Africa to calve; they're often accompanied by a "midwife" to help with the nursing. eco2 are also planning to import a **glass-bottomed boat**, which in low season will be used to educate local kids.

Both eco2 and *The Old Boma at Mikindani* also offer **canoe and dhow trips** around Mikindani Bay, giving access to various secluded beaches. Canoe rental is no more than Tsh10,000 a day.

looks even more sorry for itself after a tree fell onto its roof. The building – a rather bland three-storey construction with little decoration – was erected by the British colonial government in 1952 in memory of the famous missionary and explorer, and supposedly occupies the site of Livingstone's camp in 1866 at the start of his fifth and final expedition to the Great Lakes, which became famous for his encounter with Stanley (see p.536). Although his journal isn't too clear about the matter, it's more likely that Livingstone actually stayed in Pemba village on the northern lip of the bay, first camping, then in a house rented for four dollars a month.

When the Germans arrived, twenty years after Livingstone, slaves were still by far the town's most valuable asset, and it took them some time to eliminate the trade. Indeed, according to some accounts, it was the Germans themselves who built Mikindani's **Slave Market**. Facing the waterfront and Livingstone House across a small square, the building is said to date from the end of the nineteenth century, when the Germans were already in control. Some confusion remains about whether the building itself was used as a slave market, or if it was simply built on the site of an older one. The thick walls, some of them as deep as 60cm, seem to point to the former, which would show that slavery was at least tolerated during the early years of German occupation. Sadly, renovation has completely destroyed the charm of the previously ruined building – its wonderful pastel-shaded arches and vaults now hidden by internal walls enclosing various offices and workshops. The gaudy pink-and-turquoise colour scheme doesn't help much either. Two **crafts shops** (daily, roughly 10am–6pm) are worth a visit though, with some nice Tingatinga paintings and examples of Makonde wood-carvings on sale. More arts and crafts are for sale at the *The Old Boma* and at eco2 dive centre, with profits from either place funding various local projects.

The German Boma and Bismarck Hill

A rather more sensitive example of restoration is the **German Boma**, which has been beautifully spruced up and converted into southern Tanzania's most luxurious and atmospheric hotel. Built in 1895 as the seat of the German colonial administration, the limewashed building is the town's most distinctive and attractive landmark, combining German, Arab and Swahili architectural elements. The gardens surrounding the Boma are attractive too, with frangipani and flame trees providing splashes of colour and shade. Visitors are welcome to look around, as indeed you probably will anyway, seeing as the town's tourist office is located here. On entering, have a look at the stunning door carvings, the work of Gulum Dosa, who also carved the mosque's doorway. Inside there's a cool courtyard, with rooms arranged around it on two floors. One corner of the building has a three-storey tower with crenellated battlements, uncannily resembling an Andalusian minaret. There's an excellent view of the town from the tower, accessed by two flights of exceedingly steep steps.

Strangely enough, given their bloody colonization of Tanganyika, the Germans permitted the establishment of a separate tribal court in the Boma's grounds, which was presided over by a local chief from the raised platform at the back. The building still exists, albeit in greatly altered form, and now serves as the hotel's outdoor bar.

Just behind the Boma above the coconut groves stands **Bismarck Hill**, named after the first chancellor of unified Germany – it's well worth making the thirty-minute climb up to the top, not only for its sweeping views but also for a curious piece of history. The hill is popularly known as Baobab Hill, on account of the lone baobab (*mbuyu*) on its summit. These trees are traditionally thought to be inhabited by benevolent spirits, and so were considered safe places to bury things, like money, which gave rise to the common belief that the Germans buried treasure near baobabs when they left. In this case, the great big hole on top of the hill was made by a batty treasure-seeking *maganga* (traditional healer), who sadly failed to find anything.

Around the bay

The only real drawback to Mikindani from a tourist point of view is the lack of central **beaches**. Although the sandy shore on the other side of the road looks tempting, locals might well find sight of tourists stripping off for a dip in what is effectively their latrine rather amusing, to say the least. Cleaner, and largely out of sight, is the stretch of sand facing the **Yacht Club**, along the road to Mtwara about 1.5km south of *Ten Degrees Lodge*; entrance is free to guests of *The Old Boma* or *Ten Degrees*, otherwise buy a meal.

Heading further south – a sixty- to ninety-minute walk from Mikindani – is **Tingi Beach**, near the *Makonde Beach Resort*. Head down the road to Mtwara and turn left after the first salt pan some 3km along. Note the white pyres on your left before the salt pan, which you'll also see near the resort. These are for firing coral heads to produce lime for making mortar and paint, a practice that is sadly depleting the area's diminishing mangrove forests, which are harvested as fuel. From the salt pan follow the footpath either along the coast (low tide only) or veer right to join up with the access road for the resort, then head towards the baobab trees. Swimming is only possible at high tide unless you wade out across the shallows for several hundred metres. If you're driving, leave your car at the resort, whose *askari* will expect a tip.

More private, and definitely more romantic, is a small patch of sand on the eastern rim of the bay visible from town; both eco2 and *The Old Boma* can arrange dhow trips. On the western lip of the bay is another good stretch of sand, **Naumbu Beach**. Located beyond Pemba village, it's 7km from Mikindani (roughly thirty minutes by bike or ninety minutes on foot). To get there, head up the road towards Lindi and bear right before the bridge and past the boatyard. The track follows the old railway embankment between the bay and the electric fence of Mikindani Estate (watch out for snakes). If you stay on the track closest to the bay you'll eventually come to **Pemba**, which has the remains of an old Arab mosque (possibly from the ninth century), and some graves. The beach is on the ocean side of the village – ask for directions. Alternatively, ask at the *The Old Boma at Mikindani* for help in arranging a lift with a local *ngalawa* outrigger. The price averages Tsh10,000 there and back, or Tsh7000 one-way.

Eating and drinking

Although limited to the three hotels and a local *mgahawa*, Mikindani's **culinary offerings** are a cut above most other places in southern Tanzania, and worth splashing out on. A locally popular fish, with meaty white flesh, is *kolekole*, tasty whether grilled or stewed. The prawns are good too. **Nightlife** follows the whims of local expats; dedicated drinkers can sample traditional (if semi-legal) *gonga* hooch at the container grocery by the bus stand, but don't go overboard – most inhabitants are Muslim. Apart from the following, the Yacht Club – 1.5km along the road to Mtwara – is planning to open a restaurant and bar, on weekends initially. They have a good beach.

Makonde Beach Resort A huge menu especially strong on Indian and seafood (best ordered in advance), with mains averaging Tsh3500–6000. The bar is dead midweek but occasionally gets lively at weekends if the Indian or expat communities get it together, with all the lights and mirror-balls a dancing queen could hope for.

The Old Boma at Mikindani Consistently delicious and inventive cooking, courtesy of Mama Esther and her mates. The menu features great vegetable soups (like okra; Tsh1500), and unbeatably fresh salads (and herbs) from their own garden. There's no menu as such – the choice depends on what's available that day (around Tsh6500 for mains, Tsh15,000 for a three-course splurge with drinks), and is chalked up on a blackboard. There's always a vegetarian option, whilst evenings are often a buffet. Eat outdoors under parasols or trees, and cool off in the pool with a drink. There's also a quiet bar in the reconstructed tribal courthouse.

Samaki Restaurant In the Slave Market. A simple *mgahawa* for tea, snacks and meals (under Tsh1000), and handy for breakfasts too. Closes around 3pm. No alcohol.

Ten Degrees South Lodge Big portions of chips with everything are the style here: the seafood is particularly good, especially the Goan prawn curry, and there's lobster on the menu too, all going down a storm with expats and aid workers alike, especially for the Saturday evening barbecue. Mind you, the real attraction might be the bar – Mikindani's coolest, with good music, cold drinks, satellite TV, and often enough lively conversation. Open until the last punter falls down.

The Makonde Plateau

The area west of the southern coastal strip is covered by the **MAKONDE PLATEAU**, a river-gouged massif rising 900m above sea level, and home to Africa's most famous woodcarvers, the **Makonde**. The plateau itself is a strikingly beautiful – if largely unvisited – area, ideally suited for hiking if you have

△ A Makonde woodcarver

The Makonde

One of Tanzania's largest and most heterogeneous tribal groups, the **Makonde** are world-famous for their intricate **woodcarvings**. The birth of the tradition is entwined with the mythical origin of the Makonde themselves:

In the beginning, there was a male creature who lived alone in the bush, unbathed and unshorn. The creature lived alone for a long time, but one day felt very lonely. Taking a piece of wood from a tree, he carved a female figure and placed it upright in the sun by his dwelling. Night fell. When the sun rose in the morning, the figure miraculously came to life as a beautiful woman, who of course became his wife.

They conceived a child, but it died three days later. "Let us move from the river to a higher place where the reeds grow," suggested the woman. This they did, and again she conceived, but again the child survived only three days.

"Let us move higher still, to where the thick bush grows," the woman said. And again they moved, and a third time a child was conceived, this one surviving to become the first true ancestor of the Makonde.

The myth alludes to the Makonde's movement away from low-lying and frequently flooded areas of northern Mozambique. As a result of this, they became isolated from other tribes and developed an exceptionally strong sense of identity. They remain one of very few Bantu-speaking people in East Africa still to think that descent passes from mother to daughter rather than from father to son, and motherhood is considered a quasi-sacred state of being. Indeed, such is the female domination of Makonde society that men travelling alone still carry a carved female figure to give them protection.

Nowadays, Makonde carvings are much more abstract, in keeping with the tastes of tourists and collectors. Their best-known works are the "tree of life" or "people pole" carvings in the **Ujamaa style**: intricately carved columns of interlocking human figures representing unity, continuity, and communal strength or power – *dimoongo* in Kimakonde. *Ujamaa* has many meanings – brotherhood, co-operation, family and togetherness – and was a by-word in post-Independence Tanzanian politics. The central figure is invariably a mother surrounded by clinging children, supporting (both literally and symbolically) later generations. Lively and full of movement, rhythm and balance, these are the works that justly brought the Makonde their fame. Lesser-known styles include the naturalistic **Binadamu style**, which represents traditional modes of life: old men smoking pipes, women fetching water, and so on. The later, **Shetani style**, is much more abstract, its models being folkloric spirits presented in distorted, often fantastically grotesque forms.

For all the pre-eminence of figures in modern carvings, the most traditional form of Makonde carving is that of **masks**, representing spirits or ancestors and commonly used in dances for initiation ceremonies and harvest celebrations. There are three main kinds: face masks, body masks (which cover the dancer's torso) and helmet masks (*mapiko*), worn over the head like helmets and notable for their strong features. The masks are made in a secret bush location known as *mpolo*, which women are forbidden to approach. When not in use, the masks are taken back to the *mpolo*. *Mapiko* is also the name of a dance and the terrifying force which animates the dancers who perform it. *Mapiko* dances, together with *sindimba* dances (in which the dancers perform on stilts), still take place every year when a new generation is initiated into adulthood. For more on the Makonde, pictures and sound clips, see Ⓦ www.bluegecko.org/kenya/tribes/makonde.

Finally, when buying Makonde carvings you should be aware that the fine-grained **African blackwood** ("Mozambique ebony"), the most widely used wood for carvings, has become endangered. Please buy pieces worked in other kinds of wood, and encourage others to do likewise. The future of the African blackwood is literally in your hands.

the time and patience to sort out the practical details – not so easy, unfortunately, as the government's 1:50,000 topographical map covering the area (number 306) is out of print. The plateau's reliance on **cashew nuts** as a cash crop is the key to its economy, but despite the fickle nature of the international market (languishing in deep recession), there's a visible sense of prosperity in some places. Tandahimba District, between Mtwara and Newala, has one of the highest per capita incomes in the country, and although day-to-day poverty is as prevalent here as it is elsewhere, you can't help noticing the well-constructed houses (whether of mud and tin or cement and bricks) and numerous schools scattered about the neat and tidy villages.

The primary attraction for visitors is the fact that life on the plateau has hardly been changed by the outside world. Although Christian missionaries have made their presence felt in many ways, the Makonde themselves have remained aloof to the developments that have overtaken the rest of independent Tanzania, and – for the patient traveller willing to learn – provide a superb opportunity to explore the traditional customs that are being swept aside elsewhere. Getting to the plateau isn't too difficult, with the plateau's main towns, **Newala**, **Masasi** and **Ndanda**, being connected by several daily **buses** and pick-ups to the coastal towns of Lindi and Mtwara, running via Mingoyo. The stretch of road from Mtwara to Mingoyo is all sealed, except for a short section over the Lukuledi River between Mtama and Nanganga, which periodically gets washed away. If you're **driving during the rains**, avoid the direct road (the A19) between Mtwara and Newala via Nanyamba: the deeply rutted fifteen-kilometre section through dense *miombo* woodland that starts some 30km from Mtwara turns (literally) into a river after heavy downpours, making getting stuck in metre-deep water-filled potholes a real possibility. The longer way round, using the dirt road which cuts straight across the plateau from Mtama to Newala, is in much better condition and is generally passable all year round. Lastly, if you're continuing west towards Tunduru and on to Songea (see pp.621–623), be prepared for an exceedingly rough ride and lengthy delays during the rains, if the route is passable at all.

Newala

The town of **NEWALA**, on the southwestern rim of the Makonde Plateau, is the best base for exploring the region, and makes a pleasant stopover in any case along the rough road from Mtwara to Masasi. Its climate, although considered glacial by locals, is just about right for visitors, and there's plenty of accommodation, while its transport connections – although not extensive – are handy for getting off the beaten track.

Newala's main street, lined with tall shady trees planted by the Germans at the end of the nineteenth century, runs 1km southwest from the post office to the police station and the **German Boma**, with its strange sloping black walls, perched right on the edge of the plateau. It may be possible to visit the Boma, but bear in mind that it's currently occupied by the police, so keep your camera out of sight. Other attractions, such as **Shimu ya Mungu** ("God's Hole") west of town, where the plateau plunges into a deep chasm, and viewpoints on the plateau edge are best visited by bicycle with a local guide. *Country Lodge* can arrange for someone to accompany you (a tip would be appreciated), and you can rent bicycles at the stand facing the side of the post office at the edge of the market – it shouldn't cost more than Tsh2000 a day. A half-day trip you

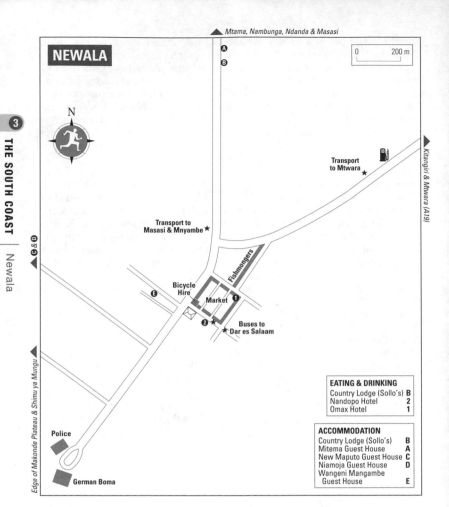

Mtama, Nambunga, Ndanda & Masasi

NEWALA

0   200 m

N

Transport to Mtwara ★

Kitangiri & Mtwara (A19)

Transport to Masasi & Mnyambe ★

Fishmongers

Bicycle Hire

Market ❶

❷ ★

Buses to Dar es Salaam

❺

Edge of Makonde Plateau & Shimu ya Mungu

Police

German Boma

EATING & DRINKING
Country Lodge (Sollo's) **B**
Nandopo Hotel **2**
Omax Hotel **1**

ACCOMMODATION
Country Lodge (Sollo's) **B**
Mitema Guest House **A**
New Maputo Guest House **C**
Niamoja Guest House **D**
Wangeni Mangambe
  Guest House **E**

could do without your own transport is to **Nambunga viewpoint** along the road to Masasi, some 10km from town. Catch a daladala towards Nangomba or Masasi and ask to be dropped at Nambunga village. From here, walk along the left fork for a few hundred metres until the road begins its descent from the Makonde Plateau, giving a fantastic view over almost 100km, including the Ruvuma River to the southwest (the beige band of sand on your left) and the isolated peaks around Masasi in the distance.

Practicalities

There are several transport stands in Newala, each serving different destinations. Coming **from Mtwara**, you're dropped almost a kilometre east of the centre; coming **from Masasi**, you finish at the junction of the Masasi and Mtwara roads. Long-distance buses **from Dar es Salaam** stop at the market, right in the centre.

There are several cheap **guest houses** in the market area, though the better ones – with the exception of the *Country Lodge* – lie off the tree-lined road that leads to the Boma. Newala has water problems, and most of its supply is trucked in, so don't drink it (and don't expect hotel showers to work). The best choice is the *Country Lodge* (also known as *Sollo's*), 1.3km north of the post office along the road to Masasi (☎023/241 0355, ℻023/241 0377; ❷–❸). Most of the rooms have bathrooms, and all come with large beds with adequately sized nets, plus a sofa, chair and table, and the luxury of cotton sheets. Cheaper options (all ❶) include the *Wangeni Mangambe Guest House* and *Niamoja Guest House*, both signposted off the road to the Boma. Even cheaper, but still acceptable, are the *Mitema Guest House*, near the *Country Lodge*, which has safe parking and a bar, and the *New Maputo Guest House*, near the *Niamoja*.

The best of the **restaurants** is at the *Country Lodge*, but skip their pricey basics and go for the specialities instead: the deep-fried kingfish (Tsh3500) is good, as are the garlic prawns (Tsh4000), but give them at least an hour to get things together. Cheaper but perfectly decent places include *Omax Hotel* and *Nandopo Hotel*, both on the edge of the market. Most of Newala's **bars** are around the corner from the post office facing the market, and range from the tawdry and dodgy to peaceful haunts popular with old men. Rather posher is the *Country Lodge*'s bar, which also has a television.

Masasi and around

The busy market town of **MASASI** lies at the western end of the 125km sealed road from Mingoyo. The reason why the authorities bothered to build an all-weather road here and nowhere else in the south is Masasi's importance as the country's major trading centre for **cashew nuts**, without which the town would undoubtedly have been little different from the small villages around it (which, incidentally, include former President Mkapa's birthplace, **Lupaso**). The cashew-nut trade peaks between October and February, when the town's bars fill up with bored traders, many of them Asian or Arab, all of them happy to make a night of it with a passing tourist. If you're heading further west, you'll probably have to spend a night here in any case, as what transport there is leaves early in the morning.

Masasi's main tribe is the **Makua**, who were also the first of the present-day tribes to arrive, coming from northern Mozambique perhaps as early as the fifteenth century. They called their new home *Machashi*, a word meaning the head of the wild millet plant, which here was said to be large and heavy with grain. The traditional culture of the Makua has all but disappeared, thanks to their relatively early contact with Christianity. If you're interested in finding out more, see the article *Excerpts of Makua Traditions* by Father Kazimierz Kubat and Brother Edwin Mpokasaye at ⓦwww.sds-ch.ch/centre/artyk/articel/makua. htm.

The first missionary to arrive was Bishop Edward Steere, who came from Zanzibar in 1876 with high hopes of abolishing the slave trade. Although there was no slavery in Masasi, the town lay along the slave route from Lake Nyasa to the coast. Between 1926 and 1944, the equally remarkable Anglican Bishop of Masasi, W.G. Lucas, made his mark, as it were, by pioneering a Christian version of the *jando* initiation ceremony for boys. The combination of traditional circumcision and Christian confirmation flew in the face of more orthodox missionary beliefs, and the new rite was even accused by some of being "little better than an orgy". But his show of respect for local traditions – which he rather unfortunately once described as "a wonderful opportunity ... to the Christian priest of getting into real personal touch with his boys" – won over the Makua. The Makua were not the first inhabitants of the region, as is shown by the prehistoric **rock paintings** which dot the isolated *inselbergs* surrounding the town, and which are not featured in any Makua tradition. The paintings are generally done in red ochre, and feature axes and geometric symbols. There are two sites close to town, the nearest on the other side of the hill behind Mkomnindo Hospital – you should ask for someone to guide you. The other site is on top of Mtandi Hill behind the Anglican church some 4km back towards Lindi; ask at the church. Before visiting either of these sites, please read the box on rock art etiquette on p.268.

Apart from the paintings, there's little else in Masasi to delay you, though you could check out either of two **Makonde woodcarvers' co-operatives**, 200m and 300m down the Nachingwea road.

Practicalities

Masasi is widely spread out and lacks an obvious focus – the most notable feature is the surfaced road, which runs east to west through the town for several kilometres, and is where you'll find most of Masasi's bars and hotels. Most **buses and daladalas** terminate at the west end of the road opposite the Nachingwea junction. Coming from the east, you may be dropped at another stand 1.6km east along the road, near the market and post office. **Leaving Masasi**, there are buses and daladalas to Mtwara until mid-afternoon, and some also to Lindi. Heading east along the adventurous route to Songea, transport leaves at 6am, so buy your ticket the day before. If you're **driving** and need repairs, a good mechanic is available near the Songea–Tunduru stand; ask for the Longino Garage. The town's **Internet café** is *Mango Net*, one block east of the main bus stand.

Accommodation

Masasi has dozens of **guest houses**, mainly catering for the cashew-nut trade. The bulk of these lie around the two bus stands and along the strip of sealed road between them. The best is the *Sayari Guest House* (☎023/251 0095; ❶–❷) at the east end of town, past the Mkuti filling station on the Lindi road. Frequently full, this has a choice of rooms with and without bathrooms, plus an excellent bar. Also good is the *Holiday Lodge* (☎023/251 0108; includes breakfast; ❷), at the west end of the road near the Nachingwea junction and bus stand, which has seven small but perfectly acceptable rooms with bathroom, plus a bar at the back serving food. Another reasonable choice is the *Saiduna Guest House* (☎023/251 0175; includes breakfast; ❶) next to the *Masasi Club*.

Eating and drinking

Masasi's restaurants are primarily bars which also happen to serve food, mainly the ubiquitous *ugali, nyama choma* and sometimes fried fish. You won't find much to write home about, but the local **relish** sold in the markets is worth searching out: ask for *kiungo cha embe* if you like mangoes, or *kiungo cha ndimo* for the version made with lemons.

For **restaurants**, the best is *Pub Le Moses*, on the highway close to the more easterly bus stand. It has continental meals for around Tsh3500, discos on Wednesday and from Friday to Sunday, and a washed out projector for European soccer matches. Cheaper are the *Masasi Club* and the relaxed *Mahenge Transit Cassino & Bravo Bar* near the *Mahenge Guest House*, the latter with famously awful service and toilets, but also with a large patio in front with plenty of seats and tables. For breakfast, try *uji*, a porridge made from millet flour.

You're spoilt for choice when it comes to **drinking**. Apart from *Pub Le Moses*, the *Mahenge Transit Cassino & Bravo Bar* has a great atmosphere, helped along by a generator which ensures a nonstop supply of eminently danceable Congolese music and Bongo Flava. The *Masasi Club* opposite is a friendly and more intimate venue, with the bonus of video shows in the back room: the quality is eye-melting and the sound is terrible, but it's great fun all the same. The *Sayari Guest House*'s bar is another good place, with a decent restaurant and upbeat music. If you're feeling brave, search out the local brew (*pombe*) made from the distilled fermented juice of the cashew fruit.

Travel details

Buses and daladalas

Around 6am is the best time to catch buses. Asterisks, below, denote routes that are open in the dry season only; during the rains (usually Nov or Dec, and most of March–May) they may be closed for weeks at a time. Buses that do attempt these routes in the rains are subject to lengthy delays, sometimes meaning days.

Kilwa Kivinje to: Nangurukuru (hourly; 30min).
Kilwa Masoko to: Dar (1–2 daily*; 14–18hr); Nangurukuru (every 30min; 30min); for southbound buses, wait at Nangurukuru.
Lindi to: Dar (2–3 daily*; 22–28hr); Masasi (3–5 daily; 2hr 30min); Mikindani (hourly; 1hr 30min); Mingoyo (hourly; 30min); Mtwara (hourly; 2hr); Nangurukuru (1 daily*; 7–9hr).
Masasi to: Dar (1–2 daily*; 25–31hr); Lindi (3–5 daily; 2hr 30min); Mikindani (3–4 daily; 3hr 30min); Mtwara (4–5 daily; 4hr); Nachingwea (1–2 daily*; 1hr 30min); Newala (hourly; 3hr); Tunduru (1 daily*; 8–12hr).

Mikindani to: Lindi (hourly; 1hr 30min); Masasi (3–4 daily; 3hr 30min); Mtwara (hourly; 20min).
Mtwara to: Dar (2–3 daily*; 24–30hr); Kalambo for Mozambique (hourly*; 1hr); Lindi (hourly; 2hr); Masasi (4–5 daily; 6hr); Mikindani (hourly; 20min); Newala (1–2 daily; 5–6hr).
Nangurukuru to: Kilwa Kivinje (hourly; 30min); Kilwa Masoko (every 30min; 30min).
Newala to: Dar (5–7 weekly*; 26–30hr); Kitangari (hourly; 1hr 30min–2hr); Masasi (hourly; 3hr); Mtwara (1–2 daily; 5–6hr).

Dhows

Commercial dhows sail irregularly between Kisiju on the mainland and Mafia Island, and along the mainland coast between Songo Songo, Kilwa Kivinje, Lindi, Mtwara and Mozambique. For more detailed information see the transport sections under Mafia Island (p.198), Kilwa Kivinje (p.220), Lindi (p.224) and Mtwara (p.232), as well as the section on travelling by dhow in Basics (p.48).

Ferries

The MV *Safari* sails once a week between Dar and Mtwara, taking around 22hr. For more details see p.232. There are no ferries to Kilwa, Lindi or Mafia.

Flights

Airline codes used below are: AT (Air Tanzania); CA (Coastal Aviation); and PA (Precisionair).

Kilwa to: Dar (CA: daily; 1hr); Mafia (CA: daily; 15min); Zanzibar (CA: daily; 1hr 35min).
Lindi to: Dar (PA: 2 weekly; 2hr 25min).
Mafia to: Dar (CA: daily; 30min); Kilwa (CA: daily; 35min); Selous (CA: daily; 50min); Songo Songo (CA: daily; 15min); Zanzibar (CA: daily; 1hr 5min).
Mtwara to: Dar (AT: daily; 55min).

Central Tanzania

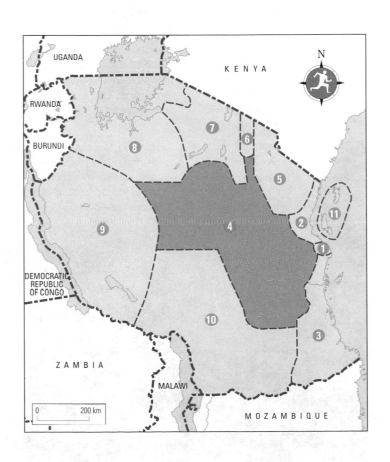

CHAPTER 4 # Highlights

* **Irangi Hills** Scattered around the hills northeast of Kondoa is one of Africa's most extensive collections of prehistoric rock paintings, the oldest possibly 19,000 to 30,000 years old. **See p.265**

* **Babati** The cultural tourism programme here offers hikes up Mount Hanang, and intimate encounters with Barbaig herders and former hunter-gatherers, the Sandawe. **See p.270**

* **Uluguru Mountains** Accessed from Morogoro, these ancient mountains offer rewarding hikes through primeval rainforest, and encounters with the Luguru tribe. **See p.285**

* **Mikumi National Park** Easily reached from Dar es Salaam, this contains a high concentration of plains game, including lions and elephants. **See p.290**

* **Selous Game Reserve** Africa's biggest wildlife sanctuary, brought alive by the Rufiji River. Best seen on foot accompanied by an armed ranger. **See p.297**

* **Udzungwa Mountains** An extremely rich rainforest habitat with several walking trails, especially good for spotting primates. **See p.307**

△ Barbaig women dressed in goatskin for a wedding

Central Tanzania

D
ry, dusty and only sparsely vegetated by *miombo* woodland, the very centre of **Central Tanzania** is an amorphous region without distinct geographical or cultural boundaries. The presence of sleeping sickness, spread by the tsetse fly, has meant that the area's main settlements are located near the forest-cloaked mountains at its fringes: the Uluguru Mountains in the east, the Irangi Hills in the north, and the Udzungwa Mountains in the south.

The exception, right in the middle of this apparently desolate land, is the planned city of **Dodoma**, which has served as Tanzania's political and administrative capital since 1973. Although the butt of many a joke, the city is pleasant enough, and provides a handy stopover for those travelling by train between the lakes and the coast. In the dry season, at least, Dodoma is also an ideal springboard for exploring the area to the north, whose attractions include a cultural tourism programme in **Babati**, hikes up the 3417m **Mount Hanang**, the prehistoric rock paintings of the **Irangi Hills** near Kondoa, and a beautiful stretch of road between Babati and the attractive district capital of **Singida**.

The lively commercial and industrial town of **Morogoro**, 279km east of Dodoma along a good sealed road, owes its existence to a fertile hinterland and to the fact that it straddles both the railway and the Tanzam Highway from Dar es Salaam to Zambia and Malawi. A few kilometres to the east, the rain-giving **Uluguru Mountains** have recently been opened up to hikers to offer outstanding scenery, encounters with the Luguru people, and hundreds of rare plant and animal species.

For the majority of visitors however, central Tanzania means one of two things: **Mikumi National Park** or the neighbouring **Selous Game Reserve**, which together contain pretty much all the Northern Circuit's wildlife but few of its crowds. For serious hikers, the rainforest of the **Udzungwa Mountains National Park**, to the west of Selous, offers unrivalled opportunities to get out into the wild, along with the refreshingly different – if nerve-racking – experience of coming face-to-face with local wildlife, mainly monkeys and, if you're especially (un)lucky, buffalo and elephant. For those really wanting to get off the beaten track, the road south of here to **Ifakara** brings you towards the swampy **Kilombero floodplain**, one of the country's least travelled areas, and accessible only by boat.

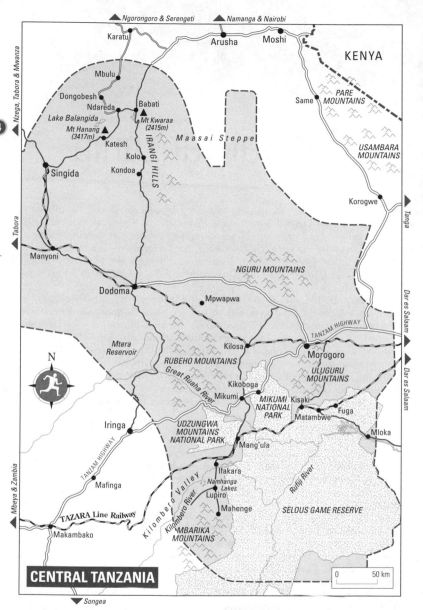

Dodoma and northwards

Situated among a desolate scatter of weathered granite outcrops, eroded gullies and sand-filled rivers, **Dodoma** is a surprisingly remote choice for a national capital, reminiscent of the similarly artificial planned capital cities of Brasília (Brazil) and Abuja (Nigeria), whose blueprints adorn the walls of the Capital Development Authority's mapping office. Unfortunately, Dodoma's unpromising location and lack of history mean that it's never really going to appeal much to visitors, though if you make the effort to explore it and the city's live-music venues, you'll experience a welcoming and vibrant side to life that no amount of town planning could ever have achieved. For a more immediately gratifying experience, a couple of places north of Dodoma come highly recommended: the prehistoric rock paintings of the **Irangi Hills**, accessible from the pleasant agricultural town of Kondoa, and a superb cultural tourism programme at **Babati**, which offers easy access up Tanzania's third-highest peak, Mount Hanang, and cultural encounters with Barbaig cattle herders and former hunter-gathers, the Sandawe, that you're unlikely to forget in a hurry.

Dodoma

Tanzania's national capital since 1973, **DODOMA** – a planned and perennially unfinished city in the middle of absolutely nowhere – is testimony to President Nyerere's perhaps overly idealistic plans for building a nation. Though he got it right most of the time, his choice of Dodoma as capital – more for its central geographical position than for anything else – was probably a mistake. In the hottest months (June–Oct), Dodoma's desert-like climate sees temperatures rising to over 40°C in the day and plummeting to 10°C at night, though the dry air makes both extremes more bearable than on the humid coast. There are no mountains or waterfalls nearby, nor any historic buildings; every time the government half-heartedly tries to shift itself from Dar es Salaam, twelve months later you'll find that most departments have stealthily snuck back to the coast. It's money that could have been better spent on less grandiose projects elsewhere, say its critics, for whom Dodoma is nothing more than a white elephant. But there's a pleasingly gentle anarchy to the city, too: Dodoma is gradually outgrowing the rigidness of its original blueprint. Large sections of the city that had been planned for government offices or open spaces are now occupied by a maze of dusty roads packed with bars, food joints and shops. The street numbering too now makes no sense whatsoever, whilst the residential nature of the city centre, with children dashing around all over the place, makes a welcome change from nocturnal Dar es Salaam's deserted central streets.

Some history

Dodoma began life in the first half of the nineteenth century as a small Gogo settlement of traditional *tembe* houses no different from the ones you can still see today along the road to Kondoa. The settlement gradually grew in importance when the ivory and slave caravans from the lakes in the west began passing through the area, from which the Gogo exacted tribute ("a tusk, a gun or a man," it's said) in return for maintaining the water wells on which the caravans depended. Come **colonization**, the settlement was sufficiently developed for the Germans to consider making it the colony's capital. Thanks to World War I, the proposal came to nought, although much of the town's modern importance stems from this period – in 1910 the Central Line Railway from Dar es Salaam reached Dodoma, bringing with it colonists and many of the missionaries whose churches now dot the city. During and after the war Dodoma was hit by two famines which killed thirty thousand people, while an outbreak of

Dodoma Region: the destruction of a fragile environment

Passing through in the 1870s, the explorer Henry Morton Stanley was enchanted by Ugogo, the old name for what comprises most of the present-day **Dodoma Region**. "In the whole of Africa", he wrote, "there is not another place whose environment has attracted me as much as this". Mr Stanley, one presumes, would have been somewhat surprised to see the changes that have occurred over the years since he was here. A large part of the region is a savannah plateau that receives little rain (around 570mm a year), most of which falls in heavy bursts in December and March or April, leaving the rest of the year hot, dry, windy and dusty. As a result, the region has long been prone to drought and famine, a natural cycle whose challenges the region's dominant tribe, the **Gogo**, mastered by developing a cyclical system of communal grazing which ensured that no one piece of land was ever exhausted.

The region's present problems can be traced back to the arrival of the Europeans, who made every effort to discourage the Gogo's nomadic lifestyle, which they considered backward (not unlike the present government's attitude to the Barbaig and Maasai). Land was confiscated, reducing the grazing ranges of Gogo cattle and encouraging the Gogo to settle and practise slash-and-burn agriculture instead. The destructive long-term environmental consequences can now be seen in the dust that billows through Dodoma for much of the year, and in the eroded run-off gullies and sand-filled rivers that scar the landscape. By clearing the land of permanent bush or tree cover, the soil in such a harsh climate quickly loses its consistency and is more easily dried out by the sun – after which the wind blows away the topsoil and the rain carries yet more of it away. And so, as cultivators clear another patch of land to replace the one which has blown to dust, the cycle repeats itself.

Politics have also had an impact. Nyerere's idealistic **Ujamaa** policy (see Contexts) had an equally catastrophic impact on this intrinsically fragile environment. Human and animal population density in critical areas increased by fifty percent as a result of the establishment of centralized "Ujamaa villages", which placed unsustainable pressure on local resources. Livestock trampling on overused pasture and, especially, around waterpoints hindered the regeneration of vegetation, which in turn lessened the soil's ability to absorb rainwater. This led to the lowering of local groundwater tables, a situation not helped by the creation of new farms on confiscated land.

With a population of over 1.3 million, the Gogo of today can hardly turn back the clock to revert to their previous way of life, even if many still dress as their ancestors did. One solution now being developed by the forestry department is to introduce sustainable modes of agriculture and plant varieties that won't leave the soil uncovered. But this will take time – and time, unfortunately, has all but run out.

rinderpest badly affected Gogo cattle herds. The British administration which replaced German rule in 1919 was less taken by Dodoma, much preferring Dar es Salaam and Arusha. In the 1960s, Dodoma's importance decreased still further with the completion of the Chinese-built Tanzam Highway from Dar es Salaam to Morogoro and Iringa, which bypassed the city.

Dodoma's slow renaissance began in October 1973, when it replaced Dar as the new **capital** of Tanzania. Although the decision was made partly through a desire to develop agriculture in the very heart of the country, the move is better understood through Nyerere's ideal of "**Villagization**". As the capital, Dodoma was to be the centrepiece of an ideology in which all tribes lived together in a shared sense of *Ujamaa* – togetherness, or brotherhood. However, the cost of physically moving the capital was exorbitant. Originally planned for completion in the 1980s, the final transfer of the ministries and state organs from Dar has been endlessly delayed, and few now believe that it will ever happen. Tanzania's National Assembly (the Bunge) has been in Dodoma since

Dodoma: origins of a name

The origin of the city's name, a corruption of the Kigogo word *idodomia* or *yado-domela*, means "sinking" or "sunk". The prosaic (and most likely) explanation is that the name was a metaphor for the fate of invaders unable to escape the bows and spears of the brave Gogo defenders. The more colourful version refers to an elephant that came to drink in the Kikuyu River near Dodoma. Arriving at the river, the elephant became stuck and began to sink, hence the name (and the inevitable "white elephant" tag that newspaper columnists gleefully attach to the city). An alternative and no less amusing tale tells of a time when Gogo warriors secretly stole a herd of cattle from the Hehe, their neighbours to the south. The Gogo feasted on the cattle, leaving only their tails, which they then stuck into the ground. When the Hehe came looking for their herd, the Gogo pointed to the tails and said, "Look, your cattle have sunk into the mud."

1996, but the government ministries which wield the real power have been loath to leave the relative comforts of Dar es Salaam, and at the time of writing only three ministries remained in Dodoma, the rest having crept stealthily back to Dar.

Arrival and city transport

Dodoma is most easily reached by **road** from Dar es Salaam, a six- to eight-hour drive (469km on a good sealed road); it's also a major stop on the Central Line Railway between Dar and Kigoma and Mwanza. The unsurfaced roads to Tabora in the west, and north to Arusha can be difficult to negotiate, and become impassable for several days at a time during and after heavy rains. The southern road to Iringa fares better, although most drivers find it quicker to take the longer route via Morogoro.

Taxis congregate outside all transport stops. The **bus stand** is on Dar es Salaam Avenue on the southeast side of town, next to a big roundabout. Scandinavian Express' terminal is on the east side of the roundabout. The **train station** is ten minutes' walk southeast of the centre. Trains from Dar (Tues, Fri & Sun) pull in the following day at around 7.35am; coming from Mwanza or Kigoma, you'll arrive at 6.10pm. The **airport** lies just north of the centre. Coastal Aviation fly in three times a week from Dar (Mon, Thurs & Sat) and Arusha (Tues, Fri & Sun).

City transport

Daladalas, locally nicknamed "Express", leave from the orderly Jamatini Stand, on Dar es Salaam Avenue just east of Zuzu roundabout, and cover the whole city (Tsh200 for most journeys). **Taxis** gather outside the Central Market, and at the junction of Kuu Street and Lindi Avenue; alternatively, call Mwani Taxi Services on ☏026/232 1360 or Muluti Car Hire on ☏0741/592641. Trips within the city cost Tsh1500–2000.

Accommodation

There's no shortage of **accommodation**, though government expense accounts have pushed prices higher than elsewhere, with the cheapest decent doubles starting at Tsh6000, and averaging Tsh12,000–20,000. Single rooms can usually be shared by couples. The main concentration of budget and mid-range hotels is in the fan-like grid of numbered streets west of Kuu Street. There are

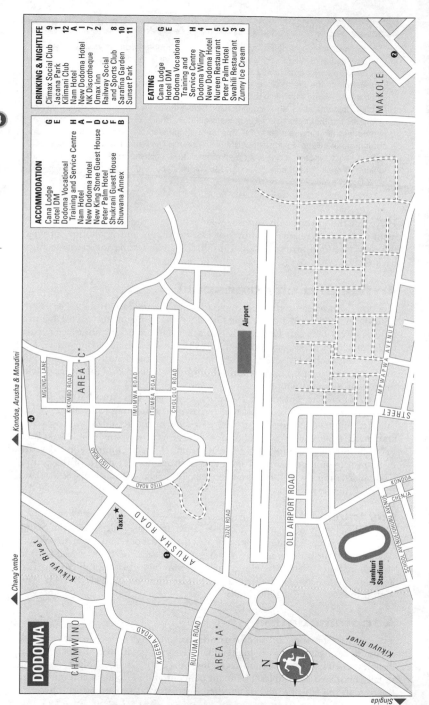

DODOMA

ACCOMMODATION

Cana Lodge	G
Hotel DM	E
Dodoma Vocational Training and Service Centre	H
Nam Hotel	A
New Dodoma Hotel	I
New King Stone Guest House	D
Peter Palm Hotel	C
Shukrani Guest House	F
Shuwana Annex	B

DRINKING & NIGHTLIFE

Climax Social Club	9
Jacana Park	1
Kilimani Club	12
Nam Hotel	A
New Dodoma Hotel	I
NK Discotheque	7
Omax Inn	2
Railway Social and Sports Club	8
Sarafina Garden	10
Sunset Park	11

EATING

Cana Lodge	G
Hotel DM	E
Dodoma Vocational Training and Service Centre	H
Dodoma Wimpy	4
New Dodoma Hotel	I
Nureen Restaurant	5
Peter Palm Hotel	C
Swahili Restaurant	3
Zunny Ice Cream	6

Kondoa, Arusha & Mnadini

Chang'ombe

Singida

Airport

Taxis

MAKOLE

Jamhuri Stadium

N

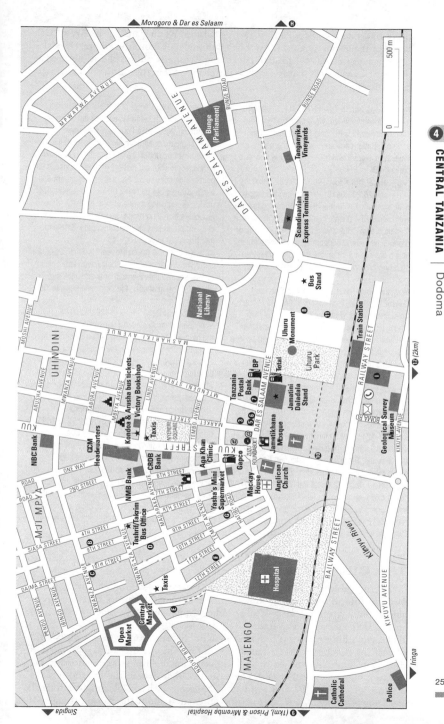

▲ *Morogoro & Dar es Salaam*

▲ **H**

Bunge (Parliament)

D A R   E S   S A L A A M   A V E N U E

BUNGE ROAD

BUNGE ROAD

Tanganyika Vineyards

Scandinavian Express Terminal ★

⊗ Bus Stand

National Library

MASHARIKI AVENUE

Uhuru Monument ⊗

8 **11**

Uhuru Park

Train Station

RAILWAY STREET

9 (2km) ▼

MPWAPWA AVENUE

MOSHI AVENUE

UHINDINI

ARUSHA AVENUE

MWANZA AVENUE

TABORA AVENUE

MBEYA AVENUE

LINDI AVENUE

MTENDENI STREET

MARKET AVENUE

Victory Bookshop
Kondoa & Arusha bus tickets

BP
Total

Tanzania Postal Bank
7

DAR ES SALAAM AVENUE

Jamatini Daladala Stand ★

Jamatikhana Mosque ✝

Geological Survey Museum

BOMA RD

KIKUYU AVENUE

10

KUU

Headquarters ⊗

NBC Bank

ONE WAY

ROAD

2ND STREET

NMB Bank

CRDB Bank

TEMBO STREET

6TH STREET

7TH STREET

Aga Khan Clinic

Taxis ★
NYERERE SQUARE

3
5 **6**

ROUNDABOUT
KUU

Gapco

Mackay House

Anglican Church ✝

MJI MPYA

ROAD

MADARAKA AVENUE

HATIBU ROAD

MVUMI ROAD

Vasha's Mini Supermarket

4TH STREET

9TH STREET

10TH STREET

12TH STREET

11TH STREET

Tashrif/Takrim Bus Office

8
D

C

SIASA STREET

9TH STREET

10TH STREET

MWANGAZA AVENUE

DAIMA STREET

MWANZA AVENUE

PAHDO AVENUE

BINGO AVENUE

NGOLO AVENUE

Taxis ★

Central Market

Open Market

MAJENGO

Hospital ✚

KINDU RIVER

RAILWAY STREET

RAILWAY STREET

KIKUYU AVENUE

Catholic Cathedral ✝

Police

E

257

▲ *Singida*

9 (1km), Prison & Mirembe Hospital ▼

▼ *Iringa*

0 _____ 500 m

more mid-range choices east off Dar es Salaam Avenue, and up in **Area "C"**, north of the airport – a shadeless thirty-minute walk from the centre. Daladalas from Jamatini Stand to Mnadani pass along Arusha Road on the western edge of the area. Dodoma's **water** supply is unreliable and in the past has been tainted by pesticides.

Cana Lodge 9th St ☎0741/786611, ℱ026/232 1716. A friendly modern place with well-kept en-suite doubles, all with cable TV, telephone, fans and nets. Better ones are upstairs. There's also a modest restaurant and bar, Internet café and safe parking. ❸

Hotel DM Ndovu Rd ☎026/232 1001, ℱ026/232 0416. A recommended place near the market with friendly staff and good rooms with satellite TV, phone, massive double beds, nice tiled bathrooms and ceiling fans. The second-floor rooms have nets; others are sprayed. There's also a bar-restaurant on the top floor with tables on a breezy terrace overlooking town. Breakfast included. ❸

Dodoma Vocational Training and Service Centre Bunge Rd, 2km east ☎026/232 2181. A training centre for chefs, waiters and hotel staff whose teachers know their stuff: rooms are clean and well kept, there's reliable hot water and service is excellent, making for a very pleasant stay. The 39 rooms have TVs and phones, singles with round nets, twins (can be pushed together) with box nets; cheaper rooms share bathrooms. There's a good restaurant and a bar. Breakfast included. ❷–❸

Nam Hotel Arusha Rd, Area "C" ☎0741/670081. Well-looked-after, quiet three-storey affair with thirty en-suite rooms, all with phones, nets, carpet, some with satellite TV (same price), and huge family suites. There's also a restaurant and bar. No single rates. Breakfast included. ❸

New Dodoma Hotel Railway St ☎026/232 1641, ℮dodomahotel@kicheko.com. Dodoma's venerable *Railway Hotel* has been superbly renovated into one of central Tanzania's best lodgings, while keeping the attractive courtyard

architecture intact. Most of the 91 rooms, mostly twins and all with cable TV, enclose the courtyard – some on the second floor have balconies. The small standard ones have big beds but small mosquito nets; better are the slightly larger deluxe rooms, some with a/c instead of fans. Service is as polished as the marble floors in the restaurant and bar, and there are plenty of tables in the courtyard next to an amusing pool and fake waterfall. Other amenities include a proper swimming pool, health club, massage parlour and steam bath. Safe parking. Breakfast included. ❺–❼

New King Stone Guest House 9th St ☎026/232 3057. An excellent budget choice, with small clean rooms, squat toilets (some rooms en suite), big box nets, cotton sheets, fan, and even satellite TV. ❶–❷

Peter Palm Hotel 10th St ☎026/232 0154, ℮pollomy@yahoo.com. Modern, clean and well-maintained three-storey affair, all en-suite doubles except for three singles on the ground floor. Some rooms have balconies (there are also shady communal balconies with seats), and all have TV, phone, hot water and fans, but no nets – rooms are sprayed. Small cool restaurant, and free Internet access for guests. Breakfast included. ❹

Shukrani Guest House 12th St ☎026/232 1895. Basic but acceptable, single rooms only, all with nets. Some marginally more expensive rooms have bathrooms (hot water comes in buckets). ❶

Shuwana Annex 9th St ☎026/232 1378. One of the better cheapies, friendly and with ground-level en-suite rooms, the doubles with TVs (local channels), all with fans, box nets, table and chair, and a whiff of detergent in their bathrooms (squat toilets). ❷

The City

Wandering around Dodoma by day can be wearying – you might invest in one of the colourful parasols that some locals have wisely taken to. Taxis are advisable at night given the lack of streetlights, though you'll be fine in residential areas if there are people around.

The city's busiest district lies west of **Kuu Street**, from where a dusty grid of partially numbered streets radiate like a fan. The mathematical logic behind the street numbering has completely broken down – the same street may have different numbers at either end. There are no "sights" here, though the area – a mixture of commercial and residential buildings – has a pleasingly informal, small town feeling, where kids getting all excited about the passing stranger is

△ Crowd waiting for a bus, Dodoma

all part of the fun. The western edge of this area is bounded by the stagnant Kikuyu River, either side of which is the lively **Central Market**, renowned throughout Tanzania for its ability to provide fruit and vegetables even out of season – mysteriously so, given the region's desolation. The heart of the market consists of two modern buildings connected by a footbridge. It's a good place to sample bitter-sweet baobab pods (*ubuyu*), which can either be sucked like sweets or pulped to make a very refreshing juice packed with vitamin C, or to enquire about buying a *marimba ya mkono* (literally "hand xylophone", also called *mbira* after the Shona word), the Gogo's famous "thumb piano" (see box on p.260).

At the south end of Kuu Street is **Zuzu roundabout**, named after a defunct ceramics factory. This area is dominated by the brick **Jamatikhana Mosque** with its strangely church-like clock tower, and the domed **Anglican Church** opposite. The most impressive of Dodoma's churches, however, is the **Catholic Cathedral**, 2km west along Railway Street. Rebuilt in 2001 in fantastic Byzantine style, the brickwork facade comes complete with overly gilded mosaic frescoes, and a pair of ornately carved Swahili-style doors. Beyond the cathedral, before you get to the *Climax Social Club*, is **Mirembe Hospital for the Insane**, Tanzania's largest such establishment and, some might say, conveniently close to the corridors of power. The hospital's name has become something of a by-word in Tanzania, in much the same way that Victorian Britain's Bedlam Asylum gave rise to a new adjective. A few hundred metres further west, a narrow track leads to the heavily guarded gate of Isanga Magereza **prison**, whose shop sells sisal (*katani*) items produced by the inmates. Back in the centre, just south of the railway tracks, Dodoma's main secular attraction (albeit only of specialist interest) is the **Geological Survey Museum** (Mon–Fri 8am–3.30pm; Tsh500) in the Ministry of Energy and Minerals on Kikuyu Avenue south of the railway station – look for the sign saying *Wizara ya Nishati na Madini*. The admission, paid at the "Sample Reception", gets you into a hall

The music of the Gogo

Mention **the Gogo** anywhere in Tanzania and you're almost certain to hear enthusiastic praise for their skills as musicians. With its polyrhythmic singing, insistent virtual bass line of *marimba ya mkono* (*mbira*) thumb pianos interwoven with the plaintive voices of one-stringed *zeze* fiddles, the traditional music of the Gogo, called **sawosi** (*ngoma ya kigogo* in Kiswahili), is some of the most beautiful, haunting and subtly rhythmical music you're ever likely to hear. *Sawosi* is a perfect blend of collective virtuosity, balancing mostly female choruses with a multipart rhythm played on a number of *marimba ya mkono*, rectangular or rhomboidal wooden hand-held sound boxes fitted with metal forks (nowadays, more often than not, the metal shafts from screwdrivers). The combined effect is utterly hypnotic, displaying a mastery of multipart polyphony, complex polyrhythms and micropolyphony comparable to that of Pygmy communities in the Central African Republic, Congo, Cameroon, Gabon and elsewhere.

Highly **recommended listening** are the two tapes of Gogo recordings sold at Radio Tanzania in Dar es Salaam (see p.124). Buying overseas or over the Internet, the best compilation is Gall's *Gogo Ritual Music*. Look out also for the following CDs: *Nyati group: L'Élégance de Dodoma – Tanzanie* (MPJ 111021); *Tanzanie: Chants des Wagogo et des Kuria* (Inedit W260041); and *The Art of Hukwe Ubi Zawose* (JVC VIGC-5011), the latter providing a distinctly modern rendition of the age old traditions. If you have time and a real interest in Gogo culture and music, the best time to seek out *sawosi* in its traditional setting is during the harvest and circumcision season from June to August, especially July, which features the *cidwanga* dance conducted by elder healers, in which ancestors are remembered and praised.

filled with display cases containing gemstones and minerals, the more valuable of which (gold, platinum, ruby, etc) are notably absent but for their labels and the patches of glue that once held them in place. Still, there's enough remaining to keep you interested for half an hour or so, including some enormous fossilized ammonites, flaky sheets of mica that resemble plastic (and are associated with emerald deposits), and a large wall map of Tanzania's minerals with blinking lights controlled from a massive Doctor Who-style dial.

Heading east from Zuzu roundabout along Dar es Salaam Avenue brings you to Jamatini daladala stand and the sorry-looking **Uhuru Park**, a dust-bowl that now serves primarily as a truck stop. The monument here consists of a spear, shield and machine-gun, together with an abstract representation of Mount Kilimanjaro topped by a replica of the Uhuru Torch that was planted at Independence. Heading 1.5km further east you'll come to the **Bunge**, Tanzania's modern Parliament building. You can watch parliamentary debates from the visitors' gallery (free; no reservations required) – proceedings are conducted in Kiswahili.

Eating

Dodoma has **restaurants** for all pockets and tastes, though many are much of a muchness, whether local places selling snacks and basic meals, or restaurants attached to mid-range hotels (good ones include *Cana Lodge*, *Peter Palm Hotel* and *Hotel DM*), whose fairly standard menus feature rice, chips or *ugali* with chicken, beef, liver or fish, plus a few continental dishes like spaghetti or steak, all for around Tsh3000–4000.

At the posher places, do sample the region's **wine**, an "art" first introduced by Italian missionaries a century ago. Something must have been lost in translation, as the output from Dodoma-based Tanganyika Vineyards is so bad that it's probably best left for those with a solid sense of humour (and stomach); faring much better is Bihawana Red, made at Bihawana Mission along the Iringa road. Both labels are sold in Dodoma's supermarkets.

Dodoma Vocational Training and Service Centre Bunge Rd, 2km east of the city centre ☎ 026/232 2181. Part of a training school, the chef is the instructor and the staff his students: they're doing good work, as both the food and service are excellent. There's a wide choice of tasty dishes (though nothing vegetarian) as well as pastries and, if you order a day in advance, a selection of set menus. Mains cost Tsh3000–3500; starters around Tsh1000. The bar outside has *nyama choma* from 7 to 11pm.

Dodoma Wimpy Zuzu roundabout. A cheap and popular outdoor meeting place serving fast-food snacks like samosas, fried chicken, chips and *kababu*, plus coffee, tea and sodas. Great for breakfast. Full meals are served at lunchtimes, but get there early for a full choice.

New Dodoma Hotel Railway St. Surprisingly affordable given the setting, its café dishes up juices, ice cream, light meals and paninis, and the more formal restaurant covers most bases, including Chinese and Indian (no pork; Tsh3500–6000 a plate including rice), fresh salads, steaks and prawns.

Nureen Restaurant Dar es Salaam Ave. A down-at-heel Indian place, but their curries can be very good (unlike their snacks). Good *mishkaki* is sold on the street outside, and there's a good unnamed bar next door. Lunchtimes only, closed Sun. No alcohol.

Swahili Restaurant Market St. An excellent establishment with a wide selection of snacks, full meals such as spiced pilau rice for under Tsh2000, and some tables outside. No alcohol.

Zunny Ice Cream Dar es Salaam Ave. Good ice cream, plus a range of light snacks, and some seats in a small garden.

Drinking and nightlife

Dodoma has a good number of attractive outdoor **beer gardens**, all dishing up excellent *nyama choma*, grilled bananas, chicken and other snacks. Some places also have live music: the big **local bands** are Saki Stars and Diamond Star Band.

Climax Social Club 3km west of the centre beyond the prison. Until Independence, this was Dodoma's main colonial hang-out, and is still favoured by expats. As well as its bar and restaurant, there's a swimming pool. Daily membership Tsh1500.

Jacana Park Arusha Rd, Area "C". A great outdoor place under a lovely stand of trees. Food includes *supu ya mbuzi* (a stew of various bits of goat in hot chilli broth), beef, chicken and *chipsi mayai*. Dala-dalas from Jamatini to Chang'ombe or Mnadani pass by.

Kilimani Club 2km south of the railway station. A broad, unmarked red building on the edge of Dodoma, this is a sleepy bar by day but has discos or live music most nights, including Diamond Star Band or Saki Stars on Sundays from 8pm (Tsh1000). Basic bar food available evenings. See the posters along Dar es Salaam Ave for details.

Nam Hotel Arusha Rd, Area "C". Two bars; the best – if it's reopened – on the roof with great views.

New Dodoma Hotel Railway St. Expensive drinks in the hotel's wonderful courtyard, or indeed at a rondavel perched over its fanciful "swimming" pool; most guests swim in the full-sized pool at the back (add Tsh5000 to the meal).

NK Discotheque Corner Dar es Salaam Ave and Mtendeni St. Occupying a former cinema, this is Dodoma's main disco, currently featuring Bongo Flava. They sometimes have live music worth asking about. Discos Fri–Sat 9pm until late, Sun from 3.30pm until late. Entry Tsh1000–1500.

Omax Inn Makole area, east of the centre. Popular local club offering free live music from the excellent Saki Stars (usually Fri & Sat). Food until midnight. Catch a taxi.

Railway Social and Sports Club East side of Uhuru Park, off Dar es Salaam Ave. A pleasant and quiet bar-cum-restaurant, somewhat in the shadow of the much busier (and shadier) *Sunset Park* next door, with a TV and good traditional Tanzanian food.

Sarafina Garden Kuu St. Friendly outdoor place, but watch you don't come a cropper on the bizarre foot-snagging woodwork beside the bar, intended to stop people stealing the stools.

Sunset Park East side of Uhuru Park. An oasis of shady trees and shrubs with plenty of secluded seating, this outdoor place is very popular with workers at the end of their shifts (and yes, there *is* a sunset, over the bus stand). Good music, *nyama* and snacks too.

Listings

Airlines Coastal Aviation tickets are booked through their Dar es Salaam office, see p.127.

Banks NBC, Kuu St, and NMB, Madaraka Ave next to CCM Building, are reliable but slow; NBC has an ATM for Visa and MasterCard. CRDB, Kuu St, is mind-numbingly inefficient.

Car rental There's no official car-rental company in Dodoma, though most taxi drivers are happy negotiating a day's use.

Car repairs CMC Land Rover, Railway St, 500m west of Kuu St ☎026/232 2205.

Cinema Paradise Theatre, Kuu St, is a real old fleapit – surely about to close – that video-projects Kung Fu and US B-movies (Mon, Tues & Fri at 7pm), and Bollywood flicks (Wed & Thurs at 7pm, Sun at 2.30pm & 7.30pm).

Hospitals Best are the private Aga Khan Health Centre, 6th St ☎026/232 2455, and Mackay House

Moving on from Dodoma

By bus

The **bus station** is along Dar es Salaam Avenue, as are most ticket offices. There's no dominant company – indeed, many only have one or two vehicles, so **safety** is hard to gauge. Ones that you should avoid though are Abood, Amit, Tawfiq, and possibly Tashriff/Takrim.

Buses travelling **east** to Dar es Salaam and Morogoro leave every 30min–1hr from 6.30am. The safest operator is Scandinavian Express (daily 9.30am & 11.15am; ☎026/232 2170), whose terminal and office is 200m east of the bus stand. Shabiby (☎0745/683976) also have a reasonable reputation; their terminal and office is adjacent to the bus stand (three times a day, last at 11am). Simba DVD Coach run to Tanga (7.30am Wed, Fri & Sun).

Going **south**, Iringa and Mbeya are covered by at least one daily bus (7.30am or earlier), operated by King Cross, Urafiki or Shabiby. Their reputations are reasonable.

Heading **west**, there are at least two daily buses to Singida (both 11.30am), continuing to Shinyanga and either Mwanza or Bukoba. Several companies alternate on the route – it's advisable to check their safety record with impartial locals before buying a ticket; Shabiby (to Mwanza on Tues & Sat) should be okay. Six buses a week make the journey to Tabora, along a newly opened dirt road along the railway line, all leaving from 5.30am to 6am – the companies are Anam, Mabruck Aleyck, Sabena and Supersonic. There are no buses to Kigoma.

Tickets for buses **north** to Kondoa, Babati and Arusha can also be bought at an office at the west end of Lindi Avenue. There are four buses a day to Kondoa in good weather (6am, 9am, noon & 1pm), the morning ones usually continuing on to Arusha. During heavy rains, the road can be blocked south of Kondoa. Mtei Express and Shabiby are probably safest, relatively speaking.

By train

Trains head to **Mwanza** and **Kigoma** at 8.10am on Monday, Wednesday and Saturday, branching at **Tabora** where there are connections to **Mpanda**. Trains for **Dar** leave on Monday, Wednesday and Friday at 6.40pm, and there are also services along the northern branch line to **Singida** (10am Wed, Fri & Sun).

The **ticket office** (Mon–Fri 8am–noon & 2–4pm, Sat 8–10.30am, and 2hr before departures) encourages tourists to take a bunk in second or first class, though if you're travelling to Tabora you'll arrive before sunset, so third class is an acceptable and much cheaper alternative (Tsh5500 compared to Tsh14,000 in second or Tsh18,200 in first).

By air

Coastal Aviation flies thrice-weekly to Arusha (Mon, Thurs & Sat) and Dar (Tues, Fri & Sun). Seats are often fully booked when parliament is in session, so book ahead.

Medical Centre, west end of Dar es Salaam Ave ☎026/232 4299; the latter has a good dental clinic. The main government-run place is Dodoma General Hospital, off Railway St ☎026/232 1851. **Internet access** Blessing Internet Café, Dar es Salaam Ave next to *Dodoma Wimpy* (daily 8.30am–9pm; Tsh500/hr); Vinkas, *New Dodoma Hotel* (daily 7.30–10pm; Tsh500/hr). Access also at *Cana Lodge*, and RAL Internet Café on Kuu St, near *Dodoma Wimpy*.
Libraries Dodoma Library, Dar es Salaam Ave, one block east of Zuzu roundabout (Mon–Fri 9am–6pm, Sat 9am–2pm; Tsh500 daily membership). National Museum and National Archives currently under construction east of Mshariki Ave.

Pharmacy Central Tanganyika Chemist, Dar es Salaam Ave, west of Zuzu roundabout ☎026/232 4506.
Police Kikuyu Ave, on the way to Iringa ☎026/232 4266.
Post Railway St.
Supermarket Yashna's Mini Supermarket, 6th St, behind GAPCO near Zuzu roundabout (Mon–Sat 8.30am–6.30pm, Sun 9am–2pm), has a small selection of imported foods.
Swimming pool *New Dodoma Hotel* charges Tsh5000.
Telephones TTCL, Railway St beside the post office (daily 7.30am–8pm).

Kondoa

Situated 158km north of Dodoma, the small and dusty town of **KONDOA** is a handy base for visiting the ancient and beautiful **prehistoric rock paintings** in the Irangi Hills, one of the finest such collections in the world. Kondoa itself has no real tourist attractions, although the weird sight of gigantic baobabs growing in the town centre is memorable enough, and there's also a **cultural tourism programme**.

Few speak English, but no matter – everyone is eager to help out, and even the taxi drivers and touts at the bus stand are uncommonly apologetic in their advances. The town's **markets** are also fun: the main one is adjacent to the west side of the bus stand, and there's also a tiny produce market a few blocks to the east of the bus stand next to a church, whose aged vendors are wholly charming and well worth the extra few shillings they'll winkle out of you.

The town's inhabitants are mainly Rangi, though there are also Gogo and Sandawe, the last of whom were hunter-gatherers until a few decades ago. Most of the town's population is Muslim: if you're awake at 5.30am, listen out for the hauntingly ethereal chanting of *dhikiri* – recitations of the 99 names of Allah,

Cultural tourism around Kondoa

Kondoa is home to the unofficial but nonetheless recommended **Irangi cultural tourism programme**. It's run by a young man named Moshi Changai, who can be tracked down at *Sunset Beach Guest House* (☎0748/948858, ⓦwww.kondoa .com). There's a welter of activities on offer, including – of course – rock art tours in the Irangi Hills, as well as birding (and bird-trapping with locals), honey-harvesting (best immediately after rains), and a marvellous hike in the Sambwa Hills to **Ntomoko Falls** where, myth has it, you might catch sight of Satu the snake, protector of the water source. Coming from Arusha, you might consider a seven-day round trip, which includes the Barbaig tribe, and Lake Eyasi: contact the programme a few weeks in advance. Accommodation is in traditional flat-topped *tembe* houses, or camping. A women's co-operative provides meals.

   Prices are higher than in other cultural programmes, primarily on account of car rental from Kondoa. In a group of four, a full day and night costs around $50 per person, dropping to $30 over three nights. Costs descend for those with their own vehicles.

which provide a soothing contrast to the more guttural calls of the muezzins which mark the passage of time during the day. Perhaps because of its common religion, the town has a strong if easy-going sense of identity, something strengthened by the feeling that the government has ignored the region for too long – in spite of years of promises, most trunk roads remain unsurfaced, and are liable to be blocked in the rains. Unsurprisingly, the region is a stronghold of the opposition Civic United Front (CUF).

Practicalities

Kondoa lies 3km west of the Arusha–Dodoma road. Whichever direction you're travelling in you'll probably have to spend a night here, as most buses terminate in Kondoa. Access is no problem in the dry season, but it's a different story in the rains, when journey times can double and the road from Dodoma especially can be impassable, usually around Mtungutu. The road from Arusha fares better and remains passable in all but the heaviest downpours, though there are a number of slippery hills where black cotton soil brings many a truck to grief, thereby blocking the road.

Buses arrive at the bus stand at the west end of Kondoa town, one block south of the main road into town. Mtei Express is the main operator from **Arusha**, continuing on to Dodoma around 2pm, weather permitting. Tashriff/ Takrim also run from Arusha but have a reputation for dangerous driving along this route; enquire beforehand about the safety of other operators. Alternatively, catch an early bus to Babati, from where you can get an onward connection to Kondoa. A few daladalas also run between Kondoa and Arusha. Coming from **Dodoma**, there's a steady stream of buses and daladalas in either direction until around noon.

Kondoa is small enough to get your bearings quickly: the "main road" referred to in our directions is the one leading west into town from the Arusha– Dodoma road. NMB **bank** at the east end of town changes travellers' cheques – be patient. The **post office** and **TTCL** phone office are close by.

Accommodation

Kondoa has over a dozen cheap and basic guest houses, as well as a couple of places geared more towards tourists and businessmen. Most of them are signposted off the main road and the bus stand. The best is the friendly and welcoming *New Planet Guest House* (℡0748/669322; ❷), 200m west of the bus stand along the continuation of the main road, which has spotless rooms, all with large and comfortable beds, round nets, and some with bathrooms. There are rooms of a similar standard, complete with spacious box nets, at *Sunset Beach Guest House* (❷), an eight-hundred-metre hike west along the road to Singida and Kwa Mtoro, which runs parallel to the main road from the south side of the bus station – follow the signposts. It also has a choice of rooms with or without private bathroom, a TV in reception and food to order (but no alcohol). Of the cheaper options (all ❶), the more salubrious is the *Kijengi Guest House and Tea House*, 200m along the Singida road.

Eating and drinking

There's not much in the way of **restaurants**, the exception being the *New Planet Guest House*, which offers a wide choice of tasty Tanzanian and continental dishes. A full meal with a soda or two costs under Tsh2500. As usual, most of the bars (see opposite) can also rustle up meals, mainly chips, chip omelettes and – if you're lucky – grilled meat. Usually with chips. There are foodstalls around

Moving on from Kondoa

Leaving Kondoa, get up early, as most buses leave at 6am, and buy your ticket a day in advance to be sure of a seat. A number of companies run daily buses from Kondoa to **Dar es Salaam** via Dodoma and Morogoro. If you're headed to **Singida**, go to Babati or Dodoma and change there, as although the direct route to Singida via Kwa Mtoro is served by occasional pick-ups, you risk being stranded if the vehicle doesn't go all the way. If you're contemplating the wild run east across the Maasai Steppe to **Korogwe and on to Tanga**, you'll need to take Mwambao Bus on Tuesday or Friday. It leaves at noon, stops overnight at a guest house along the way before Handeni, and arrives in Tanga at 2pm the following day.

the bus stand. Fresh **coffee**, served in small Omani-style porcelain cups, is sold from a stall on the west side of the bus stand.

For **drinking**, a popular local place is the cheerfully noisy 24-hour bar attached to the *New Splendid Guest House*, signposted 300m north off the main road from the bus stand, which plays good African music and has satellite TV. If you find it far from splendid, try the pleasant *Just Imagine Bar* opposite (which also has rooms; ❶), or the *Metro Garden Bar* with its agreeable shaded garden, on the main road at the junction with the street leading to the *New Splendid*. The restaurant at the *New Planet Guest House* also sells beer, but has no atmosphere whatsoever. Entertainment is limited to loud **videos** screened daily (a few hundred shillings) in the darkened front room of *Ashura's Hotel*, which faces the bus stand.

The Irangi Hills

The relatively isolated **IRANGI HILLS**, located between the Babati–Kondoa road and the low-lying Maasai Steppe to the east, are an exceptionally beautiful and rewarding area for off-the-beaten-track hiking, and also contain one of the world's finest concentrations of **prehistoric rock paintings**. The local **Rangi** tribe (also called Langi) are an extraordinarily friendly and welcoming people, and wherever you go you'll be greeted with broad smiles, effusive greetings and handshakes, and gleeful kids going berserk as you pass by. Nowadays primarily an agricultural people, the Rangi's cattle-herding past is reflected in the saying "it is better to hit a person than his cattle", so if you're driving, take extra care. Originally plains-dwelling, the Rangi moved up into the hills a couple of centuries ago to avoid the inexorable advance of the warlike Maasai. The subsequently defensive nature of Rangi society was characterized by their houses, unusual in that they were very low and built into wide natural hollows, rendering villages almost invisible to the Maasai on the surrounding steppe. Nowadays, with no more need to hide from their former enemies, Rangi villages are notable for their intricate brickwork, sometimes decorated with geometrical relief patterns similar to styles used in parts of the Sahara. The Rangi's expertise in creating earthenware objects is even more artfully shown in their beautiful **black cooking pots**, which can be bought for a few hundred shillings at any of the region's markets (there's one every day somewhere in the hills – just ask around). You'll see them perched on people's houses – the only place where they can be dried after washing without being smashed by the above-mentioned hyperactive children. In short, if you have a sense of adventure, and don't mind roughing it for a while, the rewards of any trip here are countless.

Practicalities

The easiest way to get to see the region is through Kondoa's **Irangi Cultural Tourism Programme** (see box on p.263). The gateway to both the Irangi Hills and the Kondoa-Irangi rock paintings is **KOLO VILLAGE**, 27km north of Kondoa along the Arusha road and 82km south of Babati. Coming from the north by **public transport**, there are several daily buses and daladalas from Babati, the last of which leaves around 10am. From Arusha, an early bus to Babati should get you there in time to catch the last departure to Kolo. Alternatively, catch the Mtei Express bus from Arusha to Dodoma (6am), which passes through Kolo at around 3pm. Coming from Kondoa, catch any early morning bus or daladala for Arusha or Babati, or wait for the noon Rombo Bus which continues on to Pahi, deep in the Irangi Hills, returning the next day at 4am. Cheaper but less dependable is the noon Land Rover pick-up from Kondoa, which returns from Kolo at 6am. From Dodoma, catch either the Subra Coach or Rombo Bus at 6am. Note that the road between Kolo and Kondoa consists in parts of very loose sand or black cotton soil, and may be closed during and just after heavy rains.

Unless you feel comfortable arranging lodging with local families (a few thousand shillings would be greatly appreciated; ask local shopkeepers) or are with Kondoa's cultural tourism programme, the only **accommodation** in the Irangi Hills is the *Silence Guest House* in Kolo village. The curator at the Antiquities Department, on the main road in Kolo, will be able to show you. There's no electricity and no fixed price, but it shouldn't cost more than Tsh5000 a double, and they can also arrange simple but tasty meals. The only alternative is to pitch a tent at the riverside **campsite** 4km along the track to the "Kolo B" rock paintings. However, there are no facilities whatsoever, no water for much of the year when the river runs dry, and locals advise that you should use the site only if you're in a large group (three or four tents at least), as there have been instances of robbery in the past.

There are no restaurants as such in the Irangi Hills, though each village has a handful of *mgahawa* joints – small *hotelis* serving up tea, coffee and simple dishes like rice with beans. The weekly cycle of **produce markets** is good for roasted maize cobs, freshly grilled beef and goat meat, as well as dried fish, sugar cane, live chickens and ducks, sandals made from car tyres, all manner of clothing and, of course, the beautiful Rangi cooking pots.

The Kondoa-Irangi rock paintings

The area between Singida and the Irangi Hills contains one of the world's finest collections of **prehistoric rock paintings**, with an estimated 1600 individual paintings at almost two hundred different sites, the most accessible of which are in the Irangi Hills north of Kondoa. The most recent date from just a century or two ago, but the oldest are estimated to be between 19,000 and 30,000 years old, ranking them among the world's most ancient examples of human artistic expression.

In the African context, the paintings – together with other sites in Masasi (southern Tanzania) and Bukoba (in the northwest) – form part of a wider chain of stylistically similar sites ranging from the Ethiopian Highlands to the famous San (Bushmen) paintings of southern Africa. There are also intriguing similarities with the world's most extensive rock art area in and around the Tassili n'Ajjer Plateau of the Algerian Sahara, notably the curious "round-head" style used in depicting human figures. Some of the paintings are believed to have been the work of the ancestors of the present-day Sandawe and Hadzabe

△ Kondoa – Irangi rock paintings

tribes, both of whom have preserved ritual traditions involving rock painting. The **Sandawe**, who live to the west of Kolo and Babati, were hunter-gatherers until a few decades ago, whilst the **Hadzabe**, around Lake Eyasi to the north, still adhere to that ancient way of life, albeit against increasingly unfavourable odds. It's no coincidence that the Sandawe and Hadzabe are also the only Tanzanian tribes speaking languages characterized by clicks. The parallel with the Kalahari San Bushmen – who speak a similar click language and are

Rock art etiquette

Many of Tanzania's rock paintings have deteriorated at an alarming rate over the last few decades thanks to **vandalism** – whether deliberate or unintentional – by unsupervised, irresponsible and ignorant visitors, and a lamentable lack of funds to properly safeguard this extraordinary human heritage. Most obvious is the graffiti left by both Tanzanian and foreign tourists, which at two of Kondoa-Irangi's sites has defaced almost fifty percent of paintings that had hitherto survived thousands of years. Other panels have been disfigured by misguided "cleaning" efforts that have removed much of the original paint pigments, while others have been damaged by efforts to enhance the colours and contrast of the paintings for photography by wetting the panels with water, Coca-Cola and even urine. In order to protect the paintings in the Irangi Hills, visitors are legally required to take a **guide** from the Antiquities Department office in Kolo, but other sites have no such safeguards. Experienced guides can show you most of the rock art sites and may also be able to point out many details in the paintings that you might easily miss otherwise. Whatever you do, you must adhere to the following rules when visiting any rock art site in Tanzania or elsewhere:

Do not touch paintings or the rock face around them. Traces of oil, acid and sweat from your hands destroys pigments, and any form of direct physical contact damages paintings by dislodging loose flecks of paint, in turn accelerating damage from wind and rain.

Do not wet paintings under any circumstance. This fades and dissolves the pigments and very quickly renders the paintings almost invisible, as has happened at a number of sites in the Irangi Hills.

Respect local communities and their beliefs. Many of Irangi's sites are located in traditional hunting grounds, where excess noise and off-track bush walking by tourists and researchers has in the past disturbed wildlife (one site has been partially disfigured with anti-*wazungu* graffiti because of this). Sites may also have sacred or ritual importance to locals.

themselves responsible for an astonishing array of rock art – is irresistible, and suggests that a loosely unified group of hunter-gatherer cultures covered much of southern and eastern Africa until they were dispersed, annihilated or assimilated by Bantu-speaking tribes, the first of whom arrived some two to three thousand years ago.

Most of the paintings are located in rock shelters – either vertical rock faces with overhangs, or angled surfaces that resemble cave entrances – both of which have served to protect the paintings from millennia of rain, wind and sun. All the sites give striking views of the surrounding hills, and most overlook the Maasai Steppe to the east. The paintings vary greatly in terms of style, subject, size and colour: the most common consist of depictions of animals and humans done in red or orange ochre (iron oxide bound with animal fat). Particularly remarkable are the fine elongated **human figures**, often with large heads or hairstyles, unusual in that their hands generally only have three fingers, the middle one being much longer than the other two. The figures are depicted in a variety of postures and activities, some standing, others dancing, playing flutes, hunting and – in an exceptional painting at Kolo B1 dubbed "The Abduction" – showing a central female figure flanked by two pairs of male figures. The men on the right are wearing masks (the head of one clearly resembles a giraffe's) and are attempting to drag her off, while two unmasked men on the left attempt to hold her back. Animals are generally portrayed realistically, often with an amazing sense of movement, and include elephant, kudu, impala, zebra and especially giraffe, which occur in around seventy percent of central Tanzania's sites and which give their name to the so-called **giraffe phase**, tentatively dated to 28,000–7000 BC. The later **bubalus phase** (roughly 7000–4000 BC), generally done in black (charcoal, ground bones, smoke or burnt fat), depicts buffalo, elephant and rhinoceros. Of these, the highly stylized herds of elephants at Pahi are uncannily similar to engravings found in Ethiopia. The more recent paintings of the **dirty-white phase** (kaolin, animal droppings or zinc oxide) generally feature more abstract and geometric forms such as concentric circles and symbols that in places resemble letters, eyes or anthropomorphs.

As to the meaning of the paintings, no one really knows. Some believe they held a magico-religious purpose, whether shamanistic or as sympathetic magic, where the intent was to bring to life the spirit of an animal by painting it. This was either to enable a successful hunt, or was symptomatic of a more complex belief system which summoned the spirits of certain sacred animals, especially eland, to bring rain or fertility. The latter is evidenced by the practice of San shamans "becoming" elands when in a state of hallucinogenic trance. Another theory states that rock shelters – as well as baobab trees – are Sandawe metaphors for the "aboriginal womb" of creation. Indeed, the Sandawe have a dance called *iyari* which is performed when twins are born, and part of the ritual surrounding the dance involves rock painting. Other theories, nowadays pretty much discredited, go for the simple "art for art's sake". Either way, the rock art of Kondoa gives a vivid and fascinating insight into not just Tanzania's but humankind's earliest recorded history and way of thinking. For **further information**, the expensive but extraordinarily beautiful *African Rock Art: Paintings and Engravings on Stone*, by David Coulson and Alec Campbell (Harry N. Abrams Publishers, New York, 2001; Ⓦ www.abramsbooks.com), features Kondoa-Irangi in its East Africa chapter.

Practicalities

Visitors intending to visit the rock paintings need a **permit and a guide** from the Antiquities Department on the main road in Kolo. The permit costs Tsh3000 and covers as many sites as you have time for. The congenial guide-cum-curator is not paid a fortune, so a decent tip is in order. Visits to rock paintings are also offered by some mid- and upper-range safari operators from Arusha, usually combined with a safari in Tarangire (try the East African Safari & Touring Company; p.406), and by the cultural tourism programme in Kondoa (see p.263).

The fourteen "officially" recognized sites (there are many more), each with an average of three painted shelters located within a hundred metres or so of each other, were first studied by the archeologist Mary Leakey in the 1950s, after which she had them fenced with chicken wire to deter vandalism. Inevitably, the locals found better use for the barriers, so none of the sites currently have any measure of protection, and some have – in consequence – been disfigured with graffiti from a handful of supremely moronic visitors, local and foreign. For this reason, in this guide we have deliberately omitted locations and directions for the sites – start instead at the Antiquities Department in Kolo. With the exception of "**Kolo B**", which can be visited on foot from Kolo (6km each way), unless you have strong legs, plenty of time, and a tent, **access** is most feasible with your own 4WD, as the paintings are spread out over a 35km radius to which there is little or no public transport, and no accommodation. The sites are best viewed either in the morning or late evening, depending on their orientation, when the low sunlight enhances the paintings and lends a rich orange cast to the rock, making for some wonderfully vivid photographs.

Babati and around

The fast-growing town of **BABATI**, 105km north of Kondoa, is a great place to hunker down for a few days, and enjoys a pretty location flanked by the 2415m Mount Kwaraa to the east and the freshwater Lake Babati to the south. Although there aren't any sights in the town itself, it's a friendly and lively base for visiting a number of attractions in the area, including the solitary volcanic peak of **Mount Hanang**, and local **Barbaig** and **Sandawe** communities – all of which can be done through a **cultural tourism programme**.

Babati's *raison d'être* is its position at the junction of the roads from Arusha, Dodoma and Singida and beyond to the lake region. Given the roads' historically atrocious condition, Babati has long been a stopover for travellers, so much so that it's now a thriving market centre, with a population of over forty thousand, and was recently made capital of the newly formed Manyara Region. The land around Babati is also fertile, a far cry from the forbidding semi-desert to the north, and the area is a major producer of maize, finding ready markets in Arusha, Dodoma and even Mwanza.

The town's major cultural event is the grand **monthly market** (*mnada*), held on the seventeenth of each month, 4km south of town on a hillside next to the Kondoa road. The event attracts thousands of people, many from outlying districts, and for some town-dwellers the market provides a perfect excuse to bunk off work and indulge in grilled beef, fresh sugar cane and local brews at inflated prices (many are the tall stories of hung-over revellers waking up in the early hours the next day to see packs of hyenas scavenging around the remains). The cattle auction is perhaps the day's highlight, and draws Maasai and Barbaig from all around the region. All in all, a great day out.

Babati-Hanang cultural tourism programme

The reason for the small but steady trickle of tourists who come to Babati these days is its **cultural tourism programme** (see pp.64–66 for an overview), amongst the best – although not the cheapest – in Tanzania. Their office is located in *Kahembe's Guest House* in Babati (℡0748/397477, ⊛www.authenticculture.org). **To get there** from the bus stand, walk back to the main road, then north along it for a couple of hundred metres until you reach *Ango Bar & Garden* on your right and a petrol station on your left. Turn left, and the office is 200m along on the right.

The programme offers a wide variety of flexible itineraries, ranging from a half-day of wobbly paddling in dugouts around **Lake Babati** searching for hippos (take care), to visiting a "killer bee-keeping project" (don't say you weren't warned). Also on offer are **cycling expeditions**; climbs up **Mount Hanang** (see p.274); three- to five- day walking trips in the Mang'ati Plains to a **Barbaig** community, who might put on a mock fight to illustrate how they got their name (see p.274); and encounters with former hunter-gatherers, the **Sandawe**. Local culture features heavily in all the tours, and includes enlightening meetings with respected village elders, and visits to developmental projects. Particularly recommended, if you have time, is the fourteen-day **rock art educational tour**, which features both the rock paintings in the Irangi Hills and a little-visited rock art site near Bukoba in Tanzania's far northwest – contact them well in advance.

Costs break down into group fees (the guide and some activities), and per person expenses which include meals, accommodation, bus or daladala fares, and any forest reserve or village entry fees. Overall, expect to pay $35–45 per person for a full programme lasting 24 hours, everything included, or $60–70 a day for the extended educational tours. A portion of the fees is used to improve primary school facilities in two local villages.

Practicalities

Babati lies 68km beyond the end of the sealed road from Arusha (68km of which were meant to have been surfaced years ago), to which it's connected by several daily buses. There are also daily buses from Kondoa, Singida and Tanzania's northwest, and – weather permitting – Dodoma.

The **bus stand** is just off the main road in the centre of town. Unfortunately, it's acquired something of a reputation for chaos, not helped by the **cultural tourism programme** informally employing **touts**. There's no guarantee that they're not just thieves (there have been cases of robbery), so it's best to decline their services as politely you can and make your own way there: directions are given in the box opposite.

Accommodation

Try to arrive early, as Babati's newly acquired status as regional capital means that decent **guest houses** fill up quickly. Enquire at *Kahembe's Guest House* for **camping** ($5): you can pitch a tent at the owner's house 2km east of town, or on his farm 10km away at the foot of Bambaay Hill.

Classic Guest House 200m beyond the cultural tourism programme office, on the same road, past the football ground ☎0748/390940. An excellent budget choice, with well-kept rooms (some en suite) with large box nets, and safe parking. ❶–❷

Kahembe's Guest House Behind the cultural tourism programme office ☎0748/397477, ⓦwww.authenticculture.org. Eight small and clean en-suite rooms with mosquito nets around a court-yard, a little pricey, but the manager – the affable co-ordinator of the cultural tourism programme – is a mine of information, and offers discounts if you do some of the trips. ❸

Paa Paa Motel By the bus stand ☎027/253 1111. More good budget accommodation (and often full), this safe choice has clean en-suite singles (no hot water) and doubles sharing bathrooms. Rooms have mosquito nets and fans, and there's a small restaurant, bar, and safe parking. ❶

Paris Guest House Turn right beyond *Classic Guest House* ☎0748/721958. Another good choice, similar to the *Classic*, all en-suite rooms, also with safe parking. ❷

Eating, drinking and entertainment

Lamentably, Babati's **fish** – for which it has long been famous – is currently trucked in dry from Lake Victoria, as overfishing in Lake Babati has collapsed stocks and prompted a ban on fishing. Still, there's good **food** to be had. The thatched *Ango Bar & Garden* on the highway, with a nicely atmospheric wood-and-thatch interior and some tables outside, is best at lunchtime for its regal self-service. Breakfasts are also good (tasty snacks), but evening fare is very limited. Also good for lunch, especially Indian-style, is *Abida Best Bites Café*, 100m south of the cultural tourism programme office. For dinner, you can't go wrong with the goat meat *trupa* (a particularly tasty stew of pretty much everything) at *Dolphin Bar*, between the cultural tourism programme office and *Classic Guest House*. It also does good *nyama choma*, as does *Paa Paa Motel*.

There are a multitude of **bars** to choose from. Ever popular both day and night (when the satellite TV is the big draw) is the one at *Paa Paa Motel*, which has tables facing the bus stand. *Ango Bar & Garden* is also good, whilst the large *makuti*-thatched *Dolphin Bar* is the town's main nightspot, with **live music** some nights, and tapes of *jazzi* otherwise.

Around Babati

A pleasant way to spend a day is to visit **Lake Babati**, a 2km stroll south of the cultural tourism programme office: walk down the Kondoa road, and take the

Moving on from Babati

Heading south towards Kondoa and Dodoma is no problem in the dry season, with at least two **buses** a day, but the stretch beyond Kondoa can be impassable during and after heavy rain (usually mid-March to May, sometimes also Nov & Dec). The best company for all routes is Mtei Express: their buses may be old and not overly reliable, but the company has a safer reputation than Takrim/Tashriff and some others, not that that's saying all that much. Most buses leave around 6–7am, although late risers shouldn't have too much difficulty getting a seat on one of the through buses from Arusha to Singida, Dodoma or Mwanza, which pass by between 10.30am and 1pm – you should be able to buy a ticket at the bus stand the day before. The first bus to Arusha leaves at 4am, the last around 2pm.

If you're **driving**, ensure your vehicle is in good condition before proceeding west or south, as the roads are a trial. Be sure also to leave plenty of extra time so you don't get caught out after dark – the road to Singida has been the scene of a number of nocturnal **car-jackings and hold-ups**.

track to your right that starts at an old mango tree facing the District Court. The lake – one of few freshwater bodies of water in the Rift Valley – is a paradise for **birds**: over three hundred species have been recorded so far, including flamingos. June to August is the best time for bird-watching, when migrants arrive in time for the maize, millet and sunflower harvests.

Given the lack of a known outlet, the lake's level varies wildly according to the rains: at the time of writing it was at its lowest for years, whereas during the 1997–98 El Niño rains, it rose so high that it flooded the Kondoa road in two places – a boon for fishermen who made a tidy profit ferrying people across. Parts of the town itself were also flooded, and locals joke that all they had to do for their dinner was reach out of a window to grab a fish. The event prompted an NGO to build an overflow pipeline from the lake to a river at lower altitude, which should prevent such flooding in future. The lake is said to be free of bilharzia, and kids are happy swimming in it, but not adults – the resident **hippos** are unpredictable and definitely dangerous, so swim or canoe at your own risk.

Although you don't really need a guide – you can follow the water's edge for most of the way, though a couple of swampy areas force you briefly back to the road – it's worth taking one from the cultural tourism programme as it's a good way to meet locals, and also gets you on a wobbly dugout in search of hippo (at your own risk) and, if or when the ban on fishing is lifted, chinwags with local fishermen.

Mount Kwaraa

The flat-topped mountain rising 3km east of Babati is **Mount Kwaraa**. Its 2415-metre peak is swathed in heavy forest and usually also in mist, so don't expect panoramic views if you climb it. What you will see is some fascinating and virtually untouched forest. The mountain is used by migratory herds of elephant and buffalo: you almost certainly won't see them, but the presence of fresh dung and crushed undergrowth is enough to give most spines a tingle. The lower slopes, up to around 1750m, are mainly scrub, with dry montane forest and stunted woodland dominating the higher sections, which is part of the protected **Ufiome Forest Reserve**. The mountain can be climbed in a day, but two days is preferable as you'd have much more time to explore the vegetation.

Wild Tanzania

Tanzania's national parks and reserves

Close your eyes and try to picture wild Africa. Chances are that, somewhere along the way, you'll have picked up images of wildlife thundering across dusty plains, or of lions grabbing wildebeest from behind after a breathless chase. If this is what you're expecting of Tanzania, you won't be disappointed. Its huge range of natural habitats, many little-changed by human activity, contain a vast wealth of plant and animal species – making it the fourth-most biodiverse nation on earth.

The Northern Safari Circuit

Most **safaris** set off from Arusha, capital of the "**Northern Safari Circuit**". Comprising mainly semi-arid savannah, it encompasses the country's major wildlife parks, of which the **Serengeti** – star of countless wildlife documentaries – is the jewel. Famed for its spectacular annual wildlife migration, it contains the biggest concentration of wild mammals on earth – including lions, who are fond of visiting the park's campsites at night. Almost as spectacular is the adjacent **Ngorongoro Conservation Area**, enclosing an enormous volcanic crater. Inside, beside soda lakes bedecked with pink flamingoes, lives pretty much every

Hot air balloon, Serengeti National Park

Wildlife migrations

The Serengeti serves as backdrop to an annual **migration** of millions of wildebeest, zebra and other plains game, which follow the rains up into Kenya's Maasai Mara, and back down again for calving. With hungry lions and hyenas never far behind, the migration is one of nature's most spectacular displays, especially if you time things right with the herds' perilous crossings of the Grumeti and Mara rivers – chaotic and gory scenes of panicked flesh and muddy water, during which crocodiles pick off the weak or unwary under the watchful eyes of circling vultures. Smaller in scale but still worth catching is the pulse-like migration from **Tarangire**, in which elephants also take part.

Elephants, Tarangire National Park

large mammalian species you might have hoped for, including black rhino in their natural habitat. The other northern parks are baobab-studded **Tarangire**, especially fine for elephants, birds and consummately romantic accommodation, and **Lake Manyara** at the foot of the Rift Valley escarpment, with resident flamingoes and mammals whose elusive nature makes sighting them all the more rewarding.

Ngorongoro Crater, Ngorongoro Conservation Area

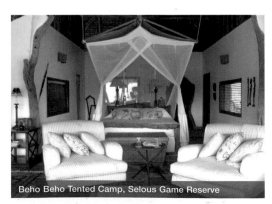
Beho Beho Tented Camp, Selous Game Reserve

The Southern Safari Circuit

The "**Southern Safari Circuit**", usually accessed from Dar es Salaam, tends to be touted as an upmarket destination; its often truly luxurious lodges can be shockingly expensive. First stop is **Mikumi**, for easy sightings of several large mammals, including – with luck – critically endangered African hunting dogs. South of Mikumi is Africa's largest protected area, **Selous Game Reserve**. Named after English elephant-hunter and all-round macho man, Captain Frederick Courteney Selous, most of the reserve is still (rather scandalously) used for trophy hunting, though a small but beautiful part in the north, including the fabulous Rufiji River floodplain, is reserved for "photographic tourism". Further south is the wild and remote **Ruaha National Park**, where the Great Ruaha River Valley plays host to tons of wildlife, and, as yet, few tourists.

Western Tanzania

Western Tanzania is either difficult or expensive to visit, its parks receiving barely a dozen visitors a day. **Gombe Stream** and **Mahale Mountains**, on the shore of Lake Tanganyika, are famed for **chimpanzees** – it was here that their use of tools was first observed, together with less attractive

Chimpanzee, Gombe Stream National Park

human traits such as warfare. Inland, **Katavi National Park**'s seasonal floodplains support huge concentrations of wildlife, including some of Africa's largest buffalo and hippo populations – often up to their necks in gigantic communal mud wallows. The other western park is **Rubondo Island**, a birder's paradise in Lake Victoria's southwest corner.

Tanzania's first conservators

For too many decades, the accepted conservationist mantra has been to exclude all human activity from protected wildlife areas, with the exception of researchers and tourists. This would make perfect sense were it not for the fact that wildlife areas had survived perfectly well before the locals were evicted. Local communities know full well that they would be destroying their own livelihoods were they to damage their environment. Often, that knowledge took the form of **taboos**: the Gorowa people believed in underground water spirits dwelling around Mount Hanang; it was said that cutting down any of the mountain's trees would cause them so much offence that they'd move away, taking the water with them. The logic was clear and unassailable: destroy trees and you destroy your water supply.

Lioness in tree, Lake Manyara National Park

Climbs and hikes

Other than wildlife, Tanzania's towering attraction is **Kilimanjaro**, the "Mountain of God". Rising to 5891m above sea level, this gigantic ice-capped dormant volcano is the roof of Africa. The considerable physical challenge of scaling it – allow at least a week – attracts tens of thousands of hikers every year, less than half of whom reach Uhuru Peak at the very top. It's an exhausting and painful experience, but a hugely rewarding one too.

Facing Kilimanjaro is another dormant volcano, the beautiful **Mount Meru** (4566m), much of which comprises **Arusha National Park**. It can be climbed over three or four days, and its lower slopes contain an eclectic spread of habitats and wildlife, including crater lakes, a miniature Serengeti, and birds aplenty.

Tanzania also has incredibly rich forest ecosystems that are perfect for hiking. Nowhere is this more obvious than when hiking at **Amani Nature Reserve**, up on the steep East Usambara Mountains, whose ancient rainforest ranks among fourteen global "hotspots" for species diversity. Another great hiking destination is central Tanzania's **Udzungwa Mountains National Park**, distinguished by its unbroken forest canopy from just 250m above sea level to over 2km up. Wildlife is exceptionally diverse, though the thick vegetation means you're more likely to hear than see its eleven primate species.

In the far south, locals know **Kitulo National Park** as "The Garden of God": over fifty varieties of unique orchids grow in and around its highland meadows, and the Highland Mangabey monkey, only discovered in 2004, resides in the fringing forest. It's a must for hikers, amateur botanists, twitchers and butterfly aficionados, especially in the rains.

Mount Kilimanjaro, Kilimanjaro National Park

Coastal Tanzania

On the **Indian Ocean coast**, an unusual combination of "beach and bush" (and croc-spotting along mangrove-lined estuaries) can be savoured at **Saadani National Park**, but Tanzania's shores are best known for their tropical **coral reefs**, providing both superb snorkelling and scuba-diving opportunities, and pristine beaches. Among the best are **Mafia Island Marine Park** (home of turtles and the almost extinct dugong), the vitually unknown **Mnazi Bay–Ruvuma Estuary Marine Park** next to Mozambique, and **Chumbe Island Coral Park** off the west coast of Unguja. The main terrestrial reserve on Zanzibar is at **Jozani Forest**, inhabited by troops of red colobus monkeys.

Fishermen, Saadani National Park

People are free to climb below the forest line, but to go higher you need a guide, and a permit from the Forestry Office in Babati, along the Kondoa road. The cultural tourism programme can arrange everything for you. If you have the energy, **Bambaay Hill** – part of Mount Kwaraa – can also be climbed, though this is better over two days, giving you time to visit the Gorowa village of Managhat, whose elders are happy to regale their guests with traditional tales and fables.

The road to Singida

The road **between Babati and Singida** is one of Tanzania's most beautiful, running for much of its 178km along the southern flank of the Rift Valley's Malbadow Escarpment and past the lone volcanic peak of **Mount Hanang**. Starting from Babati, the road crosses the floodplain of Lake Babati, then twists up into the hills amidst beautiful and ever-changing scenery before levelling out in a broad valley, with Mount Hanang to the south and the long barrier of the Malbadow Escarpment to the west. The road forks at **Ndareda**, 26km from Babati. A right turn takes you along a minor road (difficult or impassable in the rains) to the lively market town of **Dongobesh** and on to **Mbulu**, from where there's an even less-travelled but stunningly beautiful route north to **Karatu**, near the eastern entrance of Ngorongoro Conservation Area (upwards of 4hr from Ndareda). The route makes a fascinating diversion from the Northern Safari circus, but you'll need your own 4WD and ideally an experienced driver. This is the land of the **Iraqw**, a Cushitic tribe which is culturally more akin to Ethiopians and northern Kenyans than to the Bantu-speakers who dominate Tanzania; for more about them, see p.458.

Mount Hanang

Taking the left fork at Ndareda, the Babati–Singida road veers south towards Tanzania's fourth-highest mountain, **Mount Hanang**, around 60km south-west of Babati, and considered by many to be one of the most beautiful peaks in the country. Rising up from the Mang'ati Plains to three summits, the highest at 3417m, Hanang is sacred to the Gorowa (Fiome) and Barbaig tribes, since its streams feed **Lake Balangida**, one of the Rift Valley's most important watering points for cattle herders. Hanang's height means that water vapour from clouds condenses on it, making it the region's primary source of water, and the high water table around it supports a surprisingly rich groundwater forest on the mountain's lower slopes. Higher up, the groundwater forest gives way to montane and upper montane forest, with trees up to 20m tall on the wetter southern, eastern and northern slopes, and dry montane forest on the western slopes. Above 2100m the forest gives way to grassland, thicket and bushland, while above 2700m moorland dominates.

Despite recurring problems with illegal logging, much of Hanang's forest has survived intact, apparently thanks to the Gorowa belief in **underground earth spirits** called *Netlangw*. The *Netlangw* are said to live under large trees where springs emerge, which makes Mount Hanang's girdling groundwater forest of prime importance. The *Netlangw* are guardians of the water; if they are offended, say by the clearing of trees, they move away, taking the water with them. The logic is clear and unassailable: destroy trees and you destroy your water supply.

The Barbaig

The unremittingly dry expanse of savannah that stretches south of Mount Hanang, the **Mang'ati Plains**, is at first sight a deeply inhospitable place. Yet the plains are home to some 200,000 **Barbaig** (or Barabaig), a semi-nomadic, cattle-herding tribe distantly related to the Maasai. The key to their existence in such a barren land lies on the other side of Mount Hanang in the shape of **Lake Balangida**, a large freshwater expanse at the foot of the Malbadow Escarpment. The lake is fed by the mountain, which ensures that even when the lake is dry (an increasingly common occurrence), the deep wells that have been dug around its periphery still contain enough water for the Barbaig's herds.

Tall, handsome and proud, the Barbaig are at first glance very similar to the Maasai. They dress alike, and are also herders, in whose culture cattle occupy a pivotal place. Like the Maasai, their society is organized into age-sets and a clan system (**dosh-inga**) which governs rights over pasture and water sources. But for all their similarities, there's no love lost between the two peoples. The Maasai have two names for the Barbaig. One is **Mbulu**, by which many other tribes south of the Maasai are also known, and which means "unintelligent people". The other, reserved for the Barbaig alone, is **Il-Mang'ati**, meaning "the enemy", a simple tag which, coming from East Africa's most feared and warlike people, is almost akin to a compliment. The name Barbaig itself comes from *bar* (to beat) and *baig* (sticks), alluding to a unique dance that is still held today, in which fights are mimicked using sticks for weapons.

The Barbaig are one of nineteen tribes that originally made up a broader cluster of people called **Datooga** (or Tatoga). Like the Maasai and Kalenjin of Kenya, the Datooga are linguistically classed as Nilotic, meaning that they share a common origin, presumed to be in Sudan's Nile Valley. A fascinating relic from this time, which could also explain the extreme ritual importance of cattle in all Nilotic societies, is the Barbaig word for God, *Aseeta*, which is related to the Kalenjin word *Asiis*, which also means sun. Both words have their root in the name of the ancient Egyptian goddess **Isis**, who wore a solar disc and the horns of a cow and was the focus of a

Katesh

Whichever route you take to climb Mount Hanang, the first stop is **KATESH**, 76km southwest from Babati along the road to Singida, where you should visit the Forestry Department to pay $5 for every day you plan to spend on the mountain.

The **bus stand** is about halfway along the road through town, and is nothing more than a tree with the Mtei Express timetable nailed to its trunk. The ride from Babati takes about ninety minutes, and there are at least three buses a day from Arusha – basically, any service that goes to Singida or Mwanza via Singida.

The town is liveliest on the tenth and eleventh of each month during the *mnada* **market**, held 2km south of town along the Singida road. The market's popularity explains Katesh's profusion of **guest houses** (all ❶): from east to west along the Babati–Singida road, these include the *Colt* (the best, with en-suite rooms), *Matunda*, *Tip-Top* (by the bus stand, also with en-suite rooms), and *Hanang View*. *Kabwogi's Hotel* has good **food**. There's a small **daily market** on the east side of the road beyond *Hanang View Guest House*. The NMB **bank**, past the police station on the left on the way out south, may change money, but you shouldn't bank on it, as it were.

Climbing Mount Hanang

The easiest way to arrange a **climb up Mount Hanang** is through Babati's cultural tourism programme (see box on p.270), which also offers an excellent

cattle and fertility cult throughout much of antiquity. According to Roman mythology – which adopted many Egyptian cults – the beautiful Isis, whom the Romans called Io, was kidnapped by an amorous Jupiter, but her mother, Juno, gave chase. Rather than give her back, Jupiter rather unfairly turned his love into a cow. Not content with this punishment, he called down a bumble bee from the heavens and commanded it to sting the cow. Not terribly enchanted with this treatment, the miserable Io fled to Egypt, where she cried so much that her tears formed the Nile.

The Datooga's southward **migration** is believed to have started around 3000 years ago, possibly prompted by the massive climate changes that coincided with the expansion of the Sahara Desert. Around 1500, the Datooga arrived at Mount Elgon on the Kenya-Uganda border, where they stayed until the eighteenth century, when they migrated south once more into Tanzania. The Datooga first settled at Ngorongoro before being pushed further south by the Maasai, after which they separated into various tribes, many of which have now been assimilated by others. Lamentably, the Barbaig's southward migration continues even today. Loss of their ranges to commercial ranches, flower farms and seed-bean plantations, and encroachment by Maasai (who have themselves been pushed south in recent decades by the creation of the Serengeti and Tarangire national parks) mean that the Barbaig are among Tanzania's poorest people. Child mortality rates are high, as is the incidence of cattle disease. The fact that none of this used to be the case supports the Barbaig claim that nothing other than the loss of their traditional land has caused these problems, but unfortunately the scattered nature of Barbaig society means that they have largely been absent from politics, and have consequently been marginalized. Their latest efforts to regain access to their land via a series of legal actions in the courts have stalled on the absurd grounds that they lack legally recognized title to the land.

For more information on the problems Barbaig culture faces, see *Passions Lost* by Charles Lane (Initiatives Publishers, Nairobi, 1996).

four-day trip combining an ascent with a visit to a Barbaig community. They charge $35–45 per person a day depending on group size, which includes the guide, all fees, food, accommodation, and any public transport. For general **advice** on mountain climbing, read the section on Kilimanjaro in Chapter 5 (p.340).

Camping is possible on all routes, but you need to be fully self sufficient; **take enough water** as there's none near the summit and no guarantee of any further down. Don't underestimate the mountain: it gets pretty cold at 3417m so come suitably equipped. Altitude sickness isn't a major worry – you might get a headache, but nothing more serious.

The shortest and most popular ascent is the **Katesh route**, from Katesh up the southwestern ridge: five to six hours to the summit, camping at 3000m, and a three-to four-hour descent the following day. You can go up and down in one day if the physical challenge is more important than enjoyment, but do start early. Allow time to arrange transport from Babati to Katesh, and to pay the forest fee, so count on a minimum of two or three days in total.

To vary the scenery, descending via the **Ngendabi route** is recommended, or alternatively ascending along it and descending to Katesh. The route starts 16km (3hr) northwest from Katesh at Ngendabi village, which levies a $2.50 fee on visitors. Accommodation in Ngendabi may be offered informally by teachers from the primary school, but shouldn't be counted on.

The main alternative to the Katesh and Ngendabi routes is the **Giting route**, from Giting village on the northeast side of the mountain. You might need your own 4WD, as public transport is currently suspended on account of the bad road. You'll also need to visit Katesh first to pay the forest fee. Accommodation along this route has been planned for years, to take advantage of the beautiful view of Lake Balangida; enquire whether this has finally happened in Babati.

Singida

The crossroads town of **SINGIDA**, 178km southwest of Babati, sits in an alluring boulder-strewn and kopje-studded landscape flanked by two freshwater lakes. Coming from Babati, the road enters town through a natural "gate" made from two boulders on either side of the road, one emblazoned with a huge painted advert for Salama condoms.

Apart from the lakes, Singida's "sights" are limited to the granite outcrops in and around the town, and a small regional museum which, unfortunately, is usually closed. That said, the friendliness of town itself is really the main draw – even if the traffic police are the exception that proves the rule. If you're driving, ensure your papers are in order.

The main tribe here is **Nyaturu**, whose last chief, Senge Mghenyi, achieved fame during the aborted military mutiny of 1964. To pledge his support to President Nyerere, he walked all the way from Singida to Dar es Salaam's State House, accompanied by a hyena – the traditional guardian of Nyaturu chiefs.

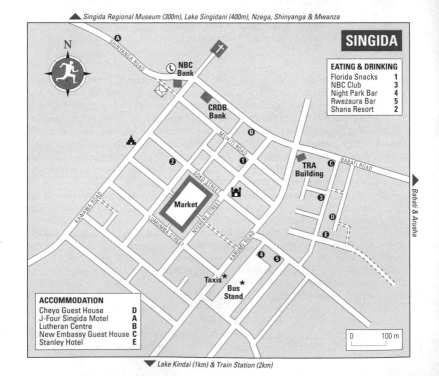

Singida Regional Museum (300m), Lake Singidani (400m), Nzega, Shinyanga & Mwanza

SINGIDA

EATING & DRINKING

Florida Snacks	1
NBC Club	3
Night Park Bar	4
Rwezaura Bar	5
Shana Resort	2

NBC Bank

CRDB Bank

TRA Building

Market

Taxis

Bus Stand

Babati & Arusha

ACCOMMODATION

Cheyo Guest House	D
J-Four Singida Motel	A
Lutheran Centre	B
New Embassy Guest House	C
Stanley Hotel	E

0   100 m

Lake Kindai (1km) & Train Station (2km)

Arrival and accommodation

Singida is a major overnight stop for trucks plying the roads between Lake Victoria and Arusha, Dodoma or Dar es Salaam, but improvements in the roads means that most **buses** no longer have to stop overnight in Singida. The town also sits at the end of a branch of the Central Line Railway, with services from Dodoma (third class only) on Wednesday, Friday and Sunday. The **train station** is 2km south of the centre along Karume Road. The NBC and CRDB **banks** are on Shinyanga Road close to the junction with Kawawa Road; NBC is the more efficient of the two, and its ATM accepts Visa and MasterCard. The **post office** is on Shinyanga Road; **TTCL** is opposite.

Singida has dozens of budget **hotels**, most of them pretty good, plus a couple of mid-range options. In most places, single rooms can be taken by couples. Make sure your bed has a mosquito net – there are zillions of those whining vampires. The following are the pick of the bunch.

Cheyo Guest House Off Babati Rd, beside the *Stanley Hotel*, entrance at the back ☎026/250 2258. A highly recommended budget option, and a bargain given that everything works: the rooms (all doubles) are clean and equipped with nets, and the shared bathrooms have powerful showers. There's also a bar with outdoor seating. ●

J-Four Singida Motel Shinyanga Rd, just past the hospital ☎026/250 2193. Close to Singidani Lake, this is often empty but still recommended and good value. It's set in a large garden with plenty of tables under parasols, children's swings and a mongoose colony. All rooms have private bathrooms with reliable hot water, table fans and box nets. There's also a big bar with a TV and good food, and breakfast is included. ❸

Lutheran Centre Shinyanga Rd (no phone). A friendly place with good twin-bed rooms (all with nets) opening onto a courtyard – the more expensive ones have private bathroom and Western-style toilet, and there's also a good restaurant. ●

New Embassy Guest House Babati Rd ☎026/250 2123. Decent rooms with shared bathrooms. ●

Stanley Hotel Off Babati Rd ☎026/250 2351, ☎026/250 2285. The most popular option in town (its entrance marked by enormous animal sculptures), offering cheap rooms with shared facilities and more expensive ones (a tad overpriced) with private bathrooms and local TV. The toilets are squat-style and clean, and there's hot water, a restaurant and safe parking. ●–❸

The Town and around

Singida's main attraction is its location, bordered by **Lake Singidani** to the north and **Lake Kindai** to the south, and set amidst a scatter of weathered granite bounders and outcrops (kopjes). On the west side of town, 100m from Lake Singidani, the **Singida Regional Museum** (ask for Makumbusho ya Mkoa; ☎026/250 2449; Mon–Fri 9am–6pm; free, but tips appreciated) might be worth a visit, although the place is usually locked and the curator out of town. It's in the unmarked building on your right some 200m beyond the *J-Four Singida Motel*, its grounds surrounded by a fence. If there's no one around, ask at the District Council offices nearby.

Eating, drinking and entertainment

Singida is best known in Tanzania for its **chickens**, which are sold as far away as Dar (hence the sorry spectacle of fowl stuffed into wicker baskets at the bus stand). The town's other speciality is its especially fine **honey** (*asali*), sold in the market. The bus stand has lots of places for filling up on fried chicken and fish, chips, grilled bananas and goat meat skewers. The main **restaurants**, all doubling as bars, are along the road just north of the bus stand. Other choices include *Florida Snacks* at the corner of Nyerere and Msikiti roads, and *Shana Resort* on Soko Street, which has a good range of dishes and is an excellent place for breakfast, with lots of snacks and freshly pressed mango juice.

   The most popular **bars** are *Rwezaura Bar* and *Night Park Bar*, both at the entrance to the bus stand, the latter with satellite TV. *NBC Club*, close to the *Stanley Hotel*, is also worth a try. **Videos** are shown in a blacked-out room at Lemmy Video Show on Soko Street.

Morogoro and the Uluguru Mountains

The town of **Morogoro**, 190km west of Dar es Salaam, is little visited by tourists, who – if they stop at all on the way down to Mbeya in southern Tanzania – generally prefer Iringa. The **Uluguru Mountains** to the east and south of Morogoro, however, provide several excellent reasons to stop. Part of the Eastern Arc chain that includes the Usambaras, the rainforests of the **Ulugurus** are similarly blessed with natural beauty, hundreds of rare plant and animal species and a wealth of cultural interest – not to mention a recently established **cultural tourism programme** based in Morogoro.

Morogoro

The first thing that strikes you as you approach **MOROGORO** is its strikingly beautiful location, nestled at the foot of the rugged Uluguru Mountains. In the morning, as the sun rises above the mist and bathes the town in warm tones of orange and gold, even the bus station is momentarily imbued with a certain charm. Although seemingly nothing remains of **Simbamwenni**, the town's nineteenth-century precursor, the legacy of that century's Muslim-dominated

MOROGORO

N

ACCOMMODATION
B One Guest House .... B
High Classic Hotel
& Guest House .... K
Hilux Hotel .... F
Hotel Oasis .... D
Kola Hill Hotel C
Lukanda Family
Lodging & Hotel I
Mama Pierina's Hotel .... E
Masinga Hotel .... H
Morogoro Hotel .... N
Mount Uluguru Hotel .... M
New Acropol Hotel .... A
New Savoy Hotel .... G
New Tegetero Hotel L
Sofia Hotel .... J

EATING, DRINKING & NIGHTLIFE
Blue Room 5
Hilux Hotel .... F
Hotel Oasis .... D
King Tom Club 1
Mama Pierina's Hotel .... E
Morogoro Hotel .... J
Mount Uluguru Hotel .... N
New Acropol Hotel .... G
New Chipukizi Club 4
New Green Restaurant 3
New Savoy Hotel .... A
Pema Bar 7
Savannah Club 6
Sofia Hotel .... J
Tushikamane Hotel 2

Train Station

KIPENGE STREET

BANDA STREET

OLD DAR ES SALAAM ROAD

STATION ROAD

MADIBIRA ROAD

Oryx

Pamba
House

Gapco

Chilunga
Cultural
Tourism

Hospital

RWAGASORE STREET

NBC
Bank

KITOPE ROAD

Clock Tower

Library

Police

Morogoro River

CRDB
Bank

KITOPE ROAD

OLD DAR ES SALAAM ROAD

NKOMO ROAD

Gapco

Daladala
Stand

Islam's Bus Office

BOMA ROAD

Pira's Cash
& Carry

Aga Khan
Clinic

MLAPAKOLO STREET

NMB
Bank

UHURU STREET

LUMUMBA STREET

JOHN MAHENGE ST

MAKONGORO STREET

MADARAKA ROAD

KONGA STREET

NGOLO STREET

Market

200 m

279

▲ Kisamvu Bus Station (3km), Dar es Salaam, Iringa & Dodoma

▲ G (4km) & ❷

▶ ⑩ (250m)

▶ Morningside

▼ ❻ & SUA

caravan trade lives on. In the town centre, the passage of time is marked by the five daily calls to prayer from the mosques, and Morogoro is one of very few places on the mainland where you'll see women wearing the black *buibui* veils which are so common in Zanzibar. The cultural compote is completed by a thriving Indian community, a welter of earnest-looking European and American missionaries and development workers, and a few Maasai warriors, with their braided hairstyles, hunkered down in the town's bars in their traditional red (or these days purple) *shuka* cloths, spears to hand.

The town has an instantly likeable and bustling feel, and an enjoyably lively nightlife, too, though its lack of obvious attractions means that it receives few visitors. Morogoro is no backwater however; the town's transport connections – it straddles both the Tanzam Highway and Central Line Railway – have ensured its prosperity. Morogoro Region is also Tanzania's second-largest producer of rice after Mbeya, and supplies the country with sizeable amounts of sugar cane, coffee, cotton, sunflower oil, millet and maize, *Arabica* coffee – introduced to Tanzania by Jesuit priests operating from Morogoro in the 1890s – and sisal, brought to the area early in the twentieth century by Greek planters whose estates still dominate the plains to the north and northeast. The town's population is growing fast, having doubled in the last decade to almost 300,000.

Some history

Morogoro's existence stems from its location on a major crossroads whose importance dates from before the arrival of the Arabs right through to the present day. Nineteenth-century Tanganyika was in a state of considerable chaos, allowing wily local leaders to carve out empires for themselves. The most unusual of these was not a tribal chief like Mirambo or Mkwawa, but **Kisabengo**, the leader of a group of fugitive slaves, who acquired power and eventually land through force of arms and the kidnapping of neighbouring tribespeople. Kisabengo's domain, although small, included part of the major caravan route from the coast to the Great Lakes region. His capital, a settlement near modern-day Morogoro which he modestly called **Simbamwenni** (the "Lion King") inevitably became an important base for traders. Kisabengo also welcomed Christian missionaries on their first forays into the interior, some of whom later settled in Morogoro on land donated by the chief. When Stanley passed through in 1871, en route to his historic encounter with Livingstone, he found a "walled town at the western foot of the Uruguru mountains, with its fine valley abundantly beautiful, watered by two rivers, and several pellucid streams of water distilled by the dew and cloud-enriched heights around". Estimating the population at up to five thousand people, Stanley was most impressed by the town's solid stone fortifications and towers. Given this unusually extensive use of stone for building away from the coast, it's a mystery why no trace of Simbamwenni appears to have survived. If you're interested in trying to find it, it should be along the Ngerengere River just west or north of town.

The present-day site was certainly known to the **Germans** when they began their push inland. When they arrived, there was but a lone Muluguru (a Luguru person) living there. The "l" became an "r", the "u"s "o"s, and lo! Morogoro.

The Germans transformed Morogoro into a base, using it as an infamous "hanging ground" during their military conquest of Tanganyika and subsequent repression of the Abushiri and Maji Maji rebellions, at which local people were forced to watch the executions. The site of the hanging ground is now perhaps fittingly occupied by the ruthless anti-riot Field Force Unit (FFU), the police headquarters and a remand prison. Morogoro was captured by the **British** on August 26, 1916, when the remnant of the German forces escaped southwards, though not before the German commander Paul von Lettow Vorbeck had taken the time to arrange a surprise for General Smuts and his army, leaving a mechanical piano playing "Deutschland über Alles" in the *Bahnhof Hotel* (now the *New Savoy*), while his soldiers deposited some rather more earthy "presents" on the chairs and tables before beating a retreat.

After Independence, Morogoro became famous, in South Africa at least, as a major base for the **African National Congress** (ANC), whose fighters were trained in the Uluguru Mountains.

Arrival and information

Morogoro lies on the **Central Line** Railway between Dar es Salaam, Tabora, Kigoma and Mwanza. The station is 1.5km northeast of the centre along Station Road; you'll arrive at night, but there are plenty of taxis, and several hotels nearby.

Morogoro's **bus station** is unhelpfully located 4km north of town at the Kisamvu roundabout ("keep lefti"), at the junction of the roads to Dar, Mbeya and Dodoma. A taxi into town costs Tsh2000, whilst a daladala charges Tsh200. Passengers are greeted by a welter of pushy touts, hustlers and taxi drivers frantically trying to grab your attention and your bags; you can reduce the hassle by retrieving your stuff from the luggage hold before arriving, and some bus drivers stop just outside Morogoro to do just this. To escape the chaos, just walk towards the main road – few hustlers will follow, as they'll miss potential pickings from other passengers.

The **Chilunga Cultural Tourism Programme** on Rwagasore Street, facing the Regional Hospital (Mon–Sat 8am–5.30pm, also Sun same hours July–Dec; ℡0741/580680 or 0744/477582, ℮chilungamg@yahoo.co.uk) functions as an informal information centre, in addition to arranging superb hikes in the Uluguru Mountains. For details, see "The Uluguru Mountains" section.

Accommodation

Morogoro has good **mid-range accommodation**, some of which could even be described as luxurious. **Budget** offerings are more limited, and for a half-decent room you're looking at upwards of Tsh6000–8000. Single rooms in cheaper hotels can be shared by couples if the beds are big enough. **Water** is a problem in many cheapies; always sterilize tap water if you're going to drink it as work has stalled on rehabilitating the town's typhoid-prone water system. **Camping** is possible at *Kola Hill Hotel*, 4km east of the centre ($5 per person; call ahead a day or two before).

Budget

B One Guest House no street name – see map ℡0748/930151. One of the better options out of a dozen lookalike choices in this neighbourhood, and ideal for sampling the nightlife hereabouts. The rooms are en-suite doubles. ❶

High Classic Hotel & Guest House Off Makongoro St ℡0741/322795. Very cheap, with decent rooms (shared bathrooms) and a good restaurant popular with locals for its TV. ❶

Lukanda Family Lodging & Hotel Off Makongoro St ℡023/260 3870. Basic and clean with a choice of twins sharing bathrooms or en-suite doubles with big beds. All have fans, but some lack nets. ❶

Mama Pierina's Hotel Station Rd ℡0741/786913. A quiet and friendly place offering en-suite twins with fans, nets and good showers. There's a garden at the back, and a pleasant restaurant and bar at the front. Breakfast included. ❷

Masinga Hotel One block east of Lumumba St (no phone). Quiet and reasonable if dark twin rooms with smallish beds, cotton sheets, and fans. The better rooms are upstairs. In café next door. ❷

New Savoy Hotel Station Rd ☎023/3041.
Currently Morogoro's main nightspot, so far from
quiet, and the eight en-suite rooms really need
a bit of loving attention (unreliable water, saggy
beds, missing nets), but it's friendly and handy if
you want to party, and some rooms have a/c. Rates
vary from room to room and have little to do with
quality, so look around before choosing. Breakfast
included. ❷–❸
New Tegetero Hotel Madaraka St
☎0744/496481. A friendly central choice: the en-
suite rooms look out over the road (and also have
a communal balcony); those sharing bathrooms

overlook *Pema Bar* at the back – needless to say,
all are extremely noisy, especially Thurs–Sun. All
rooms have fans, and the beds are clean if narrow,
making it impossible to avoid contact with the
mosquito nets. Basic restaurant downstairs. ❷
Sofia Hotel John Mahenge St ☎0741/334421. A
good central choice with a range of spotless rooms.
The cheaper ones share bathrooms and have twin
beds, fans and mosquito nets; the more expensive
en-suite rooms also have a/c, a fridge and TV.
There's also a double with a huge bed, a/c, fridge,
telephone and balcony. At the back is a bar and
cheap restaurant. Breakfast included. ❷–❹

Mid-range
The following have safe parking.

Hilux Hotel Old Dar es Salaam Rd ☎023/3946,
✉hiluxhotel@yahoo.com. A good-value but boring
modern place with plain rooms in a three-storey
block at the back, all with a/c, satellite TV, table
and chair, and spotless bathrooms, though the
mosquito nets are small. There's a restaurant and
two bars, the nicer one, under the *makuti* roof,
with a pool table. No single rates. English breakfast
included. ❹
Hotel Oasis Station Rd ☎023/4178,
✉hoteloasistz@morogoro.net. Another bland business-class place, two storeys, popular with conferences and civil servants. The 36 rooms are large
and comfortable if ageing, with nets, fridge, satellite TV, phone, fans and a/c (despite which rooms
can be musty), and tiled bathrooms. Beds in singles
are tiny. Amenities include a bar and restaurant,
Internet access, and – big cheer – a swimming
pool. Breakfast included. ❺
Kola Hill Hotel 4km along Old Dar es Salaam Rd
☎023/260 3707, ☯www.kolahill.com. In a quiet
rural location close to the Uluguru, the thirty en-
suite rooms here (twin or double) are in closely
spaced granite bungalows, all with box nets,
phones, bathtubs (with enough hot water), and
mountain-facing balconies. Most have fans, more
expensive ones have a/c and local TV, and there's
a bar and restaurant with a Harry Potter-themed
menu. Mountain guides available. Catch a daladala
towards Bigwa. Breakfast included. ❸–❹
Morogoro Hotel Rwagasore St ☎023/3270,
✉morogorohotel@morogoro.net. The town's
largest hotel, it's good value and also the most

appealing architecturally, with a cluster of buildings
designed to look like traditional Luguru homesteads, but which bear an uncanny resemblance
to flying saucers. The bedrooms – smallish but
with high ceilings and therefore cool – are in
segments of the smaller saucers, all with excellent
bathrooms, huge beds, box nets, a/c, fridge, phone
and satellite TV. The suites have bathtubs. Facilities
include tennis courts, access to the golf course
across the road (Tsh10,000 a round, but you'll
need your own clubs), a large garden with great
views of the Uluguru and plenty of trees, a good
restaurant and bar, and Internet access. English
breakfast included. ❺
Mount Uluguru Hotel Mlapakolo Rd ☎023/260
3489, ☏023/260 4079. This five-storey hotel is
the best in the town centre, the nicest rooms on
top facing the mountains. All come with twin beds
(which can be joined together) with big nets, fan,
phone, wall-to-wall carpet, fridge and bathroom,
and an either/or choice of local TV or a/c (same
price). The large downstairs bar has tables under
a hangar-like roof, and the restaurant does good
cheap food, including *nyama choma*. No single
rates. English breakfast included. ❸
🏃 **New Acropol Hotel** Old Dar es Salaam Rd
☎023/3403, ☯www.newacropolhotel
.biz. Morogoro's most stylish abode, with just six
spacious en-suite rooms including two suites, all
tastefully decorated and with big four-poster beds
(twin or double), a/c and fan, TV and fridge. There's
also a very good restaurant and bar. English breakfast included. ❺

The Town
Aside from its proximity to the Uluguru Mountains, there's not much reason
to linger in Morogoro, although the bustling pace of life is refreshing. The best

free entertainment is at the main **market** along Madaraka Road, which sees hundreds of vendors coming from the mountains each day to sell whatever they have: tomatoes, snow peas, delicious sweet tangerines, bananas, papayas and coconuts, as well as delicately woven baskets, woodcarvings and coconut-wood chairs.

With time to kill – and a bicycle – **Mindu Reservoir**, off the Iringa road (around 12km each way), makes a good day-trip. For something completely different, a local school for disabled children offers **drum and dance lessons**; ask at the cultural tourism programme office on Rwagasore Street.

Eating

Almost uniquely in Tanzania, Morogoro keeps on bustling well into the night, with dozens of bars and cheap restaurants to keep you happy. The cheapest eats are at the various **street foodstalls** in the centre, especially at the corner of Madaraka Road and John Mahenge Street, which really get going towards dusk, when the air fills with plumes of aromatic smoke spiralling from dozens of charcoal stoves: grilled goat meat, roast bananas and maize cobs, chips and eggs are the staples. Look out also for the **coconut vendors**, who chop open the fresh nuts for you to drink the juice; you then scoop out the soft rubbery flesh using a piece of the shell. There are also cheap **restaurants** by the daladala stand.

Blue Room Makongoro Rd. Cheap snacks and full meals (Tsh1500) in a dull but clean interior, or at streetside tables, where there's also a grill for *mishkaki* and *ndizi* (bananas).

Hilux Hotel Old Dar es Salaam Rd. A small selection of Chinese, Indian, seafood and continental dishes (around Tsh4000), plus the usual fried chicken and chips. The dining room is plain – it's nicer eating in the back garden.

Mama Pierina's Hotel Station Rd, next to *Hotel Oasis*. Iringa's most famous lady, whose restaurant and bar had been an institution for decades, is sadly no longer with us, but her daughter has taken things in hand. The menu pays respect to the family's Greek-Italian roots, including lasagne, moussaka, home-made pesto (with cashew nuts replacing pine kernels), great pancakes, salads, and *mezedes* – salami, cheese, olives and tomato. Eat inside or on the verandah. You're welcome just to take drinks. Main courses average Tsh5000–6000.

Morogoro Hotel Rwagasore St. Great on a sunny day, when you can eat in the garden with a great view of the mountains. The menu covers authentic Indian and Chinese as well as Tanzanian favourites like *pilau*, *uji* porridge (for breakfast; ask the day before), *matoke* banana stew and coconut-sauced fish or meat. Buffet lunches or dinners cost Tsh4000–8000; à la carte a little less.

Mount Uluguru Hotel Mlapakolo Rd. Nothing special but central, with a wide menu including pork; eat outside under a swooping corrugated roof. Mains Tsh4000–5000.

New Acropol Hotel Old Dar es Salaam Rd. Probably Morogoro's best restaurant, with a sophisticated ambience, starched linen, and good value too. The menu covers most bases, but is particularly strong on seafood and pork (around Tsh5000), along with deep pan pizzas and snacks. They also brew an excellent coffee.

New Chipukizi Club Opposite *Lukanda Hotel*. Good, cheap and filling meals throughout the day, including *supu* – a meaty broth – for breakfast.

New Green Restaurant Station Rd. Always busy, a good sign, with a wide selection of Indian dishes plus pork and seafood. Full meals cost Tsh2500 and upwards. Closed Sun evening.

Hotel Oasis Station Rd. Particularly good Indian food, but cover yourself in insect repellent if you're eating dinner in the garden – there are more mosquitoes here than elsewhere. A curry with naan bread and a drink or two shouldn't top Tsh6000.

Sofia Hotel John Mahenge St. Nothing special, but most of the short menu is available (fried liver, beef, chicken and grills, but no vegetarian), and it's cheap – around Tsh2000.

Drinking and nightlife

Morogoro is an excellent place to visit if you like a tipple or five, with **bars** pretty much everywhere, but sadly the **live music** for which it was once famous has all but disappeared. Morogoro Jazz Band and Super Volcano, two of Tanzania's most popular dance bands of the 1970s and early 1980s, are long gone, and although the newly formed Savoy Band (Fri–Sun residents at the *New Savoy Hotel*) go some way in matching them, it's a far cry from the days of music legends Mbaraka Mwinshehe Mwaruka, Juma Kilaza or Kulwa Sakum. Still, it should be worth enquiring about live **hip-hop and rap** (or Bongo Flava if you're not yet sick of it). **Venues** worth asking about for live weekend music include *Savannah Club* by the airfield, and *Tushikamane Hotel* along the road towards *Kola Hill Hotel*.

Walking at night in the town centre is generally safe if there are plenty of people about (but watch out for speeding cars, especially on Old Dar es Salaam Road), but rising crime rates on the outskirts suggest a taxi would be wiser. Clubs get busy around 10pm, and stay so until 2am or 3am.

King Tom Club Station Rd. A sprawling outdoor bar with plenty of seats under *makuti* or trees, busy at all hours, and also with good *nyama choma*.

New Acropol Hotel Old Dar es Salaam Rd. An attractive, upmarket bar with seats inside in neo-colonial comfort, or in the garden at the front. Comes complete with dartboard and pool table.

New Chipukizi Club Makongoro St, opposite the *Lukanda*. One of the largest and busiest local places, open all day and often far into the night, with a wide range of beers, good cheap food and a TV that alternates between global satellite channels and pirated videos of US movies with Arabic subtitles (daily in the afternoon).

New Savoy Hotel Station Rd. The town's biggest night-time draw, especially Fri–Sun when Savoy Band pump out a mix of jazz oldies and newer Congolese-flavoured tunes (Tsh1000 entrance, free if you're staying here). It's also busy by day, and has food.

Pema Bar Madaraka Rd, entrance beside *New Tegetero Hotel*, or from the street at the back of NMB bank. An excellent town-centre drinking hole, popular for unwinding in after work. Always lively, they play lots of (usually) good, danceable music. It gets particularly loud Thurs–Sun, when the evenings often turn into discos (free), or else host professional dancers or, worse, lip-synchers.

Listings

Banks CRDB and NBC are both on Old Dar es Salaam Rd. The cumbersome CRDB charges $10 commission, the more efficient NBC a mere 0.5%, and their ATM accepts Visa and MasterCard.

Car rental Hima Tours & Travel has a disorganized office at *Hotel Oasis*, renting 4WDs (self-drive Tsh120,000 for 100km plus Tsh650 per additional kilometre).

Courier services DHL, Boma Rd ☎023/260 4528.

Football Jamhuri Stadium currently hosts title-contenders Moro United, but they may be shifting to Tanga if the owner has his wicked way. The other team is Prisons. Tickets, costing a few hundred shillings, are sold at the stadium.

Hospital Regional Hospital, Old Dar es Salaam Rd, entrance on Rwagasore St ☎023/232 3045; better is the Aga Khan Clinic, Boma Rd (open 24hr).

Internet access A fast connection and dozens of well-maintained computers at D&S, Mlapakolo St (daily 8am–9pm; Tsh1000/hr). There are two places on John Mahenge St nearby: Matunda, on

the right (daily 8.30am–10pm; Tsh500/hr) has private booths and a generator, wisely so given Morogoro's frequent outages, but its connection is slow.

Language courses Kiswahili lessons and courses are offered by Wageni Morogoro (☎023/260 0899) and the Institute of Adult Education – Expatriate Centre (☎023/260 2988), who also have accommodation for students on their one-month courses.

Post office Old Dar es Salaam Rd.

Supermarkets Morogoro's grocery stores are just west of the daladala stand. Pira's Cash & Carry on Lumumba St is the largest (open until around 10pm). There are more on the north side of Madaraka Rd.

Swimming pool Hotel Oasis charges day guests Tsh3000.

Telephones TTCL, Kitope St beside the post office (Mon–Sat 7.30am–10pm, Sun 8am–8pm). D&S Internet Café, Mlapakolo St (daily 8am–9pm) offers cheaper Internet calls.

Moving on from Morogoro

Trains to Dar es Salaam leave at 2.15am (Tues, Thurs & Sat). Heading to Tabora, Kigoma or Mwanza, they depart at a quarter past midnight (Mon, Wed & Sat).

All **buses** leave from Kisamvu roundabout, 4km north of town. The bus station has parking bays, though destinations are only marked on the far side (away from the road). There's lots of transport in all directions, with several buses hourly to **Dar**, and roughly every hour to **Iringa** and **Mbeya**, along with less frequent buses to **Dodoma** and **Arusha**, and daily runs to **Ifakara**. The biggest companies are Hood and Abood, but both have reputations for perilous driving and are best avoided despite their "luxury" coaches. Best of the rest are Scandinavian Express (office and bus stop facing the bus stand; ℡023/260 1279) for Dar, Iringa, Mbeya, Kyela, Songea and Dodoma; Sumry and Shabiby, covering the same destinations except for Dodoma (offices at the bus stand); and Islam's Bus (office on Boma Rd opposite the mosque; ℡0748/666667) for Dar (hourly 6am–6pm), Arusha and Ifakara (both daily). Coaster **minibuses** are generally safe, and handy for getting to places within the region such as Ifakara.

It's always best to buy your ticket the day before; otherwise, get yourself down to Kisamvu early in the morning (6am latest), where you can choose your vehicle: check tyres for wear, the driver's eyes for the effects of drugs or booze, and don't let yourself be harried onto one bus or another; there's usually plenty to choose from.

The Uluguru Mountains

South and east of Morogoro, and rising to around 2743m, the spectacular **Uluguru Mountains** contain some of the most luxuriant – but sadly threatened – indigenous rainforest in the country.

Spanning 100km from north to south and 20km from east to west, the range is part of the 25-million-year-old **Eastern Arc mountain chain** (see box on p.353). The great age of the mountains and the forests that cloak them, together with high rainfall, wide altitudinal range and a climate that has remained remarkably stable over the ages, have all favoured the development of some of the world's richest and most species-diverse **rainforests**, containing eleven endemic reptilian and amphibian species and over a hundred endemic plants, including African violets, busy lizzies and begonias. **Mammals** include yellow baboons, blue monkeys, black-and-white colobus monkeys, wild pigs and duiker antelopes. But where Uluguru really comes into its own is its **birdlife**, which includes fifteen rare or unique species. Notable among these are the Usambara eagle owl, which was found here in 1993 – only its third known habitat – and the endemic Uluguru bush-shrike, critically endangered thanks to the ongoing loss of forest canopy on the lower slopes.

In the early 1960s, most of the mountains were still covered with forest, but one glance at the Ulugurus from Morogoro today tells a sorry tale of destruction, either deliberately – by timber extraction or clearance for cultivation – or accidentally, by fire (whose depressing plumes are a daily feature of the skyline). Whilst the ambitious **Uluguru Biodiversity Conservation Project** appears to have run out of steam (and into a brick wall of intransigent bureaucracy), one fortunate spin-off has been the establishment of a **cultural tourism programme** in the mountains, which aims at providing alternative sources of income to local communities through low-impact tourism, thereby lessening some of the pressure on the forests. For the visitor, this means an exciting range of **walks and hikes** combining natural attractions (forests, streams, waterfalls

For over three centuries the Uluguru Mountains have been home to the **Luguru** tribe, whose name literally means "people of the mountain" (*guru* means mountain). Although most of the 1.2 million Luguru now live in the lowlands in and around Morogoro and elsewhere, some one hundred thousand still inhabit the lower slopes of the mountains, using skilful agricultural practices like self-composting ladder terraces to make the most of the fertile soil and abundant rainfall. Apart from traditional staples like rice, maize, sorghum, vegetables and plantain, cash crops – especially coffee and fruits – are also grown to be sold to the burgeoning populations of Morogoro and Dar es Salaam.

Despite the growing influence of Islam and Christianity, Luguru society remains strongly **matrilineal**. Land is the property of women, passing from mother to daughter, either in their own name or in that of one of fifty clans to which all Luguru belong, which in turn are subdivided into around eight hundred **lineages** (essentially families). Although a man may inherit land from his mother, it reverts to his sister's children on his death, even if he has children of his own; if a man needs more land, it can only be borrowed, not bought. Naturally, possession of land gives women an uncommon independence from their husbands, and divorce is common, after which the husband is sent away with nothing more than the clothes on his back. Not surprisingly, baby girls are much preferred to baby boys.

The structure of Luguru society also does away with the need for a centralized political system, as most matters can be dealt with at the lineage level. Matters affecting several lineages are heard by a highly respected council of elders who, of course, are elected by women. The feminine touch is also apparent in the traditional system of **joking relationships** (*utani* or *ugongo*) between villages, which avoided conflict between potential rivals through an institutionalized form of friendship, good neighbourliness and humour – villages in an *utani* relationship are expected to share food with each other in times of hardship, and in return the donors are allowed to jest and jibe at their neighbours' expense. Things are changing, however: land scarcity is slowly altering the allocation of land and its inheritance, while the traditional emphasis on female sexuality and the encouragement of extramarital affairs has brought with it the devastating spectre of AIDS.

For more information on Luguru society, including lots of detail on the ceremonies that mark the lives of women from initiation to marriage, pregnancy, birth and motherhood, see Salha Hamdani's excellent *Female Adolescent Rites and the Reproductive Health of Young Women in Morogoro* at ⓦ www.hsph.harvard.edu/takemi/RP100.pdf. Also recommended – even if you manage to hear *ngoma* at Nugutu – are the two tapes of traditional music for sale at Radio Tanzania in Dar es Salaam (see p.124), in which remarkable instrumental skills are blended with voices to mesmerizing effect.

and beautiful views) with equally fascinating encounters with the Luguru tribe, all at very affordable prices.

Practicalities

Hikes and other trips should be arranged through the **Chilunga Cultural Tourism Programme** office in Morogoro, in the YMCA compound on Rwagasore Street (Mon–Sat 8am–5.30pm, also Sun same hours July–Dec; ⓣ0741/580680 or 0744/477582, ⓔchilungamg@yahoo.co.uk), a youthful, conscientious and knowledgeable set-up.

The **price structure** is relatively simple: Tsh15,000 a day for a guide for a group of up to four people (or Tsh30,000 for 24hr), plus other costs with no mark-up (transport, accommodation, food, admission fees or permits). All in all, a couple shouldn't pay more than Tsh25,000 each for a full day and night. Daily **forest permits**, required to enter protected reserves, cost Tsh5000 for tourists, Tsh3000 for locals (your guide), and can be bought at the Regional Catchment Forest Project Office (Mon–Fri 7.30am–3.30pm; ☎023/260 0992 or 023/3026) 1km north of Morogoro: it's on your left immediately after the railway crossing on the road to Kisamvu junction. A permit isn't necessary if you stay under the tree line.

Although there are a handful of **guest houses** in the mountains, a tent will greatly enhance your options – the cultural tourism programme rents out two tents for this purpose.

Hikes and tours in the mountains

The following sections cover just a selection of available trips. For other ideas and **information**, email the cultural tourism programme, or navigate to ⓦwww.africanconservation.com/uluguru, then go to "downloadable papers and articles" and look for "Tourist Information for the Uluguru Mountains". The most detailed **topographical maps**, albeit out of date in terms of forest cover, are the 1:50,000 sheets produced by the Government's Surveys & Mapping Division (see p.28 for the shop in Dar): the relevant sets are #183 for North Uluguru, and #201 for South Uluguru.

The **best time to visit** is during the dry season (July–Sept), as some of the hikes may not be possible during the rains. The main rains fall between February and June, with the lighter short rains coming between October and January. All routes are steep in places, so come with good walking boots or at least worn-in shoes with good tread, especially when wet. It's best to start off early on all treks, and you should also take water (at least a litre), some food, a light raincoat, suncream and a light fleece from June to September when temperatures can be surprisingly low, even when the sun shines brightly.

Morningside

The half-abandoned colonial settlement of **MORNINGSIDE**, a two- to three-hour walk south of Morogoro, makes a pleasant target for a hike. The views over the Uluguru and Morogoro are well worth braving the steep path for, and the cool mountain air makes a bracing and welcome change from Morogoro's often sweltering heat. Other than this, Morningside doesn't have much more to offer. The old German building, which functioned as a hotel until the 1970s, is crumbling away but still used during field trips by the Sokoine University of Agriculture. Energetic folk can continue up a steep track or along the winding road to the forest boundary, marked by an enormous eucalyptus tree planted in the 1960s – the hike from Morningside takes an hour at most. **Bondwe Peak** in the forest beyond and topped by a communications mast can also be climbed, but you need a forest permit from Morogoro.

For Morningside, leave early (about 7am) as the lower part of the walk from Morogoro's Boma Road – through open farmland – can get very hot. There's a shop halfway up which should have sodas, and a waterfall en route. If you're feeling lazy, you could rent a taxi for part of the ascent, which gets you to **Ruvuma village**, three-quarters of the way, beyond which the path is too steep for vehicles. The potter in Ruvuma is happy to receive visitors. Take a **guide** from Morogoro's cultural tourism office (see p.281), both to help you actually find Morningside (which can be obscured by cloud during the rains), and if you want to spend any time in Ruvuma, which is very much a traditional village. There's a Tsh500 **entry fee** for Morningside levied by villagers, who also charge Tsh1000 for **camping**.

Nugutu and Madola

An hour's walk east from Morogoro (Tsh2500 by taxi), the village of **NUGUTU** is an excellent place to learn about traditional **Luguru culture**. The women's group has organized a number of activities for tourists, including an excellent Luguru-style lunch (featuring various *pombe* home-brews), as well as the chance to see locals weaving and dyeing the mats and baskets that form the village's main source of income. The twine is made from the fronds of the *mkindu* tree (phoenix palm), collected in the forest or bought in Morogoro. One mat takes about two months to make, as they only have evenings in which to work on them – daylight is spent in the fields. The women are also talented musicians and for a small additional fee will introduce you to the delights of traditional Luguru **music** and dance (*ngoma ya kiluguru*). Female visitors can be taught about *ngomas* reserved exclusively for women; there's a mixed sex group that can be hired for performances. You'll also be invited to meet an ironsmith who turns scrap metal into coconut graters called *mbuzi* ("goat"). Profits are being saved to build a dispensary. There's no accommodation.

Nugutu, which is as far as you can go by vehicle, is usually combined with a visit to **MADOLA**, a ninety-minute hike further up the mountain. Madola is usually visited first, before the sun gets too hot, with lunch back down in Nugutu. The track is steep and difficult to follow in places, but you're rewarded with beautiful views, patches of forest between the fruit orchards and vegetable plots, and a small waterfall.

Madola is even tinier than Nugutu, with only six houses at the last count. The village specializes in woodwork, including dolls, figurines and combs, but is mainly known for its female **traditional healer** (Bibi Maria) – a vocation for which the Luguru have long been famous throughout Tanzania – who uses her unusual talents of premonition and clairvoyance to heal sicknesses. Her "supernatural" powers (they're considered perfectly natural by the Luguru) were first revealed to her in a series of dreams when she was six years old, the age at which she first started healing. Now, she uses her dreams to diagnose patients and determine remedies. Treatment itself involves both medicinal plants and rituals, and is said to be particularly effective in cases of insanity.

The peaks

For that top of the world feeling, set your sights on the 2150m **Lupanga Peak**, the closest to Morogoro, which can be scaled and descended in about six hours. It's a tough walk though, and inside the forest it gets dangerously slippery in the rains, but you may be rewarded by glimpses of the rare Loveridge's sunbird or Fulleborn's black boubou, or more easily seen (or heard) Livingstone's turaco and silvery-cheeked hornbill.

Longer hikes includes a challenging four-day trek from Morogoro to the range's highest point, **Kimhandu Peak**, in South Uluguru, or three days straight **across North Uluguru**, from Kinole village on the eastern side, where Morogoro's chiefs were traditionally based, back to town. All these climbs require forest permits (see p.287).

Bunduki and around

The area east of **BUNDUKI** village, a challenging three-hour drive south of Morogoro (turn left at Kipera and left again at Mgeta, which is where the Luguru first settled), offers some great **hiking** possibilities, including one of the mountains' largest waterfalls and a walk to the **Lukwangule Plateau**, which separates the northern from the southern Uluguru Mountains.

Bunduki Forest Reserve is partly natural forest, partly plantation, and home to Mrs Moreau's warbler among other rare species. No permit is needed for walking along the road, but you'll need one if you go higher up towards the ridge, from where there are superb views eastward towards Dar es Salaam. Around ninety minutes' walk from Bunduki village, are the **Hululu Falls** outside the reserve (no permit needed), where water cascades over a forty-metre drop in a cloud of spray. The site is sacred to local people, who use it for ceremonies, so you'll have to go with a local or a guide.

For **overnight stays**, either camp in Bunduki (locals are happy to rustle up food and you can swim in the nearby river), or contact Reverend Gabriel Sengo at Bunduki Mission (PO Box 640 Morogoro) who may have room in his house 2km before Bunduki Forest Reserve gate.

Matombo

On the eastern flank of the Ulugurus, accessible from Bunduki on foot (12km of very rough terrain), or from the dirt road between the Tanzam Highway and Selous Game Reserve's Matambwe Gate, is **Matombo village**, which has two very special and unusual attractions. Matombo itself takes its curious name (which means "breasts") from a cave, which contains a natural stone formation resembling a naked woman. Needless to say, the cave is considered sacred, but can still be visited. Not far away, where the river flows through **Usolo**, there's a rock bearing curious rows of circular man-made depressions resembling the traditional African board game, *bao* (or *mankala*). Though archeologists are at a loss to explain the significance of these "**cup marks**" or cupules, locals know better. They say that a long time ago, two Luguru chiefs finally made peace after having quarrelled for many years. One of them, the legendary Chief Hegga, repeatedly tapped his heel on the rock to create the depressions, then invited his former adversary to join him in a game. The site takes its name from the Kiluguru word for *bao*.

Mikumi and Selous

The southern foothills of the Uluguru Mountains mark the start of a vast ecosystem that covers a large part of central and southern Tanzania, much of it protected by **Mikumi National Park** (straddling the Tanzam Highway south-west of Morogoro) and the enormous **Selous Game Reserve**, Africa's biggest protected wildlife area. Selous extends to within 150km of Mozambique, whose Niassa Game Reserve also forms part of the ecosystem.

The extraordinary richness of wildlife encountered in this area is explained by the dry **miombo woodland** that covers almost three-quarters of it. Unlike the thorny acacia and scrub vegetation that dominates northern Tanzania's wildlife areas, *miombo* is dominated by trees of the deciduous *Brachystegia* genera. The leaves that are shed every year form the basis of a surprisingly complex food chain, creating an ideal habitat for dozens of **large mammal species** – which are the main attraction at the heart of the Southern Safari Circuit. Fortunately, from a conservator's point of view, *miombo* woodlands are also the favoured habitat for **tsetse flies**, pernicious vectors of **sleeping sickness** (*trypanosomia-sis*). Wild animals possess an acquired resistance to the disease, but domestic live-stock and humans do not (that said, as a tourist, your chances of contracting the disease in Tanzania are minute). In consequence, much of the *miombo* ecosystem survived intact until the twentieth century, when white **trophy hunters** and, more recently, African **poachers** brought devastation, resulting in the near extinction of both elephants and rhino. Thankfully, things have now improved, and **elephants** are frequently seen in both Mikumi and Selous. The ecosystem's **rhinos**, however, are still severely endangered, and are believed to be extinct in Mikumi, while their population in Selous barely numbers 150.

The *miombo* woodlands are at their most beautiful in October and November, during and before the short rains, when they put out new leaves in all shades of red, copper, gold and orange, as well as green. Mikumi National Park can easily be visited from Dar es Salaam, either driving yourself or on an organized safari. Selous is a different kettle of fish, with notoriously bad access roads, though this doesn't appear to bother the authorities too much, given that they're bent on promoting "high-income low-volume" tourism, with most visitors flying in. Nonetheless, visiting Selous on a budget is possible, and can even be done by public transport.

Mikumi National Park

Sitting astride the Tanzam Highway 286km west of Dar es Salaam, the 3230-square-kilometre **MIKUMI NATIONAL PARK** is a popular first stop on "Southern Circuit" safaris. Framed by the Uluguru Mountains to the northeast, Rubeho Mountains to the northwest, Udzungwa Mountains to the southwest, and Selous Game Reserve to the south, the park consists mainly of *miombo* woodland. Although the scenery gets a little tedious in the dry season, sightings of **plains game** like impala, buffalo and crocodile, giraffe and small migratory herds of zebra and wildebeest are common enough, especially in the swamps and grasslands of the Mkata floodplain in the centre. The absence of gazelles is curious – it seems that their ecological niche is occupied by impala. **Elephants** are common throughout the park; the best time to see them is in December and January, when the resident population is boosted by migrants from Selous and a handful that have survived massive poaching in the Rubeho Mountains. **Preda-tors** are much more elusive thanks to the woodland and grassland vegetation, though most guides will be able to locate a lion or two. Leopards are more difficult to see (your best chance is in trees along watercourses), while black-backed jackals can sometimes be seen in the evening, and the African civet is an intermittent nocturnal visitor at some of the lodges. You'd be extremely lucky to see African hunting dogs, one of Africa's rarest mammals. Mikumi's **birdlife** is profuse, with over four hundred species recorded to date, many of them Eura-sian migrants present between October and April, including red-billed oxpeck-ers, marabou storks and the attractive turquoise and blue lilac-breasted roller, which often perches on dead branches. Other commonly seen birds include black-bellied bustard, cattle egret, francolin, guinea fowl, hammerkop, hornbill, malachite kingfisher and saddle-billed stork.

For those on a really tight budget, **buses** along the Tanzam Highway pass straight through the park for 50km, which in the dry season gives you the chance of spotting a good selection of wildlife. Taking photographs from buses is difficult, given that the drivers only stop when large and potentially

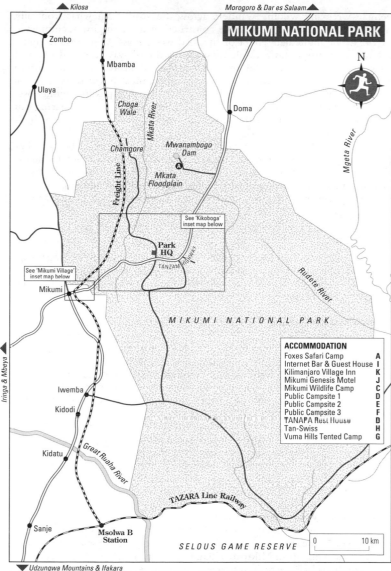

MIKUMI NATIONAL PARK

▲ Kilosa   Morogoro & Dar es Salaam ▲

N

Zombo

Mbamba

Ulaya

Choga Wale

Mkata River

Doma

Mgeta River

Chamgore

Freight Line

Mwanambogo Dam Ⓐ

Mkata Floodplain

See 'Kikoboga' inset map below

Park HQ

TANZAM HIGHWAY

See 'Mikumi Village' inset map below

Mikumi

Iringa & Mbeya ▲

MIKUMI NATIONAL PARK

Rudete River

ACCOMMODATION

Foxes Safari Camp	A
Internet Bar & Guest House	I
Kilimanjaro Village Inn	K
Mikumi Genesis Motel	J
Mikumi Wildlife Camp	C
Public Campsite 1	D
Public Campsite 2	E
Public Campsite 3	F
TANAPA Rest House	H
Tan-Swiss	D
Vuma Hills Tented Camp	G

Iwemba

Kidodi

Kidatu

Great Ruaha River

Sanje

Msolwa B Station

TAZARA Line Railway

SELOUS GAME RESERVE

0   10 km

▼ Udzungwa Mountains & Ifakara

MIKUMI VILLAGE

Buses & Daladalas to Kilosa

GAPCO

Ⓘ   Ⓗ

Ⓙ

Ⓚ

★ Buses & Daladalas to Mang'ula & Ifakara

0   1 km

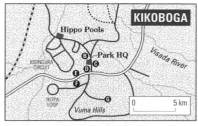

KIKOBOGA

Hippo Pools

KISINGURA CIRCUIT

Ⓑ Park HQ
Ⓓ Ⓒ

Ⓔ
Ⓕ

Ⓖ

IKOYA LOOP

Vuma Hills

Visada River

0   5 km

vehicle-wrecking wildlife wanders across the road. Somewhat ironically, Mikumi owes its protection to the construction of the highway, completed in 1954. The immediate effect of the road was a massive increase in hunting along its verges, as a result of which Mikumi was accorded national park status in 1964. The highway was asphalted in 1972. In spite of an 80kph speed limit and dozens of speed bumps, most bus drivers treat the highway as little more than a race track. Smaller creatures like mongooses and, lamentably, African hunting dogs, obviously aren't worth wearing out brake pads for, as you can tell from the assortment of flattened roadkills by the wayside.

Mikumi can be visited all year round, but many of the park roads become slippery or impassable during the long rains (March–May), and at times during the short rains (Oct–Dec).You'll find the greatest concentration of wildlife between December and March, but animals are most easily seen from mid-August to the end of October, when the last of the surface water has dried up, causing animals to congregate around the river, or at waterholes.

Arrival

Most people come on organized safaris from Dar, usually as part of longer trips to Selous or Ruaha. Driving time is around four hours. Arranging your own safari is easy and, if you rent a vehicle in Mikumi, cheaper than other options if you can find a few people to share the costs.

Organized safaris

See "Safaris from Dar" (p.132) for a list of reliable **safari companies**. Forget the one-day safaris sometimes touted from Dar: with a minimum of eight hours spent on the road, you'll invariably feel short-changed. A "two-day" camping safari – which in practice means one overnight plus a couple of game drives, one in the evening, the other the next morning – starts at around $200 per person, whilst the same with accommodation in one of the lodges or tented camps costs upwards of $350.

Alternatives to driving are either **flying** (charters only at present, though stopovers on Coastal Aviation flights to Ruaha are possible in high season), or the thrice-weekly "Safari Express" **private train** (see box on p.302), which costs $125 from Dar to Kidatu, around 60km south of the park's lodges. If you're staying at *Foxes Safari Camp* or *Vuma Hills Tented Camp*, the transfer is free; otherwise expect to pay around $50.

Arranging your own safari

Mikumi can only be visited by 4WD. Unless you're coming as part of a longer trip, in which case hiring a car in Dar (or Morogoro) makes sense, it's best to catch public transport to **Mikumi village** and arrange things there. Accommodation in the village   actually a rather dismal roadstead – is much cheaper than in the park, and you're also at the junction of the road to Udzungwa Mountains, a true hikers' paradise.

The village straggles along several kilometres of the Tanzam Highway just west of the park. Coming by **bus or daladala**, ask to be dropped at *Mikumi Genesis Motel*, 4km east of the junction to Udzungwa and Ifakara, or *Kilimanjaro Village Inn*, 1km east of the junction, both of whom rent **4WDs** ($100 a day including driver; add park fees for you and the driver), but keep an eye on the vehicle's condition. There's no fuel in the park, so fill up in Mikumi village or Morogoro.

Hiring an **official guide** at the park gate is recommended: they have an incredible eye for spotting things like a leopard's tail hanging from a tree half a kilometre away ($10–20 for a few hours; nothing fixed).

Information and entrance fees

The **park headquarters** are in the middle of the park at Kikoboga, just off the highway (PO Box 62 Mikumi ☎023/262 0487, ✉minapa@atma.co.tz). whilst the highway remains open throughout the night, driving in the park itself – speed limit 50kph – is only permitted between 6am and 7pm.

Entrance fees, valid for 24 hours, are $25 per person and Tsh10,000 for a vehicle permit. There's no charge if you're just passing along the highway. The park headquarters sells a map and an excellent **guidebook** ($10), which you can also find at the lodge gift shops, and in bookstores in Arusha, Dar and Stone Town. The park's official **website** is ⓦwww.tanzaniaparks.com/mikumi.htm.

Accommodation, eating and drinking

Most visitors only spend 24 hours in Mikumi, so the choice of **accommodation** isn't all that important given that you'll probably be spending most of your time on game drives. Nonetheless, for an extended stay, *Mikumi Wildlife Camp* is recommended for its proximity to wildlife, much of which can be seen from the bedrooms. Travellers on a budget have a choice between camping (see p.294), a rest house run by the park, and a selection of cheap hotels outside the park in Mikumi village. At present, it's possible to re-enter the park the following morning if you arrived in the afternoon, but abuse of this by dodgy tour operators (who use the same entry tickets for two groups) means that you may be limited to single entry in future. The solution is to enter the park early in the morning and spend the whole day on a game drive. All three of the park's upmarket camps serve **lunch** ($12–20) to day guests, and there are lots of cheap places in Mikumi village.

Mikumi village

Mikumi village has plenty of basic **guest houses**, most of them pretty tawdry affairs with attached restaurants, bars, and prostitutes servicing the carnal desires of truckers and safari drivers (the Tanzam Highway is dubbed the "AIDS Highway"). Luckily, there are a handful of more appetizing options. **Camping** is possible at *Mikumi Genesis Motel*.

Internet Bar & Guest House 3km east of the junction ☎023/262 0419. Best of a trio of basic guest houses in this area, with reasonably priced rooms sharing bathrooms, slightly overpriced en-suite options, and decent local food (try anything with cassava leaves). ❶–❷

Kilimanjaro Village Inn 1km east of the junction (no phone). Set in attractive gardens, this has en-suite rooms with fans and nets. ❸

Mikumi Genesis Motel 4km east of the junction ☎023/262 0461. Exploits its popularity with tourists by charging high rates, though the rooms themselves – two per cottage – are pleasant, with big beds and nets, and have clean bathrooms (cold water only). Its bar is a good place to meet fellow travellers, and the restaurant serves big portions of good food (main courses from Tsh6000). There's also a rather miserable snake park ($5). Full breakfast included. ❹

Tan-Swiss 5km east of the junction ☎0744/878752, ⓦwww.contrast.cx/tanswiss. Run by a Swiss couple, this has an affordable restaurant, including lobster when in season, fish, grills, pasta and pizza, and some times Indian and Chinese. There's also Mikumi's best bar (cocktails and South African wines), and half a dozen charming en-suite rooms at the back with digital TV and private terraces facing a garden. ❹

In the park

All-inclusive rates at the park's upmarket **tented camps** include full-board, park fees, airstrip transfer and two game drives or guided walks each day. With the exception of *Foxes Safari Camp*, be prepared to have the wilderness illusion broken by glimpses of speeding buses and trucks on the highway that bisects the park.

Much cheaper is the park's (TANAPA) rest house (book well in advance), and three **public campsites**. Campsite 1, near the park gate at Kikoboga, has running water, a pit latrine, bathroom, fireplace and fuel wood. Campsite 2, along the Kisingura Circuit nearby, is under an old baobab and has a toilet but no water. Campsite 3 is in the south of the park under a large fig tree, and also has a toilet but no water. All three cost $30 per person, paid at the gate. Be extremely wary of the resident yellow **baboons**: don't eat in their presence and keep your food in sealed containers.

In a different league is the **luxury fly-camping** offered by *Foxes* and *Vuma Hills*, where for a mere $395 per person per day (minimum two people, two days) you get everything laid on, from hot showers and champagne breakfasts to game walks and drives; the cost includes park fees.

Foxes Safari Camp Mkata floodplain, 25km north of the park gate ⓦwww .tanzaniasafaris.info (book through Foxes African Safaris in Dar; see p.133). Mikumi's classiest option, this luxury tented camp is set on a rocky kopje in prime game-viewing terrain (elephants are occasional visitors), with 360° views from its restaurant and bar. Accommodation is in eight en-suite tents with verandahs giving sweeping views over the floodplain. Guided walks, for those on full-board, cost $25–50 depending on duration. Closed April & May. Full-board $135 per person, all-inclusive $240 per person. ⓭

Mikumi Wildlife Camp Kikoboga (book through ☏022/260 0352–4, ⓔobhotel@acexnet.com). The best place for spotting wildlife from the comfort of an armchair, as several waterholes in the surrounding plain attract a large variety of wildlife including elephant, buffalo, wildebeest and impala. Accommodation is in twelve spacious African-style *bandas* (some sleeping up to six) with drapes for windows and big verandahs. Facilities include a swimming pool with sundeck and hot-tub, a look-out tower with 360° views, and bar. Decent if unspectacular meals are taken around a campfire or in a dining area overlooking a floodlit waterhole.

The downside is you'll need your own vehicle for game drives, though they do offer walking safaris to the source of the Kikoboga River by prior arrangement. Full-board $100 per person. ⓫

TANAPA Rest House At the park headquarters, Kikoboga (book through the park headquarters, or TANAPA in Arusha; see p.403). The park's cheapest accommodation, with two double rooms, shared toilets, a kitchen and sitting room. The park staff's social hall is in the same complex if you fancy a bite or a drink. Book well ahead. $30 per person. ⓬

Vuma Hills Tented Camp 7km southeast of the park gate ⓦwww.tanzaniasafaris.info (book through Foxes African Safaris in Dar; see p.133). A welcoming and relaxed place suitable for families, with good food and service, and a scatter of sixteen luxurious tents set on a low exposed hill with sweeping views of the grasslands. The tents are spacious and comfortable, and come with bathrooms and large verandahs. Facilities include a small swimming pool and sundeck overlooked by the bar and restaurant, an interesting library and gift shop. Game drives and guided walks available. Open all year. Full-board $135 per person, all-inclusive $240 per person. ⓭

The park

Mikumi boasts an impressive 200km of drivable tracks, though most become impassable during the rains. The main wildlife viewing area is the hot, low-lying **Mkata floodplain**, in the centre of the park north of the highway, which offers more or less guaranteed sightings of elephant, buffalo, herds of eland and a host of other plains game, good odds on spotting lion (sometimes in the branches of a tree) and occasionally delights in the form of a leopard (also in trees) or a pack of African hunting dogs. The floodplain's **northern section** consists of low ridges of relatively impervious "hardpan" soil separated by narrower depressions of easily waterlogged black cotton soil (*mbuga*), which turn to swamp during the rains. In the dry season when the swamps recede, hippo and waterbirds congre-

△ Baboons on safari, Mikumi National Park

gate around permanent waterholes. The **southern part** of the floodplain, which includes Kikoboga, is drier and has some slow-flowing streams. The swamp edges are characterized by baobabs and rows of borassus palms, known in the local Kivindunda language as *mikumi*, hence the park's name. Borassus palms grow up to 20m high and are easily distinguished from the often crooked *Hyphaene* palms by the strangely graceful swellings halfway up their trunks.

The floodplain can be covered in two circuits: the **Kisingura Circuit**, which covers Kikoboga and the Hippo Pools near the park headquarters; and **Chamgore, Choga Wale and Mwanambogo Dam** to the north, which can only be done in the dry season. Around the swamps is a large expanse of grassland bordered to the west and east by acacia and tamarind scrub, which in turn gives way to the *miombo* so characteristic of Selous. The grassland can be seen on the road to Chamgore and along the short **Ikoya Loop** south of the highway, whilst *miombo* woodland is at its grandest in the park's **Southern Extension**, close to the Selous Game Reserve.

Early morning and late afternoon is the best time for wildlife spotting, as most animals take cover in the noon heat. With the exception of official picnic sites and the Hippo Pools at Kikoboga, visitors must stay in their vehicles at all times. The numbered junctions in some of the descriptions below correspond to those in the TANAPA guidebook and map.

Kikoboga and the Kisingura Circuit

Kikoboga area contains most of the park's accommodation, and there's a reason: occupying the southern end of the Mkata floodplain, this is one of the best areas for spotting wildlife, and access is guaranteed all year round. Of several routes around Kikoboga, the **Kisingura Circuit** (1–2hr), near the public campsites, is recommended for an early-morning game drive, ideally before breakfast. The Kikoboga area is especially good for elephants in December and January after the short rains, since the creatures are partial to swamp grass and completely bonkers about the fruit of the amarula tree, which grows along the fringes of the floodplain. They eat the fruit – which resembles a small green or yellow plum – by the thousands, shaking the tree to get them to fall. The impressive side effects of excessive ingestion of amarula, which is a strong laxative, can be found scattered throughout Kikoboga. Other mammals you're likely to see around the floodplain include herds of eland and Liechtenstein's hartebeest (usually close to the river where it crosses the highway). The antelopes are the main prey of the endangered African hunting dogs, which are occasionally seen here in small packs. At the northern end of the circuit, 5km northwest of the park gate, are the **Hippo Pools** where, apart from hippos, you're likely to see families of yellow baboons, open-billed storks and cattle egrets.

Chamgore, Choga Wale and Mwanambogo Dam

The following circuit takes you to the north of the park, but can only be visited in the dry season. Before attempting any of the various parts of the circuit, get up-to-date information on route markers and track conditions from the park headquarters. A ranger ($20 per drive) is obligatory if you want to ride to Choga Wale, and recommended for trips to Chamgore and Mwanambogo Dam.

The road to the **Chamgore** ("Place of the Python") starts from the Hippo Pools, and heads up north between the Mkata River to the east and the freight railway line to the west. The route covers a variety of habitats, from tsetse fly-infested *Combretum* woodland and swamps to a couple of waterholes. **Mkata waterhole** is signposted off junction 32, and **Chamgore waterhole** is 1km to the north (dry season only). Birds here include saddle-billed storks either alone or in pairs, frog-eaters, hammerkops and malachite kingfishers; Bohor reedbuck are also sometimes seen. From here there's a seldom-used track onwards to **Choga Wale**, for which you'll need a ranger, and which can be impassable in the rains. This passes junctions 38 and 39 before reaching Choga Wale's glade of *Hyphaene* palms, pink jacarandas (the bark of which is used to protect against witchcraft), acacias and strangling fig trees; there's also a picnic site.

There's also a dry-season track from Chamgore over the Mkata River (near marker 32) to a dam at **Mwanambogo**, which attracts a wealth of wildlife and birdlife in the dry season. Non-venomous pythons can sometimes be seen here, either at the water's edge or coiled up in a tree, but take care – the python dispenses with poison because it doesn't need it: a single strike from this six-metre predator can knock down animals as large as impalas, whom it then asphyxiates by constriction.

From Mwanambogo, you can get back to Kikoboga by heading south along the eastern fringes of the Mkata floodplain, ending up at marker 2 just north of the park headquarters. This track is probably the best place to see Mikumi's celebrated **sunsets**, when the sun dips towards the Rubeho Mountains, lighting up the floodplain in between. However, the track is liable to be impassable about halfway along during the rains, should a tributary of the Mkata River be in spate.

Ikoya Loop

The **Ikoya Loop**, a few kilometres south of the highway west of *Vuma Hills Tented Camp*, is a short clockwise drive that shouldn't take more than an hour. The route starts at junction 71, from where it rises gently through open bush and red-oat grassland before crossing several seasonal watercourse ravines (*korongos*), so forget about Ikoya in the rains. The Ikoya Loop proper starts after the third *korongo*, at marker 73. A right turn at marker 74 takes you parallel to the **Mkata River** – marked by a strip of woodland – which is a good place for spotting giraffe and lion. Further on, **Ikoya waterhole** attracts hippo and other animals in the dry season. The best time to visit is between June and November, when the fragrant *cassia* thickets are covered in yellow flowers.

The Southern Extension

The area south of Ikoya and the highway, which extends to the boundary with the Selous Game Reserve (marked by the TAZARA railway), was added to the national park in 1975, but is seldom visited. Much of the area, including the ridges of the flanking hills, is dominated by *miombo* woodland, home to sable antelope, greater kudu, Liechtenstein's hartebeest and the black-and-white colobus monkey, as well as clouds of tsetse flies. If you're extremely lucky, you might also catch sight of African hunting dogs. Another rare animal that made its home here, the black rhino, is believed to have been hunted to extinction in Mikumi in the 1970s. Places to head for include **hot springs** and a large forest of **mikumi palms**. There are few roads, and they're liable to be closed during the rains. Hiring an official ranger for this sector is recommended – and the authorities may insist on it, given that none of the roads are marked.

Selous Game Reserve

Weighing in as Africa's biggest wildlife sanctuary, the 44,800-square-kilometre **SELOUS GAME RESERVE** – covering six percent of Tanzania's total land-

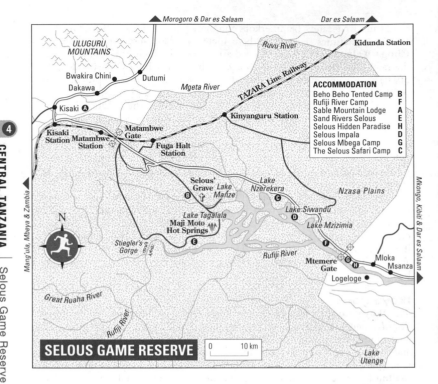

Morogoro & Dar es Salaam ▲   Dar es Salaam ▲

ULUGURU MOUNTAINS

Ruvu River   Kidunda Station

Bwakira Chini   Dutumi

Dakawa   Mgeta River

TAZARA Line Railway

Kisaki **Ⓐ**

Kinyanguru Station

ACCOMMODATION

Beho Beho Tented Camp	**B**
Rufiji River Camp	**F**
Sable Mountain Lodge	**A**
Sand Rivers Selous	**E**
Selous Hidden Paradise	**H**
Selous Impala	**D**
Selous Mbega Camp	**G**
The Selous Safari Camp	**C**

Kisaki Station   Matambwe Station   Matambwe Gate   Fuga Halt Station

Selous' Grave **Ⓑ** †   Lake Manze   Lake Nzerekera   Nzasa Plains

Lake Tagalala   Maji Moto Hot Springs **Ⓔ**

Lake Siwandu **Ⓓ**

Lake Mzizimia

Stiegler's Gorge

Rufiji River   **Ⓕ**

Mtemere Gate   **Ⓖ** **Ⓗ**   Mloka   Msanza

Logeloge ●

Great Ruaha River

Rufiji River

N

SELOUS GAME RESERVE   0   10 km

Lake Utenge

mass, or the equivalent of Ireland or Switzerland – is the highlight of Tanzania's Southern Safari Circuit. Together with the adjoining Mikumi National Park and a number of smaller reserves, Selous' rich and diverse ecosystem is home to an estimated 750,000 mammals, including the world's largest populations of elephant, African hunting dog, crocodile, buffalo and hippopotamus. Not surprisingly, the reserve is listed as a World Heritage Site by UNESCO.

The figures are impressive but are also misleading. The reserve does indeed contain more elephants than any other on earth, but given its size that's hardly surprising. Another superlative that no brochure will tell you about is that Selous is also the only place in Tanzania where the "sport" of **elephant hunting** is still permitted, even if only twenty kills are made with the fifty-odd licences granted annually. In fact, **trophy hunting** is permitted in all but three of the reserve's 45 "management blocks", while "**photographic tourism**" is limited to a small sector north of the Rufiji River, the rationale being that eighty percent of the reserve's income derives from hunting.

To be fair, the sector reserved for photographic tourism is by far the most attractive, its habitats ranging from grassy plains and rolling *miombo* woodland, to dense patches of groundwater forest and the **Rufiji River**. It's in Selous that the river – Tanzania's largest – is at its most magnificent, its labyrinthine network of lagoons, channels, islets and swamps cloaked in extensive riverine forest and attracting a mind-boggling number of bird species: over 450. Then, of course, there are the tourist lodges and tented camps, most of which are indeed as luxurious and as exclusive as their brochures claim. Such exclusivity comes at a price, and you won't find a double room inside the reserve for under $380

Selous' seasons

When to visit Selous depends on what you want to see and do, but by and large the best time for spotting large mammals is the **dry season**, most predictable from July to September or October, when vegetation is low and animals are concentrated around the river and its lakes. It's also the coolest time of year – good for walking safaris. The increasingly erratic **short rains**, generally from November to December, still see wildlife concentrated around the river, whilst the vegetation regains some of its colour. January and February enjoy a **short dry spell**, a perfect time for birds, though terrestrial wildlife is beginning to disperse and temperatures are intense and feel more so thanks to the extreme humidity. The **long rains**, peaking in April and May, are probably best avoided as roads are cut and most of the lodges and camps are closed.

(or $500 including game drives), although special offers over several days can sometimes reduce the cost slightly. Should the prices scare you off, or the all-white, neo-colonial atmosphere prick your conscience, don't despair: there *are* cheap ways of getting to see Selous, and given the fact that **walking safaris** are possible if you're accompanied by a ranger, the overall cost can – surprisingly – actually be much less than in other Tanzanian parks.

In the dry season especially, Selous' wildlife is stupendous. **Plains game** is abundant, especially elephant, wildebeest, Burchell's zebra and Maasai giraffe, which can be seen in the wooded grassland north of the Rufiji. Antelopes abound, with sizeable populations of impala, waterbuck, Roosevelt sable, Liechtenstein's hartebeest and greater kudu, though the latter – preferring dense bush – are difficult to spot. Smaller and less glamorous nocturnal mammals like lesser bushbabies and small spotted genet are often seen around the camps at night, while various species of mongoose – banded, dwarf and slender – can be seen scampering across the tracks. The forests backing the waterways are good places to spot **primates**, including vervets, large troops of olive and yellow baboons, and black-and-white colobus monkeys, as well as less frequent blue monkeys and samangos. Rare animals include Sharpe's grysbok, a tiny population of red colobus monkeys in the far northwest near the railway, and approximately 150 black rhino whose population came perilously close to extinction in the 1980s, and whose present location is a closely guarded secret. Of the **predators**, lions – often in large prides – are the most visible; leopards, despite their considerable population, are more elusive thanks to their preferred forest habitat. Cheetah and spotted hyena are also occasionally seen, but the real highlight is the African hunting dog, amongst the rarest of Africa's predators, which has found one of its last refuges in Selous.

Despite all this, Selous' wildlife can actually be rather elusive, especially if you come outside the dry season, which is part of the reason why tour operators recommend a longer stay. Even at the best of times don't expect to tick off species as you might do at Ngorongoro: much of Selous is hidden, and that, ultimately, is what gives it its charm.

Arrival

A minimum of **three nights** is recommended for Selous, up to six if you can afford it. The easiest way there is on an **organized safari**. Given the sort of clientele that can afford the reserve's hiked-up accommodation rates, most people fly in (from Dar or elsewhere), or come by train and fly back, though a handful of companies offer cheaper road safaris, the drawback being that you'll

Hunting, shooting and conservation

The history of the Selous Game Reserve is scarred with conflict. Its troubles began right at the start, when several hunting reserves were formed under German colonial rule after an epidemic of sleeping sickness gave them the excuse they needed to shift locals elsewhere. According to the popular story, the reserves were given as a wedding anniversary present from the German Kaiser Wilhelm II to his wife in 1907, and so became known as *Shamba la Bibi* – the Lady's Farm. The reserve acquired its present name after **Captain Frederick Courteney Selous**, a British explorer and hunter, was shot dead near the Beho Beho River by the Germans in January 1917, while scouting for the 25th Royal Fusiliers. His grave, covered by a simple stone slab, can still be visited. Selous spent much of his life shooting his way through a depressing array of central and southern African wildlife. Although his behaviour would be harshly judged by present-day standards, his contemporaries appear to have considered him a quasi-heroic character. One account describes how, when his horse became exhausted, he would leap from the saddle wearing (curiously enough) only a shirt and sandals, in which he would pursue his quarry on foot before, "closing in on the animals at full tilt, load his gun from a powder bag, slither to a stop and fire at point-blank range". Selous is thought to have killed over a thousand elephants in the reserve that now bears his name – all the more ironic given the decimation of the reserve's elephant population in the latter half of the twentieth century by poachers.

At the time that Selous was bagging mountains of ivory, elephants in the area were being hunted at the rate of several tens of thousands a year, which – even by early twentieth-century standards – was too much. In 1922, with Tanganyika firmly under British mandate, the various reserves established by the Germans were combined and expanded, and the remaining Africans who were unfortunate enough to live inside the new reserve's boundaries were forcibly relocated. The reserve was expanded to its present size in the 1960s, when hunting tracks were also constructed. Intended to facilitate the gentlemanly sport of elephant hunting, the tracks were used in the

---

waste a day getting there from Dar, and another going back, unless you combine Selous with Mikumi and/or Udzungwa, or are on a longer trip (Ruaha or Kitulo national parks make good targets, as does Tanzania's south coast).

Arranging your own safari is possible, and can be much cheaper. You have a choice of arriving by train (you'll need to have pre-booked at a lodge or camp), or by bus or car – the roads are deeply uncomfortable and perhaps a tad too nerve-racking if you're driving, but ultimately rewarding. Budget travellers should definitely pack a tent and enough food for the duration.

Organized safaris

Reliable **safari operators** based in Dar are reviewed on p.133, and several operators also offer fly-in safaris from Zanzibar (see p.660).

You might find it difficult convincing **budget safari companies** to take you into Selous, an indication that even they don't trust their vehicles (there are no garages or repair facilities, so a major breakdown translates into a fiasco for all concerned). If you do find a company willing to take you, at the very least check the vehicle yourself or with someone mechanically competent before parting with any money. The average cost for a budget camping safari is $130–150 per person per day – though at that price you're likely to be camping just outside the reserve.

Upmarket safaris, using a variety of expensive lodges and tented camps, usually send in their clients by plane (daily from Arusha, Dar, Manyara, Ruaha and

1980s by **elephant and rhino poachers** armed with automatic rifles. In the eight years between 1981 and 1989, they managed to obliterate over 75,000 elephants (three quarters of the population) and all but a hundred of the reserve's black rhino, whose population had started the decade at around three thousand.

Thankfully, the **Selous Conservation Programme** (now ended) – a joint venture by the Tanzanian and German governments that kicked off with some urgency in 1988 – managed to reduce poaching, and the elephant population is recovering well (55,600 were counted in a 1998 aerial survey – over half of Tanzania's total). Many challenges remain, however, the overriding one being how to involve local communities on the reserve's fringes in its activities and profits. Mistrust between the authorities and locals has long been a problem: to put it simply, locals are at a loss to understand why a handful of rich foreigners (roughly two hundred annually) are allowed to hunt in the reserve for pleasure while locals – whose land the reserve once was – are forbidden to hunt even for food.

Thankfully, the reserve authorities seem finally to have understood that the only way to significantly reduce poaching and the conflict with local people is to involve them in – and allow them to gain from – the conservation process. Consequently, a **Community Wildlife Management Programme** has been established whereby villagers agree to create Wildlife Management Areas on part of their land – effectively buffer zones – and to provide and equip village scouts to patrol the areas, in return for a sustainable hunting quota which can either be used by the villagers or sold to commercial or sport hunters, the profits being shared between the villages and the reserve. The new system has already proved its worth: over fifty villages now participate, though with the worrying side effect that crop damage by wildlife is on the increase. But it's a start at least, and the important thing is that for the first time in decades relations between the reserve and locals can now be described as constructive, a far cry from the days when a farmer trapping animals that destroyed his crops was persecuted as a poacher by rangers.

Zanzibar). However, arriving by train and flying back is an attractive alternative, giving you more of a feel for the land as you approach. Expect to pay upwards of $500 per person a day for the most luxurious lodges, or $300–400 otherwise.

Most of the cheaper places outside the reserve also offer **all-inclusive package deals** over three or more days, whilst *Selous Impala* inside the reserve usually has good fly-safari deals combining a night in Selous with Mafia Island (from $450 for two nights, plus $50 for each additional night on Mafia).

Arranging your own safari – by car

Driving yourself in to the park is by far the most adventurous approach given the atrocious state of the roads, although things have improved a little over the last few years. If you're staying at a lodge or tented camp, it's not much more expensive to arrange the transfer with them: *Selous Mbega Camp*, for instance, charge $200 per vehicle from Dar es Salaam, or $25 per person in their supply vehicle if it's running.

A **4WD** in excellent condition and with high clearance is essential, and obligatory inside the reserve. You'll also need to hire a ranger at the reserve gates ($10 weekdays, $15 weekends). There are no garage facilities, and the nearest fuel stations are at Morogoro, Ikwiriri and Kibiti, so fill up whenever you can. The reserve gates are open 6am to 6pm; driving inside is not allowed after 6.30pm.

There are **two routes** to the reserve: the track to Matambwe Gate in the far northwest of the reserve (285km from Dar, 155km from Morogoro), accessed

The Safari Express

From June to February, Dar es Salaam-based Foxes African Safaris (see p.133) operate a **private luxury train** from Dar to the Selous, the "Safari Express". It heads out of Dar at 10am on Tuesday and Friday, and 9am Sunday, arriving in Selous in the afternoon. The train terminates at Kidatuat around 5pm, half an hour's drive from Mikumi or Udzungwa national parks.

At $125 each way, it's much more expensive than the normal train, but it does include lunch and snacks, has a plush lounge car, and provides a suitably swanky introduction to the neo-colonial chic of Selous' lodges. Transfer to the lodges (except *Beho Beho Tented Camp* and *Sand Rivers Selous* – you'll have to arrange things with them) costs $55 per person.

from the Tanzam Highway near Morogoro, is the more spectacular but difficult of the two, passing along the eastern flank of the Uluguru Mountains before dropping down into a flat and often treacherously muddy plain. The easier route is to Mtemere Gate in the northeast (247km from Dar), accessed via Kibiti south of Dar, which follows the north bank of the Rufiji.

For **Matambwe Gate**, the first part involves a straight 160km drive along a sealed road from Dar to Mikese village, 30km short of Morogoro. From Mikese a minor road heads south along the eastern flank of the Ulugurus, past lively villages and patches of forest (see "Matombo"). The rocky and sometimes steep surface means that the first 80km are slow-going if passable, taking two and a half to five hours depending on the road's state of repair. If the mountain scenery grabs your attention and you have camping equipment, the gorgeously sited *Jukumu Scout Station* **campsite** ($5 per person) at Kilengezi, near Mvuha village at Mambarawe Ridge, 55km before Kisaki, has friendly locals and sweeping views over northern Selous. There are two creeks with waterfalls nearby where you can swim, and plenty of dense forest to explore. Water is available from a pump, and there are toilets, showers and firewood for sale. The site is run by community game scouts in charge of a Wildlife Management Area north of the reserve. They are, unsurprisingly, excellent guides, though there's nothing formally arranged for tourists.

Leaving the Uluguru foothills, the road descends 45km towards the swampy north bank of the Mgeta River. This route used to be terrible, and impassable after even moderate showers, but has been regraded and should now be passable in most conditions. The stretch beyond the river to Kisaki village and Kisaki train station, where the road crosses the Rudete and Msoro rivers before following the railway to the gate, is fine. Once at the gate, don't forget that there's at least another 70km to the lodge or tented camp, unless you're staying at *Sable Mountain Lodge*, 10km away. With luck, the whole drive from the Tanzam Highway can take as little as four hours.

Access is easier from the east via Kibiti, Mkongo and Mloka to **Mtemere Gate**, which should take about six hours from Dar in decent conditions. At Kibiti (see Chapter 3), 138km south of Dar, take the right fork signposted to Utete along a rough but passable road and turn right at Mkongo (also called Kirimani) after 32km. The remaining 77km via Mloka follow the north bank of the Rufiji River and can become impassable in the long rains (April & May), not that you'll be visiting at that time anyway.

Arranging your own safari – by bus

Probably to the chagrin of the reserve authorities (who are anxious to keep Selous the preserve of the monied elite), getting to see Selous on a budget is still possible. A daily **bus** leaves Dar's Temeke bus stand at the unearthly time of 4am (catch a taxi from your hotel) to arrive at **Mloka**, 10km short of the reserve's Mtemere Gate, around 2pm. Alternatively, catch any bus from Dar's Ubungo bus terminal to Kibiti, Ikwiriri, Lindi, Masasi, Mtwara or Newala, and get off in **Kibiti**, where you'll probably have to spend the night (there are some basics ❶ guest houses but nothing fancy) before catching an irregular local pick-up or the bus from Temeke on to Mloka the next day. There's a basic guest house in Mloka (❶) and tourist-oriented places between it and the reserve gate: see p.305.

Alternatively, it's theoretically possible to hire a ranger (roughly $20 for a half day, nothing fixed however) for a bush walk at Mtemere Gate, though Selous' popularity means it's pot luck whether anyone's available. Heading **back to Dar**, the bus departs Mloka between 4.30am and 7am.

Arranging your own safari – by train

Arriving by train along the TAZARA line is only workable if you've booked with a lodge or tented camp who will pick you up, as there's neither public transport nor vehicles you can rent at the stations. The transfer is usually included in the overnight cost of places inside the reserve, but those outside are likely to charge $40–50.

The information below applies to the normal TAZARA service from Dar; hugely more luxurious is the private "Safari Express" – see the box opposite. There are three weekly passenger trains from Dar, but **schedules** change constantly, and be aware that you need to leave in the morning to arrive in time to be driven to your lodge or luxury camp, as driving is not allowed after 6.30pm. Currently, only the 10am departure on Monday fits the bill. The journey takes four to five and a half hours to Fuga, Kisaki or Kinyanguru stations (which one you get off at depends on where you're staying). First or second class (around $10) is recommended if you don't want to share your body space with suitcases, sacks of pineapples, chickens, children or other people's legs. Coming **from Zambia or Mbeya**, services are unreliable and likely to deposit you in the middle of the night. For this reason, most guests arriving from Dar by train tend to fly back.

Information and entrance fees

The **reserve headquarters** and chief warden are at Matambwe Gate, but given communication difficulties, address enquiries through the "Ivory Room", close to the TAZARA station off Nyerere Road in Dar es Salaam (☎022/286 6064, ⓔsgrmp@raha.com). The best **guidebook** is the *Selous Travel Guide* ($10) by Dr Rolf D. Baldus and Dr Ludwig Siege, which should be available at the reserve's gates, camps and lodges, and in bookshops in Arusha, Dar and Stone Town. Large parts of it, periodically updated, are on the **Internet** at ⓦwww. wildlife-programme.gtz.de/wildlife/tourism_selous.html. The best **map** is the 1:500,000 *Visitor's Map of the Selous Game Reserve North of the Rufiji* published by GTZ, which shows topographical relief, vegetation type, lodges and camps, most of the walking trails, and even indicates good places for spotting given animal species. It should be available at the reserve's gates (distribution is patchy elsewhere).

Entrance fees – valid for 24 hours – are $30 per person and Tsh5000 for a vehicle pass. For **camping**, there's an additional $20 fee, plus $20 per group for a ranger to guard you overnight. If you're staying at a lodge or tented camp, fees should be included in the overall cost. The service of an **official game guide**

(likely to be obligatory if you're self-driving) is $10 on weekdays, $15 weekends. An official guide for walking safaris costs $20 for a few hours.

Accommodation

Accommodation **inside the reserve** comprises of expensive luxury tented camps and lodges, and – thankfully – a couple of much more affordable public **campsites**. There's also a small but growing number of cheaper lodges and camps just **outside the reserve**, some of which also allow camping. Do not camp without an armed guard, whether inside or outside the reserve – fatal **lion attacks** occur from time to time.

Inside the reserve

Selous' accommodation is grossly overpriced, though the standard "**fly-in**" **rates** are all-inclusive, which usually means full-board plus two 2–3 hour activities a day, entrance fees, and airstrip or station transfer. Some places also offer cheaper "**drive-in**" **rates** for full-board only. There are two **public campsites** (closed April & May), at Beho Beho bridge and Lake Tagalala (another may open at Mtemere Gate), costing $20 per person plus $20 for the obligatory armed ranger, in additional to normal entry fees. Small campfires are permitted so long as dead wood is used. The sites have long-drop toilets and water, though this needs filtering and purifying.

Beho Beho Tented Camp ⓦ www.behobeho.com (bookings in the UK on Ⓣ (+44) 020/8897 9991 or 020/8750 5655, Ⓔ reservations@behobeho. com). Very much neo-colonial in feel, and heavy on mood-setting antiques, this occupies the lower slopes of Namikwera Hill 5km from Selous' grave, with sweeping views of the plains. The guest rooms, in ten whitewashed stone-and-thatch cottages, are spacious and bright, with Zanzibari four-poster beds, open-fronted sitting area, and verandahs giving panoramic views – all very stylish without being pretentious. The attention to detail extends to the food and the experienced and flexible "white-hunter" type guides, and there's also a swimming pool, various open-sided lounges, a cocktail bar and billiards room. Children under 12 discouraged. Closed April to mid-June. All-inclusive $460 per person. ⓞ

🏃 **Rufiji River Camp** ⓦ www.rufijiriver .com (book through Hippotours in Dar; see p.133). Selous' largest, oldest and least expensive camp, attractively set on a high bank overlooking the Rufiji River and the plain beyond. Pleasingly unfussy, unpretentious and relaxed, it enjoys an excellent reputation for its guides, especially on extended wildlife walks – which include, uniquely, a combined walking and boating tour from Selous to the Rufiji Delta, with an optional continuation along Tanzania's south coast. The twenty tents, decorated in rustic style, are tucked away in secluded corners of the forest, each with a shady verandah for river and sunset views, and solar-heated open-air showers. There's also a shaded swimming pool, library,

and superb Tuscan-styled cuisine. Closed Easter– June. Full-board (including entrance fees) $190 per person, all-inclusive $250–265 per person. ⓞ
Sand Rivers Selous ⓦ www.nomad-tanzania .com (book through Nomad Tanzania in Arusha; see p.407). Overlooking a wide bend in the Rufiji River, this bills itself as Selous' most exclusive "camp", presumably referring to the price, though it is certainly one of Tanzania's most luxurious. The eight thatch-roofed cottages are secluded from each other and have views over the forest and river. The decor throughout is classy, especially in the enormous main building containing the bar, restaurant and lounge, where there's plenty of comfortable colonial-style furniture and cushions to recline on. There's also a small swimming pool on the riverbank near a baobab tree. Children under 10 discouraged. Closed May. All-inclusive $465–540 per person. ⓞ
Selous Impala ⓦ www.adventurecamps.co.tz (book through Coastal Travels in Dar; see p.133). Set amidst borassus palms and tamarinds on the north bank of the Rufiji, the six large tents here, all en suite and with two single beds, are pitched on hardwood platforms, each with colonial-style furnishings and a spacious verandah for viewing the river and forest beyond. There's also a small swimming pool with recliners, and river views from the dining room. It's a bit basic for the price, however. All-inclusive $400 per person, or $220 for "drive-in" (full-board only). ⓞ
The Selous Safari Camp (book through The Selous Safari Company in Dar, Ⓣ 022/212 8485

Luxury fly-camping excursions

It may be camping, Captain, but not as we know it: most of Selous' upmarket camps and lodges offer optional **fly-camping excursions**, involving guided walks through bush and forest, sometimes over several days, accompanied by armed rangers and a white-hunter-type chap as your guide, and often enough a Maasai warrior to lend some local colour. Vehicle access to the fly camps without walking is sometimes possible. The camps themselves are set up ahead of your arrival by a retinue of staff and are equipped with basic creature comforts like hot bucket showers hung from trees, long-drop toilets or portable chemical toilets, and enjoyable luxuries like evening banquets around a campfire and champagne breakfasts. Guests sleep on camp beds in small dome tents. Group sizes vary between two and ten; the often hair-raising proximity of wildlife means that children are not allowed. Costs, which replace room rates for the duration of the excursion, include reserve fees, meals and walks, but are mind-boggling nonetheless: $350–395 from *Sable Mountain Lodge*, *Rufiji River Camp* or *The Selous Safari Camp*, and an outrageous $565 from *Sand Rivers Selous*. *Rufiji River Camp* also offer challenging three-day walking and camping itineraries for $250–300 per person a day. All these trips must be booked in advance.

or 0748/953 551, ⓦ www.selous.com). Set in *miombo* woodland behind Lake Nzerekera, this enjoys excellent game viewing even within the camp, which is often frequented by impala, and its guides have a solid reputation. The attention to detail is unsurpassed, in fact somewhat over the top; the downside is that it's sometimes used by large tour groups. Accommodation is in thirteen huge, secluded tents mounted on platforms under thatch roofs, and dressed in classic "rustic" safari style, each with solar-powered light, lake-facing verandah and open-air shower. The thatched roof of the main building, also on stilts, rises above the trees and contains a dining room and comfortable lounge; there's another dining area in a grove of trees. Other facilities include a game-viewing hide, reference library and two shaded swimming pools. No children under 8. Closed April & May. All-inclusive $430 per person. ⑨

Outside the reserve

Accommodation **outside the reserve** is a good deal cheaper and stays open all year. Most places offer three-hour **activities** at extra cost (usually $30–35, plus entrance fees if you enter the reserve): guided walks, boat trips, game drives, and – not possible inside the reserve – night game drives. **Camping** is best at *Selous Mbega Camp* ($10 per person), who offer free pick-ups from Mloka if pre-booked – bring food, as campers aren't allowed in the restaurant (but you can use the bar). *Selous Hidden Paradise* charges $20 per person camping and isn't as nice, but has the advantage of providing meals ($30 full-board).

Sable Mountain Lodge 10km from Kisaki village outside Matambwe Gate ⓦ www.selouslodge.com (book through A Tent with a View Safaris in Dar; see p.133). Occupying three peaks of the Beho Beho Mountains above thick forest in the rarely visited northwest, this has eight simple but stylish stone cottages and four luxury tented *bandas* facing the Uluguru Mountains, all secluded and with verandahs and solar-powered light. The best – the "honeymoon bandas" – have plunge pools and beautiful views down a valley towards a waterhole. A tree house near the waterhole provides good game viewing; there's also a "snug" for star-gazing, two restaurants and bars, swimming pool, and evening campfire. Activities cost $35 per person, or $70 for a full day; night game drives are $15. No children under 6. Full-board $125–175 per person, all-inclusive $225–265 per person. ⑨

Selous Hidden Paradise 4km west of Mloka village, 7km outside Mtemere Gate (book through Family Travel & Tour Service, Libya St, Dar es Salaam ☏ 022/213 8752, ⓔ ftts@ureach.com). A lacklustre campsite (bring your own equipment) close to the Rufiji River. Facilities include bathrooms, toilets, the use of a kitchen, and a restaurant occasionally hosting *ngoma*. Bush walks cost $15, other activities $30. Breakfast included $20 per person, full-board $30. ❺

🏃 **Selous Mbega Camp** 9km west of Mloka, 500m outside Mtemere Gate ☎022/265 0250 or 0748/624664, ⓦ www.selous-mbega-camp.com. Nestled in a clearing among woodland on the north bank of the Rufiji, where colobus monkeys are sometimes seen, this has six en-suite tents with river-facing verandahs, and a restaurant under canvas. Activities, including village tours, cost $35. Specialist birding guides are available if booked in advance, and night game drives can be arranged. Backpackers arriving by bus get discounts. Full-board $95 per person. ❽

The reserve

The special thing about Selous is that you don't have to be in a vehicle to see wildlife, as both bush walks and boat trips are offered by the hotels.

Bush walks

The reserve's **bush walks**, which can be arranged at the reserve gates or through any tented camp, are an ideal way to get a feel for Selous. The walks usually involve a two- to three-hour wander through forest and savannah, during which you'll have plenty of time to observe monkeys, and perhaps experience a heart-stopping encounter with elephants or lions. Bush walks are also good for spotting details that you would otherwise miss, like the sticky black secretions that dikdiks deposit on the top of grass stems to mark their territorial latrines, or the tracks and spoors left by the animals whose strange noises kept you awake the night before.

Boat safaris

Half-day **boat safaris** are a great way of seeing the abundant wildlife of the labyrinthine channels, lagoons and islets of the Rufiji River, and make it easy to forget the ugly fibreglass-and-canvas appearance of the boats themselves. **Lake Tagalala**, actually a lagoon, is the main destination and is where most of the camps keep their boats. The lake apparently contains the densest population of crocodiles on earth, presumably fed by the profusion of wildlife that comes here to drink, and there are also plenty of hippos, though you shouldn't get too close as they will charge a boat if they feel threatened. Another good destination is **Stiegler's Gorge**, where the Great Ruaha River flows into the Rufiji. The gorge takes its name from a hunter who was killed there by an elephant in 1907, and offers a fair chance of spotting leopard.

Birdlife is plentiful throughout the wetlands: on the lagoons, look out for African skimmers, pink-backed and great white pelicans, duck and Egyptian geese, giant kingfishers and white-fronted plovers, while the shallows and sandbanks are ideal habitats for waders like herons and storks as well as kingfishers, African skimmers (again) and white-fronted bee-eaters. The groves of *mikumi* borassus palms that line the shore in many parts are also rich in birdlife, including morning warblers, palmnut vultures, red-necked falcons, nesting African fish eagles, yellow-billed storks, ibises and palm swifts. **Mammals** that can be seen from a boat are usually drinking from the river: regular visitors include waterbuck, reedbuck, bushbuck, sable antelope and elephant. Behind them in the riverine forest (best visited on foot) you might also catch glimpses of black-and-white colobus monkeys, or hear the crashing of branches as they flee your approach.

Game drives

Traditional **game drives** generally involve three to four hours of bumping and sliding around in an open-topped Land Rover or Land Cruiser. Despite the discomfort (minimized by skilful drivers), these trips have the advantage of being able to get you from place to place in rapid time, and so turn up a greater diversity of animals than walks or boat trips. If you're driving yourself, hiring an official guide at the gate is highly recommended and may be insisted on. It's impossible to recommend any one circuit or area for wildlife viewing as so much depends on the rains and the state of the roads. The best way is simply to ask your guide what's available and to decide from there. There are a couple of places that you could include in your itinerary, however. These include the sulphurous **Maji Moto hot springs** on the eastern slope of Kipala Hill near Lake Tagalala, which are cool enough in places for swimming in (the springs can also be visited by boat), and the **grave of Frederick Courteney Selous** at Beho Beho. Also at Beho Beho – apparently – is the **grave of Alexander Keith Johnston**, leader of a British expedition to find a trade route to the Great Lakes, who died here of dysentery in June 1879. His gravestone, erected in 1890, reportedly took a hundred men one year to carry from the coast, though its current location is unknown. Given its size, the stone is unlikely to have got far, and it's probably just a matter of time until someone stumbles across it.

The Udzungwa Mountains and the Kilombero Valley

Turning south off the Tanzam Highway at Mikumi village, you leave safari land behind and, after 40km or so when the road crosses the Great Ruaha River, you leave the sealed road too. The dirt road continues south, wending its bumpy and dusty way between the flat green expanse of the sugar cane plantations and rice paddies of the **Msolwa Valley** to the east, and the increasingly green and heavily forested **Udzungwa Mountains** to the west. Now a national park, the Udzungwas offer some of the most glorious hiking in the country, as well as the chance of coming face to face with some of its inhabitants, including the rare Iringa red colobus monkey, the Sanje crested mangabey, and the recently discovered highland mangabey. Further south along the track, **Ifakara** is a small but busy market town at the northern end of the vast and almost completely unvisited Kibasira Swamp, part of the **Kilombero Valley**. There are no roads in the swamp, which can only be accessed by boat, but you can access its edges by private 4WD. A trip here, assuming you have the time to get everything together – supplies, boat, fishing and camping gear and a reliable guide – is one of the most exciting, adventurous and potentially dangerous journeys in Tanzania.

Udzungwa Mountains National Park

The 1900-square-kilometre **UDZUNGWA MOUNTAINS NATIONAL PARK** was created in 1992 from several forest reserves. Its streams and rivers

④

△ Waterfall, Udzungwa Mountains National Park

form part of the Kilombero and Great Ruaha catchments, the lifeblood of the Selous. On the eastern side of the mountains in the Msolwa Valley, the waters are essential for the area's rapidly developing agriculture, especially the sugar cane which you can see along much of the road from Mikumi. By protecting the forest, the source of these waters has also been protected.

Of equal value is Udzungwa's incredible biodiversity. The mountains are part of the **Eastern Arc Mountain Range** (see box on p.353), a chain of ancient mountains which runs from the Taita Hills in Kenya, through the Pare and Usambara ranges in Tanzania to the Ulugurus near Morogoro, and finally to Udzungwa and the Mufindi Highlands just to the south. The great age and isolation of these mountains has enabled many species to evolve independently, but whereas the forests of some Eastern Arc ranges have suffered major environmental damage over the last 150 years, Udzungwa has survived in pristine condition thanks to the unusually steep terrain which limits cultivation to patches of lowland foothills. **Legends and taboos** have also contributed to Udzungwa's conservation; large swathes of forest were left untouched by locals on account of a belief that they were the abode of spirits (a belief that seems especially common in places with long-established primate populations), and so access was traditionally restricted to elders. The forests do indeed contain graves – to disturb them, locals say, will bring great calamity, while anyone who dares cut down a *mitogo* tree will be eaten by lions …

The park covers a wide range of altitudes, from 250m to 2576m above sea level, and is claimed to be the only place in East Africa with unbroken forest canopy over this entire elevation, ranging from *miombo* woodland, bamboo forest and lowland forest (the latter's canopy in places reaching heights of 50m) to distinct zones of moist montane forest and highland grassland. The upper montane forest on the eastern scarp is particularly rich in species diversity.

Given its exceptionally well-preserved forest cover, Udzungwa's **wildlife** is rich, if characteristically elusive. The park contains Tanzania's largest variety of **primates**, its eleven species including the recently discovered highland mangabey (also found in Kitulo National Park, but nowhere else), and the endemic Sanje crested mangabey, the Iringa (or Uhehe) red colobus monkey, the Matundu galago and a subspecies of the Amani mountain dwarf galago (bushbaby). Other primates include the thick-tailed galago, blue monkey and black-and-white colobus. The primates are concentrated in the east of the park, which is good news for hikers as this is where the main walking trails are located. Other commonly seen **mammals** include buffalo (keep your distance), but the elephants who apparently routinely trek up and down the mountain at night are elusive, generally given away only by their droppings or by patches of vegetation flattened by portly backsides. Rarer animals include the red-legged sun squirrel, red duiker, Abbot's duiker (also called blue duiker), Livingstone's suni, bush pig, bushbuck and the comical chequered elephant shrew, named after its unusual trunk-like snout. **Birdlife** includes the rufous-winged sunbird and Udzungwa partridge, both rare endemics.

Other endemic wildlife includes three reptile species (a gecko, a skink and a chameleon), millipedes, a tree frog and over seventy different species of spiders. For the visitor, all this makes for a superbly refreshing – if exhausting – chance to hike in an utterly unspoiled mountain wilderness.

Arrival

Access to the eastern section of the park is via **Mang'ula village**, 60km south of Mikumi village, 47km north of Ifakara and just a couple of kilometres outside the park entrance. The road is sealed between Mikumi and Kidatu on the Great

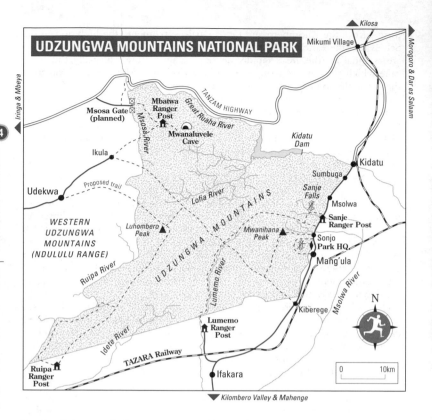

UDZUNGWA MOUNTAINS NATIONAL PARK

Kilosa

Morogoro & Dar es Salaam

Mikumi Village

Iringa & Mbeya

TANZAM HIGHWAY

Mbatwa
Ranger
Post

Msosa Gate
(planned)

Great Ruaha River

Msosa River

Mwanaluvele
Cave

Kidatu
Dam

Ikula

Kidatu

Sumbuga

Lofia River

Sanje
Falls

Msolwa

Udekwa

Proposed trail

Sanje
Ranger Post

WESTERN
UDZUNGWA
MOUNTAINS
(NDULULU RANGE)

Luhombero
Peak

Mwanihana
Peak

Sonjo
Park HQ

Ruipa River

U D Z U N G W A   M O U N T A I N S

Mang'ula

Lumemo River

Msolwa River

N

Kiberege

Idete River

Lumemo
Ranger
Post

Ruipa
Ranger
Post

TAZARA Railway

Ifakara

0   10km

Kilombero Valley & Mahenge

Ruaha River, and the remaining 24km is decent *murram*. **From Mikumi village**, catch one of the pick-ups or Coaster minibuses to Ifakara, which leave from the junction with the Tanzam Highway. The first leave Mikumi around 10am (roughly every hour thereafter), but are usually packed and badly driven, and their conductors habitually overcharge tourists (the fare should be Tsh2500). Sadly, buses **from Dar es Salaam** (departing 9–10am) fare little better, and it's also pot luck on driving skills – it's safer to catch a Scandinavian Express bus to Mikumi and change to a Coaster there. **Leaving Mang'ula**, buses for Dar pass through around 11am, and there are Coasters to Mikumi and Morogoro every hour, sometimes continuing on to Dar. Coasters also run hourly to Ifakara (8am–4pm), from where more head on over the Kilombero River to Mahenge, as do the two buses from Dar (Islam's and Tashriff).

Trains on the TAZARA line are of little use, as they tend to arrive around 3am, and the weekly Zambian service doesn't stop here. Mang'ula station is at the south end of the village, 1km from *Udzungwa Mountain View Hotel*.

Information and costs

The **park headquarters** are 200m from the junction for *Hotel Twiga* in Mang'ula (daily 8am–6pm; PO Box 99 Mang'ula ☎023/262 0224, ✉udzungwa@intafrica.com); they sell a colourful and informative **guidebook** ($10) as well as the official **map**. It's also worth checking out the official **website**, ⓦwww.udzungwa.org.

Strictly speaking, the **entrance fee** ($25 per person for 24hr) is for a single entry only, but as the various trails start at different points along the main road, the wardens don't mind visitors spending the night outside the park and returning the next morning. All of the hiking trails require an official guide or **armed ranger**, who charge $10 per group per day, more if they accompany you overnight; a generous tip would also be in order.

There's only a short trail starting from the park headquarters; for the others, pay your entrance fee first, then either drive, catch a Coaster or rent the park's vehicle to get to the starting point. The park charges $20 per group for a lift to Sanje Ranger Post, 9km north of Mang'ula, where several trails start. For longer journeys, the fare is $100 plus $1 per kilometre over 100km. If you're coming in your own vehicle, leave it at the park headquarters; they'll look after bags too. Suggested daily fees for (optional) **porters**, hired through the park headquarters, are Tsh5000 for a 16–20kg load on the Sanje Falls Circuit, Tsh8000 for the hike up Mwanihana Peak, and Tsh10,000 up to Luhombero Peak.

For information about **hiking into the park from the west**, see p.585.

Accommodation, eating and drinking

The only **accommodation** inside the park is camping (see below). Outside the park, there are two good hotels close to the park gate, and several basic guest houses in Mang'ula village, around 2km from the park gate: to get to the park, walk south along the main road, past *Udzungwa Mountain View Hotel*, and turn left at the post office. All serve **food and drinks**, and there are lots more basic bars and restaurants in Mang'ula, none of them venturing far beyond the land of *kuku na chipsi*.

In addition to **campsites** along the hiking trails, the park maintains three numbered sites close to the gate, the drawback being the cost ($30 per person plus park fees). *Campsite 2* enjoys the best location, 2km inside the park in a beautiful patch of forest, near a bubbling brook and rock pools in which you can swim. Facilities are limited to pit latrines. Much cheaper, and outside the park, is camping at *Udzungwa Mountain View Hotel* (Tsh2000).

Hotel Twiga 1km from the junction outside the park headquarters (signposted) ☏023/262 0239. Best of the lot, in shady gardens, with simple but perfectly good twin-bed rooms, some with bathrooms, all with large nets, balconies and TV. Tasty food available (around Tsh2500), and there's a bar with local TV. The hotel is due to be bought by the park, so rates may increase substantially. ❷
Mountain Peak Lodge Mang'ula village, 876 metres (so sayeth the sign) from the main road ☏0748/650392. Best of the local guest houses, clean and with safe parking. Some of its rooms

have bathrooms (squat toilets), all have ceiling fans and box nets, plus a bar and basic restaurant (chicken or beef with chips or rice). ❶–❷
Udzungwa Mountain View Hotel 600m along the road to Ifakara from the junction outside the park headquarters ☏0748/454481 or 0748/382541. Similar to the *Twiga* but overpriced. All rooms are en-suite twins (a large double and a single, both with box nets) and a choice of fans or a/c. Its restaurant charges upwards of Tsh7500 a plate, but does have prawns and, oddly, impala. There's also a bar with TV. Breakfast included. ❹

Hiking in the park

The park contains several **hiking trails**, ranging from an easy hour's walk to a serious six-day adventure across the entire park. All walks can be extremely steep in places, and a ranger or guide is obligatory. It's also possible to arrange your own itinerary: ask at the park headquarters, or – for the approach from the west – at *Little Ruaha Riverside Campsite* near Iringa (see p.579).

Equipment should include good walking shoes, a light waterproof jacket in the rains, a water bottle and sterilizing tablets or iodine (there's plenty of water along the trails), and camping equipment for overnighting. A gas or kerosene stove is also helpful. All overnight trails, with the exception of the eastern approach to Luhombero Peak, have **campsites** equipped with toilet, shelter and nearby water.

The trails

The only walk from the park headquarters, the **Prince Bernhard Trail** (1km; 40min; no guide needed), goes to the small Prince Bernhard Falls, named after the Dutch prince who, as president of the WWF, opened the park in October 1992. There's another waterfall en route. Habituated baboons are frequently seen (hide food and take care), as are red duikers.

Another short trail, the **Sonjo Trail** (2.5km; 2hr; guide needed) starts 5km north of Mang'ula at Sonjo, passing through *miombo* woodland to two waterfalls. Primates and birds are the main animal attractions there.

The most popular route is the **Sanje Falls Circuit** (5km; 4hr; guide needed), which starts from Sanje Ranger Post. The trail heads through various forest zones to the Sanje Falls, a sequence of three waterfalls which drop over 170m. The first two provide a deeply refreshing experience, surrounded with mist spray, and have splashpools you can swim in. The third and longest fall is difficult to see as you emerge from the dense forest right on top of it, though the hollows and undulating channels gouged into the rock by water are interesting. You can see the falls clearly on the way down to Sanje village, or on the bus from Mikumi for that matter. Primates are frequently seen, as are birds and butterflies.

The **Campsite 3 Circuit** (13km; 10hr; ranger or guide needed) is best for wildlife (or at least their dung). It also gives good odds on seeing bushbuck and duiker as well as primates, birds and butterflies. The trail starts at Campsite 3, 100m before *Udzungwa Mountain View Hotel* in Mang'ula, and ends on the road 3km north of Mang'ula before Sonjo.

The **Mwanihana Trail** (38km; 3 days, 2 nights; armed ranger needed) starts at Sonjo, 5km north of Mang'ula, and is the highlight of many a visit to Tanzania, taking you to Udzungwa's second-highest peak, Mwanihana (2111m). Be warned however; the walk is exhausting (19km uphill) and you need to be sure-footed. The trail follows the Sonjo River for the most part, its steep and narrow valley necessitating at least fifteen crossings; in the dry season this just means wading across, but in the rains you'll be struggling through torrents while hanging on grimly to a guide rope, so unless you're covered by ample life insurance this trek should be avoided during the long rains (March–May). At other times you have the pleasure of passing through every one of the park's forest zones, before emerging onto the grassy plateau by the peak. The park blurb promises a herd of buffalo, duiker and elephant, but you'd be lucky to see any of these. More likely are glimpses of various primates disappearing in a crackle of branches. There are also lots of butterflies and birds.

A hike up to the park's highest point, **Luhombero Peak** (2576m; 6 days; armed ranger needed), is a serious and rarely attempted undertaking. The trail from the eastern side of the park has yet to be fully opened and is difficult to follow, so access is easiest from Udekwa in the west (see p.585). In time, this will be extended into what promises to be an extraordinary cross-park trail, and with an optional northern loop to Mbatwa Ranger Post.

The park's newest walk is the **Lumemo Trail** (65km; at least 5 days, 4 nights; ranger needed), a clockwise circuit up the Lumemo River and down along the northern side of Mwanihana Peak. Access to the start of the trail is through Lumemo Ranger Post near Ifakara: driving south from Mang'ula, turn right just before Ifakara at the railway station, and it's 12km along. A vehicle from the park headquarters costs $100, or alternatively, the headquarters will contact Lumemo Ranger Post for them to pick you up from Ifakara railway station.

Ifakara

Just under 50km southwest of Mang'ula, beyond the point where the last of Udzungwa's foothills give way to the vast Kilombero floodplain stretching away to the steamy horizon, is the market town of **IFAKARA**. This is generally as far south as travellers go, and even then only a few dozen make it this far each year, though there's plenty to make the journey worthwhile: amazing birdlife attracted by the swampy floodplain; the possibility of arranging boat rides in quest of crocodiles and hippos along the Kilombero River (be careful!); and the joy of getting away from other tourists – although you will have to share the town with the steady stream of researchers who have chosen Ifakara (whose hot and humid climate is notorious for malaria) as their field base in anti-malarial research work. It's courtesy of one such project, working to popularize Zuia Mbu brand insecticide-treated mosquito nets, that you'll see street-name signs throughout town, quite a rarity elsewhere.

Arrival and accommodation

Ifakara is most easily reached by **bus**, although there are also three **trains** a week along the TAZARA railway from Dar to Mbeya, one of which continues on to New Mposhi Kapiri in Zambia. Northbound services are deeply unpredictable. The **bus stand** is on Zuia Mbu Road beside the market. NMB **bank** on Benki Road is efficient and changes travellers' cheques. The **post office** is off the south end of Kilosa Road; turn left at the Uhuru Monument. **TTCL** is beside the post office, and there are attended-call offices between Kilosa and Uhuru roads just south of the market and just up the road opposite the bank.

There's plenty of **accommodation**, all pretty basic, though all have mosquito nets. Single rooms can usually be shared by couples if the bed is big enough, though you'll only save a few hundred shillings. The best (both ❷) are the *Bambo Guest House*, at the south end of Uhuru Road, and the *Goa II Guest House*, also on Uhuru Road, both of which have reasonable en-suite rooms.

Eating and drinking

Like its accommodation, Ifakara's **eating and drinking** choices are basic but perfectly adequate, as well as cheap. Best of the **restaurants** is the *Zanzibar Restaurant* on Kilosa Road, facing the market, which could almost be described as posh. Two other good places on the same road are the unfussy *Al-Jazira Restaurant* (no alcohol); and *Paradise Restaurant*, the latter offering a decent selection of grills, stews and fish (and good juices; but avoid the snacks), and – oddly – videos. For **drinking**, there's a good unnamed bar and restaurant on the street corner facing NMB on Benki Road, especially popular whenever English Premiership football is bouncing off the satellite. Less appetizing, but with some shaded seats outside, is the *Shengena Garden Bar* near the post office. If you're feeling strong, ask around whether anyone has any *ulanzi* (bamboo wine).

The Town

The nucleus of colonial buildings from both the German and British eras is at the south end of Kilosa Road. Especially beautiful is the quasi-baroque former

Moving on from Ifakara

Take care with buses, and always ask impartial locals which company is currently slowest ("best" does not necessarily mean safest). **Dar**, via **Mang'ula, Mikumi and Morogoro**, is served by two or three buses a day, all leaving 8–9am, including Islam's and Tashriff. Islam's has the better reputation. There are also a number of Coaster minibuses, whose drivers' skills vary from suicidal to uncommonly considerate. The last of these heads off at 3–4pm, but may only go as far as Morogoro. To **Mahenge**, there are Coasters throughout the day, and two daily buses from Dar in the afternoon.

Governor's Residence just off the Uhuru Monument roundabout, a palatial structure built around a large courtyard that is now occupied by the Ifakara Rice Mill. A couple of cement lions guard the gate, in addition to a couple of policemen – ask their permission before taking photos. The **market** is a solidly rural affair, also attracting Maasai from the south side of the Kilombero River complete with their inseparable cattle. Local specialities to look for are woven bamboo *tenga* baskets. Other **handicrafts**, including cotton items, can be bought at the Ifakara Women's Weaving Association (IWWA) shop at the south end of Kilosa Road.

The Kilombero Valley

Five kilometres south of Ifakara is the narrowest point in the broad **Kilombero River**, a labyrinth of interconnecting waterways through which only experienced boatmen can find their way. Bordered by the Udzungwa and Mufindi Highlands to the north and west and the Mbarika Mountains to the east, the immense **KILOMBERO VALLEY** beyond contains East Africa's largest lowland wetland, the **Kibasira Swamp**. It's an area of exceptional biodiversity, protected by several game reserves and by virtue of having been declared a UNESCO World Heritage Site and RAMSAR Wetland (a site of global importance for birds).

With your own vehicle and a sterling sense of adventure, you might aim for the **Namhanga Lakes**, wedged between two teak plantations west of Lupiro (40km south of Ifakara towards Mahenge, then around 30km southwest to Namhanga village), whose terrestrial **wildlife** includes elephant, waterbuck, duiker, buffalo, sable, eland, elephant, yellow baboons and crested porcupines, together with two diminutive endemic characters – the yellow Kilombero tree frog, and a dwarf gecko. **Birdlife** is prolific, and includes the African fishing owl, African pitta, African fish eagle and the endemic Kilombero weaver, whilst the river is positively heaving with **hippos and crocodiles** – take all precautions possible.

Practicalities

Other than the dirt road to Namhanga, access to the swamp is very much the stuff of expeditions – access is by water (though the TAZARA railway skirts the western fringes) – but you can get a taste of the place by **walking or cycling** the 5km from Ifakara to the river, where you can browse through the riverside fish market, or watch ferry passengers, goats and the Maasai with their cattle coming and going. Bikes can be rented near the market in Ifakara, and at a number of places at the corner of Benki and Mangwale roads.

The **vehicle ferry** sails over the river to the settlement of Kivukoni: services is sometimes suspended when the river is in spate (usually March–May, sometimes also Nov & Dec), and may for that matter be dangerous at that time (the ferry capsized a few years ago). **Dugout canoes** venture across throughout the year, and their owners are the people to talk to should you fancy spending a few hours in search of crocodiles, hippos and the river's plentiful birdlife. A word of **warning**, though: dugouts are an intrinsically dangerous way to travel, given their instability, strong currents and the moody caprices of hippos and crocs – any journey here is at your own risk.

Travel details

Buses and daladalas

Asterisks denote routes that are open in the dry season only; during the rains (usually Nov & Dec and most of March–May) these routes are often closed for days, weeks or even months at a time. Buses that do attempt these routes in the rains are subject to lengthy delays, often meaning days. Journeys over 14hr are likely to involve an overnight stop.

Babati to: Arusha (5 daily; 4–5hr); Katesh (1 daily; 90min); Kondoa (2–3 daily*; 3–5hr); Mwanza (2 daily*; 28hr); Singida (2–3 daily; 4–5hr); Tabora (2 weekly*; 24hr).

Dodoma to: Dar (hourly until around noon; 6–8hr); Iringa (2 daily; 5hr); Kondoa (5 daily*; 4–5hr); Mbeya (3 weekly*; 11hr); Morogoro (1–2 hourly until around noon; 3–4hr); Mwanza (2–3 daily*; 28–30hr); Shinyanga (2–3 daily*; 25–27hr); Singida (3–4 daily*; 6–7hr); Tabora (6 weekly; 9–12hr).

Ifakara to: Dar (2 daily; 9hr); Mahenge (1 daily*; 6hr); Mang'ula (2 daily plus hourly daladalas; 1hr 30min); Mikumi (2 daily plus hourly daladalas; 3hr); Morogoro (3 daily; 6hr).

Kondoa to: Arusha (3–4 daily*; 8–9hr); Babati (2–3 daily*; 3–5hr depending on stops); Dar (3 daily*; 11hr); Dodoma (5 daily*; 4–5hr); Kolo (2–4 daily*; 1hr); Morogoro (3 daily*; 8–9hr); Pahi (1 daily*; 2hr).

Mang'ula to: Dar (2 daily; 5–6hr); Ifakara (2 daily plus hourly Coasters; 1hr 30min); Mikumi (2 daily plus hourly Coasters; 1hr 30min–2hr 30min); Morogoro (2 daily plus occasional Coasters; 4hr 30min).

Mikumi to: Dar (hourly to 4pm; 5hr); Ifakara (2 daily plus hourly Coasters; 3–4hr); Iringa (hourly; 3hr); Mang'ula (2 daily plus hourly Coasters; 1hr 30min–2hr 30min); Mbeya (hourly; 8–9hr); Morogoro (hourly; 2–3hr).

Morogoro to: Arusha (daily; 8–10hr); Dar (2–3 hourly until 4pm; 2hr 45min); Dodoma (1–2 hourly until noon; 3–4hr); Ifakara (2 daily plus occasional Coasters; 6hr); Iringa (hourly; 6hr); Mang'ula (2 daily plus occasional Coasters; 4hr 30min); Mbeya (hourly; 11–12hr); Mikumi (hourly; 2–3hr).

Singida to: Arusha (4–5 daily; 8–9hr); Babati (3–4 daily; 4–5hr); Biharamulo (5 weekly*; 10–12hr); Bukoba (5 weekly*; 14hr); Dar (1–2 daily*; 13–16hr); Dodoma (1–2 daily*; 6–7hr); Morogoro (1–2 daily*; 9–10hr); Mwanza (2 daily*; 12–14hr); Nzega (daily*; 4hr); Tabora (2 weekly*; 6hr).

Flights

Airline codes used below are: CA (Coastal Aviation) and ZA (ZanAir). Where both fly to the same destination, the one with most frequent flights or shortest journey times is listed first.

Dodoma to: Arusha (CA: 3 weekly; 3hr); Dar (CA: 3 weekly; 3hr 40min).

Selous to: Arusha (ZA, CA: 1–2 daily; 2hr 05min 6hr 30min); Dar (CA, ZA: 2–3 daily; 30min–1hr 25min); Kilwa (CA: daily; 2hr 20min); Mafia (CA: daily; 50min); Manyara (CA: 3 weekly; 5hr 50min); Pemba (ZA: daily; 2hr); Serengeti (ZA: daily; 4hr); Ruaha (CA: 3 weekly; 2hr); Zanzibar (CA, ZA: 3 daily; 1hr–1hr 50min)

Trains

The Central Line Railway connects Dodoma and Singida with Dar, Kigoma and Mwanza. The TAZARA line runs from Dar along the edge of Selous and Udzungwa and south into Zambia.

Dodoma to: Dar (3 weekly; 14hr 10min); Kigoma (3 weekly; 23hr 15min); Manyoni (3 weekly; 3hr 45min); Morogoro (3 weekly; 6hr 55min); Mwanza (3 weekly; 23hr 25min); Singida (3 weekly; 8hr); Tabora (3 weekly; 10hr 15min).

Ifakara to: Dar (3 weekly; 9–10hr); Mbeya (3 weekly; 12–14hr); New Kapiri Mposhi, Zambia (1 weekly; 31hr).

Mang'ula to: Dar (2 weekly; 7hr).

Morogoro to: Dar (3 weekly; 6hr 35min); Dodoma (3 weekly; 7hr 20min); Kigoma (3 weekly; 31hr 10min); Mwanza (3 weekly; 31hr 20min); Tabora (3 weekly; 18hr 10min).

Selous (various stations) to: Dar (2–3 weekly; 4hr–5hr 30min); Mbeya (2–3 weekly; 14–18hr). **Singida** to: Dodoma (3 weekly; 9hr 25min); Manyoni (3 weekly; 4hr 15min).

The northern highlands

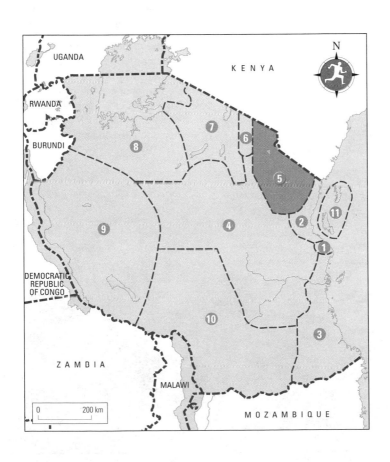

CHAPTER 5

Highlights

✳ **Coffee** A brew of Kilimanjaro's heavenly *Arabica* at Moshi's *The Coffee Shop* might just convince you to never go instant again. **See p.326**

✳ **Mount Kilimanjaro** Africa's highest mountain, its perennial snow cap makes a beautiful sight from any angle. It can be climbed – by the hardy – over five to eight days. **See p.334**

✳ **Pare Mountains** Part of the ancient Eastern Arc mountain chain, this contains patches of rich rainforest, highland meadows, and the Pare tribe,

renowned for their healers and witches. **See p.352**

✳ **West Usambara** Also part of the Eastern Arc, and home to the welcoming Sambaa tribe. Best visited through Lushoto's excellent cultural tourism programme, which blends nature and glorious views with culture. **See p.358**

✳ **Amani Nature Reserve** Dubbed "the Galapagos of Africa", the reserve contains one of the oldest and most biodiverse rainforests on earth, much of which can be seen on foot. **See p.372**

△ Herd of elephants and Mount Kilimanjaro

The northern highlands

T he lush and fertile **northern highlands** are one of the most scenically dramatic areas in Tanzania, running inland from the coast through a series of mountain chains and culminating in the towering massif of **Mount Kilimanjaro**, Africa's highest peak. The region's attractions are manifold, ranging from the arduous trek to the summit of Kilimanjaro itself to less strenuous but hugely enjoyable hikes arranged through **cultural tourism programmes** in the **Usambara** and **Pare mountains**, whose great age and climatic stability has resulted in the development of a unique and extraordinarily rich plant and animal life. The jewel is **Amani Nature Reserve** in the Eastern Usambaras, which protects some fantastic montane rainforest.

The region's main centre is **Moshi**, best known to visitors as the base for climbing Kilimanjaro, of which – clear skies permitting – it has fantastic views. The nicest town in the highlands, however, is **Lushoto**, capital of the Western Usambaras, whose friendly inhabitants, cool climate, spectacular vistas and well-established cultural tourism programme entices many visitors to stay longer than planned. Indeed the same could be said of the entire northern highlands – take your time; it's a vividly beautiful and hugely rewarding region to explore.

Kilimanjaro Region

At almost six thousand metres, the massive volcanic hulk of **Mount Kilimanjaro** is Africa's highest mountain, and dominates much of the region named after it, spiritually as well as physically and economically. Although some 30,000 tourists are drawn to "Kili" every year by the challenge of trekking to the summit, only a few spend more than a couple of days in the towns at its base, of which the bustling and friendly **Moshi** is by far the biggest. Efforts have recently been made to spread the economic benefits of tourism, with

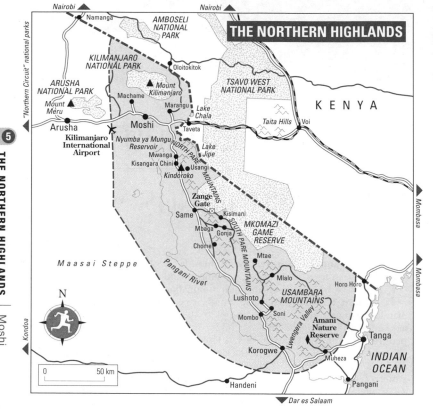

the result that community-based cultural tourism programmes have been set up in **Marangu** and **Machame**, the villages at the start of Kilimanjaro's most popular hiking routes, close to the band of tropical rainforest that skirts much of its base. The programmes include a variety of half- and full-day hikes into the forests to see waterfalls, hot-water springs, and places with spiritual or historical significance. Similar trips can be made from Moshi itself, although little is properly organized.

Moshi

An hour's drive east of Arusha is the busy commercial town of **MOSHI**, capital of Kilimanjaro Region and beautifully located near the foot of the mountain, fully five kilometres beneath its summit. The views are unforgettable, especially when the shrouding blanket of cloud that usually clings to Kili by day dissipates – with luck – just before sunset, to reveal tantalizing glimpses of Kibo and Mawenzi peaks: a subtly dramatic and ever-changing scene accompanied by the tweeting of thousands of wheeling swallows. The mountain's influence is pervasive. Meltwater streams permit year-round agriculture, especially of **coffee**, while the mountain is alluded to in the town's name: *moshi* in Kiswahili means

The Chagga

Numbering over a million, the **Chagga** occupy the southern and eastern slopes of Kilimanjaro and are among East Africa's wealthiest and most highly educated people. Their wealth stems from the fortunate conjunction of favourable climatic conditions and their own agricultural ingenuity. Watered by year-round snow and ice melt, the volcanic soils of Kilimanjaro's lower slopes are extremely fertile and are exploited by the Chagga using a sophisticated system of intensive irrigation and continuous fertilization with animal manure, permitting year-round cultivation and supporting one of Tanzania's highest human population densities. *Arabica* coffee has been the Chagga's primary cash crop since colonial times, although maize and bananas remain staple foods. The cultivation of bananas is traditionally a man's work, as is that of eleusine seed (*ulezi*), which is boiled and mixed with mashed plantain to brew a local beer (*mbege*), still used as a form of payment to elders in their role as conflict arbiters.

In the past, the potential for such conflicts was great: even today there are some four hundred different Chagga clans – indeed it's barely a century since the Chagga finally coalesced into a distinct and unified tribe. Most are related to the Kamba of Kenya, who migrated northwards from Kilimanjaro a few centuries ago during a great drought. Other clans descend from the Taita, another Kenyan tribe, and others from the pastoral Maasai, whose influence is visible in the importance attached to cattle as bridewealth payments and in the grouping of men into age-sets analogous to the Maasai system. Today, the Chagga wield considerable political and financial clout, both because of their long contact with European models of education and Christianity, both of which dominate modern-day political and economic life, and because of their involvement in the coffee business, which remains the region's economic mainstay in spite of volatile world prices. Indeed, the Chagga are the one tribe you're almost guaranteed to meet in even the most obscure corners of Tanzania, working as traders, merchants, officials, teachers and doctors.

"smoke", either from Kilimanjaro's last, minor eruption in the 1700s, or because of the smoke-like cloud that often covers the mountain. The town itself is refreshingly open and spacious, with broad, tree-lined avenues and leafy suburbs, and – despite a population of over 200,000 – it's decidedly more laid-back than Arusha. There's a wealth of good hotels to suit all pockets, and a few excellent restaurants, too, making the town an ideal base for the climb up Kilimanjaro.

Arrival, town transport and information

International **flights** land at Kilimanjaro International Airport (KIA), 34km west of Moshi off the road to Arusha. See p.381 for details about arriving there and moving on to Moshi. Most public transport stops at the combined **bus and daladala stand**, south of the clock tower between Market Street and Mawenzi Road. Some bus companies have their own terminals, including Scandinavian Express, one block south of the bus stand on Mawenzi Road, and Dar Express, on Old Moshi Road opposite NBC bank, near the clock tower. Passengers arriving on one of the **Nairobi shuttle buses** can be dropped at any central hotel: Davanu finish outside Kahawa House, facing the clock tower; Impala at their office on Kibo Road, next to *Chrisburger*; and Riverside at the THB Building, on Boma Road. **Flycatchers** touting for hotels and hiking companies are quick to spot new arrivals, but aren't as insistent as their Arushan brothers.

Town transport

Moshi's compact centre is easy to negotiate on foot and, unless you're carrying visibly tempting valuables, **safety** isn't much of an issue either. The exceptions are the Kuheshimo area, about a kilometre south of the central market, and the bus and daladala stand, which has pickpockets and bag-snatchers. The cheapest way to the suburbs is by **daladala**, nicknamed *vifordi* – alluding to the town's first-ever vehicle, a Model-T Ford. Most leave from the north side of the bus and daladala stand; journeys cost Tsh200. Daladalas heading along the Dar–Arusha highway can also be caught on Kibo Road.

Taxis park outside larger hotels, at major road junctions, around the bus and daladala stand, and on the west side of the Central Market on Market Street. A journey within town costs Tsh1500–2000; rides to the outskirts shouldn't cost over Tsh3000.

Information

Moshi lacks a **tourist office**, so don't be misled by hiking companies displaying "tourist information" signboards; it's just a ruse to get you inside. The best source of information is the annual *Moshi Guide* (Tsh2500), containing listings of pretty much everything you'll need. It's available at *The Coffee Shop* on Hill Street. There's a similarly informative **website**, ⓦ www.kiliweb.com. There are **notice boards** at *The Coffee Shop* and in the lobby of the *Lutheran Uhuru Hostel*, but be warned that not all the safari and hiking companies featured on them are reputable or licensed.

Accommodation

Town centre hotels are plentiful and generally good value, though all but the very cheapest have hiked-up "non-resident" (tourist) rates. A handful have rooftop "summit bars" for views of Kili; one or two also have views from some bedrooms. Given Moshi's low altitude (810m), **mosquitoes** and malaria are prevalent: good-sized mosquito nets are preferable to window screens and/or bug spray.

The cheapest and most characterful **campsite** is the *Golden Shower*, 2km east of town (☎027/275 1990, ⓦ www.safari-images.com; $3 per person), which also has a restaurant and bar, weekend discos, and plays host to occasional overland trucks. *Green Hostels* and the *Lutheran Uhuru Hostel* (p.327) also allow camping.

Town Centre

Budget

Buffalo Hotel New St ☎027/275 0270, ⓔ buffalohotel@yahoo.com. An affordable, clean and well-run three-storey hotel. Rooms, mostly en suite, have fans, box nets and phones; the better ones are larger, or have balconies facing Kilimanjaro. There's also a restaurant, free luggage store, and adjacent Internet café. Breakfast included. ❷–❸

Hotel Da' Costa Mawenzi Rd ☎027/275 5159, ⓔ hoteldacosta@yahoo.com. A characterful cheapie with creaky floorboards, and a good restaurant-bar on the second floor with a street-view terrace, but no Kili views. Rooms (sharing bathrooms) have fans, nets, and a table and chair. The twin-bed rooms are fine, but singles are eminently avoidable hot and stuffy cells. ❸

Green Hostels Nkomo Ave ☎027/275 3198, ⓔ greenhostels2@yahoo.co.uk. A friendly family-run place, with ten rooms in very peaceful grounds. The three en-suite ones with bathtubs are reasonably good value, even though there's not always hot water; rooms sharing bathrooms are less enticing. Food and drinks available. Breakfast included. ❸–❹

Haria Palace Hotel Mawenzi Rd, entrance on Guinea St ☎027/275 1128, ⓔ hariapalace@yahoo.com. A tatty two-storey

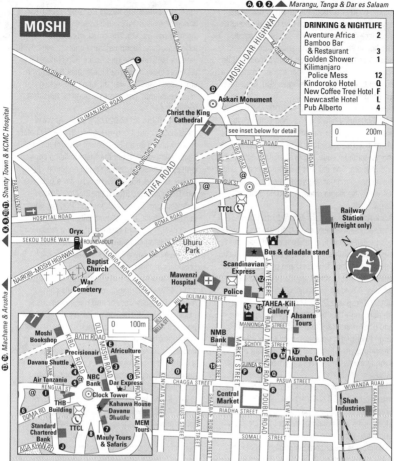

MOSHI

Marangu, Tanga & Dar es Salaam

DRINKING & NIGHTLIFE

Aventure Africa	2
Bamboo Bar & Restaurant	3
Golden Shower	1
Kilimanjaro Police Mess	12
Kindoroko Hotel	Q
New Coffee Tree Hotel	F
Newcastle Hotel	L
Pub Alberto	4

ACCOMMODATION

Bristol Cottages Kilimanjaro	J	Mountain Inn Lodge	A
Buffalo Hotel	M	New Coffee Tree Hotel	F
Green Hostels	C	Newcastle Hotel	L
Haria Palace Hotel	N	Philip Hotel	I
Horombo Lodge	E	Rose Home	H
Hotel Da' Costa	R	Siesta Inn	O
Keys Hotel	B	YMCA Youth Hostel	D
Kilimanjaro Crane Hotel	G		
Kilimanjaro Impala Hotel	K		
Kindoroko Hotel	Q		
Moshi Leopard Hotel	P		

EATING

Abbas Ally Hot Bread Shop	6	Kindoroko Hotel	Q
Central Garden	8	Lutheran Uhuru Hostel	9
Chrisburger	4	Mama Clementina's	13
The Coffee Shop	15	Mama Philips Restaurant	19
El Rancho	11	Moshi Leopard Hotel	P
Friendship Restaurant	7	New Coffee Tree Hotel	F
Hill Street Restaurant	16	Panda Chinese	10
Golden Shower	1	Salzburger Café	18
Indotalian Restaurant	17	Siesta Inn	O
Keys Hotel	B	Simple Sir Club & Restaurant	14
Kilimanjaro Coffee House	5		
Kilimanjaro Impala Hotel	K		

building containing probably the cheapest doubles in town, whilst $5 more gets you a private bathroom. It's all rather dark and depressing, and the nets are too small, but it's clean and there are ceiling fans. There's a rooftop restaurant and bar, but no Kili views. ②–③

New Coffee Tree Hotel Off Old Moshi Rd ☏027/275 2905. Popular with budget travellers, this charmless four-storey block (with lift access) is central Moshi's largest hotel, and perfectly good if you don't mind linoleum floors, saggy beds and the occasional cold shower.

Rooms (with or without bathroom; those without have washbasins) are large and breezy, though most lack fans and the nets can be too small. The hotel has one towering advantage though: matchless Kilimanjaro views from almost half its rooms, and from the top-floor bar and restaurant. Especially good value for singles ($5). Breakfast included. ❸

Newcastle Hotel Mawenzi Rd ☎027/275 3203. This four-storey building has seen better days, and its ground-floor bar isn't the most welcoming either, but it's reasonable, with huge if rather dark rooms, some en suite. There's another, better, bar and restaurant on the first floor, and another under a strange pagoda-style structure on the roof with Kili views. No single rates. Breakfast included. ❷–❸

Rose Home Ngorongoro Ave ☎0748/806662, Ⓔrosehome@kicheko.com. A private house with good-value rooms to rent, both in the main building (sharing bathrooms) and in cottages (en suite). All have TVs, fans and nets, and there's hot water, Internet access, a small plunge pool, and safe parking. Breakfast included. ❸

Siesta Inn Kiusa St ☎027/275 0158. Calm, friendly and attractive, with a shady garden and good restaurant and bar. It has ten large twin-bed rooms, some en suite (clean Western-style toilets), all with fans, but also slightly musty and with saggy beds. Breakfast included. ❷

YMCA Youth Hostel Junction of Taifa and Kilimanjaro roads ☎027/275 1754, Ⓕ027/275 1734. Breezy, welcoming and popular with backpackers. Most rooms share bathrooms, but are clean and bright and have nets, fans and good beds. The main draw is the superb swimming pool (with views of Kilimanjaro). There's also a poolside snack bar, good restaurant and curio shop. Breakfast included. ❸–❹

Mid-range

Bristol Cottages Kilimanjaro Corner of Rindi Lane and Aga Khan Rd ☎027/275 5083, Ⓦwww .kiliweb.com/bristol. This has lost some of its rustic charm since adding a three-storey accommodation block. The better rooms in the block have views of Kili (and a phone mast), and the top-floor suites are huge, and have TVs and bathtubs. Not as nice, and with no views, are the twin-bed cottage rooms, though they do have clunky old a/c units and TVs. One gripe – no mosquito nets, and the smell of bug-spray is insidious. There's also a coffee house, cheap restaurant and safe parking. Breakfast included. ❺

Horombo Lodge Old Moshi Rd ☎027/275 0134, Ⓔhorombolodge@kilionline.com. None-too-exciting high-rise (no lift). The small en-suite rooms have fans, large round nets and phones, some with satellite TV, whilst the huge suite (❺) features a teasingly tacky bedspread (puffy pink Rayon with embossed roses) as well as a bathtub. Also has a small restaurant, bar and safe parking. Breakfast included. ❹

Keys Hotel Uru Rd ☎027/275 2250, Ⓦwww .keys-hotels.com. Long-established, friendly hotel vaguely styled on an English inn. The fifteen cool, high-ceilinged rooms in the main building come with pine furniture, digital TV, phone, fan and (not always reliable) hot showers; $10 more gets you a/c. There are also fifteen unattractive African-style cottages at the back lacking TVs. Facilities include a sauna, a small and rather grotty swimming pool, a bar and restaurant, and a recommended hiking company. An annexe 3km east of town has modern houses sleeping six each. Breakfast included. ❺

Kilimanjaro Crane Hotel Kaunda Rd ☎027/275 1114, Ⓦwww.kilimanjarocranehotels.com. A large, perfectly decent and unexciting business-class hotel. The rooms, all en suite, have phone, TV, fan or a/c, and smallish nets. Doubles and suites have massive beds (and bathtubs), and some have balconies. Facilities include a rooftop bar, two restaurants, a gift shop, swimming pool and safe parking. Breakfast included. ❺

Kindoroko Hotel Mawenzi Rd ☎027/275 4054, Ⓦwww.kindoroko.com. A spotless four-storey hotel with spectacular views of Kili from the rooftop restaurant and bar. Most doubles are decently sized, and all have satellite TV, phone, fan and net. Singles are variable, so see a selection. There's another restaurant and bar downstairs (with pool table), a licensed hiking outfit, forex, curio shop, Internet café and safe parking. Breakfast included. ❹

Moshi Leopard Hotel Market St ☎027/275 0884, Ⓦwww.leopardhotel.com. Modern and calm, with clean en-suite twins and doubles, all with fridge, TV, phone and fan or a/c (same price), but no nets – rooms are sprayed. All have balconies, mainly facing neighbouring buildings. There's also a good restaurant, bar and guarded parking. Breakfast included. ❺

Philip Hotel Corner of Rindi Lane and Rengua St ☎027/275 4746. Large and well-kept but anodyne, with only singles and twins. Most have private balconies; all have nets, (local) TV, phone and clean bathrooms. Dull and expensive restaurant-bar. Breakfast included. ❺

Outside the centre

Unless you're in training for a Kili climb, you'll need to take a daladala or taxi to reach the following.

Kilimanjaro Impala Hotel Lema Rd, Shanty Town, 4.5km north of town ☎027/275 3443, ⓦwww.impalahotel.com. Moshi's most upmarket place, and excellent value too, with very stylish architecture, a calm atmosphere, international standards of accommodation, food and service, plus a large swimming pool beside the bar and restaurant, and an Internet café. The eleven superb bedrooms have wooden parquet, lots of reproduction furniture, and TVs. Some also have a/c, others have huge double beds. Breakfast included. ❻

Mountain Inn Lodge Moshi–Dar highway, 6km east of town ☎027/275 5622, ⓦwww.kilimanjaro-shah.com. A friendly place set in a beautiful garden amidst maize and banana fields, with over thirty rather basic en-suite rooms. There's the bonus of a swimming pool and sauna, plus a good Indian restaurant and two bars. Breakfast included. ❺

The Town

If you can cope with the persistent – if generally friendly – attentions of the flycatchers, especially around the clock tower and along Mawenzi Road, Moshi is a relaxing place to wander around, although there are few actual "sights", since most of the town dates from the 1930s onwards. The liveliest place is the bustling **Central market**, south of Chagga Street (Mon–Sat 8am–4.30pm, Sun 8am–noon), which sells a garish cornucopia of imported plastic and aluminium goods, as well as locally produced coffee, cardamom, spices, fruits and vegetables. Keep an eye out for traditional **herbalists** in and around the market (usually old men sitting beside vast quantities of glass jars containing multicoloured powders). One block north, Guinea Street has some **jua kali** (literally "sharp sun") craftsmen, who specialize in turning old tin cans into superb oil lamps, coffee pots, kettles and pans. Two more markets worth exploring include **Mbuyuni market**, four blocks south of the Central Market (daily by daylight; don't take valuables), and **Kiboriloni market** (Tues, Wed, Fri & Sat; best in the morning), 5km along the highway to Dar, known as far as Arusha for its cheap second-hand clothes, as well as hardware and food. There are frequent daladalas from the main daladala stand and from along Kibo Road.

Moshi's only monuments of note are the structures dominating a trio of roundabouts, including the central **clock tower**. A few hundred metres north, the **Askari Monument** rises from the roundabout at the junction with the highway. The statue of the soldier, rifle at the ready, commemorates African members of the British Carrier Corps who lost their lives in the two world wars. More amusing is the irreverent sculpture of a monkey next to it, which greets visitors coming in from Dar. On the south side of the roundabout is the Catholic **Christ the King Cathedral**, famed for its colourful Sunday Masses (6.25am, 8.30am, 10.30am & 4.30pm); the best is the 10.30am service, which attracts many children and their mothers and features plenty of traditional Chagga singing – worth catching even if you're not religious.

Kibo roundabout, 1km west along the highway (Taifa Road), is marked by a stylized **Uhuru Torch**. The original was placed atop Kilimanjaro on the day of Tanzania's Independence in December 1961 to – in the words of President Nyerere – "shine beyond our borders, giving hope where there is despair, love where there is hate, and dignity where before there was only humiliation." At the time, Kenya – whose border skirts the north and east side of the mountain – was still under colonial rule, having only recently emerged from the bloody Mau Mau Rebellion. The short walk from here to **Arusha Road Cemetery**

is worth the effort, as part of it contains the graves of British and Tanzanian soldiers who fought in World War I. It's just to the east of *Pan Africa Hotel*, and can also be reached along a path at the north end of Florida Road.

Eating

Moshi has lots of **restaurants**, one or two of which are quite outstanding. Local **specialities** include *uji*, a porridge made from finger millet (*ulezi*) and eaten for breakfast, and *mtori*, a thick mash of bananas usually served with meat. More ubiquitous, especially in bars, are *nyama choma*, *ndizi* and *chipsi mayai*: the busier the bar, the better the food. **Street food**, mainly roasted maize cobs, is found throughout town. Ambulant **coffee sellers** in and around the central market dish up small porcelain cupfuls of the scalding brew for a mere Tsh20–50.

For your own **provisions**, fresh fruit and vegetables are best at the market. See also **supermarkets** in "Listings".

Town centre

Abbas Ally Hot Bread Shop Boma Rd. Popular for snacks and light lunches, with good samosas, sandwiches, cakes, cappuccino, ice cream and waffles. There are also seats in a pleasant garden. Closed Sun.

Central Garden Facing the clock tower. Drinks, snacks or full meals in a lovely shady garden. The menu ranges from steaks and fast-food favourites to a dab of Indian. Also has good juices and coffee. Daytime only.

Chrisburger Kibo Rd. Handy for breakfast and cheap fast-food style lunches (under Tsh2000), plus burgers and hot dogs. Closes 4.30pm weekdays, 2pm weekends.

The Coffee Shop Hill St. A superb place with a warmly decorated dining room, a garden at the back with tables (and a few more on the shady streetfront terrace), and a wide range of delicious meals and snacks, including soups, pies, mouth-watering cakes, samosas and ice cream. Best of all is the heavenly Kilimanjaro *Arabica* coffee – probably the best brew in East Africa. It's also a travellers' meeting place, has a noticeboard with ads for local artists and art centres, and incorporates Our Heritage crafts shop. Mon 8am–5pm, Tues–Fri 8am–8pm, Sat 8am–6pm.

Friendship Restaurant Mawenzi Rd. Popular with

Coffee

Kilimanjaro Region produces high-quality **Arabica coffee**, characterized by its mild flavour and delicate aroma. Most of the coffee farms are smallholdings whose production is collected and marketed by the Kilimanjaro Native Coffee Union (KNCU), providing a guaranteed minimum income to farmers at times when world coffee prices slump, something that these days happens with alarming frequency.

Coffee bushes flower during the short rains (Oct–Nov), when they become covered in white blossom and give off a pervasive, jasmine-like scent. The best time to visit if you're interested in seeing how coffee is processed is between July and September, when the berries are harvested. Following harvesting, the beans' sweet pulpy outer layer is mechanically removed, after which they're fermented in water and then dried in sunlight on long tables. After a few days, the outer casing (the "parchment") becomes brittle, and is easily removed at the coffee mill, after which the beans are graded for sale according to size and weight.

Moshi's *The Coffee Shop* is the best place to sample a brew, and may also be able to point you in the right direction should you want to visit a working coffee farm. The process can also be seen as part of the cultural tourism programme at Tengeru near Arusha (see p.416), whilst Juma Kahembe, the manager of Babati's cultural tourism programme (p.270) used to be a professional coffee taster, and offers coffee-themed tours to Arusha and Kilimanjaro with otherwise difficult-to-obtain access to the tasting room at Kahawa House in Moshi.

locals throughout the day, dishing up good cheap food and drinks, including *nyama choma*.

Hill Street Restaurant Hill St. An unfailingly welcoming place serving up snacks and dirt cheap Tanzanian and Indian meals (under Tsh1000), including aromatic *pilau*, bean stews, greens and fried fish. Also has seats outdoors. Daytime only.

Kilimanjaro Coffee House Kibo House, clock tower roundabout. Tourist temptations – familiar Western grub, good coffee, a cool a/c interior, Internet café and even a small bookshop.

Kindoroko Hotel Mawenzi Rd. Almost sophisticated, the much-improved ground-floor restaurant here has a good range of Italian, Chinese and Swahili food.

Mama Philips Restaurant Selous St. Chow down on great *nyama choma* in this smoky, local *makuti*-thatched bar.

Moshi Leopard Hotel Market St. Probably has the cleanest and most modern kitchen in town (it's open plan), and is good value too, with most mains

– including tasty curried prawns – costing around Tsh4000. They also do grilled goat and chicken, and occasional buffets.

New Coffee Tree Hotel Old Moshi Rd. On the breezy top floor, the food is mainly Tanzanian, including *mtori* banana stew, and is cheap but very pedestrian, but who cares when the views of Kilimanjaro are so delectable?

Salzburger Café Kenyatta St. Pleasingly bizarre, decorated like an Austrian bar and with lots of memorabilia from the local Volkswagen Members Club. The menu is extensive and cheap (everything – including steaks – under Tsh3000), and the food is good, although not everything is always available. African dishes feature at lunchtimes, including ox liver in sweet and sour sauce, and sizzling chicken *mambo yote*.

Siesta Inn Kiusa St. The restaurant in the garden at the back dishes up some great food, including delicious curried tilapia with fried bananas (under Tsh2000).

Out of the town centre

El Rancho 200m off Lema Rd, Shanty Town, 5km from town – take the second right after the *Kilimanjaro Impala Hotel*. Tasty north Indian cuisine (plus a wide selection of European dishes) in an affluent suburb, popular with expats at weekends. A full à la carte stuffing with a drink or two costs around Tsh12,000; its famous Sunday lunch buffet costs Tsh7500. Also has evening barbecues (no beef or pork), and an excellent cocktail and wine list. There's also a pool table, minigolf and table football. Closed Mon.

Golden Shower 2km along the Dar highway. Friendly and with a pleasingly decadent feel, this is a quiet getaway (as long as overland trucks aren't in residence), with mains around Tsh3000, and game meat July–Dec.

Indotalian Restaurant New St, opposite *Buffalo Hotel*. One of the nicest places in the evening, with a cool streetside verandah, friendly service and – oddly – Indian and Italian food, including delicious pizzas and a wide range of curries (Tsh3000–4000).

Keys Hotel Uru Rd. A reasonably classy restaurant with good service, affordable prices (main courses average Tsh4000), and one of only few to feature *mtori* banana stew. Aside from this and a daily Tanzanian dish, the wide menu is mainly French style, and carries a good wine list (Tsh12,000 a bottle).

Kilimanjaro Impala Hotel Lema Rd, Shanty Town, 4.5km north of town. Fine Indian, Chinese and European fare, including fresh salads, sand-

wiches and burgers, in Moshi's foremost hotel. Most mains cost Tsh7000, with vegetarian dishes around Tsh5000. There's also a nice swimming pool (Tsh3000).

Lutheran Uhuru Hostel Sekou Touré Way, 3km northwest of town. Good grilled chicken, steaks and local Chagga dishes (under Tsh2000), and perfectly happy to satisfy the quirky needs of exhausted climbers. No smoking or alcohol. Closes 8pm.

Mama Olementina's 2.5km west of Kibo roundabout, then 500m south just after Karanga Bridge ☏ 027/275 4707. This women's vocational training centre makes some great food, with à la carte daily (full meals around Tsh5000), plus a range of three-course set menus including Mexican (Thurs), Italian (Fri) and barbecue (Sat). Eat inside or on a terrace. Best to book in advance.

Panda Chinese Off Lema Rd, Shanty Town, 500m before *Kilimanjaro Impala Hotel*, 4km from town. Excellent and authentic Chinese cuisine, with a wide selection of generous dishes. The soups and seafood are particularly good, especially the prawns. Around Tsh12,000 including drinks. Eat inside or in the garden. Open all day at weekends.

Simple Sir Club & Restaurant Arusha highway, 2km west of Kibo roundabout. A menu to please all tastes (steaks, chicken, fish, curries and sizzlers), plus a popular bar and supremely succulent roast meats and grilled bananas. Also has a pool table. Mostly Tsh2000–3500.

Drinking and nightlife

Whilst Moshi at night is not as lively as Arusha, there's plenty to keep you busy, and a couple of places host live bands. There are lots of friendly local **bars** throughout the town, few of which see many tourists. Walking around the centre at night is generally safe, although if you're going more than a few blocks, it's wiser to catch a cab. Several **hotels** – including the *Kindoroko*, *New Coffee Tree*, and *Newcastle* – have "summit bars" with views of Kili.

Aventure Africa 3km along the Dar highway. Live bands or discos (Fri & Sat), often with contests. Also has Internet access and food.

Bamboo Bar & Restaurant (no sign) Old Moshi Rd. A calm and welcoming bar popular with elderly office workers; the *nyama choma* and *ndizi* are among Moshi's best; there's also a pool table and TV.

Golden Shower 2km along the Moshi–Dar highway. This unfortunately named place makes for a good night out, especially its popular discos (Fri & Sat; Tsh1500 for men, women free), and there's food available. Catch a daladala to KDC or Kiboriloni; the last leaves town around 7.30pm.

Kilimanjaro Police Mess Mawenzi Rd. A large and friendly place for food and drinks, generally open 24hr. There's also satellite TV and a live band on Saturday from around 4pm until midnight (free).

Kindoroko Hotel Mawenzi Rd. The expensive rooftop summit bar is for hotel residents and tourists only, and has great Kili views; the distinctly more earthy but still attractive bar on the ground floor has a pool table and Internet café.

New Coffee Tree Hotel Old Moshi Rd. The top floor has unmatchable views of Kilimanjaro.

Pan Africa Hotel (no sign) Moshi–Arusha highway, 600m west of Kibo roundabout. There's a bar and *nyama choma* grill in the garden at the side of this very run-down hotel, but most people come for the discos (Fri–Sun; free), which are strangely popular with old men.

Pub Alberto Kibo Rd. Moshi's brashest nightclub, with all the loud music, lasers and spinning mirrored globes you might want, and plenty of spangled prostitutes too, though the music's pretty run-of-the-mill. There are also snacks and a pool table. Closed Mon.

Shopping

Moshi has far fewer **souvenir shops** than Arusha, but this is no bad thing – it's easier to choose, and a number of places stock stuff you simply won't find elsewhere. Local **bookshops** major on stodgy Christian texts, with little of interest for visitors except for some illustrated children's books which make great presents: try Moshi Bookshop, on the corner of Kibo Road and Rindi Lane, and the Lutheran Centre bookstore on Market Street. *Kilimanjaro Crane Hotel*'s gift shop stocks coffee table books. For Western novels, try the second-hand book stall at the corner of Mawenzi Road and Mankinga Street.

Crafts and souvenirs

Africulture Old Moshi Rd. The biggest crafts shop in town, and also happy to tailor clothes.

Kindoroko Hotel Mawenzi Rd. A small gift shop with the usual stuff, plus wire and aluminium can toys, exotic soaps and drums.

Our Heritage *The Coffee Shop*, Hill St. Carvings, batiks and "I climbed Kilimanjaro" T-shirts, plus cloth dolls from the Baptist Shangalia Women's Group, and stuff from Shah Industries.

Shah Industries Karakana St. A crafts workshop occupying an old flour mill, some of whose forty employees are disabled. They're happy to give free guided tours around the workshops and gardens, and also have a shop. Great for unusual curios fashioned out of cow horn, leather and pressed flowers, plus woodcarvings and batiks. Mon–Fri 8am–5pm, Sat 8am–1pm.

TAHEA-Kili Gallery Hill St, facing *The Coffee Shop*. More good stuff – batiks, carvings, fabrics and jewellery – this lot from a vocational training programme for young people and women.

Listings

Airlines Air Tanzania, Rengua St, near the clock tower ☏027/275 5205; Precisionair, Old Moshi Rd ☏027/275 3498. Also see "Travel agent".

Banks and exchange Reliable foreign exchanges include Executive, THB Building, Boma Rd (Mon–Sat 8am–5.30pm); Trust, corner of Mawenzi Rd and Chagga St (same hours); and Chase, Subzali Building, Rindi Lane (Mon–Fri 8am–5pm, Sat 8am–2pm; Visa cards accepted). Most banks levy hefty commissions; NBC, by the clock tower, is the exception, but takes forever. Much better is its 24hr Visa/MasterCard ATM; there's another machine at Standard Chartered on Rindi Lane.

Car rental Mauly Tours & Safaris (see p.345) charge $120–130 a day for a Land Cruiser with driver and fuel; $150 if self-drive, $1500 excess liability.

Car repairs Workshops along Bath Rd between Kaunda and Old Moshi roads. For Land Rovers, CMC is on Rengua St, opposite Air Tanzania. The *Golden Shower* campsite also has competent mechanics.

Courier services DHL, Kahawa House, by the clock tower (☏027/275 4030; Mon–Fri 8am–6pm, Sat 8am–12.30pm); EMS, at the main post office (Mon–Fri 8am–2.30pm, Sat 9.30am–noon).

Flying lessons Kilimanjaro Aero Club, Moshi Airport ☏027/275 0193, ⊛www.kilimanjaroaeroclub.com.

Hospitals KCMC (Kilimanjaro Christian Medical Centre), 6km north of town past Shanty Town

Moving on from Moshi

By bus

The **bus and daladala stand**, between Market Street and Mawenzi Road, has ticket offices in the central building, and clearly marked bays on either side: those on the north are for local daladalas, those on the south are for longer-distance minibuses and buses. The following **safer bus companies** (all running between Arusha and Dar) have their own terminals or offices: Akamba, on the corner of School and New streets (office; ☏027/275 3908; also goes to Nairobi); Dar Express, on Old Moshi Road, opposite the NBC bank (terminal; ☏0744/286847; also goes to Karatu); Royal Coach, on Kaunda Street (office; ☏0744/298274); and Scandinavian Express, on Mawenzi Road (terminal; ☏027/275 1387; also goes to Nairobi and Kampala).

The **Moshi–Arusha Highway** is extremely perilous, and the antics of the average driver are enough to kick in visions of your life in flashback; the Coaster minibuses, especially, crash with alarming – and fatal – frequency. Note that a popular Coaster scam involves having a sane and respectable-looking gentleman occupying the driver's seat whilst the vehicle is at the bus stand, only for him to be replaced by a red-eyed teenage lunatic at the exit...

Whilst the Moshi–Arusha Highway is Tanzania's most dangerous, you should also be on your guard on the run to Dar. Your safest bet is to travel only with one of the companies mentioned above. **Companies to avoid completely**, even if this means having to do a journey in two legs rather than one, include Abood, Air Bus, Air Msae, Buffalo, Hood, Kilimanjaro Express, Tashriff and Tawfiq.

Getting **to Nairobi** is easy, with three companies operating daily shuttle buses ($30) via Arusha. Safest are Impala Shuttle (☏027/275 1786, office on Kibo Rd beside *Chrisburger*; daily 6.30am & 11.30am), and Davanu Shuttle (☏027/275 3416, office at Kahawa House facing the clock tower; daily 11.30am). Either can pick you up at your hotel if you pre-book. Kenyan visas, currently $50, are easily bought at the Namanga border.

By air

The easiest way to **Kilimanjaro International Airport**, if you're flying with Air Tanzania or Precisionair, is on their free shuttle buses; contact their offices (see above) for more information. A taxi to the airport costs $25–50 depending on your bargaining skills. With more time than money, catch a bus towards Arusha and get off at the signposted airport junction 28km west, from where it's a 6km walk or hitch.

The Kenyan border at Taveta

It's possible to cross into Kenya at **Taveta**, 34km east of Moshi. Daladalas run hourly from Moshi to the border. The drawback is an hour's walk on the Kenyan side, if you can't find one of the enterprising locals running bicycle taxis from the border into town. There's a bank and plenty of decent accommodation in Taveta, which also provides access to **Lake Chala**, set in a stunningly picturesque volcanic crater on the eastern flank of Kilimanjaro – there's a hotel by the lake, but swimming is ill-advised. Onward travel in Kenya is by bus or *matatu* (daladala) to Voi or Mombasa.

(☏027/275 0748), is the best in northern Tanzania, but you need to be referred by a doctor unless it's an emergency. Blood tests can be done at Sima Hospital, Kenyatta St ☏027/275 1272 (24hr).

Immigration The Immigration Office is in Kibo House, Boma Rd, by the clock tower (Mon–Fri 7.30am–3pm; ☏027/275 2284).

Internet access Internet cafés charge Tsh1000/hr. Easy.com, Kahawa House, by the clock tower (daily 8am–8.30pm); Duma, Hill St (daily 9am–9pm); Twiga, next to *Buffalo Hotel*, (daily 7.30am–8pm); *Kindoroko Hotel* (daily 8am–11pm); TTCL (daily 8am–8pm).

Library Moshi Regional Library, Kibo Rd (Mon–Fri 9am–6pm; daily membership Tsh500).

Newspapers Newspaper hawkers hang around the bus and daladala stand; they sometimes have old copies of US or UK newspapers and magazines.

Pharmacies The dispensary at Sima Hospital, Kenyatta St, is open 24hr (☏027/275 1272) and does blood tests for malaria. Other well-stocked pharmacies include TM Pharmaceuticals, Mawenzi Rd (Mon–Sat 8am–9pm; ☏027/275 5032); and Kilimani Pharmaceutical, Hill St by Mawenzi Hospital (Mon–Sat 7am–9pm, Sun 8.30am–6pm; ☏027/275 1100).

Photography The main labs are Burhani Photographic Services and Moshi Colour Lab, both on Hill St.

Police Market St ☏027/275 5055.

Post The main office faces the clock tower. There's also a branch in a converted shipping crate on Market St, facing the police station.

Sport The Kilimanjaro Marathon (and half-marathon) is held every February: register through *Keys Hotel*.

Supermarkets Carina, Kibo Rd near *Pub Alberto* (Mon–Sat 8am–6.30pm); MDC, corner of Kawawa St and Florida Rd (Mon–Sat 7.30am–9pm); Highway Supermarket, Karanga Bridge (daily 7.30am–10pm); Mr Price, Kilimanjaro Rd (Mon–Sat 8am–9.30pm).

Swimming pools *YMCA Youth Hostel* (Tsh3000; 25m); *Keys Hotel* (Tsh3000; small and grotty, but there's a sauna for Tsh3000 for 30min); *Kilimanjaro Crane Hotel* (Tsh3000); *Kilimanjaro Impala Hotel* (Tsh3000); *Mountain Inn Lodge* (Tsh1500).

Telephones TTCL, next to the main post office on Market St (Mon–Fri 7.45am–4.30pm, Sat 9am–noon).

Travel agent Emslies, Old Moshi Rd ☏027/275 1742, ✉emslies.sales@eoltz.com.

Around Moshi

A number of flycatchers and hiking companies offer **day-trips** to various nearby sights, but there's nothing really organized. Costs average $25–40 per person per day depending on group size, mode of transport and bargaining skills. **Bicycles** can be rented informally at most hotels; the cost should be Tsh3000 a day, though Tsh10,000 is commonly asked of tourists. Possible destinations include hikes in **Kilimanjaro Forest Reserve** at Kibosho (15km north of town) and **Rau Forest** (10km northeast), and trips to see hot springs, waterfalls, and crocodiles in various locations (take care).

For something more established, consider the **cultural tourism programmes** in Marangu and Machame (see p.333) and east of Arusha (pp.414–417), most of which can also be accessed from Moshi.

Marangu

The base for most climbs up Kili is **MARANGU** village, an hour's drive northeast of Moshi. Marangu actually consists of two villages, both situated on the sealed road leading to the park gate: **Marangu–Arisi** is the section closest to the park, whilst **Marangu–Mtoni** is at the crossroads to Mamba and Rombo, 5.6km short of the park.

There's more to Marangu than just a base for climbing the mountain, however. Marangu's hotels can arrange a number of **guided walks** in the area – the scenery is superb, especially close to the park, where you get unobstructed views of the Pare Mountains, Kenya's Taita–Taveta plains and Lake Jipe, Nyumba ya Mungu reservoir and, of course, Kibo (weather permitting).

Practicalities

Frequent **daladalas** from Moshi (roughly 8am–6pm) cover the 30km to Marangu-Mtoni. If you don't fancy the walk uphill from there to the park gate, there are occasional daladalas from around 9am. **Camping** is possible at *Bismark Hut Lodge* ($3–5 per tent); *Kibo Hotel* ($5 per person, including use of kitchen and pool); *Kilimanjaro Mountain Resort* ($5; tent hire $5); and at *Coffee Tree Campsite* ($8; tent hire $10). **Hotels** are lacking in the budget range, but the price to quality ratio improves as you move upscale. Ensure your bed has adequate mosquito nets – Marangu's zillion banana plants favour the critters. All hotels have luggage stores for climbers.

Babylon Lodge 1km east of Marangu-Mtoni off the Rombo road ☎027/275 6355, ⓦwww .babylonlodge.com. Fifteen good if rather pricey en-suite twins and doubles in modern buildings scattered across a slope; functional rather than memorable. There's also a restaurant and bar, safe parking, and free guides to waterfalls. Breakfast included. ❹

Bismark Hut Lodge 4km from the park gate ☎0744/318338, ⓔbismarklodge@yahoo.com. Sad to say, but the basic rooms here (bathrooms but no running water) are the cheapest in town. There's also a somnolent bar and food. ❹

Hotel Capricorn 2.7km from the park gate ☎027/275 1309, ⓦwww.capricornhotel.com. A large, attractive option dominated by a vast conical roof and lush gardens. Rooms in the old two-storey blocks have bathtubs; new wing rooms, for $10 more, have showers but also have balconies, digital TV, fridge, phone and safe; get one facing south, as the others are very dark. Good restaurant (meals $10–12), atmospheric bar, and gift shop, but no pool (yet). A gym and Internet café are planned. Breakfast included. ❻

Coffee Tree Campsite 2km from the park gate ☎027/275 6604, ⓦwww.alpinesafari.com. The spartan but clean dorm-like accommodation here ($10–12 a mattress) is handy for a cheapish night before a climb, and paradise when you return, thanks to its sauna ($10 for 30min). Self-catering is best, as meals are expensive (Tsh10,000–15,000) and take ages in coming. Internet access. ❹

Kibo Hotel 1.4km west of Marangu-Mtoni ☎027/275 1308, ⓦwww.kibohotel.com. A rambling old hotel from German times with tons of charm, set in beautiful and slightly wild gardens. There are plenty of verandahs, nooks and crannies throughout, and the entire place is adorned with old prints, maps and antiques – and expedition flags and T-shirts in the dining room. Bedrooms are in two wings: the most atmospheric (#1–7) are in the main building, many with bathtubs; the first-floor ones have south-facing balconies with great views. Facilities include a small swimming pool, wonderfully cosy pub-like bar, a huge central fireplace in the adjacent lounge, and good meals (three-course lunch $9, dinner $14; à la carte mains around $5). Breakfast included. ❺

Kilimanjaro Mountain Resort 1.5km west of *Kibo Hotel* ☎027/275 8950, ⓦwww .kilimanjaromtresort.com. A mountain of money was used to build this vaguely Neoclassical place, more like a private mansion than hotel. The rooms – large twins or doubles – are well appointed, with parquet floors, shiny bathrooms with large bathtubs, phone and digital TV, hair-drier and fridge; the better ones have balconies, whilst two enormous triples occupy all of the second floor, one with a view of Kibo. There's also Internet access, a first-floor balcony for meals ($8–10), food also in a thatched bar at the back, tended gardens with a duck pond and kids' playground. Breakfast included. ❻

Marangu Hotel 2km south of Marangu-Mtoni ☎ 027/275 6594, ⓦ www.maranguhotel.com. Originally a coffee farm started by Czech immigrants in 1907, this became a guest house in the 1930s – though extensive modernization has robbed it of some of its charm. The rooms, mostly en-suite twins in cottages scattered around spacious gardens, are darkish and very basic for the price; some are rather worn out too, though most have views of Kili. Facilities include a good swimming pool, croquet lawn, bar, filling and tasty meals (light lunches mostly Tsh2000–2500, including lasagne, or a five-course set dinner for $10 – pre-order), gift shops and safe parking. Their hiking operation has an excellent reputation. Half-board. ❼

Walks around Marangu

You can get hassled a lot walking around Marangu, with most young men assuming you're only there to hire guides and porters for climbing the mountain; their persistent attention quickly becomes tedious. Marangu's **cultural tourism programme** circumvents some of the hassle, and of course opens the door to a side of local life you might not otherwise see. The tours are all easy half-day walks (which can be combined into one- or two-day trips) and include excursions inside the park to **Mandara Hut** (including Maundi Crater and a waterfall); **Mamba village**, 3km east towards Rombo, for traditional blacksmiths and a woodcarving school; a 120-year-old Catholic mission church at **Kilema village**, whose relics include what is purported to be a piece of Christ's own cross, and in whose grounds Kilimanjaro's first coffee tree was planted; and a nature hike up **Ngangu Hill** on the west side of Marangu, for a great view and a cave containing the remains of a former chief. Seven **waterfalls** around Marangu can also be visited. The closest are Kinukamori Falls, 1km north of Marangu-Mtoni, and Ndoro Waterfalls, 2km west of Marangu-Mtoni past *Kibo Hotel*, and in whose splashpool you can swim. The family that owns the site is planning to open a campsite and restaurant. You can visit the waterfalls on your own, as they're signposted (admission fees average Tsh3000–4000), but you'll probably be followed by a gaggle of wannabe guides.

Unfortunately, the tourism programme lacks a central office, so trips are arranged through the hotels reviewed above. **Bogus guides** are out in force, so don't arrange anything on the street, and don't necessarily believe ID cards either. **Prices** vary enormously: under $25 for one person over a full day would be reasonable (or $90 for the Mandara Hut walk, including national park entrance fee), though twice that is often quoted – definitely a rip-off. The cheapest and most reliable place to book tours is *Kibo Hotel*, which charges $5 per person for the guide (up to a day) plus entrance fees (usually $3–4 per person per site). *Coffee Tree Campsite* charges $10 per person plus entrance fees.

Lastly, if you're into culture or music, there's the modest **Chagga Life Museum**, just outside *Kilimanjaro Mountain Lodge* (daily 10am–4pm; Tsh2000). This traces the history of the Chagga, and especially of Marangu's Marealle clan, back over seventeen generations, and also displays all sorts of tools, implements and drums, all labelled in English. There's a reconstructed traditional house outside resembling a haystack, and the affable and knowledgeable curator can fill you in on the details.

Machame

On the southwestern side of the mountain, **MACHAME** – the village at the start of Kilimanjaro's second most popular climbing route – is set in a beautiful area of steep valleys, thick forests, streams and fertile farmland, and has good views of the summit to boot. Most visitors only pass through en route to climbing the mountain (the Machame route is for ascent only), so there are no tourist

Kilimanjaro on horseback

Well, not exactly. On Kili's southwestern flank, close to Machame, is the 358-acre **Makoa Farm** (☏0744/312896, ⓦ www.makoa-farm.com). Aside from producing coffee, it offers **horseback safaris** in the plains west and south of Kili, as far afield as Nyumba ya Mungu reservoir in the Maasai Steppe, should you have eleven days to spare. Of particular interest are **Kukuletwa Hot Springs** – actually cool (swimming is possible), but the sound of the water bubbling out of the ground will convince you it's boiling. Most rides give sight of small plains game and primates. To get the most out of things, prior riding experience is desirable, although beginners can try things out for half a day around the farm ($60 including lunch), and there are options for non-riders too, such as guided nature walks. **Costs** average $200 per person per day, including accommodation, either at the farm (delicious food), or under canvas.

To reach the farm, head up 5km from the highway towards Machame, turn left after Lombo (Rombo) Primary School, and it's 1km along on the far side of Makoa River.

facilities other than an infrequently visited **cultural tourism programme**, which offers a variety of guided walks and the chance to meet the locals.

Practicalities

Daladalas run hourly (7am–6pm) from Moshi's main bus stand, taking about an hour. Alternatively, catch a daladala or bus towards Arusha and get off at the signposted junction 12km west, where other daladalas connect with Machame – 14km to the north – every ten minutes or so from 8am to around 6pm. The park gate lies 4km beyond the village.

Apart from homestays arranged through the cultural tourism programme (around Tsh3000 per person), and *Makoa Farm* for horse riders (see the box above), **accommodation** is limited to the much recommended ⚹ *Protea Hotel Aishi Machame* (☏027/275 6948, ⓦ www.proteahotels.com; ❼ with full breakfast), 6km from the Moshi–Arusha Highway. The hotel boasts thirty well-equipped rooms with TVs in a stylish three-storey block with tree bark roof tiles or in bungalows, all set in lush gardens with ponds, boardwalks and hundreds of banana plants. Facilities include a good restaurant (meals $13–15), solar-heated swimming pool (Tsh5000 for day visitors), sauna and steam room. Various optional excursions include Lake Chala on the Kenyan border ($80 per person), and Arusha National Park ($95 per person).

Walks around Machame

The **cultural tourism programme**, run by Foo Development Association or FODA (☏027/275 7033, ⓔfodamachame@yahoo.com) is based at Kyalia near Foo village, about 1km beyond Machame. Costs should be no more than $25 a day, all included. Make sure you arrange things through the office itself and not through someone on the street. There are several hikes, including the fascinating **Sienye-Ngira tour** (4–6hr) through Sienye rainforest to Masama village, southwest of Machame. The trip can be extended over two days to include **Ng'uni**, upstream from Masama, with great views over the plains, where you learn about constructing traditional *mbii* houses.

A good longer trip is the **Lyamungo tour** (two to three days) to the coffee-producing village of Lyamungo, southeast of Machame, which passes through Muwe and Nkuu villages and along the Weruweru River. The trip includes hikes through rainforest, visits to the Lyamungo Coffee Research Institute and Narumu Women Pottery Centre, and overnight stays with local families.

Mount Kilimanjaro

As wide as all the world, great, high, and unbelievably white in the sun, was the square top of Kilimanjaro.

Hemingway, *The Snows of Kilimanjaro*

The ice-capped, dormant volcano that is **MOUNT KILIMANJARO**, has exerted an irresistible fascination since it was "discovered" by Europeans in the mid-nineteenth century. Rising over 5km from the surrounding plains to a peak of 5891m, Kilimanjaro – a national park, and a World Heritage Site since 1989 – is Africa's highest mountain, the world's tallest free-standing massif and one of the world's largest volcanoes, covering some 3885 square kilometres. It is also an exceptionally beautiful mountain, both from afar and close up, and fills up brochures as easily as it does the horizon.

The mountain was formed during the most recent faulting of the Great Rift Valley two to three million years ago, an event that also produced Mount Meru and Mount Kenya. Kilimanjaro has three main peaks, together with parasitic volcanic cones and craters dotted around its sides. The youngest and highest peak is the distinctive snow-capped dome of **Kibo**, actually a large crater that was formed around 100,000 years ago during the last period of major volcanic activity. Kibo's highest point is **Uhuru Peak** on the crater's southwestern rim, whose official height of 5895m was downsized to 5891.6m in 2000 after a topographical satellite survey. Eleven kilometres to the east of Kibo (to which it's connected by a broad lava saddle) is the jagged pimple-like **Mawenzi**, all that remains of a volcanic cone that lost its eastern rim in a gigantic explosion. Its highest point is Hans Meyer Peak (5149m). The oldest peak is **Shira Cone**, on the west side of the mountain, which has mostly collapsed, leaving a spectacular lava plug.

For many visitors, the prospect of scaling the mountain is as exciting as it is daunting. The fact that no technical climbing skills are required to reach the summit (it's the world's highest non-technical climb) means that Kilimanjaro has acquired something of an easy reputation – a dangerous misconception, and one which you should ignore. The high altitude and the possibility of a quick ascent mean that an average of a dozen people lose their lives every year, usually as victims of **acute mountain sickness** (see box on p.343). In addition, almost everybody gets afflicted with screaming headaches and utter exhaustion on summit day, meaning that of the 30,000 people who attempt the climb every year, less than a third make it all the way to Uhuru Peak. Having said this, if you take your time and stay attentive to your body's needs, there's no reason why you shouldn't be able to make it to the top. The mountain also offers plenty of less strenuous alternatives for those for whom the prospect of summiting smacks of a mite too much masochism: a walk on the lower slopes, through rainforest and on to the edge of sub-alpine moorland, makes no extreme fitness demands, and can be done in a day.

Some history

Contrary to the assumption of Eurocentric historians, Kilimanjaro has been known to non-Africans since at least the sixth century, when Chinese mariners reported a "great mountain" inland. The mountain may even have been known in Ptolemy's time, although the snowy "mountains of the moon" referred to in his *Geography* are more likely to have been the Ruwenzori Mountains on the border of Congo and Uganda.

△ Mount Kilimanjaro

Although a Spanish geographer writing in 1519 mentioned "the Ethiopian Mount Olympus, which is very high, and further off are the mountains of the Moon in which are the sources of the Nile", Europe remained ignorant of Kilimanjaro until 1848, when the German missionary **Johannes Rebmann**, having given up trying to convert coastal tribes to Christianity, headed inland to try his luck elsewhere. His report, published the following year, of a snow-capped mountain three degrees south of the Equator was met with scorn and ridicule back home, and it wasn't until 1861, when Kilimanjaro was scaled to a height of around 4300m by Dr Otto Kersten and Baron Karl Klaus von der Decken, that his report was accepted by the likes of the Royal Geographical Society. The first Europeans to reach the summit were the German geographer **Hans Meyer** and Austrian mountaineer **Ludwig Purtscheller**, who reached Kibo on October 5, 1889. Mawenzi was climbed in 1912.

The origin of the **mountain's name** is confusing. To some explorers, it meant "that which cannot be conquered" or "that which renders a journey impossible". To others it was the "mountain of greatness", the "spotted mountain", the "white mountain" or the "mountain of caravans". The first part of the name is actually quite simple, as in both Kiswahili and Kichagga (the Chagga language), *mlima* means mountain, while *kilima* is a hill. The use of the diminutive could be affectionate, though Chagga place names are often preceded with *ki*, as are names around Mount Kenya – whose dominant Kikuyu and Kamba tribes are related to the Chagga. The second half of the name remains vague, however: *njaro* may be related to a Kichagga word for caravan, a throw-back to the slave and ivory trade, or to an old word for God, *kyaro*. An alternative meaning stems from the Maasai word *ngare*, meaning river – Kilimanjaro, of course, being the source of life for several of these.

The Chagga have a wonderful tale about the origin of Kilimanjaro's main peaks, **Kibo and Mawenzi**, who, they say, were sisters. Kibo was the wiser of the two, and was careful to store away food for times of hardship. Her sister, Mawenzi, however, had no such cares for the future, and fell into the habit of asking Kibo for help whenever times were bad. Eventually, Kibo became angry with her sister's begging, and hit her on the head with a spoon, hence Mawenzi's ragged and broken appearance. Another Chagga legend, apparently related to distant tales of King Solomon, speaks of a great treasure on the mountain,

Meltdown: the end of Kilimanjaro's ice cap?

Incredible though it might seem, Kibo's emblematic white cap may soon be no more. Kilimanjaro is heating up, and its ice cap and glaciers are retreating at an alarming rate. In 1912, the ice cap covered just over twelve square kilometres. By 2005, it had shrunk to under two square kilometres, having diminished by a full third over the previous fifteen years.

The primary cause is **global warming**, as worryingly proven by recent research using core samples of the ice cap as a weather archive – researchers even found datable radioactive fall-out from nuclear bomb tests halfway around the globe. Hapless park and forest management has also done little to stop the ongoing **destruction of forest cover** on the mountain's lower slopes, through illegal logging and uncontrolled fires courtesy of honey-gatherers, poachers and careless farmers. Forests trap solar heat, so less forest means warmer ambient air, in turn hastening the big thaw.

Researchers believe that the ice cap will have disappeared completely sometime between 2014 and 2021 – eleven thousand years after the peak last lost its snowy crown.

one protected by powerful spirits who punished those foolhardy enough to dare climb it – extreme cold, exhaustion and altitude sickness are the very real modern forms of those spirits. This legend encouraged a curious expedition to the mountain by the Ethiopian **King Menelik II** in 1896, who is said to have been seeking the mortal remains of his thirteenth-century namesake, King Menelik I, the son of Solomon and the Queen of Sheba. According to this tale, King Menelik I was wearing King Solomon's regalia when he froze to death on the mountain.

Practicalities

Kilimanjaro National Park covers the entire mountain above the tree line (approximately 2750m), together with six forest corridors running down to around 2000m. The most popular **routes up the mountain** start at the villages of Marangu and Machame respectively. Increasingly popular, too, is the Shira route, and its longer variant, the Lemosho route.

Anyone wanting to climb Kilimanjaro must be accompanied by an officially accredited guide. Given the Soviet-style **bureaucracy** and corruption currently prevailing, going with a dedicated hiking company is by far the easiest way, saving you a lot of potential hassle in hiring guides and porters, paying park fees, dealing with obstructive officials, locating suitable equipment, booking hut space on the Marangu route, and so on. Reliable companies in Moshi and Marangu are reviewed on p.345; see also the Arusha safari company reviews in Chapter 6. Incidentally, **children under 10** are not allowed further than the tree line.

Information, guidebooks and maps

The **park headquarters** at Marangu Gate (daily 8am–6pm; ☎027/275 3195, ✉kinapa@habari.co.tz) are useless for specialized queries, but do sell maps and books. The most up-to-date **guidebook**, published by TANAPA ($10), is available in Moshi's gift shops, and bookshops in Arusha, Dar and Stone Town. Also recommended are the *Kilimanjaro New Millennium Guide* by Thomas Alexander, covering the Marangu and Machame routes; Cameron Burns' detailed *Kilimanjaro & Mount Kenya: A Climbing and Trekking Guide* (Mountaineers Books); and *Trekking in East Africa* by David Else (Lonely Planet).

There's lots of information on the **Internet**, including dozens of journey accounts. A good place to start is the Kilimanjaro Summit Log at ⓦwww.peakware.com, with hundreds of detailed tips and comments from climbers. The park's official page is ⓦwww.tanzaniaparks.com/kili.htm. See also two sites dedicated to ameliorating working conditions for Kili's long-abused porters: the Kilimanjaro Porters' Assistance Project at ⓦwww.mountainexplorers.org, and Kilimanjaro Guides and Porters Union at ⓦwww.kilimanjaro-union.com.

Given that you'll be accompanied by a guide, **maps** aren't essential, but taking one is recommended for plotting your route, putting names to geological features and gauging distances and elevations – a guide's conception of "not far" can differ radically from your own. The best is the contoured *Tourist Map of Kilimanjaro* published by the Government's Surveys and Mapping Division, although its summit plan isn't too clear; the 1:80,000 *Kilimanjaro Map and Guide* by Andrew Wielschowski is also good. The most attractive maps are the colour 1:62,500 *Kilimanjaro* map from International Travel Maps' *Mountains of the World* series, with full contours (but no heights other than peaks); and Giovanni Tombazzi's hand-painted *New Map of Kilimanjaro*, with good inserts on flora.

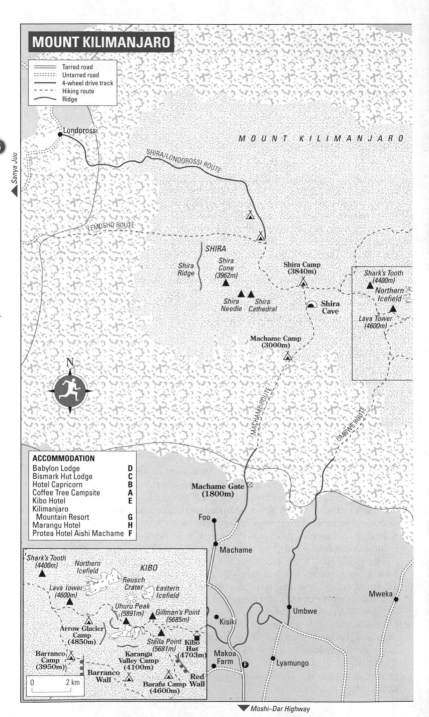

MOUNT KILIMANJARO

- Tarred road
- Untarred road
- 4-wheel drive track
- Hiking route
- Ridge

◀ Sanya Juu

Londorossi

MOUNT KILIMANJARO

SHIRA/LONDOROSSI ROUTE

LEMOSHO ROUTE

SHIRA

Shira Ridge

Shira Cone (3962m)

Shira Camp (3840m)

Shira Needle

Shira Cathedral

Shira Cave

Shark's Tooth (4400m)

Northern Icefield

Lava Tower (4600m)

Machame Camp (3000m)

MACHAME ROUTE

UMBWE ROUTE

N

ACCOMMODATION

Babylon Lodge	D
Bismark Hut Lodge	C
Hotel Capricorn	B
Coffee Tree Campsite	A
Kibo Hotel	E
Kilimanjaro Mountain Resort	G
Marangu Hotel	H
Protea Hotel Aishi Machame	F

Machame Gate (1800m)

Foo

Machame

Umbwe

Mweka

Kisiki

Makoa Farm

Lyamungo

KIBO

Shark's Tooth (4400m)

Northern Icefield

Lava lower (4600m)

Reusch Crater

Eastern Icefield

Uhuru Peak (5891m)

Gillman's Point (5685m)

Arrow Glacier Camp (4850m)

Stella Point (5681m)

Kibo Hut (4703m)

Barranco Camp (3950m)

Karanga Valley Camp (4100m)

Barranco Wall

Red Wall

Barafu Camp (4600m)

0   2 km

▼ Moshi–Dar Highway

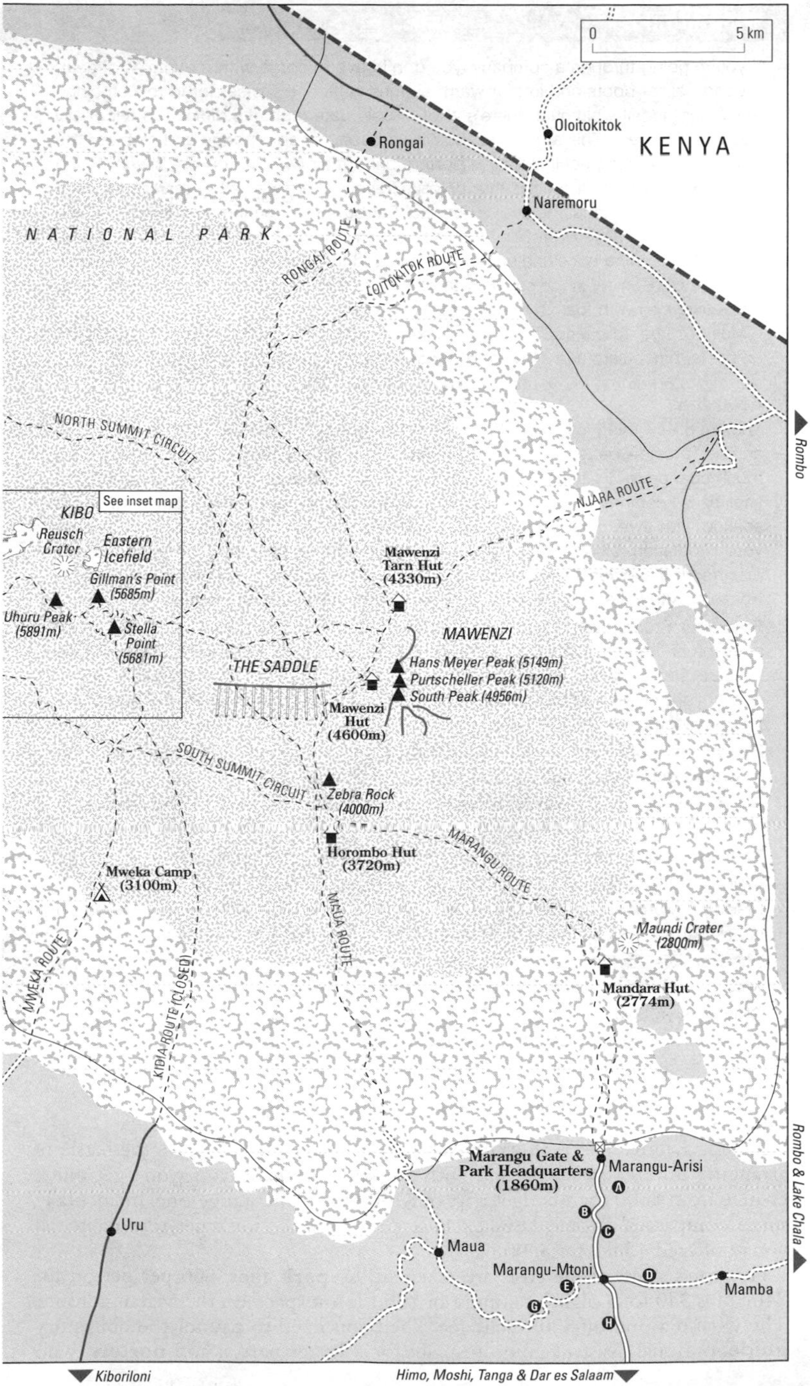

0   5 km

Oloitokitok

Rongai

Naremoru

KENYA

NATIONAL PARK

RONGAI ROUTE

LOITOKITOK ROUTE

NJARA ROUTE

▶ Rombo

NORTH SUMMIT CIRCUIT

KIBO

See inset map

Reusch
Crater

Eastern
Icefield

Gillman's Point
(5685m)

Uhuru Peak
(5891m)

Stella
Point
(5681m)

THE SADDLE

Mawenzi
Tarn Hut
(4330m)

MAWENZI

Hans Meyer Peak (5149m)
Purtscheller Peak (5120m)
South Peak (4956m)

Mawenzi
Hut
(4600m)

SOUTH SUMMIT CIRCUIT

Zebra Rock
(4000m)

MARANGU ROUTE

Horombo Hut
(3720m)

MWEKA ROUTE

Mweka Camp
(3100m)

MSIA ROUTE

KIBIA ROUTE CLOSED

Maundi Crater
(2800m)

Mandara Hut
(2774m)

▶ Rombo & Lake Chala

Uru

Maua

**Marangu Gate &
Park Headquarters
(1860m)**

Marangu-Arisi

Ⓐ

Ⓑ

Ⓒ

Ⓓ

Marangu-Mtoni

Ⓔ

Ⓖ

Ⓗ

Mamba

339

▼ Kiboriloni

Himo, Moshi, Tanga & Dar es Salaam ▼

What to take

If you're going through a company, you don't have to come with mountains of gear: a good pair of boots and lots of warm clothes suffice. It's wise not to rely on hiring equipment locally; although there's a lot of adequate stuff, it's difficult to find really good-quality gear. This applies especially to boots, sleeping bags and clothes. You don't need cooking equipment, as porters bring their own. If you don't want to lug around heaps of stuff for the rest of your travels, there's a ready market for used equipment in Marangu, Moshi and Arusha. For buying or renting gear in Arusha, see p.400. In Moshi, *Keys Hotel* has a good selection. The park headquarters at Marangu Gate sells sleeping bags and spare trousers, and the kiosk of the Kilimanjaro Guides Cooperative Society in the car park there also rents stuff: for an idea of costs, hiring a sleeping bag with foam mat costs $60 per climb.

Most of the following items are essential. Optional items include a compact umbrella, binoculars and a reflective metallic "space blanket" for emergencies.

Clothing

The important thing is to wear layers – several levels of clothing worn on top of one another provide better insulation than fewer but bulkier items. As you won't have much chance to dry things out (open fires are no longer permitted), waterproofs are vital, as is keeping spare clothes dry. Don't wear cotton next to your skin or you'll get soaked with sweat, leaving you cold and miserable. Too-tight clothing will hamper your circulation, also making you cold. Normal clothes to pack include shorts and T-shirts for the lower slopes, a couple of woolly jumpers and two pairs of comfortable trousers. A towel and scarf are also handy. Essential specialist clothing is:

Footwear Sturdy, well-broken-in and waterproof hiking boots are vital for the upper sections of the trek. Comfortable shoes with good grip are sufficient on lower slopes (in fact, some porters manage amazingly well with flip-flops). Wear two pairs of socks: light ones next to the skin, and a thick pair of wool or synthetic ones. Use thermal socks at higher altitudes.

Headwear A brimmed sun hat to avoid sunburn, and a fetching balaclava (or scarf to wrap around your head) – a godsend on summit day.

Sunglasses Essential to avoid snow-blindness; ensure they're screened against UV radiation.

Thermal underwear Long-johns and hiking socks; polypropylene works well but avoid cotton.

Fleece A warm fleece jacket is essential, and a fleece sweater wouldn't go amiss either. You could take two sets – one for hiking, the other for sleeping in.

Waterproofs Jacket and trousers or gaiters. Should be lightweight and made of a windproof, breathable material like Gore-Tex.

Gloves or mittens Ideally down-lined. Mittens are warmer; you can also buy Gore-Tex outer mittens for breathable waterproofing.

Costs

Climbing Kilimanjaro is an **expensive** business, even if you brave the hassle of arranging things yourself. Going with a hiking company, you won't get much change from $800 for a budget trip, or $1300 for a mid-range one. Incidentally, some companies' quoted rates exclude park fees, so don't get too excited if you're offered a hike for $300.

The lion's share of the costs are taken up by **park fees**: $60 per person for 24hr, plus $40 for a night's camping or $50 for hut space on the Marangu route. There's also a one-off $20 rescue fee. Then you need to pay for the obligatory **guide**, optional assistant guide (usually for a larger party), and **porters**, who

Equipment

Backpack The porters carry your main pack but tend to dash off ahead, so bring a small daypack to carry stuff you'll need by day, like water bottles, snacks, toiletries, camera, waterproofs and gloves. Don't pack too much weight, and ensure the straps don't dig into your shoulders.

Sleeping bag An insulated synthetic sleeping bag ("-10", "five-seasons" or "zero-rated") is essential: you might experience night-time temperatures of -25°C at the top. Insulating mats are usually provided by the tour operator.

Tent Essential on all but the Marangu route (where camping is banned). Your operator should provide one. If you bring your own, make sure it's light and insulated – the collapsible dome variety is ideal.

Torch With spare batteries (wrap them up well to stop the cold killing them).

Walking stick or trekking pole Saves your knees on the descent.

Water bottles Enough for three litres, and a way of insulating them. A thermos flask for soup or something hot is a boon at the top.

Miscellaneous

Camera Keep your camera dry: on lower slopes, mist and rain drenches everything, so wrap it in something soft and insulating and stash it away in a sealable plastic bag. In sub-zero temperatures, batteries die and delicate shutter mechanisms jam with frozen condensation, so don't put cameras unprotected in your pocket as body heat condenses vapour. A small tripod is helpful in low light or if you're shivering.

Money Small notes and coins for buying drinks and snacks along the Marangu route.

Plastic bags Bring more than you think you'll need to keep things dry, and to carry down rubbish.

Toilet paper A roll of toilet paper is useful – but put used paper in a bag to dispose of at the next long-drop.

Snacks Sugary, high-energy snacks are always useful: chocolate, nuts, sweets and energy drinks.

Medicine bag

Apart from your standard medicine bag (see p.36), and optional high-altitude medication (see p.343), you should take plasters, bandages and gauze, sweets (to keep your throat moist), eye drops, lip salve, and suncream (minimum factor 25) – you can be burned even through cloud. You could also take a rehydration mix, consisting of one part salt to eight parts sugar, to mix with water; the solution tastes horrible but will keep you hydrated and doesn't freeze as readily as pure water.

often double as cooks – generally one per climber plus one for the guide. Salaries are negotiable, but no more than $40 from the group to the guide for the trip, $30 to an assistant guide, and $25 for each porter. **Additional costs** include food, equipment rental, and transport to and from the park gates.

Don't forget to factor in **gratuities**. One tenth of the total cost of the trip would be about right, though exactly how much to tip is a perennial headache (leaving unneeded equipment with the guide and porters after the climb is welcome, but no substitute for a cash tip), not helped by the sour mood of some climbers who fail to reach the top or by the constant and not-so-subtle hints from the guide and porters that can plague some trips. The best way to deal with it is to say you'll pay when you get down, but don't tie the promise of tips with a successful summit attempt: you'll be encouraging the guide to take risks, and in any case success depends more on your body and attitude than on the guide and porters. On the other hand, if the guide or porters were terrible, don't tip at all – but do explain to them why.

When to go

The most popular climbing **season** is December to February, when the weather is generally clear. June to September are also good, though there's a chance of rain in June, and September can be devilishly cold. Kilimanjaro can be climbed during the intervening **rainy seasons**, but the lower slopes will be exceedingly muddy and there's no guarantee of clear skies higher up. The southeastern slopes receive most rain, meaning that the Machame and Shira/Lemosho routes are generally drier than the Marangu route. It can snow on or near the summit all year round, though chances are highest during and shortly after the rainy seasons. Try to coincide with a **full moon** on summit day – it avoids the need for flashlights, and lends an eerie beauty to the scene.

Guides and porters

If you're going through a hiking company, guides and porters are provided, so you can skip this section. Climbers must be accompanied by at least one officially licensed **guide**, who should possess a permit issued by KINAPA. The names of accredited guides are kept at Marangu and Machame entrance gates. There are dozens of guides (and even more porters) waiting for work outside the park gates – ensure that whoever you employ is experienced, especially on routes other than the Marangu. Refrain from paying until you've checked out the guide's credentials at the gate. Despite these caveats, most of the guides are superb: many have climbed the mountain innumerable times, and they're usually fluent in English.

Most climbers also hire **porters**; the guide can do this on your behalf, but settle the price beforehand and ensure that the porters receive the sum. Although unscrupulous hiking companies expect porters to carry up to 50kg of gear, it's both unethical and dangerous: just hire a few more porters to distribute the load (no more than 15kg each), and try to carry at least some stuff yourself. Incidentally, porters don't scale the summit, but stay at the last hut or campsite to pick you up on the way down. Most porters double as cooks, and rustle up some surprisingly delicious nosh.

Preparation and pacing

It cannot be said enough that the more days you have on the mountain, the higher are your chances of success – and the more time you'll have to enjoy the scenery. Small group sizes are also better, as the guide can be more attentive to your needs. A positive **mental attitude** is the key to success: climbing Kilimanjaro is difficult and usually painful, so brace yourself for a big effort and don't be overly confident – the bigger they come, the harder they fall. Being adequately equipped and in good **physical condition** also helps your attitude. You don't have to be an athlete, but cut down on alcohol and cigarettes a few weeks before the climb, go cycling to tune up your lungs, and walk or jog to get your legs in shape. If you have the time and money, a climb up Mount Meru is recommended to help your body acclimatize. On the mountain itself, **take care of your body's needs**. Your appetite may vanish at high altitude, so make the effort to eat properly. You should also drink enough to keep your urine clear (generally 4–5 litres of water a day), taken in sips throughout the hike. Also, try

Altitude sickness

Air gets thinner the higher you go; on the summit of Kilimanjaro, a lungful contains only half the oxygen you would inhale at sea level. Given enough time, the human body can adapt to an oxygen-scarce environment by producing more red blood cells. But, without weeks to acclimatize, almost everyone climbing Kili will experience the effects of high altitude, known as **altitude (or mountain) sickness**: these include shortness of breath, light-headedness, headaches, nausea, insomnia and, naturally enough, exhaustion. The symptoms appear towards the end of the second or third day. Normal altitude sickness isn't much to worry about, although vomiting should be treated seriously (staying hydrated is absolutely essential at high altitude).

Much more serious is **acute mountain sickness (AMS)**, the chronic form of altitude sickness. Symptoms of AMS include most of the above, plus one or more of the following: severe headache; shortness of breath at rest; flu-like symptoms; persistent dry cough; blood-tinged saliva or urine; unsteadiness or drowsiness; lack of mental clarity or hallucinations; and chest congestion. In these cases, **descend immediately** to a lower altitude. Be aware that mental fuzziness may convince the victim that he or she is fit to continue – they're not. A porter will usually accompany the victim, so the whole party won't have to turn back. Ignoring the symptoms of AMS can be fatal: complications like pulmonary oedema and cerebral oedema claim the lives of about a dozen climbers each year. Predicting who will get sick is impossible: AMS affects young and old alike, the fit and the not-so-fit, so don't deny the signs if you start feeling them, and heed your guide's advice.

Some **drugs** are claimed to eliminate such problems. However, opinion is sharply divided over their pros and cons, so consult a doctor before taking anything. The controversy is fiercest over the most commonly taken drug, **Diamox** (acetazolamide; available in Moshi's pharmacies at Tsh400 a tablet), since no one seems to know whether it treats the cause of AMS or just masks the symptoms, which in the latter case could hide vital warning signs (like splitting headaches) that herald potentially life-threatening conditions. The British Medical Association suggests you start taking it three days before reaching high altitude (approximately 4000m), meaning on the morning of the first day for a six-day climb, or the day before on a five-day climb. The drug has two well-known short-term **side effects**: your fingers tingle, and the drug is an extremely efficient diuretic, so you'll be urinating every few hours both day and night – drink lots of water to compensate. Some (unconfirmed) reports suggest that in rare cases the tingling or numbness in fingers may persist for several years. Nonetheless, most climbers do tend to have an easier time of things when on Diamox. As an alternative, some climbers swear by **gingko biloba** (120mg taken twice a day, starting a few days before the climb). Don't take it if you bleed easily. The occasionally touted regimen of **aspirin and codeine** tablets appears only to mask the symptoms, and could be extremely dangerous.

Given the confusion over medication, **prevention** is a better approach: let your body acclimatize naturally by taking an extra day or two when climbing the mountain (at least six days, whichever route you're taking, ideally seven or eight – or else climb Mount Meru the preceding week to help acclimatize); stay hydrated; climb slowly; and if you ascend a lot in one day, camp at a lower altitude, if possible. Lastly, don't go higher than the tree line (2700m) if you're suffering from fever, nose bleed, cold or influenza, sore throat or a respiratory infection.

to sleep properly, though this can be difficult at high altitude. For the night of the summit attempt, bring lots of energy foods and water.

The other key to success is to **take your time** – start early at a deliberately slow pace and take frequent rests and you'll find the ascent much less painful than if you charge up. On summit day, go very slowly (not that you'll feel like running), take five-minute rests every half-hour, drink plenty of fluids and breathe through a balaclava or scarf to minimize heat and fluid loss. When short of breath, inhale and exhale deeply and rapidly four or five times. Near the top, stay focused: don't be put off by grumbling climbers descending after failed attempts, and remember that the pleasure lies in the journey, not necessarily in reaching the destination. Also, be aware of your limitations, and listen to your guide – if he suggests you go no further, don't – he knows what he's talking about. Lastly, when **descending**, take it slow – the greatest risk of injury is on the way down, so use a walking stick or ski pole, and resist the temptation to slide down the scree.

The routes

There are three main routes up Kilimanjaro. Descent is usually along the Mweka or Marangu routes in the south. **Overnights** on the Marangu route are in a chain of relatively comfortable cabins; all other routes require camping, usually at recognized campsites equipped with long-drops and nothing much else. The "uniport" huts along these routes are for guides, porters and rangers only.

The **Marangu route**, approaching from the southeast, is the quickest, steepest and most popular way up (and down). Though usually offered as a five-day trek, an extra day considerably increases your chances of reaching the top.

The **Machame route**, from the southwest, is the next most popular, requiring at least six days, seven being recommended. It's slower and more sedate than the Marangu (though it has some trying hands-and-feet scrambles), has campsites instead of huts, and enjoys more varied scenery.

The third main route is the distinctly less-travelled **Shira route** from the northwest, drivable to around 3600m – it can take just five days, but six or seven are recommended, whilst eight days are required for its longer variant, the **Lemosho route**.

Other routes – requiring special permission or a specialized hiking operator – include the **Njara route** from the east up to Mawenzi Peak; the short, scenic but very difficult **Umbwe route** from the south; and the unspoiled **Rongai route** and its variant the **Loitokitok route** from the northeast. A good base for the latter is the Swiss chalet-style *Snow Cap Cottages* in Naremoru (☎027/275 2428, ⓦwww.snowcap.co.tz; half-board ❺), who also arrange hikes through other companies.

The Marangu route

Seventy percent of climbers ascend Kili along the **Marangu route**, a short, beautiful but steep trail that's anything but easy, especially if done over only five days – which probably explains why fewer than one in five climbers on this route reaches Uhuru Peak. Extending the trek over six days, as described below, or even seven days, is much preferable and greatly increases your chances of success. Depending on the season (see p.342), the Marangu route can be cloudy and muddy, and is often very busy. The route's popularity means that the path is badly eroded and trampled in many places, and the lower slopes turn into a mudfest in the rains. At times there's also a lot of litter left by dumb climbers (hence the trail's nickname, the "Coca-Cola Route"), and graffiti adorns the three large **accommodation huts**: Mandara (84 beds), Horombo (148 beds) and Kibo (58 beds). These are equipped with mattresses, twelve-volt solar lighting, kitchens, toilets and a rescue team. Snacks and drinks, including beer, are available at all the huts – but wait until you descend to indulge the booze. Bunks must be reserved through the park headquarters at Marangu Gate (a hiking company can do this for you). Camping isn't allowed.

Any company directly organizing Kilimanjaro climbs needs a current **TALA Mountaineering Licence**: the national park offices at Marangu and Machame gates have lists of licensed companies, as do the tourist offices in Arusha and Dar es Salaam.

The following are among the more reputable, licensed outfits in Moshi and Marangu. For recommended Arusha-based companies, read the safari company reviews on pp.404–407. One company not reviewed here as it only deals with tour companies, but with an excellent reputation, is African Environments (⊛www .africanenvironments.co.tz). Be wary of other companies not reviewed in this book – appearances are not everything. In addition, don't necessarily believe recommendations on the Internet: several companies are adept at plugging themselves. And if a flycatcher claims to work for one of the following, ensure that you end up at the correct address – there have been cases of disreputable outfits "borrowing" the names of other companies to snare clients. Lastly, given that the cost of climbing is so much already, **don't scrimp** by going with a dodgy company: it's not worth the saving if you're going to end up with inexperienced guides, dud equipment, or for that matter a blot on your conscience, if you use a company which exploits its porters.

Companies in Moshi
Ahsante Tours & Safaris New St ☏027/275 1971, ⊛www.ahsantetours.com. Helpful and friendly, generally coming in for praise, and cheaper than most: six-day climbs start around $750. Also licensed for wildlife safaris. TATO member.

Keys Hotel Uru Rd ☏027/275 2250, ⊛www.keys-hotels.com. Has enjoyed a solid reputation for years, though you'll pay more for their experience and thorough preparation. Also licensed for wildlife safaris. TATO member.

Kindoroko Hotel Mawenzi Rd ☏027/275 4054, ⊛www.kindoroko.com. A newcomer to the fray, so little feedback as yet. A six-day Machame climb costs $840, seven days $960; prices include two nights in Moshi. They also cover the Rongai, Umbwe and Lemosho routes. TATO member.

Mauly Tours & Safaris Next to Kahawa House, Mawenzi Rd ☏027/275 0730, ⊛www.mauly-tours.com. An Indian-run company with somewhat variable feedback; quality very much depends on the guide. A six-day Machame hike costs $820, seven-day $980, and seven days on the Lemosho or Shira routes $1070. Also licensed for wildlife safaris – it has a decent 4WD fleet. TATO member.

MEM Tours & Safari Kaunda Rd ☏027/275 4234, ⊛www.memtours.com. Professional, conscientious and keenly priced. A six-day Marangu trip costs $850, a seven-day Lemosho $1000–1100, or $1200 over eight days. Also licensed for wildlife safaris.

Companies in Marangu
Kibo Hotel ☏027/275 1308, ⊛www.kibohotel.com. One of the best mid-range companies for the Marangu route as long as you're adequately equipped (hiring stuff here is expensive), offering a six-day Marangu trip for $980–1050, a seven-day Machame for $1310–1400 plus $200/group for vehicle transfer, and seven days on the Rongai route for around $1150 plus $130/group vehicle transfer.

Marangu Hotel ☏027/275 6594, ⊛www.maranguhotel.com. Long-established, with excellent guides and a reputation for thorough preparation, offering a choice of "fully equipped" climbs, where all you need to bring is warm clothes and a good pair of boots, and "hard-way" climbs, where you supply everything and the hotel arranges guides, porters and accommodation for a $50 fee. A fully equipped six-day Marangu hike costs around $1050; a seven-day Machame hike costs $1400. TATO member.

Day 1: Marangu Gate to Mandara Hut

The Marangu route starts 5.6km north of Marangu village at **Marangu Gate** (1860m), where you pay the park fees and hire a guide and porters if you're not on an organized climb. You can also buy last-minute supplies like energy food here. Start as early as possible to give yourself plenty of time to enjoy the tangle of rainforest and to increase the odds of avoiding showers, which tend to fall in the afternoon. The entire day's walk (8km; count on around 3hr) becomes very slippery and muddy in the rains, so take care. You may get soaked along this section, even if it's not raining, as the cloying mist effectively drenches everything.

Immediately after the gate, the broad track plunges into dense forest. If time isn't a concern, the narrower signposted track to the left is a preferable but slightly longer alternative to the main track, as it follows a small stream and gives a better view of the forest, as well as being less busy. The track adds about an hour to the day's hike. Both tracks merge into a narrow and much-eroded trail after some 5km. **Mandara Hut** (2774m) is 3km further on. If you arrive early and feel up to it, there's a pleasant walk from Mandara Hut to the rim of **Maundi Crater** (2800m) 1.5km northeast, the remnant of a volcanic vent from where there are glorious views. The crater can also be worked into the next day's walk.

Mandara Hut, just inside the upper boundary of the forest, comprises a complex of comfortable wooden cabins sleeping sixty people, most containing two rooms with four bunks apiece. The exception is a large two-storey house which has a large dormitory on top and the communal dining area downstairs. Eat well, as you might lose your appetite higher up.

Mandara Hut to Horombo Hut

After an early breakfast (try for 6.30am), the trail emerges from the rainforest and veers northwest. If the sky is clear, there's a great view of the craggy Mawenzi Peak to the north and of the plains to the south from here. The trail heads up through alpine meadows and crosses a stream to emerge onto grassland, eventually thinning into surreal moorland scattered with bushes and short trees. If it's cloudy, don't fret – the vision of the plants emerging from the mist in a cocoon of silence can be magical, and you stand a reasonable chance of clear skies in the afternoon. As you approach Horombo Hut, 15km from Mandara, across a series of moorland ravines, ragged stands of giant groundsels and giant lobelia take over, lending an equally strange and unearthly quality to the scene, often complemented by magnificent sunsets from Horombo – hopefully not too clouded by the effects of altitude, which most people begin to feel on this day. **Horombo Hut** (3720m), in a rocky valley, comprises a collection of huts similar to Mandara and sleeps 120 people. There are some old-fashioned long-drops down the slope, and newer toilets flushed with piped water from a stream behind the huts. It gets cold very quickly after sunset, so wrap up well. Count on five to seven hours for the day's walk.

Day 3: Horombo Hut

Most people begin to feel the effects of altitude on the walk up to Horombo Hut, so a **rest day** at Horombo is advisable even if you're in good physical shape: no great hardship given the stunning location. You can help yourself acclimatize more easily if you spend at least a couple of hours walking to a higher altitude: most people head for **Zebra Rock** (4000m), named after its peculiar weathering pattern. If you're feeling particularly fit, you could try a day-trip to **Mawenzi Hut** (4600m), at the foot of Mawenzi Peak.

Day 4: Horombo Hut to Kibo Hut

The next stage, 13km up to Kibo Hut, can be tough if your body hasn't fully acclimatized, so keep an eye out for symptoms of acute mountain sickness beyond simple headaches, and leave Horombo early, as you'll have little time to sleep in the evening before the wake-up call for the summit attempt. The whole stage takes five to seven hours.

Just beyond Horombo, two trails diverge, both heading up to the **Saddle** – the broad lava-stone ridge between Mawenzi and Kibo peaks. The right-hand trail, which is very rocky and eroded, veers north, and is the quicker, albeit the more difficult, of the two (2–3hr compared to 3–4). From the Saddle, a track heading east takes you to the 4600-metre mark on **Mawenzi** – as far up that peak as you can get without technical gear. Ignore this track and carry straight on instead – Kibo Hut is three to four hours away, across an otherworldly alpine desert of reddish gravel and boulders. The alternative route from Horombo to the Saddle takes upwards of four hours, but leaves you little under two kilometres from Kibo Hut. Both routes have a number of steep uphill and downhill sections.

Kibo Hut (4703m) is a stone construction with a dining room and bunks for sixty people. There are long-drops outside the huts – take care at night. There's no water, so fill up near Horombo, either at one of the tarns on the eastern route, or at "Last Water" stream on the western route. Assuming you're up for the ascent the same night, try to catch some sleep in the afternoon and evening as the next stage, starting around midnight, is by far the hardest

Days 5 and 6: Horombo to the summit and back down

The summit push on **day 5** is the steepest and most strenuous part of the hike, taking around five to six hours up to Gillman's Point (and an extra ninety minutes to Uhuru Peak if you're still standing), followed by a nine- or ten-hour descent. After a generally fitful sleep due to the cold and the altitude, hikers set off between 11pm and 1am for the final ascent (the earlier you set off the better, as the icy path around the summit can become treacherously slippery after sunrise). Temperatures are well below zero, and visibility is difficult, especially if there's no moon or if flashlights conk out. The trail leads past **Hans Meyer Cave** – handy for a sheltered rest – before turning into a painful series of single-file zigzags up loose scree, for which a Zen-like mindset helps. At the top of the zigzags, a short rocky scramble gets you over **Johannes' Notch** and to within staggering distance of Gillman's Point. The thin air forces frequent stops, and means that the hike to Gillman's Point takes at least five or six hours. Most climbers get light-headed and nauseous along this stretch, and headaches afflict pretty much everyone.

Gillman's Point (5685m), on the crater rim, is where many people call an end to their attempt, to be consoled with the stupendous view and the sun rising from behind Mawenzi Peak. If you're up to it, an even more exhausting ninety-minute clockwise walk around the crater rim past **Stella Point** – where the Machame route joins up – and Hans Meyer Point brings you to the roof of Africa, **Uhuru Peak** (5891m). Those ninety minutes (or two hours if you're really whacked) may not sound like much, but are likely be the hardest, most painful and – with luck – most rewarding ninety minutes of your life. Sunrise here above a sea of clouds is unforgettable (though the majority of climbers arrive about an hour after sunrise), as is the feeling of elation, even if, right then, your only desire is to get down as quickly as possible. There's a summit log you can sign, and remember to take a photograph with that famously battered yellow sign – the pounding headache that you will more than likely be feeling means that many people forget.

It's possible to **hike into the crater** if this is arranged in advance with your guide (at extra cost). Measuring 2km in diameter and 300m deep, the crater contains another, smaller crater named after Dr Richard Reusch, who in 1926 discovered the frozen leopard later made famous by Hemingway. In the centre of this is an ash pit, and there are some small but active steam fumaroles on its northern and eastern rim. Incidentally, it's not a good idea to spend a night on the summit (**Furtwangler Camp**, 5600m) unless you're taking at least ten days for the hike, as you'll need to be totally acclimatized to avoid coming down with altitude sickness.

Most folks only spend a few minutes at the bitterly cold summit before **heading back down**. Try to avoid the temptation of "skiing" down the scree – it makes things even more difficult for climbers after you, and of course you risk a painful and potentially limb-breaking tumble. Most climbers get back to Kibo Hut around 10am, take a rest, and then retrace their steps back to Horombo, for their last night on the mountain.

The **final day** (day 6) should be bliss, but by now your knees may be complaining – take it easy, and use a walking stick. Mandara Hut is usually reached by lunchtime, and the park gate in the afternoon. Don't forget your certificate at the gate.

Kilimanjaro's high-altitude flora and fauna

Kilimanjaro is covered by a series of distinctive habitat zones, determined by altitude. Above about 1800m, farmland ceases and forests take over. Up to around 2000m, much of the forest is secondary growth, but beyond here is dense primary **cloudforest**, containing over 1800 species of flowering plants. The forest is dominated in its lower reaches by ferns, podocarpus and camphor trees, and is home to three primate species: blue monkey, western black-and-white colobus, and bushbaby (galago). Leopards also live here (though you're most unlikely to see one), preying on mountain reedbuck and members of the world's largest population of Abbot's duiker. Curiously, the belt of giant bamboo that characterizes Mount Meru and Mount Kenya is absent on Kilimanjaro.

Rainfall is less heavy at higher altitudes, so from around 2400m the forest becomes less dense. The tree line (2800–3000m) is start of the peculiar **afro-alpine moorland** (also called upland grassland), the land of the giants – giant heather, giant groundsel (or tree senecio) and giant lobelia. The cabbages on stumps and the larger candelabra-like "trees" are two forms of the **giant groundsel**, an intermediate stage of which has a sheaf of yellow flowers. The giant groundsel favours damp and sheltered locations such as stream beds; they're slow growers but, for such weedy-looking vegetables, they may be extraordinarily old – up to two hundred years. Higher up, in the alpine bogs, you'll see groundsel together with another strange plant, the tall and fluffy **giant lobelia** – the animal-like furriness insulates the delicate flowers. A number of **mammals** habitually pass into the moorland zone from the forests: grey duiker and eland are most commonly seen; bushbuck, red duiker and buffalo are rarer. There are few birds: the most common is the white-necked raven, often seen at campsites.

Above 4600m is the barren **alpine desert** zone. The sub-zero conditions here mean that few plants other than mosses and lichens are able to survive, although the daisy-like *Helichrysum newii* has been seen on Kibo's summit caldera at 5760m close to a fumarole. Even stranger was the mysterious **leopard** whose frozen body was found close to the summit in 1926 and which featured in Hemingway's *The Snows of Kilimanjaro*. No one knows what it was doing so far up the mountain.

The Machame route

Nicknamed the "Whiskey Route", presumably because of its intoxicating views (and, until a few years ago, the more upmarket trash left by the wayside), the long, winding and dramatic **Machame route** is the next most popular way up after the Marangu route, and increasingly so: encounters with eland and other wildlife are no longer so common, and you'll see dozens of other climbers along the way – the official daily limit of sixty climbers a day is apparently not enforced. Six days is usual for the ascent along this route, but seven or even eight is recommended. The walk is more difficult than the Marangu, but the advantage is that, being longer, acclimatization is easier and so the success rate is higher. There are several routes to the summit from the **Shira Plateau**, and two choices of descent: either the Marangu route or the Mweka (a mudfest in the rains), so all in all you get to see a lot of the mountain. Nights are spent camping: the campsites are usually called "huts" on maps, but the metal "uniports" there are for guides and porters only.

Day 1: Machame Gate to Machame Camp

As with the Marangu route, start early to fully enjoy the day. Count on an hour for the drive from Moshi (or an hour to walk up from Machame village), and an hour to complete formalities at the **gate** (1800m). Leave the gate no later than 11am; the day's walk takes five to seven hours.

From the gate, the trail heads up to the west of Makoa stream into dense, steamy and ever-changing **rainforest** alive with birdsong (look out for wild orchids). The trail narrows after thirty minutes to follow parts of a rocky ridge, where the vegetation becomes thicker, characterized by giant heather, and beard-like Spanish mosses hanging from the trees. The trail is steep, muddy and very slippery in places, especially beyond the two- to three-hour mark. As you approach **Machame Camp** (3000m), the vegetation thins out and the path emerges onto alpine moorland. The camp, occupying a clearing on the ridge, has long-drop toilets, water from a nearby stream and great views of the Western Breach.

Day 2: Machame Camp to Shira Camp

So long as you're in good shape, this is a very pleasant and easy day's hike (around 5hr) that brings you out of the forest (and usually above the clouds, though it can still be misty) and onto the drier and rockier **Shira Plateau**. From Machame Camp, the trail continues northeast along a steep and rocky ridge (some scrambling required) scattered with giant heather, and passes several clearings with great views of mounts Meru and Longido in the west. The top of the ridge – after three hours or so – ends in a small cliff, up which a rudimentary staircase has been built. Lunch is taken on the top. From here, the incline lessens and the trail veers northwards across several ravines, through land studded with giant lobelia and giant groundsels. This leads on past **Shira Cave** (actually more of a rock shelter), before reaching the exposed **Shira Camp** (3840m) on the edge of the Shira Plateau, an immense, gently sloping expanse of desolate moorland marked by **Shira Cone** – the remnants of Kilimanjaro's oldest peak. There's a good view of the Western Breach from the camp, and awe-inspiring sunsets over Mount Meru. Night-time temperatures usually stay a few degrees above freezing, but the wind chill makes it feel much colder – wrap up. The first symptoms of altitude sickness begin to appear here.

Day 3: Shira Plateau

The Shira Plateau is a great place to spend an extra **rest day** acclimatizing. The main attraction is **Shira Cone** at the west end of the plateau, rising some 200m above the plateau to 3962m. South of here are are two impressive pinnacles – volcanic plugs named Shira Needles and Shira Cathedral. Eland are sometimes seen on the lower reaches of the plateau.

If you're feeling OK, however, you may prefer to acclimatize later on, especially as the next day's hike – to Barranco Camp – is good for one day's acclimatization; rising to around 4400m before dropping back down to 3950m.

Day 4: Shira Camp to Barranco Camp

There are **two routes** to the summit from Shira Camp: either via Barranco Camp and Barafu Camp to Stella Point, or straight up the Western Breach. The former, described below, is by far the easier. For a description of the Western Breach route, see opposite.

The boulder-strewn trail to Barranco Camp (Umbwe Hut on some maps) takes five to seven hours and is extremely beautiful in a lunar kind of way. The walk starts with a gentle incline east towards Kibo. At the top of a ridge marked by a rock called the **Shark's Tooth** (4400m) – where vegetation is limited to lichens and mosses – the trail veers south to traverse a series of shallow up-and-down valleys at the base of the Western Breach and the 4600m **Lava Tower**, gradually descending to **Barranco Camp** (3950m). Set in alpine tundra, the camp has a great view of the icy Western Breach as well as the Barranco Wall – which you'll be climbing the next day; it appears intimidatingly vertical from here. If you're going to suffer badly from altitude sickness, it really kicks in at Barranco, so be reasonable with your expectations. Porters prefer to camp in a rock shelter at the foot of the wall, about thirty minutes' walk away.

Day 5: Barranco Camp to Barafu Camp

Although the following is a one-day route description from Barranco to Barafu Camp, this section is best done in two four-hour segments, with an overnight halfway in the Karanga Valley camp. This is especially recommended if you didn't spend a day acclimatizing at Shira. Some people attempt the walk from Shira to the Karanga Valley in a day (around 9hr), but this is exhausting and not recommended.

Although steep, only a few stretches of **Barranco Wall** require hands-and-feet climbing, and the zigzagging path is for the most part clearly marked. The path is narrow, so "experienced" climbers can get huffy about the slow pace – ignore them, and take your time. The wall normally takes ninety minutes to scale. At the top, there's a great view of the Heim, Kersten and Decken glaciers. The path follows a spectacular traverse east along the base of Kibo. The top of the icy **Karanga Valley** (4100m) is usually reached by noon, giving you a lazy afternoon to rest and sleep before heading off the next day to Barafu.

Continuing on from Karanga Valley, the track continues its eastward traverse, after about two hours reaching the crossroad with the Mweka route. Turn left for Barafu Camp – an exhausting ninety-minute climb up a steep and rocky lava ridge. It often snows, and in the rainy seasons this area can be blanketed. **Barafu Camp** (4600m) is on the ridge close to the southern edge of the Saddle, and has a great view of Mawenzi Peak. The downside is the often filthy state of the campsite – take your trash down with you. The long-drops are close to the ridge edge – take care at night, as several climbers have fallen to their deaths from here. Go to sleep no later than sunset.

Days 6 and 7: Barafu to the summit and back down

Day 6 – summit day – is the most exhausting, and involves at least seventeen hours of hiking from Barafu Camp to the summit (6–8hr) and down to

Horombo Hut on the Marangu route, or to Mweka Camp on the Mweka route. The "day" starts before midnight, when you're woken for breakfast, and most climbers set off between midnight and 1am. The trail follows an increasingly steep valley on the edge of scree fields, before passing between the Rebmann and Ratzel glaciers to emerge at **Stella Point** (5681m) on the southern rim of Kibo; the last few hundred metres are the hardest section on the climb. **Uhuru Peak** (5891m) is about an hour further along an ice-covered trail; see day 5 of the Marangu route (p.347) for a description. The trail for the most part is steep and extremely loose scree, making for painfully slow progress.

Heading **back down**, most people reach Barafu Camp around 9–11am, where an hour's rest is followed by a long hike down, either along the Mweka or Marangu routes, for your last night on the mountain. **Day 7** is generally just a few hours of relatively easy – if sometimes very muddy – downhill walking. Take it slowly.

The Shira and Lemosho routes

The extremely photogenic **Shira route** (also called the Londorossi route) approaches the mountain from the northwest, through forest used as a migration route by elephants (hence the more open canopy than in the south), and joins the Machame route on the Shira Plateau, at the end of the second day's hike. Six days is the minimum, with seven being ideal. The route is actually drivable to around 3600m, leaving you with an easy half-day walk to Shira Camp (see p.349). If you want to walk the whole way (minimum seven days, eight better), it's best to start along the **Lemosho route**, which joins the Shira route at the top of the drivable track.

If you do drive, spend at least two nights on the Shira Plateau to acclimatize before climbing further. Once patronized only by upmarket companies, the Shira or Lemosho routes now feature on most hiking company brochures, though they're still nowhere near as busy as the Machame and Marangu routes.

The Western Breach route

For experienced climbers taking the Machame or Shira/Lemosho routes, a challenging alternative to the ascent from Barafu Camp is the approach over the **Western Breach**, a steep slope flanked by glaciers that was created when the western rim of Kibo exploded. The Western Breach is sometimes touted as a short-cut to the top (theoretically feasible in five days), but don't believe the hype, which is highly irresponsible. Nicknamed "the Torture Route", the Western Breach ascent is very steep and potentially dangerous – landslides and rock falls claim victims most years, and although much of the permanent snow and ice that formerly made the route a technical climb has melted, you still risk encountering snow and ice, especially between December and February, so at the very least you'll need to pack ice picks, crampons and ropes. Another danger is that turning back on the last part is impossible without proper climbing equipment, so if you feel anything more than just a headache, turn back well before. Also be aware that the trail is unmarked and easy to lose, and most guides don't know the route well; go with a reputable hiking company.

The route starts at the **Arrow Glacier** at the foot of the Western Breach. The last **camps** for the summit attempt are either at the base of the spectacularly located **Lava Tower** (4600m), four hours from Shira Camp, or the equally dramatic **Arrow Glacier Camp** (4850m), next to an area of boulders and snow fields. It takes at least six hours to the crater rim from Arrow Glacier, and around nine hours from the Lava Tower.

The Pare Mountains and Mkomazi Game Reserve

Southeast of Kilimanjaro rise the much older but equally beautiful **Pare Mountains**, a green, fertile and infrequently visited region divided into two distinct ranges – north and south. The practical business of getting around is not as difficult as it was, thanks to the establishment of three **cultural tourism programmes** (see Basics for a general overview), two in the north at Usangi and Kisangara Chini, another at Mbaga in the south. Each programme offers a range of affordable activities based around guided walks in the mountains and their forests, and encounters with the rural culture of the **Pare** tribe, who have been living in the mountains for the last six hundred years.

The Pare are northeastern Tanzania's most traditional tribe. In the same way that the geologically separate Eastern Arc forests have developed an especially rich flora and fauna, so the isolation of the Pare from other tribes has resulted in their strong and distinctive culture and sense of identity. Whereas traditional knowledge of plants and their uses is fast disappearing elsewhere, the Pare have kept much of their knowledge intact, and are famed throughout northern Tanzania for the power of their healers, and sometimes also feared for witchcraft – witches, called *ndewa* in Kipare, are invariably associated with botanical knowledge garnered over many centuries. It's thanks to the continuity of Pare culture that many of the mountains' indigenous forests have been preserved, despite high human population densities, since the Pare consider the forests sacred places, guarded by the spirits of their ancestors. Add to all this the fact that the Pare, like their Sambaa cousins to the south (see box on p.360), are an unfailingly welcoming bunch, and you have an immensely rewarding place to visit.

In the plains between the mountains and the Kenyan border lies the **Mkomazi Game Reserve**, which became the scene of controversy following the forcible expulsion of Maasai cattle herders in 1988. It contains a rhino sanctuary, but otherwise probably isn't worth the effort if the Northern Safari Circuit figures in your plans.

North Pare

The **North Pare Mountains** are best visited through the cultural tourism programme at **Usangi**. Another programme, at **Kisangara Chini** on the Dar–Arusha highway, also offers walks into the mountains, but is better for trips to Nyumba ya Mungu reservoir in the plains to the west.

Usangi

The base for the North Pare Mountains' cultural tourism programme is **Usangi village**, 25km east of the highway in a beautiful location surrounded by no fewer than eleven peaks. Try to visit on a Monday or Thursday, when the village's **market** is held. The cultural tourism programme offers a range of trips; profits are currently used to aid a local clinic.

The Eastern Arc Mountains

The Pare Mountains are part of the **Eastern Arc Mountains**, an isolated range of ancient massifs that stretch from the Taita Hills in southeastern Kenya into Tanzania, where the range includes the Pare Mountains, East and West Usambara, the Ulugurus near Morogoro and the Udzungwa Mountains. Despite the proximity of the northern part of the Eastern Arc to the volcanic massifs of Mount Meru and Kilimanjaro, the steep crystalline ridges and peaks of the Eastern Arc are a much older and geologically separate formation. The current ranges began to take shape some 100 million years ago, and attained their present form at the start of the Miocene epoch, 25 million years ago.

The great age of the Eastern Arc Mountains, along with the physical isolation of the various ranges from one another, is one reason for their exceptional **biodiversity**. Another is the region's remarkable climatological stability over the last forty million years, thanks to the proximity of the Indian Ocean, whose monsoon system dictates weather patterns over much of the Eastern Arc, producing ample mist and rainfall from moisture-laden clouds coming in from the ocean. Together, these factors have fostered the evolution of the mountains' tremendously rich ecological systems, notably their forests, which contain literally thousands of plant and animal species found nowhere else on earth – not for nothing is the Eastern Arc often referred to as the "Galapagos of Africa".

Transport from Arusha or Moshi is on the daily Sahara Coach (10am from Arusha, passing Moshi around 11.30am; leaving Usangi at 6am). Coming from Dar es Salaam, catch a bus for Moshi or Arusha and get off in the district capital, Mwanga, 50km southeast of Moshi, from where a handful of daily buses grind uphill along a good sandy road to Usangi (90min). At Usangi, get off at Lomwe Secondary School and ask for the project co-ordinator, Mr Nelson Kangero (T0748/813787). If you get stranded in Mwanga, the school for deaf children has a good little guest house (T027/275 7727; ❷).

In Usangi, several families – most of them connected to the school – offer **accommodation** through the cultural tourism programme, and camping is possible. The school itself also has a guest house, sleeping six, and there's a guest house in the village near the mosque. **Meals** are provided by the Usangi Women's Group.

Guided walks and tours

A guided half-day walk takes in farms on the lower slopes of the Pare Mountains before climbing to **Mangatu moorland** (1600m), near the sacred forest of the Mbale clan, with superb views of Kilimanjaro and Lake Jipe on the Kenyan border. A full-day trek can be arranged up North Pare's highest peak, **Mount Kindoroko** (2113m), 9km south of Usangi, for grand views of Kilimanjaro, Mount Meru, Lake Jipe and Nyumba ya Mungu reservoir. The walk goes through the surrounding rainforest, home to blue monkeys and birds, and you can also visit a women's pottery co-operative, a traditional healer and listen to a storyteller. Another day-trip goes up **Mount Kamwala**, whose forests are sacred. Walks over several days can also be arranged; Ugweno village, near **Lake Jipe** on the Kenyan border, is a handy base both for walks and canoeing on Lake Jipe, and has accommodation at the local school. You can also camp in the mountains; bring your own gear.

If you're not up to long hikes, there are several things to do in and around Usangi, including visits to a brick-making co-operative, other artisans producing pottery, clothes and traditional beer, and – if you're lucky – a local wedding, to which you'll probably be invited. **Costs**, including food, guide and all fees, average Tsh10,000 per person for half a day, and Tsh15,000 for a full day.

Kisangara Chini

The easiest of Pare's cultural tourism programmes to visit is at **Kisangara Chini**, 12km south of Mwanga on the highway, sandwiched between vast sisal plantations in the shadow of Mount Kindoroko, North Pare's highest peak. **Buses** running between Dar and Arusha (or Moshi) pass through.

The **cultural tourism programme** (Mrs Grace Msafiri Mngara ☎027/275 7789 or 0744/487193, ✉msafirigrace@yahoo.com; see Basics for a general overview) is thirty minutes' walk east of the village. It's not signposted, so keep asking for "Mama Grace". The turning on the highway is at the sign for "Shule ya Msingi Chanjale", 100m north of the Total filling station. You pass over a small stream after 70m. Go on, then turn right at the T-junction into a square with a big tree. Keep left and exit the square. The compound is 1.5km further on, on the right as the road veers left (east) towards the mountain.

Mama Grace and her family are exceptionally welcoming, and run the project as part of a boarding school. The project offers **rooms** in cottages (cold showers; Tsh10,000 per person), and a **campsite** (Tsh5000 per person; tent hire Tsh5000). There are also two simple guest houses in the village (both ❶). Food and drinks are available. Kisangara Chini's **market days** are Thursday and Sunday.

Guided walks and tours

The "must do" is a hike up **Mount Kindoroko** (also offered by Usangi's cultural tourism programme), combined with visits to sites of ritual importance. The programme also arranges day-trips to **Nyumba ya Mungu** ("House of God") reservoir in the plains to the west, for bird-spotting, fishing excursions by canoe and encounters with local fishermen, some of whom emigrated here from Lake Victoria. Closer to Kisangara Chini, various **half-day walks** combine visits to carpentry workshops, brick and sisal factories, a traditional brewery producing beer from sugar cane or Lembeni Herbal Hospital, with traditional dancing performed by a women's group, and crash courses in Pare cookery, storytelling and Kiswahili. **Costs** depend on group size and what you do, but are under Tsh10,000 per person for half a day, or Tsh10,000–15,000 for a full day. The price includes a Tsh3000 development fee, funding the school.

South Pare

Fifty kilometres south of Mwanga, the district capital of Same sits at the western end of a lowland corridor separating North from South Pare. The mountains of **South Pare** are similar in many respects to their northern twin – just as beautiful, even from the highway down below, and also contain a superb cultural tourism programme at **Mbaga** which may well entice you to stay longer than planned. If you're just passing along the highway, a recommended **overnight stop** is *Pangani River Campsite* ($3), between the railroad and river in the shadow of the Pare's southernmost peak. Despite the river reeds, there aren't as many mosquitoes as you might fear. It's a welcoming and laid-back place, with lots of shady doum (*mikweche*) palm trees, a bar and thatched restaurant, a generator for electricity, tents for hire ($3–4) and a two-bed *banda* (❷). They can also guide you up and down the forested peak (7hr). There's another campsite, the *Tembo*, further south at Mkumbara and amply signposted, but it has little to recommend it other than its swimming pool.

Same

The district capital of the Pare region, **SAME** (pronounced *sah–mê*), straddles the highway at the foot of the South Pare Mountains. Same's main attraction is its **Sunday market**, drawing farmers from all over the mountains. A local speciality is honey (*asali*); the normal variety, called *msiku*, is from tended hives hung from trees; the sweeter and superior variety (the bee stings are also said to be more painful) is called *mpako*, and comes from wild bee hives in the ground. Another item worth seeking out is the local **scorpion and snakebite cure**, called *nkulo*, which looks to be a mineralized form of charcoal. Sold in powdered or stick form, it literally sucks venom out of wounds.

Practicalities

Same, 116km southeast of Moshi, can be reached on any **bus** travelling between Dar or Tanga and Moshi or Arusha. **Leaving Same**, most buses pass through between 7am and 3pm; see p.329 for recommended bus companies, and ones to avoid. *PADECO Bar & Restaurant*, facing the bus stand, has **information** about Mbaga's cultural tourism programme.

There's lots of **accommodation**, most of it in rather tawdry guest houses doubling as brothels. In the rains, Same gets infested by mosquitoes and malaria is present, so check bed nets carefully. The most comfortable place is *Elephant Motel*, 1.4km south of the bus stand on the highway (☎027/275 8193, ✉sgeneralsame@elct.org; ❹ including breakfast; camping $5), which has large and clean en-suite rooms with box nets and satellite TVs, safe parking, a bar and restaurant. Best of the cheapies, with safe parking, is the pious *Amani Lutheran Centre* (☎027/275 8107, ✉pd@elct.org; ❶), 200m uphill from the bus stand, with twelve en-suite rooms with round nets (but no fans) overlooking an enclosed garden. Also with safe parking is *Kambeni Guest House* (☎027/275 8186; ❶), down the side street opposite *Amani Lutheran Centre*. This is actually two hotels: "Number 1" is dingy, so go for "Number 2", with cleaner and brighter rooms, box nets (no fans), and one with private bathroom.

Same's **restaurants** are pretty basic, tending to function as "groceries" (bars) for truckers and other travellers. An exception is *Elephant Motel*, with good filling meals for under Tsh3500. For **drinks**, nicest is *Honey Port Bar*, whose pleasant shaded outdoor terrace facing the bus stand is a perfect place to watch the world go by. They also do *nyama choma*. **Change money** at NMB, near the bus stand.

Mbaga and around

South Pare's **cultural tourism programme** – one of Tanzania's best – is at **MBAGA**, a former missionary station set in a lush area of terraced cultivation up in the mountains, offering a wide variety of walks to various attractions and small villages little-changed from centuries ago, and giving you a chance to experience local Pare life and culture at first hand. Profits from the project have already paid for the construction of a pre-school building and dispensary, and now subsidize energy-efficient stoves, vocational scholarships and road maintenance. A good time to come is Wednesday, coinciding with the weekly **market**.

Practicalities

Mbaga is also known as Manka. There are two roads from Same: via the eastern flank of the Pare Mountains past Mkomazi Game Reserve, then uphill from Kisimani village (treacherous even in dry weather; 4WD essential); or, much easier, up the western flank of the mountains via Mwembe village. The latter route is advisable if you're **self-driving**, taking just ninety minutes: the road starts 2km south of Same's *Elephant Motel* along the highway; there's no sign, so ask for *njia panda kwenda Mwembe*. At Mwembe, turn left (east) and up towards Mbaga. By **public transport**, Mangare Bus leaves Same every day sometime after 2pm, taking two and a half to three hours; from Mbaga, it leaves at 5.30am. There's also an occasional daladala or pick-up, but no more than one a day.

Transport stops outside ✈ *Hill-Top Tona Lodge*, the base for the **cultural tourism programme** (Mr Elly Kimbwereza ☎0744/852010 or 027/275 8129, ✉tona_lodge@hotmail.com). The lodge's main building was the residence of a German missionary named **Jakob Dannholz**, who wrote what are still the best works on Pare culture, including *Lute: The Curse and the Blessing*, available at the lodge (Tsh2500) – it's a rare and unusually perspicacious read, and highly recommended.

Accommodation at the lodge ($10 per person including breakfast) consists of four modest rooms in the main building, and several more in brick cottages a few minutes away, each with electricity and bathroom with running water. **Camping** costs Tsh3000 (bring your own tent). Extraordinarily delicious traditional **meals** (Tsh2500) are available if ordered early; try *makande*, a light stew of maize and beans cooked with milk and vegetables, or anything with bananas. There's more basic accommodation (and food) at *Sunrise Lodge*, 5km beyond Mbaga along the road to Gonja, and *Adela Guest House* in Gonja itself.

Guided walks and tours

The cultural tourism programme (see Basics for a general overview) offers a range of walks from easy half-day hikes to treks of three days or more; they can also arrange a day's safari in Mkomazi Game Reserve, though if you don't have wheels you'll need to wait a day or two for them to rent a vehicle in Same.

One fascinating (and rather disturbing) half-day walk goes to the **Mghimbi Caves** and **Malameni Rock**. The caves provided shelter from slave raiders in the 1860s, whilst the rock, further up, was the site of child sacrifices until the practice was ended in the 1930s. The rock can be climbed, but you need to be instructed on the appropriate behaviour by an elder first – your guide can arrange this. Then there's **Ibwe Leteta** – "the Rock that Speaks" – which has three ancient trees growing from its narrow clefts. They were once maidens, says the legend, cursed for having mocked an old grandmother who wished to be anointed. You can hear them wail on stormy nights, and if you shout *Thela we!* ("You over there!"), they'll mock you with an echoed *Thela ...*

Other good half-day destinations include **Mpepera Viewpoint**, giving views – on clear days – of Kilimanjaro and Mkomazi; and the hilltop **Red Reservoir** near the Tona Moorlands; frequently covered with water plants, it's good for **birdwatching**. A recommended full-day trip is to the tiny and beautiful agricultural village of **Ikongwe**, said to have been a gift from God, or to the 136-metre **Thornton Falls**, a 1.5-hour walk from Gonja. Overnight stays in the Ikongwe village can be arranged with local families, and the trip can be combined with Mpepera Viewpoint. The most adventurous option is the three-day hike to **Shengena Peak** (2463m), the highest point in the Pare and Usambara Mountains, and the species-rich **Shengena (Chome) rainforest**, including overnights with a local family at Chome village (see opposite) and under canvas at the forest edge, before a 4am start to catch sunrise from the peak. Other options include visits to various developmental irrigation, soil conservation and reforestation projects, and a host of other weird and wonderful places.

Costs are very reasonable: Tsh2000 per person for the guide (minimum Tsh6000), Tsh2000 per person for the village, and extras like meals (Tsh2500), porter (Tsh2000) and Tsh1000 for a consultation with a traditional healer. Camping away from Mbaga costs Tsh2500, though you'll need your own tent. Tona Traditional Dancing Troupe can be hired for Tsh5000 plus tips.

Chome village

Chome village, hidden in a lush green valley at the western base of Shengena Peak, is one of Pare's gems: a small, traditional and immensely friendly place, despite having suffered the mysterious abduction of dozens of villagers in 1929 – no one knows where they ended up. The village can be visited as part of Mbaga's cultural tourism programme (it's a day's walk along narrow footpaths), or through *Kisaka Villa Inn* in Chome itself (☎027/275 6722 or 0744/288858, Ⓔkisakas@yahoo.co.uk; ❸ for en-suite double with breakfast), a large and modern two-storey alpine-style building with a rather religious atmosphere (no booze or smoking). Public transport along the 41km from Same is limited to irregular Land Rovers and pick-ups, usually leaving Same in the afternoon. If you're driving, instead of turning left at Mwembe for Mbaga, just keep going until you reach a signposted turning, leaving you with 26km. You might have to push your vehicle at the end, as the last part is very steep.

Apart from the hike up **Shengena Peak**, local attractions – most of which can be walked to in a few hours – include the Namoche Valley (scene of a victorious battle against the Maasai), warriors' graves, German ruins, local farms, waterfalls and viewpoints, and the **Kings' Stone**. This huge rocky outcrop about two hours from Chome was used for human sacrifices: victims were thrown off the top, whilst deformed or otherwise ill-starred babies were simply left there, along with many prayers, for God to take them back to the spirit world. It's a very steep and slippery climb through thick bush.

Mkomazi Game Reserve

Much of the grey-green bushland behind the Pare and Usambara mountains is covered by **Mkomazi Game Reserve**, a wild and scenic stretch of baobab-studded savannah adjoining Kenya's Tsavo West National Park. The reserve provides an ideal habitat for a wide range of wildlife, including over four hundred **bird species** and dozens of types of large mammal. Of these, antelopes, lesser kudu, dikdik, gazelle and impala are frequently seen, whilst migratory herds of elephant, buffalo, oryx and zebra are also common. There are good odds on spotting (particularly aggressive) lions, though the reserve's other predators – including leopards, cheetahs, and spotted and striped hyenas – are more elusive. A rarity is the gerenuk, an agile antelope that gets up on its hind legs to browse trees. Mkomazi's other two rare species, the **African hunting dog** and **black rhino**, have been reintroduced and are now being bred in semi-captivity, after they were wiped out in the 1980s.

Mkomazi is seldom visited by tourists and is – it must be said – a deeply controversial place, after Maasai pastoralists were forcibly evicted in 1988 on spurious environmental grounds. That said, **walking** accompanied by an armed ranger should be possible – a rare experience elsewhere.

Practicalities

Mkomazi is best visited as a day-trip. The main entrance is 7km east of Same along the road to Kisimani at Zange Gate, which is where the reserve head-quarters are located. **Entrance fees** are $20 per person, plus $5 for the obliga-tory guide. The services of an armed ranger, for game walks, cost $20 a day, but advance booking is recommended (PO Box 41 Same, ☎027/275 8248-9). **Transport** can be arranged through *Hill-Top Tona Lodge* in Mbaga (p.356), or informally in Same (ask at *PADECO Bar & Restaurant*, facing the bus stand): around $50–100 a day depending on the distance covered. There are two **campsites**: *Ibaya*, 15km from Zange Gate, which has water and toilets, and *Kisima*, 60km beyond, which has neither. Luxury camping and walking safaris are offered by the *East African Safari & Touring Company* in Arusha (p.406).

Wildlife is best during the **long rains** (end-March to May), when around a thousand elephants, as well as other species, migrate down from Tsavo, although unfortunately the reserve's roads are liable to be impassable at this time. Dindira Dam is currently waterless, so the best places for spotting wildlife are Mbula and Kavateta waterholes. The heavily guarded **Mkomazi Rhino Project Sanc-tuary** at Kisima, 76km from Zange Gate, currently houses eight rhino flown in from South Africa's Addo National Park, but can only be visited by prior arrangement: for more information, see Ⓦwww.mkomazi.com.

The Usambara Mountains

Southeast of the Pare Mountains are the granite **USAMBARA MOUN-TAINS**, known as *Shambalai* by the local Sambaa tribe. Like the Pare Moun-tains, the Usambaras are part of the Eastern Arc chain (see p.353) and, again like Pare, form two distinct ranges – east and west – divided by the Lwengera Valley. The attractive town of **Lushoto** is the main settlement in **West Usambara** and the base for the region's outstanding cultural tourism programme – the perfect way to explore one of Tanzania's friendliest and most scenic areas. In **East Usambara**, the **Amani Nature Reserve** comprises one of the most diverse ecosystems on earth: a glorious area of thick rainforest clinging to steep slopes.

West Usambara

Around halfway along the Arusha–Dar highway, the spectacularly craggy west-ern rim of the **West Usambara Mountains** rises with startling abruptness from the east side of the road, to over 1000m above the plains. Often shrouded in mist, these unexpected green mountains contain some of Tanzania's most spectacular hiking terrain, and are as friendly and as welcoming a place as you're ever likely to find.

The practical nitty-gritty of getting around the mountains is a breeze, thanks to the **West Usambara Cultural Tourism Programme**, based in the region's main town, **Lushoto**, which offers a wealth of trips accompanied by qualified

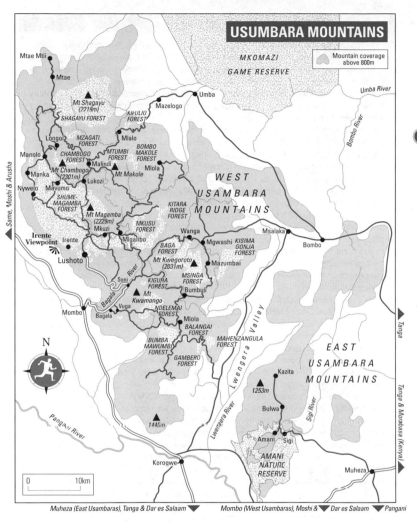

Muheza (East Usambaras), Tanga & Dar es Salaam ▼   Mombo (West Usambaras), Moshi & ▼ Dar es Salaam ▼ Pangani

local guides, from half-day walks to longer treks over several days traversing the mountains from Lushoto to Mtae, whose vertiginous views are something you're unlikely to forget. Blend in low costs and a rich and colourful history and you have what should, by rights, become one of Tanzania's leading tourist destinations, on a par with Kilimanjaro, Serengeti and Zanzibar.

Mombo

The best way to reach Lushoto is on one of the direct early-morning buses from Arusha, Dar, Moshi or Tanga. If you can't do this, access to Lushoto is easiest via the hot and humid town of **MOMBO**, 216km southeast of Moshi on the Arusha–Dar highway at the foot of the mountains (any long-distance bus passes through). **Daladalas** to Lushoto (90min) run every half-hour or so

The Sambaa and the Lion King

One reason for the survival of traditional **Sambaa culture** is that the steep Usambara Mountains were much more easily defended than the plains surrounding them – access was difficult until the construction of roads in the twentieth century. In addition, unlike most of northern Tanzania's tribes, who were originally – or still are – cattle herders, the Sambaa have always been cultivators (one possible derivation of their name is from *shamba*, a farm), resulting in settled communities and favouring intricate systems of leadership.

From around 1700 onwards, the Sambaa coalesced under a chief called **Mbega** (or Mbegha) to form a kingdom, which dominated much of Tanzania's northeast until the German conquest. Born to a Zigua chief in Ngulu, down in the plains, Mbega was cheated of his inheritance and forced to leave his birthplace. He wandered for many years, gaining fame as a skilled and generous hunter. Mbega finally settled in Kilindi in the plains, from where his reputation spread. At the time, the Sambaa were experiencing problems with an infestation of wild pigs, who were uprooting their crops, so they went to the famous hunter to ask his assistance. Mbega treated them with uncommon courtesy, and accepted the task of ridding Usambara of the problematic swine. Mbega set about his work, all the while distributing gifts of meat to the local people. Word of his skill, wisdom and fairness spread swiftly, and soon Mbega also became sought after for his skills in settling disputes. So much so that the people of Vuga, near Soni in West Usambara, asked him and his clan (family) to become their leader.

During his reign, which was characterized by intelligence and consideration, Mbega united the various rival Sambaa clans into one kingdom, the **Kilindi dynasty**. Mbega himself became known as Simbawene, **the Lion King**. The Kilindi dynasty reached its height at the start of the nineteenth century, when the Sambaa ruled not only over Usambara, but also over the Pare Mountains and much of the plains to the south and east. By the 1840s, however, the Zigua tribe of the plains was becoming dominant, thanks to their involvement in the **slave trade**, which gave them easy access to firearms. By the time the Germans arrived in the 1880s, the Sambaa's military weakness was such that they capitulated to colonial rule without a fight.

The Kilindi dynasty was granted limited power by the Germans, and the British who followed, but their rule ended in 1962 when the Tanzanian government abolished tribal chiefdoms. Nonetheless, the lineal descendants of Mbega are still known by his title of Lion King. The last, **Kimweri Mputa Magogo** (Mputa II) took office in 1947 and died in 1999. Although few people speak openly about his successor, there is little doubt that the new Lion King is known by his subjects. Although the political power of the Sambaa is long gone, the effects of the Kilindi dynasty's domination are still evident – not so much outside Usambara, but in the way the Sambaa consider themselves: with great pride and humility, in the manner of Mbega. Wherever you go, you'll be made to feel very much at home.

throughout the day, leaving from the bottom of the road to Lushoto, 100m off the highway. In the unlikely event of getting stuck in Mombo, there are some basic **hotels**, of which *Madaa Guest House* (no phone; ❶), 40m along the road to Lushoto, is the best. There are lots of **restaurants**: *Midway Express*, at the junction, is busy. Another good place is *New Liverpool Hill Breeze*, 1km north of town towards Moshi, where most long-distance buses take a break: the food – especially the grilled *mishkaki* meat skewer - is superb, as is the selection of Usambara fruit sold from the kiosks in the parking lot. The *New Liverpool Hill Breeze* is also a good place for finding safe and comfortable **transport** to Arusha or Dar on buses from companies like Dar Express and Scandinavian Express.

A word of caution: **don't hire a guide in Mombo** or on the daladala to Lushoto, no matter how genuine they appear to be. Although one or two might be reasonable, most are just in it for a quick buck, and there have also been reports of robberies. Wait until you get to the tourist office in Lushoto, and hire a guide there.

Soni

The road up into the mountains from Mombo follows the vertiginous gorge of the **Bangala River** which, if you can stop worrying about the unfenced chasm to your left, is an absolutely spectacular ride that takes you from the flat and dry expanse of the Maasai Steppe into an utterly different world: green, lush and heavily forested, with towering mountain peaks glimpsed over waterfalls and some precariously balanced ridgetop villages and farmhouses. The first major place you hit is **SONI**, a bustling village just above the **Soni Falls**, where the Mkuzu River becomes the Bangala. Soni is famed for its twice-weekly **market** (Tues & Fri) at which the entire array of West Usambara produce can be found. The plums, passion fruit, mountain papaya (sweeter and more delicate than the lowland variety), coconuts and pineapples are especially good. The prices, for tourists, aren't always as good as they should be, but you can't really complain given the quality and the taste.

There are several cheap guest houses in Soni, but the best **accommodation** is ⚒ *Maweni Farm*, 2km east of Soni (☎027/264 0426, Ⓦwww.maweni.com; half-board ❺). Occupying a 1920s German farm in the lee of a cliff, it comes complete with ornamental fish pond (and "island"), flanked by reeds topped with weaver nests. There are thirteen comfortable and well-kept rooms with box nets, most with bathrooms, in the main house and its outbuildings, plus four en-suite walk-in tents pitched on a concrete platform overlooking the pond. A luxury

△ Market, Usambara Mountains

tree house is planned. Accommodation aside, the **food** is excellent (lunches are a bargain at $5–7), much of it raised or grown organically on the farm. There's also Internet access, a telescope for star-gazing, a colonial-style wood-panelled lounge and dining room, a playgroup for young kids, and stacks of locally produced documentary films from a participatory project, also based here.

Maweni's manager, Juma Kahema, has been involved with the Friends of Usambara, and the West Usambara **cultural tourism programme**, since their inception – see "Walks around Soni" on p.367.

Lushoto

Past Soni, the scenery becomes even more spectacular as you wind further up into the mountains and through a land of forest and steep cultivated slopes to reach **LUSHOTO**, half an hour beyond Soni and 34km from Mombo. Despite being the biggest town in the Usambaras, with a population of over 100,000, this district capital is an intimate, friendly and instantly likeable kind of place, and enjoys an especially beautiful setting among high forested peaks.

The first European to reach Lushoto was the missionary **Johann Ludwig Krapf**, who in 1849 was given a warm welcome by King Kimweri I. European interest remained marginal until 1886, when arch-colonist Karl Peters – nick-named "the man with bloodstained hands" by locals and described as "a model colonial administrator" by Adolf Hitler – entered the Usambaras and "persuaded" the local chief to sign away his domain for a pittance. The subsequent German advance was made easier in that, in the latter half of the nineteenth century, Usambara was racked by chaos: the **slave trade** had begun to turn its sights to the mountains, and at the same time the Sambaa's Kilindi dynasty was caught up in a civil war against the Bondei tribe, who wanted independence.

Lushoto's altitude (1500m) ensures a cool and temperate climate all year round, and made it a favoured mountain retreat for German colonial admin-istrators, who called the town **Wilhelmstal** (after the German kaiser). For a time, it even served as the unofficial "summer capital" of German East Africa – a welcome change from the sweltering heat and humidity of Dar es Salaam.

Arrival

Lushoto is served by direct early-morning **buses** from Arusha, Dar, Moshi and Tanga, and by direct **daladalas** from Tanga. If you miss these, catch a bus between Dar or Tanga and Arusha or Moshi, and get off in Mombo (see p.359), from where there are frequent daladalas throughout the day to Lushoto. The **bus stand** is in the centre of town next to the market.

The first place to head for is the **tourist office** (daily 7.30am–6pm; ☎027/264 0132 or 0748/420310, ⓔusambaras2005@yahoo.com), behind NMB bank and signposted from the bus stand. Try not to be waylaid by guides pretending to be "official" along the way – the tourist office is clearly marked (but also read p.367). Operated by the Friends of Usambara Society, the staff are friendly and helpful, and provide up-to-date information and impartial advice on accommodation, nightlife, transport and practicalities, as well as the various locally run **cultural tourism programme** tours (see p.367) organized here.

Accommodation

Lushoto has a good spread of budget and mid-range **hotels**. The cheaper guest houses are southwest of the centre – unfortunately also the haunt of an uncom-monly abrasive and tuneless muezzin who wakes all and sundry at 5am. Out of town having a car helps, though several places are within hiking distance. The

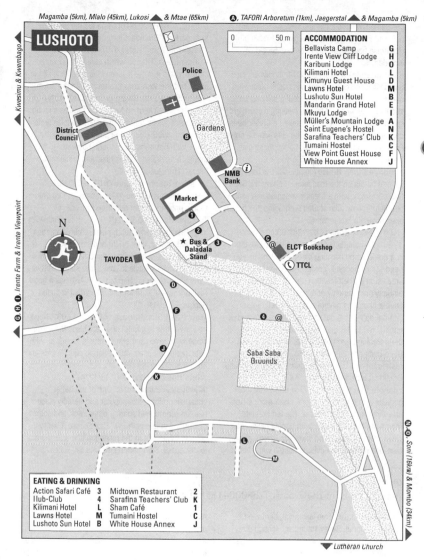

Magamba (5km), Mlalo (45km), Lukosi ▲ & Mtae (65km) | **Ⓐ**, TAFORI Arboretum (1km), Jaegerstal ▲ & Magamba (5km)

LUSHOTO

Kwesimu & Kwembago

Ⓖ, Ⓞ, Ⓘ, Irente Farm & Irente Viewpoint

0   50 m

ACCOMMODATION

Bellavista Camp	**G**
Irente View Cliff Lodge	**H**
Karibuni Lodge	**O**
Kilimani Hotel	**L**
Kimunyu Guest House	**D**
Lawns Hotel	**M**
Lushoto Sun Hotel	**B**
Mandarin Grand Hotel	**E**
Mkuyu Lodge	**I**
Müller's Mountain Lodge	**A**
Saint Eugene's Hostel	**N**
Sarafina Teachers' Club	**K**
Tumaini Hostel	**C**
View Point Guest House	**F**
White House Annex	**J**

Police

District Council

Gardens

NMB Bank

Market

TAYODEA

★ Bus & Daladala Stand

Ⓒ @ ELCT Bookshop

Ⓒ TTCL

Saba Saba Grounds

Ⓞ, Ⓞ, Soni (16km) & Mombo (34km)

EATING & DRINKING

Action Safari Café	**3**	Midtown Restaurant	**2**
Ilub-Club	**4**	Sarafina Teachers' Club	**K**
Kilimani Hotel	**L**	Sham Café	**1**
Lawns Hotel	**M**	Tumaini Hostel	**C**
Lushoto Sun Hotel	**B**	White House Annex	**J**

▼ Lutheran Church

cultural tourism programme can organize **homestays** for around Tsh6000–8000 per person. In town, **camping** is possible at *Lawns Hotel* (Tsh4500) and *Karibuni Lodge* ($5); out of town, you can pitch tents at *Müller's Mountain Lodge*, Irente Farm, and – with a gob-smacking view but no showers – *Bellavista Camp*.

In town

Karibuni Lodge 1km back towards Soni ☏0748/474026, ⓦwww.karibunilodge.com. The gorgeously luxuriant forest location, with lots of vervet monkeys and birds, is what recommends

this simple and charming colonial place, though as it has only four rooms (and a four-bed dorm), try to book ahead. The wood-floored rooms are en suite and have box nets, whilst the dorm (Tsh6000 per person) shares a bathtub with sufficient hot water to fill it. Daily set menu (around Tsh3000), otherwise book a few hours before. Breakfast included. ❸

Kilimani Hotel ☎027/264 0014, ⓔkilimaniguesthouse@yahoo.co.uk. A normally quiet place with twelve rooms (two with bathrooms; quixotic water supply for clean squat toilets) flanking a courtyard containing a somnolent bar. There's a livelier beer garden (and safe parking) at the side (can be noisy Fri & Sat), and food available. Cheap for singles. Breakfast included. ❷–❸

Kimunyu Guest House (no phone). The best of several hotels on the road looping above the Saba Saba Grounds, with a friendly welcome and simple but clean rooms with shared bathrooms (the better ones have big box nets). ❶

🏃 **Lawns Hotel** ☎027/264 0005, ⓦwww .lawnshotel.com. Over a century old, this is a quirky and charming place – as long as you heed the belligerent "complaints won't be tolerated" sign in the reception (the Cypriot owner is actually uncommonly gracious). The bedrooms have a choice of private or shared bathrooms (almost half-price) but vary greatly in style and quality: the better ones are excellent value for their creaking floorboards, fireplaces, heavy Art Deco beds and cast-iron baths. There's a good restaurant and bar, friendly dogs, and safe parking. Breakfast included. ❸–❹

Lushoto Sun Hotel ☎027/264 0082. The most popular with budget travellers, albeit more expensive than most guest houses. The ten en-suite rooms are big and bright, with double beds, nets, clean Western toilets and showers. There's also a twin-bed room, and a cheaper single with shared

bathroom. The restaurant's fine too (no alcohol). Safe parking. Breakfast included. ❸

Mandarin Grand Hotel ☎0748/533816. A half-complete hotel on which construction work stalled years ago, so it resembles a building site in parts, but the view over Lushoto – and the warm welcome – are the saving graces. The twenty rooms are well kept and spacious: singles sharing bathrooms, or better-value en-suite doubles (with box nets), twins (round nets), triples and suites, some with bathtubs *and* enough hot water to fill them. There's also a sleepy bar and restaurant. Breakfast included. ❷–❸

Sarafina Teachers' Club ☎027/264 0087. Cheap, clean and good-value rooms (shared bathrooms only) in a calm and friendly place. ❶

Tumaini Hostel ☎027/264 0094, ⓔtumaini@elct .org. This Lutheran Church place is very calm and a decent choice, with bright and simple rooms, all with box nets, some with bathrooms (good showers and Western-style toilets) and a suite with two beds that can be pushed together. Also has a good restaurant, and safe parking. Breakfast included. Rooms ❸, suites ❹.

View Point Guest House ☎027/264 0031. Nope, no view – this is a quiet and very basic family-run place with seven sometimes musty rooms, all with nets, table and chair, most sharing squat toilets and bucket showers. ❶–❷

White House Annex ☎0748/427471, ⓔwhitehouse@raha.com. One of the better cheapish options, this popular and friendly place has ten rooms, two sharing bathrooms, and some overpriced suites with TVs. There's also a bar with outside tables, TV in the reception and a restaurant (order early). Safe parking. Rooms ❷, suites ❹.

Outside town
A taxi to any of these costs Tsh8000–15,000.

Bellavista Camp Irente viewpoint, 6km west of town (no phone). Bellavista indeed, though dizzying and heart-pounding would also fit – this has several tent pitches right on the cliff edge (take care at night), and three extremely basic rooms (no guarantee of bedding). There are also some rickety two-storey wood-and-brick structures with tables on wonky terraces for views and cold drinks, including beers, but no food. Tsh3000 per person.

Irente View Cliff Lodge Irente viewpoint, 6km west of town ☎027/264 0026, ⓦwww.irenteview .com. A brand new hotel enjoying gloriously vertiginous views from its sixteen cliff-top rooms, though you'll have to hope that the owner's plans to stick iron grills outside each balcony come to nought. The best views are from the standard rooms in the

main building, all with satellite TV. The "superior" rooms, larger and with bathtubs, are in two rows, those at the front also have good views, despite the trees; the ones further back overlook a canyon and cliffs. The restaurant and bar in the main conical *makuti*-thatched building lack views. Book ahead and they'll pick you up from Lushoto. Hikes can be arranged, and there's Internet access. Breakfast included. ❺

Mkuyu Lodge Irente Farm, 5km west of town ☎027/264 0000. Intended primarily for self-catering, this has two three-bed rooms in a long green-roofed building with a kitchen (the farm sells lots of scrumptious produce, including cheese), plus an en-suite flat sleeping three, and two small doubles. ❸

Müller's Mountain Lodge 12km northeast of town ☎027/264 0204. Set in orchards and farmland close to Mkuzi Forest, this is a grand, two-storey 1930s farmhouse with steep gable roofs and a comfortably old-fashioned interior, including a cosy living room with a big fireplace and board games. There are seven bedrooms, the better ones en suite, all with big beds and fluffy pillows and duvets. Amenities include a bar and restaurant (three-course dinner Tsh10,000; full-board ❻), guides for walking trails, and mountain tours by car. To get there, turn right at Magamba and right again after 5.3km at the signpost; free lift from Lushoto if you stay two nights or more. Breakfast included. ❺

Saint Eugene's Hostel Catholic Mission of the Montessori Sisters, Ubiri (30min walk along the road to Soni) ☎027/264 0055, ℻027/264 0267. A good if pricey choice, with fourteen clean and comfortable en-suite rooms in a modern Swedish-style building, each with a balcony. There's a warm welcome, and great food. Breakfast included. ❹

The Town

Apart from its views and the cultural tourism programme, Lushoto's main attraction is its colourful **market**, liveliest on Thursday and Sunday when farmers descend from all around. Sunday is especially good for buying **traditional pottery** – either plain, or decorated with geometric incisions inspired by plants. **Fruit** is another Usambara speciality, especially apples and pears around Easter time, peaches and plums from December to February, jackfruit from March to June, tamarind from November to January, loquats in June and July, and berries all year round, but best from October to January. Look out for traditional medicinal herbs and bark (*madawa asili*), honey (*asali*) and *viungo vya chai*, which is powdered ginger (*tangawizi*) mixed with other spices for adding to tea – a small jar costs Tsh500. The best bargains can be found late evening when vendors want to go home.

In addition, many buildings survive from the period of German rule, including a bizarre construction at the top end of town whose belfry is topped by an onion-shaped steeple made from iron sheeting. Also dating from colonial times is **TAFORI Arboretum**, 1km north of town, containing botanical gardens and housing thousands of pressed plants collected from all over the country.

Eating, drinking and nightlife

The fare in local **restaurants** isn't up to much, but if you have time try to get someone to cook up *bada*, a Sambaa speciality consisting of a thick, greenish-brown porridge of pounded maize flour and dried fermented cassava, mixed with hot water and oil and served in aromatic banana leaves. It's exceedingly tasty, and is eaten like *ugali* by being dipped in sauces. *Bada* is usually served with chicken or meat, fried bananas or potatoes. Lushoto is a delight if you're **self-catering**. Your first stop for putting together a picnic should be the market for fruit and vegetables – amazingly cheap, even by Tanzanian standards. Irente Farm (p.368) is a good place to stock up on home-made jams, preserves and cheeses (also sold at *Tumaini Hostel* in town), as is the Catholic Mission of the Montessori Sisters in Ubiri (see above), who also brew and sell the surprisingly palatable Dochi **banana wine**. If you're still thirsty, the Benedictine Fathers in Sakharani, near Soni, make Tanzania's best **grape wine** (under the Sakharani label) and sell macadamia nuts and oil.

Action Safari Café Friendly and welcoming place that sees plenty of tourists, offering both local dishes (from Tsh1000) and tourist favourites like spaghetti, plus snacks and great spiced tea.

Lawns Hotel Delicious three-course lunches or dinners in a quirky dining room decorated with commemorative plates from around the globe (Tsh5000–6000; free if you bring a plate to add to the collection), plus snacks and light meals for under Tsh2000. You can also eat on a verandah.

Lushoto Sun Hotel Good cheap food (under Tsh1500), including a mixed grill, which you can eat at the streetside terrace. Also does breakfasts and snacks. No alcohol.

Midtown Restaurant Cheap local eats: *nyama choma*, fried chicken and chip omelettes. May be shifting location – ask around.

Sham Café A great little place for cheap and unfussy meals, and they're happy to rustle up something special if you contact them beforehand. They also provide hot milk – a favourite with locals and gorgeous on a cold day.

Tumaini Hostel Bland surroundings (eat in the garden) but tasty food, quite pricey for snacks, but very good value for more substantial dishes (Tsh2000–3000), including vegetarian moussaka, and a good range of meat and fish. Also has pizza, ice cream, juices and milk shakes. No alcohol.

White House Annex Not a patch on what it once was, but still serves up half-decent meals, including spaghetti and pepper steak, mostly under Tsh2000.

Drinking and nightlife

The following are the best of the town's numerous **bars**. Many sell the local sugar cane hooch, *boha*, popular with both men and women – especially the latter during festivities such as Kibwebwe, an all-night, women-only drumming celebration held after the birth of a mother's first child.

Hub-Club A normal bar by day, this hosts lively discos on Saturday nights.

Kilimani Hotel Two bars here, the one worth mentioning being the beer garden, sometimes with discos (Fri or Sat). There's a wide choice of food, including hangover-quashing *supu*.

Lawns Hotel Contains Lushoto's nicest bar, very cosy and pub-like, and equipped with satellite TV.

The Cypriot owner offers a free drink for unusual foreign coins to add to the zillions glued to the counter. There's also a verandah.

Sarafina Teachers' Club A pleasant and laid-back place open till past midnight; also does good *nyama choma*.

White House Annex Near the *Sarafina* and equally friendly and relaxed, with plenty of tables outside

Listings

Banks NMB, near the tourist office, changes cash and travellers' cheques without fuss.

Bicycles Mountain bikes can be rented through the cultural tourism programme, or via *Lawns Hotel*: no more than Tsh5000–10,000 a day.

Hospital District Hospital, 1.5km back along the road to Soni ☎027/264 0098.

Internet access Best is ELCT next to *Tumaini Hostel* (Mon–Sat 8am–6pm; Tsh2000/hour).

Souvenirs Imani Shop, next to *Action Safari Café*, sells local arts and crafts. *Tumaini Hostel* sells preserves and attractively packed flavoured teas, though there's a much wider choice at Irente Farm (see p.368).

Moving on from Lushoto

Lushoto has daily **bus** services to Arusha, Dar and Tanga, as well as Mtae. To **Arusha** (and Moshi), Fasaha VIP heads off around 7.30am – get there early as the exact time depends on when it arrives from Mtae. There's also Chakito Bus coming from Mlalo, and a minibus with less regular times. There are several daily buses to **Dar**, the better ones being Umba River Tours and Shambalai at 8am, and Mbaruku around 9–10am. For **Muheza and Tanga**, Umba River Tours and Kwekanga are the main companies, the last leaving around 10am; Tashriff also cover the route but have a very mixed safety record. Alternatively, catch a daladala down to Mombo (every 30min), and change there for another one to Tanga (the last leaves around 3pm). If you want to catch one of the better buses for Dar, Moshi or Arusha, phone their offices at the departure point (see the "moving on" sections in the Arusha and Dar es Salaam chapters) to book a seat, and tell them you'll board at *New Liverpool Hill Breeze*, 1km north of Mombo on the highway.

West Usambara Cultural Tourism Programme

Lushoto is home to one of Tanzania's most popular cultural tourism programmes, based at the tourist office (daily 7.30am–6pm; ☎027/264 0132 or 0748/420310, @usambaras2005@yahoo.com). Originally set up a decade ago by local farmers with assistance from German and Dutch NGOs, the **West Usambara Cultural Tourism Programme** offers over a dozen different guided tours around West Usambara, ranging from three-hour strolls to challenging seven-day hikes through some of Tanzania's most inspiring landscapes, and a five-day bicycle trip to Moshi via the Pare Mountains. The most popular "modules" are described below. Several can be combined into tours lasting several days.

Although you're not obliged to take a **guide**, most of them know the trails backwards, speak reasonable to excellent English, and all are of course fluent in Kiswahili and Kisambaa, making for intimate and enjoyable encounters with local people. Please do not dole out pens, sweets, money or anything else to local kids – you'll be encouraging a begging culture that is currently almost absent.

Unfortunately perhaps, the project's success has spawned a number of **copycats**: imitation may be the highest form of flattery, but it can also be confusing and gives no guarantee of quality. Given that the original programme remains reliable, and is the only one with a mechanism to guarantee that local populations benefit from your money (though all pay some sort of lip service to community involvement), there's little reason to recommend any other. However, one you might consider is TAYODEA, a self-help group for unemployed youths first established in Tanga, who claim that 20 percent of their income goes towards "youth development". They seem sincere in their efforts, and feedback has been pretty positive so far. Their office is next to *Florida Guest House* west of the bus stand (☎0748/861969, @youthall2000@yahoo.com).

Lastly, a **word of warning** – there have been a number of unpleasant incidents involving unofficial guides, ranging from shoddy service to knife-point muggings. Authorized guides from both the original cultural tourism programme and TAYODEA have photo ID cards, but these aren't infallible as others just make their own. The only sure way is to hire a guide at the tourist office or TAYODEA's office, not in hotels (excepting *Maweni Farm*, in Soni), on buses or anywhere else

Walks around Soni

There are a number of good half-day tours **around Soni**, taking four to eight hours each, and a more adventurous three- to five-day hike to West Usambara's best-preserved rainforest. Trips can also be organized through *Maweni Farm* in Soni (see p.361).

The refreshing **Bangala River Tour** starts at Mbuzi ("Goat") village between Lushoto and Soni, and follows the river downstream to the Soni Falls (you may be obliged to wade across). Costs are Tsh8000 per group plus Tsh4000 per person and the daladala fare. The **Growing Rock**, near Magila village, seems to grow taller every year, though in fact it's the soil around the base that is disappearing thanks to erosion. The tour includes **Mount Kwamongo** (good views and butterflies) and Shashui and Kwemula villages. The cost is no more than Tsh10,000 per person.

The **Mazumbai Forest** trip is more challenging, taking four or five days if you walk there and back, or three days if you return by car, taking you through a variety of terrain to Mazumbai rainforest – a great place to spot birds. Costs average Tsh35,000–50,000 per person per day.

Irente Viewpoint, Irente Farm and Orphanage

The walk to and from **Irente Viewpoint** (5–6hr) is the most popular short trek from Lushoto, and relatively easy; take a guide from the cultural tourism programme in Lushoto, as muggers have been known to prey on lone tourists (Tsh8000 per group plus Tsh4000 per person). The viewpoint, perched on the southwestern edge of the Usambaras, is reached after a six-kilometre walk through farms and small villages, and offers a truly breathtaking panorama over the Maasai Steppe below. The isolated range facing you with the knuckle-like outline is Mount Mafi, and the settlement below is Mazinde. You can **stay overnight** at *Bellavista* campsite or *Irente View Cliff Lodge* (see p.364). Both have drinks, and the latter also has a restaurant, sadly lacking views.

On the return leg, stop by the Lutheran-run **Irente Farm**, an ideal picnic break with plenty of seating in colourful shaded gardens. The farm shop sells organic produce, cheese (German-style quark curd, a kind of Camembert and one like Tilziter), pickles and preserves, macadamia nuts, *Arabica* coffee and various flavoured teas from Lutindi Mental Hospital near Korogwe, at the base of the mountains. Contact them in advance for **lunch**: they do an excellent picnic for Tsh2000 (minimum three people). Staying **overnight** is possible, either camping (Tsh2000 per pitch, including shower and toilet, plus Tsh1000 for a watchman) or at the farm's *Mkuyu Lodge* (see p.364).

Adjacent to the farm is **Irente Children's Home**, also run by the church, around which the matron will be happy to accompany you. Poverty and AIDS are the main problems affecting the age-old stability of the extended family – in some cases the latter has wiped out entire generations. The home houses over twenty orphans, disabled children and children of parents with psychiatric disorders, and also trains older girls – who look after the little 'uns – in pre-nursing care and basic schooling. The home partially funds its activities by offering **accommodation** (☏027/264 0086; ❸). Nearby are two special needs schools, also run by the church: Irente Rainbow School for autistic children, and Irente School for the Blind. You're more than welcome at either if you're sincerely interested.

Magamba Rainforest

The physically demanding but extremely rewarding walk through **Magamba Rainforest**, north of Lushoto, gives you the chance to spot black-and-white colobus monkeys, exotic birds like the paradise flycatcher, plenty of butterflies and weird fungi. The name of the forest means "fish" or "snake scales" in Kiswahili, referring to the bark of the trees which had to be stripped away before the wood could be used. Most visitors come on a round trip from Lushoto (5–6hr), though the forest can easily be combined with a trip to Irente Viewpoint. The standard **cost** is Tsh8000 per group plus Tsh9000 per person, including the Tsh5000 Forest Reserve fee.

The tour begins with a stiff uphill hike along tracks to the east of the Lushoto–Magamba road, passing through the former colonial settlement of Jaegerstal and a camphorwood forest. Just north of **Magamba village** (there's a small café here, and fruit and vegetable hawkers), a track heads west into the forest. Emerging onto a forestry road, you have the choice of delving back into the forest for a quick descent towards Kwembago (see opposite) or continuing uphill along the road to a ridge offering expansive views over Lushoto and the Maasai Steppe.

From the ridge, the track continues south to a **rest house** on top of Kiguu Hakwewa hill, whose name translates as "unclimbed by short leg", meaning steep. There are 360-degree views and a toilet. If you (literally) stomp around here, you'll notice that the hill appears to be hollow, as indeed it is: it was excavated during World War I for use as a bunker by German residents. The bunker is said to contain almost one hundred rooms: you're free to explore them, although you'll need a torch, and watch out for snakes. The entrance is 100m downhill on the southeastern flank.

From the hill, a steep and rocky path heads down through farmland to the royal village of **Kwembago**, one of the seats of the Kilindi dynasty, and which has good views over Lushoto.

Mlalo

The walk from Lushoto to **MLALO** and back takes three or four days with some sections covered by bus, but is best combined with a visit to Mtae (see below) to make a six- or seven-day round trip – expect to spend around Tsh20,000–25,000 a day. The walk includes Magamba Rainforest, followed by a bus ride direct to Mlalo, or to Malindi, from where you walk. There's simple **accommodation** in several villages along the way, including *Silver Dollar Guest House* (**①**) in Mlalo, with clean rooms sharing bathrooms, and a good restaurant.

Mlalo is a good base for a day or two. **Mtumbi Hill** – Usambara's highest – can be climbed from here, and there are several good markets in the area. **Kileti village** (also called Kwemieeti) is the main attraction, being one of the best places for meeting female potters. The Sambaa liken the art of **pottery** to the creation of life in a mother's womb, so it's no surprise that pottery is traditionally a woman's occupation, with knowledge and rituals connected with the craft being passed from mother to daughter. Although men are allowed to collect clay, they are excluded from the pot-making process itself – it's believed that their presence may anger spirits, who might crack the pots during firing or, still worse, cause sterility.

Mtae and around

The **road to Mtae**, on the far northwestern rim of the Usambaras, is the most popular long excursion from Lushoto, taking three to five days depending on how much you "cheat" by catching the bus. Although the trip can be done without a guide from the cultural tourism programme, you'll miss much of the local context and contacts that make this walk special. The views are spectacular, especially as you approach Mtae, and the villages between are as fascinating and pretty as they are friendly, offering plenty of opportunities for getting to meet locals. The **cost** of a guided trip from Lushoto is around Tsh17,000 per person per day, plus food and the Tsh5000 entry fee for Magamba Rainforest.

The goat and the leopard

Mtae's motto is *Kesi ya mbuzi hakimu ni chui haki hakuna*, which means, "In the case of the goat with the leopard as judge, there is no justice." The saying is illustrated by paintings hung up in some of the village's bars, and depicts a courtroom presided over by a leopard. The plaintiff is a lion, the defendant a goat. The saying alludes to colonial times, when there was little chance of justice for an African from a German judge when the plaintiff was a German farmer.

Passing by Magamba and **Shume rainforest** (where you might glimpse black-and-white colobus monkeys, even from the bus), **LUKOSI** is the first stop, an attractive agricultural village set in a high valley with a couple of basic **guest houses** (❶) should you want to stay. The forest has been cleared around the village, but comes back to flank the road between Lukosi and **Shume-Viti**, an equally attractive if dusty village, in a wide valley entirely covered with small plots. The village is the first place you'll see the unusual two-storey houses with intricately carved wooden balconies, accessed via external staircases, which are a feature of all the villages north of here (and in the Pare Mountains), including **Shume-Manolo**, **Shume-Kibaoni**, **Rangwi** and **Sunga**, all of which can be reached on foot. Also distinctive are the whitewashed houses, with facades and interiors painted with decorative geometric designs reminiscent of Ndebele house paintings in South Africa, or Ethiopian religious art – perhaps no coincidence, as some oral histories place the origins of the Sambaa in Ethiopia.

The village of **MTAE** itself is an enchanting place, which delights the eye with views you'll remember for the rest of your life. The location is everything; the village is isolated on a spur that juts out from the mass of West Usambara, and flanked by tiny hamlets with rust-red roofs perched along nearby ridges and peaks. At some places you have a plunging 270-degree view over the plains almost a kilometre below, giving the impression that you're hovering above them. With clear skies, especially in the evenings, you can see the Taita Hills in Kenya to the north, and the Pare Mountains and sometimes Kilimanjaro to the northwest – before the sun disappears in a kaleidoscope of colours and smoke from kitchens drifts into the air. During and just after the rains you might also wake to the extraordinary sight of being above a blanket of clouds. At any time of year, your alarm clock will be the drifting sound of cock crows and lowing cattle, followed by goats and children, while on Sundays the bells ring out from the nineteenth-century Lutheran church, complete with the church's boisterous (if not always tuneful) brass band.

Practicalities

Mtae is best visited as part of Lushoto's cultural tourism programme (see p.367), with whom you can walk all or part of the way. **Public transport** is limited to two daily buses. The ride up from Lushoto, along a narrow dirt road, often with sheer drops on one side, is one of the bumpiest (if most scenic) in Tanzania, but isn't advisable in the rainy seasons. Both buses – Fasaha VIP and the less reliable Mbaruku – leave Lushoto between 2–3pm (3–4hr), passing via Magamba, Lukosi, Shume-Viti, Shume-Manolo and Shume-Kibaoni. Arrive early to be sure of a seat.

The Fasaha VIP bus **back from Mtae** leaves at the unearthly time of 3am or 4am (double-check the day before), with Mbaruku leaving when full: anything between 4.30am and 6am. If you miss these, you'll have to spend another night in Mtae – no great hardship.

The best **restaurant** is attached to *Mwivano Guest House #1*. For **drinking**, *Mtitu wa Ndei* bar is next to the *Pendo Guest House*. If you need medical attention, try the dispensary in the Lutheran mission. Mtae's high altitude, exposed location and strong winds make it chilly at night, so bring a sweater, and wear suncream – the suns burns your skin more quickly at this altitude. **Accommodation** is limited to the following, all on the main (and only) road, within a few hundred metres of each other.

Kuna Maneno Guest House ☎ 027/264 0200. The only establishment in the village with electricity, albeit powered by a none-too-reliable generator. There are nine rooms (eight doubles and one twin; shared bathrooms only) and reliable piped water, plus a large but usually empty bar. ❶

Lutheran Mission c/o ELCT in Lushoto ☎ 027/264 0102. This has nine atmospheric rooms in a wing adjacent to the church, all of them spacious, with high ceilings and creaking floorboards. Food is available if ordered in the morning for the evening. ❷ **Mount Usambara Guest House** (no phone). Eight rooms with shared facilities (and hot water in buckets). Two rooms have fantastic views over Lake Kalimawe and the Pare Mountains beyond. ❶

Mwivano Guest House ☎ 027/264 0198. This is actually two hotels on the main road. *Number 1* has nine cell-like singles with clean shared showers and toilets, next to a restaurant. *Number 2*, 200m back on the left, is more attractive, and has double rooms with shared bathrooms and stunning views through chicken-wire mesh windows over Mkomazi Game Reserve. ❶

Mtae Mtii

A leisurely and recommended four-hour walk goes from Mtae to the small village of **MTAE MTII**, the traditional seat of the Kilindi dynasty in northwest Usambara until the chiefdoms were abolished in 1962 (the main seat was Vuga near Soni). Mtae Mtii was also the site of a semi-mythical nineteenth-century battle between the Sambaa and the Maasai, who lived in the plains below. The story goes that the Maasai believed that the king of Usambara had the power to bring rain to the plains, so one day they went to ask him for rain. He refused, and the Maasai resolved to fight. Although the Maasai were better equipped, the Sambaa vanquished their attackers by rolling boulders down the steep inclines, killing most of them. As spoils, the Sambaa seized the Maasai's cattle. Locals say they are the ancestors of all the cows you see grazing contentedly in the mountains today.

The last king of Mtae Mtii died in the late 1990s. His **compound** can be visited as part of the cultural tourism programme and has a fantastic location on a crag overlooking the Mkomazi plains. Next to the surprisingly humble (and now abandoned) hut where the king lived is an enclosure made from branches, bushes and young trees.

East Usambara

Some 40km inland from the Indian Ocean, the mountains of **EAST USAMBARA** rise abruptly from the coastal lowlands, their steep escarpments levelling off about a kilometre above sea level onto a deeply furrowed plateau. The range is separated both physically and biologically from West Usambara by the 4km-wide Lwengera Valley. With the exception of the dry lowlands to the north, the climate is warm and humid, influenced by the proximity of the Indian Ocean. Rainfall averages 2000mm a year, which together with the deeply weathered red loam soils, has created ideal conditions for the evolution of an astonishingly rich and complex tropical rainforest ecosystem – in fact, the second-most biodiverse place in Africa.

The figures speak for themselves: East Usambara's rainforests contain well over two thousand vascular plant species, over a quarter of which are found nowhere else in the world, as are sixteen of East Usambara's 230 tree species. The proportion of unique species amongst animals is even more astounding, ranging from ten to sixty percent depending on the family and genera. Other inhabitants of East Usambara include over thirty species of snakes and chameleons, amongst them the terrestrial pygmy leaf chameleon, the larger arboreal three-horned chameleon and a remarkable species of toad, *Nectophrynoides tornieri*, which gives birth to live offspring instead of eggs. There are also over two hundred species of butterfly and close to 350 types of bird.

The most famous of Usambara's endemics, however, is the **African violet**. Their botanical name, *Saintpaulia*, comes from Baron Walter von Saint Paul Illaire, the Tanga district commissioner of German East Africa, who in 1892 shipped a consignment of the small blue flowers to Berlin, thereby starting a horticultural craze which continues to this day. The African violet's hidden genetic make-up tells of the forests' immense age: blue or violet in the wild, gardeners and botanists have managed to tease out all sorts of colours from the plant's genes, from red and pink to white and even green – genetic diversity in evolution increases as time goes on.

Amani Nature Reserve

The most accessible part of the East Usambaras is **Amani Nature Reserve**. Established in 1997, this mountainous and heavily forested reserve is one of Tanzania's most attractive and under-visited destinations (*amani* means "peace" in Kiswahili), offering beautiful scenery, weird and wonderful flora and fauna, a constant chorus of cicadas and tree frogs (joined by the screeching of bush-babies at night), one of Africa's largest botanical gardens and enough hiking trails through primeval rainforest to keep you in raptures (or blister packs) for weeks. Even if your interest in things botanical is limited to the greens on your plate, the sight of the towering camphor trees festooned with vines, lianas or strangling fig trees that flank much of the drive up to the reserve is the stuff of dreams.

Bird-watchers will also be in heaven; despite difficult viewing conditions (the forest canopy conceals birds well), over 335 species have been recorded, including the endangered Amani sunbird, the long-billed apalis and the banded green sunbird which, although rare outside East Usambara, can sometimes be seen at Amani in flocks of up to sixty. Other rare species include the Usambara red-headed bluebill, long-billed tailorbird, Sokoke scops owl (named after

△ Chameleon, Amani Nature Reserve

Conserving Amani

Up until the end of the nineteenth century, East Usambara was extensively covered with forest, with a small human population. The advent of colonialism had far-reaching consequences for natural habitats in Tanzania. The main factor was the **expulsion of local people** from land that colonists wanted to use for commercial ranches and plantations. The Usambaras were an obvious destination for people displaced in the northeast of Tanzania, and very soon the forests began to shrink. The figures are sobering: from an estimated thousand square kilometres of prime forest cover in 1900, East Usambara now contains only 330, of which only a tenth remains relatively intact and undisturbed.

Apart from extensive forest clearance for commercial **tea plantations**, the single most damaging force to hit East Usambara's forests was large-scale **timber logging** between the late-1950s and 1980s. The now infamous Sikh Saw Mills was established in Tanga for processing East Usambara timber, and in the 1970s expanded its operations with funding from the Finnish government's development agency. It was only in 1986 that the Finns abruptly realized how grossly they had underestimated the damage that their rough logging methods were causing. Commercial logging was terminated, and the Finns promptly performed a perfect volte-face to espouse the cause of conservation, donating $6.1 million between 1991 and 1998 to fund the creation of **Amani Nature Reserve**.

The first of its kind in Tanzania, it both protects one of East Africa's finest surviving rainforests, and safeguards Tanga's water supply against the effects of unchecked forest clearance and unsustainable farming. To the lasting credit of the reserve's management, the **East Usambara Conservation Area Programme** has not only managed to stem the destruction of the forest (and successfully contained a 2003 **alluvial gold rush** that threatened parts of it), but has also embarked on ambitious reforestation and educational outreach programmes in sustainable agriculture for local farmers. In 2001, they achieved the long-delayed protection of Derema Forest Reserve, adjacent to Amani, and now plan to link a series of existing and planned forest reserves north to south across East Usambara to create a "biological corridor" for plants and animals.

Arabuko-Sokoke forest in Kenya), Usambara eagle owl, Tanzanian weaver and the green-headed oriole.

There are few large **mammals** in the forest, which makes sighting them all the more rewarding, though all you're likely to see of the shy black-and-white colobus monkey is a flash of black and white in the canopy as it retreats into deeper forest. Other primates include yellow baboons and blue monkeys, both pests for farmers – it's said that if you throw stones at blue monkeys to chase them off, they just pick them up and hurl them back, often with a surer eye. The Tanganyika mountain squirrel is the most common of the three squirrel species; if you're really lucky, the rufous elephant shrew may put in a fleeting appearance on the forest paths.

Access

Unless you're hiking from West Usambara, Amani Nature Reserve is accessed from **MUHEZA**, a messy little town on the highway 45km southwest of Tanga, and served by frequent daladalas from Lushoto, Mombo and Tanga, and by buses connecting Tanga with Dar and Arusha. Get to Muheza in the morning to avoid getting stranded, as public transport into the reserve can be erratic. You'll be dropped on the highway, or at the **bus stand** just off it. The "best" **accommodation** is the basic *Elephant Guest House* (❶), but don't leave valuables lying around. Friendlier, but 1km along the Pangani road east of the highway, is the run-down *Check Point Bar & Lodge* (❶), marked by a quirky statue of their "boss" in his blue suit. Some rooms are en suite, food is available, and there's safe parking.

The reserve's **Sigi Gate** is 26km west of Muheza along all-weather *murram*. The following 9km to **Amani village**, much of it hairpins, can become treacherously slippery in the rains, when 4WD may be needed. Whilst **vehicles heading to Amani** may sometimes start at the bus stand, most tend to hang around at the start of the road to Amani: walk 200m into town from the bus stand (the stand's on your left), and where the road forks bear right, and turn right again. The unmarked stand for Amani is 50m along on the left before the railway crossing, opposite the encouragingly named Death Row Electronics shop. Two buses to Amani leave Muheza between 1 and 2pm, and carry on past Amani to Kwamkoro or Bulwa. There's also usually a pick-up or two, or a lorry or occasional daladala a little later, but rarely after 4pm. If you're feeling energetic, you could catch a vehicle to **Kisiwani village**, 3km short of Sigi Gate, leaving you a very pleasant uphill walk through forest. Watch out for snakes at night.

With a few hours to kill, Muheza's busy **market** is worth a poke around; it has lots of herbalists, and sells honey (*asali*) which is especially delectable after the rains.

Entry fees and information

Entrance fees are paid at Sigi Gate or at the reserve's headquarters in Amani village (see below), depending on where you stay or start. Fees are $30 per person, with no time limit, plus Tsh5000 for a vehicle permit and $10 for a photo permit. A guide, arranged at either place, is optional but recommended, and costs $20 a day. Camping is $5. You can also pay in shillings. Keep your receipt – you may need it as proof of payment. To **book accommodation**, and for specialized queries, contact the **Chief Conservator** at the Reserve's headquarters in Amani village: PO Box 1 Amani (☎027/264 0313, ✉sawe59@yahoo.com).

The reserve's **information centre** is at Sigi Gate. It provides leaflets and maps, and sells the detailed *Guide to Trails and Drive Routes in Amani Nature Reserve*; they may also have vehicles for rent and can advise about campsites and arrange guided walks. A small shop sells attractive painted cards and the lavishly illustrated *Trees of Amani Nature Reserve* book, which details hundreds of species and has a general introduction about the reserve and its ecosystem.

The centre's main draw, though, is its thoughtfully presented **displays** on local flora, birdlife, chameleons, butterflies and moths, amphibians, plant ecology and

---

The Sigi–Tengeni Railway

The information centre at Sigi occupies the beautifully restored wooden **German Station Master's House**, at the terminus of the short-lived **Sigi–Tengeni Railway**. Built between 1904 and 1910 by the Sigi Export Gesellschaft, the narrow 75-centimetre-gauge railway opened up 120 square kilometres of forest to timber exploitation. The railway fell into disuse after World War I, and an accident in 1929 forced its closure. In 1931 the road from Muheza was opened, and the railway was finally dismantled. Apart from the Station Master's House, which later saw use as a primary school, all that remains is a diminutive freight carriage and a square block in front of the house, which housed the station bell. There's also a giant cogwheel from a demolished sawmill.

biodiversity and, of course, African violets (of which Amani has eight species). There are also a few rooms of Sambaa and Bondei artefacts.

Accommodation

Camping ($5) is possible at the rest houses reviewed below, and in campsites along various hiking trails in the vicinity of Amani village – all but one (Kiganga on the Kwamkoro trail) lack water and toilets.

Amani Conservation Centre Rest House Amani village, 9km from Sigi Gate (reservations through the Chief Conservator, see opposite). Modern and comfortable, there are nine large, triple-bed rooms with electricity, mosquito nets, hot showers and the use of a kitchen. The rooms are treated as dorms, so if there are many visitors, you'll have to share. A small bar and restaurant sells cold sodas and beers, and rustles up great meals (Tsh3000). Breakfast optional. ❸

Amani Malaria Research Centre Rest House Amani village, 9km from Sigi Gate ☏ 027/264 0311. In a medical research complex established by the Germans in 1893, this has eight beds, a cosy lounge with a huge fireplace, and food. For drinks, try the *Welfare Club* nearby. Full-board. ❺
Sigi Rest House Sigi Gate (reservations through the Chief Conservator, see opposite). Identical to *Amani Conservation Centre Rest House*. Breakfast optional. ❸

Walking trails and driving routes

There are eight walking trails and three driving routes in the reserve, some starting from Sigi Gate, some from Amani village, and others from elsewhere. The **driving routes** are intended for visitors with their own transport, although several of these trails are accessible by bus or pick-up as long as you don't mind camping (vehicles heading into the reserve generally leave Sigi Gate – or better, Amani village – in the afternoon, only returning the next morning). The reserve should have **bicycles** to rent ($5 a day), considerably expanding the possibilities for visitors without vehicles.

Information on the various trails is given in leaflets available at the information centre, as well as in the *Guide to Trails and Drive Routes in Amani Nature Reserve*. None of the trails are marked, so it's easy to get lost. If you have plenty of time this isn't a problem, but consider taking a guide, as they're also clued up on botany and ecology.

The **walking trails** – none longer than a day – go through rainforest, botanical gardens, tea plantations (and a tea factory), and past viewpoints on a ridge overlooking West Usambara across the Lwengera Valley, historical and cultural sites like sacred caves and the remains of a fortified Iron Age settlement, waterfalls, villages and farms. There's also a **butterfly breeding project** with walk-in cages, a thirty-minute walk from Amani village at Shebomeza (Tsh2500).

The rainforest is best seen along the **Amani–Sigi Mountain Trail** (3–5hr from Sigi Gate), a fairly tough and steep round trip which climbs 450m through primary and secondary lowland and submontane forest to the top of a ridge. The area has particularly tall trees (many over 60m); on the lower stretches, you may see bright orange **land crabs** hiding under fallen leaves.

Another good trail, especially for getting between Sigi Gate and Amani village, goes through **Amani Botanical Garden**, one of Africa's largest. Founded in 1902, the garden contains around three hundred tree species (both indigenous and exotic), a large expanse of original forest, a spice garden and a palmetum, whose indigenous cycads – an ancient and primitive species of palm – hint at the great age of East Usambara's forests. The garden's original function was to study the flora and fauna of German East Africa. "Any such activities that have no effect in improvement of standards to the east African culture should not be conducted," emphasized Graf von Götzen, the governor of German East

Moving on from Amani

Most transport to Muheza, including a bus from Kwamkoro and another from Bulwa, passes through Amani village between 6am and 6.30am, reaching Sigi Gate half an hour later, and Muheza in time to catch onward transport to Pangani, Tanga, Dar or Mombo (for Lushoto). If you miss the buses, you'll have to hitch – payment will be expected.

Africa, in 1904. Sadly, the fruits of this research (four thousand books and three hundred journals) were transferred to Berlin and destroyed in a 1943 bombardment. The plants are not labelled, so take a guide if you want names.

Two adventurous options are not covered by the leaflets; prices for the guide are negotiable. **Lutindi Peak** (1360m) can be climbed in a day, for jaw-dropping views over the Lwengera Valley. You'll need three days if you lack transport, as it's a day's hike to the start of the trail, and another back. There's also a five-day trail **to West Usambara** (Soni or Lushoto). You'll need a tent and a day or two to arrange guides, food and other practicalities beforehand. The route can also be done in reverse. Lastly, short **night walks** (no more than an hour; $10 per person) are also possible, and particularly recommended should tree frogs or chameleons (especially around Amani village) turn you on.

Travel details

For information on internal flights from Kilimanjaro International Airport, see the travel details in Chapter 6 (p.423). There are no scheduled flights from Moshi airport.

Buses

Lushoto to: Arusha (2 daily; 5–6hr); Dar (3–5 daily; 6hr); Mombo (daladalas every 30min until 5pm; 1hr); Moshi (2 daily; 4–5hr); Mtae (2 daily; 3–4hr); Muheza (3 daily plus daladalas until mid-afternoon; 2hr); Tanga (3 daily plus daladalas until mid-afternoon; 3hr).

Moshi to: Arusha (3 hourly; 1hr 30 min); Dar (hourly until 2pm; 8–9hr); Iringa (1–3 daily; 9–10hr); Karatu (3 daily; 5hr); Kisangara Chini (2 hourly; 1hr); Lushoto (3–4 daily; 4–5hr); Machame (hourly; 1hr); Marangu (hourly; 45min); Mbeya (1–3 daily; 15hr); Morogoro (3–4 daily; 6–7hr); Muheza (3–4 in the morning; 4hr); Mwanga (1–2 hourly; 1hr); Nairobi (3–4 daily; 6–8hr); Same (1–2 hourly; 2hr); Shinyanga (1 weekly; over 24hr); Tanga (3–4 in the morning; 5–6hr); Taveta (hourly; 45min); Usangi (1 daily; 4–5hr).

Muheza to: Amani (2 daily 1–2pm, plus irregular transport to 4pm; 1hr); Arusha (3–4 each morning; 5hr 30min); Dar (3 daily; 4–5hr); Lushoto (every 2hr until mid-afternoon; 2hr); Mombo (hourly; 1hr); Morogoro (every 2hr until 1pm; 4–5hr); Moshi (3–4 in the morning; 4hr); Pangani (2 daily except in the rains; 2–3hr); Tanga (every 30min; 45min).

Same to: Arusha (2 daily; 3hr); Mbaga (1 daily; 2hr 30min).

6

Arusha and around

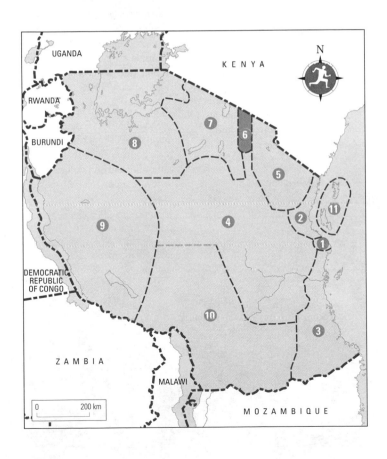

CHAPTER 6 # Highlights

✴ **Handicrafts** With vivid and
humorous Tingatinga paintings, Makonde carvings by
the thousand, beaded Maasai
jewellery and a whole lot
more, Arusha is a souvenir-
hunter's paradise. **See p.396**

✴ **Via Via** A lively restaurant-
cum-bar in the old German
Boma, this is northern
Tanzania's best place for the
performing arts. **See p.399**

✴ **Safaris** As capital of Tanzania's "Northern Safari Circuit",
most trips to Serengeti and
Ngorongoro start here. **See
p.403**

✴ **Mount Meru** Tanzania's
second-highest peak can be

climbed in three days, ideally
four, and offers stunning
scenery all the way, along
with views of Kilimanjaro. **See
p.412**

✴ **Cultural tourism** Arusha
is the base for many of
Tanzania's ground-breaking
community-run cultural tourism programmes, offering
intimate encounters with local
tribes, and dozens of walks to
local attractions. **See p.414**

✴ **Aang Serian** Based in the
village of Monduli Juu, this
local NGO offers courses in
traditional Maasai medicine,
ethnobotany and culture, from
a few days to several weeks.
See p.422

△ Cultural tourism: camel safari near Mount Meru

Arusha and around

eading west from Moshi, the last major town before the rolling savannah of the Rift Valley kicks in is **Arusha**, Tanzania's safari capital and third-largest city. The town receives around 400,000 visitors each year. Most use Arusha only as a base from which to explore the nearby wildlife parks, but the town's lively shops and markets, vibrant nightlife, cultural tourism and some excellent restaurants provide plenty to reward a longer stay.

Overlooking Arusha is the magnificent **Mount Meru**, a dormant volcanic cone which, at 4566m, is Tanzania's second-highest mountain; the three- or four-day hike to the top passes through some exceptionally beautiful (and bizarre) scenery. Another climbable mountain close by is the mist-shrouded **Mount Longido**, which can be climbed as part of a Maasai-run **cultural tourism programme**. There are more such programmes in other rural locations, giving visitors the opportunity of combining encounters with local people with hikes to unspoilt forests, rivers and waterfalls, and even camel-back safaris.

Arusha

Nestled among the lush foothills of Mount Meru, the booming town – officially now a city – of **ARUSHA** is northern Tanzania's major commercial centre and the country's undisputed safari capital. In clear weather, the sight of Mount Meru's near-perfect cone rising majestically to the north provides the town's abiding memory, while the exceptionally rich volcanic soils on and around Meru's slopes account for Arusha's prosperity – every inch of the area seems to be taken up by *shambas* and settlements, producing half of the country's wheat and substantial amounts of coffee, flowers, seed-beans and pyrethrum for export, along with bananas, maize, millet and vegetables. The rainforests on higher ground are the traditional land of the **Meru and Il Larusa (Arusha) tribes**. The former are related to disappeared hunter-gatherer communities; the latter are agricultural cousins of the Maasai who dominate the surrounding savannah.

Despite a burgeoning population of over 350,000 people, Arusha has a remarkably laid-back, small-town atmosphere, an impression accentuated by

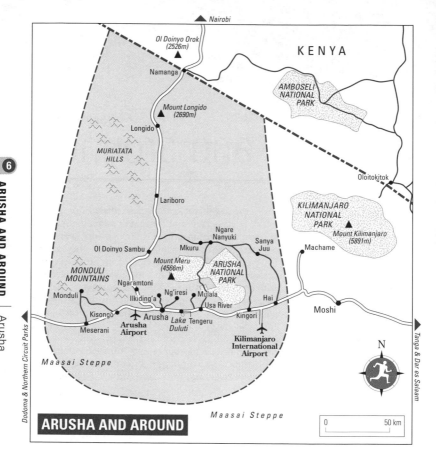

ARUSHA AND AROUND

the unexpected sight of small fields of maize and vegetables running straight through the centre of town, along the banks of the Naura, Goliondoi and Themi rivers. Even so, Arusha is a cosmopolitan and diverse place. The presence of tourists and expatriates keeps Western culture prominent, while around the market Asian and Muslim businessmen dressed in loose white or pale blue cotton garments mingle with Nike-capped youths and streetboys, and on the balconies above you might see African women in brightly patterned kangas talking to Asian neighbours dressed in lurid sarees.

And, of course, there are the **Maasai**: the men in red or purple tartan *shukas* (cloth replaced leather towards the end of the nineteenth century), the women with shorn heads and huge disc-like necklaces (*esos*) sewn with hundreds of tiny beads. Some look bewildered in the metropolitan setting, but most are as nonchalant and at ease with themselves as they are in the savannah. And then there's you, the tourist, being followed by trains of young men brandishing reams of batiks, stacks of newspapers or crumpled brochures from disreputable safari companies. If you can weather the attentions of the flycatchers for the first few days, Arusha is one of the most vibrant and ultimately enjoyable towns in Tanzania.

Arusha's altitude, at around 1500m, ensures a temperate **climate** for most of the year, and also – apparently – does away with malaria; the cold season (mid-April to mid-Aug) requires nothing thicker than a sweater, though nights can be truly chilly in July. It gets fiercely hot in November before the short rains start.

Some history

Arusha is, unsurprisingly, home to the Arusha (properly called Il Larusa) people and the related Meru. The **Meru** seem to be the original inhabitants of the foothills of the mountain that bears their name, whereas the **Il Larusa** are said to have migrated here about two centuries ago from south of Moshi. The reason for the migration remains obscure: one theory holds that they were taken or captured by Maasai to dig wells and build irrigation furrows, and later intermarried. Their Maasai heritage is evidenced by their language, a dialect of Maa, and in the fact that Il Larusa practise horticulture rather than agriculture, dispensing with ploughs – a remnant of the Maasai taboo against breaking soil: cattle are sacred, and so too is the soil that nurtures the grass that feeds them.

The town of Arusha came into existence in the 1880s during **German colonial rule**. In 1886, a military garrison was established, and the settlement that grew up around it became the main market centre for the surrounding European-owned plantations. Later, it became a stopover for vehicles travelling down from Nairobi in Kenya on what became known as the **Great North Road**, which continued south into Zambia. Arusha's increasing importance was confirmed when it was made capital of Tanganyika's Northern Province. A 1929 brochure for the province, published to coincide with the opening of the railway from Moshi, enticed prospective settlers with the offer to recreate a little piece of England, going on to explain: "Looking back ... to that period immediately after the war, Arusha was scarce a hamlet ... Those who see it today, with its railway just completed, its up-to-date hotel and its stores, see but the half-completed dream of the early settlers. *Floreat Arusha!*"

In some respects, the dream remained half-complete. The planned extension of the railway to Mwanza never happened, but Arusha's importance as a commercial and agricultural centre continued. Even so, the population remained surprisingly small, with the 1952 census putting it at just under eight thousand, of which less than half were Africans. After **Independence**, the pace of development increased dramatically, and by 1980, the population had rocketed to 100,000. The present population numbers well over 350,000, the majority of them migrants seeking waged employment.

Arrival and information

Arusha is well connected to the rest of Tanzania (and with Nairobi in Kenya) by both road and air.

By air

International flights touch down at **Kilimanjaro International Airport (KIA)**, 48km east of Arusha off the Moshi Highway. Passport formalities are efficient, and you can buy your visa at immigration if you haven't already got one ($50). There are **foreign exchange bureaux** at passport control and in the arrivals hall, offering reasonable rates for travellers' cheques, though rates for cash are about twenty percent lower than at the forexes in town. The airport has a number of gift shops, a restaurant and bar, a post office and pharmacy.

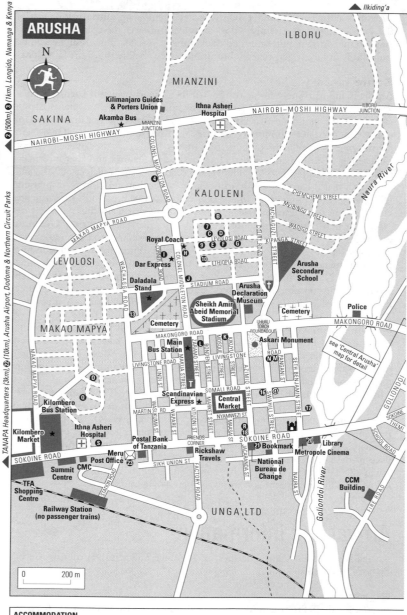

N

▲ Ilkiding'a

② (500m), ③ (1km), Longido, Namanga & Kenya

TANAPA Headquarters (3km), ① (10km), Arusha Airport, Dodoma & Northern Circuit Parks

ILBORU

MIANZINI

SAKINA

Kilimanjaro Guides & Porters Union

Akamba Bus

Ithna Asheri Hospital

NAIROBI–MOSHI HIGHWAY

ILBORU JUNCTION

MIANZINI JUNCTION

NAIROBI–MOSHI HIGHWAY

COLONEL MIDDLETON ROAD

④

KALOLENI

CHEMCHEMI STREET

Naura River

MVIBINGO STREET

WAQIGO STREET

MAKAO MAPYA ROAD

WACHAGA ROAD

MCHAGUZI ROAD

KIPANGA STREET

Ⓑ

LEVOLOSI

Royal Coach

Dar Express

Daladala Stand

LEVOLOSI ROAD

ETHIOPIA ROAD

Ⓘ Ⓗ

⑦ Ⓒ Ⓓ
⑨ Ⓔ Ⓕ Ⓖ

⑩

Ⓙ

STADIUM ROAD

Arusha Secondary School

COLONEL MIDDLETON ROAD

CORNER ROAD

⑬

Cemetery

Sheikh Amir Abeid Memorial Stadium

Arusha Declaration Museum

UHURU TORCH ROUNDABOUT

Cemetery

Police

MAKONGORO ROAD

MAKAO MAPYA

Main Bus Station

LIVINGSTONE STREET

Askari Monument

MAKONGORO ROAD

see 'Central Arusha map for detail'

GOLIONDOI ROAD

SOKOINE THEMI

MAKAO MAPYA ROAD

Ⓛ

Scandinavian Express

Kilombero Bus Station

Kilombero Market

Ithna Asheri Hospital

Ⓞ

Ⓢ

Meru Post Office

Postal Bank of Tanzania

CMC

Summit Centre

TFA Shopping Centre

Railway Station (no passenger trains)

LIVINGSTONE STREET

LINDI ST

MAKAO STREET

BONDENI STREET

KIKUU STREET

SOMALI ROAD

MARKET STREET

MARTIN RD

KITUONI ST

WAPARE ST

MASAAI ST

SIKH UNION ST

FRIENDS CORNER

Ⓣ

Central Market

Rickshaw Travels

⑯ Ⓠ

⑱

⑰

⑮

㉑

AZIMIO STREET

SETH BENJAMIN STREET

SWAHILI STREET

PANGANI ST

MOSQUE STREET

NYAMWEZI ST

SOKOINE ROAD

Bookmark

National Bureau de Change

FACTORY ROAD

STATION ROAD

JACARANDA ST

NAURA ST

⑳ Library

Metropole Cinema

CCM Building

FIRE ROAD

Goliondoi River

UNGA LTD

0 ——— 200 m

SANAWARI

Professional
Tour Guide School

SEKEI

Ng'iresi

Usa River, Arusha National Park, Lake Duluti, Kilimanjaro International Airport, Moshi & Dar es Salaam

SANAWARI
JUNCTION

Goliondoi River

NAIROBI–MOSHI HIGHWAY

AFRIKA MASHARIKI ROAD

Themi River

5   6

Mount Meru
Hospital

★ Shuttle Buses

PHILIPS
JUNCTION

Immigration
Office

AICC

Gymkhana Club

German
Boma

MAASAI
ROUNDABOUT

UZUNGUNI

KAUNDA ROAD

SIMEON ROAD

BOMA ROAD

ROAD

KANISA ROAD (CHURCH ROAD)

INDIA STREET

J. MAELI
ST

CLOCK
TOWER
ROUNDABOUT

ROAD

KENYATTA ROAD

Old Arusha
Clinic

NYERERE ROAD

AICC
Hospital

HAPE SEFASSIE

VIJANA ROAD

T

KIJENGE

ENGIRA ROAD

RIVER ROAD

25

U

NJIRO ROAD

KIJENGE
ROUNDABOUT

KIJENGE JUU ROAD

Barclay's
Bank

Sopa

SERENGETI ROAD

OLD MOSHI ROAD

28

29

30

V

Njiro

31 (100m) & Lohada (2.5km)

CLUBS

Colobus Club	31
Crystal Club	17
Hotel Saba Saba	15
Shiverz Park	9
Summit Club	6
Tembo Club	22
Triple-A	3

EATING

AICC Complex	11	Green Hut	20	Noble	S	Stiggy's	30
Arusha Crown Hotel	K	Immigration Canteen	12	The Outpost	V	Swagat	21
Big Bite	16	L'Oasis Lodge		Pizzarusha	7	Via Via	14
Dolly's Patisserie	18	& Restaurant	A	Shanghai Chinese	23	VIP Lounge	5
Dragon Pearl	28	Le Jacaranda	T	Sombrero Bar			
Everest Chinese	24	Maharaja Palace	27	& Restaurant	10		
Greek Club	26	Mount Meru Hotel	8	Spices & Herbs	25		

BARS

AICC Sports Club	29
Club Galaxy Arusha	4
Le Jacaranda	T
Matongee Arusha Club	19
Pama Bar	13
Seven Up Bar	2
Stiggy's	30
Via Via	14

For passengers arriving on Air Tanzania and Precisionair, there's a free **shuttle bus** to Arusha or Moshi; KLM passengers pay $10 for a similar service (run by Impala Shuttle, to Arusha only). Arriving on another airline, catch a lift with fellow passengers, or grab a **taxi** – the ride to Moshi or Arusha costs $50, and bargaining is difficult, so it's cheaper if you can share. There's no public transport – the closest buses are 6km away on the highway.

Arriving from elsewhere in Tanzania, most flights land at the small **Arusha airport**, 7km along the Dodoma road west of town. There are no shuttle buses, so rent a taxi (Tsh6000), or walk 1.5km to the main road to catch a daladala (every 15–30min; Tsh200).

By road

The **main bus station**, for buses coming from Nairobi and eastern Tanzania (including Tanga, Moshi and Dar) is between Zaramo and Makua streets; buses coming from the west (including Babati, Kondoa and Dodoma) drop you at the messy **Kilombero bus station** on Sokoine Road, just west of the centre. There are plenty of pushy **taxi touts** at both places, so stay cool and keep your hands on your bags. **Bus companies with their own terminals** include Scandinavian Express, on Kituoni Street just south of the main bus stand (lots of hassle and taxi touts); Akamba, beside the *Eland Motel* on the Nairobi–Moshi Highway (calm); and Dar Express, on Colonel Middleton Road (also calm).

Town transport

Daladalas (locally nicknamed *Vifordi*) cover much of the town's outskirts; most trips are Tsh200, though destinations further out cost a little more; destinations are painted on the front of the vehicles. The main **daladala stand** is north of the main bus station off Stadium Road, which should have labelled bays. At present, some vehicles **heading northwest** along the Nairobi–Moshi Highway leave from Wachagga Road one block west, whilst services **heading east** to Usa River and Tengeru (for Lake Duluti) are best caught at

Security

Given the volume of tourists that pass through Arusha each year, don't be surprised if some people treat you as little more than an easy source of income. That said, as long as you avoid booking with safari companies touted on the street by "flycatchers" (do read the section on "Safaris" and "Trouble" in Basics), there's little to worry about. If you're still uncomfortable, *Via Via* in the German Boma can fix you up with a guide to accompany you when walking around town.

As to **theft and robbery**, you'd be extremely unlucky to have problems by day, but keep a close eye on your bags and pockets in the bus stations, daladala stands and around markets. After dusk, taking a taxi is strongly advised. If you ignore this advice, there are a number of **areas to avoid after sunset**. These include bridges, which attract thieves as they give the victim little room to escape: especially notorious are the ones over the Themi River along the Nairobi–Moshi Highway, Sokoine Road where it crosses the Goliondoi River, and Nyerere Road just east of the clock tower. Indeed, the entirety of **Nyerere Road** should be avoided at night. North of town, **Sanawari** is the roughest district, though serious incidents are rare. In the town centre, **Sokoine Road** – especially the junction with Factory Road known as Friend's Corner, and the western stretch towards Kilombero Market – is known for opportunistic bag-snatchers and pickpockets. If you're driving, roll up your windows.

Sanawari junction, between Afrika Mashariki Road and the Nairobi–Moshi Highway. Daladalas to the **eastern suburbs** of Kijenge and Njiro (including *Masai Camp*) can be boarded on Sokoine Road between Swahili and Seth Benjamin streets.

Taxis – invariably white Toyota saloons – are found throughout town, and at night outside most bars, restaurants and clubs. A ride within town as far as the Nairobi–Moshi Highway costs Tsh2000. Although **taxis** are usually safe (ignoring their parlous and often comical state of disrepair), avoid taking a cab if there's already a passenger inside – although most are just friends of the driver, cases of robbery have been known.

Information and tours

The helpful **Tanzania Tourist Board tourist office** is on Boma Road (Mon–Fri 8am–4pm, Sat 8.30am–1pm; ☎027/250 3842, ✉ttb-info@habari .co.tz). They have hotel price lists covering most of Tanzania, a free town plan, an invaluable bus timetable and a list of licensed safari operators, and a sporadically updated blacklist of really bad ones. They also stock information about the various **cultural tourism programmes** in Arusha Region and nationwide (see p.414 for more details). **National parks information** can be obtained at the Ngorongoro Conservation Area Office a few doors down, and at the TANAPA headquarters (see p.403) to the west of town.

TANAPA also publish the beautiful **Arusha guidebook**, which includes Arusha National Park ($10 from bookshops, *Jambo's Coffee House* and the above-mentioned Ngorongoro office). Additional local information can be found in the often humorous *Arusha Times* (every Sat; also ⓦwww.arushatimes.co.tz), and the bimonthly *Via Via Time Out*, free from *Via Via* and larger hotels. The main travellers' **notice boards** are outside *The Patisserie* on Sokoine Road; outside *Café Bamboo* on Boma Road; and in the corridor leading to *Jambo's Makuti Garden*, also on Boma Road.

Several safari companies offer guided minibus **city tours**, averaging $20–30 per person, sometimes with lunch – Nyika Treks & Safaris (see p.405) are particularly recommended. See also the **cultural tourism programmes** on p.414. Cheaper and just as good are the **guided walks** offered by *Via Via* (see "Eating"). These take in most of the central sights, plus a range of more intimate experiences in the suburbs, including weekly markets, coffee farms and villages. Access is usually by daladala. An NGO offshoot of *Via Via* is currently active in four villages, placing the emphasis as much on education as on development of the performing and plastic arts. Costs should be no more than Tsh10,000 per person for a full day, or Tsh5000–7000 for half a day, plus (minimal) transport costs, meals and any entrance fees. For something different, Lohada, a Christian NGO caring for destitute children, welcomes visitors. Based at "Camp Moses" in Moshono, 3km along Old Moshi Road, tours last 2–3 hours; the $15 fee includes lunch and transport from town. Contact Mrs Happiness Wambura (☎0744/447640, ⓦwww.lohada.org).

Accommodation

Arusha has lots of **accommodation**, ranging from dirt-cheap town-centre guest houses with shared squat toilets and bucket showers, to mid-priced hotels and top-dollar neo-colonial places in the town's leafy suburbs and coffee plantations further out.

Town centre

The main concentration of **budget accommodation** is in Kaloleni district, north of the stadium; it's pretty safe, in spite of its dilapidated appearance, unsurfaced roads and numerous local boozers. The streets around the main bus station and Central Market are also lively and have some decent **mid-range** options. Other areas are distinctly quieter.

Power cuts are frequent (the better hotels have generators), so water supplies are also erratic: part of the town's supply depends on electric pump-powered boreholes, and many hotels use pumps to fill their tanks.

The "mid-range" and "expensive" options listed all include breakfast in their rates; the "expensive" choices all accept Visa and MasterCard, with the exception of the *New Safari*.

Budget

Annex Hotel Arusha by Night Colonel Middleton Rd, entrance on Stadium Rd (no phone). Adequate and good value for couples, with large, clean, en-suite twin-bed rooms off a dark corridor. All have nets and hot showers, and there's also safe parking and an average restaurant and bar. Can be a little noisy. Breakfast included. ❸

Arusha Centre Tourist Inn Off Swahili St ☎027/250 0421, ✉icerestaurant@yahoo.com. Eighteen recently renovated small en-suite rooms on three floors (no lift), with nets and TV. Cheap restaurant downstairs. Breakfast included. ❸

Centre House Catholic School, Kanisa Rd ☎027/250 2313, ✉angelo.arusha@habari.co.tz. An uninspiring Catholic-run hostel but good value for singles, though the 10pm curfew hampers night owls. Rooms share bathrooms, and food is available if pre-ordered. Breakfast included. ❸

Coyote Guest House Azimio St ☎027/250 5452. On the first floor, this is friendly and safe. Some rooms have cold showers and squat toilets (only shared bathrooms have hot water), and most beds have nets. There are also some large twin-bed doubles. ❷

Hanang Deluxe Guest House Levolosi Rd, Kaloleni ☎0748/544311. A basic and somnolent, if clean and safe cheapie. Rooms – all sharing showers and squat toilets are adequate, and have window nets (rooms are also sprayed), desk and chair. Safe parking. ❶

Kitundu Guest House Levolosi Rd, Kaloleni ☎027/250 9065. On three storeys, this is Kaloleni's best lodging, especially for the four east-facing en-suite rooms on each of the first and second floors, which have unobstructed views of Mount Meru beyond Kaloleni's tin roofs. All have cotton sheets and nets, but the ground-floor rooms are stuffy and overpriced. Hot running water and Western-style toilets. Safe parking. ❷, en suite ❸.

Mashele Guest House Kaloleni. Despite its popularity with travellers, this is one to avoid, given the lax security and the fact that the place is infested with flycatchers. ❷

Meru House Inn Sokoine Rd ☎027/250 7803, ⓦwww.victoriatz.com. Popular with backpackers, with small but comfortable rooms on three floors (including triples) with nets and hot showers; some have streetside balconies, others are en suite. There's also a pleasant courtyard café-bar with satellite TV but uninspiring food. The downside is the persistence of the resident Victoria Expeditions in plugging their safaris. Safe parking. ❷–❸

Minja's Guest House Levolosi Rd, Kaloleni ☎0748/707851. Basic but fine: the huge single beds can be shared by couples, and there are also twins and triples. No nets (rooms are sprayed), shared bathrooms, and Internet café. ❶

Monje's Guest House Levolosi Rd, Kaloleni (no phone). Two adequate if not hugely welcoming flop-houses, "A" and the marginally preferable and quieter "B", with no flycatchers, good mosquito nets and piping hot showers whenever there's electricity. Most rooms share bathrooms (squat toilets), but are acceptable at this level. Safe parking. ❶–❷

Palace Guest House Makao Mapya ☎0745/292780. Basic singles and twins with nets and shared bathrooms (squat toilets), and a popular bar up front with food. Little English spoken. ❶

Palm Court Inn Makao Mapya ☎0744/297495. A quirky and friendly option with decent rooms around a bar and its TV (noisy until midnight). All have desk, chair and small nets, most sharing bathrooms (hot water in buckets); the more expensive are en suite and have TVs. Food available, and basic breakfast included. ❶–❸

Williams Inn Corner Rd ☎027/250 3578. If you can deal with the desultory service and turbid atmosphere, this is pretty decent at the price, with cleanish en-suite doubles with nets and hot water morning and evening. ❷

YMCA India St ☎027/254 4032. Seedy rather than pious, but friendly. There's a local bar and drinks in a courtyard at the back. The seven tatty rooms have nets and washbasins (all share bathrooms with erratic water supply), and basic cheap meals are available. Breakfast included. ❸

Mid-range

Arusha Crown Hotel Makongoro Rd ☏027/250 8523, ⓦwww.arushacrownhotel.com. Efficiently run and oddly upmarket for the area, with lift access, electronic locks and well-kept rooms, all with cable TV, phone, window nets (bed nets on request), cotton sheets and room service. The better ones have views of Mount Meru and the football stadium. Also has a sophisticated restaurant. ❺

Arusha Resort Center Fire Rd ☏027/250 8333. The prison-like architecture scores *nul points* for atmosphere, and the standard rooms are overpriced; better are the spacious apartments with fully equipped kitchens. There's also a TV lounge, bar and restaurant, and safe parking. ❺

Hotel Fort Des Moines Pangani St ☏027/250 0277, ⓦwww.bimel.co.tz/safari.html. On four floors (no lift) and getting tatty but reasonable value. Carpeted en-suite rooms (double or twin) with ceiling fans, phone, nets and hot water; some have views of Mount Meru. Its restaurant sells alcohol. ❹

Golden Rose Hotel Colonel Middleton Rd ☏027/250 7059, ⓔgoldenrose@habari.co.tz. Friendly and decent if overpriced, with forty balconied en-suite twins and doubles, all with big beds, nets, phones, fridges and cable TV, though they get musty in the rains. There's a restaurant and bar, a pleasant patio at the back for eating, drinking or playing pool, a small shop, an Internet café next door, and safe parking. ❺

Le Jacaranda Vijana Rd, Kijenge ☏027/254 4945, ⓦwww.chez.com/jacaranda. An atmospheric colonial-era house with ten rooms, most en suite, though the flaky corridors really need some attention. The best room is on the first floor with a large balcony.There's also a good – if expensive – restaurant plus a bar and minigolf. ❺

🏃 **The Outpost** Serengeti Rd, off Nyerere Rd ☏027/254 8405, ⓦwww.outposttanzania.

com. An especially good choice for families – good value and likeable. There's a family room, bar and restaurant in the attractive colonial-era house, plus en-suite rooms including triples in fourteen bungalows and cottages around the gardens, all with huge mosquito nets, cable TV, and shared verandahs. There's also a gift shop and Internet café. ❺

Seven Eleven Zaramo St ☏027/250 1261. A wide selection of good-value en-suite twins and doubles facing the bus stand, all with large beds, hot water and satellite TV, but no nets, fans or lift. Restaurant and safe parking. ❹

Expensive

🏃 **The Arusha Hotel** By the clock tower ☏027/250 7777, ⓦwww.arushahotel. com. Established in the 1920s, this rambling hotel – the best in town – is one of Arusha's oldest and most attractive. Extensively renovated, its 65 rooms (some with a/c) coming with electronic safes, fifteen-channel TV, large box nets, and tubs in their bathrooms. An extra $10 gets you a balcony and slightly larger bed(s). Amenities include lift access, an outdoor swimming pool set in pleasant gardens (with a bar and massage parlour; $20 for 30min), another bar and terrace restaurant, slot machines, gift shops, and safe parking. ❽

The Impala Hotel Kijenge roundabout ☏027/250 8448, ⓦwww.impalahotel.com. Second-best to the *Arusha*, but good value if a little impersonal. Most of its 160 rooms are in a nine-storey block fitted with panoramic lifts running on the outside. Some have TV, others offer great views of Mount Meru; all have nets and phone. Amenities include three restaurants of varying quality (Indian, Chinese and Italian), two bars, small swimming pool, forex and Internet café. ❻

New Safari Hotel Boma Rd ☏027/250 3261, ⓦwww.newsafarihotel.co.tz. Hemingway's haunt back in 1933, unrecognizable after its latest facelift, and mainly used by large tour groups. Tiled and bright rooms are on four floors (lift access) and have TV, phone, fridge and spotless bathrooms; there's also an Internet café, and a very bland but cheap restaurant (a better one, with terrace views of Mount Meru, is planned). No alcohol. ❼

Out of town

The advantage of staying outside town is the peaceful and rural – if often somewhat neo-colonial – atmosphere. On clear days, most places also have views of Mount Meru, but take the "Kilimanjaro view" claims with a pinch of salt: it's clouded for much of the year. For a description of the Nairobi–Moshi Highway and several of Arusha's cultural tourism programmes, which also offer accommodation, see p.414; see also the reviews for Arusha National Park (p.410). The following include breakfast in their rates.

Arumeru River Lodge 15km east of town at Tengeru: 1km south of the Nairobi–Moshi Highway ⓣ027/255 3573, ⓦwww.arumerulodge.com. On a coffee estate, this has twenty large, comfortable rooms in ten angular chalets with touches of African style. Whilst the surrounding lawn is boring, there's a small reedy swamp alive with birds, and nearby forest for walks. Also has a small swimming pool and superb restaurant (buffet lunch most weekends Tsh15,000; three-course à la carte around Tsh20,000). ❼

Arusha Coffee Lodge 6.5km west of town at Burka, along the Dodoma road near Arusha airport (book through Elewana Afrika, 4th floor, Sopa Plaza, 99 Serengeti Rd, Arusha ⓣ027/250 0630–9, ⓦwww.elewana.com). Stylishly expensive, but if you have the money, the luxurious rustic-style rooms on the edge of a coffee plantation are very attractive, with individual cottages raised on wooden platforms, all with four-poster beds, lounge and fireplace, and bathtubs. Also has a very good restaurant, bar and swimming pool, plus guided walks around the estate. ❾

Karama Lodge 4km east of town at Suye Hill: 3km along Old Moshi Rd, then signposted after *Masai Camp* ⓣ027/250 0359, ⓦwww.karama-lodge.com. A cosy, stylish and keenly priced hideaway. The 22 en-suite rooms are in log cabins on stilts, with large balconies for views of Mount Meru and surrounding forest. There are similar views from the bar and restaurant (four courses $14), cute and chattery bushbabies, and lots of birdlife. A swimming pool is planned. ❼

KIA Lodge 48km east of town at Kilimanjaro International Airport: 6km south of the Nairobi–Moshi Highway ⓣ027/255 3242, ⓦwww.kialodge. com. Handy for late-night flights, this is more than just a stopover: very comfortable accommodation thatched cottages, together with a bar, good Afro-European restaurant and hilltop swimming pool with glorious views, including Kilimanjaro. Airport transfer included. ❼

Kigongoni Lodge 10km east of town at Tengeru: 1km off the Nairobi–Moshi Highway ⓦwww.kigongoni.net (book through Asilia Lodges & Camps, Arusha ⓣ027/250 2799, ⓦwww.asilialodges.com). On an uncommonly beautiful, partially forested coffee estate with views of Mount Meru, the lodge funds the adjacent Sibusiso Foundation for mentally disabled children. The fourteen attractive en-suite cottages are decked out in soft-edged, rustic simplicity, with fireplaces, four-posters, and wooden verandahs overlooking the forest and some jittery vervet monkeys. There's a swimming pool with great views, free excursions to Sibusiso, and optional guided walks through

nearby forest, the coffee farm and to waterfalls and Lake Duluti. Half-board. ❽

Klub Afriko Hotel 2km east of town at Kimandolu: 200m south of the Nairobi–Moshi Highway ⓣ027/250 9205, ⓦwww.kluba-friko.com. Hospitable and well maintained, with rooms in six attractive traditional, thatched bungalows and one huge rondavel containing a suite. There's good food, two bars (one popular with locals), a small library with lounge-verandah, and a reliable safari company for tailor-made tours. ❺

L'Oasis Lodge & Restaurant 800m north of the Nairobi–Moshi Highway at Sekei ⓣ027/250 7089, ⓦwww.loasislodge.com. Set in lush gardens in a populous area of small farms and mud houses, and within walking distance of town, this has cosy traditionally built doubles and triples. These are mostly in traditionally built ivy-festooned rondavels, though the best – with lots of sunlight – are the three large wooden houses on stilts. Their cheaper "Backpackers' Lodge" annexe ($15 per person) on the opposite side of the road is flanked by banana plants, trees and birds, and has twelve twin-bed rooms in a long house on stilts, each with a washbasin (shared bathrooms). The open-air restaurant is superb; there's also a bar, Internet café, and a swimming pool is planned. Rooms ❻

Moivaro Coffee Plantation Lodge 7km east of town at Moivaro: 1.8km south of the Nairobi–Moshi Highway ⓣ027/255 3242, ⓦwww.moivaro.com. A recommended coffee estate getaway, with 26 rustic en-suite cottages (twins or doubles), all with box nets, small verandahs and fireplace. Amenities include room service, a swimming pool with a lovely view of Mount Meru, bar and restaurant, 2km jogging circuit, children's playground and gift shop. ❼

Mount Meru Game Lodge & Sanctuary 22km east of town at Usa River: along the Nairobi–Moshi Highway ⓣ027/255 3643, ⓦwww.mountmerugamelodge.com. Founded in 1959 and recently refurbished, this welcoming choice has aged well. Styled on a colonial hunting lodge, it has seventeen large, en-suite rooms in wooden bungalows, their verandahs giving eyeball-to-eyeball views with denizens of the adjacent wildlife sanctuary. There's also a bar and good restaurant, and walks are possible through the estate, or to villages and farms. ❽

Ngare Sero Mountain Lodge 22km east of town at Usa River: 1.5km north off the Nairobi–Moshi Highway at the sign for *Dik Dik Hotel* ⓣ027/255 3638, ⓦwww.ngare-sero-lodge.com. A colonial-era farmhouse whose delightfully lush riverside location, flanked by both tended and wild gardens, is the reason to stay, with a wooden footbridge over a fishpond setting the scene. Unfortunately, the eleven bedrooms, although attractive and well kept inside, are in an uninspiring terrace row. Still, croquet anyone? Full-board. ❽

🏕 **Onsea House (Guest House)** 8km east of town at Moivaro: 3km south of the Nairobi–Moshi Highway ☎0748/833207, ⓦwww .onseahouse.com. Under construction at the time of writing, this cosy and homely Afro-colonial style place, run by a charming Belgian couple, should be an extremely stylish – and secluded – hideaway, and with excellent food to match. Swimming pool and Jacuzzi with a lovely view of Mount Meru and the Maasai steppe. ❻

Rivertrees Country Inn 22km east of town at Usa River: 300m south of the Nairobi–Moshi Highway ☎027/255 3894, ⓦwww.rivertrees.com. A stylishly rustic and homely European country house which is part of a flower and vegetable farm. There are nine en-suite rooms (can be musty in the rains), two cottages and a riverside house, all decorated with classic colonial furnishings and agricultural memorabilia. The gorgeous garden flanking Usa River (not visible from main building) is good for birdlife. Amenities include Internet access, transfers, day-trips, swimming pool, bar and excellent food (around $20). Trips on foot or horseback can also be arranged. ❽

Serena Mountain Village Lodge 13km east of town at Lake Duluti: 2km south of the Nairobi–

Moshi Highway from Tengeru (book through Serena Hotels, AICC Ngorongoro Room 605, Arusha ☎027/250 6304, ⓦwww.serenahotels.com). A homely retreat of thatched concrete bungalows (thankfully partially covered by creepers) set 300m back from the lake in tropical gardens, complete with babbling brook. The better rooms have pleasant if unspectacular lake views, and some have funny sunken baths; all have cable TV. It's a good place for lunch ($15 for the buffet), there's also a bar, and Green Footprint Adventures offer guided walks and canoeing, here or in Arusha National Park. ❽

Songota Falls Lodge 4.5km east of town at Oldadai: 1.5km north of the Nairobi–Moshi Highway from Ngulelo junction; there's another signposted turning 1km further along ☎0744/095566, ⓔjoice_kimaro@yahoo.com. Surrounded by local *shambas*, this is a great place to get a feel of village life, and also enjoys spectacular views over the forested Songota Valley below and beyond to the Pare Mountains, with Mount Meru looming up behind. Run by a Tanzanian woman, it's also a good deal cheaper than other out-of-town places, but then there's neither electricity nor hot water. The five rooms (twin or double) are in simple but beautifully decorated individual Meru cottages, and have Western-style toilets. The food is first-rate, and a guide is on hand for walks to Songota Falls ($10 per group). Half-board ❺, full-board ❻.

Camping

The following are central Arusha's only **campsites**. *Meserani Snake Park*, 30km west of town (see p.420) is also recommended. See also the accommodation reviews for Arusha National Park, p.410.

Arusha Vision Campsite Boma Rd ☎0744/040810. Nestled above the Themi River (more like a stream), this is a surprisingly central oasis. The location leaves niggling worries about safety, although there hasn't been an incident for years, but you'll get hassled by flycatchers from the three resident companies. There's a bar and basic restaurant, along with laundry and (sometimes) hot water. Tsh3000 per person.

Masai Camp Old Moshi Rd, 2.5km east of

Kijenge ☎0744/898800, ⓦwww.masaicamp .com. Set in tropical gardens, this is popular with overland trucks and has an excellent restaurant and bar, and a great children's play area; it's also the base for Tropical Trails safaris. The handful of rooms are very basic but reasonable for singles (Tsh7000), and there's also a small four-bed dorm (Tsh5000). Don't come here if dogs bristle your hair – there are plenty. Camping Tsh3000 per person.

The Town

Arusha has two distinct centres: the old **colonial quarter** between Goliondoi and Boma roads in the east, which contains most of the shops and offices you might need plus a welter of gemstone dealers; and the larger, earthier grid of streets around the **Central Market** to the west. In the east, beyond the Themi

River, is **Uzunguni** ("the place of Europeans"), a spread-out area of trees and guarded houses where the local elite live, along with a good many expats.

To the north and south of these three areas are the populous **residential suburbs** – areas like Sanawari, Sekei and Sakina to the north, Unga Limited in the south, and Kijenge to the east – where the majority live. With their dirt roads, wood-and-thatch houses, goats and chickens in the streets, impromptu markets, local bars and children both delighted and scared stiff by your presence, these typically African areas provide a welcome contrast to the largely European and Asian feel of the centre.

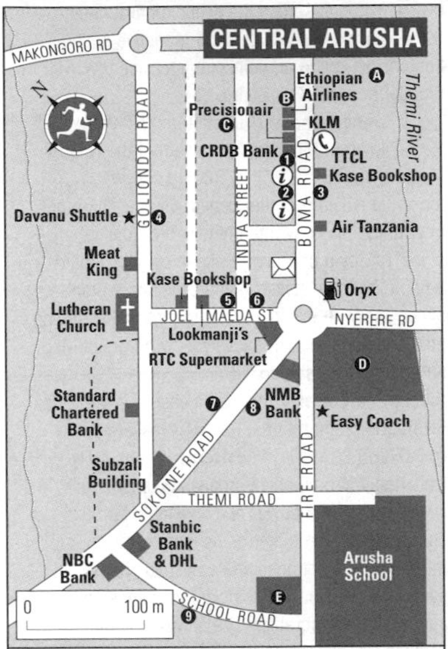

The clock tower and the German Boma

The **clock tower**, at the bottom of Boma Road by *The Arusha Hotel*, is Arusha's best-known landmark,

CENTRAL ARUSHA

(Map of Central Arusha, with labels:)

MAKONGORO RD — MAKONGORO RD
GOLONDOI ROAD
INDIA STREET
BOMA ROAD
FIRE ROAD
SOKOINE ROAD
THEMI ROAD
JOEL MAEDA ST
NYERERE RD
SCHOOL ROAD
Themi River

Precisionair — Ethiopian Airlines — KLM
CRDB Bank — TTCL — Kase Bookshop
Davanu Shuttle — Air Tanzania
Meat King
Kase Bookshop
Lutheran Church — Oryx
Lookmanji's
RTC Supermarket
Standard Chartered Bank — NMB Bank — Easy Coach
Subzali Building
Stanbic Bank & DHL
NBC Bank — Arusha School

0   100 m

ACCOMMODATION

		EATING & DRINKING			
The Arusha Hotel	D	The Arusha Hotel	D	Madini	4
Arusha Resort Center	E	Arusha Naaz Hotel	7	Onsea House	
Arusha Vision	A	Café Bamboo	3	Delicatessen	6
New Safari Hotel	B	Jambo's		The Patisserie	8
YMCA	C	Coffee House	1	Police Mess	9
		Jambo's Makuti Garden	2	Steers	5

and also where most of the town's flycatchers, second-hand newspaper vendors and "batik boys" hang out. A small plaque at the base of the tower states that Arusha is the halfway point between Cape Town and Cairo, actually something of a fib – if you draw a line between the two cities, you end up somewhere in the swamps of the Congo River basin. The story seems to have come from the megalomaniacal ambitions of the British arch-colonialist Cecil Rhodes, who dreamt of seeing the entirety of eastern Africa painted red on the map. Had his vision of a projected "Cape to Cairo" railway ever come to fruition, Arusha may well have been the mid-point.

Heading up Boma Road past the tourist office brings you to a squat white wall enclosing a number of defensive-looking whitewashed buildings. This is the **German Boma**, built in 1886 as a military and administrative headquarters during the German colonization of Tanganyika. It now houses the neglected **National Natural History Museum** (daily 9am–5pm; Tsh2000; Ⓦwww .habari.co.tz/museum). The building to your left contains a hotchpotch of dusty exhibits, mostly illustrating the evolution of mankind: hominid skulls, stone tools, and a cast of the 3.6-million-year-old footprints found at Laetoli in Ngorongoro. The questionable highlight is an amusing diorama of a cave painter looking distinctly shifty as he daubs the wall. In the smaller building with the short tower is a display tracing the history of the Boma itself. On the grassy slope east of the fortified quadrangle, the *Via Via* bar and restaurant (closed Sun; see "Eating") hosts frequent **cultural events** such as art exhibitions and music. Both the museum and *Via Via* are also accessible in the daytime from the road leading to the AICC car park – there's a gate at the end on the right.

The AICC and the Maasai roundabout

Immediately behind the German Boma are the three office blocks of the **Arusha International Conference Centre (AICC)**, built in the 1960s to serve as the headquarters of the original, ill-fated East African Community (resurrected in 2001, and which will also be based in Arusha). The triangular design of the three wings – named Kilimanjaro, Serengeti and Ngorongoro – represent Tanzania, Uganda and Kenya. The original community collapsed in the 1970s following ideological differences between Nyerere's socialist Tanzania and Jomo Kenyatta's capitalist Kenya, and sour relations with Idi Amin's Uganda.

The complex currently houses offices and the **International Criminal Tribunal for Rwanda** (Ⓦ www.ictr.org), set up by the UN in November 1994 following the horrific hundred-day genocide that same year which claimed the lives of over 800,000 people. The tribunal delivered the world's first condemnation for genocide in September 1998, when former Rwandan Prime Minister Jean Kambanda was found guilty, but has been dogged by controversy for much of its life – not the least of which being the UN's characteristically lavish and ineffectual **bureaucracy**. By 2005, over a billion dollars had been spent, and by the time the Tribunal supposedly winds up in 2010, one and a half billion dollars will have funded the trials of barely seventy suspects. The notice board outside the Press & Public Affairs Unit on the ground floor of the Kilimanjaro Wing has a weekly timetable of **court hearings**; they're usually open to the public (free).

Just southwest of the AICC, the so-called **Maasai Roundabout** at the junction of Afrika Mashariki and Makongoro roads is graced by a colourful set of statues depicting a rural family. In 2000 the roundabout became the object of local controversy when a nearby bar erected a giant beer bottle on it and had the gall to rename part of Makongoro Road after itself – Chief Makongoro had been involved in the fight against colonialism. Neither the bottle nor the road sign survived long, as they were mysteriously attacked one night. To forestall further attempts at expropriation, the municipal council commissioned the statues you see now. Designed by Charlotte O'Neal, wife of former Chicago Black Panther leader-in-exile, Pete, the monument unleashed a hail of criticism. The reason: the male figure, decked out in the traditional red *shuka* cloth of the Maasai, was carrying a heavy bunch of bananas on his head. As any Tanzanian knows, the only thing that Maasai men carry on their shoulders is a spear or walking stick, and bananas don't even feature in their diet. The furore was only quelled by repainting his *shuka* in yellow – Maasai *shukas* are always red or purple. Heading west, Makongoro Road crosses the Goliondoi and Naura rivers before reaching, after 1km, a far more imposing roundabout monument – the concrete-arched **Uhuru Torch** – symbolizing the torch that was set atop Kilimanjaro on the eve of Tanganyika's Independence (*uhuru* means freedom). Sadly, the "eternal" flame flickered out ages ago, but the relief panels in the sides of the monument have been repainted in colourful detail, and show mainly agricultural scenes. Southwest of the roundabout, a small patch of grass is home to the **Askari Monument** – a clumsy, red-painted statue of a burly soldier who has lost half of the machine gun he's brandishing. The prosaic inscription reads, "We have completed the task you assigned us", commemorating Tanzania's victory over Idi Amin's forces in the Kagera War of 1978–79.

On the northwest side of the roundabout, the **Arusha Declaration Museum** (daily 9am–6pm; Tsh2000) is worth a quick detour, assuming that the exhibits are in place – the halls are sometimes cleared for conferences. Consisting mostly of rare documentary photographs, the exhibits tell Tanzania's recent history in eloquent fashion, from just before colonial times to **Ujamaa**,

President Nyerere's economically disastrous experiment in self-reliant rural socialism. Also here is the ceremonial "Torch of Unity" used by Nyerere after Independence, recalling the original Uhuru Torch (now in Dar's National Museum) planted atop Kilimanjaro on December 9, 1961. The museum takes its name from a pivotal speech delivered here – then a social hall – in February 1967, in which Nyerere set out his policy of Ujamaa. Formally entitled "On the Policy of Self-Reliance in Tanzania", it stressed the importance of hard work and longer working hours as the key to Tanzania's future economic success, rather than dependence on foreign aid, loans and industrialization. The museum sells a limited selection of postcards and books, and attractive paintings and other artwork from an artists' co-operative.

The Central Market

The city's enjoyable **Central Market** (Mon–Sat 7am–6pm, Sun 7am–2pm) is five minutes' walk southwest from the Arusha Declaration Museum, in the thick of the Muslim district. Don't be intimidated by the swarming mass of people (but do beware of pickpockets) – the market and the streets to the west of it offer a dazzling variety of produce, from fruit and vegetables, meat and fish (fresh or sun-dried) to herbs, spices, traditional medicine, cooking implements, colourful kangas, clothing and sandals made from truck tyres, all displayed with geometric precision. Kids sell plastic bags for a few shillings, but better would be to search out one of the traditional grass baskets. A couple of other unusual things worth seeking out are pale pink baobab seeds (used to make juice, or just sucked like sweets), and fresh tamarind (at the end of the year) – also good for juices and sucking, and great for cooking with.

Eating

Visitors have a wide selection of top-notch restaurants to choose from, as well as the cheaper (but still good) local eateries. Those functioning also as bars, or marked as "licensed", also sell alcohol. The town is famed for **beef** (*ng'ombe*), whether grilled or dished up in a variety of stews, notably *trupa* (or *trooper*), which is a mix of bananas, beef (or chicken), seasonal vegetables and potatoes – it sounds weird but is rather tasty, and comes in portions sufficient for four or five people. Another speciality is a thick banana mash called *mashalali*. For your **own supplies**, check out the central market or the various supermarkets and groceries (see p.400).

There's also plenty of **street food**. Roasted maize cobs, *mishkaki* meat skewers, fried cassava and sometimes even stir-fries can be bought from vendors along Swahili Street one block south of *Big Bite*, as well as in Kaloleni, and at various other street corners in the western part of town. In addition to the restaurants below, don't forget the **bars** (see p.395), all of which rustle up cheap and filling meals, mainly based on meat, eggs and chips, and often accompanied by hangover-quashing *supu* broth in the morning.

In the centre

The Arusha Hotel Facing the clock tower. The Tsh15,000 lunchtime buffet is popular with safari groups. There's also light à la carte, such as nachos and vegetarian pie, for Tsh4000–6000. And chocolate mousse...

Arusha Naaz Hotel Sokoine Rd. Good and cheap if unexciting, with most meals around Tsh2000. They also sell snacks, and have barbecues most nights.

Café Bamboo Boma Rd. A bright, cheerful and friendly place, especially popular for breakfast – home-made cakes, ice cream, fresh juices, milk shakes, Kilimanjaro coffee and great *chai tangawizi* (ginger tea). Also serves light lunches and dinners (Tsh3500–4500): pork, pasta, crêpes, vegetarian gratin, and especially good fish and salads. Closes 4pm on Sun.

AICC Complex Off Afrika Mashariki Rd. The cafeteria in the Serengeti Wing has simple but good lunchtime buffets, including vegetarian, for Tsh4500. There are also three snack bars, including the excellent AHTI bakery for bread, pies and burgers, cakes and brownies.

Immigration Canteen Afrika Mashariki Rd. Self-service Tanzanian food, popular with office staff; full meals under Tsh1000. Lunchtimes only, closed Sun.

Jambo's Boma Rd. Two interconnected places either side of the tourist office: the unfussy *Coffee Shop* at the front (7.30am–6pm), and the beautifully decorated if dark, split-level thatch-roofed *Makuti Garden* at the back for full meals and drinks (9am–10pm). Lunches, when it's busiest, tend to be light, things like stuffed chapatis, stir-fries and salads, with more substantial evening meals (Tsh6000–8000 for two courses excluding drinks) including pork and some African dishes.

Onsea House Delicatessen Corner of Joel Maeda and India streets ⓦ www.onseahouse.com. An upmarket coffee shop with a rather delicious twist: genuine Belgian chocolate and ice cream. They have a fine delicatessen with local and imported produce, and also do waffles, fresh sandwiches, salads and patisseries. Daytimes only.

The Patisserie Sokoine Rd. Bakery-cum-Internet café popular with overlanders. The light meals and snacks are reasonably priced, and they also do cappuccino and espresso, fresh juices, ice cream, cakes, and (not always fresh) bread. Mon–Sat daytimes only.

Steers Corner of Joel Maeda and India streets. South African halal fast-food chain, not cheap (deep-fried chicken and chips Tsh4000), but the quality is fine and they have reliable ice cream.

Via Via German Boma, Boma Rd. Popular with travellers and locals alike, this is a bar, restaurant and lively cultural venue rolled into one. Nestled on the grassy bank of the Themi River, there's plenty of shaded seating, and excellent food (around Tsh4000): a cosmopolitan mix of European and African (the tilapia in white wine, and Flemish beef stew, are especially tasty). They also do toasted sandwiches, soups and salads, freshly pressed juices, milk shakes, cappuccino and espresso. Food until around 10pm. Closed Sun.

West of the centre

Arusha Crown Hotel Makongoro Rd. One of the better mid-range hotel restaurants, fresh decor, beautifully presented tables, and a mouth-watering menu. Food ranges from courgette stuffed with mince to lamb chops, steaks any way you like, grills, Indian, pizza, and a wide selection of seafood. Most mains cost Tsh5000. No alcohol, but good coffee.

Big Bite Corner of Swahili St and Somali Rd. One of the best Indian restaurants in East Africa, and reasonably priced at that (full meals upwards of Tsh8000). The naff name and the grimy street outside belie the quite exquisite Mughlai and tandoori cooking, the latter from a traditional clay oven. Both the chicken and mutton in spinach purée are unbelievably succulent, and even simple side dishes like buttered naan are saturated with subtle flavours. There's also a wide vegetarian choice and, as the name suggests, the portions are big. Ask for the day's specials. Closed Tues.

Dolly's Patisserie Sokoine Rd. Excellent cakes, buns and freshly baked bread.

Green Hut Sokoine Rd. Good fast food, with hamburgers, great samosas, *kababu*, juices and cheap full meals (around Tsh1200). Especially useful for breakfast.

Noble Under *Meru House Inn*, Sokoine Rd. Aimed at backpackers, this has rather pricey mains but is good for all manner of sweets, from cakes and buns to chocolate mousse and shakes. Also has real coffee and juices. No alcohol.

Shanghai Chinese Behind Meru Post Office, Sokoine Rd. Genuine Chinese cuisine at around Tsh15,000 for a full meal including soft drinks. Good sizzling platters, ginger crab with spring onion, and soya lemon prawns.

Swagat Sokoine Rd. Authentic and delicious Indian (including tandoori), dished up by friendly staff. Full meals Tsh6000–8000. Closed Sun.

East of the centre

Dragon Pearl Old Moshi Rd, Kijenge. Related to the *Shanghai*, and equally good and pricey (try the chicken wings). There's also a small Thai selection. Licensed. Closed Sun.

Everest Chinese Nyerere Rd. Yet another good Chinese, with seating indoors, on the terrace or in a shaded corner of the garden. The copious business lunches are good value at Tsh4500;

otherwise it's around Tsh10,000 for a main course with drinks – the sizzlers are especially good. Also has pizza.

Greek Club Nyerere Rd. Established in the 1930s by Greek planters (behold the Corinthian facade), this remains popular with expats and well-to-do-locals, especially at weekends, when it becomes a sports bar. But the main reason for coming is the superb Greek food, particularly its salads, famed moussaka, and souvlaki pitta bread rolls. Tues, Wed & Fri from 5pm, Sat & Sun from 2pm.

Le Jacaranda Vijana Rd. Set on the breezy first-floor terrace of the guest house, this is a pleasant – if very pricey – venue for a huge and remarkably sophisticated menu, ranging from stuffed crêpes, skewered lamb, fresh fish, pork and white meats to inventive salads (prawns and papaya?). Main courses average Tsh7000–10,000, and a three-course splurge could relieve you of Tsh20,000. There's also a bar, seating in the garden, and minigolf.

Maharaja Palace Njiro Rd. Generous portions of genuine Indian tandoori (try the fiery Kadhai Murg chicken and tomato curry), plus the famous *Chief's Rendezvous*, a gentlemanly kind of bar headed by the incomparable Chief Mirambo, descendant of the famous Nyamwezi empire-builder, which also does excellent grilled chicken. Eat inside or in small thatched huts.

Masai Camp Old Moshi Rd, 2.5km east of Kijenge. Excellent and very reasonably priced food majoring in smoked pork and superb pizzas, cooked in a wood-fired oven (the chef claims it possesses a perfect refractive index). Also has pasta, burgers, salads and lots of other choice, *shisha* water pipes, and an often lively bar. Mains are Tsh3500–6000.

The Outpost Serengeti Rd. Part of the family-run hotel, snacks and light meals are served throughout the day, and there's an all-you-can-eat evening buffet of mainly international favourites (7–9.30pm) for Tsh7500 (Tsh9000 with steak). There's also a quiet, relaxing bar with satellite TV, and a lush garden.

Spices & Herbs Simeon Rd. Excellent Ethiopian cuisine, also suitable for vegetarians, with a quiet and dignified atmosphere, and some seats on the lawn. Most traditional is *injera* – a huge soft pancake on which various spicy stews and pickles are placed. Most dishes cost Tsh4000–5000, and there's also Western food if you don't like spices (Ethiopian food is *hot*), plus barbecues on request. Live band Thurs–Sat from 7pm.

Stiggy's Old Moshi Rd, Kijenge. A well-regarded place which is popular with expats and specializes in Thai and South Seas seafood. There's also a pool table and bar. Closed Mon

North of the centre

L'Oasis Lodge & Restaurant Sekei: 800m north of the Nairobi–Moshi Highway. Whether you eat by the bar, in the garden with its crowned cranes, or up in the tree house, this is one of Arusha's tastiest gastronomic experiences, with the seafood especially (anything from unshelled prawns to flambéed lobster) gaining plaudits from even the most jaded of palates. The menu also nods towards eastern Asia, including delicately spiced beef teriyaki. Most mains cost just Tsh6000.

Mount Meru Hotel Nairobi–Moshi Highway. Good-value lunchtime buffets ($8) in this rather bland package hotel, though they do have a swimming pool (Tsh4000). A la carte in the evenings.

Pizzarusha Kaloleni. "The best damn pizza in Africa" they say, and despite the exaggeration it's a firm favourite with backpackers, not least for its early breakfasts, rustic decor and

candlelit dinners. Apart from Italian favourites, the menu features curries and other dishes, all at under Tsh4000. Also has sandwiches, ice cream and alcohol. The *Arusha Pizza Hut* nearby is more expensive and not as good.

Sombrero Bar & Restaurant Ethiopia Rd, Kaloleni. This claims to be the birthplace of *trupa* (a filling stew of beef, bananas and vegetables), and is certainly one of the best places to try the dish (daily 1–9pm); there's standard bar food at other times.

VIP Lounge 100m north of the Nairobi–Moshi Highway, Sekei. Once *the* bar to hang out in north of the centre, the crowds have waned but it remains popular for its famously succulent *nyama choma*, grilled *ndizi* and chicken, accompanied by fiery home-made chilli sauce.

Out of town

Most of the out-of-town hotels also have perfectly good tourist-standard restaurants, but only two of them are really worth a special trip:

Arusha Coffee Lodge 6.5km west of town at Burka: along the Dodoma road near Arusha airport. Especially popular on Sundays and cheaper than you might fear, with light meals averaging Tsh6000, and main courses Tsh8000. Choose from among lasagne, pizzas, lots of fresh inventive salads, or "pick 'n' mix" from a selection of meat and fish, cooking styles and accompaniments. Finish off with one of their famous chocolate desserts, including a chocolate samosa with orange and cardamom. You're free to use the small swimming pool.

Mount Meru Game Lodge & Sanctuary 22km east of town at Usa River: along the Nairobi–Moshi Highway ☎027/255 3643. Especially popular with weekenders, the main draw here is the game sanctuary (daily 7am–5pm; Tsh1000), which started off as a zoo for ill or orphaned animals, and also has a pond with flamingos, pelicans and herons and gardens grazed by eland, zebra and a lone buffalo – perfect for a lazy Sunday afternoon with the kids. Lunch $16. Catch a daladala towards Usa River or Kikatiti.

Drinking and nightlife

Arusha's main **nightlife** happens along the Nairobi–Moshi Highway, which has a slew of bars from Sakina in the west, to Sekei in the east. Places go in and out of fashion frequently, so if one of the following has fallen out of favour, you shouldn't have problems finding somewhere better nearby. The ever-changing scene makes tracking down what's really hot an enjoyable challenge. The owners of *Via Via* in the grounds of the German Boma keep up with the latest, and also offer an innovative guided **nightlife tour** in the populous outskirts (Tsh5000 excluding drinks and taxis, though you may have to carry your guide home). Check out ⓦ www.arushamuzik.com for the latest **bands and rappers** to make it big in "A-Town", or tune into Triple-A FM (88.5Mhz) for lots of Bongo Flava.

For **live music**, *Triple-A* and *Via Via* are the most likely venues for rap and hip-hop. *Via Via* also has traditional music, whilst for dance (jazz) bands, the *Summit Club* is currently cooking and *Saba Saba Hotel* is also worth keeping an eye on. For information about the "Trance Africa" **full moon raves** – all-night parties in the bush somewhere in the Arusha region – contact Timothy Leach at *Ngare Sero Mountain Lodge* near Usa River (☎0748/362682, ⓔngare -sero-lodge@habari.co.tz).

Worth trying at least once is Meru banana wine, which comes in two varieties (sweet and dry). You'll find it at *Via Via*, in some of the more local bars, and in supermarkets, or you can find locally brewed versions in villages closer to Mount Meru, visitable as part of the cultural tourism programmes; see p.414. Don't walk at night but catch a taxi; for getting back, you'll find them outside virtually every bar and club that's still open.

Bars

AICC Sports Club Old Moshi Rd, 150m east of Kijenge roundabout. Remains a favourite among local drinkers attracted by good *nyama choma*, grilled bananas, and roast gizzards (*filigisi*); especially popular with families on Sunday afternoons.

Club Galaxy Arusha Colonel Middleton Rd. A spacious local bar open 24 hours, also serving good cheap food including *supu*, stews and other basic meals (mostly Tsh1500). The staff are quick to defuse potential hassle, even at 4am.

Jambo's Makuti Garden Boma Rd. A stylish bar

under a thatched roof beside the tourist office, also a good restaurant (see "Eating").

Le Jacaranda Vijana Rd. Whether you drink in the garden or on the first-floor terrace, this is a lovely afternoon hideaway. There's also minigolf (Tsh500), and live music at weekends.

Madini Goliondoi Rd. Busy in the afternoons, especially for its pool table, and with a cosy little patio at the back that serves good *nyama choma*.

Masai Camp Old Moshi Rd, 2.5km east of Kijenge. One of the best, especially lively whenever the overland tour trucks are in town. Also has pool tables, darts, satellite TV and Internet café.

Matongee Arusha Club Nyerere Rd. Next to the Themi River, this is a good local bar with plenty of outdoor seating, and great *nyama choma* too.

Pama Bar Wachagga St, by the daladala stand. Popular with locals, especially after work, with loads of streetside tables, animated conversations, and also good *nyama choma*.

Police Mess School Rd, off Sokoine Rd. Forget the indoor bar and head to the beer garden beside it, a lovely relaxing place that, yes, also has superb *nyama choma*.

Seven Up Bar Nairobi–Moshi Highway, 1.2km west of Colonel Middleton Rd, Sakina. One of the best of the highway's bars, with great food (nothing much over Tsh1500), fast service and a more mentally stable clientele than in some neighbouring joints.

Stiggy's Old Moshi Rd. One of the main expat meeting places, both for its restaurant and its bar and beer garden (open until 11pm). There's satellite TV, a pool table and occasional live music on Friday. Closed Mon.

Via Via In the grounds of the German Boma, top end of Boma Rd. One of the nicest and friendliest bars in town, with great music (including a stack of traditional *ngoma*), good food, a pool table, and a grassy lawn to chill out on. There's always some special event on Thursday. Closed Sun.

Clubs

Colobus Club Old Moshi Rd, 500m east of Kijenge roundabout. The Friday and Saturday discos (10pm until late; Tsh3500) are brash, lively and extremely loud, heavy on techno and Western pop (there are actually two venues, both with state-of-the-art light shows, so you can always jump ship if the music in one doesn't appeal). Also has pool tables and Internet access.

Crystal Club Seth Benjamin St. A large old club that still pulls 'em in, with lots of dancing, a young, easy-going crowd, and Kiswahili rap and hip-hop after midnight (sometimes also on Sun afternoons). Open nightly; entrance Tsh1500–3000.

Hotel Saba Saba Simeon Rd. If it hasn't yet been knocked down to make way for a long-planned upmarket hotel, the legendary discos here (nightly except Mon) feature almost entirely African music (DJs from Clouds FM) and a largely African crowd. Busiest Fri–Sun.

Shiverz Park Kaloleni. The latest addition to Kaloleni's several nightspots, hosting a boisterous but friendly crowd well into the wee hours, together with prospecting prostitutes.

Summit Club 200m north of the Nairobi–Moshi Highway, Sekei. Currently the favoured venue out of the several bars along this road, especially for its live dance bands (Fri–Sun nights).

Tembo Club 10km west of Arusha along the Dodoma road. Top marks for architectural inspiration – this new grass-roofed club takes the form of an elephant head, and even has tusks. Whether or not it catches on is another matter – ask around.

Triple-A Nairobi–Moshi Highway, Sakina; opposite Nairobi Rd. Arusha's favourite disco, more mellow than *Colobus Club*, and with a more African feel too, especially on Thursday. Discos are held nightly, but the club is best known for its live bands (usually Fri & Sat), including rap and Bongo Flava, and music contests. Family show Sunday afternoons.

Shopping

Arusha has a vast range of **souvenirs** to choose from, bringing together arts and crafts from all over the country, as well as from Kenya (especially luridly coloured soapstone carvings) and reproduction tribal masks from Central and western Africa. Typical items include Makonde woodcarvings, bright Tingatinga paintings, batiks, musical instruments (the metal-tongued "thumb pianos" of the Gogo, from around Dodoma, are great fun, as are the slender *zeze* fiddles), Maasai bead jewellery and a whole lot more.

The main concentration of **souvenir shops** is in the eastern part of the centre between Goliondoi and Boma roads, and there are also dozens of stalls at the **CCM Building** on Fire Road, south of the *Arusha Resort Center*. Most of the salesmen have mastered the "but how am I going to feed my family" line of patter, so you might like to pay a first visit with no money to get a feel

397

△ Souvenirs, Arusha

Not everything that sparkles is tanzanite ...

Northern Tanzania – specifically the Mererani Hills between Arusha and Moshi, and an as-yet undeclared location in the Pare Mountains – is the only place on earth known to contain **tanzanite**, a precious transparent gemstone discovered in 1967. In its natural form, the stone is an irregular brownish lump, but when heated to 400–500°C it acquires a characteristic colour and brilliance, predominantly blue, with other shades ranging from violet to a dullish olive green. Determining the real colour isn't too easy however, as the stone is trichroic, meaning it shows three different colours when viewed from different angles: blue, purple or red. The facets are made by gemologists.

Arusha is the main marketing (and smuggling) centre for tanzanite and other gemstones – ruby, green garnet (locally called tsavorite), green tourmaline, emerald and sapphire – some of them spirited in from Congo and Mozambique. After initial interest in the 1970s, the international market for tanzanite almost vanished, not helped by unfounded allegations in the US that the trade was a major source of revenue for al-Qaeda. These claims apart, you should think twice about the consequences of the tanzanite trade before buying. Local miners have gradually been pushed out of the most productive areas by large-scale operations, including a couple of multinational enterprises whose heavy-handed tactics in dealing with "scavengers" – as they refer to artisanal miners – are frequently reported in the press. The mines themselves are primitive by international standards, and have a lamentable safety record: in 1998 over fifty miners drowned in a flood after heavy rain, and in June 2002, 42 more suffocated when a fresh air pump failed.

There's no official **grading system** for tanzanite, although unofficially stones are classified into five main grades – AAA, AA, A, B and C (with AAA being finest). The price depends on colour (deep and radiant is most expensive), size and grade – minor flaws like faults or inclusions will halve the value, at least. A-grade stones cost $250–500 per carat, B-grade $150–200, and C-grade $100–150. The bigger the stone, however, the higher the per carat price (a really large stone, say ten carats, would cost well over $500 per carat). If you're buying, be aware that you're likely to get ripped off unless you're clued up on gemstones. Tanzanite's many shades makes **scamming** easy; a common trick is to pass off iolite (which costs $10 per carat) as tanzanite, and there are all sorts of cheaper stones that could pass for the rare "green" variety of tanzanite (which costs upwards of $500 per carat). There's also the matter of "fosterite", a synthetic Russian imitation.

for it. **Prices** are rarely, if ever, fixed, and depend entirely on your bargaining skills. Luckily, getting a decent final price isn't too difficult thanks to the welter of competing stalls (you can play them off against each other). For advice on bargaining techniques, see p.73. Also worth mentioning is Msumbi Coffees at the TFA Shopping Centre on Sokoine Road, for beans and freshly ground Arabica from Kilimanjaro.

Aang Serian's Native Cave *Jambo's Coffee House*, Boma Rd. A small store run by a local cultural NGO (see the section on "Monduli"). Their stock is mainly Maasai-oriented, and includes *esos* – women's beaded neck discs (Tsh15,000–25,000 depending on size). They also have CDs of traditional music, also sold at their office at Mollel House, Stadium Rd (☏0744/318548, ✉enolengilo@yahoo.co.uk). Closed Sun.
The Craft Shop Goliondoi Rd. A good place to get an idea of prices, with loads of Makonde carvings, some Tingatinga paintings, and a carver at the

back who makes boxes and small chests. Closed Sat pm and Sun.
Cultural Heritage 5km along the Dodoma road, catch a daladala from the main stand to Majengo. Huddled inside an electric fence, this is Arusha's largest – and most expensive – tourist emporium, with stacks of stuff at prices that leave you reeling. Closed Sun pm.
Le Jacaranda Vijana Rd. Rummage through excellent Tingatinga paintings at the hotel's entrance, under a wonderful old candelabra euphorbia.

Lookmanji Curio Shop Joel Maeda St. One of the best selections in town, especially for carvings, and keenly priced. They also stock carvings from Kenya's Kamba tribe, who make good figurines. Other stuff includes Congolese and Malian masks, and – occasionally – a circumcision mask from Tanzania's Luguru. Closed Sun pm.

"Maasai market" Corner of Joel Maeda St and Boma Rd by the clock tower. An impromptu pavement market where Maasai women make and sell beadwork necklaces and bracelets, and men hawk scary-looking daggers and spears. Most days except Sun.

Real Arts Centre Boma Rd, next to *Jambo's Coffee House*. Mainly Tingatinga paintings, banana-fibre collages and locally made batiks, some tailored into clothes. Closed Sun.

Via Via German Boma, Boma Rd. Hosts occasional exhibitions, from wooden sculptures to paintings, each lasting two weeks. They have good contacts with local artists too. Closed Sun.

Arts and culture

After lying dormant for decades, Arusha's **arts scene** has woken up with a satisfying jolt. The main venue for performances and art exhibitions is *Via Via* in the grounds of the German Boma, which has an outdoor stage beside the Themi River (seating is in a grassy amphitheatre). There's at least one event each week (currently Thursday), whether traditional music or hip-hop, cinema, theatre or the opening of an exhibition, together with a talent contest at least once a month (currently the last Saturday). Hands-on activities at *Via Via* include drumming lessons (Tsh5000 an hour), a three-day **drum-making workshop** (Tsh45,000), and courses in batiks and Tanzanian cooking. If you're around at the end of August or early September, ask about the annual **Arusha Street Festival**, which is held along Boma Road and combines music with a carnival atmosphere.

A new **cinema** is due to open at the TFA Shopping Centre on Sokoine Road, which will probably hasten the demise of Arusha's old and very characterful fleapit, the Metropole – also along Sokoine Road. For now, it screens pirated DVDs at 6pm Monday to Saturday (Tsh1500).

Listings

Air charters The following airlines also operate air charters: Coastal Aviation, Air Excel, Precisionair and Regional Air.

Airlines Air Excel, Subzali Building (over Exim Bank), Goliondoi Rd ☎027/254 8429, ⓔreservati ons@airexcelonline.com; Air Tanzania, ATC House, Boma Rd ☎027/250 3201, ⓦwww.airtanzania .com; Coastal Aviation, ATC House, Boma Rd ☎027/250 0087, ⓦwww.coastal.cc; Ethiopian Airlines, *New Safari Hotel*, Boma Rd ☎027/250 4231, ⓦwww.flyethiopian.com; Kenya Airways, see Precisionair; KLM, *New Safari Hotel*, Boma Rd ☎027/250 8062, ⓦwww.klm.com; Northwest Airlines, see KLM; Precisionair, *New Safari Hotel*, Boma Rd ☎027/250 6903, ⓦwww.precisionairtz .com; Regional Air, Nairobi Rd – turn north after Kilombero Market ☎027/250 2541, ⓦwww .regional.co.tz; ZanAir, Summit Centre, Sokoine Rd ☎027/254 8877, ⓦwww.zanair.com. Tickets for other airlines can be booked through travel agents.

Airport information Kilimanjaro International Airport ☎027/275 4771; Arusha Airport ☎027/250 5980.

Ambulances AAR ☎027/250 8654 or 0741/510079.

Banks and exchange There are banks and foreign exchange bureaux throughout town. Bank rates are around ten percent better than forexes, but check the commission first. The best is NBC, at the corner of Sokoine Rd and School St, which takes under 20min and charges no commission, and also has a 24hr Visa/MasterCard ATM. There are also machines at Standard Chartered on Goliondoi Rd, at Barclays on Serengeti Rd, and inside the *Impala Hotel*. Forexes are quicker than banks but many only change cash: for travellers' cheques, Exchange Centre on Joel Maeda St is the most helpful (Mon–Fri 8am–4.30pm, Sat 8am–1pm). On Sundays, Northern Bureau de Change on Joel Maeda St is handy (Mon–Sat 8.30am–5.30pm, Sun 8.30am–4pm); the *Impala Hotel*'s forex also opens on Sunday (daily until midnight). Cash advances on Visa and MasterCard are made at TMCS Ltd at *Arusha Resort Center*, Fire Rd (℡027/250 0825; up to $500 a week); for Amex cards, go to Rickshaw Travels on Sokoine Rd, near Friend's Corner (℡027/250 6208).

Books and maps The best bookshop for locally published works is Bookpoint on Swahili St, which also has a good selection of coffee table books, maps and some Tanzanian novels in English. Also worth a rummage are either of Kase Bookshop's branches (Boma Rd and Joel Maeda St). For imported works, go to The Bookmark – branches on the southern extension of Swahili St, and in the TFA Shopping Centre, Sokoine Rd.

Camping equipment Tents, sleeping bags and hiking boots can be rented from *Pizzarusha* restaurant in Kaloleni (daily 8.30am–9.30pm; ℡0744/366293). Equipment can be bought from Xplorer on Boma Rd (Mon–Sat 8am–6pm; ℡027/254 8830), and at ShopRite in the TFA Shopping Centre, Sokoine Rd. The latter also stocks camping gas canisters.

Courier services DHL, Sokoine Rd beside Stanbic Bank ℡027/250 6749; EMS, at the clock tower and AICC post offices.

Dentists Dr Dhirany at Ithna Asheri Hospital, Sokoine Rd (℡0744/287350) has a good reputation and isn't too expensive. The AICC Hospital on Nyerere Rd is also good.

Football Matches are held at Sheikh Amri Abeid Memorial Stadium; the local team is Arusha FC. Tickets (Tsh500) at the gate on Makongoro Rd.

Hospitals and clinics AICC Hospital, Nyerere Rd ℡027/254 4113 is the best, and also has a good paediatrician. For minor ailments and tests, visit the Old Arusha Clinic, Nyerere Rd ℡0744/888444, Ⓦwww.oldarushaclinic.org.

Immigration office Afrika Mashariki Rd (Mon–Fri 7.30am–3pm; ℡027/250 3569).

Internet access Arusha has loads of Internet cafés, one on virtually every street in the centre. Connections are generally fast and reliable, and prices average Tsh500–1000 an hour.

Language courses *Via Via*, at the north end of Boma Rd, offers basic lessons at Tsh3000 an hour, and advanced tuition for Tsh5000 an hour.

Library Arusha Regional Library, Sokoine Rd (Mon–Fri 9am–6pm, Sat 9am–2pm; Tsh500 daily membership). Also has Internet access.

Newspapers and magazines Newspaper hawkers congregate along Boma Rd, especially the clock tower, and will pester you with old copies of *USA Today*, *Newsweek* and *The Guardian*. The best stands, with a wide selection of Tanzanian and Kenyan dailies, weeklies and magazines, are at the east end of Joel Maeda St by the clock tower outside the supermarket, and on Goliondoi Rd near Makongoro Rd.

Opticians Sunbeam Optical Centre, Sokoine Rd, next to Benson Shop ℡027/250 7757.

Pharmacies Moona's, Sokoine Rd, just west of NBC Bank (Mon–Fri 8.45am–5.30pm, Sat 8.45am–2pm; ℡027/250 9800).

Photography Film stocks are usually fresh. Passport photos, battery and film sales, developing and camera repairs (no guarantee) are offered by Astab ("Fuji Shop"), by the clock tower on Sokoine Rd. Professional slide film can be bought and developed at Burhani Photographic Services ("Kodak Shop") next to *Impala Hotel* on Simeon Rd, and also at TFA Shopping centre on Sokoine Rd, but they can be sloppy cutting film.

Police Emergency ℡112. Report thefts for insurance paperwork at the station on the north side of Makongoro Rd ℡027/250 3641. Facing it is the regional police headquarters.

Post The main post office is on Boma Rd (Mon–Fri 8am–12.30pm & 2–4.30pm, Sat 9am–noon), and has a stationery shop and philatelic bureau. For sending international parcels, arrive before 10am (Mon–Fri), when the customs officer is on duty. There are two branches on Sokoine Rd, and another in the AICC complex.

Sports and health clubs AICC Sports Club, Old Moshi Rd, has squash, tennis, darts and volleyball. The nine-hole Arusha Golf Course is part of the irksomely snobbish Gymkhana Club; membership policy is strict but the adjacent *Mount Meru Hotel* can get you in. There's minigolf at *Le Jacaranda* (Tsh500). *Stiggy's* on Old Moshi Rd is the venue for the Hash House Harriers' weekly runs (Fri 5.30pm; usually 5km, with or without beers to start with).

Supermarkets and groceries Largest is ShopRite in the TFA Shopping Centre, Sokoine Rd (Mon–Fri 9am–7pm, Sat 9am–5pm, Sun 9am–1pm). Smaller but more central are RTC (Mon–Fri 9am–5pm, Sat 9am–noon)by the clock tower, and Rushda (same hours, also open Sun), under *Coyote Guest House* on Azimio St. Meat King (Mon–Fri 9am–5pm, Sat 9am–noon), Goliondoi Rd, is favoured by expats for imported beef, cheese, smoked hams, sausages and salami. Newly opened is the Onsea House Delicatessen on Joel Maeda Rd (Ⓦwww.onseahouse .com), where you can buy Tanzanian, Belgian home-made and imported delicatessen which you can't find in the regular supermarkets and groceries.

Swimming pools Nicest is the outdoor pool at *The Arusha Hotel* (Tsh5000). *Mount Meru Hotel* charges Tsh4000, but is shaded for much of the day. The pool at the *Impala Hotel* (Tsh5000) is small. All are open daytime only.

Telephones TTCL is on Boma Rd (daily 7am–8pm). Be very careful with phone services offered by some foreign exchange bureaux, which can charge exorbitant fees. The cheapest way of ringing abroad is via Internet call: try L&D Internet Café, corner of Swahili and Somali streets.

Travel agents Reliable agents for arranging rail, bus and plane tickets, car rental, safaris and trekking include Easy Travel & Tours, *New Africa Hotel*, Boma Rd ☎027/250 3929, ⓦwww .easytravel-tanzania.com, and Emslies, Subzali Building (over Exim Bank), Goliondoi Rd ☎027/254 8048, ⓔemslies.ark@eoltz.com.

Moving on from Arusha

Arusha is northern Tanzania's transport hub, with several daily **bus connections** to all major towns in the north and east, and to Nairobi and Kampala. There are frequent **flights** to most national parks, northwestern towns, Dar and Zanzibar. For approximate **journey times and frequencies**, see "Travel details" at the end of this chapter.

By road

Road conditions to Dar, Ngorongoro, Tanga and Nairobi are surfaced, but the stretch up to Namanga on the Kenyan border is prone to flooding during heavy rains. Conditions on routes heading west vary with the season, as the sealed road only goes as far as Tarangire National Park before the road splits: northwest towards the Northern Circuit parks (sealed until Ngorongoro), and southwest towards Dodoma via Babati and Kondoa. The section south of Babati is extremely tricky, if not totally impassable, during the rains (heaviest March–May), as is most of the road network west of Singida.

The main hazard on sealed roads is **reckless driving**, especially between Arusha and Moshi – for which reason, avoid the large Coaster minibuses on that route. If you're driving yourself, be on your guard when the road swoops down towards bridges, as fatal high-speed crashes and collisions are depressingly common. The route is safest in the morning when drivers are less tired. **Safer bus companies** mentioned below include Akamba, beside the *Eland Motel* on the Nairobi–Moshi Highway (☎027/250 9491); Dar Express, on Colonel Middleton Road (☎027/250 4620); Royal Coach, next to *Golden Rose Hotel* on Colonel Middleton Road (☎027/250 7959); and Scandinavian Express, Kituoni Street south of the main bus station (☎027/250 0153). Companies with particularly **dangerous reputations** include Air Bus, Air Msae, Buffalo, Hood, Kilimanjaro Express, Tashriff and Tawfiq.

Bus tickets for most companies can be bought at the main bus station, and companies heading west also maintain offices at Kilombero bus station. Buy tickets the day before, or leave very early: most buses are gone by mid-morning.

Buses eastwards

To **Dar es Salaam**, some twenty buses head off between 6 and 8.30am; safest are Dar Express, Scandinavian Express and Royal Coach. These are also useful for getting to the **Usambaras** (change at Mombo) or the **Pare Mountains** (change at Mwanga or Same), though there are also direct buses to Lushoto (6am with Fasiha VIP and Chakito) and Usangi (10am with Sahara Coach). For **Tanga**, buses leave between 7.30 and 10.30am; Simba DVD Coach is the safest company.

For **Morogoro**, safest is probably Islam Bus (7am), but as none of the companies have particularly safe reputations, it's best to go to Dar and move on the next day. The only company covering **Iringa and Mbeya** is the perilous Hood.

Buses westwards

Heading west, things become bone-bashing and time-consuming, as the road network beyond Babati is in a pitiful state, often impassable in the rains, although things are gradually improving. To **Babati** (throughout the day), **Kondoa** and **Singida** (7–9am), Mtei and possibly Takrim are safest, though both have been known to overspeed. **Dodoma** is most easily covered in two legs, changing at Babati or Kondoa; of the direct buses, Shabiby (Tues and Fri; 6am) are safe. **Tabora** is covered twice a week (Wed and Sat; 6am) by NBS; the journey can take as little as twelve hours, but if the road's bad, count on a day and night. For towns around the **national parks**, there are three buses a day to Mto wa Mbu and Karatu (most leaving in the afternoon) as well as daladalas. There are three approaches to the **Lake Victoria region**: via Singida, via Ngorongoro and Serengeti, and via Kenya. Via Singida, buses to Mwanza (safest are Takrim on Tues, Thurs & Sun, and NBS on Wed; all 9am) can now cover the route in a day, but if there are breakdowns, you'll end up spending the night in a cheap guest house or on the bus. The other two routes are expensive for non-Tanzanians: either straight through Ngorongoro and Serengeti, adding $100 to the fare in park fees (the companies are Mtei, Kimotco, City Mist and Coast Line; all 6am), or via Kenya (Scandinavian and the cheaper Akamba are best, avoid Tawfiq and Spider; all leave around 3–4pm), which costs an extra $70 or $90 in visas (a new Tanzanian one, a $20 transit visa for Kenya and, going to Bukoba, for Uganda) but has the advantage of being a sealed road for most or all of the way.

Buses to Kenya

Mombasa is served by four buses a day: Takrim and the avoidable Tawfiq at 2pm (Tsh18,000), and Perfect and Doliphine at 7am (Tsh7500) via Taveta. **Nairobi** is covered by mainline operators (Scandinavian is safest; daily 3pm & 3.30pm; Tsh17,000) and by **shuttle minibuses**. The latter leave at 8am and 2pm from the *Mount Meru Hotel* parking lot, but can pick you up at your hotel if you buy the ticket in advance, and drop you at your hotel in Nairobi. They include: Impala, at *Impala Hotel* (☎027/250 7197; $20); Davanu, at *Mount Meru Hotel* and on Goliondoi Rd (☎027/250 7452; $20); and Easy Coach, on Fire Road behind *The Arusha Hotel* (✉easycoach@cybernet.co.tz; Tsh10,000), who claim to have functional speed-limiters. Easy Coach have onward connections to western Kenya. **Kenyan visas** are issued without fuss at Namanga ($50 for most nationalities, or $20 for a transit visa; bring dollars in cash).

By air

Airline offices are listed on p.399. A $6 **departure tax** is levied on internal flights; the $30 tax on international flights is included in the fare. Most domestic flights take off from **Arusha Airport**, 7km along the Dodoma road: catch a Monduli daladala (6am–3pm) and get off at the airport sliproad, a 1.5km walk away, or catch a taxi, which should be no more than Tsh6000. **Kilimanjaro International Airport (KIA)** lies 48km east of Arusha, 6km off the Moshi Highway. Air Tanzania and Precisionair operate free **shuttle buses** for their passengers; KLM charge $10 – enquire at their offices on Boma Road. For other airlines, a taxi is the only way: you'll do well if you bargain it down to

Tsh30,000. Buses to Moshi can also drop you at the airport turning, leaving you 6km to walk or hitch. KIA closes after the last flight, reopening at 6am, so you can't spend the night there – the upmarket *KIA Lodge* is nearby; see p.388.

Safaris from Arusha

Arusha is Tanzania's **safari capital**, and the best place for arranging safaris to the "Northern Circuit" (covered in Chapter 7). No matter what your budget, the longer the trip, the better it's likely to be. Although some operators offer **one-day trips** to Manyara or Ngorongoro, travel to and from Arusha will take up half the day, giving only few hours for spotting wildlife (the exceptions are Arusha and Tarangire national parks, both of which are within a couple of hours' drive of Arusha). The same applies to **two-day trips**, which usually only give you time for two game drives: one in the afternoon when you arrive, the other the next morning before heading back to Arusha. Over **three days** (one full day and two half-days), trips become more rewarding and flexible: a good combination would be Ngorongoro and either Lake Manyara or Tarangire. The former is good for birdlife, the latter for elephants. Over **four days**, the Serengeti is a possibility, though five or six days are recommended.

Other trips on offer include canoeing on Lake Manyara or in Arusha National Park, hikes up Mount Meru and Kilimanjaro, visits to cultural tourism programmes, and six-day Crater Highlands treks from Ngorongoro to Lake Natron via Ol Doinyo Lengai volcano; see p.405 for more details.

Information

The headquarters of the **Tanzania National Parks Authority (TANAPA)** are unhelpfully located 5km along the Dodoma road (Mon–Fri 8am–4pm; PO Box 3134 ☎027/250 3471, ⓦwww.tanzaniaparks.com). A taxi from town costs around Tsh4000, but it's cheaper to catch a daladala towards Monduli and get dropped off a few hundred metres beyond African Heritage. TANAPA's **booking office** deals with reservations and pre-payments for "special campsites" (essential for Tarangire, Lake Manyara and Serengeti) and bedspace on Mount Meru. Travel agents can also handle bookings for a fee.

TANAPA publishes a series of illustrated **guidebooks**, currently covering Kilimanjaro, Ngorongoro, Serengeti, Ruaha, Udzungwa and Arusha ($10). Though the older black-and-white series ($5) are out of date on practicalities, they include more detailed information about wildlife and ecology; you can find them in Arusha's bookshops, at park gates and in lodge and hotel gift shops. TANAPA also produces excellent **maps** of Lake Manyara, Ngorongoro and Serengeti. Also available in town is a series of very attractive, painted national park maps by Giovanni Tombazzi, each of which contains two versions: one for the dry season, the other for the rains. Ensure you get the "New" versions (part of the title), as some of the old ones are out of date in terms of game-viewing tracks.

For information about **Ngorongoro**, the Ngorongoro Conservation Authority Office is a few doors down from the tourist office on Boma Road (Mon–Fri 8am–5pm, Sat 8am–1pm; PO Box 776 ☎027/254 4625, ⓦwww .ngorongoro-crater-africa.org). They sell the latest guidebook to Ngorongoro, older ones for the national parks, and an accurate map. They're also happy to screen wildlife videos for you, and may have VCDs for sale.

Arranging your own safari

Arranging your own safari is an attractive alternative to an organized safari, and gives you much more flexibility, though you'll need a vehicle for Serengeti, Manyara and Tarangire. Still, it works out comparatively cheap if you can fill all the seats (five or seven in a 4WD, nine or more in a minibus). That said, a good chunk of Ngorongoro and Arusha National Park are visitable on foot with access by public transport, and Manyara has canoeing options. All parks have official **guides** for hire, but for something more personal, the Professional Tour Guide School in Sanawari, just off the Nairobi–Moshi Highway, is happy to provide students as guides for a maximum of two weeks. The fee is a negotiable daily allowance, but certainly no more than $20 a day; a written recommendation from you is appreciated if the student deserves one. Contact the Principal, Vedasto Izoba, PO Box 12582, Arusha ☎0744/894077, ⓦwww .protsonline.com.

Car rental

First, read the section on car rental in Basics. The following companies are reliable and have the requisite TALA licence for entering national parks if you're with a driver. Prices quoted include VAT, and insurance if self-drive.

Arusha Naaz Rent A Car *Arusha Naaz Hotel*, Sokoine Rd ☎027/250 2087, ⓔarushanaaz @yahoo.com. Land Cruiser self-drive from $100/ day, including 120km ($300–800 excess liability); with driver $110/day.

Avis Skylink Travel & Tours, Bushbuck Building, Simeon Rd ☎027/250 9108, ⓦwww .skylinktanzania.com. Suzuki Vitara self-drive $125/day, including 120km ($500 excess liability); Land Cruiser $180/day ($1000 excess). With driver, $120 and $160 respectively, excluding fuel.

Fortes Nairobi Highway, Sakina ☎027/250 8096, ⓦwww.fortessafaris.com. Land Rover self-drive

$110/day ($1500 excess liability) with unlimited mileage; add $25 for driver. Internet booking rates are considerably cheaper, from $70/day self-drive for a short-wheelbase Land Rover or Land Cruiser.

Hertz Leisure Tours & Holidays, *Mount Meru Hotel*, Nairobi–Moshi Highway ☎027/250 9150, ⓦwww .hertz.com. Land Cruiser self-drive $180/day including 100km. Excess liability $1200.

Serena Car Hire India St ☎027/250 9833, ⓦwww.serenacarhire.com. Land Cruiser with driver $150/day, including fuel and unlimited mileage for Northern Circuit. No self-drive.

Safari operators

The importance of taking your time in choosing a reliable and trustworthy safari operator cannot be stressed highly enough – do read the section on safaris in Basics, and on no account buy a safari that has been touted by flycatchers without being absolutely certain of the company's credentials.

Prices depend on the type of accommodation, group size, where you're planning to visit (park fees for Serengeti and Ngorongoro are considerably higher), and – to a lesser extent – the type of vehicle used. Reliable "budget" camping trips start at $120–140 a day; mid-range safaris with accommodation in lodges cost $200–300 a day depending on the lodges used, and luxury safaris staying in exclusive tented camps or mobile camps anything up to $700 a day. These prices are only approximate: a lot depends on **park fees**, which may increase substantially in 2007. The companies reviewed below have been carefully selected, and are in our opinion among the most reliable in their respective price ranges. At the time of writing, all held TALA licences for wildlife parks unless otherwise stated. Where companies are licenced for mountaineering (necessary for Kilimanjaro climbs), this is noted in the reviews – otherwise, assume that offers of Kili climbs will be channelled through another company. Membership of TATO (p.68) gives you some leverage in case of complaints.

If you choose to go with a company not reviewed here, common sense and a healthy dose of cynicism are vital. Fellow travellers are of course great sources of up-do-date advice, but be aware that even bad companies occasionally come up with the goods, so don't trust everything you hear. *Bamboo Café*, *Jambo's Coffee House*, *The Patisserie* and *Via Via* are all good places to meet up with travellers, as is the Kaloleni area. The tourist office can be rather partial in its recommendations, however.

Budget

The following companies are recommended primarily for their own **budget camping safaris**, though most will farm out clients to other operators if they can't fill enough seats to make a trip profitable. You should be informed of this at the very least, and be given a chance to back out – keep your options open by paying only on the day of departure. If you're short of time, arrive in Arusha before Friday, as the better companies tend to close on Saturday afternoon and all day Sunday.

Whilst offers of even cheaper safaris abound, simple mathematics means that corners are inevitably being cut; needless to say, steer clear. Incidentally, don't assume that companies behind the ads and offers pinned to the wall of the tourist office are necessarily reliable.

Duma Explorer *Sinka Court Hotel*, Swahili St (PO Box 56 Usa River) ☎027/250 0115, ⓦwww .dumaexplorer.com. A US–Tanzanian company licensed for both mountaineering and wildlife parks. They're one of only three to bring both oxygen cylinders and portable altitude chambers for their Kili climbs. Mount Meru hikes and Crater Highlands treks (around $160/day, with vehicle backup) are other specialities. TATO member.

Easy Travel & Tours *New Safari Hotel*, Boma Rd (PO Box 1912) ☎027/250 3929, ⓦwww .easytravel-tanzania.com. Large, long-established company offering a wide range of trips from budget camping to an eleven-day luxury mobile camping expedition. They also have scheduled departures – the longest is six nights. They're also licensed for Kili. Southern Circuit safaris, beach breaks and scuba-diving are handled by their Dar and Zanzibar branches. Online payment facility. TATO member.

IntoAfrica *Manor Hotel*, Nairobi Highway, Sakina (PO Box 12923) ☎0745/880078, ⓦwww .intoafrica.co.uk. A conscientious Tanzanian–British operation with the emphasis on fair trade and community involvement; many trips include cultural tourism. They also offer hikes up Kili and Mount Meru, but their main business is a seven-day "Tanzania Explorer", which includes two days of cultural activities.

Kilimanjaro Guides and Porters Union Diplomat House, Mianzini, off the Nairobi–Moshi Highway ☎027/250 9215, ⓦ www.kilimanjaro-union .com. Concerned by the exploitation of porters by

safari companies (too much to carry, too little or no payment), 120 porters and guides got together in 2003 to form a union. Now with over 200 members, it's the best place to arrange your own Kilimanjaro or Mount Meru climb (they're licensed), or indeed a Crater Highlands trek, safe in the knowledge that no one's being ripped off. They have branches at Kili's Marangu and Machame gates, and are well versed in northern Tanzania's cultural tourism programmes.

Nature Discovery 5km west along the Nairobi–Moshi Highway from Sanawari junction, Sakina (PO Box 10574) ☎027/254 4063, ⓦwww .naturediscovery.com. An efficient, safety-conscious, ethical and keenly priced firm offering 4WD camping and lodge safaris, plus a number of interesting hiking options in the Crater Highlands, donkey trekking from Longido, birding, and walks along the eastern side of Lake Eyasi. Mountain climbing is another speciality – they're licensed and enjoy an outstanding reputation for Kilimanjaro, on which they carry oxygen and a portable altitude chamber. TATO member.

Nyika Treks & Safaris *Arusha Resort Center*, Fire Rd (PO Box 13077) ☎0744/393331, ⓦwww .nyikatreks.com. With a long-standing reputation for good, basic safaris and honest service, this outfit comes highly recommended. If you want to see a bit of everything, their six-night combo featuring Arusha, Tarangire, Manyara, Serengeti, Ngorongoro and a spot of cultural tourism is very good value. They also cover "semi-luxury" camping (with walk-in tents, hot showers and toilets and lodge safaris, but specialize in Crater Highlands treks ($120/day) and culturally oriented forays, especially to the Pare and Usambara mountains.

Safari Makers India St, above *Mirapot Restaurant* (PO Box 12902) ☎027/254 4446, ⓦwww.safarimakers.com. A US–Tanzanian outfit with good vehicles and a wide choice of flexible itineraries, from budget camping to extended lodge-based itineraries including the Southern Circuit. Their hikes range from a day's walk in Ngorongoro to up to ten days in the Crater Highlands. Also available are Mount Meru and Kili climbs, for which they're licensed (they also treat their porters decently). Many options can be combined with cultural tourism programmes. TATO member.

Shidolya Tours & Safaris Room 218, Ngorongoro Wing, AICC (PO Box 1436) ☎027/254 8506, ⓦwww.shidolya-safaris.com. A long-established Tanzanian company offering something for all pockets, particularly strong for budget tours, cultural tourism and Crater Highlands treks can be appended. TATO member.

Sunny Safaris Colonel Middleton Rd, facing *Golden Rose Hotel* (PO Box 7267) ☎027/250 8184, ⓦwww.sunnysafaris.com. A long-established and competitively priced outfit specializing in both camping and lodge safaris, with transport in 4WDs with roof hatches and guaranteed window seats. They also offer trips staying in walk-in tents at special campsites, Crater Highlands treks, and Kilimanjaro climbs (licensed). TATO member.

Mid-range

There are plenty of **mid-range operators** offering comfortable safaris in the $200–300/day range, with accommodation in lodges, permanent tented camps or in large "Meru" tents pitched on public or special campsites; the tents are fitted with camp-beds, linen and sometimes showers and toilets. Take care with transport, however – some big companies ferry their clients around in convoys of minibuses, which definitely detracts from the charm.

Prices for lodge safaris depend on the standard of **lodge** used: the cheapest should be those operated by Hotels & Lodges Ltd, but their prices have been fluctuating. Next up is the semi-luxury Sopa chain, followed by the luxurious Serena chain. More expensive still are a handful of privately run lodges and tented camps; most are reviewed in Chapter 7. Safari costs fall during the long rains, especially April–June, when lodge prices drop.

Dorobo Tours & Safaris Olasiti: 6km along the Dodoma road, then 3km south (PO Box 2534) ☎027/250 9685, ⓔdorobo@habari.co.tz. A small, socially responsible and personable outfit run by three American brothers. Their exclusive tailor-made trips feature an enjoyable and instructive blend of culture and wildlife in mostly untravelled locations, and excel in rugged treks outside the national parks. If you have enough time and money, a two- or three-week trip is recommended to really get under the skin of rural Tanzania. TATO member.

East African Safari & Touring Company Goliondoi Rd, entrance beside Meat King (PO Box 1215) ☎0744/741354 or 0744/312189, ⓦwww.eastafricansafari.info. This Australian outfit is highly recommended: efficient, customer-oriented, flexible and pleasingly offbeat, with an excellent reputation for trips to suit all pockets, especially in off-the-beaten-track destinations. Their speciality is traditional game drives combined with walking, particularly in Tarangire Conservation Area (where they own *Naitolia*, *Boundary Hill Lodge* and *Sidai Camp*; night game drives are also possible), the Crater Highlands and Lake Natron (from $160/day),

and Tanzania's northwest. More unusual offerings include birding, mountain biking and a bumper 21-day "Tanzania Explorer".

Green Footprint Adventures Sekei (PO Box 2551) ☎027/250 2664, ⓦwww.greenfootprint.co.tz. Dutch/South African company offering mid- to high-end trips featuring smaller, out-of-the-way lodges and mobile camps. They also operate various activities (mostly 2–3hr) from their bases at the Serena lodges, including mountain biking, canoeing, hiking and microlight flights over Lake Manyara, and run eight-day wildlife/guide courses in April, May and November, based at Ndarakwai in West Kilimanjaro: currently $495 full-board. TATO member.

Tropical Trails *Masai Camp*, Old Moshi Rd (PO Box 223) ☎027/250 0358, ⓦwww.tropicaltrails.com. A highly respected firm offering affordable camping safaris as well as personalized safaris, either by vehicle or on foot outside the parks (anything up to two weeks), with knowledgeable guides. They also offer Crater Highlands hikes, cultural treks in the Rift Valley with Maasai guides, and a range of specialist activities arranged through other companies. They're also experts on Kili (licensed). TATO member.

Expensive

At the bank-breaking level, you'll usually have a "white hunter" chap as your guide, and although you'll be largely removed from Africans and the "real" Africa (excepting a few token Maasai warriors as picturesque guards), the quality of the guiding and service is invariably superb. Accommodation is in top-notch luxury tented camps or mobile luxury camps, catered by a retinue of staff who will set up everything before your arrival each evening.

Amazing Tanzania Based at Gibb's Farm in Karatu, 140km west of Arusha (PO Box 6084) ℡027/253 4302, ⓦwww.amazingtanzania.com. Attention to detail and personal service is the hallmark here – as it should be, given that their luxury camping safaris average $350–600 per day (including flights; a little less for lodge safaris). Most options are tailor-made and feature a mobile camp; they also have plenty of experience with elderly clients. They also offer flying safaris to the southern parks. TATO member.

Coastal Travels ATC House, Boma Rd ℡027/250 0087, ⓦwww.coastal.cc. Primarily an aviation company, Coastal also offer entirely tailor-made flying safaris, specializing in lesser-known destinations like Rubondo Island National Park, which can be combined with Serengeti. They also do last-minute holiday deals to Pemba and Zanzibar – handy if you're short of time. From $300/day. TATO member.

Hoopoe Adventure Tours India St (PO Box 2047) ℡027/250 7011, ⓦwww.hoopoe.com. Specialists in off-the-beaten-track safaris, often staying in intimate luxury tented camps such as *Naitolia* in Tarangire Conservation Area, their own concessions at Loliondo next to Serengeti, Ngorongoro, and West Kilimanjaro, or in searingly expensive mobile camps. Their subsidiary, Tropical Trekking, offers a wide range of hiking and (licensed) mountaineering expeditions, including "luxury" $3000 Kili hikes. Upwards of $400/day. TATO member.

Nomad Tanzania Usa River, 300m from *Ngare Sero Mountain Lodge* (PO Box 681) ℡027/255 3819, ⓦwww.nomad-tanzania.com. Extremely stylish flying safaris conceptualized on the colonial vision of untamed Africa, and based in a number of associated, quirky and truly luxurious tented camps: *Sand Rivers Selous*, *Greystoke* (Mahale), *Chada* (Katavi), *Serengeti Safari Camp*, *Loliondo Safari Camp*, and in mobile safari camps. $400–700 a day, depending on location, season, and whether you have exclusive use of a vehicle. TATO member.

Around Arusha

For all the hundreds of thousands of tourists passing through Arusha each year en route to the Northern Circuit, only a tiny proportion see much more of **Arusha Region** than the highway. Yet there are lots of things to keep you occupied.

The fertile lands either side of the highway, east of Arusha, were among the first in northern Tanzania to be colonized by Europeans, who grew tobacco to barter with Maasai for livestock. **Coffee** took over later, and remains the area's major crop – you can stay on a coffee estate, or see the coffee-making process as part of a cultural tourism programme based at Tengeru, close to the bird-filled **Lake Duluti**. There are several more **cultural tourism programmes** in the vicinity of Arusha, providing intimate glimpses into rural life among the Maasai, Meru and Il Larusa (Arusha) tribes. Another good destination for hikers is **Mount Meru**, part of **Arusha National Park**. The mountain is Tanzania's second-highest peak, and achingly attractive, whether you want to scale it or nose around its lower slopes, either on foot or on a game drive.

Arusha National Park

In spite of its proximity to Arusha town, **ARUSHA NATIONAL PARK** is little-visited – which is good news for visitors who do make it here, as they can enjoy the park's stunning volcanic scenery, expansive views (especially of its giant neighbour, Kilimanjaro), hauntingly beautiful rainforest and plentiful wildlife in relative solitude.

Dominating the park is the volcanic **Mount Meru** (4566m), Tanzania's second-highest mountain. While Meru appears as an almost perfect cone when viewed from Arusha, from the east it shows the effects of the cataclysmic volcanic event which a quarter of a million years ago blew away the entire eastern side and top of the mountain – which was once taller than Kilimanjaro – in a series of gigantic explosions which hurled boulders over 70km to the east and unleashed a devastating flood of water, rocks, mud, ash and lava. Although the volcano is now classed as dormant, earth tremors still occur, and a series of minor eruptions were recorded in colonial times, the most recent in 1910.

The national park and its fringing forest reserve encloses much of the mountain, including the 3.5km-wide **Meru Crater** on the summit and the entire shattered eastern slope, as well as the mountain's eastern foothills. Here you'll find **Ngurdoto Crater**, an unbroken three-kilometre-wide caldera whose wildlife has earned it the nickname "Little Ngorongoro", and the shallow, alkaline **Momela Lakes**, known for their birdlife, especially flamingos. **Wildlife** you're likely to see includes buffaloes (especially in forest glades), elephants (who are responsible for creating the glades), hippos, giraffes, warthogs, antelopes, zebras, black-and-white colobus and blue monkeys. Leopards and hyenas are present but rarely seen (there are no resident lions), and while there are also some extremely rare black rhinos, the park authorities are understandably loath to make too much noise about them, given the ever-present risk from poachers. There are also 575 bird species, and butterfly fanatics are in for a treat, too.

Arrival and information

Access to the park is easiest through **Ngongongare Gate**, 7.5km north of Usa River and the Arusha–Moshi Highway. **Momela Gate**, 17km further north, is the starting point for hikes up Mount Meru, and also houses the park headquarters.

Most visitors come on organized safaris, but visiting the park **independently** is feasible, given that hiking is possible in the western sector as long as you're accompanied by a ranger – they can be hired at Momela Gate. To reach the park by **public transport**, catch the daily Urio Bus from Arusha towards Ngare Nanyuki; it leaves Arusha at 1pm, and returns back through Momela Gate at around 7am. Alternatively, catch a daladala to Usa River, from where Land Rovers and trucks run every hour or two up to Ngare Nanyuki . If you're **hiring a car**, 2WD is sufficient for most roads in the east of the park during the dry season, but 4WD is nonetheless advisable, and essential during or shortly after the rains.

The **best time to visit** depends on what you want to do. Mount Meru can be climbed throughout the year, but is best avoided during the long rains (March–May), when you can get very wet, cold and muddy. Skies are clearest in September (when the mountain is bitterly cold), and again from December to February (when the temperature is marginally more clement). Bird-watching is best between May and October, when migrants visit.

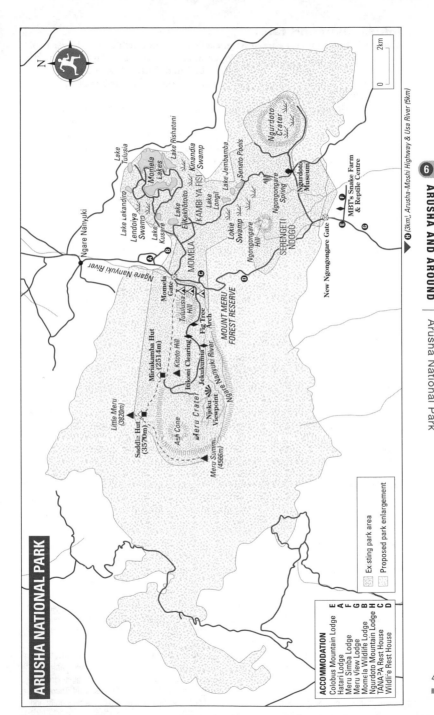

ARUSHA NATIONAL PARK

ACCOMMODATION
Colobus Mountain Lodge	E
Hatari Lodge	A
Meru Simba Lodge	F
Meru View Lodge	G
Momela Wildlife Lodge	B
Ngurdoto Mountain Lodge	H
TANAPA Rest House	C
Wildlife Rest House	D

Existing park area

Proposed park enlargement

0   2km

Information and fees

The **park headquarters** are at Momela Gate, 24km north of Usa River (daily 6.30am–6.30pm; ☎027/255 3995, ⓦwww.tanzaniaparks.com/arusha.htm); this is where rangers, guides and porters can be hired. **Entry fees** are paid here or at Ngongongare Gate: $35 per person for 24 hours, plus Tsh10,000 for a 24hr vehicle entry permit.

If you're **driving**, the services of an official guide ($10–20) are optional. If you're **hiking** (only possible west of Momela Gate), an armed park ranger is obligatory ($20 per group per day; tips expected), whilst climbers also pay a one-off $20 rescue fee if going beyond Miriakamba Hut. The total cost for a self-arranged four-day ascent and descent of the mountain works out at $320 including hut or camping fees but excluding transport, food, porters and additional guides. **Porters** come from nearby villages: the set daily rate is $5 for carrying a maximum of 15kg of clients' luggage, though $10 seems more fair. You'll also need to pay their entrance fees and accommodation (Tsh4500). A four-day hike arranged through a safari company in Arusha averages $450–500 per person.

The beautifully illustrated *Arusha* **guidebook** ($10), published by TANAPA, contains lots of information about the park, and is especially recommended if butterflies are your thing. The only decent **map** is Giovanni Tombazzi's painted version – ensure you get the "New" one. Both are available at the park gates, Arusha's bookshops, *Jambo's Coffee House* and the Ngorongoro Conservation Authority office on Boma Road.

Accommodation

The two **mountain huts** ($30 per person) along the Mount Meru climbing route are clean and have bunk beds and toilets. Water is also available, but at Saddle Hut you may have to collect it from the lower gorges during the dry season. Although the huts are rarely full, the park advises climbers to book ahead, either at the gate or at TANAPA's headquarters in Arusha (see p.403). **Camping** is possible outside the huts and at three park-run campsites a kilometre or two southwest of Momela Gate (all $30 per person), and at three special campsites ($50) with no facilities. You can also camp at *Colobus Mountain Lodge*, outside Ngongongare Gate ($5 per person).

In the park

Hatari Lodge and *Momela Wildlife Lodge* are currently just outside the park, but access is usually through the park so park fees are payable. If adopted, the park's new boundary will include them both .

Hatari Lodge 1km north of Momela Gate ☎027/255 3456, ⓦwww.hatarilodge.com. Welcoming and nicely idiosyncratic place decked out in 1960s and 1970s style – a refreshingly funky change from the neo-colonial mood of most lodges. There are just eight en-suite rooms, spacious and peaceful and with fireplaces. Good "John Wayne" bar, delicious food, library and verandah with views of Meru and Kili. Immediate wildlife interest is good, too: giraffes frequently come right up, bushbabies and genets are seen at night, a boardwalk accesses a clearing with buffalo, waterbuck, eland and giraffe, and there's a hippo pool within walking distance. Other walks (also outside the park with Maasai), game drives and canoeing can be arranged. Full-board with or without game package. ❾

Momela Wildlife Lodge 2km north of Momela Gate ☎0748/400131, ⓦwww.lions-safari-intl .com. Large and far from intimate but cheap, with 55 faded rooms in a series of mundane wooden thatch-roofed *bandas* supposedly styled after an African village. Still, there's hot water and good views of Mount Meru, while for film buffs, this is where the cheesy John Wayne movie *Hatari* was shot – quite literally, as the bow-legged strongman bagged an elephant on celluloid. There's a bar and lounge with a fireplace, a restaurant and

a big swimming pool (guests only). Breakfast and early-morning bird walks included. ⑥
TANAPA Rest House 1.3km south of Momela Gate; turn east at the signpost for "Halali" (book through TANAPA in Arusha; see p.403). Perfectly decent bunks and bathrooms. $30 per person.

Wildlife Rest House 6km south of Momela Gate (book through Mweka College of African Wildlife Management, ☎027/275 6451, ⓦwww .mwekawildlife.org). In a grassy forest clearing beside the roadside, this has just two beds, solar electricity, a toilet and bucket shower. $10 per person.

Outside the park
The following include breakfast.

Colobus Mountain Lodge 300m west of Ngongongare Gate, 7.3km north of Usa River ☎027/255 3621 (book through Shidolya Tours & Safaris, p.406). Next to an unsightly sawmill, this centres around a large *makuti*-thatched bar and restaurant, and also has Internet access. Rooms – including triples and others accessible to wheelchairs – are in two-room thatch-roofed stone *bandas*, perhaps a tad spartan but otherwise fine, and with fireplaces and verandahs. Half-board ($7 per person extra) also gets you a walking safari outside the park. ⑥

Meru View Lodge 6.5km north of Usa River on the right ☎027/255 3876, ⓦwww .meru-view-lodge.com. A quiet, charming and well-priced option run by a Tanzanian–German couple, set in sunny and colourful gardens containing a number of aviaries and wild birds. There are seven simple but comfortable en-suite rooms in individual cottages, all with big double beds. Great food and drinks are available, there's also a swimming pool, and hiking can be arranged. ⑤

Ngurdoto Mountain Lodge 2.5km north of Usa River, then 1km east ☎027/255 5217, ⓦwww .thengurdotomountainlodge.com. The area's best-appointed and biggest hotel (it's more like a resort), whose rooms – decked out in classic Africana, most with Jacuzzis – house 350 guests. Its size, overly landscaped gardens and ugly Disneylandish architecture detract from the experience, but it's good value, and comes with golf course, some rooms for disabled guests, three restaurants, a coffee shop, two bars, a swimming pool and various sports facilities. ⑦ (half-board ⑧)

Ngurdoto Crater and Momela Lakes

The highlights of the **eastern section** of the park, covering the forested foothills of Mount Meru, are the Momela Lakes and Ngurdoto Crater. Both can be visited on an organized day-trip from Arusha. **Walking** may be possible in the area if accompanied by a park ranger, but things have still not been fixed despite years of promises – ask at the park headquarters.

The **Momela Lakes** in the northeast of the park comprise seven shallow, alkaline lakes formed from the volcanic debris created when Mount Meru blew its top 250,000 years ago. The alkalinity is ideal for various forms of algae, which account for the lakes' opaque shades of emerald and turquoise and provide an ideal habitat for filter-feeders like flamingos. Other birds include pelicans, ducks, and a host of migrants, especially between May and October. Glimpses of black-and-white colobus monkeys are virtually guaranteed in the forests around the lakes, and you may also catch sight of blue monkeys, bushbucks, buffaloes, hippos, giraffes and zebras. **Canoeing** is possible on Little Momela Lake; contact Green Footprint Adventures at *Serena Mountain Village Lodge* at Lake Duluti (☎027/253 9267; see p.389). They charge $40 per person, and there's also a $20 canoeing fee payable to the national park, in addition to standard park fees and transport.

Three more lakes and Lokie Swamp flank the drivable road south from Momela Lakes to **Ngurdoto Crater**, an unbroken, 3km-wide, 400m-deep volcanic caldera (inevitably dubbed "Little Ngorongoro") produced when two volcanic cones merged and finally collapsed – you can walk along the crater's western and southern rims. Like Ngorongoro, Ngurdoto plays host to a rich variety of wildlife, including buffaloes, elephants, baboons and occasionally rhinos. To protect this little Eden, especially the highly endangered rhinos (which were hunted to the brink of extinction in the 1980s), visitors aren't allowed to descend to the crater floor. Instead, you can view the crater's denizens from a series of viewpoints on the south side of the rim, which also gives good views of Kilimanjaro, weather permitting.

Two kilometres west of the crater is **Ngurdoto Museum** (daily 8am–5pm; free), which has modest displays of butterflies, moths, insects, birds and – more worryingly – snares used by poachers. The most startling exhibit is a rhinoceros skull with a wire snare embedded several centimetres into it; the rhino survived several years before the wire finally killed it. Back on the main Usa River–Momela road, 1km south of Ngongongare Gate, **MBT's Snake Farm & Reptile Centre** (daily 8am–5pm; Tsh3000) breeds snakes, turtles and reptiles for export. There's an extensive collection of scaly critters on display, including chameleons and crocodiles.

Heading back towards Momela, keep an eye out for wildlife in the diminutive patch of grassland to the right. Dubbed **Serengeti Ndogo** ("Little Serengeti"), it contains a variety of plains game, including a population of zebra introduced following the collapse of an export scheme.

Mount Meru

MOUNT MERU is sometimes treated as an acclimatization trip before an attempt on Kilimanjaro, and although the summit is over a kilometre lower, the climb can be just as rewarding, with spectacular scenery and dense forest. The mountain's **vegetational zones** are similar to Kilimanjaro's, though the high-altitude glaciers and ice fields are absent – not that they'll survive much longer on Kili. Evergreen forest begins at around 1800m, moist, cool and thick at first, then thinning as you rise. The higher forest, including giant bamboo thickets (up to 12m tall), offers an ideal habitat for small duiker antelopes and primates, notably blue monkeys and black-and-white colobus monkeys, which are often seen by climbers. The forest disappears at around 2900m, giving way to floral meadows where you might spot buffalo, giraffe or warthog. The meadows are followed by a zone of giant lobelia and groundsel, and finally – above the last of the trees at 3400m – bleak alpine desert where the only sounds, apart from your breathing, are the wind and the cries of white-necked ravens.

The ascent

The ascent starts at Momela Gate (1500m), where rangers, guides and porters can be hired. The trek is usually done over three days (two up, one down), but an extra day will help you acclimatize, and in any case the views are something to be savoured. Climbs of Mount Meru are usually done through a safari company, though if you're suitably equipped (see "What to take" on p.340), you can save a modest amount of money by arranging things yourself. **Altitude sickness** isn't as much of a problem on Mount Meru as on Kilimanjaro, but symptoms should nonetheless be treated seriously. If you come down with the mild form of altitude sickness, Little Meru Peak, also on the crater rim but 750m lower than Meru Summit, is an easier target than Meru Summit itself. Be aware of a malingering **scam** involving rangers who don't wish to ascend all the way: they set too fast a pace to deliberately tire out their charges, who are consequently only too happy to turn back if given the chance.

Day one (4–5hr) goes from Momela Gate to **Miriakamba Hut** (2514m). There are two routes; the steeper and more direct one heads up due west

△ Meru people carrying water

(and is mainly used by walkers when descending), and the longer and more picturesque route follows a drivable trail to the south which begins by hugging the boulder-strewn **Ngare Nanyuki** (Red River); look for tawny eagles in the yellow-bark acacia trees here. The trees were called "fever trees" by early explorers, as they were believed to cause malaria – in fact, it's the swampy ground they favour that attracts the mosquitoes which carry the disease. The trail curves around **Tululusia Hill** (Sentinel Hill), in the lee of which stands an enormous strangling fig tree whose aerial roots have formed a natural arch; there's a waterfall on the Tululusia River near the tree. A kilometre beyond the tree is **Itikoni Clearing**, a popular grazing area for buffaloes (there is also a "special campsite" here), and 1km further on is Jekukumia, where a small diversion takes you to the confluence of Ngare Nanyuki and **Jekukumia** rivers. At around 2000m both routes enter the rainforest, characterized by the African olive tree (rare elsewhere thanks to its useful timber). Bushbuck may be seen here. Buffalo and elephant droppings mean you should be careful when walking around Miriakamba Hut at night

Day two heads on up to the **Saddle Hut** (3570m) below the northern rim of the summit's horseshoe crater (2–3hr). If you have time and energy, a short detour to **Little Meru Peak** (3820m) is possible (5–6hr from Miriakamba Hut), though the symptoms of altitude sickness kick in on this day, so spending an extra day at Saddle Hut if you're going to climb Little Meru is recommended. **Day three** (or day four if you spent an extra day at Saddle Hut) starts no later than 2am for the 4–5hr ascent to **Meru Summit** (4566m), following a very narrow ridge along the western rim of the crater, to arrive in time for sunrise over Kilimanjaro. Lunch is taken on the way down at Saddle Hut, and Momela Gate is reached by late afternoon. Alternatively, you could take it easy and spend an extra night at Miriakamba Hut, some four to five hours' walk from the summit.

Cultural tourism programmes around Mount Meru

Although Arusha National Park covers only the eastern flank and summit of Mount Meru, the southern and northern slopes can also be visited through a number of **cultural tourism programmes**, combining beautiful views, encounters with rural communities and hiking.

Cultural tourism programmes around Arusha

Arusha is the base for many of Tanzania's ground-breaking community-run cultural tourism programmes (see Basics for more details), which offer intimate encounters with the local Maasai, Il Larusa (Arusha) and Meru tribes, and dozens of walks to local attractions. Access to some can be a little awkward, given their rural locations off main roads: luckily, the mountain biking trips offered by Escape Maasai Biking (no office; ☎0744/207504 or 446158, ✉allysaid@hotmail.com) incorporate some of the programmes around Mount Meru. Costs are very reasonable: around $25 per person per day including the cultural tourism fees, or $40 with overnight. They also offer longer trips with their own tents, including camping at the Il Larusa village of Ilkushini, 2km before Ngaramtoni.

Ilkiding'a

On the southern slopes of Mount Meru, seven kilometres northwest of Arusha, is the Il Larusa village of **ILKIDING'A**. Its **cultural tourism programme**, most of whose members perform in the Masarie Cultural Dance Group, offers half- to three-day guided tours, including walks through farms, visits to a healer and local craftsmen, and hikes along the thickly vegetated Njeche Canyon (which has caves to explore) and up Leleto Hill. The three-day hike (or one day by mountain bike) also features forest reserves and local markets, with nights spent camping or in family homes. Profits benefit the local primary school.

There's no public **transport**, but as it's only 7km from Arusha, walking is the best way there: turn north at the signpost for *Ilboru Safari Lodge* on the Nairobi–Moshi Highway and follow the signs – the lodge and Arusha's tourist office can fix you up with a guide, though these are not necessarily part of the project. The road is bad, so taxi drivers charge up to Tsh20,000 for the return trip.

Costs for the programme depend on group size, ranging from Tsh10,000–17,000 per person for half a day, to Tsh45,000–60,000 for three days and two nights including meals and accommodation. Mountain bike rental is an extra Tsh10,000 a day. Arrange **bookings** through Eliakimu Ole Njeche ☎0741/520264, ✉enmasarie@yahoo.com.

Mkuru

On the north side of Mount Meru, some 70km from Arusha, the Maasai settlement of **MKURU** is famed for its camels, which were introduced in the early 1990s, as they fare better in semi-arid conditions than cattle. Mkuru's **cultural tourism programme** offers **camel rides** (from a few hours to a week-long expedition to Ol Doinyo Lengai and Lake Natron), **bird-watching** in acacia woodland guided by warriors, encounters with Maasai, and a short but stiff climb up the pyramidal Mount Ol Doinyo Landaree (3hr 30min return trip). Profits fund a nursery school.

At least one overnight is needed, preferably several; **accommodation** is in three two-bed cottages at the camp (bring your own bedding, food and drink). **Access** is expensive unless you're coming as part of a regular safari to Arusha National Park. The cheapest but fiddliest route is via Kingori, 5km before the Kilimanjaro International Airport turning, from where daladalas and pick-ups head to Ngare Nanyuki, 5km north of Arusha National Park (most leave in the afternoon). Much easier is to catch the daily Urio Bus service from Arusha (1pm) to Ngare Nanyuki: it goes through the park, so you'll have to pay the $35 entrance fee. From Ngare Nanyuki, walk the remaining 5km (signposted) west to Mkuru or rent a pick-up (Tsh20,000). Arrive the day before to give yourself time to arrange things.

Costs are more expensive than other programmes: the guide charges Tsh5000–9000 per group, and each visitor also pays Tsh8000 in fees, Tsh5000 per meal (if you haven't brought food), Tsh2500 for camping, Tsh3000 for visiting a Maasai *boma*, and Tsh10,000 for a day's camel hire. **Bookings** can be made through Mr Isaya Ishalavel ☎0748/756162, or with *Momela Wildlife Lodge* (p.410).

Mulala

On the southeastern slopes of Mount Meru, 34km from Arusha, is the beautifully located Meru village of **MULALA**. The cultural tourism programme is run by a women's group, who will show you their cheese dairy (which supplies a good many tourist hotels), bakery, stores, farms, and perhaps a few nifty dance moves. You can also visit a school, explore **Mount Meru Forest Reserve** (birds and monkeys), and hike through coffee and banana farms to Lemeka Hill (views and a traditional healer), along the Marisha River (thick tropical vegetation, birds and monkeys), or to **Ziwa la Mzungu** – White Man's Lake – where legend recounts that a European disappeared while fishing, after frightening demonic sounds came from the lake. The lake also has a colony of fruit bats. The various walks can be combined into a full day, or spread over two days if you have a tent – a better option.

To get to Mulala by **public transport**, catch a daladala towards Usa River and get off 1km before at the signboard for "Dik Dik Hotel". From here, catch a pick-up or Land Rover for the nine kilometres to the Ngani (pronounced *njani*) Cooperative Society. Ask for Mama Anna Palangyo (⊕0748/378951, ⓔagapemulala@yahoo.com), whose house is nearby.

Costs depend on group size, but shouldn't be more than Tsh10,000–15,000 per person for half a day, or Tsh20,000–25,000 for a full day and night. Profits have improved a playschool and dispensary, and are now funding Mulala Primary School.

Ng'iresi

Six kilometres north of Arusha on the verdant southern slopes of Mount Meru, **NG'IRESI** village and the Il Larusa tribe are currently in transition from cattle-herding and life in Maasai-style *bomas* (cattle corrals) to agriculture and permanent stone buildings. Several easy tours are offered as part of the cultural tourism programme, from half-day walks to three-day camping trips (bring your own equipment), and include an encounter with a traditional healer, hikes through Olgilai Forest Reserve, Songota and Navaru waterfalls, viewpoints on the Lekimana Hills, a climb up Kivesi Hill to the crowning forest, and visits to development projects. The local women's group provides meals. Profits fund a cattle dip and improvements to the primary school.

To get there, walk 5km up the road that goes past the *Summit Club* from the Nairobi–Moshi Highway, just east of *Mount Meru Hotel*, or arrange transport via the tourist office in Arusha (Tsh20,000 there and back). Other **costs** depend on group size, from Tsh14,000–18,000 per person for half a day and Tsh27,000–37,000 for a full day and night, to Tsh38,000–62,000 for a three-night stay. **Bookings** can be made through Mr Loti Sareyo of Kilimo Youth Group: ⊕0744/320966, ⓦwww.ngiresischool.org.

Tengeru and Lake Duluti

Twelve kilometres east of Arusha lies **TENGERU** and its bustling, recently modernized market – busiest on Wednesday and Sunday (all day). Tengeru's **cultural tourism programme** is five minutes' walk north of the highway: head down the road facing the Natoil petrol station where daladalas from Arusha drop you (ones to Usa River and Kikatiti also pass by), turn right after 350m, then left at the signpost for "Tengeru Campsite". The **campsite** has hot water (the Tsh5000 fee includes breakfast), they also have a tent for hire (an extra Tsh5000), and a self-catering apartment (❸). Mountain bikes and good food are also available. For **bookings**, contact Mr Brightson Pallangyo ⊕0744/960176, ⓔtengeru_cultural_tourism@yahoo.com. **Costs** – sometimes variable – should be around $13–18 for a full day, $30–35 with overnight, and $50–65 for two nights and three days. Profits are used to educate AIDS orphans, and also benefit the primary school.

△ Lake Duluti

Other than seeing **village life** and visiting a traditional healer, the programme is good for getting your hands dirty – stone grinding finger millet (*ulezi*) to make *uji* porridge, visiting coffee farms followed by coffee roasting (you can take some home), and tree planting, where you can get your name on a plaque. They also offer a hike along the **Malala River**, whilst the three-day tour includes a visit to the gruesome spot where hundreds of Maasai drowned in a war with the Meru in the nineteenth century. If you have time to arrange things, though, **horseback** – arranged through the cultural tourism programme – is the way to go ($50–80 a day).

The main reason for coming to Tengeru, however, is **LAKE DULUTI**, a small crater lake 2km to the south, visits to which can be made through either the cultural tourism programme, *Jambo's Coffee House* and *Via Via* in Arusha, or independently. Formed at the same time as Mount Meru, which feeds it underground, it's partially flanked by a thin slice of forest through which wends a nature trail. It's a very pretty place, probably best savoured at the end of your trip – if you have the money, at *Serena Mountain Village Lodge* near the east shore (see p.389 for review; ❽). Sunsets are a particular joy, both for the sky-show and the many birds. Unfortunately, **swimming** is out of the question: the floating papyrus beds suggest bilharzia, whilst volcanically induced currents may also be dangerous.

The lake and its forest are a reserve managed by Arusha Catchment Forestry (☏027/250 9522, ⊜tourismduluti@yahoo.com), who charge $7 **entry**, plus $2 per person for a guide and $5 for an inflatable canoe or fishing gear. Their office is next to the (signposted) Duluti Club on the lake's western shore, a lovely 1.5km walk from the Natoil junction on the highway through a coffee plantation and patches of woodland. The office also has a **campsite**, and the adjacent Duluti Club charges nominal daily membership and has drinks and views.

The road to Kenya

The bus ride from **Arusha to Kenya** is a delight, especially early in the morning when the mist shrouding Mount Meru begins to dissipate. The rolling hills and acacia-studded plains beyond can be fantastically green after the rains, but the lush appearance is illusory: like the area to the west of Arusha, the plains north of Mount Meru suffer from massive erosion as a result of overgrazing by Maasai cattle herds, itself a consequence of their expulsion from traditional pastures following the establishment of the region's wildlife parks and commercial ranches.

Ngaramtoni

Rounding the southwestern flank of Mount Meru, the first major settlement you come to is **NGARAMTONI**, 12km from Arusha (daladalas from Arusha's daladala stand or the main bus station). Signposted from Ngaramtoni is the **Osotwa cultural tourism programme**, a two-kilometre walk east of the highway. You may be met by guides – ensure they're carrying an ID card. The best time to come is Thursday or Sunday, when you'll coincide with **Ngaramtoni market**, where you'll find fantastic spherical pots at throwaway prices.

Rather than being a place, *osotwa* means "good relations between people", and the project covers nine neighbouring villages. On offer are various walks accompanied by Il Larusa guides and visits to traditional healers, crafters, and a sacred fig tree ("strangling fig" vines have long been venerated by East Africa's peoples). You can also walk along the Ngarenaro River, or clamber up the 2000m Sambasha Hill to its crater and forest for great views, and to spot birds, butterflies, and both colobus and blue monkeys.

At present, the longest trip is just a day and night – there are various **campsites**, or you can stay in a **guest house** on the edge of a forest plantation. **Costs** vary according to group size: Tsh8000–14,000 per person for half a day; Tsh11,000–18,000 for a full day; Tsh23,000–30,000 for a day and night. Profits subsidize energy-efficient stoves. For **bookings**, contact the Chairman on ☏0744/960905, ✆osotwa_cbco@yahoo.com.

Ilkurot

Whereas Ngaramtoni is largely inhabited by settled Maasai, the drier terrain further north is the domain of their cattle-herding cousins. One of the best places to get to know their culture is through the **Ilkurot cultural tourism programme** (contact: Jeremia Laizer ☏0748/459296, ✆kinyorilomon@yahoo.com), 8km towards Nairobi from Ngaramtoni, or 20km from Arusha.

Thoroughly recommended are visits to (or overnights in) Maasai *bomas*, and a three- to five-day walking or **riding trip** (by camel or donkey) for a unique insight into semi-nomadic life, as well as glimpses of plains game and sweeping views of mounts Meru, Kilimanjaro, Longido and Kilimamoto. Shorter trips include a half-day hike up **Ngorora Hill**, followed by a visit to a blacksmith, women's handicrafts groups and a *boma*; for a full day, there's also time to climb **Kilimamoto mountain** to its crater, or to visit bee-keepers. Saturday is market day at nearby **Ol Doinyo Sambu** (no photos). Should you wish to witness a Maasai-style goat slaughter (and subsequent transformation into succulent *nyama choma*), just ask.

Access by daladala is easy: take one first to Ngaramtoni, then change to another for Ol Doinyo Sambu and drop at Sitau: the project is based at the campsite 400m west of the road from here. A taxi from Arusha might charge

Tsh25,000. If you're not staying under canvas (you'll need to bring your own tent), **accommodation** is available on traditional skin-and-grass beds in a Maasai *boma*, or in a guest house (❸). **Costs** are reasonable: Tsh9000–15,000 per person for half a day depending on group size; Tsh12,000–18,000 for a full day; Tsh19,000–26,000 for a day and night; and Tsh56,000–79,000 for three days and two nights. The included "boma fee" benefits elderly widows and orphans, and the "development fee" pays for primary schools and health care.

Longido

Located 80km north of Arusha along the Nairobi Highway in the heart of Maasai land, **LONGIDO** is the most distant but probably the most popular of the **cultural tourism programmes** around Arusha.

Rising abruptly in the east, **Mount Longido**'s 2690-metre elevation makes for a dramatic change of vegetation, winding up through dense cloudforest before following a series of buffalo trails across drier montane forest and scrub. The climb is possible in a day (8–9hr return trip), but two days, with overnight camping at Kimokouwa (bring your own tent), is recommended. With clear skies, the views from the summit are stunning; good weather is most likely from May to October. **Other walks** are possible in the plains around the mountain, including a half-day hike to Maasai *bomas* at Ol Tepesi, and a day-trip to Kimokouwa's "Valley of Wells" (the wells lead to an underground river used by Maasai herders), both of which offer the chance of sighting gerenuk (common in southern Kenya but rare in Tanzania), lesser kudu and klipspringer, giraffe, zebra, gazelle and buffalo. The guides are all young Maasai warriors, and most speak reasonable English.

The best **day to visit** is Wednesday, to coincide with the weekly cattle market, where you can also buy *kiloriti*, a root taken as an infusion for its stimulating properties – which may explain the astonishing ability of the Maasai and other pastoral tribes to cover enormous distances on foot, seemingly without fatigue. **Buses** and Peugeot shared taxis leave from Arusha's main bus station every hour or so, and take ninety minutes. The **cultural tourism programme** office is signposted a short distance from the highway in Longido. There's a basic and clean **guest house** (❶) in the village, and three **campsites** connected to the tourism programme. **Food** is available from local *hotelis* (restaurants) and the FARAJA Women's Group. **Costs** depend on group size, from Tsh9600–16,000 for a half day to Tsh18,000–24,500 for a full day plus overnight stay. The cost for climbs up Mount Longido varies but shouldn't be much more than Tsh30,000. Profits fund the construction and maintenance of cattle dips. **Bookings** can be made via Mr Ally Mwaiko of Longido Village Committee on ☎027/253 9209 or 0748/648202, ✉touryman1@yahoo.com.

Namanga

Passing Mount Longido, the road veers northeast towards **Ol Doinyo Orok** mountain (2526m), sacred to the Maasai. At its base, 110km north of Arusha, is the bustling settlement of **NAMANGA**, straddling the Kenyan border. **Buses, daladalas and Peugeot pick-ups** to Namanga run once or twice an hour throughout the day from both Nairobi and Arusha; the trip from Arusha takes ninety minutes to two hours. Locals pass between Kenya and Tanzania with impunity, but tourists wishing to **cross the border** have to complete formalities, which can take up to half an hour on each side. **Visas** (currently $50 for either country) are usually paid in dollars cash; you may be able to pay in sterling, but don't rely on it. There's a KCB **bank** on the Kenyan side, and an

NBC in Tanzania within the customs area. Tsh10,000 should get you about 700 Kenyan shillings. Don't be suckered into changing money on the street, and if someone says you need to have Tanzanian/Kenyan shillings to enter Tanzania/Kenya, ignore it – it's just a ruse leading to a money-changing scam.

The Kenyan side of the border is famed for its admirably tenacious Maasai women, who sell trinkets and pose for photos. The Tanzanian side is marginally calmer if you can avoid the red-eyed daladala touts, but watch your luggage on both sides – there are a lot of drugged-up male youths hanging about. If you want or need to spend the night at Namanga, there's a slew of cheap **guest houses** (all ❶) on either side, the better ones in Tanzania. For something more comfortable, try the *Namanga River Lodge* in Kenya, a colonial oddity composed of wooden cabins set amidst pretty gardens (❺).

West of Arusha

Heading **west from Arusha** along the Dodoma road, towards the wildlife parks and central Tanzania, the landscape changes with startling abruptness from Mount Meru's lushly forested foothills, into a broad and largely featureless expanse of savannah. Although it turns green in the rains, for much of the year it's an unremittingly dry and unforgiving area, where the disastrous effects of **overgrazing** are depressingly apparent. With little plant cover left, the soil no longer absorbs rainwater as it should, and the resulting floods have gouged deep, lunar gullies across the land, which in the dry season are the playground of spinning dust devils. Often taken as an indictment of the Maasai obsession with cattle, the massive erosion is actually more the result of the eviction of Maasai herders from their traditional ranges further west, which has created unnaturally high population densities elsewhere.

Kisongo and Meserani

KISONGO village, 16km from Arusha, is the first settlement of any size along the highway west, and hosts a lively cattle market on Wednesdays (all day) attended by herders from all over the area. To catch the best of it, you'll have to stay over the night before: there are cheap and basic **rooms** (❶) at *Sinya Bar* and *2000 Millennium Bar*, on the left of the main road at the west end of the village; both places also have food and drink. The Kisongo Maasai Gallery and Cultural Centre, 800m east of the village, is one of several **souvenir emporiums** along the road to the parks: you'll have to bargain hard, and bear in mind that if you're on safari, your driver will be paid a twenty to thirty percent kickback on anything you buy. Credit cards are accepted, but whether you can trust them with your card details is another matter. **Daladalas** from Arusha's main bus stand to Monduli (6am–3pm, to 6pm on Sun) also pass through.

Past Kisongo, the landscape becomes increasingly bleak, especially in October before the onset of the short rains, when the flat brown plains and distant inselbergs are edged by mirages under a leaden sky, and danced over by spiralling dust devils. The next major settlement is **MESERANI**, 30km from Arusha, which holds livestock auctions on Tuesdays (all day; mornings are best). There are several cheap and basic **guest houses** with bars and restaurants: try the *Vulilia*, *Engigwana* or *Parselian* (all ❶), but don't expect anything more than a grubby bed under a roof. Much better, if you have a tent, is **Meserani Snake Park** beside the highway at the west end of the village (☎0744/440800 or 0744/445911, ✆snakepark@habari.co.tz). Started by a South African family in

1993, the park was almost wholly desert when they arrived, but the judicious planting of drought-resident indigenous trees has now created an oasis. Most of the snakes are collected from local farms and villages; in return for not killing them, locals benefit from free antivenin. Highlights include black and red spitting cobras, several green mambas and one black – it's actually steel-grey, but the full name is black-mouthed mamba – not that you'd have much time to savour the sight. There are also lizards, chameleons and a crocodile pool, the fence serving mainly to keep out drunken overlanders.

Adjacent to the snake park and run by the same people is an excellent **Maasai Cultural Museum**, containing dozens of dioramas of figures in various situations (daily life, dance, an *orpul* meat feast, circumcision, and "milking" blood from a cow, amongst others). The guide will explain anything that catches your eye. Entrance to the museum and snake park costs $10, and **camping** is free. There's good, touristy grub and one of East Africa's funkiest bars (cold beers, cool cocktails, good atmosphere and zillions of flags), which becomes something of a riot whenever overland truck groups are in residence.

Behind the museum are a dozen thickly thatched houses built by Maasai, who sell **handicrafts**; there's little hassle, so take your time. If you don't find something to your liking, there's more choice at Tingatinga Art Gallery in the centre of Meserani, and Oldonyo Orok Arts and Gallery (both open daily; free admission) at the north end of the settlement. The Maasai outside the snake park can also arrange **camel rides** (Tsh1000 for a short jaunt, Tsh5000 for a few hours), and guided walks through the village. To get to Meserani from Arusha, catch a **daladala** from the main bus station towards Monduli.

Monduli

The **Monduli Mountains**, north of Meserani, act as condensers for rainfall, and so are of obvious importance to the Maasai, providing year-round water and pasture. The area's main town is **Monduli Chini** (Lower Monduli; usually just called Monduli), 12km north of Meserani and the highway, at the foot of the mountains. **MONDULI JUU** (Upper Monduli), 10km further into the mountains, is actually a cluster of four Maasai villages: Emairete, Enguiki, Eluwai and Mfereji. Emairete is the main one, and occupies a crater that was once considered sacred. If you can, it's worth coinciding with Emairete's weekly market on Saturday. **Maasai** are of course the main reason to visit – made relatively easy thanks to a cultural tourism programme, and – better – a culturally inclined NGO, Aang Serian.

Access, however, is a problem: whilst there are roughly hourly daladalas from Arusha's main bus station to Monduli Chini until 3pm, there's no onward public transport to Monduli Juu. Ask for Mama Ester in Monduli Chini, who works with the tourism programme and may be able to fix you up with a bicycle or a lift – though the latter may cost up to Tsh20,000. Alternatively, contact Aang Serian in advance – they have a vehicle.

Accommodation can also be arranged through Aang Serian. Camping is possible at four family-run sites; the best is *Esserian Maasai Camp*, which has running water (the others have long-drops and firewood but nothing else).

Monduli Juu cultural tourism programme

Monduli's **cultural tourism programme** is sadly not one of the best-run, with fluctuating management and reports of overcharging. Their various tours, from half a day to four days or more, all feature visits to Maasai *bomas* (semi-permanent settlements formed around protective cattle corrals). The half- and full-day walks include a hike up **Kona Saba escarpment** for great views over the Rift Valley, a clamber up through rainforest to **Kilete Peak**, excursions to various small dams popular with birds, a trip to a herbal doctor and a visit to a small jewellery "factory". With more time, the two-day Olkarya tour includes an *orpul* "meat feast" (a feasting and socializing camp traditionally reserved for Maasai warriors and their friends) and a visit to **Olkarya**, where warriors collect the red ochre with which they adorn themselves. The trip can be extended to three days, with a beautiful walk in the **O'Liyamei Valley**, and over four or five days with hikes up mounts Komoloniki or Tarosero.

All tours start at Naramatu Maasai Jewel Market in Emairete. **Costs** are not fixed, but really shouldn't be more than Tsh30,000 for a full day and night excluding transport. The programme's contacts change constantly: try ⓔctpmonjuu@yahoo.com, or enquire through Arusha's tourist office.

Aang Serian at Monduli Juu

Monduli Juu is also home to another cultural project, the peerless **Aang Serian** (Maasai for "House of Peace"; ☎0744/673368 or 0744/318548, ⓦwww.aangserian.org.uk), run by Lesikar and Gemma Enolengila. Their Arusha office is at Mollel House, 3rd floor, room 110, on Stadium Road. Founded in 1999, it's advanced in leaps and bounds on its central aim of preserving the indigenous cultures of northern Tanzania (especially music and orature), whilst instilling pride among the youth in their heritage at a time when westernisation risks sweeping away many of the old beliefs and values. The project is currently building a school, and has already organized several arts festivals in Arusha, produced books and CDs (it has a recording studio) and initiated a fair-trade programme with the UK. You can buy Aang Serian's output from their offices, through their website, or at their small shop in *Jambo's Coffee House* in Arusha.

Aang Serian runs **summer schools** (and winter courses) in anthropology, indigenous knowledge and medicine, and environmental studies; the cost is around £550 ($1000) for a three-week programme, including full board. They also offer "flying visit" **tours** (2–5 days), focusing on Maasai culture, with night-time visits to Maasai *esoto* (a traditional forum for young people to meet) and short ethno botanical walks. Costs are no more than $40 per day.

Travel details

Full details on moving on from Arusha are given on p.401.

Full details on moving on from Arusha are given on p.401.

Buses

Routes marked with an asterisk are liable to delays or cancellations during the rains.

Arusha to: Babati (5 daily; 4–5hr); Bukoba via Kenya and Uganda (2 weekly*; 26–30hr); Bukoba via Tanzania (3 weekly*; 16–18hr); Dar (20 daily; 9–11hr); Dodoma (1–2 daily*; 12–15hr); Iringa (1 daily; 12hr); Karatu (3 daily plus hourly daladalas; 3hr); Kondoa (1–3 daily*; 8–9hr); Lushoto (2 daily; 6–7hr); Mbeya (1 daily; 15hr); Mombasa (4 daily; 6hr); Mombo (20 daily; 5hr); Morogoro (4 daily; 8–10hr); Moshi (20 daily plus Coasters; 1hr 20min); Musoma via Nairobi (2 daily; 16–18hr); Musoma via Serengeti (3 weekly; 10hr); Mwanza via Nairobi (6 daily; 18–20hr); Mwanza via Serengeti (4 weekly; 10hr); Mwanza via Singida (1–2 daily; 12–14hr); Nairobi (12 daily; 4–6hr); Namanga (14 daily plus daladalas; 2hr); Ngorongoro (1–2 daily; 4hr); Same (21 daily; 3hr); Singida (4–5 daily; 8–9hr); Tabora (2 weekly*; 12–13hr); Tanga (6 daily; 6hr); Usangi (1 daily; 4hr).

Flights

Airline codes used below are: AE (Air Excel), AT (Air Tanzania), CA (Coastal Aviation), PA (Precisionair), RA (Regional Air) and ZA (ZanAir). Where more than one airline flies to the same destination, the one with most frequent flights and/or shortest journey times is listed first.

Arusha Airport to: Dar (PA, CA, AE, ZA: 5 daily; 2hr–3hr 30min); Dodoma (CA: 3 weekly; 2hr); Kilimanjaro (RA: daily; 10min); Kilwa (CA: daily; 4hr); Mafia (CA: daily; 3hr 15min); Manyara (AE, RA, CA: 5 daily; 20–30min); Mwanza (CA: daily; 3hr 30min); Ngorongoro (CA: daily; 1hr); Pemba (ZA, CA: 2 daily; 2hr 15–2hr 50min); Ruaha (CA: daily; 3hr 30min); Rubondo (CA: 2 weekly; 4hr 30min); Selous (CA: 1–2 daily; 3–5hr); Serengeti (AE, RA, ZA, CA: 6 daily; 1hr–2hr 40min); Tanga (CA: daily; 3hr 20min); Zanzibar (PA, CA, ZA, AE: 5 daily; 1hr 10min–1hr 35min).

Kilimanjaro International Airport to: Arusha (RA: daily; 10min); Dar (AT, PA: 3–4 daily; 1hr–3hr); Manyara (RA: daily; 55min); Mwanza (PA: 6 weekly; 1hr 20min–2hr 5min); Serengeti (RA: daily; 2hr–2hr 35min); Shinyanga (PA: 3 weekly; 1hr 10min); Zanzibar (PA: 1–2 daily; 2hr–2hr 30min).

6

The Northern Safari Circuit

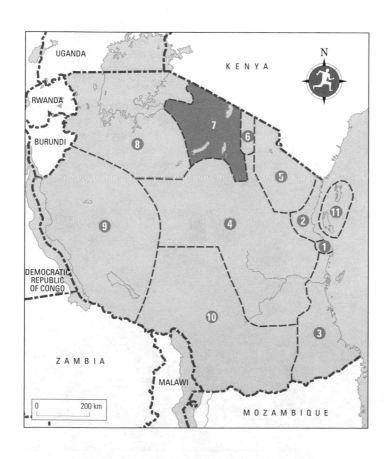

CHAPTER 7 # Highlights

* **The Maasai** East Africa's emblematic tribe, and one of the most traditional. Aside from their imposing appearance, their singing is among the continent's most beautiful. **See p.446**

* **Ol Doinyo Lengai** The Maasai's "Mountain of God", this near-perfect cone is East Africa's only active volcano, and can be climbed in a day, or as part of an extended "Crater Highlands" hike. **See p.452**

* **Lake Natron** A gigantic sump of soda and salt, much of it caked with crystals, and home to the world's largest breeding colony of flamingos. **See p.453**

* **Ngorongoro Crater** When a volcano collapsed 2.5 million years ago, it left a huge crater, which now contains the world's biggest concentration of predators. **See p.464**

* **Oldupai Gorge** The archeological site that revealed the cranium of 1.75 million-year-old "Nutcracker Man", and many other hominid fossils and stone tools. **See p.466**

* **The Serengeti** The name says it all. When the migration of 2.5 million wild animals is at home, the Serengeti Plains contain the world's largest number of mammals. **See p.471**

△ Ol Doinyo Lengai and Maasai tribesman

7

The Northern Safari Circuit

Head west out of Arusha and the land quickly turns to dry and dusty savannah, marking the start of traditional Maasai pastureland, and the journey to paradise for hundreds of thousands of safari-goers each year – eighty percent of Tanzania's visitors. The pride of the country's blossoming tourist industry is a quartet of wildlife areas between Arusha and Lake Victoria, collectively known as the **Northern Safari Circuit**.

The most famous of its destinations, known worldwide through countless wildlife documentaries, is **Serengeti National Park**. Its eastern half comprises the Serengeti Plains, which in the popular imagination are the archetypal African grassland. If you time your visit right, they offer one of the most spectacular wildlife spectacles on earth: a massive annual **migration** of over 2.5 million wildebeest, zebra and other animals, from the Serengeti Plains north into Kenya's Maasai Mara Game Reserve and back down, following the life-giving rains. Even if you can't coincide with the migration, there's abundant wildlife, and the plains are as good a place as any for seeing lions, often in large prides, and packs of hyenas.

The Northern Safari Circuit's other undeniable jewel is the **Ngorongoro Conservation Area**, the centrepiece of which is an enormous volcanic caldera – one of the world's largest – whose base, comprising grassland, swamp, forest and a shallow alkaline lake, contains an incredible density of plains game, and a full complement of predators. Ngorongoro is also one of few Tanzanian wildlife areas to tolerate human presence beyond tourism: the undulating grasslands around the crater are the land of the cattle-herding **Maasai**, whose red-robed, spear-carrying warriors are likely to leave an indelible impression. To cynics, Ngorongoro's popularity makes it resemble little more than a zoo, with the presence of dozens of other safari vehicles all looking for that perfect photo opportunity. Nonetheless, Ngorongoro is the highlight of many a trip, and its popularity is a small price to pay for the virtually guaranteed sight of lion, buffalo, leopard, cheetah, and highly endangered black rhino.

East of the Serengeti and Ngorongoro, in the **Great Rift Valley**, are two more national parks, less well known, but each with its own appeal. **Lake Manyara**, at the foot of the valley's western escarpment, is one of Tanzania's smallest national parks, despite which its wide variety of habitats attracts disproportionately dense wildlife populations. The bushy terrain, while not as immediately gratifying as

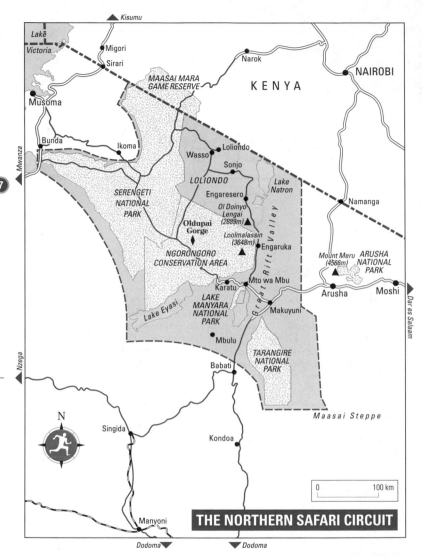

428

the wide-open dramatic spaces of Serengeti and Ngorongoro, can still make for sudden, heart-stopping encounters with animals. The lake itself is a popular feeding ground for large flocks of flamingos, and has a series of picturesque hot-water springs on its shore. Southeast of the lake, only two hours by road from Arusha, is **Tarangire National Park**, a likeably scruffy place, whose millenarian baobab trees dwarf even the park's substantial elephant population; in the dry season, this is probably the best place in all of Africa to see pachyderms. Adjoining the park's northeastern boundary is **Tarangire Conservation Area**, a vast conjunction of community-managed wildlife areas, where the main attractions are guided bush walks, night game drives illuminated by spotlights and some consummately romantic accommodation.

But it's not all about wildlife. Three **cultural tourism programmes**, at Mto wa Mbu near Lake Manyara, Karatu near Ngorongoro, and at Engaruka, a remote Maasai settlement, offer intimate and enlightening encounters with local communities, and there are also a number of **archeological sites** worth visiting. Engaruka contains the ruins of seven villages and their irrigation network, while the Serengeti's weathered granite outcrops have **rock paintings** of shields and animals daubed by Maasai warriors, and an enigmatic **rock gong**, part of a huge boulder that was once used as a musical instrument. Ngorongoro, for its part, was where the **origin of mankind** first began to make sense, in the paleontological paradise of **Oldupai Gorge**.

Fans of really wild places also have a couple of destinations to head to. **Lake Natron**, in the desolate north, is an enormous soda sump, much of its surface covered by a thick crust of pinkish-white soda crystals. At its southern end rises the perfectly conical and supremely photogenic **Ol Doinyo Lengai**, the Maasai's "Mountain of God", which is East Africa's only active volcano. It can be climbed in a day, or as part of a longer hike from Ngorongoro's **Crater Highlands**.

Almost everyone comes on an **organized safari** from Arusha, though companies in Mwanza (p.500), Moshi (p.345) and Dar (p.133) also offer trips, albeit at a slight mark-up – ensure they have the requisite TALA licence for safaris or tour operators. It is possible to visit the parks under your own steam, the easiest way being to **rent a vehicle** (preferably with an experienced driver worked into the bargain) – the price is competitive if you fill all the seats. There are car rental companies in Arusha, Dar and Mwanza, and vehicles can also be rented in Karatu, close to Ngorongoro.

Access to the parks by **public transport** is limited, given that you'll need a car in any case to enter Tarangire or Lake Manyara, or to see more of the Serengeti than the highway between Arusha and Lake Victoria, covered by a few buses each week. Ngorongoro is more viable – take the bus from Arusha to the conservation area headquarters, from where you can arrange guided walks from a few hours to several days, as long as you have a tent.

Guidebooks and **maps** are sold at the park gates and lodges, but are not always in stock: buy them beforehand in Arusha, Dar es Salaam or in Stone Town. For practical advice on arranging safaris and avoiding dodgy companies, and for information on what to expect, see pp.67–71.

The Great Rift Valley

The **Great Rift Valley**, which furrows its way clean across Tanzania from north to south, is part of an enormous tectonic fault that began to tear apart the earth's crust twenty to thirty million years ago. This geological wonderland runs from Lebanon's Bekaa Valley to the mouth of the Zambezi River in Mozambique, passing through a network of cracks across Kenya and Tanzania – a distance of 6600km.

The gigantic fracture is at its most dramatic in East Africa, where the valley reaches up to 70km in width, and whose floor has sunk more than a kilometre beneath the surrounding plains in places. There are actually two distinct rift valleys in Tanzania: the western branch, which includes depressions occupied by Lake Tanganyika and Lake Nyasa; and the eastern Great Rift Valley, which is at its most spectacular west of Arusha, where it's marked by a long and almost unbroken ridge. In places, however, the exact limits of the fault are blurred by associated volcanic activity: mounts Kilimanjaro, Meru and Hanang are products of these cataclysms, as is the still-active Ol Doinyo Lengai.

Three major lakes fill depressions within the Great Rift Valley: Natron, Manyara and Eyasi. The southernmost is **Lake Eyasi**, at the base of the Ngorongoro Highlands. The surrounding woodland is home to one of Africa's last hunter-gathering tribes, the **Hadzabe**, whose future looks as bleak as the lake itself. Increasing encroachment on their territory, the conversion of scrubland around their habitat into farmland and ranches, and insensitive tourism hyped around "Stone Age" images, may soon consign their way of life to oblivion – stay away.

Less morally challenging is **Lake Manyara**, at the foot of the highest and most spectacular section of the escarpment, whose northern extent is protected as a national park. The lake's water, though alkaline, is fresh enough for animals, including dense populations of plains game and large flocks of flamingos. **Mto wa Mbu**, the village serving as the base for visits here, has a popular cultural tourism programme that provides a good way of getting to know some of the dozens of tribes that have settled here, attracted – as with the wildlife – by the year-round water supply. There's another cultural tourism programme at **Engaruka** to the north, an excellent place for getting to know Maasai in a genuine context. The village lies within walking distance of one of Africa's most enigmatic archeological sites: the ruins of a city about which little is known other than that it was founded around six hundred years ago and abandoned in the eighteenth century.

North of Engaruka is the bleak and windswept terrain around **Lake Natron**, a vast and largely lifeless soda lake that will appeal to desert aficionados. At the lake's southern end rises **Ol Doinyo Lengai** ("The Mountain of God"), one of the few volcanoes in the world to spew out sodium carbonate (soda), with the result that the water is exceedingly alkaline – a thick, pinkish-white crust forms on its surface in the dry season. The unremittingly dry and desolate nature of the lake and its shore excludes most forms of life, the major exception being **flamingos**, who thrive on the soda-loving diatom algae; the lake is their most important breeding ground in the world. At times, literally millions of birds paint the horizon with a shimmering line of pink; Lake Natron is protected as an Important Wetland Area under the international RAMSAR Convention.

Safari operators usually offer trips to Lake Manyara as an either/or choice with **Tarangire National Park**, southeast of the lake. But the two parks actually complement each other, both for wildlife and visually. Tarangire is the more open of the two, with lots of (partly seasonal) plains game and an immense variety of birds – over 550 species at the last count. It is also one of the best places in Africa to see elephants, especially in the dry season when animal densities in the park are second only to those of the Serengeti–Ngorongoro ecosystem.

Tarangire

Occupying almost four thousand square kilometres of pure Rift Valley wilderness southeast of Lake Manyara, **TARANGIRE** comprises **Tarangire**

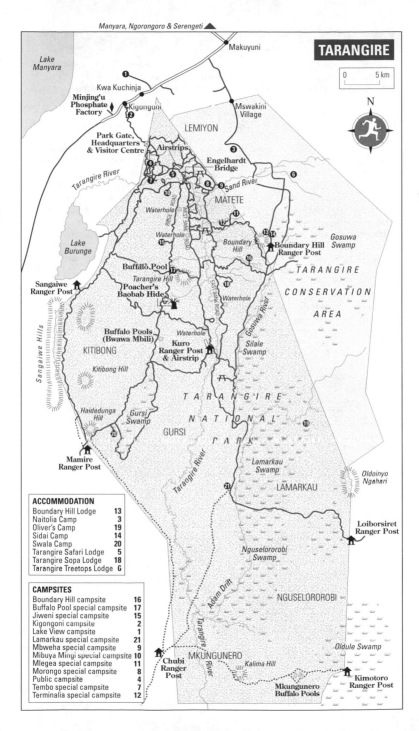

TARANGIRE

0   5 km

N

Manyara, Ngorongoro & Serengeti

Lake
Manyara

Makuyuni

Kwa Kuchinja

**Minjing'u
Phosphate
Factory**

Kigongoni

Mswakini
Village

**Park Gate,
Headquarters
& Visitor Centre**

LEMIYON

Airstrips

Tarangire River

Engelhardt
Bridge

Sand River

MATETE

Waterhole

Lake
Burunge

Waterhole

Waterhole

Boundary
Hill

Boundary Hill
Ranger Post

Gosuwa
Swamp

**Sangaiwe
Ranger Post**

Buffalo Pool

Tarangire Hill

**Poacher's
Baobab Hide**

T A R A N G I R E

C O N S E R V A T I O N

A R E A

Buffalo Pools
(Bwawa Mbili)

KITIBONG

Kitibong Hill

Waterhole

Kuro
Ranger Post
& Airstrip

Silale
Swamp

Gosuwa River

Haidedunga
Hill

Gursi
Swamp

GURSI

T A R A N G I R E

N A T I O N A L

P A R K

**Mamire
Ranger Post**

Lamarkau
Swamp

Oldoinyo
Ngahari

LAMARKAU

Loiborsiret
Ranger Post

Tarangire River

Nguselororobi
Swamp

Adam Drift

NGUSELORORBI

Oldule Swamp

**Chubi
Ranger Post**

MKUNGUNERO

Kalima Hill

**Kimotoro
Ranger Post**

**Mkungunero
Buffalo Pools**

ACCOMMODATION

Boundary Hill Lodge	13
Naitolia Camp	3
Oliver's Camp	19
Sidai Camp	14
Swala Camp	20
Tarangire Safari Lodge	5
Tarangire Sopa Lodge	18
Tarangire Treetops Lodge	G

CAMPSITES

Boundary Hill campsite	16
Buffalo Pool special campsite	17
Jiweni special campsite	15
Kigongoni campsite	2
Lake View campsite	1
Lamarkau special campsite	21
Mbweha special campsite	9
Mibuya Mingi special campsite	10
Mlegea special campsite	11
Morongo special campsite	8
Public campsite	4
Tembo special campsite	7
Terminalia special campsite	12

Sangaiwe Hills

WEST BANK ROAD

EAST BANK ROAD

Bird-watching in Tarangire

With its wide variety of habitats and food sources, **bird-watching** in and around Tarangire is a major draw, with over 550 species recorded to date, the highest count of any Tanzanian park, and about a third of all Tanzania's species. In the swampy floodplains in the south and east, Tarangire also contains some of earth's most important breeding grounds for **Eurasian migrants**. Wherever you are, you'll rarely be left in silence: birdsong starts well before dawn, and continues deep into the night.

It's impossible to give a full list of what's around, but to give an idea, the **woodlands** are particularly good for hoopoes and hornbills, brown parrots and the white-bellied go-away-bird (named after its curious call), and for game birds like helmeted guinea fowl, yellow-necked spurfowl and crested francolin. Other commonly sighted birds include yellow-collared lovebirds and lilac-breasted rollers, barbets and mouse-birds, swifts, striped swallows and starlings, bee-eaters, hammerkops, owls, plovers and cordon bleus. There are also four **bustard species**, including the kori, the world's heaviest flying bird, albeit usually seen on the ground. High above, especially close to hills, soar bateleur eagles, their name – "tumbler" in French – aptly describing their aerobatic skills. Over fifty more species of **raptors** (birds of prey) have been recorded, from steppe eagles (migrants from Russia) and giants like lappet-faced vultures, to the tiny pygmy falcon.

The **best months** for bird-watching are from September or October to April or May, when the winter migrants are present, though access – especially to the swamp areas – can become impossible at the height of the long rains from March to May. A recommended safari company offering **specialist birding safaris** is The East African Safari & Touring Company in Arusha (p.406), whose trips are based at *Naitolia Camp* or *Boundary Hill Lodge* in the conservation area, and cost a very reasonable $120–180 per person per day.

National Park and the adjacent **Tarangire Conservation Area**. Uncrowded and unspoiled, they possess a wild and unkempt beauty, and contain pretty much every animal species you're likely to see on safari with the exception of rhino, which were wiped out here by poachers in the 1980s. Tarangire's signature attractions are **elephants** (head counts of several hundred a day are not unusual), and **baobabs**, weird, ungainly and hugely impressive trees that can live for several thousand years, providing wonderful silhouettes for sunset photographs.

The area's ecological importance stems from the **Tarangire River**, which loops through the park in an anticlockwise direction, emptying into the shallow and alkaline **Lake Burunge** just outside the park's western boundary. A bare string of isolated waterholes in the dry season, the river is in spate during the rains, the catalyst for an annual **wildlife migration** (see box opposite). Many animals stay all year round however, including significant numbers of elephants, buffaloes, giraffes, zebras, ostriches and warthogs, and a full range of **antelopes**. Also present are **predators**; lions can usually be viewed lazing around by the river and, with luck, you might also catch sight of a leopard (best seen in the adjacent conservation area, where night game drives by spotlight are allowed). Cheetahs exist but are rare, as the long grass doesn't favour their hunting technique, and you'd also be lucky to see hyenas, whether spotted or striped.

The **best time to visit** is July to October or November for the national park, when wildlife concentrations are second only to the Serengeti–Ngorongoro ecosystem. The conservation area is also good at this time, but even better when

Tarangire's wildlife migration

Albeit nowhere near as grand as Serengeti's world-famous migration, Tarangire is the centre of an annual **migration** that includes up to 3000 elephants, 25,000 wildebeest and 30,000 zebras, as well as large numbers of gazelles and antelopes, including the fringe-eared oryx – rare elsewhere. The migration follows a pulse-like motion, expanding outwards from Tarangire National Park and to a lesser extent from Lake Manyara National Park during the rains, and contracting during the long dry spell that equates to the European summer.

In the dry season, from July to late October or early November, animals concentrate along the Tarangire River and its waterholes, before the onset of the short rains prompts wildebeest and zebra to head off north towards Lake Manyara, and east into the Simanjiro Plains of the Maasai Steppe. Over the following months, the short rains give way to a short dry spell and the wildebeest and zebra give birth to their calves, before the arrival of the long rains bring with them large herds of other animals. By April or May, when the long rains are at their height, the migration is also at its peak, with animals scattered over an area ten times larger than Tarangire, some even reaching Kenya's Amboseli National Park, 250km northeast on the northern side of Kilimanjaro.

When the rains come to an end, usually between mid-May and early June, the plains dry up quickly and lose their colour. Eland and oryx turn back towards Tarangire, followed by elephants, and then, by July, zebra and wildebeest. In August, with the weather now hot and dry, the bulk of the migrants are back in Tarangire, where they will stay a few months before the whole cycle begins anew.

the migration is passing through, meaning December–March and May and June, though long grass immediately after the rains may hinder visibility.

Practicalities

The main **national park** entrance gate is 7km south of the highway from Arusha. The first 104km to the junction at Kigongoni village are on a fast sealed road; the remaining 7km are all-weather gravel. The gate is open 6.30am–6.30pm and driving is not allowed after 7pm. **Entrance fees**, valid for 24 hours, are $35 per person and Tsh10,000 for a vehicle. An optional **wildlife guide**, handy if you're self-driving, can be hired at the gate for $20 per drive.

Special permission is required to enter or leave through other gates (marked on our map as ranger posts); the most useful of these is Boundary Hill in the northeast, for access to **Tarangire Conservation Area** (no entrance fees at present). To access the conservation area otherwise, turn south off the Arusha highway 3km west of Makuyuni, the village at the junction to Lake Manyara, Ngorongoro and Serengeti. The start of the dirt track is marked by a sign for Naitolia School. Self-drive is difficult as there are few other signposts along the way. The track is passable by 2WD as far as *Naitolia Camp* (18km), but you'll need 4WD to get in deeper, or in the rains. It's possible to enter the national park at Boundary Hill, but you'll need to have paid the entrance fee at the main gate first – a fine example of bureaucratic logic.

All of Arusha's **safaris operators** cover Tarangire, usually tacked on to a trip to Ngorongoro and/or Serengeti. Day-trips are possible, but bear in mind that you'll be spending at least two hours on the road in either direction. Particularly good value is an overnight trip offered by the East African Safari & Touring Company (see p.406) for $120 per person, which includes a night at *Naitolia Camp* in the conservation area, a five-hour guided walk and night game drive; the minor catch is that you have to make your own way from Arusha to Makuyuni (several daladalas and buses cover the route daily, including Mtei Coach), where they'll pick you up. A similar trip over two nights costs $330, and can be extended.

The national park headquarters are 1km inside the gate; nearby is the **Tarangire Visitor Centre**, which has loads of information, a viewing platform built around a baobab tree, and an artificial waterhole for wildlife. The official **website** is ⓦ www.tanzaniaparks.com/tarangire.htm; for the conservation area, see ⓦ www.tarangireconservation.com. For more detail on the park, get one of TANAPA's **guidebooks**, which can bought in bookshops in Arusha, Dar and Stone Town, or at the park gate. The old black-and-white version ($5) is comprehensive but out of date for roads; the new full-colour version costs $10. The best map is Giovanni Tombazzi's beautiful hand-painted version, with two plans, one each for the dry and rainy seasons; ensure you get the "New" version, as the road network on the old one is wrong.

Accommodation, eating and drinking

Apart from some very basic guest houses along the highway at Makuyuni and Kigongoni, the cheapest **accommodation** is camping, either outside the park in some very average campsites, or – much better – inside the park. There are lodges and tented camps in both the park and adjacent conservation area; the latter has the edge in being able to offer night game drives and bush walks, though walks should eventually also be possible inside the park (currently only from *Oliver's Camp*), but probably only for overnight visitors.

For **food**, most safari-goers pack a picnic (or a lunch box, available at all the lodges and tented camps). There are some basic *hotelis* and bars in the villages along the highway, and you're welcome for drinks or lunch ($20–25) at *Tarangire Sopa Lodge* and *Tarangire Safari Lodge*, both of which also have swimming pools.

Accommodation in the national park
See also "campsites", opposite.

Oliver's Camp East of Silale Swamp, 70km inside the park ⓦ www.oliverscamp.com (book through Asilia Lodges & Camps, Arusha ☎ 027/250 2799, ⓦ www.asilialodges.com). Nestled around a hillside with good views of the nearby swamps, this is painfully expensive but highly rated for its wildlife guides – especially if birds are your thing (the location is a twitcher's paradise). It's currently also the only place inside the park to offer bush walks. Accommodation is in comfortable en-suite tents, and game drives are in open-topped vehicles; fly-camping is possible if pre-booked. Closed mid-March to mid-June. All-inclusive $400 per person. ❾

Swala Camp Close to Gursi Swamp, 67km inside the park (book through Sanctuary Lodges, Njiro Hill, Arusha ☎ 027/250 9816–7, ⓦ www.sanctuarylodges .com). Sheltered in a grove of acacias, this is another financial shocker, with nine luxurious en-suite tents stuffed with period furniture, each with an elevated terrace overlooking a waterhole frequented by

waterbuck, the said *swala* (impala), lion, elephants, and the occasional leopard. The dining tent (with silver service) and library are stylish, and game drives are in open-topped vehicles. Closed April & May. All-inclusive $550 per person. ❾

🏃 **Tarangire Safari Lodge** High above the Tarangire River, 10km inside the park ⓦ www.tarangiresafarilodge.com (office: 50 Serengeti Rd, Arusha ☎ 027/254 4752). The only affordable lodge within the park, and none too quiet or private given its 86 rooms and popularity with package tours, but the location is superb, allowing wonderful wildlife viewing around the river below (binoculars recommended). The rooms and permanent tents are fine (but lack nets), and have verandahs facing a lawn, often browsed over by dikdiks at night. There's also a large swimming pool. Half price April & May. Half-board $80 per person. ❽

Tarangire Sopa Lodge South of Matete, 32km inside the park (book through Sopa Lodges,

4th floor, Sopa Plaza, 99 Serengeti Rd, Arusha ⓣ027/250 0630–9, ⓦwww.sopalodges.com). A large and functional rather than beautiful 150-bed lodge on a wooded hillside east of the Tarangire River. There's not a lot of wildlife interest, but the views are good, and the bedrooms (some designed for disabled people) are spacious and comfortable if a little dark. There's also a small pool. Half price April & May. Half-board $135 per person. ➒

Accommodation in the conservation area

🏃 **Boundary Hill Lodge** 47km from the highway ⓦwww.tarangireconservation. com (book through The East African Safari & Touring Company in Arusha; see p.406). Perched high on the rocky hillside, this is a truly eco-friendly lodge – relying on rainwater, solar panels and wind turbines – and the Maasai village of Lokisale owns fifty percent of the venture. The eight spacious rooms – out of sight from each other – are built of natural materials, each with spectacular (and vertiginous) views over Silale and Gosuwa swamps; some even have bathtubs on their balconies. The dining area has similarly blessed views, as does the large swimming pool built into the rock. Included in the cost are game drives (also at night with spotlights), visits to Maasai *bomas* and sundowners on Sunset Hill. All-inclusive $235 per person. ➒

🏃 **Naitolia Camp** 18km from the highway ⓦwww.tarangireconservation.com (bookings as for *Boundary Hill Lodge*). Located in baobab- and acacia-studded woodland, this is a small, informal place with friendly staff. Accommodation is in four secluded stone-and-canvas rooms, or in an achingly romantic tree house fronted only by a (white) mosquito net, and so with spectacular views of the savannah from your bed. All have flush toilets and bucket showers – if elephants haven't drunk the water – but no electricity. Same activities as at *Boundary Hill Lodge*, plus fly-camping ($285 per person). All-inclusive $175 per person. ➒

Sidai Camp Close to *Boundary Hill Lodge* (same booking information). This really is just a camp – two large and luxuriously fitted tents on a ridge overlooking Gosuwa Swamp, each with a cast-iron bathtub on its terrace, plus a dining tent and little else – intended for those who want a really exclusive experience. Same activities as for *Boundary Hill Lodge*, plus game drives in the national park (included). All-inclusive $325 per person. ➒

Tarangire Treetops Lodge 37km from the highway (book through Elewana Afrika, 4th floor, Sopa Plaza, 99 Serengeti Rd, Arusha ⓣ027/250 0630–9, ⓦwww.elewana.com). This gets close to the ultimate in bush chic, though at prices that leave you seeing stars, with twenty quirkily romantic tree house tents. Each has two beds, stone bathrooms, electricity and sweeping 270° views from their balconies. In similar style are the dining room and bar, built around a baobab close to a small swimming pool and waterhole used by elephants. Optional extras include short wildlife walks, night game drives and bush dinners. Closed April & May. Full-board $335–425 per person. ➒

Campsites

The park's **public campsite** ($30 per person) is 4km south of the main gate. There's plenty of shade, few tsetse flies, flush toilets and cold showers. Deeper in the park are several **special campsites** ($50 per person), which should be booked and paid for in advance at TANAPA headquarters in Arusha (see p.403), though you may strike lucky if you just turn up. None has facilities of any kind, and are often unnervingly close to wildlife; hiring an armed ranger ($20) at the park headquarters may be necessary for staying at some of them. Firewood collection is forbidden, so bring gas cans, or buy charcoal at Kigongoni or Kwa Kuchinja before entering the park. There are also a few **privately run campsites** outside the park, none of them anything special but handy for a cheap night ($5 per person), the best being the following:

Kigongoni Campsite 1km south of Kigongoni towards the park gate ⓣ0744/460539. Well placed for trying to hitch around the park with safari drivers, this occupies a shadeless, stony and dusty site, but is adequate. Hot showers mornings and evenings, and a bar and kitchen (but no food).

Lake View Campsite 2km east of Kigongoni along the sealed road, then 1km northwest – bear left at the first fork (no phone). Fenced and shadeless but with a fine sweeping view of Lake Manyara, under an hour's walk away. Has toilets, showers and soft drinks, but no kitchen.

Tarangire National Park

Tarangire contains a range of different habitats, from grassland and woods in the north, to low hills, scrub and swampland further south. Cutting through these habitats is an evergreen corridor, the **Tarangire River**, which empties into Lake Burunge in the west. The river is the key to life here, and its northern extent – close to the park gate and *Tarangire Safari Lodge* – is the most popular area for game drives. In the dry season, when the bulk of the migration congregates around the river and its water pools, the area is phenomenal for game viewing. Fauna on the gently inclined grassland and woodland either side of the river is thinner, but the chance of spotting rarer animals like klipspringers and Bohor reedbuck, and rich birdlife, makes up for this, and the **baobab forests** in both areas are a big attraction.

With an extra day or two, you can venture farther afield. The shallow and saline **Lake Burunge** is an attractive destination, and usually has flocks of pink flamingos. South of here is **Gursi Swamp**, one of many marshes dominating the park's southern half and a paradise for birds. The **far south** is extremely remote, with access only guaranteed in dry weather. **Walking in the park** is theoretically possible, but currently only allowed for guests of *Oliver's Camp* – enquire at the park headquarters or with a safari company. You'll almost certainly need a vehicle to reach the walking zone, as it's likely to be in the south.

Lemiyon and Matete

The park's northern sector consists of **Lemiyon** and **Matete areas**. Their proximity to the park gate makes them easy to visit, and there's an extensive network of roads and tracks throughout the area. Together, they encompass a broad range of habitats, from grassland plains (where fringe-eared oryx can be seen), umbrella and flat-topped acacia woodland (great for birds) and more open woodland to the east, dominated by **baobab trees**. The acacia woodland is always good for wildlife viewing, providing year-round shelter and food, and there's abundant birdlife. Vervet monkeys and olive baboons are common in both areas, especially around picnic sites where they scavenge for food – be wary of the **baboons**, which can be dangerous, especially if you have food in view.

The Tarangire River

The park's peerless attraction is the **Tarangire River**, which forms Lemiyon's southern and Matete's western boundary. Although good for wildlife all year round, the river is at its most special in the dry season, when the migration is at home around the river's water pools. The section where the river flows from east to west has sandy cliffs along much of its northern bank, where there are several **viewpoints** and a picnic site – bring binoculars.

This east–west section of the river can be crossed at two points: across a concrete **causeway** in the west (dry season only) towards Lake Burunge, and over **Engelhardt Bridge** close to *Tarangire Safari Lodge*, which offers access to two south-running routes: Ridge Road down to Gursi Swamp, and West Bank Road which hugs the river. Following the east bank is another road, accessed from Matete, which heads down to Silale Swamp. Any of these riverside drives is ideal for getting close to wildlife. In the dry season, a number of **water pools** attract large numbers of thirsty zebra, wildebeest, elephant (who are responsible for creating a good many pools themselves by digging up the dry riverbed with their tusks), giraffe, eland, gazelle, impala, warthogs and buffalo.

Baobab trees

The one thing that never fails to amaze visitors to Tarangire is its giant **baobab** trees. Known in Kiswahili as *mbuyu* (plural *mibuyu*), to botanists as *Adansonia digitata*, and popularly as the calabash tree, the baobab is one of Africa's most striking natural features. With its massive, smooth silver-grey trunk and thick, crooked branches, it's the grotesque and otherworldly appearance of the trees that impresses more than anything. The **trunk's circumference** grows to ten metres after only a century, and by the time the tree reaches old age, it may be several times more. Most live to at least six hundred years, but exact dating is difficult as the tree leaves no rings in its often hollow trunks. Carbon radio-dating, however, suggests that the **oldest** can reach three thousand years or even more.

Needless to say, the baobab is supremely adapted to its semi-arid **habitat**, its range stretching right across Africa and eastwards to Australia, where it's known as the bottle tree. One of the secrets to its longevity is its fibrous wood, which is extremely porous and rots easily, often leaving a huge cavity in the trunk that fills with water during the rains. The immense water-carrying capacity of the trunks – anything from three hundred to a thousand litres – enables the tree to survive long spells of drought. For this reason alone, the baobab has long been useful to humans, and the Kamba tribe of Kenya, who migrated north from Kilimanjaro five centuries ago, say in their legends that they moved in search of the life-giving baobabs: the Ukambani Hills, where they settled, are full of them.

The tree's shape has given rise to several **legends**. Some say that baobabs used to be in the habit of walking around the countryside on their roots, until one day God got tired of their endless peregrinations and resolved to keep them forever rooted to the soil, replanting them upside-down. On the Tanzanian coast, a pair of baobab saplings were traditionally planted at either end of the grave of an important person, which in time grew together to form one tree, enclosing the tomb within their roots. Baobabs were also, therefore, a propitious place to bury treasure, as the spirits of the ancestors would ensure their safe-keeping.

The baobab has myriad other more **practical** uses. The gourd-like seed pods or calabashes, which grow up to 25cm long, form handy water containers and bailers for boats, and the seeds and fruit pulp ("monkey bread") are rich in protein and vitamin C, and effective against dysentery and circulatory disease. They're also a source of "cream of tartar". When soaked in water, the seeds make an invigorating drink (you can buy baobab seeds, *ubuyu*, at Arusha's market); when roasted and ground, they taste similar to coffee. Young leaves are edible when boiled, and also have medicinal uses, and the bark, when pounded, yields a fibre suitable for making rope, paper and cloth, while glue can be made from the pollen. It's not just humans who benefit from the baobab though. Bees use the hollow trunks for hives, hornbills nest in their boughs, and elephants like to sharpen their tusks by rubbing them against the trees. In exceptionally dry seasons, they gouge deeper into the trunk to get at the water stored in the fibrous interior: the scars left by these activities are clear wherever you go in Tarangire.

Olive baboons are resident, and lions too are often found nearby. The bush on either side is ideal for hartebeest, lesser kudu and leopard, which usually rest up in the branches by day, their presence given away by little more than the flick of a tail. This part of the river, before it veers west, can be crossed along various dry season causeways and small bridges.

There's a pleasant **picnic site** by the river south of Matete, about 6km north of the turning for *Tarangire Sopa Lodge*. The site, by a huge mango tree, gives a good view of the river, which at this point provides a popular mud wallow for elephants.

Lake Burunge

The Tarangire River empties into **Lake Burunge**, a shallow soda lake just outside the park's western boundary, which is home to flocks of flamingos from July to November. The lake is surprisingly large, and makes a pretty picture with the Great Rift Valley's western escarpment in the background. There's no outlet, so salts and other minerals washed in by the river have turned the lake inhospitably saline, although during the rains the water is fresh enough to serve as a watering point for animals, including elephants and lions (look for their tracks in the mud). The lake's shallowness (barely 2m) means that its extent fluctuates widely. It tends to dry up completely at the end of the dry season, leaving only a shimmer of encrusted salt on its surface.

The road from the north – the last 3km of which are impassable in the rains – crosses the Tarangire River south of the park gate. It's not the most spectacular game-viewing area, but you may catch glimpses of lesser kudu or eland, steinbok in undergrowth, and small herds of shy and rare fringe-eared oryx. Closer to the lake are plains of tussock grass and clumps of fan palms, hemmed in by acacia woodland and scattered baobabs, and weirdly imposing cactus-like "trees" – **candelabra euphorbia**. Their sap is extremely corrosive, so the trees are usually left well alone by wildlife: the exception were the rhinos, which sadly were poached to extinction in the park in the 1980s.

The plains are best for wildlife at either end of the migration, when they fill up with large herds of wildebeest and zebra. But the main species to leave a mark, literally, are **tsetse flies**, clouds of them, especially in the vicinity of wildebeest.

Ridge Road

A right fork just south of Engelhardt Bridge marks the start of **Ridge Road**, a superb 40km drive south through acacia woodland to Gursi Swamp, which in places offers beautiful vistas over much of the park and further afield. While wildlife is not as dense as around the river, there's still a pretty decent selection, with mostly solitary elephants, giraffe, eland, warthog and buffalo. They're best seen at two sets of signposted **buffalo pools** along the way.

The other main attraction here is **Poacher's Hide**, its name possibly explaining the unusual jumpiness of the area's elephants. The hide is an enormous old baobab tree out of whose hollow trunk a small door has been carved, to resemble the dwellings of elves and sprites in children's books. The artificial doorway has led to lots of speculation about the original use of the hide: it seems likely that hunter-gatherers, possibly ancestors of Lake Eyasi's Hadzabe tribe (see box on p.457), used it as a shelter or for keeping honey-bee hives. The hide was certainly used by poachers in the 1970s and 1980s, hence its name – thick grass around the site, and a boulder that could be rolled across the entrance, completed the disguise. The hide is now used by animals: hyena cubs, bats and bat-eared foxes have all been seen inside – take care.

The swamps

In the dry season, access to the **swamps** of central and southern Tarangire is possible. The swamps, which feed the Tarangire River, are among the richest areas in Tanzania for **birdlife**, especially water birds from November to May. During the dry season as the swamps begin to dry, the receding waterholes and remaining patches of marshland also offer superb game viewing, including large buffalo herds up to a thousand strong, and elephants longing for mud baths. The easiest to visit are Gursi Swamp, at the end of Ridge Road close to *Swala Camp*, and Silale Swamp at the end of the East Bank Road on the park's eastern border.

A game track runs all the way around **Gursi Swamp**, much of the grassland on its periphery studded with tall termite mounds. Bushy-tailed ground squirrels are common, as are giraffes in the woodland. **Silale Swamp**, which should be accessible all year round, is perhaps even better for birdlife, and lions, preying on herds of zebra and wildebeest, are often seen on the western side in October. The fringing woods are said to contain huge tree-climbing pythons.

At its southern end, Silale merges into the enormous **Lamarkau Swamp** (whose name comes from *il armarkau*, Maasai for "hippo"), which itself merges into **Nguselororobi Swamp** (Maasai for "cold plains"). Both areas, together with Ngahari Swamp and Oldule Swamp in the park's southeastern extremity, are exceedingly remote and virtually unvisited.

Tarangire Conservation Area

Contiguous to the national park's northeastern boundary is Tanzania's first community-controlled wildlife area, **Tarangire Conservation Area**. Formerly used (and abused) by trophy hunting safari misfits, local villages were finally given official title to the land at the turn of the millennium, who turned it over to photographic tourism. The communities derive income from various lodges and camps, one of which (*Boundary Hill*) is half-owned by villagers – another admirable first.

Although the conservation area lacks the perennial flow of the Tarangire River, a number of seasonal "sand rivers" turn into a series of water pools during the dry season, at which time wildlife viewing can be better than in the park. Likely sightings include impala, Thomson's gazelle, oryx and dikdik, ostrich, giraffe and wildebeest, and of course **elephants**, which inhabit the area all year round. But the area's real magic lies both in some wonderfully romantic accommodation, and in not being tied by park regulations: **guided bush walks** are offered by all the camps and lodges – a perfect way of getting a feel for the wild. Just as unusual are **night game drives**, giving you the chance of seeing otherwise elusive animals like leopards and fringe-eared oryx. Strangely, they seem unfazed by the spotlights. To visit the area, you'll either need to come on an organized safari, or stay overnight at one of the lodges or camps.

Lake Manyara and Mto wa Mbu

One of Tanzania's most dramatically located wildlife areas is **Lake Manyara**, a shallow soda lake at the foot of the Great Rift Valley's western escarpment. The lake's northwestern section may be one of Tanzania's smallest national parks, but its varied shoreline habitats shelter a wide variety of animals, including elephants, great flocks of pink flamingo, large hippo pods, and much-hyped "tree-climbing lions". The park has been a UNESCO World Biosphere Reserve since 1981.

Although the park is usually tacked onto the end of a safari, after Ngorongoro or Serengeti, the grandiose nature of those places means that Manyara is best visited at the start of a trip, before you become too jaded with wildlife – unless birds are your thing, in which case Manyara can be a grand finale. A day is sufficient to see most of the park's sights.

The park is accessed through the bustling town of **Mto wa Mbu**, which has a wide range of accommodation and a good **cultural tourism programme** – perfect for getting up close with the town's many tribes, including the Maasai. For a bird's-eye view of the lake, strap yourself into a **microlight** (see p.445), or content yourself with the drive up from Mto wa Mbu to the top of the escarpment en route to Ngorongoro and the Serengeti. It's a spectacular road, with every hairpin giving increasingly breathtaking views of Lake Manyara and the green expanse of vegetation around its shore. There's a **viewpoint** on top, complete with curio shops, as well a number of lodges and a recommended campsite.

Mto wa Mbu

The verdant, oasis-like area around **MTO WA MBU**, whose name means "River of Mosquitoes", was a thinly populated patch of scrubland until the 1950s, when the colonial government began an ambitious irrigation project aimed at controlling Lake Manyara's cyclical floods, and to turn "unproductive" swampland into farmland. The project was a big success, attracting farmers from all around. In the 1960s, Mto wa Mbu was declared a collective **Ujamaa village** as part of Tanzania's ultimately disastrous experiment in "African socialism", into which thousands of people were sometimes forcibly resettled from outlying rural areas. In Mto wa Mbu, the main effect of the Ujamaa period is its extraordinary **ethnic diversity**: the population represents almost fifty tribes, including Hehe from Iringa; Gogo, Gorowa, Mbugwe, Nyamwezi and Rangi from central Tanzania; Barbaig, Hadzabe and Maasai from close by; Ha from Kigoma on the shore of Lake Tanganyika (who introduced oil palms); and the Il Larusa, Chagga, Iraqw and Meru from the north and northeast. Some of these tribes can be visited as part of a **cultural tourism programme**. Also recommended, as much for colour as for culture, are several **markets**.

Arrival

The 113km from Arusha is all sealed road. Three **buses** leave Mto wa Mbu in the morning (the last around 10am), and turn back in Arusha in the afternoon; they take around two and a half hours. The bus stop is outside *Red Banana Café* on the highway, the base for the cultural tourism programme.

Accommodation

Mto wa Mbu and its surroundings has a wide range of **accommodation**, from cheap (and not-so-cheap) campsites and guest houses in town, to mid-range places in woodland and expensive safari lodges atop the escarpment overlooking the town and the lake. None of the escarpment places have much in the way of wildlife except for birds, but the views can be great – make sure your room has one, as not all do. Nonetheless, at the price, there are much better pampered retreats elsewhere. See also the accommodation reviews for the national park on p.434.

Camping ($5 per person) is possible at *Kiboko Bushcamp* (forest), *Panorama Safari Camp* (matchless views), *Twiga Campsite & Lodge* (popular with overlanders) and at *Wild Fig Lodge & Campsite* (includes use of swimming pool).

Budget and mid-range

Kiboko Bushcamp 2.5km east of town along the highway, then 2km south ☏027/253 9152, ⓦwww.equatorialsafaris.co.tz. On the edge of a thick fever tree forest, this is dominated by a huge *makuti*-thatched dining room and bar. There are six big walk-in tents raised on platforms under thatched roofs, each with two beds, big box nets, bathroom, and amusing decor (an animal painted on the door, and elephant-dung sculpture of said animal's head on the verandah railing). Views are of the camp and its trees. There's also a fake Maasai village for those with no time for the real thing, and mountain bikes to rent. Closed April & May. Breakfast included. ❻

Lodge (*Camp Vision*) In town on the third block south of the highway; turn in at the Oryx petrol station ☏027/253 9159. More inspiring than its name suggests, this is actually three guest houses, almost adjacent. The main ones have basic but good-value twin-bed rooms with fans and nets, some with bathrooms, but much more characterful – and lived in by the friendly owners – is the one with en-suite rooms around a narrow but extremely lush garden courtyard. Safe parking. ❶–❷

Mashanga In town ☏027/253 9153. This is two hotels: *International Mashanga* on the second block south of the highway starting at the Oryx petrol station; and *Mashanga Guest House*, one block south of the highway (turn in at Oryx, then first left, past *Rembo Bar* and continue to the end). Both are good for safe and cheap, no-frills accommodation, all rooms with huge nets and fans, some with attached bathrooms. Little English spoken. Drinks available, and safe parking. ❶

🏃 **Panorama Safari Camp** On the escarpment, 500m north of the highway beside the mobile phone mast ☏0745/417838. Kudos to this gorgeously -sited campsite, especially for providing tents with bedding for those without – free of charge. Some of the pitches have great views, as does the bar (food needs pre-booking; there's also a pool table). There's electricity, piped water and hot showers, and guided walks can be arranged through Mto wa Mbu's cultural tourism programme. Bookings advisable. $5 per person.

Twiga Campsite & Lodge 1.5km east of town ☏027/253 9101, ✉twigacampsite@hotmail.com. The best of the moderately priced places, this has ten good en-suite twin-bed rooms with hot water mornings and evenings, and some triples ($25). There's a bar and restaurant, and a lounge with satellite TV and "wild video shows" (wildlife documentaries), plus traditional dances whenever it's busy. Rates are bargainable. Breakfast included. ❹

Wild Fig Lodge & Campsite In town, 200m north of the highway just west of *Red Banana Café* ☏027/253 9102. Lots of good large rooms in this peaceful and relaxed place, all with nets, electricity and hot water, and some with fans. The big draw is the swimming pool. There's also a quiet "bar" (no alcohol) with TV, a restaurant, gift shop, and a talented Tingatinga artist in residence. Breakfast included. ❹

Expensive

E Unoto Retreat 10km north of Mto wa Mbu, accessed off the road to Lake Natron starting 4km east of town ☏027/254 8542, ⓦwww

.maasaivillage.com. On a ridge overlooking the small Lake Miwaleni, this is aimed at upmarket package tours, with 25 bungalows styled after Maasai homesteads – some with disabled access (and golf buggies for carting weary guests around), and personal butlers for your every need. There's also a swimming pool, and guides for walks and birding. Full-board $204 per person. ❾

Kirurumu Tented Lodge On the escarpment, 6km northeast of the highway (book through Kirurumu Tented Camps & Lodges, Joel Maeda St, Arusha ☏027/250 2417, ⓦwww.kirurumu.com). Twenty large, mostly twin-bed en-suite tents spread out over the ridge, some but not all with lake views from their shady verandahs. Service is formal but friendly and efficient, and it's good value compared to the other options. Facilities include an excellent restaurant (fruit and vegetables from their organic garden), and ethno-botanical walks accompanied by Maasai warriors. Full-board $215 per person. ❾

Lake Manyara Hotel On the escarpment, 3km southeast of the highway (book through Hotels & Lodges Ltd, 2nd floor (Block B), Summit Centre, Sokoine Rd, Arusha ☏027/254 4595, ⓦwww .hotelsandlodges-tanzania.com). A 1970s concrete hulk with a hundred rooms, complete with a giant chess set in the bar. The only real attraction is the spectacular location, with magnificent views over the lake from most bedroom balconies, but it's all rather bland at the price. There's also a swimming pool. Full-board $180 per person. ❾

Lake Manyara Serena Safari Lodge On the escarpment, 2km northeast of the highway (book through Serena Hotels, AICC Ngorongoro, Room 605, Arusha ☏027/250 6304, ⓦwww.serenahotels .com). Poshest of the lot, but with 67 rooms (in two-storey "rondavels"; only a few of them with lake views) and overly formal service, it's hard to remember you're on safari, whilst the asking price is hard to justify. Still, the swimming pool has good views. Full-board $210 per person. ❾

Migunga Forest Camp 2.5km east of town along the highway, then 2km south, 200m before *Kiboko Bushcamp* (book through Moivaro Lodges & Tented Camps, *Moivaro Coffee Plantation Lodge*, Arusha ☏027/255 3242, ⓦwww.moivaro.com). Snug in a forest of yellow-bark acacia trees, this has seven tents and three bungalows, all with balconies facing a central lawn. There's a pleasant open-sided bar and dining room, seating in the garden, a gift shop, and activities (at extra cost) include wildlife safaris and nature walks. Full-board. ❼

The Town

Given Mto wa Mbu's ethnic diversity, it's no surprise that the town's **markets** are among the liveliest and most colourful in the country. The **central market** on the south side of the highway is a happy dog's breakfast of shops and stalls where you'll find pretty much anything that's produced locally, including many of the town's estimated eighty varieties of **bananas**. One corner of the market, the so-called "Maasai Central Market", is a tourist trap flogging the usual trinkets like Maasai beadwork jewellery and tartan *shuka* cloth, but an enjoyable one at that. Much more authentic is the Thursday **animal auction** held at the roadside 5km east of Mto wa Mbu (1km beyond the junction for Engaruka), and a **monthly market** (*mnada*) on the same site on the 22nd of each month, which attracts buyers and herders from as far away as the Zanaki tribe of Mara Region. Some of these herders continue to Arusha and a handful even make it to Dar es Salaam – an epic journey of at least 900km.

Mto wa Mbu's ethnic diversity is best experienced through the town's **cultural tourism programme** (☎027/253 9303 or 0748/606654, ⓔmtoc ulturalprogramme@hotmail.com), based at *Red Banana Café* on the highway. Their **guides** are former pupils of Manyara Secondary School and speak good English; to avoid hustlers and conmen, do not hire guides on the street or elsewhere, and ensure you get a receipt. Incidentally, the cultural tours offered by some upmarket tour operators and lodges are not necessarily the same thing, and can't guarantee that locals will profit from your visit.

The various **guided tours**, each lasting a few hours, can be combined into longer excursions. Some are offered as optional extras on standard wildlife safaris from Arusha. While the tours are not as immediately exciting as those of similar projects elsewhere, they are good for getting to know a wide variety of **tribes**, as all include visits to farms, local artisans and small-scale development projects. There are three main tours. Starting at the market, the **farming tour** covers a number of *shambas* north of town, where you'll meet farmers and see banana beer being brewed, and taste the result. The papyrus-fringed **Lake Miwaleni**, 5km north of town at the foot of escarpment, together with a waterfall, is accessed by trails along small streams. **Njoro hot-water springs** can be visited as part of a short trek up **Balaa Hill** to the northwest (30min to the top), which has good views. Other options, including visits to a Maasai *boma* and treks over several days, can also be arranged.

Costs are Tsh23,500 per person for a half- or full-day village tour, plus Tsh5000 if you combine it with another option. Traditional meals, provided by a women's group, cost Tsh2500. **Bicycle rental** is Tsh4000 a day (or a mean Tsh25,000 for a mountain bike). **Canoeing** on the east side of Lake Manyara (outside the park boundary) is Tsh15,000 per canoe, assuming there's sufficient water.

Eating and drinking

Mto wa Mbu has lots of basic **restaurants**, especially south of the market and highway, most doubling as bars. One of the best, despite appearances, is the *Rembo*, one block south of the market (turn south at Oryx and then left), which rustles up tasty and filling meals for under Tsh1000. The more touristy hotels also have restaurants: try *Wild Fig Lodge & Campsite* (meals $5, but allow two hours; use of their swimming pool costs Tsh4000 more) or *Twiga Campsite & Lodge* (meals around Tsh6000, but sometimes limited to the chickens running around its grounds). Meals at the upmarket lodges average $15–30.

The main cluster of **bars** is one block south of the Oryx petrol station, and east from there along the road to *Mashanga Guest House*: the *Rembo* and *Fiesta Complex* are both lively. Also good, and popular with tourists and locals alike, is the cavernous *Red Banana Café* on the highway.

Lake Manyara National Park

Set against the impressive 600m-high backdrop of the Great Rift Valley's western escarpment, **LAKE MANYARA NATIONAL PARK**, which covers the lake's northwestern corner – is a rare flash of green in an otherwise unremittingly dry land. Much of the park's land area is covered by groundwater forest or thick bush, which – though it makes spotting wildlife harder – allows an intimate and heart-stopping sense of being in the wild when an animal suddenly appears as you turn a corner.

For its small size, the park contains a wide range of **habitats**: evergreen groundwater forest in the north fed by springs; a swampy fan delta crowning the top of the lake; acacia woodland at the foot of the scarp scattered with baobab trees; a small grassy plain; and, of course, the lake itself. Together, they provide an oasis for wildlife, and the presence of year-round water also makes the lake part of the same migratory system of which Tarangire is the heart (see box on p.433).

Manyara is perhaps most memorable for its **elephants**, which number around 160 individuals – down from 640 in the 1960s but recovering well from the disastrous poaching of the 1980s. Other impressive denizens include **buffalo**, sometimes in large herds, which feed on sedge by the lakeshore, and two hundred **hippo**, seen in water pools in the northern fan delta. **Antelope** include impala, bushbuck and waterbuck, and agile klipspringers on the rocky escarpment wall. Other plains game are zebra, giraffe, mongoose and warthog, together with their predators: leopards and, famously, **tree-climbing lions**, which are sometimes seen resting up in the boughs of acacia trees south of the groundwater forest – your best bet for this is between June and August. The reason for their arboreal prowess is a mystery, though there's no shortage of possible explanations, the most plausible of which is their attempt to avoid the unwelcome attention

△ Pelicans, zebra and wildebeest at waterhole

Lake Manyara's ailing ecosystem

For all Lake Manyara's riches, all is not well. Migratory **wildlife routes** have been blocked by Mto wa Mbu in the north and, progressively, by commercial ranches and farms (the same problem that afflicts the Hadzabe hunter-gatherers to the south), whilst **lake levels** have dropped drastically over recent years due to recurring droughts and unsustainable water use by Mto wa Mbu's burgeoning population (now around 30,000, compared to 3500 in the early 1970s). Coupled with **land clearance** of swamps, woodlands and forest for arable land, continued **poaching**, and the insidious **pollution** of lake waters from both commercial and subsistence farms in its catchment area, the balance of the entire ecosystem has never been more precarious.

Even before the millennium was out, human interference had exacted a terrible toll – the **local extinction** of at least nine mammalian species: lesser kudu in 1957, wild hunting dogs in 1963, cheetah in 1980, mountain reedbuck and hartebeest in 1982, eland and oribi the following year, black rhino in 1985 and the common reedbuck in 1991. And if that was not enough, in 2004 ten thousand of the lake's emblematic flamingos perished en masse, victims of **toxins** accumulated in algae that had reached deadly levels following several years of drought. Alas, short of wholesale changes in the entire region's farming methods, there's little real hope that the lake's gradual degradation can be halted, never mind reversed.

of tsetse flies. The phenomenon isn't unique to Manyara – lions have also been seen up in trees at Tarangire, Serengeti, Ngorongoro and Selous.

Primates are represented by blue monkeys and vervet monkeys in the forest, and numerous baboon troops. The vervets are preyed on by crested hawk eagles, one of Manyara's over 380 **bird species** – for many visitors, the park's great highlight. Birdlife is at its most spectacular in the form of large flocks of flamingos feeding on the lake's algae. The algae are supported, in turn, by a series of picturesque **hot-water springs** along the shoreline, heated by geothermal activity associated with the Rift Valley's ongoing expansion.

Arrival, information and entrance fees

The park gate is 2km west of Mto wa Mbu, 115km west of Arusha. If you've come on public transport you'll still need a vehicle for visiting the park as walking is not allowed: the main tourist hotels can help out, or contact the cultural tourism programme (see p.442). 4WD is recommended although 2WD will get you to most places in dry weather.

The national park is open all year round, but best avoided during heavy rains (most likely March–May), when road access can be limited to the far north. The **best time to visit** for big mammals is June or July to September or October, and again in January and February. For birds, November to May is best. The best source of information is the TANAPA **guidebook** to Manyara, available in Arusha ($10). The park's **Internet** site is ⓦ www.tanzaniaparks.com/manyara .htm. There's an accurate **map** published by harms-ic-verlag in association with TANAPA, not that you really need one for getting around, and a more attractive hand-painted one by Giovanni Tombazzi.

Park **entry fees**, valid for 24 hours, are $35 per person and Tsh10,000 for a vehicle. It's possible to exit and re-enter the park on the same ticket, given that most accommodation is outside.

Accommodation

Accommodation inside the park is limited to park-run campsites and *bandas*, and an obscenely overpriced tented camp that has not been reviewed.

TANAPA Bandas Just inside the park gate (bookings – not always required – through TANAPA in Arusha; see p.403). A complex of ten basic brick cottages which, although basic for the price, are nonetheless comfortable, and have hot showers, proper toilets and electricity but no nets. There's no food, but firewood is supplied free of charge, and there's a kitchen and dining room. $30 per person.

TANAPA Public Campsites Just inside the park gate (bookings not required; pay at the park gate). Three sites close to the *bandas*, each occupying a lovely forest clearing, and with toilets and cold showers. Although camping in Mto wa Mbu is much cheaper, the beauty and intimacy of these sites can't be matched. Don't bother with the three "special" campsites further into the park ($50), which are nothing special at all. $30 per person.

The park

From the gate, a small network of tracks covers most of the vegetational zones in the northern section, and a single track (with some short game-viewing loops) heads south along the narrow strip of land between the lake and the escarpment.

The groundwater forest

Heading west out of Mto wa Mbu and over its eponymous river, the abruptness with which thick green forest appears to your left is quite startling. This is part of Manyara's evergreen **groundwater forest**, a soothingly cool, refreshing and very special habitat that dominates the northern section of the park next to the escarpment. Although it looks and feels like rainforest, Manyara's average annual rainfall of 760mm would be nowhere near sufficient to sustain trees of this size on its own. Instead, groundwater forest, as the name suggests, is fed by water from mineral springs which seeps through the ground's porous volcanic soil.

The tall mahogany, croton and sausage trees, tamarind, wild date palms and strangling fig trees, are home to a variety of wildlife, including blue monkeys, vervet monkeys and baboons (all of whom are fond of crashing around in the branches, especially at the park gate's picnic site), and there's plenty of **birdlife** too, though seeing anything more than a flitting form disappearing into the foliage is a challenge. More easily seen are ground birds, including two species of guinea fowl, and the large silvery-cheeked hornbill, which lives in the canopy but is often seen on the ground. Forest plants which benefit from the shade of the trees include orchids. **Elephants** are occasional visitors, and partial to using larger trees as back-scrubbers, much to the anguish of the park authorities who have tried to deter them by dressing some trees in prickly corsets of chicken wire.

The fan delta and hippo pools

About 4km southwest of the park gate along the main track is a signposted left turn towards a loop road around **Mahali pa Nyati** – the Place of Buffaloes

---

Activities at Lake Manyara

A number of "soft adventures" inside Manyara National Park are offered by Green Footprint Adventures, based at *Lake Manyara Serena Safari Lodge* (ⓦwww .greenfootprint.co.tz). Apart from short canoeing excursions ($60 excluding park fees) and mountain biking (outside the park), worth doing at least once if you don't have the chance elsewhere is a **night game drive** (3hr; $130–170 including park fees), which can be combined with a romantic bush dinner. But the highlight – quite literally – is to fly off the escarpment and over the lake whilst strapped into a **microlight aircraft**: $125 for twenty minutes, or $250 for an hour for die-hard thrill-seekers. Only one passenger per flight.

The Maasai

Exotic, noble, aristocratic, freedom-loving, independent, savage, impressive, arrogant and aloof ... you'll find these adjectives scattered all over travel brochures whenever they talk of the **Maasai**, one of East Africa's most emblematic tribes.

Meeting a Maasai warrior, with his red robe, spear and braided ochre-smeared hair, is one of the high points of many a safari holiday. Depending on the tour company or your ability to haggle, **visits** to spend half an hour in a "genuine" Maasai village (*boma*) in Ngorongoro, or along the road coming from Arusha, cost anything from a few dollars to $50. The money buys the right to take photographs and perhaps witness a dance or two, though you may also be mercilessly pestered by old ladies selling beaded jewellery and other trinkets. Depending on your sensibilities, the experience can either be an enlightening and exciting glimpse into the "real" Africa, or a rather disturbing and even depressing encounter with a people seemingly obliged to sell their culture in order to survive.

Some history

In the popular imagination, the Maasai – along with South Africa's Zulu – are *the* archetypal Africans, and as a result a disproportionate amount of attention, and nonsense, has been lavished on them, ever since the explorer Joseph Thomson published his best-seller *Through Maasailand* in 1885. In those days, the Maasai were seen as perfect "noble savages", but their story is much more complex.

What we know of their distant **history** is little more than conjecture proposed by romantically minded Western scholars. Some say that they are one of the lost tribes of Israel and others that they came from North Africa. Still others believe that they are the living remnants of Egyptian civilization, primarily, it seems, on account of their warriors' braided hairstyles. Linguistically, the Maasai are among the southernmost of the Nilotic-speaking peoples, a loosely related group that came from the north, presumably from the Nile Valley in Sudan. It's thought that they left this area sometime between the fourteenth and sixteenth centuries, migrating southwards with their cattle herds along the fertile grasslands of the Rift Valley. The Maasai eventually entered Kenya to the west of Lake Turkana, and quickly spread south into northern Tanzania, whose seasonal grasslands were ideal for their cattle. They reached their present extent around the eighteenth century, at which time they were the most powerful and feared tribe in East Africa. Their tight social organization, offensive warfare and deadly cattle raids, and mobility as semi-nomadic cattle herders, ensured that they could go where they pleased, and could take what they wanted. Their military prowess and regimentation meant that they were rarely defeated. As a result, their history before the arrival of the British was one of ceaseless expansion at the expense of other people.

Their combined Kenyan and Tanzanian territory in the seventeenth century has been estimated at 200,000 square kilometres. But all this is just one side of the story. The other is told by their territory today, which is less than a quarter of what it was before the Europeans arrived. The Maasai have been progressively confined to smaller and smaller areas of land. The British took much of it away to serve as farms and ranches for settlers, and in recent decades the land expropriations have continued, this time to form the wildlife preserves of Serengeti, Tarangire, Mkomazi, and part of Ngorongoro, to which the Serengeti Maasai were relocated when they were evicted.

– which, as you might expect, is a good place for spotting those rather cantankerous and temperamental beasts, who are invariably accompanied by ox-peckers and buff-backed herons feeding on insects disturbed by the passing of their hosts. South of the buffalo circuit is another loop leading to the mouth of Mto wa

The Maasai today, and in the future

Politically and economically, the Maasai remain marginalized from the Tanzanian mainstream, having stubbornly refused to abandon their pastoralist way of life, or their traditions, despite repeated attempts by both colonial and post-Independence governments, and missionaries, to cajole or force them to settle. Many men persevere with the status of **warriorhood**, though modern Tanzania makes few concessions to it. Arrested for hunting lions, and prevented from building *manyattas* for the *eunoto* transition in which they pass into elderhood, the warriors (*morani*) have kept most of the superficial marks of the warrior without being able to live the life. The ensemble of a red or purple cloth *shuka* tied over one shoulder, together with spear, sword, club and braided hair is still widely seen, and after circumcision, in their early days as warriors, you can meet young men out in the bush, hunting for birds to add to their elaborate, taxidermic headdresses.

But the Maasai **lifestyle** is changing: education, MPs and elections, new laws and new projects, jobs and cash are all having mixed results. The traditional Maasai staple of curdled milk and cow's blood is rapidly being replaced by cornmeal *ugali*. Many Maasai have taken work in the lodges and tented camps while others end up as security guards in Arusha and Dar es Salaam. A main source of income for those who remain is provided by the **tourist industry**, which gives the Maasai a major spot in its repertoire. Maasai dancing is *the* entertainment, while necklaces, gourds, spears, shields, *rungus* (knobkerries), busts and even life-sized wooden warriors (to be shipped home in a packing case) are the stock-in-trade of the curio and souvenir shops.

For the Maasai themselves, the rewards are fairly scant. **Cattle** are still at the heart of their society but they are assailed on all sides by a climate of opposition to the old lifestyle. Sporadically urged to grow crops, go to school, build permanent houses and generally settle down, they face an additional dilemma in squaring these edicts with the fickle demands of the tourist industry for traditional authenticity. Few make much of a living selling souvenirs, but enterprising *morani* can do well by just posing for photos, and even better if they hawk themselves on the coast; one or two can even be seen in Zanzibar.

For the majority, who still live semi-nomadic lives among a growing tangle of constraints, **the future** would seem to hold little promise, although a promising recent development has been the creation of various community-run conservation areas outside the parks and reserves, which generate income from annual land rents paid by tourist lodges and tented camps, and often enough a percentage of profits or overnight receipts. That stubborn cultural independence may yet insulate the Maasai against the social upheavals that have changed the cultures of their neighbours beyond recognition.

Unless you're really short on time, a much more satisfying and less voyeuristic way of meeting Maasai than in the touristic "cultural *bomas*" is via Tanzania's community-run cultural tourism programmes, several of which are run by Maasai: see Engaruka (p.451), and pp.414–416, 418–419 and 421–422 for projects around Arusha. In addition, the cheaper Crater Highlands treks (see p.465) from Ngorongoro to Lake Natron are usually guided in part by Maasai, and may include overnights in genuine, non-tourist-oriented *bomas*. For **more information**, see Ⓦ www.bluegecko. org/kenya/tribes/maasai, a comprehensive resource about Maasai culture, including their marvellously hypnotic singing.

Mbu River, and a series of **hippo pools**. This naturally swampy area is part of a **fan delta** formed by river-borne sediment, though massive flooding in 2001 and prolonged drought ever since has wrought havoc with the area, forcing the hippos upriver. The shallow lakeshore is especially favoured by **water birds**,

△ Maasai tribesmen

including pelicans, storks, herons, ibis, jacanas, egrets, plovers and lots of ducks and geese. But the undoubted avian stars are the vast flocks of pink **flamingos**, attracted by the profusion of algae in the lake's shallow, alkaline waters.

The acacia woodland, Msasa and Ndala rivers

To the south and east of the groundwater forest is more open **woodland**, dominated by umbrella acacias and dotted here and there by ancient baobab trees. It's a good habitat for all sorts of big game, especially elephant, giraffe and buffalo, and is good for spotting **birdlife** too, including various species of plover and kingfishers, larks and wagtails.

South of the groundwater forest, the park's main track crosses a series of small rivers, sometimes by bridge, other times by causeways which can become impassable if the rains hit hard. The main watercourse in the park's northern section is the **Msasa River**. This area is good for seeing solitary old male buffaloes, and if you're going to see lions in trees, it'll be here. There's a signposted **picnic site** under a big tree with benches, tables, a lake view and often uncomfortably close sightings of buffalo. There are two more picnic sites near the **Ndala River**, 9km south of the Msasa River, one of which has good lake views. The presence of buffalo, often in large herds, means tsetse flies start to be a nuisance south of the Msasa River.

The hot-water springs

Flamingos can also be seen on the western shore, close to a series of pungently sulphurous **hot-water springs**, of which there are two main groups. The smaller but most accessible are **Maji Moto Ndogo**, 22km south of the park gate, which keep to a very pleasant 33°C and get covered whenever the lake level is high. Just over 17km further south, past the patch of grassland formed by the modest delta of the Endabash River, are the bigger and more scalding **Maji Moto Kubwa** springs, whose temperature averages 76°C – hot enough to give you a nasty burn and to melt the soles of your shoes if you wander too close. They're at their most impressive when the lake level is low, and then especially in the rains (higher water pressure), when the water erupts in a series of highly pressurized flumes. Even when the lake level is high, however, there are some small springs closer to the road, which are remarkable for the beautiful colours and patterns formed by the heat- and sulphur-loving algal blooms, lichens and assorted slime moulds growing in and around the shallow pools.

Engaruka

The most enigmatic of northern Tanzania's attractions is a complex of stone ruins at **ENGARUKA**, at the foot of the Great Rift Valley's western escarpment north of Mto wa Mbu. Standing in the shadow of the forested eastern rim of Ngorongoro's Crater Highlands, the ruins comprise at least seven villages and a complex irrigation system of stone-walled canals, furrows and dams. Being in a naturally dry and stony environment, where natural vegetation is limited to thornbush and spiny acacias, the most amazing thing about the site is that it existed at all.

First recorded in 1883 by the German naturalist, **Dr Gustav Fischer**, the ruins extend over 9km of the escarpment base and cover twenty square kilometres. Various dating methods indicate that the site was founded early in the fifteenth century, but was mysteriously abandoned between 1700 and 1750.

The question of who was responsible for creating what must have been an extraordinary sight amidst this dry and desolate wasteland, and which at its height supported a population of over five thousand people, continues to leave archeologists largely baffled.

Most of Engaruka's present-day occupants are Maasai, but the absence of any tradition mentioning Engaruka indicates that the settlement had already been abandoned when they arrived, at most two centuries ago, and consequently little is known of Engaruka's original inhabitants. Research, however, shows that they were most likely to have been the ancestors of the **Iraqw** tribe (see box on p.458), who now live around and to the south of Karatu, and whose techniques of intensive, self-contained agriculture are uncannily similar to the remains of systems found at Engaruka. Iraqw oral history also recounts their last major migration, some two hundred to three hundred years ago, which followed a **battle with Barbaig** cattle herders (who, until the arrival of the Maasai, occupied the "Crater Highlands" above Engaruka). This fits in perfectly with the presumed date of Engaruka's desertion. Another present-day tribe that has been linked to Engaruka is the numerically small **Sonjo**, who presently live 100km north of Engaruka west of Lake Natron (see p.482). Their last migration also coincides with Engaruka's dates, and their traditional method of building houses on raised stone platforms is identical to remains found at Engaruka.

Apart from the Iraqw's story of the Barbaig war, a likely factor contributing to Engaruka's desertion was environmental. Engaruka's very success at irrigation in such a dry land may have proved counter-productive, when the demands of a vastly increased human population became too much for the area's limited water supplies. There's also evidence that the flow of the Engaruka River, and of other streams descending from the Ngorongoro highlands, began to diminish three hundred to four hundred years ago, perhaps due to the presence of pastoralists like the Barbaig, and then the Maasai, for whom forest clearance to make way for cattle pasture (and subsequently trampling and overgrazing) was and is a way of life. With luck, the recent introduction of more eco-friendly camels means that modern Engaruka won't go the same way.

Despite – or perhaps because of – its uncertainties, Engaruka provides a fascinating and thought-provoking glimpse into the history of pre-colonial Tanzania, and a reminder that we still remain ignorant about much of the continent's history.

Arrival

Getting to Engaruka can be a hassle, and impossible in the rains, when the road is impassable. Unless you're coming from the Serengeti's Klein's Gate across Loliondo, the only access is from the road junction 4km east of Mto wa Mbu, leaving you with a wild 64km ride. The first section, to **Selela village**, is decently graded, but beyond there you need a measure of luck to stay on track, as well as experience of 4WD in rough and sandy conditions, as the road disappears into a number of poorly defined trails. If you're driving yourself, bear in mind that the road to Engaruka initially veers away from the escarpment to avoid gullies and hills. The ride from Mto wa Mbu takes two to four hours depending on the state of the road and how often you get lost.

Public transport is limited to Land Rover pick-ups every day or two from Mto wa Mbu, and the daily "Kiazi Kitamu" bus (its name means sweet potato) from Arusha. Both leave for Engaruka in the afternoon, and head back the following morning before 7.30am.

The place for finding a guide for visiting the ruins is *Jerusalem Campsite*, which doubles as the base for Engaruka's **cultural tourism programme** (☎0744/507939, ℮engaruka@yahoo.com). Apart from the ruins, **options** include a day's climb of Mount Kermasi, a two-day hike to Ol Doinyo Lengai (see p.452; you'll need a vehicle), visits to Engaruka Juu's farms (one of few places where the Maasai have become cultivators) and a "Rift Valley Escarpment Walk", providing a good way of getting to know the flora and fauna of the area, as well as Maasai.

Costs are not particularly cheap, and unfortunately not as fixed as they should be, so get up-to-date prices from the tourist office in Arusha before setting off. Group costs are currently Tsh5000 for the guide and Tsh10,000 for visiting a Maasai *boma*. To this add Tsh6000 per person a day in other fees, plus a $5 tax (roughly Tsh5000) levied by the district council. Food and accommodation cost extra; lunch or dinner prepared by the women's group costs Tsh5000.

The **best days to visit** are Thursday and Sunday, when Engaruka Juu's market is at its liveliest. At least two days is recommended to do more than just scratch the surface of Maasai life.

Accommodation and eating

There are actually two Engarukas in addition to the ruins – a dusty spread of huts at Engaruka Chini along the road from Mto wa Mbu to Lake Natron, and the bustling Maasai market centre of Engaruka Juu, spreading 2–4km west of here towards the escarpment (along the way to the ruins), which is much livelier and greener, its fields watered by the Engaruka River.

The only **accommodation** is at the basic *Mlezi Guest House* (❶) in Engaruka Juu (2km west of Engaruka Chini and the main road), or camping at *Jerusalem Campsite*, 6km west of Engaruka Chini and close to the escarpment, in the grounds of Engaruka Primary School. Despite being signposted, the campsite is awkward to find: turn left just beyond *Mlezi Guest House*, cross the river immediately, and take the right fork on the opposite bank; the campsite is 1km on along a rough track. The site itself is pleasantly shaded, thanks to the proximity of the Engaruka River. You're best bringing your own food, though the local women's group can rustle up meals given enough time. The site may have tents for hire for those without.

The site

Old Engaruka can only be visited on foot; *Jerusalem Campsite*, which provides guides and has two helpful and informative **site custodians** provided by the Antiquities Department, is the departure point.

Several paths from the campsite go to the ruins; the best follows the Engaruka River's south bank, rising quickly towards the escarpment and the closest remains, 1km away. The site's extent and lack of obvious landmarks makes it impossible to give directions beyond here, but you can find a representative selection of the main structures throughout the area, notably the extensive network of stone-walled irrigation and drainage ditches, and small dams. When visiting the ruins, take care not to dislodge any stones, and certainly avoid climbing on them.

Two curious features characteristic of Engaruka are cairns and stone circles. The **cairns**, particularly well preserved in the west where they measure up to 5m long and 2m high, appear to be little other than places where rocks and stones cleared from fields were gathered, although their carefully arranged square or angular faces suggest something rather more useful, or spiritual, than just a heap of stones. A human skeleton was found under one cairn, but other than that, excavations have yielded few other clues as to their real purpose. More readily explained are the large **stone circles**, especially on the south side of the river, which measure up to 10m in diameter and functioned as cattle pens – manure was used to fertilize the fields (a trick also used by the Iraqw).

Look out also for clusters of **raised stone platforms** on ground unsuitable for irrigation, which mark the sites of Engaruka's seven villages. The platforms served as bases for houses; the Sonjo tribe still build their homes the same way. Excavations in these areas have revealed an iron-working forge and remains of meerschaum pipes, thought to have been used for smoking **cannabis** (*bangi*); cannabis remains an important part of many northern Tanzanian cultures, including that of the Hadzabe and Kuria.

For **more information**, John Sutton's exhaustive and scholarly work about Engaruka is available at *Jerusalem Campsite*, at Kase bookshop in Arusha, and at A Novel Idea bookshop in Dar.

Ol Doinyo Lengai

Rising up at the south end of Lake Natron is East Africa's only active volcano, **OL DOINYO LENGAI**, whose Maasai name means "The Mountain of God". Despite its active status, very little is known about the mountain other than that it tends to erupt explosively every twenty to forty years, and manages smaller **eruptions** every decade or so (the last major explosive eruption was in 1966, with a minor one in 1993). If history is a guide, a major explosive eruption is due any time now.

For **geologists**, the special thing about Ol Doinyo Lengai is that it is one of few volcanoes worldwide to emit sodium carbonate and potassium, whose run-off accounts for the extremely alkaline and corrosive swill of neighbouring Lake Natron. For **photographers**, Ol Doinyo Lengai's perfectly conical shape is a delight, especially if you can get Maasai cattle herders in the foreground, whilst the lava flows on the summit – when seen before sunrise – can be every bit as terrifyingly awe-inspiring as you might imagine or fear. **Climbers** are also in for a treat, despite the volcano's summit (2889m) being but a pimple compared to the majesty of its giant but dormant brothers to the east, Meru and Kilimanjaro. Admittedly, any pleasure gained by climbing the mountain (which can be done without any special equipment) is distinctly masochistic: the searing sun, the notoriously prickly vegetation and rough surface, reported sightings of spitting cobras near the summit (and leopard tracks), and the almost 45° slope. But as a reward for your travails, there's the weird, wonderful, eggily pungent and quite positively perilous sight and sound of **lava flows** bubbling at 510°C on top. There are two summit craters: the southern one is dormant or extinct and almost filled to the brim with ash, but the northern one, over 200m deep, remains active (occasionally lobbing lava bombs into the sky) and should be treated with **extreme caution**, particularly so given the highly fluid and hence potentially quick moving (or explosive) nature of natrocarbonatite lava. Similarly, keep your distance from fissures, vents and cones, and tread cautiously – the ground under your feet may well be hollow. Lava pools may also produce spatter – wear sunglasses for a minimum of protection for your eyes, and hiking boots for your feet. Ⓦ www.mtsu.edu/~fbelton/lengai.html is a great **Internet**

site dedicated to the mountain, with lots of up-to-date practical info, photos and links.

Practicalities

Climbing must be done with a guide who knows the mountain and its caprices. There are two ways of going about it: the easiest is simply to tackle the mountain as part of an extended "Crater Highlands" trek (see box on p.465) from Ngorongoro to Lake Natron. Many of Arusha's safari operators offer this as a regular trip, but do check that they have both their own experienced guides, and that – if you need it – there's adequate back-up (vehicles rather than donkeys, and HF radio for emergencies). For more modest budgets, it's perfectly feasible to arrange things at the campsites in Engaresero (see p.454). **Costs** are variable, and may include an official camping fee ($30) plus the wage paid to a porter (Tsh30,000–40,000); either way, it shouldn't really be more than $30–40 per person.

The climb starts about 10km south of Engaresero village, and takes at least seven hours: four hours up and three back down. If you don't have a vehicle and don't fancy walking from Engaresero to the start of the trail, you'll have to wait until a vehicle is available. The ride shouldn't cost more than a few thousand shillings. The ascent is steep and mostly on loose and uncompacted soil, and there's no shade, so set off before dawn to arrive at the summit by mid-morning. It's possible to camp on the summit – the inactive southern crater makes a distinctly safer campsite than the active northern one.

With your own vehicle, you also could try searching out one of several **volcanic cones** and craters on the eastern side of the mountain, the biggest of which is called *Shimo la Mungu* ("God's Hole").

Lake Natron

To desert rats, the land around **LAKE NATRON** – a vast, shallow soda lake bordering Kenya in Tanzania's far north – is something of a dream: hellishly hot, dry, desolate and bizarrely beautiful, especially with the grandiose peak of Ol Doinyo Lengai rising at its southern end. This volcano is the cause of the lake's

---

Security around Lake Natron and Loliondo

The wild and remote territory all around Lake Natron, eastern Loliondo, and south between the lake and Engaruka, is known for **bandits**, many of them allegedly Somali, who in the past have attacked travellers, herders and villagers. The problem peaked in the 1990s, and although no major incidents have been reported since 2000, there have been reports of failed hold-ups as recently as 2004, and the wild and remote nature of the terrain means that travelling here remains potentially dangerous.

Whether you're coming on an organized safari or are driving yourself, check and double-check the latest situation with as many people as possible (police, safari companies and drivers). When driving, beware of stopping for anyone except soldiers and police; stories circulate of bandits dressed up as Maasai disguising their AK-47s as millet stalks, and of others trying to spike vehicle tyres. If you do get **held up**, common sense is to give in to their demands, and never, ever try to resist. Lastly, remember that it's not just you taking the risk, but your driver too, so make sure you're clear about where you want to go before finalizing car rental.

extreme alkalinity, which forms a pinkish-white crust of soda crystals across much of its surface in the dry season, cracked into a polygonal patchwork.

Covering over 1300 square kilometres, the lake, like the smaller Lake Magadi just over the border in Kenya, lacks any outlet, and receives only 400mm of rain a year, part of it falling as "phantom rain", meaning that the raindrops evaporate before hitting the surface. The amount lost by **evaporation** is eight times that; the shortfall is made up by volcanic springs and temporary streams, whose waters leach through Ol Doinyo Lengai's caustic lava flows before reaching the lake. The concentration of salt, sodium carbonate (soda, or natron) and magnesite in the lake water is highly corrosive and the surrounding land isn't much more hospitable.

Not surprisingly, the lake isn't the most conducive to life, the big exception being a flourishing population of sometimes several hundred thousand **lesser flamingos**, who feed on the lake's microscopic diatom algae, and who have made the lake the most important flamingo breeding ground in the world.

Practicalities

The only settlement of any size is **ENGARESERO** (also called Ngara Sero or Natron Village), near the lake's southwestern shore, 56km north of Engaruka and 124km from Mto wa Mbu. The name means "river forest", referring to the wood-flanked river just south of town. Engaresero contains a handful of poorly stocked **stores**, a **bar** (the *Lake Side*) – and that's about it. There's no petrol or diesel, and the place has all the charm of a frontier outpost, which of course it is.

The easiest way to get to Lake Natron is on an **organized safari**. Companies running trips through this area include The East African Safari & Touring Company (p.406), who have a seasonal camp near Engaresero; Dorobo Tours & Safaris (p.475), who offer walking and camping trips to Loliondo; and the cultural tourism programme in Karatu (p.456). The lake also features on a growing number of **Crater Highlands treks** from Ngorongoro; see the box on p.465.

The next easiest way to Lake Natron is to rent a vehicle with a driver in Arusha or through the cultural tourism programme in Mto wa Mbu (p.442), as there's **no public transport** north of Engaruka. Theoretically, the drive from Mto wa Mbu should only take a few hours, but the road is in a terrible state (impassable in the rains) and difficult to follow, so count on a full day. Locals either walk or wait around, sometimes for a day or three, for a lift on one of the very few private vehicles that make it up here, usually carrying supplies for Engaresero's shops. Alternatively, if you're planning to stay at *Lake Natron Camp*, they can arrange a ride up from Mto wa Mbu.

Ngorongoro District Council has a **toll gate** 3km south of Engaresero, which charges tourists $15 for entering the area; this covers Engaresero, the lake and Nguruman Escarpment, and Ol Doinyo Lengai. New arrivals must **sign in** at the police station at the north end of town.

For information about the rough route to Lake Natron **from Loliondo**, see p.481.

Accommodation

Accommodation is limited to the following; all are marked on the map on p.456

Lake Natron Camp 2.5km south of Engaresero, 1km north of the toll gate (book through Moivaro Lodges & Tented Camps, *Moivaro Coffee Plantation* : *Lodge*, Arusha ☎027/255 3242, ⓦ www.moivaro .com). Set in a bone-meltingly hot and dusty grove of trees 4km from the lake, this has the lakeside's only guest rooms, in permanent luxury tents with solar powered light. There's also a campsite ($8 per person), a bar and good simple food, and even a swimming pool, but the main reason for staying is to organize excursions, including hikes up Ol Doinyo Lengai and visits to Maasai *bomas* (Tsh2000 per person). Full-board. ❽

🏃 **Riverside Kamakia Campsite** In a ravine beside the Engaresero River; turn left at the toll gate, then right as you approach the escarpment (no phone). Despite being less shady than *Lake Natron Camp*, this has a much nicer and marginally cooler location, and there are rock pools in the adjacent river where you can cool down. Cool drinks and meals are available, and there's a full range of guided walks. $8 per person.

🏃 **Waterfall Kamakia Campsite** Engaresero Gorge, 2km upstream from the *Riverside* campsite, and run by the same people – perfect for splashing around in the waterfall. $8 per person.

Around Engaresero

Engaresero itself has little to detain you, but is the only base for visiting a number of attractions. The most obvious, of course, is the **lakeshore**, currently 4km away across scorching grey sand (the level varies). As you approach the edge, soda and salt crystals appear, concealing a foul-smelling slurry of mud, which can burn your skin. To reach the **hot-water springs** on the eastern shore calls for 4WD and a driver experienced on loose sand. Take care not to drive too close to the shore, where you're likely to get bogged down. The soda flats in the southeastern corner are used by **flamingos** to mate and nest between August and October; the nests, which you can see from a distance, are made from mud and resemble miniature volcanoes – rather fittingly, given the location. Flamingos can usually also be seen in Moniki area, roughly 10km north of Engaresero village. Other birds you might see include pelicans, ibis, ducks and geese, together with eagles and plovers. **Terrestrial wildlife** is also present, especially close to the springs, albeit in small numbers, and includes zebra, wildebeest, gazelle, ostrich and golden jackal, and – more rarely – fringe-eared oryx, lesser kudu and gerenuk.

The **Nguruman Escarpment**, within walking distance of Engaresero, contains a number of attractions, including a volcanic implosion crater, ravines containing nesting sites for Ruppell's griffon vultures, and several waterfalls along **Engaresero Gorge**. Swimming is possible, though women are expected to cover up while bathing – shorts and a T-shirt. Walks further up the escarpment can be arranged at the campsites, who can also fix up visits to a Maasai *boma*.

Ngorongoro and around

One of Tanzania's best-known wildlife refuges is **Ngorongoro Conservation Area**, which together with the adjoining Serengeti National Park forms an immensely rich ecosystem. Ngorongoro's highlight is an enormous volcanic crater, providing one of Africa's most stunning backdrops for viewing a glut of wildlife, especially lion, elephant and highly endangered black rhino. There's plenty of upmarket **accommodation** inside the conservation area and more affordable campsites, plus a good range of hotels in **Karatu town**, outside Ngorongoro's eastern gate.

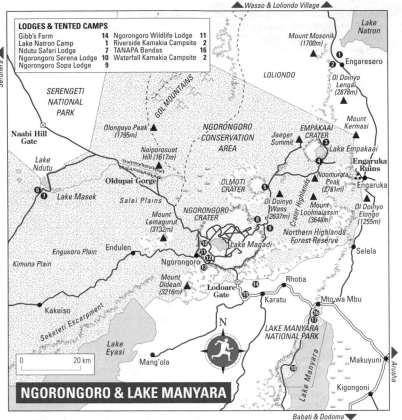

LODGES & TENTED CAMPS

Gibb's Farm	**14**	Ngorongoro Wildlife Lodge	**11**
Lake Natron Camp	**1**	Riverside Kamakia Campsite	**2**
Ndutu Safari Lodge	**7**	TANAPA Bandas	**16**
Ngorongoro Serena Lodge	**10**	Waterfall Kamakia Campsite	**2**
Ngorongoro Sopa Lodge	**9**		

NGORONGORO & LAKE MANYARA

CAMPSITES

Doffa Camp	**15**	Lemala special campsite	**8**	Nyati special campsite	**13**	TANAPA public campsites	**17**
Empakaai special campsite 1	**3**	Nanokanoka special campsite	**5**	Simba A public campsite	**12**	Tembo A special campsite	**8**
Empakaai special campsite 2	**4**	Ndutu campsite	**6**	Simba B special campsite	**12**	Tembo B special campsite	**8**

Karatu

The dusty town of **KARATU** – periodically swept by red twisters in spite of the new sealed road – is the main supply base for Ngorongoro Conservation Area, 18km to the northwest, and an obvious base if you can't afford Ngorongoro's lodges and don't want to camp there. Capital of a densely populated district, the town has little of interest in itself other than a new **cultural tourism programme**, which offers a range of walks and drives in the area and encounters with Barbaig, Iraqw and Maasai.

Given the steady stream of safari vehicles passing through, tourists are generally seen as a source of money: most hotels have shamelessly hiked-up their rates for non-Tanzanians, and local children are unusually insistent in their demands for not just pens and shillings, but dollars too.

The **best day to visit** is on the seventh of each month, for a big market and livestock auction (*mnada*) that attracts thousands of Maasai and Barbaig cattle herders, and Iraqw farmers.

Lake Eyasi and the Hadzabe

Occupying a shallow trough in the shadow of Ngorongoro's Mount Oldeani is **Lake Eyasi**, another of the Rift Valley's soda lakes. In the dry woodland around its edges live the **Hadzabe** tribe. Numbering between 500 and 2500, depending on how "purely" you count, the Hadzabe are Tanzania's last hunter-gatherers, a status they shared with the Sandawe further south until the latter were forced to settle forty years ago. Sadly, the Hadzabe appear to be heading the same way: much of their land has been taken by commercial plantations and ranches, which also form effective barriers to the seasonal wildlife migrations on which the hunting part of the Hadzabe lifestyle depends, whilst the unwelcome attentions of outsiders – notably tourists – is rapidly destroying their culture.

Being absolutely destitute in monetary terms, the Hadzabe are in no position to resist the more pernicious elements of modernity, with its trade, evangelical missionaries, enforced schooling, the cash economy, AIDS and indeed tourists, the majority of whom consider the Hadzabe to be little more than primitive curiosities – not surprisingly, given the blurb accorded them in holiday brochures. The supposedly backward and primeval form of Hadzabe society has also attracted a welter of researchers, whose dubious activities range from the "discovery" that grandmothers are useful for feeding their grandchildren, to thinly veiled attempts by multinational pharmaceutical companies to patent their DNA.

In 2000, a news report stated that the Hadzabe were preparing to leave their land and way of life for the brave new world of Arusha. Though at that time the story turned out to be a hoax, within five to ten years it may sadly become a reality. Short of convincing the Tanzanian government to protect Hadzabe land and its wildlife routes (most unlikely given the government's previous attempts to forcibly "civilize" the Hadzabe), the best thing you can do is to help preserve their culture. In the absence of any kind of tourism that directly benefits and is controlled by them, this means leaving them well alone.

Practicalities

Karatu is about three hours' drive from Arusha along a good sealed road. **Buses** leave Arusha between 3–4pm, arriving in Karatu before sunset: Dar Express, which starts in Dar, is probably the safest. Others include Sai Baba (also from Dar), and Lakrome Bus from Moshi. All leave Karatu at daybreak. You can change money at NBC **bank**, which also has a Visa/MasterCard ATM. To **rent a 4WD**, ask at Karatu's hotels, petrol stations or the cultural tourism programme; prices average $120 for a day's rental including driver and fuel, but excluding food and entry fees.

Accommodation

A rare beast is a Karatu hotel that doesn't charge **outrageous rates** to tourists, putting it on a par with Zanzibar but without the attractions. As such, **camping** is the way to stay flush, though there are still some basic local guest houses charging standard rates. Karatu has **mosquitoes** if not malaria; get a room with a net.

Bushman (BM) Camp 700m south of the highway, signposted at the west end of town ☎0745/814579, ✉faidabushmancamp@yahoo .com. One of few sanely priced tourist places, with several double rooms sharing bathrooms set in pleasant flowery gardens, and camping too, with hot and cold showers ($5 per person). Meals $5. Breakfast included. ❸

Crater Rim View Inn 500m south of the highway opposite *Bytes* (no phone). Friendly, clean and well run, with eight beautifully appointed double rooms, and a good restaurant. Breakfast included. ❹

The Iraqw

Karatu's main tribes are the cattle-herding Barbaig (see pp.274–275) and the agricultural Iraqw. The history of the 200,000-strong **Iraqw**, who occupy much of the area between Karatu and Mbulu town in the south, is a fascinating enigma, though the theory that they originally came from Mesopotamia (Iraq, no less) is too simplistic to be likely. Nonetheless, the Iraqw language is related to the "southern Cushitic" tongues spoken in Ethiopia and northern Kenya, meaning that at some point in their history they migrated southwards along the Rift Valley, something you can also tell by their facial features, which are finer than those of their neighbours and similar to those of Ethiopians.

Exactly when the Iraqw arrived in Tanzania is not known, but a number of clues offered by their agricultural practices – the use of sophisticated terracing to limit soil erosion, complex irrigation techniques, crop rotation and the use of manure from stall-fed cattle – provide uncanny parallels to the ruined irrigation channels, terraces and cattle pens of Engaruka (see p.449), at the foot of the Great Rift Valley's escarpment.

Iraqw **oral legend** makes no mention of a place called Engaruka, but that's hardly surprising given that Engaruka is a Maasai word. Instead, legends talk of a place called **Ma'angwatay**, which may have been Engaruka. At the time, the Iraqw lived under a chief called **Haymu Tipe**. In what is suggestive of a power struggle or civil war, the legend says that Haymu Tipe's only son, Gemakw, was kidnapped by a group of young Iraqw warriors and hidden in the forest. Finally locating him, Haymu Tipe was given a curious ultimatum: unless he brought the warriors an enemy to fight, his son would be killed. So Haymu Tipe asked the cattle-herding **Barbaig**, who at the time occupied the Ngorongoro highlands, to come to fight, which they did. Many people were killed, and it seems that the Iraqw lost the battle, as Haymu Tipe, his family and his remaining men fled to a place called Guser-Twalay, where Gemakw – who had been released as agreed – became ill and died. Haymu Tipe and his men continued on to a place called Qawirang in a forest west of Lake Manyara, where they settled. The legend then becomes confusing, but it appears that Qawirang is the same as the most recent Iraqw "homeland", Mbulu in the **Irqwar Da'aw Valley**, 70km south of Karatu, where the Iraqw settled at least two hundred years ago, shortly after Engaruka was abandoned. Subsequently, population pressure in Irqwar Da'aw led to further migrations; the first Iraqw to settle in Karatu arrived in the 1930s. For more about Iraqw **history**, see Bjørn-Erik Hanssen's "Three stories from the mythology of the Iraqw people" at ⓦ www.leopardmannen.no/hanssen/tanz-eng.htm.

Doffa Annex Camp & Garden Just off the highway beside *Paradise Garden Restaurant* ☎ 027/253 4305. A pleasantly grassy campsite with hot showers and basic restaurant: meals cost around Tsh2000 (no alcohol), and they have *supu* for breakfast. Their main site is 8km west of town, a lovely breezy place under jacaranda trees and with a bar, but no views thanks to the surrounding hedge. Both $5 per person.

🏃 **Gibb's Farm** (*Ngorongoro Safari Lodge*) 5km off the highway northeast of town ☎ 027/253 4040, ⓦ www.gibbsfarm.net. This working farm – surrounded by dry forest and coffee plantations – is by far the nicest place around Ngorongoro, despite (or perhaps because of) the slightly formal colonial atmosphere. The eight best rooms are in the 1930s farmhouse,

while seven more occupy a row of garden bungalows. Included in the price are guided walks, and the food is top-notch. Upmarket safaris can be arranged. Closed mid-April to mid-May. Breakfast included. ❽

Karatu Lutheran Hostel At the west end of town, 100m north of the highway ☎ 027/253 4230 or ☎ 0744/550569. A nice, peaceful choice with large en-suite rooms in a curved brick building. All have nets, screened windows, hot water and electricity. There are also two suites. Soft drinks and meals (Tsh5000) available, but order before 4pm for dinner. Breakfast included. ❹

Kudu Campsite & Lodge 500m south of the highway, signposted at the west end of town (same junction as for *Bushman Camp*) ☎ 027/253 4055, ⓦ www.kuducamp.com. Set in character-

Karatu cultural tourism programme

The best place to learn more about the Iraqw is through the **Karatu cultural tourism programme**, whose office is next to *Paradise Garden Restaurant* on the highway (☏027/253 4451 or 0748/828684, ⓔsandemutraditional@yahoo.com). The project has its roots in the independent **Sandemu Iraqw Art & Culture Promoters Centre**, roughly one and a half hours' walk west of Karatu. The centre (entry Tsh15,000 per group) is built in the form of a traditionally painted and fortified house, nestling so snugly into the hillside that it only needs a front wall (a construction that is remarkably similar to the former fortified houses of the Rangi; see p.265). Historically, fortification and camouflage was essential to avoid the warlike attention of the Maasai and Barbaig. The centre contains displays of weapons, tools, grinding stones and furniture, and sell mats, baskets, traditional clothes and jewellery, clay pots, gourds and calabashes. Given enough time, they can also arrange performances of traditional music and theatre, and lay on traditional meals. **Camping** costs $5, and overnight *bandas* are planned.

Other tours, most of which need a vehicle unless you're used to walking longer distances, include a 5km (2–3hr) hike up and down **Gyekurum Hill** for views over Karatu (no car needed); a 25–30km circuit to **Baray Gorge** south of Sandemu centre for forest, birds and hides excavated in living baobab trunks; and a half-day excursion to the western escarpment of the Great Rift Valley for views and the **Kambi ya Simbi caves**, whose nine chambers are home to bats, porcupines and insects. This trip can be extended to a full day to include waterfalls, Mto wa Mbu town and Lake Miwaleni. Two-day trips include one to the Iraqw heartland of **Mbulu** to see rock paintings and climb Mount Guwangw, and another covering Engaruka, Ol Doinyo Lengai and Lake Natron in the **Rift Valley**.

Costs average $20–30 per person per day plus transport, which usually means a car as buses and pick-ups rarely have useful timings: vehicle rental for a half-day, 60km round trip shouldn't be over $50. Part of the profits fund a kindergarten and soil conservation measures.

---

ful gardens, this has fifteen nicely decorated but wilfully overpriced rooms. Campers fare better at $10 per person in the flowery gardens, with clean bathrooms and cooking huts. There's a curio shop, bar and decent restaurant (meals $15, snacks around $4), and Internet access (Tsh4000/hr). Breakfast included. ❼

Msimbazi B Guest House Turn south off the highway just east of *Bytes*, then left after 50m ☏027/253 4098. A good cheapie, rooms either en suite or sharing bathrooms, and with safe parking. ❶

Muungano Guest House On the highway 300m west of *Bytes* ☏027/253 4385. One of several decent local guest houses around here to have resisted the temptation to overcharge tourists, and with good en-suite rooms. ❷

Ngorongoro Safari Resort On the main road ☏027/253 4287, ⓔsafariresort@yahoo.com

Vastly overpriced and very average rooms. Better is the campsite, mostly used by overland trucks, as belied by their supermarket: everything from Red Bull and Marmite to Pringles and champagne. There's also a gift shop, bar and garden bar, and restaurant. Rooms ❻, camping $5.

The Octagon Lodge 1.2km south of the highway, off the same road as for *Bushman Camp* and *Kudu* ☏027/253 4525, ⓦwww .octagonlodge.com. Run by an Irish–Tanzanian couple, this new place has twelve bright rooms in individual raised wooden chalets vaguely resembling garden sheds, all with a verandah facing the garden lawns (complete with a few crowned cranes, flamingos and a pond). There are also large cottage suites for four people, a nice Irish-themed bar, and good fresh food. Closed mid-April to May. Full-board. ❽

Eating and drinking

Karatu has lots of cheap and basic **restaurants and bars**, and most hotels also provide sustenance.

Bytes Crater Highlands Service Station on the highway, 300m east of *Karatu Lutheran Hostel*. Karatu's best restaurant, with great food in a polished, pub-like interior. Its several menus wander all over, from paninis and lasagne to an extensive selection of snacks from pizza melts to toasts, but are strongest on English and American country cooking, with sterling favourites like cottage pie, fried breakfasts and chocolate fudge – and inventive takes on the theme, such as a tilapia and prawn "shepherd's pie" topped with mashed potato and cheese. Prices are reasonable, with most mains around Tsh5000–6000. There's also an Internet café (Tsh4000/hr), a sophisticated bar (and great coffee), gift shop and dairy produce store.

Gibb's Farm 5km northeast of town. Something of a time warp back to the happier days of the British Empire – and pleasingly so. With Nouvelle Cuisine presentation, natural farm-grown ingredients (and some game meat like eland), and lots of flair like sorbet served in a croquant cup (for the starter), a meal here is always an experience. Lunch $19, dinner $26; digest it all with a guided walk around the coffee farm, or up to some waterfalls. Book ahead (⏂027/253 4040).

Paradise Garden Restaurant Around the corner from the cultural tourism office. Good cheap meals (Tsh1500; mainly rice with stews or *nyama choma*), eaten either at tables on a lawn or in funny little conical *bandas*. There's also a bar.

Ngorongoro Conservation Area

"The eighth wonder of the world" is the clarion call of the brochures, and for once they're not far wrong. The spectacular 8288-square-kilometre **NGORONGORO CONSERVATION AREA** occupies the volcanic highlands between the Great Rift Valley and the Serengeti Plains. It's the product of the volcanic upheavals that accompanied the formation of the Rift Valley, and its varied habitats virtually guarantee sightings of "the big five" – elephant, lion, leopard, rhino and buffalo. For animals, the place is a haven, while for tourists, it's something close to heaven.

Coming from the east, the magic begins the instant you pass through Lodoare Gate. The road begins to climb up through the tall and liana-festooned Oldeani Forest, giving way to an unforgettable view of **Ngorongoro Crater**, a fluid and ever-changing patchwork of green and yellow hues streaked with shadows and mist. At its centre Lake Magadi reflects the silvery sky, while on the western horizon, there's the seemingly endless shimmer of the Serengeti Plains. The 19km-wide crater is Ngorongoro's incomparable highlight, a vast, unbroken caldera left behind when an enormous volcano collapsed. Its grasslands, swamps, glades, lakes and forests contain vast numbers of herbivores, together with Africa's highest density of predators. **Game viewing**, needless to say, is phenomenal, as is the abundance of photo opportunities, the crater's deep, bluish-purple sides providing a spectacular backdrop to any shot. The crater also contains a few highly endangered **black rhino**, which despite their disastrously reduced population (now a lucky or unlucky thirteen), are easily seen. **Birdlife** is pretty decent, too, and includes ostriches, Verreaux's eagles, Egyptian vultures, kori bustards and lesser flamingos, the latter feeding on soda lakes occupying Ngorongoro and Empakaai craters, and at Lake Ndutu on the border with Serengeti.

Although the crater is often all that tourists see of Ngorongoro, there's much more besides. In the west, the rolling hills give way to the expansive grassland of the **Salei Plains**, which receive a good part of the Serengeti's annual wildlife migration between December and April. Both hyena and cheetah are frequently seen here, though in the dry season the plains resemble a desert. Right on the edge of the plains is a remarkable geological fissure, **Oldupai Gorge**, famous among paleontologists as the site of important hominid finds dating back millions of years. To the northeast, close to the edge of the Great Rift

Ngorongoro's ecology: a precarious balance

Ngorongoro is a wilderness, but one that has also long been inhabited by humans, originally by hunter-gatherers collectively known as **Dorobo**, and later by cattle herders, including the ancestors of the Barbaig (see pp.274–275) and then the Maasai (see p.446). As with the Serengeti, humans were and are very much part of Ngorongoro's delicate **ecological balance**, a balance that has become increasingly precarious since the end of the nineteenth century, when Europe began to colonize East Africa.

The first *mzungu* to set eyes on Ngorongoro and its famous crater was the German explorer, **Dr Oscar Baumann**, who in March 1892 reported a magnificent abundance of game, and promptly went on to bag three rhinos. So began a long history of European involvement, first for hunting, then for conservation, and which, for all their efforts and theories, has witnessed a massive decline in animal numbers.

Originally heavily exploiting the area for hunting, the British administration soon realized that their activities were having a detrimental effect on Ngorongoro's wildlife, and in 1921 Ngorongoro became a **Game Reserve**. Seven years later, locals were prohibited from hunting and cultivating in the crater, although – hypocritically – Europeans continued to do as they wished until the end of the 1930s, when trophy hunting was finally banned. In 1951, Ngorongoro became part of Serengeti National Park, and in 1958 the Maasai – under formidable pressure – formally renounced their claim to Serengeti. The following year, they were evicted and moved into Ngorongoro, which was declared a **multiple land use area**. This special status still allows Maasai to settle and graze their cattle in coexistence with wildlife, but this admirable idea conceals a more disturbing reality.

Although the **law** states that in cases of human-wildlife conflict in Ngorongoro, Maasai rights are to take precedence, this has rarely been the case, and relations between the authorities and the Maasai have at times been extremely bitter. Settlement in the crater itself was banned in 1974, and cultivation, which the Maasai were increasingly having to adopt, was prohibited throughout Ngorongoro in 1975, and only periodically allowed since. Livestock too has been excluded from the crater since the early 1990s, denying the Maasai a critical dry-season pasture for their cattle, and the last decade has been peppered with deeply troubling allegations. For more details see Ⓦwww2.warwick.ac.uk/fac/soc/law/elj/lgd/2000_1/lissu.

The underlying problem is that the Maasai presence is barely tolerated by Ngorongoro's authorities, who have progressively made it harder for them to scrape a living from their diminishing resources. Having lost water and pasture rights to the crater (and eighty percent of the land they controlled until a century ago), and been forbidden from hunting or cultivating, an estimated forty percent of Ngorongoro's Maasai are considered destitute, owning less than two livestock units per household. Some conservationists see **tourism** as the solution, but to date the Maasai have seen little of Ngorongoro's gate receipts beyond the construction of a few wells, dams and dispensaries.

Ngorongoro's problems aren't just with the Maasai, however. The changing ecological balance caused by the ban on subsistence hunting and the exclusion of cattle from large areas has favoured increased wildebeest and buffalo populations, with the unfortunate knock-on effect of an increased incidence of **malignant catarrh fever**, which is fatal to cattle. Diseases affecting wildlife have also become more common, disastrously so in 2000 and 2001, when an outbreak of tick-borne Babesiosis claimed the lives of over six hundred animals, including three rhino. The changing ecological balance may also have been responsible for swarms of aggressive blood-sucking flies, *Stomoxys calcitrans*, which in March 2001 killed at least six lions and injured 62 more.

It can only be hoped that Ngorongoro's authorities can find the wisdom to settle their differences with the Maasai once and for all. As has been shown in several other protected areas in Tanzania, the key to successful wildlife conservation lies in fully involving local communities, in both the running and the profits of wildlife areas.

Valley's escarpment, are two smaller craters, **Olmoti and Empakaai**, which are also rich in wildlife yet see very few visitors. The craters form part of the so-called **Crater Highlands**, which can be visited on foot if accompanied by an armed ranger – an exciting if hair-raising prospect. For those with more time, and a sturdy pair of legs, it's also possible to walk across the highlands from Ngorongoro to Lake Natron via Ol Doinyo Lengai volcano, a journey that can take anything from two to seven days (see p.465).

Another attraction, especially for visitors with limited time, is the chance to meet the red-robed **Maasai** for whom the conservation area provides year-round pasture. Package tours are catered for by **cultural bomas** – "traditional" Maasai villages set up expressly for tourists. The experience can feel uncomfortably staged and voyeuristic at times, but for many it's the only time they'll be able to meet one of Africa's traditional tribes. With more time, much better would be a Crater Highlands walk, which passes clean through Maasai territory, or a visit to one of Tanzania's cultural tourism programmes; see p.64.

Given these manifold attractions, Ngorongoro is Tanzania's most visited wildlife area, attracting over three hundred thousand tourists annually, and this, in fact, is the main drawback. To some, large numbers of visitors make Ngorongoro resemble a zoo, and spoils the experience of being in a true wilderness – something the authorities are now attempting to tackle with massive increases in entrance fees. Nonetheless, for all the tourists, the hype and the expense, Ngorongoro – designated a World Heritage Site in 1979 – is still a place that enchants, and few people leave disappointed.

Arrival

Pretty much every tour operator in Tanzania offers **safaris** to Ngorongoro, and with the new sealed road running all the way from Arusha to Ngorongoro's Lodoare Gate, most safari vehicles cover the 160km in under three hours. If you're adept at bargaining and have access to enough backsides to fill seats, it's cheaper to arrange **car rental in Karatu** (see p.457). **Self-drive** is possible as everything is signposted, but you won't be allowed into the crater without an officially licensed **guide** or driver-guide; they can be hired at the park gate for $20 a day. Open-topped vehicles are not admitted.

It's not possible to get around the conservation area by **public transport**, but there is a bus run by the Ngorongoro Conservation Area Authority (NCAA) from Arusha (10am Mon–Fri; returning in the afternoon) to their headquarters close to the crater (and a few buses each week between Arusha and Musoma or Mwanza), where you should be able to hire a ranger for walks, and possibly a vehicle. There's no guarantee of either however, so enquire at the conservation area's office on Boma Road in Arusha before heading out.

Entrance fees and information

Entry fees, paid at Lodoare Gate if you're coming from the east or at Naabi Hill Gate coming from Serengeti, are currently $50 per person for 24 hours, plus $5 for a vehicle permit, and $100 per vehicle for a morning or afternoon spent inside Ngorongoro Crater (the "crater fee"). **Armed rangers**, obligatory for Crater Highlands treks, cost $20 a day.

There are **tourist information centres** at Lodoare Gate and at Oldupai Museum. The conservation area **headquarters**, mainly useful for research queries, are at Ngorongoro village, southwest of the crater (☎027/253 7046, ⓦ www.ngorongoro-crater-africa.org). They also have an office in Karatu (turn

7

south opposite *Bytes* and then left after 400m), and in Arusha on Boma Road (see p.403). The latter has brochures and also sells books, maps and films.

The **guidebook** published by Ngorongoro Conservation Unit ($10) contains a wealth of information about the region, its history, geology and inhabitants (animal and people), and is accompanied by a number of other booklets covering geology, birdlife, wildlife, tree and plants, and prehistory. The most detailed and accurate **map** is harms-ic-verlag's 1999 edition. Not as detailed but more visually attractive is the painted dry-season/wet-season map by Giovanni Tombazzi. The guidebooks and maps are sold at Ngorongoro's entrance gates, lodges and Oldupai Museum, and also at bookshops in Arusha, Dar and Stone Town, and at Ngorongoro's tourist office in Arusha.

Accommodation

The only regular **accommodation** inside Ngorongoro is at a number of expensive **lodges**, all but one on the crater rim – the latter often fully booked for months in advance. Environmentally and ethically, however, none of the crater-rim lodges enjoys an unblemished reputation, and anyway, much cheaper – and superior in many other ways, especially for the feeling of being in the wild – is **camping**, which costs $30 or $50 per person depending on the site; see below. There are more campsites, and also much cheaper hotels, outside the conservation area in Karatu; see p.457. All of the following are marked on the map on p.456.

Lodges

Day-visitors can take **lunch** at the lodges: prices range from $20 (*Ndutu*) to $30 (*Serena*). Room **rates** drop considerably April–June.

Ndutu Safari Lodge Next to Lake Ndutu on the border with Serengeti ⓦwww .ndutu.com (Arusha office: 50 Haile Selassie Rd ⓣ027/250 6702). A welcoming and friendly place well off the beaten track, this has 32 comfortable bungalows, the best at the front facing the lake, which becomes a starkly beautiful salt-pan in the dry season – wonderful at sunrise. With no fences, wildlife can come and go: mammals are best Feb–June, water birds Dec–March. There's an open-sided bar, a lounge and dining room with superb food (perhaps explaining the resident genet's nocturnal visits). Evening meals can also be taken around a camp fire within earshot of roaring lions. Full-board $85–230 per person. ❽–❾

Ngorongoro Serena Lodge On the crater rim (book through Serena Hotels, AICC Ngorongoro, Room 605, Arusha ⓣ027/250 6304, ⓦwww .serenahotels.com). The usual high standards of creature comforts from this chain make this a very stylish yet impersonal place. Most of its 75 rooms overlook the crater from their verandahs. There are various bars and lounges, a restaurant and a terrace with views. Full-board $210 per person. ❾

Ngorongoro Sopa Lodge On the crater rim (book through Sopa Lodges, 4th floor, Sopa Plaza, 99 Serengeti Rd, Arusha ⓣ027/250 0630–9, ⓦwww .sopalodges.com). The only hotel on the eastern rim, this is perfect for sunsets, but also the largest and least personal of the lodges, with 90 mostly twin-bed rooms. The external architecture is an eyesore, but the views are fantastic, whether from public areas, the balconies of most of the rooms or the swimming pool. Full-board $175 per person. ❾

Ngorongoro Wildlife Lodge On the crater rim (book through Hotels & Lodges Ltd, 2nd floor (Block B), Summit Centre, Sokoine Rd, Arusha ⓣ027/254 4595, ⓦwww.hotelsandlodges-tanzania.com). Another architectural mess, this one – nicknamed the "ski lodge" – was government-owned for years, but has since raised its rates rather more than its standards. On the positive side, the views are superb, whether from the 75 bedrooms (just four with balconies), or from the lounge. Full-board $180 per person. ❾

Camping

Campers can choose between one public campsite, which doesn't require reservations, and several "special campsites" which are often block-booked by safari companies months if not years in advance. In Arusha, you can enquire about availability – and book – at Ngorongoro's tourist office in Arusha; see p.403.

The **public campsite** ($30 per person, paid at the gate) is *Simba A* on the southwestern rim of Ngorongoro Crater, which has toilets and showers, but gets packed, noisy and often filthy in high season. Nonetheless, the views of the crater are jaw-dropping, and the Woodstock/Glastonbury feel appeals to many, despite the discomforts.

The **special campsites** ($50 per person), where you're guaranteed to be the only campers, are usually in very scenic locations but have no facilities at all. The only one to be avoided is *Nyati*, near Ngorongoro Crater, which lacks any kind of views. The rest, all recommended if you can find them free for a night, are: *Simba B*, which has similarly good views to *Simba A* 1km away; *Nanokanoka*, close to Olmoti Crater and Nanokanoka village, which means you can wander in for a chat with local Maasai; two sites next to Empakaai Crater, perfect for descending into it the next day; and three sites on the wooded northeastern rim of Ngorongoro Crater, *Tembo A*, *Tembo B* and *Lemala*, all of which occasionally see elephants. There are also seven special campsites around Lake Ndutu in the west, often very crowded.

Ngorongoro Crater

Some 2.5 million years ago, the reservoir of magma under an enormous volcano towering over the western flank of the Great Rift Valley emptied itself in an enormous explosion, leaving a vacuum which caused the mountain to implode under its own weight. In its wake, it left an enormous 600m deep crater (caldera), its 19-kilometre diameter now making it the world's largest unbroken and unflooded caldera. This is **Ngorongoro Crater**, one of Tanzania's wonders, covering approximately three hundred square kilometres and providing a natural amphitheatre for the wildlife spectacle on its floor. The crater contains 25,000 to 30,000 large mammals, which when viewed from the rim are a blur of pulsating specks arranged in fluid formations, while above the crater, eagles, buzzards, hawks and vultures circle.

The main feature on the crater floor is the shallow and alkaline **Lake Magadi**, whose extent varies according to the rains. Flocks of flamingos feed here in the dry season. On the western shore is an enigmatic scattering of stone **burial mounds**, believed to have been left by the Datooga (Tatoga), ancestors of Barbaig cattle herders who occupied the crater until they were pushed out by the Maasai. At the lake's southern edge is **Lerai Forest**, a large patch of acacia woodland that takes its Maasai name from the dominant yellow-barked acacia (or fever trees). The forest is a good place for seeing waterbuck and flitting sunbirds. Swamp, thorn scrub and grassland fill the rest of the crater, and provide the bulk of the game viewing.

The majority of the animals are **herbivores**, supported by year-round supplies of water and fodder, and include vast herds of wildebeest (up to 14,000), zebra, buffalo, Grant's and Thomson's gazelle, eland, hartebeest and mountain reedbuck, warthog and hippo, and two of Africa's giants: elephants, of which a handful of bulls are always present, and a small population of **black rhino**. Once common across all of eastern and southern Africa, rhino poaching in the 1970s and 1980s took a terrible toll on this magnificent creature, decimating the population from 108 in the 1960s to only fourteen in 1995. Although poaching is now under control (if not completely eradicated), Ngorongoro's rhino suffered a major blow in 2000–2001, when tick-borne Babesiosis killed three of them. There are now just thirteen.

The Crater Highlands

The Crater Highlands is the informal term for the mountainous eastern part of Ngorongoro that forms the lush forested ridge of the Great Rift Valley's western escarpment, and which the Maasai call Ol Doinyo Ildatwa. The area includes Ngorongoro Crater, the 3216m Mount Oldeani to its south, the isolated Gol Mountains in the north, Olmoti and Empakaai craters in the northeast, Mount Loolmalassin (the range's highest point at 3648m) and Ol Doinyo Lengai, East Africa's only active volcano (see p.452), which rises in a perfect cone just outside the conservation area's northeastern corner.

One of Ngorongoro's major attractions is a **Crater Highlands trek**, which can be as short as half a day, or as long as a week, giving you ample time to get to Lake Natron, perhaps including a climb up Ol Doinyo Lengai along the way. The exact distance, and number of days required, depends on where you start and whether you're being driven part of the way. For example, a two-day (44km) trek to Lake Natron starts at Empakaai Crater, while a seven-day trip allows you to amble at your leisure from the rim of Ngorongoro Crater to the desolately beautiful Lake Natron, overnighting at Maasai *bomas* or camping wild. Most safari companies offer five-day trips as standard.

Costs vary according to the level of service and back-up: count on between $120–300 a day. Upmarket operators offer something close to bush luxury, where a full camp attended by plenty of staff is set up ahead of your arrival, including mess tents, furniture, chemical toilets and ingenious bucket showers. On these trips you'll generally be guided by a white-hunter kind of chap. Much cheaper, more adventurous and definitely more "authentic" are humbler trips where the gear (dome tents, usually) – and you if you're tired – is carried by donkey. These trips are often guided by Maasai warriors (or "worriers", as a number of brochures amusingly have it), who make up for their sometimes limited knowledge of English with tremendous practical botanical know-how and an uncanny ability to spot all sorts of wildlife.

For **one-day trips**, contact the conservation area headquarters (see p.462), who can fix you up with an armed ranger, or Green Footprint Adventures (ⓦwww .greenfootprint.co.tz) at *Ngorongoro Serena Lodge*. For **longer forays**, see the safari company reviews for Arusha (p.345); some of Moshi's hiking companies (pp.403–407) also offer Crater Highlands treks.

Apart from rhino, the big draw is the transfixing sight of Africa's densest population of **predators** in action. Lions are very common and easily seen (best in the dry season), as are hyenas and jackals. Cheetahs are also sometimes present, while leopards require some patience to spot, as they rest up in trees or thick bush by day.

There are three **access roads**. The eastern Lemala route, from *Lemala* and *Tembo* campsites, can be driven in either direction. In the south, the steeper Lerai route from Lerai Forest on the crater floor is for ascent only, while the Seneto route in the west is only for descent. A **crater fee** of $100 per person for six hours applies (in practice, a morning or afternoon's game drive), in addition to standard entry fees, and you'll need to hire an official guide if you're driving yourself (this doesn't apply if your driver is licensed by the authorities, or if you're on an organized safari). Only 4WD vehicles are allowed in the crater, and in theory they need to carry a heavy-duty jack, chains or a tow rope, a shovel or hoe, and an axe or *panga*. The speed limit is 25kph, and you must be out by 6pm, so start ascending no later than 5.30pm. Visitors must stay in their vehicle except at two **picnic sites**: one next to Lerai Forest at the foot of the Lerai ascent route, the other at Ngoitokitok Springs in the east next to a small lake.

Olmoti and Empakaai craters

North of Ngorongoro Crater are two smaller craters, Olmoti and Empakaai. The rims of either can be reached by vehicle, but are best seen on foot, ideally prearranged as part of a Crater Highlands trek. Though ranger posts are close to both craters, if you're intending to walk it's best to organize in advance with the conservation area headquarters (see p.462) for a ranger to accompany you.

The shallow and grassy **Olmoti Crater**, accessed from Nanokanoka village (there's a special campsite there), contains several antelope species, and there are waterfalls nearby on the Munge River. Accompanied by an armed ranger (the post is in the village), the crater rim and its fringing forest can be explored on foot, taking anything from two to seven hours.

Northeast of here is the stunningly beautiful, 6km-wide **Empakaai Crater**, much of which is filled with a forest-fringed soda lake. This is better for wildlife than Olmoti, and resident species include bushbuck, reedbuck and waterbuck, buffalo, monkeys and an abundance of birds, including flamingos. You can walk along the rim (again, if accompanied by an armed ranger – the post is about 5km southeast) and into the crater itself (at least 7hr). There are two special campsites on the rim, and plans to allow canoeing on the lake: enquire with a safari operator, or Green Footprint Adventures (Ⓦ www.greenfootprint.co.tz).

Oldupai Gorge

Gouged into the edge of the Salei Plains is **Oldupai (or Olduvai) Gorge**, a steep-sided, 48km-long ravine whose depth reaches 150m in places. Furrowed out of the volcanic land by the capricious Oldupai River, the rock strata on either side of the gorge have exposed the fossilized remains of animals and over fifty hominids dating back almost two million years, and – when taken together with finds from Lake Turkana in northern Kenya, Ethiopia and elsewhere in Africa – comprise an archeological trove of inestimable importance for understanding the origins of humankind.

The fossils were first noted in 1911 by **Professor Kattwinkel**, a German butterfly collector, who stumbled across them quite by chance, and took the fossilized remains of a three-toed horse back to Berlin's Museum für Naturkunde. Two decades later, his findings aroused the curiosity of a Kenyanborn British anthropologist, **Louis Leakey**, whose name now features in almost any discussion on human prehistory. In 1931, inspired by nothing more than a gut feeling that Africa was the "cradle of mankind", Leakey began excavating at Oldupai Gorge.

For almost thirty years, Louis and his wife, Mary, found only stone tools, the oldest belonging to the so-called **Oldowan industry** (1.2 to 1.8 million years ago). Spurred on by the belief that the remains of the hominids that had created the tools could not be far behind, they persevered, and their patience was finally rewarded in 1959 by the discovery of two large human-like teeth and a piece of skull. Further digging provided over four hundred additional fragments, which were painstakingly reassembled to form the 1.75 million year-old skull of *Australopithecus boisei* ("southern ape"), nicknamed **Nutcracker Man** on account of his powerful jaws. The tool-maker had been found, and the discovery – at the time, the oldest known – provoked a sea-change in paleontological circles, especially as the skull's size and dentition displayed uncanny similarities with modern man. The unavoidable conclusion was that the Leakeys had unearthed a direct ancestor of modern man, and in fact that the much vaunted "missing link" had been found.

The theory was accepted until disproved by much older finds from Ethiopia, and from Laetoli south of Oldupai (see box on p.468), and since then poor old Nutcracker Man has been consigned to history as an evolutionary dead end. His importance remains, however, in showing that hominid evolution was not a simple linear progression. The find also spurred on a flurry of **further excavations** at Oldupai, which showed conclusively that two other hominid species, almost certainly our ancestors, lived contemporaneously with Nutcracker Man – *Homo habilis* ("handy man") and *Homo erectus* ("upright man").

Over the years, various claims have been made for one place or another being the "cradle of mankind", but it's way too early to say this with any certainty (indeed, a recent find of seven-million-year-old hominid fossils in Chad makes the East African fossils look positively juvenile, though the dating is disputed), and of course fossil beds are usually revealed by geological chance, which in East Africa was the Rift Valley. What is certain, however, is that the incredible journey into our prehistory first began to make sense at Oldupai, and it's a journey that, if it can be traced at all, should happily continue to baffle humankind for many years to come.

Practicalities

Oldupai Gorge can be seen on foot or by vehicle, and even if old bones and stones don't appeal, the gorge itself is a pleasant diversion off the road to Serengeti, and there's also a range of fast-moving black sand dunes to explore. The entrance to the gorge, next to a small but fascinating museum documenting the finds, lies about 30km west of Ngorongoro Crater, and 7km north of the road to Serengeti. The Tsh3000 **entrance fee** also gives access to the museum; in theory, this includes the services of an **official guide** for the gorge, but in practice they won't join you unless you pay a fairly hefty tip, anything from $2–25 depending on their perception of your ability to pay; $10 per group would be reasonable. That said, the guides do know their stuff – they reel off entertaining lectures and can put a context to even the most mundane-looking of rocks or fossil fragments. The average tour lasts thirty minutes to two hours if you're in a car. Walking down into the gorge is not permitted after 3pm, and may cost extra.

Oldupai Museum

Despite its modest size, **Oldupai Museum** (daily 8am–4.30pm; ☎027/253 7037) packs in a bewildering amount of information, too much in fact for non-experts to digest comfortably in a single visit, though the museum shop usually has copies of a guidebook covering Ngorongoro's prehistory. The three rooms are full of bones, tools and skilful reproductions of skulls (the original Nutcracker Man is at Dar es Salaam's National Museum; see p.107), all well documented so long as you turn a blind eye to the uncomfortably hagiographic praise for the Leakey family. Should museum fatigue strike, there's a shady picnic area outside, with soft drinks, beers and sweets for sale, and *nyama choma*.

The gorge

As you head into the gorge, its stratified nature is immediately apparent, each clearly-defined stratum ("**bed**") containing a rich record of fossils and tools.

The oldest and lowest stratum is the 60m-thick **Bed I** (2.1 to 1.7 million years old), where the fossilized remains of both *Homo erectus* and *Australopithecus boisei* (Nutcracker Man) were found, proving that two species coexisted at the same time. The spot where Nutcracker Man was unearthed is marked by a metal plaque. Bed I also contained stone tools, remains of animals (especially

Laetoli

For all Oldupai's paleontological wonders, perhaps Tanzania's most astonishing prehistoric find occurred at **Laetoli** (or Garusi), 40km south of Oldupai, which offered up its first fossils in 1938. The most spectacular discoveries came in the 1970s, the first of which were thirteen jaw fragments dating back 3.6 million years. They belonged to a species called *Australopithecus afarensis*, taking its Latin name from the first finds of the species in Ethiopia's Afar desert, which in 1974 introduced the world to "Lucy" – a half-complete female skeleton which circumstantial evidence suggested had been bipedal, and which was dubbed Dinquenesh ("you are amazing") by Ethiopians.

In 1979, Laetoli offered up something equally amazing: a trail of **fossilized footprints** that had been left in wet volcanic ash by two adults and a child. The discovery was dated to around 3.75 million years ago, and attracted worldwide attention as it provided incontestable proof that hominids were walking (and running) upright way before anyone had imagined. Further research suggested that *Australopithecus afarensis* stood fully erect, was about 100–150cm tall, and weighed up to 50kg. The skull, although only fractionally larger than that of modern chimpanzees, had dentition similar to modern humans.

Access to Laetoli is not possible, and the footsteps have been covered up again, but plaster casts are on display at Oldupai Museum, both museums in Arusha, the National Museum in Dar and Nairobi's National Museum.

---

antelopes) whose bones had been split and broken, and a circular shelter made from lava-stone – one of the world's oldest houses.

Hot on the heels of Nutcracker Man came a series of hominid finds in the 1960s in **Bed II** (1.7 to 1.2 million years old) that were markedly different from *Australopithecus*. The new species, small and compact, and with a dentition approaching that of modern man, was named *Homo habilis* ("handy man"), and is believed to be one of our ancestors. The upper strata of Bed II also yielded a partial skull of *Homo erectus* (dubbed OH 9), a more recent ancestor, together with more advanced stone tools, and the bones of giant tusked pigs the size of hippos. But the strange thing about Bed II is that the more primitive *Australopithecus boisei* is also found throughout, showing that *Australopithecus* coexisted with both hominid species for a considerable time before becoming extinct.

Moving up, the narrower and more recent **Bed III** (1.2 million to 850,000 years old) revealed more remains of *Homo erectus*, but not many: an unusually hot climate at the time is the suggested cause for the scarcity of human remains. **Bed IV**, whose top level dates back 600,000 years, revealed more finds of *Homo erectus*, and plenty of stone tools: cleavers, knives and scrapers, and throwing stones.

Overlying these beds are several more recent ones. The **Masek Beds** (600,000–400,000 years old) record a time of explosive volcanic activity, and revealed only tools, and the later **Ndutu Beds** (up to 32,000 years old) are similarly poor. The most recent are the **Naisiusiu Beds** (to 15,000 years old), which came up with more tools and a skeleton of *Homo sapiens* – modern man – who appeared on earth at least 50,000 years ago.

The Shifting Sands

Providing an appropriate metaphor for Oldupai's immense sweep though time are the **Shifting Sands**, roughly 15km northwest of the museum and beyond the northern edge of the gorge, which are a range of elegant black sand dunes forever being pushed eastward by the wind (an estimated 17m a year). Taking a guide is obligatory as you have to pass through the gorge to get there, and the authorities also discourage folk from clambering over the dunes, which destroys their fragile plant cover and hastens their onward advance.

The Serengeti and around

As one of the world's most famous wildlife areas, the **SERENGETI** needs little introduction. Bordering Ngorongoro in the east, Kenya's Maasai Mara Game Reserve in the north, and reaching to within 8km of Lake Victoria in the west, the Serengeti is also Tanzania's largest national park, and any safari here promises wildlife galore, especially when the **annual migration** of plains game – mainly wildebeest and zebra and their natural predators – is in residence. The migration, which swings up to Maasai Mara, also passes through **Loliondo**, a remote and little-visited wilderness sandwiched between Serengeti, Ngorongoro, Lake Natron and the Kenyan border. Loliondo contains a number of upmarket tented camps offering much of Serengeti's wildlife in exclusive wilderness concessions, and if you're coming by rented car, a rough road through the area from Serengeti gives an alternative – and highly adventurous – way of getting to and from Lake Natron.

Serengeti National Park

As Tanzania's oldest and largest national park, and one of the world's best-known wildlife sanctuaries, the 14,763-square-kilometre **SERENGETI NATIONAL PARK** is one of the jewels in Tanzania's wildlife crown. Protected since 1929, at a time when white trophy hunters were wreaking havoc on wildlife populations, and declared a national park in 1951, the Serengeti is also – together with Ngorongoro – a UNESCO World Heritage Site and International Biosphere Reserve. And with good reason; the Serengeti lies at the heart of the world's largest and most impressive **wildlife migration** (see box on p.471), at the peak of which it contains the highest concentration of mammals on earth.

Serengeti takes its name from the flat **grassland plains** that cover the eastern section of the park next to Ngorongoro, which the Maasai called *siringet*, meaning "endless plain". Along with the Kalahari, these plains are the Western imagination's archetypal African landscape, and the highlight of many a visit, certainly when the migration is in full swing. Even outside the migration, there's plenty to see, including large clans of hyenas and thriving lion prides, and a series of weathered granite outcrops called **kopjes** (pronounced kop-yees; from the Afrikaans for "little head"), one of which contains rock paintings, and another a mysterious "rock gong".

There's more to Serengeti than the plains though, which cover only one third of the park. In the hilly centre, around **Seronera** – where a good deal of the park's accommodation is located, and an excellent visitors' centre – a series of lightly wooded valleys provide excellent year-round game viewing, while

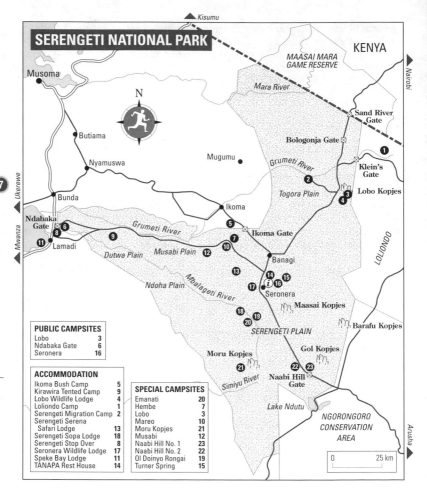

SERENGETI NATIONAL PARK

Kisumu

KENYA

MAASAI MARA
GAME RESERVE

Musoma

Mara River

Narobi

N

Butiama

Sand River
Gate

Bologonja Gate ⊠

❶

Nyamuswa

Mugumu ●

Grumeti River

Klein's
Gate

❷

Togora Plain

Lobo Kopjes

❸
❹

Bunda

Ikoma

LOLIONDO

Ndabaka
Gate ⊠ ❻

Grumeti River

❺

Ikoma Gate ⊠

Ukerewe

❽
❶❶

Lamadi

❾

Banagi

Dutwa Plain

Musabi Plain ⓬ ❿

❼

Mwanza

Ndoha Plain

Mbalageti River

⓭

⓮ ⓯
ⓘ ⓰

❶❼

Seronera

Maasai Kopjes

⓲

⓳

Barafu Kopjes

⓴

PUBLIC CAMPSITES

Lobo	3
Ndabaka Gate	6
Seronera	16

SERENGETI PLAIN

Gol Kopjes

Moru Kopjes

ACCOMMODATION

Ikoma Bush Camp	5
Kirawira Tented Camp	9
Lobo Wildlife Lodge	4
Loliondo Camp	1
Serengeti Migration Camp	2
Serengeti Serena	
Safari Lodge	13
Serengeti Sopa Lodge	18
Serengeti Stop Over	8
Seronera Wildlife Lodge	17
Speke Bay Lodge	11
TANAPA Rest House	14

㉑

㉒ ㉓

Naabi Hill
Gate ⊠

SPECIAL CAMPSITES

Emanati	20
Hembe	7
Lobo	3
Mareo	10
Moru Kopjes	21
Musabi	12
Naabi Hill No. 1	23
Naabi Hill No. 2	22
Ol Doinyo Rongai	19
Turner Spring	15

Simiyu River

Lake Ndutu

NGORONGORO
CONSERVATION
AREA

Arusha

0   25 km

in the **north**, along a 40km-wide corridor connecting with Kenya's Maasai Mara Game Reserve, rolling hills and thorny acacia woodland dominate. To the west, another corridor runs along the **Grumeti River** to within 8km of Lake Victoria. The river's flanking evergreen forests are another special habitat, providing a home for primates as well as lurking leopards, whilst the river itself and its swamps are as perfect for water birds as they are for crocodiles preying on thirsty wildlife, a sight as enthralling as it is gruesome when the migration is passing through.

Wildlife, of course, is why people come to Serengeti, and the figures are flabbergasting. Of the five million animals to be found during the migration (double the resident population) there are wildebeest, who numbered 1.7 million at the last count, gazelle, both Grant's and Thomson's, who are estimated at around half a million, and some three hundred thousand zebra. But even when the migration is up in Maasai Mara, or spread out across Ngorongoro and Loliondo, the park contains substantial populations of **plains game**, including

The Great Migration

The Serengeti owes its hallowed place in our imagination to the annual 800km **migration** of over 2.5 million animals, the largest mammalian migration on earth. A continuous, milling and unsettled mass, including 1.7 million wildebeest and close to a million other animals, the migration offers visitors one of nature's most staggering displays, one in which the ever-vigilant predators – lions, cheetahs, African hunting dogs and spotted hyenas – play a vital part. The river crossings are the biggest obstacle, namely the Grumeti in Serengeti, and the Mara along the border with Kenya in the north, and both can be the scene of true carnage as the panicked herds struggle across the raging flows in a writhing mass of bodies while the weak, injured or careless are picked off by crocodiles and lions.

The migration's ceaseless movement is prompted by a seasonal search for fresh water and pasture dictated by the rains. It moves in a roughly clockwise direction, concentrating in the national park from **April to June**, towards the end of the long rains, before leaving behind the withering plains of the Serengeti and journeying northward towards the fresh moisture and grass of Kenya's Maasai Mara Game Reserve, which the migration reaches in August. By **September** and **October**, the bulk of the migration is concentrated in Maasai Mara. By **late October** and **early November**, the Mara's grasslands are approaching exhaustion, so the migration turns back towards northern and eastern Serengeti, following the fresh grass brought by the short rains. In this period, the migration is widely spread out, and a large part of it circles through Loliondo and into Ngorongoro, beyond the Serengeti's eastern border. From **December to March**, the migration settles in the Serengeti Plains and western Ngorongoro, where it remains until the onset of the long rains. The wildebeest take advantage of this temporary pause to give birth (especially from late Jan to mid-March), accounting for half a million calves annually. The timing of this mass birthing provides security in numbers: predators will eat their fill, but within a few months, the surviving calves are much stronger and able to outrun their pursuers; nonetheless, the hazards of the migration are such that only one in three calves makes it back the following year. By April, the migration is once more concentrated inside Serengeti, and the whole cycle starts again.

The exact time and location of the migration varies annually, depending on the rains and other factors, so coinciding with it cannot be guaranteed; in 2000 for example, prolonged drought shifted the whole cycle forward by two months, flat-footing thousands of safari-goers. Nonetheless, as a general rule, the **best months** for seeing the migration in the Serengeti are from December to July, especially February and March in the plains when the wildebeest herds are dotted with new-born, and April to June when animal concentrations are at their highest. June is also the best time for catching the migration's perilous crossing of the Grumeti River, while the spectacular Mara River crossing, best seen from Kenya but also in northern Serengeti, is at its most awesome (and gruesome) in July and August.

buffalo, giraffe and warthog, and a wide range of antelopes, including dikdik, bushbuck, waterbuck and mountain reedbuck, eland and impala, and the rarer oryx and topi. Some 1500 elephants, too, are present, though they are largely migratory and can easily be missed.

But all this is to forget perhaps the most memorable of Serengeti's animals, its **predators**, who thrive off the regal banquet on offer. Indeed, apart from Ngorongoro, Serengeti is probably the best place in Tanzania to see predators in action. Foremost are nearly eight thousand much-maligned spotted hyenas, who live in clans of up to eighty individuals. Also very visible are the park's three thousand or so lions, whose males have characteristic black manes. Other predators include cheetahs, which have been the subject of ongoing research

△ A busy waterhole, Serengeti National Park

since 1975, leopards and bat-eared foxes. Scavengers, apart from hyenas (who also hunt) include both golden and side-striped jackals and vultures. There are six species of the latter, a fraction of Serengeti's 520 **bird species** (including Eurasian winter migrants) – the country's second-highest count after Tarangire National Park. Keen birders can expect to see several hundred species in a two- or three-day safari, including many of the park's 34 raptors.

The **best time to visit** depends on a combination of weather and the extent of the migration. All things considered, June and July are probably optimum. The Serengeti is at its busiest from December to February and, to a lesser extent, in July and August. Still, it's a big park, so you won't get anything like the congestion that beleaguers Ngorongoro. The driest months are June to October and mid-December to January or early February. The scattered **short rains** fall between November and December, while the **long rains** are from February or March to the end of May. The wildlife migration passes through Serengeti between December and July; see box on p.471 for more information.

Arrival

Serengeti's eastern entrance, shared with Ngorongoro Conservation Area, is **Naabi Hill Gate**, 17km inside Serengeti, 45km southeast of Seronera Visitor Centre and approximately 300km from Arusha. The western entrance, 145km from Seronera, is **Ndabaka Gate**, next to the Mwanza–Musoma Highway. Two other, less used, gates are **Ikoma Gate** north of Seronera (see pp.514–515 for a description of the road from Bunda), and **Klein's Gate** in the northeast, which gives access to Loliondo and the wild road to Lake Natron (see p.481). You can't visit Serengeti in any meaningful way using public transport, though you can get a feel for the place on one of the roughly daily **buses** between Arusha and Musoma or Mwanza; you'll still have to stump up the entrance fee, though (and another $50 for Ngorongoro), so it's an expensive glimpse.

The **Sand River border** crossing between the Serengeti and Kenya's Maasai Mara Game Reserve is only open to private vehicles, and – being unofficial – may leave you open to having to pay bribes on the other side: anything up to $50 in *chai*, in addition to visa and nature reserve fees. Tanzanian immigration is at Seronera Visitor Centre; in Kenya, the nearest is in Narok. The closest **official border crossing** is at Sirari along the Mwanza–Kisumu road in the west; there's a rough road on the Kenyan side into Maasai Mara.

All this means that most visitors come either on an organized safari from Arusha (p.403), Moshi (p.345) or Mwanza (p.500), whether by road or, for upmarket packages, by light aircraft, or in a rented 4WD.

Renting a 4WD vehicle, in either Arusha, Karatu or Mwanza, gives you more flexibility than a standard safari, and works out pretty cheaply if you can fill all five or six seats. **Self-drive** is possible, although in theory this restricts your movements to the main roads through the park, so it's better to rent a vehicle with a driver (who usually doubles as a wildlife guide), or to hire an official guide at the park gate ($20 per day), pretty essential in any case given that Serengeti's roads aren't particularly well signposted. Fill up on **fuel** wherever you can, as supplies are limited and expensive. The cheapest fuel is at Seronera village in the centre. Much costlier, and sometimes reluctant to sell it except in emergencies, are the garages at *Lobo Wildlife Lodge, Serengeti Migration Camp, Serengeti Serena Safari Lodge* and *Serengeti Sopa Lodge*.

Entry fees and information

Park entry fees, valid for 24 hours, are $50 per person and Tsh10,000 for a vehicle; fees may increase to $100 in 2007 or 2008.

The park's **administrative headquarters** are just outside Ikoma Gate and of little use to tourists, but the park also maintains more useful offices behind the excellent **Seronera Visitor Centre** (see p.479) There's also tourist information at **Naabi Hill Gate**, which has a viewpoint over the plains, and an informative park office at *Lobo Wildlife Lodge*.

Maps and guidebooks can be bought at the park gates (if they're not out of stock), in Arusha, Dar and Stone Town, or at the park's lodges. The best **guidebook** is the full-colour pocket-size edition published in 2000 by TANAPA. Given that driving off the main routes is only allowed with a professional guide or driver-guide, finding a decent **map** isn't that important. As ever, a good bet is Giovanni Tombazzi's hand-painted version. For Seronera, the park publishes an A4 leaflet (available at the gates) containing a detailed map showing all the routes and road junction markers. There are lots of **Internet sites** dedicated to Serengeti; the official one is Ⓦ www.serengeti.org.

Accommodation

There's plenty of accommodation both inside and outside the park, but the **luxury tented camps** and **lodges** inside the park are often fully booked months ahead, even for low season, despite their prohibitive prices. For most visitors, the choice just depends on how close you want to be to the wildlife migration (see the box on p.471 for an idea of where the migration is at any time of year, though be aware that it all depends on the rains – dates can differ by a month or even two from one year to the next). When choosing,

Balloon safaris

From the ground, the wildebeest migration is a compelling phenomenon, bewildering and strangely disturbing, as you witness individual struggles and events. From the air, in a **hot-air balloon**, it resembles an ant's nest. At $400 for the sixty- to ninety-minute flight (including a champagne breakfast), **balloon safaris** are the ultimate in bush chic. The inflation and lift-off at dawn from the launch site near *Seronera Wildlife Lodge* is a spectacular sight, and the landing is often interesting, to say the least, as the basket may be dragged along before finally coming to rest.

You don't need to stay at the lodge to fly; they'll pick you up from any of the central lodges or campsites before dawn. There are only two balloons, one for twelve people, the other for sixteen, so book in advance, whether through a lodge or safari company, or directly with Serengeti Balloon Safaris (ⓦ www.balloonsafaris.com).

don't forget *Ndutu Safari Lodge* (p.463), in Ngorongoro right on the Serengeti border.

If you have at least three days to spare, it's best to stay in two **different places** to give you a better chance of getting close. But the most atmospheric (and nerve-jangling) way of spending a night is to **camp**, whether on the cheap or on an all-frills, included jamboree; see p.476.

Inside the park

Wildlife and scenery vary greatly from one lodge and tented camp to the other, but don't believe the hype about the **migration** passing right under your nose. A rough indication of the best months for each of the following places is included, but as you'll have a vehicle in any case, you can always catch up with the herds elsewhere. Room rates can drop by half in low season, which varies according to the lodge's location on the migratory route.

Kirawira Tented Camp Kirawira Hills, 100km west of Seronera (book through Serena Hotels, AICC Ngorongoro, Room 605, Arusha ☏ 027/250 6304, ⓦ www.serenahotels.com). On a hilltop overlooking the savannah in the western corridor, this place will pamper you silly with its valets, luxurious double tents, "plunge pool" and refined cuisine. Massively overpriced, but ideally placed for catching the migration May–July. Full-board $550 per person. ⑨

Lobo Wildlife Lodge Lobo Kopjes, 76km north of Seronera (book through Hotels & Lodges Ltd, 2nd floor (Block B), Summit Centre, Sokoine Rd, Arusha ☏ 027/254 4595, ⓦ www .hotelsandlodges-tanzania.com). Built around the crest of a high kopje, this enjoys awesome views, especially eastwards where the land drops away to a vast game-filled plain that receives a small part of the migration: northbound July–Sept, and southbound Nov–Dec; there are also large resident lion prides nearby. Each of the 75 rooms has views, as has the swimming pool and its terrace. Facilities aren't up to the standards of other lodges, but frankly who cares with views – and doorstep wildlife – like this. Full-board $180 per person. ⑨

Serengeti Migration Camp Ndassiata Hills, 80km north of Seronera (book through Elewana Afrika, 4th floor, Sopa Plaza, 99 Serengeti Rd, Arusha ☏ 0027/250 0630–9, ⓦ www.elewana.com). Built into a kopje overlooking the Grumeti River, this is a good location for wildlife and has a friendly atmosphere. There are 21 super-luxurious tents, an open-sided bar that's great for sunsets, and a small swimming pool. The African-style meals are good, with dinner usually served around a camp fire. A small floodlit waterhole attracts resident wildlife including hippos, and the migration normally passes by June–Aug and returns late-Oct and Nov. Like *Lobo* nearby, the rocky location doesn't favour disabled visitors. Closed April & May. Full-board $335–425 per person. ⑨

Serengeti Serena Safari Lodge Mbingwe Hill, 24km northwest of Seronera (book through Serena Hotels, AICC Ngorongoro, Room 605, Arusha ☏ 027/250 6304, ⓦ www.serenahotels.com). An architecturally inventive lodge hidden behind acacia trees, with 23 two-storey rondavels topped with spiky thatch roofs, and natural materials and local decor throughout. The best views are on the upper floors of the rondavels lower down the

Luxury camping around the Serengeti

A handful of safari companies operate blindingly expensive **luxury tented camps** in and around the Serengeti, mainly on private concessions in neighbouring Loliondo. All offer walking safaris, game drives in open-topped vehicles, and optional fly-camping in small dome tents. Recommended, if you have the money ($350–600 per person per day) and don't mind the neo-colonial feel, are:

Asilia Lodges & Camps Ⓦ www.asilialodges.com. Operates *Sayari Camps*, which shift location to keep up with the migration. One site is close to the Mara River inside the park, the others in Loliondo.

Dorobo Safaris (see Arusha safari operators, p.406). A socially responsible operator with a temporary camp in Loliondo, part of its adventurous cultural and walking trips. Local communities are involved throughout, and take a cut of the profits.

Kirurumu Tented Camps & Lodges Ⓦ www.kirurumu.com. Operates the semi-permanent *Loliondo Camp*, catching the migration Oct & Nov. At other times, a nearby waterhole draws animals. Oloipiri village nearby takes a share of the profits. March–Oct only.

Nomad Tanzania (see Arusha safari operators, p.407). Operates *Serengeti Safari Camp*, changing position three times a year to follow the migration. The tents are huge, and service second to none.

---

hill. Service is attentive, there's a kidney-shaped swimming pool with a telescope, two rooms for disabled guests, and bush dinners for an extra $30. The migration passes April & May, with stragglers continuing until July – nothing overly spectacular, though. Full-board $210 per person. ❾

Serengeti Sopa Lodge Nyarboro Hills, 46km southwest of Seronera (book through Sopa Lodges, 4th floor, Sopa Plaza, 99 Serengeti Rd, Arusha ☏ 027/250 0630–9, Ⓦ www.sopalodges.com). Occupying a ridge, this is an architectural blot, but things perk up considerably inside where warm, soft ochre tones and forms dominate the public areas, complete with chunky armchairs with big cushions. The 79 rooms are large and comfortable, and have balconies with sweeping views over acacia-studded hills and plains. Service is friendly and efficient, the food is good, and there's a swimming pool on a panoramic terrace. Feb–June is the main migration time, especially April. Full-board $175 per person. ❾

Seronera Wildlife Lodge Seronera (book through Hotels & Lodges Ltd, 2nd floor (Block B), Summit Centre, Sokoine Rd, Arusha ☏ 027/254 4595, Ⓦ www.hotelsandlodges-tanzania.com). This breezy place has aged well and still looks good, though the 75 rooms, as with *Lobo*, are a little basic. The best, and with better views, are at the back. The bar, restaurant and terrace have beautiful views over the Seronera Valley. The migration is in Seronera April–July. Full-board $180 per person. ❾

TANAPA Rest House 1km from Seronera village and the Visitor Centre (bookings advisable: contact TANAPA in Arusha, p.403; pay at the park gate). This park run place has three en-suite rooms each with two beds, but lacks any kind of "in the wild" feeling. Still, it benefits from the proximity of Seronera village, which has three *hotelis* dishing up cheap meals, some local bars and shops selling everything from chocolate to champagne. $30 per person. ❺

Outside the park

Ikoma Bush Camp 3km outside Ikoma Gate (book through Moivaro Lodges & Tented Camps, *Moivaro Coffee Plantation Lodge*, Arusha ☏ 027/255 3242, Ⓦ www.moivaro.com). In a great location on the edge of the western migratory routes (May–July & Nov–Jan), plus resident herds of impala and topi, distant lions and lots of birdlife. There are sixteen large and comfortable en-suite tents, a relaxed, peace-

ful and friendly atmosphere and good food. The camp also offers reasonably priced excursions on foot (outside the park) or by vehicle, and – if you're staying – a night game drive ($20 per person), giving the chance of seeing genet, civet and serval cats, lesser bushbabies, white-tailed mongooses, African and spring hares and, if you're really lucky, aardvarks, porcupines and hyenas. Full-board. ❽

Serengeti Stop Over On the highway 2km south of Ndabaka Gate 027/253 7095 or 0748/422359, ⓦ www.serengetistopover .com. A pleasant if largely shadeless place within walking distance of Lake Victoria (no swimming, alas, due to bilharzia). Rooms are in eight small, clean *bandas*, each with two beds, big nets and bathrooms (good showers). Good food available (meals $3–8), and there's also a beer garden, playground for kids, a gift shop funding local developmental projects, and traditional Sukuma dancing at weekends (and on request), but the main reason for staying is for its cultural tours, destined to turn the place into a (Sukuma) cultural centre. Excursions include Serengeti safaris, consultations with a traditional healer ($20 per group), a combined forest and village walk ($5), and an hour's fishing and birding with local fishermen in their canoes (also $5). A snake park and swimming pool are planned. Breakfast included ❹

Speke Bay Lodge 13km south of Ndabaka Gate; the turning is 6km south of Lamadi ☎ 028/262 1236 ⓦ www.spekebay.com. On the lakeshore (no swimming due to bilharzia), this occupies a lovely, lightly wooded plot with lots of birdlife, and great sunsets over the lake. Accommodation is in a series of stuffy tents lacking bathrooms and views, or in eight attractive bungalows on the shore. There's a bar and restaurant, plus lake excursions, mountain biking and canoe rental. Breakfast included: tents ❺, bungalows ❼.

Camping

Apart from TANAPA's rest house, **camping** is the only cheap way to stay in Serengeti, at $30 a person for a pitch in a public campsite, and $50 in a "special campsite". Outside the park, camping is possible off the Mwanza–Musoma Highway at *Serengeti Stop Over* and *Speke Bay Lodge*, both charging $5.

The park's **public campsites** – one at Ndabaka Gate, another at Lobo in the north and the others in a tight cluster a few kilometres northeast of Seronera Visitor Centre – have water, toilets and showers (which don't always work). The **special campsites** are spread all over the park, have no facilities whatsoever, and need to be booked months if not years ahead through TANAPA in Arusha (see p.403), who can give details on locations. However, you may strike lucky if you enquire at the park gate on arrival.

Neither style of campsite is fenced, so wildlife comes and goes. As a result, Seronera's public campsites have become notorious for nocturnal visits by **lions**. Though the last attack on humans was in 1965, needless to say, take extreme care. The lions are generally just curious, so the rule is to stay calm and remain inside your tent. Similarly, take care with **baboons**, who are well used to people and quite capable of mauling you: don't tempt or tease them, and keep food in air-tight containers.

Collecting **firewood** in the park is prohibited, so bring your own fuel for cooking. If you're staying at Seronera, you're permitted to drive along the shortest route to *Seronera Wildlife Lodge* in the evening for dinner, so long as you're back by 10pm (driving elsewhere is forbidden after 7pm).

Eating and drinking

Picnic lunches are the norm. Lodges provide guests with "lunch boxes", either as part of a full-board package, or for an extra $10–20. For little more, it might be better splashing out on an all-you-can-eat **buffet** at one of the lodges. With the best views, and use of their swimming pools included in the price, are *Lobo Wildlife Lodge* ($15) and Serengeti Sopa Lodge ($25). Cheap **local meals** (no more than Tsh2500) are cooked up at three *hotelis* in Seronera village.

The park

Serengeti National Park has four main sectors: the Serengeti Plains and their kopjes; Seronera in the centre; the Western Corridor; and the north. Each

△ Hot air balloon, Serengeti National Park

warrants at least half a day, meaning that two or three days overall is recommended to see a bit of everything. Coming from the east, the road from Ngorongoro Crater to central Serengeti is one long game drive in itself, passing through the heart of the **Serengeti Plains**. Scattered around the plains are a number of weathered granite outcrops called kopjes, which are miniature ecosystems, providing some shade, and limited water supplies in pools left in the rock after the rains. **Moru Kopjes** are the most visited.

Before starting a game drive, check the latest rules regarding **off-road driving** with the park authorities, which is allowed only in certain areas (mainly the western edge of the plains). The rule when off the main roads is never to follow tracks left by other vehicles, as this hastens soil erosion. However, at the time of writing all off-road driving had been banned for environmental reasons following recurring droughts. **Restricted areas** which require special permission to visit ($10) include Gol Kopjes in the east, which is a vital habitat for cheetah (whose hunting patterns are easily disturbed by safari vehicles), and sometimes Moru Kopjes.

The Serengeti Plains

The cornerstone of Serengeti's ecosystem are the undulating semi-arid **Serengeti Plains**. For a bird's-eye view, walk up the kopje behind **Naabi Hill Gate**, whose viewpoint and picnic site are ideal for observing the **migration** (see box on p.471) between January and April, especially February and March, when literally hundreds of thousands of wildebeest, zebra and gazelle munch their way across the grasslands below. The popularity of the plains with wildlife appears to owe something to the alkaline nature of the soil, whose volcanic ash was laid down during the eruptions of Ngorongoro's Crater Highlands, and is therefore rich in **minerals** – something accentuated by the annual cycle of rain and evaporation, which sucks minerals to the surface. The main ones are calcium, potassium carbonate and sodium carbonate, which recent studies have shown are an essential component of many animal's diets, especially when lactating (and which explains why eighty percent of Serengeti's wildebeest give birth on these plains).

Even when the migration moves out of the area, and the plains turn into a dry and dusty shimmer of straw, there's still plenty of resident **wildlife** around, including lion prides, unusually large clans of hyenas (up to eighty strong), plus hartebeest, topi, warthog and ostrich. **Birdlife** is richest during the rains, through you'll see secretary birds and kori bustards throughout the year. Another bird worth looking for is the **black-throated honey-guide**, which has a remarkable symbiotic relationship with the ratel (honey badger). The honey-guide, as its name suggests, leads the ratel to wild bee hives in trees, which the ratel – seemingly immune to the stings – pulls down and breaks open. The ratel eats the honey, and the honey-guide treats itself to beeswax.

Moru Kopjes

The flat plains are broken in several places by isolated and much-eroded granite "islands" called **kopjes**. Also known as inselbergs ("island hills"), the kopjes were created millions of years ago when volcanic bubbles broached the surface and solidified, and were subsequently eroded by rains and floods, carving out the singularly beautiful and sensuous forms you see today. Rainwater run-off from the kopjes and permanent water pools caught in rocky clefts make them particularly good for spotting wildlife in the dry season, when **lions** like to lie in wait for other animals coming to feed or drink – for this reason, take care when walking around kopjes.

Humans, too, have long been attracted to kopjes, both hunter-gatherers like the Dorobo, who were evicted in 1955, and seasonal "migrants" like Maasai cattle herders. The latter, evicted in 1959, left their mark – literally – in a rock shelter on one of the **Moru Kopjes** 32km south of Seronera. Here, a natural rock shelter is daubed with **rock paintings** (in red, white and black) of Maasai shields identical to ceremonial shields still used today. The paintings, accompanied by drawings of elephants and less distinct animal and human forms, were left by young Maasai warriors (*morani*) for whom the site was the location of an *orpul* meat-feasting site – as you can tell from soot lining the shelter's ceiling. According to Maasai custom, junior warriors were prohibited from eating meat, at least in public, so they'd steal a cow and bring it here. As with all rock art, the paintings are perishable and should be treated with respect: read the box on p.268.

One kilometre away is another thoroughly enigmatic kopje containing **rock gongs**, which are an ensemble of three loose boulders. One in particular – a large lemon-shaped wedge – bears dozens of circular depressions, created by people repeatedly striking the rock with stones to produce weirdly reverbative and metallic sounds (the sound differs depending where you strike the rock). Although rock gongs are nowadays played only by tourists, the wedge-shaped one was certainly used as a instrument way before the Maasai arrived a couple of centuries ago, as they lack any musical tradition involving percussive instruments, and similar gong rocks have been found as far south as Zimbabwe. However, as little is known of the now vanished hunter-gatherers who presumably made and used the gongs, their exact age and purpose remains a mystery. Incidentally, time spent poking around the boulders may turn up a surprise – in 1992, a species of **tree frog** hitherto unknown to science was discovered in one of the rock gong's depressions.

Seronera

The central part of Serengeti is **Seronera**, which comprises the wooded valleys and savannah of the Grumeti River's main tributaries. There are a large number of drivable circuits in the area, which your driver or guide should certainly know well, and the wildlife is representative of most of Serengeti's species. For many, the highlight is Seronera's famous **black-maned lions**, the cause of sleepless nights at the campsites. **Leopards** also abound, though you'll need a dash of luck, as they chill out by day in the leafy branches of yellow-barked acacias close to the rivers. The migration usually moves up to Seronera from the plains in April, before continuing on north and west.

A great place to head for after an early-morning game drive is **Seronera Visitor Centre** (daily 8am–4.30pm; T & F 028/262 1515), close to Seronera village, the public campsites and *Seronera Wildlife Lodge*. This brilliantly designed centre is a real pleasure, combining permanent exhibits, displays and wildlife video screenings at lunchtime (if the generator's working), with a humorous **information trail** up and around a nearby kopje. There's also a picnic site where semi-tame rock hyraxes and birds, including hoopoes and adorable Fischer's lovebirds, eye up your lunch, and a shop with drinks and snacks. The centre's gift shop should have a booklet containing the information presented on the trail, and also a leaflet with a map and detailed descriptions of the various game drives around Seronera. The staff can usually fill you in on recent predator sightings and road conditions, and a number of park wardens are also based here for more detailed queries.

A quick rundown of the **main trails** follows. Most have numbered road junctions corresponding to those on the leaflet. The **Seronera River Circuit** (junctions 1–26) starts at Seronera Hippo Pool and follows the river, and offers sightings of lions, leopards, crocodiles and waterbuck, as well as hippos, giraffes, vervet monkeys, baboons and many birds. The circuit can be combined with the **Kopjes Circuit** (junctions 52–62; enter at junction 18 on the east bank of the Seronera River), which goes anti-clockwise around Maasai, Loliondo and Boma Kopjes. Climbing on the rocks is forbidden. **The Hills Circuit** (junctions 27–29) cuts through grassland to the wooded foothills of the Makori and Makoma Hills west of the Seronera Valley, and is good for hyena, zebra, ostrich, warthog, gazelle, topi and hartebeest. A drive along this circuit is best combined with the **Songore River Circuit** (junctions 30–34), which loops into the plains south of the Seronera River. Thomson and Grant's gazelle, topi, hartebeest and ostrich are frequent, as are cheetah during the dry season. Lastly, the **Wandamu River Circuit** (junctions 40–49) covers similar habitats to the Seronera River Circuit, and hugs the banks of the Wandamu River, especially popular with buffaloes.

The Western Corridor

The **Western Corridor** is the unlovely name given to the forty-kilometre-wide strip that reaches out from Seronera to within 8km of Lake Victoria. The forests and swamps of the **Grumeti River** mark the northern boundary, while to the south is an area of grassland flanked by low wooded hills. The area receives the annual migration between May and July, after which time the bulk of the herds head on north over the Grumeti River towards Maasai Mara. This is the best time to visit the area, especially if the river is in flood, when the crossing is extremely perilous. At first hesitant, the herds surge headlong with a lemming-like instinct into the raging waters, while crocodiles and lions lie in wait for those injured in the effort, too weak for the strong currents or who get stuck in the muddy quagmire at the river's edges. You can find the crossings just by looking for vultures circling overhead.

A small part of the migration forgoes the pleasures of the river crossing to stay behind in the grasslands in the western part of the corridor, which also contains substantial populations of **non-migratory animals**, including some wildebeest and zebra, and smaller populations of giraffe and buffalo, hartebeest, waterbuck, eland, topi, impala and Thompson's gazelle. Hippo are present in large numbers, and in the dry season can always be seen at **Retima Hippo Pool**, 20km north of Seronera. Given the abundance of food, predators flourish, too, **leopards** in the lush tangled forests and thickets beside the river, and **crocodiles** – especially around Kirawira in the west – for whom the migration's river crossing provides a Bacchanalian feast. A speciality of the forest is a population of **black-and-white colobus monkeys**, though you'll need time and patience to track them down. The forests are also rich in **birdlife**, especially during the European winter. With luck, a rare species you might see is the olive-green bulbul.

Northern Serengeti

The patches of acacia woodland at Seronera begin to dominate the rolling hills of northern Serengeti. The area contains at least 28 acacia species, each adapted to a particular ecological niche, and the change in species is often startlingly abrupt, with one completely replacing another within a distance of sometimes only a few dozen metres. The undulating nature of the landscape makes it easy to spot animals from a distance and, further north, especially around **Lobo Kopjes**, higher ground provides fantastic views of the migration in the grasslands to the east (the best months are July–September when it heads north, and November and December when it turns back). Elephant, buffalo, zebra, gazelle and warthog can be seen all year. There's a game-drive circuit to the east of *Lobo Wildlife Lodge*, whose waterholes attracts a variety of wildlife, although the natural spring mentioned on older maps has now been capped by a pump.

Loliondo

Located outside the Serengeti's northeastern boundary, and hemmed in by Ngorongoro, Lake Natron and the Kenyan border, is **Loliondo**, a wild and little-visited region. Nowadays offered by a handful of mainly upmarket safari companies (see "luxury camping around the Serengeti" on p.475) as a venue for off-the-beaten-track wildlife trips, Loliondo will also appeal to lovers of wild and desolate landscapes, especially if you've rented a vehicle – the drive across Loliondo, from Serengeti's Klein's Gate to Lake Natron (see below), is spectacular and, in places, hair-raising (especially the hairpins down Nguruman Escarpment in the east). It's also potentially dangerous, thanks to past incidents involving **armed bandits** – read the warning on p.453.

Yet for all its aridity and wild frontier feeling, Loliondo is also a subtle land, even in the dry season, when – if you look carefully – even the leafless trees and bushes are full of colour, from the blue or yellow bark of some acacias, through violet and rusty orange bushes, and the mauve and green of thorn trees.

The area is especially good for **wildlife** in November and December when a good part of the annual migration heads back down from Maasai Mara. In consequence, Loliondo has long been favoured by **trophy hunters**, most notoriously over the last decade by a brigadier of the Dubai army, whose activities – including the alleged use of machine guns – have prompted much controversy.

Klein's Gate to Wasso

There's no reliable public transport to or within Loliondo, so other than buying a safari, you'll need your own 4WD, an experienced local driver and plenty of petrol and water. A decent map would be helpful, too; all but the *Kenya & Northern Tanzania Rough Guide Map* are completely wrong on Loliondo. Note that the western section of the route, between Klein's Gate and Wasso, goes across patches of **black cotton soil**, which can make it impassable in the rains, while the zigzagging road down the Nguruman Escarpment in the east sometimes loses entire sections of road.

Leaving Klein's Gate, the road heads southeast towards Wasso, 70km away, passing through impressively craggy hills, heavily wooded save for clearings made by Maasai for their cattle and limited agriculture. The road is easy to follow for the most part, although there are some confusing forks: just keep asking for Wasso. Along the way you pass many Maasai who, unlike their cousins in Ngorongoro, are not accustomed to tourists, so make a point of always obtaining (or paying for) permission before taking photos.

Wasso, about two hours from Klein's Gate, is the first major settlement. A government building on the left with a flag, and a transmitter on the right, marks the entrance. There's a small river crossing beyond here, then a junction. Bear left for Loliondo village, or turn right into Wasso itself and the road to Lake Natron and Ngorongoro Conservation Area. Wasso Hospital has three **guest rooms** (❸ with breakfast), and there's a campsite in the village.

Loliondo village

Before the sealed road from Kenya to Tanzania via Namanga was built, Loliondo was a major stop on the Great North Road from Nairobi to Arusha, which ultimately went on to Cape Town in South Africa. The sight of **Loliondo village**, about 6km northeast of Wasso, is probably the biggest surprise you'll have in the region. Amidst such desolate terrain, the village is a cool oasis of lush vegetation, and its high altitude gives it a pleasantly breezy and cool climate, which can be quite nippy at night. A handful of Europeans settled here early on, and the village still has an old colonial feeling to it, both in the style of its buildings, and the wide main road which some thoughtful soul long ago planted with beautiful purple-flowered jacaranda trees. There's a post office, a branch of NMB bank, fuel and a **campsite**: ask for *Saimon Kamakia's Oloolera Holiday Campsite* (Tsh5000 per person).

Wasso to Sonjo

Entering Wasso from the west (Serengeti), turn right after the river crossing, where a decently graded road heads south. If you're on the right road, you'll pass the entrance to Wasso airfield on your right after 2km. Bear left at any road fork, and continue for another 13km (15km from Wasso), where the road forks again. The right fork heads on down to Ngorongoro Conservation Area, while the left one continues south/southeast for 8km before turning east into a valley. Follow this until the road turns south again (there's a beautiful viewpoint near the top).

Sonjo village, a large cluster of round thatched huts in the lee of an escarpment, is 5km south of the viewpoint, and the main settlement of the agricultural **Sonjo tribe**. The Sonjo, who supplement their subsistence agriculture by hunting, may be one of the peoples responsible for having constructed the now-ruined villages and intricate irrigation complex at Engaruka, 100km to the south (see p.449), and have similar stone bases for building houses on. They settled in their present location at least three hundred years ago, but their more distant origins remain unknown, and academics can't agree on whether their language – quite distinct from Maasai – is Bantu or Cushitic, though it's probably a bit of both. There's no accommodation, and you should certainly not take pictures without permission.

Sonjo to Lake Natron

From the north side of Sonjo village, the road veers east once more, starting a long, straight and very dusty drive due east to the edge of the Nguruman Escarpment. The low craggy mountain that gradually appears to the southeast is **Mount Mosonik**, rising on the southwestern side of Lake Natron. Beyond its peaks is the distinctive pyramidal mass of Ol Doinyo Lengai. The road is extremely sandy in places, and 4WD is helpful even in dry weather. Along the way, there are fantastic candelabra euphorbia trees to admire, as well as bizarre giant aloe, which resemble palm trees with upturned fronds. With luck, you'll also see ostrich.

At the edge of the escarpment, the road – now a narrow rocky trail barely wider than a Land Rover – twists down a frightening stretch known as **Seventeen Corners**. Some sections get washed away in the rains, so check on the road's condition at the army post before Sonjo (or at Engaresero if you're coming from the lake). Once down, the road heads south across a weird and extremely beautiful moonscape pitted with craters and gullies, before skirting the lake to arrive at Engaresero, an hour's drive from Seventeen Corners. Engaresero, and the route from Mto wa Mbu to Lake Natron, is covered on pp.454–55.

Travel details

Buses

Engaruka to: Arusha (1 daily; 4–5hr); Mto wa Mbu (1 daily; 2hr).

Mto wa Mbu to: Arusha (3–4 daily plus daladalas; 2hr 30min–3hr); Engaruka (1 daily; 2hr).

Karatu to: Arusha (3 daily; 4hr); Dar (2 daily; 13hr); Moshi (3 daily; 5hr 30min).

Kigongoni to: Arusha (4 daily; 2hr); Babati (4 daily; 2–3hr); Singida (3–4 daily; 6–7hr).

Flights

Airline codes used below are: CA (Coastal Aviation), AE (Air Excel), RA (Regional Air) and ZA (ZanAir). Where more than one airline flies to the same destination, the one with most frequent flights and/or shortest journey times is listed first. Most flights to Serengeti land at both Seronera in the centre and Grumeti in the west; some also go to Klein's Gate in the north, or to Serengeti South.

Manyara to: Arusha (AE, RA, CA: 5 daily; 20–25min); Dar (AE: daily; 2hr 45min); Kilimanjaro (RA: daily; 45min); Mwanza (CA: daily; 2hr 45min); Ruaha (CA: 3 weekly; 3hr); Selous (CA: 3 weekly; 4hr 35min); Serengeti (AE, RA, CA: 5 daily; 30min–1hr 30min); Zanzibar (AE: daily; 2hr 10min).

Ngorongoro to: Arusha (CA: daily; 1hr); Mwanza (CA: daily; 2hr 15min); Serengeti (CA: daily; 1hr).

Serengeti to: Arusha (AE, RA, ZA: 6 daily; 1hr 5min–2hr 20min); Dar (AE, ZA: 2 daily; 3hr 30min–5hr 20min); Kilimanjaro (RA: daily; 1hr 35min–2hr 15min); Manyara (AE, RA, CA: 5 daily; 30min–2hr); Mwanza (CA: daily; 1–2hr); Pemba (ZA: daily; 4hr); Rubondo (CA: 2 weekly; 2–3hr); Selous (CA: daily; 5hr); Zanzibar (ZA, AE, CA: 3 daily; 3–4hr).

8

Lake Victoria and northwestern Tanzania

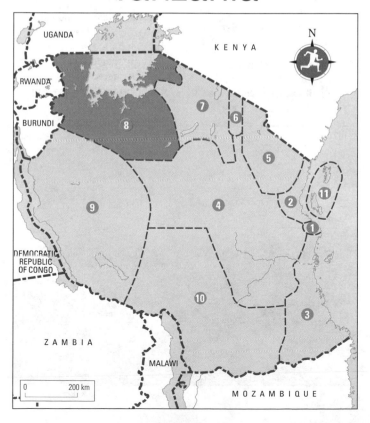

CHAPTER 8 # Highlights

✳ **Lake Victoria** The world's second-largest freshwater lake is also the fabled source of the Nile, an enigma that baffled Europeans until Speke stumbled upon it in 1858. **See p.487**

✳ **Sukuma Village Museum** At Bujora near Mwanza, a great place for getting to know the Sukuma, Tanzania's largest tribe, and seeing their annual dance competitions. **See p.502**

✳ **Ukerewe and Ukara** Long-inhabited and heavily agricultural, these lake islands are way off the beaten track, and ideal for getting a feel for an existence largely untouched by the twenty-first century. **See p.503**

✳ **Bukoba** A pleasant port town connected to Mwanza by ferry and by road to Uganda and Rwanda. A lovely beach, laid-back feel and lots of cultural activities are the reasons to linger. **See p.516**

✳ **Rubondo Island** Snug in the lake's southwestern corner, difficult (or expensive) access is compensated for by a host of endangered animals and breeding bird colonies. **See p.524**

△ Bismarck Rock, Lake Victoria

Lake Victoria and northwestern Tanzania

Dominating Tanzania's northwest is **LAKE VICTORIA** (Lake Nyanza), which fills a shallow depression between the Western and Eastern Rift Valleys. Covering an area of 69,484 square kilometres, and with a shoreline of 3220km, the lake is Africa's largest, and the world's second-largest freshwater lake. It's also the River Nile's primary reservoir, providing it with a steady, year-round flow.

The lake region is densely inhabited by farmers and cattle herders, and also by people living in the major cities on its shores, including Kampala and Jinja in Uganda, Kisumu in Kenya, and **Mwanza**, **Bukoba** and **Musoma** on the Tanzanian side. Bukoba is especially worth visiting as a base for exploring the hitherto virtually inaccessible northern reaches of Kagera Region bordering Uganda and Rwanda. Several islands also warrant exploration, notably **Ukerewe** and **Ukara** between Mwanza and Musoma, and **Rubondo Island** in the lake's southwest corner, whose diverse birdlife – along with elephants, chimpanzees and sitatunga antelopes – is protected as a national park.

The most enjoyable way of getting to, and around the region is on one of Lake Victoria's **ferries** (from Mwanza to Bukoba or Ukerewe Island), or by train from Dar and Tabora. But whilst the region's trunk roads have improved massively, cutting driving times from Arusha to under a day, unsurfaced roads can still become impassable during heavy rains, and getting **off the beaten track** by public transport can be an interesting experience to say the least, one that's definitely not recommended for those with old bones or claustrophobia: daladalas and buses really pack 'em in. If you're **driving**, bring plenty of spare petrol, food, water, and mechanical expertise, and ensure your vehicle's in good shape. A rental car's **PSV licence** should explicitly state the regions you're intending to visit, or else the daily routine of roadblocks and bribes will quickly become tiring.

Whichever way you travel, you will need plenty of **time**, as connections aren't guaranteed. But then, getting stranded in the back of beyond is all part of the fun …

LAKE VICTORIA AND NORTHWESTERN TANZANIA

Lake Victoria's troubled waters

Just over a century ago, Lake Victoria contained one of the richest freshwater ecosystems on earth, with an estimated five hundred fish species, including many brilliantly coloured cichlids. Today, only two hundred remain, the rest having vanished in the biggest mass extinction of vertebrates since the demise of the dinosaurs, while the lake itself is being systematically polluted, starved of oxygen and invaded by infestations of water hyacinth – all of which offers a bleak prospect for the thirty million people who depend on it for survival.

The alarming collapse of Lake Victoria's ecosystem can be traced back to the arrival of the railways in colonial times and the subsequent development of lakeside cities – Mwanza in Tanzania, Kisumu in Kenya, Kampala in Uganda – which began to place unsustainable pressure on the lake's resources. The Europeans also started commercial fishing, which rapidly depleted traditional fish stocks, until by the 1950s, catches of the two main edible species of tilapia fish had fallen to uneconomic levels. In a bid to find an alternative, moves were made to introduce non-native **Nile perch** (*mbuta*) into the lake, whose size (up to 250kg) and carnivorous habits, it was hoped, would convert smaller and commercially worthless cichlid species into profitable dinner-table protein. The proposal was fiercely opposed by scientists, who correctly predicted ecological disaster. Nonetheless, Nile perch found their way into the lake, having either been surreptitiously introduced, or having swum in along the Victoria Nile from Lake Kyoga in central Uganda. From a commercial point of view, the arrival of Nile perch in the lake was an enormous success, and catches spiralled, fuelling a lucrative export trade to Europe and Asia. Ecologically, however, the Nile perch was an unmitigated disaster: by the 1970s, Lake Victoria's cichlid populations, which had previously constituted eighty percent of the lake's fish, had fallen to under five percent (they're now estimated at just one percent). The Nile perch were quite literally eating their way through the lake's native species.

Sadly, the Nile perch are only part of the problem. **Pollution** on a massive scale is the major cause of the lake's oxygen depletion, and another legacy of colonial rule. Both the British and Germans were keen to use the lake's fertile hinterland for commercial plantations, and set about clearing vast areas of forests and other natural vegetation. With no permanent cover, soil erosion became an acute problem, as shown today in the sludge-brown colour of many of the region's rivers. In addition, the drainage of lakeside swamps (which are natural filters of silt and sediment) removed the barrier between the lake and rain-carried chemical residues from farms (especially pesticides and fertilizers) and gold mines, whose slurry is poisoned by mercury and other heavy metals. Add to this vast quantities of untreated effluent from the lakeside cities (Mwanza alone discharges an estimated 65 million litres of sewage into the lake every day) and you have some idea of the scale of the problem.

The result – unnaturally high levels of nutrients in the lake water, especially nitrates – has caused the proliferation of algae near the lake surface and the acidification of the water, which in turn has provided an ideal habitat for another unwanted species, **water hyacinth** This pernicious (albeit beautiful) floating weed is native to South America, and was introduced to Africa as an ornamental pond species. Apart from hindering shipping, the blanket of weed cuts off sunlight to the water beneath, creating stagnant areas of lake and leading directly to an increased incidence of diseases like cholera, malaria and bilharzia. The weeds also deplete oxygen levels, which has much the same effect on cichlid populations as the jaws of the Nile perch.

Now, the vicious cycle of destruction appears to have turned full circle: Nile perch stocks are dwindling for want of food – a singular irony for a lake that, at its height, produced half a million tons of fish a year. The whole sorry mess features as the subject of the documentary film, **Darwin's Nightmare** (ⓦ www.coop99.at/darwins-nightmare), by Austrian director Hubert Sauper, which parallels the lake's ecological catastrophe with the dire social consequences of untrammelled capitalism in Mwanza.

Mwanza Region

⑧

Mwanza Region, on the south side of Lake Victoria, is dominated by the port city of **Mwanza**. The region, much of it undulating plain scattered with large granite outcrops called kopjes, is home to the **Sukuma**, cattle herders by tradition, though many are now subsistence farmers. Mwanza is a handy base for a number of nearby attractions, including the **Sukuma Museum** and the islands of **Ukerewe** and **Ukara**, and also serves as a potential base for visiting Serengeti National Park, whose western border is barely 5km from the lakeshore.

Mwanza

Located on Mwanza Gulf on the southeast shore of Lake Victoria, the scruffy and weather-beaten but lively and friendly city of **MWANZA** is Tanzania's second-largest metropolis, one of Africa's fastest-growing cities (by twelve percent annually), and the country's busiest inland port, handling most of Tanzania's trade with Uganda.

The city was founded in 1892 as a cotton-trading centre, and although cotton has declined in importance as a result of low world prices, erratic rains and mismanagement, fishing, trade, some light industry, and – especially – receipts, legitimate or otherwise, from the region's **gold and diamond mines** have stepped in to fill some of the economic gap. Mwanza's inhabitants, many of them economic migrants, now number around one and a half million, seventy to eighty percent of whom live in insalubrious slums on and around the hills on the city's outskirts. The pace of population growth has now far outstripped the development of the city's infrastructure, much of which – water and sewerage, solid disposal and electricity – is in a pitiful state, where it exists at all. For many, the main source of protein is "punky" – fishbone waste sold off by fish-processing factories. Still, things are looking up: the city's streets, until recently notorious for having more holes than asphalt, have finally been patched up and even expanded, and the location – snug among rolling lakeside hills with great views – is handsome indeed.

Arrival and information

Mwanza has good **transport connections**, whether by road, plane, ferry (to Bukoba) or train (to Tabora and Dar, and, indirectly, to Kigoma).

Most buses terminate at the chaotic **bus stand** in the centre of town, where taxi drivers compete for your attention (and bags) – take care. Exceptions include Scandinavian Express, which stop at their office at the south end of Rwagasore Road, and Akamba, under *Majukano Hotel* at the west end of Liberty Street. There's another major bus stand at **Buzuruga**, 5km east of the city along the Musoma highway, where services coming from the north call in. Buzuruga is slated to replace the central bus stand; should this finally happen, there are plenty of daladalas from there to the daladala stand in the centre.

If you're **driving from the west**, you'll have to catch a **ferry** across Mwanza Gulf. The quickest is the northern crossing from Kamanga to the city centre (Mon–Sat from 8am until 6pm, Sun until 5pm; every hour or so; Tsh3000 for a car with driver, plus Tsh500 each passenger; 1hr). There's another roll-on roll-off ferry from Busisi to Kigongo further to the south (daily from 8am until 9pm; every hour or two; same prices), although this leaves you with a 30km drive into the city once you're across. Arriving at night, vehicles are supposed to travel in convoy, with armed policemen at the front and rear.

Most **ferries** dock at the ferry port in the city centre. The exceptions are the Kamanga ferry, which arrives just to the south, and the MV *Airbus* from Ukerewe, which ties up at Kirumba Mwaloni 3km north along Makongoro Road. Despite the welter of people and hawkers that greet ferry passengers, there's not much hassle, but keep an eye on your bags.

Mwanza Airport lies 8km northeast of the centre. Daladalas into town cost a few hundred shillings. The normal taxi fare is Tsh5000–7000, but drivers will try it on for Tsh10,000.

Mwanza is the terminus of the **Central Railway Line**'s northern branch, served by three trains a week from Dar (a fascinating if exhausting 37hr ride) via Dodoma, Tabora and Shinyanga. The station is 500m south of the centre on Station Road, and within walking distance of most hotels, although you could always catch a taxi.

The city centre is small enough to walk around. **Taxis** can be found everywhere: a short ride costs Tsh1000–1500, though tourists may be overcharged. A comprehensive source of **tourist information** is ⓦ www.mwanza-guide.com. Tap water needs purifying for drinking.

Accommodation

There's lots of central **accommodation** in all price ranges, and most hotels will let couples share a single room.

Budget

Deluxe Hotel Corner Uhuru St and Kishamapanda St ☎028/254 0543. A welcoming four-storey place with bright and breezy rooms, especially higher up. The mattresses are sagging, but otherwise the rooms – all en suite and with large box nets and writing tables – are pretty good value. There's also a bar and restaurant. Breakfast included. ❶

Kishamapanda Guest House Corner Uhuru and Kishamapanda streets ☎0745/083218. The entrance – shared with the *New Geita* – is through a bar that's fortunately not as rough as it looks. There are eight clean rooms, all with fans; the cheaper ones share bathrooms. It might be best to skip on the food, since the kitchen – shared with the *New Geita* – is none too salubrious. ❶

Lake Hotel Station Rd ☎028/250 0658. A funny old place near the train station whose rooms are accessed through a dark and sprawling bar popular with elderly gents. There are 47 en-suite rooms (singles, twins and triples), and though they're pretty simple, they're good value if you don't mind the noise (upstairs rooms are marginally quieter). Food available in the bar. Breakfast included. ❷

New Binza C Guest House Uhuru St (no phone). Good, cheap, basic and clean rooms (shared bathrooms only) in the thick of a busy local area, with lots of cheap restaurants and foodstalls nearby. If it's full, the similar *New Binza B* is on the same road closer to the centre. ❶

New Geita Lodging Corner Uhuru and Kishamapanda streets ☎028/254 0033. Sharing

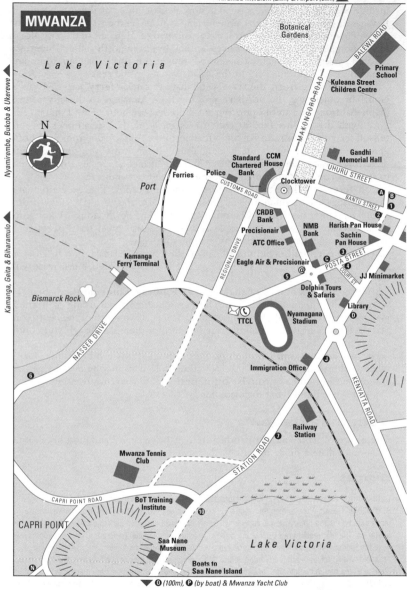

MWANZA

Kirumba Mwaloni (2km) & Airport (8km) ▲

Lake Victoria

Botanical Gardens

BALEWA ROAD

Primary School

Kuleana Street Children Centre

MAKONGORO ROAD

Gandhi Memorial Hall

UHURU STREET

N

Port

Ferries

Police

Standard Chartered Bank

CCM House

Clocktower

BANTU STREET

A B
1
2

CRDB Bank

Precisionair

ATC Office

Eagle Air & Precisionair

NMB Bank

Harish Pan House

Sachin Pan House

3

POSTA STREET

4

JJ Minimarket

Kamanga Ferry Terminal

REGIONAL DRIVE

5

C

@

COURT ST

Dolphin Tours & Safaris

Library

D

Bismarck Rock

NASSER DRIVE

TTCL

Nyamagana Stadium

6

Immigration Office

J

KENYATTA ROAD

STATION ROAD

7

Railway Station

Mwanza Tennis Club

CAPRI POINT ROAD

BoT Training Institute

10

CAPRI POINT

Saa Nane Museum

Boats to Saa Nane Island

Lake Victoria

N

▼ ⓞ (100m), ⓟ (by boat) & Mwanza Yacht Club

LAKE VICTORIA AND NORTHWESTERN TANZANIA | Mwanza (left margin, vertical) — 8

Nyamirembe, Bukoba & Ukerewe (left margin, vertical)

Kamanga, Geita & Biharamulo (left margin, vertical)

---

its dissolute entrance with the *Kishamapanda*, the twenty en-suite rooms here finally got their much-needed renovation, and are now quite decent – all tiled, and with large double beds, TV (local stations), ceiling fan, net, and fine squat toilets. Breezier rooms are upstairs. ➋

Nyanguge Guest House Lumumba Rd ☎0744/310820. Probably the best on this road, with simple but decent rooms on four floors – the better and brighter ones are on top – with large nets and two beds. All but one share bathrooms (bucket showers). ➊

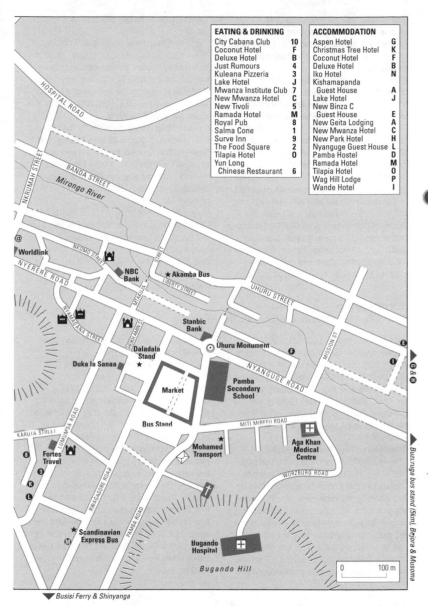

Pamba Hostel Station Rd, by Fourways roundabout (no phone). Run by the Nyanza Cooperative Union, this is a good, calm and exceedingly dusty budget choice, with decent shared showers, clean sheets and nets. Rooms lack nets but catch any lake breezes. ❶

Mid-range

All of the following include breakfast in their rates.

Aspen Hotel Uhuru St ☏028/250 0988. A large, modern place with well-appointed en-suite rooms (doubles or twins), all with cable TV, phones, fans, nets and cotton sheets, most with balconies. Safe parking. ❸–❹

Christmas Tree Hotel Off Karuta St ☏ & ℗028/250 2001. Good-value and often full, all 27 rooms have cable TV, phone, fan, a big double bed and well-kept bathroom. A handful (best on the third floor) have great views of the inlet and Saa Nane Island. There's also a bar. No single rates. ❸

Coconut Hotel Liberty St ☏028/254 2373. A clean, modern choice overlooking the filthy Mirongo River. All rooms are en suite with TV, fan, carpet and reliable hot water. Has a stuffy restaurant downstairs, and a nicely breezy bar (also with food) on the first and second floor terraces. No single rates. ❸

Iko Hotel Capri Point ☏0745/668354. A somnolent (or relaxing?) place in the posh Capri Point district, with 52 increasingly tatty en-suite rooms including gigantic doubles with a/c and fridge; the even bigger suites have TV, a/c and bathtubs.

There's a basic restaurant (pre-order) and quiet bar. ❸

🏃 **New Park Hotel** Uhuru St ☏ & ℗028/250 0265. Spotless en-suite "singles" (that can be shared by couples) with huge double beds and box nets, fan and cable TV, and some with bathtubs in addition to showers. The best rooms – breezier and with views over town – are on top. There's also a posh bar and restaurant. ❸

Ramada Hotel Rwagasore St ☏028/254 0223. Good and secure, despite the noisy location, with bright and breezy rooms, some with views over the bay, others with balconies, all with TVs, phones, big beds and fans but no nets (rooms are sprayed instead). There's a nice restaurant and bar on the first floor. ❸

Wande Hotel Off Uhuru St ☏028/250 3373. A friendly place, all rooms en suite with TV, fridge and fan; singles have huge beds, doubles have two beds and are a bit dark. Food and drink is available, and there's the *Hai Bar* nearby if you fancy a change. Safe parking. ❸–❹

Expensive

The following include breakfast in their rates.

New Mwanza Hotel Posta Rd ☏028/250 1070, ⓦwww.newmwanzahotel.com. A rather soulless but perfectly adequate "international" class hotel that smells of wood polish, with 54 en-suite rooms (double or twin), all with minibar, phone, a/c, satellite TV and wall-to-wall carpet. Facilities include a swimming pool, room service, 24hr coffee shop, bar and restaurant, health club, casino and lift access. ❺

Tilapia Hotel Capri Point ☏028/250 0517, ⓦwww.hoteltilapia.com. A posh bayside place that's been popular with expats and package tourists for years (hence the upmarket hookers in the bar). Rooms come with cable TV, phone, big bed(s), fan, a/c, minibar, safe, and Internet access; the better ones have lake views, whilst the more atmospheric are on a houseboat called the *African Queen*. Suites have fully equipped kitchens. Amenities include several restaurants and bars, a swimming pool, curio shop, safaris

and yacht cruises. Rooms ❻, suites and houseboat ❼.

🏃 **Wag Hill Lodge** On the west side of Mwanza Gulf; accessed by boat from Mwanza Yacht Club ☏028/250 2445 or 0744/777086, ⓦwww.waghill.com. Up above the western shore of Mwanza Gulf in a small protected patch of indigenous forest, this romantic lodge enjoys a gloriously lush forested location teeming with birds, including fish eagles and various kingfisher species. It's also extremely intimate, with just three secluded, cosy bungalows in what could be called "Indo-Alpine" style – a refreshing change from the *makuti*-roofed school of lodge architecture. Each has balcony views of both forest and lake. There's also a swimming pool, fine food, and an open fire in the evenings with views across the lake's twinkling lights. Rates include guided forest walks, fishing trips, and boat transfers. All-inclusive $500 (double) ❾.

The City and around

Most of Mwanza's burgeoning population lives in the outskirts, most visibly in unplanned slums spread all over various boulder-strewn hills and outcrops, the most famous of which is **Bugando Hill**, crowned by the Government hospital. The area at the hill's base, stretching westwards towards the city centre, is a lively hive of industrious activity, reaching a crescendo in the **market area** centred around the bus and daladala stands. Facing the latter is the **Duka la**

The riddle of the Nile

Africa's Great Lakes – Victoria (Nyanza), Tanganyika and Nyasa – remained virtually unknown outside Africa until the second half of the nineteenth century, when they suddenly became the centre of attention amidst the scramble to pinpoint the **source of the Nile**. This was no mere academic exercise, for whoever controlled the Nile, controlled Egypt.

Yet it was a riddle that had bamboozled geographers and travellers alike since ancient times, when **Herodotus**, the "Father of History", had wrongly stated that West Africa's Niger was a branch of the Nile. Pliny the Elder compounded the confusion with his belief that the Nile had its head in a "mountain of lower Mauretania, not far from the [Atlantic] Ocean", whilst early Arab geographers didn't help matters by calling the Niger *al-Nil al-Kebir*, meaning the Great Nile.

In February 1858, the English explorers **John Hanning Speke** and **Richard Francis Burton** became the first white men to set eyes on Lake Tanganyika. The impetuous Burton instinctively believed Lake Tanganyika to be the Nile's source, but Speke argued – correctly, it turned out – that the lake lay too low. Leaving behind a grumbling and poorly Burton, Speke headed south, having been told of Lake Victoria by an Arab slave trader. As soon as he reached the shore, where Mwanza is now, in August 1858, Speke was convinced that the millennial quest was finally over.

To verify his theory, Speke returned to the lake in October 1861, accompanied by the Scottish explorer **James Augustus Grant** and, after circling half the lake in a clockwise direction, sailed down the Nile in 1863 all the way to Cairo. "The Nile is settled," he wrote in a telegram from Khartoum to the Royal Geographic Society. Many people remained sceptical of Speke's claim, however, while Burton himself continued to insist that Lake Tanganyika was the true source of the Nile. In the end, it took a circumnavigation of Lake Victoria by Stanley in 1875 to prove Speke right. Sadly, Speke didn't live to enjoy his triumph, having died in a hunting accident in 1864.

Sanaa handicraft shop (Mon–Fri 8am–5.30pm), much of its wares made by the Mwanza Women Development Association. There's some especially good bright and chunky jewellery, plus pottery from the Jita and Sukuma tribes. Nearby, just north of the Uhuru Monument on both sides of a footbridge straddling the foul Mirongo River, are several **Maasai herbalists**, who apart from locally-esteemed medicinal concoctions also sell cowrie-shell necklaces and other trinkets you won't easily find elsewhere.

Close to the ferry ports, a plaque next to the **clock tower roundabout** at the west end of Nyerere Road commemorates the "discovery" of Lake Victoria and hence the source of the Nile in 1858 by the English explorer Speke, who first saw the lake "from Isamilo Hill one mile from this point" – see the box above. The traffic island also contains a small **memorial** to men who died in the two world wars; the British as soldiers, the Africans as conscripted porters.

Four hundred metres north of here off Makongoro Road are Mwanza's neglected lakeside **Botanical Gardens**, nonetheless a pleasant target for a short walk. The **lakeshore** is, of course, Mwanza's main attraction, best savoured on either side of the hilly **Capri Point peninsula** south of the centre – the city's most affluent district, home to millionaires grown fat off diamonds and gold, and the fishing, processing and export of the lake's remaining tilapia and Nile perch stocks. None of these have done any favours for the environment, or to locals dispossessed of their land by mining conglomerates, or pushed out of their fishing grounds by trawlers.

△ Igogo slum, Mwanza

Tanzania
in celebration

Celebrations are an integral part of life for Tanzanians. From the birth of a child to its being named; a girl's or a boy's ritual passage into adulthood; marriage; the cyclical seasons of rains and harvests; death; and the remembrance of the dead – every step in life's journey is marked and celebrated.

Maasai boys after the Eunoto ceremony

Ritual and religion

Usually, Tanzanian celebrations mean music, dancing, much feasting and drinking, and all-round merry-making, in addition to any ritual or religious aspect. By bringing together communities, celebrations forge and strengthen ties that are important in life, both among the living, and between the living and the dead: music and sweet smoke drifting up to the sky from a sacrificed animal also entice deceased ancestors to come and partake. With the ancestors satisfied, matters outside peoples' control, such as the provision of sufficient rain, were also assured: the ancestors would – the reasoning went – be more willing to intercede with God if they'd been pleasured and fed.

New Year celebrations

One of the most extraordinary Tanzanian celebrations is Zanzibar's Mwaka Kogwa festival, held in celebration of the Persian New Year every July. The four-day festival – introduced by Zoroastrian immigrants over a millennium ago – is at its most exuberant in Makunduchi on Unguja, where the rituals that take place on the first day cleanse the old year and bless the new. The proceedings begin with houses being swept clean, and a ritual bath in the sea (*mwaka kogwa* means "washing the year"). By mid-morning, most of Makunduchi's inhabitants descend on the centre of town, where a medicine man (*mganga*) erects a thatched hut accompanied by the singing of women. A group of elders enter the hut, upon which the *mganga* sets it alight. The men's subsequent "escape" gives a fine opportunity to the more theatrically inclined, and the smoke that issues at this moment indicates the direction in which the fortunes of the following year will blow. The rituals complete, the following three days consist of feasting, dancing and drumming, during which time women and girls appear in all their finery, their hands and feet painted with henna.

Mwaka Kogwa festival, Makunduchi

The dance season

For Tanzania's more traditional tribes, the end of the harvest heralds the dance season.

Based predominantly around the Makonde Plateau deep in southern Tanzania, the Makonde's famed woodcarving skills come to the forefront at this time in the Mapiko dance. The *mapiko* dancer performs on stilts, and wears a carved mask that completely covers his head, like a motorbike helmet. He represents evil, and is the most feared figure in Makonde ritual; despite this, the dance is also performed on happy occasions that involve entire villages.

Several other tribes hold musical contests (*mashindano*) in the dance season, of which a superb example is given by northwestern Tanzania's Sukuma tribe. Coinciding nowadays with the Christian festival of Corpus Christi, their annual

Sukuma *bulabo* dance competition

Mock fights...

Of course, celebrations would be pointless were there any bad blood still hanging around; mock fights serve as a means of settling old grievances publicly. In Makunduchi, this involves two groups of men who flail each other with sticks and banana stems while spurred on by raucous insults and jokes from the ever-vocal women. On the mainland, mock fights gave a name to the cattle-herding **Barbaig** tribe: from *bar* (to beat) and *baig* (sticks). For the Barbaig, pretend fights by young warriors were also a vital part of the tribe's security: their warlike northern neighbours, the related Maasai, called the Barbaig *Il-Mang'ati* – "the enemy" – and little love was lost between the cousins.

... and bull fights

A most unusual Zanzibari celebration is **bull-fighting**. A relic of Portuguese times, the fights take place on Pemba from around September to February and feature up to six specially trained bulls. Initially tethered, the bulls are provoked by jostling crowds and

pipe music until, sufficiently enraged, they're untethered, the crowd scatters and the "matador" takes over. Completely unarmed, he goads the bull with a white cloth, his skill lying in artfully avoiding the bull's charges and in overt displays of machismo, while the pleasure for the spectators lies both in the fighter's deft movements, and in seeing him shimmy up the nearest tree whenever things gets hairy.

Bull fighting, Pemba

Bridal henna tattoos

cycle of *bulabo* dance competitions pits dance societies against each other in gladiatorial-style displays of crowd-pulling prowess. The contests began in the nineteenth century when rival healers could not agree about which of them possessed the most powerful medicine (*dawa*). The format, which remains unchanged, is for the dance societies to perform at the same time, with the crowd being free to move between the two – the bigger the crowd, the better the medicine.

The Maasai's Eunoto ceremony

Historically, the success of the Maasai in warfare (and territorial expansion) was due to a rigidly hierarchical society characterized by regimented "age-groups" and "age-sets", which persists today. Every seven to twelve years, the age groups shift up a notch to make room for a younger generation of inductees. The **Eunoto ceremony** is when boys become junior warriors, junior warriors are promoted to senior warriors, and the latter are pensioned off to become elders, effectively marking the end of their youth. Their promotion into elderhood entitles them to take wives and raise families, but for many it also marks the end of the most privileged time of their lives. The songs sung by warriors at this time are competitive in nature, both in the lyrics – with singers bragging about how they killed a lion or rustled cattle from a neighbouring tribe – and in the leaping that passes for Maasai dancing, in which the higher and more graceful the leap, the better (and sexier in the eyes of unmarried girls).

Modern festivals

A couple of annual festivals provide the perfect excuse to get over to Zanzibar: both the **Sauti za Busara** music festival in February, and the **Festival of the Dhow Countries** in July are excellent entertainment, and feature music from all over East Africa, and in the case of the latter, from the Arabian Peninsula and the Indian subcontinent as well. On the mainland, particularly good is Dar es Salaam's two-day **B-Connected Festival** in the city's Mnazi Mmoja Grounds at the end of May. Fast on the way to cult status, it's a great showcase for up-and-coming talent on the hip-hop, rap and "Bongo Flava" scenes.

Festival of the Dhow Countries

Heading south from the clock tower or ferry port is the city's most photographed landmark, **Bismarck Rock**, a weathered granite kopje just offshore. Although kids are fond of swimming around it, it's not recommended due the city's lamentable lack of sewage treatment, and sadly the same applies to all the beaches close by. Continuing beyond Bismarck Rock, the road veers away from the western shore and across Capri Point to the eastern shore. A right turn here (along Station Rd) gets you to the gloomy **Saa Nane Museum** (Mon–Fri 9am to around 5pm; free), which contains enough wacky oddities to make the walk worthwhile. Aside from various decaying trophies and manky stuffed animals, questionable highlights (collected by a foot fetishist, it seems) include a giant hippo's foot, a chair fashioned from an elephant's foot and table lamps made from ostrich and eland legs.

Opposite the museum is a small jetty used by ferries going to the ninety-acre **Saa Nane Island Game Reserve**, sitting in the inlet between Capri Point and Bugando Hill. The island is attractive, and the big rocks that stud it make popular picnic spots, but the "game reserve" itself – established in 1964 as a quarantine station during the creation of Rubondo Island National Park – encapsulates all that's most dismal and depressing about zoos, as exemplified by a thoroughly depressed caged chimpanzee, who has endured decades of taunts from visitors. The **ferries** sail daily at 11am, 1pm, 3pm and 5pm (returning half an hour later); the Tsh800 return fare includes entry to the reserve. Alternatively, rent a whole boat from the museum (11am–4pm) for Tsh10,000.

To get to **the top of Capri Point**, walk on past the museum and turn right before *Tilapia Hotel*. Take the first left, then right – ascending all the time. You should pass an enormous yellow mansion on your left (the road here is surfaced). Keep going straight up until the drivable road stops. From here, a footpath wends along the edge of the summit, giving fantastic views of Mwanza Creek, Lake Victoria and dozens of islands.

Eating

At night, Uhuru Street is a good place for **street food**, with numerous stalls dishing up grilled meat (goat is best), fish and bananas cooked on smoky charcoal *jikos*. For a taste of *paan* (see p.104), try either *Harish Pan House* or *Sachin Pan House*, both at the junction of Nyerere Road and Posta Street.

Deluxe Hotel Kishamapanda St. Popular at lunchtimes, this has the usual range of Tanzanian favourites plus an excellent bean *matoke* (a stew made primarily from bananas). Around Tsh1000 a plate.

The Food Square Bantu St. A reliably good cheap place in the centre, on two floors, with great *pilau* and other full meals (Tsh1200–1500), plus *supu*, various snacks, fresh juices, and grills in the evening. No alcohol.

Kuleana Pizzeria Posta St. Semi-outdoors, this cheerfully decorated place is as popular with locals as with travellers, so get there early to be sure of a table. The food – strictly vegetarian – is invariably delicious, once the sullen waitresses finally get round to you: large pizzas for around Tsh4000, good sandwiches, and a good range of cakes, biscuits and fresh bread. There's also a TV and notice board. Daily to 8pm.

Ramadd Hotel Rwagasorc Rd. A pleasant first-floor restaurant and bar, with most dishes costing around Tsh2500. The bar is open daily until midnight, and has satellite TV.

Salma Cone Bantu St. Snacks like samosas, cakes and buns, ice creams and good juices, including sugar cane. In the evenings, a mobile *mishkaki* place sets up on the pavement outside: Tsh200 per skewer, with very juicy salad, tamarind sauce and chilli accompaniment. No alcohol.

Surve Inn Lumumba Rd. A good, calm and clean *hoteli* which is especially good for breakfast, with decent *supu*, tea, samosas and even espresso. Daytime only; closed Sun. No alcohol.

Tilapia Hotel Capri Point. The hotel houses various restaurants serving up Italian, Chinese, Indian and (especially good) Thai cuisine, with tables by the lakeside, others on breezy terraces or by the pool. Starters average Tsh4000 (includ-

By road

Mwanza's bus stand is a brash and chaotic place, so buy tickets a day or two before when unencumbered by bags. You should also enquire about the correct fare with your hotel, as you'll almost certainly get ripped off otherwise. For an approximate idea, hopefully the 2003 prices displayed on black signboards at the stand's southern end are still there (or have even been updated). To avoid the touts, tell them you're just after information: "Naomba maelezo tu" is the phrase to use. Incidentally, if a tout offers a "discount", you'll still be charged over the odds. If you're heading into Kenya, you can avoid all this as the best companies have their own offices and terminals: **Akamba**, *Majukano Hotel*, west end of Liberty Street (☎028/250 0272); and **Scandinavian Express**, Rwagasore Road (☎028/250 3315). On surfaced roads or mostly surfaced routes (Arusha, Kenya, Musoma, and west from Shinyanga), avoid Spider, Tawfiq and Zuberi buses, all known for speeding.

Heading north to **Nairobi** (or back into Tanzania via Namanga to Arusha and Dar), Akamba and the more expensive Scandinavian Express are safest. To the fare, add $100 in visa fees ($70 if you can wangle a Kenyan transit visa) if you're re-entering Tanzania and lack a multiple-entry visa. There are two other ways of reaching **Arusha**: the main one (dry season, but should soon be all-weather) passes through Shinyanga, Nzega and Singida, and takes a full day (around Tsh18,000). The other is **through Serengeti and Ngorongoro**, which will add $100 to the fare in park entrance fees; the companies are Mtei on Monday and Friday, Kimotco on Wednesday, and Coast Line on Friday.

The road to **Biharamulo** via the gold-mining town of Geita starts at Kamanga on the west side of Mwanza Gulf, accessed by vehicle ferry from the end of Posta Street (Mon–Sat 8.30am, 10.30am, 12.30pm, 4pm & 6pm, fewer on Sun; Tsh3000 per vehicle and Tsh500 per person). Two buses cover the route daily (Zuberi and Nyahunge); board the bus at the ferry terminal but buy your ticket at the bus stand the day before.

There are no buses to **Bukoba** – go to Biharamulo and change there (next day), or catch the ferry. Services to **Kigoma** are sketchy and prone to change, and to delays and cancellations in the rains. At the time of writing, two buses – Adventure Connection and Saratoga Line – operated on alternate days, both leaving at 5am to arrive late the same day. **Tabora** has two or three buses daily, including Mohamed Transport (☎0748/566501), whose office is off Miti Mirefu Road.

ing the classic Thai prawn, lemongrass and lime soup), with main courses Tsh7000–10,000. A Japanese-style *teppinyaki* blow-out, where you cook your own meal at your table, costs Tsh8500 for the vegetarian version, Tsh15,000 with meat or fish.

Yun Long Chinese Restaurant Nasser Drive, beyond Bismarck Rock. The only completed part of an abandoned project to build a posh resort-style hotel on the lakeshore. Despite this, it's Mwanza's most attractive eating venue, its delightful lakeside terrace offering unmatched views. The menu is strictly Chinese or "neo-traditional" Tanzanian (chips, rice or *ugali* with chicken, fish or stews). For Chinese, most plates cost Tsh7000 including rice. Daily to midnight.

Drinking and nightlife

The most popular **discos**, for the latest Bongo Flava or whatever style is making waves, are in the northern suburbs. Currently humming are *Hotel La Kairo*, 2km north off Makongoro Road (taxi Tsh2000) which also has a swimming pool and access to a grubby beach; the *Hot Pot Disco* in Bwiro area (taxi Tsh3000); and *Casanova Disco* in Kiroreri area east of the airport (taxi at least Tsh5000).

By ferry

A more comfortable and sedate approach to **Bukoba** is on the MV *Victoria*, currently sailing at 10pm Tuesday, Thursday and Sunday, stopping en route at **Kemondo**, 21km south of Bukoba. There are also daily ferries to **Ukerewe Island** (see p.503 for details), and tentative plans to resume the twice-weekly service to **Port Bell** in Uganda.

The **tourist fare** to Bukoba is Tsh21,500 first-class (two bunks per cabin), Tsh19,500 second-class (six bunks), Tsh16,300 second-class seated, and Tsh15,600 in third. Cabins are recommended if you want to arrive refreshed, so buy your ticket several days before. For **information**, contact Marine Services Ltd: ☏028/250 0880, ✉marine@africaonline.co.tz.

By train

A leisurely if tiring way to **Dar es Salaam** (almost forty hours) is by train: currently 6pm on Tuesday, Thursday and Sunday. Change in **Tabora** for **Mpanda** or **Kigoma**: the Tuesday and Sunday trains from Mwanza will give you a full day in Tabora (you arrive before dawn and leave after dusk); the Thursday service gives you two days and a night before the next train to Mpanda or Kigoma.

The **station** is on Station Road (☏028/254 2202, ⓦwww.trctz.com). **Fares** from Mwanza to Dar are Tsh44,600 first-class sleeper, Tsh32,600 second-class sleeper, and Tsh14,800–17,700 second-class seating or third-class. For sleepers, buy your ticket a few days before to be sure of a compartment.

By plane

The **airport** is 8km north of town. Daladalas cost a few hundred shillings, or taxis charge Tsh5000–10,000. There are daily **flights** to Arusha, Bukoba, Dar, Lake Manyara, Ngorongoro and the Serengeti, and less frequent flights to Entebbe, Kilimanjaro and Rubondo Island. At the time of writing, Coastal Aviation were proposing a useful western loop from Mwanza to Tabora, Mahale, Katavi and Kigoma and back. See "Travel details" at the end of the chapter for more route details, and "Airlines" (p.500) or "Travel agents" (p.500) for booking information. For an idea of **fares**: Mwanza–Arusha one-way on Coastal Aviation costs $200, and Mwanza–Rubondo Island is $70.

City Cabana Club Station Rd, Capri Point. Beside the inlet near *Tilapia Hotel*, but without the latter's tourists and pretence. Indeed, it can feel deserted, but does host one-off events like beauty contests and live bands.

Coconut Hotel Liberty St. Great open-sided rooftop bar on two levels, and with food: a big portion of rice or chips with chicken for Tsh2500; pre-order for fish.

Just Rumours Corner of Posta and Court streets. Something like a wine bar (lots of mirrors, glass and polished wood), and with Castle lager on tap. There are discos on Friday and Saturday from around 10pm (Tsh3000), when the dancing continues until daybreak. Open from 3pm; closed Mon.

Lake Hotel Station Rd. A large and dark, friendly and popular old-timers' bar, fitted with satellite TV. There's also a reasonable restaurant (meals around Tsh2500), but eat in the bar rather than in the glum, strip-light-lit dining room.

Mwanza Institute Club Station Rd. Another pleasant and peaceful place, with seats in a shady garden at the back.

New Mwanza Hotel Posta St. The first-floor *Kipepeo Bar* terrace is the city's most reliable venue for live music, with Jambo Stars playing every Saturday (9pm–3am; Tsh3000). There's a casino upstairs.

New Tivoli Posta St. The first-floor streetside balcony attracts workers at the end of the day. Also has food.

Royal Pub Off Karuta St. Popular throughout the day and well into the night, this is an excellent example of a Tanzanian beer garden, and with mellow music to boot. It also does good nourishing breakfasts of chapati and *supu*, and also sells cakes and sweets.

Tilapia Hotel Capri Point. The well-stocked bar here has a great view over the inlet to Bugando Hill and Saa Nane Island, and is the main weekend hang-out for the well-to-do. Big TV screen for sports.

Yun Long Chinese Restaurant Nasser Drive. A lovely place for a lakeside drink, and with good service.

Listings

Air charters Auric Air, corner of Posta and Kenyatta streets ☏ 028/250 0096, ⓦ www.auricair .com; Precisionair, Kenyatta Rd ☏ 028/250 0819, ⓦ www.precisionairtz.com; Renair, Mwanza Airport ☏ 028/256 2069, ⓦ www.renair.com.

Airlines Air Tanzania, Kenyatta Rd ☏ 028/256 1846, ⓦ www.airtanzania.com; Coastal Aviation, Mwanza Airport ☏ 028/256 0441, ⓦ www.coastal .cc; Precisionair, Kenyatta Rd ☏ 028/250 0819, ⓦ www.precisionairtz.com.

Banks and exchange Quickest for cash or travellers' cheques are the forexes at the *Mwanza Hotel* (also Sunday) and Serengeti Services & Tours on Posta St. NBC bank on Nkomo St, and National Bureau de Change, on the same street, give better rates but are slow. Both NBC and Standard Chartered, at the CCM Building by the clock tower roundabout, have 24hr Visa/Master-Card ATMs.

Car rental See "Safari companies", below.

Courier services DHL, Kenyatta Rd ☏ 028/250 0890; Skynet, *New Mwanza Hotel*, Posta St ☏ 028/250 2405.

Hospitals Bugando Hospital, Bugando Hill, top of Würzburg Rd (☏ 028/250 0513), is government-run. Better for non-emergencies is Aga Khan Hospital Medical Centre, corner Würzburg and Miti Mirefu roads ☏ 028/250 2474.

Immigration Station Rd, before the train station ☏ 028/250 0585.

Internet access Most reliable are Karibu Corner Internet Café, corner of Kenyatta and Posta streets (Mon–Fri 8am–8.30pm, Sat 8am–6pm, Sun 9am–5pm), and Barmedas.com, Nkrumah St

(Mon–Sat 8am–8pm, Sun 9am–8pm). Both charge Tsh1000/hr. Access also at the post office, and *Tilapia Hotel*.

Library Mwanza Regional Library, Station Rd (Mon–Fri 9am–6pm, Sat 9am–2pm; Tsh500 daily membership).

Mechanics There are lots of car workshops along Pamba Rd, and spares at the Land Rover garage at Fourways roundabout, between Station and Kenyatta roads.

Pharmacy FDS Pharmacy, *New Mwanza Hotel* building, Posta St (☏ 028/250 3284), is reasonably well stocked.

Police Customs Rd outside the ferry port.

Post office Posta St; branch also at Pamba Rd near the bus stand.

Supermarkets Mwanza's supermarkets are expensive. Imalaseko, CCM Building by the clock tower, has the best selection. Try also JJ Minimarket on Station Rd.

Swimming pools *New Mwanza Hotel* charges day-guests Tsh1000 to use its pool; *Tilapia Hotel* Tsh4000.

Telephones TTCL, Posta St beside the post office. Barmedas.com, Nkrumah St, offers Internet calls: Tsh500/min to the UK, US or Canada, Tsh1000 to most other international destinations.

Travel agents Fourways Travel Service, corner Station and Kenyatta roads ☏ 028/250 1853, ⓦ www.fourwaystravel.net; Serengeti Services & Tours, Posta St ☏ 028/250 0061, ⓦ www .serengetiservices.com; Worldlink Travel & Tours, corner of Nyerere Rd and Nkrumah St ☏ 028/250 0214, ⓔ worldlink.mwz@mbio.net.

Safari companies

Mwanza can be an alternative base to Arusha for **Northern Circuit safaris**, since it's better placed for Serengeti and has good connections to the little-visited bird haven of Rubondo Island National Park. Prices depend on the cost of car rental and the style of accommodation used. A "budget" camping trip starts at $150 per person per day. Plain **car rental** averages $150–200 per day, depending on the distance covered, for a 4WD with driver, fuel, and the driver's expenses (park fees, food and accommodation). Self-drive outside Mwanza is generally not possible. The following companies are licensed for safaris; it's worth shopping around, as none have fixed prices.

The Sukuma

The lake's southern and eastern hinterland, strewn with impressively eroded granite boulders, is the land of the six-million-strong **Sukuma**, Tanzania's largest tribe. Their long-horned Ankole cattle – startlingly different from the short-horned Maasai race – provide the first inkling that central Africa is near. But the region is far from being a rural Nirvana: the area is notorious for its modern **witch-slaying** tradition, usually poor old ladies with red eyes caused by one too many years of hunkering over smoky kitchen fires. In Shinyanga Region alone, one old woman has been murdered every day, on average, since the mid-1990s. Fear of witchcraft is part of the problem, but so is greed for land: an old lady's soil, once inherited, may yield more than just crops: **diamonds** have been mined in the region since the 1920s, and the region's **gold reserves** – currently exploited (in every sense of the word) by foreign mining corporations – are also staggering.

Whilst the slayings are the most notorious facet of Sukuma superstition, the age-old Sukuma belief in magic is also more cheerfully expressed through **dance competitions**. Held in June and July, and sometimes also in August after the harvest that follows the long rains, they're particularly exuberant examples of a successful synthesis between old and new. The two oldest **dance societies** (*wigashe*), both of which perform annually at Bujora, are the Bagika and Bagalu, founded in the mid-nineteenth century by **rival healers** (good witches, if you like), Ngika and Gumha. As the two could not agree about which of them had the most powerful medicine (*dawa*), a dance contest was organized to decide the issue.

The format, which remains unchanged, is for two competing dance societies to perform at the same time, with the crowd being free to move between the two. The better the medicine, the bigger the crowd. Obviously, good preparation is the key to success, and nothing is more important than **good luck medicine** (*samba*). This is dispensed by each dance society's healer (*nfumu*), and is intended to make the dancers, especially the dance leader (*mlingi*), appealing to the crowd. The *samba* can be applied in many ways – buried or placed on the dance ground, worn in amulets, applied to the body in a lotion, rubbed into skin cuts or inhaled through smoke. Given that crowd size is the key to success, each passing year sees new and innovative dance routines, tricks and costumes – in 1995, one group won by using a toy plastic monkey given by a Japanese traveller. Others used articulated wooden puppets as props, others stilts or fire breathing, while all dancers possess the most outrageous gymnastic agility. Although dance moves and lyrics change annually, there are some enduring favourites, notably the *Bugobugobo* **snake dance**, a speciality of the Ngika Society, hugely theatrical affairs starring live pythons.

The dance contests are best experienced at Bujora's two-week **Bulabo festival** following the Christian festival of Corpus Christi (usually early or mid-June). Alternatively, the Sukuma Museum at Bujora can arrange dances at any time of year. **Tapes** of traditional Sukuma music (*ngoma*) can be found in Mwanza if you're particularly determined, and more easily at Radio Tanzania in Dar es Salaam (see p.124).

Dolphin Tours & Safaris Corner of Posta and Kenyatta streets ☎028/250 0096, ⊛www.auricair .com. Reliable and keenly priced Northern Circuit safaris by road or light aircraft (the company is owned by a charter airline), plus various Ugandan options, including a four-night white water rafting trip on the Nile, flying there and back from Mwanza, for $555–750. Straight 4WD rental costs $80/day including 150km, driver and driver's allowance, but excludes fuel; the same but with a camping vehicle (a tent folds out of the bodywork) costs $150/day.

Fortes Car Hire Lumumba Rd, near Karuta St ☎028/250 1804, ⊛www.fortessafaris.com.

Primarily a car rental firm, the fact that it has its headquarters in Arusha is very useful if you want to cover the Northern Circuit without having to backtrack to Mwanza.

Worldlink Travel & Tours Corner of Nyerere Rd and Nkrumah St ☏028/250 0214, ℮ worldlink.mwz @mbio.net. A general travel agent able to arrange pretty much anything, including gorilla trekking.

Around Mwanza: the Sukuma Museum

The **Sukuma Museum** (Bujora Cultural Centre, Mon–Sat 8.30am–6pm, Sun 1–6pm; ☏0748/592172) at Bujora makes an excellent day-trip from Mwanza. Eighteen kilometres east of the city just off the Musoma highway, it covers in great detail the culture and traditions of Tanzania's largest tribe, the Sukuma. The museum is in the compound of the **Bujora Catholic Mission**, founded in 1952 by a Canadian missionary, Father David Clement. Clement's open-minded approach saw Sukuma music, dance and history introduced into the mission's religious services, and is also reflected in the mission's **church**. Modelled on Sukuma lines, it has a round peaked roof resembling a traditional Sukuma house, and is decorated inside with symbols of chiefly power: the altar is in the shape of a royal throne, and the tabernacle resembles a chief's house (*ikulu*), complete with a shield and crossed spears on the door.

The **museum** entrance is marked by a monument depicting a painted royal drum placed on a bas-relief map of Tanzania. The exhibits, which cover every aspect of Sukuma life from the humdrum to the ritual, sacred and chiefly, are contained in a number of startlingly designed and colourfully painted pavilions. A reconstruction of a traditional family house and compound incorporates material artefacts from daily life; the thatched dwelling of the blacksmith (*malongo*) contains the tools of his trade, as does the replica of a traditional doctor's house (*iduku*). The "Dance Society Pavilion" has a wealth of information on the competing Bagika and Bagalu dance societies, whilst Sukuma history is presented in the "Royal Pavilion", designed in the form of a royal throne and containing a mass of genealogy, as well as royal drums, fly whisks, headdresses and other objects donated by the descendants of former chiefs.

Practicalities

Buses and daladalas run approximately every half-hour from Mwanza to Kisesa, 16km along the Musoma road. The museum is a 2km walk north of here – turn in at the sign for "Shule ya Msingi Bujora". A taxi from Mwanza won't cost more than Tsh10,000, though the driver may need convincing to cover the last 2km from Kisesa. **Accommodation** is available at the centre, either in small rooms with nets (❷, or ❸ full-board) or at a large campsite (Tsh1500 per person).

The MV Bukoba disaster

Eleven kilometres along the Musoma road from Mwanza, just before Kisesa, is a small gate on the left surmounted by a scale model of a ferry, the **MV Bukoba**. Grossly overloaded and badly maintained, it capsized near Mwanza on May 21, 1996. Most of the passengers were trapped inside the hull as the ship keeled over. Some were rescued through a hole burned into the hull by rescue workers, but a second hole proved catastrophic: air trapped in the hull escaped, the vessel lost its buoyancy and disappeared beneath the calm surface of the lake. The graveyard behind the gate contains the remains of some of the victims; the exact number of fatalities was never established, but was somewhere in the region of 550 to 800.

Performances of **traditional drumming and dancing** can be arranged with a day's notice (Tsh40,000), and you can take lessons in traditional arts. For more about the museum and its activities, log on to Ⓦ www.mwanza-guide.com /bujora.htm or Ⓦ www.photo.net/sukuma, the former with practical information, the latter featuring hundreds of jaw-droppingly gorgeous photographs and reams of text.

Ukerewe and Ukara Islands

Lake Victoria's largest island is **UKEREWE ISLAND**, due north of Mwanza and separated from it by Speke Gulf. Nicknamed "U.K." by locals, this densely populated island of low wooded hills, craggy outcrops, granite boulders and subsistence farms is the district capital of an archipelago comprising 26 other islands and islets, including **Ukara Island**. Despite its proximity to Mwanza, Musoma and the tourist traffic in the Serengeti, these islands are among the least-known areas in Tanzania. Don't come expecting anything really exceptional – there are few sights apart from the views – but do expect to encounter a kind of rural Arcadia that has remained virtually unchanged from before colonial times. The isolation, in fact, is a good part of the attraction, though it makes travelling here – and around the islands – something of an adventure.

Arrival

There are two ways of **reaching Ukerewe**, either by road from Bunda with a short ferry crossing over the narrow Rugezi Channel, or by ferry from Mwanza.

By ferry from Mwanza

Daily **ferries** connect Mwanza with Ukerewe's main town, Nansio, taking two and a half to three hours (seats Tsh3000–3500). From the ferry port at the end of Customs Road, there's the MV *Serengeti* (9am Tues, Wed, Fri & Sun; returning 2pm), which can take vehicles, and the MV *Butiama* (Mon 8am & 4pm, Thurs 9am, Sat 8am & 4pm; returning from Nansio Mon noon, Tues 8am, Thurs 2pm, Sat noon and Sun 8am). The smaller MV *Airbus* departs daily from Kirumba Mwaloni, 3km north of Mwanza, at 2.30pm, having set out from Nansio at 8am.

By road from Bunda

The unsurfaced 83km from Bunda, on the Mwanza–Kenya highway (see p.514) to the ferry at **Masahunga** (or Kisoria) passes through attractive countryside scattered with the small homesteads of the Luo tribe, between which marshy areas attract a wealth of **birdlife**, including grey herons, egrets, marabou storks, vultures, fish eagles and weavers. The trip is a two-hour drive in good weather if you have your own vehicle, or three to four hours by **bus**. Two companies – Bunda Bus and Trans Africa – cover the route daily, continuing on to Nansio after the ferry crossing; Bunda Bus is the more reliable, leaving Bunda every day at 10.30am to arrive in Nansio around 3.30pm. Their office in Bunda is 150m from the highway at the start of the road to Masahunga.

The **ferry** from Masahunga on the mainland to **Rugezi** on Ukerewe takes twenty to thirty minutes and can carry up to six cars (Tsh3000 for a car with driver, Tsh200 for each passenger or pedestrian). The ferry leaves Masahunga daily at 9.30am, 11.30am, 1.30pm, 3.30pm and 6pm, and Rugezi at 8.30am

(Tuesday 8am), 10.30am, 12.30pm, 2.30pm and 5pm. The ferry is met in Rugezi by daladalas going to Nansio. Should you get stranded in Masahunga, there are a couple of hotels (both ❶): the *Bwanza* is very basic; much better is *Deo Guest House*, on the left before the jetty. For food, try the *Tata Taigo Café*, on the right just before the colourful fishing canoes beside the jetty, which serves great *maini rosti* (liver stewed with tomatoes, green peppers and onions).

Information and accommodation

The island's capital, **Nansio**, is one of Tanzania's doziest towns – even the market is a low-key affair. Travellers are rare, and people are quite visibly startled to see tourists. You can **change money** at NMB between the bus stand and the market. There's no Internet access.

Unless you're planning to decamp to the even sleepier "town" of Bwisya on Ukara, Nansio will be your base for the duration as it contains Ukerewe's only guest **rooms**.

Island Guest Inn Posta St, facing the Uhuru Monument (no phone). The cheapest rooms in town, some en suite, and all clean, well kept and with friendly management. They're often full, so arrive early. ❶

Kazoba Lodging & Boarding Posta St, near the *Island Guest Inn* ☏028/251 5146. Quiet and peaceful (indeed almost dull), with basic rooms (some en suite) with nets. Avoid the stuffy singles with no external windows. ❶

Monarch Gallu Beach Hotel 600m west of the ferry jetty on a headland facing Nansio Bay ☏028/251 5303. Not to be confused with the *Gallu Beach Hotel* restaurant that organizes tours, this is Nansio's best lodging, a breezy place on the lakeshore with wide lawns, an attractive view and a bar and restaurant. The rooms (with or without bathroom) are spacious, but overpriced at Tsh20,000 per person. Electricity (from a generator) runs from 7 to 10pm, but there's no running water. Breakfast included. ❺

Eating and drinking

Apart from a couple of *mishkaki* stalls along the main road between the ferry jetty and *Monarch Gallu Beach Hotel*, and a couple of basic cafés at the west end of town, the following are virtually the only places on the island where you can buy **cooked food**. All three also serve alcohol. Other places for **drinks** include *Picnic Villa* (or *Sunset Beach*), 50m from the ferry jetty, which has some tables in a small lakeside garden, and a good number of "groceries": semi-legal joints hidden behind net curtains which cater for the more alcoholically challenged members of society.

Gallu Beach Hotel On the main street, off on the right when walking towards the *Monarch*. Ukerewe's best cuisine (and breakfasts), and with some tables outside under thatched parasols. But the main reason for chewing the cud here is to organize tours, and chat with the manage-

ment, who are knowledgeable about all things concerning "UK".

Monarch Gallu Beach Hotel A nice location, and good meals for around Tsh5000. It's also a civilized place for a drink, with tables under parasols in the garden by the lake.

Exploring the islands

Public transport on the islands is scant, so **hiring a bicycle** is the best way around: ask at Nansio's market, or arrange things through *Gallu Beach Hotel* restaurant (see above; ☏028/251 5094, ✉gallubeachhotel@yahoo. com), the base for a number of enticing **day-trips** around Ukerewe and Ukara. These are organized in collaboration with the **Ukerewe Tourist Association**, whose first objective is to establish a network of sign-

The journey of Lukanga Mukara

The Journey of Lukanga Mukara into the innermost of Germany is the title of a bitingly satirical book by the German explorer and pacifist, **Hans Paasche** (1881–1920), who was posted to Tanganyika during the brutal repression of the Maji Maji Uprising. The book, published in instalments in 1912 and 1913, seems to have been Paasche's way of expunging the guilt he felt about his role in the conflict. In it, an imaginary character from Ukara Island, one **Lukanga Mukara**, recounts his often hilarious impressions of the Fatherland in a series of letters to his chief back home. The following extract, concerning the nature of German women, gives a flavour of his style.

Here it becomes difficult for me to follow things to the heart of the matter. Only this one thing I already know for sure: the women of the Wasungu are artificially deformed and their crippled bodies are dressed in furs, woven material skins and feathers of wild creatures, so that a new figure is created which has nothing in common with the natural, beautiful woman-sculpture as we know it with the Watinku. Nude girls and women are nowhere to be seen, not on the streets, nor at the harvest work. Also, they do not all bathe, and those who do bathe, wear suits and it is not allowed to take a close look at them. Only in the evenings when the Wasungu eat and dance together, the girls are as good as nude and only a part of their body is covered with clothing. They do not dare to come completely without clothes because their body consists of two parts which are only loosely connected and are held together with a stiff outer construction. This construction, they cover up in the evening with a little clothing. But of course, not more than absolutely necessary. If the women did not have this construction they could not walk upright and would collapse. This construction is most likely to be an ancient invention of the men. They forced it onto the women in order to remain superior to them in health and stamina, in spite of their own laziness and bad habits. This frame is designed in such a way that the women cannot breathe, so that a part of the lung rots and dies. They lack the deep breath. Consequently, the women cannot run or move. So the flesh under the frame withers away and the body becomes grossly fat on the upper and lower parts, which is something the Wasungu find beautiful.

Paasche was arrested for treason in 1917, having resigned his commission in the navy, and was locked away as insane in the Berlin Sanatorium. He was released during the chaos of the November Revolution of 1918, but was shot dead in mysterious circumstances in May 1920 after having been anonymously denounced as "a known pacifist and antimilitarist". There's an English translation of Paasche's book on the Internet at Ⓦ www.cs.ucl.ac.uk/staff/a.steed/lukanga.html, from where this extract is taken.

---

posted bicycle routes around the island. They also facilitate volunteering to primary schools for English and maths teachers, and can organize private accommodation: contact the Association's chairman on ☎ 0748/317078 or Ⓔ utalii_ukerewe@yahoo.com.

Tours currently in place include all of the attractions detailed below, organized into neat thematic packages such as "The chiefs of Ukerewe", "Independence and *Ujamaa*", "Heights and Conservation", and, of course, "the Dancing Stone and traditions of Ukara". **Costs** are roughly $20 per person per day, or $40 if there's some driving and there are only two of you. Full details are given on the **Internet** at the excellent Ⓦ www.gallu.net.

Bukindo palace

The closest "attraction" to Nansio is the semi-ruined **Bukindo Palace**, 8km to the north (and 2km north of Bukindo village), and which features on *Gallu Beach Hotel*'s "The Chiefs of Ukerewe" cycling tour. It's a few hundred metres to the right of the road in a stand of trees, but isn't signposted so you'll have to ask directions: ask for Kasale Victor Mazura Rukumbuzya, the grandson of the last king of Ukerewe, who owns the place.

Built in 1928, apparently by an Italian architect named Tonerro, the palace is a grand, colonial-style two-storey construction, surrounded on both levels by a wide balcony. It served as the palace of **Chief Gabriel Ruhumbika** (who died in 1938) and then of his son, **Chief Rukumbuzya**, who was the last king of Ukerewe. After his death in 1981, the palace was abandoned by the family, most of whom emigrated to North America. The gardens, which contain two of the biggest mango trees you're likely to see, have become gloriously overgrown, but the building itself is beginning to collapse. There's talk of renovation, but for the time being it's just a pretty ruin buzzing with the sound of cicadas. Some of the ground-floor rooms are used by a local family: they'll appreciate a tip to show you around, not that there's much to see. To get there, catch a **pick-up** from Nansio to Bugolora, which run at irregular intervals throughout the day.

Handebezyo Museum

Ten kilometres west of Nansio, **Handebezyo Museum** is not so much a museum as a glorified picnic site, but an entertaining excuse for a day-trip nonetheless. The site, to which you'll be accompanied by dozens of hyperactive children, is perched on top of one of several low granite hills in the centre of the island, distinguished by the rather charming christening of its "peaks" after 1960s African leaders: Nyerere, Karume, Kaunda, Kenyatta and Kawawa. Until Independence, the hills were fully forested, having wisely been protected by royal mandate in order to preserve the island's water supply. Sadly, the abolition of tribal chiefdoms after Independence encouraged **tree felling**, so the hills are now bare. The small **cave** at the base of the highest hill was placed under guard by the kings (*watemi*) of Ukerewe, so that their subjects could deposit valuables in cooking pots for safe-keeping – a kind of bank. Concrete steps have been built all the way to the top (at 172m above the lake surface, Ukerewe's highest point), giving sweeping views over much of the island and lake.

Access is easiest via **Mahande**, about 10km northwest of Nansio. If you're driving, head 2km along the road towards Bukindo then turn left at the school. At Mahande, ignore the main road running north–south but continue due west along a less-used road. This crosses a river planted with rice paddies (look for herons, open-billed storks and egrets) before curving right to join another north–south road. Turn right (north), and the site is signposted on the left after 1km. By **public transport**, catch the first daladala from Nansio to Rubya (currently 11.30am) and get off at Mahande, leaving you with a pleasant three-kilometre walk. Ensure you get back to Mahande before 4pm to catch the last daladala on the Rubya–Nansio route, but double-check all times before setting off to avoid getting stranded.

Beaches

Bilharzia is a problem around Ukerewe, though no one seems to know exactly where. The most accessible beaches, such as the one beside the *Monarch Gallu Beach Hotel*, may or may not be infected, so swimming is at your own risk. The only beach that is definitely free of bilharzia is beyond **Rubya Forest** in the far west. Two daladalas cover this route: if you're not planning on camping overnight at the beach, the 11.30am run is your only option, giving you around

Leaving Ukerewe is easiest on the daily **ferries** from Nansio to Mwanza; see p.503. By **road**, the Trans Africa **bus** departs around 7am to catch the 8.30am ferry, followed by Bunda Bus Service at around 9am to catch the 10.30am ferry. If you miss these, catch a **daladala** from Nansio to Rugezi before 3.30pm for the last ferry (but don't bank on transport on the other side). A local departure tax is levied at Rugezi: Tsh50 per person and Tsh200 for a vehicle and driver.

three hours by the lake before the last daladala returns from Rubya (around 4pm); again, double-check times with daladala drivers in Nansio before setting off. If you do camp overnight, the first daladala back to Nansio leaves at 6am. The journey takes just under an hour in good weather.

Ukara Island

Even further off the beaten track is **Ukara Island**, an hour's boat ride north of Ukerewe, and home to the Kara tribe. Like Ukerewe, it's heavily populated and has few attractions you can pin down, other than the isolated rural ambience and a clutch of distant legends.

The most vivid of these concerns the **Dancing Stone of Butimba**, on the western shore, which is a boulder balanced on top of another boulder. The story goes that once upon a time, a man fell into a cave that suddenly opened up beneath the stone. His friend dashed away just in time, but left his footprint for all posterity. Being balanced one atop the other, the topmost boulder can indeed "dance" if pushed in exactly the right way, revealing the "footprint" underneath, although traditionally it only dances when people are singing: Butimba was a sacred place for making offerings.

Ukara and the Dancing Stone are offered as a thirteen-hour **day-trip** by *Gallu Beach Hotel* in Nansio, and this is the recommended approach, but give them two days' notice. If you want to try getting there under your own steam, Ukara Island is accessed by boat from **Bugolora**, on the north side of Ukerewe Island. One DCM minibus and two Hiace daladalas run daily from Nansio, the first leaving around 7am, the last heading back to Nansio at 4pm. If you arrive before 11am, chances are that you'll be able to get a ride on a "ferry" with locals (around Tsh1000 per person). The boat lands at **Bwisya** on Ukara, which has a couple of basic guest houses (**①**) and a beautiful beach. You may be able to rent a bicycle in Bwisya, though it's ultimately more rewarding to get one in Nansio and do most of the 70km round trip by pedal-power. **Returning from Ukara**, there's usually a passenger boat just after sunrise. The boats can't take cars, and there's only one on the entire island.

Mara Region

The eastern shore of the Tanzanian portion of Lake Victoria is part of **Mara Region**, named after the **Mara River**, which rises to the north of Kenya's

Maasai Mara Game Reserve. The river is famed as the scene of the carnage that results every year when massive herds of wildebeest and zebra attempt to cross the raging river on their great migration (see p.471), providing a feast for countless crocodiles, lions and other carnivores. By the time the river approaches the lake, however, it has become one of the most sedate and beautiful of East Africa's rivers, creating a labyrinthine network of lazy waterways bounded by papyrus and reeds. While there's not currently an awful lot to actually do in the region (a cultural tourism programme or two certainly wouldn't go amiss), the area's natural beauty makes any journey here a pleasure in itself.

Musoma

Mwanza's expansion has been at the expense of **MUSOMA**, a small port town located on a peninsula in Mara Bay, 120km south of Kenya. What the town lacks in terms of cosmopolitan delights it makes up with its instantly likeable, laid-back charm, its gorgeous setting and a refreshingly different climate from the strength-sapping humidity of Mwanza. Other than informally arranged **boat trips** to various isles for fishing, bird-watching and just lazing around, there aren't any sights as such, though a walk to the end of the peninsula is always fun, both for the views and for the local **birdlife**, especially waders and raptors which can be found around the papyrus beds that fringe the beaches, kingfishers, and all sorts of wonderful, garishly coloured birds. There are also a couple of small **markets**: one by the lakeshore to the east of town close to where fishing boats are repaired, the other a more generic affair next to the bus stand in the centre.

Unfortunately, **swimming** – although popular with local children – doesn't appear to be terribly safe, despite local assurances to the contrary. The papyrus and reed beds at the waterline offer an ideal habitat for bilharzia-infected blood flukes, so take local advice with a pinch of salt.

Practicalities

The **bus stand**, just off Kusaga Street in the centre, is an orderly affair, and there are taxis on hand. Scandinavian Express have their office and stop on

---

The Lukuba Archipelago

Visible from the west side of Musoma Peninsula is the **Lukuba Archipelago**. It consists of three large islands and several smaller ones roughly 15km offshore, and is traditionally used as a base by fishermen – who account for the twinkling necklace of lights strung across the lake at night. Being too rocky for extensive agriculture, they're rich in wildlife, especially **birds**, and – a rarity elsewhere – **spotted-neck otters**.

Other than informally arranging things with fishermen at Musoma town's eastern beach, there are two ways of **visiting** the archipelago. Either rent a large motorboat for a few hours via *Tembo Beach Hotel* (a bargainable $80–90 depending on where you go; space for up to thirty people), or contact *Lukuba Island Lodge* (☏027/250 2283 in Arusha, ⓦwww.lukubaisland.com) who offer day-trips from Musoma for $40 per person including lunch, for a minimum of four people. The cost of **staying overnight** in one of the lodge's five stone-walled lake-facing bungalows is $235 per person, to which you should add the cost of guided hikes and (expensive) water sports, including Nile perch fishing. There's also a swimming pool and sundeck.

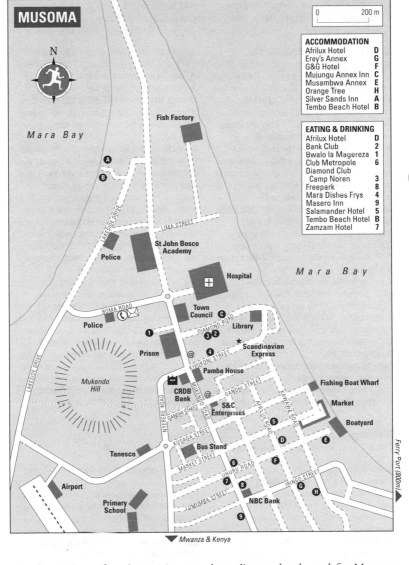

MUSOMA

ACCOMMODATION
Afrilux Hotel	**D**
Erey's Annex	**G**
G&G Hotel	**F**
Mujungu Annex Inn	**C**
Musambwa Annex	**E**
Orange Tree	**H**
Silver Sands Inn	**A**
Tembo Beach Hotel	**B**

EATING & DRINKING
Afrilux Hotel	**D**
Bank Club	**2**
Bwalo la Magereza	**1**
Club Metropole	**6**
Diamond Club Camp Noren	**3**
Freepark	**8**
Mara Dishes Frys	**4**
Masero Inn	**9**
Salamander Hotel	**5**
Tembo Beach Hotel	**B**
Zamzam Hotel	**7**

Mara Bay

Fish Factory

St John Bosco Academy

Police

Hospital

Mara Bay

Town Council

Library

Police

Prison

Scandinavian Express

Mukendo Hill

Pamba House

CRDB Bank

Fishing Boat Wharf

S&C Enterprises

Market

Boatyard

Tanesco

Bus Stand

Airport

Primary School

NBC Bank

Mwanza & Kenya

Ferry Port (800m)

Kivukoni Street. If you're coming on a long-distance bus bound for Mwanza or Nairobi, chances are it'll drop you at **Makutano junction** 10km from town, from where you can catch a shared taxi for a modest Tsh1000. There are currently no scheduled **flights**. Should they resume, the airport is 500m west of the town centre.

Accommodation

Musoma has dozens of **guest houses**, most to the east of Mukendo Road; some grotty, most perfectly sound. Two hotels – *Silver Sands Inn* and *Tembo Beach Hotel*

– are on the **beach**, which might entice you stay longer, even if swimming isn't a very good idea. Both places allow **camping** ($5), the *Tembo*'s sandy, unfenced plot being preferable. The following include breakfast unless otherwise noted.

Afrilux Hotel Afrilux Rd ☎028/262 0031, ✉afriluxhoteltz@yahoo.com. At four storeys Musoma's highest building, this is also the town's largest hotel, and the best mid-range choice, albeit pretty impersonal. Rooms are en suite, most with cable TV, and those from the upper floors have good views of Mara Bay. There's also a bar and restaurant, room service and safe parking. ❹

Erey's Annex Iringo St (no phone). A modern two-storey building with eight tiled en-suite rooms: three twins and five smallish singles (which can be shared by couples), all spotless, and with TVs and round nets. Fine, if a little soulless. ❷

G&G Hotel Uhuru St ☎028/262 0601, ☎028/262 0602. Another bland but adequate option, the better rooms on the first floor, all with box nets, TVs, phones, decent bathrooms and hot water. There also a reasonable restaurant, a bar, and safe parking. ❸

Mujungu Annex Inn Diamond Rd ☎028/262 0017, ✉mujunguinn@yahoo.com. Cheap, clean, calm and obliging family-run guest house, all rooms en suite, the better ones with TVs, all with big beds and adequately sized box nets. As with all the cheaper hotels, they have water problems. Secure parking. ❷

🏃 **Musambwa Annex** Uhuru St, next to where fishermen pull up their boats ☎028/262 0190. A good compromise for being close to the lake and in town, this calm, friendly and good-value place has nine en-suite rooms, seven of them singles that can be shared by couples. The bathrooms and Western-style toilets are well kept, there's reliable electricity, and a TV lounge. ❶

Orange Tree Kawawa Rd ☎028/262 0021. Clean rooms with or without bathroom, a sleepily attractive saloon-style bar with a TV, and food (wait up to an hour). ❷

Silver Sands Inn 1km north of town, off Lakeside Drive ☎028/262 2740. Occupying a large scrubby plot, the location's the thing here, with lovely views west over Mara Bay (albeit through a fence; the beach on the other side is popular with kids). The rooms, with showers and Western-style toilets, are generally fine but check the mosquito nets for size and holes, and the condition of the bathroom: the better ones are further along the corridor. Beers and sodas available, but food is limited to *chipsi mayai*. Breakfast not included. ❶

🏃 **Tembo Beach Hotel** 1km north of town, two plots from *Silver Sands Inn* ☎0741/264287, ✉tembobeach@yahoo.com. What recommends this is the fenceless location right on the (grey sandy) beach. There are six spankingly new en-suite rooms in a graceless two-storey block. All have side-on views of the beach and bay from their windows, and one also has front-facing views. Also has a bar (tables on the sand) and meals in the *kuku na chipsi* tradition (Tsh3000). No single rates. ❸

Eating

There's not a big choice for **food**, but what there is is good.

Afrilux Hotel Afrilux Rd. Relatively upmarket and expensive, with a huge menu (including Indian dishes), and shady outdoor seating.

🏃 **Mara Dishes Frys** Kivukoni St. Escape from *chipsi*-land: this self-service place cooks up big vats of inexpensive traditional food including a tasty brown *ugali* made from cornflour and cassava, banana *matoke*, and good bean, liver and tripe stews. Tsh2500 will get you fed handsomely, and a soda or juice. No alcohol.

Masero Inn Mukendo Rd. A slightly tawdry bar and guest house by night, by day the ladies dish up some truly delectable finger-licking whole broiled fish (Tsh1500 with *ugali*).

Salamander Hotel Corner of Market St and Afrilux Rd. A great local place, both for snacks (including Musoma's take on a *kababu*, a meatball wrapped in a pancake), and combo-plates of tasty African food, whether fresh fish, meat, chicken or liver, all for Tsh800–1500. No alcohol.

Zamzam Hotel Mukendo Road. A little place with brusque service (and oft-unsteady clients from nearby bars) but great *supu ya samaki* in the morning – a fishy broth containing a great chunk of tilapia. No alcohol.

Drinking and nightlife

Most **bars** also serve limited food; often good for *nyama choma*.

There are neither scheduled flights nor ferries (formerly to Kisumu in Kenya) from Musoma. Should they resume, the **airport** is 500m west of town at the end of Kusaga Street, and the **ferry port** 2km southeast of town.

Most minor **bus companies** have offices at the bus stand, while the larger ones have their offices on Uhuru Street either side of Mukendo Road, and Scandinavian Express (℡028/262 0006) have theirs on Kivukoni Street. There's transport to **Mwanza** every half-hour or so from 6am to around 3pm (Scandinavian leave around 7am, but you can't buy tickets the day before; VIP at 9am is fine, but avoid Zuberi), and frequent daladalas to **Tarime** and on to Sirari on the **Kenyan border**, where you can catch a *matatu* (daladala) to Migori or Kisii, or a bus to Kisumu. The border formalities don't take too long, though you'll need to pay the $50 visa fee ($20 if you're in transit) in cash if you don't have one already. Scandinavian run daily to Nairobi (you can buy those tickets in advance).

For **Arusha**, you have three options. Quickest is straight through Serengeti and Ngorongoro (add $100 in entry fees to the Tsh18,000 fare). There are buses most days at 5am: the better companies are City Mist, Kimotco and Mtei Express. Just as expensive is to stay on the sealed road and go through Kenya (add $70 in visas). The safest companies are Scandinavian (see above) and, considerably cheaper, Akamba – but the latter only have an office in Mwanza – both leave in the afternoon. Much cheaper is to go to Mwanza and catch a bus via **Shinyanga** and **Singida** from there.

Bank Club and **Diamond Club Camp Noren** Diamond Rd. Two adjacent bars, rather run-down but still popular. *Bank Club* has a pool table and food (*nyama*, *supu* and *mtori* banana soup), and both can have lively weekends.

Bwalo la Magereza (Prisons Club) Beside the prison off Mukendo Rd. A friendly, partially outdoor place frequented by prison wardens, with good food and music. The inmates are often seen around town working in (unchained) chain gangs.

Club Metropole Mukendo Rd. The only real nightclub, jumping from Friday to Sunday (admission Tsh1500; women free).

Freepark Down a little cul-de-sac off Mukendo Rd. A great place to meet people; in addition to a wide range of drinks and bar food (succulent grilled goat meat and bananas, or *ugali* with chicken), this has tables under shady trees – lovely by day, and atmospheric at night.

Tembo Beach Hotel Off Lakeside Drive, 1km north of town. If it's beach you're after, this – or adjacent *Silver Sands Inn* – is the place. Apart from cold beers and sodas, there also basic but good food, and they can rustle up *nyama choma* and sandwiches. The tables are on the beach.

Listings

Airlines The agent for Precisionair and Air Tanzania is S&C Enterprises, Gandhi St ℡0741/264294.
Banks CRDB and NBC, both Mukendo Rd; NBC charges lower commission and has a 24hr Visa/MasterCard ATM.
Internet Koko Internet Café, Mukendo Rd (daily 8am–7pm); Musoma Communications Centre,

Gandhi St (same hours); both Tsh1000/hr.
Telephones TTCL at the post office, Boma Rd. The bus station has call offices, and there are card phones at the *Afrilux* and *Orange Tree* hotels. Cheaper Internet phone calls can be made through Musoma Communications Centre, Gandhi St.

North to Kenya: Tarime

Heading north from Musoma, the landscape becomes hillier and very beautiful as the road drops down into the valley of the Mara River, which begins

Straddling the border with Kenya, the ancestors of the **Kuria tribe** were among the first Bantu-speaking peoples to have settled in East Africa, possibly over two thousand years ago. Although traditionally cattle herders, larger and more power-ful groups – such as the Luo on the lakeshore, and the Maasai in the plains – have restricted the Kuria to the hill country just east of **Lake Victoria** and forced them to adopt a settled, agricultural way of life. Nonetheless, cattle remain ritually important, especially in marriage negotiations, where hefty dowries – paid for in cattle – remain the norm. Rainfall is generally favourable, allowing the cultivation of cash crops such as coffee, sugar cane, tobacco and maize. Another cash crop is **marijuana** (*bangi*), which serves the same purpose as locally brewed beer elsewhere, being taken communally by elders when discussing tribal affairs. Disputes over marijuana-producing areas, however, have been the main cause of recent and bloody clashes between rival clans, which have claimed dozens of lives.

Music and dance accompany almost every traditional ceremony and rite of passage for the Kuria, especially weddings and circumcisions, and also serve as entertainment in their own right. The music itself is characterized by one of Afri-ca's largest lyres, the *iritungu*, which gives a distinctly metallic timbre, the strings' deep and resonant buzzing providing a hypnotic impetus. For more information about Kuria music and culture, see ⓦwww.bluegecko.org/kenya/tribes/kuria, which includes music from the Kuria, as well as the Luo and Maasai, and has full-length sound clips. You can also buy tapes locally, and at Musoma's bus stand.

---

life north of Kenya's famous Maasai Mara Game Reserve. Much of the valley here is occupied by the **Masura Swamp**, consisting of extensive papyrus beds through which the river meanders. The river marks the southern border of Tarime District, an area of rolling hills scattered with small homesteads and plenty of granite crags, outcrops and boulders, the latter sometimes balanced on top of one another. The drive is the main reason to come to the friendly hill-top agricultural town of **TARIME**, 24km south of the Kenyan border, which is the main market town for the **Kuria tribe**. Although there are abso-lutely no "sights" as such, the main attraction are the Kuria themselves, who – despite modern attire – have kept much of their traditional culture intact; see box above.

Tarime lies 4km to the east of the highway into Kenya. **Daladalas** run roughly every hour from Musoma and Sirari, on the Kenyan border, pulling in at the bus stand one block south of the market. There are some **guest houses** around the market, but better are the handful of places back along the road towards the highway (Nyerere Road). The best is the friendly *AMA Hotel*, 300m from the bus stand (☎028/269 0371; ❷), with eight en-suite doubles, all with TV, fan and net, plus a garden bar and a good restaurant. A little cheaper is the *CMG Motel*, 450m from the bus stand and then 500m along Ngombe Road (☎028/269 0149; ❷), with large and bright en-suite rooms, each with two beds, running hot water in the morning (and in buckets in the evening), a nice garden, and also food. NMB **bank** is on the south side of the bus stand – be patient.

South of Musoma

The hilly country inland from the lake between Musoma and Tarime to the north and Serengeti's "Western Corridor" to the south is home to several small

Tanzania's first and much-loved president, **Julius Kambarage Nyerere**, was born in 1922 to a chief of the small Zanaki tribe in Mwitongo village, near Butiama, when Tanganyika was under British rule. Nyerere was educated at Tabora Secondary School in central Tanzania and at Uganda's celebrated Makerere College before going on to study history and economics at Edinburgh University. He returned to Tanganyika in 1952, where he became leader of the pro-independence **Tanganyika African National Union** (TANU). In this capacity, Nyerere preached a creed of non-violence and succeeded in securing Tanzania's peaceful transition to Independence in 1961 (in sharp contrast to neighbouring Kenya, whose road to freedom was long and bloody), following which he was elected Tanganyika's first president. Affectionately known to Tanzanians as **Mwalimu** ("Teacher") and **Baba wa Taifa** ("Father of the Nation"), his unpretentious, softly spoken and light-hearted style (his wonderful smile features in pretty much every photo ever taken of him) perfectly complemented his political vision of tolerance, courtesy, modesty and non-violence, words that could equally be applied to the nation as a whole.

Nyerere's legacy is mixed, however. His decade-long experiment in self-reliant "African socialism", **Ujamaa** (see p.733), ended in economic disaster, while his insistence that Zanzibar remain part of the 1964 Act of Union that created Tanzania is seen by many, especially in Zanzibar, as a mistake. Nonetheless, the one unassailable achievement over his 24-year tenure as president was his role as a nation builder. From 129 different tribes, he forged a cohesive state completely free of the divisive tribalism that has plunged many other African countries into chaos.

Nyerere died of leukaemia at St Thomas' Hospital, London, on October 14, 1999, and is buried in the family graveyard close to the museum in Butiama. He ranks with Nelson Mandela as one of the twentieth century's great African statesmen.

tribes, most of them agricultural. One of these tribes (the Zanaki) provided Tanzania's first president, **Julius Nyerere**, who was born – and is now buried – in the town of **Butiama**, where there's a museum dedicated to his memory. East of here is an infrequently travelled dirt road offering access to Serengeti's remote **Ikoma Gate**.

Butiama

Apart from Musoma, Mara Region's other major town is **BUTIAMA**, about 45km southeast of Musoma, which would be an unremarkable place were it not the birthplace of Tanzania's revered founder, **Julius Kambarage Nyerere** (see box above), whose life is commemorated by the **Mwalimu Julius K. Nyerere Memorial Museum** (daily 9.30am–6pm; $3), which opened in July 1999, a few months before his death. The guided tour (included in the entry fee, though a tip is always welcome) starts with a short talk about the president's life before you're taken around the exhibits. These are a mixture of personal items like clothing, shoes, his favourite (and very battered) radio, presents from official tours and archival material documenting his presidency, including plenty of photos, an *Ujamaa*-style Makonde carving (see p.242) depicting the founding members of TANU who had spearheaded the drive to Independence, and an oddly beautiful set of carved plaques commemorating the 1978–79 Kagera War with Idi Amin's Uganda. You should also be able to visit his **grave**, close to the museum, which has been enclosed in a mausoleum, contrary to his wish to be buried in a simple manner.

Access by **public transport** is easiest from Musoma, from where daladalas run every hour or two; the visit can be done as a half-day trip. If you're driving from Musoma, head along the sealed road towards Mwanza. Ignore the first signposted junction to Butiama (which leads you along 17km of bad road) and take the second instead, leaving you with only 11km of rough road. The museum itself is signposted at several places along the highway, but these disappear in Butiama itself, so you'll have to ask: it's at Mwitongo, about 1km west of the centre along a tree-lined avenue that passes a transmitter mast. Hang around, or ask at the army base just before the museum, and the curator will come to let you in. Butiama has a few simple few places to stay and eat.

Bunda

The bustling town of **BUNDA**, on the Mwanza–Musoma highway 30km north of Serengeti National Park's Ndabaka Gate, owes its importance to a couple of unsurfaced side roads which originate here: one heading west to Masahunga and the ferry to **Ukerewe Island** (see p.503); the other running east around the northern boundary of **Serengeti** to the park's Ikoma Gate, east of Bunda (described below).

The **bus stand** is about 1km west of the highway. There's no shortage of good, cheap **accommodation**, the best being the friendly *Bhukenye Bar & Guest House* (no phone; ❶): from the bus stand head north, and then first right back towards the highway, and it's on the second road left (signposted). From the highway, take the side road by the post office (look for the transmitter) and then the third right. Some rooms have bathrooms (bucket showers and spotlessly clean squat toilets), and there's a friendly bar at the front which also serves roast meat, chips and omelettes. There are plenty more choices lining the Mwanza–Musoma highway, including *CN Hotel* at the north end of town (☏028/262 1298; ❸), which has en-suite rooms with fans, nets and clean Western-style bathrooms. The town's only real **restaurant** is the *A&B Restaurant*, behind *Hotel Inchage Galaxy* and the NMB bank, 50m east of the highway. It has a big choice of Tanzanian food (superb *pilau*, good liver stew and delicious stewed fish), and nothing costs over Tsh1500. There's a good **bar** at the *Hotel Inchage Galaxy*.

Nyamuswa and Issenye

The *murram* road east from Bunda to Serengeti's Ikoma Gate (the turn-off isn't signposted, so you'll have to ask) passes through a rural area full of small villages, cassava fields, mango trees and banana plantations – rainfall, as you can tell, is uncommonly reliable in this corner of the country. **NYAMUSWA**, 24km from Bunda at the junction of a minor road to Butiama, is the first settlement of any size. There are basic **rooms** at *Wakuru Guest Bar & Hotel* (❶), 50m from the junction by a huge amarula tree under which the village's elderly *wazee* (elders) like to while away the day.

The next major town is **ISSENYE**, the end-point for most of the pick-ups from Bunda. There's **accommodation** in several cheap guest houses on the main road and at the *Issenye Serengeti View Campsite*, situated in the grounds of the Anglican Issenye Secondary School, signposted 2.5km south of the main road. You can either camp here or stay in the school's bizarrely misnamed *Savoy Game Lodge*, which comprises two very basic rooms with nets and shared bathroom. Costs aren't fixed and are treated as donations: Tsh4000 per person is about right. The school is a good base for **hiking**, and the headmaster is happy to fix you up with a suitable pupil as guide. They can also arrange **traditional dance** (*ngoma*) concerts for around Tsh30,000.

The only regular transport along the road from Bunda is the daily **bus** to Mugumu, beyond Ikoma, which leaves Bunda at around 11am. In the other direction, it passes through Issenye at 7.30am. Land Rover **pick-ups** also cover the route from Bunda to Issenye: these leave Bunda after noon, and head back to town the next morning between around 6am and 7am.

Ikoma

Forty kilometres further along the road from Issenye, and roughly 110km east of Bunda, is **IKOMA**, named after the local tribe. It's not a village as such, but rather a collection of small settlements which form part of the four-hundred-square-kilometre Ikoma Wildlife Management Area, one of several buffer zones around the Serengeti. **Public transport** from Bunda is on the daily bus for Mugumu, which leaves Bunda at around 11am and passes through Ikoma on the way back at around 6am. There's **accommodation** at *Ikoma Bush Camp*, 3km outside the park's Ikoma Gate; it's reviewed on p.475. They also have a **campsite**: $20 per person, including a $10 conservation fee.

Apart from wildlife safaris, either on foot or by vehicle (see p.475), other possible excursions include the ruins of **Ikoma Fort**, situated on top of the most easterly of the Nyabuta Hills. The fort was built by the Germans in 1900 and controlled by them until 1917, when it was shelled and taken by a Kenyan detachment of the King's African Rifles. The nearby **Ikoma Refuge** comprises a series of stone walled corrals where the Ikoma and their cattle used to hide from advancing Maasai. With more time, you could also visit **Nyagoti gold mine** (a 64km round trip from Ikoma); officially abandoned, the mine is still worked by locals using traditional methods – they'll happily sell you nuggets, should they have found any.

Kagera Region

The thickly forested hills, raincloud-filled skies and vibrant red laterite soil of **KAGERA REGION** in Tanzania's far northwest provide a very welcome, beautiful and truly tropical contrast to the unremitting scrub of central Tanzania. However, mere mention of the region sends a shiver down many a spine: bordering Rwanda and Burundi as well as Uganda, Kagera has become synonymous with armed incursions and rebel attacks. Though Burundi remains unstable, the northern half of Kagera, bordering Rwanda and Uganda, is now safe to visit; if you're worried though, check your government's travel advice for Tanzania and Rwanda (see p.29). Visits are more easily done from the harbour town of **Bukoba**. Connected to Mwanza by passenger steamer, the town is an attractive and lively base, with some delightful beaches and an innovative tour company offering dozens of trips in northern Kagera, including prehistoric rock paintings, and ruined palaces that were part of eight traditional kingdoms.

With more time, there's also the little-visited **Rubondo Island National Park** in the lake's southwest corner to explore – a wonderland if birds are your thing. The park's isolation, and hence inaccessibility to poachers, has also made it a preferred place for relocating species endangered elsewhere, including chimpanzees, black rhinos and even elephants.

The Haya

Properly called Bahaya, the **Haya** of Tanzania's northwestern Kagera Region number around two million people. Their history is complex, mirroring that of Rwanda and Burundi, thankfully without the tragedy of their neighbours.

The region's original inhabitants, whose descendants constitute the Haya's present-day **Iru clan**, were Bantu-speaking farmers and fishermen who excelled in steel production. Excavations have revealed 1500-year-old forges that were capable of producing a higher grade of steel than that produced in eighteenth-century Europe, and using a fraction of the fuel. But the **kingdoms** for which Haya later became famous were founded by aristocratic cattle-herding northern immigrants in the fifteenth or sixteenth centuries, **the Hima**. Imposing a rigidly hierarchical social structure upon the Iru, the Hima feudal kingdoms effectively oppressed the Iru in much the same manner as the Tutsi had dominated the Hutu in neighbouring Burundi and Rwanda. Although the German and British colonial powers tacitly favoured the Hima, rising tensions between the two groups were thankfully defused after Tanzanian Independence. President Nyerere's emphasis on equality and togetherness across all tribes, and his **abolition of traditional chiefdoms and kingdoms**, brought an abrupt but peaceful end to the social divisions that had threatened to go the same way as Burundi and Rwanda, even if some curious stereotypes persist: pale-skinned women (usually the Hima) are still considered more attractive, to the extent that darker-skinned girls frequently resort to skin bleaching creams, sometimes with sadly toxic results. Either way, far preferable to the disasters that engulfed Burundi and Rwanda.

For more on Haya culture, especially music and epic poetry, see the excellent and wide-ranging "The Last of the Bards: The Story of Habibu Selemani of Tanzania (c. 1929–93)" by M.M. Mulokozi, at ⓦ www.iupjournals.org/ral/ral28-1.html.

Bukoba

Tanzania's only major town on Lake Victoria's western shore is **BUKOBA**, a bustling, upbeat and friendly place, even if it's become infamous for the lazy service offered in its hotels and restaurants. Most tourists who come here are generally passing to or from Uganda, but it really is worth hunkering down for a while: the surrounding region contains a feast of attractions, whilst the gorgeous lakeshore location backed by boulder-strewn and thickly vegetated hills, and plentiful birdlife in the surrounding swamps, make it a pleasant destination in its own right.

Arrival and information

The **bus stand** is at the west end of town off Kawawa Street; there are plenty of taxis. The **airport** is near the lakeshore at the end of Aerodrome Road; there are rarely any taxis there, but the walk into town is very pleasant. The **ferry port** lies 2.5km southeast of town. There's a bar and canteen at the port, but beware of pickpockets and thieves. A taxi into town from here costs Tsh2000–3000, but a cheaper and funnier way in, as long as you don't have mountains of luggage, is to catch a **bicycle taxi** for a few hundred shillings. These can also be rented at the bus stand or at the west side of the market.

Bukoba's unofficial **tourist office** is Kiroyera Tours on Sokoni Street (Mon–Sat 8am–6pm; ☎028/222 0203, ⓦ www.kiroyeratours.com), who can recommend hotels, and offer a huge range of trips around Bukoba and Kagera Region – see "Around Bukoba" on p.521.

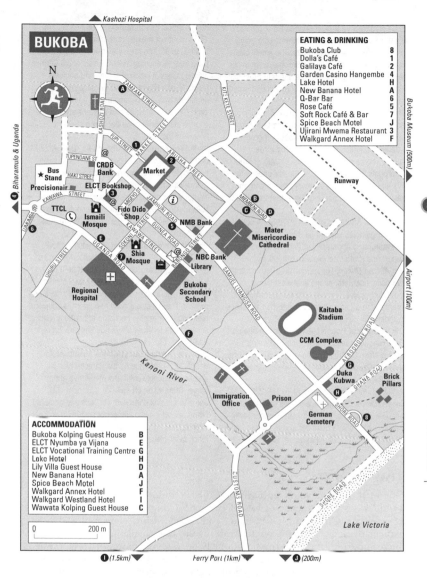

EATING & DRINKING

Bukoba Club	8
Dolla's Café	1
Galilaya Café	2
Garden Casino Hangembe	4
Lake Hotel	H
New Banana Hotel	A
Q-Bar Bar	6
Rose Café	5
Soft Rock Café & Bar	7
Spice Beach Motel	J
Ujirani Mwema Restaurant	3
Walkgard Annex Hotel	F

ACCOMMODATION

Bukoba Kolping Guest House	B
ELCT Nyumba ya Vijana	E
ELCT Vocational Training Centre	G
Lake Hotel	H
Lily Villa Guest House	D
New Banana Hotel	A
Spice Beach Motel	J
Walkgard Annex Hotel	F
Walkgard Westland Hotel	I
Wawata Kolping Guest House	C

Accommodation

The main concentration of budget **guest houses** is on Miembeni Street, about 600m east of the bus stand. Mid-range places are situated closer to the lake, with one right on the shore. **Camping** is possible at the *Lake Hotel* (Tsh3000 per person).

Bukoba Kolping Guest House Miembeni Rd, opposite the *Wawata Kolping* ☏028/222 1461. Secure if dull and not overly welcoming, with eight good en-suite doubles, each with tiled

bathroom, cable TV, fan and telephone. The rooms have two beds, which can be put together. Soft drinks and food (to order) are available. Breakfast included. **③**

ELCT Nyumba ya Vijana Uganda Rd ☏028/222 0069. This Lutheran youth hostel has little going for it other than dirt-cheap rates. The small, clean, cell-like rooms, all sharing bathrooms, have either two or four unduly narrow beds, the latter functioning as dorms (Tsh2000 per person). Food to order. No smoking. ❶

ELCT Vocational Training Centre Aerodrome Rd ☏028/222 3121. Also run by the Lutheran Church, this enjoys large and beautiful grounds with lawns, mature trees and many birds. The 22 rooms range from doubles with shared bathrooms, to en-suite twins (better ones with TVs and box nets) and suites. All are clean and have phones. Safe parking. Breakfast included. ❸–❺

Lake Hotel Shore Rd ☏0744/773956. A colonial survivor going to seed in gardens near the lakeshore, and apparently where Humphrey Bogart and Katherine Hepburn stayed for the film *African Queen*. The rooms, all huge, contain two beds, box nets, phone and washbasin; the better ones have lake views or bathrooms. There's also a basic restaurant and bar. Breakfast included. ❸

Lily Villa Guest House Miembeni Rd (no phone). Cheap and welcoming place. Twin-bed rooms sharing clean bathrooms with surprisingly powerful showers. Check the mosquito nets – some are too small. ❶

New Banana Hotel Zamzam St ☏028/222 0892. Good-value rooms with decent beds and nets, cable TV and phone, and well-kept Western-style toilets. There's also a quiet bar and restaurant, and secure parking. Breakfast included. ❸

Spice Beach Motel On the beach 2km south of the centre ☏0741/451904 or 0741/270795. The breezy lakeside location's the thing here, occupying a neat cluster of old German buildings near a patch of kopjes and boulders facing Musila Island. The six en-suite rooms, double or twin, are big and bright, with box nets, cable TV, clean showers and Western-style toilets. There's also a beachside bar and restaurant. Breakfast included. ❸

Walkgard Annex Hotel Uganda Rd ☏028/222 0626, ⓦwww.walkgard.com. A two-storey business-style option with a range of good-value rooms, all but one with private bathroom. All have TV, hot water and phone, and some also have balconies or fridges. The suite-like doubles come with large beds, box nets, sofa and TV. Breakfast included. ❹

Walkgard Westland Hotel 3km south of town ☏028/222 0935, ⓦwww.walkgard.com. An architectural mish-mash occupying a high bluff overlooking the lake, this has Bukoba's best accommodation, all thirty rooms with cable TV, phone and minibar. There's also a good restaurant, a couple of bars and a swimming pool, and the hotel arranges similar tours to those offered by Kiroyera Tours. Half-board. ❺

Wawata Kolping Guest House Miembeni Rd ☏028/222 1289. Run by the Catholic Church, and with a fittingly calm and meditative atmosphere. There's one en-suite double room (❶), and a single-sex dorm with six beds and a shared bathroom, which you can either rent in its entirety (Tsh9000) or by the bed (Tsh1500). Breakfast and lunch available.

The Town

One of the things you'll notice in Bukoba – aside from zillions of harmless lake flies – is the presence of lots of earnest-looking *wazungu* working for aid agencies and Christian NGOs, many concerned with dealing with AIDS – a particularly acute problem on this side of the lake thanks to the presence of the road into Uganda and the traditionally open sexual mores of Haya women. The aid workers are merely the latest in a long line of *wazungu* – the influence of their predecessors, the European missionaries, is visible throughout town in the form of several very large churches. The biggest and most grandiose is the Catholic **Mater Misericordiae Cathedral** (Africa's first Cardinal, Laurian Rugambwa, was from Bukoba), at the corner of Barongo Street and Samuel Luangisa Road, whose enormous, architecturally adventurous and presumably very expensive concrete spire and roof has obviously brought it close to bankruptcy – construction stopped in 2001 with the structure only half-complete. It currently serves as a roost for a raucous colony of hadada ibis.

Daily life centres around the bus stand and the lively and colourful **market** to its east, right in the middle of town. It's a good place to buy *Robusta* coffee, the region's major cash crop (and cultivated here long before the arrival of the

Europeans), which you might also find prepared for chewing (dried after being boiled in herbs). Also admire the many shapes and colours of bananas, which form local inhabitants' staple food – some are used for steaming, others for stewing, grilling or roasting, and some just for eating raw (the small finger-sized ones, and the big red ones, are usually best).

About twenty minutes' walk east of the market area, along Uganda or Samuel Luangisa roads, is the **lakeshore**, the southern part backed by pretty freshwater swamps full of papyrus and reed beds which are a good place to see water birds. There's also a narrow but attractive stretch of beach between the swamp and the lake – *Spice Beach Motel*, at its south end, is a wonderful base, and has a bar and food. According to locals, **swimming** is safe and bilharzia is said to be absent, though you might like to treat this assertion with a pinch of salt, since the swamps behind the beach could be a possible breeding ground for the parasite-carrying flukes. There are no reports of crocodiles, but be aware that the Ugandan section of the lake saw a spate of crocodile attacks during 2001–2002, and also note that there are hippos in the waters around the rocky **Musila Island**, facing the beach. The island can be visited by boat, most easily through Kiroyera Tours ($7 per person; minimum five people; lifejackets provided).

There's an untended and overgrown **German cemetery** on Shore Road opposite the *Lake View Hotel*, and another reminder of colonial rule at the corner of Shore and Aerodrome roads in the form of **Duka Kubwa** ("Big Shop"). Now mostly abandoned and covered by truly spectacular mosses and dust-encrusted spider webs (as are most of the trees around here – quite surreal), it served as the town's first general store in German times. Also ruined are the three **brick pillars** behind the nearby *Bukoba Club*, which are said to have been built during the 1978–79 Kagera War with Uganda for use as look-out posts (the soldiers simply stood on top), or as firing range observation towers to gauge the accuracy of tank artillery.

Lastly, enquire with Kiroyera Tours about the fledgling **Kagera Museum** (daily 9.30am–6pm; $2), currently north of the airport (walk up Sokoni Street and keep going as it veers right; or take a guide from Kiroyera Tours; $2 per person). It currently contains a collection of traditional tools, Haya artefacts, and an extensive photographic display of the region's wildlife by Dick Persson. If all goes as planned, it could become quite a buzzy cultural centre along the line's of Bujora's Sukuma Village Museum.

Eating

Restaurants in Bukoba close when their supply of food for the evening is finished, meaning that whatever's on offer is cooked in a great big pot, and when it's empty, that's your lot. This means you should either find a place early, or risk encountering locked doors and an empty stomach. The local speciality is **ebitoke** (or *matoke*), a thick banana stew which, when well made, is similar to a sticky potato stew.

Dolla's Café Market St. This has a limited menu of Tanzanian dishes, even fewer of which are actually available, but what there is is good. Full meals, like *pilau* or meat with *ugali* or rice, cost Tsh800–1500. Closed Sat evenings and Sun. No alcohol.

Galilaya Café Arusha St. A small and unassuming place that serves some of the best food in town – it's also pretty much the only cheap place guaranteed to be open at night or on Sunday. Stuff yourself silly with a gorgeously aromatic *pilau*

with steamed or broiled fish, for under Tsh1000. They also have fresh milk (hot or cold) and real juices. No alcohol.

New Banana Hotel Zamzam St. This has a big menu of both Tanzanian and European dishes and is handy for breakfast, though not everything is always available. Meals around Tsh2500.

Rose Café Jamhuri Rd. A long-standing favourite, with good breakfasts and snacks, and simple but filling full meals, including *matoke* and – a sop to

tourists – hamburgers. Daytime only; closed Sun. No alcohol.
Spice Beach Motel On the beach 2km south of the centre. A brilliant location and very good food, served under parasols facing the beach (there's no dining room as such). *Nyama choma* is available all day, but you'll have to wait for stuff from the menu: mains cost Tsh2500–3000.

Ujirani Mwema Restaurant Market St. The large dining room here is popular for quick bites or a cup of tea or coffee, though arriving at a time when they have full meals is pot luck. Erratic hours; closed Sat evenings. No alcohol.
Walkgard Annex Hotel Uganda Rd. The usual – roast chicken, fried tilapia and chips – plus burgers. Mostly around Tsh4500.

Drinking and nightlife

The unfinished (and now abandoned) CCM complex along Samuel Luangisa Road is the unlikely venue for beauty contexts and **visiting bands**; check posters around town for details of upcoming events. It's also worth asking for performances by Bukoba's big star, **Saida Karoli** (of Saida Group), whose song *Maria Salome* was one of Tanzania's biggest hits in 2001, despite being sung in the local language, Kihaya. The local **banana beer** is *olubisi*; distilled, it becomes *nkonyagi* ("Cognac").

Bukoba Club Shore Rd. This former colonial social club is now mainly a bar, charming in a dusty and tattered way (even the trees are encased in spider silk), with seats inside and out in the garden. There's also a snooker table, dartboard, table tennis and lawn tennis. Food is limited to good *nyama choma* and chip omelettes.
Garden Casino Hangembe 3km along the Biharamulo road. Currently the most popular Sunday disco, from mid-afternoon onwards.
Lake Hotel Shore Rd. The lake view from the terrace or the tables on the lawn is the main draw in this calm, dignified and increasingly dilapidated place. Food is available, but isn't up to much.

Soft Rock Café & Bar Corner of Uganda Rd and Sokoni St. One of the better places in the centre, with lots of space and seats in or out, a TV and *nyama choma*.
Q-Bar Lumumba Rd. A busy local bar, even by day.
Spice Beach Motel On the beach 2km south of the centre. A stunning lake view, brisk breezes, sandy shoreline, lots of booze, good food, and it's open until midnight too – languorous bliss.
Walkgard Annex Hotel Uganda Rd. This has a good bar open until midnight – nothing special, but it does the trick – and there's an old-timers' (*wazee*) disco on Saturday.

Listings

Banks and exchange NBC, corner Barongo St and Jamhuri Rd, is helpful and efficient for travellers' cheques, and has a 24hr Visa/MasterCard ATM.
Bookshop ELCT Bookshop, corner of Kawawa and Market streets, has a good book on Haya proverbs, and also sells beads, necklaces, basketry and carvings.
Car repairs ELCT Garage and the adjacent Naushad Auto Works, both on Kawawa St.
Hospital Hospitali ya Mkoa, Uganda Rd ☎028/222 0927, is reasonably well equipped.
Immigration Immigration office on Uganda Rd, ☎028/222 0067.
Internet access Best at the post office, Barongo St (Mon–Fri 8am–8pm, Sat 8am–6pm, Sun 10.30am–4pm; Tsh600/hr). There's also New

Bukoba Cyber Centre at the corner of Kashozi Rd and Tupendane St (Mon–Sat 8.30am–9pm; Tsh500/hr), and Kadé Café beside the ELCT bookshop on Kawawa St (Mon–Sat 8am–5.30pm, Sat 8am–12.30pm; Tsh500/hr).
Library Barongo St (Mon–Fri 9am–6pm, Sat 9am–2pm; Tsh500 daily membership).
Pharmacy MK Pharmacy, opposite *Rosé Café*, Samuel Luangisa Rd ☎028/222 0582; also open Sun.
Post office Corner of Kawawa and Barongo streets.
Supermarket Fido Dido Store, Jamhuri Rd.
Swimming pool *Walkgard Westland Hotel* charges day-guests Tsh2500.
Telephones TTCL, Uganda Rd near the bus station.

Moving on from Bukoba

Heading to Mwanza, it makes sense to catch the overnight MV *Victoria* **ferry**, which sails from Bukoba at 9.30pm on Monday, Wednesday and Friday. The ticket office is at the port 3km south of town. For a $3 mark-up, Kiroyera Tours on Sokoni Street will buy the ticket for you – get it a few days in advance to be sure of a berth rather than just a seat. Tickets cost Tsh21,500 first-class (two bunks per cabin), Tsh19,500 second-class (six bunks per cabin), Tsh16,300 for a second-class seat, and Tsh15,600 in third.

Bus services from Bukoba are sketchy and usually deeply uncomfortable experiences, but if you're up for a lash or two of masochism, note that bus frequencies and schedules change frequently; the following is just a rough guide. For **Biharamulo**, there's a daily bus except Sunday; do catch a bus rather than a daladala, which really *is* painful. For **Arusha** via **Nzega** and **Singida**, Classic Bus is the company, heading off on Tuesday, Thursday and Saturday. The improved road means that the journey now takes one day, with no overnight stop. For **Kigoma** (all 6am), Visram Bus leaves on Monday and Wednesday, and Saratoga Line on Tuesday and Saturday, both arriving before midnight the same day. There are no direct buses to **Mwanza**: change in Biharamulo (next day) or catch the ferry.

Tanzania's only overland crossing into **Uganda** is at Mutukala (Mutukura), 80km northwest of Bukoba. There's the daily Dolphin Bus at 7am for Kampala (roughly six hours), and several uncomfortably packed daladalas and pick-ups every hour or so to the border. Work is currently under way to asphalt the road. **Immigration** can be awkward if the official decides to be, well, officious – be patient and polite. There are money-changers at the border: the rate should be around 1500 Ugandan shillings for Tsh1000. There are no ferries to Uganda.

The only **flights** out of Bukoba are a twice-daily service to Mwanza operated by Precisionair, whose office is on Karume Street (℡028/220 0545 or 0741/316806).

Around Bukoba

Kagera Region is both a political boundary, sharing its borders with Uganda, Burundi and Rwanda, and a natural one, marking the transition from east African flora and fauna, to vegetation more typically Central and West African. It's also a wildly beautiful region, with scattered lakes, hills cloaked in deep forests, impressive escarpments (and caves), and villages built in traditional style with artfully designed beehive-shaped grass houses (*mushonge*) thatched down to the ground. Add in a cornucopia of attractions, from game reserves to prehistoric rock paintings and ruined palaces, and there's more than enough to keep you busy for weeks.

Yet the region sees very few tourists, not least because for much of the last decade, Rwanda's troubles rendered the area too dangerous to visit. With the situation in Rwanda now as normal as it could be given the post-genocidal context, **Kiroyera Tours** in Bukoba (Sokoni St; ℡028/222 0203, ⓦwww .kiroyeratours.com) – owned and ably managed by five local women – offers quite possibly the largest number of trips and activities of any Tanzanian tour operator: a pleasingly bewildering assortment, and with something for all interests, from history and archeology to wildlife, culture and cooking. Itineraries can be customized, and trips extended over several days. **Costs** largely depend on transport: half-day bicycle trips around Bukoba work out very cheap (upwards of $7 per person), while a two-day tour of Kagera's far northwest could easily

△ Ankole horned cattle, Kagera Region

relieve you of $200 per person between transport and game reserve entrance fees. On average, though, expect to pay $25–35 per person per day, plus $35 per group for transport: not especially cheap, but reasonable given the cost of car rental otherwise.

Some sample tours (see Kiroyera's excellent website for more) include **Lake Ikimba**, 40km southwest of Bukoba, which shares a curious Sodom and Gomorrah-style myth with several other lakes around Lake Victoria, in which the disobedience of a newly-wed bride caused the lake to emerge from a cooking pot. The trip includes **hippo-watching** at Engono River. South of here is the steep but climbable **Nyamilyango escarpment**, which has caves, freshwater springs and waterfalls. The trip can be extended over two days to include Muleba Palace, Kishaka Island and tea farms.

The far northwest of Kagera Region is **Karagwe district**, home to Rumanyika and Ibanda Game Reserves, the latter on the border with Uganda and Rwanda at the edge of gorilla country. Trips here include visits to the palace of a famous iron-working monarch, hot water springs, and the sobering **mass graves** of victims of the 1994 Rwandan genocide, whose bodies were fished out along the Tanzanian stretch of the Kagera River. The tour can be extended into **Uganda** for chimpanzee or gorilla tracking (book well in advance).

Other options include **fishing** with locals and **boat trips** to various islands (great for birds), walks through banana, coffee and tea **plantations**, visits to more **palaces** (some ruined) that belonged to the despotic kings of yore, a **pilgrimage** to a Catholic shrine at Nyakijoga where the Virgin Mary put in an appearance in the 1950s, and visits to prehistoric **rock paintings** in natural shelters all around (please read the section on rock art etiquette on p.268).

Biharamulo

Set on a high ridge crowned by an unusually well-fortified **Boma** founded by the Germans in 1902 (now a hotel), the small, lively and friendly town of **BIHARAMULO** – only recently endowed with electricity and direct-dial phones – is a handy overnight stop if you're heading to Bukoba by bus, or are self-driving. It's also a possible jumping-off point for visits to Rubondo Island National Park, via the fishing village of Nyamirembe (see p.525).

Sadly, the three **game reserves** immediately north of Biharamulo – Kimisi, Burigi and Biharamulo – have had their wildlife populations and forests decimated over the last three decades, first during the Kagera War with Idi Amin's Uganda, and then as a result of the conflicts in Burundi and Rwanda; the presence of refugee camps on both sides of the border has placed a destructive burden on bush meat and firewood. All three reserves are effectively out of bounds at present, while locals live in fear of attack by armed Burundian rebels and bandits from both countries; as a result, road travellers are accompanied by armed escort.

Practicalities

The **bus stand** is at the bottom of town on the road in. There are buses to Bukoba on Tuesday, Thursday and Saturday afternoons, and Monday morning, as well as hugely uncomfortable daladalas every morning (get there for 7am to be sure of a seat), though these may only go as far as Muleba, where you'll have to change (plenty of daladalas from there). There's also at least one daily bus (except Sat) between Biharamulo and Mwanza, at 6am. Buses to Kigoma start in Bukoba, and whilst the companies – Visram Bus on Monday and Wednesday, and Saratoga Line on Tuesday and Saturday – have agents at Biharamulo's bus stand, there's no guarantee of a seat until you reach Kibondo, so it might be better starting your journey in Bukoba.

If you're **driving north**, pick up an armed guard at the police post north of town, who will accompany you as far as Kyamnyarwa on the northern boundary of the Burigi and Biharamulo Game Reserves. **Heading south**, there's a good unsurfaced road as far as Lusahunga (31km) at the junction of the sealed road into Rwanda. The road south of here towards Kigoma is in a bad shape until you reach the first of the refugee camps near Kibondo. Depending on the security situation in these and in Burundi, you may have to pick up an armed escort at **Nyakanazi**, at the junction with the sealed road that goes most of the way to Shinyanga. If you get delayed, there are several guest houses in both Kibondo and Kasulu.

Change money at NMB **bank**, 800m uphill from the bus stand. TTCL is nearby; turn left along Makongoro Road just before reaching the bank. The post office is at the northwest corner of the bus stand. There's **Internet access** beside *Robert Hotel*.

Accommodation, eating and drinking

The town has a good spread of cheap **hotels**. Hot water is provided on request in buckets. There's not much in the way of **restaurants**: the best place for food or drinks is *Robert Hotel*; the *Sunset Inn* next door is also fine. Both also do breakfast – try the *supu* broth. **Street food** is limited to roast maize cobs sold at the bus station until around 10pm.

Boma Guest House 1.5km uphill (west) from the bus stand, at the end of the District administration offices ☏ 028/222 3486. Occupying the fortified German Boma, this is Biharamulo's classiest option, if still far from luxurious. Rooms come in pairs: two en-suite rondavels in the courtyard, two singles and two doubles sharing bathrooms, and a couple of "VIP" suites. Breakfast included, but other meals need pre-arranging. ❷–❸

Robert Hotel On the main road facing the bus stand ☎028/222 3432. The best place in the centre (so often full), with en-suite rooms with big double beds, nets and Western-style bathrooms. There's also an excellent beer garden up front,

together with very tasty and cheap grilled goat meat. Breakfast included. ❷

Victoria Guest House ☎028/222 3418. Ntare Road: walk down Mwinyi Street, on the west side of the bus stand, and take the second right. Friendly and clean, and extremely cheap, with good- sized beds and nets, and shared bathrooms (water from buckets). ❶

Rubondo Island National Park

Tucked-in snugly into the lake's southwestern corner, **RUBONDO ISLAND NATIONAL PARK** is one of Tanzania's least-visited and best-preserved wildlife areas. It covers 457 square kilometres, little more than half of which is land, and includes eleven minor islets in addition to Rubondo Island itself. Most of the main island is scattered with the granite outcrops so characteristic of the lake region, and covered by moist evergreen forest – butterfly paradise. The rest is grassland, open *miombo* woodland, sandy beaches and papyrus swamps. The variety of habitats favours high species diversity in both plants and animals, something that is especially evident in **birdlife** – close to four hundred species have been recorded so far. Among the more easily identifiable species are hammerkops, cormorants, Goliath herons, saddle-billed storks, egrets and sacred ibises, kingfishers, geese, darters, bee-eaters, flycatchers, parrots, cuckoos, sunbirds and birds of prey, including martial eagles and the world's highest density of African fish eagles. A particular highlight is an unnamed islet to the east, which serves as a breeding ground for tens of thousands of birds.

In addition to the park's birdlife, a number of **endangered mammals** have been introduced, since the island's isolation makes it inherently safer from poachers. While attempts to introduce black rhinos and roan antelopes haven't met with much success, the introduced populations of elephants, chimpanzees, black-and-white colobus monkeys, suni antelopes and African grey parrots are flourishing and – with the exception of the elephants – can be seen with relative ease. The forest-dwelling **chimpanzees** descend from a population of seventeen individuals rescued from smugglers and introduced in the late 1960s. Most had been kept in cramped cages, some for as long as nine years. It speaks for the adaptability of chimps (like humans) that these ragged survivors apparently had few problems in establishing themselves on Rubondo, and their population now numbers around 35. The chimps are habituated, so can be visited (but see the box on chimp etiquette on p.548).

Of the native species, the undoubted stars (together with the birds) are the amphibious **sitatunga antelopes**, an unusual species with splayed and elongated hooves, though unless you catch a glimpse of one straying into the forest, you probably won't see them in all their glory, as they spend much of their lives partly submerged in the marshes and reed beds along the shore. Other frequently seen native mammals include vervet monkeys, bushbucks, large numbers of hippos and crocodiles and a number of small predators including genets, spotted-neck otters and marsh mongooses. There are no large predators.

The **best time to visit** depends on how important clear skies are to you: the best weather is in the dry season from June to the end of September or October, but butterflies and flowers – most spectacularly forest orchids, fireball lilies and red coral trees – are at their showiest during the rains (Oct–Nov and March–May), at which time migratory birds also arrive in abundance.

Arrival

The easiest access – and not prohibitively expensive if you start from Mwanza – is by **plane**: Coastal Aviation fly to Rubondo every Tuesday and Friday from Arusha ($300 one-way) via Serengeti ($110–165) and Mwanza ($70), heading back the following morning.

The alternative approach, by **boat**, can be divinely awkward. The place to aim for is **Maganza**, 25km north of **Nyamirembe** (itself 43km northeast of Biharamulo), leaving you with a roughly ten-kilometre boat crossing to the park headquarters at Kageye. If you're booked at the upmarket *Rubondo Island Camp* they'll organize the crossing; otherwise either arrange things locally with fishermen in Maganza, or well in advance through TANAPA in Arusha (see p.403). There are two or three daladalas most days from Biharamulo to Maganza via Nyamirembe. There's no accommodation in Maganza, so catch the first **daladala** (currently 11am), which – should you be unsuccessful in arranging a boat ride that day – gives you the chance to catch the last daladala back to Nyamirembe where there's the basic *Maendeleo Guest House* (**❶**), 1km from the lake. Nyamirembe also has a small dairy which makes delicious cheese (Tsh2500 a kilo): it's the last building on your left before the lake.

Information and accommodation

The **park headquarters** are at Kageye, halfway up the island. **Entry fees** are $25 for 24 hours. The park's **Internet** site is ⓦwww.tanzaniaparks.com /rubondo.htm and TANAPA's **guidebook**, available in Arusha, Dar and Stone Town, also covers Lake Victoria.

You have three choices for **accommodation**: a campsite, simple park-run *bandas*, and a luxury tented camp. The campsite ($30 per person) is close to the park headquarters, and offers unnervingly close contact with grazing hippos at night (never position yourself between them and water, which panics them and usually prompts an attack). The *bandas* ($20–30 per person) only have six beds, so you're advised to book ahead at TANAPA in Arusha (see p.403). Bring enough food and drink for the duration whether you're camping or staying in the *bandas*. The upmarket option is *Rubondo Island Camp*, overlooking the lake (book through Tanganyika Swiss Hotels in Switzerland ⓣ+41 32/392 5450, ⓦwww.flycat.com; full-board **❾**), which has ten large, twin-bed tents under thatched roofs between forest and shore, each with attached bathroom, electricity and lake views from a terrace. There's a bar and swimming pool, and bathing in the lake is also possible.

There are no vehicles, so **getting around** the park is either on foot or by boat. **Guides** are obligatory ($15–20 per walk per group). There are several walking trails from the park headquarters, including forest and crocodile and sitatunga habitats. **Boats** for excursions (no more than $50 for a few hours) can be rented at *Rubondo Island Camp* or the park headquarters.

Travel details

Buses, daladalas and pick-ups

The following journey times are minimums; breakdowns, washed-out roads and bridges and prolonged stops play havoc with timetables. Routes that are especially prone to delays and cancellations during the rains are marked with asterisks.

Biharamulo to: Bukoba (4 weekly plus daladalas*; 3–5hr); Kigoma (4 weekly; 12–14hr); Maganza (3 daily; 3hr); Nyamirembe (3 daily; 1hr 30min).

Bukoba to: Arusha via Tanzania (3 weekly*; 16–18hr); Arusha via Uganda and Kenya (2 weekly*; 26–30hr); Biharamulo (1–2 daily plus daladalas*; 3–5hr); Dar via Uganda and Kenya (2 weekly; 34–40hr); Kigoma (4 weekly; 15–18hr); Nzega (3 weekly*; 8–10hr); Singida (3 weekly*; 10–12hr); Uganda border (hourly; 2hr).

Musoma to: Arusha via Kenya (2 daily; 16–18hr); Arusha via Serengeti (4–6 weekly; 9–11hr); Dar via Kenya (2 daily; 25–27hr); Butiama (every 2hr; 1hr 30min); Mwanza (hourly; 3–4hr); Shinyanga (daily; 10–11hr); Sirari (hourly; 2hr); Tarime (hourly; 2hr).

Mwanza to: Arusha via Kenya (6 daily; 18–20hr); Arusha via Serengeti (4 weekly; 10–12hr); Arusha via Singida (1–2 daily; 12–14hr); Biharamulo (2 daily*; 9–11hr); Bunda (hourly; 2hr); Dar via Kenya (3–4 daily; 27–29hr); Dodoma (1 daily*; 22–25hr); Kigoma (1 daily*; 14–18hr); Morogoro (4–5 daily*; 22–27hr); Moshi via Kenya (2–3 daily; 20–22hr); Musoma (hourly; 3–4hr); Nairobi (6 daily; 14–15hr); Nzega (3–4 daily; 10–12hr); Shinyanga (5 daily; 5hr); Singida (2 daily*; 20–22hr); Sirari (hourly; 5–6hr); Tabora (2–3 daily*; 8hr).

Ferries (Lake Victoria)

Bukoba to: Mwanza (3 weekly; 11hr).
Mwanza to: Bukoba (3 weekly; 11hr); Nansio (2–3 daily; 2hr 30min–3hr).

Nansio (Ukerewe Island) to: Mwanza (2–3 daily; 2hr 30min–3hr).

Flights

Airline codes used below are: AA (Auric Air), AT (Air Tanzania), CA (Coastal Aviation) and PA (Precision-air). Where more than one airline flies to the same destination, the one with most frequent flights and/or shortest journey times is listed first.

Bukoba to: Mwanza (PA: 2 daily; 45min).
Mwanza to: Arusha (CA: daily; 3hr 5min); Bukoba (PA: 2 daily; 45min); Dar (AT, PA: 3-4 daily; 1hr 30min-2hr 15min); Entebbe (AA: 2 weekly; 1hr); Katavi (CA: proposed); Kigali (CA: proposed); Kigoma (CA: proposed); Kilimanjaro (PA: 6 weekly; 1hr 20min); Mahale (CA: proposed); Manyara (CA: daily; 2hr 45min); Ngorongoro (CA: daily; 2hr 15min); Rubondo (CA: 2 weekly; 30min); Serengeti (CA: daily; 30min-1hr 15min); Tabora (CA: proposed).

Rubondo Island to: Arusha (CA: 2 weekly; 4hr 5min); Mwanza (CA: 2 weekly; 30min); Serengeti (CA: 2 weekly; 1hr 30min-2hr 35min).

Trains

Mwanza to: Dar (3 weekly; 39hr); Dodoma (3 weekly; 24hr 10min); Morogoro (3 weekly; 31hr 35min); Tabora (3 weekly; 10hr).

Lake Tanganyika and western Tanzania

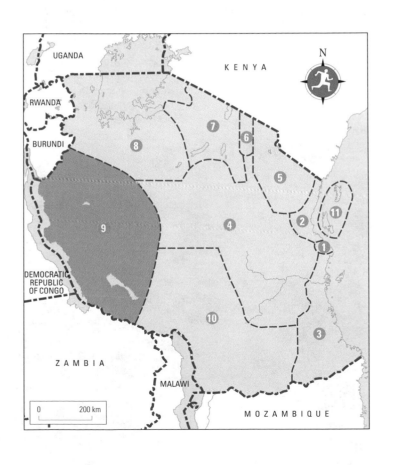

CHAPTER 9

Highlights

* **Ujiji** Now a fishing village, Ujiji was at the start of a 1200-kilometre slave route to Bagamoyo, and where Stanley gave the world those immortal words, "Dr Livingstone, I presume?" See p.536

* **MV Liemba** Lake Tanganyika, the world's second deepest, is best savoured from the venerable MV *Liemba*, an old German troopship. See p.542

* **Gombe Stream** Tanzania's tiniest national park and accessible only by boat; Gombe's chimpanzees have been studied since 1960. See p.544

* **Katavi National Park** A remote wilderness where biomass really looks like it means something as thousands-strong hippo pods gather in the same pool of mud. See p.564

* **Rukwa Region** The Mbizi Mountains and Lake Rukwa offer a glimpse into this enchanting and almost unknown region. See p.570

△ Hippo, Katavi National Park

Lake Tanganyika and western Tanzania

Western Tanzania is as fascinating and rewarding to explore as it can be frustrating to get around, especially during the rains, when most roads become impassable. The region is dominated by **Lake Tanganyika**, which separates the semi-arid *miombo* woodland of Tanzania's Central Plateau from the lush forests of Central Africa. The lake also marks the border with Burundi, Zambia and the Democratic Republic of Congo (formerly Zaïre), and as such is a veritable cultural crossroads. This mixture is best seen in the region's largest town, **Kigoma**, on the northeast shore of the lake, though for tourists Kigoma's main attraction is **Ujiji**, the former slave-trading centre nearby where Stanley and Dr Livingstone famously met. Kigoma is also the starting point for the weekly ferry to Zambia, calling at a string of fascinating places along the way, and the most convenient base for visiting **Gombe** and **Mahale national parks**, both of which contain **chimpanzees**.

Heading away from the lake to the east, the Central Line Railway follows the line of the old caravan routes across the Central Plateau, bringing you to the large and bustling town of **Tabora**. Occupying the historically strategic junction of routes from Lake Tanganyika and Lake Victoria, Tabora controlled much of the **slave trade** in the latter half of the nineteenth century, though like Kigoma it owes its modern importance to the railway. The region **south of Kigoma and Tabora** is seldom visited, mainly because of the difficulty of getting around, although a branch line of the Central Line Railway runs to Mpanda, just beyond which is **Katavi National Park**, dominated by tsetse-fly-infested *miombo* woodland and rich wildlife, especially hippo, buffalo, crocodiles and birds. Further south, **Lake Rukwa** and the **Mbizi Mountains** are completely off-the-beaten track destinations for adventurous travellers, both reached from the area's only significant town, **Sumbawanga**.

Getting around

Travel in western Tanzania is for the most part a wild, adventurous and hugely time-consuming affair. **Language** is limited to Kiswahili and local tongues, though if you really get stuck some bus drivers and hotel managers can usually muster a few words in English. **Road conditions** throughout the region are dreadful. In the **dry season** you can get through to anywhere if you don't mind

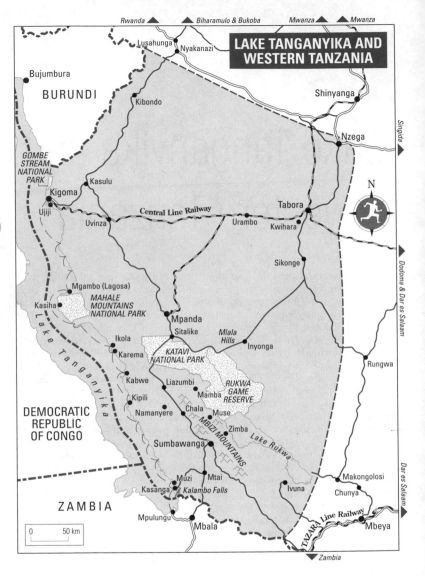

9

LAKE TANGANYIKA AND WESTERN TANZANIA

a slow, dusty, bumpy – and, on public transport remarkably body-crunching – ride. During the **short rains** (Oct–Dec) you can still get to most places but may be delayed waiting for the road to dry out; in the **long rains** (March–May), however, you can forget about roads, as most routes are closed for weeks on end. The only half-decent stretches are between Tabora and Mwanza, and south from Mpanda to Sumbawanga, but these are likely to become impassable if not properly maintained. Wherever you're driving, always seek local advice about the state of the road before heading off, as well as **security**: there's a slight but ever-present risk of attack from armed bandits, especially around Kigoma and northwards. If things are considered risky, you'll be offered armed escorts at roadblocks when leaving towns. The one all-weather route is the **Central Line Railway**, from Dar es Salaam to Tabora and Kigoma, with a southward branch to Mpanda (timetables on Ⓦ www.trctz.com). The land border with **Burundi** is for local traffic only.

Lake Tanganyika

Occupying the southern end of the Western Rift Valley, and bordered by Tanzania, Burundi, Congo and Zambia, **LAKE TANGANYIKA** is the **world's longest freshwater lake**, measuring 677km from north to south. Fed by the Malagarasi and Kalambo rivers on the Tanzanian side, and the turbulent Ruzizi River from Lake Kivu, the lake's maximum recorded depth of 1436m (the lake bottom at its deepest lies 358m below sea level) also makes Tanganyika the **world's second-deepest lake** after Siberia's Lake Baikal, though lake life only inhabits the top two hundred metres, as there's little or no oxygen further down. Covering some 32,900 square kilometres, Lake Tanganyika is also **Africa's second-largest permanent lake** (Lake Victoria is the biggest) and, last but not least, is also one of the **world's oldest lakes**, having been formed around twenty million years ago during the tectonic upheavals that created the Rift Valley. Its great age, size, freshness, ecological isolation and geological and climatological stability have fostered the evolution of a remarkably diverse local flora and fauna. Animals which can be spotted there include various species of crabs, molluscs and crustaceans, the usual hippos and crocodiles, and over 250 species of fish, most of which are small and often brightly coloured cichlids.

The main settlement on the Tanzanian shore is the lively harbour town of **Kigoma**, at the end of the Central Line Railway from Dar es Salaam, which has a weekly ferry south to Zambia via a string of little Tanzanian fishing villages, some of which have road access inland towards Mpanda and Sumbawanga. Ten kilometres south of Kigoma is the old Arab slave-trading town of **Ujiji**, the place where the immortal words "Dr Livingstone, I presume?" were uttered by Henry Morton Stanley. Accessible by boat from Kigoma are two expensive but very special national parks – **Gombe Stream**, and **Mahale Mountains**, both famous for their chimpanzees.

Kigoma

Tucked into the southeastern corner of Kigoma Bay at the end of the Central Railway line, the bustling harbour town of **KIGOMA** is Lake Tanganyika's busiest port, handling most of Burundi's foreign trade and serving as the main arrival point for refugees fleeing Central Africa's interminable conflicts. Head out of town and you're bound to come across a long-term UN refugee camp. In town you'll hear plenty of French, the lingua franca of Burundi, Rwanda and Congo, and many business signs include French translations in addition to Kiswahili and English. The refugee presence also means that people are well used to seeing pale-skinned foreigners, the majority of whom work for one of the plethora of international aid organizations based here.

The town itself is very attractive, its lush tropical vegetation providing a welcome contrast to the monotonous *miombo* woodland which covers much of central Tanzania. For tourists, the town serves as the base for the **Gombe Stream** and **Mahale Mountains** national parks, and for day-trips to **Ujiji**, scene of Stanley's famous meeting with Livingstone. There are also a few beautiful beaches if you want to escape the strength-sapping heat and humidity.

Some history

In the nineteenth century, Lake Tanganyika was the major source of the Zanzibari-controlled **slave trade**. Slaves were captured as far west as the Congo Basin, from where they were transported across the lake to a number of transit centres on the Tanganyikan shore, of which **Ujiji** was the most infamous. For much of this time, Kigoma was a small fishing village, and it wasn't until towards the end of the nineteenth century that its importance grew, just as Ujiji's began to wane. The slave trade was at an end, and Germany controlled much of what is now Tanzania, Rwanda and Burundi. Kigoma's sheltered location inside Kigoma Bay gave it the edge over Ujiji, and the site was consequently developed into the regional headquarters. The town really took off in February 1914, when the 1254-kilometre **Central Line Railway** from Dar es Salaam finally reached the lake nine years after construction had begun, establishing a reliable and rapid connection between the Indian Ocean and Lake Tanganyika which has ensured the town's livelihood to this day. The Germans had little time to enjoy the fruits of their labour however: World War I erupted, and in 1916 they were ejected by troops from the Belgian Congo.

The indigenous population of Kigoma (and of Kasulu and Kibondo districts to the north) is the **Ha tribe**, who number nearly a million. They call their country Buha, which before the arrival of the Germans contained six independent chiefdoms organized into elaborate hierarchies of subchiefs and headmen similar to that of the Haya (see p.516) and Nyamwezi (p.555). Oral traditions state that the Ha have always lived in Buha: if true, it's likely that their ancestors were among the first Bantu groups to arrive in eastern Africa from Central Africa, some two thousand years ago. Over the last three centuries the Ha have developed close ties with Burundi's **Tutsi**. Through intermarriage and commerce, the two tribes have come to share a good part of their language, and the Ha have adopted the Tutsi cattle-herding culture in the grasslands south of Kigoma, where tsetse flies are not so much of a problem. Although primarily still an agricultural people, their long-horn Ankole cattle play a vital social role as tokens of inter-family bonds and friendship, especially in marriage, when cattle are exchanged as bridewealth paid to the bride's family.

Arrival

The easiest way to reach Kigoma is by **train** from Dar es Salaam or Tabora. The **bus station** – for services from Bukoba and Mwanza – is 4km uphill at Mwanga, from where there are taxis (you'll probably arrive too late to catch a daladala). Kigoma **airport** lies 1km beyond Mwanga; Precisionair fly in daily from Dar es Salaam via Tabora, and at the time of writing Coastal Aviation were proposing a clockwise loop from Mwanza via Tabora, Katavi, Mahale and Kigoma.

Daladalas start at the Central Market off Lumumba Avenue. **Taxis** can be rented at the airport, at the bus and daladala stands, and along Lumumba Avenue. Short journeys cost Tsh1000–1500.

KIGOMA

ACCOMMODATION

Aqua Lodge	G
Diocese of Kigoma	A
Community Centre	I
Diplomatic Villa	B
Furaha Guest House	H
Kigoma Hilltop Hotel	C
Lake Tanganyika Beach Hotel	D
Mwanga Hotel	E
Mwanga Lodge	F
Zanzibar Lodge	

EATING & DRINKING

Ally's Restaurant	5
Kigoma Hotel & Guest House	2
Lake Tanganyika Beach Hotel	C
Lake View Hotel	3
Magereza (Prisons) Club	7
Mwanga Lodge	F
New Stanley's Restaurant & Bar	4
Sandra Restaurant & Bar	1
Sangara Restaurant	I
Website Pub	6

Kibirizi (3km) ▲

Colonial Building

BURTON ROAD

School

MWANGA ROAD

Panjatan
@ Bureau de Change

TTCL

Railway Station

TRA Building

Police

DRC Consulate

KAYA ROAD

STANLEY ROAD

Kigoma Port

Ferry Port

Customs & Immigration

Daladalas

LUMUMBA AVENUE

MIDDLE ROAD

Central Market

NBC Bank

Precisionair

UJIJI ROAD

NMB Bank

Kaiser House

BANGWE ROAD

Red Cross

Burundi Consulate

Refugee Reception Centre

TANESCO Power Station

Mahale Mountains Wildlife Research Centre

Lake Tanganyika

H, **I**, Kitwe Point & Katanga ▲

250 m

N

9

LAKE TANGANYIKA AND WESTERN TANZANIA | Kigoma

533

Accommodation

Kigoma's town centre **guest houses** are pretty basic, but fine if you're used to that kind of thing. In better condition are those up in Mwanga district, 3km up Ujiji Road. But as you're on Lake Tanganyika, much nicer – unless you're on a really tight budget – is to stay at one of the three **lakeshore hotels**. In the cheaper places, "single" rooms can be shared by couples, as "double" means two beds. **Water supplies** are erratic, so shower when you get the chance. The town also suffers regular and sometimes prolonged **power cuts** – the better places have generators.

Aqua Lodge Bangwe Rd ☎0744/953429. If it weren't for TANESCO's thunderous electric generator across the road, this beachside place would be especially recommended, though to be fair, with the bedroom door closed, the noise is easily forgotten. The nine twin-bed rooms, all en suite (hot water in the evenings), are reasonably well maintained and face the lake and the hotel's red sandy beach through caged-in verandahs. Food and drinks are available, and the hotel is the base for Sunset Tours, for trips to Gombe and Mahale. Safe parking. ❸

Diocese of Kigoma Community Centre Kiezya Rd, close to the railway station ☎028/280 2520. A friendly and quiet choice with basic and very cheap rooms sharing bathrooms (with rather dingy showers and toilets, though they do have running water). Singles are like cells, doubles (twins) fare little better. The beds are droopy but have mosquito nets, and all rooms have a sink. ❶

Diplomatic Villa 2.5km southwest of town, signposted from Lumumba Ave and Bangwe Rd ☎028/280 4597. Up on a dusty hillside, this is an odd, vaguely colonial-style place, with a nice garden (and *banda* for drinks), and six reasonable if not immaculately tended en-suite rooms in the main house, which you share with the family: big beds and box nets, local TV, fan and window screen. Good food to order, and breakfast included. ❸

Furaha Guest House Burton Rd ☎028/280 3665. Another acceptable and calm central cheapie, all with fans and nets, saggy beds, and clean squat toilets (either sharing or en suite), plus one "special" en-suite room with Western-style toilet. ❶

Kigoma Hilltop Hotel 4km southwest of town on a headland high above the shore ☎028/280 4435

or 280 4436 or 280 4437, Ⓦwww .chimpanzeesafaris.com. Kigoma's poshest by miles, but the electric fence, armed guards and wildlife trophies gracing the lobby hardly make for a happy first impression, and the service isn't all it could be. There are thirty rooms in chalets strung out across the headland, giving spectacular views over the lake from their balconies. All have a/c, satellite TV, phone and fridge. Facilities include two restaurants, swimming pool (with lake views), sandy beach down below, tennis court and gym, and (at extra cost) jet-skiing, water-skiing, parasailing, snorkelling and moonlight cruises. The hotel also runs Chimpanzee Safaris, for trips to Mahale and Gombe. Full-board. ❼

Lake Tanganyika Beach Hotel West of the ferry port, signposted off Bangwe Rd ☎028/280 4894. Enjoying a fantastic lakeshore location (the garden drops right down to the shore), the hotel is set for extensive renovation, which will hopefully not detract too much from its aged charm. Of the standard rooms, all but the singles have lake views (albeit through wire mesh), and cottages are planned. Some should have a/c, the rest fans. There's also a bar and restaurant, and shady tables by the lakeside. Breakfast included. ❸

Mwanga Hotel, Mwanga Lodge and **Zanzibar Lodge** Ujiji Rd, Mwanga (no phone). Kigoma's best budget guest houses, under the same management and within 150m of each other. The beds have big nets, but not all rooms have fans. Bathrooms, either shared or en suite, are relatively clean and have showers and squat toilets. *Mwanga Hotel* and *Zanzibar Lodge* also have restaurants, and some of the latter's upper-floor rooms give glimpses of the lake. All sell soft drinks, and have generator power from 6pm to midnight. ❶–❷

The Town and around

Kigoma's most impressive building is the German-built **railway station**, completed shortly after the Central Railway arrived in 1914, and which boasts a colonnaded first-floor balustrade with horseshoe arches. According to some sources, **Kaiser House**, 700m southwest along Bangwe Road, is connected to the station by a tunnel, which is plausible given that it was constructed just after the outbreak of World War I. It's now where the President stays when in town, and comes complete with painted red "carpet" up the staircase (no photography).

Heading along Lumumba Avenue from the station, about 2km along behind the CCM building on the right is the neglected **Church Missionary Society graveyard**, adjacent to a similarly overgrown Muslim cemetery. Among the graves are those of reverends J.B.Thompson and A.W. Dodgshun, ministers from the London Missionary Society under whose auspices Livingstone had worked in Africa. The pair were on an expedition to establish a string of missions along Lake Tanganyika when they succumbed to illness at the end of the 1870s. Another grave contains the remains of an eccentric French clergyman named Michel Alexandre de Baize ("Abbé de Baize"), who reached Ujiji in 1878 with two suits of armour, a portable organ and 24 umbrellas, before passing away in December 1879.

Further up the road is **Mwanga** district, occupying a ridge along the road to Ujiji. This is Kigoma's liveliest area, boasting several video lounges screening second-rate pirated films, and the excellent **Mwanga Market** at the junction of the roads to Kasulu and Ujiji. Aside from normal produce (the pineapples are especially delicious), the market offers an eye-opening insight into the infamous corruption that afflicts many United Nations agencies. Military-style "Compact Food Rations", presumably diverted en route to Kigoma Region's refugee camps, are sold openly at stalls sheltered from the sun by plastic hessian sheeting stamped with the initials of the UNHCR, beside which you might find piles of rice and flour sacks bearing legends from a variety of aid agencies.

The lakeshore

Lake Tanganyika's surface water is a very pleasant 23°C, and according to locals, **swimming** near Kigoma is safe as long as there's no reedy vegetation nearby, in which case there might be a risk of bilharzia. **Crocodiles** are sometimes sighted in the area, although there have been no reports of attacks, but **water-snakes** may dwell near rocks. If you want the take the risk (and plenty do, including tourists), then the *Lake Tanganyika Beach Hotel* is a lovely place for a dip, or just to spend a blissfully lazy afternoon doing nothing more energetic than watching crows and distant dhows while sipping a beer. If you don't want to chance it, *Kigoma Hilltop Hotel* charges Tsh2000 for the use of its pool. **Women should cover up** when bathing to avoid offending Islamic sensibilities – indeed, this applies to the whole lake. There are two private beaches 7km south of town near Kitwe Point. The best is **Jacobsen's Beach** (Tsh2000), which has coarse red sand and a few parasols in a small secluded cove, but no facilities. Just to the south, less sheltered and with pebbles instead of sand, **Zungu Beach** (Tsh500) has three parasols, a couple of shelters and some warm sodas and cans of Castle lager for sale, but no food. Tsetse flies can be a pain but don't carry sleeping sickness. To get to either beach, take a taxi (Tsh3000) or catch a daladala to Katonga village from outside the TRA Building at the start of Bangwe Road – these will leave you at the junction for the track leading to the shore (there's a green sign to Zungu Beach); it's a sweltering three-kilometre walk over the hills to either beach. The intermittent signposts aren't much help – for Zungu, turn left at the first fork after about 2km and bear right at the next junction; for Jacobsen's, just keep right at every fork.

Kibirizi, 3km north of town (follow the rail tracks, catch a daladala, or take a taxi), is the best place to see how **dagaa** – the lake's main commercial catch – is dried. These diminutive fish, which measure between 2cm and 10cm, live in immense shoals near the surface, and are caught at night using pressure lamps mounted on wooden boats. At a given moment, the fishermen beat on the sides of the boat to panic the fish into tight shoals, which are then scooped up in nets. The flotilla leaves Kibirizi late in the afternoon in pairs, the lead boat towing the other to conserve fuel, and you can see their lights bobbing up and down from the coast at night; the season peaks in the second half of September. The fish are spread out the following morning to dry, either on gravel or over a suspended wire mesh.

Ujiji

The pleasantly relaxed atmosphere of **Ujiji**, 10km southeast of Kigoma, belies a terrible past when, as the main Arab trading post on Lake Tanganyika, it was the place from where tens of thousands of shackled slaves began their gruelling 1200-kilometre march towards the Indian Ocean. The journey from Ujiji to Bagamoyo, Saadani or Pangani took anything from three to six months, and many died along the way, perishing either from exhaustion or being shot when they became too ill to move or tried to escape – it's thought that during the fifty years when Zanzibar controlled the route, over a million Africans (mostly from eastern Congo) were enslaved, though the true figure may have been much higher, as estimates are based on those who survived the arduous journey to the coast. Now little more than a suburb of Kigoma, Ujiji has few visible reminders of its infamous past other than its distinctive Swahili-styled houses (more typical of the Indian Ocean coast) and a profusion of mango trees, said to have grown from stones discarded by slaves.

From the 1850s onwards, **European explorers** venturing into the interior also used the slave routes, and – so long as they were armed with letters of recommendation from the sultan in Zanzibar – generally had little to fear. The first to visit Ujiji and set eyes on Lake Tanganyika were Richard Burton and John Hanning Speke, who arrived in February 1858 during their search for the source of the Nile (see p.495). Ujiji was also the scene of Henry Morton Stanley's legendary meeting with David Livingstone, which is commemorated by a memorial and small museum. The alleged site of the famous encounter is marked by the **Livingstone Memorial** (ask for "Livingstone"), halfway along Livingstone Street some 500m before the harbour; coming into town along Kigoma Road, the junction for Livingstone Street is on the right before the *Matunda Guest House*. A plaque beside two mango trees – said to have been grafted from the tree under which the duo allegedly met – marks the spot. Ironically enough, the original tree died when Belgian authorities laid out a concrete platform around the trunk as a memorial, promptly starving it of moisture. It was cut down in 1930. The small **museum** (daily 8am–5.30pm; Tsh2000) contains amusing local paintings depicting the famous encounter, some equally offbeat larger-than-life sculptures of Livingstone and Stanley raising their hats to each other in greeting, and nothing much else.

Frequent **daladalas** run to Ujiji from the east side of the market in Kigoma, dropping you along Kigoma Road, from where it's a ten-minute walk to the Livingstone Monument. A taxi from Kigoma costs Tsh4000–5000.

Eating

The local delicacies are **migebuka**, which looks like a thin mackerel and tastes similar, and of course **dagaa**, which is best roasted in palm oil (*mawese*, which gives it a nutty taste) and served with dark *ugali* made from cassava. **Street food**, especially fried cassava, roasted maize cobs and seasonal fruit, is best along

△ Statues of Livingstone and Stanley, Ujiji

David Livingstone, missionary-turned-explorer, first made his name with a bestseller, *Missionary Travels and Researches in South Africa*, but lasting fame came from his serialized *Journals'* graphic and impassioned tirades against the horrors of the slave trade, particularly the massacre of hundreds of market women at Nyangwe in Congo by Arab slavers:

"Shot after shot continued to be fired on the helpless and perishing. Some of the long line of heads disappeared quietly; while other poor creatures threw their arms high, as if appealing to the great Father above, and sank [...] As I write, I hear the loud wails on the left bank over those who are there slain, ignorant of their many friends now in the depths of Lualaba."

Livingstone's words obliged the British Government to blockade Zanzibar, forcing a reluctant Sultan Barghash to close Stone Town's slave market, thus hastening the end of the slave trade, and ultimately of slavery, in East Africa.

Born on March 19, 1813, near Glasgow in Scotland, the introspective **David Livingstone** turned to a religious life at a young age, and joined the London Missionary Society, under whose auspices he travelled to Cape Town in 1841, where he married a missionary's daughter and set to work as a preacher and doctor. On his early expeditions he crossed the Kalahari Desert and "discovered" Lake Nyasa, but his most famous discovery, in November 1855, was that of Mosi oa Tunya – the "Smoke that Thunders" – which he dutifully rechristened the **Victoria Falls**. His fourth major expedition (1858–64) covered the area between the Lower Zambezi River and Lake Nyasa.

After a brief sojourn in Britain, he returned to Africa in 1866, having been commissioned by the Royal Geographical Society to explore the country between Lake Nyasa and Lake Tanganyika and to solve the riddle of the source of the Nile. So began the five-year odyssey that was to end with the famous **encounter with Stanley**. At the time of the meeting, Livingstone was suffering from dysentery, fever and foot ulcers, but within two weeks had recovered sufficiently to explore the northern shores of Lake Tanganyika with Stanley, before returning to Kazeh near Tabora, where Stanley headed back to the coast and world-wide acclaim.

Livingstone stayed behind awaiting supplies, and then set off on his fifth and final expedition in August 1872, during which he again fell ill with dysentery and died at **Chitambo** village close to Lake Bangweulu (in present-day Zambia) in May 1873. His heart and viscera were removed by his African servants **James Chuma and Abdullah Susi** and were buried in a tin under a tree at the spot where he died. Susi and Chuma embalmed the missionary's body with brandy and salt, then dried it, wrapped it in calico and encased it in a bark cylinder. This in turn was sewn into a large piece of sailcloth, and tarred shut. Thus wrapped, they attached the bundle to a pole and carried the body back to Bagamoyo – an epic eleven-month, three-thousand-kilometre journey. From Bagamoyo the body was transferred to Zanzibar for shipment to London, and Livingstone was buried as a national hero at Westminster Abbey on April 18, 1874.

Lumumba Avenue between the daladala stand and the train station. There are also plenty of dirt-cheap grilled meat and *chipsi mayai* places around the daladala stand and market. Mwanga, a few kilometres uphill along Ujiji Road, is especially good in the evenings, with dozens of stands serving up fried *dagaa* and tasty *mishkaki* goat-meat skewers. There are also cheap *hotelis* facing the railway station.

... and Stanley

Among Livingstone's pallbearers was **Henry Morton Stanley**. Twenty-eight years Livingstone's junior, Stanley was born John Rowland at Denbigh, Wales, on January 29, 1841. His childhood included nine years in a workhouse, before – at the age of 17 – he took work on a ship from Liverpool to New Orleans. Here, his new employer – a cotton merchant – gave him his new name. Always the self-assured self-publicist, eleven years later he was working as the *New York Herald*'s scoop journalist when the paper's eccentric manager, James Gordon Bennett (he of "Gordon Bennett!" fame), commissioned him to cover the inauguration of the Suez Canal and then find Livingstone, who had been "missing" for five years. Arriving in Zanzibar, he borrowed a top hat from the American consul and paid a visit to Sultan Barghash, who issued him with letters of recommendation, the nineteenth-century version of a passport. In keeping with Stanley's larger-than-life character, the expedition set off with 192 men and six tonnes of stores, including glass beads, reams of American cloth, coral and china for trading, as well as two silver goblets and a bottle of champagne for the day he met Livingstone.

Exactly 236 days later, 76 pounds lighter and having buried eighteen porters and guards, his two European companions, both his horses, all 27 donkeys and his watchdog, Stanley arrived in Ujiji, having heard in Tabora that an elderly white man was there. The date was November 10, 1871. "I would have run to him," wrote Stanley, "only I was a coward in the presence of such a mob – would have embraced him, but that I did not know how he would receive me; so I did what moral cowardice and false pride suggested was the best thing – walked deliberately to him, took off my hat, and said: 'Dr Livingstone, I presume?'"

The studied nonchalance of those now legendary words was well in keeping with Stanley's character. Following his successful encounter with Livingstone, Stanley abandoned journalism and dedicated himself to exploring Africa, which he subsequently recounted in a series of derring-do books bragging about his adventures. Receiving a commission to find the southernmost source of the Nile, Stanley returned to Zanzibar in September 1874, this time for an epic 999-day journey across the breadth of Africa following the Lualaba and Congo rivers to the Atlantic, which he reached on August 12, 1877. His third and fourth trips, from 1879 to 1884, were commissioned by King Leopold II of Belgium and laid the foundations of the **Congo Free State** (subsequently the Belgian Congo) by establishing settlements, constructing roads and negotiating land deals with local leaders, effectively robbing them of their territory. The 450 treaties which Stanley agreed during these expeditions effectively laid the ground for one of the most glaring examples of European misrule ever witnessed. The Congo Free State, despite its name, was little more than a gigantic slave colony, in which order and production quotas were maintained by means of officially sanctioned torture, summary executions, assassinations, the taking of hostages and myriad other abuses.

Stanley – an "ugly little man with a strong American twang", as Queen Victoria privately described him – was knighted in 1899, and died in London on May 10, 1904. His summation of Livingstone: "He is not an angel, but he approaches to that being as near as the nature of a living man will allow."

Ally's Restaurant Lumumba Ave. A friendly place busy with locals at lunchtime. Some of the pre-cooked snacks are a bit grim (especially the egg *chops* and "pizzas", which are actually greasy stuffed chapatis), but the aromatic cinnamon-laced tea is wonderful, the chicken *supu* a delight, and full meals (Tsh1000–2500), including birianis if

ordered in advance, are also good. No alcohol.
Kigoma Hotel & Guest House Lumumba Ave. Limited to rice or *ugali* with fish or chicken (Tsh1500), though with a breezy if loud (blaring music) streetside terrace.
Lake View Hotel Lumumba Ave. Snacks, beers and a TV, with *supu* for breakfast, good mashed

potato *chops*, and a nice shady terrace. No lake view, incidentally.

Lake Tanganyika Beach Hotel West of the ferry port, signposted off Bangwe Rd. Offers a wide selection of rather average Tanzanian, Chinese, Indian and European dishes, and charges Tsh2500–4000 for main courses. The food's nothing special, and service is achingly slow, but who cares – the lake view shouldn't be rushed.

Mwanga Lodge 3km up Ujiji Road, Mwanga. The *migebuka* fish here is usually good, as is their *dagaa*, and it's very cheap, costing under Tsh1000 for a meal. No alcohol.

Sangara Restaurant *Kigoma Hilltop Hotel*, 4km southwest of town on a headland high above the shore. Expensive Continental and Indian-style meals in an anodyne atmosphere, compensated for by superb lake views and a swimming pool (Tsh2000). There's also an ice-cream parlour. No alcohol, but they don't mind if you bring your own.

Drinking and nightlife

Unsurprisingly, considering Kigoma's location, **Congolese music** rather than Bongo Flava reigns supreme, with the sound of long-established stars Koffi Olomide, Le General Defao *et al* strutting their stuff pouring from radios and tape players in the streets and in a number of bars, which sometimes double as discos. Incidentally, **don't walk** around Kigoma at night, but catch a taxi.

Lake Tanganyika Beach Hotel West of the ferry port, signposted off Bangwe Rd. Idyllically located on the breezy lakeshore with seats under thatched parasols, this is the best bar in town, and

---

Moving on from Kigoma

By train
Trains to Dar via Tabora, Dodoma and Morogoro (change in Tabora for Mwanza or Mpanda) depart at 6pm (Tues, Thurs & Sun). The ticket office is open 8am–noon and 2–6pm on these days, and 8am–noon and 2–4.30pm on others; buy your ticket in advance to be sure of a first- or second-class bunk. **Fares** to Dar es Salaam are Tsh45,200 in first-class sleepers, Tsh33,100 in second sleeping, and Tsh15,000–18,000 for a seat. The **timetable** is posted at ⊛www.trctz.com.

By plane
Scheduled flights are limited to the Precisionair service to Dar es Salaam every evening; $200 one-way. Coastal Aviation may start running a service to Mwanza.

By road
The only practical **road** out of Kigoma is north via Kasulu and Kibondo to Biharamulo and Bukoba (Visram Bus Wed & Fri, Saratoga Line Thurs & Sun), or to Shinyanga and Mwanza (six weekly: Adventure Connection and Saratoga Line), either of which takes a full day, or two days with breakdowns or rain. Minimum **journey times** are given at the end of this chapter. During heavy rains, the stretch between Kibondo and Nyakanazi, at the junction with the sealed road from Shinyanga, can be impassable. Buy tickets – from the offices at the bus stand in Mwanga – at least two days in advance to avoid having to stand, though even seated, it can be an uncomfortable and very cramped journey.

Forget about getting to **Mpanda** by road unless you've got 4WD and it's bone-dry weather, as there's no public transport and you may have to wait a week or more in Uvinza for a lift on a truck. The first 100km to Uvinza are fine, but the remaining 190km – with their loose sand, black cotton soil and precarious log bridges – can take twelve hours or more, if they're passable at all.

By boat
Open-topped **lake taxis** (nicknamed *kigoma-kigoma*) leave from Ujiji for ports to the south, and from Kibirizi, 3km north of Kigoma, for ports to the north. There are

has a popular and tacky 70s disco on Saturday (9.30pm–3am; Tsh2000) with swivelling lights and simmering whores. The rest of the week, the bar closes around 11pm.

Magereza (Prisons) Club 2km along Bangwe Rd, just before the prison on the right. Another popular place on the beach – its Sunday afternoon discos give the prisoners next door something to dance to.

New Stanley's Restaurant & Bar Kakolwa St. The restaurant serves food and drinks all day, but most people come for the disco, sometimes featuring live bands (Wed & Fri from 9pm, Sun from 3pm).

Sandra Restaurant & Bar Stanley Ave. Handy place if awaiting a train or ferry, with a pleasant beer garden at the back, and good *nyama choma* and fried bananas.

Website Pub 1.5km south, off Ujiji Rd (turn right after NMB bank). Currently Kigoma's liveliest nightspot, an open-air bar with professional dancers nightly except Wed and Thurs, satellite TV for football, a pool table, food and a great atmosphere.

Listings

Airlines Precisionair, Mlole Rd, facing the Central Market ☎028/280 4436, ⓦ www.precisionairtz.com.

Consulates Burundi, Bangwe Rd ☎028/280 2865, ⓔ consbdi@africaonline.co.tz; Congo, corner of Bangwe and Kaya roads ☎028/280 2401. Travelling to either country is currently not recommended, and there's no regular public transport into either.

Hospitals Kigoma's hospitals are in Mwanga. The best is the mission-run Baptist Hospital (☎028/280 2241) about 1km from Kasulu junction: turn left at the junction then first right. A check-up costs $15. The government-run Maweni Hospital (☎028/280

no lake taxis from Kigoma itself. Their unpleasant reputation is due not so much to the risk of sinking, nor because they can be massively uncomfortable and offer no shade, water or toilets, but because they sometimes carry "dangerous passengers", meaning anything from mild drunks to the armed bandits who shot dead two passengers and drowned twenty others between Kigoma and Mgambo by throwing them overboard, in January 2001.

Much safer and more comfortable if you're heading south is the **weekly ferry** (Marine Services Company ☎ & ⓕ 028/280 3950, ⓔ marine@africaonline.co.tz), either the historic **MV Liemba** or the **MV Mwongozo**. This sails from the ferry port southwest of the commercial harbour every Wednesday at 4pm for Mpulungu in Zambia, if all goes well arriving around 10am on Friday, turning around at 2.30pm the same day to arrive back in Kigoma on Sunday. It stops more or less everywhere, offering a number of feasible if rough-going overland connections in the dry season to Mpanda, Katavi National Park and Sumbawanga – see "Port-hopping along Lake Tanganyika" on p.542 for full details. The MV *Liemba* is also helpful for getting to Mahale Mountains National Park – see p.542 for more information. There are currently no ferries to **Burundi** or to **Congo**.

Tickets for non-Tanzanians must be paid in dollars cash. First-class cabins on both boats are small but have two bunks, a window and fan. Second-class (in cabins with four to six berths) get hot and stuffy – given the meagre price difference, you may as well go for first-class. Third-class is seating only. **Fares** (1st/2nd/3rd class), including $5 harbour tax, are: Mgambo (also called Lagosa) $25/$20/$15; Karema $30/$27/$22; and Mpulungu (Zambia) $55/$45/$30. The galley cooks are very able, and drinks are also available. Berths can be reserved by fax or email, at least in theory.

Tanzanian **immigration and customs formalities** are dealt with on board when the ferry arrives at Kasanga, next to Zambia. There's no Zambian consul in Kigoma (the nearest is in Dar es Salaam), but Zambian visas are usually given without fuss at Kasanga, or aboard. Should ferries to Burundi and DR Congo resume, visit their respective consuls in Kigoma first; see above.

2671) on Ujiji Road beyond Kasulu junction and Mwanga Market lacks resources.

Immigration Exit formalities for Zambia are done on the ferry. The main immigration office is on Ujiji Road in Mwanga, 100m beyond Maweni Hospital on the left.

Internet access KamNet, and Baby Come & Call are on Lumumba Ave (both daily 8am–8pm; Tsh2000/hr). *Kigoma Hilltop Hotel* charges Tsh4000/hr.

Money NBC Bank, corner of Lumumba Ave and Mlole Rd, changes cash and travellers' cheques and has a 24hr Visa/MasterCard ATM. The only forex, handy for changing cash quickly (but watch out for fake notes) is Panjatan Bureau de Change, Lumumba Ave (erratic hours, usually Mon–Sat 10am–1pm & 3–4pm).

Pharmacy Kigoma Pharmacy, Lumumba Ave facing the market.

Police Bangwe Rd, near the TRA building, and in the train station.

Post office Kiezya Rd.

Telephone TTCL, beside the post office on Kiezya Rd (Mon–Fri 7.45am–12.45pm & 2–6pm, Sat 9am–1pm).

Port-hopping along Lake Tanganyika

For the truly adventurous, **port-hopping** along Lake Tanganyika south of Kigoma is a time-consuming yet strangely rewarding exercise. Given that the **ferry** (usually the MV *Liemba*; see p.541 for fares and departure times) sails only once a week, to "hop" more than one port means either hunkering down in a lakeside village for a week to await the ferry's return, or risking local **lake taxis** – a potentially dangerous form of transport. Most of the villages that the ferry calls at also have road access to Mpanda or Sumbawanga (both covered later in this chapter), so bailing out is also an option, at least in the dry season – in the rains, none of these roads is recommended, or even passable.

Ikola and Karema

Sailing south from Kigoma, Thursday morning sees the ferry drop anchor off **IKOLA**, famed among tropical aquarium fanatics for giving its name to a highly prized family of cichlid fish. There's connecting road transport to

> ## The MV Liemba
>
> A much-loved feature of Lake Tanganyika is the **MV Liemba**, which has been ferrying passengers and cargo up and down the lake once a week for over eighty years. Originally christened the **Graf von Götzen** (after a former governor of German East Africa), the 1300-tonne steamship was constructed in Germany in 1913, then cut apart and transported by train from Dar es Salaam to Kigoma in the early stages of World War I, where she was reassembled for use as an armed troop transport. In June 1916 the ship was bombed by Belgian aircraft but escaped with light damage. However, when the British took control of the Central Line Railway the following month, the Germans **scuttled** the ship at the mouth of the Malagarasi River south of Kigoma rather than have her fall into enemy hands. The *Graf von Götzen* remained submerged for eight years until, following an unsuccessful effort by the Belgians in 1921, the British finally salvaged the vessel in March 1924 and renamed her the MV *Liemba*, after the lake's original name.
>
> Any journey on the MV *Liemba* (or the MV *Mwongozo* for that matter) is a memorable one – gorgeous sunsets over Congo's eastern highlands, and the frenetic activity that erupts in the port villages along the way whenever the ferry arrives: the ferry drops anchor offshore, with passengers, luggage and cargo carried to and from land in small lighters, invariably eliciting chaotic scrambles as people jostle to get on or off.

Mpanda (at least 5hr), a **guest house** (❶) owned by local taxman Mr Mollo, and a basic "restaurant" – buy the ingredients at the market and let the chef work his magic.

If the lake – or its history – appeals, rent a bike from Ikola's guest house or stay on the ferry until **KAREMA** (or Kalema), 15km to the south. During the nineteenth-century **slave trade**, the lake region was convulsed by war and slave hunting. As a regular staging post, the Europeans were inevitably attracted to Karema, the first to occupy it being the Belgian Comité d'Études du Haut Congo in 1879, who named the place **Fort Leopold** in honour of King Leopold II, whose notoriously tyrannical rule over Central Africa only recently made it onto Belgium's school curriculum. Belgium went on to claim the sardonically named Congo Free State as its African domain, but was obliged to relinquish Karema in 1885 following the European partition of Africa, when Germany took over Tanganyika. With the slave trade effectively at an end, it was the **Missionaries of Africa** ("White Fathers") who inherited the fort, and who ransomed four or five hundred slaves to found the village proper. Their church was erected in 1890, and the fortified mission house – which still stands – was completed in 1893.

The Catholic Mission in Karema has a **rest house** (❶), and there are regular **Land Rovers to Mpanda** (upwards of 6hr) most days around noon, and certainly when the ferry calls.

Kasanga and Muzi

KASANGA is the last Tanzanian port before Zambia, and is where **Tanzanian border formalities** are dealt with. The immigration officer is unusually helpful, and boards the ship on arrival. In German times, Kasanga was known as **Bismarckburg** – the ruins of their fort are just outside the village but on military land, so there's no access. With time, the **Kalambo Falls** (see below) are an attractive target from here. The ferry usually arrives at Kasanga between midnight and dawn on Friday. For **accommodation**, there's the *Mwenya Guest House* (❶) on the hill behind the harbour, with a bar and – novelty of novelties – a TV.

Five kilometres north of Kasanga is the tranquil fishing village of **MUZI** (90min on foot, or squeeze into a local boat for Tsh1000–1500), which also has a hotel – *Muzi Guest House* (no nets but plenty of mosquitoes; ❶), a small *mgahawa* restaurant, nice views and plenty of friendly people.

Daily Land Rovers and pick-ups **to Sumbawanga** leave Kasanga around 6–7am, the badly rutted road taking four to five hours in the dry season and nine hours in the rains. Returning from Sumbawanga, they head off around 9am.

Kalambo Falls

Sitting square on the border with Zambia a few kilometres east of Lake Tanganyika, the breathtaking 215-metre **Kalambo Falls** are Africa's second-highest uninterrupted falls, their waters plunging into the canyon of the river that forms the border with Zambia. Aside from the falls' natural beauty, they're also a breeding ground for the giant marabou stork, and several sites in the vicinity have great archeological importance: 300,000-year-old Stone Age tools have been uncovered, as well as some of the oldest evidence for the use of wood in construction, dating back sixty thousand years. Excavations of early Iron Age villages and campsites have also revealed a wealth of earthenware pottery – mainly globular pots and shallow bowls – the earliest of which have been dated to around 350 AD.

Access to the falls, which lie 130km southwest of Sumbawanga, is easiest from Kasanga: catch a pick-up at around 6am to Kalambo village, 5km north of the falls, from where you'll have to walk. If you're coming by road from Sumbawanga, catch a pick-up towards Muzi or Kasanga but get off in Kawala, from where it's an exhausting fifteen-kilometre walk to the falls through Kalambo village. A tent would be useful as there's no accommodation either in Kalambo or Kawala, nor any regular transport back to Sumbawanga after 9am, though a few pick-ups run from Kawala to Muzi until late afternoon. Seek local advice about **crocodiles** if you want to swim.

Gombe Stream National Park

Just 16km north of Kigoma, **GOMBE STREAM** is the smallest but one of the most inspiring of Tanzania's national parks – and also the most expensive. Its 52 square kilometres cover a narrow strip of hilly country rising from Lake Tanganyika to the eastern ridge of the Western Rift Valley escarpment, cut by thirteen steep-sided river valleys running east to west. The variation in altitude

Gombe's chimpanzees

Chimpanzees are our closest living relatives: they share 98.5 percent of our genome, and of course – unless you're a Creationist – we share common ancestors. Like us too, chimpanzees are intelligent social creatures who feel and share emotions, and are able to adapt to different environments and foods, pass on knowledge, and make and use simple tools. They also hunt in a human way, use plants medicinally, raid each other's communities and sometimes descend into a state of war. We owe much of our knowledge of chimpanzees to two ongoing research projects in Tanzania, one at Gombe, the other at Mahale (p.552), both of which started in the early 1960s. **Dr Jane Goodall** began a fifteen-year study of Gombe's chimpanzees in June 1960, having been encouraged by the Kenyan palaeontologist Louis Leakey, who believed that by observing the behaviour of great apes we could reconstruct something of the early life of mankind. The studies continue under the patronage of the Jane Goodall Institute (Ⓦ www.janegoodall.org).

The study's first surprising discovery was that chimpanzees were capable of making and using simple **tools**. This is best seen in November at the start of the rains, when they go "fishing" for termites by inserting sticks into termite mounds, and then withdraw the probe to lick it clean of insects. The study has also demonstrated chimpanzees' knowledge and use of **medicinal plants**, in their use of *Aspilia mossambicensis* to clean their intestines of worms. The leaves contain an antibiotic and worm-killer, and are eaten in the morning before moving on to other foods. The method of eating the leaves is as important as their chemical content: using their lips, the chimps carefully remove one of the rough and hairy leaves from the plant and pull it into their mouths using their tongue. This causes the leaves to fold up like an accordion, which are then swallowed without chewing, thereby not only killing but physically removing worms.

Altogether, Gombe's chimps have been observed to eat 147 different plants, but contrary to what had previously been thought, both the Mahale and Gombe studies revealed that chimpanzees are omnivorous rather than vegetarian. Indeed, their success rate at **hunting** – primarily of red colobus monkeys, young bushpigs and bushbuck – is far higher than that of some specialized predators such as lions. The secret of their success is co-operative hunting, as several chimps can block any possible escape routes; it has been estimated that chimps may be responsible for

and the variety of habitats make the park one of the country's most rewarding places for observing wildlife and flora, but you can forget about the "Big Five" – the Gombe ecosystem is a far more subtle affair. Lake Tanganyika and the unremitting *miombo* woodland which stretches to the east have acted as a natural barrier for the last twenty million years, and as a result Gombe contains several plant and animal species common in West Africa but unknown further east. The evergreen riverine forests are especially diverse, and are the abode of the park's famous **chimpanzees** which have, since 1960, been the subject of what is now the world's longest-running study of a wild animal species; one troop has been habituated to humans and can be visited. Other **primates** include the olive baboon, along with less common red colobus, redtail and blue monkeys. The redtail and blue monkeys are unusual in that, despite their striking physical differences, they have only recently diverged as separate species, and hybrids occur, usually with the redtail's white nose and the blue monkey's dark tail and larger size. Other **mammals** include grey duiker antelope, bushbuck and marsh mongoose, as well as the chequered elephant shrew, which eats insects and can be seen patrolling the forest floor – it's named on account of its comical trunk-like snout and long legs. Over 230 **bird species** have been recorded, along with 250 species of butterfly.

killing fifteen percent of the red colobus population every year. Goodall's study also found that most of the dominant "**alpha**" **males** in the studied community were not necessarily big or physically strong, but gained their status through persistent or inventive macho displays of power. In one case, the alpha male used empty fuel-cans to terrify his peers; in another, two brothers – one of whom had lost an arm through polio – worked as a team to intimidate their competitors; others use family connections to gain influence. All in all, uncomfortably human. The parallels became even more unsettling when the study revealed that chimps also engaged in **warfare**, which had all the depressing hallmarks of our own conflicts. There are presently three communities, Mitumba, Kasakela and Kalande, whose borders are patrolled every few days by male groups. On occasion these groups invade neighbouring territories, attacking and sometimes killing any strangers encountered, with the exception of young females without young who are taken into the community. In a series of raids between 1974 and 1977, the males of the Kasakela community exterminated those of the Kahama community, with whom they had formerly been allied. The males also attacked strange females, and in three cases the stranger's child was killed and later eaten. **Cannibalism**, which was first seen in Mahale, was also observed in a Kasakela female and her daughter, who calmly went around killing and eating the new-born infants of other females belonging to their own community. And in one infamous alleged incident in 2002, a male snatched and killed the baby of the wife of a park ranger. It would appear that these behavioural extremes may be related to **environmental pressures**, certainly in Gombe: hemmed in by humans on three sides and the lake on the fourth, forest habitat suitable for chimpanzees is limited – and shrinking. Indeed, all is far from well: human viruses have killed several chimps since the new millennium began, and the feeding station has been abandoned due to the increasingly aggressive behaviour of the chimpanzees.

Good books include the lavishly illustrated *40 Years at Gombe* (1999) by Stewart, Chabori and Chang, and numerous works by Jane Goodall, including: *In the Shadow of Man* (1971); *The Chimpanzees of Gombe: Patterns of Behaviour* (1986); *Through a Window: My Thirty Years with the Chimpanzees of Gombe* (1991); and *Reason for Hope* (2002).

Gombe's diminutive size, and dense human population surrounding it on three sides, make it highly vulnerable to **environmental degradation**, something that sadly appears to be coming to a head, thanks in part to the unsustainable needs of **refugees** from Burundi, barely 20km to the north. Despite efforts by various authorities both inside and outside the national park to keep deforestation in check, it seems destined to be a losing battle for as long as Burundi's troubles continue, and the refugees stay.

Arrival and information

Gombe can only be reached by **boat** (half an hour to three hours), and visitors get to see the place on foot, accompanied by an official guide – nothing too strenuous, but you need to be reasonably fit.

Organized safaris are the easiest way in, offered by a handful of safari operators based in Arusha (p.403), Mwanza (p.500) and Dar (p.132), who generally fly their guests into Kigoma on upmarket packages, and by two in Kigoma: Chimpanzee Safaris at *Kigoma Hilltop Hotel* (p.534), who run Gombe's tented camp and charge $300–400 per person all-inclusive, and Sunset Tours at *Aqua Lodge* (p.534), who are better for lower-end safaris, with nights spent camping or in the park *bandas*, and – if you're really on a shoestring – with transport there and back by lake taxi.

Arranging your own safari is possible but fiddly (you may need to book a chimp-trekking slot, and a *banda* if staying over, through TANAPA in Kibirizi; see below) and not necessarily cheaper. As a rough guide, a boat holding 10–12 passengers costs $150–170 return through Sunset Tours or *Lake Tanganyika Beach Hotel*, or $250 for one of Chimpanzee Safaris' speedboats. **Lake taxis** are overcrowded, potentially dangerous (see p.541) and offer limited if any shelter from the sun, but are cheap. They leave for Gombe from Kibirizi, 3km north of Kigoma, between 8am and 11am (Mon–Sat; 2–3hr; Tsh1500, for locals at least). To boat costs add park fees, food and accommodation. Returning to Kibirizi, park staff can help you find a boat; 5–6pm appears to be the best time.

Entrance fees and information

Entrance fees cost a whopping $100 per person per 24 hours, plus $20 per group for the obligatory guide, and are slated to increase to $150 per person, possibly in 2007.

The **park headquarters** are on the shore at Kasakela where the boats tie up; TANAPA also have an office in Kibirizi, 3km north of Kigoma (PO Box 185 Kigoma, ☎028/280 3040). **Chimp tracking** is limited to four groups a day (maximum six people each including the guide), so if you're arranging things yourself, enquire at the office in Kibirizi beforehand to be sure of a free slot. They'll also be able to tell you whether camping on the beach is still allowed (ie safe from baboons), and if there's room in the overnight *bandas*. The best source of **information** is the excellent guidebook published by TANAPA, available in Arusha, Dar and Stone Town. It contains masses of information on the park's wildlife and the chimpanzees, and also covers Mahale Mountains National Park. The park's official **website** is ⓦ www.tanzaniaparks.com/gombe.htm.

The **best time to visit** depends on your interest. Photography is best in the dry season (July to mid-Oct and mid-Dec to Jan), but the chimps are easier to see in the rains (roughly Feb–June and mid-Oct to mid-Dec), when the vegetation on the higher slopes is at its greenest and most beautiful. There are occasional windy thunderstorms during April and May and from August to September.

Monkey trouble

Wherever you stay or are in Gombe, **beware of baboons**, which can be extremely dangerous if teased or tempted as they're completely unfazed by humans. The golden rules for avoiding hassle are to keep all food (and valuables) out of sight, keep tents and rooms closed, never eat outdoors, and never stare at a baboon (if threatened, look away, turn your back, and move away slowly). Should a baboon snatch something from you, don't resist but alert the park staff instead, who'll try to get it back. The same might be said of Gombe's **chimpanzees**, which have become increasingly violent towards humans of late.

Special **equipment** to bring includes dull-coloured clothes, a pair of shoes which have a good grip in wet conditions, rain gear, a torch for walks along the beach at night and bottled water if you're planning long hikes. Binoculars are pretty much de rigueur, and take plenty of fast film if not on digital, to handle the subdued forest light (800 ASA at least; buy it at home) – flash photography is not permitted. For swimming, a face-mask and snorkel are an advantage. If you plan to cook, take a kerosene or gas stove. Fish can be bought from fishermen on the beach, but bring all other food, and conceal it in sealed containers to avoid unpleasantness with baboons.

Accommodation

Despite the white sandy beach and glorious lake views, neither of Gombe's **accommodation** options are perfect, mainly thanks to increasingly threatening behaviour from both chimps and baboons, which has led to communal eating areas being screened with wire mesh. Whilst **camping** – either in the campsite near the *bandas*, or on the beach – is still allowed ($30 per person), it appears to be a mite dangerous these days, and you'll need permission first from the park warden in any case – enquire at the TANAPA office in Kibirizi.

Gombe Luxury Tented Camp (aka *Mitumba Tented Camp*) ⓦ www.chimpanzeesafaris.com (book through Chimpanzee Safaris at *Kigoma Hilltop Hotel* in Kigoma; see p.534). On a wide sandy beach at the mouth of the Mitumba stream in the north, this is a rather simple tented camp whose rates would be unjustifiable were it not Gombe's only upmarket place. Its eight, twin-bed tents are pitched on raised wooden platforms under shady trees, and have verandahs with lovely lake views, but aggressive baboons mean that the windows and verandah of the dining *banda* are caged in wire mesh. Evening sundowners and dinner can be taken around a campfire though, and there's also a small library, shop, bar and lounge. Rates ($250–300 per person) include park fees. ⓞ

TANAPA Bandas Kasakela. Very basic and uninspiring breeze-block *bandas* near the beach, which – like the tented camp – have their verandahs fitted with wire mesh to keep out chimps and baboons. It should have bed sheets and mosquito nets, but you'll need to be self-sufficient food-wise. $30 per person. ❺

The park

Whilst **chimp-trekking** is the main reason for visiting Gombe, there are a number of other possible **hikes** in the park, both along the shore and up through the forest to the crest of the mountain ridge – attractions in their own right, and handy for filling in the time whilst waiting for a slot with the chimps. **Night walks** are an exciting novelty, especially around full moon when you can dispense with a torch, giving glimpses of nocturnal animals such as genet, white-tailed mongoose, the slow-moving giant rat (up to 90cm long, including the tail),

Chimpanzee etiquette

Despite living in a national park, Gombe's chimpanzee population has dwindled from 150 in the 1960s to around a hundred today, thanks to poaching and outbreaks of human-transmitted diseases. The following rules are designed to protect both you and the chimps.

Do not visit chimpanzees if you are ill: chimpanzees are susceptible to many of our diseases without necessarily possessing our immunity: an epidemic of infectious pneumonia killed almost a third of Gombe's main study community in the 1980s.

Keep your distance: never approach closer than 10m. If approached by a chimp, move away quietly or, if you can't, ignore it.

No food: visitors are not allowed to eat or display food in front of chimpanzees, nor to feed them.

Sit while observing chimps: standing upright can intimidate.

Stay with your group: do not spread out, as surrounding chimpanzees disturbs them.

Respect chimp feelings: don't follow chimps who appear to be shy or are avoiding you, and talk quietly.

Photography: be patient and don't try to attract the chimps' attention. Flash photography is not allowed.

Safety: chimpanzees are much stronger than us and can attack humans. Never come between a mother and her child. Should a chimp charge you, stand up, move quickly to a tree and hold on tightly to signal that you're not a threat. Do not scream or run away.

porcupine and bushbuck. You might also hear the loud cracking of palm nuts, a favourite with the hairy bushpig and also popular with palm civets.

The shore

You can walk along the **beach** without a guide. The temporary camps along the sand are occupied by *dagaa* fisherman, who spend about ten days here every month in the dry seasons around the full moon, when the catches are best. The mango trees and oil palms in the bays are human introductions, the latter a familiar sight in West Africa, but largely unknown in Tanzania. In parts, the forest reaches down to the beach, but there's little other permanent vegetation along the shore. As a result, hippos and crocodiles are rare if not completely absent; seek advice from park staff before **swimming**. Bilharzia is also believed to be absent. If you're given the all-clear, head to the river mouths or the rocky shore just north of Mitumba beach, where a mask and snorkel will reveal many beautifully coloured cichlid fish. In deeper water you may see the harmless Lake Tanganyika jellyfish, a tiny (2cm diameter) semi-transparent pulsating disc. Many beach strollers here are spooked by the sight of harmless **Nile monitor lizards**, which look like little crocodiles, but these skittish fellows are just as easily spooked as you and dash off into the water when approached. Gombe's most common primate, the stocky and thick-furred **olive baboon**, is generally the only mammal seen by day on the shore, where they scavenge for fish and occasionally swim and play in the water – keep your distance.

The lack of mud flats, weeds or perches means there's little **birdlife**, though the reeds at the mouths of streams are good habitats. Pied kingfishers, African pied wagtails and common sandpipers are most frequently seen, the giant kingfisher less so, while fish eagles are comparatively rare. Palm-nut vultures can sometimes be seen over the lake angling for fish. Winter migrants include white-winged black terns, hobbies and the lesser black-backed gull.

Evergreen riverine forest

Of Gombe's various habitats, the narrow **evergreen riverine forests** are the undoubted highlight, especially in the north. These originally formed part of the great forests of Central and West Africa, but became isolated by climatic change during the last eight thousand years, and more recently from each other by human activity. The nearest is straight up the Kakombe Valley from Kasakela: a high, tangled canopy of trees and vines, the cool obscurity below – where you'll see butterflies and flowers amidst the shrubs and ferns – illuminated here and there by narrow shafts of sunlight. As you walk along, crushed undergrowth marks the hasty retreats beaten by chimpanzees, red colobus, redtail or blue monkeys. Your guide should know where chimpanzees were last seen. The walk terminates at the beautiful twenty-metre **Kakombe waterfall**.

Forest birdlife is melodious but difficult to see, usually no more than a brief flash of colour disappearing into the undergrowth or up into the canopy. The more easily seen birds are crimson-winged turacos: the mainly green Livingstone's; and Ross's, the latter with a blue body, yellow face and red crest. Both have raucous calls. Of the four species of fruit-eating barbets, the only one you're likely to see is the tiny yellow-rumped tinkerbird, which has black-and- white facial stripes, a yellow rump and a monotonous "tink, tink, tink" call. More pleasant to the ear are the flute-like calls of the tropical boubou, a black-and-white shrike that duets in dense foliage. The African broadbill gives itself away by periodically flying up from its perch to do a somersault, emitting a small screech. The ground-feeding Peter's twinspot is an attractive finch with a red face and a white-spotted black belly. Winter migrants include various species of cuckoo, Eurasian swifts, bee-eaters and rollers, and four species of flycatcher. With a good deal of luck, you might also spot the pennant-winged nightjar, or one of two species of warbler (icterine and willow).

Dry woodland and upper ridges

The drier valleys and higher slopes, especially in the south of the park, are neither as rich nor as interesting as the forest, and the semi-deciduous woodland and thorn scrub that covers them can look rather bleak in the dry season, the result of fires which formerly devastated large areas. Firebreaks have now been made by the park authorities by lighting controlled fires at the start of the dry season, at which time damage to young trees is minimal because the still moist grass burns at lower temperatures than when completely dry. In the wet season it's a different world, with the vivid green grass being scattered with pink gladioli and giant heather. The poor soil and lack of year-round food supports few mammals however, the exceptions being olive baboons, vervet monkeys and bushbuck. Even so, a hike to the top of the escarpment (over 700m above the lake) rewards the effort with sweeping views over the park, a luxuriant contrast to the dry and crowded farmland to the east. On ridges, you might also see **crowned eagles** circling over the forests in search of imprudent monkeys. There are several routes to the top, all of them steep; leave early in the morning, and don't expect to be back until around nightfall.

Mahale Mountains National Park

Located 120km south of Kigoma on a wide peninsula jutting out into Lake Tanganyika, **MAHALE MOUNTAINS NATIONAL PARK** is one of the

Mahale's first conservationists: the Batongwe and Holoholo

The Mahale Mountains are the traditional home of the **Batongwe** and **Holoholo** (the latter also known as Horohoro or Kalanga) tribes. Following the establishment of the Mahale Mountains Wildlife Research Centre in 1979, however, all human habitation was demolished to make way for the new national park (created 1985), despite the fact that the Batongwe and Holoholo's lifestyle was highly adapted to the local environment. The Batongwe lived in compact communities of around forty people and practised a sustainable form of shifting cultivation over a cycle of thirty to fifty years, giving ample time for forest regeneration. They practised little or no commercial hunting, and what fishing they did was with nets whose mesh size was no smaller than 12cm, while some parts of the land – especially rivers, waterfalls, large trees, and the entirety of Sinsiba Forest and the forest fringing the summit of Mount Nkungwe – were considered the sacred abodes of guardian spirits, and so were left completely untouched. As such, it is deeply ironic that whilst proponents of "high- cost, low-impact tourism" stretch moral boundaries to the limits to justify five hundred dollars a night, the real conservators of the Mahale Mountains, the Batongwe and Holoholo, who lived in near-perfect symbiosis with their environment, have been completely excluded from their ancestral land, and their traditional livelihoods.

country's least- visited (and indeed least accessible) parks. Covering 1613 square kilometres, it's dominated by the heavily forested **Mahale Mountains**, which rise up from the pristine sandy beaches on the lakeshore to the 2462-metre peak of Mount Nkungwe.

Like Gombe, the park's ecology is characterized by a curious **mixture of habitats and species** typical of both the East and West African biogeographical zones, and includes forest, mountain, savannah, *miombo* woodland and lake environments. As might be expected, Mahale is exceptionally rich in **birdlife**, and also has lots of **butterflies**, including over thirty species of fast-flying charaxes that feed on animal dung. **Mammals** include elephant, buffalo, lion and leopard, giraffe, kudu and eland, as well as rarer species such as roan and sable antelope and the brush-tailed porcupine, but it's for the nine species of primates that Mahale has gained international renown – especially its **chimpanzees**, of which one group has been habituated and can be visited.

Arrival and information

Given its remote location, visiting Mahale is either **very expensive**, or just **plain awkward**. And as with Gombe, there are no roads into or within the park, so **walking** is the only way around – a sometimes heart-stopping but always memorable experience.

The easiest way of seeing Mahale is on an **organized safari**, either flying in from Arusha or Mwanza, or by boat from Kigoma. Chimpanzee Safaris at *Kigoma Hilltop Hotel* (p.534) has a number of trips to Mahale, with a five-day excursion costing $1600–2200 per person depending on group size and where you stay. Sunset Tours, also in Kigoma at *Aqua Lodge* (p.534), can be cheaper if you find enough people to share the cost of hiring a boat, and can also arrange access via the MV *Liemba*.

Alternatively, you can arrange things yourself. **Flights** are currently limited to charters from Arusha and Mwanza, but Coastal Aviation may soon be introducing **scheduled flights** to Mahale from Mwanza via Tabora, returning via Katavi and Kigoma. The airstrip is close to the park headquarters.

Otherwise, the only access is by **boat from Kigoma**, 130km to the north, which takes up to ten hours. Given spiralling fuel costs, hiring a motorboat is bitterly expensive unless you can muster a large enough group, with costs starting at $900 for a vessel seating eight or ten people. Kigoma's *Lake Tanganyika Beach Hotel* (see p.540) is currently the cheapest place for arranging this. You could also check with the TANAPA office in Kibirizi, 3km north of Kigoma (T028/280 3040), or the Mahale Mountains Wildlife Research Centre on Bangwe Road in Kigoma (T028/280 2072) whether they have a trip heading down to Mahale, as they may have spare seats.

Considerably cheaper, but not for everyone, is to catch the **MV Liemba** ferry on Wednesday at 4pm (see p.541), or the military vessel **MV Burombora** from Kibirizi (Mon & Fri at 5pm; an extremely reasonable Tsh3500), both of which drop anchor off **Mgambo** (also called Lagosa), 15km north of the park, before midnight the same day. You'll need onward boat transport from there to the park headquarters, which should ideally be arranged in Kigoma: contact the Mahale Mountains Wildlife Research Centre or TANAPA's office in Kibirizi, either of which should be able to **radio call** the park to let them know you're coming. If you arrive in Mgambo without having contacted the authorities, you'll need to rent a local boat for the trip (2–3hr) to the park headquarters at Kasiha. You might strike lucky at night, but it's far safer to await sunrise before setting off. Getting back to Kigoma is just as awkward, with the MV *Liemba* passing Mgambo in the wee hours of Sunday morning.

Lastly, whilst it's possible to catch a **lake taxi** all the way from Kibirizi or Ujiji to the park (locals pay Tsh4000; you almost certainly won't), the lengthy (16–24hr) trip is anything but comfortable, and is also potentially dangerous – see p.541.

Entrance fees and information

Park fees are $80 per person for 24 hours, though if TANAPA have their wicked way there may eventually also be a substantial chimp-trekking fee (anything up to $100 per trek, possibly from 2007 onwards). The obligatory guide/armed ranger costs $20 per walk, more if you're fly-camping and he stays overnight. **Children** under ten are not allowed on chimp treks, and may not be admitted inside the park in any case.

The park is **best visited** during the dry season (May to mid-Oct). A good source of information is the **Mahale Mountains Wildlife Research Centre** on Bangwe Road in Kigoma (T028/280 2072), or check out the park **website** at ⓦwww.tanzaniaparks.com/mahale.htm. TANAPA's *Gombe* **guidebook** has a good section on Mahale, and is available in Arusha, Dar and Stone Town; alternatively, a good **coffee table book** is *Mahale: a photographic encounter with chimpanzees* by Angelika Hofer *et al* (Sterling, 2000).

Accommodation

Accommodation in Mahale is either basic and comparatively cheap ($30 per person in *bandas* or camping, plus park fees), or scaldingly expensive but beautifully pampered.

Mango Tree Park Bandas At Kasiha near the park headquarters. Run by TANAPA (bookings rarely if ever required), this former guest house 100m from the shore provides Mahale's cheapest rooms and perfectly reasonable ones at that, with eight en-suite twin-bed rooms and a kitchen. Bring cooking equipment, fuel, food, drinks and bed sheets. $30 per person. ❺

Nkungwe Luxury Tented Camp On the beach between the Kasiha and Sinsiba streams, 2km south of the park headquarters ⓦwww.chimpanzeesafaris.com (book through Chimpanzee Safaris at *Kigoma*

Mahale's chimpanzees

The Mahale Mountains are one of the world's last strongholds for **wild chimpanzees**, with a population estimated at seven hundred to a thousand individuals in fifteen to twenty communities; several more of which are believed to exist outside the park. Despite their number, the chimps can be difficult to see, so be patient. **Visits** are limited in length to an hour, and group sizes to ten people, five being preferable. Read the box on "Chimpanzee etiquette" on p.548.

Wildlife research in the Mahale Mountains has been dominated by Japan's **Kyoto University** since 1961, when primate expert Junichiro Itani and his colleagues began exploring the shoreline south of Kigoma. The primatologists' work has focused on two communities in the northwest of the park in the Kasoge area, close to the tourist accommodation. Areas of research include their use of medicinal plants, predatory behaviour, infanticide and cannibalism, temporary adoption of infants and "dialects" in their gestural language (there's an excellent essay on chimpanzee communication at ⓦ www.mnsu.edu/emuseum/cultural/language/chimpanzee.html).

Mahale's chimps have been separated from Gombe's for quite some time, as their social behaviour, use of tools and diet differ markedly – Gombe's chimps eat termites by probing the mounds with sticks, for example, but do not eat tree ants, whereas Mahale's chimps catch tree ants in the same way but leave the termites alone. Mahale's chimps also have a unique "handshake". For more **information** about chimp research at Mahale, see ⓦ http://jinrui.zool.kyoto-u.ac.jp/ChimpHome/mahaleE.html (keep the mixed case or it won't work).

Hilltop Hotel in Kigoma; see p.534). If you've got this kind of money ($700 per double room), spend a little more to stay at *Nomad Mahale*, as *Nkungwe* doesn't really compare – unless you get a good price for it. There are six lake-facing twin-bed tents on wooden platforms, each with attached bathroom, an attractive reception area on the beach, beach loungers, and evening campfires. Canoes and snorkelling gear available. Closed March & April. ❾

Nomad Mahale Camp (aka *Greystoke Mahale* and *Zoe's Camp*) Two hours by dhow from the airstrip ⓦ www.nomad-tanzania.com (book through Nomad Tanzania in Arusha; see p.407). This English-run set-up inspires travel hacks into penning ecstatic thesauri of purple prose, some of it possibly justified, as well it should be given the shocking cost: the main reason for which being the idyllic location on a small sandy bay backed by palm trees and forested slopes. The guides are good too, as are meals (breakfast and sushi on the beach), and the attractively bizarre main building, a play of triangular forms, is as close as grass architecture gets to sci-fi. Guests stay in six twin-bed tents pitched on wooden decks, with a chill-out zone above each reached by a ladder built into a canoe – all in all satisfyingly theatrical if extremely pretentious "glamour in the wild". Rates ($850–970 double) include chimp tracking, forest walks, dhow trips (in search of hippo), snorkelling and fishing. Closed mid-March to mid-May. No children under 6. ❾

TANAPA Campsite The most atmospheric way of staying over, close to the park headquarters; facilities are limited to long-drops and water. Camping in the bush is possible elsewhere, but has to be arranged with the park headquarters. Bring enough food for the duration. $30 per person. ❺

The park

Mahale offers a wide range of **walks**. You must be accompanied by an armed guard, who will be able to advise you about recent sightings of chimps and leopards. The **lakeshore**, with its reeds, swamps and grassland is good for birds, including nesting speckled mousebirds in the stands of oil palms around Kasiha. Large game is rare on the shore, although antelopes come here to drink and African hunting dogs are also seen from time to time. Mahale's richest habitat, however, is the lowland **gallery forests** in the northwest of the park, where the mountains rise from close to the shoreline, ascending to around 1300m. Apart from the famous chimpanzees and the leopards, the forest – like Gombe's

△ Young chimpanzee, Gombe Stream National Park

– contains several animal and plant species more typical of western than eastern Africa, including the brush-tailed porcupine, the red-legged sun squirrel, the giant forest squirrel and the bushy-tailed mongoose. Forest birds to look out for are the crested guinea fowl and Ross's turaco – the latter is evasive, despite its vivid coloration, as it spends all its time in the forest canopy.

The misty **mountains** themselves are also home to a small population of black-and-white colobus monkeys. Their range is restricted to the belt of bamboo and montane forest above 2000m on Mount Nkungwe. Above 2300m the forests give way to grassland. One- or two-night camping hikes up and down **Mount Nkungwe** are possible, but must be arranged in advance with the park authorities or the tented camps; longer trips can be arranged to explore the drier **eastern slopes** of the mountains, which are covered by *miombo* woodland, acacia and "terminalia" savannah (characterized by termite mounds). Plains game is abundant, and includes elephant, giraffe, zebra, buffalo and warthog, together with rare roan antelopes and their predators – lion, spotted hyena and the endangered African hunting dog.

Unyamwezi

Occupying much of the tsetse-fly-infested *miombo* woodland of the Central Plateau, Tabora Region – popularly known as **Unyamwezi** after the dominant tribe – used to straddle two of East Africa's most lucrative and heavily travelled nineteenth-century ivory and slave caravan routes to the Indian Ocean: from Ujiji on Lake Tanganyika, which was the main transit port for slaves from the Congo Basin, and from Lake Victoria in the north. The routes converged on **Kazeh** ("Kingdom"), 15km southwest of Tabora, which at its height in the 1860s saw an estimated half a million porters and uncounted slaves pass through each year. Later, the focus of trade shifted to Arab-controlled **Tabora**, now a bustling town of two hundred thousand people and the regional capital. Tabora's importance as a trading centre has remained, thanks to the **Central Line Railway**, which follows the routes of the old caravan trails almost exactly, and provides easy access westwards to Kigoma on Lake Tanganyika and north to Mwanza on Lake Victoria. The legacy of the slave and ivory caravans lingers on in the form of Islam, which is becoming the region's dominant religion, and in the name of the region's major tribe, the million-strong **Nyamwezi**, which means "of the moon" in Kiswahili – an appellation used by the coastal Swahili and Arabs to describe a number of tribes to the west, where the moon sets.

Tabora

Whereas Kazeh has all but disappeared, its hot and dusty neighbour **TABORA** has continued to prosper as a major trading centre thanks to its position on the Central Railway line. Like the old slaving routes, the railway branches at Tabora, the northern line heading to Mwanza on Lake Victoria, the western one going on to Kigoma on Lake Tanganyika, and to Mpanda. Except for a handful of German buildings, there's not all that much to see in town, but it's a friendly place, and the shady, tree-lined streets provide an attractive and soothing break from the blistering *miombo* woodland that stretches for hundreds of kilometres around, making it a good place to break the exhausting (37–39hr) train journey from Dar es Salaam to Kigoma or Mwanza. There's also a pleasant side trip to the **Livingstone Museum**, 15km southwest of town at Kwihara, the modern incarnation of Kazeh.

Tabora's **climate** is hot all year round, with temperatures peaking at an average of 32°C in September and October before the arrival of the short rains. Still, it's perfectly bearable if you've arrived from the sweltering humidity of Kigoma or the coast. The long rains – scattered heavy showers rather than continuous downpours – generally fall from February to May.

Some history

The history of Tabora and its forerunner Kazeh is very much the history of the **Nyamwezi people**, who by the mid-1700s had come to dominate the

Chief Mirambo

It was only in the nineteenth century that the Nyamwezi coalesced into a unified state, **Unyanyembe**, largely built on wealth accrued from the ivory trade, much of which was controlled by the Nyamwezi themselves. The appearance of wealthy Nyamwezi traders in the coastal ports soon aroused the avarice of the Zanzibari sultanate, which from the 1850s onwards launched increasingly confident incursions along Nyamwezi caravan routes, dealing not only in ivory but increasingly in slaves. As a result, the balance of power between hundreds of central Tanzanian clans and tribes broke down, and a new generation of leaders with little respect for the established way of things rose to prominence.

One of these was **Chief Mirambo-ya-Banhu**, who by 1871 had managed, mainly through conquest, to establish a rival state to Unyanyembe called **Unyamwezi**, which at its zenith between 1876 and 1881 extended as far as northwest Tanzania and Congo. Mirambo controlled the entire western caravan route from Tabora to Ujiji, including the valuable salt workings and Malagarasi river crossing at Uvinza, as well as another caravan route heading up the western shore of Lake Victoria towards Uganda's powerful Buganda empire, whose hegemony he briefly threatened – not without reason did Stanley dub him "this black Bonaparte". And like Napoleon, Mirambo's rule was very much a product of his character: "Throughout all my travels in Africa I have not yet met such disinterested kindness as I have received from the great bandit Mirambo", effused Stanley in 1876. "He is tall, large chested and a very fine specimen of a well-made man [and] as quiet as a lamb in conversation, rather harmless looking than otherwise, but in war the skulls which line the road to his gates reveal too terribly the ardour which animates him."

Mirambo's success was manifold. Geographically, his empire effectively blocked the Arab trade routes to Lake Tanganyika. Militarily, the vast wealth that the Nyamwezi had gained from the ivory and slave trade enabled the purchase of firearms from Zanzibar and the hiring of *Ruga-Ruga* mercenaries from the Ngoni tribe, who had conquered their way up from southern Africa since the 1820s, all of which meant that Mirambo's empire was engaged in **incessant warfare**, be it against Arabs or neighbouring chiefs. To consolidate his power, Mirambo reappointed governors of captured territories as agents and consuls, and even made an alliance with Sultan Barghash of Zanzibar, who had been trying to extend his own influence into the interior.

The fact that the empire was held together largely by war, and the force of Mirambo's personality, meant that it quickly disintegrated following his death in December 1884, paving the way for the arrival of the Germans a few years later. Nowadays, Mirambo is considered something of a national hero, not so much for his empire-building skills as for the fact that he managed to trump the Arabs over so many years.

ivory trade of central Tanzania. A century later, with the Omani-dominated slave trade eclipsing ivory, Nyamwezi traders and porters were commonly seen on the coast, having followed the trading routes that they had developed, while the Nyamwezi themselves also organized slave hunts. By the 1850s, under the rule of chiefs Swetu I and Saidi Fundikira I, both Tabora and Kazeh were well established, and over the following decade an estimated half-million porters passed through the twin towns every year. The towns – and the Nyamwezi – grew rich on taxes levied on caravans, as well as from the profits of caravans operated by the Nyamwezi themselves, whilst their increasing power was typified by the establishment of a short-lived but extremely powerful new state established by Chief Mirambo (see box on p.555), which successfully challenged Arab hegemony over the slaving routes in the 1870s.

During the **German conquest** of Tanganyika, an outpost and then a fort (the still-existing Boma) were raised in Tabora, surviving an armed rebellion in 1891 led by Chief Isike "Mwana Kiyungi" of Unyanyembe – defeated the following January, Isike chose to blow himself up in the armoury of his fort rather than surrender. The German victory made a considerable impression on lesser chiefs, some of whom took to sending envoys to Tabora for help in local conflicts. In signing treaties with the Germans, they effectively handed over their land to the colonists, and with the Nyamwezi "pacified", the Germans set about developing Tabora itself. The **Central Line Railway** (*Mittelland Bahn*) from Dar es Salaam reached Tabora in 1912, and before the outbreak of World War I had been extended to Kigoma. German efforts to open up the territory were in vain, however: in September 1916 they were ejected from Tabora after a fierce ten-day battle with Belgian troops from Congo, under the command of Colonel Tombeur. The British took control of Tabora after the war, and in 1928 gave the go-ahead for the extension of the railway from Tabora to Mwanza, thereby assuring the continued prosperity of both towns.

Arrival

The **train station** is at the east end of Station Road, 1.5km from the bus stand – taxis converge on the station whenever a train is due. Trains from Dar and Dodoma should arrive at 6.30pm; coming from Mwanza or Kigoma, you should pull in just before sunrise. The train from Mpanda rolls in at 2.45am, at least in theory; the *Orion Tabora Hotel*, 400m from the station, will let you in at this time. If you're looking for somewhere cheaper, hang around for a few hours until sunrise – there's a café inside the station, while the 24-hour *Police Mess* on Boma Road sells food and drinks.

Buses use the new central bus stand beside the open-air market. There are daily buses from Mwanza and Nzega, and less frequent services from Arusha, Dodoma, Singida and Mbeya. Tabora **airport** lies a few kilometres south of town; the only flight is the daily Precisionair service from Dar. **Taxis** can be found at the junction of Market and Lumumba streets, outside the market, and at the bus station.

Accommodation

Reviewed below is Tabora's only mid-range **hotel**, plus the best of the budget ones – there are many other cheap **guest houses** (all ➊) spread out around the junction of Boma Road and Manyema Street. Excepting the *Moravian Church Hostel* and *Orion Tabora Hotel*, "single" rooms can be shared by couples. Tabora's

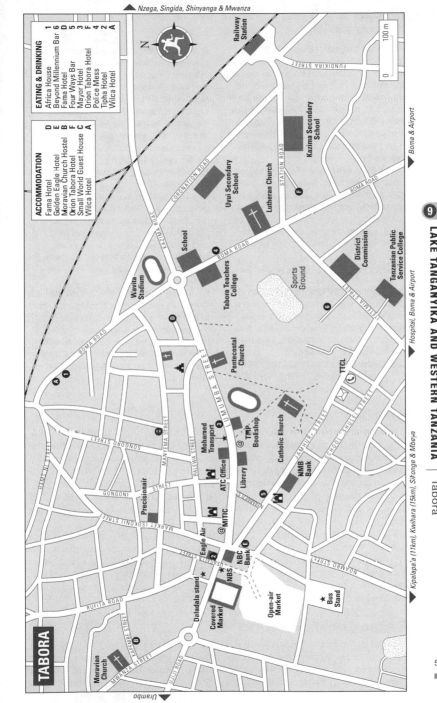

TABORA

ACCOMMODATION
Fama Hotel	D
Golden Eagle Hotel	E
Moravian Church Hostel	B
Orion Tabora Hotel	F
Small World Guest House	C
Wilca Hotel	A

EATING & DRINKING
Africa House	1
Beyond Millennium Bar	6
Fama Hotel	D
Four Ways Bar	5
Mayor Hotel	3
Orion Tabora Hotel	F
Police Mess	4
Tipha Hotel	2
Wilca Hotel	A

Nzega, Singida, Shinyanga & Mwanza

Railway Station

Kazima Secondary School

Uyui Secondary School

Lutheran Church

Tabora Teachers College

Wavita Stadium

Pentecostal Church

Catholic Church

District Commission

Tanzanian Public Service College

Sports Ground

TTCL

TMP Bookshop

Mohamed Transport

Library

NMB Bank

NBC Bank

Eagle Air

Precisionair

ATC Office

Moravian Church

Daladala stand

Covered Market

Open-air Market

Bus Stand

CORONATION ROAD
STATION ROAD
BOMA ROAD
KAZIMA ROAD
FUNDIKIRA STREET
LUMUMBA STREET
SONGORO STREET
MANYEMA STREET
BALEWA STREET
HAMISI STREET
GONGONI STREET
MARKET (SOKONI) STREET
KIVAILA STREET
RUFITA ROAD
KAPEMBE STREET
MWANZA STREET
ULULI ROAD
JAMHURI STREET
SCHOOL (SHULE) STREET
NKRUMAH STREET
NDABO STREET
LUMUMBA STREET
LELEMA STREET

Boma & Airport

Hospital, Boma & Airport

Kipalapa'a (11km), Kwihara (15km), Sitonge & Mbeya

Urambo

0   100 m

9

LAKE TANGANYIKA AND WESTERN TANZANIA | Tabora

557

tap water is, on the rare occasions it flows, highly discoloured but drinkable if properly purified.

Fama Hotel Signposted off Lumumba St ☎026/260 4657. A lovely little place tucked away in a quiet corner with a few shady Indian almond (*mkungu*) trees. The rooms are getting tatty and not everything works, but all have fans and box nets, private bathrooms with Western-style toilets, clean beds with cotton sheets, and running water. The "single" rooms have huge beds. The restaurant is good, and there's also safe parking. Breakfast included. ❷

Golden Eagle Hotel Corner of Market and Jamhuri streets, entrance through the car park ☎026/260 4134. Another good-value place, especially if you want a TV (though cheaper rooms lack TVs, and also share bathrooms). The rooms are getting tatty, but all have fans, and some also have box nets and bathtubs. There's also a first-floor bar and restaurant. ❶–❷

Moravian Church Hostel Corner of Kapembe and Mwanza streets ☎026/260 4822, ✉mcwt@taboraonline.com. This friendly and pleasant place is the best-value budget option in town, with clean and cool rooms with mosquito nets and washbasins. There are only ten of them though, so you'll need to arrive early. Food available if ordered well in advance. ❶

🏃 **Orion Tabora Hotel** Station Rd, 400m from the station ☎026/260 4369, ✉oriontbrhotel@spidersat.net. This charming German railway hotel has been completely renovated and expanded, but still retains its allure. Best value are rooms in the old Kaizer Wing, with high ceilings, big beds, net, fan, carpet, phone, digital TV, and screened-off balconies facing the gardens. Rooms in the other wings are not all that different, but may lack balconies and are more expensive. There's also a restaurant and two bars (live music Fri, discos Wed & Sat), tortoises on the lawn, and safe parking. Breakfast included. ❺

Small World Guest House Manyema St (no phone). One of the better budget places, this has a choice of clean rooms with squat toilets and bucket showers, or cheaper ones with shared bathrooms. The beds are large and have nets, and there's a TV in the bar, though food is limited to the usual *chipsi mayai* and *mishkaki*. ❶

Wilca Hotel Top of Boma Rd ☎026/260 4106. This has ten en-suite rooms in a calm and peaceful atmosphere, all with large double beds, nets on request (rooms are usually sprayed), ceiling fans and running hot water; some also have TVs (same price), but not all have toilet seats. There's also a bar, restaurant, and safe parking. Breakfast included. ❷

The Town

There's nothing much to see in Tabora itself, but the plentiful mango and flame trees shading many of its streets provide a pretty spectacle when in bloom – the mango trees are believed to have been unwittingly introduced by slaves who discarded the stones during their painful trek to the coast. Relics from German times include the **train station**, with its steep central gable and lime-green roof, and the imposingly robust **German Boma** (or fort) at the south end of Boma Road, overlooking a small valley to the east. It's now occupied by the military, so a visit (and photography) is sadly out of the question.

The lively **central market**, both covered and outdoors, is also worth a wander, with distinct areas set aside for anything from bicycle parts and tyre recyclers, to a huge section dedicated to the diminutive dried *dagaa* fish which is brought in by rail from Kigoma. For *kangas* (the colourful wraps worn by Tanzanian women), try any of the shops on Balewa Street off Market Street.

Eating and drinking

Tabora's perked up considerably in the food department, and isn't too bad either for nightlife, especially **live music**: Nyamyembe are worth seeking out, whilst the famous and eminently danceable **Tabora Sound Band** (formerly Tabora Jazz; also known by their *Sensema Malunde* dance style) perform several times a week. Apart from *Africa House*, reviewed below, two other places that host visiting big-name bands (and edifying events like beauty contests) are the Tabora Teachers College on Boma Road, and UHAZILI – the Tanzania Public Service College – on Itetemia Street.

Africa House Boma Rd. A dozy bar for most of the week (it sometimes closes mid-afternoon), things gets busy on Wednesday and Saturday when Tabora Sound Band are in residence. Food consists of the usual grills and chip omelettes.

Beyond Millennium Bar Off Itetemia St. Currently the most popular of several local beer garden-style bars, also with cheap food.

Fama Hotel Signposted off Lumumba St. The pleasantly calm bar here (even the TV volume is kept down) also serves up some superb food for under Tsh2500 – their *maini* (ox liver) in particular is delicious.

Four Ways Bar Jamhuri St. A long, dusty garden which hosts discos or live music most Saturdays (from 8pm), often enough Tabora Sound if they get displaced from *Africa House* by touring groups. Grilled meats, chips and eggs are available throughout the day.

Mayor Hotel Lumumba St. This makes a pleasant change from the usual fare as long as you don't look too closely at what's crawling around on the counter. The food is self-service Indian-Tanzanian (you can fill up for Tsh1500) and includes snacks like soft ice cream, fruit juices and weirdly tasty vanilla-laced tea (flavoured with last week's ice cream?). Despite the dubious hygiene, it's popular for breakfast and gets packed at lunchtimes. No alcohol.

Orion Tabora Hotel Station Rd, 400m from the station. Set in pleasant gardens, this renovated old hotel is good for both food and drinks, with an extremely well-stocked bar. The food – if you order a day in advance – is particularly accomplished, with local dishes (around Tsh5000) featuring stuff like cassava leaves (*kisamvu*) and pumpkin leaves (*msusa*). There's also a selection of Indian and Chinese dishes (Tsh6000–7000 a plate). Eat or drink inside or out. Entertainment comprises Tabora Sound Band (Fri from 8pm; Tsh2500) and free discos (Wed & Sat).

Police Mess Boma Rd. This 24-hour outdoor bar also dishes up good food (oxtail soup, *mtori* banana stew and *nyama choma*), and hosts live bands every so often, usually Saturdays, including the danceable Nyanyembe Stars: check whether there's a banner announcing a forthcoming gig.

Tipha Hotel Ujiji Rd, facing the daladala stand. Great snacks like *sambusa* and *kababu*, even better meals (banana, *ugali*, or rice with fish or beef) and totally superb *supu* for breakfast. And cheap too.

Wilca Hotel Boma Rd. A very calm place with a wide choice of well-prepared food, all for around Tsh3500 – the roast chicken is especially good, and there are also a few cheap vegetarian dishes, but the "pizzas" are actually stuffed chapatis (*mantabali*). There's also a pool table and shaded seating under trees.

Listings

Airlines Precisionair, Old Bhakhresa Building, Market St ℡026/260 4818 or 0744/496766.

Bookshops TMP Bookshop, Lumumba St, has one or two interesting books on proverbs, some nicely illustrated children's books, and a ton of stodgy Christian texts.

Football Local matches are played at the small Wavita Stadium at the corner of Boma and Kazima roads most Saturdays. Entrance is a few hundred shillings.

Hospital The government-run district hospital is on Kitete St, west of the Boma ℡026/260 3269.

Internet access Can be awkward. Of the three places on Lumumba St only Tabora Online (daily 9am–8pm; Tsh1500/hr) is regularly open, but it has very badly maintained computers infested with viruses and malware.

Library The municipal library, Lumumba St (Mon–Fri 9am–6pm, Sat 9am–2pm; daily membership Tsh500) is well stocked with English-language works on Tanzania and Africa.

Money NBC Bank, at the corner of Market and Lumumba streets, is the most efficient, taking around forty minutes to process travellers' cheques, less for cash, and also has a Visa/Master-Card ATM.

Police Jamhuri St, near the junction with School St.

Telephones TTCL by the post office, Jamhuri St. Cheaper Internet calls through Tabora Online, Lumumba St (daily 9am–8pm; Tsh1000/minute internationally).

By road

Improvements on the roads between Tabora and Dodoma or Mwanza mean that **buses** are slightly more predictable these days, if only in the dry season; in the rains, huge delays (overnights stuck in tiny villages) or cancellations are still the norm, so factor in plenty of time for travelling. The new bus stand is beside the open-air market: tickets can be bought there or at a few offices elsewhere (noted below). Most buses get fully booked days in advance, so buy your ticket as early as possible. Buses are invariably overcrowded, making for intensely uncomfortable journeys, even if you're seated. Avoid seats at the back – the bumpy roads will toss you all over the place.

The road to **Mwanza** is unlikely to be cut except in the very worst weather. Daily 6am services are operated by Mohamed Transport (office on Lumumba St; ☎0748/566505) and NBS (Ujiji Road, behind NBC bank; ☎026/260 5132). For **Dodoma**, buses use a "short cut" along the railway (5.30–6am). The companies are Anam, Mabruck Aleyck, Sabena and Supersonic. For **Dar es Salaam**, buy a ticket to Dodoma and move on from there the following day on Scandinavian or Shabiby. For **Singida** and **Arusha**, the only direct bus is NBS (Wed & Sat 6am). Alternatively, catch a bus to **Igunga** and change there (next day – try the *Booksellers Lodge*; ❶), or a Mwanza- or Kahama-bound bus (daily except Sun; NBS and Supersonic are the companies) as far as the dusty and fly-ridden town of **Nzega**, where you'll likely spend the night before moving on: *Nzega Motel* (❶), on the Singida road, 1km northeast of the bus stand, is decent. Lastly, you could go instead towards Dodoma, getting off at **Manyoni**, a major yet friendly truck stopover with several guest houses, of which the *Victoria Falls* and *Nile Falls* (both ❶) are fine, and from where there's onward transport – possibly the same day – to Singida.

Heading west, there are daily buses to Urambo (around noon), but nothing whatsoever further west, so for Kigoma catch a train or plane, or – for a time-consuming detour – go to Mwanza and move on from there. Heading south to **Mbeya** is a bone-rattling, dry-season-only adventure, with luck taking as "little" as eighteen hours: Sabena's (☎0744/825776) buses run from Tabora on Wednesday and Sunday at 5.30am.

By train

The ticket office at the train station is open daily 8am–noon & 2–4.30pm, and for two hours before departures. **Eastbound trains** for Dodoma and Dar leave at 7.25am (Mon, Wed & Fri). **Westbound** services (Mon, Wed & Sat) leave at 8.10pm for Kigoma and 9.30pm for Mwanza. Trains to **Mpanda** head off at 9pm (Mon, Wed & Fri). The fare to Dar is Tsh32,700 (1st class), Tsh24,200 (2nd sleeper) and Tsh11,000–13,000 (seat); for Kigoma, it's Tsh18,000 first-class, Tsh14,000 in a second-class sleeper, and around Tsh6000 for a seat. The **timetable** is at ⓦwww.trctz.com.

By plane

The only **scheduled flights** from Tabora are the daily Precisionair service to Kigoma and thence to Dar es Salaam. At the time of writing, Coastal Aviation were toying with a loop from Mwanza, going clockwise via Tabora, Mahale, Katavi and Kigoma.

Kwihara

Fifteen kilometres southwest of Tabora is **KWIHARA**, known to nineteenth-century explorers as **Kazeh**. Until the German development of Tabora, Kazeh was by far the more important of the two towns, serving as a major caravanserai – a stop for caravans – along the slave route from Ujiji to the coast. Speke and Burton passed through in 1857, and visited the town again in June 1858, having "discovered" Lake Tanganyika. But the most famous of Kazeh's visitors were undoubtedly Stanley and Livingstone, who arrived here in 1872 following their legendary meeting in Ujiji (more on the duo on p.538). Stanley was most impressed by Kazeh: "On my honour, it was a most comfortable place, this, in Central Africa."

It seems incredible that all that remains of this famous town is a handful of crumbling earth houses, a few mango trees and coconut palms introduced by the Arabs, and a quirky **museum** dedicated to Livingstone. Despite all this, the place's historical importance, as well as the rural scenery scattered with flat granite outcrops, repays the hassle of reaching it.

The Livingstone Museum

The **Livingstone Museum** (Tembe la Livingstone; no set times; Tsh2000), which boasts a beautiful Swahili-style carved door frame, is a 1957 reconstruction of the fortified house (*tembe*) where the good doctor stayed following his meeting with Stanley at Ujiji. The pair arrived in Kazeh on February 18, 1872, and while Stanley went back to the coast, Livingstone stayed on awaiting supplies. He left Kazeh on August 25 for what proved to be his final journey, dying eight months later at Chitambo, near Lake Bangweulu in present-day Zambia.

The curator will show you a box containing a lock of hair from the famous missionary, and a piece of the Ujiji mango tree under which Stanley allegedly met Livingstone. There's a room containing photocopies of pages from Livingstone's journals, reproductions of hand-drawn and later maps, and copies of contemporary US newspapers. The other rooms are empty but bear labels: Donkeys, Kitchen, *Askaris*, Bombay. The latter refers to Saidi Mbarak Mombay, the leader of Stanley's "exceedingly fine-looking body of men" during his quest for Livingstone; he'd previously worked for Burton, Speke and Grant. During the expedition, Stanley was also accompanied by **John William Shaw**, who fell ill repeatedly and finally died in Kazeh in 1871. During their journey, Stanley and Shaw had travelled for a time with an Arab army, thinking it would offer safe passage further west; unfortunately for them it was routed by Chief Mirambo at Wilyankuru. In typically obtuse form, Stanley blamed Shaw for the defeat, calling him "base and mean" in his memoirs, though the phrase is surely more applicable to the racist, murderous and implacably heartless Stanley himself, as amply evidenced by his own writings (*How I Found Livingstone* – Epaulet in the US; also free at ⓦwww.gutenberg.org/etext/5157). Shaw's grave lies 100m from the museum under a coconut tree.

Practicalities

There's no accommodation in Kwihara, so it can only be visited as a day-trip from Tabora. Taxis charge around Tsh10,000 for the return trip, though the last few kilometres can be a struggle in the rains. Alternatively, if you don't mind walking, catch a bus bound for Sikonge and ask to be dropped off at **Kipala-pala village**, 11km south of Tabora, from where Kwihara is a very pleasant (if largely shadeless) four-kilometre hike though villages and farmland; at Kipala-pala, turn right at the sign for Kwihara School (there's also a small, easily missed sign for Tembe la Livingstone). Heading back to Tabora, there's no guarantee of public transport from Kipalapala, so you might have to hitch. The museum is the large red building on the left just after Kwihara village – the children will alert the curator for you.

Rukwa Region

South of the Central Railway Line between Lake Tanganyika and the western arm of the Great Rift Valley, **Rukwa Region** offers a refreshing change of scenery from the dusty *miombo* woodland to the north. The *miombo* continues to **Katavi National Park** but gives way to open rolling hills as you approach the fresh and relaxing town of **Sumbawanga**, only a few hours from the Zambian border. To the east of Sumbawanga, the **Mbizi Mountains**, still virtually unknown to the outside world, provide a picturesque backdrop. Further east, a shallow depression holds **Lake Rukwa**, a desolate, hot, humid but enchanting destination for those who really want to get away from it all – assuming you can get there at all. For details of boat travel around the southern part of **Lake Tanganyika**, see p.541.

Mpanda

Sprawling over several kilometres at the end of the Central Railway's southern branch, the dusty town of **MPANDA** serves as a transit point for travellers heading between Sumbawanga and Mbeya in the south and Tabora in the north. For the trickle of tourists who make it here by train, the town also acts as a springboard for visits to **Katavi National Park**, 35km to the south.

As might be expected from its strategic location, Mpanda served as a collective village during the failed **Ujamaa** experiment of 1967–77 (see p.733), into which numerous small agricultural tribes such as the Konongo, Bende, Pimbwe and Rwira were forcibly relocated, followed in 1979 and 1998 by people evicted from Katavi National Park. Given the vastly increased population and the district's low rainfall and poor soil, the environmental outcome has been predictably destructive. The continued use of unsustainable **slash–and–burn agriculture** has removed all tree and shrub cover in many areas, causing flooding and massive soil erosion during the rains. This in turn has led to the silting up and disappearance of Lake Chada in Katavi National Park, and billowing clouds of dust in the dry season, which account for the unusually high rate of eye disease among Mpanda's inhabitants. Things haven't been helped by an influx of Sukuma **cattle herders** from the north, who have placed even greater pressure on the region's meagre natural resources. For all their woes, the people are exceptionally friendly and welcoming, and deserve much better than they've got.

Practicalities

Most people arrive on the **train from Tabora**; this theoretically pulls in at 10.30am, but is often delayed by an hour or two. Make sure you get up at sunrise on the train to catch the evocative sight of the subtly coloured and misty deciduous woodland between the railway and Ugalla River Game Reserve in the east, and the tiny settlements of bark gum-tappers and honey collectors by the rail tracks. The train station is at the west end of town. To get to the centre, follow the stream of passengers back along the rail tracks and turn left onto the first road. *Super City Hotel* is 100m ahead, and the roundabout referred to in our reviews is 50m further on.

Arriving **by road** you're most likely to come in from the south, as the roads north and east (from Uvinza and Inyonga respectively) are in a dire state and become impassable during the rains, and the road from Inyonga to Sikonge is subject to occasional bandit attacks. Buses, trucks and pick-ups arrive at the **bus stand** outside *Super City Hotel*, apart from some pick-ups coming from the south, which stop at the Tawaqal petrol station on the west side of town. To get to the main guest houses from here, turn right and walk 200m up the avenue, then take the second left. Continue straight for 800m and you'll arrive at the roundabout beside the *Super City Hotel*. For details on getting to Mpanda from the **Lake Tanganyika port** of Karema, see the box on p.541.

NMB **bank** takes forever but does eventually change travellers' cheques; it's about 1.5km from the market on the northeastern fringes of town. The **post office** is close to the main market in the centre of Mpanda, and the **TTCL** phone office is close to the police station at the northwestern edge of town – alternatively, there's a card phone at *Super City Hotel*.

Accommodation

There are plenty of perfectly decent cheap **hotels** scattered around town. Running water is erratic, so you'll probably have the pleasure of bucket showers (again).

Super City Family Guest House Mjimwema area, 400m northeast of the *Vatican Guest House* (no phone). Fifteen spotless rooms with ceiling fans, nets, showers and Western-style toilets; there's also a small bar, and food available. **❶**

Super City Hotel By the transport stand ☏025/282 0160. This long-standing favourite has rooms with fans, nets and either private or shared bathrooms – the toilets lack seats, but there's running water most of the time. There's also a good bar in front, although service is somnolent. **❶**

Vatican Guest House Immediately behind *Super City Hotel* ☏025/282 0065. A friendly, family-run budget option with large clean rooms, some with private bath, and all with ceiling fans and nets. Go down the alley on the right side of *Super City Hotel*, or walk around the parking lot by the roundabout. **❶**

Eating, drinking and nightlife

Mpanda's most atmospheric **restaurant** is the *Garden Club*, close to the *Paradise Discotheque* (see below). The nameless restaurant next to *Super City Hotel* serves up tasty if somewhat dentally challenging grilled chicken, together with *ugali*, beans or rice, all for under Tsh2000. The little brick café facing it is handy for an early breakfast and does a lovely cup of tea; cups of *uji* finger-millet porridge are served up by women outside. For your own supplies, head to one of the town's **markets**, both of which are extraordinarily cheap. The larger one (ask for the *sokoni kuu* – large market) is in the Majengo area: walk northeast from the roundabout and follow the road around to the left after 700m, then take the first right and turn left after the Free Pentecostal Church, and the market is behind the buildings on your right. There's a smaller market on the north side of town off the avenue between Tawaqal petrol station to the south, and TTCL and the police station to the northeast.

Mpanda's **bars and nightlife** revolve around four very different places. You can break into a sweat at the *Paradise Discotheque*, southwest of the large market (open Fri & Sat nights, and on Sun from mid-afternoon). Unfortunately, walking back isn't advisable after midnight and there are next to no taxis, so take a reliable local with you if you want to stay out late. The *Super City Hotel*'s bar, with seats under thatched parasols, is the most dignified place for a drink, and also has a TV, but the barmaids have a propensity to overcharge if you don't keep count. Equally pleasant is the *Garden Club*, close to the *Paradise Discotheque*,

Moving on from Mpanda, the **train** heads back to Tabora at 1pm (Tues, Thurs & Sat), arriving just before 3am. Heading to Kigoma by train, get off at Tabora rather than Kalilua, where the lines meet, as you'll arrive at the latter at midnight and the onward connection leaves at 11pm the next night (or two nights later if you take the Saturday train); much better to kick around in Tabora.

Buses, trucks and pick-ups leave from the stand outside *Super City Hotel*. Buses also meet arriving trains at the station. For **Sumbawanga**, the most reliable transport is Sumry Bus (☎025/282 0464), which runs daily, and continues on to **Mbeya**. A handful of **pick-ups** also go to Sumbawanga, the first around 7–8am. The drive south to Sumbawanga goes via Katavi National Park and takes five hours in a private car or pick-up, or six or seven hours by bus. The road is all-weather *murram*, though be warned that if it's not properly maintained it will give way to a quagmire of black cotton soil.

Excepting one or two lorries a month, there's no road transport to **Uvinza** or **Kigoma**; catch the train via Tabora instead. Self-driving, leave before sunrise to have any hope of reaching Uvinza by nightfall (forget about Kigoma in one day), and count on an average speed of 15–20kph.

which has a shady garden and also does food. At the other end of the scale, *Soweto Bar (Kalambo Falls Club)* promises an adventurous night elbow to elbow with local men inebriated on local hooch; again, a reliable local companion is helpful to avoid drunken hassle. To get there, walk northeast from the roundabout by *Super City Hotel*, and turn right just before the road bends left.

Katavi National Park

Thirty-five kilometres south of Mpanda and 143km north of Sumbawanga, **KATAVI NATIONAL PARK** covers 4471 square kilometres, making it Tanzania's fourth-largest protected wildlife area. Given its poor soil and the presence of tsetse flies, the area has always been sparsely inhabited, although it attracted small numbers of hunters in the days before the park's creation, after which all human settlement was prohibited – the last expulsions having taken place in 1998. Some of those evicted now live in Sitalike on the park's northern boundary. Like Mpanda, Sitalike is a former *Ujamaa* village but is a good deal poorer, its inhabitants relying on subsistence farming, along with fishing whenever the Katuma River is in spate. The injustice of excluding locals from parks and restricting their activities in game reserves, whilst accommodating a handful of tourists is rendered starkly apparent by the adjacent Rukwa Game Reserve, whose regulations permit trophy hunting by tourists while forbidding hunting for food by locals.

Whilst the national park doesn't have especially spectacular scenery, its extraordinarily rich **dry-season wildlife viewing**, when vast quantities of game concentrate around rapidly receding water sources, easily makes it one of the gems of Tanzania's wildlife crown. Three species in particular offer stunning photo opportunities: one of Africa's most extensive **buffalo** herds, estimated at the last count to number around sixty thousand; and **crocodiles and hippo** packed into a handful of muddy lake-swamps, whose populations can reach several thousand in each. Other **wildlife** you're likely to see includes elephant (there are well over four thousand), giraffe, zebra and lion, gazelle, large herds of roan and sable antelopes, topi, eland and – in reed beds near the swamps – the southern reedbuck. **Birders** are in for a treat too, with over four hundred recorded species recorded, including eagles, hawks, marabou storks and palm-nut vultures. But the main attraction for many is simply the park's remoteness, and the fact that – given that it attracts a mere 1200 visitors each year – you're pretty much guaranteed to have the place to yourself.

Arrival and information

Most visitors **fly in** to Katavi either direct from Arusha on light aircraft chartered by the upmarket tented camps or safari companies, or – usually as clients of Foxes African Safaris (p.133) – by five-seat Cessna from Ruaha National Park. At the time of writing, Coastal Aviation were proposing scheduled flights from Mwanza to Katavi via Tabora, heading back via Mahale and Kigoma. As walking inside the park is allowed, arriving by **public transport** is a perfectly feasible alternative: **from Tabora**, catch the train to **Mpanda**, from where there are daily road connections to Sitalike, just 1km north of the park headquarters; for details of bus companies and pick-ups, see "Moving on from Mpanda" opposite. You might also get a lift from one of the vehicles used by the tented

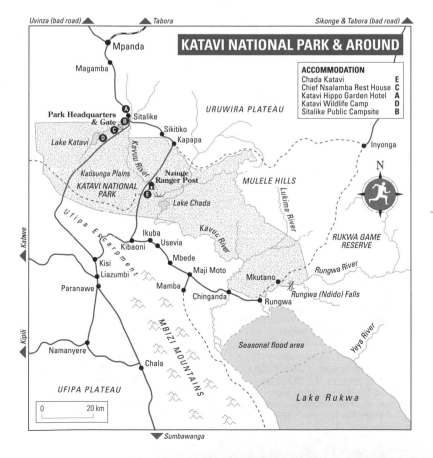

KATAVI NATIONAL PARK & AROUND

ACCOMMODATION

Chada Katavi	E
Chief Nsalamba Rest House	C
Katavi Hippo Garden Hotel	A
Katavi Wildlife Camp	D
Sitalike Public Campsite	B

camp or park staff; they usually park next to the *Super City Hotel* in Mpanda. The ride takes under an hour, and passes through desolate terrain whose few villages are notable for some beautifully decorated houses painted with geometric and floral motifs. Coming **from Mbeya**, catch a bus to **Sumbawanga**, and on from there (if there's no direct service) towards Mpanda, getting off at Sitalike. The road is decently graded and should be open year round. Incidentally, the fifty-kilometre stretch of road which bisects the park is open 24 hours and doesn't require the payment of park fees if you're just passing through. Sitalike village has a few sparsely stocked shops, lots of little bars and soda joints, a couple of basic restaurants and a mid-range hotel.

Entrance fees and information

Entry fees, valid for 24 hours, are $25 per person, and Tsh10,000 for a vehicle permit. Although hiring a **guide** when driving is not compulsory, it's advisable given the lack of proper roads, signs or maps – the cost is $10–15 for a few hours.

The **park headquarters** are 1km south of Sitalike: follow the road out of the village, cross the bridge which marks the park's northern boundary (look for hippos wallowing in the Katavi River below), and turn right after 100m, where you'll pass a number of metal huts; the park headquarters occupy a cluster of brick buildings just beyond. The official **website** is Ⓦ www.tanzaniaparks.com /katavi.htm. There are no park maps other than four adjoining sheets from the Government's Surveys and Mapping Division in Dar (see p.28), which are way out of date – there's a copy on the wall of the principal park warden's office. The **best time to visit** is during the dry season (May–Oct, especially from July, and less so from mid-Dec to Feb). At other times the park is liable to be inaccessible due to the rains, and much of the plains game migrates beyond the park boundaries or into hillier and less accessible terrain. **Tsetse flies** are present all year round, but are especially bad in the rains.

Accommodation

For those with obese bank accounts, a couple of **luxury tented camps** provide a handy means of losing excess wealth; their guests fly in, and rates include game drives, bush walks and park fees. There's more sensibly priced accommodation at **Sitalike** on the park's northern boundary. A recommended alternative is **camping**, which enables you to do walks over several days, though you'll need to be entirely self-sufficient. Pitches are limited to *Sitalike Public Campsite* near the park headquarters ($30 per person plus park fees) and informal sites elsewhere which rangers can recommend ($50 per person if considered "special"). Basic supplies can be bought in Sitalike.

Chada Katavi (aka *Katavi Luxury Tented Camp* or *Roland's Camp*) On a wooded rise northwest of the Chada flood plain Ⓦ www.nomad-tanzania .com (book through Nomad Tanzania in Arusha; see p.407). Travel hacks tie themselves in knots talking this one up, but one fact remains: it's just a bunch of tents (six, to be precise), the pleasure of staying in one of which – three nights minimum – costs more than the average rural Tanzanian earns in five years. Park fees, walks and game drives included. No kids under 10. Closed March–May. All-inclusive ($850–1080 double per night). ❾

Chief Nsalamba Rest House Under 1km south from the park headquarters, off the main road. Basic park-run rooms; book ahead as there are just three (most easily done at TANAPA headquarters in Arusha, see p.403). You'll have to say whether you're bringing your own food or want park staff to arrange meals or cooking equipment. There's no problem walking from the rest house to the village along the main road. $30 per person. ❺

Katavi Hippo Garden Hotel Outside the park at Sitalike (no phone). Several dozen rooms in en-suite *bandas* overlooking the Katama River. They should be able to arrange transport around the park for around $120 a day including driver but excluding park fees. ❹

Katavi Wildlife Camp Katisunga Plains, at the mouth of the Katama River ⓦ www.tanzaniasafaris .info (book through Foxes African Safaris in Dar; see p.133). Similar to *Chada Katavi*, with its six tents set under trees and fronted by green gauze mosquito screens. Most guests fly in by Cessna from Ruaha National Park, where Foxes have another camp. Closed Dec–May. All-inclusive "fly-in" rate ($700 double). ❾

The park

Walking in Katavi is possible as long as you're accompanied by an armed ranger ($20 per walk, more if you camp overnight; they also double as guides). There are no set routes or itineraries, so arrange things with the ranger. You should plan for at least two days, camping overnight, to really get anywhere. A good place to head to is the viewpoint over Lake Katavi and its flood plain, a forty-kilometre round trip from Sitalike. If you're strapped for time, it's possible to do a day's walk from the gate along the Katavi River and back through *miombo* woodland. If you've come by public transport and don't want to walk, the authorities might oblige with a lift or a spare vehicle, though there's nothing formal about this, so you certainly shouldn't count on it, and payment will of course be expected.

The dusty *miombo* and acacia **woodland** that skirts much of the highway through the park is a favoured haunt for giraffe, antelope and elephant. But the park's main attraction is the **seasonally flooded grassland** occupying the area around Lake Katavi (20km southwest of Sitalike), the Katisunga Plains in the centre flanking the Kavuu River, and much of the eastern extension. In the dry season, the grasslands support vast herds of buffalo and plains game, and when still flooded attract waterbirds in their thousands (though driving around the grasslands in the rains is treacherous if not impossible). If you're exceptionally lucky, you may see the shy and rare puku antelope (*Kobus vardoni*), about which very little is yet known – it's also found in Mahale, the Kilombero Valley and in isolated pockets across southern Africa. The **thickets and short grasses** around the edges of the flood plains are inhabited by leopard, lion and elephant, and various antelope species: roan and sable, southern reedbuck, eland and topi. The leopards are, as ever, difficult to spot, but your guide or ranger should be able to point out most of the antelopes.

The park's **lakes** – the palm-fringed Lake Katavi, and Lake Chada at the confluence of the Kavuu and Nsaginia rivers in the centre of the park – are nowadays little more than seasonal flood plains. Their gradual disappearance is due to river-borne silt deposits from the arid badlands between Mpanda and the park – a vivid example of the environmentally damaging consequences of concentrating human settlement in marginally productive areas, the result both of Nyerere's failed *Ujamaa* programme and of evicting people from the

Katabi the hunter

Katavi National Park takes its name from a semi-legendary ancestor of the Pimbwe, Fipa and Bende tribes, **Katabi**. A famed hunter in his time, his spirit is said to reside near Lake Katavi, in a small clearing around two tamarind trees. The site remains sacred, and locals still come here from outside the park to leave offerings, seeking Katabi's intercession with God in worldly matters like asking for rain. The vast hippo pods at either of the park's lakes are said to be Katabi's herds, and if you look really carefully, you might even catch a glimpse of him driving them along the shore...

park. Nonetheless, both lakes retain some extraordinary wildlife viewing, most famously in the form of enormous herds of buffalo, birds in flocks of biblical proportions, and – most amazing in the dry season – literally thousands of hippos squashed together in the park's few remaining **mud pools**, lending visible meaning to the word biomass. At the edges of these glorious mud baths, and along riverbanks, large crocodiles also seek shelter from the dry-season sun by burrowing out nests, often stacked one atop the other. The hippos are best seen at Lake Chada, particularly at the pool close to Nzinge Ranger Post, whilst buffaloes, pelicans and marabou storks yanking out catfish from the mud are best seen from the observation hut overlooking Lake Katavi.

With your own transport, you could visit the permanent streams, small cascades and year-round springs of cooler and wetter escarpment of the forested **Mulele Hills** (also spelled Mlala or Mlele), at the eastern boundary of the park beside Rukwa Game Reserve, while in the far southeast you might head to the **Rungwa (Ndido) Falls** on the Rungwa River, a thundering 100-metre drop into a hippo- and croc-filled pool. If you get this far down, instead of retracing your steps you could follow the dirt road outside the park west from Rungwa village to Kibaoni, where a right turn takes you back into the park. Roughly 40km west of Rungwa you'll pass through the village of **Maji Moto** ("hot water"), just before which there are – no surprise – hot-water springs.

Sumbawanga

The capital of Rukwa region is **SUMBAWANGA**, a pleasantly unimposing sort of place set in the lee of the Mbizi Mountains, whose breezes lend the town a refreshing climate – chilly at night, and just right by day. As a bonus for travellers emerging battered and bruised from a bumpy journey, there's no hassle either. The town's main attraction is the cosy **market** off Mpanda Road – just the place for cheap seasonal fruit and vegetables, *dagaa* fish from Lake Tanganyika and the traditional assortment of imported plastic and aluminium

---

The Fipa

Numbering over two hundred thousand, the **Fipa** (also called the Ichifipa or Fiba) are the largest tribe in Rukwa Region. The majority are farmers who practise an inventive method of cultivation using *ntumba* ("bales" or "packages"). In preparation for the short rains, small mounds 40–60cm high are made from soil and grass, with vegetables sown on top. Following the rains and the harvest, the now highly composted mounds (mixed with the leaves and stems of the vegetables) are levelled and the main crops – finger millet (*ulezi*) and maize – are planted for the long rains. The method minimizes soil erosion, retains moisture long after the rains are gone, ensures the continued fertility of the soil season after season, and dispenses both with fertilizers and the destructive slash-and-burn techniques that have laid waste to much of Mpanda district to the north.

The Fipa's knowledge of soil is also shown by the many brick kilns on the outskirts of town, and by their skill in iron-smelting and iron-working, which they and several other tribes have possessed for at least two millennia. Knowledge of iron-working in Africa is often associated with witchcraft, and the Fipa are no exception, with Sumbawanga being especially famous for it. This is mirrored by the town's name, which appears to be a combination of *sumba*, meaning to light or to kindle, and *mwanga*, which is an enlightened person as well as a witchdoctor.

household goods from China and Taiwan. For cheap second-hand clothes and sandals made on the spot from recycled truck tyres, have a browse through the stalls outside Nelson Mandela Stadium on the way out of town on Mpanda Road. There's really nothing else to see in town, so unless you've got the patience and the stamina to arrange a hike in the **Mbizi Mountains** or down to **Lake Rukwa**, most people just stay a night before heading on towards Mpanda, Katavi National Park, Mbeya or – in the dry season – Kasanga on the shore of Lake Tanganyika.

Practicalities

NBC **bank** on Mpanda Road changes travellers' cheques and has a 24-hour Visa/MasterCard ATM.

Accommodation

The **guest houses** immediately adjacent to the bus stand are pretty grim; the ones a few minutes' walk away in the grid of streets to the south are much better.

Lupila Lodge Kalangasa St ☎025/280 2418. Simple but well-kept rooms, some with private bath, all with nets. ❶

Moravian Conference Centre Mpanda Rd ☎025/280 2853. Large, clean and calm if not overly welcoming Christian guest house, some of its 75 rooms with bathrooms (and hot water). There's also a restaurant, its chapatis as flat as the overall atmosphere. Breakfast included. ❸

New Kisumu Guest House Maendeleo St ☎025/280 2927. A decent budget option similar to the *Lupila* – it's well kept, and some rooms have private bathrooms. ❶

Upendo View Inn Corner Kiwelu Rd and Kalangasa St ☎025/280 2242, ☎025/280 2502. The town's best hotel, with large clean twins (no single rates) with private bathrooms, reliable running water, Western-style toilets and even toilet paper. There's also a restaurant and bar, but the adjacent nightclub is exceedingly noisy. ❷

Zanzibar Annex Off Kiwelu Rd ☎025/280 0010. An excellent choice should the *Upendo* be full, with a choice of rooms with or without private bathroom (the latter are much cheaper). Beds have nets, bathrooms have running water and clean, tiled squat toilets. ❶

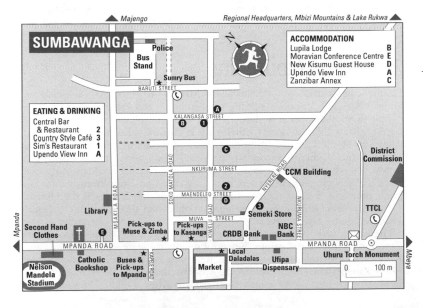

Despite the welter of (boarded-up) bus company offices in and around the now defunct bus stand, only two companies currently operate from Sumbawanga: Air Bus has a perilous reputation; much safer is Sumry (☎025/280 2747) on Baruti Street, which goes daily to **Mbeya and Dar es Salaam** (6.30am), and to **Mpanda** (1pm). There are also daily pick-ups and trucks to Mpanda from the petrol station on the corner of Mpanda and Kapele roads. Pick-ups to **Muse**, on the eastern flank of the Mbizi Mountains north of Sumbawanga, and **Zimba**, near the shore of Lake Rukwa, leave from Mpanda Road: see below for more details. In the dry season, there's at least one vehicle heading to **Kasanga** on Lake Tanganyika at 9am, sometimes later. There's no regular transport to Mbala in **Zambia** (the usual border crossing is via Tunduma along the road to Mbeya), so it's a matter of asking around at the petrol station at the corner of Mpanda and Kapele roads for a truck.

Eating and drinking

The main concentration of **restaurants** is on Maendeleo Street, where the competition keeps standards fairly high. For your own supplies, Semeki Store, at the corner of Nyerere Road and Muva Street, has a reasonable selection of imported produce including tasty South African Ceres juices.

Central Bar & Restaurant Maendeleo St. Friendly local restaurant which is good for cheap breakfasts (great savoury *supus*; take your pick of goat, chicken or liver) and lunches (under Tsh1000), while the attached bar is great for an afternoon drink, its TV tuned to Discovery Channel and CNN during the day to keep locals riveted to the screen.
Country Style Café Nyerere Rd. A neat little café and restaurant with a wide range of snacks and affordable meals.
Sim's Restaurant Corner Kiwelu Rd and Kalangasa St. Long-established place serving up delicious and

filling meals for under Tsh1000, with a choice of meat stew, roast chicken, fish or liver with *ugali* or rice, plus beans and greens. No alcohol.
Upendo View Inn Kalangasa St. This is the most kicking nightspot in town, especially on Wednesday, Friday and Saturday. Entertainment features live music from the Rukwa International Band, plus a "*wazee* disco" (*wazee* are old men), with Tanzanian golden oldies (possibly Fri), some *ngoma ya kiasili* (traditional music) and a children's disco (Sun 2–7pm) followed by one for adults. There's good and reasonably priced food too.

The Mbizi Mountains

Sumbawanga is the base for hikes in the **MBIZI MOUNTAINS**, which are almost completely unknown outside Sumbawanga – and indeed to a good many people in Sumbawanga as well. You'll need to be completely self-sufficient and have a tent, as the only **guest houses** are at **Zimba**, a former German camp (now run by the Catholic Mission) an hour's drive from Sumbawanga on the eastern slopes of the range overlooking Lake Rukwa, and 100km to the north at Mamba, which lies 10km south of the hot-water springs at Maji Moto (see p.568). When camping, make sure you get permission from locals before you pitch your tent. A good source of **information** before leaving is the District Commissioner's Office in Sumbawanga (100m beyond TTCL), or the Regional HQ, 1km along Nyerere Road.

The easiest way to reach the mountains is to take one of the **pick-ups** to Zimba, which leave daily from the petrol station at the corner of Mpanda and Kapele roads between 10am and noon, returning to Sumbawanga around 4pm. From Zimba, you could explore the western shore of Lake Rukwa before heading northwest along a little-used road to Muse (40km). Pick-ups back to Sumbawanga from Muse leave around 4pm. If you want to go directly to Muse, pick-ups depart from Sumbawanga at the same place and time as those for Zimba. For something even more adventurous, the sixty- to seventy-kilo-metre trek northwest towards **Mamba** takes you along the eastern ridge of the mountains via the villages of Nkwilo, Mfinga, Finga and Kilida. The Amour Video Coach **bus** runs from Mamba to Mpanda, 120km north, on Monday, Wednesday and Friday, arriving in time to catch the train to Tabora the following day. **Coming from Mpanda**, they leave around noon on Tuesday, Thursday and Saturday, arriving in Mamba before nightfall.

Lake Rukwa

Occupying the lowest part of the Rukwa Rift Valley (also called the Rukwa Trough), **Lake Rukwa** follows the same northwest–southeast faultline as Lake Nyasa to the south. The water is extremely alkaline, and there are salt pans at **Ivuna**, 15km from the lake's southern shore, fed by hot brine springs. Excavations have established that Iron Age people lived on the lakeshore from as early as the thirteenth century, working the salt, cultivating cereals, keeping cattle, goats, chickens and dogs, and hunting zebra and warthog for food. The trade in Ivuna's salt was sufficiently important to have made the southern shores of Rukwa figure as a stopover on a slaving caravan route to Bagamoyo during the nineteenth century.

Crocodile, hippopotamus and fish abound, of which tilapia provide the basis for a flourishing fishing industry that exports its dried catch as far away as Congo and Zambia's Copperbelt – strange, given the plentiful lake resources in those countries, unless you know that Rukwa's alkaline water makes for tastier and more tender fish. Despite the fishery, the lake could hardly be more different from its western neighbour, Lake Tanganyika: the latter's enormous depth contrasting with Rukwa's average of a mere 3m, while given the lack of an outlet and the unreliability of the streams feeding it, the lake's size is prone to wild variations – at times it actually splits into two lakes separated by a narrow belt of swamp. During the 1820s and 1830s the lake almost dried up, and when the explorer John Hanning Speke passed by in 1859 he saw only an impassable swamp. The lake's chronic siltation over recent decades, hastened by deforestation in its catchment area, appears to have bucked the trend by permanently flooding large expanses of formerly seasonal flood plain, an effect that has grown worse since the exceptionally heavy 1998 El Niño rains. The **Uwanda Game Reserve**, established in 1971 and still marked on maps, has for all practical purposes ceased to exist, as over half of it now lies permanently under water.

Rukwa's main natural attraction is its **birdlife**, with over four hundred species recorded, many of them waterfowl. The disappearance of much of the flood plain and grassland ecosystem has greatly reduced the numbers of **plains game** that once frequented the area, especially after the short rains from November onwards. Still, you might still see zebra and buffalo, rarer animals such as topi and puku antelopes, and – at least according to rumour – an albino giraffe or spotted zebra.

Practicalities

Lake Rukwa can be accessed either from the northwest or the southeast, but whichever route you choose, take everything you'll need with you, and be prepared for the lake's unpleasantly hot and muggy atmosphere. The easiest of the two routes is from **Sumbawanga** in the northwest, which has daily pick-ups to Zimba (see p.570), about 5km from the lakeshore. Access along the **southeast route** from Mbeya via Chunya is much more difficult and really only feasible in your own 4WD, and even then only in the dry season. There are no restrictions on **camping** at the lakeshore (or as near as you can get without becoming stuck in a swamp), but you should seek permission from any locals you can find and keep an eye out for crocodiles and hippos. Swimming is not advisable for this reason, especially on the southeast shore, where the crocodiles are known to be particularly dangerous.

Travel details

Buses and pick-ups

Full details are given in the "moving on" sections throughout this chapter. An asterisk denotes that transport may not run in the rains, or may be hugely delayed.

Kigoma to: Biharamulo (4 weekly*; 7–9hr); Bukoba (4 weekly*; 15–18hr); Kibondo (1–3 daily*; 4–6hr); Mwanza (daily*; 14–18hr); Shinyanga (weekly*; 10–12hr).

Mpanda to: Karema (pick-ups*; 6hr); Mamba (3 weekly; 3–5hr); Sumbawanga (daily; 5hr).

Tabora to: Arusha (2 weekly; 12–13hr); Dodoma (6 weekly*; 9–12hr); Kahama (6 weekly; 4–5hr); Mwanza (2–3 daily; 8hr); Nzega (3–4 daily; 3hr); Singida (2 weekly; 6hr).

Ferries (Lake Tanganyika)

Full details of ferries and lake taxis are given in "Moving on from Kigoma" on p.540.

Flights

PA is Precisionair. Upmarket tented camps at Katavi and Mahale Mountains national parks can organize charter flights from Arusha, Mwanza or Kigoma.

Kigoma to: Dar (PA: daily; 2hr 40min).

Tabora to: Arusha (charters); Dar (PA: daily; 4hr); Kigoma (PA: daily; 55min).

Katavi to: Arusha (charters).

Mahale to: Arusha (charters).

Trains

See p.46 for general information on Tanzania's train network. Times and days are given in the relevant arrival and moving on sections.

Kigoma to: Dar (3 weekly; 39hr); Dodoma (3 weekly; 24hr 10min); Morogoro (3 weekly; 31hr 35min); Tabora (3 weekly; 10hr 30min).

Mpanda to: Tabora (3 weekly; 13hr 45min).

Tabora to: Dar (3 weekly; 25hr 35min); Dodoma (3 weekly; 10hr 45min); Kigoma (3 weekly; 11hr 15min); Morogoro (3 weekly; 18hr 10min); Mpanda (3 weekly; 13hr 30min); Mwanza (3 weekly; 10hr 5min).

Southern Tanzania

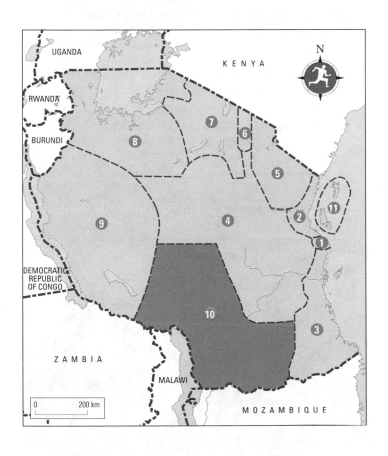

CHAPTER 10

Highlights

❋ **Kalenga** The historical seat of the Hehe tribe, who under Chief Mkwawa famously resisted the Germans in the 1890s. A museum tended by his descendants contains his skull. **See p.583**

❋ **Isimila** Quietly spectacular series of eroded gullies near Iringa, resembling the Grand Canyon in miniature, and site of numerous finds of prehistoric stone tools and fossils. **See p.585**

❋ **Ruaha National Park** "Tanzania's best-kept secret", Ruaha contains all of the Northern Safari Circuit's wildlife minus the crowds. **See p.587**

❋ **The Southern Highlands** Guided walks and day-trips are possible from Mbeya or Tukuyu to waterfalls, volcanic crater lakes, a lava-stone bridge, a meteorite, and up the forested peaks of several mountains. **See p.593**

❋ **Kitulo National Park** Known as "God's Garden", this highland plateau contains an immense diversity of flowers, especially orchids, best experienced during the rains. **See p.602**

❋ **Lake Nyasa** The most beautiful of the Rift Valley lakes, best seen from the weekly ferry from Itungi Port to Mbamba Bay; the latter also has a beautiful beach. **See p.609**

△ Guliies, Isimila

Southern Tanzania

Much of **southern Tanzania,** from the volcanic Southern Highlands to scenic Lake Nyasa, is mountainous and wildly beautiful terrain, perfectly suited for hiking.

Travelling along the Tanzam Highway, the first major town after Morogoro is charming **Iringa**, 500km southwest of Dar es Salaam. It's an excellent base for exploring numerous cultural and natural attractions, including the forested **Western Udzungwa Mountains**, historical **Kalenga**, the Stone Age site of **Isimila**, and **Ruaha National Park**, equal to the Northern Circuit parks in terms of animal numbers, but with only a fraction of the crowds.

Further south are the verdant **Southern Highlands**, created during the volcanic upheavals that formed the Rift Valley. The area is paradise for hikers, with crater lakes aplenty, hot springs, patches of ancient rainforest and even a meteorite. Access to these attractions is simple, thanks to the establishment of **cultural tourism programmes** in **Mbeya**, the region's capital, and in the agricultural town of **Tukuyu** to the south, at the base of the dormant **Mount Rungwe volcano**.

To the east of Mount Rungwe lies the ruggedly beautiful **Kitulo Plateau**, dubbed "God's Garden" by locals and now a national park, whose flowers – including over fifty species of rare orchids – put on an impressively colourful display during the rains (Nov–May).

South of Tukuyu, straddling the border with Malawi and Mozambique, the eastern and western branches of the Rift Valley converge to form **Lake Nyasa**, a stunning deep-water trough flanked to its east by the soaring Livingstone Mountains. There are a couple of beautiful beaches, at **Matema** in the north, and **Mbamba Bay** in the south, from where local boats connect with Malawi's Nkhata Bay. From Mbamba Bay, a road heads east to **Songea**, a large and exceedingly remote town from where **Tanzania's worst road** heads east towards the Indian Ocean.

Overland routes into southern Tanzania

There are three main **routes into southern Tanzania**: the fast Tanzam Highway from Dar es Salaam to Zambia (a branch also goes to Malawi); the TAZARA Line Railway, which follows much the same route; and the more adventurous approach from western Tanzania via Sumbawanga (covered in Chapter 9). Even more adventurous is the approach from the Indian Ocean, along a rarely travelled and extremely rough dry-season-only road to Songea via Masasi and Tunduru.

Tabora ◣   ◣ Singida

Mtera
Reservoir

N

Rungwa

Dodoma ▶

RUAHA
NATIONAL
PARK

Great Ruaha River

Kalenga
Iringa
Tungamalenga   Isimila

Morogoro, Western Udzungwa Mountains & Dar es Salaam ▶

Lake
Rukwa

Makongolosi

Usangu Flats

Mafinga

Chunya
Loleza Peak
(2656m)
Mbeya Peak
(2834m)

TAZARA Line Railway   Makambako

MUFINDI HIGHLANDS

Pango la Popo ▲

Utengule
Mbozi
Mbeya

Chimala
Matamba

KITULO
NATIONAL PARK

Mount Mtorwi (2961m)

Mbozi
Meteorite

Ngosi
Crater Lake

Mount
Rungwe
(2952m)

KIPENGERE RANGE

Makete

Sumbawanga & Mpanda ◣

Nakonde
Tunduma

SOUTHERN HIGHLANDS

Tukuyu   Bulongwa

Njombe

Ipinda   Matema

Mwandenga   Itungi
Kyela   Port

LIVINGSTONE

Karonga

Lupingu

Ludewa

MOUNTAINS

Chilumba   Manda

ZAMBIA

L
a
k
e

N
y
a
s
a

Songea

MALAWI

Mbinga

0   50 km

Mzuzu

Mbamba Bay

SOUTHERN TANZANIA

Nkhata Bay

MOZAMBIQUE

Tunduru ▶

▼ Lilongwe   ▼ Mozambique & Monkey Bay

Iringa and around

The only major settlement between Morogoro and Mbeya is the pleasingly relaxed town of **Iringa**, set amidst appealingly bare and jagged hills which are scattered with weathered granite boulders, and covered here and there with deep green patches of ancient forest – wild country ideal for hiking. There are plenty of worthwhile destinations here, from the beautiful forests of the **Western Udzungwa Mountains** and **Mufindi Highlands**, to sites of historical importance related to the Hehe Chief Mkwawa's long and – for several years – successful stand against German conquest. For most visitors, however, Iringa is only a stepping stone to **Ruaha National Park** – a beautiful and infrequently visited wilderness rich with wildlife.

Iringa

Gloriously perched atop an escarpment overlooking the Little Ruaha River Valley, and backed by a range of undulating hills and cracked boulders, **IRINGA** is one of Tanzania's most attractive towns, and is friendly, laid-back and welcoming, although not many people speak English. Travellers will appreciate the cool climate brought by the relatively high altitude (1600m) – it gets positively chilly in June and July. Apart from the surrounding views, and its proximity to Ruaha National Park, the town's main attraction is its small but atmospheric market, which has an unusually wide range of produce, including handicrafts.

Arrival, information and accommodation

Iringa lies 3km north of the Tanzam Highway, 309km southwest of Morogoro, and 362km northeast of Mbeya. The **bus stand** is in the centre of town; however, buses en route to other destinations do not enter town but stop at **Ipogoro** (nicknamed Ruaha), next to the junction on the Tanzam Highway; a taxi into town from there costs Tsh2000. As ever, keep an eye on your bags when arriving. Catch taxis at night.

The best source of **information** about Iringa is the owner of the *Hasty Tasty Too* restaurant on Uhuru Avenue (☎026/270 2061, ✉shaffinhaji@hotmail .com). For information about Ruaha and regional attractions, talk with Iringa Safari Tours on Kawawa Road (☎0744/315948, ✉cdjmungai@hotmail.com). Sadly, the **tourist office**, 500m east of the bus station at the Natural Resources Office, on the corner of Mkoa Street and Old Dodoma Road (Mon–Fri 8am–5pm; ☎026/270 2246, ✉dlnro.idc@twiga.com), is virtually defunct.

Accommodation

There's plenty of good budget and mid-range accommodation, as well as a couple of attractive rural places out of town; both have **campsites**, as does *Huruma Baptist Conference Centre* – all charge Tsh3000. Apart from the following, there are cheap and very basic guest houses throughout town, but reports of thefts from rooms at some of them invite caution. Iringa's **tap water** needs sterilizing before drinking.

Town centre

Annex Staff Inn Lodge Uhuru Ave ☎026/270 1344. Pricey but secure, with cool if cramped en-suite rooms (hot water) with good beds, nets and TVs, some with phones. Good restaurant. No smoking. ❸

Dr Amon J. Nsekela Bankers Academy Uhuru Ave ☎026/270 2431, ☏026/270 2563. Former college offering clean en-suite rooms (couples can share singles) with sporadic hot water, plus suites with bigger beds and fridges. Check nets for size. Safe parking. Breakfast included. ❷–❸

Huruma Baptist Conference Centre 2.5km north of town: turn left 2km along Uvinza St opposite Mkwawa Secondary School; daladalas until 7pm ☎026/270 0184, ✉hbcc@maf.or.tz. Set in expansive gardens complete with small golf course. Lots of clean, comfortable and well-kept rooms, ranging from dorms to en-suite twins and huge four-bed apartments with kitchens. Good restaurant. No smoking. Safe parking. Breakfast included. ❷–❹

Iringa Lutheran Centre Kawawa Rd ☎0748/348457. The town's best cheapie, quiet and adequate if extremely dull, with tiny singles, better twins (some en suite), and dorms. Bed sheets are too small, but nets are okay; hot water comes in buckets. "It is forbidden to use loin cloths

SOUTHERN TANZANIA | Iringa

10

IRINGA

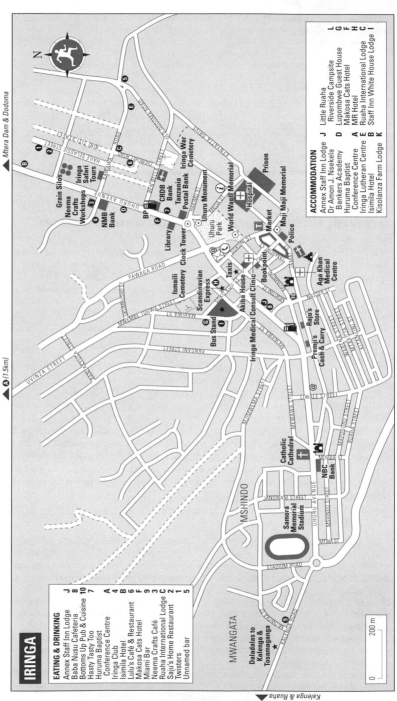

EATING & DRINKING

Annex Staff Inn Lodge	J
Baba Nusu Cafeteria	8
Bottoms Up Pub & Cuisine	10
Hasty Tasty Too	7
Huruma Baptist	
Conference Centre	A
Iringa Club	4
Isimila Hotel	B
Lulu's Café & Restaurant	6
Makosa Cats Hotel	F
Miami Bar	9
Neema Crafts Café	3
Ruaha International Lodge	C
Saju's Home Restaurant	2
Twisters	1
Unnamed bar	5

ACCOMMODATION

Annex Staff Inn Lodge	J
Dr Amon J. Nsekela	
Bankers Academy	D
Huruma Baptist	
Conference Centre	A
Iringa Lutheran Centre	E
Isimila Hotel	B
Kisolanza Farm Lodge	K
Little Ruaha	L
Riverside Campsite	G
Lupombwe Guest House	F
Makosa Cats Hotel	H
MR Hotel	C
Ruaha International Lodge	I
Staff Inn White House Lodge	

Mtera Dam & Dodoma

Kalenga & Ruaha

Ipogoro Bus Stand, Isimila, Tosamaganga, Mbeya & Morogoro

Daladalas to Kalenga & Tosamaganga

0   200 m

to dust the body" is one of their rules. Wake the *askari* to get in after 10pm. Safe parking. ❶

Isimila Hotel Uhuru Ave ☏026/270 1194. Friendly and calm with 48 en-suite rooms including suites, in several big blocks surrounded by cypress and bottlebrush trees. Despite being a bit damp and forlorn, it's comfortable and well priced. There's also a restaurant, bar and safe parking. Breakfast included. ❸

Lupombwe Guest House Mahiwa St (no phone). Simple and basic, conveniently close to the bus stand for early departures. ❶

Makosa Cats Hotel Uhuru Ave ☏0748/425781. Two small and unexceptional en-suite doubles, though another seven, with bathtubs, should be good if ever they get completed. There's also a bar and restaurant, and live music most nights. Safe parking. Breakfast included. ❷

MR Hotel Mkwawa Rd ☏026/270 2006, ⌨www.mrhotel.co.tz. Near the bus stand and aimed at the business market, this has bright and spotless rooms on three floors; ones higher up are less noisy. All have satellite TV, phone, balcony and hot water; there's also a restaurant (no alcohol), Internet café and safe parking. Breakfast included. ❹

Ruaha International Lodge Corner of Kawawa and Churchill roads (no phone). A basic place that fills up with couples after its weekend discos. The rooms, some en suite, are pretty decent, having recently been renovated. Safe parking. ❶

Staff Inn White House Lodge Mahiwa St ☏026/270 0161. A reasonable budget choice facing the bus stand, with lots of clean, mostly en-suite rooms. Singles are tatty; better are the doubles with box nets, phones and bathtubs. ❷

Out of town

See also the section on Mtera Reservoir, p.586.

Kisolanza Farm Lodge 59km southwest of Iringa towards Mbeya (no phone) ⌨kisolanza@bushlink.co.tz, ⌨www.kisolanza.com. This delightful colonial-era farm is a major stopover for overland tourist trucks, but this shouldn't put you off: overlanders have their own area, and apart from camping, there are attractive twin-bed chalets sharing bathrooms with reliable hot showers, and more expensive en-suite cottages with log fires. There's also a bar, and a farm shop with fresh bread. Email reservations essential for rooms. Chalets ❹, cottages (half-board) ❺.

Little Ruaha Riverside Campsite 14km east of town: 12.5km towards

Morogoro then 1.5km south ☏026/272 5280 or 0748/414514, ⌨phillips@africaonline.co.tz. Set beside the Little Ruaha River, this lovely hideaway has a campsite (tent rental Tsh2000) and three chalets with kitchen for up to three adults and two children (Tsh10,000 per person). Meals are available if ordered in advance (from Tsh2500). The main attraction is a welter of activities, including several kilometres of walking trails, swimming in the river, village tours, mountain biking, horse-riding, visits to Lugalo, Isimila and Kalenga, and safaris to Ruaha National Park. Hikes in the Western Udzungwa Mountains and Kising'a Lugalo Forest require prior arrangement. ❹

The Town

Iringa's main attraction is its **market**, a colourful and vibrant shambles built in 1940, on the south side of town between Jamhuri and Jamat streets. You could spend hours rummaging amongst the many oddities on offer, including beautifully woven (and sometimes aromatic) baskets made from reeds or sisal, pumice stones, local honey, bath sponges and loofahs from the coast, and even cow bells. There's also a riotous selection of *kanga* wraps, *kibatari* oil lamps, pungent dried fish from Mtera Reservoir, and pottery from a variety of places, including – if you're lucky – examples of the gorgeous cream-and-red ware from the Kisi tribe of Lake Nyasa. For medicinal herbs, especially bark, have a mooch down the alleyway that runs up past the post office and TTCL office, where several Maasai sit behind their wares, together with others making and selling beaded jewellery.

The historic streets of the compact **German quarter** around and to the **west of the market** are also worth exploring, since these are where most of the town's surviving colonial buildings are located – look for the tall, Bavarian-style building with the clock tower on Jamat Street, originally the town hall, now the Ismaili mosque.

△ Iringa town

On the south side of the market in front of the police station (no photography) is the **Maji Maji Memorial**, honouring African soldiers who died while in the service of Germany during the uprising (see p.729). Similarly poignant is the **Iringa War Cemetery**, 600m northeast at the junction of Old Dodoma Road and Ben Bella Street, which contains both British and German graves from World War I, and those of locals and Europeans who fought in World War II. The cemetery gate is not always open.

Two blocks northwest, just off Uhuru Avenue facing NMB bank, are the **Neema Crafts Workshops** (Mon–Fri 9am–5pm, Sat 10am–2pm; ☎026/270 1988, Ⓔneemacrafts@hotmail.com). Established by the Anglican Church, this is a great vocational handicrafts training project for deaf and otherwise physically disabled youths. You're welcome to tour the workshops, which includes weavers, and even try your hand at making paper from elephant dung. A shop sells all the project's output, which ranges from the said dung paper, to cards and lamps made from maize or pineapple leaves, paintings, collages, screen prints, beaded jewellery, patchworks, cushions, rugs and wall-hangings. There's also a coffee shop and gallery on the first floor, and a book exchange.

One more attraction is **Gangilonga Rock** – a large, orange-streaked boulder nestling in a vale between two peaks east of town, where Chief Mkwawa – the celebrated leader of the Hehe tribe – is said to have come to meditate. The rock's name means "talking stone", alluding to a legend that the rock gave advice when asked – perhaps inspired by the whistling sound which cracks in the boulder emit when the wind blows in the right direction. Either way, it's a nice walk (45min each way) which rewards you with a panoramic view of Iringa, though a few isolated cases of muggings means you should get a local to accompany you – ask at your hotel, or at *Hasty Tasty Too*. It's best visited in the afternoon to catch the sunset. You can see the rock to your right as you walk north along Uhuru Avenue, past the grain silos.

Eating

Iringa Bakery on Churchill Road bakes good **bread** and does cakes to order. Fresh **milk** is sold at the petrol station at the junction of Uhuru Avenue and Miomboni Street.

Annex Staff Inn Lodge Uhuru Ave. Busy local eatery with a nice streetside terrace; the liver stew is excellent. No smoking or alcohol.

Baba Nusu Cafeteria Uhuru Ave. Good cheap Tanzanian food (*ugali*, rice, beans and meat), and open late. International football screened. No alcohol.

Bottoms Up Pub & Cuisine Miomboni St. Nothing to write home about, but perfectly reasonable, with the usual meaty mains and a touch of Indian and Chinese dished up in a bright dining room. Mains around Tsh3500. Opens 6.30pm on Mon, 2.30pm Tues–Thurs, and 11.30am Fri–Sun.

🏃 **Hasty Tasty Too** Uhuru Ave. Something of an Iringan institution, both for meals and snacks and as a place to meet friends and catch up on the latest. Its cooked breakfasts (from Tsh2000) are uncommonly good, full meals (around Tsh3000) are tasty too, and they also have treats like chocolates, jam, cakes, fresh coffee and juices. Closes 2pm on Sun.

Huruma Baptist Conference Centre 2.5km north of town. A bit of a hike if you're not staying overnight, but perhaps the prospect of pork or tortillas will tempt you. There's a big menu averaging Tsh3000 for mains, but arrive early and be patient if you order their Indian, Chinese or Mexican dishes.

Isimila Hotel Uhuru Ave. The second-floor restaurant here is usually empty and has a limited choice (Tanzanian staples, meaning rice or chips with everything), but the food can be excellent. Around Tsh3000.

Lulu's Café & Restaurant Churchill Rd. Like *Hasty Tasty Too*, a favourite with travellers and expats, though it's more expensive (mains Tsh3000–4000) and not as cosy. Breakfasts are good, as are snacks – toasted sandwiches, burgers and ice cream, together with excellent coffee. Full meals, mainly Euro-Asian with a touch of Greek, are hit and miss. Closed Sun.

Makosa Cats Hotel Uhuru Ave. Forget the dismal bar and dining room at the front and get them to move a table into the enchanting *Alice in Wonderland*-style garden at the back, where the shady magnolia trees, yellow-bark fever trees and bougainvillea bushes make for a blissful setting. The food (Tsh1500–2000) is slow in coming, but when it does is often superb.

🏃 **Neema Crafts Café** Above the workshop, facing NMB just off Uhuru Ave. A gallery and coffee shop rolled into one, perfect for locally -grown quality teas and coffee, juices and ice cream, snacks and even chocolate cake. Mon–Fri 9am–5pm, Sat 10am–2pm. No alcohol.

Saju's Home Restaurant Haile Selassie St. An attractive and peaceful split-level place with a good selection of Tanzanian, Indian and Chinese options (main courses upwards of Tsh4000; allow an hour), plus good pizzas. The chicken soup is a meal in itself, and the naan bread freshly baked, but avoid the seafood. Also does snacks. Best for lunch, as the street is unlit at night.

Twisters Haile Selassie St. Next to *Saju's* and serving similar fare (mains around Tsh3500), including vegetarian and pizzas (Tsh3000), though quality is variable. There are seats under para-sols at the back. International football screened. Closed Mon.

Drinking and nightlife

Lots of bars and "groceries" throughout town serve alcohol, but few are particu-larly enticing. More attractive are the following.

Bottoms Up Pub & Cuisine Miomboni St. The town's only upmarket bar, with a TV (shows inter-national football), dartboard, two pool tables (one L-shaped), plus a good restaurant. You can also sit on the narrow balcony overlooking the street.

Iringa Club Off Uhuru Ave. Ignore the "members only" sign – someone forgot to take it down – this genteel place is happy to serve everyone.

Makosa Cats Hotel Uhuru Ave. Apart from the prospect of a quiet afternoon drink in the wonderful garden, the big attraction is the rather excellent Makosa Sounds dance band, who play Wed–Sun from 8pm into the wee hours (free entry, but beers at that time cost more). Busiest after 11pm. The big

hall next door is used for one-off events, including boxing matches.

Miami Bar Kalenga Rd. A lively, friendly and often packed local bar, with – weirdly – an excellent selection of Scotch whiskies.

Ruaha International Lodge Corner of Kawawa and Churchill roads. This normally sleepy bar and restaurant hosts loud discos Fri & Sat; it's a good place to meet new friends, but keep an eye on your valuables.

Unnamed bar Corner of Kawawa and Old Dodoma roads. A nice local place around a converted container crate, with seating under big trees in a garden. Bar food available.

Listings

Banks and exchange CRDB, NMB and NBC are all on Uhuru Ave; NMB is the least inefficient, though NBC has a 24hr Visa/MasterCard machine.

Courier services DHL, near Samora Memorial Stadium in Mshindo area ☏ 026/270 0110.

Hospital Best is Aga Khan Medical Centre, Jamat St near the market ☏ 027/270 0581. Iringa Medi-cal Consult Clinic, Akiba House, Soko Kuu St (daily 8am–8pm; ☏ 026/270 2819), does blood tests and handles minor ailments.

Internet Cheapest (Tsh500/hr) are Planet 2000 in Akiba House, Soko Kuu St, and Iringanet, Uhuru Ave, both open daily until 9pm. Other good places include Cyber Internet Centre, under *Bottom's Up* on Miomboni St, and *MR Hotel* on Mwembe Togwa St.

Language courses *Huruma Baptist Conference Centre* (p.577) offers two- to four-month courses:

$450 a month including tuition and full board. *Little Ruaha Riverside Campsite* (see p.579) offer two-week to four-month courses, with tuition costing $65 a week. For something less intensive, enquire at *Hasty Tasty Too* (see p.581).

Library Iringa Regional Library, Uhuru Ave by the clock tower (Mon–Fri 9.30am–6pm, Sat 8.30am–2pm; Tsh500 daily membership).

Newspapers There's a good stand on Uhuru Ave just west of the clock tower, and another at the east end of Miomboni St.

Pharmacy Acacia Pharmacy, Uhuru Ave ☏ 026/270 2335 (Mon–Sat 8am–8pm, Sun 8am–2pm).

Post office Just west of the clock tower.

Supermarkets Premji's and Raju's supermarkets, both Jamhuri St.

Telephones TTCL, beside the post office (Mon–Sat 7.30am–10pm, Sun 8am–8pm).

The Tanzam Highway is a good sealed road and terrifyingly fast in places. The unsurfaced road to Dodoma, in contrast, is always in bad shape, despite periodic regrading. The condition of other regional routes, such as the road to Ruaha National Park, varies according to the severity of the last rains and how quickly repairs are completed. Nonetheless, they're rarely impassable.

Long-distance buses coming from Mbeya leave from the bus stand in the centre of town; ones passing by en route from somewhere else call only at Ipogoro, 3km away on the highway; most companies have ticket offices at both places.

There are frequent buses northeast to **Morogoro** and **Dar**, and southwest to **Mbeya**. For these, as well as **Kyela** and **Songea**, safest is Scandinavian Express, whose office is on Soko Kuu Street near the bus stand (☏026/270 2308). Their buses to Dar leave from the central bus stand, and tickets for these can be bought a day or two in advance, but for their other routes – where buses only call en route at Ipogoro – you'll have to book at 9.30am on the day of departure. Mbeya, Songea and Kyela are also covered by packed Hiace minibuses, but their safety record isn't great. The only daily bus to **Moshi** and **Arusha** is run by the notoriously reckless Hood; better to catch Scandinavian Express to Dar and head on the next day. **Dodoma** is served by three daily buses (Urafiki Bus 8am, Upendo Coach 10am & King Cross noon).

Around Iringa

There are loads of things to do and see around Iringa, including hikes through **rainforests** rich in birdlife, the Stone Age site of **Isimila**, and the historic villages of **Kalenga** and **Tosamaganga**, which played a pivotal role in Chief Mkwawa's confrontations with the Germans. For all the following options, the best starting point should by rights be Iringa's **tourist office** (see p.577), which is supposedly developing low-impact tourism. Unfortunately, the project appears to have stalled, so you might find the folks at *Hasty Tasty Too*, Iringa Safari Tours (see p.577 for both) and, especially, *Little Ruaha Riverside Campsite* (p.579) more enlightening. **Vehicle rental** with driver averages $50–60 for half a day.

Kalenga and Tosamaganga

An easy half-day trip from Iringa is to the small and dusty village of **KALENGA**, 15km along the bumpy road to Ruaha National Park. Kalenga was the headquarters of **Chief Mkwawa** (see p.584) until he was driven out by the Germans in 1894. The history of Mkwawa's struggles is recorded in the **Mkwawa Memorial Museum** (no set hours – someone will open it up for you; Tsh1500), signposted 1.5km from the village. The museum, tended by the great warrior's descendants, contains an assortment of clubs, spears and shields, as well as the shotgun with which Mkwawa committed suicide. The chief exhibit is Mkwawa's skull, which was returned to the Hehe in 1954 after a 56-year exile in Germany. Outside the museum are **tombs** of Mkwawa's descendants, including his son, Chief Sapi Mkwawa, and his grandson, Chief Adam Sapi Mkwawa. Five hundred metres away is another tomb, containing the body of **Erich Maas**, a German commando who attempted to infiltrate the fort and capture Mkwawa alive; the unfortunate Maas was discovered by Mkwawa, at whose hands he met his fate.

Public transport for Kalenga leaves Iringa from Kalenga Road on the west side of town. Most locals catch pick-ups (6am–6pm; every 30min–1hr), whilst

The Tanzanian interior in the latter half of the nineteenth century was in a state of chaotic flux. Incursions by **Arab slave traders** from the coast had disrupted the balance of power between clans and tribes, while the militaristic **Ngoni tribe's invasion** in the south had triggered several mass migrations. This uncertain climate provided ideal soil on which opportunistic leaders such as Chief Mirambo of the Nyamwezi (see p.555) could plant their own personal kingdoms.

Another leader who emerged triumphantly from this confusion was a Hehe chief named Mtwa Mkwawa Mwamnyika ("Conqueror of Many Lands"), better known as **Chief Mkwawa**. Born near Kalenga in 1855, Mkwawa's ambitious character was well suited to his time. By 1889, he had become undisputed leader of the Hehe, whom he made the region's dominant tribe by uniting – though force or diplomacy – more than one hundred clans and smaller tribes. It was not just numbers, but regimented **military organization** that formed the basis of Hehe power, and which gave Mkwawa the ability to stem the hitherto inexorable south-ward advance of the Maasai. Mkwawa also began to threaten Arab control over the lucrative slave and ivory-carrying caravan routes that passed through his territory, though declining Arab power meant that it was not against the sultans of Zanzibar that the showdown eventually came, but against the **German colonial war machine**.

At first, Mkwawa tried to secure treaties with the Germans, but when they refused, the Hehe turned their arms against the arrogant newcomers. On August 17, 1891, a year after the Germans had placed a garrison in Iringa, Mkwawa's troops surrounded and ambushed a German expeditionary force led by Lieutenant Emil von Zelewski in the **Lugalo Hills** east of Iringa, killing nearly five hundred soldiers and capturing a vast quantity of firearms and munitions. Only two German officers and fifteen men escaped.

Mkwawa was no fool, and anticipated German revenge – by building a thirteen-kilometre, four-metre high wall around his palace and military base at **Kalenga**. The Germans took their time to reorganize, and it wasn't until October 1894 that they made their move, establishing themselves on a hill overlooking Kalenga, now the site of **Tosamaganga**, and beginning a two-day bombardment of Kalenga (the name *tosamaganga* means to "throw stones"). On October 30, 1894, the Germans under **Tom von Prince** stormed and took Kalenga with relative ease. The extent of Mkwawa's wealth can be gauged by the fact that it took four hundred porters to carry all his ivory away. The Germans also found 30,000 pounds of gunpowder, which they used to level the town. For Mkwawa, the loss of Kalenga was a double tragedy, since his mother – who had been told that her son had been captured – committed suicide.

In fact, Mkwawa escaped into the forests west of Kalenga, from where he waged a four-year **guerrilla war** against the Germans. He was finally cornered in 1898, having been betrayed by informants attracted by a five-thousand-rupee reward. Rather than surrender, he shot his bodyguard, and then himself. The Germans, arriving on the scene shortly after, placed another shot into Mkwawa's head just to be sure, then severed it. The chief's headless body was buried by his family at Mlambalasi, 12km south of the road to Ruaha National Park, while his **skull** was sent on to Berlin and then on to the Bremen Anthropological Museum. There it remained until 1954, when it was finally returned to the Hehe – it's now the star exhibit of Kalenga's Mkwawa Memorial Museum.

Mkwawa's death marked the end of two decades of resistance to German rule across Tanganyika, and the end of the Hehe Empire, but the ensuing peace was short-lived. Seven years on, the Maji Maji Uprising erupted. For more on Chief Mkwawa and the Hehe, see ⓦ www.mkwawa.com.

the daily Kiponza Bus (1pm) to Tungamalenga also passes through. **Taxis** charge around Tsh15,000 for the return journey.

If you like the area, Kalenga can be combined with a visit to the Catholic mission at **Tosamaganga**, a pleasant six-kilometre (2hr) walk southwest. It's another 5km from there to the Tanzam Highway, where there are frequent dala-dalas back to Iringa. There's no accommodation in Kalenga or Tosamaganga.

Isimila

Just over 20km southwest of Iringa, 1km off the Tanzam Highway, is **ISIMILA**, one of Africa's richest Stone Age sites. Since 1958 excavations have uncovered thousands of stone tools dating from the **Acheulian period**, some 60,000 years ago. Even if archeology isn't your thing, the scenery – small but spectacular canyons studded with bizarrely eroded pink and orange sandstone needles – makes the trip worthwhile, as do the rock hyrax, swifts and sand martins.

The Isimila River created the strange natural **sandstone sculptures** you see today, and was also responsible for uncovering hundreds of **stone tools**. Pear-shaped hand-axes and cleavers are most common; there are also cutters, hammers, picks and scrapers, and spherical balls whose use has never been fully explained. At the time the tools were made part of the site was occupied by a shallow lake, attracting both wildlife and hunters. The **fossil remains** of various animals hint at an environment not too different from today: elephants and antelopes, and various extinct mammals, including a giant hog, a short-necked giraffe and a weird species of hippo, which appears to have been even more boggle-eyed than its modern form.

The curator's hut is signposted 1km southeast of the highway, and sits at the edge of a low escarpment overlooking the eroded gully where the stone tools were found. There's a small **museum**, which also sells a short but informative guidebook. **Admission** to the site and museum costs Tsh1500 (tip appreciated), which gets you an entertaining two-hour tour of the gully. The tools cover much of the area – you're allowed to handle but not remove them.

Udekwa and the Western Udzungwa Mountains

East of Iringa, the forested foothills of the **Western Udzungwa Mountains** have recently been opened to small-scale tourism by the establishment of walking trails. The foothills are especially rich in endemic and near-endemic **birds** (over three hundred species), including the Udzungwa partridge, rufous-winged sunbird, dappled mountain robin, spot-throat, Nduk eagle owl, and Iringa akalat. The **best time** for birding is September to early December. Apart from birds, the forests are an attraction in their own right, as are the expansive views from the peaks and ridges. For more on **Udzungwa Mountains National Park**, which covers the central and eastern section of the range, see Chapter 4.

Access is easiest by arranging a hiking tour with Iringa-based Hehe Hikes (℡026/270 0424 or 0748/400783, @kforrester@iringanet.com), who charge a very reasonable $100 per group for day- trips, including food, guides and transport from Iringa; overnight trips can also be arranged. They have no office, so contact them in advance – *Hasty Tasty Too* is the usual venue for meeting up. Also clued-up on the area (and a handy base for longer trips) is *Little Ruaha Riverside Campsite* (see p.579), who also rent out tents. If you're making your own way to Western Udzungwa, drive or catch a bus along the Tanzam Highway 45km northeast from Iringa to **Ilula** village and, shortly after, turn right on to an unsurfaced road to **Udekwa** (at least 2hr) – there should be pickups at the junction covering this stretch. If you're driving, ask for directions whenever you can as there are no signposts. With your own wheels, a day-trip from Iringa is feasible, but it would be much better to spend a few days in the area. It can get chilly at night, so bring warm clothes, and rain gear. Most of the foothills are protected as forest reserves and you'll need a **permit** to enter (available from the Natural Resources Office in Iringa, see p.577; Tsh 5000 per day). Show the permit to the village government officer near the school in Udekwa. You'll also need a **guide** and (optionally) porters if you're hiking for more than a day; contact Masumbo Ltd (Ⓔmasumbo@masumbo.co.tz) through *Little Ruaha Riverside Campsite*, whose excellent guides are completely passionate about birds. Costs shouldn't be more than $40 a day, including guide, permits and porters, though if you enter Udzungwa Mountains National Park, park fees are extra.

There are no guest houses in Udekwa, but there are three **campsites** in the area. Easiest to reach is *Chui Campsite*, 7km into the forest reserve. *Luala Valley Campsite* is set on a grassy glade in the forest on Ndundulu ridge (5–6hr walk from *Chui Campsite*). From *Luala*, you can birdwatch along forest trails northeast towards **Mount Luhombero**, Udzungwa's highest point. It's a good place to find the Udzungwa partridge and rufous-winged sunbird. The third campsite is *Mufu Camp*, a six-hour walk from *Chui* along a steep trail. The camp is right in the heart of the forest, and has a wealth of birdlife around it.

Mtera Reservoir

Roughly 100km north of Iringa along the unpaved road to Dodoma, **MTERA RESERVOIR** is the source of most of Iringa's fish, and much of southern Tanzania's hydroelectric power. It's also home to a **cultural tourism programme**, based at *Chapuya Camp* (reservations through *MR Hotel* in Iringa, see p.579) in Migoli village, a few hundred metres off the road. Buses between Iringa and Dodoma pass by, taking around three hours from Iringa. **Accommodation** (❹, or ❺ full-board) is in simple but attractive and comfortable open-sided *bandas* on a hillside amidst scrubby vegetation and trees, with great sunsets over the reservoir. There's no bar, but drinking water – and food – are available.

The $15 **admission fee** goes towards various local development projects. **Activities** cost extra, and include boat trips for angling (tiger fish and tilapia; hiring a long-prowed fishing boat costs $25 for half a day), visiting a fishermen's camp ($10), messing about in wobbly dugouts, exploring bird walks and an elephant trail ($5 per guide), meeting a blacksmith, carpenter or basket-maker ($5 each), and visiting a Maasai *boma* for cow-milking and dancing ($20). You can also enter the sacred **Chamdindi Caves**, but only after a traditional cleansing ceremony is performed by village elders ($45 per group).

The Mufindi Highlands

The tea estates and forests of the **Mufindi Highlands** south of Iringa are exceptionally scenic: bright green tea estates, scattered lakes and rainforests, and dramatic views from peaks and ridges over the Kilombero Valley to the east. The forests are especially rich in **birdlife**, with rare species including blue swallows, the Uhehe fiscal, short-tailed pipit, the mountain marsh whydah and Iringa akalat.

Access is via **MAFINGA** (John's Corner), 90km southwest of Iringa along the Tanzam Highway. If you're driving and fancy a pleasant side trip, the dirt road into the Mufindi Highlands from Mafinga loops around at Kibao (Kibaoni), coming back to the highway at Nyororo (James' Corner), 80km in all.

Accommodation is at ⚶ *Mufindi Highland Lodge* (book through Foxes African Safaris in Dar, see p.133; full-board ❽), 40km south of Mafinga. Located in a six-square-kilometre estate, the main building is a rustic two-storey granite-and-timber affair containing a bar, dining room, TV lounge, snooker room and a large verandah with great views of the surrounding forests. The bedrooms are in eight en-suite log cabins; room rates include guided forest walks, birding, mountain biking, horse-riding, a cultural tour to local villages and fishing for rainbow trout, and as such represent excellent value for money. Two nights at least are recommended. The easiest way to get there is for the lodge to pick you up at Mafinga ($50 per person). If you're driving, turn off the highway at Mafinga and head south into the hills until Sawala, then turn left along the road to Lupeme Tea Estate and follow the signs for 15km.

Ruaha National Park

Straddling the Eastern Rift Valley west of Iringa, and covering almost thirteen thousand square kilometres, **RUAHA NATIONAL PARK** is one of Tanzania's largest wildlife areas. The **Great Ruaha River**, which runs along much of the southeastern boundary, is the park's lifeblood, attracting great numbers of wildlife in the dry season (July–Oct), when all else around is parched and yellow. Since 1993, however, the river has dried up completely in the dry season, each time for longer periods, thanks to unsustainable water use for rice paddies in the Usangu Flats north of Mbeya, and overgrazing by an estimated 1.5 million cattle belonging to migrant Sukuma cattle herders, who enter the flats during the dry season. In response, the **Friends of Ruaha Society** (Ⓦ www.friendsofruaha.org) is spearheading a project to reduce water wastage in Usangu, though its confidence

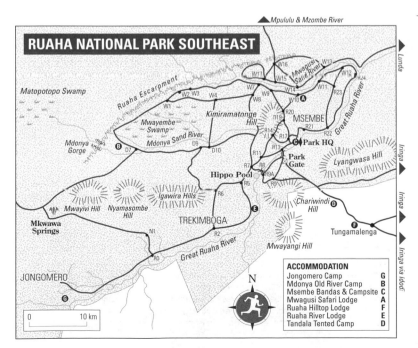

in restoring the Ruaha's perennial flow by 2010 seems hopelessly optimistic. In the meantime, the animals are still around, albeit in reduced numbers.

Although most visitors are confined to the lower southeastern section of the park around the Great Ruaha River – separated from the rest of the park by the Ruaha Escarpment – the area is representative of most of Ruaha's habitats, including *miombo* woodland plateau and isolated hills in the west, undulating plains, acacia and baobab bushland, palm-fringed swamps, grassland, evergreen forest around the main rivers, seasonal "sand rivers" whose water pools draw wildlife in the dry season and, of course, the Great Ruaha River itself.

The area is also a **transitional zone** between eastern and southern African plant and animal species, explaining its unusually rich biodiversity: the park contains over 1650 plant species. In turn, this attracts a wealth of **wildlife** – pretty much every species you're likely to see on the Northern Circuit with the exception of **black rhinos**, whose whereabouts are a well-guarded secret given the predations wrought by poachers in the 1970s and 1980s. Also targeted by poachers were Ruaha's **elephants**, though their present population of around twenty thousand is the largest and densest of any Tanzanian park. Ruaha is also noted for **antelopes**, being one of only few areas where you can see both greater and lesser kudu, and the elusive sable and roan antelopes, the latter sometimes in groups of up to twenty. Other denizens include zebra, the shy bushbuck, Grant's gazelle, eland, giraffe, impala, reedbuck, Defassa waterbuck, Liechtenstein's harte-beest, klipspringer, Kirk's dikdik, mongooses (slender, banded and dwarf) and large herds of buffalo near water. With so much potential food around, it's no surprise to find **predators** out in force, including lions, leopards, cheetahs, jack-als, crocodiles and several packs of highly endangered African hunting dogs; the park is also the southernmost range of the striped hyena. **Nocturnal animals**, which may be glimpsed in the early morning or late evening, include the aard-wolf, ratel, lesser galago (bushbaby), porcupine and bats.

Ruaha's **birdlife** is equally rich and colourful, with 526 species recorded to date, many of them migrants (especially mid-Nov to March). Two special species to look out for are the rare sooty falcon, which breeds in the Sahara and the Middle East, and Eleonora's falcon, which breeds further north in the Mediterranean. Other **raptors** include the African hawk, Pel's fishing owl and eagles: bateleur, martial, long-crested and snake.

The **best time to visit** for mammals is the dry season (July–Oct), when animals concentrate around the Great Ruaha River and the receding water-holes of the park's seasonal sand rivers. The park is best avoided at the height of the **long rains** in April and May, when many tracks are cut.

Visiting the park

The park lies 112km west of Iringa along all-weather *murram* (2–3hr). **Park fees**, paid at the gate 9km inside the park, are $25 per person for 24hr, and Tsh10,000 for a vehicle permit.

Walking in Ruaha National Park

A great way of getting to experience Ruaha is on a **bush walk**, accompanied by an armed park ranger. Costs are $25 per person for up to three hours, or $50 for longer walks, plus $20 per group for the ranger. Walks can be arranged through any of the park lodges, or – with at least one week's advance notice – through the park head-quarters. You'll need a vehicle, however, both to access the park headquarters and to get to the walking zone, the exact location of which depends on the season.

The **park headquarters** are in Msembe area, 6km beyond the entrance gate (PO Box 369 Iringa, ⓦwww.tanzaniaparks.com/ruaha.htm); they can fill you in on road conditions. The best sources of **information** are either of TANAPA's guidebooks, which can be bought at the gate, at the lodges, or in bookshops in Arusha, Dar and Stone Town. The older monochrome booklet describes game drives in scientific detail, while the full-colour edition makes an attractive souvenir.

Organized safaris from Arusha and Dar

Several Arusha-based safari companies, and most in Dar, offer **road safaris** to Ruaha. Arusha-based Dorobo Safaris are particularly recommended for combined driving and walking trips between June and October. Trips from Dar are cheaper given the shorter driving distance, though you'll still be spending most of your first and last day whizzing along the Tanzam Highway (it's roughly 10hr from Dar). Avoid this problem by arranging things in Iringa, by flying in, or by combining Ruaha with Mikumi, Selous, Udzungwa or the newly formed Kitulo National Park. For this to be worthwhile, count on at least six days. Expect to pay upwards of $130–150 a day for a basic camping safari, often staying in cheap hotels or camps outside the parks, and upwards of $250–300 per day if sleeping in lodges or luxury tented camps.

Flying safaris

Most visitors come on **all-inclusive flying safaris**. These can be arranged through Ruaha's lodges and camps, or with safari companies in Arusha and Dar: Coastal Travels tend to have good-value special offers. Normal rates are $300 each way for the daily flights on Coastal Aviation (from Arusha, Dar, Zanzibar, Selous or Lake Manyara), plus $200–300 a day for accommodation and game drives.

Organized safaris from Iringa

Currently, only two Iringan companies (plus the lodges inside and outside the park) have the requisite TALA licence for taking tourists into the park. Their prices are based on the cost of 4WD rental with driver, and are therefore much cheaper if you can fill all the seats (four or five passengers).

Iringa Safari Tours (see p.577). $145 per vehicle for the return trip from Iringa, plus $90 for each extra day spent driving inside the park (or $250 for a day-trip). Park fees, meals and accommodation cost extra.
Little Ruaha Riverside Campsite (see p.579). $120 a day for the vehicle, to which add park fees,

meals and accommodation. During high season weekends, you can get a lift to the park for $30, though to venture further you'll probably have pre-book game walks or game drives with either TANAPA (see p.403) or one of the lodges (usually around $35–50 per person for a few hours, plus park fees).

Self-drive

Self-driving around Ruaha is only recommended if you're experienced at driving on rough roads, especially during and after the rains. Only high-clearance 4WDs are admitted. There's no **petrol** in the park, although the lodges or park headquarters can help out in an emergency. It's impossible to arrange self-drive in Iringa; do it in Arusha or Dar.

Accommodation

Ruaha's **luxury tented camps and lodges** are mostly neo-colonial in feel and searingly expensive, though their all-inclusive "fly-in" rates do include full board, park fees, airstrip transfers and two game drives a day. If you're coming by road, ask for the cheaper full-board rates (still ❾, however), as obviously you won't need their vehicles. None of them are fenced, providing an exciting chance of seeing (or hearing) wildlife pass through at night. TANAPA maintains more sanely priced accommodation in the form of **bandas** near the park headquarters, and there's also relatively cheap accommodation outside the park. All accommodation is best reserved in advance.

The main **campsite** is on the Great Ruaha River near the park headquarters at Msembe ($30 per person, paid at the gate), with pit latrines but nothing else, though you can use the showers at the nearby *bandas*. There are also **special campsites** scattered around ($50 per person) – the locations change every few years; those at Mbagi and Mdonya especially are recommended, but tend to be block-booked by safari companies.

At a different level, both *Mwagusi Safari Lodge* and *Ruaha River Lodge* offer luxury **fly-camping excursions**, starting at $400 per person per night (minimum two nights and two clients); this includes everything from personal butlers and guided walks (if allowed), to champagne breakfasts in the bush.

In the park

Jongomero Camp 63km southwest of Msembe (book through The Selous Safari Company in Dar, ☏022/212 8485 or 0748/953 551, ⊛www.selous .com). Gloriously isolated but ingloriously expensive, this offers classic safari luxury in a grove of acacias, on the north bank of the (usually dry) Jongomero River. The eight spacious and comfortable en-suite tents on raised platforms under thatched roofs, each with a verandah for wildlife viewing. There's also a swimming pool with uninterrupted views of the river and yonder bush. No children under 8. Closed mid-March to end-May. All-inclusive $335 per person. ❾

Mdonya Old River Camp 40km west of Msembe ⊛www.adventurecamps.co.tz (book through Coastal Travels in Dar; see p.133). Set in a dry area amidst large sycamore figs and acacia beside the Mdonya Sand River, it's the isolation, intimacy and wildlife you're paying for rather than creature comforts, as the camp itself is decidedly plain – perhaps deliberately so, placing the emphasis squarely on the bush rather than swanky trimmings. The eight candlelit twin-bed tents have private verandahs and al fresco showers, and a resident genet entertains guests at night. Closed April & May. Full-board $180 per person, all-inclusive $270 per person. ❾

Msembe Bandas Msembe (book through TANAPA in Arusha; see p.403). Several basic park-run

chalets sleeping two to five people each. Sheets, blankets and firewood are provided, and there's a kitchen, dining area, toilet and shower. Bring your own food and drink. The roofs are corrugated metal, so suffocatingly hot by day. ❺

Mwagusi Safari Lodge 27km north of Msembe ⊛www.ruaha.org (book through TropicAfrica, 14 Castelnau, London, SW13 9RU, UK ☏ & ⊕ +44 (0)208 846 9363). In prime game-viewing territory on the banks of the Mwagusi Sand River, which are especially popular with buffalo. The ten large and comfortable en-suite tents (twin or double) are pitched inside thatched *bandas* with shady verandahs overlooking the river, solar-powered lights and hurricane lamps. Meals are taken in a stylish *banda* decorated with branches and skulls, or on the sandy river bed. All-inclusive $300 per person. ❾

Ruaha River Lodge 18km southwest of Msembe ⊛www.tanzaniasafaris.info (book through Foxes African Safaris in Dar; see p.133). Built on and around a granite outcrop overlooking rapids with hippos and crocodiles, this is another fine place for wildlife (seen from armchairs on your private verandah, no less). Room are in riverside cottages, and facilities include two bars with glorious views, lounges, evening campfires and library. Full-board $135 per person, all-inclusive $250 per person. ❾

Outside the park

Without your own transport, to reach **Tungamalenga village**, 20km shy of the park gate, catch the daily Kiponza bus, leaving Iringa at 1pm (get there at noon) from Kalenga Road in Mwangata area. You'll have to walk or hitch from Tungamalenga.

Ruaha Hilltop Lodge 2km west of Tungamalenga ☎0745/685275 or 026/270 1806,
✉ruahahilltoplodge@yahoo.com (Iringa office in
IFCU Building, Uhuru Ave, opposite the library). On
a scrubby hill with nice views over the bush, this is
a pretty basic set-up with several en-suite cottages
and a brick-and-thatch building lower down,
containing the restaurant and bar. Game drives
available ($100 per vehicle, excluding park fees),
and walks in Ruaha can be arranged. Full-board
$80 per person. ❽
Tandala Tented Camp 15km west of Tungamalenga ☎026/270 3425, ✉tandalacamp
@yahoo.com. An attractively simple place beside

the Mdekwa Sand River, with ten comfortable
en-suite tents on wooden platforms, each with a
verandah. A big draw is the swimming pool (occasionally doubling as a waterhole for elephants),
and there's also a thatched bar and restaurant
featuring French, Greek and Tanzanian cuisine.
Game drives are available ($50 per person for a
full day, $35 a half-day, excluding park fees),
plus nature walks, hikes up Mount Idelmele, visits
to a Maasai village and to hot-water springs
(all $15 per person), and night game drives are
planned. Part of the profits benefit Mbomipa
village, which can also be visited. Full-board $110
per person. ❽

The park

The park's 400km of tracks mainly cover the southeastern sector around the
Great Ruaha River, within reach of the lodges. Access to the western *miombo*
woodlands is difficult and time-consuming, but there are plans to expand the
road network to 1500km. Unless they've been trashed by elephants looking for back scrubbers, road junctions are marked by **numbered signposts**,
corresponding to the ones marked in the park's guidebooks. The guidebooks
are essential for exploring beyond the Msembe area, unless you're with a guide.
During and after the rains, always enquire beforehand as to which roads are
open. **Driving** is only allowed between 6am and 7pm, and remember that off-
road driving is illegal and environmentally destructive.

If you're short on time, the tracks along the Great Ruaha River downstream
from Msembe are always good for a broad range of wildlife. With more time, the
roads along the Mwagusi and Mdonya sand rivers are rewarding, as is the long
drive southwest to the Jongomero River. Early morning and late afternoon are
the best times for spotting wildlife, as many species take shelter at noon.

The park's pristine condition owes a lot to the humble if deeply irritating
tsetse fly, which transmits sleeping sickness. The disease doesn't affect wildlife
but does bring down domestic animals and humans, so herders have traditionally avoided the area. Don't worry about contracting the disease yourself
– infections are extremely rare, and the main tsetse-infested area is in the infrequently visited *miombo* woodland. If you do go there, the usual precaution is to
keep car windows closed.

Lastly, a word of warning about Ruaha's **elephants**. The inaccessibility of
huge swathes of the park, especially in the rains, makes it ideal territory for ivory
poachers, an ongoing problem, albeit nowhere near as bad as it was in the 1980s.
However, the massacres of that decade have made older elephants nervous and
sometimes aggressive whenever humans are present, particularly if they're with
calves. Treat any elephant you encounter with uncommon courtesy and caution,
and back off if they show signs of irritation.

Msembe

The most accessible game drive is the web of tracks in and around Msembe
area. The dominant tree species is the tall **acacia albida**, which has bright
orange sickle-shaped seed pods. These trees play an important ecological role in
providing shade in the dry season, thereby limiting the evaporation of moisture
from soil, and binding the riverbank with their roots. Elephant poaching in the

1980s had a unfortunate side effect on this area however: the presence of the national park headquarters meant that elephants learned that Msembe was their only safe haven, and so congregated there, unwittingly damaging the acacia groves. Things haven't been helped by the drying up of the Great Ruaha River in the dry seasons since 1993, which has vastly increased pressure on the areas surrounding the few remaining waterholes.

Highlights include a **Hippo Pool** close to junction R8, which also has crocodiles; the drive west from Msembe to junction D7 for views of the river and escarpment; and the circuit around **Kimiramatonge Hill** to the north, where you might see klipspringers.

The Great Ruaha River and Mwagusi Sand River

An excellent circular drive heads northeast from Msembe. The first section, from junction R21 to R24, takes you along the north bank of the **Great Ruaha River** to its confluence with the Mwagusi Sand River, passing tamarind and palm woodland, patches of thorn scrub and grassy plains scattered with candelabra trees. There are lots of animals all year round, including elephants, lions, leopards and most of the park's ungulates. Hippos and crocodiles also put in appearances, but you'll need luck to see sable antelopes, cheetahs or hunting dogs. There's a **picnic site** in a grove of acacia trees by junction R24.

Head back west to Msembe by following the south bank of the **Mwagusi Sand River**. Like many of the park's rivers, the Mwagusi only sees water in the rains, when floods wash down vast quantities of silt and soil. Elephants and plains game are frequent visitors to its dry-season waterholes, as are predators – easily camouflaged in the flanking vegetation.

Ruaha Escarpment and Mdonya Sand River

In dry weather only, a recommended circuit for seeing a variety of habitats (and which can be tacked onto the circuit described above) covers the foot of the Ruaha Escarpment and Mdonya Sand River. The first part of the drive, west from junction W8, hugs the base of the **Ruaha Escarpment**. After some 10km you reach **Mwayembe Spring**, whose salty residue makes it a popular salt lick for elephant and buffalo. In the surrounding swamp, you might spot the rare Bohor reedbuck. The road continues along the escarpment base to the Mdonya Sand River, just below **Mdonya Gorge**.

To return to Msembe, turn southeast and follow the southern bank of the Mdonya Sand River, passing tamarind woodland and evergreen riverine forest (with good birdlife). Keep an eye out for eland and black-backed jackals. The longer way back from Mdonya Gorge is from junction D7 to Mkwawa Springs in the west, then downstream along the Great Ruaha River.

Msembe to Jongomero

A good long drive, giving the advantage of seeing wildlife even at noon when in other places animals stay hidden, follows the north bank of the Great Ruaha upstream from Msembe to Mhawa then past **Trekimboga** ("the cooking of meat" in Kihehe, the Hehe language). A right turn at junction R2, 9km beyond *Ruaha River Lodge*, offers a scenic drive to the Mdonya Sand River (junction D9) or a loop back to junction R5 near Trekimboga. Carrying straight on instead for another 36km through acacia and commiphora woodland takes you to **Jongomero**, where the Jongomero River joins the Great Ruaha. This riverside trees are a good place to nose around for leopards.

The road to Mpululu

This route starts at the Mwagusi Sand River (junctions W14, W15 or W17) and heads up 95km northwest to the Mzombe River. Crossing the Mwagusi Sand River is impossible in the rains, but should be feasible at other times – check with the park headquarters before trying. Up the escarpment, the road passes through undulating woodland where you should see small groups of elephants, and perhaps also sable antelope or Liechtenstein's hartebeest. There are some **walking trails** at Mpululu by the Mzombe River, which marks the border with Rungwa Game Reserve. The river is dry from July to September, when hippos congregate in pools. Walkers need to be accompanied by a park ranger or guide.

The Southern Highlands

North of Lake Nyasa, the fertile **SOUTHERN HIGHLANDS** extend from around Mbeya in the west to the Kipengere Range, close to Njombe, in the east. Despite the region's high population density and reliance on cash crops like coffee, cocoa and bananas, many of the highlands' **forests** have survived, providing one of the region's highlights, along with other natural attractions including impressive waterfalls, crater lakes and hot springs. Given the mountainous terrain (and often stunning views), the highlands are ideally suited for **hiking** – at its most spectacular and beautiful in Tanzania's newest protected area, **Kitulo National Park**, over two and a half kilometres above sea level and famed for its orchids and a hitherto unknown species of monkey.

The prosperous town of **Mbeya**, which lies on both the Tanzam Highway and the TAZARA Railway, makes a good base for exploration, and is also an important gateway to both Malawi and Zambia. Another good base is the agricultural town of **Tukuyu** next to Mount Rungwe volcano. All of these sites, and much more besides, are beautifully covered on the **website** of the Southern Highlands Conservation Programme, Ⓦ www.southernhighlandstz.org.

Mbeya and around

Some 140km north of Lake Nyasa, the regional capital of **MBEYA** nestles on a small highland plateau between the Mbeya Range and Panda Hills. Founded in 1927 as a supply town during the gold rush at Lupa, Mbeya's importance was assured by its position on the **Great North Road** (now the Tanzam Highway), which is still the major overland route from eastern to southern Africa, covering over five thousand kilometres from Nairobi to Cape Town. The town's importance increased still further during the 1960s with the construction of the TAZARA Line Railway from Dar to Zambia. With a population of over 400,000, Mbeya is southern Tanzania's biggest town, yet remains an easy-going and laid-back sort of place, once you've extricated yourself from the assorted hustlers and con-artists at the bus stand or train station. Although there's nothing

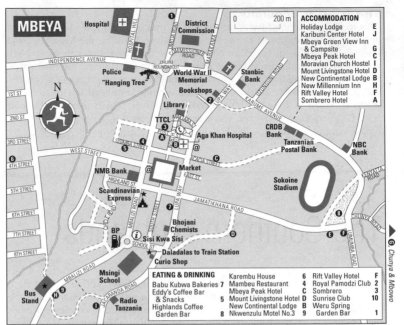

Map labels:

MBEYA

Hospital
HOSPITAL HILL
District Commission
JUHURU ROUNDABOUT
COMMISSIONER ROAD
Police "Hanging Tree"
INDEPENDENCE AVENUE
World War II Memorial
Stanbic Bank
Bookshops
Library
KARUME AVENUE
MZUZNGINI ROAD
TTCL
MAKANBAKO ROAD
Aga Khan Hospital
CRDB Bank
Tanzanian Postal Bank
NBC Bank
SISIMBA STREET
1ST ST
2ND ST
3RD STREET
WEST STREET
4TH STREET
ACACIA STREET
NMB Bank
Market
EAST ST
Sokoine Stadium
LUMUMBA ROAD
KIVATTA ROAD
5TH STREET
HIGHLAND ROAD
Scandinavian Express
JAMATIKHANA ROAD
6TH STREET
MBALIZI ROAD
CIRCLE ROAD
LUPA WAY
7TH STREET
Bhojani Chemists
8TH STREET
KHINYA BUTAN
BP
Sisi Kwa Sisi
Daladalas to Train Station
SCHOOL ST
Curio Shop
Msingi School
JACARANDA ROAD
Bus Stand
Radio Tanzania

ACCOMMODATION

Holiday Lodge	E
Karibuni Center Hotel	J
Mbeya Green View Inn & Campsite	G
Mbeya Peak Hotel	C
Moravian Church Hostel	I
Mount Livingstone Hotel	D
New Continental Lodge	B
New Millennium Inn	H
Rift Valley Hotel	F
Sombrero Hotel	A

0   200 m

EATING & DRINKING

Babu Kubwa Bakeries	7	Karembu House	6	Rift Valley Hotel	F
Eddy's Coffee Bar & Snacks	5	Mambeu Restaurant	4	Royal Pamodzi Club	2
Highlands Coffee Garden Bar	8	Mbeya Peak Hotel	C	Sombrero	3
		Mount Livingstone Hotel	D	Sunrise Club	10
		New Continental Lodge	B	Weru Spring	
		Nkwenzulu Motel No.3	9	Garden Bar	1

G, Chunya & Mbowo

Tanzam ▼ Highway (2km), Train Station, Mbalizi & Tunduma   Tanzam Highway (2km), Airport (2.5km), Mafiati, ❿ (4km) ▼ & ❿ (4km)

much to see in the town itself, the local **cultural tourism programme** and its imitators offer a wide range of activities in the vicinity – including hikes up the nearby Loleza and Mbeya peaks, trips to hot-water springs, waterfalls, and even a giant meteorite – making a longer stay well worthwhile.

Except for the rare days when dust storms cloud the horizon and billow up through town from the east, Mbeya has a refreshing **climate** and can be very pretty when the many jacaranda and bottle brush trees are in blossom (Nov–March).

Arrival

Buses coming in from the east along the Tanzam Highway stop first at Mwanjelwa – get off there for *Karibuni Center Inn*, otherwise stay on the bus to finish up at the **bus stand** on Mbalizi Road, just south of Mbeya town centre. The **train station** is 5km south of the centre on the Tanzam Highway; a taxi into town costs around Tsh3500. **Daladalas** arrive on School Street at the top end of Jacaranda Road. **Taxis** can be caught on Mbalizi Road just south of the centre, either at the bus stand or at the BP petrol station.

Accommodation

Mbeya's cheapest **guest houses** are a sorry lot, often with unwashed sheets, and incidents of thefts from locked rooms common enough. Sisi kwa Sisi (see p.597) can point you to reliable places. In spite of the altitude, **mosquitoes** abound, so ensure that nets fit the beds and that window screens, if they have any, are intact (or use bug spray or smoke coils). Mbeya's **tap water** may carry typhoid – sterilize it before drinking. **Camping** is possible at *Mbeya Green View Inn & Campsite* and *Karibuni Center Hotel* – both $3.

Mbeya is amazingly laid-back for a town of its size, but first impressions are often quite the opposite. Whether you arrive by bus or train, you'll be greeted by self-appointed **guides and hustlers** eager to escort you and your baggage to a hotel. Although some of these characters are genuine, unwary travellers get conned or robbed frequently, so stay cool, and keep a close eye on your bags and valuables while you get your bearings. At the **bus stand**, you can shake the hustlers by heading to the *New Millennium Inn*, facing the stand on Mbalizi Road, where at least you'll have the chance to collect your thoughts. If you do need a guide (necessary only for hikes around Mbeya) make sure you arrange things at the **cultural tourism programme** (Sisi kwa Sisi; see p.597) at the corner of Mbalizi Road and School Street, or with Tanzannature beside Sokoine Stadium (p.598). Some other operators sell themselves as "cultural tourism programmes", and while some might be okay, it's wise to be cautious.

In the **town centre**, walking around by day is fine, but at night it's best to catch a cab. This applies especially to Jacaranda Road (for the *Moravian Church Hostel*), even at dusk or dawn. Other areas to avoid walking in after dark include Chunya Road (for *Mbeya Green View Inn*), all of Jamatikhana Road, and the side streets coming off the bus stand.

Holiday Lodge Jamatikhana Rd ℡025/250 2821. A friendly place with big, bright rooms in a two-storey block with showers, the more expensive ones with TVs. There are also very cheap rooms behind the restaurant, sharing bathrooms, slightly shabby but clean and with excellent beds. The restaurant is average, but there's no bar. Safe parking. ❶–❸

Karibuni Center Hotel Off the Tanzam Highway, 4km from town ℡025/250 3035, ⓦwww.twiga .ch/TZ/karibunicenter.htm. Run by the Swiss Mbalizi Evangelistic Church, this has good en-suite rooms with hot showers, safe parking and a decent restaurant (meals Tsh2000–5000). Catch a taxi the first time. ❷

Mbeya Green View Inn & Campsite Off Chunya Rd, 1km east of town ℡025/250 0175. An appealing place built in vaguely Scandinavian style with plenty of pinewood furniture, offering four doubles with shared bathrooms and three bright en-suite rooms upstairs with bathtubs and hot water, all with satellite TV. Food, sodas and beers are available, and there's an attractive rooftop verandah and a communal kitchen. Don't walk here at night. Breakfast included. ❸

Mbeya Peak Hotel Acacia St ℡025/250 3473. Good-value mid-range place with showers and telephones in its standard rooms, and cable TV for Tsh3000 more. Breakfast included. ❸

Moravian Church Hostel Jacaranda Rd ℡025/250 3263. The main backpackers' choice, with small but decent rooms, clean communal showers and squat toilets. The downside is the lack of single rooms, and too-small mosquito nets.

Food is occasionally available. Don't walk here at night. ❶

Mount Livingstone Hotel Off Jamatikhana Rd ℡0741/350484, ⓔmtlivingstone@hotmail.com. Mbeya's leading tourist-class hotel, if usually pretty empty, with 47 mostly twin-bed rooms, but overpriced given the lack of TV and phone – and you'll have to ask for a mosquito net. There's also a somnolent bar and restaurant, gift shop, Internet access, and safe parking. Breakfast included. ❺

New Continental Lodge North St ℡025/250 2511. A reasonable, central option accessed through its bar and restaurant, but with only six rooms. The cheapest share bathrooms (hot showers and Western toilets), others have TVs, and the best have narrow balconies overlooking the street. The bedding could do with a bit more care, and check the nets for size. No access after midnight. ❷–❸

Rift Valley Hotel Corner of Jamatikhana Rd and Karume Ave ℡0748/355141. If you don't mind the slightly forlorn feel and saggy beds, this four-storey business-class hotel is a reasonable choice, with clean en-suite rooms with nets and phones, some also with balconies. "Executive doubles" have satellite TV, and there are also some (overpriced) suites, as well as two bars and a restaurant. Breakfast included. Rooms ❸, suites ❹.

Sombrero Hotel Post St ℡025/250 3636, ⓕ025/250 0663. The town's newest and biggest (if still not quite complete) hotel, with twenty very small rooms and two suites, all with hot showers, Western toilets, wall-to-wall carpet, TV, phone and piped music. Great views of Loleza Peak from the upper front rooms. ❹

The Town

The abiding memory of Mbeya is of its views, especially the 2656-metre **Loleza Peak** looming over town from the north. From some places, the sharper outline of **Mbeya Peak** (2834m) can be seen protruding from behind it. Both can be climbed; see p.600 for details.

As most Mbeyans live in crowded, slum-like suburbs some kilometres out of town, the centre itself is eerily quiet at times. The main focus is, of course, the **market** which – although modest in size – is always interesting. The northwest corner has vendors selling medicinal herbs, beans, bark and assorted powders, and there are usually also some beautiful cream-and-ochre Kisi pots from Ikombe near Matema on Lake Nyasa. North of here, at the top end of Mbalizi Road by Uhuru roundabout, is the "**hanging tree**" over the river, which it's believed was used by the Germans during the 1905–07 Maji Maji Uprising to execute opponents of their oppressive rule. The tree in question has a strange metal winch with a hook attached to its largest branch, but the slender wire that ties it to the tree seems too thin to have supported the weight of the condemned. More certain is the sacrifice made by local people during World War II while fighting for the British: the names of the dead are commemorated on a small **memorial plaque** by the roadside just along Karume Avenue.

Eating

Mbeya's subtly aromatic **rice** is prized throughout the country, and its Arabica coffee isn't bad either, but unfortunately Mbeya's culinary mantra as far as restaurants are concerned appears to be *kuku na chipsi* (chicken and chips), pretty much all that's ever available, especially in the evening; lunchtimes provide a happier hunting ground. See also "Drinking and nightlife".

Babu Kubwa Bakeries Lupa Way. Run-of-the-mill snacks and meals, but the reason to come is for the shady streetside terrace – one of few places where you can just sit and watch the world go by.

Eddy's Coffee Bar & Snacks Sisimba St. Popular with locals and tourists alike, this remains a nice central place for a meal or a drink despite flagging standards, with *supu* for breakfast, full meals for lunch and dinner, *nyama choma*, and seating both in round huts at the side and on a leafy streetside verandah. Closed Sun.

Mambeu Restaurant Corner of Mbalizi Rd and Sisimba St. This characterful and very basic place does good snacks (especially *sambusas*), an excellent tripe *supu* for breakfast if you like that kind of thing, *mtori* banana soup, as well as very cheap lunches and dinners (under Tsh1000) – the liver is particularly good.

Mount Livingstone Hotel Off Jamatikhana Rd. The massive à la carte menu has almost a hundred dishes from all over the world, from Chinese and Italian to Bourguignonne fondues, kedgeree chicken and seafood paellas. It's expensive for Mbeya (mains from Tsh4000, and a bottle of imported wine upwards of Tsh12,000), but gets consistently good reports. There's also a rather empty bar with tables outside.

New Continental Lodge North St. Walk through the standard restaurant-cum-bar to the smoky courtyard at the back for some of the best *nyama choma* in town.

Rift Valley Hotel Corner of Jamatikhana Rd and Karume Ave. If you don't mind the slightly dreary surroundings, this can be good, though to be sure of finding your favourite (the menu includes pork and pasta; mostly Tsh3500), best order the day before.

Sombrero Restaurant Post St. One of the town's better lunch spots (meals Tsh3000–4000), with good pasta and curries – the kidney stew is an especial wow – fresh juices and milkshakes; evenings are more limited, and the atmosphere then is stultifying. Check your bill.

Drinking and nightlife

Mbeya is considered Tanzania's second city on the **rap** scene, but unfortunately anyone who makes it big absconds to Dar. It might be worth asking around though. **Live bands** (and beauty contests) are sometimes hosted at Dando Hall, down on the Tanzam Highway – ask at Sisi kwa Sisi (see below), or check out the posters adorning town. Wherever you're going, use a taxi at night.

Highlands Coffee Garden Bar East end of Jamatikhana Rd, entrance opposite the stadium. A lovely outdoor place for a drink or food (*nyama choma* and filling Tanzanian dishes), with plenty of tables along the long grassy plot, plus slides, see-saws and swings for kids. And yes, it also serves real coffee (Arabica from Mbinga).

Karembu House 4th St. A great local bar, always busy, with a TV for European football and a popular dartboard.

Mbeya Peak Hotel Acacia St. A nicely relaxing garden bar with shaded *bandas* for a daytime drink or meal, including delicious *nyama choma* with grilled bananas.

New Continental Lodge North St. A laid-back local bar, with satellite TV, a "cosier" area at the back beside a *nyama choma* kiosk, and a couple of streetside tables.

Nkwenzulu Motel No.3 Mbalizi Rd, opposite the bus stand. A large bar, busiest at night, with grim toilets and pushy barmaids. Things are much better outside, where there are plenty of seats (food also available), and a pool table.

Royal Pamodzi Club Lupa Way. Currently the in place for shaking those hips, it plays a wide range of music. Fri–Sun only.

Sunrise Club Tanzam Highway. A popular local disco open nightly, but especially lively at weekends. Plays all kinds of music, from Congolese and Tanzanian Jazz to Bongo Flava, pure hip-hop and reggae.

Weru Spring Garden Bar Umoja Rd, 250m north of the roundabout. A gorgeously relaxing and hassle-free outdoor bar like *Highlands Coffee Garden*, but in an even nicer location, next to a small stream overgrown with datura trees and bamboos. It has a wide range of drinks, a pool table, kids' playground and bar food (Tsh1500 a plate).

Listings

Banks and exchange Quickest for changing cash or cheques (under 10min) is Stanbic on Karume Ave, who whack you with $20 commission. You'll pay much less at NBC down the road, but you'll need patience for the pointless paperpushing – they also have a 24hr Visa/MasterCard ATM.

Bookshops The best of Mbeya's pathy bookshops are Tanzania Elimu Supplies and Volile Investment, beside each other on Lupa Way. They both have a few books in English, and there are second-hand bookstalls outside.

Car repairs CMC Land Rover on Karume Ave have skilled mechanics and genuine spare parts, and also deal with Nissan, Volvo and Volkswagen. Spare parts can also be found at Mbeya Spares and Hardware, South St.

Courier services DHL, at Scandinavian Express office, Mbalizi Rd ☎025/250 0250.

Football Mbeya's local team, Prison, play at Sokoine Stadium, as do the far more popular second-division Tukuyu Stars, much to the chagrin of their home fans in Tukuyu, who face a 140km round trip to support their side.

Hospitals The Aga Khan Health Centre, corner North and Post streets, is the first port of call ☎025/250 2896. Mbeya Regional Hospital is on Hospital Hill north of town ☎025/250 2985.

Immigration Behind the District Commissioner's Office off Karume Ave ☎025/250 3664, though they're not much help.

Internet access Nane Information Centre, Mbalizi Rd (daily 8am–10pm), and ATMA Internet Café, Lupa Way (daily 8am–9pm), charge Tsh500 an hour for fast connections.

Library Maktaba St (Mon–Fri 9am–6pm, Sat 9am–1pm; Tsh500 daily membership).

Pharmacy Bhojani Chemists, south end of Lupa Way (Mon–Sat 8am–8pm, Sun 10am–2pm; ☎025/250 4084).

Police Independence Ave ☎025/250 2037.

Post Corner of Lupa Way and Post St.

Supermarkets Idete Store, a large grocery, is at the corner of Lupa Way and Acacia St.

Telephones TTCL, corner Maktaba and Post streets beside the post office (daily 7.45am–8pm). Nane Information Centre (see "Internet access") does Internet calls.

Around Mbeya

Mbeya Region's attractions can be visited as part of the **cultural tourism programme** run by Sisi kwa Sisi Youth Group, at the corner of Mbalizi

Mbeya is well connected, with plenty of road transport around the region and along the Tanzam Highway to Iringa and Dar, plus connections for getting to Zambia and Malawi. There's also a weekly train into Zambia, and three a week to Dar. There are no flights, though an airport is under construction.

By bus

Most long-distance buses leave Mbeya from 5 to 7am; buy your ticket the preceding morning to be sure of a seat. The large buses leave from the bus stand on Mbalizi Road in the centre, but many Coasters and daladalas – especially those bound for Tukuyu, Kyela and the Malawian border – then stop along the Tanzam Highway at **Mwanjelwa** to pick up more passengers, which can take over an hour; for these, it's always quicker to board them there. Mwanjelwa is a chaotic place, but the ever-helpful folks at Sisi kwa Sisi are happy to escort you.

Don't buy tickets from touts, but only from bus company offices – locals are amused at stories of gullible tourists shelling out wads of cash for non-existent rides to Zimbabwe or South Africa. Also, be very careful about **safety**: long-distance daladalas are overcrowded and often drive dangerously. The larger Coaster minibuses fare better, though Super Feo can be dangerous. Of the big buses, the **best reputations** are with Scandinavian Express (ticket office on Mbalizi Rd in town; ☎025/250 4305; Dar, plus 2pm to Lusaka) and Sumry (office at the bus stand; ☎025/250 0112; Dar, Songea and Sumbawanga). **Ones to avoid** include Abood, Air Bus, Hood, Kilimanjaro Express, Super Feo, Takrim, Tashriff and Tawfiq.

There are at least fifteen daily buses to **Dar** via **Iringa and Morogoro**. Getting to **Arusha** in one ride isn't guaranteed unless you gamble your life with Hood (not wise); Scandinavian Express used to cover the route every other day – it's worth asking whether they've restarted. Otherwise, catch a bus to Dar and continue the following morning. For **Dodoma**, the Urafiki International Coach (daily) and Shabiby (3–4 weekly) are the most reliable. The rough and wild road to **Tabora** via Chunya, Rungwa and Sikonge is travelled by Sabena (5am) on Wednesday and Sunday during the dry season, taking at least 18hr. Going south, **Tukuyu** and **Kyela** (for access to Lake Nyasa's MV *Songea* ferry; see p.614) are connected to Mbeya by Coaster minibuses roughly hourly from around 6am until late afternoon. You might also find a seat on one of the big buses coming in from Dar in the evening. Most daladalas only go as far as Tukuyu; some tourists are conned into buying tickets to Kyela only to be dumped in Tukuyu. The safest company for **Sumbawanga** is Sumry, also best for **Songea** (both 6am); if you miss this or the later Shabiby bus (around 8am), catch a Coaster to **Njombe** (until around 1.30pm from Mwanjelwa; those run by Mchape Express and Upendo seem fine) and change there, or stay the night and move on the next day.

By train

Mbeya is the last Tanzanian stop on the TAZARA line before it enters Zambia. The **train station** is 5km southwest of the centre on the Tanzam Highway (tickets Mon–Fri 7.30am–12.30pm & 2–4pm, Sat 8am–12.30pm, Sun 7.30–11am). A taxi from town shouldn't cost over Tsh3500; daladalas to the station leave from School Street at

Road and School Street (daily 8am–6pm, closed for lunch; ☎0744/463471 or 0744/087689, ✉sisikwasisitours@hotmail.com). Be wary of other operators and guides; some have no experience while others are just out to rob you – if someone tells you that they're with Sisi kwa Sisi, believe them only when you get to the office. An exception is Arusha-based Tanzannature, who have an Mbeya branch beside the stadium facing the *Highlands Coffee Garden Bar* (☎0744/651721, ⓦwww.tanzannature.com).

the top end of Jacaranda Road. **Timetables** change with dogged stubbornness. At the time of writing, trains to Dar left at noon on Tuesday, Wednesday and Saturday, whilst the mysteriously named "Express" into Zambia crawled out at 1pm on Saturday. The fare to Dar is Tsh12,000–24,500, depending on the class and whether it's the "Express".

Overland into Zambia or Malawi

Crossing into either country, be prepared for **hassle and pickpockets** at the borders, and keep an eye (or hand) on your luggage in buses and daladalas. Also, avoid **money-changers** if you can, as they're notorious con-artists (read the warning on p.77). In September 2005, **exchange rates** were Tsh1000 for 3700 Zambian kwacha, or 70 Malawian kwacha. If you must change money on the street, keep it small.

The safest way into **Zambia** is on the daily Scandinavian Express bus from Dar to Lusaka, which passes through Mbeya around 2pm. Alternatively, there's a daily Sumry bus (and plenty more Coasters and nerve-wracking daladalas) from Mbeya to the border at **Tunduma**, 114km southwest along a reasonable surfaced road, through which buses from Sumbawanga to Mbeya also pass. The Zambian border town is **Nakonde**, infamous for con-artists and thieves – luckily, there's plenty of onward transport from there. The border is open from 7am to 6pm. **Zambian visas** can be bought at the border. Most travellers pay $25, except Brits (£35) and Americans ($40). At present, Australians, Canadians, Irish and Kiwis do not require visas, but given the ever-changing situation, bring enough dollars just in case.

Arriving in Tanzania, other than changing money (NMB bank at the start of the road to Mbeya – allow an hour for travellers' cheques), there's no reason to stay in Tunduma and, given the pushy hawkers, you'll probably be glad to jump on the next bus out anyway.

There are currently no ferries from Tanzania to **Malawi**, but things keep changing, so ask in Mbeya or Kyela. There are no safe bus companies running all the way to Lilongwe, and in any case cross-border services can be delayed for hours if one of its passengers gets held up at customs. Instead, catch a bus or Coaster from Mbeya towards Kyela, and get off at the border ("Bodaboda") at **Mwandenga** on the Songea River. Avoid the Hiace daladalas. If you're driving or cycling, the turning is at Ibanda, 11km before Kyela and 7km from the border. There's plenty of onward transport on the Malawian side. If you fancy a **ferry** ride, get to Chilumba, from where the MV *Ilala* sails weekly to Monkey Bay in the far south, via a string of Malawian and Mozambican ports. It should leave Chilumba at 2am on Monday, but rarely respects its schedule. (See ⓦwww.tourismmalawi.com, or ring ☏000265 (Malawi) 1/587 221 or 1/829 9840. **Malawian visas** are currently not required for EU, US and most Commonwealth citizens, but check this beforehand as the rules keep changing, and visas cannot be bought at the border. The nearest Malawian Embassy is in Dar (p.128). You will, however, need a **yellow fever vaccination certificate**. Corrupt immigration officials on both sides are a nuisance; be patient and polite and you'll eventually get through unscathed. There are simple but none too savoury **guest houses** (❶) on the Malawian side, and better accommodation at Karonga, 40km on.

On offer are a wide range of day-trips and hikes, although many will be cheaper if arranged in Tukuyu, where Sisi kwa Sisi have recently opened a branch (these trips are covered on pp.600–602). Some trips include a modest "village development fee", which has so far paid for a small dispensary and books for a primary school. Sisi kwa Sisi are also the most reliable place to fix up **off-the-beaten track tours** not normally covered, for instance a ten-day hike around the highlands and down to Lake Nyasa, or east from Tukuyu and Mount Rungwe into and around Kitulo National Park.

Loleza and Mbeya Peaks

Dominating the skyline north of Mbeya are the highest points in the Mbeya Range, Loleza and Mbeya peaks, both of which can be climbed. Looming over town is the 2656-metre **Loleza Peak** (also called Kaluwe), which is covered in beautiful flowers in the rainy season. Security concerns mean that taking a guide is advisable ($15 per person from Sisi kwa Sisi, see p.597). The walk starts from Hospital Hill off Independence Avenue and follows a forested ridge up towards the peak, a steep three- to four-hour climb, plus two hours back down. The summit itself is topped by an array of transmitters.

Slightly higher (2834m) is **Mbeya Peak**, to the west of Loleza Peak. There are at least seven routes to the summit. A **guide** is recommended: Sisi kwa Sisi charge no more than $20 per person, excluding transport if required. The quickest approach is from a path northwest of Mbeya, within walking distance of town. Shorter and easier is to climb from the north, starting at the end of a drivable track that begins in **Mbowo** village, 13km along the Chunya road; a taxi to the top of the track costs Tsh12,000. From there, the path to the summit takes around two hours, passing through eucalyptus forest. Look out for flowers in the rains, and for rare butterflies at other times. An alternative route, best done over two days (either camp, or spend the night at *Utengule Country Hotel*; see below), is more strenuous but more rewarding, involving steep and difficult scree in parts. It starts at a coffee farm 20km northwest of Mbeya; there's public transport as far as **Mbalizi** on the Tunduma Highway, leaving you with a nine-kilometre walk past *Utengule Country Hotel* to the start of the trail; from there it's six hours to the summit. The **traverse** along the 7km ridge joining Loleza and Mbeya peaks is possible but rarely attempted. Lastly, you can combine a hike with a **homestay** at Iziwa village ($30 for a full day and night), where you can meet a healer, learn local culinary tricks, and get on down to some *ngoma* (traditional music) should you coincide with a celebration.

Utengule

For those with transport (or a bicycle), a pleasant alternative to Mbeya as a base for visiting the Southern Highlands is **Utengule**, a village and district roughly 20km northwest of town at the western edge of the Mbeya Range. It's worth seeking out one of the district's **pitagos** – ritual sites next to ravines from where the **Sangu tribe** threw their dead (and, sometimes, the living, if they had been convicted of certain crimes, including philandery). The exceptions were chiefs, who were treated to lavish burials which reportedly included the interment of retainers or slaves. The explorer Captain James Elton, visiting in the 1870s, described the scene at the base of one *pitago*: "... now over a heap of skeletons, scattered leather aprons and beads, hovered flocks of vultures and gigantic storks ... gorged with their loathsome feast". *Pitago* sites are still considered with apprehension by locals, although the practice itself survives only in words: the polite way of referring to burial in Kisangu is *kitaga umunu* – which means "to throw away a person". For more information, see *Throwing Away the Dead* by Martin Walsh at ⓦwww.museums.or.ke/mvita/walsh.html.

Unless you arrange a day-trip with Sisi kwa Sisi in Mbeya, the only practical way to get to know Utengule is to **stay overnight** at the upmarket *Utengule Country Hotel*, 3km from Utengule village (☎025/256 0100; ❻). Turn right at Mbalizi, 11km along the highway to Tunduma, and follow the signposts. The hotel is set in lovely gardens on a coffee estate and offers a wide choice of colourfully decorated rooms and bungalows, some with views over the Rift Valley. There's also a restaurant and bar, and guided walks and excursions are available to Kimani Falls and Pango la Popo. If you're staying overnight, the hotel offers free transfers from Mbeya.

Pango la Popo

Thirty-nine kilometres west of Mbeya are a couple of unusual attractions: **Pango la Popo** (the "cave of bats"), and the nearby **hot-water springs**. They're best visited in your own 4WD or in a group, as there's no public transport for the last 14km, and taxis won't take you as the road is too rocky. Head along the road to Tunduma for about 25km until Songwe, where there's a dust-belching cement factory, and turn north. Sisi kwa Sisi in Mbeya can arrange a 4WD vehicle for around $50 there and back, plus $20 for a guide. There's an entrance fee of Tsh3000, covering both places.

Mbozi Meteorite

Weighing in at a cool twelve tons, the irregularly shaped **Mbozi Meteorite** – which lies on the southwestern slope of Marengi Hill, 70km west of Mbeya off the road to Tunduma – is the world's eighth largest known. The meteorite is a fragment of interplanetary matter that was large enough to avoid being completely burned up when entering earth's atmosphere, and small enough to avoid exploding; of the estimated five hundred meteorites that fall to earth each year, only thirty percent strike land, and less than ten are reported and recorded. Mbozi has been known for centuries by locals, who call it **Kimwondo**, but the absence of legends recounting its sudden and undoubtedly fiery arrival indicate that it fell to earth long before the present inhabitants arrived, a thousand years ago. The meteorite was officially discovered in 1930. At the time only the top was visible. To reveal the whole meteorite, the hillside around it was dug away, leaving a pillar of soil under the meteorite, which was then reinforced with concrete to serve as a plinth. The irregular notches on the pointed end were caused by souvenir hunters hacking out chunks – no easy task given the strength of the nickel-iron of which it's made. Most meteorites consist of silicates or stony irons, so Mbozi is uncommon in that it's composed mainly of iron (90.45 percent) and nickel (8.69 percent), with negligible amounts of copper, sulphur and phosphorus.

The turn-off from the highway is signposted 4.5km before Mbozi village; catch one of the frequent minibuses plying the highway between Mbeya and Tunduma. Bicycles can be rented at the junction (Tsh3000 is a fair price) to cover the remaining 13km. Sisi kwa Sisi combines trips to the meteorite with visits to coffee farms (five hours in all), but at $30 per person it's much cheaper to visit on your own. Entrance costs Tsh1000; the guardian also sells photocopies of Hamo Sassoon's brief but informative *Guide to the Mbozi Meteorite*. If you want to stay overnight, arrange things with Sisi kwa Sisi, who have a **campsite** 7km from the site, in a plot donated by the government to enable unemployed youths to start profitable agricultural projects ($5 per person; tent rental $5).

Ngosi Crater Lake

Some 35km southeast of Mbeya in the Poroto Mountains, **Ngosi Crater Lake** (marked as Poroto Crater Lake on some maps) is the most popular destination for day-trippers from both Mbeya and Tukuyu. In the local Kisafwa language, Ngosi means "very big", referring to the lake rather than the conical mountain that contains it. The two-kilometre lake occupies the crater floor 200m beneath the highest point of the 2620-metre Mount Ngosi. Although the lakeshore is tricky to reach (it's 200m down in the crater along a steep and potentially dangerous footpath), the walk there is really the attraction, winding uphill through tropical rainforest, stands of giant bamboo and wild banana plants. Among the forest denizens are black-and-white colobus monkeys, many colourful birds, and particularly vocal tree frogs. Local legend speaks of the lake's magical powers, and of a **lake monster** that has the ability to change the colour of the water from time to time. Though quaint, the tale should urge caution, as such stories usually have some basis in real-life perils such as man-eating crocodiles or dangerous volcanically induced currents – and note that locals don't swim in the lake.

Ngosi is most easily visited with a guide from Mbeya or Tukuyu, although it's quite feasible to visit on your own. Coming from either place, catch a bus or daladala to Mchangani (nicknamed "Mbeya Moja"), where there's a sign-posted turn-off. From here it's 6km west along a rough road (4WD only) to the bottom of the mountain, then an hour's strenuous walk up the southeastern slope to the crater rim. You could walk all the way from Mchangani (2–3hr each way). A **guide** is recommended for the last bit up the forest on Ngosi Hill, as the path isn't marked: guides offer their services at Mchangani. From Mbeya, the cost is $12 per person if you can find a few other tourists to share the cost. Hiring a car in Tukuyu for the round trip costs around Tsh25,000. There's a **ticket office** in Mchangani at the start of the road to the lake which collects Tsh1000 per visitor and Tsh3000 per vehicle, and a **campsite** at Ngosi; it's free if you've paid the entrance fee, though you'll have to stump up the cost of a night watchman if locals advise it (Tsh3000 seems fair).

Kitulo National Park

The **Kipengere Mountain Range**, comprising much of the region between Mbeya and Njombe, contains areas of immense ecological importance, notably the remote grasslands of the highland **Kitulo Plateau**, which recently became Tanzania's newest protected area, **KITULO NATIONAL PARK**. Comprising some 135 square kilometres of the plateau's northern section, and twice as much montane forest on its western and southwestern flanks (412 square kilometres in all), the park promises more than just a taste of paradise for botanists, bird-watchers and hikers alike.

Known locally as *Bustani ya Mungu* ("God's Garden"), the plateau – which lies around 2600m above sea level – contains great numbers of endemic wild flowers, including over fifty species of **orchids** (and counting), many of which are unique to the region. Their protection was the primary impetus behind the park's creation, as a growing illegal trade in orchids with Zambia – where orchids were traditionally a famine food source but had become more of a staple – was threatening their extinction: at the start of the millennium, an estimated four million Tanzanian orchids were being smuggled out of southern Tanzania each year.

Unusually for a national park, the **best time to visit** is during the rains (more or less continuous from November to May), when the plateau erupts in a glorious show of colour, contrasting beautifully with the lingering morning mists, ominous storm clouds and deep, enveloping silence. The flowers attract insects aplenty – notably moths and butterflies – in turn providing food for frogs, chameleons and lizards. The park is also home to breeding colonies of rare **birds**, including the pallid harrier, Njombe cisticola, Denham's bustard, blue

△ Highland Mangabey monkey, Kitulo National Park

swallow, and Kipengere seed-eater. There are few large mammals on the plateau, although some may be reintroduced: the plateau's grasslands owe their existence to the grazing habits of large herbivores, whether indigenous eland, impala and montane reedbuck, or the cattle that replaced them in the 1980s – though a small population of reedbuck remain. Although degraded and still under pressure from illegal logging, in December 2003 the **fringing montane forest** gave rise to a startling discovery: the hitherto unknown **highland mangabey** monkey (*Lophocebus kipunji*). In 2004 another group of researchers at Ndundulo Forest Reserve in the Western Udzungwa Mountains, 400km away, discovered the same species there. The total population is estimated at under a thousand, and will probably be classified as critically endangered. See ⓦwww.kipunji.org for more information.

Practicalities

At the time of writing there was no infrastructure at all. Campsites, overnight *bandas*, an interpretation centre, hiking trails and possibly driving routes are likely to be in place by 2007; in the meantime, you'll need to be fully self-sufficient.

Getting to the park independently requires 4WD or a good pair of legs, though the park can also be reached through a combination of public transport and hiking, as well as on tours organized by Sisi kwa Sisi in Mbeya and Tukuyu. Eventually, safari companies operating "Southern Circuit" trips out of Dar should also include the park in their itineraries. **Entry fees** are likely to be $20 for 24hr, plus $30 for camping, and guide fees – likely to be obligatory – pegged at $15–25 a day.

The **main access route** is from the Tanzam Highway, where there's a signposted turning 3km west of Chimala village, some 70km east of Mbeya. Coming by bus or daladala (Tsh1500 from Mbeya), ask to be dropped at *njia panda ya Matamba* ("the junction for Matamba"). From here, Land Rovers (Tsh2000) head south and begin grinding up a spectacular dirt road, which includes an eye-popping 57 hairpin bends in its first 9km, arriving an hour or two later at **MATAMBA**, a sizeable trading centre also known as Uwanji. The TANAPA park office is currently located here, but will be shifted further along the road beyond the 2750m Matamba Pass. Matamba itself has lots of cheap restaurants, and four surprisingly good **guest houses**, the best of which is the *Zebra* (no phone; ❶). Given the altitude (2200m), malaria is absent.

A **western access route** is also in the works, linking the park's western forested ridge with adjoining Mount Rungwe (p.607) and the Mbeya–Tukuyu road, thus making extended hikes from Tukuyu a tantalizing prospect. At present, the road is virtually undrivable from February until the end of the rains.

For now, you're free to hike pretty much anywhere. Recommended is the fifteen- to twenty-kilometre hike from Matamba village up to **Matamba Ridge** overlooking the plateau. The hike is for the fit only, as it's a pretty strenuous up-and-down affair. A tent would be wise too, giving you plenty of time to explore at your leisure. Once at the ridge, you can either follow it eastwards, or descend into the flower-bedecked **Numbe Valley**, which slopes down along the ridge towards **Numbe Juniper Forest**, many of whose trees reach a ripe old height of over 50m, making them amongst the world's tallest junipers. Further east is **Mount Mtorwi**, at 2961m southern Tanzania's highest.

For more **information**, contact TANAPA in Arusha (see p.403; ⓦwww .tanzaniaparks.com/kitulo.htm), or the Wildlife Conservation Society's **Southern Highlands Conservation Programme** in Mbeya, whose office is in a colonial-era building off Karume Avenue, 100m along a path starting opposite

CRDB Bank (PO Box 1475 Mbeya; ☎025/250 3541, Ⓦwww.southernhigh-landstz.org). The office also sells the recommended *A Guide to the Southern Highlands of Tanzania* by Liz de Leyser, which includes Kitulo and much more besides. The book is also available at Iringa's *Hasty Tasty Too* restaurant. Sisi kwa Sisi in Mbeya and Tukuyu are also clued up on the new national park.

Tukuyu and around

The ride south from Mbeya to Lake Nyasa is one of Tanzania's most scenic, wending up through the lush volcanic foothills of Mount Rungwe before descending into the tropical humidity and forests hugging Lake Nyasa's northern shore. Close to the highest point of the road, 71km southeast of Mbeya, is the rural town of **TUKUYU**. Founded just over a century ago by the Germans as a replacement for the mosquito-ridden lakeshore town of Matema (Langenburg), Neu Langenburg – as they called Tukuyu – became an administrative headquarters. The **German Boma**, whose ramparts have been incorporated into today's municipal buildings, date from this time. Tukuyu could scarcely be more different from prosperous Mbeya. There's none of the latter's cosmopolitan feeling, and the atmosphere is decidedly small town (or big village). Yet Tukuyu is certainly an attractive and refreshing place to spend some time, with wonderful views over the lushly vegetated hillocks and valleys far below, many of them extensively cultivated with tea, banana groves and sweet potatoes.

The main reason for staying is to visit various natural attractions surrounding the town (many can also be visited through Sisi kwa Sisi in Mbeya – see p.597 – but are more expensive from there). Foremost among the local sights are the dormant volcanic mass of **Mount Rungwe** (which can be climbed), various associated **crater lakes** in the Poroto Mountains to the west, **waterfalls**, a natural **lava-stone bridge** over a river, and – possibly – an epic hike all the way into the newly established Kitulo National Park.

The best months to visit are September and October, as for much of the rest of the year it rains ... and rains. With annual precipitation sloshing around the 3m mark, Tukuyu is Tanzania's wettest place. Tukuyu itself is best visited between August and November, to coincide with the **drumming season** following the year's main harvest.

Age villages of the Nyakyusa

The **Nyakyusa** are the dominant ethnic group between Tukuyu and Lake Nyasa, numbering well over a million in Tanzania, and around 400,000 in Malawi, where they're called Ngonde (or Nkonde). A unique but now extinct feature of traditional Nyakyusa society was their **age villages**, brand-new villages established by boys between the ages of 11 and 13, to which they would later bring wives and start families of their own. The villages died upon the death of their last founding member, after which the land was reallocated by the district chief. Age villages served both to preserve the privileges and land of the older generation, and also to spread population pressure on the land more evenly, thereby avoiding unsustainable agricultural use. However, with each generation the available land was repeatedly divided amongst the sons of each chief, until the system finally collapsed when the land plots became too small to subdivide (a problem that also afflicts the Chagga around Kilimanjaro).

Practicalities

There are frequent **daladalas** between Mbeya and Tukuyu; safer would be to catch a Coaster or bus to Kyela, which all pass through. Tukuyu's **bus stand** is on the west side of the highway. A word on **safety**: there have been instances of tourists being robbed by newly-made "friends" – don't let strangers into your room, and insist on carrying your own bags from the bus stand. For **information and tours**, visit Sisi kwa Sisi (a branch of Mbeya's cultural tourism programme) on the highway 100m south of the bus stand, on the same side.

Accommodation

There are few mosquitoes and malaria is absent, so none of the **hotels** have mosquito nets. The places reviewed below are all east of the Mbeya–Kyela highway: from the bus stand, turn left (north) along the sealed road so that the market is on your left, and take the first right after 100m or so: the directions given below ("from the highway") are from this junction.

Sisi kwa Sisi, and Tanzannature in Mbeya (p.518) can organize **homestays** around Tukuyu: the cost for a full-day's activities plus accommodation is $20–30 per person.

Landmark Hotel 500m east from the highway ☏0748/247373. Newest and best by far, with attractive en-suite rooms, the more expensive ones higher up with grand views over Mount Rungwe, the Livingstone Mountains, and – on clear days – Lake Nyasa. Also has good food and a bar, and an Internet café across the street. ❹–❺
Langboss Lodge 1.5km east from the highway: go past the *Landmark* and turn right after a clothes market and school playing field

☏025/255 2080. Best of the budget places, the better rooms here are its large en-suite doubles; singles share grim toilets and showers, and everything is rather scruffy. There's also a bar and restaurant. ❶–❷
Laxmi Guest House Just off the roundabout near the *Landmark* ☏025/255 2226. Humble, but clean and usually calm, with a choice of singles and doubles with or without bathroom, plus a bar and restaurant. ❶–❷

Eating and drinking

Tukuyu's **restaurants** mostly double as bars and are mostly pretty tawdry affairs in which some knowledge of Kiswahili is helpful to overcome small-town reticence. There are two **local brews**: *kimpuno* (made from millet), and *kyindi* (millet mixed with maize).

Landmark Hotel The best restaurant, with a good choice of local and international dishes (including cheese to go with pasta), and even wine (around Tsh8000 a bottle). The upstairs bar has great views.
Langboss Lodge Perfectly decent meals under Tsh2000, though you'll have to wait at least an hour. The bar is pretty boring, but dispenses with the *Laxmi*'s prostitutes, and also has a TV – making it a popular venue for watching European football matches.

Laxmi Garden Centre Bar & Restaurant Just past the post office; turn left opposite the petrol station 250m east of the highway. Downmarket but pleasant and cheerful, this is good for roast meat in the garden at the back, breakfast *supu*, and even fresh pork (*kiti moto*, meaning "hot chair". Its bar is the town's liveliest, and gets packed at weekends and whenever it hosts live music promotions.
Topcut Garden & Bar Behind the football ground opposite the bus stand. An exceedingly somnolent

Moving on from Tukuyu

Leaving Tukuyu, the first vehicles to Mbeya and Kyela (every half-hour or so to either) leave at 6am, the last around 7pm. Scandinavian Express (☏025/255 2041), for the long ride to Dar, have an office at the bus stand. The route from Tukuyu to Matema is covered on p.622.

outdoor joint with a few open-sided *bandas*, serving the usual grills, rubbery chicken, fish, chips and somewhat better liver, though you'll have to wait for ages. Good *supu* for breakfast.

Around Tukuyu

There are lots of things to see around Tukuyu, most of them – including crater lakes, a natural lava-stone bridge and waterfalls – associated with **Mount Rungwe**'s more excitable volcanic past. Its last eruption was about two centuries ago, but **earthquakes** are still a common occurrence, frequently rendering thousands homeless. All the sights can be visited through Mbeya's cultural tourism programme, but it's cheaper to arrange things in Tukuyu, either with Sisi kwa Sisi's branch office (see p.598) or – less expensive but also less organized – through *Langboss Lodge* (about Tsh15,000 per group per day, excluding transport and entry fees). Some of the sites don't need a guide, though transport can be tricky; details are given below. Incidentally, you'll have trouble hiring a car in Tukuyu at short notice, but bicycles are no problem – ask at your hotel, and expect to pay upwards of Tsh2000 a day.

Mount Rungwe

With a full day or preferably two, a climb to the 2960-metre summit of **Mount Rungwe**, a dormant volcano, is an enticing prospect, passing through wild and varied scenery. Formed 2.5 million years ago, the volcano – which comprises at least ten craters and domes – dominates the skyline for miles around. Part of its forested eastern flanks have been incorporated into Kitulo National Park, and are an important wildlife habitat, whose denizens include a unique subspecies of black-and-white colobus monkey, the newly discovered highland mangabey monkey, and the threatened Abbot's duiker.

There are two approaches to **the summit**, both passing through several habitat zones, from montane forest at 1500m, through upper montane forest and grassland, to higher-altitude bushland and heath. The summit itself gives breathtaking views of the Nyasa Trough to the south and the Kitulo Plateau to the east.

Practicalities

Hikers will need a **guide**: either from Sisi kwa Sisi or *Langboss Lodge*, both in Tukuyu. Locals in Rungwe village are also knowledgeable about the hiking route, but speak little or no English.

The easiest route to climb, but difficult to access without your own vehicle, is **from the northeast**, starting 10km along the track from Isongole (on the highway towards Mbeya) to Ndala, passing by Shiwaga Crater. The longer route, more heavily forested and therefore more scenic, is **from the west**, starting at Rungwe village, 7km off the Mbeya highway. To get to this trail from Tukuyu, catch the 7am **daladala** to Kikota, from where it's a ninety-minute walk east to Rungwe Secondary School. The base of the climb is another hour's walk east. Alternatively, rent a **taxi** from Tukuyu to the school (around Tsh20,000 each way; you'll have to make it worth the driver's while to wait for you, or arrange for him to pick you up the next day). The climb itself takes at least four to five hours up to the southern rim of the summit crater, and around two and a half hours back down. The Wildlife Conservation Society in Mbeya (see p.604) are planning to build a **log cabin** on Rungwe as part of their efforts to link the area with Kitulo National Park.

The last daladala **back to town** from Kikota leaves no later than 7.30pm – if you get stranded, Rungwe Secondary School has a **hostel** (Tsh3000 per person), and there's a **campsite** run by the Moravian Mission. If you're coming from Mbeya, leave no later than 7am, and allow at least twelve hours for the round trip. The **best time to visit** is September or October, when there's less chance of rain.

Masoko Crater Lake

An attractive by-product of Mount Rungwe's volcanic rumblings is **Masoko Crater Lake** (also called Kisiba Crater Lake), 15km southeast of Tukuyu along the unsurfaced road to Ipinda and Matema. It's easy to find, being right next to the road (on the right coming from Tukuyu). Like Ngosi Crater Lake near Mbeya, Masoko also has a legend, this one more explicable: the stone building on the crater rim housed the German Fifth Field Garrison before and during World War I, and was afterwards occupied by British troops, who later turned it into a courthouse (*mahakama*). In common with similar legends all over Tanganyika, locals believe that before the Germans were routed by the British, they buried treasure here – or, more precisely, dumped it in the lake – a theory borne out by the old German and Austro-Hungarian coins periodically washed up on the shore, encouraging intrepid locals to dive in for more (the coins are sold to tourists for under Tsh1000, though these days you're more likely to be offered coins from the British colonial period).

Access to the lake is relatively easy: catch the first of the two crowded daily pick-ups (8–9am) which head from Tukuyu to Ipinda and get off when you see the lake on your right. There's no entrance fee or facilities of any kind. There should be a pick-up or two in the opposite direction in the afternoon, but check in Tukuyu before leaving – there's more transport on Friday and Saturday, the market days in Ipinda and Ntaba respectively. From Mbeya, the only practical way of visiting the lake as a day-trip is by private car: the cultural tourism programme charges $20–40 per person, including a walk in a tea plantation.

Kaporogwe Falls

Twenty-five kilometres south of Tukuyu, the 25-metre **Kaporogwe Falls** (also called Kala Falls) on the Kala River, a tributary of the Kiwira River, are a good target for a day-trip. Apart from swimming, you can walk between the tumbling torrent and the cave behind it, home to a concrete wall where Germans are said to have hidden during World War I. The discovery of **stone tools** above the waterfall – knives, scrapers, picks and core axes from the "Kiwira Industry" – indicate that the place was intensively occupied during the Stone Age. It was later abandoned, possibly when it became covered by pumice and volcanic debris from one of Mount Rungwe's eruptions.

Transport from Tukuyu is most convenient by private vehicle, though a combination of public transport and bicycle rental can work out well too. Catch one of the frequent daladalas or Coasters from Tukuyu towards Kyela and get off at **Ushirika**, 10km south, at the junction to the falls 12–15km west of the highway. You should be able to rent a bicycle in Ushirika (no more than Tsh3000). Alternatively, Sisi kwa Sisi in both Tukuyu and Mbeya can organize trips (5hr return; roughly $30 per person), which also includes a visit to tea, banana or coffee plantations. A Tsh1000 **entrance fee** is collected in the car park near the falls on behalf of the local village.

The Kiwira River

The **Kiwira River**, about 20km north of Tukuyu, has three distinct attractions: God's Bridge and the Kijungu Pot Falls, which can be visited together as a day-trip, and the Marasusa Falls, which have to be visited separately. **God's Bridge** (Daraja la Mungu) is a natural lava-stone archway over the Kiwira River that was formed a few hundred years ago during one of Mount Rungwe's eruptions, and acquired its unusual shape when river-water cooled a lip of lava before it could collapse. Three kilometres away, on the same river, are the **Kijungu Falls**. Their name, meaning "cooking pot", alludes to the impressive pothole into which the river falls and disappears, before reappearing downstream. The sites are about 20km west of Tukuyu.

To reach God's Bridge and the Kijungu Falls by **public transport**, catch a daladala from Tukuyu or Mbeya to **Kyimo**, leaving you with an eleven-kilometre walk or bicycle ride west from the highway (Kyimo's villagers rent out bikes for around Tsh3000). There's a basic guest house in Kyimo, should you miss the last daladala back (around 4 to 5pm). A taxi from Tukuyu and back costs around Tsh20,000. There's no entrance fee, but you'll need your passport because the sites are on military prison land: register first at the gate by the prison near God's Bridge, where you'll be assigned a prison guard to escort you to the river (a tip is appreciated). Sisi kwa Sisi offers the trip (roughly 8hr) for $15 per person.

Further upstream are the impressively thunderous **Marasusa Falls**. From Tukuyu or Mbeya, catch a daladala to **Kiwira** village, 20km north of Tukuyu, from where it's a forty-minute walk to the river ($15 per person with Sisi kwa Sisi). The last daladala back to Tukuyu passes Kiwira at 7pm. If you miss it or want to stay, *Mapembero Guest House* is the best of several here (all ❶).

Lake Nyasa and eastwards

Straddling the border between Tanzania, Malawi and Mozambique, the 31,000-square-kilometre **LAKE NYASA** (also called Lake Malawi) is East Africa's third largest, and one of the most beautiful. The first European to hear about it was the Portuguese explorer Gaspar Bocarro in 1616, but it took until the 1770s for the first non-Africans to reach it, when Arab slavers began following a caravan route developed by the Yao tribe, making Nyasa a major source of slaves for the Omani empire.

Geologically, the lake is similar to Lake Tanganyika, having been formed in the same period of Rift Valley faulting some twenty million years ago.

The Nyasa ecosystem

Although eclipsed in absolute size and depth by Lake Tanganyika, Nyasa (meaning "great water" in Kiyao) trumps its big brother in terms of **biological diversity**. Whilst Tanganyika boasts a hugely impressive two hundred cichlid species, Lake Nyasa contains over four hundred, an astonishing figure, representing no less than one-third of the world's known species, most of which exist only here. However, commercial **overfishing** has wrought havoc on the lake's ecology. Catches of the freshwater *dagaa* sardine have declined drastically, and stocks of catfish, carp and the large Malawi bass have also fallen, giving rise to fears of environmental disaster if strict quotas aren't imposed.

△ Fishing canoes at Matema, Lake Nyasa

Like Lake Tanganyika, Nyasa is long and narrow, measuring 584km from north to south, but only 80km at its widest. A maximum depth of almost 700m was recorded at the northern end near the Tanzanian shore, where the jagged and largely unexplored **Livingstone Mountains** rise precipitously to over 2500m, providing an unforgettable backdrop, especially if you take the weekly ferry from Itungi Port to Mbamba Bay – one of Africa's great journeys.

Snorkellers are in for a treat, as most of the lake's four hundred colourful cichlid species favour the clear waters just off the rocky northeastern shoreline, easily reached by dugout or motorboat from the village of **Matema**, which also has one of Tanzania's most alluring beaches. Equally relaxing is the diminutive and exceptionally friendly town of **Mbamba Bay**, near the Mozambican border. Unfortunately there's a price to pay for paradise in the form of plagues of mosquitoes, which are especially ravenous in the first few hours after sunset. **Cerebral malaria** is a big problem around the lake, so make sure you're adequately protected.

East of the lake, the small agricultural settlement of **Njombe** makes for a pleasant if nondescript stop. South from here is the remote town of **Songea** – a surprisingly populous place given its distance from anywhere else, and one of the focal points of the 1905–07 **Maji Maji Uprising**. From here, rough roads continue west to Mbamba Bay, and east to Lindi and Mtwara on the Indian Ocean. For details of **ferry services** on Lake Nyasa, see p.614.

The **best time to visit** the lake region is September to November, when the weather is hot and dry, and June to August, which is cooler, sometimes windy, and has fewer mosquitoes. At other times it can get unbearably humid.

Matema and around

Tucked into the northeastern corner of Lake Nyasa between the Lufilyo River floodplain and the Livingstone Mountains, the fishing village of **MATEMA** enjoys both an inspiring location and a magnificent beach. There's superb snorkelling on the rocky shoreline just to its east, and for the energetic a waterfall in the mountains can be explored, as can the thick forest and *shambas* (farms) at their base. In short, it's a perfect place to unwind in.

The village served for a brief time as the regional headquarters under **German colonial rule** before the mosquitoes forced them out. Matema's oldest building is the **Lutheran mission house**, which looks somewhat like a Bavarian barn. Another reminder of colonial rule is the bay on which the village sits, named after the nineteenth-century explorer Hermann von Wissmann, whose two successful crossings of Africa spurred on his country's colonization of East Africa. Later, in his capacity as imperial commissioner of German East Africa, Wissmann brutally fought and won the Abushiri War (1889–91). Matema is now inhabited mainly by members of the Nyakyusa tribe – see p.605.

Matema's diminutive **market**, in the area known as Lyulilo, is 2.5km east of the *Lutheran Beach Resort* across a river ford. If you're feeling especially lazy, a dugout ride costs Tsh1000–3000 depending on its size and your bargaining skills (you'll see men carving out trunks to make the boats en route). The market itself has only the barest necessities, though the clearing at the end by the beach usually has piles of Kisi pots (see Ikombe village, p.613) awaiting transport, which you should be able to buy. There are also a couple of people selling skewers of grilled goat meat, fish and bananas, but other than that there's little else to it other than the fun of either amusing or inadvertently terrifying the local kids.

Practicalities

Given the cramped conditions on local road transport (whether from Tukuyu or Kyela), **getting to Matema** can be a deeply uncomfortable experience. The easier, dry season route is **via Kyela**. Catch an early-morning daladala or bus from Mbeya or Tukuyu to Kyela, and change to a pick-up there: with luck, you'll get one all the way to Matema, but you're more likely to be dumped in Ipinda, 30km north of Matema, where you'll have to change again (see below). Kyela to Ipinda should take about two hours in good weather.

The alternative approach, recommended for its scenery, is **direct from Tukuyu**: catch an early-morning pick-up or truck along the dirt road to Ipinda, passing by Masoko Crater Lake. The pick-ups (usually two daily, though some days nothing runs) leave from the roundabout beside NBC bank, 500m east of the Mbeya–Kyela highway; the first heads off at 8–9am, the second at noon. If there's nothing going, ask at the petrol station beside the bank or at the Lutheran Church offices next door – someone might have a vehicle heading down. The best day for lifts is Friday – market day in Ipinda. In good weather, the journey takes two and a half hours.

With luck, you might find a vehicle going all the way, but chances are that you'll have to change in the hot and dusty town of **Ipinda**, 30km north of Matema, from where a handful of vehicles head down to Matema daily, generally after noon. The ride is very crowded and uncomfortable: Land Rovers and Toyotas are best, though breakdowns are common. 4WD might be necessary in the rains. Should you get stuck in Ipinda, there are two basic guest houses and lots of bars and restaurants. Matema also lacks mains electricity, restaurants, telephones and bank, so bring enough **money** for your stay. Should you need it, Matema's mission-run **hospital** enjoys a good reputation.

Accommodation

Matema's **accommodation** is two modest but good-value church-run places a couple of kilometres west of the village at Matema Beach. **Camping** is also available at both of these places, or better, *Roger's Camping Site* 1km beyond *Matema Lake Shore Resort* on the beach (Tsh3000 per person), with toilets, a fully equipped kitchen, campfire area (firewood available), and meals if ordered in advance.

Lutheran Beach Resort 600m west of Ipinda junction in the mission school's compound (c/o Tukuyu Lutheran Mission ☎ 025/255 2130). Idyllically located in the grounds of the historic mission, the rooms and *bandas* (some en suite) are getting run-down, but remain comfortable, and some are right on the beach. There's a small shop, meals and soft drinks available, and a generator until 10pm. Spartan breakfast included. ❷

Matema Lake Shore Resort 2km west of Ipinda junction ☎ 025/250 4178, ⓦ www.twiga .ch/TZ/matemaresort.htm. A modern place with 22 nice, spotless rooms in four two-storey beach-front buildings (top floor rooms have balconies), each with large box nets, and most with Western toilets. The beach has been cleared though, so there's no shade. There's also a communal kitchen, barbecue area, cheap meals to order, snorkelling equipment, and various day-trips. ❸

Around Matema

The coarse grey sand of **Matema Beach** starts at Ipinda junction beside the hospital, a little over 2km west of the market. The water is apparently free of bilharzia, and crocodiles – which elsewhere have a habit of lunching on locals – are thankfully absent, but take any advice to the contrary seriously. The walk to the mouth of the **Lufilyo River**, 4km west of the hotels along the beach via a small lagoon, is recommended, but take care along the river itself, which is home to both crocodiles and hippo. If you're too lazy for the return trip, catch a ride back in a dugout.

A number of other **hikes and day-trips** from Matema are possible, should you feel the need to rouse yourself from your Arcadian reverie. The walk back along **the Ipinda road** passes through satisfyingly thick tropical vegetation agog with birdlife. Some of the vegetation is wild (look for vervet monkeys in the tall and bushy palms), but much is planted with banana and papaya plants, mango trees, stands of giant bamboo and sugar cane. Many of the houses in the clearings are built in traditional Nyakyusa fashion, using straight bamboo stalks lashed together for walls, and reeds for their pointed roofs. Look out too for the curious toadstool-like granaries made from woven reeds and topped by broad straw thatch roofs.

Matema lies tantalizingly close to the northernmost spur of the **Livingstone Mountains**, which run most of the way along the Tanzanian side of the lake. The mountains' thick forests and steep slopes are sparsely inhabited, and the

> ### Moving on from Matema
>
> Leaving Matema, get to the Ipinda junction by the hospital before 6am to catch the first **pick-ups** to Ipinda and Kyela. For Tukuyu you'll probably need to change in Ipinda. *Matema Lake Shore Resort* has a **Land Rover** for rent.

entire range is little explored. For a taste, there's a **waterfall** a couple of hours' walk from Matema, for which you'll need a guide: *Matema Lake Shore Resort* should be able to arrange one.

Ikombe and the lake

IKOMBE village, a few kilometres southeast of Matema on a small peninsula, is populated by the **Kisi tribe**, whose women have long been famed for their skills as potters – you can find Kisi pots in the markets at Matema, Ipinda, Kyela, Tukuyu, Mbeya and sometimes even in Iringa and Dar. Unlike other Tanzanian potters, the Kisi women use wheels – actually thick, ash-sprinkled plates – which help create the pots' characteristically rounded forms. When the pot is ready, it's smoothed with pebbles or maize cobs and rubbed with a greyish clay to give a creamy colour after firing. After a few days of drying, the pots are decorated with red ochre and sometimes incised with motifs. The final firing is done in a shallow depression in the ground lined with dry banana leaves. The resulting pottery is ideal for cooking or storing cool liquids. The **best time to visit** is on Friday to coincide with the weekly market.

Access to Ikombe is either on foot along a narrow path along the lakeshore, or by dugout canoe from Matema, which takes just over an hour and costs Tsh2000–4000. Alternatively, *Matema Lake Shore Resort* has a small **motorboat** (Tsh10,000 an hour).

For **full-day trips** on the lake, negotiate a discount for the motorboat, or rent a **dugout** – ideally through the hotels or campsite. **Snorkelling** (equipment at *Matema Lake Shore Resort*) is best off the rocky eastern shore, where you'll see many of the lake's cichlid species in the crystalline water. There are shoreline **caves** nearby but access depends on the lake level, the best time being towards the end of the dry season (Oct & Nov), when the water is lower.

Kyela

The hot, loud, dusty and mosquito-infested town of **KYELA** is no one's favourite place, with the possible exception of cyclists, for whom the 55km descent from Tukuyu is something close to heaven. For non-Africans, the town also has the dubious honour of being one of only very few places in Tanzania where the insistent shouts of "*mzungu*", "*mchina*", "*mhindi*" (or whatever applies to you) repeated *ad nauseam*, make visitors feel like little more than zoological curiosities. Not surprisingly, most travellers just pass through, at most spending a night on their way to or from the Lake Nyasa ferry at Itungi Port, the Malawian border, or the beach at Matema, 46km to the east. Having said that, the generalized tourist-baiting is at least partly offset by soothing choruses of "good morning, teacher!" and "*Shikamoo*" (a respectful greeting to which you should reply "*Marahaba*") from the town's children – or at least the ones who aren't totally petrified by your mere appearance – so turn a deaf ear and take it all in good spirit, and you'll hopefully find that Kyela provides a bearable, if not wholly enjoyable, experience.

Practicalities

There was a helpful but short-lived **tourist office** next to the *Steak Inn*; it might be worth checking whether it's reopened. NMB **bank** on Msitikini Road changes cash and travellers' cheques. The **post office** is between Posta and Mwakalinga roads. You can **phone** from TTCL and several call centres on Itungi Road.

There's currently only one ferry on the Tanzanian side of Lake Nyasa, the **MV Songea**, supposedly sailing weekly from Itungi Port to Mbamba Bay and back. However, **sailing times** are erratic and prone to cancellation, so check first with Sisi kwa Sisi in Mbeya or Tukuyu (they're happy to answer emailed queries), with the daladala and pick-up drivers in Kyela, or ring the Marine Services Company in Itungi Port on ☏028/250 3074. For what it's worth, MV *Songea* officially sails from Itungi Port on Thursday, calling at a string of minor ports before docking at Mbamba Bay around Friday lunchtime. It turns back to Itungi Port on Sunday or Monday.

The MV *Songea* has **first-class cabins** on top, each with two bunks and a table, and numbered **third-class seating** below. There's no second class. If you opt for third class, get your ticket as soon as the ticket office opens (three hours before departure) or you might be stuck in the steamy windowless confines of the dungeonlike lower deck. First class to Mbamba Bay costs just over Tsh20,000; third-class is around Tsh7000. There's also a Tsh500 port charge. Cheap meals and drinking water are available.

Itungi Port

The ferry starts at **Itungi Port** (also called Ziwani), 15km east of Kyela at the Kiwira River estuary. The road from Kyela is usually in a dreadful state, and the port itself has only a handful of buildings and a pontoon jetty where motorboats take passengers to the ferry moored offshore. **Access** from Kyela is by pick-up or daladala (Tsh500–700, plus charges for large baggage), taking about an hour. Both pick-ups and daladalas circle around Kyela in the morning angling for passengers, but get up early in case your vehicle takes ages to fill up. You can also board them on Mwakalinga Road facing the market. The touts are pests, so go for the vehicle that seems most likely to leave – minibuses are preferable to the deeply uncomfortable open-backed pick-ups.

Along the lake

The ferry stops at a number of villages and small towns along the way, including **Lupingu** (6–7hr from Itungi Port; also accessible by bus from Njombe), **Manda** (13hr), **Lundu**, **Nindai**, **Mango** and **Liuli**, the latter with some impressive boulder outcrops: the shape of the one furthest from the shore to the south inspired the Germans to call the place Sphinxhafen. At Lupingu, the boat is greeted with a wonderfully surreal spectacle of women and kids who have perfected the art of selling meals (fish and cassava) to hungry passengers by using plastic jugs strapped to long poles to reach up to the deck while wading up to their necks in the water. The ferry reaches Mbamba Bay roughly 22–24 hours after leaving Itungi Port.

Across to Malawi

Unfortunately, there are currently no ferries from **Mbamba Bay to Nkhata Bay** in Malawi, although there are open-topped wooden boats. The crossing takes up to ten hours, and you'll need a sense of adventure and confidence in your swimming skills. Needless to say, they're not officially recommended. There, is however, a sturdier cargo boat, the MV *Karonga*, which crosses over roughly once a week – it may (or may not) take passengers. It's also worth asking whether either of the MV *Songea* or MV *Ilala* have resumed the route (Sat & Mon respectively).

Before **leaving Tanzania**, get an exit stamp in Mbamba Bay. There's no office, but the official is on hand to greet the MV *Songea*. Information on Malawian visas is given on p.599. There are no banks in **Nkhata Bay**, so keep your wits about you when dealing with **money-changers**: the exchange rate in September 2005 was 70 Malawian kwacha for 1000 Tanzanian shillings. Nkhata Bay's best **accommodation** is the backpacker-friendly *Mayoka Village* (❷), ten-minutes' walk north of Nkhata Bay, with a lively atmosphere (and bar) and great food. Canoeing, snorkelling and scuba-diving are possible.

Accommodation

Kyela has loads of **accommodation**, mostly quite reasonable. Inspect several rooms or hotels before choosing though: if a bed lacks an adequately sized **mosquito net**, forget it – this is malaria country. In Kyela, a double room means it has two beds, so "singles" can be shared by a couple if the bed's big enough.

Gwakisa Guest House Corner of Itungi and CCM roads ☎025/254 0078. The large rooms here have ceiling fans and share clean toilets, showers and a laundry area, but do check the nets. ❶

Makete Half London Guest House Corner of Itungi and CCM roads ☎025/254 0459. Six en-suite "singles" with clean squat toilets and showers, nets, fans, carpet, table and chair. ❶

Pattaya Centre Guest House Itungi Rd ☎025/254 0015. The best central choice, so a little pricier than others, with good clean en-suite

rooms (including triples) and a separate bar and lounge. ❷

Side Villa Hotel Mwafongo Rd, 100m west of the road in from Mbeya ☎025/254 0348. A surprisingly rural part of town, so quieter and calmer than elsewhere. The hotel is a welcoming family-run affair, and all rooms are en suite with Western toilet, double bed, net and ceiling fan. It can be loud in the evenings thanks to the adjacent bar: get a room at the back on the right. ❶

Eating and drinking

Kyela's best **food** is served by women at the stalls off Posta Road between the bus stand and the market, who are also refreshingly friendly and polite compared to their male counterparts. Meals are basic but can be delicious, featuring fresh fish, fried cassava, bananas, grilled goat meat and boiled cakes, all for a few hundred shillings. Breakfasts are good too, whether you go for *supu*, fried cassava with chilli sauce, or porridge. Of the proper restaurants, best are *Mummy Classic Restaurant* on Itungi Road, who serve good and very filling lunches and dinners (around Tsh1000) and have CNN on the telly, and *New Karuma Restaurant*, facing the southeast side of the market, which does good cheap fish with *ugali*, rice or chips, and other dishes (well under Tsh1000). The poshest-looking place – *Steak Inn Hotel & Bar*, on the same street as the *New Karuma* – has horrid toilets, abrupt service and the quality varies, though the fish is usually good (Tsh800–2000).

Kyela has scores of **bars**, mostly pretty tawdry dives where manhood – and occasionally womanhood – seems to be measured by the quantity imbibed. There are no taxis, so if you want a night out, drink close to your hotel to avoid a potentially hazardous walk back. An ability to humour the town's dipsomaniacs would also be an asset. One of the more salubrious places is *Pattaya Centre* next to the guest house of the same name on Itungi Road, whose TV screens European football.

Moving on from Kyela

Buses generally leave from outside their ticket offices on Itungi Road. There are daily services to Dar via Mbeya, Iringa and Morogoro, all leaving around 6am: Scandinavian (☎025/254 0514) and Sumry are safest, and Hood the most perilous. Ipinda and Matema are served by irregular pick-ups that cruise around town in the morning looking for passengers. Ask the touts on Mwakalinga Road next to the market. Route details and information on getting to Matema are given on p.611. There are pick-ups and daladalas throughout the day to Tukuyu, Mbeya and the Malawi border (see p.599).

Mbamba Bay

MBAMBA BAY is currently the last port of call for the MV *Songea*, and the nation's southernmost town, although that word is a tad generous for such a hot, small and dusty place lacking running water, electricity or a bank, and which until recently had its road to the rest of the world cut off annually during the rains. Although Mbamba Bay serves as a border town of sorts for travellers arriving from or going to Malawi, the present lack of a ferry service between the two nations (there are local boats though; see p.614) means its sees few travellers. Still, if the long-mooted Mtwara Development Corridor Master Plan finally sees the light of day, a major shipping port is apparently in the offing – just don't hold your breath.

For now, the feeling of laid-back isolation is all part of Mbamba Bay's charm, and there are miles of sandy beaches to loll about on to either side of town – the enormous **Mohalo Beach** begins about 5km south of the centre. You'll see drying racks for *dagaa* sardines everywhere, plenty of shady mango and coconut trees, and even a few baobabs, but there's one thing that really makes Mbamba Bay special: the people. Even the children, instead of running away in terror like some do in Kyela and Matema, become delighted whenever they elicit a "*Marahaba*" from tourists in reply to their chirpy "*Shikamoo*".

Practicalities

The **MV Songea** beaches itself next to Mbamba Bay's ruined jetty some 22–24 hours after leaving Itungi Port. The ferry is met by two or three Land Rover **pick-ups** headed to Mbinga and Songea, but there's no reason to rush, and the daily 5am **bus** is in any case more comfortable. Services are run by Madamba Video Transport and Kisuma Pai Bus on alternate days – buy your ticket the day before.

Getting to Mbamba Bay **by land** means coming from Songea. The road has been widened but is still dirt and thus liable to be impassable during and after heavy rains. From Songea's bus stand, catch the daily bus (departure times vary; check the day before), or board a minibus to **MBINGA**, a wealthy coffee-growing centre 66km short of Mbamba Bay, where you might have to spend the night before heading on down through the forests and farms of the Matengo Highlands to the lakeshore by bus or pick-up. There are several basic guest houses around Mbinga's bus stand, but the best hotel is *MBICU Lodge* (℡025/264 0168; ❷), 1.5km towards Songea, run by Mbinga Co-operative Union, which has en-suite doubles, a bar and restaurant.

There's a **bank** in Mbinga. In Mbamba Bay, **money-changers** (dollar banknotes only) hang around to meet the ferry, but otherwise track down one of the bus owners.

Accommodation, eating and drinking

There's a cluster of very cheap **lodgings** signposted a few hundred metres from the beach near the bus stand, the best of which is *Tumaini Hotel*, also called *Satellite Hotel* (℡ Mbamba Bay 24; ❶), a friendly place with good clean rooms with big mosquito nets, but primitive shared toilets and bucket show-ers. Other choices include the *New Bay Annex Guest House*, 50m south of the roundabout (no phone; ❶), with good simple rooms, and the welcoming but grotty *Mabuyu Guest House*, 200m east of the roundabout (no phone; ❶). Much better than any of these, but awkwardly placed for the early bus, is *Neema Beach Garden Guest House*, 2km south of the centre at the foot of the boulder-strewn headland (☎ Mbamba Bay 3; ❷), with six good en-suite rooms with mosquito nets, and the advantage of being right on the beach. To get there, walk south along the Mbinga Road (it starts on the right just before the bus stand if you're looking from the shore), turn right after 1km just after the bridge, and follow the track.

Restaurants are limited to the *Neema*, which offers salads, chicken, fish and rice if ordered in advance, and a small unnamed *mgahawa* tea room on the corner of the street leading to *Tumaini Hotel*, which serves delicious and very filling meals for around Tsh700 (usually fish with *ugali* or rice). The only real **bars** are a small packed room on your left just before the bus stand if you're coming from the beach, and the *Neema*, which sometimes has **discos** on Saturday and Sunday. There's no problem walking back to the centre at night, but you'll need a torch if there's no moon.

Njombe

Perched atop a ridge at the eastern end of the Kipengere Range, midway between Mbeya and Songea, is the agricultural centre of **NJOMBE** – one of Tanzania's highest, coolest and breeziest towns. The fresh climate and expansive views are the main attractions, making Njombe a likeable sort of place to break a journey at, something you'll have to do if you arrive late from Mbeya. If you've a few hours to spare, there are two easily accessible patches of **rainforest** just outside town, one on a small hill less than a kilometre east of the cathedral, the other occupying several vales and low hills, starting 1km northwest of *Chani Hotel*, from where there's a footpath. There are also a couple of **waterfalls** next to the highway: one 800m north of NBC bank; the other 2km south of town. The **market**, one street west of the highway at the end of both Mlowezi and UWT streets, is a good place to buy naturally dyed **woven baskets** made from a reedlike grass called *milulu*; the baskets are at their freshest and most aromatic after the long rains. On Sundays, the imposing **Catholic Cathedral of St Joseph** at the south end of town next to the bus stand celebrates Mass (7am, 9am, 10.45am & 3pm) in effervescent musical style.

Practicalities

The Mbeya–Songea highway runs north to south through town. The **bus stand** is on the west side of the highway at the south end of town, near the Catholic cathedral. The **post office** and **TTCL** office are behind the cathedral. **Internet access** is possible at Ngewe.com (daily 8am–8pm), next to *Wasia Hotel* one block east of the highway opposite the bus stand. The most efficient **bank** is NBC, 1km north along the highway, which has a 24hr Visa/MasterCard ATM.

Njombe has some great-value **accommodation**. The best of the budget places, actually mid-range in standard, is the excellent ⚑ *Impoma Garden Lodge* off Kinyozi Street (☎026/278 2570, ✉impomalodge@yahoo.com; ❷ including breakfast); turn left at the Total petrol station 600m north of the bus stand and it's 300m along. It's a modern place with sixteen clean and fresh en-suite rooms (including three enormous doubles), all with cotton sheets, good nets, satellite TV and phone, and hot running water; there's also safe parking. More upmarket, but still very good value, is the *Chani Hotel* (☎026/278 2357; ❸ including breakfast) off Usunguni Road; turn left at *Edina Hotel* 700m north of the bus stand, then right after *Mpoki Hotel* – 1.5km in all. It sits on the edge of the lower, partially forested part of town, its twelve comfortable rooms with wall-to-wall carpet, big beds and spotless toilets and showers. There's also a TV lounge and safe parking. Best of the really cheap places is *New Magazeti Highland Green Inn* (☎026/278 2913; ❶), 100m along Usunguni Street heading towards *Chani Hotel*, whose somnolent atmosphere conceals some cheerful rooms decorated with woodcarvings and Tingatinga paintings; some are en suite (so-so squat toilets and showers).

All three hotels have very reasonably priced **restaurants and bars**, the *Chani Hotel* benefiting from a lovely garden and, amazingly, silver service.

Songea

If you can ignore the often reckless driving, the long, swooping descent from Njombe to **SONGEA** is gloriously exhilarating, passing through majestic granite scenery reminiscent of the Scottish Highlands, complete with rushing mountain streams, misty moorlands and incredibly long views over the hills. Songea itself, 237km southeast of Njombe, is – despite its remoteness – a large and dirty market town you probably won't want to settle into. The only reason to come here is if you're either travelling on to Mbamba Bay, or attempting the adventurous overland route eastwards to the Indian Ocean.

Arrival and accommodation

Songea's **bus stand** is at the west end of town on Sokoine Road, where there are taxis. There are dozens of cheap **guest houses** scattered about, most of them very basic and uninviting, and Songea's low altitude compared to Njombe also marks the unwelcome return of **mosquitoes** – ensure your bed has a good net. Songea also experiences frequent and prolonged **power cuts**, which affect the pumped water supply of many hotels – **tap water** is unsafe to drink.

Annex Yapender Lodge Deluxe St ☎025/260 2855. Almost catatonically calm and getting tatty, the ten en-suite doubles here are nonetheless the best in town, so arrive early. The related *Yapender Lodge* on the same street is less enticing, but has the enjoyable *Yapender Mtini Pub* in front. Safe parking. Breakfast included. ❷

Golani Bar & Guest House At the bus stand ☎025/260 2023. The most secure of a grotty (and

noisy) set of hotels by the bus stand, with cheap but gloomy rooms sharing smelly bathrooms. There's a good bar and restaurant up-front with outdoor tables. ❶

New Star Guest House & Bar Deluxe St (no phone). Clean and friendly, with slightly shabby rooms sharing bathrooms, all with nets, some with fans. There's a small verandah at the front with a couple of tables for drinks, and a restaurant inside. ❶

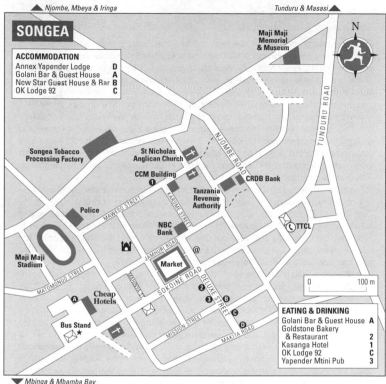

SONGEA

ACCOMMODATION
Annex Yapender Lodge **D**
Golani Bar & Guest House **A**
New Star Guest House & Bar **B**
OK Lodge 92 **C**

N

Maji Maji
Memorial
& Museum

TUNDURU ROAD

Songea Tobacco
Processing Factory

St Nicholas
Anglican Church

NJOMBE ROAD

CCM Building ❶

CRDB Bank

Tanzania
Revenue
Authority

Police

MAWESO STREET

KARUME STREET

NBC
Bank

⌚ TTCL

Maji Maji
Stadium

MATOMONDO STREET

JAMHURI ROAD

@

Market

SOKOINE ROAD

DELUXE STREET

0   100 m

MACHINA ST.

Cheap
Hotels

❷ ❷ Ⓑ
❸ Ⓒ

Ⓓ

EATING & DRINKING
Golani Bar & Guest House **A**
Goldstone Bakery
   & Restaurant **2**
Kasanga Hotel **1**
OK Lodge 92 **C**
Yapender Mtini Pub **3**

Bus Stand ★

MISSION STREET

MAKITA ROAD

▼ Mbinga & Mbamba Bay

OK Lodge 92 Deluxe St ☎025/260 2640. The travellers' favourite for years but shoddily maintained, with holier-than-thou mosquito nets. On the positive side the beds are comfortable, the better rooms have bathrooms and TVs, and cheap if uninspiring food is available, and drinks. Safe parking. ❶–❷

The Town

Songea's main attraction is the **Maji Maji Memorial and Museum** (daily 8am–7pm; donation expected), northeast of the centre. The memorial ground is a large square lawn flanked on three sides by the cement busts of twelve Ngoni chiefs who were captured and executed by the Germans during the Maji Maji Uprising. The centre of the ground is dominated by a bulky statue of a soldier with a machine-gun in his hand, while facing the ground in a pagoda is a large cement statue of Nyerere looking uncharacteristically solemn. Though crudely fashioned, the busts are rendered poignant by garlands hung around their necks. Three of the chiefs are depicted with turbans, an unwitting reminder of the Arab-dominated slave trade in which the Ngoni also participated, both as traders and as captives. One of the busts represents **Chief Songea Luwafu Mbano**, from whom the town takes its name. As the most famous of the Ngoni resistance leaders, the Germans honoured him with decapitation rather than hanging – his cranium presumably lies in a German museum's storeroom, awaiting DNA identification and eventual repatriation – as is the case with over fifty other skulls of executed Tanzanian tribal leaders.

The Ngoni invasions

Songea is the main town of the **Ngoni** tribe, who occupy much of southwestern Tanzania (they are also found in Malawi, and in scattered groups as far north as Lake Victoria). The Ngoni are relatively recent immigrants, having arrived only in the 1840s, at the end of a remarkable twenty-year, 3500-kilometre migration from KwaZulu-Natal in southern Africa.

At the beginning of the nineteenth century, the militaristic **Zulu empire** under King Shaka (or Chaka) began to make its presence felt, until by the 1830s many of southern Africa's people were on the move, either fleeing the Zulu armies or the famine and drought that accompanied the conflict. Twelve major migrations out of South Africa occurred during this period, half of which resulted in the creation of new kingdoms elsewhere: the Basotho in Lesotho; Ndebele in Zimbabwe; Gaza in Mozambique; Kololo in Zambia; and the Ngoni in Malawi and Tanzania.

The Ngoni were led by **Zwangendaba**, a former Zulu commander who had fallen out of favour. Copying the regimented military organization and strategies of the Zulu, in 1822 Zwangendaba and the Ngoni crossed into southern Mozambique, and subsequently followed the course of the Zambezi River into Zimbabwe, where in 1834 they destroyed the 300-year-old Changamire empire of the Shona people. The following year, the Ngoni crossed the Zambezi and headed into Malawi, and by 1840 they had reached the Ufipa Plateau in southwestern Tanzania.

On Zwangendaba's death in 1845, the Ngoni split into several groups and continued their odyssey of conquest and migration. One group, known as the **Tuta**, headed north and settled between Lake Tanganyika and Unyamwezi, where they were welcomed by Chief Mirambo (see p.555), who took advantage of their military skills by hiring them as mercenaries for his own expansionist plans. Other groups went southwest to Malawi and eastern Zambia, while others headed east to set up independent states at Songea and Njombe in Tanzania, displacing the indigenous Ndendeule and Matengo tribes respectively, and all the while waging war against other tribes, and amongst themselves. The ensuing chaos that enveloped southern Tanzania greatly eased the German conquest of the country fifty years later – although the Germans themselves would later meet with serious opposition from the Ngoni during the 1905–07 Maji Maji Uprising.

The curator speaks no English, but is happy to take you around. Inside are photographs and full-length paintings of the twelve chiefs, some of them pictured in the style of Ethiopian Christian icons. The upper floor contains three drums (two still playable), a couple of grinding stones, bellows used in iron-working, a beautiful tobacco horn (which might also have been used for storing marijuana, traditionally smoked by Ngoni elders), weapons and some surprisingly light hide shields. A mass grave from the uprising lies behind the building, marked by an obelisk and a low rectangular wall. Chief Songea's grave is 50m away.

Other than the museum, there's really only the **market** to keep you occupied. It's a good place for sampling or smelling the dried fish from Lake Nyasa, but for *kangas* and *kitenges*, rummage through the shops and stalls at the west end of Jamhuri Road.

Eating and drinking

Songea's eateries are a sorry lot, serving up dentally-challenging chicken with chips, and little else. Still, the best local **restaurant** is the friendly and unassuming *Kasanga Hotel* on Maweso Street, which dishes up good cheap meals and also sells beers and sodas. Try also *Goldstone Bakery & Restaurant* on Deluxe

All **buses** leave between 6 and 7am; thereafter it's Coasters and more dangerous Hiace minibuses (to Njombe, Iringa and Mbeya). Of several bus companies running to **Dar es Salaam**, passing Njombe, Iringa and Morogoro, safest are Scandinavian Express (℡025/260 0443) and Sumry. **Mbamba Bay** is served by one daily bus. If you miss it, plenty more buses and minibuses go roughly hourly to Mbinga, where you can stay the night before heading on. For **Tunduru**, see p.622.

The only official land border crossing between Tanzania and **Mozambique** is south of Mtwara on the coast. From Songea, the easiest way in is via Lake Nyasa: from Mbamba Bay to Nkhata Bay in Malawi by local boat, then back across the lake on the weekly MV *Ilala* via the Malawian islands of Chizumulu and Likoma to the Mozambican ports of Cobué and Metangula.

Street, which makes reasonable pizzas. On the same street, *OK Lodge 92* has filling meals, but arrive early to avoid the *kuku na chipsi* (chicken and chips) syndrome. Other than these, there's little other than the town's drinking holes for the usual chip omelettes and grilled meat.

Songea's most enjoyable **bar** is the large, *makuti*-thatched *Yapender Mtini Pub* on Deluxe Street, which plays good music and has the town's best *nyama choma*. Best of the places around the bus station is *Golani Bar & Guest House*, which screens CNN and European football.

Listings

Banks NBC, corner of Jamhuri and Karume roads, is helpful and averagely efficient, and has a 24hr Visa/MasterCard ATM; CRDB, Njombe Rd, is slower.

Clinic China Medical Clinic, Deluxe St in same building as Valongo Internet Café (Mon–Sat 8.30am 5.30pm, Sun 8 30am–4pm; ℡0748/371348).

Internet access Valongo Internet Café, Deluxe St (daily to 8pm; Tsh1000 an hour).

Post office Main one at bottom of Tunduru Rd; branches in the bus stand and along Sokoine Rd.

Telephones TTCL is beside the main post office; attended-call offices in the bus stand and throughout town. Cheapest for international calls is the Net2Phone service at Valongo Internet Café.

From Songea to the coast

A wickedly adventurous and infrequently travelled route from Songea is the rough road east to the **Indian Ocean**, almost 700km. Easily one of Tanzania's worst roads, travel along it is determined by the **weather**: best in the dry season from June or July to late October or November, before the short rains kick in. At other times, **mud** can block the road for days or weeks at a time (even experienced Tanzanian drivers get bogged down), and the route is completely blocked between March and May at the height of the long rains. The journey is done in three legs: from Songea to Tunduru, on to Masasi, and then on to Lindi, Mtwara or Mikindani on a good sealed road or to Newala along reasonable dirt.

A **warning**: do not attempt self-drive in anything other than bone-dry weather if you're not an expert off-road driver (for basic off-road driving tips, see p.45), or if you lack advanced mechanical skills or suitable equipment: shovel, tow-rope, plenty of spare oil, water and brake fluid, and a full tank of fuel, as there's none between the towns. You should also be fully confident in your vehicle, as the bone-shaking, gear-grinding, mud-drenching road will test it to the limit. Needless to say, high-clearance 4WD is essential. Still, with good luck, the whole journey takes three days.

Songea to Tunduru

The 273km **Songea to Tunduru** road, mostly through thick, tsetse- fly-infested *miombo* woodland, is probably the worst in the country, and covered by buses only in the dry season. More "reliable" (a distinctly relative concept around here) are the daily Land Rover daladalas ("one tens"), departing either town at 6am (Tsh18,000), and whose drivers are capable of astonishing prowess behind the wheel. In dry weather, these can take as little as eight hours, but from November to February (after which the road becomes impassable), and also after the long rains, fifteen to twenty hours is considered good going. If you're **self-driving** outside the dry season (during which loose sand is the main problem), getting stuck in mud is a certainty, so it's best to fill up with as many passengers as you can to provide the necessary muscle power when horse power fails. Alternatively, travel in convoy.

Food and drink at inflated prices can be bought at a handful of isolated villages along the way. The only **accommodation** between the two towns is the *Malinyi Hotel and Guest House* (❶) at **Namtumbo**, 72km east of Songea.

Tunduru

The reward for your efforts is a night at the rough gemstone mining town of **TUNDURU**, which should give you the necessary resolve to move on the following day. Several gemstone dealers and hardware stores line the main street, and that's really about it.

You'll probably have to stay overnight, unless you're headed to Masasi and are happy cat-napping on the next bus out at the bus stand (stash your bags somewhere safe; there are plenty of wild types around). Unfortunately, the town's **guest houses** (all ❶) are a sorry lot, with particularly rank squat toilets-cum-showers, though most guest houses do at least have some en-suite rooms with large mosquito nets and ceiling. The best is *Annex Hunters Guest House* (no phone), 100m from the bus stand off the road towards Songea, which is friendly and secure, but has no running water.

Tunduru's man-eaters

Apart from terrible roads, Tunduru district's other claim to ignominy is its **man-eating lions** (for which reason you should avoid camping wild, and, if you've broken down, stay close to your vehicle whilst awaiting help). The gruesome attacks have been occurring on and off for three decades, even in town – in 1986, a single lion claimed the lives of 42 inhabitants before stopping its killing spree. The problem has been given a surreal slant by superstitious locals. One belief is that witches – especially in neighbouring Mozambique – are able to invoke evil in the form of lions. The tale goes that a man had a quarrel with a neighbour, and so consulted a witch, who gave him a rope that could be turned into a lion to attack his neighbour if he followed strict instructions. The man created the lion, but forgot the instructions and was himself gobbled up by the lion, who thereby acquired a taste for humans. A more prosaic explanation is simply that the district lies in the path of the wildlife migration from southern Selous to Mozambique's Niassa Game Reserve, and where grazers go, big cats are sure to follow.

Similarly uninspired are Tunduru's **restaurants**: the best is *The Mainland Hotel*, 300m from the bus stand towards Songea, whose menu is fanciful but at least their stock dish of rice with meat or beans makes a welcome change from carbonized chicken and chips. Two other places between here and the bus stand you might try are the *Graceland* and the *Amazon Hill*, both also doubling as the town's more appetizing **bars**.

Tunduru to Masasi

The 196-kilometre road from **Tunduru to Masasi** is better, with public transport being a daily 6am bus from either town (Tsh6000), taking five hours in good weather, or up to twice that if it's been raining. If you miss the buses (buy your ticket the day before), you may find yourself having to pay for a lift in the back of a lorry. The route skirts the southern boundary of Selous Game Reserve, beyond which huge, eroded boulder-like hills dominate. Masasi, and the final leg to the coast, is covered in Chapter 3 (pp.245–247).

Travel details

Buses, daladalas and pick-ups

Although Iringa, Njombe and Tukuyu lie on main routes, most buses passing through are already full, so only frequencies for buses starting their journeys in those towns are mentioned. Routes liable to long delays or cancellation in the rains are marked with asterisks.

Iringa to: Arusha (1–2 daily; 12hr); Dar (7 daily; 6–7hr); Dodoma (3 daily; 5–6hr); Kalenga (hourly daladalas; 20min); Mbeya (hourly; 3hr 30min–4hr); Morogoro (2 hourly; 3–4hr); Moshi (1–2 daily: 11hr); Songea (hourly Coasters; 8hr); Tunga-malenga (1 daily; 2–3hr).

Kyela to: Dar (4 daily; 13hr); Ipinda (2–3 pick-ups daily*; 1–1hr 30min); Iringa (4 daily; 6hr); Itungi Port (pick-ups on ferry days; 1hr); Malawi border (hourly pick-ups and daladalas; 30min); Matema (2–3 pick-ups daily*; 2–3hr); Mbeya (4 daily plus hourly daladalas; 2hr 30min–3hr); Morogoro (4 daily; 10hr); Tukuyu (4 daily plus hourly daladalas; 1hr 30min).

Mbamba Bay to: Mbinga (1 daily plus occasional pick-ups*; 3hr 30min); Songea (1 daily plus occasional pick-ups*; 6hr).

Mbeya to: Arusha (1–2 daily; 15–17hr); Chunya (half hourly Coasters; 2hr); Dar (15–20 daily; 11–13hr); Dodoma (3 weekly; 11hr); Iringa (11 daily; 3hr 30min–4hr); Kyela (hourly pick-ups and daladalas; 2hr 30min–3hr); Lilongwe, Malawi (1 weekly; 18hr); Lusaka, Zambia (6 weekly; 20–22hr); Mikumi (hourly; 8–9hr); Morogoro (11 daily; 11–12hr); Njombe (hourly minibuses; 4hr); Rungwa (2 weekly*; 8–10hr); Songea (2 daily;

8–9hr); Sumbawanga (2–3 daily; 6–7hr); Tabora (2 weekly*; 18hr); Tukuyu (hourly minibuses; 1hr 30min); Tunduma (hourly pick-ups and daladalas; 1hr 30min–2hr).

Njombe to: Dar (1 daily; 9hr); Iringa (1 daily plus hourly minibuses; 4hr); Mbeya (hourly minibuses; 4hr); Morogoro (1 daily; 7–8hr); Songea (hourly Coasters; 4hr).

Songea to: Dar (3–4 daily; 13hr); Iringa (3–4 daily plus hourly daladalas; 8hr); Mbamba Bay (1 daily plus occasional pick-ups*; 6hr); Mbeya (2 daily; 8–9hr); Mbinga (3 daily plus hourly daladalas and pick-ups*; 4hr 30min); Morogoro (3–4 daily; 10hr); Njombe (hourly 3–4 daily plus hourly minibuses; 4–5hr); Tunduru (2 Land Rovers daily*; 8–24hr).

Tukuyu to: Mbeya (hourly minibuses; 1hr–1hr 30min); Kyela (hourly daladalas; 1hr 30min); Ipinda (1–3 daily pick-ups*; 1hr 30min–2hr 30min); Matema (1 daily pick-up*; 4–8hr).

Tunduru to: Masasi (1 daily*; 5–10hr); Songea (2 Land Rovers daily*; 8–24hr).

Ferries (Lake Nyasa)

For more details, see p.614.

Itungi Port to: Mbamba Bay (MV *Songea* Thurs noon; 22–24hr).

Mbamba Bay to: Itungi Port (MV *Songea* Sun or Mon; 22–24hr).

Flights

All flights are operated by Coastal Aviation.

Ruaha to: Arusha (daily; 4hr 15min); Dar (daily; 2hr 15min); Kilwa (daily; 4hr 35min); Mafia (daily; 3hr 45min); Manyara (daily; 3hr 35min); Pemba (daily;

3hr 20min); Selous (daily; 1hr 20min); Zanzibar (daily; 2hr 35min).

Trains

Mbeya to: Dar (3 weekly; 19hr 15min–22hr 30min); Ifakara (2–3 weekly; 11hr 40min–14hr 10min); Mang'ula (2 weekly; 12hr 20min–15hr); New Kapiri Mposhi, Zambia (1 weekly; 19hr 10min); Selous Game Reserve, various stations (2–3 weekly; 15hr–18hr 10min).

Zanzibar

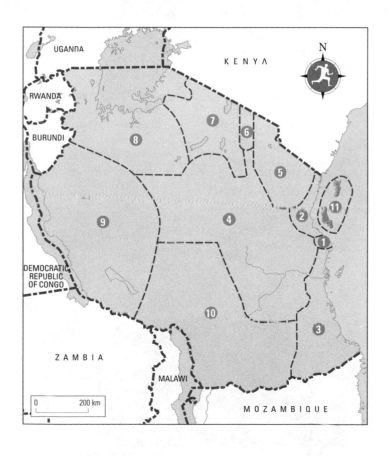

CHAPTER 11

Highlights

✱ **Stone Town** Africa meets the Orient in the most atmospheric town south of the Sahara. **See p.629**

✱ **Forodhani Gardens** Stone Town's nightly waterfront street food market, with a choice of chow that would spoil a sultan. **See p.650**

✱ **Jozani Forest** Ideal for escaping the heat, a soothingly cool and shady forest that contains troops of endangered red colobus monkeys. **See p.671**

✱ **Spice tours** See, touch, smell and taste Zanzibar's famous spices, followed by a slap-up meal. **See p.662**

✱ **Nungwi** A former hippy beach now discovered by mainstream tourism, but still offering a lively and enjoyable beach holiday. **See p.694**

✱ **Misali Island** Gorgeous beaches, nature trails through mangroves, flying foxes, snorkelling and some of East Africa's best scuba-diving. **See p.710**

✱ **Bull-fighting, Pemba** One of the few reminders of the Portuguese occupation, but don't worry, the bull isn't killed, just mightily annoyed. **See *Tanzania in celebration***

△ Children sitting on a cannon, Zanzibar

Zanzibar

This is the finest place I have known in all of Africa ...
An illusive place where nothing is as it seems. I am mesmerized ...

David Livingstone, 1866

Lying 35km off the coast of mainland Tanzania, the **Zanzibar archipelago** is one of Africa's best-known and most enticing destinations, one whose very name evokes images of an exotic paradise replete with coconut palms, multicoloured coral reefs and, of course, miles and miles of white sands lapped by warm, turquoise waters.

The image is not without justification, of course, but there's a whole lot more to Zanzibar than beaches and tropical languor. Its history, for a start, has seen more than its fair share of invasions, empires and intrigues, and Zanzibari culture reflects this mixture of influences, not just in the colourful architecture of Stone Town and the ruined cities and palaces scattered across the islands, but in its delicious cuisine and a wealth of festivals ranging from Islamic celebrations to bull-fights. If Zanzibar feels like a different country to mainland Tanzania, it's because it is – or at least it was until 1964, when it united with mainland Tanganyika to form the present-day nation of Tanzania. The awkward terms of this union, in which Zanzibar retains a good deal of autonomy (too much for the liking of mainlanders, too little for Zanzibaris), has been a source of political unease and unrest ever since.

The archipelago's biggest and most important island is **Unguja**, 1651 square kilometres of low-lying fossilized coral separated from the mainland by the Zanzibar Channel. **Stone Town**, on the west coast, is centred on an alluring Arabian-style labyrinth of crooked narrow alleyways, packed to the rafters with nineteenth-century mansions, palaces and bazaars. The town itself has enough of interest to merit several days of aimless wandering, and is a good base for visiting the rest of the island. The wetter western side of Unguja is where most of the island's famous **spice plantations** are located, easily visited on an

Zanzibar: one name, many uses

Technically, the name **Zanzibar** applies to the entire archipelago, including Unguja and Pemba islands, although, rather confusingly, **Unguja** is also known as **Zanzibar Island**. To add to the conundrum, the capital of Unguja, **Zanzibar Town**, is often referred to as **Stone Town** (as we have done) – although properly speaking this name refers only to the older sections of Zanzibar Town, rather than to the entire city.

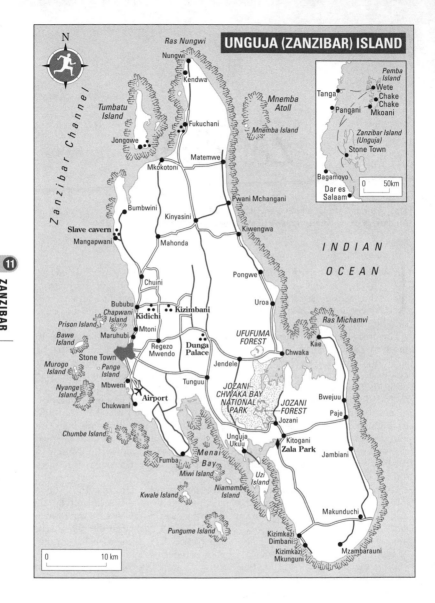

organized tour, as are a number of other attractions including ruined Omani palaces, Persian baths, and a number of uninhabited islands whose surrounding coral reefs are ideal for snorkelling. Another viable day-trip is to **Jozani Forest**, Zanzibar's largest tract of indigenous evergreen forest, which shelters several endemic wildlife species including red colobus monkeys; it's usually combined with a boat excursion off Kizimkazi on the south coast in search of dolphins. But Unguja's main attraction after Stone Town is its **beaches**. The most beautiful are on the east and northeast coasts, and either side of Unguja's northernmost tip, Ras Nungwi. Although parts of the coast, notably the northeast, have been swamped by monstrous package resorts, development remains for the most part low-key, with a selection of beach accommodation ranging from homely bungalow-style set-ups to plush five-star resorts. As well as standard water sports, **scuba-diving** is offered by an increasing number of PADI-accredited dive centres and schools.

Unguja's sister island of **Pemba**, 48km to the north, is quite a contrast. Few tourists come here, facilities are extremely limited, and its beaches are less numerous and less accessible – though you're at least likely to have them to yourself. The island's main attraction is its fringing **coral reef**, offering exhilarating scuba-diving and snorkelling, whilst terrestrial attractions include the pristine Ngezi Forest, and a host of medieval ruins dating from the height of the Swahili trading civilization.

Zanzibar's climate is typically **tropical**, making for hot and humid weather most of the year. There are two **rainy seasons**. The "long" *masika* rains (dubbed the "Green Season" by some hoteliers) run from March to May, and are especially heavy from April onwards, when some of the larger hotels close. The lighter "short" *mvuli* rains fall between October and early December. The rest of the year is hot and dry, with temperatures gradually increasing from July until the onset of the short rains. **Ramadan** (see p.60 for dates) is not the best time to visit, as most restaurants are closed by day and the atmosphere, especially in Stone Town, is not at its brightest.

Stone Town

Located on Unguja's west coast, STONE TOWN is the cultural and historical heart of Zanzibar. Known locally as *Mji Mkongwe* (Old Town), Stone Town in many ways resembles the medinas of the Arabian Peninsula and North Africa with its magical labyrinth of narrow, twisting streets, bustling bazaars and grand Arab mansions. In spite of the neglect which followed Tanzania's independence, the town's original **layout** and fabric remain intact, making it the finest and most extensive example of the Swahili trading settlements that dot the islands and coastline of East Africa. Most of the town was built in the nineteenth century at the height of the monsoon-driven dhow trade, when Zanzibar was the most important commercial centre in the western Indian Ocean, acting as a conduit for all manner of goods shipped in from the mainland, most notoriously ivory and slaves. The pitiful cells under the last slave market can still be seen, as can two former palaces (now museums), an early eighteenth-century Omani fortress, two cathedrals and some Persian-style baths, along with a wealth of less important but no less impressive buildings.

Above all, Stone Town is a cosmopolitan city, its ability to absorb and blend outside influences and cultures discernible in the faces of its inhabitants: African, Indian, Arabian, European, and every possible combination in between. It's a place of contrasts: in the harbour, wooden dhows bob up and down beside modern hydrofoil ferries; women in black *buibui* veils chat on mobile phones, with kids dressed in baseball caps in tow; and Internet cafés offer broadband access from glorious old mansions with crumbling facades. Yet somehow every-thing, even the tourists, seems to fit.

Some history

In spite of Stone Town's centuries-old aura, most of its buildings date only from the last 150 years or so. Although the **Portuguese** established a small trading post at Shangani Point in 1503, Stone Town's history only really starts after their expulsion by the **Omani Arabs**. Fearing a counter-attack by the Portuguese, or from rival Mazrui Arabs based in Mombasa, the Omanis quickly constructed a fort, largely unaltered today, which was completed in 1701. It wasn't until the start of the nineteenth century, however, that the town began to grow up around the fort. The first **stone buildings** were constructed during the reign of the Omani sultan, **Seyyid Saïd**, who in 1832 shifted his capital from Muscat to Stone Town. Helped by the establishment of clove plantations, Zanzibar grew rich, and the town's mud houses were replaced with multi-storeyed construc-tions made from coral stone quarried from nearby islands. This period coin-cided with the rising importance of the **slave trade**, which at its height saw the transportation of sixty thousand slaves annually from the mainland to Zanzibar, from where they found ready markets in Arabia, India and French Indian Ocean possessions. The sultan received a tax on every sale, and as the town expanded and his revenues multiplied, so did his palaces.

The building boom lasted almost sixty years and was responsible for most of what we see today. But behind the waterfront facade of palaces all was not so grand. An English physician, Dr James Christie – who arrived in 1869 at the start of a devastating cholera epidemic which claimed ten thousand lives in Stone Town alone – described the town as "a closely-packed, reeking suffoca-tion of dirt-caked stone and coral-lime houses, whose open drains, abundant night-soil and busy vermin help erase any image of oriental glamour". The end of the epidemic, in 1870, coincided with the accession of **Sultan Barghash**, who must have felt particularly ill-starred when, only two years into his reign, a violent cyclone swept across the island, devastating his fleet and decimating the clove plantations on which much of his revenue depended. The **slave trade** too was increasingly being hindered by British warships, and was banned in 1873, effectively marking the end of Zanzibar's economic independence. Nonetheless, Stone Town continued to grow and the sultan embarked on the construction of several monumental palaces and civic buildings.

When the **British Protectorate** over Zanzibar was imposed in 1890, the development of Stone Town was more or less complete, though the water-front gained an involuntary facelift after a **British bombardment** in 1896, undertaken to ensure that their choice of sultan took power. The bombard-ment, known as the shortest war in history, lasted all of 45 minutes, destroyed two palaces and was sufficient to elicit the prompt surrender of the usurper. British influence in Stone Town itself, however, was negligible, although their gradual sanitization of the city meant that by the 1920s a more romantic vision of Zanzibar had begun to replace the images of filth, squalor and slavery that epitomized the nineteenth century.

The **1964 Revolution** was the single most important event in modern-day Stone Town's history. In one night of terror, some twelve thousand Indians and Arabs were massacred by a ragtag army of revolutionaries, prompting the mass exodus of all but one percent of Stone Town's non-African population. The new government, steeped in the socialist ideology of the Eastern Bloc, had neither the money nor the political inclination to concern itself with Stone Town's upkeep. Tenants of the palaces and merchants' houses that had been

△ Stone Town street

converted into low-cost state housing could not hope to keep the lavish build-ings in any decent state of repair, and so the old town was left to crumble into the advanced state of decay and disrepair in which it languishes today.

The **economic liberalization** ushered in by President Mwinyi's election in 1985 finally brought hope to Stone Town; by the early 1990s, a sizeable number of Indians and Arabs had returned, and several restoration projects had got off the ground. It's hoped that the recent addition of Stone Town to UNESCO's World Heritage list will attract further funding to help restore the town to its original magnificence.

Arrival and information

Most people arrive by plane or by ferry from Dar es Salaam. **Zanzibar Inter-national Airport** – known by the delightful Kiswahili phrase *Uwanja wa Ndege*, the Stadium of Birds – is 7km south of town. There are several foreign exchange bureaux in the arrivals hall, which also change travellers' cheques. Daladalas on the #505 route start from the north end of the traffic island outside the airport, and charge Tsh300 to the terminus on Creek Road. Taxi drivers will lie shame-lessly about their fares, and might even angle for $20 at first. A fair price would be $5 (around Tsh5000), so bargain hard. Alternatively, upmarket hotels and tour operators can pick you up if arranged in advance: you'll pay $15–20 for a vehicle seating six or seven.

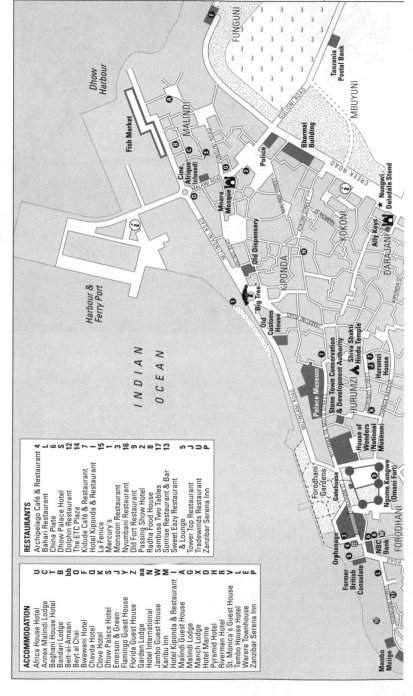

INDIAN
OCEAN

Dhow
Harbour

Harbour &
Ferry Port

Fish Market

FUNGUNI

Tanzania
Postal Bank

MBUYUNI

CREEK ROAD

GULIONI ROAD

Bharmal
Building

Police

MALINDI

Cine
Afrique
(closed)

Mnara
Mosque

Old Dispensary

KIPONDA

Old
Customs
House

"Big Tree"

Nungwi
Daladala Stand

Ally Keys

BARAJANI

KOKONI

HURUMZI

Shiva Shakti
Hindu Temple

Hurumzi
House

Stone Town Conservation
& Development Authority

Palace Museum

House of
Wonders
(National
Museum)

Forodhani
Gardens

Gatehouse

Ngome Kongwe
(Omani Fort)

FORODHANI

Orphanage

NBC
Bank

Former
British
Consulate

Mambo
Msiige

ACCOMMODATION

Africa House Hotel	U
Annex Malindi Lodge	C
Baghani House Hotel	T
Bandari Lodge	B
Beit-al-Amaan	bb
Beyt al Chai	O
Bwawani Hotel	F
Chavda Hotel	Q
Clove Hotel	K
Dhow Palace Hotel	S
Emerson & Green	J
Flamingo Guest House	Y
Florida Guest House	Z
Garden Lodge	aa
Hotel International	N
Jambo Guest House	W
Karibu Inn	M
Hotel Kiponda & Restaurant	I
Malindi Guest House	A
Malindi Lodge	G
Manch Lodge	X
Hotel Marine	D
Pyramid Hotel	H
Riverman Hotel	R
St. Monica's Guest House	V
Tembo House Hotel	L
Warere Townhouse	E
Zanzibar Serena Inn	P

RESTAURANTS

Archipelago Café & Restaurant	4
Bahari Restaurant	L
China Plate	6
Dhow Palace Hotel	S
Dolphin Restaurant	12
The ETC Plaza	14
Kidude Café & Restaurant	7
Hotel Kiponda & Restaurant	I
La Fenice	15
Mercury's	1
Monsoon Restaurant	3
Nyumbani Restaurant	16
Old Fort Restaurant	9
Passing Show Hotel	2
Radha Food House	8
Sambusa Two Tables	17
Sunrise Restaurant & Bar	13
Sweet Eazy Restaurant & Lounge	5
Tower Top Restaurant	J
Tradewinds Restaurant	U
Zanzibar Serena Inn	P

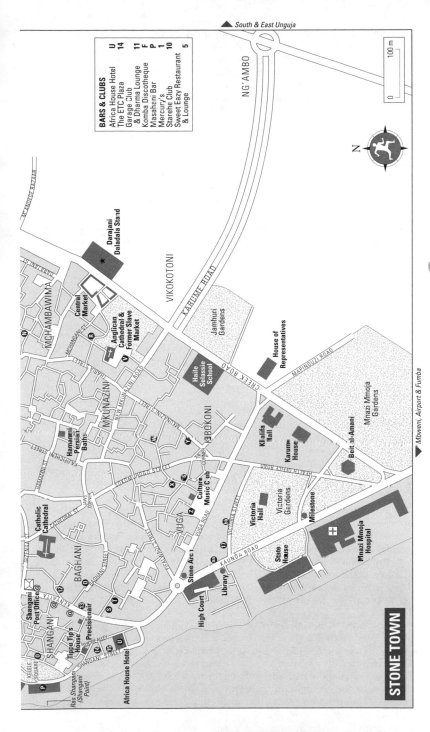

STONE TOWN

BARS & CLUBS

Africa House Hotel	U
The ETC Plaza	14
Garage Club	
& Dharma Lounge	11
Komba Discotheque	F
Masaheni Bar	P
Mercury's	1
Starehe Club	10
Sweet Eazy Restaurant	
& Lounge	5

▲ South & East Unguja

NG'AMBO

Darajani
Daladala Stand

VIKOKOTONI

KARUME ROAD

Jamhuri
Gardens

House of
Representatives

MAPINDUZI ROAD

Mnazi Mmoja
Gardens

Beit al-Amani

Central
Market

Anglican
Cathedral &
Former Slave
Market

MCHAMBAWIMA

MKUNAZINI

Hamamni
Persian
Baths

Haile
Selassie
School

CREEK ROAD

KIBOKONI

Culture
Music Club

Khalifa
Hall

Karume
House

VUGA

BAGHANI

Catholic
Cathedral

Shangani
Post Office

Tippu Tip's
House

Precisionair

SHANGANI

Ras Shangani
(Shangani Point)

Africa House Hotel

Stone Arc 1

High Court

Library

KAUNDA ROAD

State
House

Victoria
Hall

Victoria
Gardens

Milestone

Mnazi Mmoja
Hospital

▶ Mbweni, Airport & Fumba

N

0   100 m

ZANZIBAR | Arrival and information

11

633

The **ferry port** is at the north end of town. Depending on the political climate in semi-autonomous Zanzibar, passengers arriving from Dar es Salaam may be expected to visit immigration and customs before leaving the port, a farcical procedure given that Tanzanian visas are valid for Zanzibar. It's best just to walk past, unless there's some kind of barrier (there isn't normally) and it's obvious that some kind of paperwork is needed. Taxi drivers hang around outside: using one to find a hotel on your first day is recommended if only to avoid the clouds of commission-hunting *papasi* (hustlers who target tourists). If you're walking, the easiest way to a hotel is to stay on one of the main roads flanking Stone Town for as long as possible before diving into the labyrinth.

The main stands for **daladalas** (the local term for them is *gari ya abiria*) are along Creek Road in Darajani, opposite and alongside the Central Market. Coming from Unguja Ukuu in the south, or from Chwaka, Pongwe or Uroa in the northeast, you'll be dropped short at Mwembe Ladu, east of town, from where there are frequent onward daladalas to Darajani. There are few if any hustlers at Darajani, as hardly any tourists travel by daladala, and finding a taxi is easy.

Information

The Zanzibar Tourist Corporation (☎024/223 8630, ✉ztc@zanzinet.com) has two **tourist offices**, neither of which are particularly useful or impartial: one at the port (Mon–Fri 8am–4pm, Sat 9am–1pm; no phone), the other at the top of Creek Road (Mon–Fri 7.30am–5pm; ☎0747/482356 or 0747/438851). Bookshops (see p.657) sell **maps**: the best for Stone Town are insets in Giovanni Tombazzi's hand-painted *New Map of Zanzibar (Unguja Island)*, and harms-ic-verlag's *Zanzibar*. Printed practical information is limited to the quarterly *Recommended in Zanzibar*, a free glossy listings booklet that includes some interesting articles as well as tide tables helpful for timing trips to the beach, and the similar *The Swahili Coast* magazine. They're available at the tourist office in the port and various hotels, restaurants and tour operators around town.

City transport and tours

The best way of getting around Stone Town is **on foot**. Distances are relatively short and, in any case, most of the streets are too narrow for cars (though not for scooters – be prepared to leap out of the way). Still, if you're feeling lazy in the midday heat or need a ride back at night, there are plenty of **taxis**. You'll always find some outside the port, by the Central Market, parked alongside Forodhani Gardens, at the top of Kenyatta Road, and outside the busier night-time venues. Drivers are happy to escort you on foot to your hotel inside Stone Town for an additional tip. A ride across town currently costs Tsh2000 (Tsh2500–4000 at night).

Stone Town's tour operators (see p.661) all offer half-day **guided walks** through the town – a good way to get your bearings – going to all the major sights, and costing $15–35 per person. Alternatively, your hotel should be able to fix you up with a reliable guide for much less. For something different, Kawa Tours offer a couple of unusual walking tours for Tsh10,000 per person: cultural tournées to the Michenzani housing estate in Ng'ambo, and "Stone Town at night", which includes a short introduction to the art of drumming. They have an office just inside the entrance of the Old Dispensary on Mizingani Road (daily 9am–4pm; ☎024/223 3105).

Accommodation

There's a huge range of **hotels** to choose from in and around Stone Town, fitting all tastes and pockets – though (as throughout Zanzibar) it's almost impossible to find a double room for much under $20. **Bargaining** is possible, however – in fact expected – at all the cheaper places, particularly during the rains (March–May). At that time, rooms can be extremely damp, with mildew on bedroom walls and towels that never dry, so take especial care with your personal hygiene at that time.

The advantage of staying in the labyrinthine old part of town is that you'll be in the thick of things, though actually finding your hotel can be a challenge at first – most hotels are at least five minutes from the nearest drivable road. Many rooms come equipped with traditional Zanzibari **semadari beds**: indestructible four-poster affairs often inlaid with painted panels, and draped with voluminous **mosquito nets**. Always check nets for size and holes, as Zanzibar has a lot of mosquitoes and malaria is present. "Box nets" hung from rectangular frames are far preferable to round nets as they give you more space, but check whether box nets reach the ground all around the bed. If not, see whether it's possible to tuck it in around the mattress – the island's mosquitoes are experts in finding even the smallest aperture.

Breakfast is normally included in the price. **Credit cards** are generally not accepted; exceptions are noted.

Budget

Annex Malindi Lodge Between *Warere Townhouse* and *Bandari Lodge*, Malindi ☎024/223 0676. A budget option near the port with twelve rooms in a rambling old house shared with the owner's charming family. Second-floor rooms are best, arranged around a sunny courtyard where breakfast is served, and are good value if a little tatty. The hotel arranges trips and vehicle rental but you'll have to haggle. ❹

Bandari Lodge 100m north of the port gate, Malindi ☎024/223 7969. One of Malindi's better budget choices, and especially cheap for singles. The nine high-ceilinged rooms, all with bathrooms except for one double, are in better condition than those in nearby *Annex Malindi Lodge*, and are fresh and clean, all with *semadari* beds and box nets. Guests have use of a kitchen, but breakfast is not included. ❹

Bwawani Hotel North of Gulioni Rd between the ocean and a saltwater swamp, Funguni ☎0747/486487. An ugly concrete hulk built by the government in 1972, with 108 suites accessed off depressingly dark hospitalish corridors. Thankfully it's not all bad: the north-facing rooms (forget the decrepit south-facing ones) have balconies and distant glimpses of the ocean, and tiled floors rather than manky wall-to-wall carpets. All have clean bathrooms, phone, TV and a/c. Facilities include the adjacent *Komba Discotheque*, a basic restaurant and bar (closes 9pm), and a swimming pool. Breakfast included. ❹

Flamingo Guest House Mkunazini St, Kibokoni ☎024/223 2850, ⓔflamingoguesthouse@yahoo .com. One of the cheapest, with six good if simple rooms around a small courtyard with a fountain. All rooms have box nets and fans; $4 more gets you a private bathroom with Western-style toilets, and another $4 gets you a triple. Breakfast is served on the roof. ❸

Florida Guest House Vuga Rd, Vuga ☎024/223 3136, ⓕ024/223 1828. Also very cheap, with eight clean rooms, mostly en suite. There's also a suite for two or three people, with two beds, satellite TV, a fridge and a spotless modern bathroom. Breakfast not included. ❸

Garden Lodge South of Stone Town on Kaunda Rd ☎024/223 3298, ⓔgardenlodge@zanlink.com. Good budget accommodation and friendly staff. Its eighteen rooms, including triples, are all en suite and equipped with *semadari* beds and cotton sheets, box nets and ceiling fans. The ground-floor rooms are cheaper, and have bathtubs but no hot water; the cooler but more expensive rooms on the two floors above have bigger beds and do have hot water, but showers only, and they smell of air "freshener". The better ones have street-facing balconies, there's a TV lounge and food is available, which you can eat on the roof. ❹

Jambo Guest House Signposted west off Mkunazini St, Mkunazini ☎024/223 3779 or 0747/415948, ⓔjamboguest@hotmail.com. Popular with backpackers, with a friendly feel and cheap rates. The nine rooms (some triple, six with a/c) have shared bathrooms, and are large and clean if rather spartan, with ceiling fans and box nets. Internet access is available for guests and there's satellite TV in the lounge. No food other than breakfast, but the jungly *Green Garden Restaurant* is opposite (closed April & May). ❸

Karibu Inn Off Forodhani St, Forodhani ☎024/223 3058, ⓔkaribuinn@zanzinet.com. Partly renovated but still a little shabby, this is still a decent – and clean – budget choice, and enjoys a good location close to the sea front. It has almost twenty en-suite rooms, scattered over four half-storeys, some on the ground floor. All beds have cotton sheets, round if adequately sized mosquito nets and fans, and some of the doubles and triples (just $10 more) also have a/c. There are also three dorms ($10 per person), each with a/c and bathroom, and two of them with fridges. ❷

Hotel Kiponda & Restaurant Behind the Palace Museum on Nyumba ya Moto St, Kiponda ☎024/223 3052 or 0747/411653, ⓔhotelkiponda@email.com. Quiet and comfortable, this well-kept former mansion has fourteen rooms, including some triples. The walls are unusually thick, so the interior stays cool even in midsummer. Rooms vary in size and price, the cheapest ones little more than cells, the larger and more expensive ones with day beds and private bathrooms. Most have box nets, all have ceiling fans, and the renovated bathrooms have clean Western-style toilets complete with seats and paper. An average breakfast is served on the roof. Credit cards accepted. ❹–❺

Malindi Guest House 200m north of the port, Malindi ☎024/223 0165, ⓔmalindi@zanzinet.com. One of the best of Stone Town's budget houses, enjoying a friendly ambience, helpful service and wonderful decor. The rooms are excellent, all with nets, fans and safes, and some with bathrooms; the only minor niggle is that some beds might be too short for tall people. The manager can help arrange reliable tours with no mark-up on prices, and the rooftop (where breakfast is served) has good views over the harbour. ❹

Malindi Lodge Funguni Rd, Malindi ☎024/223 2359, ⓔinfo@sunsetbungalows.com. An attractive budget option near the port, its entrance prettily adorned with brass plates. The nine rooms, including one triple, are in good condition, all with nets and a/c. Bathrooms, whether shared or private, have Western-style toilets and reliable hot water. The hotel makes up for the lack of a rooftop terrace with a common balcony on both floors. ❹

Manch Lodge Between Vuga Rd and Sokomuhogo St, Vuga ☎024/223 1918, ⓔmoddybest@yahoo

.com. A large, good-value hotel ($10 per person), with twenty rooms including three with bathrooms and some with three or four beds, all with fans. The tiled Western-style toilets are clean, and there's a pleasant first-floor balcony with recliners. ❸

Pyramid Hotel Kokoni St, Kokoni ☎024/223 3000, Ⓔ pyramidhotel@yahoo .com. A long-standing backpackers' favourite, boasting a TV lounge, rooftop terrace for its excellent breakfast, a laundry service and friendly and knowledgeable staff. The eleven rooms (one with bathroom) have two *semadari* beds with crisp cotton sheets, box nets, fans and high ceilings, and some have balconies. Steep staircases. ❹

Riverman Hotel East of Tharia St, Mchambawima ☎024/223 3188, Ⓔ rivermanhotel@yahoo.com. This three-storey place just north of the Anglican Cathedral is good value ($10 per person) if you don't mind sharing bathrooms. All rooms, including some triples, have tiled floors, small fans, box nets, and table and chair. There's a pleasant courtyard for dining. ❸

St. Monica's Guest House Off New Mkunazini Rd by the Anglican Cathedral, Mkunazini ☎024/223 0773, Ⓔ monicaszanzibar@hotmail .com. Run by the Anglican church, this basic but cheap and clean hostel has seen better days but can't be matched for chilling historical atmosphere, as one of its two buildings – formerly the mission hospital – was constructed directly on top of the slave market's infamous underground cells. All fourteen rooms have fans, and one has a/c – they can get a little musty, something that seems to add to the historical weight of the place. The rooms over the slave chamber share a wooden verandah. Has a plain but good restaurant (for breakfast and lunch) and a small gift shop. No alcohol or smoking. ❹

Warere Townhouse Behind *Annex Malindi Lodge*, Malindi ☎024/223 3835 or 0747/478550, Ⓦ www .wareretownhouse.com. A simple, decent and welcoming option, with ten smallish rooms on three floors, all with fans and traditional *semadari* beds, and most with private bathrooms, a/c, cable TV and a minibar. The best rooms are at the front with balconies, and there's a rooftop terrace for breakfast. ❹

Moderate

Baghani House Hotel Signposted east off Kenyatta Rd, Baghani ☎024/223 5654, Ⓔ baghani@zanzinet.com. An attractive choice in a big old house handsomely furnished with antiques, masks and archive photographs. The hotel is popular with families (and often full in high season), and its eight clean, high-ceilinged rooms – singles or doubles – have private bathrooms (some with bathtubs), cable TV, minibar and fans. Credit cards accepted. ❺

Beit-al-Amaan Victoria St, Vuga ☎0747/414364 or 0747/411362, Ⓦ www .houseofpeace.com. Run by the same people as the *Monsoon Restaurant*, this occupies a converted two-storey town house. It's the business both in terms of comfort and (authentic) Zanzibari style, and for the pocket, with its six large rooms offering the best value in Zanzibar (book well in advance). The hotel is decorated throughout with colourful and pleasing Swahili artwork, seashells, Persian carpets and all sorts of antiques. The beds, predictably enough, are big old *semadari* four-posters; all but the huge downstairs room have private bathrooms, and there's a kitchen on top. ❺

Chavda Hotel Baghani St, Baghani ☎024/223 2115 or 0745/363738, Ⓔ chavdahotel@zanlink .com. A lovely, well-maintained former Indian merchant's mansion adorned with its original Indian fittings, plenty of reproduction furniture, and Chinese vases. The sixteen rooms, arranged on three floors, have *semadari* beds, satellite TV, a/c, a minibar and clutter of furniture; doubles have bathtubs, whilst twin-bed rooms have balconies. There's a great restaurant, the *Kisimani*, upstairs (particularly good breakfasts), and free airport pick-up. Credit cards accepted. ❼

Clove Hotel Hurumzi St, behind the House of Wonders ☎0747/484567, Ⓦ www .zanzibarhotel.nl. Run by a very helpful and welcoming Dutch lady who formerly made hats in Amsterdam, this wonderfully located and laid-back hotel contains eight unfussy but very comfortable rooms, the better ones higher up, all with fans, fridges and Western-style bathrooms. There's a lovely roof terrace with a sea view and lovely sunsets, and drinks available; the hearty breakfast is also taken there. Closed May. ❺

Dhow Palace Hotel Signposted east off Kenyatta Rd, Shangani ☎024/223 3012, Ⓦ www .tembohotel.com. A beautiful and tranquil Omani mansion from the 1870s that preserves much of its original Arabian flair. Service is smart and efficient, and the spacious rooms (including triples) are good value, with bathrooms featuring blue-tiled sunken baths, and bedrooms a/c, phone, cable TV, minibar, big *semadari* four-posters or brass beds, Persian rugs and a smattering of antiques. The better rooms and suites have balconies, and amenities include a swimming pool in the main courtyard, and an attractive rooftop restaurant with panoramic views (à la carte works out cheaper than taking half- or full-board; no alcohol). Credit cards accepted. Closed April & May. **6**–**8**

Hotel International Just south of Kiponda St, Mchambawima ✆024/223 3182, @hotelinter@zanlink.com. This four-storey former palace, restored to resemble a giant cuckoo clock, is an attractive option. The twenty rooms are arranged around a big atrium and have bathrooms, box nets, a/c, cable TV, phone, hair dryer, fridge and plenty of windows. Six rooms also have balconies (same price), one with a distant sea view. There are a few tables and chairs on a rooftop gazebo giving great views over the town, but no restaurant (or alcohol). Has a foreign exchange bureau. **6**

Hotel Marine Corner of Mizingani and Malawi roads facing the port entrance, Malindi ✆0747/411102 or 0747/496615, @hotelmarine@

africaonline.co.tz. The 24 en-suite rooms, arranged around an airy atrium dominated by a wooden staircase, have large cable TVs, minibar, phone, a/c and small but mighty fans, wall-to-wall carpet and hot water. Triple rooms are available for $10 more. There's the *Indiano Restaurant & Bar* at the side by the street, and a pool table. **5**

Tembo House Hotel Shangani St, Shangani ✆024/223 3005, @www.tembohotel.com. Built in the 1830s to house the American Embassy, this is now a busy package tour hotel. Whilst not as stylish as other options, and with famously shoddy service verging on the disagreeable, the beach-front location and lovely swimming pool are undeniable draws. The rooms too are fine: spacious, with all mod cons, and filled with Oriental and Zanzibari antiques. Get one with an ocean view or ocean-facing balcony to justify the expense. There's the shoreline *Bahari Restaurant* (no alcohol) with tables under Indian almond trees, and a rooftop terrace for sunbathing. **6**–**7**

Expensive

The following all accept credit cards.

Africa House Hotel Suicide Alley, Shangani ✆0747/432340, @www.theafricahouse-zanzibar .com. Formerly the English Club, this grand colonial shoreline building contains fifteen elegantly furnished rooms, all with a/c, cable TV, phone and fridge (hidden in the furniture), the better ones with ocean views. The claimed "regal" ambience expresses itself through plentiful antiques, Persian carpets, old photographs, gilded mirrors, and golden tassels and brocade adorning the heavy green drapes hung around the four-poster beds. Facilities include a good library, travel shop and gift shop, two restaurants, and its famous terrace bar, ever-popular at sunset. Airport transfer included. **7**–**8**

Beyt al Chai (aka *Zanzibar Stone Town Inn*) Kelele Square ✆0747/444111 or 0747/413996, @www .stonetowninn.com. One for the luvvies: six small-ish wooden-floored rooms occupying a gorgeous nineteenth-century three-storey building, stylishly decked out with silk and organza draperies and comfy antiques, though it's all rather basic for the price. All have a/c, and the two on the top have sea views over Kelele Square. **7**–**9**

Emerson & Green 236 Hurumzi St ✆0747/423266 or 0747/438020, @www .emerson-green.com. Set in Tharia Topan's magnificent Hurumzi House (p.647), this is East Africa's most atmospheric hotel, an utterly delightful and bewitchingly beautiful place offering heaven on earth for incurable romantics, and – a rarity on

Zanzibar – very reasonable rates for what's effectively a self-indulgent foray into the semi-mythical world of *The Arabian Nights*. Style is everything: an assured reinterpretation of classic Zanzibari (Afro, Arabian and Indian) themes – heavy carved teak doors, Omani bronzes, stained glass, opulent drapes, Persian rugs, Venetian Murano chandeliers, heavy roof beams of Burmese teak, and lots of fittingly camp touches courtesy of its American owners, Emerson Skeens and Tom Green. Each of its sixteen rooms (accessed by steep staircases, so not suitable for wheelchairs) has its own quirky character, unobtrusive a/c and fans, and there are no TVs or phones. There's the famous *Tower Top Restaurant* on the roof, and *Kidude Restaurant* next door. Closed mid-April to end-May. Needless to say, book well in advance. **7**–**8**

Zanzibar Serena Inn Kelele Square, Shangani ✆024/223 3587, @www.serenahotels.com. Located at the westernmost tip of Stone Town, this occupies the former Cable & Wireless Telegraph House and the adjacent Chinese Doctor's House. Service is friendly and faultless, standards are at international five-star levels, and the rooms – all sea-facing – come with all mod cons. However, whilst there are plenty of amenities, including several bars and restaurants, a beauty salon, and a large outdoor swimming pool by the shore, it's impossible to justify the price ($300–400 per room) unless you get discounted rates as part of a package. **9**

The Town

Stone Town divides into several distinct sections, centred on the grandiose **waterfront**, whose monumental buildings run south from the port to the Forodhani Gardens. To the south is **Shangani Point**, the site of an early fishing village and later the city's principal European quarter. East of here is the leafy residential and administrative suburb of **Vuga**. Heading inland from the waterfront brings you to the most atmospheric of the city's districts, **central Stone Town**, a bewildering, souk-like labyrinth of narrow streets and alleyways, flanked with crumbling mansions and mosques. On its east side, the labyrinth is bounded by Creek Road, beyond which is **Ng'ambo**, a packed and tumbledown area where the majority of Zanzibar Town's inhabitants now live.

The waterfront

Stone Town's **waterfront** is the town's showpiece, a glorious strip of monumental architecture through which the nineteenth-century sultanate expressed its wealth and power. The bulk of the buildings you see today were erected by **Sultan Barghash** (1870–88), whose reign coincided with the end of the slave trade. The approach by ferry from Dar es Salaam gives you the best view over the waterfront panorama, starting with the port to the north, then south along Mizingani Road past the Palace Museum and the jewel-box House of Wonders to the squat bulk of Ngome Kongwe (the Omani Fort) and the grassy Forodhani Gardens.

The northern continuation of Mizingani Road, past the port, takes you to a streetside **fish market** which is every bit as pungent as you might fear. The **dhow harbour** is accessed from the northern end of the road, and is mainly used as a fishing wharf. There are only few of the large commercial *jahazi*

△ Dhow, Stone Town waterfront

dhows left nowadays; your best chance of seeing them is during the *kaskazi* monsoon season between December and March.

Although you'll see kids swimming off the **beach** in Stone Town, the water is very polluted, especially during the rains; the nearest clean beaches are north of Bububu (p.669), and around the islands off Stone Town (p.663).

The Old Dispensary and "Big Tree"

About 200m south of the port entrance is one of Stone Town's most beautiful landmarks, the **Old Dispensary**. A grand four-storey building, the sumptuousness of the dispensary's design and decoration is reminiscent of British colonial architecture in India – no coincidence, really, given that it was constructed by craftsmen brought in from India by the dispensary's founder, **Sir Tharia Topan**. An Ismaili businessman, Topan was one of the wealthiest men in Zanzibar at the end of the nineteenth century, much of his wealth having accrued from his multiple functions as head of customs, financial adviser to the sultan, and banker for the most infamous of slave traders, Tippu Tip (see p.645). Perhaps to atone for his relationship with the latter, Topan's charity financed the building of the

The doors of Zanzibar

The traditional modesty shown in Islamic architecture mattered little to Stone Town's richer inhabitants at the height of the slave trade. Social standing, largely determined by wealth, was far more important, and thus **doors and door frames** became the favoured means of expressing the opulence and grandeur of the mansions they guarded. Unsurprisingly, Zanzibar's largest and heaviest door guards the entrance to Sultan Barghash's House of Wonders, whose interior contains another twelve spectacular examples.

Many of Stone Town's original doors are over 150 years old. Their longevity – they've often outlasted the houses whose entrances they once formed – is the result of the hardwoods they're made of, which are resistant to termites, water and decay. Local tree species used included jackfruit or breadfruit, while teak and sesame were imported from as far away as India (the use of sesame perhaps lending sense to Ali Baba's "Open Sesame"). The brass studs with which many doors are decorated also originated in India, where they're said to have protected houses against marauding elephants. Further symbolic protection is given by a chain or rope motif carved around the door frame, to guard against bad luck and the evil eye.

Residential doors are the most elaborate. Divided into two panels, the male (*mlango mdume*) on the right and female (*mlango jika*) on the left, many also have a smaller door inset into the left-hand panel for the use of children. The oldest, in the **Persian or Omani style**, are characterized by carved rectangular frames, massive plain panels and rectangular lintels with floral and geometric patterns. Over time, the **frames and lintels** became more intricate and ornate, often with an Arabic arch or semicircular panel above. The arch usually contains a rectangular frieze with a date, the owner's monogram and inscriptions from the Koran. Both door leaves are studded with brass bosses. Decorative motifs include fish (a symbol of fertility), smoke (prayers rising to heaven) and lotus flowers, which represented fertility in ancient Egypt and peace in India. More common are doors in the plainer and smaller **Indian style**, many of them serving as entrances to shops. Their abundant floral motifs represent God's presence in the natural world: pineapples are a variation of the fish symbol, and palm leaves are another ancient symbol, inferring good health and plenty. A startling variant of the Indian style are Gujarati doors, invariably made of teak imported from Kutch, distinguished by their coffered panels, many studs and delicately carved frames.

dispensary, as well as a non-denominational school, the first in Zanzibar. The **foundation stone** was laid with a golden trowel by Topan in 1887 to mark Queen Victoria's Golden Jubilee.

The dispensary itself occupied the ground floor, while the first and second floors – whose galleries overlook a U-shaped courtyard – were converted into apartments for the doctor and his family. Following the 1964 Revolution, the building was abandoned and fell into disrepair until, in 1990, the Aga Khan Trust for Culture embarked on an ambitious restoration programme. Now beautifully and sensitively returned to its former glory, visitors are welcome (daily 9am–5pm, sometimes later; free), though there's not much of interest other than the architecture, as most of its rooms are either empty or occupied by offices.

A hundred metres beyond the Old Dispensary, opposite *Mercury's* restaurant, is the **"Big Tree"** – a gigantic Indian banyan planted by Sultan Khalifa bin Haroub in 1911. It has grown so large that it's now home to a family of vervet monkeys. The ample shade offered by its boughs and aerial roots has also long been a favourite with dhow builders. Although these are no longer much in evidence, it's still a good place to enquire about day-trips to the islands off Stone Town (see also "tour operators" on p.661).

The Palace Museum

Continuing along the waterfront you reach the whitewashed **Palace Museum** (Mon–Fri 9am–6pm, Sat & Sun 9am–3pm; Ramadan daily 8am–2.30pm; Tsh3000 or $3), which served as the sultanate's official residence from 1911 until the Revolution. After 1964, the building – renamed the Peoples' Palace – was used for gatherings of the Revolutionary Council, during which time it was stripped of most of its internal fittings (which presumably now beautify the houses of former politicians).

The bulk of the museum's collection comprises the furniture and fittings that survived the Revolution, a selection as eclectic as the tastes of the sultans who lived here. The **lower floors** are dominated by a wealth of ebony furniture, gilt Indian chairs, Chinese recliners, formal portraits and boxed international trade treaties and other documents, whilst the **top floor** gives way to the surprisingly proletarian taste of the last sultan, Jamshid bin Abdullah, including a Formica wardrobe captioned "A style much favoured in the Fifties". The real **highlight**, though, is the room recreated from the memoirs of Princess Salme (see p.668), a daughter of Seyyid Saïd, whose elopement in 1866 with a German merchant caused such a scandal that she was effectively ostracized by her family until the end of her life.

The House of Wonders – Beit al-Ajaib

The next major building along the waterfront is Zanzibar's most distinctive and emblematic landmark, the Beit al-Ajaib or **House of Wonders**, which houses the **Zanzibar National Museum of History and Culture** (daily 9am–6pm, closes at 5.30pm April–June; Tsh3000 or $3). With its balconies, colonnaded facade and large clock tower, this ceremonial and administrative palace, completed in 1883, was the culmination of Sultan Barghash's extravagant building spree. Its statistics amply justify its name: it was the tallest building in East Africa at the time (and remains the tallest in Stone Town); it was the first to have running water and electric lighting (installed in 1906 as a sweetener by an American company in return for the contract to construct the Bububu railway); and it was also the first to have an electric lift (long since broken).

The entrance is guarded by two sixteenth-century bronze **Portuguese cannons**, captured by the Persians at the siege of Hormuz in 1622. One of them bears an embossed Portuguese coat of arms: an armillary sphere (a

△ House of Wonders, Stone Town

globe encircled with bands), and both guns bear later Persian inscriptions. The cannons didn't much help the Portuguese, but they do appear to have worked magic in protecting the House of Wonders during the 45-minute **British bombardment** of the waterfront on August 27, 1896, when two adjacent palaces were reduced to rubble, and a lighthouse that had been constructed in front of the House of Wonders was so badly damaged that it had to be pulled down. The House of Wonders itself escaped the bombardment virtually intact, and even the crystal chandeliers in its salon remained in place. The decision was made, nonetheless, to reconstruct the front facade, which was fitted with a new tower containing the old lighthouse clock.

Stylistically, the building is a jumble, perhaps owing partly to the fact that a British marine engineer had a hand in its design. The cast-iron pillars that support the surrounding tiers of balconies are really far too thin for the building's grandiose proportions, centred around a huge roofed atrium. This is dominated by a sewn *Jahazi la Mtepe* **dhow**. Last built for real in the 1930s, this replica (2000–4) was constructed in Zanzibar under the supervision of craftsmen from Kenya's Lamu Archipelago. The accompanying displays chronicle efforts to preserve traditional forms of boat-building and seafaring in East Africa, navigation, and the evolution of the monsoon-driven dhow trade. In a side room is a smashed up 1950s **Zephyr** automobile, once driven by President Karume – Tanzanian driving skills obviously being much the same back then.

The museum's **other displays** occupy two more floors, are exceptionally well presented, with good photographs and detailed information in both Kiswahili and English, and cover most aspects of Zanzibari life, culture and history. Some highlights are a whole room dedicated to *kangas* (the colourful cloth wraps worn by women); David Livingstone's medicine chest; bicycle lamps that run on coconut oil; an exceptionally thoughtful display on traditional Swahili music; several rooms on Zanzibari food and cooking; and a fascinating section dedicated to **traditional healing**, which includes a *pini* (charm) containing herbs and, so it is said, a dog's nose – just the thing to help exorcize evil spirits, though sadly the famous bottle containing a genie that's also part of the collection appears to have been spirited away.

Ngome Kongwe (the Omani Fort)

Just southwest of the House of Wonders, **Ngome Kongwe**, or the Omani Fort (daily 9am–8pm or later; free entry except evenings when performances are held) comprises four heavy coral ragstone walls with squat cylindrical towers and castellated defences, and makes for a calm and hustler-free place to sit for an hour or two. The fort dates back to the years following the expulsion of the Portuguese by the **Omanis** in 1698. The victorious Omanis quickly set about defending their gains, completing the fort in 1701. Its **walls** incorporate the last remnants of two hundred years of Portuguese rule: the foundations of a chapel (erected 1598–1612) and an adjoining merchant's house which were incorporated into the wall of an early fortification.

Omani and later Zanzibari control over the western Indian Ocean was so complete that for much of its life the fort served mainly as a jail, and as the venue for public executions, which were held outside the east wall. In the **twentieth century** it became a market, then a customs house and, in the 1920s, a depot and shunting yard for the Bububu railway (p.669), which was routed directly into the courtyard through the main entrance. In 1949 the fortified entrance was removed and the courtyard found a new vocation as the Zanzibar Ladies' Tennis Club. After an inevitable period of neglect following the Revolution, the fort was restored in 1994 and now functions as the **Zanzibar Cultural Centre**, containing various craft shops, an open-air amphitheatre that hosts live music concerts several evenings a week (announced on a sign outside the fort), a couple of tour companies, the *Old Fort Restaurant* (p.651), and – in the gatehouse – the office for the Festival of the Dhow Countries (p.655).

Forodhani Gardens

The neglected **Forodhani Gardens** were the original site of the two cannons now outside the House of Wonders, part of a battery of guns which gave their name (*mizingani* means cannons) to Mizingani Road. The name *forodhani* – meaning a ship's cargo or a reloading place – alludes to the slave trade, when slaves would be landed here before being taken to the market. The site was occupied by customs sheds until 1935, when the gardens were laid out in honour of King George V's Silver Jubilee. The following year, coinciding with the Silver Jubilee of Zanzibar's Sultan Khalifa bin Haroub, the central bandstand, fountain, seats and the small and currently derelict pier were added. The bland "ornamental arch" facing the pier was erected in 1956 for the arrival of the Queen of England's sister, Princess Margaret, who as it turned out landed elsewhere.

The gardens are a pleasant, shady place to relax under the midday sun, and there are a handful of curio stalls and Maasai waiting to have their pictures taken (for a fee), but Forodhani really comes alive after sunset when it hosts a great **street food market** (see p.650). If you're around in January, ask about the **dhow races**, usually involving *ngalawa* outriggers, which sail from Forodhani to Prison Island and back.

Shangani and Vuga

The westernmost point of Stone Town is **Ras Shangani**, a triangular promontory flanked by a narrow beach where, in the mid-nineteenth century, Seyyid

Saïd gave Europeans land for building their embassies and consulates. Towards the end of the century, when the British became the dominant force, the area served as the nucleus of their administration, whilst the area to its south, Vuga, was developed into a residential and diplomatic district, its wide boulevards and green spaces providing a soothing contrast to the claustrophobic hustle and bustle of Stone Town itself. Nowadays, Shangani is where you'll find most of Stone Town's upmarket hotels, restaurants, bars and – inevitably – a good deal of *papasi* too.

Shangani Post Office and Kelele Square

From Forodhani Gardens a footbridge leads to the Zanzibar Orphanage. Passing through the tunnel under the orphanage, Forodhani Street continues on to the junction of Kenyatta Road and Shangani Street. Taking a left up Kenyatta Road (be wary of traffic), the impressive colonnaded green-and-white building on your left beyond the junction with Gizenga Street is **Shangani Post Office** (1906), one of several buildings designed by **J.H. Sinclair**, who came to Zanzibar in the wake of the British bombardment of 1896 as an administrator, and gradually worked his way up the ranks to become British Resident (Britain's "advisor" to the sultan; effectively Zanzibar's political governor). His early work is characterized by an easy blend of Islamic forms and classical detail, but over time his style – dubbed "Saracenic" – became increasingly detached from European tradition, so much so that his contemporaries joked about him having "gone native".

Heading down Shangani Street, the **Tembo House Hotel** on your right occupies what used to be the American Embassy, constructed in 1834. A hundred metres further on is the leafy **Kelele Square**. Now one of Stone Town's most peaceful areas, its name – which means "shouting", "noisy" or "tumultuous" – hints at a terrible past, when it was used as Zanzibar's main **slave market**. The first building on your right is **Mambo Msiige** (not open to visitors), meaning the "Inimitable Thing", its name apparently deriving from the extravagance of the construction, for which thousands of eggs and – allegedly – the bodies of slaves, were used to strengthen the mortar. Dating from 1847–50, the building later served as headquarters for the Universities Mission to Central Africa – a sombre irony given that they had come to Africa to eradicate the slave trade. **Sir John Kirk**, an abolitionist luminary, lived in the house from 1874 to 1887 in his capacity as the British Consul General, and the explorer **Henry Morton Stanley** spent time here too. After 1913 the building became a European hospital, and presently houses a number of government departments.

The **Zanzibar Serena Inn** next door occupies two buildings restored in the 1990s by the Aga Khan's luxury *Serena* hotel chain. The main building (you can get inside as long as you don't look too scruffy) was the Cable & Wireless Building, which was connected via Bawe Island to Aden (Yemen) by telegraphic cable. A room on the first floor next to *The Terrace Restaurant* contains phones and relays from the period. The smaller adjacent building was built in 1918 and is popularly known as the Chinese Doctor's House.

Tippu Tip's House

The riches to be had from the slave trade are perhaps best understood (with a little imagination, admittedly) by visiting **Tippu Tip's House** along the poetically named Suicide Alley, south of Kelele Square. Although the home of the infamous slave trader (see box opposite) is now in an advanced state of decay, its door is one of Stone Town's most elaborate. The house is currently occupied by local families, evidently undaunted by stories that the house is haunted by the spirits of slaves. A polite enquiry may elicit an invitation to have a look around; a tip (no pun intended) would be appreciated.

Africa House Hotel and the High Court

Continuing down Suicide Alley you come to a small square dominated by the **Africa House Hotel**, a grand old building with a heavy carved door studded with brass spikes. The building was erected in 1888 as the exclusive English Club, though in time membership was opened to Americans and other Europeans, for whom it provided gin and tonics on the terrace, a library, wood-panelled committee rooms, billiard halls and powder rooms for the ladies. Social activities included cricket, golf, hockey and a New Year fancy dress ball, which attracted sizeable crowds of excited locals eager to witness this amusing manifestation of *wazungu* culture. After the Revolution, the building was predictably neglected, and has only recently been restored as a luxury hotel. The club remains famous for its ocean-facing terrace bar; non-guests are welcome to have a look around, and a sunset drink on the outdoor terrace is always a delight.

Suicide Alley finishes at Kenyatta Road (watch out for traffic here), which opens into a small roundabout at the junction with Vuga and Kaunda roads. The **High Court** on the right (1904–8) is another of J. H. Sinclair's syncretic creations, and perhaps the most successful. The domed tower was apparently originally fitted with a golden ring so that the Archangel Gabriel could carry the structure up to heaven on the day of reckoning, although quite why heaven would need a courthouse remains a mystery.

Victoria Hall and Gardens and the State House

Along Kaunda Road on the left are **Victoria Hall and Gardens**, which once housed Sultan Barghash's harem. The hall was built over the harem baths and functioned as Zanzibar's Legislative Council Chamber from 1926 until the Revolution, and was restored in 1996 to house the all-too-necessary Zanzibar Sewerage and Sanitation Project. The gardens contain some graves of the Barwani family of Omani Arabs, and many exotic plant species like tea, cocoa and coffee. The south end of the hall and gardens is marked by an octagonal marble **milestone**, showing London as 8064 miles away – the distance by ship after the Suez Canal was opened in 1869. The marble came from the ruins of Sultan Barghash's Chukwani Palace south of town, destroyed by fire in 1899.

Set back from Kaunda Road opposite the Victoria Gardens is the **State House**, another of Sinclair's works, which originally housed the British Resident. The building is now home to the President's Office and is out of bounds. Photography of any part of the building is forbidden.

Central Stone Town

Away from the waterfront, Stone Town is a labyrinth of narrow, twisting streets dotted with faded mansions and mosques, and criss-crossed by serpentine alleyways that unexpectedly open out onto semi-ruined squares alive with food vendors, hawkers and, at night, crowds of people enjoying coffee on the stone *barazas*. Getting lost is unavoidable – and part of the pleasure. If you really get stuck, any local will show you the way, or just keep walking along the busiest street and you'll emerge onto one of the main roads that bounds the old town. Safety is not a problem by day, though you should take care at night since parts of the town lack street lights; although still rare, muggings and other incidents involving tourists have been reported.

The slave market and Anglican Cathedral

On the eastern edge of Stone Town, the Anglican Cathedral occupies the site of Africa's last **slave market**, closed in 1873 by a reluctant Sultan Barghash under pressure from the British. Stone Town's original slave market had been at Kelele Square, but it's here in Mkunazini, where the market shifted in the 1860s, that the appalling cruelty of the trade hits home. Beside the cathedral, in the basement of the former mission hospital (now part of *St Monica's Guest House*), are two tiny, dingy **slave chambers** that each housed up to 75 people until market day. Conditions were squalid in the extreme: the cells are so small that most people couldn't stand upright; the only furnishings were a pit in the centre and a low platform around the sides; and there were no windows. One of the cells is now lit by artificial light; the other has been left unlit save for two slits at one end that hardly make a dent in the gloom. The cells are visited as part of a **guided tour** run by the church (daily 9am–6pm; Tsh2000), which also includes the cathedral.

The juxtaposition of the cells with the imposing **Anglican Cathedral Church of Christ** might appear grimly ironic but, in the spirit of Christian evangelism, replacing the inhumanity of the slave trade with the salvation of God made perfect sense. The cathedral's foundation stone was laid on Christmas Day 1873, the year the market closed, and was funded by Oxford's Universities Mission in Central Africa. Construction proceeded under the supervision of **Bishop Edward Steere**, third Anglican bishop of Zanzibar and a tireless individual, whose other achievements included the compilation of the first English–Kiswahili dictionary, and the first Kiswahili translation of the Bible. Steere conducted the first service, on Christmas Day, 1877. The cathedral's design follows a basilican plan, blending the perpendicular neo-Gothic form popular in Victorian England with Arabic detailing. The unusual barrel-vaulted roof was completed in 1879, and the spire was added in 1890. The clock in the cathedral's steeple was donated by Sultan Barghash on condition that the spire's height did not exceed the House of Wonders. A stark and pensive modern **sculpture** by Clara Sornas in the cathedral courtyard shows five bleak figures placed in a rectangular pit, shackled together with a chain brought from Bagamoyo – the most notorious of the mainland slave-trading ports. It's a devastatingly poignant memorial to the horrors of the slave trade.

The cathedral's **interior** is also full of reminders of the slave trade. A red circle in the floor beside the altar marks the position of a post to which slaves were tied and whipped to show their strength and resilience before being sold, while behind the altar is the grave of Bishop Steere. The small crucifix on a pillar beside the chancel is said to have been fashioned from a branch of the tree under which David Livingstone's heart was buried. Livingstone is also remembered in a stained-glass window, as are British sailors who died on anti-slaving patrols in the western Indian Ocean. The cathedral organ, made by Henry Willis & Co. of Ipswich, England, can be heard during Sunday services (weekly in Kiswahili, monthly in English), together with joyous gospel singing.

Hamamni Persian Baths

The contrast between the misery of the slave market and the slave-trade-financed luxuries of the **Hamamni Persian Baths** (daily 10am–4pm, ask for the caretaker across the road to let you in; Tsh2000 including a short guided tour – tip expected; guidebook Tsh2000), 250m to the west, comes as something of a shock. Commissioned in the early 1870s by Sultan Barghash, the baths are surprisingly plain, the only decoration of note being the red-brick pattern above the lime stucco rendering outside, which is topped by a crenellated parapet. The baths were open to the public (though only the rich could afford them), with the proceeds benefiting a charitable trust managed by the sultan. They ceased functioning in the 1920s and despite partial restoration remain bone-dry. The guided **tour** isn't up to much, but the baths are a good place to head for in the midday sun, the dry air, thick walls and stone floors providing a welcome respite from the sweltering heat outside.

The Catholic Cathedral of Saint Joseph

The twin towers of the **Catholic Cathedral of Saint Joseph** can be seen from pretty much every rooftop in Stone Town, but the cathedral isn't all that easy to locate on foot. The best way is to start on Kenyatta Road, head down Gizenga Street, and take a right down Cathedral Street. Although the site lacks the historical significance of the Anglican Cathedral, the Catholic Church was equally involved in the struggle against the slave trade, its main memorial being the Freedom Village for slaves in Bagamoyo (see p.153). The cathedral's foundation was laid in July 1896, and the first Mass was celebrated on Christmas Day, 1898, two years before completion. The design is loosely based on the Romano-Byzantine cathedral of Notre Dame de la Garde in Marseilles, while the interior is painted with badly deteriorated frescoes depicting scenes from the Old Testament. Masses are held regularly and are the best time to visit. The main entrance is usually closed at other times, though you may be able to get in through the small passageway leading through the convent at the back of Shangani Post Office.

Hurumzi House

Running a short distance west to east from behind the House of Wonders is **Hurumzi Street**, one of Stone Town's best places for rummaging around souvenir and antique shops. Near the end on the right, an unassuming sign marks the entrance to the beautifully restored and opulent **Hurumzi House**, now Stone Town's best hotel, *Emerson & Green* (see p.638). The house was constructed by the wealthy Ismaili businessman Tharia Topan (also responsible for the Old Dispensary, see p.640), to serve as both the sultanate's customs house and his private residence. Topan's good relations with Sultan Barghash allowed him to make it the second-highest building in Stone Town, after the House of Wonders. Its name comes from its use by the British after 1883 to buy the freedom of slaves, to ease the pain of Arab slave owners following the abolition of slavery; *hurumzi* literally means "those shown mercy". The conversion into the present hotel has been gloriously done, and it's well worth looking around even if you've no intention of staying there.

Mnara Mosque

Most of Stone Town's 51 **mosques** are surprisingly restrained and unobtrusive, certainly compared to the ostentation of the waterfront palaces, but then few if any of the sultans were much given to religious contemplation. Indeed, you won't even notice the majority of the mosques unless you walk past their entrances and glimpse their simple prayer halls (strictly no photography). There are few embellishments, and only four have minarets, one of which is the Sunni community's curious **Mnara Mosque** near the northern tip of Stone Town; its strange minaret (*mnara*) is one of only three conical minarets in East Africa (the other two are on the Kenyan coast), and is decorated with a double chevron pattern. It's best seen from Malawi Road; non-Muslims aren't allowed inside.

Creek Road and eastwards

The fume-filled **Creek Road** running up the east side of Stone Town was, until the twentieth century, a saltwater creek. The area's name, Darajani, means "bridge", alluding to one that was erected across the creek in 1838. The creek separated Stone Town from the mud-and-thatch district of Ng'ambo to the east, which remains much more African in feel than the oriental alleyways and grand buildings of Stone Town. The British reclaimed the southernmost portion of the creek in 1915 to make way for the English Club's playing fields, now known as **Mnazi Mmoja** ("one coconut tree"), and which serve as a focus for the Idd al-Fitr celebrations at the end of Ramadan. The rest of the creek was drained in 1957, leaving only a small reed-filled marsh between Gulioni Road and the ugly 1970s *Bwawani Hotel* in the north.

At the south end of Creek Road stands the **Beit al-Amani** ("House of Peace"), which was until recently the Peace Memorial Museum, whose collection is now in the House of Wonders. The building is currently unoccupied but is worth the walk for its external architecture: a squat but elegant octagonal construction topped by a Byzantine-style dome. Opened in 1925, it was the last of J. H. Sinclair's creations, and is his most Islamic work, dubbed "Sinclair's mosque" by detractors, and the "House of Ghosts" by locals, for whom the concept of a museum was a strange novelty.

Central Market

Zanzibar's lively, colourful and pungent **Central Market**, also called Darajani Market, is about halfway up Creek Road. Liveliest in the morning from 9am onwards, the market and streets around it have pretty much everything you might need, from meat and fish, cacophonous bundles of trussed-up chickens and seasonal fruit and vegetables (and some exotic fruits like apples) to herbs and spices, radios, TVs and mobile telephones, bicycles, shoes and sandals, swaths of brightly patterned cloth and – years after the fad subsided elsewhere – Teletubbies. The main building opened in 1904 as the Seyyidieh (or Estella) Market, and was probably the second of J. H. Sinclair's constructions. Actually little more than a glorified shed under a tin roof, it houses the meat and fish sections, the smell of which announces the market's presence from a fair distance.

The Bharmal Building, Blue Mosque and Livingstone House

Constructed around 1900, the **Bharmal Building**, towards the top of Creek Road on the left, is the earliest and most European of Sinclair's buildings (the comparison with his last work, the Peace Memorial Museum, which bears nary a wisp of his classical training, is startling). Stylistically somewhere between an Arab palace and English manor house, the Bharmal Building is not Sinclair's best creation, though the profusion of plaster mouldings hints at the Orientalist direction his work was to take, and one should bear in mind that when built it would have been facing the creek rather than a fume-filled highway. Previously the office of the British provincial commissioner, the building currently houses the offices of Zanzibar Municipal Council.

Reaching the north of Creek Road, a left turn takes you down Malawi Road to the roundabout by the port entrance, while a right skirts the reed-filled salt-water swamp between Gulioni Road and the *Bwawani Hotel* – the only remnant of Darajani Creek. Some 700m along Gulioni Road is a modern mosque built out over a small artificial lake, which goes by the name of the **Blue Mosque**. A left here, which leads to the service entrance of the *Bwawani Hotel*, takes you past patches of mangroves and tidal mud flats where **dhows** are still built, or repaired. The occasional spice tour stops here, and the workers should be happy to show you round if they're not too busy.

Back on Gulioni Road, the old two-storeyed house on the opposite side of the road, almost surrounded by modern apartment blocks, is the fine two-storeyed **Livingstone House**. Now the headquarters of the Zanzibar Tourist Corporation, it was built in 1860 by Sultan Majid and saw use as a rest house for various European explorers and missionaries, most famously David Livingstone, who spent time here in 1865–66. The proximity of the swamp presumably inspired the good doctor to note that the town might be called "Stinkibar rather than Zanzibar" – a far cry from the celebrated scent of cloves that sailors could allegedly smell from far out at sea.

Ng'ambo

Beyond Livingstone House, a right turn off Gulioni Road onto a dual carriage-way takes you into to the poorer but vastly more populous half of Zanzibar Town, **Ng'ambo**. The name is a throwback to the days when Stone Town was still bounded by Darajani Creek. As Stone Town filled up, its poorer inhabitants, mostly African, were forced to decamp to the main island opposite, which the Arab elite patronizingly referred to as *ng'ambo*, "the other side". The centre-piece of Ng'ambo (also reachable along Karume Road from Creek Road) is **Michenzani**, whose pretty name ("tangerine trees") spectacularly fails to disguise a dismal experiment in socialist urban housing. Flanking each of the four roads radiating from a vast roundabout are the kind of grey, numbered and deeply neglected multi-storey blocks of flats one would expect to see in Stalin-ist Russia. No surprise, then, to learn that their design and construction were supervised by East German engineers in the late 1960s and early 1970s, during Tanzania's economically disastrous experiment with African socialism, *Ujamaa*. Nonetheless, the mildewed housing blocks – and the ramshackle slums around them – do provide an abrupt return to reality for those who have become jaded with the tourist trap some consider Zanzibar to have become.

The best way to get a feel for how "the other side" lives is on a **cultural walking tour** (Tsh10,000 per person) organized by Kawa Tours; see p.634.

Eating

Stone Town is Tanzania's culinary apotheosis, offering an embarrassment of choice when it comes to **eating out**, from the glorious nightly food market in the Forodhani Gardens and some very good local restaurants, to dozens of sophisticated or romantic establishments, including several right by the shore (great sunsets), and others on rooftops within the old town for good views over the city and, if the view isn't blocked by other buildings, the Zanzibar Channel beyond. Menus generally feature traditional **Zanzibari cuisine**, combining subtle use of the island's spices and coconuts with seafood including prawns, crab, octopus and lobster, while more conservative tastes are catered for with pasta, pizzas, Indian and Chinese dishes, and even burgers and chips.

Apart from the Forodhani Gardens, the market on **Creek Road** and the daladala stand opposite are also handy for street food, especially in the morning for cups of scalding *uji* (eleusine) porridge, and *supu*. Another good spot is the **Big Tree** on Mizingani Road, where there's usually someone selling *mishkaki* skewers of grilled goat meat, and another with a sugar cane press for juice. In the evenings, the west end of **Malawi Road** near the port is popular with passengers catching night ferries. For something more traditional, seek out one of the **coffee barazas** inside the old town, where the beans are roasted, ground and brewed on the stone benches (*barazas*) that line the streets: a tiny cup of piping *Arabica* costs a negligible Tsh20–50. One of the liveliest *barazas* is in Sokomuhogo Square – popularly known as **Jaws Corner**, possibly after the

Forodhani Gardens

For all its refined restaurants, the best place for eating out in Stone Town is at the open-air street food market held in the waterfront **Forodhani Gardens** after sunset, which combines a magical twilight atmosphere with a variety and quality of food to put many a five-star hotel to shame, though check seafood carefully before ordering in low season, when it's not always as fresh as it should be. It's also one of the cheapest places to eat, where a couple of thousand shillings will leave you well and truly stuffed, though you will have to contend with that ever-endearing Zanzibari habit of asking a "special price, my friend" of tourists.

Every evening, seven dozen *baba lisha* ("feeding men") set up trestle tables, charcoal stoves and gas and oil lamps and prepare the food. The **choice** is regal, ranging from grilled or stewed seafood caught that morning and sauced with local spices, to goat meat served with a superb home-made chilli sauce and, more rarely but deliciously, tamarind sauce. The market is also a great place to try "Zanzibari pizzas" (*mantabali*), actually chapatis stuffed with egg, vegetables or whatever takes the cook's fancy, and resembling fat spring rolls. Other **snacks** worth sampling include spiced *naan* bread and *andazi* doughnuts, grilled cassava, fried potato and meat or vegetable balls, samosas filled with meat or vegetables, and salads. You can even get grilled bananas topped with melted chocolate.

Non-alcoholic **drinks** are abundant too, with sodas, freshly pressed seasonal juices (including sugar cane, wrung noisily out of hand-operated iron presses), gently spiced *zamzam* tea (named after a sacred well in Mecca), Turkish coffee, coconut milk (*dafu*) and – at the start of the year – tangy tamarind juice.

△ Street food market, Forodhani Gardens

film once shown on its TV – where locals spend the evening glued to a **television screen**, usually featuring pirated movies, more often than not bizarrely dubbed or subtitled into Chinese.

Eating out during **Ramadan** can be quite expensive as the government bans restaurants not attached to hotels from opening during the day. There are some exceptions, though the cloth screens with which the proceedings are often covered lend a furtive aspect to dining at that time; the restaurants reviewed below remain open during Ramadan unless otherwise indicated.

Budget

The following restaurants are among the cheapest in Stone Town, most of them aimed as much at locals as tourists. Unless you're splurging on prawns or lobster, a full meal with soft drinks shouldn't cost more than Tsh5000.

Dolphin Restaurant Halfway along Kenyatta Rd, Shangani. An attractive place with a mangrove pole ceiling, turtle shells on the walls, and a noisy African grey parrot. The speciality is grilled red snapper with coconut sauce, though the daily specials are worth tasting – things like crab claws, biriani or *pilau*, octopus, or green lentils with fish – even if portions aren't overly generous. Finish your meal with a *shisha* water pipe. Daily 9am–9.30pm; closed Ramadan daytimes.

Old Fort Restaurant Ngome Kongwe (Omani Fort), Forodhani St. A relaxed place for lunch, with two menus: a rather humdrum printed one for fish *pilau*, vegetable curry, chicken *ugali* and beef stroganoff, and more interesting daily specials chalked

up on a blackboard for things like grilled prawns and seafood platters (Tsh8500). Also has snacks, milkshakes, coffee, and booze from the attached bar. Daily 9am–10pm; closed Ramadan daytimes.

Passing Show Hotel Malawi Rd, Malindi. This looks like a typical local restaurant, with dirty floors, metal-legged furniture and TVs in the corner, and so it is, but the ruckus of diners that make it difficult to find a table at lunchtime also says something about the food: that it's excellent, cheap, and comes in huge portions. The *pilau*, biriani and stews are particularly good, including fish or cashew nuts in coconut sauce, and chicken – you pay more for the tougher but tastier free-range variety than for bland battery farm broilers.

Nothing much over Tsh2000. No alcohol. Daily 6am–10pm; closed Ramadan.

Radha Food House Off Forodhani St beside *Karibu Inn*, Forodhani. A vegetarian Indian restaurant famed for its *thali*, and also offering tasty samosas, spring rolls, lentil or chickpea cakes, and perfumed sweets for dessert. There's a small but well-stocked bar too. Daily 9am–10pm.

Sunrise Restaurant & Bar Kenyatta Rd, Shangani. A local *hoteli* aiming at the tourist trade and which, apart from its awful toilets, comes recommended. The food, a mixture of local and international, is well priced, and you can also eat on its sunny streetside terrace, or in a courtyard at the back. Daily 10am–11pm.

Moderate

With Tsh5000–10,000 to spend on a main course and perhaps a starter, most of Zanzibar's manifold delights lie within reach (lobster being the expensive exception), and there are some truly fabulous restaurants to choose from.

Archipelago Café & Restaurant Off Forodhani St, south end of Forodhani Gardens. On an open-sided first-floor terrace with expansive ocean views, it's not just the location that's fresh but what they conjure up in the kitchen. The menu is an attractive blend of Swahili, African and international dishes (including pizzas), all very reasonably priced for generous portions: try the spicy *pilau*, the excellent kingfish with chilli and mango sauce, or red snapper simmered in orange. They also do great breakfasts (and divine cakes) and various kinds of fresh coffee. No alcohol. Daily 8am–11pm; closed Ramadan daytimes, and April & May.

Bahari Restaurant *Tembo House Hotel*, Shangani St. The menu here flirts briefly with most cuisines and is pretty affordable, with a four-course set menu costing Tsh10,000. Service can be very slow, however, and there's no alcohol, but it is Stone Town's only proper beach restaurant, and you can also use the swimming pool. Daily 8am–10pm; closed Ramadan daytimes.

China Plate Forodhani St, at the south end of the tunnel, Forodhani. On the open-sided second floor, the menu provides the habitual head-scratching selection of Chinese dishes: the seafood is good, there are also a number of tofu dishes, and they also offer fresh fruit and vegetable juices. Daily noon–2.30pm & 6–9.30pm.

Dhow Palace Hotel Signposted east off Kenyatta Rd, Shangani. An attractive rooftop restaurant with panoramic views and a small but affordable menu, including octopus and fish in coconut sauce, and some European dishes. Free escort to and from your hotel at night. No alcohol. Daily noon–3pm & 6–9pm; closed Ramadan daytimes.

The ETC Plaza Corner of Suicide Alley and Shangani St, Shangani. A congenial and comfortable bar and restaurant on three floors, the top floor being open air with views over the ocean, and with good music. Good by day or at night,

when candles add to the atmosphere. The food's not half bad either, whether moussaka, sandwiches or seafood: the bouillabaisse is highly recommended as a starter, followed by a seafood casserole simmered in creamy coconut sauce, or crab pilipili with ginger, fresh basil and pepper. They also do milkshakes, and freshly brewed coffee served from brass samovars. Daily noon–late; closed mid-April to mid-June.

Kidude Café & Restaurant Beside *Emerson & Green*, Hurumzi St, Hurumzi. Named after Zanzibar's much-loved nonagenarian *taarab* singer and suitably kitted out in neo-Arabian style, this cosy, air-conditioned place is open for drinks, cakes and snacks and throughout the day, and for light Mediterranean-style lunches and more substantial à la carte dinners, though prices are rather hiked up. Daily 11am–10pm; closed mid-April to end-May.

Hotel Kiponda & Restaurant Behind the Palace Museum on Nyumba ya Moto St, Kiponda. Perched at the top of the hotel with a fine view between the houses, the daily specials can be enticing, such as chicken in tamarind and ginger, though at other times the something-with-chips style isn't so hot. Evening à la carte is good, though. No alcohol. Daily 7–10am, 11am–3pm & 6–9pm; closed Ramadan daytimes.

Mercury's North end of Mizingani Rd near the Big Tree. Named after the rock star, this stylish yet informal bar and restaurant has a beautiful oceanside setting to recommend it, especially the sunset (there are plenty of tables on wooden decking over the beach). The fun menu covers both classic Zanzibari dishes and international favourites, and includes plenty of fresh salads and pasta, excellent pizzas, seafood seasoned nicely with saffron, chilli, ginger and garlic, and an ample "Seafood Extravaganza", where Tsh18,000 gets you grilled lobster, fish, squid, prawns, octopus and crab, served with roast potatoes and salad. Desserts are hearty: chocolate cake, mango crumble or sticky almond *halua* goo, or finish with a *shisha* pipe. There's live *kidumbak* music on Friday from 7pm, more tourist-oriented melodies on Saturday (from 8pm), and – ineluctably – good odds on hearing "Bohemian Rhapsody" and Freddie's other hits at other times (see box p.654). Pizzas and drinks all day, other meals 12.30–3pm & 7–10pm; closed Ramadan daytimes.

Monsoon Restaurant Forodhani Gardens ☎0747/410410. One of Zanzibar's most atmospheric restaurants (with good food too), where meals are served in a pillared dining room with cushions on woven rugs replacing seats, though if you wish you could sit outside instead under a thick canopy of palm trees and bougainvillea, as long as it's not Ramadan. The light lunches are refreshing, featuring dishes like hummus, guacamole and falafel, and whilst the short main menu concentrates on seafood (four-course set menus under Tsh12,000), there's plenty for other tastes too, such as tasty vegetarian grilled stuffed aubergine. All meals are accompanied by side dishes and condiments you won't find elsewhere, such as pumpkin cooked in creamy coconut, mangetout in peanut sauce, and home-made mango chutney, and there's a good wine list. Reservations advisable, especially Wednesday and Saturday evenings when there's live *taarab* or *kidumbak* music (7.30–10pm). Daily 10am–midnight.

Nyumbani Restaurant Off Sokomuhogo St, Vuga ☎0744/378026 or 0747/413622, ⓔamirbatikstudio@yahoo.com. A private home belonging to an artist and his wife that doubles as a restaurant in the evenings. The $7 set menu, all traditional Swahili, is guaranteed to fill you up and tickle your taste buds. Book ahead; deposit required. Mon–Sat evenings only.

Sambusa Two Tables Victoria St, just off Kaunda Rd, Vuga ☎024/223 1979 or 0747/416601. Highly recommended family-run place situated on the first-floor verandah of a private house. The traditional Zanzibari food just keeps on coming (samosas, fishcakes, marinated aubergine and superb octopus), and costs around Tsh10,000. Phone or pass by beforehand. No alcohol. Open for lunch and dinner; closed Ramadan daytimes.

Tradewinds Restaurant *Africa House Hotel*, Suicide Alley, Shangani. On the second floor above the famous sunset terrace bar, the dining room here is rather dreary (and afflicted with horrible muzak) but you can always sit on the wooden seafacing balcony. Seafood is the predictable speciality, including a great spicy seafood soup, good marinades and grills, and Zanzibar's classic fish or octopus with coconut sauce combos. Desserts could do with a bit more inspiration however. Daily 7.30am–10pm.

Expensive

Over Tsh10,000 for a "basic" (fish or octopus) main course is not uncommon at Stone Town's posher places, where full three- or four-course meals with a few drinks may lighten your pocket by anything up to Tsh50,000. It's worth enquiring whether someone's opened another **dhow restaurant**. There have been several in the past; the last one caught fire and sank. All offered two-hour sunset cruises, either with drinks and snacks, or a full-on meal, and charged $25 to $40 per person. The folks at *Sweet Eazy Restaurant & Lounge* should know the latest, as the dhows set sail from the landing beside it.

La Fenice Shangani St, one block north of *Africa House Hotel*, Shangani. Italian restaurants can usually be relied on for style, and this one's no exception, with its decor a cross between neo-African and classical European. The menu is thoroughly refined, with the full raft of Italian and French Riviera aperitifs, first starters including fried avocado, then pasta as a second starter, and some inspired main courses such as dorado cooked with saffron, courgettes and balsamic vinegar, or lobster flambée (Tsh23,000). It's not hard to succumb to their ice creams as well, hot chocolate dressing optional. And of course the coffee is *perfetta*, as is the wine list. Daily 10am–10.30pm.

Sweet Eazy Restaurant & Lounge Kenyatta Rd, close to NBC bank, Forodhani. Sadly lacking sea views, this nonetheless comes highly recommended, offering a mouth-watering selection of outstandingly good and totally authentic Thai and African cooking that makes particularly effective use of Zanzibar's ingredients. A few examples are the tamarind casserole, featuring prawns and crab, fish and squid, cooked in coconut milk flavoured with tamarind, green pepper, tomato, onion and garlic; and an inspired take on lobster, cooked with red curry, sweet basil, lime and lemongrass (Tsh23,000). Well-stocked bar, a good wine list and live music

Freddie Mercury

Farok Bulsara, better known as **Freddie Mercury**, the flamboyant lead singer of the glam-rock group Queen, was born in Stone Town on September 5, 1946, to a family of wealthy Zoroastrian Parsee immigrants from India. Various **houses** around Shangani claim that Freddie lived there. If you're into tracing his roots, the *Mercury's* restaurant on Mizingani Road is the place to start – they're nuts about him.

At the age of nine, Farok was sent to boarding school in India, and never returned to Zanzibar. He ended up studying graphics at Ealing College in London, where in 1970 he formed Queen and adopted his stage persona. Somewhat ironically, given that the Bulsaras fled Zanzibar in the aftermath of the bloody 1964 Revolution, Queen's song "Bohemian Rhapsody" – which contains the phrase "Bismillah [in the name of God], will you let him go?" – was embraced by Zanzibari secessionists campaigning for independence from the mainland.

Freddie Mercury died on November 24, 1991, a day after making public his battle with AIDS.

Friday nights (except April & May) complete the experience. Daily 11am–late.

Tower Top Restaurant *Emerson & Green*, 236 Hurumzi St, Hurumzi ☎0747/423266 or 0747/438020, ⊛www.emerson-green.com. Effortless sophistication and inspirational views from the roof of Stone Town's second-highest building, dinner here is a good excuse to have a poke around East Africa's most atmospheric hotel, before you settle down, minus shoes, on the giant pillows and Persian rugs to watch the sunset, cocktail in hand. The six-course menu changes daily and offers something for everyone (including vegetarians). The cost, excluding drinks, is $25 Monday–Thursday, and $30 otherwise, when live music completes the mood (traditional African

ngoma on Friday, *kidumbak* on Saturday, and *taarab* on Sunday). Reservations required. Dinner only; closed mid-April to end-May.

Zanzibar Serena Inn Kelele Square, Shangani. This five-star hotel contains two restaurants, the elegant *Baharia*, and the outdoor *The Terrace* on top, though you can also eat by the swimming pool; book ahead or arrive early for tables with ocean views. The various menus are designed to pamper, and feature French haute cuisine blended with Swahili flavours and clever use of spices, for example deep-fried crab claws coated with mustard seeds and served on a tomato and saffron coulée. In addition to the restaurants, there's also a coffee shop with a limited but well-balanced choice of light meals, including smoked sailfish. Daily for lunch and dinner.

Drinking and nightlife

Tourism has brought with it a small but growing number of **bars and nightclubs**, which sit somewhat uncomfortably in what's still very much a Muslim town – part of the reason why police have a whimsical habit of bringing an abrupt end to proceedings after midnight (if that should happen, just be polite and go home).

Africa House Hotel Suicide Alley, Shangani. For decades this has been the favoured haunt of expats, tourists and mainlanders, drawn to its first-floor terrace *Sunset Bar* to watch the sun slip behind the ocean. There's a good range of drinks, including a fine South African wine list and particularly imaginative cocktails, many incorporating Konyagi, Tanzania's home-grown papaya gin. There's also a good snack menu and all-day breakfast, whilst darts, a pool table and *shisha* pipes are available. At night, the basement *Pirate Cove* disco boogies to state-of-the-art lighting and strobes. Be careful walking in

the surrounding area after dark. Daily 10am–10pm.
The ETC Plaza Corner of Suicide Alley and Shangani St, Shangani. One of the most appealing bars in the city (and with superb food; see p.652), with three levels, the best on top with nice ocean views. The staff are friendly, the mood chilled out, there's good music, and milkshakes and juices are also available along with cocktails. Daily noon–late; closed mid-April to mid-June.
Garage Club & Dharma Lounge Shangani St, Shangani. Two interconnected places: the very mellow *Dharma Lounge* at the front, which is an

upmarket bar that doesn't admit prostitutes, and the club at the back (Tsh2000 entry), which does. The latter is currently Stone Town's leading disco, with plenty of strobes and spinning mirrored globes, and a lively mixture of music ranging from modern *taarab* to rave and Bongo Flava. Daily 9pm–3am.

Komba Discotheque *Bwawani Hotel*, Funguni. Stone Town's oldest disco and popular with locals, with a large swimming pool beside it. No smoking. Tues–Sun 9pm–3am; closed Ramadan.

Masahani Bar *Zanzibar Serena Inn*, Kelele Square, Shangani. A sophisticated Arabic ambience with lots of period decor, and food and drinks available throughout the day, plus tea and cakes. Daily 11am–midnight.

Mercury's North end of Mizingani Rd near the Big Tree. Along with *Africa House Hotel*, this enjoys the best sea views, and is especially blissful for sunset. It can get really busy at night, particularly on Friday when there's live *kidumbak* (7–11pm), and on Saturday, when there's another live band (8pm–midnight). The bar's well stocked, with a ton of cocktails too (try the "Zanzibarbarian": tropical juice, Bacardi, Malibu and clove syrup), and they have *shisha* water

pipes (Tsh3000). Great food too; see p.652. Daily 8.30am–late; closed Ramadan daytimes.

Starehe Club Shangani St, Shangani. Formerly the European Yacht Club, this is now an unpretentious outdoor bar accessed through a curio shop, with a terrace overlooking the beach and harbour, albeit through a chickenwire fence. Drinks and food are cheap, though the blackboard menu is hopelessly out of touch with the kitchen's actual contents; you're usually limited to chicken with chips or *ugali*, or *nyama choma* (grilled meat). Weekends are good for music: *kidumbak* on Friday, reggae on Saturday (both from 9pm), and – sometimes in high season – a live band on Sunday from 4pm. Daily 8am–midnight.

Sweet Eazy Restaurant & Lounge Kenyatta Rd, close to NBC bank. A nicely chilled-out bar (and superb restaurant; see p.653) popular with well-to-do Zanzibaris, expats and tourists. There are no sea views, but you can sit outside under palm trees, and it's very cosy inside. Also plays great retro rock (Velvet Underground, The Doors, Hendrix), and – except in April and May – hosts the rather more touristy Coconut Band on Fridays from 10pm (free entry). Daily 11am–late.

Live music

Stone Town's **live music scene**, although vibrant, can be difficult to find as a lot of bands only play for weddings and other social functions, with few

Annual festivals in Stone Town

Established in 1997, the **Festival of the Dhow Countries** (formerly the Zanzibar International Film Festival) is a firm fixture on the African cultural calendar, and provides as good a reason as any to try to get to Zanzibar in the first half of July. No longer restricted to cinema, the festival has been growing steadily, featuring dozens of groups of musicians from all over East Africa and the western Indian Ocean, almost as many films and art exhibitions, together with acrobats, film and video workshops, special activities for women and young people, and an innovative mobile wide-screen cinema that brings the magic of cinema to outlying villages on Unguja and Pemba. The **music** menu is especially alluring, having in recent years featured rare and beautiful sounds from Sufi dervishes, Egyptian Nubian drummers, an Ethiopian circus, and sacred Islamic praise songs from Gujarat. The main **venues** are the Forodhani Gardens and Ngome Kongwe (the Omani Fort) for film, music and dance, the House of Wonders for exhibitions and children's activities, and the Old Dispensary. For information and exact dates, contact ZIFF, Ngome Kongwe (in the gatehouse), PO Box 3032 Zanzibar, ☎0747/411499, ⓦwww.ziff.or.tz.

Since 2004, a welcome addition to the music scene has been the **Sauti za Busara** ("Sounds of Wisdom") festival, held over four nights in February, its scope ranging from *taarab*, rap and hip-hop to big-name bands from Zimbabwe and Mozambique, but especially from Tanzania. For more information, contact the Dhow Countries Music Academy (p.656), or Busara Promotions, PO Box 3635 Zanzibar, ☎024/223 2423 or 0747/428478, ⓔbusara@zanlink.com.

venues for more public performances. Apart from groups mentioned below, ask about performances by Nadi Ikhwan Safaa (also called Malindi Taarab), which celebrated its centenary in 2005. See also the bar reviews for *Mercury's*, *Starehe Club* and *Sweet Eazy Restaurant & Lounge*.

Culture Music Club Vuga Rd, Vuga. Headquarters of one of Zanzibar's best-loved *taarab* orchestras, who practise here and occasionally put on concerts. **Dhow Countries Music Academy** Old Customs House, Mizingani Rd (Mon–Fri 9am–7pm, Sat 9am–5pm; ☎0747/416529, ⍟www.zanzibarmusic .org). If anyone knows about upcoming events, it'll be this lot. Their various student orchestras also give performances, and they offer tuition to tourists in music and dance; $5 per 45-minute lesson. **Haile Selassie School** Creek Rd, opposite Jamhuri Gardens. Unlikely as it sounds, this school

is a good place to catch performances of *taarab*. **Khalifa Hall** Ben Bella School, corner of Creek and Vuga roads. Another school that likes hosting *taarab*. **Ngome Kongwe (Omani Fort)** Forodhani St. The open-air amphitheatre here hosts "A Night at the Fort" two or three times a week (7–10pm), being rather flaky interpretations of traditional dances from around Tanzania. Entry costs $5, or $10 including a sometimes mediocre barbecue. A sign outside the fort announces the next performance.

Shopping

Stone Town is a veritable Aladdin's Cave for souvenirs, with hundreds of shops containing a huge variety of handicrafts, Arabian and Indian antiques and local products. Prices can be reasonable if you're into bargaining, and competition makes it easy to play one shop's prices off against another's. Local items to look out for include all manner of **jewellery**, modern and antique **silverwork**, and hefty brass-studded Zanzibari **chests**. More portable are henna, incense, soaps and even bubble bath. Also typically Zanzibari are woven **palm-leaf items** like mats (*mkeka*) and baskets (*mkoba*), the latter often containing a selection of spices. **Aromatic oils**, which use coconut oil as a neutral base, also make good souvenirs. **Clothing and fabrics** are another speciality: these include colourful cotton *kangas* and more simple woven *kikois*, together with intricately embroidered *kofia* caps for men.

The biggest concentration of souvenir and craft shops is along **Gizenga Street** behind the Omani Fort and House of Wonders, and its continuation **Changa Bazaar**. **Hurumzi Street**, which runs parallel to Changa Bazaar, is also good and has several henna "tattoo" parlours and chest-makers. **Kiponda Street**, east of Changa Bazaar, has more antique shops and places specializing in silverwork, while **Tharia Street** and its continuation **Mkunazini Street** is where most of the gold jewellers are. Shops generally open Monday to Saturday 9am to noon and 2pm to 6pm, and Sunday 9am to 1pm. The following is a tiny selection of the more unusual places.

What not to buy

It's illegal, both in Tanzania and internationally, to buy or export items made of **ivory**, **coral**, **turtle shell**, unlicensed **animal skins** and **furs**. Trade in several species of **seashell** is also illegal, especially larger species such as tritons, and in any case their collection has dire consequences for the marine environment. Please don't buy any of these products.

Abeid Curio Shop Cathedral St, opposite the Catholic Cathedral. One of several antique shops between the Cathedral and Sokomuhogo St (Jaws Corner), good for antiques like Zanzibari chests, silverwork, clocks and British colonial kitsch.

Capital Art Studio Kenyatta Rd. Established in 1930, this sells a huge selection of archive black-and-white photos (both on display and in boxes you can rifle through), covering pretty much every aspect of Zanzibari life and history.

Dhow Countries Music Academy Old Customs House, Mizingani Rd. Virtually every Swahili music CD ever published. Mon–Fri 9am–7pm, Sat 9am–5pm.

Forodhani Gardens Best in the evening when the food market is held and there are a dozen or so stalls selling mainly Makonde woodcarvings, together with cheap wooden and beaded jewellery in the style of the Maasai, who are among the stall-holders.

Kanga Bazaar Mchangani St, behind Central Market, off Creek Rd. The whole street here is stuffed with shops and stalls selling *kangas*, *kitenges* and *kikois*, in a glorious feast for the eyes.

Kibiriti Gallery Boutique Gizenga St. Hand-painted batiks – the stock is limited and expensive, but lovely.

Lookmanji Arts & Antiques Off Forodhani St, next to *Archipelago Café & Restaurant*. A large selection covering most bases, especially good for woodcarvings, masks and batiks.

Memories of Zanzibar Kenyatta Rd, opposite Shangani Post Office. A huge souvenir shop: choose from reproduction maps, banana leaf collages, batiks, rugs, some very luxurious and expensive Indian fabrics, masks (some more authentic-look-ing than others) and loads of jewellery. There's also a good selection of coffee-table books, and CDs of Zanzibari music. Daily 9am–6pm, closed weekends March–May.

Ngome Kongwe (Omani Fort) Forodhani St. A very calm place to browse for an hour or two, with a handful of souvenir shops, a gold jeweller, and the exceptional "Art Gallery" (Mon–Fri 8am–7.30pm, Sat & Sun 8am–9pm) in the west tower on the far side of the grassy quadrangle for quality paintings, batiks and tie-dye. There's also a bar and restaurant.

Zanzibar Curio Shop Changa Bazaar. A glorified junk shop, packed to the rafters with fascinating stuff from old marine compasses and Omani astrolabes to gramophones and novelty tin models from British times. One of the best places to get an idea of the opulence and decadence enjoyed by Zanzibar's wealthy before the 1964 Revolution.

The Zanzibar Gallery Mercury House, Kenyatta Rd at the corner with Gizenga St. Zanzibar's best curio shop, selling everything from clothes to pickles, lovely reproductions of ancient maps, Indian fabrics, masks, studded wooden chests, bao games and scented toiletries. Best of all, it's also the best bookshop on the isles. Mon–Sat 9am–7pm, Sun 9am–2pm, shorter hours March–May.

Zanzibar Secrets Kenyatta Rd at the top end of Shangani St. Not all that much choice here but extremely stylish, and a must for homemakers. Currently popular are weirdly fluid Moroccan leather lampshades, and fabulously warm and colourful fabrics. Massage oils, flavoured teas, reproduction masks and candles are also stocked. Mon–Sat 9am–8pm, Sun 8.30am–2pm.

Listings

Air charters Reliable companies include Precisionair and ZanAir; see "Airlines" for both. Expect to pay around $3 per kilometre for a 5-seater Cessna 206.

Airlines Air Excel, in Arusha on the mainland ☏024/254 8429, ⊜reservations@airexcelonline.com; Air Tanzania, beside *Wings* restaurant off Shangani St ☏024/223 0297, ⓦwww.airtanzania.com; Coastal Aviation, Kelele Square, Shangani ☏024/223 9664, ⓦwww.coastal.cc; Emirates, south of Gulioni Rd – head east from the top of Creek Rd and it's on the next dual carriageway on the right ☏024/223 4956, ⓦwww.emirates.com; Precisionair, *Mazson's Hotel*, Kenyatta Rd, Shangani ☏024/223 4521, ⓦwww.precisionairtz.com; ZanAir, off Malawi Rd behind *Passing Show Hotel* ☏024/223 3670, ⓦwww.zanair.com. See also "Travel agents", most of whom deal with airlines.

Bicycle rental Most cheap hotels can fix you up with a bicycle for $5 a day. If you want to arrange things yourself, Maharouky Bicycle Hire, Creek Rd just north of the market, has plenty. You may be asked for a deposit, of anything up to $50; get a receipt.

Books and maps Zanzibar's best bookshop is The Zanzibar Gallery, Kenyatta Rd (see above), and there's also a good if slightly more expensive choice at Memories of Zanzibar (above) on the same road.

Car and motorbike rental A normal saloon suffices for most of Unguja's roads, but if you plan on driving extensively along the coast (sandy roads), 4WD might be better. Prices with unlimited mileage but excluding fuel average $50/day for a saloon, $70–80 for 4WD. Add $10–20 a day for the services of a driver. Arranging things informally with a taxi driver can work out marginally cheaper. Unlike car rental on the mainland, there's no or very limited excess liability in Zanzibar, meaning you're largely covered in case of an accident, but do read the small print. For motorbikes (*pikipiki*), previous experience is strongly recommended for safety. The main place is Ally Keys in Darajani (see the map on pp.632–633); ☎0747/411797, ✉allykeys768@yahoo.com), where $25/day gets you a 250cc motorbike, helmet and full insurance.

Embassies and consulates The nearest are in Dar es Salaam; see pp.632–633.

Hospitals and medical centres The main hospital is the poorly equipped government-run Mnazi Mmoja Hospital, Kaunda Rd ☎024/223 1071, 024/223 1072 or 024/223 1073. Much better are Afya Medical Centre, between Kenyatta Rd and Baghani St ☎024/223 1228, and Zanzibar Medical Group, Kenyatta Rd near Vuga Rd ☎024/223 3134.

Internet There are lots of Internet cafés around town, charging a standard Tsh1000/hr. Easiest to find are those on Kenyatta Rd: Cross Road Internet Café opposite *Sunrise Restaurant & Bar* (Mon–Sat 9am–8pm, Sun 10am–8pm); the large but unfriendly Shangani Internet Café a short distance north (daily 9am–9pm); and Two Shot Internet, beside Malkia Minimarket on Forodhani St (daily 9am–11pm).

Language courses The Institute of Kiswahili and Foreign Languages (Taasisi ya Kiswahili na Lugha za Kigeni), Vuga Rd, Vuga ☎024/223 1964 or 024/223 3337 is the place for tuition, charging $5/hr. The usual course is a one-week, 20hr affair; cheaper deals are available for longer courses, and there's the possibility of arranging accommodation too. Try also KIU, based at the *Salvation Army Hostel* in Dar es Salaam ☎022/285 1509, ⊛www .swahilicourses.com, who offer a two-week, four-hour-a-day course in Zanzibar for $120.

Moving on from Stone Town

Daladalas

All Unguja's **daladalas** (*gari ya abiria*) start in or around Stone Town. The routes are numbered (according to no logic whatsoever), but thankfully vehicles are also marked with their destinations. Details are given throughout this chapter. Most start at "Darajani", meaning Creek Road on the eastern flank of the old town, either opposite the Central Market or – for services headed north – a short distance north of the market. A handful of routes, notably to Unguja Ukuu, Chwaka, Uroa and Pongwe, start at Mwembe Ladu 2km east of town: there are frequent daladalas to there from Darajani, and from "Hospitali" at the south end of Creek Road. Another major terminal, handy for east coast departures (many daladalas start there rather than at Darajani) is "Mwana Kwerekwe", 5km southeast of town beside a huge, chaotic, dirty and very enjoyable market. Daladalas run every few minutes from Darajani, especially #510 (marked "M/Kwerekwe").

Minibuses

An easy way of accessing the east coast (Paje, Jambiani or Bwejuu), or Nungwi in the north, is on a daily tourist **"beach transfer" minibus**, which will deposit you directly outside your hotel. Most tour operators and budget hotels in Stone Town can fix you up with a seat. The ride costs Tsh3000–5000 depending on the season and who you talk to, or more if you can't be bothered to bargain or if the minibus leaves almost empty. Be clear where you want to go, otherwise the driver will take you to a hotel that pays him the best commission. It's best to pay when you arrive, though giving a small advance for fuel is fine. Upmarket hotels and travel agents run a similar service but milk their captive audience for $50–100 for a four-to-six-seat vehicle (and sometimes per person). **Hiring a taxi** is cheaper (starting price $40–50). If you choose this approach, you'll have to buy a permit for driving outside Stone Town: it costs Tsh2500, and is bought without fuss at a police-run office inside *Bwawani Hotel* at the top end of Creek Road.

Flights

To reach the **airport**, catch daladala #505 (marked "U/Ndege"; Tsh300) from Dara-

Library The library occupies the former *Zanzibar Gazette* office, Kaunda Rd next to High Court (Mon–Fri 9am–6pm, Sat 9am–2pm).

Money NBC Bank, Forodhani St (Mon–Fri 8.30am–4pm, Sat 8.30am–1pm) takes ages but has the best rates, minimal commission, and a 24hr ATM for Visa, MasterCard and Delta. Barclays Bank, ZSTC Building, Gulioni Rd, also has a machine. Rates at forex bureaux are bad, hotel forexes even more so, but service is much quicker: try Malindi Bureau de Change, Malawi Rd (Mon–Sat 8am–4pm, Sun 8am–3pm), one of few to also change travellers' cheques. There are other places on Kenyatta Rd near NBC Bank. Credit cards (Master-Card, Visa, Delta and JCB) can be used for cash withdrawals at Coastal Travels, next to *Zanzibar Serena Inn* on Kelele Square (Mon–Sat 9am–2pm & 3–5pm). Western Union money transfers can be picked up at the Tanzania Postal Bank on Gulioni Rd (Mon–Fri 8.30am–4pm, Sat 8.30am–noon).

Pharmacies Keriy's Pharmacy, Shangani St opposite *Tembo House Hotel* ☎0748/445454 (daily 9am–9pm, closed 4–8pm during Ramadan); Fahud

Pharmacy, Creek Rd, Darajani ☎024/223 5669 (daily 8am–midnight).

Police Stone Town's police station is at the corner of Malawi Rd and Creek Rd in Malindi ☎024/223 0771 or 024/223 0772; for driving permits (if you're hiring a taxi for outside town, or are driving with a national, not international licence), the office is inside *Bwawani Hotel* off the top end of Creek Rd.

Post, couriers and freight Shangani Post Office, Kenyatta Rd, has a not entirely reliable poste restante service (ensure letters are addressed "Shangani Post Office, Kenyatta Rd, Shangani"). For sending parcels home couriers are the only reliable method: DHL, Kelele Square ☎024/223 8281; EMS, Shangani Post Office, Kenyatta Rd ☎024/223 0889.

Snorkelling equipment For buying, there's an unnamed shop on Shangani St, under *Africa House Hotel*. For rental, any tour operator or boat owner will fix you up.

Supermarkets and groceries The main supermarket is Shamshuddin, off Creek Rd behind

jani, or use a taxi: it should cost no more than Tsh5000, though of course they'll try for more. Departure taxes, paid in cash, apply if not included on your ticket: $6 or Tsh6000 including safety levy on flights within Tanzania, or $25 plus $8 safety levy on international flights. Airlines are listed on p.657, and routes and journey times are summarized in "Travel details" at the end of this chapter.

Ferries

Ticket offices for most **ferry companies** (for Dar es Salaam and Pemba) are inside the port, and tend to be open all day until 6pm, though tickets for night ferries can be bought until departure time. Ensure it's you and not the commission-hunting *papasi* who will undoubtedly have latched on to you who does the talking when buying. Fares for tourists ("non-residents") are priced in dollars. You can pay the shilling equivalent, but the exchange rate is bad. The fare should include $5 port tax. Don't try for cheaper "resident" fares, or you'll run into trouble with the ticket inspector and will have to pay full whack plus a bribe/fine to smooth things over. Boats and schedules for **Dar es Salaam** change frequently, but there are at least seven daily sailings, including the overnight MV *Flying Horse*, leaving at 10pm to arrive at 6am. The most reliable boats are the MV *New Happy* ($20 including port tax), and the MV *Sea Express*, MV *Sea Star*, MV *Sea Bus* and MV *Sepideh* (all $35 in economy or $40 first-class, including port tax), all taking two to three hours. For **Pemba**, the quickest ferry is the MV *Sepideh* (Wed, Fri & Sun; $40 second-class, $50 first), taking under three hours to reach Mkoani. At the time of writing, all other ferries were overnight, leaving at 8pm or 10pm to arrive at 6am ($30 first-class, $25 second, $20 in third): the MV *Serengeti* on Tuesday, Thursday and Saturday; the government-run MV *Mapinduzi* or MV *Maendeleo* on Thursday; the MV *New Happy* on Friday; and the MV *Aziza I, II* or MV *Mudathir*, also on Friday (their office is 100m south of the port on Mizingani Road). The MV *Mudathir* or *Aziza* continues on to **Tanga** on the mainland; the MV *New Happy* may also cover this route.

Central Market (Mon–Sat 9am–8pm, Sun 9am–2pm; closed Fri noon–2.30pm). Malkia Minimarket, with less choice, is at the south end of the tunnel in Forodhani (Mon–Sat 10am–10pm; closed 3–7pm during Ramadan). There's an unnamed supermarket on Gizenga St, one block from the post office. Alcohol is sold in various shops along Kenyatta Rd. **Swimming pools** Nicest of the lot is the beachside pool at *Tembo House Hotel* (Tsh3000). *Bwawani Hotel* at the top end of Creek Rd asks just Tsh1000 for use of its huge pool with swim-up bar and sun loungers.

Telephones The cheapest way to call abroad is through the Internet: Shangani Internet Café, Kenyatta Rd (daily 9am–9pm) charges Tsh500/minute to terrestrial lines and Tsh1500/minute to mobile phones; line quality isn't up to much, but at a quarter of the price of normal calls you can't complain. For normal international calls, expect to pay over $2 a minute: try Zantel, Kaunda Rd beside the High Court (Mon–Fri 8am–5pm, Sat 8am–1pm), or *Dolphin Restaurant*, Kenyatta Rd (daily 9am–9.30pm; closed Ramadan daytimes). More practical, but not always reliable, is to use a card-operated phone outside Shangani Post Office; cards, sold inside, cost Tsh5000 or Tsh10,000.

Travel agents Coastal Travels, Kelele Square, Shangani ☎ 024/223 9664, ⓦ www.coastal.cc; Easy Travel & Tours, Malawi Rd opposite *Hotel Marine* ☎ 024/223 5372, ⓦ www.easytravel-tanzania.com; Tabasam Tours and Travel, Kenyatta Rd facing *Dolphin Restaurant* ☎ 024/223 0322, ⓦ www.tabasamzanzibar.com; ZanTours, off Malawi Rd behind *Passing Show Hotel*, Malindi ☎ 024/223 3670 or 024/223 3768, ⓦ www.zanair.com. All can arrange wildlife safaris on the mainland.

Around Stone Town

There's a wealth of possible **day-trips** from Stone Town, all of which can be arranged through the tour operators reviewed opposite. Their mark-up isn't always that much more than the cost of arranging things yourself, and of course it's much less hassle. Half-day **spice tours** are virtually obligatory, and include a visit to **Kidichi Persian Baths**, and sometimes also to the creepy slave chambers at **Mangapwani** (which can also be visited by daladala). Other possibilities include half-day **dolphin safaris** from Kizimkazi in southern Unguja, and soothing walks through **Jozani Forest** in search of red colobus monkeys.

Recommended boat trips are a half or full day to **Changuu (Prison) Island**, during which you can snorkel and feed a colony of giant tortoises, and **Chumbe Island Coral Park** for some of the world's most stunning snorkelling reefs and virtually untouched coral rag forest. Other islands, which could be combined with a trip to Prison Island, are **Chapwani**, which has a lovely beach, and **Bawe Island**, with another good beach and snorkelling. **Scuba-diving** is possible around all the islands with the exception of Chumbe. Apart from the islands, the best clean **beaches** close to Stone Town are Fuji Beach near Bububu, 8km to the north, and Mbweni, 7km to the south.

Organized tours

There are dozens of **tour operators** in Stone Town, most of them offering a standard selection of excursions at pretty standard prices. At the budget level you'll almost certainly be sharing the trip with up to eight other tourists, and may be travelling by daladala or minibus. For private trips in an air-conditioned Land Rover or Land Cruiser, expect to pay three times more than the prices quoted in our reviews. Unfortunately, a lot of companies are unreliable and quote ludicrously inflated "starting prices"; if this happens, look elsewhere. Similarly, ignore approaches by *papasi*. For more flexibility, **rent a car** (see p.658) or a taxi for the day.

Tour companies

Apart from dedicated tour operators, budget **hotels** can also arrange trips; be careful though, as some deal with dodgy companies and aren't averse to overcharging. A reliable exception is *Jambo Guest House*. **Prices** below are per person. Where two prices are given (eg $15/35), the first is for a person in a group of four, the second in a couple. Discounts are available for larger groups. Most tour company offices are open daily until sunset.

Blue Dolphins Tours & Safaris East end of Changa Bazaar ☎0747/424858, ⓦwww.bluedolphinstours .com. Useful for day-trips to Tumbatu Island (otherwise almost impossible to access), combining ancient ruins with encounters with fishermen, farmers and other locals ($40/60, excluding food and drinks). No beach lounging, given Tumbatu's Islamic ethics. A trip to Jozani Forest costs $25/30.

Eco+Culture Tours Hurumzi St, facing *Kidude Restaurant*, Hurumzi ☎024/223 0366 or 0747/410873, ⓦwww.ecoculture-zanzibar.org. A recommended company which promote ecological and cultural tours, plus more standard options. Their wide "menu" includes a spice tour with a medicine man ($20/30 including a superb lunch), day-trips to Nungwi ($35/50 including lunch), Jambiani village ($30/45 including lunch) and Unguja Ukuu ($40/60), and – in planning – a cave tour.

Madeira Tours & Safaris Facing *Baghani Hotel*, Baghani ☎024/223 0406 or 0747/415107, ⓦwww.madeirazanzibar.com. Efficient, responsible, and with a wide range of options: spice tour ($30/40), a half-day Prison Island trip ($25/35), Jozani ($40/50), dolphins ($50/70 excluding lunch), a trip combining a spice farm visit, Mangapwani and Nungwi beach ($55/65), and a full day's fishing with locals off Mkokotoni ($80/100).

Mitu's Spice Tour Off Malawi Rd, Malindi ☎024/223 4636 or 0747/418098. Self-proclaimed inventor of the spice-tour industry, former taxi driver Mr Mitu has now retired but his sons continue to offer reliable and entertaining shared tours at a standard $10 per person for over six hours, including Kidichi and Mangapwani.

Sama Tours Gizenga St, behind the House of Wonders ☎024/223 3543 or 0747/430385, ⓦwww.samatours.com. Noted for the unhurried nature of its trips, standard options include a spice tour ($25/45), Jozani ($20/35) and a full-day Prison Island excursion ($20/35). Other trips include a full day on the east coast ($20/35) and one-day cultural tours of Jambiani or Nungwi ($20/45). A full day combining dolphin-spotting with a trip to Jozani Forest costs $41/71 including lunch and fees.

Tabasam Tours and Travel Kenyatta Rd, facing *Dolphin Restaurant* ☎024/223 0322, ⓦwww .tabasamzanzibar.com. Calm, unhurried and professional, the choice including half-day spice tours ($21/25 with lunch), a day-long dhow and snorkelling trip combining Prison Island, Bawe Island and Chapwani Island ($46/56 with lunch), and a full day with snorkelling at Chumbe Island ($75 including lunch). They also offer a good-value combined spice and city tour for $30/36.

Tropical Tours & Safaris Kenyatta Rd ☎024/413454 or 0747/411121, ⓔtropicalts@hotmail.com. Cheap and reliable: they offer spice tours ($15/25), trips to Prison Island ($20/25) or Jozani Forest, and the east coast (both $25 per person in a couple), and dolphins ($25 per person).

ZanTours Off Malawi Rd, behind *Passing Show Hotel*, Malindi ☎024/223 3670 or 024/223 3768, ⓦwww.zantours.com. Expensive if thoroughly reliable, offering a variety of unusual trips, including full days on Chumbe Island (around $100), live-aboard diving, and flying safaris to Selous Game Reserve on the mainland. Their standard trips include spice tours ($25), Prison Island ($30), and a combined dolphin safari and Jozani Forest excursion for $50–80.

Spice tours

Spice tours are by far Zanzibar's most popular excursion. All leave in the morning (9.30am latest) to return around 2pm, unless the tour includes Mangapwani. The guides know their stuff, even on cheaper tours, but ensure you have a responsible driver. The trips centre on a **guided walk** around a spice farm where you're shown herbs and spices, fruits and other crops, and are given fascinating descriptions of their uses, with plenty of opportunities for smelling and tasting. Things to look out for include the "lipstick tree", whose pods produce a vibrant red dye, the "iodine tree", whose clear sap is used as an antiseptic, and a "soap bush", whose berries lather like soap. **Lunch** is generally included in the price, as is a visit to Kidichi Persian Baths – it's worth paying extra to have the slave caves at Mangapwani included in the tour. Some itineraries include the Maruhubi ruins and/or Livingstone's House, though neither are particularly interesting. The tours finish with a stop at a roadside kiosk selling packaged spices, essential oils and trinkets.

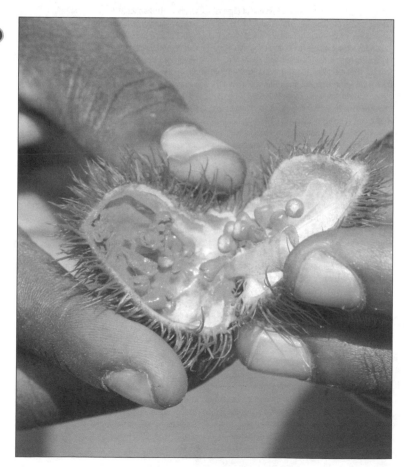

△ Guide holding a "lipstick tree" pod on a spice tour

For an introduction to scuba-diving and snorkelling in Tanzania, see pp.61–63.

Southwest Unguja's waters aren't Zanzibar's cleanest, and with underwater visibility averaging a humble 10m, experienced **scuba-divers** don't have much to look forward to other than wreck dives. The sheltered nature of the area's reefs do make them suitable for novices, however.

Murogo Reef is the highlight, its dramatic pinnacles and gullies filled with colourful hard corals and some soft growths, which attract a wide variety and quantity of fish. **Boribo Reef**, further south, is good for large pelagics. The shallower reef east of **Bawe Island** has brain corals and, a little deeper, gorgonian sea fans; sand sharks and blue-spotted stingrays may be seen. **Pange Reef** surrounds a sandbank handy for sunbathing. Another favourite is **Turtles Den**, which lives up to its name thanks to its turtle-friendly barrel sponges. The main **wrecks** are the *Great Northern* (see p.664) at Fungu Reef, and – for history buffs only given the poor visibility – the remains of I IMS *Glasgow*. A present from Britain to Sultan Barghash, it was sunk in 1896 by the Royal Navy during their bombardment of Stone Town and, in 1912, was dynamited and the resulting pieces dumped into deeper water.

Dive centres

Stone Town has two PADI-accredited dive centres, both open daily until around 6.30pm.

Bahari Divers Forodhani St, just south of the tunnel ☏0748/254786, ⓦ www.zanzibar-diving.com. A small, friendly and flexible outfit with whom a four-day Open Water course costs $320; Advanced Open Water $250; and Dive Master $650. Two dives with lunch cost $75. Night and wreck dives possible.

One Ocean (The Zanzibar Dive Centre) Kenyatta Rd, beside *Sweet Eazy Restaurant & Lounge* ☏024/223 8374, ⓦ www.zanzibaroneocean.com. Highly experienced and knowledgeable outfit offering the full range of PADI courses (same prices as Bahari Divers), plus instructor training and underwater camera rental. Night and wreck dives possible, and novices can learn the ropes in a swimming pool. They also have dive centres on the east and northeast coast.

Islands around Stone Town

A number of small islets within a few kilometres of Stone Town can be visited as day-trips. **Prison Island**, the most popular destination, is famous for giant tortoises, and snorkelling is also possible. The larger **Bawe Island** is infrequently visited but also has good snorkelling. There are also a couple of privately owned islands: the incomparable **Chumbe Island**, in the heart of a protected marine area which boasts one of the world's most beautiful snorkelling reefs, virtually untouched coral rag forest and a lovely upmarket lodge; and **Chapwani Island**, also with a lodge, lovely beaches and dikdik antelopes.

Changuu Island (Prison Island)

A trip to **Changuu Island**, a narrow kilometre-long strip 5km northwest of Stone Town, is a popular, enjoyable and cheap way of getting out of town. There's a beautiful beach, good snorkelling on the shallow fringing reef, a nineteenth-century ruin, patches of coral rag forest, and the giant tortoises (*changuu*) from which the island gets its Kiswahili name.

Once used as a transit camp for slaves, the island's English name comes from a **prison** that never was. Following the abolition of the slave trade, the British built what was supposed to be a prison, but which only saw use as a yellow fever quarantine camp. Its ruins are now inhabited by a colony of showy peacocks. A narrow trail behind the ruins leads into a patch of forest, home to a herd of diminutive **suni antelope** – spotting them isn't too difficult as long as you tread softly. The forest is also good for **birdlife**; look for the intricately woven sock-like nests of weavers hanging from the trees.

The fenced enclosure behind the restaurant contains a colony of **giant tortoises**, some of them the descendants of four tortoises from Aldabra Atoll in the Seychelles, which were presented to the British Regent in 1919. They breed from January to May; the male copulatory organ is in the tail. At over two hundred kilograms in weight, the biggest – aged anything up to 100 years – are second in size only to Galapagos tortoises, and like their cousins are real dinosaurs, having evolved some 180 million years ago. Tsh500 buys you a bowl of spinach and some quality bonding time, but watch out for sharp beaks, and don't sit on them as some tourists like to do – they're hot enough as it is already.

Practicalities

A **lodge** with 25 cottages is currently being built on the island (Stone Town's tour operators will know the score). In the meantime, half- or full-day **excursions** are the only way of seeing the place. The boat ride, from the landing next to *Sweet Eazy Restaurant & Lounge*, takes 30–45 minutes. Hotels and tour operators can arrange things for you, but you can also deal directly with the boatmen; the ride itself shouldn't cost more than Tsh5000 there and back. More expensive are the smart modern boats, with sunscreens usually adorned with advertising; apart from these there's little difference in the quality of service on offer. An entrance fee of $4 (or shilling equivalent; not included in tour rates) is paid at a small shack near the landing on the island. Snorkelling gear can be rented for around Tsh2000 in Stone Town or on the island if not included in the cost. Most people bring **picnics**, but food and drinks are available at a **restaurant** facing the beach where the boats arrive (meals from Tsh3500).

Bawe Island

Lying 6km west of Stone Town, **Bawe** is the largest of the islands near Stone Town and is popular with scuba-divers. Uninhabited for want of fresh water, the island acquired modest fame in the 1880s when it served as a base for East Africa's first underwater telegraphic cable. The cable ship, *The Great Northern*, arrived in Zanzibar in 1882 and eventually laid 1950 nautical miles of cable between Aden (Yemen) and Mozambique via Zanzibar. The ship's wreck lies off Fungu Reef.

The easiest way of **getting to Bawe** is to combine the trip with a visit to Prison Island; most tour operators can arrange this. The more interesting way of getting here is to rent a boat at the dhow harbour (turn right 50m inside Stone Town's harbour entrance). The journey takes thirty to ninety minutes depending on the seaworthiness of your conveyance. There are no facilities whatsoever on Bawe, so if you plan on snorkelling, eating or drinking, bring everything you'll need with you from Stone Town

Chumbe Island Coral Park

Chumbe Island Coral Park, 6km off Chukwani south of Stone Town, was Tanzania's first marine protected area, and encloses one of the richest and finest coral gardens in the world, as well as rare coral rag forest. The island's name aptly encapsulates the notion of a rich ecosystem as a living entity; it means a creature, or a being.

The coconut crab

The **coconut crab** (also known as the robber crab) is the world's largest land crab, reaching 60cm–1m in length and weighing three to four kilograms. Originating in Polynesia, it appears to have made its way to the western Indian Ocean by being carried by ocean currents while in its plankton stage, or was introduced by early sailors as a source of food. The crabs are crimson or bluish black in colour, and their unusual name comes from their amazing ability to climb trees, a skill popularly believed to be used for wrenching off coconuts. True or not, they do climb trees and certainly feed on fallen coconuts, as well as on hermit crabs, to which they are related. The main differences between the two species, other than size and an aptitude for arboreal gymnastics, is that the coconut crab sheds its shell and is nocturnal. By day, you might see them hiding in rocky crevices on the coral cliffs or burrowed in the roots of palm trees; at night, they emerge to forage for fruit and coconuts, which can be stored in their burrows.

Coconut crabs have long been considered a delicacy and aphrodisiac throughout the Indian Ocean, and so have been hunted to the point of extinction. On Zanzibar, the crabs were also used as bait in fish traps – their struggles attracted fish – though the crabs drowned after two days in water. In Tanzania, the species is limited to Chumbe and Chapwani islands (see p.666), Misali Island off Pemba, and Mbudya Island north of Dar es Salaam.

Coral growth and diversity along the shallow **reef** is among the highest in East Africa, and marine life diversity is astonishing, with more than two hundred species of stone corals and around ninety percent of all East African fish species, over four hundred in all. Needless to say, **snorkelling** is superb (scuba-diving is prohibited), and several snorkelling trails have been established. If you're really lucky, you may get a glimpse of blue-spotted stingrays, dolphins, or a couple of batfish who like following snorkellers. There's also a resident hawksbill turtle, and Oscar, a large cave-dwelling potato grouper.

It's not just marine life that makes Chumbe special. Most of the island is covered with pristine **coral rag forest**, which contains a surprisingly rich variety of flora and fauna given the lack of permanent groundwater. The survival of the forest is largely due to the absence of humans on the island, settlement having been limited to temporary fishermen's camps and the keeper of the lighthouse (which was built in 1904 and fitted with its present gaslight in 1926; its 132 steps can be climbed). The forest, which can be explored via several carefully laid **nature trails**, is one of the last natural habitats of the rare coconut crab and endangered Ader's duiker, reintroduced in 1997 after being wiped out by hunters in the 1950s. It's also possible to walk around the island at low tide, a good way of seeing **mangroves** and for poking around intertidal rock pools for crabs, starfish and shellfish. Over on the bleak and rocky eastern side of the island, look out for petrified corals and fossilized giant clams.

The island and its reefs are explored either in the company of one of the park's rangers (a friendly and informative bunch of former fishermen), or by using laminated route plans and leaflets. If you have $200 per person to spare, the superb and truly eco-friendly **lodge** offers a memorable investment. All profits are channelled back into conservation and environmental education. There's no beach, but with so much other natural beauty around you'll hardly miss it.

Practicalities

You can visit the island on a day-trip, or by staying at its intimate and justifiably pricey lodge. The **boat** leaves from the beach at *Mbweni Ruins Hotel* (see p.667), 7km south of Stone Town, every day at 10am, taking thirty to forty minutes for the nine-kilometre crossing. The transfer is free for overnight guests; day-trippers pay $75, which includes entry fee, lunch (on a beautiful sea-view terrace) and activities. It's best to **reserve in advance**, as day-trips may not be allowed if the lodge is full: Chumbe Island Coral Park ☎024/223 1040 or 0747/413582, Ⓦwww.chumbeisland.com.

Accommodation at ⚘ *Chumbe Island Eco-Lodge* (closed mid-April to mid-June; full-board ❾) is in seven romantic split-level *bandas* overlooking the ocean, with casuarina poles for walls and palm fronds for roofs. All have a large living room, handmade furniture and hammock. The "ecotourism" tag is more than just an advertising gimmick: rainwater is filtered and stored under the floors, hot water and electricity are provided by solar power, and ventilation is achieved naturally with cleverly designed roofs. There are no TVs or phones and, apart from the activities on the island, entertainment is limited to watching the palm trees sway in the breeze. Meals are a mixture of Zanzibari, Arabic, Indian and African cuisine, with good options for vegetarians too. Rates may be cheaper if booked though a reputable travel agent in Stone Town.

Chapwani Island (Grave Island)

Like Chumbe, **Chapwani Island** – 3km due north of Stone Town (rather too close for any desert island make-believe) – is privately owned, and you're only allowed to land if you buy a meal or are spending a night in the lodge, both of which require reservations. The island is tiny, measuring barely 600m by 60m, with a beautiful sandy beach on one side and a series of coral inlets dotted with tidal swimming pools on the other. Though it lacks the quantity and quality of Chumbe's reefs and terrestrial flora and fauna, Chapwani still has plenty to make it a pleasant hideaway, including dikdik antelopes, a colony of fruit bats, hermit and coconut crabs, interesting birdlife, and good swimming and snorkelling at all tides. There's also the **cemetery** from which the island draws its English name, among whose untended tombs are those of sailors from the HMS *Pegasus*, which was attacked by the German cruiser *Königsberg* at the start of World War I (see p.198).

The fifteen-minute **boat** ride from Stone Town costs $15 per person each way if arranged through *Chapwani Island Lodge* (☎024/223 3360 or 0747/322102, Ⓦwww.chapwaniisland.com; closed April & May; full-board ❾), which has five thatched **cottages** with two large, cheerfully kitted-out guest rooms each ($300 for a double) on the south side of the island, each with a verandah and secluded beach. Rooms are pretty simple, but do have generator-powered ceiling fans and solar-heated water. The beachside **restaurant** does mainly Italian-inspired dishes, and is particularly strong on seafood. **Activities** include canoeing, snorkelling and boat trips to Changuu or Bawe islands.

Mbweni

On the coast 7km south of Stone Town, **MBWENI** makes for a good day-trip, thanks to its botanical gardens, the poignant ruins of a nineteenth-century Christian mission, and a great restaurant at the *Mbweni Ruins Hotel*.

The hotel is set amidst the ruins of a nineteenth-century **Anglican mission** that housed and schooled girls freed from captured slave dhows, and daughters of freed slaves. The church, in late English Gothic style, was built in 1882. Aptly complementing the ruins are the glorious cascaded **botanical gardens** founded by the Scottish physician, Sir John Kirk, during his lengthy stint as Britain's Consul General. A botanist by profession (in which capacity he had accompanied Livingstone up the Zambezi), Kirk introduced many of the 650 species found in the garden, including sausage trees, Madagascan periwinkle, devil's backbone and over 150 palms. Many of the plants are labelled, and there's a nature trail which you can walk on your own (the hotel has bird, plant and butterfly lists) or accompanied by a guide from the hotel.

Practicalities

There's no problem walking or cycling the 7km from Stone Town, but it's far easier to catch a taxi – Tsh7000 would be good going. Alternatively, catch a #505 daladala from Darajani (for the airport) and get off at Mazizini police station next to the signposted junction for Mbweni. Follow the Mbweni road for 800m and turn right: the ruins and the hotel are 900m along.

Accommodation is at the *Mbweni Ruins Hotel* (T024/223 5478, W www. mbweni.com; breakfast included ❸), a peaceful and cosy place beside the ocean with thirteen spacious suites, including one with a rooftop terrace. All have air conditioning, sea- and garden-facing verandahs, and are furnished in traditional style with four-poster beds, but are rather plain for the price. The narrow beach isn't Zanzibar's best, either, as there are plenty of mangroves and the sand is coarse, but this at least attracts a rich variety of birdlife. Facilities include a fresh-water swimming pool overlooking the sea, a beach bar, and an excellent clifftop restaurant where you might be joined by bushbabies for dinner. Barbecues are sometimes held in the ruins, or on a dhow, and trips to Changuu, Bawe and Chumbe islands can be arranged.

North of Stone Town

Attractions north of Stone Town include a couple of ruined palaces at **Maruhubi** and **Mtoni** and the Persian baths at **Kidichi**, all of which can be visited as part of a spice tour (see box on p.662). Some tours also include **Mangapwani**, about 20km north of town, which apart from a lovely beach, has a natural cave and a man-made cavern that was used for holding slaves. All these places can be visited under your own steam. There's also a good beach near Bububu at **Fuji Beach**.

Maruhubi

Just off the road to Bububu, 3km north of Stone Town amidst mango and coco-nut trees, are the ruins of **Maruhubi Palace**, built by Sultan Barghash in 1882 to house his harem of 99 concubines and one wife. Dark legends tell of the former being killed if they did not satisfy the sultan, and of others being put to death after having fulfilled the carnal desires of visiting dignitaries. The largely wooden palace, one of the most beautiful of its time (there's a photo in the House of Wonders), was gutted by fire in 1899 and the marble from its Persian-style bath house was subsequently stolen, leaving only the foundations of the bath house, an overgrown collection of coral stone pillars and a small aqueduct that carried water from a nearby spring to cisterns, which is overgrown with lilies. To get here, walk or catch one of the frequent #502 Bububu daladalas from Darajani. Access is free.

Mtoni

About 2km beyond Maruhubi is the bustling village of **Mtoni** and the ruins of **Mtoni Palace**. Built by Seyyid Saïd between 1828 and 1832 as his first official

Princess Salme

Princess Sayyida Salme bint Saïd bin Sultan was born in 1844 to the Sultan of Oman, Seyyid Saïd, and a concubine named Jilfidan. Although Salme's early childhood, much of which was spent at Mtoni, was by her own account idyllic, her adult life was to be much more turbulent. Sultan Saïd died when Salme was 12, beginning a period of rivalry which ended with the creation of the separate sultanates of Zanzibar and Oman. In the former, Salme's brother **Barghash** unsuccessfully attempted to usurp the throne from his half-brother Majid. In 1859, Salme's mother died in a cholera epidemic, and Salme went to live with her half-sister, with whom she played a minor role in Barghash's second and equally doomed attempt to seize power. For her part in the plot, Salme spent several years in internal exile before making peace with Majid – something that permanently soured her relations with Barghash.

Salme returned to Stone Town in 1866, where she lived next door to a German merchant named **Rudolph Heinrich Ruete**. The couple soon fell in love, but Heinrich's Christianity meant that problems were inevitable and when, in the same year, Salme became pregnant, Heinrich realized the danger and made arrangements to smuggle her out of Zanzibar to Aden. On May 30, 1867, Salme converted to Christianity, being baptized as Emily, and married her lover – all on the same morning. In the afternoon, the couple and their child set sail for Hamburg. Tragically, Heinrich was killed in a tram accident in 1870. Following his death, Salme spent much of her time campaigning for the restitution of the "rights" she had forfeited by converting to Christianity, but her family remained deaf to her entreaties. Finally, in 1885, the German government sent her to Zanzibar aboard the *Adler*, escorted by five warships, the idea being to use her as a pawn in obtaining Zanzibar as a German protectorate. The attempt backfired, and Sultan Barghash refused to see her. When Barghash died in March 1888, Salme hoped for a change of heart from his successor, Seyyid Khalifa bin Saïd, and once more returned to Zanzibar, only to be shunned again. The rest of her life was one of restless travel, and writing, in which she expressed what were, for her time, visionary ideals about healthcare, literacy, education, and cross-cultural understanding. Her most famous work is her autobiography, *Memoirs of an Arabian Princess*, originally written in German, in which she beautifully describes the opulence of palace life at Mtoni in the 1850s and 1860s, where she spent her early childhood; Stone Town's bookshops have copies.

When Salme died in 1924, the dress she had been wearing during her elopement, and a bag of sand taken from the beach at Mtoni, were among her possessions. The Palace Museum in Stone Town has an entire room dedicated to the errant princess.

residence, the palace at one time housed the sultan's three wives, 42 children and hundreds of concubines. The main building had two floors with elegant balconies, and other buildings included baths, a mosque and an unusual conical tower that served both as a meeting place and a place for meditation, while the gardens contained a menagerie of wildlife, including ostriches, flamingos and gazelles. Like Maruhubi, much of Mtoni Palace was destroyed by fire in 1914, leaving only the mosque intact. The advent of World War I saw the mosque converted into a warehouse, and it was later destroyed when the present oil depots were constructed. Nowadays nothing more than a few walls and collapsing roofs remain, and the ruins would be unremarkable were it not for their association with **Princess Salme** (see box above), whose elopement with a German merchant caused a colossal scandal.

Practicalities

The remains of the **palace** can be seen off the path that goes beside the oil depot to the beach; route #502 daladalas from Darajani (for Bububu) pass by the junction. **Accommodation** is at ✈ *Mtoni Marine Centre* (℡024/225 0140, Ⓦwww.mtoni.com; breakfast included ❸–❼), a laid-back and welcoming hotel which caters for all budgets, set in palm-tree-studded lawns with good views of Chapwani Island and Stone Town over the ocean. All rooms have air conditioning and private bathrooms. Amenities include a swimming pool, recliners and parasols on the sandy beach, aromatherapy, a kids' playground, dhow cruises and other day-trips, and – reason enough for coming – good **restaurants**. The stylish *Mtoni Marine Restaurant* is famed for its fusion of local and international styles, seafood being the predictable speciality. It has tables right on the beach, and is particularly romantic at night, what with your toes in the sand, candles on the tables and the stars twinkling above (reservations recommended; ℡024/225 0140). There's live music most nights, including *taarab* (and a barbecue) on Tuesday for Tsh10,000. The more casual *Mcheza Bar & Bistro* has wood-fired pizzas, chargrills, burgers, cocktails and sports on TV, whilst *Zan Sushi Bar* on the beach excels at sushi and sashimi (raw fish, including lobster).

Bububu

The first clean beach north of Stone Town is at **Bububu**, a densely populated area 10km north of the city beyond a none-too-attractive industrial suburb. There's a reasonable range of cheapish guest houses and one exceptionally atmospheric upmarket option, but if it's a beach holiday you're after you'd be better off elsewhere, where the beaches are nicer and there's a wider choice of accommodation.

Practicalities

Daladalas (#502) to Bububu run every few minutes throughout the day from Stone Town's Darajani (Creek Rd) terminal. **Fuji Beach** is 300m off the main road down a track from Bububu police station, and takes its name from *Fuji Beach Bar*, which was set up here a couple of decades ago by a Japanese expatriate. He's long gone, but the bar, which also serves cheap meals, still exists and remains popular with locals and day-trippers from Stone Town, and hosts a beach disco on Saturday and Sunday nights (to midnight; don't leave items unattended).

There are two good **hotels**, facing each other off the main road from the police station. The most atmospheric is *Salome's Garden* (℡024/225 0050,

---

Zanzibar's steam trains

Bububu may have inherited its name from the sound of a nearby spring, or, it is said, from the whistle of East Africa's first train, when a two-foot-gauge track was laid from Stone Town to Sultan Barghash's summer palace at Chukwani, south of the city, in the 1880s. The railway saw little use and was pulled up after the sultan's death, but between 1905 and 1909, a second line – the Bububu Light Railway – was constructed by an American company, Arnold Cheney & Co. It consisted of seven miles of three-foot gauge and connected Stone Town's Omani Fort with Sultan Ali bin Hamoud's clove plantation at Bububu. The railway quickly became infamous, as a government official recounted in 1911: "The whole width [of the railway] is blacked, while the engines, which belch forth clouds of smoke and sparks into the front upper storey windows, cover the goods in the shops below, not to speak of the passengers, with large black smuts. Funeral processions are interrupted, old women are killed, houses and crops are set on fire ... and no redress can be obtained." Thankfully for locals, the advent of the motorcar scuppered plans for the railway's extension to Mkokotoni, and the track was pulled up in 1927.

www.salomes-garden.com; **❼**), a restored mid-nineteenth-century country house set in colourful gardens that drop down to the beach; the surrounding wall gives the place an enchanting Alice in Wonderland feel. The building itself, with four large, high-ceilinged bedrooms stylishly furnished with original antiques, was built by Seyyid Saïd and is claimed to have been the last place that Princess Salme slept before her elopement and escape. In July and August, you can only rent the whole house ($800 for up to ten guests); rates include full house staff and cook. Facing *Salome's Garden* is *Imani Beach Villa* (☎024/225 0050, Ⓦwww.imani.it; **❻**), an Italian-run mini-resort set in a garden with lots of whitewash and *makuti* thatch. The restaurant in the small, enclosed garden is good for seafood (try the barracuda carpaccio or kingfish ravioli), and a full range of excursions is offered.

Kidichi Persian Baths

Included in most spice tours are the well-preserved **Kidichi Persian Baths** (daily 8am–4pm; Tsh1000 plus guide's tip) 2.5km east of Bububu, which once formed part of a palace built in 1850 by Seyyid Saïd for the use of his second wife, a granddaughter of the Shah of Persia named Binte Irich Mirza, also known as Sheherazade. The baths' ornamental stucco decorations depicting lotus flowers, peacocks, cloves, coconut palms and dates were made by Persian Zoroastrians, as Muslims were forbidden by the Qur'an from depicting Allah's worldly creations.

Daladalas (#511, marked "K/Spice") run directly to the baths from Stone Town's Darajani (Creek Rd) terminal, or catch a #502 to Bububu and walk the remaining 2.5km east; the baths are on the right side of the road. About 2.5km further east, at **Kizimbani**, are another set of baths, less elaborate and in a more ruinous state, also dating from Seyyid Saïd's reign. His estate at Kizimbani was where, in 1818, clove trees were first planted in Zanzibar. At its height, the estate is said to have contained three hundred thousand of them.

Mangapwani

Some 25km north of Stone Town is **Mangapwani** village, with a lovely stretch of clean beach and a couple of caves in the coral ragstone facing the sea. The name means "Arabian Shore", possibly alluding to one of the caves, a man-made chamber used for hiding slaves after the trade with Oman was outlawed in 1845. The cave saw even more use after the rest of the slave trade was abolished in 1873, when black market prices took off (the trade only finally stopped after the Abushiri War of 1888–89, which gave Germany total control over the mainland coast). The dank and claustrophobic **slave chamber** is one of the most shocking of Zanzibar's sights and, like the underground cells beside Stone Town's last slave market, conveys the full horror and misery of the East African trade. The chamber consists of two rectangular cells hewn out of the soft coral rock, accessed along a deep and narrow passage and sealed by a heavy door, which was originally covered with coral ragstone, all of which served to hide slaves from the prying eyes of British anti-slavery patrols. For the slaves, being shut up here would have been a terrifying experience, as no light – and not much air – could penetrate from the outside.

Two kilometres south is a **coral cavern**, this one natural and larger than the slave chamber, and of interest for its spiritual importance to locals. The cavern, which contains a pool of fresh water, was discovered in the early 1800s by a plantation slave boy when one of the goats he was herding fell through the entrance. Like other caves in Zanzibar and on the mainland, it contains offerings to ancestors left by locals seeking their intercession in mortal affairs – a good example of the syncretic nature of Zanzibari Islam.

Mangapwani can be visited as part of a spice tour if the entire group agrees, though operators can be reluctant given the bad state of the road and the extra distance involved. It can also be incorporated in one of the north coast day-trips offered by many tour operators, which include a spice tour and Nungwi beach.

To reach Mangapwani by **public transport**, catch a #102 ("Bumbwini") daladala from Darajani terminal (Creek Rd) in Stone Town. Some daladalas turn left off the main road into the village and continue towards the coast, which is preferable if you don't fancy walking too much. If you're dropped on the main road, which is more likely, walk northwest through Mangapwani village. The turning for the **coral cavern** is 600m along on the left – it lies 1km south of there along a narrow track. For the **slave chamber**, ignore the turning and continue on to the coast. Just before the coast (roughly 1.5km from the main road, or 1km beyond the coral cavern turning), the road veers north – the slave chamber is 500m further on.

If you're taking lunch at the *Mangapwani Serena Beach Club* you can catch their complimentary shuttle bus from Stone Town: it leaves from outside the *Zanzibar Serena Inn* at 8.30am and 11.30am, and returns at 4pm or 5pm. The club's **restaurant**, half way between the two caves, blends high style and service with a relaxed atmosphere, beautiful location and view, and a private beach. The food is pricey but worth every shilling: the catch of the day, or a mixed seafood salad, costs Tsh10,000, whilst a regal seafood grill will set you back Tsh24,000. It's open daily for lunch, and for dinner by reservation through the *Zanzibar Serena Inn* in Stone Town (p.654). The club has a **water sports** centre for snorkelling, canoeing and catamaran sailing. There's no accommodation.

South Unguja

For most visitors, Unguja's **south coast** means only one thing: dolphin tours. Visits to the resident pods off the fishing village of **Kizimkazi** are Zanzibar's most popular excursion after spice tours, and the opportunity of swimming with dolphins exerts an irresistible allure. A fine alternative to Kizimkazi for spotting dolphins is a boat tour in **Menai Bay Conservation Area**, either from Fumba Peninsula or from Unguja Ukuu, the latter also containing some of Zanzibar's oldest ruins. Another highlight is **Jozani Forest**, where walks give good odds on seeing otherwise endangered red colobus monkeys. East of Kizimkazi lies **Makunduchi**, a sleepy fishing community that comes alive once a year for the vibrant Mwaka Kogwa festival.

Jozani–Chwaka Bay National Park

Lying 38km southeast of Stone Town, just north of the road to the east coast beaches and Kizimkazi, is the magnificent **Jozani Forest** (daily 7.30am–5pm; $8), the largest remnant of the indigenous groundwater forest that once covered most of Unguja. Originally protected by an NGO, the forest now lies at the

Red colobus monkeys

Jozani is best known for its large and characterful population of **Kirk's red colobus monkeys**. The species is endemic to Unguja, as it has been isolated from other red colobus populations on the Tanzanian mainland for at least ten thousand years, during which time it has evolved different coat patterns, food habits and calls.

A decade or so ago, the monkeys were on the road to extinction, but the protection of the forest in the 1990s appears to have reversed the trend. Their current population is estimated at around 2500 in and around Jozani, accounting for one-third of their total number. The local population is steadily increasing, perhaps not so much because of conservation but through the continued destruction of their natural habitats elsewhere.

The monkeys are known locally as *kima punju* – poison monkeys – as it was believed that dogs who ate them would lose their fur, and trees and crops would die if the monkeys fed off them. The name may also come from their inability to digest sugars from ripe fruit: however, their four-chambered stomachs can tackle unripe and potentially toxic fruit with ease, helped along by their habit of eating charcoal.

Two troops of thirty to fifty individuals are frequently seen, one inside the forest (usually flashes of red accompanied by the crashing of branches) and another that frequents a patch of open woodland just outside the gate. The latter are habituated and completely unfazed by human presence, making them incredibly photogenic. However, for your own and their **safety**, do not approach closer than three metres, avoid eye contact and noise, and do not feed or otherwise interact with the monkeys. Also, don't visit Jozani if you're ill: monkeys are susceptible to infectious human diseases and have little resistance.

heart of the fifty-square-kilometre **Jozani–Chwaka Bay National Park**, the island's only terrestrial nature reserve. The forest is home to a variety of wildlife once common all over the island, including Sykes' (blue) monkeys, red colobus monkeys, bush pigs, diminutive Ader's duiker and suni antelopes, elephant shrews, chameleons and lots of birds. There are several **nature trails**, ranging from an easy hour's stroll to a half-day hike. Route descriptions are given in a leaflet available at the gate, though taking an official **guide** is recommended (no fee but tip expected), and obligatory if you want to see monkeys inside the forest – those outside the gate can easily be spotted on your own.

Apart from the forest, the park contains several other types of interconnected habitats, including swamp forest, evergreen thickets, mangroves and salt-tolerant grassland. These environments can be seen along the **Pete–Jozani Mangrove Boardwalk**, which loops through coral thicket vegetation, mangrove forest and across a creek in the north of Pete Inlet. The walk starts in a car park under a large tamarind tree, 1km south of the forest gate, and finishes nearby. An informative leaflet containing a sketch map is available for free from the forest entrance gate; the boardwalk entrance fee is covered by the ticket for Jozani. Typical thicket **fauna** includes snakes, lizards, mongooses, Ader's duikers and the nocturnal civet cat. Birdlife is also good, ranging from purple-banded and olive sunbirds to kingfishers and blue-cheeked bee-eaters.

Practicalities

Jozani is usually visited as part of an organized day-trip to see Kizimkazi's dolphins, but the forest can easily be visited by **public transport**: daladalas (Tsh700) from Stone Town's Darajani terminal on Creek Road to Bwejuu (#324), Jambiani (#309) and – most frequently – Makunduchi (#310), drive past the gate throughout the day, the last back to Stone Town passing at around sunset. Alternatively, taxi or car rental from Stone Town costs around $40 for half a day.

The best **time to visit** Jozani is early morning or late afternoon, when there are fewer visitors. The evening light is superb for photographing the troop of red colobus monkeys near the gate, whilst the morning light is deliciously soothing.

There's an **information centre** at the gate, a snack bar, and a community-run gift shop that stocks CDs, postcards and woven baskets made from dried and bleached palm fronds called *ukindi*. Barely 100m away, just outside the park boundary, is the locally run *Jozani Tutani* **restaurant** (daily 8am–4pm), surrounded by trees and coconut palms, and the songs of birds and cicadas. Its meals are tasty and cheap, and include fried octopus, garlic prawns and seafood pizza. They also make good juices, and sell sodas and beers.

Menai Bay

Unguja's only protected marine zone is the 420-square-kilometre **Menai Bay Conservation Area**, which covers most of the coastline and islands between Fumba Peninsula in the west and Kizimkazi in the east. The area is famed for dolphins, which you have a good chance of seeing from boat trips, especially from Kizimkazi where dolphin tours have become an industry. Should Kizimkazi's tourist circus turn you off, an alternative way of seeing dolphins – and virtually no other tourists – is either from **Unguja Ukuu** or **Fumba Peninsula**, the latter also with a scuba-diving centre.

Kizimkazi

At the south end of Unguja, 53km from Stone Town, is the pretty fishing village of **KIZIMKAZI**, known to tourists for its **dolphin tours**, and to historians as the one of the oldest continuously inhabited settlements on Zanzibar, one that served as the capital for Zanzibar's traditional rulers at various times before the Omani conquest.

The village actually comprises two places: **Kizimkazi Dimbani**, which contains East Africa's oldest standing mosque and is where most dolphin tours depart from; and **Kizimkazi Mkunguni** (sometimes called Kizimkazi Mtendeni), 3km to the south, which has a fledgling hotel strip, and a couple of ancient **baobab trees**, the oldest and biggest of which is thought to be over 600 years old, and was used as a transmissions mast during World War II when communications gear was strapped to its crown.

The **beaches** at both places are beautiful, and swimmers are likely to share the water with easily amused local children; be wary of stepping on sea urchins, however. Kizimkazi and Pungume Island also offer excellent but largely unexplored **diving**. Knowledgeable dive centres for the area include Scuba Do in Kendwa (p.695), who also have a base at Fumba in the south (p.676), and Rising Sun Dive Centre in Dongwe (p.677).

Arrival and accommodation

Most tourists come to Kizimkazi on a dolphin tour (see p.674), but it's easy to get there by **public transport**: catch a #326 daladala from Stone Town's Darajani terminal on Creek Road. Few people stay **overnight**, but if you do you'll have the chance to get out on the water the next morning before the crowds arrive. Kizimkazi Dimbani is the more beautiful of the two villages, with a lovely sheltered bay in which dozens of outrigger canoes are moored, but there's only one hotel. All of the following include breakfast.

Kizidi Restaurant & Bungalows Kizimkazi Dimbani ☎0747/417053. On the northern headland flanking the bay, this has glorious views from each of its five large and clean rooms. There's also a bar and a huge, expensive restaurant that gets packed with day-trippers for lunch. In the evening, you're likely to have the place to yourself. **❺**

Kizimkazi Coral Reef Village Kizimkazi Mkunguni, 500m south of the baobabs beside an ugly cottage resort ☎0747/479615 or 024/223 1214, ✉mkazi_coreevi@yahoo.com. Six cramped but clean rooms in three *bandas* at the back of large beachside plot (no views from the rooms), all

with a/c, fan, box nets and Western-style bathrooms with hot water. There's a good restaurant, *Pomboo's Grill*, and the staff are friendly. **❺**

Kizimkazi Dolphin View Cottage Kizimkazi Mkunguni, 1.5km south of the baobabs ☎0747/434959. A somewhat down-at-heel place with several cottages on a low cliff (the water comes right up at high tide), whose staff seem surprised to have visitors. Its double rooms, all en suite, are large and breezy, and $15 more gets you a sea view. Singles can be shared by couples. Its bar and restaurant have waned in popularity with day-trippers. **❹–❺**

Dolphin tours

The waters off Kizimkazi are home to several pods of bottlenose and humpback **dolphins**. For many tourists, the chance to swim with them is the experience of a lifetime; the odds of sighting dolphins on any given day are claimed to be eighty percent (calm days are best), but for some people, the experience comes depressingly close to Disneyland, with dozens of noisy boats crowding and hounding the dolphins on a daily basis, the tourists encouraged to leap into the water just as pods are passing by. The potentially detrimental effects of this regular disturbance are the subject of ongoing research, so think twice before taking part in the melee. If you do decide to go, follow these **guidelines**: encourage your skipper not to chase the pods; if you enter the water, do so away from the dolphins and with as little disturbance as possible; when in the water, stay close to the boat; avoid sudden movements; allow the dolphins to come to you and do not under any pretext attempt to touch them.

Dolphin tour practicalities

Buying a place on a **prearranged dolphin safari** in Stone Town, or from east coast beach hotels, is the easiest way to go about things. Prices quoted generally exclude lunch (anything from Tsh1500 to Tsh25,000), and a $3 conservation area entry fee. Some trips include snorkelling on an extensive reef fringing Pungume Island, 13km offshore. Most of the boats are shared between companies no matter what you're paying. If combined with Jozani Forest, an extra $8 to cover the forest entry fee is charged; any extra payment over this is really just a gratuity.

Arranging things yourself in Kizimkazi has the disadvantage of having to contend with some offensively pushy touts, but the advantage of costing considerably less than an organized tour (especially if you travel by daladala), and – by staying overnight in Kizimkazi – being able to sail off early in the morning before the masses arrive. The main cost is boat rental, generally Tsh35,000–40,000 per boat for around two hours. To that, add Tsh3000–5000 per person for snorkelling equipment, and $3 (Tsh3000) per person for the conservation area fee, which your boatman will collect for you. To avoid hassle with the touts, it's best to arrange things through a hotel or restaurant: *Cabs Restaurant*, *Kizimkazi Coral Reef Village* and *Kizidi Restaurant & Bungalows* are all reliable. Whatever the deal, ensure the boat has adequate shade.

Dimbani Mosque

Kizimkazi's other claim to fame – and usually included in dolphin tours – is **Dimbani Mosque**, on the main road 100m back from the bay at Kizimkazi Dimbani. Founded in the year 500 of the Islamic Hegira calendar (1107 AD), it's East Africa's oldest standing mosque, and direct proof of the Persian migration which led to the establishment of the Shirazi civilization and people, and, ultimately, of the Swahili themselves. From the outside, the mosque – which is still in use – doesn't look too different from any other building in Dimbani: it has the same rusty corrugated metal roof, and there's little other than a roadside plaque to indicate its importance. Indeed, most of the mosque was completely rebuilt in 1770, but the atmosphere inside could hardly be more different, having retained the simple but graceful form and style typical of medieval Persian mosques. In the north wall – the only part that definitively dates from the twelfth century – is an ornate *mihrab* prayer niche indicating the direction to Mecca. To its left, a florid Kufic inscription carved in coral ragstone contains verses from the Qur'an and commemorates the mosque's establishment. An Arabic inscription to the right records its eighteenth-century rebuilding.

Admission to non-Muslims is prohibited during prayer times, and to women at all times. Visitors should remove their shoes and cover up bare limbs before entering, ask permission before taking photographs, speak quietly, and leave a donation in the box provided.

The **graves** outside the mosque, one with a headstone resembling a toadstool, another with a curious checkerboard engraving, include those of – in the words of the signpost – "pious single-handed Sheikh Ali Omar, one-legged Sayyid Abdalla Saïd bin Sharif, Mwana bint Mmadi and her son Mfaume Ali Omar the Guard of the Town Drum". With luck, this drum – which would have been used on ceremonial occasions as a symbol of kingly authority – should be on display in the House of Wonders in Stone Town in the near future.

Eating and drinking

With the exception of *Jichane Restaurant* the following places remain open during Ramadan.

Cabs Restaurant & Dolphin Safaris Kizimkazi Dimbani. An enticing menu, with seafood a speciality: try the seashell meat with potatoes, spices and ginger. Most fish dishes are very good value at Tsh4000. Evening barbecues are held whenever there are enough punters.

Jichane Restaurant Kizimkazi Mkunguni, near the big baobab. The only really local place, with basic meals for Tsh1500 (at least that's what locals pay). If you want something other than rice with fish or chicken – prawns or lobster, for example – ask what's available in the morning.

Kizidi Restaurant & Bungalows Kizimkazi Dimbani. Larger, more sophisticated but considerably more expensive than *Cabs* across the beach, this nonetheless gets packed for lunch (evenings are a complete contrast). Meals start at Tsh7000, though at that price the pasta and omelettes are very poor

value. Better are prawns at Tsh10,000 and lobster for Tsh15,000. A seafood platter will relieve you of Tsh25,000.

Kizimkazi Dolphin View Cottage Kizimkazi Mkunguni, 1.5km south of the baobabs. No fixed menu, just what you arrange with the cook. Standard dishes (chicken or fish with chips or rice) cost Tsh3000–4000, spaghetti is just Tsh2500, and fancier things like prawns and octopus Tsh5000.

Pomboo's Restaurant Kizimkazi Mkunguni, 500m south of the baobabs at *Kizimkazi Coral Reef Village*. A good wide menu, most of it available as they tend to be busy with day-trippers at lunchtimes, and with a lovely beachfront location in which to enjoy it. Grilled or marinated fish of the day goes for Tsh5000, grilled calamari with tamarind sauce is Tsh6000, and the seafood grill is good value at Tsh10,000.

Unguja Ukuu

Just under thirty kilometres southeast of Stone Town, the fishing village of **Unguja Ukuu** is more used to archeologists than it is to tourists, thanks to the **ruins** of an ancient town at the neck of Ras Kitoe Peninsula, 1km beyond the village. Nowadays little more than rubble, nothing much is known about the place other than it was probably one of the first settlements on Zanzibar: excavations have unearthed **sixth-century** Sasanian pottery from pre-Islamic Persia, and a gold dinar dated 798 AD, that was minted during the reign of Harun bin Rashid, the anti-hero of *The Thousand and One Nights*. In later years, Unguja Ukuu – "Great Unguja" – served as the island's main port, and briefly also as capital of the island under the Hadimu tribe. The rapacious **Portuguese** captain Ruy Lourenço Ravasco put an end to the town by sacking it in 1503, after which the Hadimu moved their capital inland to Dunga.

To get to Unguja Ukuu, catch one of the frequent #308 **daladalas** (Tsh1000) from Mwembe Ladu or Mwana Kwerekwe, both just outside Stone Town (frequent daladalas to either from Darajani terminal). If you're staying overnight the bungalows can pick you up for $30 per vehicle each way. **Accommodation** is available at ⅔ *Menai Bay Beach Bungalows* (☏0747/411753, Ⓦwww .menaibaybungalows.com; half-board ❻), recommended not so much for its rooms (which are pretty basic but fine) but for the matchless location in a palm grove on the edge of a gorgeous west-facing beach. The rooms, two in each of five large bungalows, have bathrooms and verandahs for sunsets. Sunsets are also rather wonderful from the romantic **restaurant** nestled under a giant baobab tree – you can also eat at a table on the beach. A wide variety of half- and full-day **tours** are organized in conjunction with Stone Town's Eco+Culture Tours (see p.661) and – apart from the usual itineraries - include mangrove tours, boat trips, a visit to Uzi Island, and a **sailing and snorkelling excursion** to various uninhabited islands. If arranged through Eco+Culture Tours in Stone Town, the latter trip costs $60 per person in a couple and includes a seafood barbecue.

Fumba Peninsula

The northwestern side of Menai Bay is bounded by **Fumba Peninsula**, the tip of which lies barely 18km south of Stone Town. Surprisingly, given the beautiful beaches, tourism has largely passed it by, though a new upmarket **beach hotel** may be a sign of things to come. This is the *Fumba Beach Lodge* (☏0747/860504, Ⓦwww.fumbabeachlodge.com; half-board ❾), which boasts an impressive two kilometres of coastline containing three sandy coves. There are 26 rooms, so it's not as exclusive as the price (upwards of $340) would warrant, and the style is an odd blend of clean Scandinavian lines and Swahili style. All have sea views, and the suites have rooftop terraces. There's a cliff-top swimming pool, a bar built into an old dhow, and a branch of Kendwa's well-regarded Scuba Do **dive centre**.

Excursions are run through Adventure Afloat (☏0747/423162, Ⓦwww .safariblue.net if you want to arrange things yourself from Stone Town), whose speciality is an enjoyable day's sail from Fumba to Kwale Island, for dolphin-watching, mucking about on *ngalawa* outriggers, and lazing on or snorkelling around sandbanks, complete with a delicious seafood lunch. This costs $43 per person from Fumba, more if you start in Stone Town. To **get to Fumba**, the hotel charges $50 per minibus from Stone Town (one way). Daladalas aren't too frequent: ask at Darajani stand on Creek Road.

Makunduchi

Despite its proximity to Kizimkazi and Jambiani, the nebulous settlement of **MAKUNDUCHI** in the far southeast hardly receives any visitors, and its last hotel closed years ago. Most of Makunduchi's inhabitants survive on fishing and seaweed farming, colourful piles of which you'll find laid out to dry all over the place. The settlement is for the most part modern, with a few large blocks of Soviet-style flats. But despite the veneer of modernity, Makunduchi remains a very traditional sort of place, something best seen during the exhilarating **Mwaka Kogwa festival** in July (see the "Tanzania in celebration" colour section). The 69 kilometres from Stone Town are covered by #310 **daladalas** from the Darajani terminal throughout the day.

East Unguja

Unguja's **east coast** is a major tourist destination, its magnificent white sandy **beaches** lined for the most part with swaying coconut palm and casuarina trees. Despite the attention of sun-worshippers, the coast retains a much more local, isolated and meditative feel than the north and northeast coasts – Unguja's other big beach areas – and with the exception of a handful of expensive resorts at Dongwe on Michamvi Peninsula, tourist development remains low-key. There are no tall buildings, nor many walls to keep locals out, and in fact

Diving off Unguja's east coast

For an introduction to scuba-diving and snorkelling in Tanzania, see pp.61–63.

Unguja's east coast is fringed by a long barrier reef whose soft corals make any dive extremely photogenic. The shallow and sheltered coral gardens inside the lagoon offer ideal conditions for **novices**, whilst the deeper and exposed drop-offs outside the barrier attract more **experienced divers** (calm weather only). Visibility is best between November and January, when 40m is common; it can drop to around 10m from July to September. The best time for **dolphins** is from October to March, whilst humpback and sperm **whales** on their southward migration might be seen (or, more likely, just heard) in September and October.

As the name suggests, **Turtle Garden** is good for turtles; the barrel sponges so beloved of them also attract giant eels, whilst the sandy bottom is populated by guitar sharks, eagle rays and stingrays. For exquisite corals, **Unicorn (Jambiani) Reef** is hard to beat. Also recommended is the clear and calm **Stingray Alley**, where you may witness shoals containing literally hundreds of blue-spotted stingrays.

Dive centres

The following dive centre is PADI-accredited; check others out thoroughly before diving with them.

Rising Sun Dive Centre Breezes Beach Club, Dongwe ☎0747/415049, ⓦwww .risingsun-zanzibar.com. Highly experienced and knowledgeable, also about sites off south Unguja. They're well equipped and have solid safety standards (and small groups), and offer one of Zanzibar's most exhaustive Open Water courses, with four pool dives and six in the ocean when just four or five in all is the norm elsewhere. They teach up to Instructor level. For experienced divers, exploration dives to uncharted reefs are possible by prior arrangement, as are night dives and trips to Mnemba Atoll.

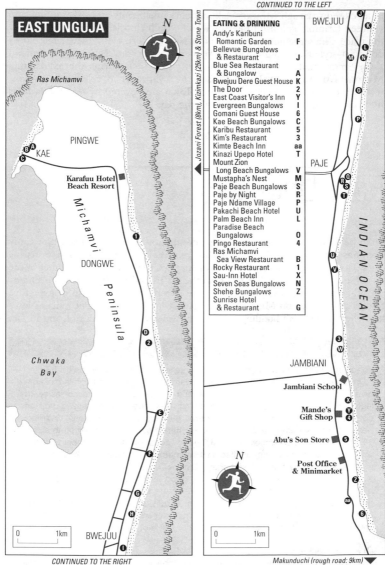

EAST UNGUJA

N

Ras Michamvi

PINGWE

A **B**
C KAE

Karafuu Hotel
Beach Resort

Michamvi

DONGWE

Peninsula

Chwaka
Bay

1

O
2

E

F

G

H

0   1km

BWEJUU

I

Jozani Forest (8km), Kizimkazi (25km) & Stone Town

EATING & DRINKING

Andy's Karibuni Romantic Garden	F
Bellevue Bungalows & Restaurant	J
Blue Sea Restaurant & Bungalow	A
Bwejuu Dere Guest House	K
The Door	2
East Coast Visitor's Inn	Y
Evergreen Bungalows	I
Gomani Guest House	6
Kae Beach Bungalows	C
Karibu Restaurant	5
Kim's Restaurant	3
Kimte Beach Inn	aa
Kinazi Upepo Hotel	T
Mount Zion Long Beach Bungalows	V
Mustapha's Nest	M
Paje Beach Bungalows	S
Paje by Night	R
Paje Ndame Village	P
Pakachi Beach Hotel	U
Palm Beach Inn	L
Paradise Beach Bungalows	O
Pingo Restaurant	4
Ras Michamvi Sea View Restaurant	B
Rocky Restaurant	1
Sau-Inn Hotel	X
Seven Seas Bungalows	N
Shehe Bungalows	Z
Sunrise Hotel & Restaurant	G

BWEJUU **J**
K
L
M **N**
O
P

PAJE

Q **R**
S
T

INDIAN OCEAN

U
V

3
W

JAMBIANI

Jambiani School

Mande's
Gift Shop **X**
Y **4**

Abu's Son Store **5**

Post Office
& Minimarket

Z

aa

6

0   1km

Makunduchi (rough road: 9km)

ACCOMMODATION

Andy's Karibuni Romantic Garden	F	Kae Beach Bungalows	C	Ras Michamvi Sea View Restaurant	B
Arabian Nights Hotel	Q	Kimte Beach Inn	aa	Robinson's Place	H
Bellevue Bungalows & Restaurant	J	Kinazi Upepo Hotel	T	Sau-Inn Hotel	X
Blue Oyster Hotel	W	Mount Zion Long Beach Bungalows	V	Seven Seas Bungalows	N
Blue Sea Restaurant & Bungalow	A	Mustapha's Nest	M	Shehe Bungalows	Z
Breezes Beach Club	E	Paje Beach Bungalows	S	Sunrise Hotel & Restaurant	G
Bwejuu Dere Guest House	K	Paje by Night	R		
East Coast Visitor's Inn	Y	Paje Ndame Village	P		
Evergreen Bungalows	I	Pakachi Beach Hotel	U		
Hotel Sultan Palace	D	Palm Beach Inn	L		
		Paradise Beach Bungalows	O		

in most places you'll be sharing the beach with women collecting seaweed, fishermen hunting for squid and octopus with spears, and children invariably delighted to kick a football around with you.

The main beaches are at Paje, Bwejuu and Jambiani, the most beautiful at **Paje** village, at the end of the asphalt road from Stone Town. Strung out a few kilometres to the north, **Bwejuu** has a wider choice of accommodation, and some seriously good restaurants. The longest of the beaches is at **Jambiani**, which starts 5km south of Paje and whose sands roll on for another 5km. Small affordable hotels are scattered all along. North of Bwejuu is a spread of large beach resorts at **Dongwe**, but for those who really want to get away from it all, **Kae**, at the top of the peninsula facing Chwaka Bay, has just three very modest guest houses.

The entire coast is protected by a fringing **coral reef**, so the calm conditions inside the shallow lagoon make for safe paddling for small children, and superb **snorkelling**, which can be arranged almost everywhere. At **low tide**, the ocean recedes for hundreds of metres. **Scuba-diving** is also memorable, both inside and – for more experienced divers – outside the barrier beef. Most hotels offer **excursions** similar to those run from Stone Town (see p.661): spice tours are more expensive ($25–35 per person), trips to Jozani Forest are cheaper, and dolphin safaris are pretty much the same. **Bicycles** can be rented at most hotels.

Paje

The friendly fishing village of **PAJE**, 51km east of Stone Town at the end of the asphalt road, is easy to reach by public transport. The village is a nondescript shamble of houses, but also one of the more tranquil and characterful places on the island, and its white sandy **beach** is gorgeous, backed by postcard-perfect swaying palms. In common with Jambiani, it's also refreshing to share the beach with locals, including some of Paje's five hundred female seaweed farmers, and fishermen cycling to work. The proximity of the village makes some holiday-makers feel awkward about donning swimming costumes, but the locals are a tolerant lot and, so long as you don't go topless or canoodle in public, there's no problem (off the beach, please do cover up – some hotels provide *kangas* or *kitenges* for this). At low tide, the sea can recede by up to a kilometre, so **swimming** is restricted to two six-hour periods each day.

Practicalities

Coming from Stone Town, either buy a seat on a "beach transfer" **minibus** (see p.658), or catch a #324 **daladala** for Bwejuu from Darajani terminal on Creek Road (Tsh1000). These leave roughly hourly between 9am and 2pm. **Leaving** Paje, the first daladala passes through around 6.30am, the last no later than 4.30pm.

Accommodation

Some of Paje's **hotels** are decidedly average, but with such a nice beach, frankly who cares. Most are clustered together at the south end of the village and the majority also offer massages, hair plaiting and henna tattoos. The following hotels are marked on the map on opposite; all include breakfast in their rates.

Arabian Nights Hotel On the beach at the south end of Paje ☎024/224 0190, ⓦwww .pajedivecentre.com/arabiannights. Two rooms in each of four very closely spaced modern bungalows, somewhat Scandinavian in style, with big floor-to-ceiling windows, bathtubs and verandahs, but little privacy given the cramped layout; $10 more gets you a sea view. The indoor restaurant is similarly functional, but overall it's fine for the price. Facilities include 24hr Internet access, snorkelling, water-skiing and use of kayaks. ❻

Kinazi Upepo Hotel On the beach at the south end of Paje ☎0748/655038, ⓦwww.kinaziupepo .com. Locally run, this has eight bungalows set in a coconut grove containing very ordinary rooms (some with round mosquito nets rather than square). Much better, albeit more basic (bed, net, and that's about it) are five cute coconut wood and *makuti* thatch *bandas* on stilts (shared bathrooms) which, unlike the bungalows, have good sea views. For triple rooms, add $10. There's also a characterful beach bar and good restaurant. ❹–❺

Paje Beach Bungalows On the beach at the south end of Paje ☎0747/461917 or 0747/497876, ⓦwww.pajebeachbungalows.com. Basic but adequate, this is a cluster of closely spaced modern bungalows plus an architecturally infelicitous two-storey house, all with steep thatched roofs. Twenty rooms in all, the better ones – for $10 more – with sea views. The restaurant/bar is on the beach, flanked by day beds and thatched parasols. ❺

🏃 **Paje by Night** Behind *Kitete Beach Bungalows* ☎0747/460710, ⓦwww.pajebynight .net. An excellent bar and sublime restaurant are the main attractions here, together with a friendly, funky and laid-back atmosphere and Italian-style hospitality – all of which makes it easy to ignore the lack of beach or sea views (the beach is 100m away). There are 24 simple but well-kept rooms in colourfully painted rows, some with a/c; rates depend on how big they are and whether there's hot water. There's also a couple of quirky two-floor "jungle bungalows" likely to pit parents against their kids about who's going to sleep upstairs; these also have rooftop terraces. Fishing trips with locals can be arranged. Closed May. ❺–❻

Paje Ndame Village On the beach 2km north of Paje village ☎0747/865501, ⓦwww.ndame.info. A small resort set back in a grove of coconut palms; its 24 rooms (not all with sea views) are small and not terribly inspiring, but they're comfortable enough. There's also a bar, gift shop, coconut rope loungers and parasols on the beach, a good Italian/Swahili seafood restaurant, and expensive snorkelling trips (Tsh10,000 per person including boat ride). ❺

🏃 **Paradise Beach Bungalows** On the beach 3.5km north of Paje village ☎024/223 1387 or 0747/414129, ⓦwww.geocities.jp /paradisebeachbungalows. A friendly, peaceful and likeable place snuggled into a grove of coconut palms, this is one of the east coast's nicest hotels if you can do without electricity, and is famed for exquisite and affordable food. Its ten Swahili-styled bedrooms, all en suite (seven with sea views) are large and comfortable, and there are three stand-alone cottages at the back with covered roof terraces. Facilities include a bar, a good library, cultural tours and dhow trips (Tsh5000), and courses in cooking and Kiswahili. Bicycles and snorkelling equipment available. ❹–❺

Eating and drinking

Most of Paje's **bars** and **restaurants** are in its hotels.

Kinazi Upepo Hotel On the beach at the south end of Paje. Right on the beach, this has an airy and friendly bar and restaurant (with hammocks and beach loungers too), open throughout the day for drinks and snacks, including fresh juices, smoothies, milkshakes, ice cream and real coffee. The lunchtime menu is the usual blend of Swahili, European and seafood; evenings meals vary, but always include seafood, something spicy, and a vegetarian option. Around Tsh5000.

Paje Beach Bungalows On the beach at the south end of Paje. Not the most rousing menu, and the lovely sea view is sadly through glass windows (to avoid monsoon winds), but prices are cheaper than most: fish or octopus (or burgers, for that matter) costing just Tsh3500, and prawns from Tsh4000. Alcohol is limited to beer.

🏃 **Paje by Night** Behind *Kitete Beach Bungalows*. Zanzibar's best bar, with good music, laid-back vibes and good company. Uniquely, it's also open 24 hours. The food (10am–10pm) is well up there too, and many of the ingredients are home-grown: the wood-fired pizzas (Tsh5000–6000) please even Italians, the lasagne is excellent, and where else could you sample home-made ravioli stuffed with fish and almonds? It's also very good value at Tsh7000 or under for most dishes, with a three-course Swahili dinner costing Tsh10,000–15,000. There's always a vegetarian option, and a good wine list.

Paje Ndame Village On the beach 2km north of Paje village. Reasonably priced Italian and Swahili dishes, including octopus and potato salad with basil and garlic (Tsh4500), pasta with crab sauce (Tsh6000), mixed fish grills (Tsh10,500) and grilled prawns with spinach (Tsh9000). Shoots itself in the foot with instant coffee.

Paradise Beach Bungalows On the beach 3.5km north of Paje village ☎024/223 1387 or 0747/414129. An unusual and successful mix of Swahili and Japanese cuisine, and excellent value at Tsh4000–5500 for a three-course lunch or dinner. The Japanese cuisine is especially recommended, whether classic sushi and sashimi (raw kingfish, squid and tuna; both Tsh12,000), or chicken teriyaki seasoned with ... Coca-Cola! (Tsh7000). There's also a small bar, and – for that extra thrill – a table in a tree house. Book ahead if you're not staying overnight.

Bwejuu

Five kilometres north of Paje is the even smaller village of **BWEJUU**. The beach north of here is highly rated, as you can tell from the string of bungalow hotels that back it. As at Paje, the tide heads out a long way, so there's no swimming at low tide unless you're up for a long hike across coral flats and tidal pools. There are, however, some excellent **snorkelling** spots within walking distance. Most hotels have **bicycles** for their guests, either free or for a nominal sum.

Practicalities

Bwejuu is covered by roughly hourly #324 **daladalas** from Stone Town's Darajani terminal on Creek Road, the first leaving at around 9am, the last at 2pm. The ride takes just over an hour, and costs Tsh1000. Beach transfer **minibuses** (see p.658) also go to Bwejuu. **Leaving** Bwejuu, the first daladala (coming from Kae) passes through at around 6am, and the last leaves Bwejuu at 4pm.

△ Bwejuu beach, East Unguja

Accommodation

There's a huge choice of **accommodation**, mostly small bungalow "resorts", and most are reasonably priced. Breakfast is usually included. Distances given below assume *Bwejuu Dere Guest House* to be the centre of the village. See map on p.678.

Andy's Karibuni Romantic Garden On the beach 3km north of the village ☎0748/430942, ⓦwww .eastzanzibar.com. Run by a charming Hungarian woman, this simple, laid-back place on a sandy beachside plot has seven bungalows (all with showers and Western-style toilets) sleeping two to seven people each. The food, cooked to order, is exquisite. Stay away if you don't like big dogs, even soppy and friendly ones. ❺

Bellevue Bungalows & Restaurant 500m north of the village ☎0747/465271, ⓦwww.geocities .com/bellevue_zan. A friendly, locally owned place on a hill on the land side of the road, with good views and the beach just a minute away. The four rooms in two bungalows come with private bathrooms, big heavy beds and nets. There's excellent food too (half-board is an extra $5 for two people), and activities including sailing trips by *ngalawa*. ❹

Bwejuu Dere Guest House Village centre ☎0747/434607. Four lacklustre but cheap guest houses in one, two of them (#1 and #2) on the beach. The small rooms are cleanish and share bathrooms, but only worth it if you're on a strict budget ($10 per person). ❸

Evergreen Bungalows On the beach 800m north of the village ☎024/224 0273 or 0748/408953, ⓦwww.evergreen-bungalows.com. The beach-front plot is the best thing here, though the seven recently renovated thatched bungalows (ten rooms) are good value, and there's also a cheaper but very basic first-floor *banda* with a verandah, accessed up very steep steps. They offer a wide variety of trips (run themselves), including mangrove boat tours. Food available. ❹–❺

Mustapha's Nest 700m south of the village on the west side of the road ☎024/224 0069, ⓦwww .fatflatfish.co.uk/mustaphas. A long-established and very welcoming place run by local Rasta Mustapha and his family. Accommodation is in several coral-walled thatched-roof *bandas* set in beautiful gardens, and the bar is as good a place as any to learn African drumming. ❹

Palm Beach Inn On the beach 200m south of the village ☎024/224 0221 or 0747/411155, ⓔmahfudh28@hotmail.com. An intimate clutter

of buildings beside the beach, well run and with good service, but rather pricey. Rooms have a/c, fridge, hot showers and *semadari* beds, and there's a large bar, painfully expensive restaurant, and inexpensive excursions. ❻

Robinson's Place On the beach 1.3km north of the village ☎0747/413479 or 0748/595572, ⓦwww.robinsonsplace.net. A small, whimsical and highly recommended place run by a Zanzibari-European couple, where the lack of electricity is billed as an attraction (lighting is by kerosene lamps). There are only five rooms (so book well ahead), all equally eclectic in design, though the best is at the top of a two-storey Robinson Crusoe-style house by the beach. There's also the "main house" at the back, with a huge en-suite room decorated with lots of trinkets. Other rooms share bathrooms. Meals, drinks and siestas are taken in a cool beach "banda", a circular architectural take on the traditional Swahili coffee *barazas* (the benches that line buildings) complete with stained cement and soft, adobe-like forms. Meals are limited to a sumptuous breakfast and dinner (guests only; around Tsh7000). ❺

Seven Seas Bungalows On the beach 600m south of the village ☎0747/481767. A peaceful, cheap and very friendly Tanzanian-run place on a lovely scrubby beach (a refreshing change from the water-guzzling lawns common elsewhere), with just seven rooms in four bungalows, each with fan, Western-style toilet and shower. There's also a good restaurant and friendly bar. ❸

Sunrise Hotel & Restaurant On the beach 2km north of the village ☎024/224 0170, ⓦwww .sunrise-zanzibar.com. A cheerfully offbeat choice run by a charming Belgian, with a friendly, unfussy atmosphere, recommended restaurant, swimming pool (with sun loungers), and even a dovecote. The en-suite "garden" rooms at the back are dark and not particularly good value; for an extra $15, much better to get a room in one of the thatched, beach-facing bungalows (two rooms in each), for more privacy and sea views. The usual range of tours can be arranged, and Internet access is available. ❻

Eating and drinking

Most of Bwejuu's **restaurants** are attached to hotels, and some are outstandingly good.

Andy's Karibuni Romantic Garden On the beach 3km north of the village. Superb Hungarian cooking plus Zanzibari delights in a laid-back venue. The speciality is *lecso*, a Hungarian stew with onion, tomato, chili, garlic and spices. Full meals around Tsh5000.

Bellevue Bungalows & Restaurant 500m north of the village. Another good place for home cooking, with good seafood (full meals around Tsh5000, including succulent fish and crab) and freshly roasted coffee (natural, spiced or laced with ginger). Meals take up to two hours to arrive.

Bwejuu Dere Guest House Village centre. Fairly average but cheap restaurant (fish Tsh3500, prawns Tsh6000), plus a more attractive beer garden behind the main building with mainland favourites like grilled goat meat (*nyama choma*) with bananas (*ndizi*). Closed Ramadan.

Evergreen Bungalows On the beach 800m north of the village. Eat by the beach, or take a drink on a swing. Has a broad menu; lunches cost around Tsh5000, whilst something more substantial for dinner, for example grilled tuna with tamarind sauce or garlic prawns, averages Tsh6500–8500.

Mustapha's Nest 700m south of the village on the west side of the road. A great option for drinks or meals, with lunch (Tsh3000) and candlelit dinners (Tsh4000) featuring fresh seafood (fabulous octopus). Mellow jam sessions some nights.

Palm Beach Inn On the beach 200m south of the village. Overpriced for standard dishes (for example fish at Tsh8000), but worth trying for its less common offerings, such as fried gazelle (Tsh10,000) or whole fried duck (Tsh18,000). Also has a friendly bar, and you may catch traditional dancers in the evening.

Seven Seas Bungalows On the beach 600m south of the village. This is Bwejuu's main local bar, a pleasantly cheerful sort of place. There's good simple food (Tsh3500–4000; full meals around Tsh8000), and snacks, too.

Sunrise Hotel & Restaurant On the beach 2km north of the village. Quirky surroundings to suit an attractively quirky menu, covering seafood plus unusual treats like gazpacho, puffed crab pancakes and fish soup with rouille and croutons, plus – make room – superb desserts such as fried banana in pancake with melted chocolate, and an acclaimed Belgian chocolate mousse (the owner being Belgian, it's a matter of national pride). There are also good vegetarian options, such as okra with black mustard seeds, coriander, cumin and tomato. Prices are reasonable, with most mains courses costing Tsh7000–9000, and there's a good choice of cocktails and South African wines.

Dongwe

As you head up Michamvi Peninsula north of Bwejuu, the last of the bungalows give way to **Dongwe**. Sparsely populated, dusty and rather dull when seen from land, the beautiful sandy beaches that lie hidden behind the walls and thickets have attracted an ever-increasing number of wilfully expensive **beach hotels**, most of them dealing mainly with pre-booked package tours. If you have the money, and are happy foregoing local authenticity for pampered service and mod cons, they may be worth considering, though none are anything like intimate, and are poor value compared to similarly priced places elsewhere. As at Bwejuu, the ocean recedes into the far distance at low tide; the sheltered lagoon is fine for children.

Practicalities

The only daladala that runs along the peninsula leaves Kae, at its northern tip, early in the morning, and returns in the afternoon. So, without a car, the only practical way of getting around is by **bicycle**: most hotels in Bwejuu, Paje and Jambiani can fix you up.

Accommodation

The following are marked on the map on p.678.

Breezes Beach Club ☏0747/415049, ⓦwww .breezes-zanzibar.com. A large and somewhat

impersonal beach resort behind a forbidding wall, whose hidden extras (including water sports and sea views) can come as a nasty surprise. Still, the seventy rooms – in bland two-storey blocks – have all mod cons, and there are tons of amenities and a great beach. Half-board. **❽–❾**

Hotel Sultan Palace ☎024/224 0173, ⓦwww.sultanzanzibar.com. Overlooking a narrow beach, this is small for a "palace", but standards of service and its architecture are

suitably sultanic, and the fifteen idiosyncratically designed rooms are spacious and have everything you'd expect for the price (though only eight have sea views). Meals – mainly Swahili and Mediterranean – can be taken on the beach or one of the secluded terraces in the main building. Closed April & May. Full-board. **❾**

Eating and drinking

There are a couple of great **restaurants** in Dongwe that make it well worth the trip. For upmarket dining, try the hotels.

The Door Just south of *Hotel Sultan Palace*, Dongwe ☎0747/414962 or 0748/374930, ⓔthedoor_zanzibar@hotmail.com. Named after the channel in the barrier reef opposite, this is a classy but informal clifftop restaurant run by a Swahili-Italian couple, whose excellent cooking is both sophisticated and affordable. The menu – which changes daily (there's always a vegetarian option) – is a blend of Italian classics punctuated by inventive Swahili-inspired touches such as spiced sauces or lemongrass tea. Grilled fish of the day is a bargain at Tsh6000, as is the grilled lobster in ginger and garlic (Tsh12,000). Apart from food, there's also a beach down a long and particularly steep flight of steps, and good snorkelling within swimming distance: locals rent masks and snorkels

for Tsh3000, and can fix you up with a *ngalawa* outrigger for around Tsh15,000 per boat for two or three hours. Open lunchtimes until 4pm; dinner by reservation only.

Rocky Restaurant Kijiweni Beach, 2km south of *Karafuu Hotel Beach Resort*, Dongwe ☎0747/435191. Sitting on a small, breezy coral outcrop 3m above sea level (at high tide you wade out to it), this has one of the nicest locations in Tanzania, and is well priced. They have a small but enticing menu (order a few hours ahead): rice with grilled fish, squid or octopus (all extremely fresh; Tsh4000). For prawns or lobster, it's best to order the day before. No guarantee of alcohol. Order at least two hours in advance. Closed Ramadan lunchtimes.

△ Fish market

Kae

The road at the top of Michamvi Peninsula becomes diabolically rocky as it heads 2km west towards the village of **Pingwe**, the entrance to which is marked by a grove of coconut palms. There's nothing to see there, and the handful (literally) of tourists who come here generally continue on to the beach at the tiny fishermen's settlement of **KAE**, 1km further on, 13km beyond Bwejuu. As long as your idea of a perfect beach isn't of the sanitized, seaweed-cleaned, cocktail-on-a-sunbed-and-disco-in-the-evening variety, this is, well, the perfect **beach**: powdery white sand, leaning coconut palms, beautiful shades of blue, turquoise and green in the water, scuttling ghost crabs, irregular grids of staves for collecting seaweed, dozens of wooden *ngalawa* outriggers moored offshore, hardly any other beach-goers, nor *papasi* trying to sell their grandmas, and – for now – silence. Of course, it's probably only a matter of time before the developers move in and trash the magic by prettifying the place with lawns, tall walls and higher prices, so enjoy it while you can.

Practicalities

Public transport is limited to one daladala a day. It leaves Kae at 5am, and heads back from Stone Town's Darajani terminal on Creek Road at 3.45pm. Confusingly, the vehicle is marked "Bwejuu" (#324), so in Stone Town ask for the one for Pingwe. The ride costs Tsh1000 and takes two to three hours. Given the timing, the daladala is useless for day-trips, so if you're coming from Bwejuu, Paje or Jambiani, rent a bicycle. Incidentally, the **ferry** from Kae to Chwaka that's still marked on some maps has never existed, though you may find octopus fishermen willing to take you at high tide, when they set off for Chwaka's fish market. There are no fixed prices for the thirty-minute crossing – Tsh4000 per person would be very good going. There are just three **guest houses**:

Blue Sea Restaurant & Bungalow 200m north of *Kae Beach Bungalows* ☎ 0747/464398. Two single-room bungalows and one double, set back from the beach in a palm grove with no direct sea views. **⑤**

Kae Beach Bungalows At the end of the road beside the beach ☎ 0747/475299 or 0747/487723, ⓦ www.kaebeachbungalows.com. In a beautiful location, this has just three en-suite bungalows, not really with views as they're side-on, and whilst basic, they're airy and perfectly comfortable, and also come with a day bed and solar-powered lights (there are also day beds on the beach). The restaurant, which does have views, takes two hours to deliver, and you should pre-order for coolish beers and sodas. Rice with fish or Kae's speciality, octopus, costs Tsh5000. With a bit of patience, they can arrange various boat trips, including cruises around mangroves, or snorkelling (Tsh30,000 per *ngalawa* for a few hours, plus Tsh3000 per person for snorkelling equipment). Breakfast included **④**

Ras Michamvi Sea View Restaurant 150m north of *Kae Beach Bungalows* (no phone). The beach here is a total heart-stopper, with sand so soft you could rub a baby's bottom with it. There are just three rooms around a courtyard in the manner of mainland guest houses – all pretty basic, the rooms with twin beds, box nets, modern bathrooms and nothing much else. Breakfast included, and meals available (count on at least an hour). **⑤**

Jambiani

The long stretch of beach at **JAMBIANI**, 9km south of Paje, possesses a wild, windy and fascinating beauty. The fringing reef lies several kilometres out, and the intervening area is a mix of sandbanks, coral reefs and shallow water, which at low tide can turn up a surprising variety of marine life. The people of Jambiani have long been involved in **fishing**, and at times dozens of *ngalawa* fishing boats are moored together just offshore, while in the evenings there's the joyous spectacle of young boys racing after their handmade model dhows, painstakingly made from sandals or bits of wood with plastic bags for sails. It's the community feeling of Jambiani that makes it special, something worth exploring further through the highly recommended **local cultural tourism programme**, which offers visits to traditional herbalists, seaweed farms and a sacred local cave.

Practicalities

The tourist "beach transfer" **minibuses** take about ninety minutes to cover the 56km from Stone Town, and shouldn't charge more than Tsh4000. **Daladalas** – #309 from Stone Town – are infrequent and unpredictable; enquire the day before at Darajani terminal on Creek Road. The daladalas take two to three hours, and leave no later than 3pm. **Returning** to Stone Town, the first heads off at 6am and the last at 3pm.

The post office and minimarket (daily 6am–10pm) on the main road opposite *Karibu Restaurant* rents out **bicycles**, as does *Abu's Son Store*, also on the main road. There's no official **money-changing** facility, so get this sorted in Stone Town before arriving. **Internet access** is possible at the *East Coast Visitor's Inn*.

When choosing a room, note that **hotels** on the northern part of the beach are pretty isolated from most of the bars and restaurants. All the following are shown on the map on p.678; distances given below refer to the distance from Jambiani School. **Breakfast** is included unless otherwise noted.

Accommodation

Blue Oyster Hotel 800m north ☏ 024/224 0163, ⊛ www.zanzibar.de. An architecturally clumsy two-storey affair, but good value, with friendly service and ten clean rooms, five en suite (the others are considerably cheaper). They can also arrange excursions, and there's a restaurant and bar on the ocean-facing terrace. ❹–❺

East Coast Visitor's Inn 900m south ☏ 024/224 0150, ⊛ www.visitorsinn-zanzibar .com. An affordable, functional set-up with fifteen en-suite bungalows around a parking area, most with sea views, and ten en-suite rooms in a guest house set back from the beach. The rooms are well kept and there's a large open-sided restaurant and bar offering reasonable if unexciting food, Internet access and various activities. Rooms ❹, bungalows ❺.

Kimte Beach Inn 3.2km south ☏ 0747/430992 or 024/224 0212, ⊜ kimte@lycos.com. Rasta-run place with Zanzibar's best beach bar, seven en-suite rooms, a dormitory ($10 per person), and a basic but fun *banda* raised on tall stilts beside the bar. Dhow trips with snorkelling can be arranged (from $7 per person). ❹

Mount Zion Long Beach Bungalows 3.8km north, halfway between Jambiani and Paje ☏ 0747/439034 or 0747/439001, ⊛ www .mountzion-zanzibar.com. Another friendly Rasta place, with four good, simple cottages (eight rooms) on top of a grassy headland with partial sea views, and – a real distinction – uniquely designed thatched *bandas* on the gorgeous beach below (beds, nets and electric light; shared bathrooms) in the form of two pyramids, one on top of the other – very cool. As might be expected, the bar's good too, as is the food, and the whole atmosphere is imbued with a very relaxing vibe. ❺

Pakachi Beach Hotel 4km north, just north of the *Mount Zion* ☏ 024/224 0001 or 0747/423331, ⊛ www.pakachi.com. Three rooms and a large family house ($100) on the land side of the road, all en suite and with *semadari* beds. There's a bar and restaurant on a low headland on the other side of the road beside the beach. Run by young Rastafarians, the reggae-fuelled atmosphere is suitably laid-back. They also have fishing equipment, canoes, and an *ngalawa* for snorkelling ($10 per person including equipment). ❺

Sau-Inn Hotel 600m south ☏ 024/224 0205 or 0747/457782, ⊛ www.sauinn.net. This medium-sized resort is the only place with a swimming pool (Tsh5000 for day guests), and also the only place where you're likely to get bothered by *papasi* (beach boys). The forty rooms in thatched cottages have a/c, satellite TV and spotless bathrooms, and most overlook the pool. Facilities include a bar and restaurant, and Internet access. **6**

Shehe Bungalows 2.8km south ☎024/223 3949 or 0747/418386, ✉shehebungalows@hotmail .com. This place has a great view from its first-

floor bar and restaurant, and the rooms, in a row of cottages facing the ocean on both sides of the main building, are fine and have bathrooms. Breakfast not included. **4**

Eating and drinking

There are a lot of **restaurants** to choose from, and not just in the hotels, so prices are keen by Zanzibari standards. The following are marked on the map on p.678; distances are from Jambiani School.

East Coast Visitor's Inn 900m south. Reasonable value if you choose carefully, with some mouthwatering dishes like banana fritters, marinated prawns in coconut sauce and a large number of crab and jumbo prawn dishes for Tsh5000–6000. They also do milkshakes.

Gomani Guest House 3.5km south, by the mobile phone mast. A good range of cheap and filling dishes, with fish of the day for Tsh2500 and grilled lobster in lemon butter for Tsh8000. There's a great view of the ocean from the headland. Order an hour in advance. No alcohol.

Karibu Restaurant 1.9km south ☎024/223 3545. Everything here is literally home-cooked, as the restaurant is in a family home. The food – all local Swahili dishes – is good as well as cheap: drop by a good few hours before to discuss what you'd like to eat.

Kim's Restaurant 1km north, near *Blue Oyster Hotel*. One of a growing number of

locally run places, this one decorated with shells and with particularly good – and cheap – food, from snacks and starters (fish cakes, succulent fried octopus, garlic soup; all Tsh1000–2000) to the classic coconut-crusted fish with mango chutney, or baby octopus grilled with ginger and chilli (both Tsh3500).

Kimte Beach Inn 3.2km south. Zanzibar's most chilled-out beach bar (Rastafarians know a thing or two about this), very well stocked including single malts and cocktails, and with excellent music – from reggae and The Doors to danceable club sounds, plus evening campfires and even swings at the bar. Meals are well priced at around Tsh4500–5500, with pizzas a little cheaper.

Mount Zion Long Beach Bungalows 3.8km north. Romantic candlelit dinners, nice music, the sound of the waves ... The food's not half bad either, particularly anything fishy. There are vegetarian options too, and they'll jump through hoops to please. Well priced at around Tsh5000.

△ Fishermen coming into port

Jambiani Cultural Village Tour

Zanzibar's first community-run tourism programme, the **Jambiani Cultural Village Tour**, offers a highly recommended half-day diversion for exploring aspects of local life and culture. Part of the $10 fee goes into a village development fund to finance primary healthcare, a children's nursery and various educational projects.

The **tour** guide fills you in on Jambiani's history before taking you round a subsistence farm; to a *mganga* (herbalist) to learn the medicinal uses of various herbs and plants; and on to a seaweed farm. There's also the option – arrange this in advance – of visiting a sacred limestone cave, which may have been used to hide slaves after abolition in the late 1800s. The project's **office** is at Mande's Gift Shop (℡0747/469118; open most days, no fixed times) on the main road. They also offer a selection of other tours across Unguja, and the shop stocks a small selection of curios, including spices and essential oils. For further information and reservations for day-trips from Stone Town, contact Eco+Culture Tours (see p.661).

Pakachi Beach Hotel 4km north, halfway between Jambiani and Paje. Mellow Rasta place on a low headland by the beach, good music and a wide choice of food, including pizzas and pasta (Tsh4500–5500). Weekend evenings feature a Swahili three-course buffet for $15.
Pingo Restaurant 700m south, just off the beach. Simple, open-sided bar and restaurant with a choice of snacks and tasty seafood (around Tsh3000). Leisurely service but generous portions.

Sau-Inn Hotel 600m south. A breezy restaurant and bar with a sea view and a choice of seafood, European or Zanzibari, ranging from Tsh4000–5000, and there are occasional "Swahili Night" buffets for Tsh8000.
Shehe Bungalows 2.8km south. The first-floor open-front bar enjoys a fantastic view over the beach and lagoon. The limited choice of dishes should be ordered well in advance, and range from average to excellent depending on who's cooking.

Northeast Unguja

As you approach Unguja's **northeast** coast, the vegetation becomes scrubbier, with coconut palms, baobabs and thorny thickets replacing the lush spice plantations of the interior, before giving way to a broad swath of fine white sand backed by a line of waving palm trees. Much of the coast retains an attractively isolated feel, in spite of the road connecting it with Stone Town, and – with the exception of Kiwengwa, which is blighted by all-inclusive package holiday resorts – receives few tourists.

The main **beaches**, from south to north, are Uroa, Pongwe, Kiwengwa, Pwani Mchangani and Matemwe; the sprawling expanse of sand at Matemwe and the coves at Pongwe are especially beautiful. All can be adorned by pungent **seaweed** between December and February. A host of **activities** is offered by most of the larger hotels, including reef walks, sailing and water sports, while **snorkelling** gear can be rented locally. **Scuba-divers** will find their nirvana, especially off Mnemba Atoll, though you'll need a measure of luck regarding sea conditions and seasons.

Daladalas serve all these places, but for getting around there's nothing better than hiring a bicycle and heading off along the beach, which serves as a highway for locals.

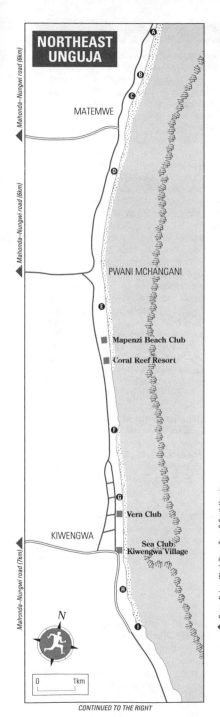

NORTHEAST UNGUJA

MATEMWE

PWANI MCHANGANI

■ Mapenzi Beach Club

■ Coral Reef Resort

KIWENGWA

■ Vera Club

Sea Club
■ Kiwengwa Village

Mahonda–Nungwi road (6km)

Mahonda–Nungwi road (6km)

Mahonda–Nungwi road (7km)

0 — 1km

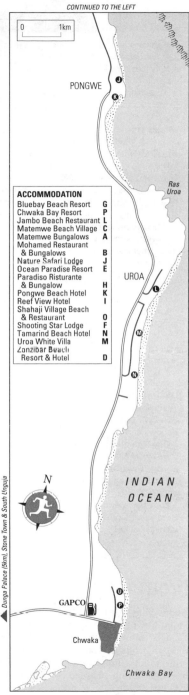

0 — 1km

PONGWE

Ras
Uroa

ACCOMMODATION

Bluebay Beach Resort	G
Chwaka Bay Resort	P
Jambo Beach Restaurant	L
Matemwe Beach Village	C
Matemwe Bungalows	A
Mohamed Restaurant & Bungalows	B
Nature Safari Lodge	J
Ocean Paradise Resort	E
Paradiso Risturante & Bungalow	H
Pongwe Beach Hotel	K
Reef View Hotel	I
Shahaji Village Beach & Restaurant	O
Shooting Star Lodge	F
Tamarind Beach Hotel	N
Uroa White Villa	M
Zanzibar Beach Resort & Hotel	D

UROA

INDIAN
OCEAN

Dunga Palace (5km), Stone Town & South Unguja

GAPCO

Chwaka

Chwaka Bay

11

ZANZIBAR | Northeast Unguja

689

Diving off Unguja's northeast coast

For an introduction to scuba-diving and snorkelling in Tanzania, see pp.61–63.

At the heart of northern Zanzibar's dive scene is **Mnemba Atoll**, a broad, shallow reef enclosing Mnemba Island. Sometimes dismissed for its modest underwater visibility (20m on average, dropping to 10m or less in July and August), the atoll is nonetheless a divers' paradise, both on account of the variety of **corals** and associated fish life, and for reasonable odds on sighting turtles, dolphins and other big species. There's also a slim but ever-tantalizing possibility of seeing or hearing **whales** between September and October. The barrier reef further north is described on p.694. **Visibility** is best in January but sea conditions are calmest in late October and November, when you're less likely to have problems with swells.

The wide depth range of **Kichwani Reef**, on the south side of the atoll, suits all levels of divers and snorkellers. Dolphins are often seen from the boat, attracted by the huge diversity and abundance of fish. Running west from Kichwani, **Aquarium Reef** has a wide range of corals, both soft and hard, inhabited by all sorts of colourful species, whilst sponges attract turtles, the whole lot arousing the appetite of white- and black-tipped reef sharks. The reef is suitable for novices. Also on the south side and suitable for novices is **Wattabomi Reef**, dominated by brain and plate corals. It's a great place for chancing upon green turtles; other biggies that may put in an appearance include peppered moray eels, dolphins and, most likely, blue-spotted ribbontail rays. The lovely **Coral Garden** in the west is one of the best dives for corals, with a wide and beautiful variety, including large fans. Given its wide depth amplitude, there's plenty of variety in fish life too, from octopus and eels to swarms of reef fish, rays, turtles and, lower down, circling barracuda and occasional black-tipped reef sharks. For advanced divers (in perfect conditions only), **The Big Wall** on the atoll's eastern side is a deep, near-vertical coral face pitted with small caves: an incredible drift dive with plenty of game fish (rays, tuna) and, frequently enough, reef sharks, though reported sightings of gigantic whale sharks are as rare as the animals are extraordinary – the best odds are in September or October.

Dive centres

The following are recommended PADI-accredited **dive centres** in Matemwe. Rising Sun Dive Centre in Bwejuu (see p.677) also covers Mnemba, as do all outfits in Kendwa and Nungwi on the north coast; see p.694.

One Ocean (The Zanzibar Dive Centre) *Matemwe Beach Village*, Matemwe ☏0747/417250; *Bluebay Beach Resort*, Kiwengwa ☏024/224 0241; *Ocean Paradise Resort*, Pwani Mchangani ☏0747/439990; ⓦwww.zanzibaroneocean.com. Highly experienced and knowledgeable, with centres throughout Unguja – read the review on p.663.

Zanzibar Beach Hotel & Resort Matemwe ☏0747/417782, ⓦwww.zanzibar-beachresort.com. Costly but experienced and strong on safety, offering thorough training for PADI courses up to Dive Master (training dives are done in the hotel's pool).

Uroa

About 9km north of the small fishing town of Chwaka, itself 32km east of Stone Town, is the spread-out village of **UROA**. The welcoming cries of "Jambo" from excited toddlers are more appealing than the village itself, but the beach, albeit bleak and windswept at times, is certainly refreshing. Despite some modest hotel developments, life for the villagers continues as it always has, with fishing, seaweed collection and some cultivation comprising the main livelihoods.

Getting to Uroa, catch one of the hourly #214 **daladalas** from Mwembe Ladu, 2km east of Stone Town (there are frequent daladalas to there from the Darajani/Creek Road terminal); the last leaves around 6pm. Several **hotels** – all with restaurants – are spread along the coastline; see the map on p.689.

 Jambo Beach Restaurant 500m north of Uroa village ☎0747/460446. A really friendly, locally run place on a lovely stretch of beach, with seven basic but beautiful twin-bed *bandas* with sandy floors made from natural materials like banana thatch and coir rope, plus one en-suite bungalow. There's also a good beach restaurant (most meals around Tsh4500, pasta is cheaper at Tsh3000), snorkelling equipment is available (Tsh2000; not fins), and sailing trips can be arranged (Tsh15,000–20,000 per *ngalawa* outrigger). Breakfast included. ❹

Tamarind Beach Hotel 1.5km south of Uroa village ☎0747/411191 or 024/223 7154, ⓦwww .tamarind.nu. An informal and good-value if slightly

tatty resort-style hotel, with fourteen clean rooms (all with private bathroom) in attractive stone cottages, each with a small roof terrace. The gardens adjoin the beach, and there's a breezy bar and restaurant. Snorkelling and boat trips available. Breakfast included. ❺

Uroa White Villa In the centre close to Uroa Primary Health Care Unit; follow the signs ☎0741/326874, ⓦwww.uroawhitevilla.net. A modern, German-run place on the beach with comfortable, spotless accommodation (mostly en suite). The restaurant does good Swahili dishes (mains Tsh4500–7000) – the *pilau* with fresh tuna is especially tasty. Boat trips and snorkelling are available, and there are discounts on rooms if booked ahead. ❻

Pongwe

There's nothing much to the tiny fishing village of **PONGWE**, six kilometres north of Uroa, but its handful of small sandy coves with unbelievably clear water and lots of swaying palm trees are the stuff of dreams.

Getting here by **daladala** (#209 from Mwembe Ladu just east of Stone Town) can be awkward, as it doesn't run every day, so enquire the day before. Don't confuse Pongwe with Mwera Pongwe (#225 daladalas), which is a different place entirely. If it is running, the #209 leaves Stone Town at 7am, and turns back in Pongwe at 10am, unfortunately ruling out the possibility of a day-trip. There are two **hotels**. Both use generator power for electricity, which is switched off at night, so rooms can get rather hot when ceiling fans are still.

Nature Safari Lodge ☎0747/415613 or 0747/419070, ⓦwww.pongwevillage.com. On a low shady cliff beside a small sandy cove, the beach here lacks palm trees but is still gorgeous. Rooms, slightly dilapidated, are in two rows of four bungalows. The three at the front are used by staff, so there's only one with a sea view ("Pongwe III", with three beds). There's a cheap bar and plain restaurant with an entirely African menu (order 2–3hr before), including vegetarian options. Canoe rental costs Tsh10,000 per day (for two people). Free transport from Stone Town if prebooked. Breakfast included. ❺

 Pongwe Beach Hotel 100m south of *Nature Safari Lodge* ☎0748/336181,

ⓦwww.pongwe.com. The tight security here comes as an unpleasant shock but if you can live with that, the beach really does just blow every-thing else away. Scattered around the mature gardens are thirteen spacious rooms in thatched bungalows, with carved wooden doors and *semadari* beds, but where the place comes into its own is its exquisite seafood restaurant (Tsh15,000–20,000 for three courses). There's also a bar, pleasant lounge area, and various pricey tours and activities including snor-kelling (from $15 per person), which should be arranged the day before. Book ahead. Breakfast included. ❼

Kiwengwa and Pwani Mchangani

As Zanzibar's main package holiday resort, **KIWENGWA** is dominated by enormous all-inclusive resorts catering almost entirely to the Italian package tour market, though there are thankfully a few places more in tune with local life, and these are reviewed below.

Kiwengwa is actually rather difficult to pin down, seeing as it sprawls along almost 10km of coastline. The package hotel strip hotels fizzles out a couple of kilometres south of **PWANI MCHANGANI**. Still very much a traditional fishing village, it has so far managed to avoid selling its soul – and shoreline – to the developers, surviving instead on fishing, coconut cultivation and the farming of seaweed, which you'll see hung out to dry everywhere. The village receives few visitors, though Italians have left their mark in the way local kids greet you: the habitual "Jambo!" has become "Jao!", their way of saying "Ciao!"

Practicalities

Kiwengwa is 40km northeast of Stone Town along a good surfaced road. Route #117 **daladalas** finish at Kiwengwa village. Others go to Pwani Mchangani, the last 8km being unsurfaced. Both start at "Nungwi stand" in Stone Town, being the west side of Creek Road just north of the Central Market. The ones to Kiwengwa run every ten minutes or so throughout the day, but those to Pwani Mchangani are infrequent, so find out about them the day before. At Kiwengwa, the daladalas stay on the asphalt, so if you're heading to *Bluebay Beach Resort* or *Shooting Star Lodge*, try and get the daladala driver to drop you there – an extra Tsh2000 or so should suffice; if not, you face a long, dusty and very hot walk. If you're **driving from Pongwe**, note that the unsurfaced road to Kiwengwa is extremely rocky in places and may require 4WD in some sections.

Bluebay Beach Resort 2km north of Kiwengwa ⓣ024/224 0241, ⓦ www.bluebayzanzibar.com. Similar in size to the brash all-inclusives on either side, this slick five-star resort has made some efforts to minimize its environmental impact. There's a fine stretch of beach, a nice swimming pool, and a wide range of activities on offer, while accommodation is in 88 luxurious rooms. Perhaps inevitably with a place this size, service – and indeed food – can be variable. Water sports and diving are offered by One Ocean (see p.690). Day visitors are admitted on condition of buying lunch. Rates include windsurfing, tennis and fitness centre. Half-board. ❽–❾

Ocean Paradise Resort 2km south of Pwani Mchangani ⓣ0747/439990, ⓦ www .oceanparadisezanzibar.com. Newest and best of the big five-star beach resorts on this part of the coast, this is very stylish and makes good use of local materials in both its rooms and common areas. Facilities include Zanzibar's largest swimming pool, tons of water sports including scuba-diving, a fitness centre and tennis courts, ocean-view restaurant, various bars and disco. Half-board. ❾

Paradiso Risturante & Bungalow Behind the school in Kiwengwa village (no sign) ⓣ0747/415351, ⓔ alimcheni@hotmail.com. Two very good-value bungalows with two rooms in each, all en-suite doubles, on a scrubby patch of land next to a beach lined with coconut palms.

There are also two huge houses for monthly rental (from $500), each with two bedrooms. *Ngalawa* trips ($10 per boat including snorkelling equipment) are available, and food and drinks can be arranged (usually Tsh4000 for a plate of fish; prawns Tsh8000). Breakfast included. ❹

Reef View Hotel 1.5km south of Kiwengwa at Kumba Urembo ⓣ0747/413294. The southernmost of Kiwengwa's hotels, somewhat seedy these days but still good value for its five thatched *bandas* with shared bathrooms, and one two-room bungalow, all with sea views through strange *mikadi* palm trees. Facilities include a pleasant bar and a good restaurant. Breakfast included. ❹–❺

🏃 **Shooting Star Lodge** 4km north of Kiwengwa ⓣ0747/414166, ⓦ www .zanzibar.org/star. Occupying a cliff top with wonderful sea views (the beach is accessed down a steep flight of steps), this is Kiwengwa's most romantic, intimate and effortlessly stylish option, and benefits from a small but lovely "infinity" pool (it has no raised edge, so the horizon just goes on and on), the absence of nearby resorts to spoil views or the silence, and one of Zanzibar's best restaurants (Tsh15,000–20,000 for three courses). All fifteen rooms are attractively furnished, though at this price, invest in a cottage with private sea-view verandah rather than a "garden lodge" room. Day guests can use the pool if they buy lunch. Activities are run through *Bluebay Beach Resort*. Closed from mid-April to mid-June. Half-board. ❽

Matemwe

The beautiful palm-fringed beach either side of the fishing village of **MATEMWE**, 5km north of Pwani Mchangani, is the last of the northeast coast resorts, and one of the more intimate. **Swimming** at low tide is impossible unless you fancy a very long hike, but no matter – the walks across the lagoon to the barrier reef a kilometre offshore are part of the attraction. The hotels have kayaks and can organize sailing trips, though it's cheaper to arrange things yourself with locals. The main reason for coming here is for the superb **diving and snorkelling**, both in the lagoon and around Mnemba Atoll; see below.

Practicalities

Matemwe lies 50km from Stone Town, with #118 **daladalas** running throughout the day from Stone Town's "Nungwi stand" on Creek Road, just north of the Central Market. The road is all asphalt, and ends at the shore. The rough and sandy road from Pwani Mchangani, 5km to the south, can be slow going, and there's no public transport along this stretch.

There are only a handful of **hotels** at present, though the latest – the large *Zanzibar Beach Resort & Hotel* – may be indicative of further large-scale development. Book ahead for *Matemwe Beach Village* or *Matemwe Bungalows*, both of which fill up quickly in season.

Matemwe Beach Village 1km north of the village ☏024/223 8374 or 0747/417250, ⓦwww .matemwebeach.com. Located amid palm trees on a large beachside plot, this welcoming place is considerably cheaper than the rest but could still do with a bit of work (a lot's been done already), as its seventeen spacious *makuti*-thatched bungalows (few if any with sea views) are rather basic and spoiled by an insidious smell of mould. There's a cosy bar and good restaurant, and water sports and diving are offered by One Ocean (see p.690). No swimming pool. Free transfers from Stone Town. Half-board. ❼–❽
Matemwe Bungalows 3.5km north of the village ☏0747/425788, ⓦwww.matemwe.com. Upmarket yet personal and unpretentious place on a rocky outcrop overlooking Mnemba Atoll, and the beach at one end. The fourteen rooms, all suites, are in individual thatched cottages strung out along the cliff, each with a verandah, hammock and dreamlike views. All have solar-powered light and hot water. Superb seafood is the speciality of the gloriously positioned restaurant. Non-guests are welcome for lunch but should book ahead. There's a swimming pool, kayaks, and boat trips or snorkelling can be arranged; diving is run through *Zanzibar Beach Resort & Hotel*. Closed April & May. Full-board. ❾
Mohamed Restaurant & Bungalows 2km north

of the village ☏0747/431881. Don't expect much of the rooms here, which are tatty if adequate and clean (big blue mosquito nets, "cold" water only, and neither fans nor views), and the plot is narrow and cramped. But the gate in the fence at the end opens on to a beach that was surely made in paradise. It's also one of the few beaches that isn't "cleaned" of seaweed, a plus if you're not keen on the overly sanitized versions elsewhere. Also has good, fresh and simple food (including fish with coconut sauce, crab with salad; main courses around Tsh5500), snorkelling equipment and motorbikes. Breakfast included. ❹
Zanzibar Beach Resort & Hotel 2km south of the village ☏0747/417784, ⓦwww .zanzibarbeachresort.com. Matemwe's newest and largest hotel lacks the intimacy of the other options, but is very well endowed, coming with a raft of amenities (including lots of stuff for kids), a beautiful swimming pool, the beach, and several restaurants and bars. It's also the base of a recommended scuba-diving outfit. Accommodation is in smallish chalets or four villas (up to six people in each) with kitchens, some of them with a prefabricated appearance. All are decorated in a neo-colonial theme, have a/c and balconies, most with sea views. It should be just right for families. Rates include non-motorized water sports. Half-board. ❽

Mnemba Atoll

Off the coast between Matemwe and Nungwi, **Mnemba Atoll** is a shallow expanse of coral reef with a tiny heart-shaped island on its western fringe.

Contrary to Zanzibari law which states that beaches cannot be privately owned, landing on the island itself is not allowed unless you're super-rich and are staying at the obscenely priced *Mnemba Island Club* ($1700 a double). No matter – the atoll is a "must do" for many visitors if snorkelling or scuba-diving appeals (see p.690). Day-trips can be arranged from both Matemwe and Nungwi. The fairly standard price of $30–35 includes transport, lunch, snorkelling equipment, and a $5 entry fee paid to the Mnemba Island Marine Conservation Area.

North Unguja

Life for tourists on Unguja's **north coast** centres on the beach at **Nungwi**, at the northernmost tip of the island. A favourite with backpackers, it combines beautiful beaches with Zanzibar's liveliest nightlife, some excellent restaurants, and snorkelling and scuba-diving. If the place feels too touristy, there's an equally beautiful stretch of beach a few kilometres to the south at **Kendwa**.

Nungwi

From humble beginnings as a little fishing village and dhow-making centre known only to a handful of hippies, **NUNGWI** has become, in little more

---

Diving and snorkelling off Unguja's north coast

For an introduction to scuba-diving and snorkelling in Tanzania, see pp.61–63.

Strong currents and coral damage means that the reefs just off Nungwi aren't the best for diving or snorkelling. However, with a boat, there are over a dozen better reefs within easy reach.

Boat trips for **snorkelling** are offered by virtually everyone, though for locations on the east coast or off Tumbatu Island, safety considerations mean you should go through one of the dive centres reviewed below. Prices depend on location and duration, and also whether you can tag along with a group of divers, which works out cheaper. Trips to reefs just offshore, where Kendwa Coral Garden is the highlight, cost $15; a day-trip to Mnemba Atoll (average price $30–35; see above) is highly recommended.

For **scuba-diving**, there are a handful of reasonable reefs just offshore, though visibility is a modest 15m. The best of these is **Hunga Reef**: its soft and hard corals contain a wide variety of schooling tropical fish, and give occasional sightings of reef sharks, blue-spotted stingrays and barracuda. The water is clearer off **Mnemba Atoll** (see p.690 for reef descriptions), trips to which are offered by all of Nungwi's dive centres. Together with Mnemba, the one reef that's touted everywhere is the spectacular **Leven Bank** in the Pemba Channel. However, its depth and **dangerously strong currents** limits it to experienced divers only, and even with the best preparations there's always a risk of getting swept out to sea, so for this one – more than others – choose your dive centre with safety foremost in your mind. Safer locations are scattered along the **barrier reef** to the east, and include Ametatu, Mbwangawa (good for novices, with occasional reef sharks), Haji and – best of all – Kichafi Reef, suitable for all levels and good for night dives too, as well as being home to all sorts of life including blue-spotted stingrays, marbled groupers, turtles and crocodile fish.

than a decade, Zanzibar's most popular beach resort – there are even a handful of Maasai warriors in all their red-robed glory mining the lucrative ethnic photography market. The place is positively infested with tourists, and much of the western flank of the cape has been overrun by a flurry of development, behind which the actual village is practically invisible. But things aren't as bad as they sound: the buildings are for the most part modest, locals remain unfazed by the invasion, and the atmosphere is remarkably easy-going. As long as you're not pursuing the "real" Zanzibar, you're almost guaranteed to have a good time.

The **beach** is of course the main enticement; it's narrower on the western side and gradually gets wider as you round the cape to the east, while the sea is resplendent in all directions, especially when dhows drift into view. As along the east coast, the wide tidal range here, especially around the top and to the east of the cape, means that swimming isn't possible at low tide, and note that the shoreline east of *Smiles Beach Hotel*, including the entire eastern cape, can be covered in **seaweed** between November and January. Apart from the beach, there's a natural tidal aquarium that is home to **marine turtles**, plus a number of other activities including sunset dhow cruises, scuba-diving and snorkelling. When swimming, be wary of treading on **sea urchins**.

Arrival

Nungwi is 59km from Stone Town, 8km beyond the end of the asphalt. **Daladalas** (#116) run there throughout the day (roughly 2hr; Tsh1200–1500) from the west side of Creek Road, north of the Central Market. Most tourists, however, come on **shared minibuses** (see p.658). These leave Stone Town at 8am and sometimes also at 3pm, most dropping their passengers at

---

Dive centres

The following **dive centres** are PADI-accredited and reliable. Use others at your own risk. When comparing prices, check for VAT (twenty percent) and per dive or per day supplements for Mnemba Atoll ($15–40) and Leven Bank ($15–20).

East Africa Diving & Watersports Center *Jambo Brothers Bungalows*, Nungwi ☎0747/416425 or 0747/420588, ⓦwww.diving-zanzibar.com. A cheap German-run company running courses up to Dive Master. Basic costs excluding supplements: Open Water $350, ten dives $230.

Ras Nungwi Diving *Ras Nungwi Beach Hotel*, Nungwi ☎024/223 3767, ⓦwww.rasnungwi.com/diving. Experienced with novice divers, and, though expensive, you get high safety standards and well-equipped boats. Basic costs without supplements: Open Water $430, Advanced Open Water $330, ten dives $390.

Scuba Do Between *Kendwa Rocks* and *Sunset Bungalows*, Kendwa ☎0747/417157 or 0748/415179, ⓦwww.scuba-do-zanzibar.com. Kendwa's only dive outfit, and highly recommended. Courses up to Instructor, using prescriptive computer-teaching methods. Good equipment and very safety-conscious. They also dive on the south coast from *Fumba Beach Lodge* (p.676). Basic costs without supplements: Open Water $385, Advanced Open Water $275, ten dives $300.

Sensation Divers Opposite *Amaan Bungalows*, with a branch at *Nungwi Village Beach Resort*, Nungwi ☎0745/863634, ⓦwww.sensationdivers.com. Zanzibar's only dive centre with Nitrox facilities (enabling longer dives), but with tricky pricing – read the small print. Basic costs without supplements: Open Water $360, Advanced Open Water $300, ten dives $270, Nitrox course $198.

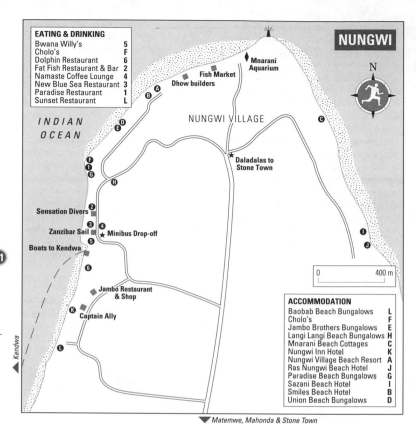

Matemwe, Mahonda & Stone Town

Amaan Bungalows, whose services the drivers (and *Amaan*'s "bouncers") can be extremely pushy in plugging. A **taxi** from Stone Town costs $50–60; renting a daladala (minibus) costs the same and works out cheaper if you're in a large group. **Day-trips** to Nungwi are offered by a number of Stone Town tour operators; see p.661.

Accommodation

Nungwi has almost two dozen **hotels**, mostly clusters of whitewashed bungalows with standard-issue *makuti*-thatched roofs. Most are pretty bland, overpriced even by Zanzibar's standards, and sometimes not especially welcoming. Don't be swayed by recommendations from minibus drivers or touts, who only push hotels that pay them commission. Most places also want payment in dollars: although you can legally pay in Tanzanian shillings, the hotel's conversion rates are so bad that you'll end up paying fifteen to twenty percent more. Still, it's not all gloom: the good news is that there's still a handful of more decent places to choose from, though if you're on a budget, neighbouring Kendwa (see p.701) is looking ever more enticing. Incidentally, the presence or absence of water sports doesn't really matter as you can arrange them virtually anywhere.

The cheaper options are scattered along the cape's **western shore**, which is good for sunsets, eating out and nightlife. Unfortunately, the stretch of beach from *Union Beach Bungalows* to beyond *Nungwi Village Beach Resort* has been trashed by clumsy attempts at hindering erosion; concrete sea walls and piles of stones aren't really what the doctor ordered. The **eastern cape** has more upmarket hotels, better beaches and benefits from sunrises. It's generally quieter than the western side but has no restaurants or bars other than in the hotels, and walking along the beach east of the lighthouse can be unsafe at night. All hotels include breakfast in their rates. See the map opposite for locations.

Baobab Beach Bungalows ☎ 024/223 6315 or 0747/429391, ⓦ www.baobabbeachbungalows .com. At the south end of the western shore next to a beautiful little cove and nice stretch of sand, this contains fifty decent if unexciting rooms, most set well back from the beach on an uninteresting lawn – check them out before paying, as some can be smelly. The cheapest, in rows of bungalows at the back, have verandahs. Next up are lodge rooms, in thatch-roofed two-storey buildings containing four rooms each, all with satellite TV, whilst the spacious deluxe rooms at the front have sea-view verandahs, a/c and fridges. All have good bathrooms and ceiling fans. There's also Internet access, and the superbly positioned *Sunset Restaurant* (and bar). ❻–❼

Cholo's ☎ 0748/705502, ⓔ fox708@yahoo. com. Run by a friendly bunch of Rastas, this is Nungwi's most chilled-out set-up, right on the beach (not on a small cliff like places to the south). Accommodation is in just three small, open-fronted *bandas* (security doesn't seem to be a problem) and there's a great "Mad Max"-style bar, with good food. The music goes on till late, so it's not ideal for early risers. ❸

Jambo Brothers Bungalows ☎ 0747/498380. One of Nungwi's oldest hotels, with a lovely nearby beach, but the reception staff are rather frosty and there's a lingering weariness throughout. The rooms too are tired, with cracked toilet seats and holey nets. Still, it's cheap, and most rooms have limited sea views. ❹

Langi Langi Beach Bungalows ☎ 024/224 0470, ⓔ langi_langi@hotmail.com. The "beach" bit is actually across the road past their restaurant, but the fourteen rooms in semi-detached bungalows have clean modern bathrooms, a/c, fans and balconies, and the management are friendly. ❺

Mnarani Beach Cottages ☎ 024/224 0494, ⓦ www.mnaranibeach.com. There's always a warm welcome at this small, intimate and efficiently run mini-resort on the quieter eastern flank of the peninsula, set beside a wonderful cove-like beach in lush gardens full of labelled plants and trees. The twelve smallish *makuti*-thatched cottages have private bathrooms, a/c and sea views. Larger, and better for families, are four

two-storey apartments with kitchens and open-air upstairs bedrooms. There are sun loungers and hammocks on the beach, a bar nestled among coconut palms, and a wonderful restaurant specializing in seafood – dine on a terrace or, at night, on the beach. Snorkelling equipment is available and they have a motorized dhow for cruises and fishing. Good value. ❻–❼

Nungwi Inn Hotel ☎ 024/224 0091. An unexceptional place on the west side where you'll have to haggle to get a decent price, with a jumble of small cottages scattered around a dishevelled "lawn" doubling as a car park. Still, the rooms are well kept, have good bathrooms, and the beds even have cotton sheets. One or two rooms have limited sea views, and there's a basic restaurant. ❺

Nungwi Village Beach Resort ☎ 022/215 2187 (Dar es Salaam), ⓦ www.nungwivillage.com. Facing a broad and formerly picturesque stretch of beach, this is now fronted by an unsightly concrete sea wall, against which the waves collide at high tide. This design malfunction aside, it's a pretty good place: the staff are friendly and helpful, and the rooms – all with a/c – are reasonable, standard ones in a courtyard at the back, and – at almost twice the price – sea-view ones in a number of two-storey thatched buildings by the beach, in front of a garden with hammocks slung between palm trees. The restaurant and bar are both good. ❺–❼

Ras Nungwi Beach Hotel ☎ 024/223 3767 or 024/223 2512, ⓦ www.rasnungwi.com. Nungwi's only proper resort (it's the only place with a swimming pool), this 32-room complex is set on a palm-dotted outcrop beside a lovely stretch of sand. Prices depend on room size and proximity to the beach – at these prices, you might as well cough up the extra for a sea-view chalet. All rooms have a/c, fans and balconies, and are attractively decorated. The hotel also boasts several bars and restaurants (occasional live music, and seafood buffets twice a week), Internet access and plenty of water sports. Closed April to mid-June. Half-board. ❾

Sazani Beach Hotel ☎ 0747/491747, ⓦ www .sazanibeach.com. A small, relaxed place on a lovely east coast beach, miles from the western tourist hub. There are ten well-equipped, en-suite rooms (they call them "snuggeries") in the colourful gardens, most with sea views from their verandahs. There's also a good beachside bar and restaurant. Half-board. **7**

Smiles Beach Hotel ☎024/224 0472, ℮ smilesbeachhotel@zanzinet.com. An amusing foray into kitsch, with four two-storey Toytown houses with red tin roofs and external spiral staircases facing the sea (the beach lies beyond an unsightly seawall, as with *Nungwi Village* next door). The sixteen rooms, including triples, have

a/c, sea views, phone, satellite TV and spotless bathrooms. There's a restaurant by the ocean, a boat for snorkelling or sunset cruises ($10 including drinks), and the staff are helpful and friendly. Closed April & May. **6**

Union Beach Bungalows ☎0747/454706. Next to *Jambo Brothers Bungalows* and similarly run-down but more welcoming, with ten basic twin-bed rooms, and a small restaurant (no alcohol). The scatter of rocks on the beach are a clumsy attempt to stop beach erosion. **4**

Along the western shore

In spite of the tourist trade, Nungwi itself is still very much a traditional fishing village, whose history of sea-faring and dhow building remains a source of pride to many. The **dhow builders** use the stretch of beach beyond *Nungwi*

Village Beach Resort; the craftsmen are used to inquisitive tourists, but ask before taking photos. Nearby, at the back of the beach, is a cluster of wooden structures that become the daily **fish market** whenever the fishermen return (times depend on the tides). Moored just offshore here are dozens of *ngalawa* outriggers.

At the northernmost tip of Unguja, Ras Nungwi, stands a **lighthouse** built in 1886. Just before it is **Mnarani Aquarium** (daily 9am–6pm; Tsh2000), a small natural pond surrounded by porous coral ragstone into which seawater seeps at high tide. It contains dozens of endangered hawksbill and green turtles. The first were introduced in 1993, both for study and to provide a sanctuary for injured animals. New arrivals are bought from fish-

△ Sunset dhow cruise, Nungwi

Dhows

The art of sailing has been known to East Africans for at least two millennia, but it was the Arabs who introduced the lateen-rigged vessel that became the maritime emblem of East Africa: the **dhow**. The main dhow-building centre on Unguja was the north coast, though its teak (*mvule*) forests are now sadly almost all gone. Also now vanishing are the **jahazi** dhows, the largest and grandest of East Africa's sailing ships, which reach up to fifteen metres in length. Their construction took up to half a year, and launches were accompanied by animal sacrifices and much celebration. Few *jahazis* are built today (having been superseded by freighters and tankers), but one or two examples can still be seen, including one at Nungwi that has been converted for sunset cruises.

Still common, however, are the smaller **mashua** dhows that shuttle between Zanzibar and the mainland, and the delightful sail-powered **ngalawa** outriggers, whose design is said to have come from Indonesia. The lowliest of the lot are the paddle-powered **mtumbwi** canoes, traditionally dug out from a single trunk, but nowadays made from planks. Dhows were originally sewn or lashed together with coconut-fibre coir rope, and, apart from iron nails, modern **construction methods** and tools remain unchanged from those used a thousand years ago.

ermen who occasionally catch them in their nets. Males are retained, whilst females are released when sexually mature. There's a walkway over the pond from where you can feed seaweed to the denizens; the murky water, whose level varies according to the tide, also contains grey mullet and trevally.

All these attractions are included in the locally run **Nungwi Cultural Village Tour**, which you can book at a hut outside the aquarium ($10 per person; ☎0747/863611, ✉nungwicvt@yahoo.com). The two-and-a-half hour walk includes visits to old mosques, medicinal trees and plants, markets, basket-weavers, and a curious haunted saltwater well only used for washing in the morning – the spirits evidently being late-risers.

Water sports and cruises

All of Nungwi's hotels can arrange **snorkelling trips** or find you equipment to rent ($5 a day is about right), though for longer trips it would be safer to go through one of the **dive centres** reviewed on p.694. As to other water sports, it's really just a question of asking around, as outfits start up and disappear on an almost seasonal basis. For an idea of maximum prices, *Ras Nungwi Beach Hotel* charges $20 an hour for **kayaking** or **windsurfing**, and $40–65 for half- or full-day trips to **Mnemba Atoll** for snorkelling. You should be able to get the same things for about half those prices elsewhere. *Ras Nungwi Beach Hotel* is the only place to offer **water-skiing** however: $50 for fifteen minutes.

A place on a **sunset dhow cruise** can be booked through any hotel; the cost is generally $10–15 without drinks or snacks, $15–20 with.

Eating and drinking

Nungwi's **nightlife** is Zanzibar's liveliest, with plenty of bars to choose from along the western cape, and impromptu moonlit drumming sessions on the beach. The string of **restaurants** along the same section are one of Nungwi's main attractions, where – unlike the hotels – competition has succeeded in keeping standards high and prices low. Overall, they're quite similar both in their *makuti*-roofed appearance and menus (pizzas, pasta, seafood with rice), so choose by location. The best are directly on the beach or on small rocky headlands with wooden terraces, both with beguiling views. Most restaurants have daily specials chalked up on boards by the beach.

Bwana Willy's On wooden decking extending over the beach from a low headland on the western shore, this is a great bar for chilling out: delicious views, great cappuccino, huge comfy sofas, and even swings at the bar. Food should be available once the adjacent *Kigoma Hotel* is rebuilt.

Cholo's Right on the beach, this is Rasta heaven, and easily Nungwi's weirdest and funkiest place, constructed almost entirely from flotsam. The seats are canoes, the bar is a dhow's prow, and there's a cool "chill-out" zone on stilts above it. Drinks, including beers, fresh juices and cocktails (including a very good "Banana Blowjob") are reasonably priced, and the limited seafood menu is good, whether for lunch (Tsh4000–6000 a plate, including *pilau* with fish of the day) or, better, for dinner, when you can eat on the beach by a campfire (Tsh7000) or in the chill-out zone above (Tsh10,000) – dinner should be booked by lunchtime.

Dolphin Restaurant One of the cheaper places for eating out with Swahili favourites like banana curries, together with seafood and pizzas (mostly around Tsh3000–3500), and toasted sandwiches. There's also a bar, and reggae prevails.

Fat Fish Restaurant & Bar Wonderful views from the wooden terrace, and – if you're missing it – satellite TV. This tends to be one of the main nightspots in high season (discos most likely Tues & Fri). The menu isn't too spectacular, and slightly more expensive than elsewhere.

Namaste Coffee Lounge Next to *Amaan Bungalows* on the land side of the road (no views), this is a fine place for breakfast or snacks (up to 8pm), with juices and smoothies, freshly ground Kilimanjaro *Arabica* served as espresso or cappuccino, North American-style cookies and brownies, and great chocolate cake.

New Blue Sea Restaurant Like the adjacent *Fat Fish*, this enjoys a wonderfully romantic view from its wooden terrace, and has plenty of tables with unobstructed sea views. The big speciality is pizza, courtesy of a wood-fired oven (mostly Tsh4500), though other dishes (around Tsh5500) are alluring too, including a wide variety of barbecued fish, Thai-style calamari (with lemongrass, garlic and soy sauce), typical mainland Tanzanian *mishkaki* (grilled skewers of goat meat) served with peanut butter or hot sauce, and half lobsters from Tsh13,000 to Tsh23,000 depending on size. Drinkers are welcome, and they also do cocktails. Closed May.

Paradise Restaurant *Paradise Beach Bungalows.* The menu here is identical to that at *New Blue Sea* and by and large similarly priced, though crab or prawns will cost you Tsh8000. Particularly good is the grilled seafood platter, which includes lobster, crayfish, crab, calamari, octopus and fish (Tsh20,000; enough for two people). The sea-view terrace, looking north and west, is smaller than at other places, so come early for a table right at the edge. It also functions as a bar, with a preference for Tanzanian sounds.

Sunset Restaurant *Baobab Beach Bungalows.* Another gorgeously sited place under a huge *makuti* roof by the beach and with sweeping views. There are also tables under parasols on the low bluff beside it, and sun loungers on the beach. Drinks are slightly over the odds for Nungwi, but meals cost a little less, and include an excellent three-course seafood platter (Tsh17,000; or Tsh27,000 for four courses including lobster) and good starters (Tsh2500–3000: the pumpkin soup and crab or bisque soup are both worth trying). Good wine list.

Listings

Bicycles can be rented cheaply from locals and hotels. Tourist prices average $10 a day; more reasonable would be $5.

Car and motorbike rental Nungwi Travel, *Amaan Bungalows* (daily 8am–6pm; ☎024/224 0026, ⓦwww.amaanbungalows.com) sublets vehicles:

Buying souvenirs

Please do not buy seashells, sea horses or other **marine souvenirs** in Nungwi, or elsewhere, no matter what the growing number of vendors might tell you. Apart from the trade being illegal, both internationally and in Zanzibar (not that you'd ever guess it), the collection of shells for the tourist trade kicks off a very damaging chain reaction on the already brittle coral ecosystem.

$50/day for a car ($65 with driver), $35/day for a motorbike. Needs to be arranged at a day in advance to give them time to sort out licences. However, they're not transparent about insurance arrangements in case of an accident – read the small print, and ensure that everything agreed is explicitly mentioned in the contract.

Health The larger hotels have doctors on call. For anything complicated go to Stone Town.

Internet Internet Club, *Amaan Bungalows* (daily 8am–8pm; $1 for 30min).

Money Exchange rates in Nungwi are ten to fifteen percent worse than in Stone Town. If you're stuck, Internet Club at *Amaan Bungalows* changes cash and travellers' cheques (daily 8am–8pm). Cash advances on credit cards, at similarly bad rates plus seven percent commission, are made at Nungwi Cards Assistance Point beside *Nungwi Inn Hotel* (Mon–Sat 9am–5.30pm) – you're paid in shillings.

Telephones Nungwi Cards Assistance Point at *Nungwi Inn Hotel* (Mon–Sat 9am–5.30pm) charges $3/min for international calls, Tsh300–500 for national.

Travel agent Nungwi Travel, *Amaan Bungalows* ☎024/224 0026, ⓦ www.amaanbungalows.com (daily 8am–6pm).

Kendwa

Compared to Nungwi, **KENDWA** – a few kilometres southwest – is refreshingly low-key, with a lovely wide beach deep enough for swimming at all tides, several hotels geared to budget and mid-range travellers, and monthly full-moon beach parties. There are no noisy water sports, and nothing much to do except swim, snorkel or dive, and lounge around in a hammock, although things may not remain like this forever: one developer has seen fit to blot the northern part of the beach with an all-inclusive package resort (thankfully largely out of sight). With Zanzibar running after tourist dollars, enjoy Kendwa now before it's too late.

Practicalities

Kendwa lies 1km west of the road to Nungwi along a very rocky track. Daily tourist **minibuses** are operated by *Kendwa Rocks* and *Sunset Bungalows* (both Tsh5000); they leave Stone Town in the morning at 8am, and turn back at 10.30am. Cheaper is to catch a #116 Nungwi **daladala** from the west side of Creek Road in Stone Town (roughly 2hr; Tsh1200 1500); get off at the sign posted junction for Kendwa and walk the remaining kilometre.

Getting there **from Nungwi**, 3.5km to the north, is easiest on *Kendwa Rocks'* motorboat, which leaves from the beach next to *Bwana Willy's* between 10am and 10.30am, coinciding with the arrival of tourist minibuses from Stone Town. It's free if you stay with them, Tsh1000 otherwise. Private boats – just ask around – sometimes sail to Kendwa (Tsh3000 per person). There are no boats when sea conditions are rough. **Walking along the beach** is possible at low tide, but tourists have been mugged in the past, so don't walk if you're carrying valuables.

Accommodation

With the exception of the ugly *La Gemma Dell' Est* resort, Kendwa's **hotels** are all quite intimate, even if they've been busy adding more bungalows and edging up their prices, and a good deal of the old hippy bliss style still survives. For snorkelling and **scuba-diving**, there's the recommended Scuba Do dive centre (see p.695). The hotels can also arrange snorkelling, and dhow cruises with local fishermen. **Internet access** is possible at *Kendwa Rocks* (Tsh2000/30min).

The following hotels are listed from north to south, and cover just under one kilometre of beachfront. Breakfast is included in room rates.

Les Toits de Palme ☎0747/418548. Kendwa's cheapest, with eight or nine basic, palm-thatched beach *bandas* (four of which are for guests) sharing a bathroom, plus six rooms in three small and spartan en-suite bungalows on the coral bluff, facing the sea. Cheap meals available (Tsh2500–3500). ❹

White Sands Beach Hotel ☎0747/480987, ⓦwww.zanzibar-white-sands-hotel.com. A nicely relaxing, unpretentious and well-run place with stylishly decorated if rather bare rooms. There are three kinds, all on top of the coral bluff behind the beach: small and cosy ones in thatched cottages at the back with "cold" water, slightly bigger cottages with hot water, and – the biggest – four rooms in two cottages at the front with huge double beds and good views. There are hammocks slung between tamarisk trees on the beach, and a beautifully designed beach restaurant and bar. ❺–❻

Sunset Bungalows ☎0747/414647, ⓔinfo@sunsetbungalows.com. Six two-room bungalows facing each other at the back of the sandy beach (no real sea views though as they're side-on), and more atop the coral bluff. The rooms, decorated with colourful *kangas*, are small but have enough space for four-poster beds. Triples cost just $5–10 more. Bar and restaurant on the beach. ❺

Kendwa Rocks ☎0747/415475 or 0747/415527, ⓦwww.kendwarocks .com. Mellow Rastafarian-run place for a quiet and affordable getaway, with a range of accommodation including cheap "dorms" in very basic palm-thatch *bandas*, the best being the two at the back of a sandy clearing behind the beach. Also in the clearing are eight coconut wood bungalows on stilts, whilst on the coral headland at the back are slightly more expensive stone bungalows (some triples too) with the benefit of fans, reproduction antiques, four-posters with box nets and verandahs, but not all with sea views. The bar and restaurant is on the beach. "Dorms" ❹, bungalows. ❺

Amaan Kendwa Beach Resort ☎0747/492552, ⓔamaankendwa@hotmail.com. Thirty-eight rooms, most in large two-room cottages sharing terraces in a scrubby garden on the coral cliff above the beach. Although the hotel claims that most rooms have sea views, only ten in the front row (also with a/c) are worth spending the extra $15 on. Good beach restaurant and bar (the *Titanic*), Internet access ($2/hr) and a forex with bad rates except for dollars cash. ❺–❻

Eating and drinking

Each hotel has its own bar, restaurant and musical tastes; you're welcome at any. The following are directly on the beach, and have wonderful views from their open sides. **Full-moon beach parties** are held at *Kendwa Rocks* (free entry), who also offer a distinctly provocative "booze cruise" most evenings at 5.30pm, for $15. As with hotels, the following restaurants are listed from north to south.

White Sands Beach Hotel A very stylish place with upbeat music split into three areas: the bar, which also has swings; dining tables on the circular building's perimeter; and a wonderful lounge around a sandpit in the centre, with big rustic-style cushions, comfy loungers, and drapes for lampshades to create a magical nocturnal mood. Tingatinga painters ply their art in an adjacent building. The menu is short but well thought out, and always includes a decent vegetarian option. Expect to pay Tsh6500–8000 for things like crab claws with chilli, baked sea perch, or octopus in coconut sauce. To start, try the pleasingly tingly marinated fish, whilst to finish there's cake with whipped cream. Cocktails available.

Sunset Bungalows Another good beach restaurant-cum-bar with a youthful vibe, the menu here – just four or five dishes (usually Tsh5000) – is displayed on a blackboard. Dishes are well picked: things like grilled calamari in

ginger sauce, marinated chicken skewers, or pan-fried beef, and there's chocolate cake to finish. In addition to tables and comfy sofas, there are lounges and hammocks under the thatched roof, and a pool table.

Kendwa Rocks Run by reggae-loving Rastafarians, this youthful split-level *makuti*-thatched bar and restaurant is surprisingly plush in appearance, though prices remain in touch with the roots (around Tsh4000–4500 for main courses). The limited menu is based on the day's catch, and makes full use of Zanzibar's spices, though you can also be less adventurous and just go for fish and chips or seafood pasta. Barbecue buffets are held on the beach whenever it's busy. The starters are refreshingly different, and include falafel, and fish-stuffed chapati. There's always a vegetarian dish too. The attached *Mermaid Bar* is well stocked so perfect for cocktails (Tsh3000), and has South African wines.

A few kilometres off the northwestern Unguja is the dagger-shaped **Tumbatu Island**, whose inhabitants are famed for their pride in having kept to their Swahili traditions, and for their aloofness when dealing with strangers. Tumbatu's society is tightly knit, and whilst visitors with a genuine interest in history and traditions will find the place fascinating, the majority of tourists are definitely not welcome. Day-trips are best arranged through Blue Dolphins Tours & Safaris in Stone Town (see p.661).

There's also a pool table, darts, and a traditional *bao* game.
Titanic Restaurant *Amaan Kendwa Beach Resort* This has tables on the sand rather than on a wooden terrace, and a menu (averaging Tsh6000–

8000) ranging from pasta, burgers, sandwiches, grills and curries to the rather more inventive "Surf & Turf", which is tuna stir-fried with coconut, peanuts, cashews, pineapple and oyster sauce. The music is middle of the road.

Pemba

The island of **PEMBA**, 48km northeast of Unguja and 56km off the Tanzanian mainland, is Zanzibar's forgotten half, traditionally conservative, deeply religious, and far removed from the commercialization of Unguja. With its low hills gouged by gullies and snaking, mangrove-lined creeks, the island presents a lush and fertile contrast to much of Unguja and aptly fits the name given it by the Arab geographer Yakut ibn Abdallah al-Rumi (1179–1229), who called it *Jazirat al-Khadhra*, the Green Island. Despite a wealth of attractions, including a primeval forest, atmospheric ruins dating from the dawn of the Swahili civilization, a handful of deserted if difficult to access beaches, beautiful offshore islets and great scuba-diving, there are rarely more than a few dozen tourists on the island at any one time.

Pemba has three main towns, all on the west coast: the capital **Chake Chake** in the centre close to the airport; **Mkoani** in the south, where the ferries land; and **Wete**, a dhow port in the north. There's not an awful lot to do in any of these, but they are good bases for exploring further afield. **Tourist facilities** are extremely limited. Almost half the island's **restaurants** have closed down over the last few years, leaving barely more than a dozen, and by any standards Pemba is a gastronomic wilderness for those without a *mama* to cook for them. Given that affordable bed space is limited too, **accommodation** should be booked before arrival. Public **transport** is limited to shared pick-ups and mini-buses along the main asphalt roads; beyond these, you'll need to walk, or rent a car, taxi or bicycle. The **long rains**, during which time it can pour constantly for weeks, fall between March and June, a little later than on Unguja. Pemba's

Changing money on Pemba

Change all the money you'll need before coming, as changing cash can take half a day, and there's no way of changing travellers' cheques or getting cash advances on credit cards, though payment for scuba-diving and upmarket accommodation can be made by cheque or plastic as long as this is arranged beforehand.

opening hours are notoriously capricious, even for banks: the best time for finding things open is in the morning.

Sadly, whilst Unguja is experiencing an economic boom, Pemba – which has always been peripheral to the concerns of the Zanzibari Government based on Unguja – is going back in time and **poverty** is widespread. Per capita income is Tanzania's lowest, and the child mortality rate among the country's highest.

Meanwhile, the island's lamentable infrastructure continues to deteriorate: most roads are pitted with potholes, the airport's only fire tender recently bade the world adieu, and there's not a single working streetlight on the island. Power cuts too are a daily reality, and the water supply is more likely to be trucked in than arrive through pipes. Not surprising, then, that Pemba is the main stronghold of the opposition party, the **Civic United Front (CUF)**, support for which has only deepened Pemba's marginalization. **Political unrest** and related violence as a result of all these factors has been considerable, especially in the run-up to elections, the next of which are due in 2010.

Chake Chake

Pemba's capital and largest town, **CHAKE CHAKE** ("Chake" for short), lies about halfway up the west coast at the end of a mangrove-lined creek. The town is lively by Pemba's standards, and contains a small and busy **market** along with a well-preserved **Arab quarter** that resembles a very miniature Stone Town (two streets and a few alleyways). Chake's history dates back at least to the Portuguese occupation, as evidenced by the style of the town's **fortress**, now a museum. The main reason for coming to Chake though is for **scuba-diving** off the west coast, and for **snorkelling** at Misali Island, an unspoilt gem of a place. Other possible excursions include the ruins of a tyrant's citadel at **Pujini**, and the ancient city of **Quanbalu** on Ras Mkumbuu Peninsula, possibly the first Muslim settlement in East Africa.

Arrival, information and accommodation

All flights to Pemba land at **Karume Airport**, 6km southeast of Chake Chake; taxis wait outside and charge Tsh3000–5000 for a ride into town. There are also a few daladalas (#105 or 106 marked "U" or "U. Ndege") to Chake Chake, but no guarantee of your arrival coinciding with them. Arriving by **daladala** from Wete or Mkoani, you'll be dropped in Chake Chake either at the junction by the Esso petrol station, or at the stand behind the market. The *Old Mission Lodge* is a good source of **information**.

Accommodation
Room rates include breakfast.

Government Hotel (*Hotel ya Chake Chake*) In the centre ⓣ024/245 2069. Seven large but decrepit twin-bed rooms, often full, all with fans and nets. There's also a bar, and an achingly slow restaurant. ❹

Le-Tavern Hotel 200m north of the *Government Hotel* ⓣ024/245 2660. This modern two-storey place is a reasonable option, despite its non-communicative staff, with en-suite or shared bathrooms, the better rooms with views over town. ❸

Mamy Hotel & Restaurant Machomane; turn right at the junction 2km north of town, right at *Pattaya Guest House*, left after 200m ⓣ0747/432789. A little out of the way, this basic but pleasant and friendly family-run guest house is one of Zanzibar's cheapest, and perfectly decent if

you can live with its horrid green light bulbs. There are just four large rooms, all with big beds, round nets and small ceiling fan. The one en-suite room isn't worth spending double on, especially as its bathtub serves as the hotel's water tank. Also has safe parking, and food to order. ❷–❸

Old Mission Lodge (Swahili Divers) 300m north of the *Government Hotel* ⓣ024/245 2786, ⓦ www.swahilidivers.com. Set in a restored Quaker Mission, this is Chake's most atmospheric choice, though the dorm beds are very pricey at approximately $24 (prices are in euros). Other rooms are much better value and it's these that are recommended. Facilities include a bar, massage, use of bicycles, an excellent library, good food, and – above all – their diving centre. ❺–❻

For an introduction to scuba-diving and snorkelling in Tanzania, pp.61–63.

Surrounded almost entirely by reefs, atolls and coral-fringed isles, Pemba's spectacular underwater kingdom – which contains almost half of Tanzania's coral reefs – is one of the world's most exhilarating **scuba-diving** destinations. The caverns, drop-offs, swim-throughs and immense coral gardens contain a Bacchanalian profusion of marine life, of all which attracts the larger pelagics (open water fish) in abundance. Diving companies will know the best places for turtles (all year), dolphins (best Dec–April), and – with a good deal of luck – migrating whale sharks (June–Aug) or whales (Aug–Sept). The calmest conditions and clearest visibility are from October to March. **Snorkelling** is best off Misali Island and at Uvinje Gap and Njao Gap in the north, though it's not cheap as Pemba's snorkelling reefs require boat access: count on $40 per person for a half or full day.

Underwater **visibility** is generally excellent, averaging 20–40m and often increasing to 60–70m on incoming tides, even during the rains. However, the steep drop-offs and **strong currents** that make such exciting drift drives out of most of Pemba's sites are also potentially **dangerous**, and mean that beginners or inexperienced divers should stick to Unguja's more sheltered reefs. The disappearance of five divers off Misali Island in 2005 was a tragic reminder of the dangers inherent in scuba-diving.

Probably the best reef for novices is **Uvinje Gap** southwest of Wete, which has lots of fish around shallow coral heads (*bommies*), and magnificent gorgonian sea fans lower down. Another good all-round site is **Njao Gap** in the north, which gives good odds on seeing turtles. For experienced divers, Pemba has two indisputable highlights. The dreamlike **Manta Point** west of Wete is the tip of an underwater mountain that rises to within five to eight metres of the surface; its dense coral formations, including brittle leaf and gorgonian sea fans, attract a teeming profusion of life including turtles and the occasional reef shark, though unconscionable fishermen from Kojani Island on Pemba's east coast have annihilated the eponymous giant mantas that used to scratch their bellies on the peak to rid themselves of parasites. Also good, but with strong currents lower down are a number of places around **Misali Island**, which enjoy exceptional visibility, pristine corals and the chance of spotting sharks, manta rays and either green or hawksbill turtles. Although this is where the divers were lost in 2005, the sites had been dived virtually every day for years before then without incident, so you shouldn't let safety fears prevent you from diving here. Exhilarating drift dives include **Emerald Reef** in the very south (giant barracuda and

---

Pattaya Guest House Machomane; turn right at the junction 2km north of town and it's 100m on the left ☏ 0747/852970. Six largish twin-bed rooms with fans and decent-sized nets, all but one room sharing bathrooms. It's a bit run-down and nylon bedsheets aren't too clever in this climate, but it's okay and the Western-style toilets still have their seats. ❹

The Town

Chake Chake contains a strange but attractive fusion of buildings and is well worth a wander. The atmosphere is relaxed and friendly, and people are genuinely pleased – and curious – to see tourists poking around. Starting in the centre, head for the **market** (daily from 7am). Aside from a selection of herbs and spices, you can buy aromatic essential oils and tasty clove honey (*asali*). You can also purchase colourfully painted straw plate covers that look like hats, and aromatic *halua* – a sticky boiled goo (think Turkish Delight) inherited from the Omanis, made from wheat gluten, nuts, spices, and a whole lot of sugar. At one corner of the market

hammerhead sharks), the southern wall of **Fundo Reef** southeast of Manta Point (superb corals, shallow caverns and spectacular overhangs from 5m to below sport diving depth), and **Kokota Reef** in the same area, which lends itself to night-time drift dives for spotting Spanish dancers, a species of nudibranch that gets its name from its reddish fringed "skirt" and graceful movements.

Lastly, there are a couple of wrecks at **Panza Point** in the south, the more photogenic one – a Greek freighter that foundered in 1969 – lying in shallow water. Strong currents are present at both sites.

Dive centres

Pemba has three PADI-accredited **diving centres** offering tuition, and one live-aboard. Single dives average $40–50, and two dives in one day $80–100. It's best to book before arrival.

Dive 710 *Fundu Lagoon*, Wambaa Beach in the south ☎024/223 2926, ⓦwww. fundulagoon.com. Solid reputation, state-of-the-art equipment and good instructors for PADI courses at all levels, but you'll have to stay at the sadistically expensive *Fundu Lagoon* (see p.714). Closed mid-April to mid-June.

One Earth Diving *Manta Reef Lodge*, Ras Kigomasha in the far northwest ☎0747/423930, ⓦwww.mantareeflodge.com. Very well-regarded and reliable operator offering the full range of PADI courses; staying at the lodge is expensive (from $240 a double), but Jambo Tours & Safaris (p.710) can arrange daily transport from Chake Chake. Open Water costs $465; Advanced Open Water $340; ten dive package (accommodation not included) $350.

Pemba Afloat Moored at Njao Inlet west of Wete ⓦwww.pembaisland.com. Based in three twenty-metre ketches, this is a great live-aboard operation (with good dive sites almost under your feet) where full-board accommodation costs $100 per person. Diving is extra: $40–60 per dive, or $350 for Open Water tuition, $250 for Advanced Open Water.

Swahili Divers *Old Mission Lodge*, Chake Chake ☎024/245 2786, ⓦwww.swahilidivers.com. Experienced and reliable, and reasonably priced if you buy a package that includes accommodation. They offer all PADI courses up to Dive Master, and tuition in underwater photography. Prices are quoted in euros: Open Water with five nights full-board costs €500 (approx $600); a combined Open Water and Advanced Open Water course with seven nights full-board is €750 (approx $900); and a ten-dive package with six nights full board costs €445–545 (approx $535–655).

is an **old mosque** with a softly rounded minaret. Following the narrow road past the mosque brings you to the **Chief Minister's Office**, a bizarre, pale blue building dominated by a round tower studded with protruding hollow cylinders. Opposite is the glorious colonial-era **Omani Court House**, with an impressive carved door and clock tower with a defunct clock.

Continuing along the same street and turning right at the junction brings you to the diminutive **Nanzim Fort**, with its commanding view over the creek. Walking downhill towards the creek are the remains of the fort's battery on your right, comprising some rubble and a couple of rusty cannons. The current fort was built in the eighteenth century by the Omanis, but incorporates the foundations of a Portuguese fortress built in 1594. Much of the fort was demolished in the early 1900s to make way for the present hospital; part of what's left has been converted into a small but charming **museum** (Mon–Fri 8.30am–4.30pm, Sat & Sun 9am–4pm; Tsh2000). It consists of just three small rooms, containing well-presented displays in both English and Kiswahili on

△ Scuba-diving off Pemba

most aspects of Pemban life: Room 1 covers the island's archeological sites in surprising detail, and has medieval pottery, coins and other finds; Room 2 is dedicated to dhows and seafaring; and Room 3 covers Zanzibar's rulers, the accent being on their work – or lack of – in Pemba.

Eating and drinking

The following **restaurants** and **bars** are pretty much all there is, other than **street food stalls** on the main road between *Old Mission Lodge* and the *Government Hotel*. Busiest at night, this is where you can find everything from the usual *chipsi mayai* (chip omelette) and goat meat *mishkaki* (served, if you're lucky, with a spicy potato stew) to grilled octopus, squid and fish, bite-sized fishcakes and juices. To finish off, track down one of the **coffee vendors** for scaldingly hot and bitter brews in tiny Omani-style porcelain cups.

Afay Restaurant & Take Away In the town centre, this is the only local restaurant in Chake. It makes good simple food (little over Tsh2500), but the menu is in the weary "rice with fish, chicken with chips" tradition. Order early for a little more choice or for special requests. No alcohol.

Government Hotel Most people (well, a handful) come for the relatively cheap beer – it's one of only three bars in town. More fun when there's a power cut and people can't tell you're a tourist.

Pemba Island Hotel 50m west of the People's Bank of Zanzibar. The third-floor restaurant here has good views and the typically Swahili menu is reasonably priced (mostly Tsh4000–5000), including octopus with coconut sauce and chicken *pilau*.

No alcohol.

Police Mess 1km along the Mkoani road. Has beer and Konyagi (papaya gin). Don't indulge too much as you'll have to walk back, and keep your opinions on Zanzibari politics under your hat. May not admit tourists whenever the political situation is incendiary.

Swahili Divers Run by a friendly bunch of *wazungu* well attuned to foreign tastes, with meals taken at a long table on the verandah. Lunch is limited to a salad and sandwich (Tsh5000). Dinners (Tsh11,000) are more substantial three-course affairs, nothing fancy but filling and always with a vegetarian option. Tasty seafood buffets feature on Wednesday and Saturday. Beer available, making this the town's finest bar.

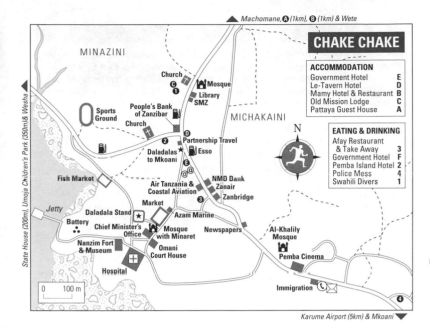

Machomane, **A** (1km), **B** (1km) & Wete

CHAKE CHAKE

ACCOMMODATION
Government Hotel	E
Le-Tavern Hotel	D
Mamy Hotel & Restaurant	B
Old Mission Lodge	C
Pattaya Guest House	A

EATING & DRINKING
Afay Restaurant & Take Away	3
Government Hotel	F
Pemba Island Hotel	2
Police Mess	4
Swahili Divers	1

Karume Airport (5km) & Mkoani

Listings

Airline tickets Air Tanzania (☏024/245 2162) and Coastal Aviation (☏0747/418343) are both opposite NMB bank; ZanAir is beside NMB bank (☏024/245 2990 or 0747/420760, ✉zanairpemba@zanzinet.com).

Cinema Pemba Cinema, despite its mind-bogglingly dilapidated appearance, is still open and provides a unique and highly recommended experience. Amazingly, it still manages to get hold of real celluloid: weekday evenings (6pm) feature Bollywood flicks and weekends have third-rate American dross; a great night out for Tsh500.

Ferry tickets The one-stop shop is Partnership Travel on the main road near the *Government Hotel* (☏024/245 2278), who deal with all ferries, though you may pay a small mark-up. To book direct: SMZ (☏024/245 2349) next to the library, for the MV *Mapinduzi* and MV *Maendeleo*; Zanbridge (☏0747/420132), 200m south of the Esso filling station, for the MV *Sepideh*; Azam Marine (no phone) by the market for the MV *Serengeti*.

Hospital The government-run Chake Chake Hospital beside Nanzim Fort (☏024/245 2311) is very run-down; the one in Mkoani is better. There's a good pharmacy nearby. For diagnostic tests, the Public Health Laboratory in Machomane (☏024/245 2473) is reliable.

Internet access Adult Training Centre, on the main road just north of Air Tanzania (daily 7.30am–4pm; Tsh1000/hr); ZCF Internet Café, beside the *Government Hotel* (erratic hours; Tsh1000/hr).

Library The public library (Mon–Fri 8am–4pm, Sat 8am–2pm; during Ramadan closes 2 hrs earlier; free) has lots of English language works on Zanzibar and Tanzania.

Money Chake's banks are dog-slow and can chew up to half a day for changing cash. The "best" is NMB bank on the main road.

Telephones TTCL is on the main road near the Esso petrol station (Tsh2500/min for international calls).

Around Chake Chake

Chake Chake is a good base for **excursions** to anywhere on Pemba. Recommended is a full day in the **north**, combining Ngezi Forest and Vumawimbi Beach

When arranging half- or full-day trips, go through one of the companies below, as Chake's self-appointed guides are far from reliable, and reports of theft by some of them circulate. Prices are based on the cost of car rental ($50–60 a day including fuel and driver) plus lunch and additional expenses. The following can also fix you up with a motorbike (*pikipiki*) for around $25 a day excluding fuel.

Jambo Tours & Safaris Under *Le-Tavern Hotel* ℡0747/437397 or 0747/468809. Well priced and reliable; can also book scuba-diving at *Manta Reef Lodge* on Ras Kigomasha in the northwest for no mark-up. Daily 8am–4pm.

Partnership Travel On the main road near the *Government Hotel* ℡024/245 2278. Long-established; negotiable prices but not unreasonable to start with. Daily 8am–4pm.

Swahili Divers *Old Mission Lodge* ℡024/245 2786, ℺www.swahilidivers.com. More expensive but the most experienced for matters aquatic; a day's snorkelling at Misali Island costs around $40. They can help you find a reliable driver-guide.

---

with Tumbe fish market and nearby ruins. Other than **Misali Island**, a paradise for snorkellers, the easiest **beaches** to get to are beyond Vitongoji on Pemba's east coast. Historical interest is provided by the **ruins** at Pujini and Quanbalu.

Vitongoji

The nearest good beaches to Chake Chake are a series of sandy coves beyond **VITONGOJI** on the east coast, which offer excellent swimming at high tide and reef walking at low tide. Chake's tour operators can arrange transport, but it's much cheaper and more fun to rent a **bicycle** from one of the tour operators. Heading out from Chake Chake, take the road to Wete for 2km and turn right (southeast) at Machomane. At the end of the sealed road (1km from the junction) turn left. Vitongoji village is 5km further on. Follow the main track beyond Vitongoji to get to Liko la Ngezi beach, or branch left 2km beyond the village to reach Liko la Vumba and Makoba beaches. The alternative approach is by #316 **daladala** from Chake Chake to Vitongoji, but this leaves you with a 3km walk to the nearest beach.

Misali Island

The island of **Misali**, 17km off the coast west of Chake Chake, is one of Pemba's highlights, offering idyllic beaches, nature trails for spotting flying foxes (bats), good snorkelling and superb diving. It also has a touch of historical romance, as the legendary pirate **Captain Kidd** is said to have buried booty here. The island's name is explained by the legend of the prophet **Hadhara** (his name meaning "knowledge" or "culture"), who appeared before Misali's fishermen and asked them for a prayer mat (*msala*). There was none, so Hadhara declared that since the island pointed towards Mecca, it would be his prayer mat. Misali's real treasure is its rich **ecosystem**, which boasts 42 types of coral, over three hundred species of fish, a rare subspecies of vervet monkey, endangered colonies of flying foxes (bats), nesting sites for green and hawksbill turtles, and a large if rarely seen population of nocturnal coconut crabs. In 1996, the island and its reefs became Pemba's first (and as yet only) **marine sanctuary**; it's uninhabited except for the sanctuary's rangers and passing fishermen.

A $5 **entrance fee**, generally not included in tour prices, is payable at the island's **visitor centre** on Baobab Beach, where the boats pull up. It has good displays on ecology and wildlife, and information sheets that you can take with you while snorkelling or walking along one of the island's **nature trails**, which covering mangroves, other intertidal zones, and coral caves. The shallow reef around Misali is good for **snorkelling**, though the current can be trying for weaker swimmers and you should stay close to the shore as currents further out can be dangerously strong; ask the folks at the visitor centre for advice. The reef off Baobab Beach, which starts a mere 10–40m from the shore, is easily accessible. The shallower part features conical sponges, traditionally collected by fishermen for use as hats; further out, the reef is cut by sandy gullies and teems with life. Misali lacks accommodation, camping is prohibited and so is alcohol.

Ras Mkumbuu and Quanbalu

The long and narrow peninsula north of Chake Chake Bay is **Ras Mkumbuu**, its name, meaning a belt or sash, aptly describing its shape. At its far western tip are the remains of East Africa's oldest-known Muslim town, **Quanbalu** (or Qanbalu), which may have been founded as early as the eighth century. The town was mentioned by several early writers as one of two major trading centres on Pemba (the other being **Matambwe Mkuu**, 30km north).

The **ruins**, mostly from the thirteenth and fourteenth centuries but built on older foundations, include a large congregational mosque which was the largest in sub-Saharan Africa until the Great Mosque at Kilwa Kisiwani on the mainland pipped it in the fourteenth century. Quanbalu's has an especially fine arched *mihrab*, as well as a minaret. Other remains include houses and at least fourteen tombs, some of them surmounted by chimney-like pillars and decorated with Chinese porcelain. Both the pillars and inclusion of chinaware are common throughout the Swahili coast. For reasons as yet unknown, the town fell into decline in the sixteenth century and was eventually abandoned.

Access is cheapest by road from Chake Chake (upwards of $30–40 per vehicle), though the extremely rocky trail along the peninsula means that many drivers are reluctant to take you: try Jambo Tours & Safaris (opposite). More romantic but much more expensive (up to $150 per group) is to come by sea: Swahili Divers (p.707) can sort you out.

Pujini ruins

Some 10km southeast of Chake Chake, the **Pujini ruins** provide an enjoyable and fascinating half-day excursion. Pujini is the site of a citadel built during the heyday of the **Diba tribe**, who ruled eastern Pemba from the fifteenth to seventeenth centuries, by the tyrant Muhammad bin Abdulrahman, a merchant and pirate whose nickname, **Mkama Ndume**, means "grasper of men". The ruins (also known as Mkama Ndume) are defensively located on a hilltop and are now mostly rubble, though the presence of several old tamarind and baobab trees makes them singularly photogenic. The **mosque** is the best-preserved building. Also noteworthy is the **well**, half-filled with rubble, in the enclosure's northeastern corner. Legend has it that Mkama Ndume had two wives who were jealous of each other, so to prevent them meeting at the well he had a dividing wall built inside it. One of the wives would use a bucket and rope whilst the other descended by a staircase – still partially visible – to reach the water. More likely though is that the small chamber at the foot of the staircase was a shrine to spirits (*majini*). Carved out of the soft limestone, it contains a lamp niche and a small plaster relief of a **siwa horn** – a symbol of sovereignty and authority all along the Swahili coast. Another

staircase leads up to the battlements, beyond which what looks like a dried moat was actually a canal that enabled dhows to be pulled inland for loading and offloading.

The ruins aren't signposted and are difficult to find without a guide – just make sure that whoever accompanies you knows the place. **Renting a car** is the simplest approach; half-day rental with driver costs $30–35 from Chake Chake. Alternatively, rent a **bicycle**. From Chake Chake head towards the airport along the road and turn right after 5km (1km before the airport). Pujini village lies 4km along a rough dirt road.**Guides** can be hired informally in Pujini, though few people speak English, and they'll need their own bicycle. The site lies a few kilometres southeast of the village, south of a football field.

Mkoani

MKOANI is where most visitors to Pemba arrive, as ferries from Stone Town dock here. The town itself is very dull, though the fish and produce market on the beach south of the jetty is always worth a look. However, Mkoani is a handy base for **boat trips** and **snorkelling**, and for visiting Kengeja, one of several places in Pemba that adopted **bull-fighting** from the Portuguese (see the "Tanzania in celebration" colour section).

Practicalities

Ferries dock at the port 1km downhill from the centre along Uweleni Street. **Daladalas** drop you along Uweleni Street (there's no stand); leaving Mkoani, #603 daladalas run frequently throughout the day to Chake Chake (Tsh700–800). Given the limited hours and slothsome endeavour of The People's Bank of Zanzibar (Tues & Thurs 8.30am–1.30pm), forget about **changing money** – Chake Chake is better. If you get ill, the town's **hospital** (℡024/245 6075 or 024/245 6011) is Pemba's best.

Accommodation, eating and drinking

With precisely two hotels, one restaurant, and a couple of stalls selling grilled and fried fish in the market, Mkoani doesn't exactly spoil its visitors. Local culinary passions centre around octopus (*pweza*).

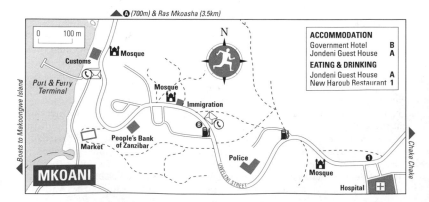

Government Hotel (*Hotel ya Mkoani*) 1km uphill along Uweleni St ☎024/245 6271. Identical in every respect to the government hotels in Chake Chake and Wete, giving a weird sense of déjà vu. Rooms are tatty twin beds (and no single rates, at least officially), but they do have private bathrooms, fans and nets, and it's the only place that serves alcohol. Breakfast included. ➍

Jondeni Guest House 1km north of the port ☎024/245 6042, ⓔjondeniguest@hotmail.com. Set on a hill high above the sea, this is Pemba's best-value budget hotel, and is well used to backpackers, offering a wide range of affordable boat and snorkelling excursions. Accommodation ranges from dorms ($8 per person) to rooms with bathrooms, all with big *semadari* beds. There's a pleasant garden at the back with inspiring sea views, and there's always something cooking for lunch and dinner ($5): the spiced octopus in coconut with mashed potatoes is particularly good, and they're happy to conjure up something more fancy like prawns if you order early. Breakfast included: dorms ➌, rooms ➍.

New Haroub Restaurant Uweleni St. A limited choice to say the least, but if you order in the morning they should be able to rustle up something more exciting than rice with fish. Closed Ramadan.

Around Mkoani

Mkoani is ideal for **boat trips**, as there are several places within an hour's sail. Between September or October and February, don't miss the **bullfighting** at Kengeja on the south coast (see the "Tanzania in celebration" colour section). To get there, catch a #215 daladala from Mkoani marked "Mwambe". Tickets for seats in the sexually segregated grandstands cost a few hundred shillings; it's free to join the crowds around the arena. There's no accommodation.

Boat tours and snorkelling

Ignore Mkoani's handful of *papasi* and arrange things instead at *Jondeni Guest House*, whose costs are reasonable, and which has its own *mashua* dhow (with twin outboard motors and sun canopy) for trips. **Makoongwe Island**, 3km off Mkoani, has a roost of Pemba flying foxes (bats), while minuscule **Kwata Islet**, 7km west off Mkoani, is practically all beach and has decent snorkelling and a patch of mangroves nearby. The isles can be visited individually, or combined as one trip for $20 per person (minimum two). Snorkelling at Misali Island (see p.710) costs $35 per person including entrance fee, and snorkelling over a shallow wreck at Panza Point in the south is $45. *Jondeni* also offers high-tide **mangrove tours** by dugout canoe ($5 per person) for birding and swimming, and **sailing** in *ngalawa* outriggers ($10 per person).

Wambaa Beach

The sheltered western shore of **Wambaa Peninsula**, north of Mkoani, has several kilometres of dreamy white sand of the kind that upmarket lodge developers dream about, though at present there's only one such place. In addition, the untouched mangrove forests at either end are a bird-watcher's delight. The place is most easily visited on a boat trip arranged through Mkoani's *Jondeni Guest House*, which gives you the chance to spot dolphins along the way. Public transport is limited to infrequent #230 daladalas from Mkoani, and #330 daladalas from Chake Chake.

Staying on the cheap is not possible, as the only **hotel** is the woefully expensive *Fundu Lagoon*, 2km north of the village (ⓦ www.fundulagoon.com; $530–1050 depending on the room and season; closed mid-April to mid-June).

Wete

The friendliest and most likeable of Pemba's main towns, **WETE** counts a dhow port and two markets among its attractions (the reason for its having two markets, incidentally, is to divide local fishermen from competitors from Tumbe in the northeast: the former occupy the central market; the latter the one near the *Government Hotel*; both are open daily from 10am to 6pm). The **port** still sees the occasional *jahazi* trading dhow, and – should the service not have been suspended yet again – a weekly ferry to and from Tanga on the Tanzanian mainland. The main reason for coming here is to visit Ngezi Forest, the beaches further north, and a number of fascinating ruins to the northeast.

Practicalities

There are **two roads** from Chake Chake to Wete: the old and more direct one (30km; daladala #606 marked in red) to the west, whose surface has all but

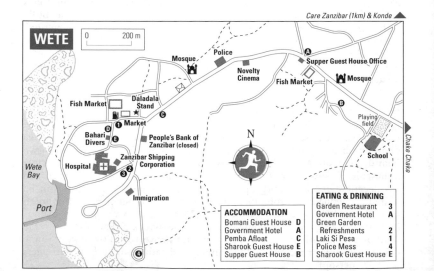

Care Zanzibar (1km) & Konde ▲

WETE   0   200 m

Mosque

Police

Supper Guest House Office

Novelty Cinema

Mosque

Fish Market

Fish Market

Daladala Stand

Market

Fish Market

Bahari Divers

People's Bank of Zanzibar (closed)

Playing field

Zanzibar Shipping Corporation

Wete Bay

Hospital

School

N

Chake Chake

Immigration

Port

ACCOMMODATION
Bomani Guest House   D
Government Hotel   A
Pemba Afloat   C
Sharook Guest House   E
Supper Guest House   B

EATING & DRINKING
Garden Restaurant   3
Government Hotel   A
Green Garden
   Refreshments   2
Laki Si Pesa   1
Police Mess   4
Sharook Guest House   E

vanished, and the fast Pemba North Feeder Road (35km; daladala #606 marked in black), which starts 7km north of Chake Chake at Melitano junction. The drive takes about an hour. Wete's **daladala** stand is next to the market near *Sharook Guest House*; you can also catch vehicles along the main road.

Change **money** before coming as there's no bank. **Plane** and **ferry tickets** can be bought at a number of ever-changing agents along the main road. If you're **ill**, Wete Hospital (☎024/245 4001) between the centre and the port is in reasonable shape, and Clove Island Pharmacy opposite *Garden Restaurant* is well stocked.

Accommodation

All except *Bomani* include breakfast in their rates.

Bomani Guest House Between the market and *Sharook Guest House* ☎024/245 4384. A sleepy, friendly and pleasingly prim and proper Muslim place with eight rooms (singles and doubles), all but one sharing bathrooms. All have good box nets, ceiling fans and a table and chair. ④
Government Hotel (*Hotel ya Wete*) Junction of the Chake Chake and Kondo roads ☎024/245 4301. The third of Pemba's identikit government-run hotels, this one still with some broken windows from a bomb blast following the 2000 elections. All rooms are large en-suite twins, rather dilapidated but acceptable if you get one with a decent net and clean sheets; there's also a TV lounge, bar and restaurant that requires plenty of patience on your part. ④
Pemba Afloat ⊛www.pembaisland.com. Not exactly *in* Wete, this is a trio of yachts moored in Njao Inlet, two of which have berths for overnight

guests. Mainly used by scuba-divers (see p.706), other excursions are also available, and the food's good. Full-board. ⑧

Sharook Guest House In the centre ☎024/245 4386 or 0747/431012. Run by a friendly and very helpful family, this calm place is used to tourists, and offers a range of tours. Rooms are large and have fans, most also have bathrooms complete with toilet seats and paper. Check the nets for size though. There's satellite TV in the entrance, and very good food if ordered early. ③
Supper Guest House (aka *North Lodge*) Behind the Soviet-style apartment blocks west of the Chake Chake road ☎0747/427593 or 0748/427459. Half-asleep staff and just four rooms, two (same price) with showers and cleanish squat toilets, but the mosquito nets are too small, and some rooms are stuffy. All have ceiling fans and a table and chair. Food available. ③

Eating and drinking

There's not a lot of choice for **eating out**, but one or two good places turn up trumps if you order several hours before you intend to eat. Best of the lot is *Sharook Guest House*, with a good range of very well-prepared dishes for around Tsh5000. Several basic restaurants along the main road provide cheaper meals, the best being *Garden Restaurant* (for full meals) and *Green Garden Refreshments* (better for snacks), both at the west end of town. Near the western market, the dingy-looking *Laki Si Pesa* is reliable for *pilau* and *supu ya kuku* (chicken broth). Food stalls by the post office sell juice, octopus, meat balls, fish and chapati, and there's a place with fresh sugar cane juice facing the *Government Hotel*. **Drinkers** are catered for by the *Government*

Ferries from Wete

Since 2004, a weekly passenger **ferry** has replaced the rickety cargo boat between Wete and Tanga on the Tanzanian mainland, though if history be a judge, this is liable to be suspended at any time. The vessel is either the MV *Mudathir* or the MV *Aziza I* or *II*. Sailing times change on an almost weekly basis, the mostly likely being Sunday morning at either 7.30am or 9am. Also worth enquiring about is the MV *New Happy*, which occasionally continues from Stone Town via either Mkoani or Wete to Tanga.

Hotel and the *Police Mess*, the latter likely to be closed to visitors at times of political tension.

Around Wete

Northern Pemba contains a scattering of atmospheric medieval **ruins**; those at Hamisi near Chwaka are especially beguiling. There are plenty of **beaches** too, Pemba's best (all spectacularly wide, blindingly white and just about perfect), but getting to them can be tricky. Easiest to reach is Vumawimbi on Ras Kigomasha peninsula, just north of Ngezi Forest, another worthwhile destination. As Wete is Pemba's main dhow harbour, there are lots of possible day-trips by **boat**, notably to the casuarina-covered Uvinje Island, Fundo Island (overnight stays possible), Misali Island for snorkelling, and ancient Shirazi ruins at **Matambwe Mkuu**, three hours' sail south of town. **Scuba-diving** is offered by Pemba Afloat (see p.707), a trio of twenty-metre ketches moored at Njao Gap.

Tours can be arranged through the *Sharook* and *Supper* guest houses, who offer much the same trips at much the same prices. The standard cost for visiting Ngezi Forest is $25 per vehicle plus entrance fees; spice tours, at a farm south of Wete, are no more than $40 per person including lunch and transport. Wete's speciality, though, is a trip to **Fundo Island** by *mashua* dhow; you can either camp for the night or stay with a family for around $50–60 per person (this can also be arranged through Jambo Tours & Safaris in Chake Chake; see p.710). Both guest houses can arrange **vehicle rental** ($40 a day for a car with driver, excluding fuel; $25 for a motorbike) or fix you up with a **bicycle** (Tsh5000/$5 a day).

Ngezi Forest

Until the introduction of cloves in the early 1800s, sixty percent of Pemba was covered by forest. Nowadays the only sizeable remnants are small patches at

---

Cloves

Pemba's low hills, fertile soil and tropical climate are ideal for growing **cloves** (*karafuu*). Cloves are the dried flower buds of the dark-leafed evergreen *Syzygium aromaticum*, a tall thick-trunked tree – the buds are picked from the tree and laid out to dry by the roadside. The pungent but pleasant **smell** derives from a high concentration of *eugenol*, an essential oil used medicinally as a local anaesthetic (especially for toothaches), in perfumes, and, of course, in cooking (especially in *pilau*). Eighteenth-century French traders smuggled cloves from the Dutch East Indies to Madagascar, from where, in 1818, Seyyid Saïd transplanted several thousand saplings to Zanzibar, and by the 1850s Zanzibar had become the world's largest clove producer. Unguja's plantations exceeded Pemba's until 1872, when a hurricane destroyed two-thirds of Unguja's clove trees and the balance shifted. Nowadays, Pemba accounts for ninety percent of production from a combined total of three and a half million clove trees.

Recent times have been hard for Pemba's clove producers however, due to the Zanzibar State Trading Corporation's monopoly. With the corporation paying well under open-market rates, a large proportion of each harvest is smuggled by dhow to Mombasa in Kenya, where producers receive up to three times as much (this smuggling is the reason for the many roadblocks north of Chake Chake). Unfortunately, the only visible signs of the government revenue from cloves are the seaside mansions built by local politicians and "big men".

Ras Kiuyu and Msitu Mkuu in the northeast, and in the 29-square-kilometre **Ngezi–Vumawimbi Nature Reserve** straddling the neck of Ras Kigomasha Peninsula in the northwest. Protected as a forest reserve since the 1950s, Ngezi (also written Ngesi) is a veritable ecological island, of which about a third is incredibly lush tropical forest characterized by unusually tall hardwood trees – notably endangered *mvule* teak species, that grow to over 40m. Most of the trees are festooned with vines and creepers, and their canopies conceal a thick tangle of undergrowth as well as a few small ponds. Other habitats in the reserve include coastal evergreen thickets, mangroves, swamps and a central heathland, the latter dominated by a species of heather (*Philippia mafiensis*; in Kiswahili, *ndaamba*) unique to the islands of Pemba and Mafia.

The major attraction for naturalists is the chance of spotting the endemic Pemba **flying fox**, which is a large species of bat that feeds on figs, mangoes, papaya and tree blossoms, and thereby plays an important pollinatory role. Other mammals include the **marsh mongoose** – Pemba's only indigenous carnivore – and the endemic Pemba **vervet monkey** (or green monkey, locally called *tumbili*). With luck, you might also see the diminutive **Pemba blue duiker** (*chesi* or *paa wa Pemba*), feral pigs introduced by the Portuguese, and the Zanzibar **red colobus**, introduced in 1970 when fourteen monkeys were relocated from Unguja's Jozani Forest. The forest's **birdlife** should interest keen twitchers, with rare sightings including the Russets scops owl, the Pemba white-eye, Pemba green pigeon and the violet-breasted sunbird.

Locals consider the forest sacred, and Ngezi contains at least six **ritual areas** called *mizimu* that are periodically swept clean for the benefit of the ancestral spirits who dwell there. Two of these, containing the tombs of *shariffs* (people claiming descent from the Prophet Muhammad), lie along the road that transects the reserve and can be visited as part of a two-kilometre **nature trail** from the gate, which also passes by ponds that are popular with birds. With time for arranging things, you could also go looking for flying foxes (two days' notice required), or scouting for scops owls at night (half a day's notice).

Practicalities

Getting to Ngezi is easiest on an organized tour; around $30 per person including entrance fees from Wete, or $40 through Chake Chake's tour operators or *Jondeni Guest House* in Mkoani. Access by daladala is awkward, as they terminate in the scruffy market town of **Konde**, 4km short of the reserve (#601 from Wete, #602 from Chake Chake); there's neither accommodation there or in the reserve. Daladala drivers are usually happy to earn a few thousand extra shillings by taking you up to the gate though. Alternatively, you could cycle from Wete, a 36-kilometre round trip.

The office at the gate (daily 7.30am–4pm) collects a Tsh4000 **entry fee**; there's no charge if you're cycling or driving through to get to the top of Ras Kigomasha Peninsula. Although you can walk around Ngezi unaccompanied, it's best to hire a **guide** at the gate, both for their knowledge, and for security as muggers have frequented the forest in the past. The guides are free, but tips are expected.

Ras Kigomasha

Passing through Ngezi Forest, the forest ends quite abruptly, giving way to scrub, patches of cultivation, a neglected rubber plantation started by the Chinese, and a couple of fabulous and virtually deserted beaches on either side of Pemba's northernmost point, **Ras Kigomasha**. On the western side is a fabulous five-kilometre stretch of sand known as **Panga ya Watoro**, a curious name meaning "the knife of the refugees". To the east, **Vumawimbi** ("roaring surf") beach consists of 4km of gently curving bay.

Practicalities

Public transport stops at Konde, so access is limited to car rental or organized tours. Cycling isn't really a possibility unless the sixty-kilometre round trip from Wete leaves you unfazed; remember that camping is illegal on Zanzibar. There are just two **hotels** in the area, both with delightful beaches.

Kijiwe Beach Resort Ngezi Beach, southwest of Ngezi Forest ☎0747/866027. A new locally run hideaway, with basic *bandas* on the beach, and better-appointed cottages behind. Also has a restaurant. A day-trip from Wete, arranged through *Supper Guest House*, costs $20 per person including lunch. ❹

🏃 **Manta Reef Lodge** Panga ya Watoro beach ☎0747/423930, ⓦwww .mantareeflodge.com. Sitting on a completely unspoiled and utterly magical beach that's worth the asking price alone, this is particularly recom-

mended if you've come to Pemba for scuba diving or snorkelling – the hotel has an excellent dive centre (One Earth Diving; see p.707), a relaxed and unpretentious atmosphere, and fifteen marvellous and very large, open-fronted (breezy) timber-floored cottages lining the hillside between the ocean and forest, most with sea views. There's also a beach bar, hammocks, and a welter of activities (most $25–60), including nature and bird walks, fishing from inflatable kayaks, road and sea excursions, and of course diving and snorkelling. Full-board. ❽

Tumbe and the Hamisi ruins

Heading east from Konde, a sandy track to your left after 6km leads to the sprawling village of **TUMBE**, known for its lively fish market and skilful dhow builders. Beyond the village, the road heads on to the beach, where Tumbe's fishermen land and auction their catch. The best times to visit are at low tide (especially in the afternoon) and early in the morning, when there's a lively assortment of traders from Wete and elsewhere. Tour operators in Chake Chake include Tumbe in most northern itineraries. By **public transport**, things are easiest from Chake Chake: catch a #602 daladala and get off at the junction 1.5km beyond Chwaka. From Wete, catch a #601 daladala to Konde and change there for a #602, and get off at the same junction. The village is 1km from there, and the beach another 1km beyond.

East of Tumbe are several **medieval ruins**, of which the sixteenth-century **HAMISI RUINS** (also known as the Haruni or Chwaka ruins), close to the bay, are the most impressive and easiest to find. Tradition has it that the fortified town and palace were the seat of Harun bin Ali, son of Muhammad bin Abdulrahman (see p.711). Tyranny appears to have been a family trait, as hinted at by Harun's nickname, *Mvunja Pau: mvunja* means destroyer, and *pau* is the pole that takes the weight of a thatched roof. Hamisi is signposted on the main road about 2km east of the junction for Tumbe. The first building you see is a small **mosque**, much of it reduced to blocks of collapsed masonry. The *mihrab* remains more or less intact, in spite of a tree root growing into it. The mosque was built for Harun's wife and gets its nickname of *Msikiti Chooko* ("Mosque of the Green Bean") from the ground beans or peas that were blended with the mortar to strengthen it. Some 100m southeast of the mosque are the remains of a particularly large **tomb**, surmounted by a ten-sided pillar bearing curious upside-down shield-like indents on one side. On the other side of the pillar is an incised eight-petalled floral motif, oddly off-centre. The tomb is said to be that of Harun. Fifty metres south of here is a large **Friday mosque** that appears

to be raised by a metre or so above the ground, a false impression caused by the amount of rubble covering the original floor. Its *mihrab* is in almost perfect condition; the five circular depressions on either side of it originally held Chinese porcelain bowls, and people still leave offerings here.

Travel details

Ferries

Schedules to and from Pemba and Tanga change, or are cancelled, with amazing frequency, and travel agents outside the port towns are often ill-informed, so don't rely on them.

Pemba (Mkoani) to: Dar es Salaam (3 weekly; 6hr); Stone Town (8 weekly; 3–6hr by day, 8–10hr overnight).

Pemba (Wete) to: Stone Town (1 weekly; 8hr 30min); Tanga (1–2 weekly; 6hr).

Unguja (Stone Town) to: Dar es Salaam (7 daily; 2–3hr); Pemba (8 weekly; 3hr by day, 8–10hr overnight).

Flights

Airline codes used below are: AE (Air Excel), AT (Air Tanzania), CA (Coastal Aviation), PA (Precisionair) and ZA (ZanAir). Where more than one airline flies to the same destination, the one with most frequent flights and/or shortest journey times is listed first.

Pemba to: Dar (ZA, CA: 2–3 daily; 1hr); Saadani (ZA, 1–2 daily; 30min); Tanga (CA: daily; 20min); Zanzibar (ZA, CA: 3 daily; 30min).

Zanzibar (Unguja) to: Arusha (ZA, AE, CA: 3 daily; 1hr 20min–2hr); Dar (CA, PA, ZA, AT: hourly; 20–25min); Kilimanjaro (PA: daily; 2hr 5min–2hr 15min); Kilwa (CA: daily; 2hr 20min); Mafia (CA: daily; 1hr 30min); Pemba (ZA, CA: 3 daily; 30–35min); Ruaha (CA: daily; 3hr 30min); Selous (ZA, CA: 3 daily; 1hr–1hr 15min); Serengeti (ZA: daily; 1hr 20min); Songo Songo Island (CA: daily; 1hr); Tanga (CA: daily; 1hr).

Contexts

Contexts

History

anzania's history is one of many themes, with the main distinction being between inland Tanganyika, and Zanzibar and the coast. Of the former, little is known beyond four or five centuries ago other than some vague notions about mass migrations and what little can be deduced from archeological finds. The history of Zanzibar and the coast, however, can be traced with considerable accuracy over several thousand years, thanks to chronicles left by ancient Greeks, Romans and Egyptians, and later by Persians, Arabs and even Chinese.

The coast's turbulent and often brutal history has been shaped both by its geographical position on the edge of Africa, and by the monsoon system of the western Indian Ocean, which brought it within reach of sailing ships from Arabia, India and the Far East. The first historical link connecting Tanganyika with Zanzibar was the ivory and slave trade, which took its primary materials from the mainland but was dominated by Zanzibar. The second was the unification of Tanganyika and Zanzibar in 1964 to create the present **United Republic of Tanzania**. A marriage of convenience, some say, and indeed the united parties have shown little affection towards one another over their four-decade-old union. In spite of this, Tanzania continues to be held up as an example of mutual co-operation between different peoples and cultures, showing that ethnic conflict ignited by the artificial national boundaries imposed by the Europeans can be overcome.

Tanzania's first inhabitants

Mainland Tanzania has been inhabited since the dawn of humankind. Some 3.75 million years ago, a family of hominids with chimpanzee-like faces strode across an area of wet volcanic ash in **Laetoli** in Ngorongoro; at the time of their discovery in the 1970s, the fossilized footprints of these three *Australopithecus afarensis* provided the first absolute proof that our ancestors were walking upright way before anyone had imagined. Fossilized hominid remains and stone tools found at **Oldupai Gorge** nearby trace the evolution of man from those first faltering steps to the genesis of modern humans.

Tanzania's "modern" historical record starts with a modest collection of **ostrich shell beads** recently unearthed in the Serengeti. Should their tentative date of 70,000 years turn out to be true, they are among the very earliest manmade items found to have been made for a purpose other than pure survival, and as such indicate that modern man – *Homo sapiens* – had evolved much earlier than previously thought. Indisputable evidence of modern man comes in the form of **rock paintings**, especially in the Irangi Hills of north-central Tanzania, the oldest of which may be up to 30,000 years old, and the youngest just a century or so. Comprising one of the most extensive rock art complexes on earth, the thousands of paintings, many remarkably well preserved, depict a land of wild animals and everyday domestic life not too different from today.

The people who left those paintings were small groups of **hunter-gatherers**, living from game meat, honey, wild berries, fruits, nuts and roots, and possibly also from limited agriculture – who arrived in Tanzania as early as three thousand years ago. Most of these "aboriginal" hunter-gathering cultures have long since disappeared, having been either annihilated or assimilated by more powerful newcomers. Two exceptions are the **Hadzabe and Sandawe**

△ Laetoli footprints, Ngorongoro Conservation Area

tribes of central Tanzania, both of whom have traditions of rock painting. The Sandawe abandoned their ancient way of life a few decades ago, but the Hadzabe persist, albeit under immense adverse pressure which will probably consign their way of life to oblivion within the next decade. Both tribes speak unusual languages characterized by clicks, similar in sound to that spoken by southern Africa's San (or "Bushmen"), who were also hunter-gatherers until recently and also had a strong tradition of rock painting. The similarities point to the existence of a loosely linked and widely dispersed hunter-gathering culture across much of sub-Saharan Africa, before the arrival of the Bantu turned their world upside-down.

The Bantu

Cameroon is considered to be the cradle of the loosely connected ethno-linguistic group known as the **Bantu**. Nowadays spread over much of Africa south of the equatorial rainforest belt, the Bantu are primarily an agricultural people, and have been for thousands of years. Their success at agriculture in their original homeland led to an increased population and, ultimately, to overpopulation. So started the first of several waves of **Bantu migrations** in search of fresh land. The first to reach Tanzania arrived at least two thousand years ago, possibly much earlier, and the last settled just a few centuries ago. Over time the migrants split into a myriad distinct tribes, each developing their own individual cultures, belief systems and languages. Elements common to most Bantu societies, apart from their shared linguistic roots, are their agricultural way of life, the belief in a unique God, and a knowledge of **iron working**. Excavations in Ufipa in southwestern Tanzania, and in the land of the Haya west of Lake Victoria, have led to the astounding conclusion that, until the European method of mass-produced steel was perfected, Tanzania's deceptively simple furnaces produced the world's highest quality steel, fired at temperatures that were unthinkable in eighteenth-century Europe. Nowadays, Bantu-speakers comprise all but a handful of Tanzania's 129 officially recognized tribes.

Early coastal trade

Little is known about the coast's early history other than that its first inhabitants, African fishermen who also populated Zanzibar and the Mafia archipelago, arrived almost six thousand years ago. The first non-Africans to visit the coast, sometime before 2000 BC, were **Sumerian traders** from Mesopotamia, followed a millennium later by the **Phoenicians**, who used Zanzibar as a stopover en route to Sofala (Mozambique), whose main commodity was gold. Around this time, **Assyrian traders** were also active on the East African coast. The earliest coins found on Zanzibar are over 2000 years old, and come from ancient Parthia (northeast Iran), Sassania (Iran/Iraq), Greece and Rome. Egyptian coins and a dagger have also been found, as have Roman glass beads, all proving that trading connections between East Africa and the **Mediterranean** were strong. At that time it would appear that Zanzibar and the coast were controlled by Sabaeans from the kingdom of Sheba (modern Yemen), who brought weapons, wine and wheat to exchange for ivory and other East African goods.

The **monsoon weather system** of the western Indian Ocean meant that traders, coming by boat, were obliged to stay for part of the year in East Africa, before the monsoon winds changed direction and gathered enough strength for the journey home. In due course, **trading towns** grew up along the East

African coastline. The second-century *Periplus of the Erythraean Sea*, which calls the coast Azania, mentions one such place called **Rhapta**, which scholars have tentatively identified with Pangani or an as yet unknown location in the Rufiji Delta. Also mentioned, two days' sail away, is the island of **Menouthias**, probably Pemba or Unguja. Both places, says the *Periplus*, were under Arabian sovereignty.

Swahili civilization

In later centuries, the East African coastline became part of a vast trading network that included China, Malaysia and Indonesia. Malay and Indonesian influence lasted from the sixth century to at least the twelfth, and the **Indonesians** are believed to have introduced coconuts, bananas, and possibly the Polynesian-style outrigger canoes (*ngalawas*) still used today. Chinese presence is seen in numerous finds of coins and porcelain, and in written accounts.

The first outsiders to establish a permanent presence in East Africa were **Persian traders** who, by the end of the first millennium AD, ruled a series of settlements along the coast, from Somalia in the north to Mozambique in the south. According to legend, they arrived in 975 AD after the king of Shiraz dreamt that a giant iron rat destroyed the foundations of his palace. Taking it as a bad omen, the king set sail with his six sons in seven dhows. Separated in a storm, each son founded a city along the East African coast, including Kizimkazi in Zanzibar, and Kilwa on the mainland. Whatever the historical truth of the tale, Persian traders were already well acquainted with the East African coast – which they knew as Zang-I-Bar or the "sea of the blacks" – and the influx of a ruling class encouraged many to settle.

The Persians were not averse to intermarrying with indigenous inhabitants, and in so doing gave rise to East Africa's **Shirazi culture** – a blend of African and Persian elements that was later to receive sizeable Arab input, becoming the **Swahili**. The birth of the Swahili (from the Arabic *sahel*, meaning "coast") coincided with an upsurge in the Indian Ocean trading network. **Gold** and **ivory** were the main African exports, though slaves, turtleshell, leopardskin, rhinoceros horn, indigo and timber also found ready markets. The Swahili civilization reached its peak in the fourteenth and fifteenth centuries, when its coastal towns – especially **Kilwa** – controlled the flow of gold from mines near Sofala; mines that some scholars believe to have been the original "King Solomon's Mines".

The main legacy of Swahili civilization is its language, **Kiswahili**; essentially a Bantu tongue enriched with thousands of loan-words from Persian and Arabic, and nowadays also Portuguese, Hindi, English and German. Kiswahili spread into the interior along trade routes over following centuries, and is now the official language of Tanzania and Kenya, and the lingua franca of eastern Africa.

The Portuguese period

The growth and prosperity of the Swahili came to an abrupt end on the arrival of the **Portuguese**. The first to visit was **Vasco da Gama** in 1498, en route to discovering the ocean route to India, which would circumvent the need to trade across a series of Arab middlemen in the Middle East.

Although Portuguese involvement in East Africa was initially limited to its use as a staging post, the riches of the Swahili trade soon kindled a more avaricious interest. In 1503, part of Unguja Island was sacked by the Portuguese captain

Ruy Lourenço Ravasco, who exacted annual tribute in gold from Unguja's traditional ruler, the Mwinyi Mkuu. Kilwa Kisiwani on the mainland – by then East Africa's most prosperous city – was sacked two years later, and within a decade the Portuguese had conquered most of the Swahili coast. However, the Portuguese presence disrupted the ancient western Indian Ocean trading network so badly that the entire coast fell into decline, and formerly prosperous cities were abandoned and crumbled away.

The collapse of the trade network deterred further Portuguese interest in East Africa other than maintaining a number of harbours to act as stepping stones along the route to India. This lack of attention, coupled with their increasingly stretched military resources, opened the way for a new power to take control of the abandoned trade routes – **Oman**. In 1606 Pemba was taken by Omanis based in Malindi, Kenya, and in 1622 the Portuguese suffered a monumental defeat at the **Battle of Hormuz**. The defeat signalled the de facto ascendancy of Oman power in the region, although the Portuguese held onto Unguja until 1652, when the Omani sultanate sent a fleet at the request of the Mwinyi Mkuu. The modest Portuguese garrison at Stone Town was captured and burned, and the Europeans expelled. The last Portuguese stronghold in East Africa north of Mozambique, Mombasa's Fort Jesus, fell to the new rulers in 1698.

Omani domination and the slave trade

Having ejected the Portuguese, Oman was the western Indian Ocean's major trading and military power, and was swift to assert its control over East Africa. The only real threat to Omani sovereignty was from a rival Omani dynasty, the Mazrui family, based in Mombasa. The Mazruis seized Pemba in 1744, but were unsuccessful in their attempt to take Unguja eleven years later. In spite of the rivalry, Zanzibari trade flourished, and key to its wealth was the **slave trade**. The establishment of sugar and clove plantations in European Indian Ocean possessions boosted demand, and by 1776 – when the French joined the trade – some three thousand slaves were being traded annually at Zanzibar and Kilwa. The increased demand, and rocketing prices for ivory, encouraged Oman to extend its control over the mainland trade routes.

Given its increasing economic independence, Zanzibar was becoming politically autonomous from Oman. The pivotal figure in Zanzibari history was **Seyyid Saïd** (full name Saïd bin Sultan bin Ahmad bin Saïd al-Busaïdi; ruled 1804–1856), who at the age of 15 assassinated his cousin to become the sole ruler of the Omani empire. The sultan (*seyyid*) recognized the economic potential of Zanzibar and East Africa, and spent most of his reign developing and consolidating it, encouraging merchants to emigrate from Oman, and continuing incursions on the African mainland. In 1811 he opened Stone Town's notorious **slave market**, which during the following sixty years traded over a million lives. Shrewd diplomacy with the British – who were increasingly pushing for the abolition of the slave trade – allowed Seyyid Saïd to wrest Mombasa from the Mazruis in 1827. The sultan also cultivated trading relationships far beyond the Indian Ocean: the United States opened a consulate in Stone Town in 1837, and European nations were swift to follow. With the entire East African coast now under his control, and backed by the Western powers, Seyyid Saïd took the unusual step of moving the Omani capital from Muscat to Zanzibar in 1841, and a short-lived but immensely prosperous golden age began, bankrolled not just by ivory and slaves, but by cloves – for which Zanzibar accounted for four-fifths of global output.

Seyyid Saïd was succeeded by **Sultan Majid**, and after a brief power struggle between him and his brother, the Omani empire was split into two: the Arabian half, and the vastly more prosperous African one centred on Zanzibar. In spite of the efforts of the British to stop it, the slave trade was now booming, as was the clove trade, and Omani control of the inland trade routes also made Zanzibar the logical base for European explorers of the "dark continent".

The age of exploration

Apart from a trip to Lake Nyasa by the Portuguese explorer Gaspar Bocarro in 1616, the first Europeans to travel through Tanzania were the German missionaries, **Johann Ludwig Krapf** and **Johannes Rebmann**, who in the 1840s tried to convert several tribes to Christianity, without much success. In 1848, Krapf – who considered Africans as "the fallen man, steeped in sin, living in darkness and [the] shadow of death" – moved inland to try his luck elsewhere, and became the first European to describe Mount Kilimanjaro (to the incredulity of the bigwigs back home, who ridiculed the idea of a snow-capped mountain on the Equator). Hot on his heels came a train of other explorers and missionaries, among them such Victorian heroes as Sir Richard Francis Burton, James Augustus Grant, Joseph Thomson, Samuel White Baker and John Hanning Speke. Many of them set out to locate **the source of the Nile** (see p.495), a riddle that had baffled Europeans since Herodotus in the fifth century BC. The search for the Nile's source was not just an academic exercise, but had geo-political importance: whoever controlled the Nile's waters would control Egypt and from 1869 the Suez Canal, giving quick access to India and the Far East. The "riddle of the Nile" was finally solved by the British explorer, **John Hanning Speke**, who reached the shore of Lake Victoria in 1858, and went on to sail down the great river. The most famous explorers to have graced East Africa though are a duo whose names have become inseparable: the journalist-turned-adventurer **Henry Morton Stanley**, and the missionary-turned-explorer **Dr David Livingstone**. Their famous "Dr Livingstone, I presume?" meeting took place in 1871 at Ujiji, on the shore of Lake Tanganyika in western Tanzania (see p.536).

Although Livingstone was careful about how he went around preaching the gospel of the Lord, he was very much an exception among a motley bunch of conceited missionaries who believed that Africans were primitive and inferior and therefore in need of being "civilized". But with competition heating up between rival European powers for new markets and natural resources, the supposedly backward nature of Africans and the handy excuse of wanting to stamp out the slave trade (in which Europeans had freely participated) gave them the perfect reason to begin the conquest of the continent by force.

German and British colonization

The **partition of Africa** was rendered official in a series of conferences and treaties in the 1880s between various European powers. Through the 1886 **Anglo–German Agreement** finalized in 1890, Germany took nominal control of Tanganyika, while Britain gained Kenya, Uganda and Zanzibar.

The German colonization of Tanganyika

The arrival of the militaristic **Ngoni tribe** in the 1830s had plunged vast swathes of southern Tanganyika into chaos, while in the north the equally warlike **Maasai** (see box on pp.446–447) were busy carving out their own terrain. This turbulent state of affairs should have made the German conquest of Tanganyika an easy matter, but in fact their problems began the instant they arrived, when in 1888 local slave traders – who were none too appreciative of Germany's intention to abolish their livelihoods and wrest away control of the caravan routes – rose up in arms. Led initially by a slaver named Abushiri ibn Salim al-Harthi – from whom the uprising got its name, the **Abushiri War** – the conflict dragged on for over a year before the Germans finally gained control.

With the coast subdued, the Germans set their sights inland, but immediately ran into opposition from those tribes whom they had failed to convince to sign over their land; a series of farcical treaties were cooked up by arch-colonist **Karl Peters**, whom locals knew as "the man with bloodstained hands", and who was later lauded as a "model colonial administrator" by Adolf Hitler.

In central Tanzania, two tribal chiefs in particular were able to take advantage of the crumbling status quo, and of Zanzibar's waning power, by taking military control of portions of the trade routes, which they used to exact tributes from passing caravans. The tributes in turn financed the purchase of arms on the coast, which enabled them to expand their budding empires. **Chief Mirambo** (see p.555) of the Nyamwezi built a short-lived empire between central Tanganyika and what is now Burundi, Rwanda and Uganda. Luckily for the Germans, Mirambo's empire disintegrated shortly after his death in 1884, but the more southerly Hehe tribe, under **Chief Mkwawa** (see p.583), were a formidable adversary to German rule, which they proved in 1891 by annihilating an attacking German force. Mkwawa's resistance only ended in 1898, when he killed himself rather than surrender to the surrounding German troops.

Mkwawa's suicide signalled a temporary lull in armed resistance. But in 1905, frustrated with the harsh rule of the colonialists, a vast swath of central and southern Tanganyika rose up once more, in what became known as the **Maji Maji Uprising**. The war gets its name from a soothsayer named Kinjikitile (see p.222), who claimed to have discovered a spring from which magic water (*maji*) flowed. If sprinkled on a person, he said, the water would protect the wearer from bullets.

This time using brutal scorched-earth and terror tactics, the German army (the *Schutztruppe*) finally crushed the uprising in 1907, and began the colonization proper of Tanganyika. Work included the construction of a railway from their Indian Ocean capital of Dar es Salaam to Kigoma port on Lake Tanganyika, following almost exactly the route of one of the most infamous of nineteenth-century slave roads.

The railway arrived in Kigoma in February 1914, too late to be of much help to the Germans, however, as **World War I** was about to erupt. Although the war's main focus was Europe, the German troops posted in Tanganyika, ably led by Paul von Lettow-Vorbeck – chief architect also, it must be said, of the genocide perpetrated against Namibia's Herero tribe in 1904–08 – began a guerrilla-style conflict against the British based in Kenya and Zanzibar, and Belgians in Burundi and Rwanda. Von Lettow-Vorbeck's purpose was not to defeat the numerically superior Allied forces, but to tie down resources that would have been more productively used back in Europe. The strategy worked, and Von Lettow-Vorbeck's force remained undefeated when, in 1918, the Armistice brought an end to the slaughter and forced his surrender.

The British Protectorate of Zanzibar

In 1870 Sultan Majid's successor, **Sultan Barghash**, inherited vast wealth – much of it squandered on opulent palaces and civic buildings that grace Stone Town today – but also an empire that had little real power, not least over the mainland trade routes that had made its fortune.

Barghash's accession also coincided with a devastating cholera epidemic that killed ten thousand people in Stone Town alone, whilst in April 1872, a violent cyclone swept across Zanzibar, destroying all but one ship in Stone Town's harbour (around three hundred in all), and levelling 85 percent of Unguja's clove plantations. This string of disasters was compounded in 1873 when the sultan was forced by the British to ban the slave trade between the African mainland and Zanzibar (slavery itself was only abolished in 1897). With both its main sources of income in tatters, it became increasingly clear that Zanzibar was at the mercy of British.

Barghash tried briefly to reassert his authority on the mainland, but by 1882 European plans for the colonization of Africa were in full flow. Barghash's protests fell on deaf ears, and he retreated from international affairs, while Europe proceeded with the partition of Africa. Zanzibar's mainland possessions – with the exception of a six-kilometre coastal strip – were taken from it in 1886.

Barghash died in 1888 a bitter man, to be succeeded by his son, Khalifa bin Saïd, who had little choice but acquiesce in whatever the Europeans wanted. He died just two years later, and on November 1, 1890, Zanzibar was declared a **British Protectorate**. The sultanate was allowed to continue in a ceremonial capacity, but the real shots were called by the British – quite literally, in August 1896, upon the death of Sultan Hamad bin Thuwaini bin Saïd. Two hours after the sultan's death, the palace complex in Stone Town was seized by Khalid, a son of Sultan Barghash, who, urged on by 2500 supporters, proclaimed himself sultan. The British, who preferred Thuwaini's cousin, Hamud ibn Mohammed, issued an ultimatum which Khalid ignored. At precisely 9.02am on August 27, the **shortest war in history** began when three British warships opened fire on the palace complex. By 9.40am the British had reduced two palaces to rubble, killed five hundred people and forced the surrender of Khalid, who took refuge in the German consulate from where he fled into exile.

The road to Independence

At the end of World War I, the British were given control of Tanganyika, though the administration remained separate from that of Zanzibar, which was nominally still a sultanate. British rule in Tanganyika (1919–61) was relatively benign compared to the German period and the British oppression of neighbouring Kenya, which culminated with the Mau Mau Uprising in the 1950s. In Tanganyika, the British just picked up where the Germans had left off: the city of Dar es Salaam was expanded, agricultural "up-country" towns like Arusha and Morogoro flourished, and the railway was extended to Mwanza on Lake Victoria. The five-decade British Protectorate over Zanzibar was similarly uneventful. Zanzibar's sultans were nothing more than puppets, and the real rulers set about consolidating their administration with a new judicial system, refinements to the rubber-stamping parliament and the installation of a sewerage system for Stone Town.

World War II was a major turning point in the history of Tanzania and of Africa. Many Tanzanians had been conscripted as soldiers and porters for the British and expected something in return when the war was over. Opposition to colonial rule began across the continent, and with the new world order now dominated by the United States and the Soviet Union, change was inevitable.

In Tanganyika, the Independence movement was headed by the Tanganyika African National Union – **TANU** – founded as the Tanganyika African Association in 1929. From 1954 onwards, TANU was led by **Julius Kambarage**

731

△ Presidents Julius Nyerere

Nyerere (see p.513), a mild-mannered former schoolteacher from Butiama in northern Tanganyika, and graduate of Edinburgh University. Professing a peaceful path to change inspired by Mahatma Gandhi, Nyerere's open-minded and down-to-earth style won TANU widespread support, and the grudging respect of the British, who, faced with the inevitability of Independence sooner or later, saw in Nyerere a figure that they could trust. Following a number of legislative elections in which TANU were kept at bay with a rigged system of "reserved seats", in August 1960 mounting tension finally forced free elections for 71 seats of the Tanganyika Legislative Council. TANU won all but one, Nyerere became chief minister, and in that capacity led the move towards **Tanganyikan Independence**, which was officially proclaimed on December 9, 1961.

Zanzibari Independence – and revolution

In Zanzibar the situation was more complicated, as there were effectively two colonial overlords: the British, who wielded political and judicial power, and the Omanis, who still owned the land and the island's resources, and whose sultans retained their importance as heads of state. The first rumblings of **discontent** came in 1948, when African dockers and trade unionists publicly protested against both British and Arab domination. Britain eventually allowed the formation of political parties to dispute elections held in 1957 for the Legislative Council. Africans were represented by the **Afro-Shirazi Party (ASP)**, while the Arab minority supported the Zanzibar Nationalist Party (ZNP). Between 1959 and 1961 a series of increasingly rigged elections gave the ZNP, in coalition with the Zanzibar and Pemba People's Party (ZPPP), disproportionate representation in the council, while the ASP was consistently denied power. Heedless of the rising tension, the British instituted limited self-government in June 1963, and the following month another round of elections was held, which again saw the ASP lose, despite having polled 54 percent of the vote. Nonetheless, Britain went ahead with plans for Independence, and on December 10, 1963, the **Sultanate of Zanzibar** came into being.

African resentment of the Arabs on Zanzibar – who made up just twenty percent of the population but controlled most of the wealth and power – grew steadily until, on January 12, 1964, barely four weeks after Independence, **John Okello**, a Ugandan migrant labourer and self-styled Field Marshal, led six hundred armed supporters in a bloody **Revolution**. In one night of terror, some twelve thousand Arabs and Indians were massacred, and all but one percent of Stone Town's Arab and Indian inhabitants fled the country. Among them was Zanzibar's last sultan, Jamshid ibn Abdullah, who ended up in exile in England. Despite having started the Revolution, Okello lacked the support to create a government, and the ASP's leader, Sheikh Abeid Amani **Karume** made himself Prime Minister of the Revolutionary Council of the **People's Republic of Zanzibar and Pemba**.

The United Republic of Tanzania

As President of Tanganyika, Nyerere's first moves were to promote a sense of national consciousness: Kiswahili was made the official language and was to be taught in every school, while tribal chiefdoms – a potential source of divisive conflict – were abolished. In 1962 Tanganyika adopted a republican constitution, and elections returned Nyerere as president. The following year, Tanganyika became a **one-party state** under TANU.

The chaos of the Zanzibari Revolution coincided with the height of the **Cold War**, and came shortly after Nyerere had survived an army mutiny, for which he had recourse to help from British marines. Feeling threatened by the possibility of extremists taking power in Zanzibar, Nyerere sought to defuse the threat through an **Act of Union** between Tanganyika and Zanzibar, which would give him the power to intervene militarily on the Isles. Karume, for his part, was in a quandary, as the exodus of Arabs and Indians after the bloody revolution instantly devastated Zanzibar's economy, and few international organizations were willing to help a left-wing regime that had come to power through such violent means. The solution, which he soon came to regret, was to accept Nyerere's overtures for the Union, which was signed on April 26, 1964, bringing into existence the **United Republic of Tanzania**. Nyerere became Union president and Karume one of two vice-presidents. Zanzibar retained political and economic autonomy, a separate administration and constitution, and its own president and judicial system, while gaining fifty of the 169 seats in the Tanzanian National Assembly. In spite of these concessions, Karume came to view the Union as a mainland plot to take over the island, and even now – four decades down the road – few people on either side are happy with the marriage.

Ujamaa

As first President of the Union, Nyerere faced huge challenges. The entire country was one of the poorest on earth, with just twelve doctors and 120 university graduates to its name. Life expectancy was 35, and 85 percent of the adult population was illiterate. The outside world was willing to help out, but the inevitable strings would compromise Tanzania's independence. The task of developing the country was made harder as over ninety percent of the population lived in remote rural settlements.

In February 1967, at the height of an extended drought, Nyerere delivered a famous speech that became known as the **Arusha Declaration**, in which he laid out his vision of self-reliant, non-Marxist "African socialism" for Tanzania: "The development of a country is brought about by people, not by money. Money, and the wealth it represents, is the result and not the basis of development... The biggest requirement is hard work. Let us go to the villages and talk to our people and see whether or not it is possible for them to work harder."

In practice, those noble ideals translated into "villagization": the resettlement of rural households into centralized and collective **Ujamaa villages**, *ujamaa* being the Kiswahili word for brotherhood or familyhood – togetherness. Until 1972 the resettlement programme was voluntary, and around twenty percent of the population had moved. This, however, wasn't enough, so **forcible resettlement** started and by 1977 over thirteen million people, or about eighty per cent of the population, resided in some eight thousand Ujamaa villages.

Unfortunately, the policy was an **economic disaster**. Vast areas of formerly productive land were left untended and the communal system proved to be more fertile for corruption and embezzlement than for agriculture. Yet the policy did have its successes: access to clean water, health care and schools was vastly improved, and by the 1980s adult **literacy** had soared to over ninety percent. Equally important, throwing everyone together in the same, sinking boat, forged a strong and peaceful sense of **national identity** that completely transcended tribal lines, and created a nation of people justifiably proud of their friendly relations with each other, and with outsiders. Tanzania is one of few African countries wholly unaffected by ethnic or religious conflict, and is unique in having a population that takes pride in both its tribal and national identity.

Depression, collapse and conciliation

By the mid-1970s, both mainland Tanzania and Zanzibar were in a terrible state. *Ujamaa*, while forging a healthy sense of national identity, had completely wrecked the country's economy, and by 1979 Tanzania's jails contained more political prisoners than in apartheid South Africa. Over on Zanzibar, Karume, who had courted the USSR, Cuba and China for help in establishing state-run plantations (many of which now lie abandoned), had brought about similar ruin but without much sense of unity: the Isles remained, and still remain, bitterly divided, the most obvious political gulf mirroring geography, with pro-government Unguja Island and pro-opposition Pemba Island.

Karume became increasingly paranoid and dictatorial. He deported Asians whom he believed were "plotting" to take over the economy, elections were banned, arbitrary arrests and human-rights abuses became commonplace and there were even allegations that Karume himself had arranged the murder of leading politicians and businessmen in the late 1960s. In April 1972, after two previous attempts on his life, an **assassin's bullet** finally found its mark.

Big changes came in 1977. The failure of *Ujamaa* to address Tanzania's economic problems had become glaringly apparent, and the same year the **East African Community** between Tanzania, Kenya and Uganda, founded in 1967, was finally buried when rock-bottom relations with capitalist Kenya closed the border between the two countries. With both sides of the Union increasingly isolated, closer ties between them seemed to be the way forward. In February 1977, the Afro-Shirazi Party – under Karume's more moderate successor, Aboud Jumbe – merged with Tanganyika's TANU to form **Chama Cha Mapinduzi** (CCM – The Revolutionary Party), which remains in power today. Nyerere became chairman, and Jumbe vice-chairman.

The Kagera War and the road to change

While relations with Kenya were bad, things were worse with **Idi Amin**'s brutal dictatorship in Uganda. Matters came to a head in October 1978, when Uganda invaded Tanzania's northwestern **Kagera Region**. Tanzania barely had an army worth the name, so it took a few months to train up a force of some fifty thousand men, who responded, assisted by armed Ugandan exiles, with a counter-attack in January 1979. Much to the surprise of seasoned military observers, they completely routed the supposedly better-equipped and better-trained Ugandan army, and pushed on to Uganda's capital, Kampala, driving Idi Amin into exile. The war, although brief, was something that Tanzania could ill afford, and the estimated $500-million cost ensured further economic misery back home.

As Tanzania sank deeper into **debt** and resorted to international donors for aid, Nyerere found himself increasingly at odds with his stated socialist ideals. Far from being self-reliant, Tanzania was more dependent than ever. The economy had collapsed, agriculture barely sufficed for subsistence, and the country was saddled with a crippling debt burden. In 1985, with the donors demanding economic reforms, **Nyerere resigned** from the Union presidency. It was time for change.

The **1985 elections** ushered in a Union government headed by pragmatic reformer **Ali Hassan Mwinyi**, whose ten-year tenure was characterized by the wholesale desertion of Nyerere's socialist *Ujamaa* policies. Instead, capitalist economic reforms and liberalization were the order of the day – literally so in the case of IMF-imposed austerity measures. Another condition of donor support was the scrapping of the one-party political system.

The multiparty era

Independent Tanzania's first **multiparty elections** were held in 1995. There were two polls: one for the Union parliament and presidency, the other for Zanzibar's separate executive. On the mainland, things passed off smoothly with the ruling CCM and their presidential candidate, former journalist **Benjamin Mkapa**, easily winning the race. Steady economic improvement since then, and a hopelessly divided mainland opposition, handed Mkapa and the CCM a second term in 2000, whilst – to no one's surprise – the 2005 elections once again saw the CCM romp to power, this time under the charismatic leadership of **Jakaya Kikwete**.

Things could not have been more different over on **Zanzibar**, its experience of multiparty politics marred by bitterly disputed elections, condemnation from international observers, withdrawal of foreign aid, outbursts of violence, political repression, and a whole lot of bad blood between the two feuding parties, CCM and CUF, that was only barely contained by a peace accord – the *Muafaka*, or Agreement – signed in 2001.

Zanzibar since 1995

While the 1995 election on the mainland was generally free and fair, the contest for Zanzibar's separate executive plunged the Isles into chaos. There, the CCM was pitted against a formidable foe, the **Civic United Front (CUF)**. As heir to the ZNP and ZPPP parties that had given way to the ASP in 1963, CUF favoured looser ties with the mainland, even secession, and had at one time vaunted the possible imposition of Islamic sharia law. Needless to say, CCM viewed their challengers as extremists to be kept out of power at all costs.

The run-up to the elections was marred by unrest, and although polling itself was peaceful, violence erupted again when CCM was declared victorious by the slenderest of margins: winning 26 seats in Zanzibar's parliament to CUF's 24. Despite condemnation from international observers, who reported serious discrepancies, **Salmin Amour** was duly reinaugurated as Zanzibari president, responding to his critics with police harassment and arbitrary arrests, causing around 10,000 CUF supporters to flee and the European Union to cut off aid.

After the election, CUF activists were charged with treason after speaking out against police harassment. Amnesty International adopted the accused as prisoners of conscience. Arrests of CUF MPs followed in 1998, and international pressure mounted against the repeatedly postponed **treason trial**, which finally got under way in March 1999. As was becoming habitual with Zanzibar's embattled leaders, Amour claimed that the Isles' troubles were being orchestrated by an external "plot". More arrests followed in 1999, despite which CCM and CUF signed a Commonwealth-brokered **reconciliation pact** to resolve their differences through peaceful means. It was not to be.

There had been high hopes that the **October 2000 elections** would be free and fair but, in a repeat of 1995, the Zanzibari vote was a dangerous farce. Trouble erupted immediately after polling, with both CUF and CCM claiming irregularities, and international observers calling the vote a shambles. The new Zanzibari president, **Amani Karume** – son of Zanzibar's first president – attempted to defuse the tension by acquitting the treason trial suspects. The gesture was not enough to appease CUF, who felt they had been cheated once again and demanded a re-run. Tensions increased when CUF issued a ninety-day ultimatum in November calling for fresh elections, failing which, "extraordinary action" was promised.

In **January 2001**, just days before CUF's ultimatum was to expire, mass demonstrations in Zanzibar and Dar es Salaam were held, and the ensuing violence saw the deaths of at least 26 demonstrators and one policeman. News footage clearly showed police brutality, but Karume went on the offensive, blaming CUF for having started the violence, and publicly praising the police for their handling of the "heavily armed demonstrators". Mass arrests were widely reported, as were allegations of intimidation, torture and rape, especially in the CUF stronghold of Pemba.

Public condemnation of the killings came from all sectors of Tanzanian society, finally prompting the government to talk with CUF. Much to everyone's surprise this resulted in a peace accord. Called the **Muafaka** ("Agreement"), CCM agreed to incorporate other parties in their government, release political detainees, and reform the judiciary and widely derided Zanzibar Electoral Commission. And as a possible sop to CUF's nationalist leanings, Zanzibar has had its own flag, and international soccer team to boot, since 2004.

The October **2005 elections** – which once again saw CCM claim a slender victory on the Isles – were a predictably chaotic and contentious affair, marred by violence and allegations of vote-rigging by the ruling party. For much of the year, CCM and CUF had traded inflammatory threats during which the spirit of *Muafaka* seemed all but buried. The Electoral Commission had indeed been reformed, but unfortunately for CUF, so had constituency boundaries: three seats were transferred from their Pemba stronghold to Unguja, CCM's powerbase, a decisive move as CCM won by only one seat. The establishment of a **permanent voters' register** was not without controversy either, with allegations that mainland police and soldiers – traditionally CCM supporters – had been drafted into the Isles to be inscribed as voters.

As has now become traditional, the elections completely buried the remaining vestiges of *Muafaka*'s spirit, and there has been little real change to give cause for hope. The two parties are as bitterly divided as ever, corruption is pervasive, the Isles' basic infrastructure remains inadequate, freedom of the press is not all that it could be, and the gap between the haves and have-nots has widened: the average Zanzibari is poorer than his Tanganyikan cousin, earning well under a dollar a day.

For now, the fragile *Muafaka* accord survives, but at some point the status of Zanzibar as part of the Union will have to be renegotiated or clarified. And for the islands to have a genuine chance of lasting peace and prosperity, it's clear that CCM and CUF will have to continue working together, whether they like it or not.

The Union since 1995

While **Benjamin Mkapa's presidency** was largely overshadowed by events in Zanzibar, his tenure saw a number of quiet but positive changes, continuing Ali Hassan Mwinyi's reformist legacy. Most obvious was the further liberalization of the **economy**. The results are certainly impressive from a macro-economic stance: inflation has stabilized at four percent, down from 27 percent in 1995; GDP grew by seven percent in 2005; the ten percent target for 2008 and beyond appears reasonable; and per capita income has doubled to over $500 a year, with civil servants earning at least $70 a month.

But figures can be misleading. Per capita income may have increased, but only for those working. Averaged out across all people of working age, the figure barely tops $200, and over one third of rural Tanzanians live on less than a dollar a day (the UN's laughably derisory "poverty line"). The increase in GDP also isn't as rosy as it looks: a large chunk is accounted for by tourism and mining, both sectors largely owned by foreign companies, with little "trickle-down" to the masses.

Yet Mkapa's success at taming Tanzania's macro-economic ills is unequivocal, and brought with it renewed donor confidence and recently, substantial relief from Tanzania's crippling **foreign debt burden**. In 2001, China wrote off the entirety of the debts owed her, and in 2005 the G8 finally decided that enough was enough, and also cancelled their debts – albeit with various long-term conditions attached. With luck, Tanzania's 2005 budget will be the last one where the servicing of debt repayments accounted for a quarter of total government expenditure, or three times the country's health budget.

One of the first fruits of debt forgiveness has been an ambitious and so far successful programme to place Tanzania back on the path towards **universal primary education** (and literacy), last achieved during Nyerere's tenure. The scheme makes primary education free and compulsory. Mkapa also addressed the country's woesome **infrastructure**: an ambitious road construction programme is now well under way, and even with projects habitually finishing years behind schedule, the benefits are beginning to be felt, particularly along the north–south corridor from Dar to Mozambique, and west to Mwanza and the lake region.

Internationally, Tanzania has forged closer ties with Kenya and Uganda. In 2001, the **East African Union** was resurrected, its 27-member legislative assembly based in Arusha. The three nations also agreed on a Customs Union, the first step towards political federation. Although the 2010 target for this seems a mite optimistic, there's little doubt that regional cooperation is the way forward.

The future

Whilst the future of Zanzibar is nigh impossible to predict, that of Tanzania as a whole is easier to divine. The cancellation of a large part of Tanzania's foreign debts, and hence the debt servicing payments that have crippled Tanzania's economy for decades, should hopefully see the focus shift from macro-economics to more immediate **social concerns**, as funds are freed up for further improvements in health care, education and basic infrastructure. But Tanzania's greatest challenge is its fight against **poverty**: the economy may have been rescued from the fires of *Ujamaa*, but the benefits still need to reach ordinary people, the *wananchi*. Yet with President Kikwete's burden lightened by debt forgiveness, this is probably the most optimistic time in Tanzania (at least on the mainland) since Independence.

Wildlife and habitats

D
espite tremendous losses over the last century, Tanzania teems with wildlife and is considered to be one of the twelve most bio-diverse nations on earth, with at least 310 mammalian species, 1100 varieties of birds, 1370 species of butterfly, 380 reptilian and amphibian species and over 10,000 distinct plants, a quarter of which are unique to the country.

Even outside the protective boundaries of the national parks and game reserves, it's possible to see a lot of **wildlife** if you travel fairly widely, including gazelles, antelopes, zebras, giraffes, monkeys and baboons, and even hippos, buffaloes, crocodiles and elephants. On the reptile front, snakes are rarely sighted, but lizards skitter everywhere, and geckos can be seen clinging upside down on ceilings at night. Other innocuous denizens include giant millipedes up to thirty centimetres long, which live on rotten fruit. The country's **birdlife**, ranging from the thumb-sized cordon bleu to the ostrich, is astonishingly diverse and attracts ornithologists from all over the world, as well as making converts of many visitors.

If this impression of abundant wildlife alarms you, rest assured that any **danger** is minimal. The big cats, for example, are hardly ever seen outside the parks and reserves. Buffaloes, though plentiful, are only really dangerous when solitary. The main species to be wary of are **hippos** and **crocodiles**, who inhabit many of the lakes and rivers, meaning you should always seek local advice before swimming in inland waters.

This introduction to Tanzania's habitats, mammals, birds, reptiles and amphibians complements the full-colour guide to the mammals of East Africa at the front of this book, which will prove useful in identifying the main species likely to be seen on safari. For more detailed coverage, a field guide is a must – some recommended **books** are listed on p.763.

Habitats

Tanzania contains a huge range of **habitats**, from scrub and bushland to a wide range of woodland, rainforests, lakes, rivers, swamps, marshes, mangroves and coral reefs. Tanzania has a higher percentage of protected wildlife areas than any other country on earth, with over a quarter of its surface area covered by national parks and game and forest reserves.

Savannah and semi-arid habitats

Savannah, consisting of patches of grassland, bushland and some lightly wooded areas, covers vast areas of Tanzania, most famously in the Serengeti. Nowadays largely protected by national parks and reserves, the **grasslands** owe a good part of their existence to human presence over the centuries: bush fires set by hunter–gatherers and cattle herders regularly cleared the land of scrub (and tsetse flies), and the trampling of cattle inhibited new growth, thereby making humans an integral part of the ecological balance. Over the last century, humans have been excluded from vast swathes of the country, and a new balance has yet to be found. The Serengeti's famous wildebeest herds are now 1.7 million strong – compared with a few hundred thousand until the 1950s when the Maasai were evicted from the Serengeti – while other species have seen their numbers plummet.

In areas with more erratic rainfall, a thin scattering of flat-topped acacia trees, along with shorter acacias, occurs among the grassland, producing the archetypal imagery of the East African landscape. In drier areas, these wooded grasslands give way to the typical semi-arid flora of **thornbush and thicket**, characterized by an often impenetrably thick growth of stunted, thorny trees, which are grey for most of the year, but become green during the rainy season. Scaly-barked species such as acacia and euphorbia also occur. The true **desert** habitat around Lake Natron is drier still and plant life is very limited; many of the trees and bushes are dwarf, and large areas are bare, stony desert with a thin and patchy growth of desert grasses and perhaps a few bushes along dry watercourses.

Woodland and forest

Roughly one third of Tanzania is covered by some form of **woodland**, including deciduous and evergreen woods, rainforests and high-altitude montane forest. Open deciduous woodland covers a large part of central Tanzania, and is known as **miombo** (the local name for the dominant *Brachystegia* tree species). Despite its dry appearance for much of the year, the woodlands are particularly rich in plants and animals and are the cornerstone for the migratory ecosystem of Selous and Mikumi, which stretches down as far as Mozambique. The pristine state of much of the *miombo* woodlands owes a lot to the presence of **tsetse flies**, which are vectors for sleeping sickness. Though wild animals have developed immunity to the disease, it strikes down livestock and humans with impunity, leaving areas of infestation largely unpopulated. For more information on the *miombo* environment, see p.289.

The most important areas of natural woodland are **rainforests**, at their most spectacular and diverse along the isolated ranges of the ancient **Eastern Arc Mountains** (see p.353), which include North and South Pare, East and West Usambara, Uluguru and Udzungwa. The isolated nature of the forests over millions of years has enabled the evolution of an incredible diversity of plants and animals, and one place in particular – Amani Nature Reserve in East Usambara – fully deserves its unofficial tag of the Galapagos of Africa.

At higher altitude, generally over 1500m, the rainforest gradually gives way to cloudy **montane forests**. Reaching 2900m, these are characteristically interspersed with grassy meadows, which add to their conservation value. The **main highland forest areas** are to be found on Mount Kilimanjaro and Mount Meru. Higher up, beyond the tree line, the so-called **Afro–Alpine zone** bears strong similarities to those of other high East African mountains, and includes giant heather, protea and groundsel and desolate high-altitude tundra: see p.348 for a full description.

Inland wetlands

Tanzania has more **inland waters** than any other country in Africa, ranging from enormous freshwater and caustic salt-rimmed soda lakes in the Rift Valley, to both permanent and seasonal rivers scattered with water pools, marshes and swamps.

There are several **permanent rivers**, the main ones being the Ruvuma, Ruaha/Rufiji, Wami and Pangani. All drain eastwards into the Indian Ocean. Their permanent nature makes them extremely favourable dry-season habitats for wildlife, when the surrounding savannah and woodlands become too dry. Particularly rich are the section of the Great Ruaha as it flows through Ruaha National Park; the estuary of the Ruvuma, now protected as part of Mnazi Bay-Ruvuma Estuary Marine Park; the Wami estuary, part of Saadani Game Reserve; the Kilombero Valley; and the Rufiji, as it flows through the northern part of Selous Game Reserve. **Seasonal rivers**, which only flow during the rains, are also known as sand rivers; permanent vegetation along their banks, and water pools in their beds during the dry seasons (which are sometimes deliberately excavated by wild animals such as elephants) are particularly good places for seeing wildlife.

Where rivers pass through flat land, **marshes and swamps** dominate, and are exceptionally rich for wildlife, especially birds, whether in the rains when water levels are at their height, or in the dry season when the waters drain into permanent water pools. Two superb and easily visited areas for seeing these habitats are Selous Game Reserve and Tarangire National Park.

In the far west, three big **freshwater lakes** – Africa's Great Lakes – dominate the scene, both ecologically and economically. Lake Victoria, in the northwest, is the world's second-largest freshwater lake, and the main source of the River Nile; sadly, the lake has become a perfect example of catastrophic environmental damage caused by man, having been the scene of the mass extinction of hundreds of fish species in the last few decades (see p.489). Still, the lake retains its beauty, along with a good deal of terrestrial and avian wildlife, particularly at Rubondo Island National Park. In the west, Lake Tanganyika occupies a deep Rift Valley fissure, making it the world's second-deepest lake. It contains an amazing profusion of fish species, especially the tiny and very colourful cichlids. Even richer is Lake Nyasa in the southwest, another deep Rift Valley lake, which contains over four hundred cichlid species – one third of the world total – many of which are unique. Apart from their fish life, the lakes also mark the eastern boundary of central and west African flora and fauna, and their shores contain many plant and animal species absent elsewhere in Tanzania, most famously Lake Tanganyika's chimpanzees.

Most of Tanzania's other inland water bodies are shallow **soda lakes**, occupying Rift Valley depressions that over the ages have been filled with sediment, making them extremely shallow. Their alkalinity isn't overly conducive to wildlife, though they are important as drinking points, especially during and after the rains when the water is fresher. Their most spectacular inhabitants are lesser flamingos, usually in flocks of tens of thousands, for whom the soda-loving algal blooms in the lakes are the staple food.

The coast

The islands of the Zanzibar and Mafia archipelagos, and the narrow, low-lying coastal strip itself between the shore and higher ground inland, receive ample rainfall, as their weather patterns follow the monsoon cycle of the western Indian Ocean. As a result, they contain a range of rich habitats, including coastal plain, forest and woodland, beaches, sandbanks and mudflats, mangrove swamps and – offshore – some of the finest coral reef systems on earth.

Large areas of the **coastal plain** are covered in moist, tree-scattered grasslands, and higher areas – ideally placed to break rain clouds as they roll in from the ocean – are covered by **coastal forests**, which at Amani Nature Reserve are among the world's richest. However, the extent of the forests has declined massively over the last century, due to commercial logging, wood collection for making charcoal, clearance for agriculture and ensuing soil exhaustion and uncontrolled fires. Nonetheless, a good many coastal forests survive, albeit in isolated patches. On the beach itself, tall **coconut palms** and the rather weedy-looking **casuarina** (known as "whistling pine") dominate the high-tide line.

Most of the coastline though is not the white sandy beaches of the holiday brochures, but humid and silty **mangrove swamps**, which play a vital part in offshore marine ecology by acting as gigantic filters for fresh water washed in by rivers, and as impediments to coastal erosion. The largest tract is in the Rufiji delta, but all the coastal tidal creeks and estuaries are more or less bordered by mangroves (*mikoko* in Kiswahili). There are also areas of saline grassland on the landward side of some of the mangrove thickets. Although fun to travel through by boat, mangrove forests are not noted for their faunal diversity, although the mangrove trees themselves – characterized by spiky aerial roots through which they breathe – are uniquely adapted to their salty, water-logged environment. One unusual animal you're bound to see is the **mudskipper**, a fish on the evolutionary road to becoming an amphibian.

Far and away the coast's richest habitats, and the country's most colourful, are **coral reefs** which form a fringing barrier along much of the shore between Kenya and Mozambique, and also surround the offshore islands of Zanzibar and Mafia. Corals, which only thrive in warm, shallow tropical waters, are a strange mix of animal and mineral: the coral that we know as jewellery is actually an external skeleton (exoskeleton) excreted by coral polyps (microscopic animals). Growing together in colonies of billions, the excretions of these polyps eventually forms gigantic reefs, which provide a perfect habitat for all kinds of marine life, from micro-organisms, sea cucumbers, sea stars and crustaceans, to a dazzling array of fish, dolphins, sea turtles and whales.

Corals are very vulnerable to small changes in ocean temperature, however. The 1997–98 El Niño event, which fractionally increased ocean temperatures, killed off large numbers of symbiotic algae called *zooxanthellae*, without which the coral polyps also die – in places wiping out up to ninety percent of corals. Tanzania's reefs have recovered well, and much of the coast still offers some extraordinarily inspiring snorkelling and diving.

Wildlife

For further information, see "The mammals of East Africa colour section.

Mammals

Tanzania has 310 species of **mammals**, of which 31 are endangered and fourteen are endemic, meaning that they occur here and nowhere else. The majority are vegetarian grazers, browsers and foragers at the lower end of the food chain – animals such as monkeys, rodents and antelopes. The big predators are fewer in species and tend to be the dominant topic of conversation at game lodges. Tour operators make a big song and dance about the **Big Five** – elephant, rhino, buffalo, lion and leopard or cheetah – and in consequence some safari-goers feel short-changed if they fail to see these emblematic species. But don't ignore the less glamorous animals: there can be just as much satisfaction in spotting a shy, uncommon antelope or in quietly observing a herd of gazelle. Once you get the bug, you'll be looking out for a lone-striped hyena rather than the common and gregarious spotted version, or for a serval cat rather than a cheetah.

Primates

Tanzania contains dozens of primate species. One you're certain to see almost anywhere with a few trees, is the small and delicately built **vervet monkey**, which has no difficulty adjusting to the presence of humans and, if possible, their food. Vervets are characterized by long tails, black faces, white cheek tufts and grey fur, and are perfectly adapted to a life on the prowl for fruits, leaves, insects and just about anything else small and tasty. The males have pale blue genitalia. Their main predators are leopards and large eagles, hence their constant and nervous skyward glances.

Almost as common in certain areas, notably on the coast and in lowland rainforests, are agile **blue monkeys**, whose predilection for agricultural crops makes them a pest. Other than colour, the species is very similar to smaller **red tail monkeys** (whose tails are actually orange), from whom they diverged only recently; male blue monkeys who fail to gather their own "harem" can be accepted into red tail troops, and hybrids of the two species are common enough. Their main predator is the crowned eagle.

The beautiful, leaf-eating and effortlessly acrobatic **black–and–white colobus monkeys**, with attractive bushy white tails, can be seen all across northern Tanzania's forests, albeit in isolated habitats. They are usually found high in the tree canopy, swinging from tree to tree in family groups and they rarely descend to the ground. Anatomically, they're distinguished by their lack of thumbs. Rare colobus offshoots include several isolated populations of **red colobus monkeys**, notably in the Udzungwa Mountains, in Zanzibar's Jozani Forest, in northwestern Selous and at Gombe and Mahale.

If you stay in a game lodge, you're quite likely to see **bushbabies** (galagos) at night, as they frequent dining rooms and verandahs. There are two species, the cat-sized greater galago and the kitten-sized lesser galago. Both are very cute, with sensitive, inquisitive fingers and large eyes and ears to aid them in their hunt for insects and small animals.

Chimpanzees live right across Africa's tropical rainforest belt, from the Gambia and Sierra Leone to Lake Tanganyika, and are the stars of Tanzania's primates; there are several communities at Gombe Stream and Mahale Mountains national parks on the east shore of Lake Tanganyika, and a translocated population on Lake Victoria's Rubondo Island. Chimpanzees are our closest living relatives, sharing 98.5 percent of our genes, and exert an irresistible fascination. Like us, they're intelligent and complex (and sometimes temperamental) social creatures who feel and share emotions, and are able to adapt to different environments and foods, pass on knowledge learned from experience and make and use simple tools, like probes for fishing ants and termites from their nests. They also hunt in a human way, use plants medicinally, raid each other's communities and sometimes descend into states of war. Their **communities** consist of fifteen to eighty individuals, dominated by "alpha males", whose dominance depends not so much on physical strength as an ability to form and keep strategic alliances with other males. Chimps are endangered, their African population having dropped from two million a century ago to around 150,000 today. Continuing worries are the on going loss of tropical forests outside the parks, subsistence hunting and the killing of mothers to capture infants for the pet trade, entertainment industry and – notoriously – biomedical research.

Equally gregarious are **baboons**, which you'll see wherever you go on safari. There are two species in Tanzania: yellow baboons in the centre and south, and the slightly larger olive baboons in the north. Like chimps, baboons form complex, hierarchical and highly territorial troops of between twenty and a hundred individuals. Rank and precedence, physical strength and kin ties all determine an individual's position in this mini-society led by a dominant male. The days are dictated by the need to forage and hunt (baboons will consume almost anything, from a fig tree's entire crop to a baby antelope). Grooming is a fundamental part of the social glue during times of relaxation. Large males can be somewhat intimidating in size and manner, and should always be treated with wary respect, as they're quite capable of mauling humans: never feed or tease them, or tempt them with visible food.

Rodents and hyraxes

Rodents aren't likely to make a strong impression on safari, unless you're lucky enough to do some night game drives – or preferably walks; Tarangire and Selous are good places for this. If you partake of either, you may see the bristling back end of a **crested porcupine** or the frenzied leaps of a **spring hare**, dazzled by headlights or a torch. In rural areas off the beaten track you occasionally see hunters taking home **giant rats** or **cane rats** – shy, vegetarian animals, which make good eating. Tanzania has several species of **squirrel**, the most spectacular of which are the giant forest squirrel – with its splendid bush of a tail – and the nocturnal **flying squirrel** – which actually glides, rather than flies, from tree to tree, on membranes between its outstretched limbs. Very widespread are the two species of **ground squirrel** – striped and unstriped – which are often seen dashing along the track in front of the vehicle.

The bucktoothed, furry **rock hyraxes**, which you're certain to see on the kopjes and around the lodges of the Serengeti, look like they should be rodents, but in fact are technically ungulates (hoofed mammals) and form a classificatory level entirely their own. Incredibly, their closest living relatives, apart from tree hyraxes, are elephants. Present-day hyraxes are pygmies compared with some of their prehistoric ancestors, which in some cases were as big as bears. Rock hyraxes live in busy, vocal colonies of twenty or thirty females and young, plus a male. Away from the lodges, they're timid in the extreme – not surprising in view of the wide range of predators that will target them. The related **tree hyraxes**, as is obvious, prefer trees; they're also common around Serengeti's lodges.

Carnivores: the big cats

Tanzania's predators are some of the most exciting and easily recognizable animals you'll see. Although often portrayed as fearsome hunters, pulling down plains game after a chase, many species do a fair bit of scavenging and all are content to eat smaller fry when conditions dictate or the opportunity arises.

Of the large cats, **lions** are the easiest to find. Lazy, gregarious and large – up to 1.8 metres in length, not counting the tail, and up to a metre high at the shoulder – they rarely make much effort to hide or to move away, except on occasions when a large number of tourist vehicles intrude, or if elephants are passing through. They can be seen in nearly all the parks and reserves. Especially good photo opportunities are in the Serengeti, where they form particularly large prides; at Ngorongoro, Mikumi and Ruaha you may well also see them hunting. Normally, lions hunt co-operatively and at night, preferring to kill very young, old or sick animals, and make a kill roughly once in every three attacks. When they don't kill their own prey, they will steal the kills of cheetahs or hyenas. "Man-eating" lions appear from time to time, and though usually one-off feline misfits, there are two regions that have had persistent trouble with man-eaters for decades: Kondoa, north of Dodoma, and anywhere around Selous, particularly Tunduru.

Leopards are among the most feared animals in Tanzania. Intensely secretive, alert and wary, they live all across the country except in the most treeless zones. Their unmistakable call, likened to a big saw being pulled back and forth, is unforgettable. Solitary and mainly active at night, they're difficult to see by day, when they rest up in trees or thick bush. They also sometimes survive on the outskirts of towns and villages, carefully preying on different domestic animals to avoid a routine. They tolerate nearby human habitation and rarely kill people unless provoked. For the most part, leopards live off any small animals that come their way, including small mammals, primates and birds, pouncing from an ambush and dragging the kill up into a tree where it may be consumed over several days, away from the attentions of scavengers. The spots on a leopard vary from individual to individual, but are always in the form of rosettes.

While the leopard hunts by stealth, the **cheetah** uses speed. Often confused with leopards because of their spots, once you get to know them, they're impossible to confuse: more lightly built, more finely spotted, with small heads, long legs and distinctive "tears" under their eyes. Cheetahs prefer open ground where they can hunt. Hunting is normally a solitary activity, reliant on eyesight and an incredible burst of speed that can take the animal to 100kph for a few seconds. Cheetahs are most common in the Serengeti and as they hunt by day, they're highly sensitive to human presence; careless driving and noisy tourists will ruin their chances of success. Never drive directly at a cheetah (do a series of zigzags instead), pause frequently as you approach, keep quiet, don't crowd around and don't move or start engines when they're stalking prey.

Other large Tanzanian cats include the beautiful part-spotted, part-striped **serval**, found in most of the parks, though its nocturnal nature means it's usually seen scavenging around lodges at night. Up to a metre long including the tail, it uses its large ears to locate and approach prey – game birds, bustards, rodents, hares, snakes or frogs – before pouncing. The heavily built grey-black **African civet** resembles a large, terrestrial genet. It was formerly kept in captivity for its musk (once a part of the raw material for perfume), which is secreted from glands near the tail. Being nocturnal, they're infrequently seen, but are predictable creatures, wending their way along the same paths at the same time night after night, preying on small animals or looking for insects and fruit. Also nocturnal but much rarer is the aggressive, tuft-eared **caracal**, a kind of lynx that favours drier zones like Mkomazi and Tarangire.

Carnivores: hyenas, dogs and other predators

The biggest carnivore after the lion is the **spotted hyena**; it's also, apart from the lion, the meat-eater you will most often see, especially in the Serengeti. Although considered a scavenger par excellence, the spotted hyena – with its distinctive sloping back, limping gait and short, broad muzzle – is also a formidable hunter, most often found where antelopes and zebras are present. In fact, their success rate at hunting, in packs and at speeds up to 50kph, is twice that of some specialized predators. Exceptionally efficient consumers, with strong teeth and jaws, spotted hyenas eat virtually every part of their prey in a matter of minutes, including bones and hide and, where habituated to humans, often steal shoes, unwashed pans and refuse from tents and villages. Although they can be seen by day, they are most often active at night – when they issue their unnerving, whooping cries. Socially, hyenas form territorial groups of up to eighty animals. These so-called clans are dominated by females, who are larger than males and compete with each other for rank. Curiously, female hyenas' genitalia are hard to distinguish from males', leading to a popular misconception that they are hermaphroditic. Not surprisingly, in view of all their attributes, the hyena is a key figure in mythology and folklore, usually as a limping, heartless bad guy, or as a symbol of duplicitous cunning. In comparison with the spotted hyena, you're not very likely to see a **striped hyena**. A usually solitary animal, it's slighter and much rarer than its spotted relative, though occasionally glimpsed very early in the morning. You have reasonable odds of seeing them at Tarangire, and at Ruaha, which marks their southernmost extent.

The unusual and rather magnificent **African hunting dogs**, also called wild dogs or "painted wolves" (in Latin, *Lycaon pictus*), have disappeared from much of their historical range in Africa. Their remaining strongholds are at Mikumi, Selous and Ruaha, and there are smaller and more endangered populations at Mkomazi and Tarangire. Canine distemper and rabies have played as big a role in their decline as human predation and habitat disruption. They are efficient pack hunters, running their prey in relays to exhaustion before tearing it apart, and live in groups of up to forty animals, with ranges of almost eight hundred square kilometres.

The commonest members of the dog family in Tanzania are the **jackals**, one of few mammalian species in which mating couples stay together for life. The black-backed or silver-backed jackal and the similar side-striped jackal, can be seen just about anywhere, usually in pairs. The golden jackal is most likely to be seen in the Serengeti. All three species are scavengers, feeding off grubs and the remains of kills made by predators. **Bat-eared foxes** live in burrows in the plains, and while not uncommon, are rarely seen as they're most active at dawn and dusk. Their very large ears make them unmistakable.

The unusual **honey badger** or **ratel** is related to the European badger and has a reputation for defending itself extremely fiercely. Primarily an omnivorous forager, it will tear open bee hives (to which it is led by a small bird, the honey-guide), its thick, loose hide rendering it impervious to their stings. The solitary and nocturnal **genets** are reminiscent of slender, elongated black-and-white cats, with spotted coats and ringed tails. They were once domesticated around the Mediterranean, but cats proved better mouse hunters, and in fact genets are related to mongooses. They're frequently seen after dark around national park lodges. Most species of **mongoose**, attractive animals with elongated bodies and long tails, are also tolerant of humans and, even when disturbed out in the bush, can usually be observed for some time before disappearing. Their snake-fighting reputation is greatly overplayed: in practice they are mostly social foragers, fanning out through the bush, rooting for anything edible – mostly invertebrates, eggs, lizards and frogs. The most common are the dwarf, banded and black-tipped (also called slender mongoose), the latter often seen darting across tracks as you approach. Rarer are the marsh mongoose (frequent at Gombe) and white-tailed mongoose (also Gombe, and Serengeti).

Elephants

African **elephants**, larger than their Asian cousins and rarely domesticated, are found throughout Tanzania, and almost all the big plains and mountain parks have their populations. These are the most engaging of animals to watch, perhaps because their interactions, behaviour patterns and personalities have so many human parallels. They lead complex, interdependent social lives, growing from helpless infancy, through self-conscious adolescence, to adulthood. Babies are born with other cows in close attendance, after a 22-month gestation, and suckle for two to three years. Elephants' basic family units are composed of a group of related females, tightly protecting their babies and young and led by a venerable matriarch. It's the matriarch that's most likely to bluff a charge – though occasionally she may get carried away and tusk a vehicle or person. Bush mythology has it that elephants become embarrassed and ashamed after killing a human, covering the body with sticks and grass. They certainly pay much attention to the disposal of their own dead relatives, often dispersing the bones, spending time near the remains, and returning to the site for several years. Old animals die in their seventies or eighties, when their last set of teeth wears out and they can no longer feed.

Seen in the flesh, elephants seem even bigger than you would imagine – you'll need little persuasion from those flapping, warning ears to back off if you're too close – but are surprisingly graceful, silent animals on their padded, carefully placed feet. In a matter of moments, a large herd can merge into the trees and disappear, their presence betrayed only by the noisy cracking of branches as they strip trees-and uproot saplings. Relatively quiet they may be to our ears, but researchers have discovered that vibrations from stamping elephant feet can be picked up 50km away, and are almost certainly a form of communication, complementing their equally remarkable language of very low frequency rumbles.

Until the 1950s, elephants inhabited almost ninety percent of Tanzania, but their range now covers just half that original area. Apart from habitat loss, elephant populations also suffered from **ivory poachers**, especially in the 1970s and 1980s, when three quarters of the national population were massacred. The more peaceful 1990s managed to bring their Tanzanian population back to a healthy hundred thousand of which sixty thousand or so are concentrated in Selous Game Reserve.

Rhinos

The **rhino** is one of the world's oldest mammalian species, having appeared on earth some fifty to sixty million years ago, shortly after the demise of the dinosaurs. Nowadays, it's also one of the most critically endangered, as a result of catastrophic poaching for their valuable horns in the 1970s and 1980s, which completely wiped out the populations at Tarangire, Mikumi and Mkomazi. There are five species worldwide, the Tanzanian one being the hook-lipped or **black rhinoceros**. The name is a misnomer, having been given in counterpoint to the white rhino, where "white" was a mistranslation of the Afrikaans for "wide", referring to its lip: the white rhino's broad lip is suitable for grazing, whereas the black rhino's is adapted for browsing. Both species are actually greyish in colour.

Until the mid-1970s, black rhinos were a fairly common sight in many Tanzanian parks and reserves. In the 1960s, for example, the Selous contained over three thousand, some with long upper horns over a metre in length. Today, the Selous **population** is barely 150, accounting for three- quarters of Tanzania's total (which had started the 1960s at around ten thousand). The driving force behind the poaching, which began in earnest in the 1970s, was (and is) the high price for rhino horn on the black market. The horn is actually an agglomeration of hair, and has long been used to make status-symbol dagger handles in Arabia and an aphrodisiac medicine in Far Eastern countries. Contributing factors to the decline are their long gestation period (15–18 months), and the fact that calves remain dependent on their mothers until the age of five, when the next one comes along.

The **location** and size of most surviving populations is, understandably, a closely guarded secret, and the only rhinos that can readily be visited by tourists are fewer than a dozen at Ngorongoro Crater, and a handful on Rubondo Island.

Hippos

Hippopotamuses are among the most impressive of Africa's creatures – lugubrious pink monsters that weigh up to three tons and measure up to four metres from their whiskered chins to their stubby tails. Despite their ungainly appearance they're highly adaptable and found wherever rivers or freshwater lakes and pools are deep enough for them to submerge in and also have a surrounding of suitable grazing grass. They are supremely adapted to long periods in water, a necessity as they need to protect their hairless skin from dehydration; their pinkish colour is a natural secretion that acts as a sunblock. In the water, their clumsy feet become supple paddles, and they can remain completely submerged for six minutes, and for hours on end with just their nostrils, eyes and ears protruding. They communicate underwater with clicks, pulses, croaks and whines, and at the surface with grunts, snorts and aggressive displays of fearsome dentition. After dark, and sometimes on wet and overcast days, hippos leave the water to spend the whole night grazing, their stumpy legs carrying them up to 10km in one session.

Hippos are thought to be responsible for more human deaths in Africa than any other animal except malarial mosquitoes. Deaths mainly occur on the water, when boats accidentally steer into hippo pods, but they can be aggressive on dry land, too, especially if you're between them and water, or when they're with calves. They can run at 30kph if necessary, and their enormous bulk and steel-crunching jaws advocate extreme caution. Yet if they pass through a campground at night, nary a guy rope is twanged.

Zebras

Zebras are closely related to horses and, together with wild asses, form the equid family. Burchell's zebra is the only species in Tanzania, and is found throughout the country. In Serengeti and Tarangire, zebras gather in migrating herds up to several hundred thousand strong, along with wildebeest and other grazers. Socially, they're organized into family groups of up to fifteen individuals led by a stallion. The stripes appear to be a defence mechanism for confusing predators: bunched up in a jostling herd, the confusion of stripes makes it very difficult to single out an individual to chase; the stripes are also said to confuse tsetse flies.

Pigs

The commonest wild pig in Tanzania is the comical **warthog**. Quick of movement and nervous, warthogs are notoriously hard to photograph as they're generally on the run through the bush, often with the young in single file, tails erect like antennae, though you can catch them browsing in a kneeling position. They shelter in holes in the ground, usually old aardvark burrows, and live in family groups generally consisting of a mother and her litter of two to four piglets, or occasionally two or three females and their young. Boars join the group only to mate, and are distinguishable from sows by their longer tusks, and the warts below their eyes, which are thought to be defensive pads to protect their heads during often violent fights.

Also common but rarely seen is the nocturnal **bush pig**, which inhabits forest and dense thickets close to rivers and marshes. They're brownish in colour, resemble European boars, and weigh up to 80kg.

△ Young reticulated giraffes

Giraffes

Tanzania's national symbol, and the world's tallest mammal (up to five metres), is the **giraffe**, found wherever there are trees. The species in Tanzania is the irregularly patterned Maasai giraffe. Both sexes have horns, but can be distinguished by the shorter height of the females, and by the tufts of hair over their horns. Daylight hours are spent browsing on the leaves of trees too high for other species; acacia and combretum are favourites. Non-territorial, they gather in loose leaderless herds, with bulls testing their strength while in bachelor herds. When a female comes into oestrus, which can happen at any time of year, the dominant male mates with her. She will give birth after a gestation of approximately fourteen months. Over half of all young fall prey to lions or hyenas in their early years, however. Oddly, despite the great length of their necks, they're supported by only seven vertebrae – the same as humans.

Buffaloes

The fearsome African or Cape **buffalo**, with its massive flattened horns and eight-hundred-kilogram bulk, is a common and much-photographed animal, closely related to the domestic cow. They live in herds of several hundred, which can swell to over a thousand in times of drought. Though untroubled by close contact with humans or vehicles, they are one of Africa's most dangerous animals when alone, when their behaviour is unpredictable. Their preferred habitat is swamp and marsh, though they have also adapted to life in highland forests. Buffaloes are often accompanied by **ox-peckers** and **cattle egrets**, who hitch rides on the backs of buffalo and other game. They have a symbiotic relationship with their hosts, feeding off parasites such as ticks and blood-sucking flies. The ox-peckers also have an alarm call that warns their hosts of danger like lurking predators.

Plains-dwelling antelopes

Plains-dwelling antelopes are common throughout Tanzania, even outside protected areas. Large herds of white-bearded **wildebeest** or gnu are particularly associated with the Serengeti; their spectacular annual migration is described in the box on p.471. The blue wildebeest (or brindled gnu) of central and southern Tanzania lack beards and are paler in colour. The strong shoulders and comparatively puny hindquarters of both species lend them an ungainly appearance, but the light rear end is useful for their wild and erratic bucking when attacked. Calves begin walking within minutes – a necessity when predators are always on the lookout.

There are two main species of **gazelles**: **Thomson's** ("Tommies"), which can survive extremely arid conditions, and the larger **Grant's**. Both are gregarious, and often seen at roadsides. Almost as common is the **impala**, seen either in breeding herds of females, calves and one male, or in bachelor herds. They're seldom far from cover and, when panicked, the herd "explodes" in all directions, confusing predators. Only males have horns. Also putting in frequent appearances is the huge, cow-like **eland**, which weighs six hundred to nine hundred kilograms and has a distinctive dewlap. Females are reddish, males are grey; and both have corkscrew-like horns. Equally imposing is the **fringe-eared oryx**, present in small numbers throughout the country but best seen at Tarangire, and whose long straight horns may explain the unicorn myth. They live in herds of up to forty animals, and are migratory. Also plains-dwelling is the elegant **gerenuk**, an unusual browsing gazelle able to nibble from bushes standing on its hind legs (its name is Somali for "giraffe-necked"); in Tanzania, its range is restricted to the semi-arid north, around Lake Natron, Longido and Mkomazi, and a few in Tarangire.

Two more species, these favouring rocky islands rising from the plains, are the surprisingly aggressive **steinbok** which, despite a height of only 50cm, defends itself furiously against attackers (best seen at Tarangire), and the grey and shaggy **klipspringer** (Afrikaans for "stone jumper"; p.xvi), whose hooves are wonderfully adapted for scaling near-vertical cliffs. Like dikdiks, both are monogamous, giving birth to one offspring each year; their territory is marked by secretions from glands near the eyes. Klipspringers can easily be seen at Ruaha, Tarangire and Manyara, and sometimes in Udzungwa.

Bushland and forest-dwelling antelopes

The rather ungainly, long-faced **hartebeest** family, with its distinctive S-shaped horns, has three representatives in Tanzania: the reddish **Liechtenstein's hartebeest** is the most common, especially in *miombo* and acacia woodland (Saadani is a good place to spot them); the paler **Coke's hartebeest**, with a longer, narrower head, is rarely found in the north; and, resembling hartebeest, the **topi**, whose males often stand sentry on top of abandoned termite mounds in the Serengeti and in Katavi. The striped **kudu** are also very localized, and their preference for dense bush makes them hard to see; your best chance is at dawn or dusk. There are two species, both browsers: **greater kudu**, with eight to ten lateral stripes, are best seen at Selous, Mikumi and Saadani; the smaller **lesser kudu**, which has more stripes, can be seen in Mkomazi and Tarangire. Both can be seen at Ruaha. The spiralled horns of the male greater kudus can grow up to 180cm, and have long been used by local people for making musical instruments.

Other large bushland antelopes include the massive **roan antelope**, with their backward-sweeping horns, large ears and black-and-white faces, found mainly in Katavi, Ruaha and Mahale and often seen close to water in the mornings, and the related **sable antelope**, with their handsome curved and swept-back horns. Males are black with white bellies and face markings; females are all brown. They thrive in *miombo* woodland, making them regular sightings at Mikumi, Selous, Ruaha, Mahale and Katavi. There's also a lighter and smaller subspecies at Saadani on the coast. The large **bushbuck** is nocturnal, solitary and notoriously shy – a loud crashing through the undergrowth and a flash of a chestnut rump are all most people witness.

Top marks for Bambi-like features goes to **Kirk's dikdik**, a miniature antelope found all over the country. Measuring no more than 40cm in height (4kg in weight), they're most active in the morning and evening. Usually seen in monogamous pairs (the males are horned, the females are slightly larger), their territories are marked by piles of droppings and secretions deposited on grass stems. Their name mimics their whistling alarm call when fleeing. The forest-loving **suni** antelope is even daintier, measuring up to 32cm in height, but rare and with a scattered distribution: you have very good odds on seeing them on Prison Island in Zanzibar, and a reasonable chance at Zanzibar's Jozani Forest, the Pugu Hills near Dar, in the Udzungwa Mountains and on Rubondo Island where they've been introduced. The **duikers** (Dutch for "diver", referring to their plunging into the bush) are larger – the **common duiker** is around 60cm high – though they appear smaller because of their shorter forelimbs. It's found throughout the country in many habitats, but most duikers are more choosy and prefer plenty of dense cover and thicket. Their isolation from other communities means that they've evolved into several subspecies which still confuse taxonomists: the most common family is that of the **blue duiker** (and related **Abbot's duiker**), which ranges from Mount Rungwe in the south to the world's largest population in the forests of Kilimanjaro. Rarer subspecies include the tiny **Ader's duiker** on Zanzibar (Chumbe Island and Jozani Forest); the **Pemba blue duiker** (Ngesi Forest on Pemba Island); a relict population of blue duikers on Juani Island in the Mafia archipelago; **red duikers** (Kilimanjaro and Udzungwa) and **grey duikers** (Gombe and Kilimanjaro).

Antelopes found in or around water

Easily confused with impala, the **Bohor reedbuck** prefers long grass and reedbeds near swamps, where they're easily concealed. Only males have horns; short, ringed and forward-curving. They're most easily seen in Mikumi, Selous and Ruaha, but are also present in Saadani, Katavi and Tarangire. **Mountain reedbuck**, common in Ngorongoro, are similar. The related brownish-grey **common waterbuck** has a much wider distribution; they have a distinctive white ring around their rump, and are seen in mixed herds controlled by a dominant male. Like reedbucks, they're often seen near water, in which they can seek refuge from predators. The semi-aquatic **sitatunga** is found in Tanzania only in remote corners of Lake Victoria's shoreline, notably Rubondo Island.

Other terrestrial mammals

That much-loved dictionary leader, the **aardvark**, is one of Africa's strangest mammals, a solitary termite-eater weighing up to 70kg. Its name, Afrikaans for "earth pig", is an apt description, as it holes up during the day in large burrows, excavated with remarkable speed and energy, and emerges at night to visit termite mounds within a radius of 5km. It's most likely to be common in bush country well scattered with tall termite spires. **Ground pangolins** are equally unusual – nocturnal, scale-covered mammals, resembling armadillos and feeding on ants and termites. Under attack, they roll into a ball.

In wooded areas, insectivorous **elephant shrews** are worth looking out for, simply because they are so weird (the elephant bit refers to their trunk-like snout). They're extremely adaptable, as their habitat ranges from the semi-desert around Lake Natron to the lush forests of Amani, Gombe, Jozani and Udzungwa. Tanzania's many **bats** will usually be a mere flicker over a water-hole at twilight, or sometimes a flash across headlights. The only bats you can normally observe in any decent way are fruit bats hanging from their roosting sites by day; there are visitable roosts on Chole Island in the Mafia Archipelago, at Misali and Makoongwe islands off Pemba Island and in Pemba Island's Ngesi Forest (the endemic Pemba flying fox or Mega Bat). For more "traditional" bat viewing, visit the incredible colonies of the Amboni Caves near Tanga.

Marine mammals

Of the three main marine mammals of the western Indian Ocean, the most common are **dolphins**, which need no introduction. They're most easily seen off Kizimkazi in Zanzibar, though the as-yet unknown psychological effects of dozens of tourists chasing them around day after day may put you off. **Whales**, both humpback and sperm, pass along the coast from October to December on their vast migrations around the world's oceans, and – if you're exceptionally lucky – can be heard singing when you're diving. The rarest of all of Tanzania's mammals, rarer even than the rhino, is the **dugong**, the original mermaid prototype which resembles a cross between a seal and walrus. The mermaid legend probably had something to do with the dugong's habit of floating around on its back, letting a pair of bobbing and rather ample breasts work their magic on the mariners of yore. Their only known breeding ground in Tanzanian waters lies between the mainland and Mafia Archipelago, but the population there is on the brink of extinction.

Reptiles and amphibians

The **Nile crocodile** can reach six metres or more in length. You'll see them, log-like, on the sandy shores of most of Tanzania's rivers and lakes. Although they mostly live off fish, they are also dangerous opportunists, seizing the unwary with disconcerting speed. Once caught, either by the mouth or after being tossed into the water by a flick of their powerful tails, the victim is spun underwater to drown it, before massive jaws make short work of the carcass.

Tanzania has many species of **snakes**, some of them quite common, but your chances of seeing a wild specimen are remote. In Tanzania, as all over Africa, snakes are both revered and reviled and, while they frequently have symbolic significance for local people, that is quite often forgotten in the rush to hack them to bits when found. All in all, snakes have a very hard time surviving in Tanzania: their turnover is high and their speed of exit from the scene when humans show up is remarkable. If you want to see them, wear boots and walk softly. If you want to avoid them completely, tread firmly and they'll flee on detecting your vibrations. The exception is the **puff adder**, which relies on camouflage to get within striking distance of prey, but will only bite when threatened (or stood on); around ten percent of its bites are fatal. Other common **poisonous species** include black mambas (fast, agile and arboreal; properly called black-mouthed mambas), the boomslang, the spitting cobra and blotched forest cobra, night adder, bush snake and bush viper. Common **non-poisonous snakes** include the constricting African python (a favoured partner of the Sukuma tribe's dance societies; see p.501), the egg-eating snake and the sand boa.

Tortoises are quite frequently encountered on park roads in the morning or late afternoon. Some, like the leopard tortoise, can be quite large, up to 50cm in length, while the hinged tortoise (which not only retreats inside its shell but shuts the door, too) is much smaller – up to 30cm. In rocky areas, look out for the unusual pancake tortoise, a flexible-shelled species that can put on quite a turn of speed but, when cornered in its fissure in the rocks, will inflate to wedge itself inextricably to avoid capture. Terrapins or turtles of several species are common in ponds and slow-flowing streams. On the coast, **sea turtles** breed and it's not unusual to see them from boats during snorkelling trips, though their populations have declined drastically and all three nesting species – the Olive Ridley, green, and hawksbill – are now endangered. Trade in turtle products (including "tortoise shell") is illegal.

Lizards are common everywhere, harmless, often colourful and always amusing to watch. The commonest are **rock agamas**, the males often seen in courting "plumage", with brilliant orange heads and blue bodies, ducking and bobbing at each other. They live in loose colonies often near human habitation; one hotel may have hundreds, its neighbours none. The biggest lizards, **Nile monitors**, grow to nearly 2m in length and are often seen near water. From a distance, as they race off, they look like speeding baby crocodiles. The other common monitor, the smaller **Savannah monitor**, is less handsomely marked and often well camouflaged in its favoured bushy habitat.

A large, docile lizard you may come across is the **plated lizard**, an intelligent, mild-mannered reptile often found around coastal hotels, looking for scraps from the kitchen or pool terrace. At night on the coast, the translucent little aliens on the ceiling are **geckos**, catching moths and other insects. Their gravity-defying agility is due to countless microscopic hairs on their padded toes, whose adhesiveness functions at an atomic level. By day, their minuscule relatives the day geckos (velvet grey and yellow), patrol coastal walls. In the highlands you may come across prehistoric-looking three-horned **Jackson's chameleons** creeping through the foliage, and there are several other species, most also in the highlands.

Night is usually the best time for spotting **amphibians**, though unless you make an effort to track down the perpetrators of the frog chorus down by the lodge water pump, you'll probably only come across the odd toad. There are, however, dozens of species of frogs and tree frogs, including the diminutive and unique Kihansi spray toad, whose discovery in the spray at the bottom of a waterfall in 1996 scuppered the profitability of a hydroelectric dam in the Southern Highlands, which now has to divert part of its flow to keep the toads moist.

Birds

Tanzania boasts one of Africa's highest counts of **bird species**, with over 1100 recorded so far (compared with around three hundred for Britain and six hundred for North America). This huge variety, spread across 75 families and very roughly split across northern and southern Tanzania, is made possible by the lack of climatic extremes, and a wide range of habitats in every conceivable altitudinal range, from montane forest to semi-desert, lakes, rivers and estuaries.

Nearly eighty percent of Tanzania's birds are thought to breed in the country. The remainder are **migratory species**, breeding during the northern summer but wintering in tropical Africa. Many of these are familiar British summer visitors, such as swallows, nightingales and whitethroats, which have to negotiate or skirt the inhospitable Sahara on their migration. The extent of the migration is astonishing: an estimated six billion birds make the journey each year.

The mammals of East Africa

This field guide provides a quick reference to help you identify the larger mammals likely to be encountered in East Africa, together with their Kiswahili names. Straightforward photos show easily identified markings and features. The notes give you clear pointers about the kinds of habitat in which you are most likely to see each mammal; its daily rhythm (usually either nocturnal or diurnal); the kind of social groups it usually forms; and general tips about sighting it on safari, its rarity and its relations with humans. For further details and background, see p.738.

✿ HABITAT   ◑ DAILY RHYTHM   ▢ SOCIAL LIFE   ✓ SIGHTING TIPS

Yellow Baboon
Papio cynocephalus (Nyani)

 open country with trees and cliffs; adaptable, but always near water

◐ diurnal

✧ troops led by a dominant male

✓ common throughout East Africa; two species, *P. cynocephalus* (illustrated) and *P. anubis* (Olive); both species adapt quickly to humans, are frequently a nuisance and occasionally dangerous

---

Black-and-White Colobus Monkey
Colobus guereza (Mbega)

 thick forest, both in highlands and along water courses in otherwise arid savannah; almost entirely arboreal

◐ diurnal

✧ small troops

✓ two species of black and whites, *C. angolensis* on the Indian Ocean coast and in northern Tanzania, and the much larger *C. guereza*, in up-country Kenya; troops maintain a limited home territory, so easily located, but can be hard to see at a great height

---

Red Colobus Monkey
Procolobus badius (Kima punju)

 thick forest, both in highlands and along water courses in otherwise arid savannah; almost entirely arboreal

◐ diurnal

✧ troops of several dozen individuals

✓ limited distribution and highly endangered; most common in Jozani Forest on Zanzibar (*P. b. kirkii*), Tanzania's Udzungwa Mountains (*P. b. gordonorum*) and the Tana River Primate National Park in Kenya (*P. b. tephrosceles*)

Patas Monkey
Erythrocebus patas (Ngedere)

 savannah and forest margins; tolerates some aridity; terrestrial except for sleeping and lookouts

◐ diurnal

✧ small troops

✓ endangered and infrequently seen; can run at high speed and stand on hind feet supported by tail

---

⚜ HABITAT   ◐ DAILY RHYTHM   ✧ SOCIAL LIFE   ✓ SIGHTING TIPS

Vervet Monkey

Cercopithecus aethiops or C. pygerythrus (Tumbili)

🏵 most habitats except rainforest and arid lands; arboreal and terrestrial

◑ diurnal

🗪 troops

✓ widespread and common; occasionally a nuisance where used to humans (will steal food and anything else to hand)

Blue or Sykes' Monkey

Cercopithecus mitis (Nyabu)

🏵 forests; arboreal and occasionally terrestrial

◑ diurnal

🗪 families or small troops

✓ widespread; shyer and less easily habituated to humans than the Vervet; can be a pest for farmers

Lesser Bushbaby or Galago

Galago senegalensis (Komba)

🏵 woodland; arboreal

◑ nocturnal

🗪 solitary or in small family groups

✓ unfazed by humans, these small foragers often frequent lodge restaurants; call is a distinctive wail like a baby's; huge eyes, inquisitive fingers, fondness for bananas

Aardvark

Orycteropus afer (Mhanga)

🏵 open or wooded termite country; softer soil preferred

◑ nocturnal

🗪 solitary

✓ rarely seen animal, the size of a small pig; old burrows are common and often used by warthogs

🏵 HABITAT   ◑ DAILY RHYTHM   🗪 SOCIAL LIFE   ✓ SIGHTING TIPS

Pangolin or Scaly Anteater
Manis temminckii (Kakakuona)

🦋 termite savannah and woodland; terrestrial

◐ nocturnal

♀ solitary or in pairs; baby carried on mother's back

✓ armoured ant and termite eater resembling an armadillo; when frightened, they secrete a smelly liquid from anal glands and roll into a ball with their scales erect (*pangolin* is Malay for "rolling over")

Spring Hare or Cape Jumping Hare
Pedetes capensis (Kamendegere)

🦋 savannah; softer soil areas preferred

◐ nocturnal

♀ burrows, usually with a pair and their young; often linked into a network, almost like a colony

✓ fairly widespread rabbit-sized rodent; impressive and unmistakable kangaroo-like leaper

Crested Porcupine
Hystrix cristata (Nungu or Nungunungu)

🦋 adaptable to a wide range of habitats, often in caves

◐ nocturnal and sometimes active at dusk

♀ family groups

✓ large rodent (up to 90cm in length), rarely seen, but common away from croplands, where it's hunted as a pest, or for its quills

Bat-eared Fox or Cape Fox
Otocyon megalotis (Mbweha masikio)

🦋 open country

◐ mainly nocturnal; diurnal activity increases in cooler months

♀ monogamous pairs

✓ distribution coincides with termites, their favoured diet; they spend many hours foraging using sensitive hearing to pinpoint their underground prey

🦋 HABITAT   ◐ DAILY RHYTHM   ♀ SOCIAL LIFE   ✓ SIGHTING TIPS

Black-backed Jackal
Canis mesomeles (Bweha)

🌼 broad range from moist mountain regions to desert, but drier areas preferred

◐ normally nocturnal, but diurnal in the safety of game reserves

💬 mostly monogamous pairs; sometimes family groups

✓ a common, bold scavenger the size of a mid-sized dog that steals even from lions; three species in East Africa: black-backed with a "saddle" (illustrated); the shy side-striped (*C. adustus*); and golden (*C. aureus*) – the commonest species in Tanzania, restricted in Kenya to the Rift Valley and Laikipia

African Hunting Dog or Wild Dog
Lycaon pictus (Mbwa mwitu)

🌼 open savannah in the vicinity of grazing herds

◐ diurnal

💬 nomadic packs

✓ extremely rare and rarely seen, but widely noted when in the area; the size of a large dog, with distinctively rounded ears and blotchy orange and brown fur

Honey Badger or Ratel
Mellivora capensis (Nyegere)

🌼 very broad range of habitats

◐ mainly nocturnal

💬 usually solitary, but also found in pairs

✓ widespread, omnivorous, badger-sized animal; nowhere common; extremely aggressive

African Civet
Civettictis civetta (Fungo)

🌼 prefers woodland and dense vegetation

◐ mainly nocturnal

💬 solitary

✓ omnivorous, medium-dog-sized, short-legged prowler; not to be confused with the smaller genet

🌼 HABITAT   ◐ DAILY RHYTHM   💬 SOCIAL LIFE   ✓ SIGHTING TIPS

Genet
Genetta genetta (Kanu)

✾ light bush country, even arid areas; partly arboreal

◑ nocturnal, but becomes active at dusk

♀ solitary

✓ quite common, slender, cat-sized omnivore, often seen at game lodges, where it easily becomes habituated to humans

Banded Mongoose
Mungos mungo (Nguchiro)

✾ thick bush and dry forest

◑ diurnal

♀ lives in burrow colonies of up to thirty animals

✓ widespread and quite common, the size of a small cat; often seen in a group, hurriedly foraging through the undergrowth. The main East African species are the banded (illustrated); dwarf (*Helogale parvula*); and black-tipped or slender (*Galerella sanguinea*)

Spotted Hyena
Crocuta crocuta (Fisi madoa)

✾ tolerates a wide variety of habitat, with the exception of dense forest

◑ nocturnal but also active at dusk; also diurnal in many parks

♀ highly social, usually living in extended family groups

✓ the size of a large dog with a distinctive loping gait, quite common in parks, especially early in the morning; carnivorous scavenger and cooperative hunter; dangerous; not to be confused with the shy, solitary and rarely seen striped hyena (*Hyaena hyaena*; Fisi miraba)

Caracal
Caracal caracal (Simba mangu)

✾ open bush and plains; occasionally arboreal

◑ mostly nocturnal

♀ solitary

✓ lynx-like wild cat; rather uncommon and rarely seen

✾ HABITAT   ◑ DAILY RHYTHM   ♀ SOCIAL LIFE   ✓ SIGHTING TIPS

Cheetah
Acinonyx jubatus (Duma)

❀ savannah, in the vicinity of plains grazers

◐ diurnal

☖ solitary or temporary nuclear family groups

✓ widespread but low population;
much slighter build than the leopard, and
distinguished from it by a small head, square
snout and dark "tear mark" running from eye
to jowl

Leopard
Panthera pardus (Chui)

❀ highly adaptable; frequently arboreal

◐ nocturnal; also cooler daylight hours

☖ solitary

✓ the size of a very large dog; not
uncommon, but shy and infrequently seen;
rests in thick undergrowth or up trees; very
dangerous

Lion
Panthera leo (Simba)

❀ all habitats except desert and thick forest

◐ nocturnal and diurnal

☖ prides of three to forty; more usually six
to twelve

✓ commonly seen resting in shade;
dangerous

Serval
Felis serval (Mondo)

❀ reed beds or tall grassland near water

◐ normally nocturnal but more diurnal than
most cats

☖ usually solitary

✓ some resemblance to the cheetah but far
smaller; most likely to be seen on roadsides or
at water margins at dawn or dusk

❀ HABITAT   ◐ DAILY RHYTHM   ☖ SOCIAL LIFE   ✓ SIGHTING TIPS

Rock Hyrax
Procavia capensis (Pimbi or Wibari)

🌸 rocky areas, from mountains to isolated outcrops

🌓 diurnal

🔲 colonies consisting of a territorial male with as many as thirty related females

✓ rabbit-sized; very common; often seen sunning themselves in the early morning on rocks

African Elephant
Loxodonta africana (Tembo or Ndovu)

🌸 wide range of habitats, wherever there are trees and water

🌓 nocturnal and diurnal; sleeps as little as four hours a day

🔲 almost human in its complexity; cows and offspring in herds headed by a matriarch; bulls solitary or in bachelor herds

✓ look out for fresh dung (football-sized) and recently damaged trees; frequently seen at waterholes from late afternoon; dangerous

Black Rhinoceros
Diceros bicornis (Faru/Kifaru)

🌸 usually thick bush, altitudes up to 3500m

🌓 active day and night, resting between periods of activity

🔲 solitary

✓ extremely rare and in critical danger of extinction; largely confined to parks and heavily protected wildlife reserves; distinctive hooked lip for browsing; bad eyesight; very dangerous

White Rhinoceros
Ceratotherium simum (Faru/Kifaru)

🌸 savannah

🌓 active day and night, resting between periods of activity

🔲 males solitary, otherwise small same-sex herd or nursery group

✓ Not found in Tanzania; confined to protected reserves; distinctive wide mouth (hence "white" from Afrikaans *wijd*) for grazing; docile

🌸 HABITAT   🌓 DAILY RHYTHM   🔲 SOCIAL LIFE   ✓ SIGHTING TIPS

Burchell's Zebra
Equus burchelli (Punda milia)

✿ savannah, with or without trees, up to 4500m

◐ active day and night, resting intermittently

♡ harems of several mares and foals led by a dominant stallion are usually grouped together, in herds of up to several thousand

✓ widespread and common inside and outside the parks

Grevy's Zebra
Equus grevyi (Punda milia)

✿ arid regions

◐ largely diurnal

♡ mares with foals and stallions generally keep to separate troops; stallions sometimes solitary and territorial

✓ easily distinguished from smaller Burchell's Zebra by narrow stripes and very large ears; rare and localized but easily seen; not found in Tanzania

Bush Pig
Potamochoerus porcus (Nguruwe mwitu)

✿ forest and dense thickets close to water

◐ nocturnal

♡ groups (sounders) of up to twenty animals

✓ resembles a long-haired domestic pig with tasselled hair on its ears and white-crested back

Warthog
Phacochoerus aethiopicus (Ngiri or Gwasi)

✿ savannah, up to an altitude of over 2000m

◐ diurnal

♡ family groups, usually of a female and her litter

✓ common; boars are distinguishable from sows by their prominent facial "warts"

✿ HABITAT   ◐ DAILY RHYTHM   ♡ SOCIAL LIFE   ✓ SIGHTING TIPS

Hippopotamus
Hippopotamus amphibius (Kiboko)

🏵 slow-flowing rivers, dams and lakes

◐ principally nocturnal, leaving the water to graze

🛡 bulls are solitary, but other animals live in family groups headed by a matriarch

✓ usually seen by day in water, with top of head and ears breaking the surface; frequently aggressive and very dangerous when threatened or when retreat to water is blocked

Giraffe
Giraffa camelopardalis (Twiga)

🏵 wooded savannah and thorn country

◐ diurnal

🛡 loose, non-territorial, leaderless herds

✓ common; many subspecies, of which Maasai (*G. c. tippelskirchi*, left), Reticulated (*G. c. reticulata*, bottom l.) and Rothschild's (*G. c. rothschildi*, below) are East African

African or Cape Buffalo
Syncerus caffer (Nyati or Mbogo)

🏵 wide range of habitats, always near water, up to altitudes of 4000m

◐ nocturnal and diurnal, but inactive during the heat of the day

🛡 gregarious, with cows and calves in huge herds; young bulls often form small bachelor herds; old bulls are usually solitary

✓ very common; scent much more acute than other senses; very dangerous, old bulls especially so

🏵 HABITAT   ◐ DAILY RHYTHM   🛡 SOCIAL LIFE   ✓ SIGHTING TIPS

Red Hartebeest
Alcelaphus buselaphus (Kongoni)

 wide range of grassy habitats

◗ diurnal

♈ females and calves in small, wandering herds; territorial males solitary

✓ hard to confuse with any other antelope except the topi; many varieties, distinguishable by horn shape; most common is the Red or Cape (illustrated); others include Coke's (*A. cokei*), Lichtenstein's (*A. lichtensteinii*), and Jackson's (*A. jacksoni*), found only in Kenya

Topi or Sassaby
Damaliscus lunatus (Nyamera)

 grasslands, showing a marked preference for moist savannah, near water

◗ diurnal

♈ females and young form herds with an old male

✓ widespread, very fast runners; male often stands sentry on an abandoned termite hill, actually marking the territory against rivals, rather than defending against predators

Blue Wildebeest or Brindled Gnu
Connochaetes taurinus (Nyumbu)

 grasslands

◗ diurnal, occasionally also nocturnal

♈ intensely gregarious; wide variety of associations within mega-herds which may number over one million animals

✓ unmistakable, nomadic grazer; long tail, mane and beard

Gerenuk
Litocranius walleri (Swala twiga)

 arid thorn country and semi-desert

◗ diurnal

♈ solitary or in small, territorial harems

✓ not uncommon; unmistakable, its name is Somali for "giraffe-necked"; often browses standing upright on hind legs; the female is hornless

 HABITAT   ◗ DAILY RHYTHM   ♈ SOCIAL LIFE   ✓ SIGHTING TIPS

Grant's Gazelle
Gazella granti (Swala granti)

 wide grassy plains with good visibility, sometimes far from water

◑ diurnal

♀ small, territorial harems

✓ larger than the similar Thomson's Gazelle, distinguished from it by the white rump patch which extends onto the back; the female has smaller horns than the male

Thomson's Gazelle
Gazella thomsoni (Swala tomi)

❀ flat, short-grass savannah, near water

◑ diurnal

♀ gregarious, in a wide variety of social structures, often massing in the hundreds with other grazing species

✓ smaller than the similar Grant's Gazelle, distinguished from it by the black band on flank; the female has tiny horns

Impala
Aepyceros melampus (Swala pala)

❀ open savannah near light woodland cover

◑ diurnal

♀ large herds of females overlap with several male territories; males highly territorial during the rut when they separate out breeding harems of up to twenty females

✓ common, medium-sized, no close relatives; distinctive high leaps when fleeing; the only antelope with a black tuft above the hooves; males have long, lyre-shaped horns

Common (or Southern) Reedbuck
Redunca arundinum (Tohe)

❀ reedbeds and tall grass near water

◑ nocturnal and diurnal

♀ monogamous pairs or family groups in territory defended by the male

✓ medium-sized antelope, with a plant diet unpalatable to other herbivores; only males have horns

---

❀ HABITAT   ◑ DAILY RHYTHM   ♀ SOCIAL LIFE   ✓ SIGHTING TIPS

Common Waterbuck
Kobus ellipsiprymnus (Kuro)

🐾 open woodland and savannah, near water

🌓 nocturnal and diurnal

📋 territorial herds of females and young, led by dominant male, or territorial males visited by wandering female herds

✓ common, rather tame, large antelope; plant diet unpalatable to other herbivores; shaggy coat; only males have horns

Kirk's Dikdik
Madoqua kirkii (Digidigi or Dika)

🐾 scrub and thornbush, often far from water

🌓 nocturnal and diurnal, most active morning and evening

📋 monogamous pairs for life, often accompanied by current and previous young

✓ tiny, hare-sized antelope, named after its alarm cry; males are horned, females slightly larger; found next to or in bushes, and almost always in pairs; territory marked by piles of droppings and black secretions deposited on grass stems

Common Duiker
Sylvicapra grimmia (Nysa)

🐾 adaptable, prefers dense scrub and woodland, some subspecies prefer mountainous forests

🌓 nocturnal and diurnal

📋 most commonly solitary; sometimes in pairs; occasionally monogamous

✓ widespread and common small antelope with a rounded back, up to 70cm tall; seen close to cover; rams have short straight horns.

Suni *Neotragus moschatus* (Suni)

🐾 forest, or dense, dry bush

🌓 nocturnal and crepuscular

📋 monogamous pairs, sometimes with additional non-breeding females

✓ even smaller than dikdiks, no higher than 32cm; extremely isolated populations scattered throughout East Africa including Zanzibar, particularly forested coastal hills; hide in shade by day; freeze when threatened before darting into undergrowth

🐾 HABITAT 🌓 DAILY RHYTHM 📋 SOCIAL LIFE ✓ SIGHTING TIPS

Sitatunga
Tragelaphus spekei (Nzohe)

✿ swamps

◑ nocturnal and sometimes diurnal

♈ territorial and mostly solitary or in pairs

✓ very localized and not likely to be mistaken for anything else; usually seen half submerged; females have no horns

Bushbuck
Tragelaphus scriptus (Kulungu or Mbawala)

✿ thick bush and woodland close to water

◑ principally nocturnal, but also active during the day when cool

♈ solitary, but casually sociable; sometimes grazes in small groups

✓ medium-sized antelope with white stripes and spots; often seen in thickets, or heard crashing through them; the male has shortish straight, spiralled horns

Eland
Taurotragus oryx (Mpofu or Mbungu)

✿ highly adaptable; semi-desert to mountains, but prefers scrubby plains

◑ nocturnal and diurnal

♈ non-territorial herds of up to sixty with temporary gatherings of as many as a thousand

✓ common but shy; the largest and most powerful African antelope; both sexes have straight horns with a slight spiral

Greater Kudu
Tragelaphus strepsiceros (Tandala mkubwa)

✿ semi-arid, hilly or undulating bush country; tolerant of drought

◑ diurnal when secure; otherwise nocturnal

♈ territorial; males usually solitary; females in small troops with young

✓ impressively big antelope (up to 1.5m at shoulder) with very long, spiral horns in the male; very localized; shy of humans and not often seen

✿ HABITAT   ◑ DAILY RHYTHM   ♈ SOCIAL LIFE   ✓ SIGHTING TIPS

Lesser Kudu
Tragelaphus imberbis (Tandala mdogo)

❀ semi-arid, hilly or undulating bush country; tolerant of drought

◖ diurnal when secure; otherwise nocturnal

▽ territorial; males usually solitary; females in small troops with young

✓ smaller than the Greater Kudu; only the male has horns; extremely shy and usually seen only as it disappears

Fringe-eared Oryx
Oryx gazella callotis (Choroa)

❀ open grasslands; also waterless wastelands; tolerant of prolonged drought

◖ nocturnal and diurnal

▽ highly hierarchical mixed herds of up to fifteen, led by a dominant bull

✓ the *callotis* subspecies is one of two found in East Africa, the other, in northeastern Kenya, being the Beisa Oryx (*Oryx g. beisa*)

Sable Antelope
Hippotragus niger (Palahala)

❀ open woodland with medium to tall grassland near water

◖ nocturnal and diurnal

▽ territorial; bulls divide into sub-territories, through which cows and young roam; herds of immature males; sometimes pairs in season

✓ large antelope; upper body dark brown to black; mask-like markings on the face; both sexes have huge curved horns

Roan Antelope
Hippotragus equinus (Kirongo)

❀ tall grassland near water

◖ nocturnal and diurnal; peak afternoon feeding

▽ small herds led by a dominant bull; herds of immature males; sometimes pairs in season

✓ large antelope, distinguished from the Sable by lighter, greyish colour, shorter horns (both sexes) and narrow, tufted ears

Steinbok
Raphicerus campestris (Dondoo or Dondoro)

�֎ dry savannah

◑ nocturnal and diurnal

♈ solitary or (less often) in pairs

✓ widespread small antelope, surprisingly aggressive towards attackers but shy with humans; males have horns

Grysbok
Raphicerus melanotis sharpei (Dondoo or Dondoro)

✖ thicket adjacent to open grassland

◑ nocturnal

♈ rams territorial; loose pairings

✓ small, rarely seen antelope; the East African subspecies is Sharpe's (illustrated); distinguished from more slender Steinbok by light underparts; rams have short horns

Oribi
Ourebia ourebia (Kasia)

✖ open grassland

◑ diurnal

♈ territorial harems consisting of male and one to four females

✓ localized small antelope, but not hard to see where common; only males have horns; the Oribi is distinguished from the smaller Grysbok and Steinbok by a black tail and dark skin patch below the eye

Klipspringer
Oreotragus oreotragus (Mbuzi mawe)

✖ rocky country; cliffs and *kopjes*

◑ diurnal

♈ territorial ram with mate or small family group; often restricted to small long-term territories

✓ small antelope; horns normally only on male; extremely agile on rocky terrain; unusually high hooves, giving the impression of walking on tiptoe

✖ HABITAT   ◑ DAILY RHYTHM   ♈ SOCIAL LIFE   ✓ SIGHTING TIPS

No surprise, then, that Tanzania is a superb place for **bird-watching**, whether you're a novice or a dyed-in-the-wool twitcher, so make a point of bringing binoculars. Even on a standard wildlife safari, taking in all or some of the major game-viewing areas, the birds provide a superb added attraction. The keenest independent bird-watchers can expect to encounter over three hundred species in a ten-day trip, while some of the organized tour groups can hope for a hundred more.

Many bird-watchers are attracted to Tanzania by the large number of rare species: some forty **endemics** (of which 26 are endangered), meaning that they are found only in Tanzania and often only in one or two locations there, and many more **near-endemics** confined to East Africa. Pretty much every location has a few endemics or near-endemics, but three places stand out in particular: the Kilombero floodplain of central Tanzania, which recently gave three new species to science; the ancient and disjointed Eastern Arc Mountains, especially in the western Udzungwas and at Amani Nature Reserve near the coast; and Tarangire National Park and its adjacent conservation area in the north, whose count tops 550 species.

It's impossible to give an adequate rundown of the main bird species, but the following are some of the more frequently seen and easily identified species. For a full list, consult the comprehensive ⊛ www.tanzaniabirdatlas.com, or get hold of a dedicated birding guidebook to Tanzania or East Africa; see p.763. Another good source of information is the *African Bird Club* ⊛ www.africanbirdclub.org, which publishes an excellent regular bulletin and occasional monographs and itineraries. For practical advice, see "Birding" in Basics on p.63.

Large walking birds

Several species of large, terrestrial (or partly terrestrial) birds are regularly seen on safari. The flightless **ostrich** is found in dry, open plains and semi-desert in the far north, namely Tarangire, Ngorongoro, Serengeti, and around Lake Natron. At up to 2.5m high, it's the world's biggest bird and one of the fastest when need be. The females are neutral in colour, whilst courting males wow the ladies with their naked pink necks and thighs. Contrary to popular belief, they don't bury their heads in the sand, but do hide them in their plumage while resting.

The large, long-tailed **secretary bird** is also easily identified, and gets its name from its head quills, which resemble pens propped behind its ears. It's often seen in dry, open bush and wooded country, usually in pairs, and feeds on beetles, grasshoppers, reptiles and rodents.

The **marabou stork** is another easy one to spot – large and exceptionally ugly, up to 1.2m in height and with a bald head, long pointed funnel-like beak and dangling, pink throat pouch. The marabou flies with its head and neck retracted (unlike other storks) and is often seen in dry areas, including towns, where it feeds on small animals, carrion and refuse. If you're lucky, you'll see them roosting in trees.

Another reasonably common walking bird is the **ground hornbill**. This impressive creature lives in open country and is the largest hornbill by far, black with red face and wattles, bearing a distinct resemblance to a turkey. It's not uncommon to come across pairs, or sometimes groups, of ground hornbills, trailing through the scrub on the lookout for small animals. They nest among rocks or in tree stumps. The Maasai say their calls resemble humans talking.

Not really walking birds, but usually seen in flocks on the ground before scattering ahead of your advance in a low swooping flight, are several species of **guinea fowl**. These game birds have rather comical and brightly coloured heads, and a luxurious covering of royal blue feathers, often spotted white. The **vulturine guinea fowl** is found in very arid areas, while the **helmeted guinea fowl**, found in wetter areas, has a bony yellow skull protrusion (hence its name).

The world's heaviest flying bird, the greyish-brown **Kori bustard**, is also frequently seen; males weigh up to 12kg. Another commonly seen ground-lover is the **black-bellied bustard**. Both distinctive and elegant is the **crowned crane**, its head topped with a stunning halo-like array of yellow plumes. They're often seen feeding on cultivated fields or in marshy areas; Lake Victoria is a good place.

Flamingos and ibises

Many visitors to Tanzania are astounded by their first sight of **flamingos** – a sea of pink on a soda-encrusted Rift Valley lake (Natron and Manyara are the best places). There are two species: the greater flamingo, and the much more common lesser flamingo, which can usually be seen in flocks of tens of thousands, and sometimes several hundred thousand. The **lesser flamingo** is smaller, pinker and with a darker bill than its greater relative. The Rift Valley population – which only nests at Lake Natron but migrates to feed, notably to Lake Manyara and, most famously, at Kenya's Lake Nakuru – numbers several million, and is one of only three groups in Africa. Flocks can leave or arrive at an area in a very short period of time, the movements depending on all sorts of factors including the water's alkalinity and the presence of algal blooms, so sighting big flocks is impossible to predict. Lesser flamingos feed by filtering suspended aquatic food, mainly blue-green diatom algae that occur in huge concentrations on the shallow soda lakes of the Rift Valley.

Greater flamingos may occur in their thousands but are considerably fewer in number than the lesser, and are bottom feeders, filtering small invertebrates as well as algae. Although greaters tend to be less nomadic than their relatives, they are more likely to move away from the Rift Valley lakes to smaller water bodies and even the coast.

The most widely distributed **ibis** species (stork-like birds with down-curved bills) is the **sacred ibis**, which occurs near water and human settlements. It has a white body with black head and neck, and black tips to the wings. Also frequently encountered is the **hadada ibis**, a bird of wooded streams, cultivated areas and parks in northern Tanzania. It's brown with a green-bronze sheen to the wings, and calls noisily in flight.

Water birds

Most large water bodies, apart from the extremely saline lakes, support several migratory species of **ducks, geese, herons, storks** and **egrets**. The commonest large heron is the black-headed heron, which can sometimes be found far from water. Mainly grey with a black head and legs, the black heron can be seen "umbrella-fishing" along coastal creeks and marsh shores: it cloaks its head with its wings while fishing, which is thought to cut down surface reflection from the water, allowing the bird to see its prey more easily. The **hammerkop** or hammer-headed stork is a brown, heron-like bird with a sturdy bill and mane of brown feathers, which gives it a top-heavy, slightly prehistoric appearance in flight, like a miniature pterodactyl. Hammerkops are widespread near water and build large, conspicuous nests that are often taken over by other animals, including owls, geese, ducks, monitor lizards or snakes. Another common stork is the **saddlebill**, sporting an elegant red bill with a yellow "saddle" and black banding.

Birds of prey

Tanzania abounds with **birds of prey** (raptors) – kites, vultures, eagles, harriers, hawks and falcons. Altogether, over a hundred species have been recorded in the country, several of which are difficult to miss.

Six species of **vulture** range over the plains and bushlands of Tanzania and are often seen soaring in search of a carcass. All the species can occur together, and birds may travel vast distances to feed. The main differences are in feeding behaviour: the lappet-faced vulture, for example, pulls open carcasses; the African white-backed feeds mainly on internal organs; the hooded vulture picks the bones.

Two other birds of prey that are firmly associated with East Africa are the **bateleur**, an acrobatic eagle that is readily identified by its silver wings, black body, chestnut red tail, stumpy body shape and wedge-shaped tail; and the elegant **African fish eagle**, generally found in pairs near water, often along lakeshores.

Go-away birds and turacos

These distinctive, related families are found only in Africa. Medium-sized and with long tails, most **go-away birds** and **turacos** have short rounded wings. They are not excellent fliers, but are very agile in their movements along branches and through vegetation. Many species are colourful and display a crest. Turacos are generally green or violet in colour, and all are confined to thickly wooded and forest areas. Open-country species, such as the widely distributed and common **white-bellied go-away bird** (go-aways are named after their call), are white or grey in colour.

Rollers, shrikes and kingfishers

A family of very colourful and noticeable birds of the African bush, **rollers** perch on exposed bushes and telegraph wires. They take their name from their impressive courtship flights – a fast dive with a rolling and rocking motion, accompanied by raucous calls. Many have a sky-blue underbody and sandy-coloured back; long tail streamers are a distinctive feature of several species. The **lilac-breasted roller** is common and conspicuous.

Shrikes are found throughout Tanzania. Fierce hunters with sharply hooked bills, they habitually sit on prominent perches, and take insects, reptiles and small birds. Particularly rare is the **Uluguru bush-shrike**, found only in the Uluguru Mountains.

There are around a dozen species of colourful **kingfishers** found in Tanzania, ranging in size from the tiny **African pygmy kingfisher**, which feeds on insects and is generally found near water, to the **giant kingfisher**, a shy fish-eating species of wooded streams in the west of the country. Several species eat insects rather than fish and they can often be seen perched high in trees or on open posts in the bush where they wait to pounce on passing prey. One of the more common is the **malachite kingfisher**, which stays true to its roots by catching small fish: it swallows its prey head first after killing it by whacking it against branches.

Hornbills

Named for their long, heavy bills, surmounted by a casque or bony helmet, **hornbills** generally have black and white plumage. Their flight consists of a series of alternate flaps and glides. When in flight, hornbills may be heard before they are seen, the beaten wings making a "whooshing" noise as air rushes through the flight feathers. Many species have bare areas of skin on the face and throat and around the eyes, with the bill and the casque often brightly coloured, their colours changing with the age of the bird. Most hornbills are omnivorous, but tend largely to eat fruit. Several species are common open-country birds, including the silvery-cheeked and red-billed hornbills. Hornbills have interesting breeding habits: the male generally incarcerates the female in a hollow tree, leaving a hole through which he feeds her while she incubates the eggs and rears the young. The unusual ground hornbill is covered on p.753 under "Large walking birds".

Sunbirds and starlings

Sunbirds are bright, active birds, feeding on nectar from flowering plants, and distributed throughout Tanzania wherever there are flowers, flowering trees and bushes. Over forty species have been recorded, with many confined to discrete types of habitat. Males are brightly coloured and usually identifiable, but many of the drabber females require very careful observation to identify them. A particularly rare species is the **Amani sunbird**, which can be seen in small flocks at Amani Nature Reserve.

The glorious orange and blue **starlings** which are a common feature of bushland habitats – usually seen feeding on the ground – belong to one of three species. The **superb starling** is the most widespread of these, found everywhere from remote national parks to gardens in Arusha, and often quite tame. It can be identified by the white band above its orange breast. Of the thirty-odd other starling species present there is a handful of near-endemics, including Kenrick's, Hildebrandt's, Fischer's and Abbott's.

Weavers and whydahs

These small birds are some of the commonest and most widespread of all Tanzanian birds. Most male **weavers** have some yellow in the plumage, whereas the females are rather dull and sparrow-like. In fact, many species appear super-ficially very similar; distinctions are based on their range and preferred type of habitat. Weavers nest in colonies and weave their nests, many situated close to water or human habitation, into elongated shapes which can be used to help in the identification of the species. Unique to the Kilombero floodplain in central Tanzania is the **Kilombero weaver**, while the **Usambara weaver** is endemic to the Usambara Mountains, and the best place for the rufous-tailed weaver is Tarangire.

Whydahs are also known as widowbirds. The **paradise whydah** has extremely ornate tail feathers, with the central pair of tail feathers flattened and twisted into the vertical. Male paradise whydahs are mainly black in colour, and perform a strange bouncing display flight to attract females.

Adapted from the *Rough Guide to Kenya* by Richard Trillo, with additional material from Tony Stones and Tony Pinchuck

Books

T here's woefully little published about Tanzania other than glossy coffee-table tomes on wildlife or Maasai. Locally produced books are mostly in Kiswahili, a notable exception being the output of Zanzibar's Gallery Publications. Apart from these publications, a handful of other English-language works do trickle onto the market each year, mostly self-published collections of oral fables and proverbs with very limited distribution – snap them up wherever you can, as specific titles are often simply impossible to track down in Tanzania.

Tanzania's best **bookshops**, which can also order titles for you, are A Novel Idea in Dar es Salaam and the Zanzibar Gallery in Stone Town. These and other bookshops are mentioned in the "Listings" sections at the end of town accounts. You can usually also find a decent selection of titles in the gift shops of larger beach hotels and safari lodges. A good online store is ꩜www .africabookcentre.com. Most of the UK-, US- and Zanzibar-published books reviewed below can also be bought through ꩜www.amazon.co.uk or ꩜www .amazon.com. Books marked with a 🏃 are highly recommended.

Travel and general accounts

🏃 **Peter Matthiessen** *The Tree Where Man Was Born* (Harvill, UK/NAL-Dutton, US). Wanderings and musings of the Zen-thinking polymath in Kenya and northern Tanzania. Enthralling for its detail on nature, society, culture and prehistory, and beautifully written, this is a gentle, appetizing introduction to the land and its people.

🏃 **George Monbiot** *No Man's Land* (Picador, UK). A journey through Kenya and Tanzania providing shocking expos of Maasai dispossession and a major criticism of the wildlife conservation movement.

Shiva Naipaul *North of South* (Penguin, UK). A fine but caustic account of Naipaul's travels in Kenya, Tanganyika and Zambia. Always readable and sometimes hilarious, the insights make up for the occasionally angst-ridden social commentary and some passages that widely miss the mark.

Explorers' accounts

Copies of nineteenth-century explorers' journals are often difficult to track down unless they've been recently reprinted, or scanned and posted on the Internet (try ꩜www.gutenberg.org or ꩜www.blackmask.com). Apart from the following, ask your bookshop for anything on or by David Livingstone, John Hanning Speke, Verney Lovett Cameron, James Elton, Samuel White Baker or Johann Krapf.

Richard Francis Burton *The Lake Regions of Central Africa: From*

Zanzibar to Lake Tanganyika (Narrative Press, US); *Zanzibar: and Two*

Months in East Africa (o/p; ⓦwww
.wollamshram.ca/1001/Blackwood/
zanzibar.htm): *Zanzibar: City, Island
and Coast* (o/p). Entertaining but
extremely bigoted accounts of the
explorer's adventures.

🏃 **Martin Dugard** *Into Africa:
The Epic Adventures of Stanley
and Livingstone* (Broadway, US). A
compelling, blow-by-blow biographi-
cal account of the explorers' travels
before and after their famous meeting. The text relies heavily on both
the explorers' published and unpub-
lished works, and is a riveting read.

Henry Morton Stanley *Autobiography of …* (Narrative Press, US). A

suitably bombastic autobiography by
the famous explorer. The title of his
bestseller, *How I Found Livingstone*
(Epaulet, US; also ⓦwww.gutenberg
.org/etext/5157), needs no explanation.

Joseph Thomson *Through Maasai-
land: To the Central African Lakes and
Back* (1885, 2 vols; Frank Cass/avail-
able in the US through International
Specialized Book Services). A best-
seller at the time, Thomson was the
originator of "Maasai-itis" and the
nonsense that has been written about
them ever since. To his credit, he was
one of few explorers to have preferred
the power of friendly relations with
the locals to that of the gun.

Coffee-table books

🏃 **Mitsuaki Iwago** *Serengeti*
(Thames and Hudson, UK/
Chronicle, US). Simply the best
volume of wildlife photography ever
assembled, this makes most glossies
look feeble. If any aesthetic argument
were needed to preserve the parks
and animals, this is the book to use.

🏃 **Javed Jafferji** *Images of Zanzibar* (Gallery, Zanzibar). Superb
photos by Zanzibar's leading photog-
rapher.

Javed Jafferji & Gemma Pitcher
Safari Living (Gallery, Zanzibar). A

photographic tribute to Tanzania's
top safari lodges and camps. By
the same authors are *Recipes from
the Bush*, a collection of posh nosh;
Zanzibar Style, inspiring eye-candy
for budding interior decorators; and
Zanzibar Style: Recipes.

🏃 **Javed Jafferji & Graham
Mercer** *Tanzania: African Eden*
(Gallery, Zanzibar). Very much a
brochure in book form but stunningly beautiful, with over two
hundred photos from all over the
country, many taken over the air.

History

Extremely little of a non-academic nature has been written about the history of
mainland Tanzania; most of what's available covers Zanzibar and the Swahili coast.

Africa in general

Christopher Hibbert *Africa
Explored: Europeans in the Dark Continent 1769-1889* (Penguin, UK). An

entertaining read, devoted in large
part to the "discovery" of East and
Central Africa.

John Iliffe *Africans: the History of a Continent* (Cambridge UP, UK). Available in abridged form in Tanzania, this is the standard and recommended overview of Africa's history.

Roland Oliver & J.D. Fage *A Short History of Africa* (Penguin, UK/Viking, US). Dated, but still the standard paperback introduction.

Tanzania and East Africa

Aga Khan Trust for Culture *Zanzibar: A Plan for the Historic Stone Town* (Gallery, Zanzibar). Hefty but entertaining academic tome covering Stone Town's architecture and history in detail.

British Institute in Eastern Africa *Azania* (BIEA, Kenya/London). Annual academic journal containing a wealth of research articles, abstracts and book reviews about all aspects of East African archeology. Subscribe through ⊛www.britac .ac.uk/institutes/eafrica.

Heinrich Brode *Tippu Tip & the Story of his Career* (Gallery, Zanzibar). The semi-autobiographical story of East Africa's most notorious slave trader.

Richard Hall *Empires of the Monsoon* (HarperCollins, UK). A recommended sweep across the history of the western Indian Ocean.

John Iliffe *A Modern History of Tanganyika* (Cambridge UP, UK). A mammoth work and the definitive textbook on mainland Tanzania's history.

I.N. Kimambo & A.J. Temu (eds) *A History of Tanzania* (Kapsel, Tanzania). A comprehensive round-up from various authors, and the only one widely available in Tanzania. The modern period finishes at *Ujamaa* (1967), making it a little dated, but it's still a great resource.

Alan Moorehead *The White Nile* (Penguin, UK/Harper Perennial, US). A riveting account of the search for the source and European rivalries for control in the region. Good for a quick portrayal of nineteenth-century European attitudes towards Africa, with plenty of contemporary quotes and extracts from explorers' journals.

Kevin Patience *Zanzibar: Slavery and the Royal Navy*; *Zanzibar and The Bububu Railway*; *Zanzibar and the Loss of HMS Pegasus*; *Zanzibar and the Shortest War in History*; *Königsberg – A German East African Raider* (all self-published, ⊛www .zanzibar.net/zanzibar/zanzibar_ books). Various short, informative and pleasurable reads about Zanzibar. Most are available in Zanzibar and Dar.

Emily Ruete *Memoirs of an Arabian Princess from Zanzibar* (Gallery, Zanzibar). The extraordinary memoirs of the runaway Princess Salme, who eloped in the 1860s with a German merchant. Also available in the German original, and translated into French, Italian and Spanish.

Abdul Sheriff *Slaves, Spices and Ivory in Zanzibar* (James Currey, UK/Ohio University, US). Covers the immensely profitable eighteenth- and nineteenth-century slave trade. Abdul Sheriff is also editor of *Zanzibar under Colonial Rule* (James Currey, UK) and *Historical Zanzibar – Romance of the Ages* (HSP, UK).

Gideon S. Were & Derek A. Wilson *East Africa through a Thousand Years* (Evans Brothers, Kenya/UK). An authoritative sweep, including the cultures and traditions of several tribes, and illustrated with plenty of black-and-white photos, etchings and drawings.

Tanzania's people

Aside from the glossy and usually very superficial coffee-table splashes on the Maasai, decent material on any of Tanzania's tribes is difficult to come by, and there's no general overview.

James De Vere Allen *Swahili Origins* (Nkuki na Nyota, Tanzania). Masterful treatment of a potentially thorny question: exactly what, or who, are the Swahili?

Jakob Janssen Dannholz *Lute – The Curse and the Blessing* (private publication, Germany). Written almost a century ago by a German missionary, this is still the best work on Pare culture and society, both for content, and in its approachable and non-judgemental style.

Gregory H. Maddox (ed) *The Gogo: History, Customs and Traditions* (M.E. Sharpe, UK/US). Covers most facets of central Tanzania's Gogo tribe, including very detailed histories of separate clans, and transcriptions of songs.

Sarah Mirza & Margaret Strobel *Three Swahili Women* (Indiana UP, UK/US). Born between 1890 and 1920 into different social backgrounds, these biographies of three women document enormous changes from the most important of neglected viewpoints.

David Read *Barefoot over the Serengeti* (self-published, Kenya). No colonial rose-tint here – the author tells of his early Kenyan childhood and later upbringing in northern Tanzania with his Maasai friend. Contains fascinating tales of both colonial and later life told in a riveting matter-of-fact way and is a superb source of information on Maasai culture.

Frans Wijsen & Ralph Tanner *Seeking a Good Life* (Paulines, Kenya). Religion and society among the Sukuma of northern Tanzania, with a Christian undertone.

The arts

Anon *Tribute to George Lilanga* (East African Movies, Tanzania). Gorgeously illustrated tome collecting many works by one of Tanzania's leading Tingatinga painters.

Manfred Ewel & Anne Outwater (eds) *From Ritual to Modern Art: Tradition and Modernity in Tanzanian Sculpture* (Mkuki na Nyota, Tanzania). A collection of authoritative and scholarly essays on all aspects of Tanzanian sculpture, illustrated with black-and-white reproduction of works in the National Museum.

Yves Goscinny (ed) *East African Biennale* (Tanzanian Publishers, Tanzania); *Art in Tanzania* (East African Movies, Tanzania). Gloriously illustrated catalogue for the East African Biennale contemporary art exhibition (formerly "Art in Tanzania"): fantastic and inspiring stuff, from Tingatinga to the brilliant woodcarvings of Bagamoyo's artists.

Jens Jahn *Tanzania – Meisterwerke Afrikanischer Skulptur* (Haus der Kulturen der Welt, Germany). Even if you don't read German, this mammoth work is a must; blissfully comprehensive on all kinds of traditional Tanzanian woodcarving. It's also available at the German Embassy in Dar.

Uwe Rau & Mwalim A. Mwalim *The Doors of Zanzibar* (Gallery, Zanzibar/HSP, UK). Gorgeously illustrated glossy tome.

Fiction, poetry and orature

Fiction

Tanzanian novels or short stories in English are rare animals indeed, as most popular fiction is written in Kiswahili; books go out of print quickly, too, so snap up anything you find. Strangely, you're more likely to find Tanzanian fiction in Nairobi's bookshops.

 Aniceti Kitereza (tr. Gabriel Ruhumbika) *Mr Myombekere and His Wife Bugonoka. Their Son Ntulanalwo and Daughter Bulihwali* (Nkuki na Nyota, Tanzania). First published in 1945, this epic novel from Lake Victoria's Ukerewe Island tells the story of a couple's deepening devotion to one another despite the social stigma of infertility. Superbly translated from the original Kikerewe by a descendant of both Kitereza and the Ukerewe chiefs, the descriptions of local life remain as fresh as ever.

A.M. Hokororo *Salma's Spirit* (Nkuki na Nyota, Tanzania). Boy meets girl, except the girl has been dead for three years ... An interesting window into the Tanzanian conception of life after death.

Various *Voices: An Anthology of Short Stories from Tanzania* (Macmillan, UK). The only collection of contemporary Tanzanian fiction you're likely to find outside the country, with just four stories, enough to give a flavour of life and society but nothing more

Poetry

The oldest form of written poetry in Tanzania is from the coast. Inland, poetry in the sense of written verse is a recent form. But oral folk literature was often relayed in the context of music, rhythm and dance.

Ali A. Jahadmy *Anthology of Swahili Poetry* (Heinemann o/p). Rather wooden translations of classical compositions, and pertinent background.

Jonathan Kariara & Ellen Kitonga (eds) *An Introduction to East African Poetry* (Oxford UP). An accessible collection categorized into broad subjects like "love and marriage", and "yesterday, today and tomorrow".

 Shaaban Robert (tr. Clement Ndulute) *The Poetry of Shaaban Robert* (Dar es Salaam UP, Tanzania). The only English translation of works by Tanzania's foremost poet and writer, with the Kiswahili original on facing pages; a great tool if you're learning the language.

Various *Summons* (Tanzania Publishing House, Tanzania). The only collection of modern Tanzanian poetry written originally in English, offering an intimate insight into the concerns of post-Independence Tanzania.

Oral traditions and proverbs

Oral traditions (orature) are one of the jewels of Africa, encapsulating every aspect of myth, morals and reality with ogres, flying trees, strange worlds and lots of talking animals, who symbolize all manner of vices and virtues – the hare is invariably cunning, the hyena greedy and stupid, the elephant power-

Kiswahili proverbs

Proverbs (*methali*) are an important part of daily life, and find all sorts of uses. Proverbial knowledge is respected, and speakers alluding to appropriate proverbs at the right time are much lauded. The following is a selection that you might find useful yourself. The pithier ones also find their way onto *kangas* – the cotton wraps worn by women – which are used to display a woman's disapproval of her husband's actions, as a reminder of a woman's worth, or as a declaration of tenderness from a lover who gave the *kanga* as a present.

Asifuye mvuwa imemnyea.	He who praises rain has been rained on.
Atangaye na jua hujuwa.	He who wanders around by day a lot, learns a lot.
Fadhila ya punda ni mateke.	Gratitude of a donkey is a kick.
Fumbo mfumbe mjinga mwerevu huligangua.	Put a riddle to a fool, a clever person will solve it.
Haba na haba, hujaza kibaba.	Little and little, fills the measure.
Haraka haraka haina baraka.	Hurry hurry has no blessings.
Hata ukinichukia la kweli nitakwambia.	Hate me, but I won't stop telling you the truth.
Heri kujikwa kidole kuliko ulimi.	Better to stumble with toe than tongue.
Kila ndege huruka na mbawa zake.	Every bird flies with its own wings.
Kizuri chajiuza kibaya chajitembeza.	A good thing sells itself, a bad one advertises itself.
Maji ya kifufu ni bahari ya chungu.	Water in a coconut shell is like an ocean to an ant.
Mchumia juani, hilla kivulini.	He who earns his living in the sun, eats in the shade.
Mgeni ni kuku mweupe.	A stranger is like a white fowl (ie noticeable).
Mjinga akierevuka mwerevu yupo mashakani.	When a fool becomes enlightened, the wise man is in trouble.
Moyo wa kupenda hauna subira.	A heart deep in love has no patience.
Mtumai cha ndugu hufa masikini.	He who relies on his relative's property, dies poor.
Mwenye pupa hadiriki kula tamu.	A hasty person misses the sweet things (because they cannot wait for the fruit to ripen).
Nazi mbovu harabu ya nzima.	A rotten coconut in a heap spoils its neighbours.
Pekepeke za jirani, hazinitoi ndani.	Unwarranted spying by a neighbour does not take me out of my house.
Penye nia ipo njia.	Where there's a will there's a way.
Tulia tuishi wazuri haweshi.	Calm down and live with me, pretty ones are never in short supply.
Ulimi unauma kuliko meno.	The tongue hurts more than the teeth.
Usisa firie Nyota ya Mwenzio.	Don't set sail using somebody else's star.

ful but gullible, the lion a show-off. Anthologies of transcribed stories are extremely thin on the ground, so buy what you can.

George Bateman *Zanzibar Tales: Told by the Natives of East Africa*

(Gallery, Zanzibar). A delightful collection of fables and legends first published in 1908.

A.C. Hollis *Masai Myths, Tales and Riddles* (Dover, US). Collected and translated over a century ago, this is a very welcome reprint of a superb work. Time has done little to dampen the Hollis' evident enthusiasm and respect.

🏃 **Naomi Kipury** *Oral literature of the Maasai* (East African Educational Publishers, Kenya). A lovely selection of transcribed narratives, proverbs, songs and poetry.

Jan Knappert *Myths & Legends of the Swahili* (East African Educational Publishers, Tanzania). An entertaining selection of tales similar to stories told across the Muslim world, with strong echoes of the *Arabian Nights*.

🏃 **Joseph M. Mbele** *Matengo Folktales* (Infinity Publishing, US). Ably translated traditional tales from Lake Nyasa featuring that lovable trickster, the hare, and hungry monsters.

Amir A. Mohamed *Zanzibar Ghost Stories* (Good Luck, Zanzibar). A collection of weird and wonderful ghost stories from Zanzibar. Available in Zanzibar only.

O. Mtuweta H. Tesha *Famous Chagga Stories* (Twenty First Century Enterprises, Tanzania). A short but sweet collection, giving a pleasant insight into Tanzania's most prosperous tribe.

Criston S. Mwakasaka *The Oral Literature of the Banyakyusa* (Kenya Literature Bureau, Kenya). Tales and proverbs from southern Tanzania.

🏃 **R.A. Mwombeki & G.B. Kamanzi** *Folk Tales from Buhaya* (self-published, Tanzania). A hugely enjoyable collection of over sixty stories, representative of many other African oral traditions: a flying tree, ogres, and the classic tale of how the hare managed to get it on with the leopardess. Wonderful stuff.

Guidebooks and field guides

Helpful **guidebooks** to individual parks are published by the parks authority, TANAPA. There's also a series of guidebooks to Ngorongoro published by the Ngorongoro Conservation Area Authority. All can easily be found in Tanzania, as can many of the following.

Mammals

🏃 **Richard Estes and Daniel Otte** *The Safari Companion: A Guide to Watching African Mammals* (Chelsea Green Pub Co, UK). Beautifully illustrated, especially detailed on social behaviour.

D. Hoskings and M. Withers *Collins Field Guide: Handbook to East African Mammals* (HarperCollins, UK). Handy, pocket-sized and readily available in Tanzania.

Birds

🏃 **Ber van Perlo** *Collins Illustrated Checklist of the Birds of East and Southern Africa* (HarperCollins, UK). An essential pocket guide, providing clear colour illustrations and distribution maps for every species in East Africa, though little in the way of descriptive text.

Dave Richards *Photographic Guide to the Birds of East Africa* (New Holland, UK). Over three hundred colour photos.

John Williams *The Field Guide to the Birds of East Africa* (Collins, UK). The most commonly used book on safari, also available in German, but outdated.

🏃 **Nigel Wheatley** *Where to Watch Birds in Africa* (Helm, UK/Princeton UP, US). Tight structure and plenty of useful detail make this a must-have for serious birders in Africa.

Zimmerman, Turner and Pearson *A Field Guide to the Birds of Kenya and Northern Tanzania* (Helm, UK). Comprehensive coverage in hardback.

Flora

Michael Blundell *Wild Flowers of East Africa* (HarperCollins, UK). The most readily available botanical companion for a safari.

Scuba-diving and snorkelling

🏃 **Anton Koornhof** *The Dive Sites of East Africa* (New Holland, UK). Highly recommended if you're at all interested in snorkelling or diving, beautifully illustrated and with thoughtful sections on environmental matters.

Ewald Lieske and Robert Myers *Coral Reef Fishes: Caribbean, Indian Ocean, and Pacific Ocean* (Princeton UP, US). Another beautifully illustrated guide, although not everything applies to Tanzania.

Music

M
usic is very much part of Tanzanian life, and with 129 officially recognized tribes and an open attitude to foreign influences, the country presents an extremely broad and rich musical panorama. On the coast, Islamic influences find expression in **taarab** – a blend of Bantu drum rhythms and Indian and Arabian chamber orchestras – while brassy Cuban beats underlie the lively sounds of Dar es Salaam's dance bands, dreadlocked rastas groove along to home–grown reggae, church choirs sing the praises of the Lord through translated European hymns, and rappers evoke urban woes over Stateside backing tracks and breakbeats. But all these are contemporary genres. Much older – and musically often much more sophisticated – is *ngoma*, or traditional music, which, although gradually disappearing, can still be heard if you're patient in your quest.

Ngoma ya kiasili – traditional music

Music, songs and dance play a vital role in traditional culture, not least in providing a sense of continuity from the past to the present, as can be seen in the Kiswahili name for traditional music, **ngoma ya kiasili** – "music of the ancestors". Traditional music is also a cohesive social force: *ngomas* involve everyone present, whether as singers, dancers, instrumentalists, or in combination.

Ngoma is often drum-based (the word also means drum), and tends to keep to its roots, hence giving each tribe's musical output a distinctive sound. The **lyrics**, often poetry that makes full use of tribal riddles, proverbs and metaphoric language, change according to the occasion, and are used to transmit all kinds of information from reciting family histories and advising youngsters of their responsibilities, to informing newly-weds of the pains and joys of married life and to seeking the intervention of the spirits of the deceased to bring rain.

The powerful **hypnotic quality** characteristic of many Tanzanian musical traditions (the Maasai and Gogo are superb examples) is not merely aesthetic, but has its purpose: the mesmerizing rhythms of work songs help reduce fatigue, while the ethereal rhythms and intricate harmonies of ritual dances aim to bring the living and the dead together to communicate in a mental limbo. This astonishing shifting of the senses can be done for all sorts of reasons: at funerals, for the living to accompany the departed to the spirit world, or for warriors preparing for battle to come into direct contact with their proud history of success in war. But the underlying idea is that of **continuity**, that a person is never completely "dead" until forgotten by the living – a crucial concept for understanding the basis of virtually every traditional African society.

Despite damaging outside influences, to a large extent Tanzania's traditional values remain unchanged, though the structures of traditional societies themselves are changing fast. Increasingly bereft of its original context, traditional music is gradually disappearing. Nevertheless, even the most "developed" tribes, like the Chagga, still prefer traditional music for special events like weddings and, nowadays, baptisms and other Christian and Muslim ceremonies. It's only

The heart of Tanzania's live music scene is **Dar es Salaam**, where dozens of bands perform in an ever-changing rota in bars and clubs in the city's suburbs. Economic liberalization from the mid-1980s onwards has made things harder for less popular bands, so things elsewhere have become pretty quiet: Arusha and Dodoma are the main places, whilst Mwanza, Morogoro, Mbeya and Tabora sometimes receive big-name bands whenever they're on tour.

The best time for catching live music on **Zanzibar** is early February for the Sauti za Busara Festival, and early July for the ZIFF Festival of the Dhow Countries (see p.655 for both). The Muslim festival of Idd al-Fitr, at the end of Ramadan, is also a great time to be around; it can last up to five days, with a nonstop feast and much music and dancing.

in remote areas that you're likely to come across traditional festivities, but if you're patient and reasonably adventurous in your travels, you'll be able to witness something more authentic than the usual tourist fare and listen to some of the most extraordinary sounds you'll ever hear.

There is another way of getting to hear traditional music. Though the *Ujamaa* period of the 1960s and 1970s destroyed a good deal of the old ways, it also limited radio airtime for non-Tanzanian music, with the result that sound engineers from Radio Tanzania Dar es Salaam (RTD) set off to record traditional music. The result is a priceless **archive** housed at their headquarters in Dar es Salaam, of which over a hundred recordings – covering almost as many tribes – are for sale; see p.124 for more details. Although the recordings aren't perfect in terms of acoustics, they're a national treasure and the following are some highlights. There are dozens of playable, full-length **sound clips** of Kuria, Luo, Maasai and Makonde *ngoma* at ⓦwww.bluegecko.org/kenya.

Gogo

Central Tanzania's **Gogo** are among Africa's most skilled musicians. At the heart of their musical repertoire, known in Kigogo as *sawosi*, is the **marimba ya mkono** (or *mbira*), a hand-held xylophone with strung metal tongues that resound in a small wooden resonator when struck. The instrument, examples of which can be bought in the souvenir emporiums of Arusha and Dar es Salaam, provides a light but insistent bassline, which becomes immensely complex when several musicians are playing (several rhythms at a time, not quite overlapping and known as polyrhythm). Interwoven with equally polyrhythmic singing, and the plaintive voices of one-stringed *zeze* fiddles, the result is both beautiful and haunting. For more information, see "The Music of the Gogo" on p.260.

Kuria

The music of the **Kuria**, who straddle the border with Kenya, is characterized by one of Africa's largest lyres, the *litungu* (or *iritungu*), which has a distinctly metallic and incredibly deep timbre, with the resonant buzzing of the strings providing the hypnotic impetus. The musical tradition remains strong, even if the elaborate trappings that were once employed – such as giant "clogs" worn by dancers – have become museum pieces. See also p.512.

Luguru (Ruguru)

The instrumental genius of Luguru women – one of few matriarchal societies remaining in Africa – has entered something akin to folklore in Tanzania. RTD has one outstanding recording for sale. The dominant instrument is a kind of flute, whose constant rising and falling immediately captures the imagination. You might be able to see a live performance of Luguru music in the Uluguru Mountains near Morogoro; see p.288.

Luo

The Luo are the largest tribe on Lake Victoria's Kenyan shore, but a minority also live on the Tanzanian side around Musoma and between Bunda and Ukerewe Island. Despite having been almost wholly converted to Christianity, the Luo still play traditional music and instruments. They are best known for the *nyatiti*, a double-necked eight-string lyre with a skin resonator which is also struck on one neck with a metal ring tied to the toe. It produces a tight, resonant sound, and is used to generate sometimes long and remarkably complex hypnotic rhythms. Originally used in fields to relieve workers' tiredness, a typical piece begins at a moderate pace, and quickens progressively throughout, over which the musician sings. The lyrics cover all manner of subjects, from politics and change since the *wazungu* arrived, to moral fables and age-old legends. Look out also for recordings of the *onand* (accordion) and *orutu* (a single-stringed fiddle).

Maasai

The nomadic cattle-herding traditions of the **Maasai** precluded the carrying of large instruments, meaning that their music is entirely vocal (with the exception of kudu horns blown during one or two ceremonies). The result, similar to the music of other pastoral peoples in Kenya, Sudan and Ethiopia, is an astonishing multipart singing, sometimes with women included in the chorus. The best are the polyphonic songs of the *morani* warriors, where each man sings part of a rhythm, often produced in his throat, which together with the calls of his companions creates an incredibly complex rhythm (the buzzing from the vocal chords themselves are hypnotic to the singers). The songs are usually competitive, expressed through the singers leaping as high as they can, or bragging about how they killed a lion or rustled cattle from a neighbouring tribe. The Maasai have retained much of their traditional culture, so singing is still very much used in traditional ceremonies, most spectacularly in the *eunoto* circumcision ceremony in which boys are initiated into manhood to begin their ten- to fifteen-year stint as *morani*. See also box on p.446

Makonde

RTD has a couple of tapes of the powerfully rhythmical drumming of the **Makonde** (see p.242), but they're best known for the visual aspect of their dances, especially the *Sindimba*, in which the protagonist – a masked dancer embodying a spirit called *Mapiko* – performs on stilts (*machopila*) to the terrified delight of the kids.

Nyasa (Nyanja)

Over on Lake Nyasa, musical groups from various districts in **Mbamba Bay** (see p.616) compete in a series of musical contests (*mashindano*) in the dance season, roughly at the end of the harvest following the long rains. The music is quite unlike anything else in Tanzania, with weirdly wonderful rasping pipes accompanied by big drums. When not competing, the groups practise in the evenings.

Sukuma

In similarly competitive vein, the **Sukuma** on the opposite side of Tanzania around Lake Victoria, also have an annual cycle of dance competitions, rooted in a nineteenth-century dispute between two witchdoctors about whose medicine was more powerful. They resolved to test the strength of their skills by trying to influence the crowd to favour one or another group of competing musicians and dancers; for more information, see p.501.

Zanzibar

The influence of Arabic and Indian music is particularly evident on the coast, especially Zanzibar, where *taarab* (see p.770) is the dominant form. *Ngoma* does exist, though being of spiritual or supernatural significance it's rarely performed in public. There are many styles, but the one you're most likely to come across is **chakatcha**, in which drums provide a fine rhythmic base for dancing. Other dances worth enquiring about include *msondo, beni, bomu, kyaso, gonga, lelemama, msewe, tukulanga* and *kirumbizi*. **Unyago**, traditionally played for girls' initiation ceremonies, has been popularized by *taarab* singer Bi Kidude. If you're around during Ramadan, the drumming and singing you might hear between midnight and 4am is **daku**, which urges people to take their last meal of the night before the next day's fast begins.

Popular music

Nowadays, *ngoma* has all but disappeared from the street and other popular venues. Taking its place is **popular music**: jazz or dance, Christian *kwaya* gospel, reggae, rap, hip-hop, Bongo Flava, and *taarab* on the coast and on Zanzibar.

Dance music – Muziki wa dansi

For most people, Tanzania's most enjoyable musical genre is what's locally known as *jazzi* or **muziki wa dansi** – dance music. The usual line-up includes several electric guitars and basses, drums, synthesizers, a lead singer (often also a guitarist) and often female dancers whose stage antics leave little to the imagination. Band sizes can be big – anything up to thirty members – a necessity given the almost nightly performances, and all-too-frequent defections of musicians to rival bands.

Congolese and **Cuban** rhythms and styles have had an especially pervasive influence on the scene since its inception in the 1930s, especially Cuba's pre-Revolution big bands and Congo's enormously successful Afro-Cuban brand, and styles like rumba, cha-cha-cha, salsa, marimba, soukous, kwasa kwasa, ndombolo and mayemu are recognized everywhere.

Most bands are known by two names: their proper name, like African Stars, and their *mtindo*, or dance style, which for African Stars is Twanga Pepeta. What follows is a brief rundown of the most popular bands; for an exhaustive round-up, see Volume 1 of the encyclopaedic *Rough Guide to World Music*. See also ⓦwww.members.aol.com/dpaterson, which has lots more information on East African music, with articles by Rough Guide contributors Doug Paterson and Werner Graebner.

The Congo connection

The **Congolese influence** began between the world wars, when 78s of Cuban rumba began to make their way into East Africa. These shellac recordings made a huge impression on Congolese musicians, and started a marriage that is still going strong today. The scene was especially lively in Kinshasa (then Léopold-ville), which was quick to adapt the imported Latin rhythms to a more African beat and style, and in time it was Congolese recordings that were wending their way into Tanzania.

The Congo connection reached its height in the 1970s, after a number of Congolese musicians fled their war-torn country to settle in East Africa, where they established a number of extremely popular bands. The greatest of the lot – gathering the cream of Congo's expatriate musicians – was **Maquis du Zaïre**, which later became **Orchestre Maquis Original**. Their first *mtindo*, "Kamanyola bila jasho", aptly describes their cool, laid-back style: it means "dance Kamanyola without sweating". After the death of their charismatic lead singer and saxophonist, Chinyama Chiaza, in 1985, the band began to disinte-grate. Many of its musicians went off to form their own bands, of which – since the demise of **Bana Marquis** in 1999 – there's now only one survivor, **Kili-manjaro Connection**, whose arrangements include rhythms borrowed from traditional Tanzanian *ngomas*. Although the Congolese period was dominated by big bands, an individual musician that made it big was **Remmy Ongala**, admired for his powerful political and social lyrics over driving guitar riffs, though his fan base has diminished since he become a born-again Christian, after recovering from paralysis.

OTTU Jazz Band and DDC Mlimani Park Orchestra

A throw-back to traditional *ngomas* and their competing dance societies is the habit of Tanzanian dance bands to come in rival pairs. In the early 1980s, Orchestra Safari Sound sparred off with Maquis, while in the late 1980s, and throughout much of the 1990s, the big rivals were Ottu Jazz and Mlimani Park.

OTTU Jazz Band is Tanzania's longest-established band (their nickname is *baba ya muziki* – father of music), having been formed in 1964 as NUTA Jazz, the acronym for the National Union of Tanzanian Workers. The band changed its name to Juwata in 1977, after the defection of various band members, and takes its present name from the Organization of Tanzanian Trade Unions. Under their *mtindo* of Msondo (a kind of drum and a style of music performed during girls' initiations), they reached their first peak of fame in the 1970s, and have provided the model for a welter of copycat bands ever since. Their music now, as then, is dominated by supremely fluid guitar licks and rough, brassy horns, and although the vocals can get lost at times, is still the most danceable live music you'll hear in Dar.

Their big rivals are **DDC Mlimani Park Orchestra**, who have been strong since 1978 after a number of musicians from Juwata defected. Despite suffer-ing waves of defections themselves over the years, Mlimani Park – under their *mtindo* of Sikinde (the name of a Zaramo *ngoma*) – produced a string of hits in the 1980s (the best known is *Neema*, "My comforter"), and their tight, cohesive sound, blissful harmonies and famously poetic lyrics have made them one of Tanzania's best-loved bands.

African Stars and African Revolution

The latest big name Congo-style bands are African Stars and African Revolu-tion. **African Stars**, better known by their *mtindo*, Twanga Pepeta, are forth-right about their Congolese influences, and play a version of whatever style is currently making waves in Kinshasa. From the same stable (see ⓦwww .africanstars.net) are **African Revolution**, catering for a more upmarket crowd. Their output, under the *mtindo* Tam Tam, is barely distinguishable from that of the **Mchinga Sound** band.

Taarab and Kidumbak

Taarab is the quintessential music of the Swahili coast, from Somalia in the north to Mozambique in the south. It's actually barely a century old, but has roots stretching way back to pre-Islamic Arabia, Persia and India – a quixotic synthesis easily discernible in its sound. The soloist – in Zanzibar usually female – sings in a high-pitched and distinctly Arab-influenced nasal twang, and is accompanied by an orchestra of up to fifty musicians, often dressed in full European-style dinner suits (the name *taarab* derives from the Arabic for "civilized"). The main instruments are cellos and violins, Arab lutes (*udi*), the Egyptian *qanun* (a 72-string zither called *taishokoto*), *zumari* (*nay*) clarinets and sometimes drums (*dumbak*). Most groups nowadays also include accordions, a double bass or cello, electric guitars and synthesizers, all in all lending modern *taarab* an uncannily "Sonic the Hedgehog goes to Bollywood" kind of quality. No coincidence – modern *taarab* is also influenced by Indian movie scores, and by a touch of Latin verve borrowed from the jazz bands.

Taarab is usually performed at weddings and other social gatherings, when the poetic lyrics – composed in Kiswahili and laced with Arabic – come into their own. Dealing with love, jealousy and relationships, they are often composed especially for the occasion. Some of the songs, called *mipasho*, are requested by one person specifically to criticize or upbraid another, and although the "accused" is never named, his or her identity is easily understood by the parties involved. *Taarab* is danced almost entirely by women, who shuffle along in a conga while shaking their bottoms rhythmically in a complex pelvic movement called *kukata kiuno*, meaning "to cut the waist" – it looks lazy, but drives men crazy.

The doyenne of Zanzibari *taarab* was the hugely influential **Siti Bint Saad**, Zanzibar's first female *taarab* singer and also the first to perform in Kiswahili rather than Arabic. In so doing, she did more than anyone else to popularize *taarab* across the social spectrum, reaching the peak of her fame in the 1930s and 1940s, when her voice became synonymous with Swahili culture.

Equally beloved, and still going strong after a career now spanning eight decades, is **Bi Kidude** (real name Fatuma Binti Baraka), who began her career in the 1920s under the tutelage of Siti Bint Saad. Like her mentor, Bi Kidude was not afraid to broach controversial topics in her songs, including the abuse of women, and as her fame grew, she did away with the veil that she and Siti Bint Saad had been obliged to wear for public performances. Old age has done nothing to temper her independence: she has experimented with *taarab* and jazz/dance fusion, and has also popularized drum-based *unyago* (which she plays in "hobby horse" style), formerly reserved for girls' initiation ceremonies. With her deep, bluesy and mesmerizing voice, the "little granny" (her nickname) is a giant among African musicians.

The main *taarab* orchestras are based in Stone Town, here the big two are the traditionalist **Ikhwani Safaa** (Malindi Taarab) founded in 1905, who remain close to the Arabic roots of *taarab*; and **Culture Music Club** (Mila na Utamaduni), the largest and most successful, who began life in the Afro-Shirazi Party in the years before Independence. In Dar es Salaam, the two big orchestras – both contemporary in style – are **Zanzibar Stars Modern Taarab** and **East African Melody**.

Hiring a full *taarab* orchestra is an expense that most cannot afford. A cheaper alternative is a smaller **Kidumbak** orchestra, which features more drums (*dumbak*) and a peculiar bass made from a tea chest, giving it a much more African feel. **Makame Fakis** is the main exponent of this genre.

Rap, hip-hop, R&B and Bongo Flava

It's taken a decade for hip-hop, rap and R&B to establish themselves as a major force in Tanzanian music. The scene is constantly changing: whilst you'll hear plenty of it on the radio, live performances are rare, not helped by the fact that acts form, split, rename, disappear or even emigrate with bewildering frequency.

Having spent the 1990s as the poorer cousins of the dance band scene, rap and hip-hop emerged from the underground in the new millennium to take the country – and East Africa – by storm. **Hip-hop** is the purest, underground form of the styles, sometimes with no backing track at all, and its conscious lyrics often broach social issues such as poverty, AIDS, politics and identity. **Rap** is more commercial, its lyrics – usually US-inspired or-produced backing tracks – leaning more towards love songs and postured "gangsta rap" copied from MTV – nothing you can't hear anywhere else. But the huge commercial hit – propelled by ample airtime on Tanzania's FM radio stations – has been **Bongo Flava**, which combines rap with R&B. Perhaps the most eclectic of the styles, the sound varies greatly between performers – sometimes irritatingly sugary and repetitive "I love you so"-type songs, other times mind-bendingly inventive in its combination of traditional rhythms, samples and computer-generated riffs.

Attempting to recommend current **performers** for each style is a thankless task, and perhaps rather pointless for a guidebook, given the ever-changing scene. The fans, too, are a fickle lot: a crew ruling the airwaves one month might be completely forgotten the next. As a result, performances are difficult to locate, not helped by the fact that even the big names only perform a dozen times or so a year. For the low-down on the latest, get to the **Internet** and navigate to ⊛www.africanhiphop.com, for up-coming events, a welter of band reviews, features, and a webcast; or go to ⊛www.afropop.org for lots of excellent feature articles, including reviews of festivals and gigs. The subject of ⊛www.bongoflava.com is self-evident, and has audio and video clips, and an events section; there's also a good introduction to the genre at ⊛www.artmatters.info/bongo.htm.

Nonetheless, for what it's worth, **big names** in Bongo Flava at present include Juma "Sir" Nature, Solo Thang, T.I.D., Man Dojo and Domo Kaya, Mr Nice, and Professor Jay. Also worth seeking out are recordings by the granddaddies of Tanzanian rap and hip-hop, **Kwanza Unit** ("First Unit"; now disbanded), formed by veterans K.B.C. and Rhymson in 1990 – Rhymson has now taken his career to Canada. For the R&B roots of Bongo Flava, winkle out early (1995–96) recordings of **Afro Reign**, also now disbanded. But when it comes to staying power, it's a sassy woman you need: mingling modern preoccupations with stylishly raunchy delivery is **Lady Jay Dee**. Also a contender in career longevity, albeit now in the UK, is Bongo Flava pioneer **Sugu** (formerly **Mr II** and **2 Proud**). Some of the most inventive recent output comes from **X Plastaz**, three Arushan brother and two kids, the first to have experimented with fusions of traditional music; their Maasai rap has gone global.

Reggae

Reggae is under-represented, historically because of government disapproval, and nowadays because of hip-hop's and Bongo Flava's massive popularity. The official distrust of reggae was based on the fact that Rastafarians smoke marijuana as part of their religion, which to the simple and always sober President Nyerere was plain immoral. The story goes that during the celebrations for Zimbabwe's Independence, Nyerere refused to shake hands with Bob Marley. Come evening, Marley's rendition of *Africa Unite* was persuasion enough, and Nyerere got on stage to shake hands with the great musician, to huge applause. The government hasn't bothered with crackdowns on reggae since 1995. **Roots & Culture** is the main outfit.

Kwaya

With its roots mostly in American gospel and European hymns, **kwaya** ("choir") is perhaps the least Tanzanian of the popular music styles, though if the blaring wattage from mobile tape vendors is any indication, *kwaya* cassettes far outsell other musical genres. The best make superb use of traditional *ngoma* rhythms, vocal power and instruments; the worst use horribly synthesized tinny backing tracks – no fun if you're stuck on a bus blasting it out.

Each *kwaya* forms part of a church community; Sunday Mass is the best time and place for listening to it live, usually marked by plenty of uplifting singing, sometimes of Latin hymns in Kiswahili, more often totally African, all interspersed by fiery admonitions from a crazed preacher. The cassettes can be bought everywhere, especially on Sundays outside churches.

Discography

A good **Internet store** with a decent selection of Tanzanian music is ⊛www .natari.com. A good compilation is the two-volume *Music from Tanzania and Zanzibar* (Caprice). The following are all CDs.

Ngoma ya kiasili

One performer that doesn't quite fit into any category is Hukwe Ubi Zawose (*Tanzania Yetu and Meteso*, Triple Earth; *The Art of Hukwe Zawose*, JVC; *Chibite*, RealWorld), who plays a modernized form of traditional Gogo *marimba ya mkono* music.

The best place for buying **cassettes** of traditional *ngoma* is RTD in Dar es Salaam (see p.124), who have almost eighty different tapes for sale at Tsh1000 a pop.

Bondei *Ng'anga Ngoma – Wabondei drumming by Fred Ng'anga* (⊛www .aangserian.org.uk).

Gogo *Tanzanie: Chants des Wagogo et des Kuria* (Inedit); *Tanzanie: Musiques rituelles Gogo* (VDE Gallo); *Nyati group: L'Élégance de Dodoma* (MPJ).

Iraqw *Safari Ingi* (⊛www.leopard mannen.no/hanssen/safari.htm).

Maasai *Music of the Maasai* (⊛www .laleyio.com); *Maasai Warrior Chants*

and *Namayana* (both ⊛www .aangserian.org.uk).

Rangi *Rhythms of the Rangi* (⊛www .aangserian.org.uk).

Sukuma *Tanzania: Music of the Farmer Composers of Sukumaland* (Multicultural Media).

Various *Ouganda, Kenya, Tanzanie – Musiques de Cérémonies* (Nonesuch).

Zanzibar *Imani Cultural Troupe: BAPE, Songs and Dances from Zanzibar* (Felmay).

Taarab and kidumbak

The following, and much more, can be bought at Stone Town's Dhow Countries Music Academy; see p.656.

Bi Kidude *Zanzibar* (RetroAfric); *Machozi ya Huba: Bi Kidude, Zanzibar 2003* (HeartBeat Records, Zanzibar).

Culture Musical Club *The Music of Zanzibar* (Globestyle); *Spices of Zanzibar* (Network); *Bashraf: Taarab Instrumentals from Zanzibar* (Dizim); *Waridi – Scents of Zanzibar* (Jahazi Media/EMI).

Ikhwani Safaa *Taarab: The Music of Zanzibar. Vol 2 Ikhwani Safaa Musical Club* (Globestyle).

Kidumbak Kalcha *Ng'ambo – The other side of Zanzibar* (Dizim).

Makame Fakis Various locally produced CDs available in Zanzibar.

Various artists *Soul & Rhythm: Zanzibar* (2 CDs, Jahazi Media/EMI); *Zanzibar: Music of Celebration* (Topic).

Jazz and muziki wa dansi

The best place for buying cassettes of dance classics is RTD in Dar es Salaam (see p.124), which has over a hundred recordings.

Bana Maquis *Leila* (Dakar Sound).

Mbaraka Mwinshehe & The Morogoro Jazz Band *Masimango* (Dizim).

Mlimani Park Orchestra *Sikinde* (World Music Network/Africassette); *Sungi* (Popular African Music).

Remmy Ongala & Orchestre Super Matimila *Nalilia Mwana* (WOMAD); *Songs for the Poor Man* (Real World/Womad); *The Kershaw Sessions* (Strange Roots).

Shikamoo Jazz Band *Chela Chela Vol.1* (RetroAfric).

Various Dada Kidawa, Sister Kidawa – Classic Tanzanian Hits from the 1960s (Original Music); The Tanzania Sound (Original Music); Musiki wa Dansi: Afropop Hits from Tanzania (World Music Network/Africassette); The Tanzania Sound (Original Music).

Rap, hip-hop and Bongo Flava

Kwanza Unit *Kwanzanians* (Madunia/RAHH, ☻www .africanhiphop.com).

Lady Jay Dee *Machozi* (Benchmark Productions); *Binti* (Smooth Vibes); *Moto* (Smooth Vibes).

Mr II *Bongo Flava* (Kwetu Entertainment).

Sugu *Sugu* (Social Misfit Entertainment).

X Plastaz *Maasai Hip Hop* (out here rec, ☻www.xplastaz.com).

Various artists Bongo Flava – Swahili rap from Tanzania (out | here rec).

Language

Language

A beginner's guide to Kiswahili

Kiswahili is a Bantu language, incorporating thousands of foreign words – the majority of them Arabic – and is, perhaps surprisingly, one of the easiest languages to learn. Even with limited knowledge you can make yourself understood, and people are delighted if you make the effort, though you'll rarely have problems in tourist areas with English. Zanzibar is acknowledged as being the source of the "standard" dialect of Kiswahili that is spoken throughout East Africa, even if the inhabitants of Kenya's Lamu Island would beg to differ.

The best **phrasebook** is the *Rough Guide Swahili Phrasebook*. A good **dictionary**, available in Tanzania's better bookstores and some lodge gift shops, is the two-volume edition published by Oxford University Press. For **language courses** and tuition, see this book's Index.

Pronunciation

Kiswahili is pronounced exactly as it's written, with the stress nearly always on the penultimate syllable. Each vowel is syllabic, and odd-looking combinations of consonants are often pronounced as one syllable, too. **Shauri** (advice) for example, is pronounced "sha-oo-ri". Nothing is silent. Where an apostrophe precedes a vowel, e.g. **ng'ombe** (cattle), the vowel is accentuated, something like a gulping sound.

A as in appetite

AO sounds like "ow!"

B as in bed

CH as in church, but often sounds like "dj"

D as in donkey

DH like a cross between dhow and thou

DJ as in pyjamas

E between the "e" in bed and "i" in bid

F as in fan

G as in good

GH at the back of the throat, like a growl; nearly an "r"

Tribal and national prefixes

For the sake of clarity, we've ditched the Kiswahili prefixes for tribal names in this book. For example, we refer to "Gogo" when "Mgogo" (a Gogo person) or "Wagogo" (Gogo people) are the correct forms. We have, however, kept the "Ki" language prefix ("Kigogo"). The other prefix, handy for describing areas, is "U", as in "Ugogo" – the land of the Gogo. The same prefixes apply to nationalities (for English: "Mingereza", "Waingereza", "Kiingereza" and "Uingereza" respectively). Similarly, prefixes commonly used in northwestern Tanzania ("Bu", "Ba", "M" and "Mu") have also been omitted.

H as in harmless
I as in happy
J as in jug
K as in kiosk
KH as in loch
L as in lullaby. Often pronounced "r"
M as in munch; preceding a consonant, it's one syllable, eg **mnazi** (coconut), "mna-zi"
N as in nonsense; preceding a consonant, it gives a nasal quality
NG as in bang

O as in orange
P as in paper
Q Same as K
R as in rapid, or rolled. Often pronounced "l"
S as in silly
T as in tiny
TH as in thanks
U like **oo**, or "ou" in the French **tous**
V as in victory
W as in wobble
Y as in you
Z as in zero

Elementary grammar

Kiswahili **grammar** is confusing at first, but relatively simple once you grasp (and memorize) the basic building blocks. The main idea is that nouns, adjectives and verbs change their prefixes according to the context. The following sections cover the most common grammatical rules. Don't worry about getting things wrong: really correct Kiswahili isn't much spoken except on the coast.

Nouns and adjectives

Nouns fall into eight or nine classes, each with different prefixes for their singular and plural forms, and with the same prefix applied to any associated adjective.

Each class covers certain areas of meaning. For example, words beginning "m" (singular) or "wa" (plural) are people, eg **mtalii/watalii** tourist/s. Also beginning "m" (singular) or "mi" (plural) are trees and plants or things connected with life, eg **mti/miti** tree/s. Words beginning "ki" or "ch" (singular) or "vi" or "vy" (plural) are generally "things", eg **kiti/viti** chair/s. Most abstract nouns, and place names derived from a people's name, begin with "u", eg **uhuru** freedom, **Uingereza** England.

The same noun prefixes are added to the associated **adjective**, so you get **mtalii mzuri** – a nice tourist; **miti mizuri** – lovely trees; **viti vizuri** – good chairs.

Pronouns

mimi	I, me
wewe	you (sing.)
ninyi	you (pl.)
yeye	he/she, him/her
sisi	we, us
wao	they, them

Verbs

The **verb** system is reasonably simple, though there's a lot to memorize at first. You begin with a personal prefix, then a marker for the tense, then the verb root, eg I (**ni-**) am (**-na-**) be happy (**furai**) is **ninafurai**.

Personal prefixes

(negative **si-**)	I **ni**
(negative **hu-**)	you (sing.) **u**
(negative **ham-**)	you (pl.) **m**
(negative **ha-**)	he/she **a**
(negative **hatu-**)	we **tu**
(negative **hawa-**)	they **wa**

Tenses

na	present
li	past
ta	future
me	just past, or still going on

Some verb roots

The following are common verb roots. Except for irregular verbs, the infinitive gets a "ku" prefix (eg *kutaka* to want, *ninataka* I want).

fanya	do
wa	be/become
weza	be able (can)
wa na	have
taka	want
jua	know, understand
ikiri	think
penda	like
kupenda (irregular)	love
tazama	look
sikia	hear
sema	say or speak
ona/onana	see/meet
kuja (irregular)	come
toka	come from
kwenda (irregular)	go
kaa	stay
nunua	buy
leta	bring
pa	give
kula (irregular)	eat
nywa (irregular)	drink
sikia njaa	be hungry
wa na kiu	be thirsty
choka	be tired
lala	sleep
ota	dream
andika	write
soma	read
cheza	play
furai	be happy

Examples of pronouns, verbs and tenses

The hyphens in the examples below illustrate how the word is constructed. Hyphens are not used in written Kiswahili.

she wanted	**a-li-taka**
I am tired	**ni-me-choka**
we will sleep	**tu-ta-lala**
Did you hear?	**u-li-sikia?**
they like...	**wa-na-penda...**
are you (pl.) going?	**m-na-enda?**
has he come?	**a-me-kuja?**
have they gone?	**wa-me-kwenda?**
she said...	**a-li-sema...**
can I...?	**ni-na-weza...?**
I will bring	**ni-ta-leta**
we are staying (at/in)...	**tu-na-kaa...**
I know	**ni-na-jua**

Words and phrases

Greetings

Hello **Jambo**; reply **Jambo**. Used mainly for tourists. The correct form is **Hujambo**; reply **Sijambo** ("problems?", "no problems")

How are things? **Habari?** ("news?"); can be qualified, eg **Habari gani?** ("your news?"), **Habari yako?** ("what news?"), **Habari za kazi?** ("news of work?") or **Habari za safari?** ("news of the safari?"); reply **mzuri** ("good"), **mzuri sana** ("very good"), or other adjective

"I show my respect" (said to an elder on the mainland) **Shikamoo** (**Shikamooni** when greeting several), usually qualified by a title (eg **Shikamoo bibi** for an old woman); reply **Marahaba**

Peace be on you (Muslim, mainly Zanzibar) **Salaam mualaikum**; reply **Mualaikum salaam**

Peace **Salaam** or **Salamu**

Good morning/evening (Zanzibar) **Sabalkheri/Masalkheri** (polite greetings for elders)

What's up? (informal) **Vipi?** or **Mambo?** reply **Poa**, **Bomba** or **Gado** (all slang, meaning "cool")

Hello? May I come in? **Hodi** or **Hodi hodi!** (said on knocking or entering)

Come in, enter, welcome (also said when offering something) **Karibu** (**Karibuni** when speaking to several)

Goodbye **Kwaheri** (**Kwaherini** when speaking to several); literally "with blessings"

Good night (when leaving) **Usiku mwema**

Sleep well **Lala salama**

Come back again **Rudi tena**

We shall meet again **Tutaonana**

Thank you **Asante** (**Asanteni** when speaking to several people) or **Ushukuru**; in Zanzibar, say **Shukrani**

And the same to you **Na wewe pia**

My name is/I am called... **Jina langu/Nina itwa**...

Where are you from? **Unatoka wapi?**

I am from... **Ninatoka**...

I'm British/American/German/French/Italian **Mimi Mwingereza/Mwamerika/Mjerumani/Mfaransa/Mwitalia**

I don't understand **Sifahamu**

sorry, pardon **Samahani**

Sorry, I don't understand Kiswahili **Samahani, sifahamu Kiswahili**

My Kiswahili is bad **Kiswahili changu ni kibaya**

Do you speak English? **Unasema kiingereza?**

How do you say ... in Kiswahili? **Unasemaje kwa kiswahili ...?**

Could you repeat that? **Sema tena** (literally "speak again")

I don't know **Sijui**

God willing **Mungu akipenda** or **Inshallah** (Muslim)

Praise God **Tunamshukuru mwenyezi Mungu** or **Alhamdullilah** (Muslim)

OK **sawa** or **sawa sawa**

please **tafadhali**

Excuse me (let me through) **Hebu**

No problem **hamna shida**, **hakuna matata** or **wasiwasi**

It's nothing **Si kitu**

really? **I say?** (one of the funnier English loan words)

I want to take a photo **nataka piga picha**

May I take your picture **Naomba nikupige picha?**

May I take a picture? (not a person) **Naomba nipige picha?**

friend **rafiki**

child **mtoto** (pl. **watoto**)

father **baba** (also used for a man)

mother **mama** (also used for a woman)

brother **kaka**

sister **dada**

grandfather **babu** (also an old man or elder)

grandmother **bibi** (also an old woman or elder)

mister **bwana**

sir **mzee** (a term of respect for an old or important man); pl. **wazee**

teacher (also a term of respect) **mwalimu**

Basics

na	and/with
kwa	with
za or **ya**	of
ya	by
au	or
ndio or **naam** (on the coast)	yes
hapana (a general negative); **la** (on the coast)	no
hakuna or **hamna**	none, there isn't
nani?	who?
nini?	what?
gani?	which?
kwa nini?	why?
wapi?	where?
lini?	when?
kwa sababu...	because...
ni	(it) is/(they) are
hii	this/these
langu	mine
siyo?	isn't it?
kweli?	really?
kabisa (used as positive emphasis)	exactly
labda	maybe
sana (follows adjective)	very
-zuri (with prefix)	good, pretty, tasty
-baya (with prefix)	bad
si mbaya	not bad
-kubwa/-dogo (with prefix)	big/small
-ingi (with prefix)	a lot

safi	clean, pure, fresh
moto/baridi	hot/cold

Getting around

Iko wapi...?	Where is...?
lini?	when?
gari (pl. magari)	vehicle
teksi	taxi
basi (pl. mabasi)	bus
daladala or gari ya abiria	communal minibus
kituo cha teksi/basi/ daladala	taxi/bus/daladala stand
baisikeli	bicycle
treni	train
stesheni	train station
mvuko (pl. mivuko)	ferry
kivuko	ferry port/landing
chombo (pl. vyombo)	boat
mtumbwi (pl. mitumbwi)	canoe
ngalawa	outrigger (with sail)
jahazi	trading dhow (large)
mashua	trading dhow (smaller)
ndege	plane
uwanja wa ndege (lit. "stadium of birds")	airport
manamba	ticket tout
dereva	driver
petroli, mafuta	petrol, oil
fundi	mechanic
barabara	highway
njla or ndia	road, path
njia panda ya...	junction for...
keep lefti (from old English signs)	roundabout
kwa miguu	on foot/walking
Inaondoka lini?	When does it leave?
Tutafika lini? or Tutafika saa ngapi?	When will we arrive?
pole pole	slowly
taratibu	carefully, methodically
haraka	fast, quickly
Ngoja!/Ngoja kidogo	Wait!/Wait a moment
Simama!	Stop!
Unaenda wapi?	Where are you going?

Mpaka wapi?	To where?
Kutoka wapi?	From where?
Kilometa ngapi?	How many kilometres?
Ninaenda...	I'm going to...
Songa kidogo	Squeeze up a little
Twende	Let's go
Twende tu	Keep going
moja kwa moja	straight ahead
kulia	right
kushoto	left
juu	up
chini	down
Nataka kushuka hapa	I want to get off here
Gari imevunjika	The car has broken down
Safari njema	Have a good journey

Accommodation

hotel, gesti or nyumba ya wangeni	Hotel
Naweza kukaa wapi?	Where can I stay?
Naweza kukaa hapa?	Can I stay here?
mapokezi	reception
chumba (pl. vyumba)	room
Napenda kuona chumba	I'd like to see a room
Nataka chumba kwa wasiku mbili	I want a room for two nights
self containa or chumba self	en-suite room
common	room sharing bathroom
Choo/bafu kiko wapi?	Where's the toilet/ bathroom?
maji moto/baridi	hot/cold water
kitanda (pl. vitanda)	bed
shiti	bedsheet
mto	pillow
chandarua	mosquito net
kiti na meza	table and chair
televisheni	television
mshumaa	candle
ufuaji	laundry
kuni	firewood

Shopping

duka	shop
machinga	street vendor
biashara	business, commerce
fungua	open
funga	closed
mfuko or rambo (plastic bag)	bag
pesa or hela	money
Ngapi?	How much? (quantity)
Pesa ngapi?, Bei gani? or Shillingi ngapi?	How much? (price)
Mingi zaidi	That's too much
ghali sana	expensive
rahisi	cheap
Punguza kidogo!	Reduce the price!
Nipe...	Give me (can I have?)...
Nataka...	I want...
Naomba... (more polite)	May I have...
Sitaki...	I don't want...
Sitaki biashara	I don't want to do business

Health and toiletries

Mimi mgonjwa or Ninaumwa	I'm ill
homa	fever
daktari	doctor
hospitali	hospital
duka la dawa	pharmacy
kidonge	pills
dudu	insect
dawa ya waddudu	insect repellent
dawa (dawa baridi Western, dawa kali traditional)	medicine
sembe	razor
sabuni	soap

Numbers (*Namba*)

moja	1
mbili	2
tatu	3
nne	4
tano	5
sita	6
saba	7
nane	8
tisa	9
kumi	10
kumi na moja	11
kumi na mbili	12
ishirini	20
ishirini na moja	21
thelathini	30
arbaini	40
hamsini	50
sitini	60
sabaini	70
themanini	80
tisini	90
mia or mia moja	100
mia moja na ishirini na moja	121
elfu	1000
milioni	1,000,000

Time and calendar

Saa ngapi?	What time?
Saa ngapi sasa?	What time is it now?
saa kumi	ten o'clock (4am or 4pm)
saa kumi na robo	quarter past ten
saa kumi na nusu	half past ten
saa kumi kasorobo	quarter to ten
dakika	minutes
leo	today
jana	yesterday
jusi	day before yesterday
majusi	several days ago
kesho	tomorrow
kesho kutwa	in two days
kila siku	every day
alfajiri	dawn
asubuhi	morning
mchana	daytime
usiku	night time
wiki ilioyopita/ hii/ijayo	last/this/next week
mwaka huu	this year
mwezi huu	this month

sasa	now
bado	not yet, still
sasa hivi	soon
baadaye	later
-subiri (has prefix)	wait
Jumatatu	Monday
Jumanne	Tuesday
Jumatano	Wednesday
Alhamisi	Thursday
Ijumaa	Friday
Jumamosi	Saturday
Jumapili	Sunday
Januari	January
Februari	February
Machi	March
Aprili	April
Mei	May
Juni	June
Julai	July
Agosti	August
Septemba	September
Oktoba	October
Novemba	November
Desemba	December

Signs

Hatari	Danger
Angalia/Onyo	Warning
Mbwa mkali (literally "sharp dog")	Fierce dog
Hakuna njia	No entry

Animals

Animal is **mnyama** (pl. *wanyama*). Most species' names are the same in singular and plural; it's noted where they differ.

mhanga (pl. **wahanga**)	aardvark
fisi mdogo (pl. **fisi wadogo**)	aardwolf
nyani	baboon
popo (pl. **mapopo**)	bat
mbweha masikio	bat-eared fox
nyuki	bee
ndege	bird
nyabu	blue monkey

nyati or **mbogo**	buffalo
komba	bushbaby (galago)
kulungu or **mbawala**	bushbuck
nguruwe mwitu	bush pig
kipepeo (pl. **vipepeo**)	butterfly
ndezi	cane rat
simba mangu	caracal
paka	cat
ng'ombe or gombe (pl. **magombe**)	cow, cattle
kinyonga (pl. **vinyonga**)	chameleon
duma	cheetah
kuku	chicken
sokwe	chimpanzee
fungo	civet
mbega	colobus monkey
mamba	crocodile
digidigi or **dika**	dikdik
mbwa	dog
mbwa mwitu	dog (wild, or African hunting)
pomboo (pl. **mapomboo**)	dolphin
punda	donkey, ass
bata (pl. **mabata**)	duck
nguva	dugong (manatee)
nysa (common), mindi (Abbot's), funo or kiduku (red; pl. **viduku**), paa (blue)	duiker
mpofu or **mbungu**	eland
tembo or **ndovu**	elephant
sange	elephant shrew
samaki	fish
chura (pl. **vyura**)	frog
swala (**granti** Grant's, **tomi** Thomson's)	gazelle
kanu	genet
swala twiga	gerenuk
twiga	giraffe
mbuzi	goat
kanga	Guinea fowl
sungura	hare
kongoni	hartebeest
kiboko (pl. **viboko**)	hippopotamus

farasi	horse	kifaru (pl. **vifaru**)	rhinoceros
fisi (**madoa** spotted, **miraba** striped)	hyena	kirongo (pl. **virongo**)	roan antelope
		pimbi or **wibari**	rock hyrax
swala pala	impala	palahala	sable antelope
dudu (pl. **madudu**)	insect	siafu	safari ant
bweha	jackal	mondo	serval
mbuzi mawe	klipspringer	papa	shark
tandala (**mkubwa** greater, **mdogo** lesser)	kudu	kondoo	sheep
		nyoka	snake
		kamendegere	spring hare
chui	leopard	kindi or **chindi**	squirrel
simba	lion	dondoo or **dondoro**	steinbok, grysbok
mjusi (pl. **mijusi**)	lizard	nyamera	topi
nguchiro	mongoose	kobe (pl. **makobe**)	tortoise
tumbili	monkey	pelele or **perere**	tree hyrax
kenge	monitor lizard	kasa (**kikoshi** Olive Ridley, **mwamba** hawksbill, **uziwa** green)	turtle
kasia (pl. **makasia**)	oribi		
choroa	oryx		
mbuni	ostrich		
fisi maji	otter	tumbili	vervet monkey
kakakuona	pangolin	ngiri or **gwasi** (pl. **magwasi**)	warthog
nguruwe	pig		
nungu or **nungunungu**	porcupine	kuro	waterbuck
		nyangumi	whale
panya	rat	mbwa mwitu	wild dog
nyegere	ratel (honey badger)	nyumbu	wildebeest
tohe	reedbuck	punda milia	zebra

Food and drink

General

chakula	food
hoteli	restaurant
mgahawa	tea house (very basic restaurant)
mama/baba lisha or **mama/baba ntilie**	streetfood vendor
Mnauza chakula hapa?	Do you serve food here?
Nakula mboga tu	I am vegetarian
meza	table
Iko...? or **Kuna...?**	Is there any...?
Iko... or **Kuna...**	Yes, there is...
Haiko... or **Hakuna...**	No, there isn't
nusu	half (portion)

tosha/basi	enough
choma	grilled
mchemsho	boiled
rosti	stewed
kufurahia chakula or **karibu chakula**	enjoy your food

Drinks (*Vinywaji*)

kinywaji	a drink
glasi or **bilauri**	glass
chupa	bottle
kopo	can
kiroba (contains a tot of spirits)	sachet
moto/baridi	hot/cold
barafu	ice

bia (commercial); **pombe** or **busa** (local brew)	beer		**mtindi** or **maziwa mgando**	curdled milk
gongo or **changaa**	local spirits		**chai** (ginger tea **chai tangawizi**, spiced tea **chai masala**, black tea **chai rangi**, tea with milk **chai maziwa**)	tea
tuwi	coconut juice			
kahawa	coffee			
juice (pronunced "juwiis")	juice		**maji** (drinking water **maji ya kunywa**)	water
maziwa	milk			

Menu Reader

Snacks

andazi	doughnut
biscuti	biscuits
chapati	chapati, a floury pancake
chop	mince meat or egg in a mashed potato pasty, or a rib of mutton or chicken leg in batter
kababu	fried meatball
kitumbua	deep-fried rice cake
mahindi	maize cob
mantabali	"Zanzibari pizza", stuffed chapati like a spring roll
mayai	eggs (singular **yai**)
mishkaki	grilled goat meat skewers
sambusa	samosa (triangle of pastry stuffed with minced meat, onion and pepper, or vegetarian)

Meat (*Nyama*) and Fish (*Samaki*)

dagaa	tiny freshwater sardines, sun-dried
filigisi	tripe, innards, sweetmeats
kamba	prawns
kamba coach	lobster
kolekole	kingfish
kondoo	lamb
kuku	chicken
maini	liver
ngisi	squid
ng'ombe	beef
pweza	octopus
sangara	Nile perch

Vegetables (*Mboga*)

biringani	aubergine (eggplant)
chipsi	chips
dengu	lentils
kabichu	cabbage
karoti	carrots
kiazi kitamu	sweet potato
kitunguu	onion
mabamia or **mabinda**	okra
maharage or **maharagwe**	beans
mahindi	maize
mchicha	kind of spinach
mdewere	spinach
mtama	millet
muhogo	cassava
ndizi	banana (plantain)
nyanya	tomatoes
pilipili mboga	sweet pepper
saladi	salad or lettuce
tango	cucumber
ujaka	kind of spinach
viazi	potatoes
wali	rice

Typical dishes

Most dishes take the form *samaki na wali* (fish and rice) or *kuku na chipsi* (chicken and chips)

biriani	peppery and highly spiced dish of meat and rice
chipsi mayai	chip omelette
matoke	banana stew
mchanganyiko	a mixture of more or less everything
mtori	a light banana soup, in Arusha and westwards
nyama choma	char-grilled meat, best accompanied with grilled bananas and chilli
pilau	rice spiced with cardamom, cinnamon, cloves and pepper, and whatever else comes to hand
pweza na nazi	octopus cooked in gently spiced coconut sauce (Zanzibar)
supu	spicy meat broth served with lemon and chilli, eaten for breakfast (and as a hangover cure): *supu ya makongoro* is with animal hooves, *supu ya utumbo* is with intestines
ugali	East Africa's staple food, a stodgy cornmeal polenta usually served with a stew of fish, meat or vegetables
uji	millet porridge, eaten for breakfast

Condiments, herbs and spices

pilipili manga	black pepper
pilipili hoho	chilli pepper
hiliki	cardamom
mdalasini	cinnamon
karafu	cloves
gilgilani	coriander
uzile	cumin
tangawizi	ginger
limao	lemon
mchaichai	lemon grass
kungu manga	nutmeg
mafuta	oil
chumvi	salt
gigiri	sesame
sukari	sugar
mrehani	sweet basil
manjano	tumeric

Fruit (*Matunda*)

tunda la kizungu	apple
pea	avocado
ndizi	banana
sheli sheli	breadfruit
nazi	(*dafu* is a young coconut for drinking) coconut
korosho	cashew
tende	date
duriani	durian
zabibu	grape
pera	guava
kungu	Indian almond
chongoma	Indian plum
fenesi	jackfruit
limau	lemon
shoki-shoki	litchi
embe	mango
chungwa	orange
papai	papaya
pasheni	passion fruit
nanasi	pineapple
kungumanga	pomegranate
mratab	sapodilla
danzi	sour orange
stafeli	soursop
mtopetope	sweetsop (custard-apple)
kwaju	tamarind
chenza	tangerine
tikiti	watermelon

Glossary

askari security guard, soldier

banda any kind of hut, usually rectangular and with a sloping thatched roof (pl. **mabanda**)

baraza stone bench, a sitting or meeting place

benki bank

boma Maasai village; also colonial German headquarters

boriti mangrove poles used in building

buibui the black cover-all cloak and veil of Shia Muslim women

chai a tip or bribe, literally "tea"

choo toilet (**wanaume** is gents, **wanawake** is ladies)

imam the man who leads prayers in a mosque

jengo building (pl. **majengo**)

kabila tribe (pl. **makabila**)

kanga or **khanga** printed cotton sheet incorporating a proverb, worn by women

kanisa church

kaskazi northeast monsoon (Dec–Mar)

kitabu book

kitenge double-paned cotton cloth (pl. **vitenge**)

kofia embroidered cap worn by Muslim men

korongo ditch or ravine, often erosional

kusi southwest monsoon (June–Sept)

makuti palm-leaf thatch, used for roofing

malaika angel

malaya prostitute

mama kubwa big lady

mbuga black cotton soil, impassable by motor vehicles in rains

mchina Chinese or oriental-looking person (pl. **wachina**)

mhindi Indian person (pl. **wahindi**)

mihrab prayer niche set in a mosque's qibla wall facing Mecca

msikiti mosque

mtaa ward or neighbourhood; street

mtalii tourist (pl. **watalii**)

Mungu God

murram red clay and gravel road

mzungu white person (pl. **wazungu**)

ngoma dance, drum, music, celebration

ngoma ya kiasili traditional music

panga machete or knife

polisi police

posta post office

rondavel round hut or cottage, often thatched

safari any journey

sahil coast

semadari traditional Zanzibari four-poster bed

serikali government

shamba farm

shisha water pipe

shule (**skule** in Zanzibar) school

sigara cigarette

simu telephone

soko market

soko kuu main market

tembe flat-roofed hut, common in central Tanzania

Ulaya Europe

Travel store

TRAVEL

& MORE

Visit us online

www.roughguides.com

Information on over 25,000 destinations around the world

- **Read** Rough Guides' trusted travel info

- **Share** journals, photos and travel advice with other readers

- Get exclusive Rough Guide **discounts** and travel deals

- Earn membership points every time you contribute to the

  Rough Guide community and get free books, flights and trips

- Browse thousands of **CD reviews** and artists in our music area

ONLINE

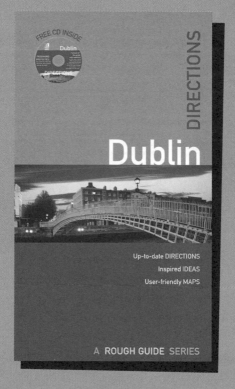

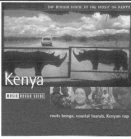

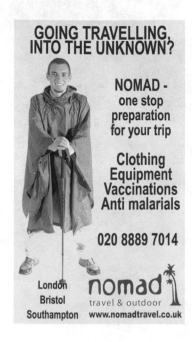
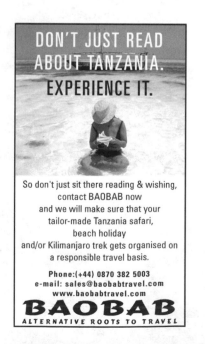

ETHICAL SPONSORED SAFARIS TO TANZANIA

Our treks offer the opportunity to understand and support local communities, their lives, struggles and ideas for the future, while enjoying the diverse environment and wildlife.

Peasant farmers ~ Maasai pastoralists ~ Hadza hunter-gatherers

Community Empowerment,
Social Justice

"In Maasai, women are seen as children. Individual empowerment will come through education - and I have education. I know my rights and how to fight. I am self confident and self controlled. We need to push and kick away our inferiority complexes that we are under men. We are equal and we need to be seen as equal."

www.african-initiatives.org.uk info@african-initiatives.org.uk
+00 44 (0)117 9150001
Registered Charity No: 1064413

THE EAST AFRICAN SAFARI AND TOURING COMPANY

Safari of a lifetime

wildlife
adventure

comfort

Experience the sensation of being alone in Africa amongst the very core of wildlife!

EASTCO can take those with a desire for the remote wilderness to areas far away from the well-beaten tracks of the main circuits.

Since 1992 EASTCO has provided private and exclusive safaris for discerning travelers.

Whether it be a walking safari, night drive in Tarangire, camping on the Serengeti plains or relaxing in a lodge overlooking the Ngorongoro Crater, EASTCO offers a variety of safari options from standard camping safaris and lodge safaris to full service luxury camps, in any and all combinations.

With a fleet of 4WD vehicles and an average group size of between two and three our proficient safari crew ensures your safari experience goes beyond any adventure you may have had.

adz@work AFR5807

 TARANGIRE CONSERVATION COMPANY LTD

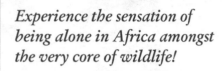 Naitolia   BoundaryHill lodge

Contact us today for more information:
PO Box 1215 Arusha Tanzania East Africa
Email: eastafricansafaris@habari.co.tz
naitolia@tarangireconservation.com

 www.eastafricansafari.info   www.tarangireconservation.com

Small print and
Index

A Rough Guide to Rough Guides

Published in 1982, the first Rough Guide – to Greece – was a student scheme that became a publishing phenomenon. Mark Ellingham, a recent graduate in English from Bristol University, had been travelling in Greece the previous summer and couldn't find the right guidebook. With a small group of friends he wrote his own guide, combining a highly contemporary, journalistic style with a thoroughly practical approach to travellers' needs.

The immediate success of the book spawned a series that rapidly covered dozens of destinations. And, in addition to impecunious backpackers, Rough Guides soon acquired a much broader and older readership that relished the guides' wit and inquisitiveness as much as their enthusiastic, critical approach and value-for-money ethos.

These days, Rough Guides include recommendations from shoestring to luxury and cover more than 200 destinations around the globe, including almost every country in the Americas and Europe, more than half of Africa and most of Asia and Australasia. Our ever-growing team of authors and photographers is spread all over the world, particularly in Europe, the USA and Australia.

In the early 1990s, Rough Guides branched out of travel, with the publication of Rough Guides to World Music, Classical Music and the Internet. All three have become benchmark titles in their fields, spearheading the publication of a wide range of books under the Rough Guide name.

Including the travel series, Rough Guides now number more than 350 titles, covering: phrasebooks, waterproof maps, music guides from Opera to Heavy Metal, reference works as diverse as Conspiracy Theories and Shakespeare, and popular culture books from iPods to Poker. Rough Guides also produce a series of more than 120 World Music CDs in partnership with World Music Network.

Visit www.roughguides.com to see our latest publications.

Rough Guide travel images are available for commercial licensing at www.roughguidespictures.com

Rough Guide credits

Text editor: Helen Marsden
Layout: Ajay Verma
Cartography: Ed Wright
Picture editor: Sarah Cummins
Production: Julia Bovis
Proofreader: Karen Parker
Cover design: Chloë Roberts
Editorial: London Kate Berens, Claire
Saunders, Geoff Howard, Ruth Blackmore,
Polly Thomas, Richard Lim, Clifton Wilkinson,
Alison Murchie, Karoline Densley, Andy Turner,
Ella O'Donnell, Keith Drew, Edward Aves, Nikki
Birrell, Alice Park, Sarah Eno, Joe Staines,
Duncan Clark, Peter Buckley, Matthew Milton,
Tracy Hopkins, Ruth Tidball; **New York** Andrew
Rosenberg, Richard Koss, Steven Horak,
AnneLise Sorensen, Amy Hegarty, Hunter
Slaton, April Isaacs, Sean Mahoney
Design & Pictures: London Simon Bracken,
Dan May, Diana Jarvis, Mark Thomas, Jj Luck,
Harriet Mills; **Delhi** Madhulita Mohapatra,
Umesh Aggarwal, Jessica Subramanian, Amit
Verma, Ankur Guha
Production: Sophie Hewat, Katherine Owers

Cartography: London Maxine Repath, Katie
Lloyd-Jones; **Delhi** Manish Chandra, Rajesh
Chhibber, Jai Prakash Mishra, Ashutosh
Bharti, Rajesh Mishra, Animesh Pathak, Jasbir
Sandhu, Karobi Gogoi
Online: New York Jennifer Gold, Suzanne
Welles, Kristin Mingrone; **Delhi** Manik
Chauhan, Lalit K. Sharma, Narender Kumar,
Manish Shekhar Jha, Rakesh Kumar,
Chhandita Chakravarty
Marketing & Publicity: London Richard
Trillo, Niki Hanmer, David Wearn, Demelza
Dallow, Louise Maher; **New York** Geoff
Colquitt, Megan Kennedy, Katy Ball; **Delhi**
Reem Khokhar
Custom publishing and foreign rights:
Philippa Hopkins
Manager India: Punita Singh
Series editor: Mark Ellingham
Reference Director: Andrew Lockett
PA to Managing and Publishing Directors:
Megan McIntyre
Publishing Director: Martin Dunford
Managing Director: Kevin Fitzgerald

Publishing information

This 2nd edition published April 2006 by **Rough
Guides Ltd**,
80 Strand, London WC2R 0RL, UK
345 Hudson St, 4th Floor,
New York, NY 10014, USA
14 Local Shopping Centre, Panchsheel Park,
New Delhi 110017, India
Distributed by the Penguin Group
Penguin Books Ltd,
80 Strand, London WC2R 0RL, UK
Penguin Putnam, Inc.
375 Hudson Street, NY 10014, USA
Penguin Group (Australia)
250 Camberwell Road, Camberwell
Victoria 3124, Australia
Penguin Books Canada Ltd,
10 Alcorn Avenue, Toronto, Ontario,
Canada M4V 1E4
Penguin Group (New Zealand)
Cnr Rosedale and Airborne roads
Albany, Auckland, New Zealand

Typeset in Bembo and Helvetica to an original
design by Henry Iles.

Printed and bound in China

© Jens Finke 2006

816pp includes index

A catalogue record for this book is available from
the British Library.

ISBN 978-1-84353-531-7

The publishers and authors have done their best
to ensure the accuracy and currency of all the
information in **The Rough Guide to Tanzania**,
however, they can accept no responsibility for
any loss, injury, or inconvenience sustained by
any traveller as a result of information or advice
contained in the guide.

3   5   7   9   8   6   4

Help us update

We've gone to a lot of effort to ensure that the
2nd edition of **The Rough Guide to Tanzania**
is accurate and up to date. However, things
change – places get "discovered", opening
hours are notoriously fickle, restaurants and
rooms raise prices or lower standards. If you
feel we've got it wrong or left something out,
we'd like to know, and if you can remember
the address, the price, the time, the phone
number, so much the better.

We'll credit all contributions, and send a
copy of the next edition (or any other Rough

Guide if you prefer) for the best letters.
Everyone who writes to us and isn't already
a subscriber will receive a copy of our full-
colour thrice-yearly newsletter. Please mark
letters: **"Rough Guide Tanzania Update"** and
send to: Rough Guides, 80 Strand, London
WC2R 0RL, UK; or Rough Guides, 4th Floor,
345 Hudson St, New York, NY 10014, USA.
Or send an email to **mail@roughguides.com**

Have your questions answered and tell
others about your trip at
www.roughguides.atinfopop.com

Acknowledgements

Jens Finke: I would especially like to thank Maria Helena, for being there, keeping up with my insane working hours, and making lasagne on the day I finally finished, and Helen Marsden at the other end of the line for her superb (and for me enjoyable) work as this book's editor, and for her patience while under pressure from the almighty grandes perruques in dealing with my infamous inability to stick to deadlines. All well worthwhile, I hope.

In Tanzania, particular thanks in no particular order go to the following fine people: Kathleen and Jef "Wachizi" from Via Via, the tireless Rachel Kessi of Mawazo Gallery in Dar, Arnold and Maglan Christopher in Arusha (fine conversations), Onesmo Sanka for his endless patience with a litany of hotel visits, and – as ever – to the Kings of Arusha. Thanks also to Tim Davenport at WCS Mbeya for the scoop on Kitulo, Dirk and Inneke Janssens-Onsea for an unforgettable breakfast (and undoubtedly several previous nights I hardly recall!), Juma Kahema in Soni (great work), Mwisho and the gang at Lushoto CTP (ditto), Mohamed Yassin of TeV in Tanga, Lars Johannson, Thomas Kimaro (Marangu), E.N.M. Kasyupa in Kigoma, Christopher David Timbuka and Richard Kishe of Udzungwa NP, Corodius Sawe and Godfrey Mathew Msumari at Amani, William Haule and Rianne Koopmans (both TTB Arusha), Heri Mkunda of Chilunga cultural tourism, the ever-helpful and hugely knowledgeable Niko Ntinda and Felix Amandus at Sisi Kwa Sisi (Mbeya), Martin Guard (eco2, thanks even without the octopus gonads), Yvonne Munnichs (The Old Boma at Mikindani), Raf at Swahili Divers, David Barker (formerly A Tent With A View), Michelle Bragg at Morogoro, and – all in Zanzibar – the Machano brothers of Warere Townhouse, Rod Kayne (glad you finally got rid of me?) and Abbas Juma Mzee.

SMALL PRINT

Readers' letters

A big thanks to all the readers who wrote in with comments and suggestions about the first edition, and grovelling apologies to those whose names I've either misspelled or missed off entirely (things got very hectic):

Johan Vanden Abeele, Nick & Sarah Atkinson, Nancy Benham, Dorian Bloch, Richard Buckingham, Ian Chisholm, Dagmar Christiansen, James Clarke, Erika Cule, Claude David, Simon Davies, Julia Dinsdale, Leicester Fosse, Bruce Fox, Susan Fox, Anja Gartmann-Denz, Janice Grant, Steven Gray, Rahel Hardmeier, Mike Hartwell, Wolfgang Heep, Michael Hell, Gerard Hettema, Thomas Holden, Professor James Hough, Sue Jagger, Ilona Johnston, Marije Jongejan, Bas Kemperman, Mussa Hassan Mussa Kitambulio, Belia Klaassen, Joyce Klaassen, Christoph Kotanko, Susanne Kuehhorn Harfenstr, Laura Kyrke-Smith, Fredrik Lekström, Maisy Luk, Michela Mazier, Dr Paul McAndrew, Kris Mizutani, Laszlo Paizs, Dr Alan J. Perry, Kristina Pentland, Helen Pieper, Simon Pleasance, Alberto Poli, Val Presten, Liisa Riihimaki, Amanda Sangorski, Gillian Scoble, Ashley Seaman, Mansuetus Setonga, Ketki Shah, Jo Slater, Ype Smit, Andrew Szefler, William Visser, Mary Taylor, Adam and Anne White, Murray White, Kirsty Whitoley, Mary Wickler-Peterson, Stephanie Wynne-Jones, Andreas Zahner.

Photo credits

All photos © Rough Guides, photography by Suzanne Porter, except the following:

Cover

Main front picture: Zebra © Lawrence Worchester
Back top picture: Fisherman, Zanzibar © Jamie Marshall

Title page

Flamingos, Ngorongoro Conservation Area © Tim Davis/Corbis

Full page

Iringa market © Pat de la Harpe/Images of Africa

Introduction

Iringa market © Pat de la Harpe/Images of Africa
Locals playing Bao, Stone Town © Yadid Levy/ Alamy
Dhow © Peter Adams Photography/Alamy
Children in local bus © Alan Gignoux/Impact
Giraffes, Tarangire National Park © Javed Jafferji
Women wearing kangas © Javed Jafferji

Things not to miss

01 Maasai at edge of Ngorongoro crater © Sylvain Grandadam/Robert Harding
02 Beach, Zanzibar © Peter Adams Photography/ Alamy
03 Climbers on Uhuru Peak, Mount Kilimanjaro © Ariadne Van Zandbergen/Images of Africa
04 Stone Town © Steven Marks/Cape Photo Library
05 Lion in long grass, Serengeti National Park © Javed Jafferji
06 Bull-fighting, Pemba © Javed Jafferji
07 Forodhani Gardens, Stone Town © Ian Cumming/Axiom
08 Gereza Fort Ruins, Kilwa Kisiwani © Javed Jafferji
09 Ngorongoro Conservation Area © Bruce Coleman Inc/Alamy
10 Makonde carvings © Javed Jafferji
11 Seafood © Nicholas Pitt/Alamy
12 Tingatinga painting © Ulrich Doering/Alamy
13 Kondoa–Irangi rock paintings © Guy Marks/ Axiom
14 Chimpanzee © Nigel Pavitt/John Warburton Lee
15 Scuba-diving © Geoff Spiby/iAfrika
16 Tarangire National Park © Javed Jafferji
17 Usambara Mountains © Friedrich von Horsten/ Images of Africa
18 Indian Ocean flight © Jens Finke

Colour insert: Tanzania in celebration

Maasai boys wearing ceremonial clothing © Ralph A. Clevenger/Corbis
Mwaka Kogwa Festival, Makunduchi © Chiara Gallo
Sukuma annual dance competition © www.photo .net/sukuma
Bull-fighting, Pemba © Peter Bennett/www.ziff.or.tz
Bride awaiting her husband © Per-Anders Pettersson/iAfrika
Festival of the Dhow Countries, Uroa Dhow race © Peter Bennett/www.ziff.or.tz

Colour insert: Wild Tanzania

Hippo, Katavi National Park © Ariadne Van Zandbergen/Images of Africa
Hot air balloon, Serengeti National Park © Peter Blackwell/Images of Africa
Elephants, Tarangire National Park © Ariadne Van Zandbergen
Ngorongoro crater © Peter Blackwell/Images of Africa
Beho Beho Tented Camp, Selous Game Reserve © Ian Cumming/Axiom
Chimpanzee, Gombe Stream National Park © Ariadne Van Zandbergen
Lioness in tree, Lake Manyara National Park © David Hosking/Alamy
Mount Kilimanjaro © Javed Jafferji
Fishermen, Saadani National Park © Ariadne Van Zandbergen

Colour insert: The mammals of East Africa

All photos © Bruce Coleman Picture Library except:
Red colobus monkey © Peter Blackwell/Images of Africa
Lesser Bushbaby © Peter Davey/Bruce Coleman/ Alamy
Pangolin © Ian Michler/Images of Africa
Lion and Lioness © Peter & Beverley Pickford/ Images of Africa
White rhino © Peter & Beverley Pickford/Images of Africa
Bushpig © Nigel J Dennis/Images of Africa
Maasai Giraffe © Geoffrey Morgan/Alamy
Reticulated Giraffe © Martin Harvey/Images of Africa
Sharpe's Grysbok © Stu Porter/Alamy
Suni antelope © David Keith Jones/Images of Africa photobank/Alamy
Fringe-eared oryx © David Keith Jones/Images of Africa photobank/Alamy

Black and white pictures

p.90 Kunduchi Beach © Robert Harding
p.95 The Central Line Railway © John Warburton-Lee
p.109 Coconut vendor © Impact
p.123 Mlimani Park Orchestra © Werner Graebner
p.146 Livingstone Tower, Holy Ghost Mission, Bagamoyo © Peter Blackwell/Images of Africa
p.154 Holy Ghost Mission Church, Bagamoyo © Ariadne Van Zandbergen/Images of Africa
p.166 Sisal plantation © Daryl & Sharna Balfour/ Images of Africa
p.182 Boy and girl in traditional Swahili doorway © David Constantine/Axiom
p.190 Gereza Fort Ruins, Kilwa Kisiwani © Javed Jafferji
p.194 Aerial of the Rufiji River © Peter Blackwell/ Images of Africa
p.202 Hawksbill turtle © Danja Kohler/Images of Africa

SMALL PRINT

Index

Map entries are in colour.

INDEX

INDEX

813

Y

yellow fever
vaccination 33

Z

Map symbols

maps are listed in the full index using coloured text

Regional Maps

–·–·–	International border
– – –	Chapter division boundary
▬▬	Motorway
═══	Major tarred road
═══	Minor tarred road
——	Untarred road
- - - -	Footpath
▬▬	Railway
——	Coastline/river
– –	Ferry route
——	Wall
✕	International airport
✗	Domestic airport
▲	Point of interest
▲	Mountain peak
⌂	Mountain range
☼	Crater
⌇	Gorge
⌇	Reef rocks
⅄	Waterfall
⩊	Spring
⩊	Swamp
⩊	Viewpoint
⌓	Cave
∴	Ruins
⍭	Lighthouse
⸸	Church
⋏	Campsite
⌂	Hut
⌂	Ranger post
⊠–⊠	Gate
⊼	Picnic site
⸙	Museum

Town Maps

═══	Tarred roads
- - - - -	Untarred roads
ⓘ	Information office
⊠	Post office
ⓒ	Telephone office
@	Internet access
⊙	Statue
★	Transport stop
⊞	Hospital
⊛	Swimming pool
⌂	Mosque
▥	Sikh temple
⚲	Hindu temple
⽕	Petrol station
T	Toilets
⍚	Coconut plantation
▬	Building
⊞	Church
▭	Market
⬭	Stadium
⊡	Christian cemetery
⊓	Muslim cemetery
▦	Park

National park/nature reserve
Glacier
Forest
Mangrove swamp
Coral reef
Beach

Planning your safari in Tanzania

The devil's in the detail

When it comes to planning your safari, you can find yourself confronted with a bewildering array of choices, many of which appear to be offering something similar and often at wildly different prices. Should you go to northern Tanzania, southern or western Tanzania? How is each of the parks different and what are the different seasons like in each? As with most subjects, once you go into them in-depth, the choices aren't black and white, but shades of grey. So how do you differentiate between them and find exactly what you're after?

The answer is to take your time and ask plenty of questions. There is enough variety in Tanzania to cater for most people's tastes, so it should be possible to get a good quality safari that suits you.

Natural High Safaris is a small company specifically focused on those people who are interested in planning their safari in-depth. We encourage our clients to engage with us by phone, email or both. We will listen to you, make suggestions and then answer your questions as candidly as we can (people don't always like the answers). In our experience, this is one of the key ways we can help you to navigate the myriad choices - and decide if what we are offering is what you want.

Our consultants have an unrivalled knowledge of Tanzania, born of more than a decade's experience in the field; safari guiding, bush-flying and running small safari camps throughout the lesser known parts of the country. We have first hand knowledge of the remotest regions; Selous, Ruaha, Katavi, Mahale and the edges of the greater Serengeti amongst others. Of course we don't pretend to be all things to all people, but if you're looking to get under the skin of Tanzania and would like to plan something exceptional - a truly Tanzanian safari - then we'd very much like to help you.